ABERDEEN UNIVERSITY STUDIES SERIES

NUMBER 154

THE SULIDAE

Gannets and Boobies

Illustrations by

JOHN BUSBY

THE SULIDAE

GANNETS and BOOBIES

by

J. BRYAN NELSON

Senior Lecturer in Zoology
UNIVERSITY OF ABERDEEN

Published for the
UNIVERSITY OF ABERDEEN
by
OXFORD UNIVERSITY PRESS
1978

Oxford University Press, Walton Street, Oxford OX2 6DP

OXFORD LONDON GLASGOW
NEW YORK TORONTO MELBOURNE WELLINGTON
IBADAN NAIROBI DAR ES SALAAM LUSAKA CAPE TOWN
KUALA LUMPUR SINGAPORE JAKARTA HONG KONG TOKYO
DELHI BOMBAY CALCUTTA MADRAS KARACHI

ISBN 0 19 714104 8

Set by Western Printing Services Ltd., Bristol and printed in Great Britain
by T. & A. Constable Ltd., Edinburgh

CONTENTS

Colour plates: *Between pages* 484–485

Black and white plates *Between pages* 500–501

FOREWORD

By V. C. WYNNE-EDWARDS, C.B.E., F.R.S.

This monograph is the fruit of almost 20 years of single-minded effort, devoted to the natural history and especially the ecological and behavioural adaptations of a small but very interesting family of birds. Though it is a large and scientific volume packed with information, its language is easy and enjoyable, and the author's warmth and candour and his own personal story keep coming to the surface.

Prolonged study of seven of the nine living species of Sulidae committed Dr Bryan Nelson and his wife June to a frugal life for the first eight years of their marriage, mostly on desert islands; but the hardships they endured brought them great rewards. Their first and longest stay was on the Bass Rock, that windy, historic home of gannets in the Firth of Forth, whose 'forbidding battlements' are described below. Moving with scarcely a break from there to the tropical Galapagos they lived for a year on two uninhabited islands, Tower and Hood, where, even if they were not exactly in a Garden of Eden, at any rate they 'were Adam and Eve; there was nobody else on earth, as far as they could tell' (*Galapagos: Islands of Birds*, 1968). That venture was rounded off with a sea-trip to the prolific seabird islands of Peru.

By 1967 they were off hunting the Sulidae once more, on Christmas Island in the eastern Indian Ocean. Back in Britain again, they were out of funds. Bryan accepted a post in Jordan, and for eighteen months put his energies into starting a desert ecology programme in a new national park (*Azraq: Desert Oasis*, 1973). Not until 1969 did he settle down (more or less), teaching zoology at the University of Aberdeen, and dividing his free time between writing, turning an old Aberdeenshire granite house into, at last, a family home, and making shorter expeditions, twice more to Christmas Island, once to Aldabra, and regularly to the Bass Rock.

Arduous though the field work must have been, living at home has altered only his type of work; his tenacity allows of no remission. Editing results, drawing conclusions and putting them all down on paper usually present the researcher with his most exacting tasks. Bryan is as gifted and indefatigable a writer as he is a field observer. Not surprisingly nevertheless, it has taken years of work to produce the half-million printed words that the book contains. Its publication marks an epoch of achievement.

It was our mutual interest in gannets that led us to meet while he was a graduate student working on the Bass. In my generation I, too, had pursued the gannet, from my student days in 1925. Later, seabird ecology became one of my preoccupations, lasting over a decade. In fact, though we have no gannetry nearer than the Bass Rock, the proximity of large colonies of other seabirds was a material attraction in bringing me to Aberdeen, as it has been for many others, Bryan among them.

One expects a book like this to have a long useful life. For the tropical Sulidae in particular it provides a new survey against which future changes in breeding distribution and numbers will be checked. For the family as a whole it contains the first standard accounts of their comparative behaviour and their adaptive radiation. In so far as anything is predictable beyond that millennial curtain, 2000 A.D., I expect that, when it is long past, marine ornithologists will still consult J. B. Nelson's *Sulidae*, even as now we look up J. H. Gurney's *The Gannet*, published in 1913. What scientist could wish for more?

V. C. Wynne-Edwards

ACKNOWLEDGEMENTS

I must first thank my wife for untold hours of help, including fieldwork, typing, compiling tables, checking page-proofs etc. If anybody is more heartily tired of the book than I am, it is she. I am extremely grateful, also, to Sarah Wanless for unstinted help with the figures. I thank John Busby for taking enormous pains to draw both accurate and beautiful representations of behaviour. Joan Fairhurst generously provided extensive data from her gannet studies at Bempton, and David Powell from his work on Abbott's booby on Christmas Island. The following people kindly answered queries, provided unpublished information or helped in other ways: D. L. Anderson, R. Appleby, R. Broad, W. R. P. Bourne, R. G. G. Brown, E. Brun, H. O. Bunce, D. Cabot, R. Clapp, J. Cudworth, Th. Einarrson, P. Evans, M. P. Harris, A. C. B. Henderson, M. J. D. Hirons, P. G. Hopkins, T. Howell, R. van Halewijn, M. F. Jarvis, R. Jordan, C. Kepler, N. Kinnear, D. Nettleship, O. T. Owre, M. Plenge, C. J. R. Robertson, R. F. Ruttledge, J. B. Smart, F. Staub, P. Stein, K. E. L. Simmons, S. Wanless, K. Wodzicki, P. W. Woodward, J. G. Young. W. R. P. Bourne *et al.* and C. J. O. Harrison each contributed an appendix.

I am grateful to the following for allowing me to use one or more of their photographs (except where otherwise acknowledged the photos are my own): D. F. Dorward, G. M. Dunnet, R. van Halewijn, M. P. Harris, K. Hindwood, C. Kepler, G. Millie, G. M. Poulin, R. Reinsch, C. J. R. Robertson, R. W. Schreiber, F. Staub, R. Vaughan, S. Wanless, J. Warham, K. Wodzicki (from D.S.I.R. (Ecology Division) New Zealand). D. W. Snow, for the British Museum, kindly loaned sulid skins. I thank Mike Craig, Zoology Department, for printing most of the photographs.

I owe much to Fred Marr for friendliness and for never failing to get me onto and off the Bass these last 17 years and to successive clutches of keepers for cheerful hospitality. My debt to Sir Hew Hamilton Dalrymple for allowing me to study on the Bass is most gladly acknowledged. Aubrey Buxton of Anglia Television, and the British Phosphate Commissioners, contributed significantly to my study of Abbott's booby, and I thank them.

Throughout the long and painful preparation of this complex book, my Editor and Designer, Tom Jenkins, has been expert guide, wise counsellor and tireless labourer. Without him, I should have sunk without trace.

Finally, I am grateful to the Aberdeen University Studies Committee for taking on a book such as this in these days of soaring costs.

Professor V. C. Wynne-Edwards, a pioneer in seabird research and one of the deep thinkers in biology, has given me great pleasure, and conferred a privilege, by writing the Foreword.

GENERAL INTRODUCTION

If one is lucky enough to study spectacular seabirds in wild places, it is easy to identify with them; indeed to become mildly obsessed by them. The literature on seabirds is full of the power of the sea and the fascination of islands. The great pioneers, Martin Martin, Von Humboldt, Beebe, Chapman, Murphy, Fisher, Lockley and many others, evoke, often unconsciously, the tang of seabird colonies.

One begins to understand the subtleties of bird behaviour and ecology only after long and critical observations and many tedious measurements, and obsession can then be an essential driving force. During the past seventeen years my wife and I have watched gannets in winter, on the Bass Rock, when no amount of clothing thwarted the biting wind, sweltered in tropical sun watching red-footed boobies in the Galapagos and sought Abbott's booby in the humid forests of Christmas Island. And we have been fortunate enough to see the others—blue-footed, Peruvian, brown and masked boobies. This first-hand experience encourages me to attempt this monograph on the Sulidae.

There are only nine species, but so many aspects—morphology, taxonomy, distribution, and populations, ecology and behaviour—that it is helpful to explain the structure of the book at the outset. My twin intentions have been to make it easy to locate the facts about each species, and to place these within their biological context. It is no good simply presenting a mass of detail. One of the greatest attractions of the family is its blend of phylogenetic compactness with considerable adaptive radiation. The sulids are all closely related but yet have diverged enough to occupy widely different habitats and to exhibit substantial differences in ecology and behaviour. From them, we can learn a great deal about, for example, the significance of the colonial habit, the role of food in shaping breeding ecology, the value of ritualised behaviour, adaptation and evolution.

So, besides being able to locate descriptions of plumage, growth rates, the timing of breeding, the nature of territorial behaviour etc., the enquirer—ornithologist, ecologist, ethologist or whatever—should be able to find discussions on deferred maturity, recruitment, Clubs, synchronisation of breeding, parental care, the evolution of displays and other such topics. However inadequately these subjects may be handled, their treatment ought at least to show how the available sulid material relates to the concept in question, and thus widen the usefulness of this account.

To achieve both aims it seemed best to present the facts under the nine species and then discuss their comparative and theoretical aspects in separate sections, arranged in much the same way as the species' accounts.

Each species is dealt with under four headings of grossly disparate status: 1. Nomenclature and external features; 2. Breeding distribution and numbers; 3. Breeding ecology and 4. Breeding behaviour. Most of these sections, for each species, have an introduction which aims to lay down some guidelines. I have tried to be consistent in the order in which material is presented, but some differences are unavoidable, since each species has special features and its own areas of most detailed investigation. When looking up information for any species it will be found helpful to read the equivalent sections for the others; relevant material cannot be repeated in them all.

Style is as important as method, and presents real difficulties. The clipped, impersonal reporting enforced by the competition for space in most scientific journals is often tedious. Obviously, this book is hardly a thriller, but the idea has been to make a browsable book, with ideas and atmosphere as well as facts. This is one reason why it is far too long.

The material itself is inevitably patchy. Whilst we are fortunate in knowing many basic facts about sulid breeding regimes, breeding success, mortality rates, age of first breeding, display repertoires etc., which provide a good basis for interpretation, the different species have nevertheless been studied unequally. Furthermore, my own interests have inevitably obtruded. For example, in the account of the Atlantic gannet I would have liked to emulate James Fisher's historical treatment of the fulmar, but have instead offered breeding ecology and behaviour. Moreover, Gurney's monograph is largely historical. I have included very little anecdotal material or early accounts.

I have started with the gannet, about which most is known, and which therefore paves the way for the others. After that the order is mainly one of convenience. However, the blue-footed and Peruvian boobies are very closely related and must go together, with the blue-foot first because it is probably nearer the ancestral form which gave rise to both. The booby nearest to this pair is the brown, and should go before them because in many ways it fits next to the masked, which in turn is a good one with which to begin the booby sequence. This then leaves the two specialised arboreal species, the red-footed and Abbott's boobies, to finish the series.

Most of the behaviour sections are about behaviour at the breeding colony, arranged in chronological sequence under functional headings such as 'site establishment', 'territorial', 'pair formation and maintenance', 'incubation', 'care of young' and so on. Within such categories it is possible to describe everything the bird does and still maintain coherence. It remains, however, to comment on the word 'describe'.

When one watches a complex piece of stylised behaviour like the 'long-call' of the herring gull or the 'choking' of the kittiwake, one has to describe it so that it becomes available for other workers to use. If, instead, one could circulate a ciné record of the 'typical' sequence of events, that would be much better and all that would be required would be an attached name for shorthand reference. Better still would be a number of ciné records showing the variations in intensity at which the behaviour occurs under different conditions (say at the beginning of the breeding season and the middle or end). Even better would be a series showing how neighbouring conspecifics seemed to react. The ideal would be to consult such ciné records taken once every ten million years or so, to monitor evolutionary changes. When words are substituted for visual records, one would like:

1. A description of a typical 'specimen' of the behaviour, accurate enough to permit another observer to identify it instantly.

2. A description of the variability of the behaviour with a note about contexts, including that of the typical form.

3. Evidence for the apparent effect of the behaviour on conspecifics. From this we might be able to see its adaptive value, which is quite as interesting and important as its causal aspects.

4. Indications of the origin of the behaviour and the probable nature of the changes which have occurred as a result of natural selection acting on variability.

So, if one is to 'describe' stylised behaviour in the fuller sense, one must try to cover straight description, motivation, function and derivation, though this is often too tall an order.

'Stylised' or 'ritualised' behaviour must be distinguished from other behaviour. The distinction does not rest on form alone. Rubbing the nape on the oil gland is a highly stereotyped action in sulids, yet we would not call it ritualised, because it has no communication value. It is simply forced, by virtue of the bird's anatomy, to take that form. No nearby bird makes any response. On the other hand, acts that are not highly ritualised may communicate 'mood', so that one cannot debar non-ritualised behaviour from this function. So one cannot use 'communication' as the sole criterion for ritualisation. Assessment must rest on the frequency, degree of stylisation and the evidence for communication value, taken together.

The Morphology and Ecology and Numbers and Distribution sections are straightforward enough and require no special comment, whilst Distribution at Sea is discussed, for all species, in a single comparative section.

Finally, the comparative sections are meant to draw together the implications of much of the factual material assembled under 'species' and to discuss general issues thus raised.

I suppose I ought to apologise for the length of the book; although it is more difficult to write a short book, details do take up space and I was determined to try and make sense of them.

THE SULIDAE ....

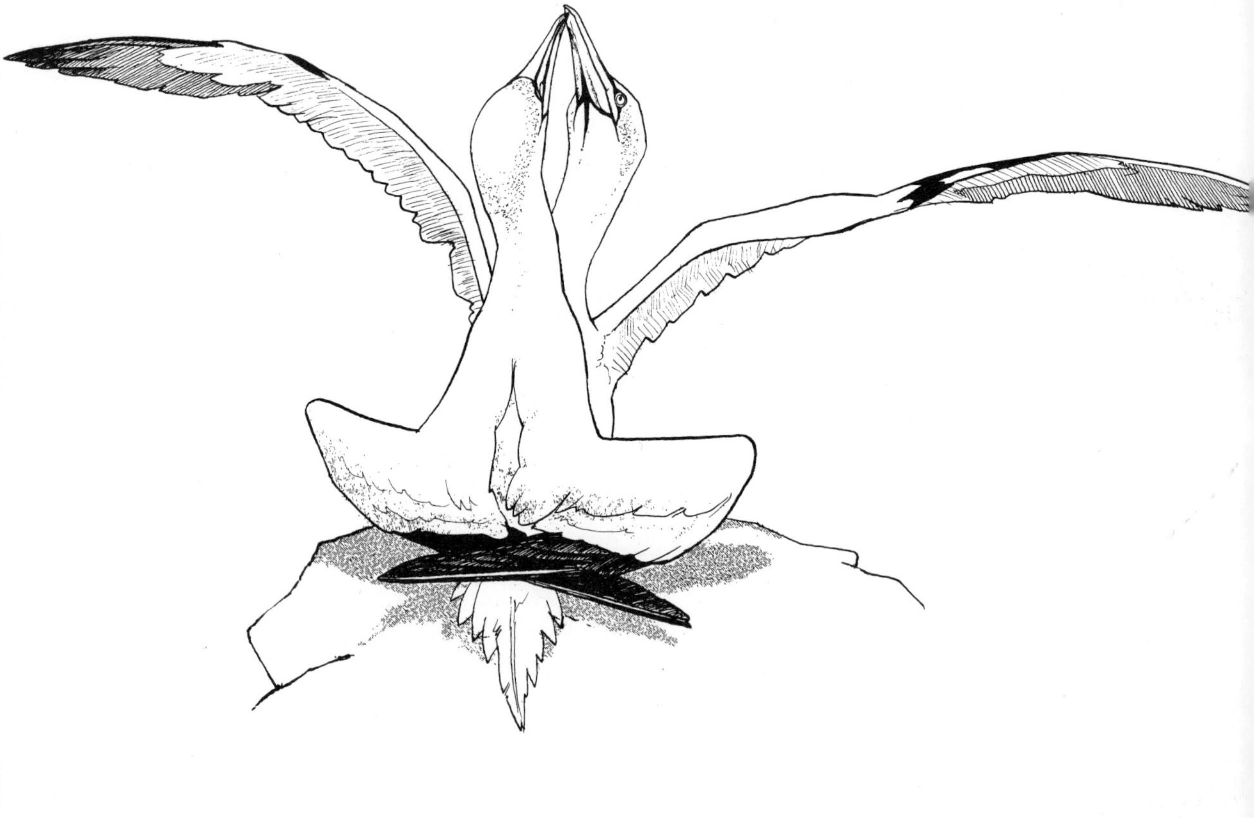

I

Sula [bassana] bassana (L.)

NORTH ATLANTIC GANNET

1. NOMENCLATURE; EXTERNAL FEATURES; MORPHOLOGY; MOULT AND VOICE

NOMENCLATURE

1. *Common*

This subject is dealt with in scholarly manner by Gurney (1913) and it is merely necessary, here, to summarise and add new names. English names for the gannet (by which is meant the Atlantic gannet) have included great booby, spotted booby (referring to juvenile plumage), saithor (Cornish for arrow)[1] and solan goose.

Gannet, gander and goose are all derived from the same germanic root and, going back to the Sanskrit, so are *anser* and *chen* (Latin and Greek for goose). Dialect words 'gant' and 'gaunt' (possibly from the Greek χασκειν = to yawn) may have been applied to the gander and later to the gannet—both birds that gape. The name 'solan (soland, solendae) goose' is most used in Scotland and Gurney favours Martin's (1698) derivation ('sou'l-er' related to Gaelic 'suil' or eye, 'suilaire', sharp-sighted, referring to the gannet's proverbially keen sight when spotting fish. However, 'solan' apparently stems from 'sūla-n' from 'sūla-hin' ('the' gannet in Icelandic).

[1] CELTIC BIRD NAMES. Extracted from 'Old Cornwall', Vol. VI (8), Spring 1965, by Mordon, revised by Dr. Eugene Graves. Mordon = Mr. Nance.

In the old vocabulary 'saithor' is given as naming a "diver" or "plunger", 'mergus vel mergulus' in the Latin, and it has been variously supposed that the bird of this name was a cormorant or a gull. The Gannet was evidently unknown to those who have so rendered 'saithor', and so one of those brilliant bits of descriptive naming that we so often find amongst popular flower or bird names has been missed. Derived from 'seth', an arrow, 'sethor' means "archer", and paints in a word the bent Scythian bow made by the bird's outstretched wings as it takes aim aloft, and the arrow-like dart and splash as it rushes with

Gurney lists 15 variants of solan. Local Gaelic names include the lovely Ian Ban an Sgadan (the white bird of the herring), Amhasan, Amhasag, Asan and the well known Guga (young gannet). Young with a 'wig' of down on the head (Fig. 1) have been called 'Parliament Goose'. Vernacular names in other languages are *Welsh* Gwydd Lygadlon (clear-eyed goose); Gwylan Wydd (gull goose) and Gans; *Icelandic* Hafssúla; *Danish* Havsula, Tossefugl; *Swedish* Sillebas, Hafssula, Bergshammar; *Finnish* Suula; *German* Bass-Tölpel, Schottengans, Seerabe (sea raven); *Dutch* Jan van Gent, Basaangans; *French* Fou de Bassan, Fou Tacheté; *Normandy French* Boubie, Harenguier, Marga (Margot); *Spanish* Alcatraz; *Portuguese* Ganso-patôla, Mascato, Facão; *Italian* Sula bianca. The Russian name is Olusha-glupish, meaning simpleton or dolt.

2. *Scientific*

The controversial matter of the taxonomy of the gannets and boobies (whether to include both in *Sula* or to separate the gannets under *Morus* and what status to give each of the three gannets) is discussed in the Comparative Section (p. 812).

Pelecanus bassanus Linnaeus, Syst. Nat. ed. x, i, p. 133 (1758 Scotland, America); *Pelecanus maculatus*; *Sula bassana* Linnaeus; *Sula alba* Meyer; *Sula americana* Bonoparte; *Sula lefevri* Baldamus; *Sula hoieri* Clusius; *Dysporus bassanus* Illiger; *Moris bassana* Leach; *Morus bassanus*

closed wings on its prey in the water. This wonderful name seems to be of Cornish invention and is not known elsewhere.

Note by Dr. Graves.

. . . Mr Nance's interpretation of 'saithor' "gannet" as derived from 'saith', 'seth', 'saeth' "arrow" was brilliant. It is found only in Cornish, the Welsh being 'morfran', Breton 'morvran', which latter words are not found in Cornish, but the Old Vocabulary has 'marburan' "raven", which should read 'marchvran', . . . (But Nance, in a later footnote modestly says; 'Lhuyd in his manuscript Cornish Vocabulary now in the National Library of Wales, gives "Zethar (i.e. Saethwr) a ganet, Larus cinereus major". He had probably heard this as a living word and it is curious that the true meaning should have been passed over in all other dictionaries, so that until I had seen this MS, at Aberystwyth I had thought that it had been left to me to discover it. Ed.)

Fig. 1. 'Parliament goose', a ten-week-old gannet with downy wig.

Vieillot. *Sula melanura, Sula vulgaris* and *Sula major* have also been used. Here the trinomial (superspecies) *Sula [bassana] bassana* (L) is used (sensu Amadon, 1966b).

Sula derived from *Sulao*—to rob or spoil, according to Morris (1848) but see 'Sula-n' (p. 5).

GENERAL FEATURES

1. *Adult*

With moderately outstretched neck, the gannet is about 90cm long and has a total wing span of some 170–180cm. Like all sulids, in flight it has a distinctive, streamlined look, pointed at both ends due to the stout, sharp beak, tapered body and long pointed tail; the wings also are long and narrow (Fig. 2). The normal flight (see p. 225) is steady and powerful (about 3 beats per second), often with distinctly shallow and rapid strokes of the slightly angled wings, quite different from the buoyant flight of a gull, but wing strokes may be deep and gannets often bank, soar and glide, characteristically lifting a wing and bearing abruptly off to one side. The body is often carried at an angle. It is pure white, except for the black primaries providing black wing tips and the pale yellow or deeper buff head and neck. The whiteness is notably brilliant, especially in sun, marking a gannet at a greater distance than other white birds. The body plumage is extremely thick and quilt-like, often lying on the breast and belly in overlapping ranks. The thick head feathers often have such a compact pile that they lie like a smooth shell. The eyes and bill are pale blue/grey, and the legs and feet dark grey or blackish with greenish-yellow or bluish lines along the digits and up the tarsus.

2. *Juvenile and immature stages*

The juvenile is predominantly blackish, variably speckled with white on wings and back and with a distinctive white V at the base of the tail (Fig. 3). Some are fairly pale below and silvery above whilst others are almost coal black. The eyes are dark, bill black and feet dark grey. Even at this age, the distinctive size and shape are diagnostic. This plumage fades during the first year of life to give a distinctly brownish one-year-old and the underparts and head may become white during this time. Subsequent development is highly variable (see Fig. 4) but typically produces second-year birds which are mainly white on the head and underparts, with black wings and back usually boldly flecked with white and showing conspicuous white epaulettes; third year birds which are as adults except with many black secondaries and tail feathers and usually some black in the scapulars and wing coverts, and fourth year birds which typically retain a few black secondaries and tail feathers.

DETAILED DESCRIPTION

1. *Adult*

The whole of the body plumage, tail feathers, secondaries and greater, median and lesser coverts are pure white. The head, nape and upper neck vary from almost white, through pale yellow to a deeper buff (see below). The primaries are black brown, paler on the inner webs. The shafts of the wing and tail feathers are blackish when new (pale at the base) fading with age to straw colour. The primary coverts and alula are black and the lesser primary coverts along the edge of the wing are white or a mixture of white and black. Primary 10 (outermost) is emarginated on inner web for approximately the distal 7cm and is the longest primary. The outer vane of primary 9 narrows markedly in the distal 10cm and the inner in the distal 7cm. Primary 10 exceeds 9 by 6mm; 9 exceeds 8 by 23mm and so on, to primary one, in the following steps: 39; 42; 39; 35; 35; 31 and 23mm.

The only difference between summer and winter (breeding and non-breeding) plumage is that the head colour becomes progressively paler (and, in the female, conspicuously spotted with white) as summer advances.

The fully buff-coloured head is virtually absent in winter. Over 90 per cent of males attending the colony in January are pale-headed, at best a pale yellowish, whereas a full buff

Fig. 2(a). Characteristic flight position, showing long, narrow wings with long humerus, torpedo-shaped body and pointed tail.

Fig. 3

Juvenile plumage and underwing pattern.

head is a smooth deep yellow with orange-brown overtones. At this time females are perhaps marginally paler but often indistinguishable. Gradually the colour deepens, until by April it is at its best and although males tend to be darker, many females are as dark or darker, and as smooth as their mates (Table 1). Then the females begin to pale and become spotted with white; by late August they are noticeably pale, very patchy, and some are almost white headed. Some males are still very dark, others much paler and a few spotted with white. Some females begin to darken again by October and presumably maintain some of this 'new' yellow throughout winter. Thus the time of year at which the head colour shows most difference between the sexes is late in the breeding season and at this stage it is usually extremely marked.

The buff colour is probably associated with the reproductive physiology, differing in male and female. It cannot be due simply to the ingestion of pigment from food, otherwise the annual and sexual patterns would not occur. Nor is the spottiness of the female due (as has been suggested) to the displacement of head feathers by the male's nape biting; some males

Fig. 2(b)

Wing, foot and tail position
when hanging in wind; underwing pattern of adult and immature.

go spotty and unmated females, who are not bitten also follow the normal course. It is clear, also, that the buff colour is not gained by rubbing the head on the oil gland.

The bill is light blue, tending to grey-blue with black indented lines (nasal grooves or sutures) running along the upper mandible on each side and merging into the black skin on the lores, which in turn encircles the eye and runs, as a line, backwards and slightly downwards from the angle of the gape. The cutting edges of the mandibles are black. A line of black skin divides the forehead feathers from the base of the upper mandible and delineates the insertion of the lower mandible becoming, in the mid-line between the rami, a wider strip extending down onto the throat. Thus, the gannet's face achieves its typical clean-cut appearance with sharp, black outline of the gape and eye area. The inside of the mouth is blackish. Fig. 367 illustrates the bill structure.

The orbital ring is cobalt blue and the iris clear, pale blue-grey, cold and arresting, with a fine, dark outer ring. The pupil appears small. Gurney records a Bass gannet which had

TABLE 1

A COMPARISON OF THE HEAD COLOUR OF MALE AND FEMALE GANNETS

Period	Male darker %	Female darker %	Equal %	Total
February–March	15	2	83	177
April–May	28	6	66	80
June–July	67	19	14	105
August–September	99	0	1	101
				463

brown pigment around the pupils making them appear star-shaped. In albinos (which are extremely rare) the eye is pink.

The legs and feet are black with conspicuous greenish lines along the tops of the toes, converging to run up and across the front of the tarsus. These lines vary in colour from a lime green with a strong hint of yellow, to a deep turquoise-green, the former tending to occur in males and the latter in females. Although the two extremes are easily distinguishable, the distinction becomes difficult in the middle range. The cases which were clearly assignable to one or other category were: yellow lines, males 93, females 13; turquoise lines, males 21, females 71. Of 43 pairs compared in good light, the male was more yellow and female turquoise in 27 cases, both were yellow in 9 and both turquoise in 7. A small proportion of young adults have pale grey webs and legs. These are birds which have recently come to the colony, probably after a prolonged period of life at sea. They darken later in the season. This feature is a useful clue to the status of the bird. Measurements are given in Table 2.

2. *Juvenile and immature stages*

The chick's appearance during development is described along with its growth etc. (p. 90). The gannet's first true plumage differs from that of the adult more than in any other British seabird. The change from the black juvenile to the white adult takes about four years, but sight records of intermediates of known age showed tremendous variation. Even in the nest, juveniles differ in the blackness of back and underparts, and at three years may be almost fully adult in plumage or indistinguishable from an advanced two-year-old. This is partly a consequence of the sulid method of interrupted moult (see p. 18).

The variability in plumage makes it pointless to attempt to match a particular stage with an age expressed in months, but neither can one refer merely to 'a two-year-old' or 'three-year-old', since a bird hatched early in June 1963, for example, is a two-year-old (i.e. in its second year) between early June 1964 and earlier June 1965. If it happens to moult[1] in late

[1] The position is further complicated by the gannet's habit of more or less continuous moult over many months, so that one cannot properly speak of moulting 'in May'.

TABLE 2

MEASUREMENTS OF THE

Area	Weight (g) Male	Weight (g) Female	Culmen Length (mm) Male	Culmen Length (mm) Female	Culmen Depth (mm) Male	Culmen Depth (mm) Female
Bass	2932 (2470 to 3470) 27 cases	3067 (2570 to 3610) 27 cases	100·1 (93·5 to 110) 66 cases	99·2 (92·5 to 104) 66 cases	35·5 (33 to 40) 27 cases	34·3 (32 to 39) 36 cases
Ailsa*	3120 (2400 to 3600) 17 cases	2941 (2300 to 3600) 18 cases	98·2 (92·5 to 104·1) 22 cases	97·7 (92·5 to 100·4) 23 cases	NR	NR
Bonaventure†	3153 38 cases	3284 24 cases	101·7 (93·5 to 107) 37 cases	101·7 24 cases	NR	NR

* S. Wanless (pers. comm.)
† Poulin 1968.

May 1965, its new plumage becomes that of a three-year-old though chronologically the bird is still two. If it moults in July 1965, its late June plumage remains that of a two-year-old though by then it is chronologically already an early three-year-old. One must therefore make what allowance one can for the time of year at which any plumage stage is observed and indicate, in the case of plumages at either extreme of the age-class spectrum, whether it was likely to be just before or just after a moult. Simply because moult is not fixed within a few weeks, there will always remain a large number of cases observed in May, June or July, which are impossible to classify accurately in these terms, even though the chronological age of the bird in question is certainly known.

It seems preferable to take the hatching (rather than the fledging) month as month one of 'plumage life', since the physiological mechanisms underlying moult probably begin before fledging and it is also chronologically month one of life.

Juvenile

The slaty grey-black upper plumage is speckled with white, the 'spots' (white tips) bigger and fewer on the back, scapulars and wing-coverts, are fine and dense around the leading edges of the wings and on head, neck and throat. The finely speckled areas whiten first. A conspicuous V-shaped white patch in the area of the upper tail coverts, lies with its apex towards the tail. The tail coverts have the tips and most of the outer webs white. The axillaries are paler than the underwing coverts, though both often appear uniformly lighter than the upper wing. The primaries and secondaries are blackish brown, glossy, with the bases of the shafts straw coloured and the inner secondaries tipped white, and the rectrices black-brown with small white tips. Beneath, and particularly on the abdomen, the juvenile is generally paler than on top. Some birds are almost coal-black, with few and small white spots. A fairly uncommon form is light silvery grey above and extremely pale beneath. I have seen one albino chick (Ailsa 1973).

Defining three 'shades' of dark (dark, intermediate and light) a sample count of 127 juveniles on the Bass in 1966 comprised 67 dark on the back and intermediate beneath; 19 intermediate both above and beneath; 14 light above and beneath; 12 dark above and beneath, 11 intermediate above and light beneath and 4 dark above and light beneath. So none were

NORTH ATLANTIC GANNET

Wing length (mm)		Tail (mm)		Tarsus (length, mm)		Toe (mm)	
Male	Female	Male	Female	Male	Female	Male	Female
513 (500 to 535) 9 cases	510·2 (484 to 522·4) 14 cases	NR	NR	50·2 (48·5 to 51) 3 cases; thickness 14×11·9 4 cases	50·8 (47 to 59) 12 cases; 14×10·5 1 case	97·7 (96·6 to 98·8) 2 cases	95·7 (92·8 to 98·4) 12 cases
NR	NR	NR	NR	NR	NR	NR	NR
501 (487 to 511·5); 10th primary 291	496 (485 to 503); 300	214·5 (189·5 to 225·5)		62·5 (59 to 65)		NR	NR

(a)

(b)

(c)

(d)

(e)

(f)

(g)

darker beneath than above, but few showed maximal contrast between dorsal and ventral surfaces, the commonest form being medium contrast (dark above and intermediate beneath). This compromise is relevant to the interpretation of juvenile plumage (p. 209). On Grassholm (1975) dark, intermediate and light or silvery feathered young were in the proportions 1:5:2.

The dark brown or black bill becomes slightly greyer in older juveniles; feet or tarsi are black, sometimes dark grey and with faint lines discernible on the webs. The middle claw is pectinated from an early age. The iris is usually dark, so that the eye appears dull blueish or black from a distance, but varies and may be light coloured (greyish), though not clear and conspicuous as in the adult.

Post-juvenile (Fledging to first birthday)

Fig. 4 illustrates the range of plumage in immature gannets. The birds that, at almost a year old, most resemble a newly-fledged juvenile, have become browner above and have lost the white spots on the back, appearing more uniform and in some cases very dark. These birds could easily be mistaken for juveniles and may be responsible for some records of unusually early fledging. Usually, the juvenile pattern of fine spots on head and neck has begun to disintegrate. Often, a light patch develops just below the lores and ear coverts, giving a capped appearance, at others the entire head, nape and neck become mottled brownish on white. Frequently there is more whitening on the throat and the sides of the neck than in the area around the upper breast and on the back of the lower neck. Since the underparts also whiten, this dark area remains as a throat band and (often) as a dark stripe on the hind neck. The throat band may continue onto the base of the neck, but even if it does, it is usually separated from the brown back by a paler patch where the neck runs into the back. In a few birds the head and neck clear completely and begin to show the yellowish suffusion. A few brown speckles, perhaps clumped, may remain anywhere on the head, or a whole tract of brownish feathers, say from the forehead, through the lores and ear coverts and right down the side of the neck, may persist in combination with the yellow suffusion. A very common feature is the retention of brown thigh and flank patches. Combinations of these features occur, so that, for example, one may have a bird, one year old, completely brown above, including neck and head, and brown on throat and extreme upper breast, but with a sharp demarcation between this and the white underparts. A new juvenile, by contrast, even if it were a pale specimen, would not show such a demarcation line. Similarly, the pale area may be only a shade lighter than the head, but indicates the beginnings of the breakdown of the uniformity which characterises the new juvenile and is enough to show that the bird is a year old rather than newly fledged. At

Fig. 4(a). Late first-year plumage; note that the forehead and hind neck have become paler (often, a pale collar is then formed), the under parts have become white, a pale patch has formed distal to the scapulars (this later extends to the leading edge of the wing as an 'epaulette') and the fine white dorsal speckling of the juvenile has been largely lost. The bird is browner than a juvenile.

(b). Late first-year plumage showing white chin and lower breast but persistence of dark feathers as pectoral band and in thigh region—the areas which, in general in sulids, stay dark longest; in many, the thigh patch persists in the adult.

(c). Early second-year plumage; the last remnants of dark on the head are disappearing and the white tail coverts are encroaching laterally and will isolate the dark rump feathers as a 'rosette'. The head may show some yellow, but the beak is not yet clear blue.

(d). Advanced second-year plumage; the erstwhile dark dorsal surface is being rapidly invaded by white, producing a boldly patterned effect.

(e). Early third-year plumage; notice that the wings are not identically patterned. The bill may now be clear.

(f). Fourth-year plumage (highly variable).

(g). Fifth-year; one or a few black secondaries and tail feathers remain. Occasionally late fifth-year birds may be fully adult.

Fig. 4(h). Advanced first-year plumage; note that the iris is already pale and the web lines bright.
(i). Second-year plumage.
(j). Typical fairly late second-year plumage.
(k). Typical fairly late third-year plumage.

the most advanced end of the one-year spectrum there are birds which, in addition to white or yellowish heads, have achieved white or whitish 'epaulettes'—the leading edge between the carpal joint and elbow—and in which the brown back is beginning to break up, particularly in the mid-back and upper rump areas. However, I have no definite, known-age records of such birds and they are so similar to some colour-ringed birds well into their second year that my estimate may be mistaken. My judgment rested mainly on the degree of uniformity of certain brown areas.

A captive bird kept by Gurney from the age of about 15 weeks (he assumed it to be 12, but it was probably slightly older, having fledged and got onto the wing before being blown inland) to about 26 months, actually grew darker at the age of about six to nine months. It began moulting in about April of its first year (at about nine months of age or six months after fledging) and just before it was fully 12 months old had acquired some white at the base of the neck and become wholly white beneath. Its head, neck and throat were brown and white, the forehead retaining many dark speckles. Two birds which I kept from before fledging to (at the time of writing) 15 and 16 months respectively started moulting from April of their first year.

The bill may show signs of blue, though it first passes through a lead to a nondescript, suffused colour. The eye may be becoming pale, though not yet clear.

Year two

From colour-ringed birds it emerges that, even when fully two years old, the least advanced individuals are still all brown above except for white epaulettes, head and neck and the rump V patch. Their underparts are white. At the other extreme I have a record of a bird hatched in June 1961 which in June 1963 had just a few dark feathers on the wing coverts and a mixture of dark and white secondaries and one or more black tail feathers, being otherwise like an adult. In this case it is probable that the bird had been moulting since March/April and just assumed the plumage most of which was to last another year. In plumage it was thus a very new third-year bird, though just about at its second birthday. Between these extremes, the 'typical' plumage of a bird during most of its second year (Fig. 4) is boldly patterned blackish (or deep brown) and white on the rump, back, scapulars and wing coverts, with a mixture of black and white secondaries and some black tail feathers. Underneath it is white; brown patches may persist on thighs and variably on the back of the head and nape, which is suffused yellow. The leading edge of the wing is broadly white. The bill, face and eyes are already blueish.

Gurney's bird became very black on the back when about one year five months, but then began to fade or abrade. Its head and neck lost almost all its remaining brown feathers around November/December (i.e. between the ages of 17 and 18 months). The conspicuous white epaulettes appeared at about 22 months (in one of my birds they had become conspicuous at 13 months) and just as the bird approached a full two years, large white blotches appeared on its dark back and wing coverts and continued to increase in size at the beginning of its third year.

Year three

The most immature-looking bird late in its third year has 'piano key' secondaries, with variably sized black blocks, conspicuously black and white scapulars, and some black or part black feathers in the wing and upper tail coverts and several black tail feathers. Thus, in flight, it retains a boldly patterned appearance, though with white predominating, whereas in the typical boldly-patterned bird late in its second year, either it is difficult to say which predominates or black does. At the other extreme, though rarely, the late third-year plumage may be almost adult. Between these extremes the typical bird during most of its third year, has several black secondaries, one or two black tail feathers and may well show a trace of black on scapulars or wing coverts.

Because most birds are back at the breeding colony in the latter half of their third year or earlier, I have a greater number of accurately aged records. Of 70 sightings, 11 had black on the scapulars; nine of these were seen before June of their third year, i.e. before they were fully three, and a moult fairly soon after the sighting could, in all cases, have disposed of the black scapulars. In addition, they all had several to many black secondaries and two or more tail feathers. 25 had several to many black secondaries and some black tail feathers (it is usually impossible to see the exact number) but no black elsewhere. Eight had several black secondaries but no black tail feathers; 14 had one, two or three black secondaries and one central black tail feather; two had a single black secondary only; two had one black or part-black tail feather only and three seemed fully adult. The remainder had various combinations of the above features, including seven with some black on upper tail coverts and two with a few small black lesser wing coverts in addition to some black secondaries and tail feathers. All the adults were, in fact, seen in the first few days of July and thus were, technically, very early four-year-olds, though it is highly improbable that they would all have been more immature a few days earlier. Nevertheless, it is likely that they had shed some immature feathers in April, May or early June.

Two three-year-old males both found in May (towards the end of their third year) showed individual differences; also right and left wings differed and presumably had not moulted synchronously.

Year four

Just under half of the fourth-year birds seen in the breeding colony before June of their fourth year (i.e. probably before the moult that would take them into their fifth year plumage) already looked adult. The remainder had a single central black tail feather (commonest), one or two black secondaries at the outer (distal) end of the row or, in a few cases, both, except for four cases with several black secondaries and more than one black tail feather. I specify 'in the breeding colony' because it is possible, though perhaps unlikely, that these represented a more advanced sample than the four-year-olds to be found in the Club, of which I have insufficient known-age records to make a direct comparison.

Year five onwards

It is unusual to find a full five-year-old with any immature plumage, but earlier, during their fifth year, traces of immaturity are not uncommon. A very few, aberrant individuals, retain a single black feather indefinitely. We know one breeding female, at least ten years old, with a single black feather in the wing coverts and a breeding male at least 15 years old with a black secondary and a voice which has never 'broken' from the high pitched squeaky one of the juvenile. However, a breeding female, just after her sixth birthday, still had a black central tail feather which she would later definitely lose, so caution in ageing such breeding birds is indicated.

To sum, a gannet may attain fully adult plumage, at the earliest, a few months before its fourth birthday, that is, when three years old. Usually, it does so during its fifth year, probably near the end, that is when four years old. Late birds do not lose the black central tail feathers and/or the remaining black secondaries until they are into their sixth year (five years old), whilst rarely a bird may be actually six years old and still retain traces, which will probably be lost a few weeks later. Gurney's estimate of two years and a half to reach adult plumage was well out!

It is useful to separate the various age classes seen at sea and in the Clubs of non-breeding birds at gannetries. The main problem areas lie at the two ends of the scale. We know that birds in their second and third years are common in our coastal waters and at colonies in the breeding season, from May to August, and their movements back from the areas to which they migrated as post-juveniles, are fairly straightforward. Similarly, they are fairly easily recognisable in the Clubs and breeding colonies, where even third-year birds will not be breeding. But the very retarded first-year birds that, by August, are beginning their second year, pose a real problem in their resemblance to some post-juveniles a few weeks old, and since there are some little-understood features of the latter's movements, it is necessary to make careful identifications. In poor light and at a distance this may be impossible, but on many occasions the browness and the demarcation lines shown by late one-year-olds on upper breast or on the head are useful. Also, anything seen on the wing before August cannot be a bird of the year and anything before mid-August is unlikely to be. It is just at this time and in September, that confusion is likely to arise and is most damaging, because there are many problems concerned with when and where most of the young from our own colonies manage to get on the wing after their days or weeks of swimming; how they learn to fish, their relations with adults at sea; their rate of progress south and so on.

At the other end, the degree of immaturity can be so slight as to be easily overlooked and the analysis of Clubs, the interpretation of immature site establishing and breeding birds and the investigation of sex differences in the plumage of birds of the same age depend on careful definition of the plumage and time of year. Particular attention should be paid to apparent adults seen very far from land in the breeding season. Records could helpfully specify the degree of immaturity by reference to the presence of black secondaries, tail feathers and scapulars in their varying degrees.

MEASUREMENTS AND WEIGHT

Adult measurements are given in Table 2. Weights are misleading unless it is realised that males, in particular, lose weight in the pre-laying period of protracted attendance at the breeding site. Thus, their overall figure is slightly reduced if several males from early in the season are included. The difference in weight between the sexes is not significant, but since wing length and bill are, the male's relatively low weight may be for the reason mentioned above; in mid-winter and when they first return to the colony, males may be expected to be significantly heavier than females. The male's larger bill may have resulted from selection pressure favouring birds with greater gripping power in site competition (p. 162).

Male culmens are 0·9mm longer than female but 1·2mm deeper even though the difference in depth operates over a mere 30mm rather than the 100mm of bill length. This should mean that male bills are disproportionately thicker at the base than those of females and therefore have greater gripping power. Expressed as an index of variability (max. minus min. over mean, multiplied by 100) the male scores 16·5 for length and 19·7 for depth, whereas the female scores 11·6 and 20·4. This implies that the male's thickness relative to length varies hardly at all and much less than does the female's, which means that some females have relatively long thin beaks whereas males do not. Both sets of differences can probably be partly explained in terms of the advantage to the male, in site competition, of a particularly strong bill, thus restricting variability in this feature compared with the female. Naturally, bill shape will confer slightly different abilities when fishing as well as when fighting, but we know nothing about sex differences in feeding habits. The gannet's web has an area of about 63sq cm, the toes (excluding claws) measuring about 95, 90, 70 and 30mm, outer to inner respectively.

Barlee (1956) makes some interesting points about the gannet's morphology in relation to flight. Apparently, its aspect ratio (long, narrow wings) is the highest of any British bird and its wing loading (3lb./sq.ft) is also high. Its pectoralis major muscles are relatively small and its sternum keel shallow. In these circumstances, good streamlining, essential for diving, is also useful in flight. The pointed tail streamlines the rear end but does not provide much surface area and, although opened and lowered when coming in to land to increase drag and enable the bird to fly more slowly without stalling (Fig. 2) it is helped out by the feet. Its shape gives the gannet poor manoeuvrability, a factor which helps skuas to take advantage of it. It is difficult for a heavy bird with narrow wings and small flight muscles to land delicately among a mass of hostile neighbours or on a tiny ledge and for this reason, among others, windy islands and cliffs are sought. Landing involves use of the emarginated outer primaries (which are spread and provide wing slots) and of the alula, which is automatically raised so that a slot is opened just before stalling angle.

The gannet's wing muscles comprise only 13 per cent of its total weight compared with 29 per cent for a turtle dove or a snipe (both birds with enormously rapid acceleration and climb). In particular, the pectoralis minor, which raise the wings during flight, are small, and so wing recovery for the next stroke is slow. Long wings exacerbate these difficulties and in calm conditions take off is very difficult and up to 20 strokes may be required. In 'eed, on the rare combination of calm conditions and a heavy swell, gorged gannets may be quite unable to take off, and there is a record of a large flock having been drifted ashore at Sennen Cove, Cornwall and clubbed to death. One local took away a cartload of corpses.

Gannets land on water either by gliding close over the surface and touching down with feet forward and tail spread and lowered or, most commonly, by a shallow dive. Its casual flight speed in windless conditions was timed over a distance of about 40m at between 34 and 40 m.p.h. (59k.p.h.). When flying over waves in windy conditions they alternate flapping and gliding, using up-currents deflected by the waves. In really strong wind, dynamic soaring is employed; gannets glide down or across wind, turn into it and with a few flaps to accelerate even further, shoot steeply upwards into a faster air layer. When enough height has been gained the process is repeated. To fly in this way is helped by good penetration, best achieved by weight and streamlining. Soaring in standing waves is common practice on the leeward side of the Bass. Probably not all rocks are equally good, for soaring columns are not as much a part of the Ailsa scene, though they do occur and Barlee noted them off Skellig too. The base of the column is about 15m above the sea and the top is often 200m. Fifty to 300 or more birds may be seen ascending, circling in the same direction. Presumably birds use the height to depart on foraging trips or to return to the nest site, but it is usually difficult to follow a bird long enough and I believe many do not make any particular use of the height but ascend for pleasure. However, they certainly do so on occasions; Barlee saw a returning forager leave the incoming skein, fly to the column, mount to the top and glide to its nest. Thus gannets use slope soaring, dynamic soaring and soaring in standing waves. Barlee sometimes saw a second column as far beyond the first as the first was beyond the rock and occasionally even a third.

MOULT

In the Sulidae (as generally in the pelecaniformes) wing moult follows an unusual pattern. Instead of the flight feathers all being renewed annually, moult is semi-continuous. Initially, it begins with the shedding of the juvenile (first generation) innermost (first) primary when the bird is about six or seven months post-fledging and continues outwards at about one feather per month (a feather probably takes 3 or 4 weeks to grow). When the bird is a year old it has already replaced primaries 1 to (about) 6; primary 7 of this, the second generation, is just growing whilst primaries 8, 9 and 10 are still the original juvenile feathers. However, primary 1 is now ready to be replaced again (by generation 3). Thus three generations co-exist in the wing—the distal feathers still belong to the first generation, the middle ones to the second and the innermost to the third. Moult is thus continuous—staged—descendant (Stresemann & Stresemann 1960).

Few, if any, adult gannets moult during the period in which they are attending the colony before egg laying; moult is suspended around January–February and resumed when the egg has hatched in June or July. Of 46 adults examined whilst incubating, 41 were full-winged and the five in moult were all late incubators (end of June) when almost all eggs have hatched. *None* of the 41 adults examined in April or May were in primary moult. By contrast, 15 out of 18 (83 per cent) birds examined in June, July and August with chicks, were moulting primaries; three birds caught in June–July with eggs were moulting, as mentioned above, and two caught on empty sites were not. However, secondaries and tail-feathers may be dropped from about mid-April (laying time) onwards, even in breeding birds. The moult of body feathers becomes extremely noticeable in late May, when eggs are hatching, and the colony is soon enveloped in a miniature snow storm (at this time the body shaking movement (p. 221) concerned with dislodging such feathers shoots up). Once resumed, moult continues at least until November, possibly December. Birds may be growing up to six feathers at a time (up to three primaries in one wing may be completely absent though this is unusual); usually one or two primaries per wing are missing or partially grown at any one time. In 65 per cent of cases wing moult was symmetrical and in 35 per cent the wings had unequal numbers of missing or growing primaries. Because of the staggered moult cycles, adjacent primaries are never absent simul-

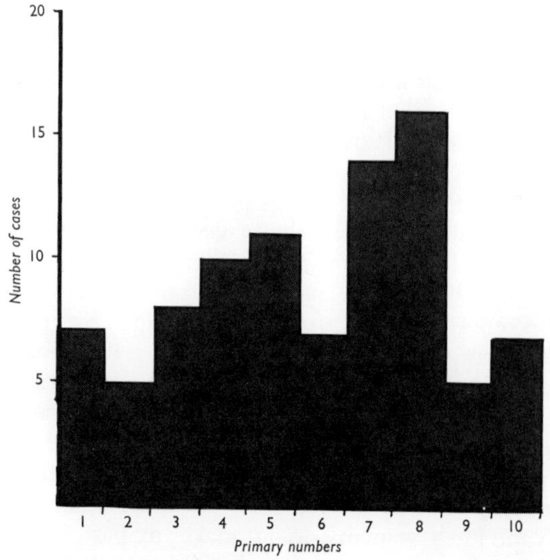

Fig. 5. Moult in the Atlantic gannet; primaries absent or growing in breeding gannets, June/July.

taneously and in fact there are always at least two fully grown primaries between the nearest missing ones. In June–July, when most of my birds were examined, the primaries most commonly missing were 7 or 8 (Fig. 5). This is because, as a result of starting its first moult in about April, the cycle of replacement falls around primaries 7 and 8 at about June and July of each year thereafter. In other words there is no special significance in resuming primary moult at 7 and 8.

The adaptive significance of the pre-laying pause in moult is the energy saving which is necessary at this, the most demanding period of the entire breeding cycle (p. 174). When the young are demanding much food, this is anyway so readily available that the extra burden of moult can easily be borne—an unusual state of affairs. However, even in those sulids in which food is not superabundant, moult is still timed to avoid the pre-laying period and coincide with the feeding of young.

VOICE

Gannets are noisy birds and the metallic clangour of a great colony in uproar imparts some of the excitement which grips the birds. I have sometimes squatted in the very heart of a dense nesting mass in the sunset of a fine July evening, when the flood of incoming birds stirred the group to a frenzy of calling as partners Fenced and single birds Bowed. Waves of harsh sound rose to a crescendo and died away whilst white plumage glowed in the serried ranks. They are noisy at sea when hunting and the old German name Seerabe (sea raven) speaks for itself (I had myself likened a soft 'krok, krok' call which gannets occasionally utter in level flight, to a raven's call). Reinsch (1969) says they call whilst actually diving as well as when swimming on the surface.

The basic call is a rasping 'arrah-arrah', given when flying in to land at the site (about 2 calls per second increasing in loudness and pace) when Bowing, Mutual Fencing, Menacing and fighting. Variations in the intensity and speed correlate with the degree of stimulus; at its loudest, at close quarters, it is a brassy note of deafening volume. It is the 'urrah' call which forms the background clamour at a gannetry. The excited calling which occurs when gannets are fishing or gathering nest material (both communal activities) is slightly different in quality; rather shorter ('rah rah') and often gruffer but less metallic.

A quite different note is uttered as the bird begins to take off or after a hop or a short run. It is a soft, attenuated 'oo-ah" and often sounds like a hollow grown and is typically accompanied by a special posture (Fig. 96) preceding movement. Because it is often given from a strained position, neck stretched and tail acutely depressed, it has been suggested to result involuntarily from physical contortion. However, it is produced by birds in all sorts of normal positions, including flight and may be absent from contorted ones. Although an expiratory sound can be produced by pressing a corpse and expelling air, I think the 'oo-ah' is produced voluntarily.

Atlantic gannets show little sex difference in the 'urrah' call. There may however be a difference detectable by the human ear (as there is in the Australasian gannet.) All the boobies except Abbott's, the red-foot and the Peruvian show a massive difference between the sexes, in some cases associated with a structural difference in the syrinx. Gannet mates recognise each other's voice and those of neighbours, and chicks know their parents' voices. White & White (1970) analysed the sound qualities of the gannet's voice. They concluded that amplitude, perhaps particularly its temporal pattern rather than amplitude as such, was the only property showing consistent individual features. They succeeded in building up an average 'profile' for each of 10 males and showed that these were distinctive. By replaying recordings White (1971) shows that mates recognise each other by their voice but neighbours do not. She gained less positive evidence for the recognition of parents by young, but my field observations show that this does occur.

2. NUMBERS AND DISTRIBUTION

INTRODUCTION

In 1939 Fisher and Vevers led a remarkable investigation into the world population of the North Atlantic gannet, whose inspiration it is interesting to note in passing, was by no means only scientific. They write 'our interest in the gannet has been largely aroused and wholly maintained by the beauty of this great seabird and the romance of its surroundings'. Theirs's was the first accurate assessment ever attempted of the world population of a common bird, and it fulfilled Gurney's prediction that it could be done. Gannetries are few, discrete and conspicuous, large but not impossibly huge. The big white birds, often nesting in regular rows, can be counted from photographs and most recent censuses have used this method. Furthermore, there is a useful body of historical information which together with the series of counts made in the last forty years, gives a uniquely complete picture of the gannet's population over a long period. Fortunately, too, there is now a detailed assessment of the numbers of the Australasian gannet and a reasonable one of the Cape gannet, so the relative standing of these three and their joint world population compared with that of the boobies, can be established. The Atlantic gannet in fact outnumbers the other two by a factor of about six and two respectively

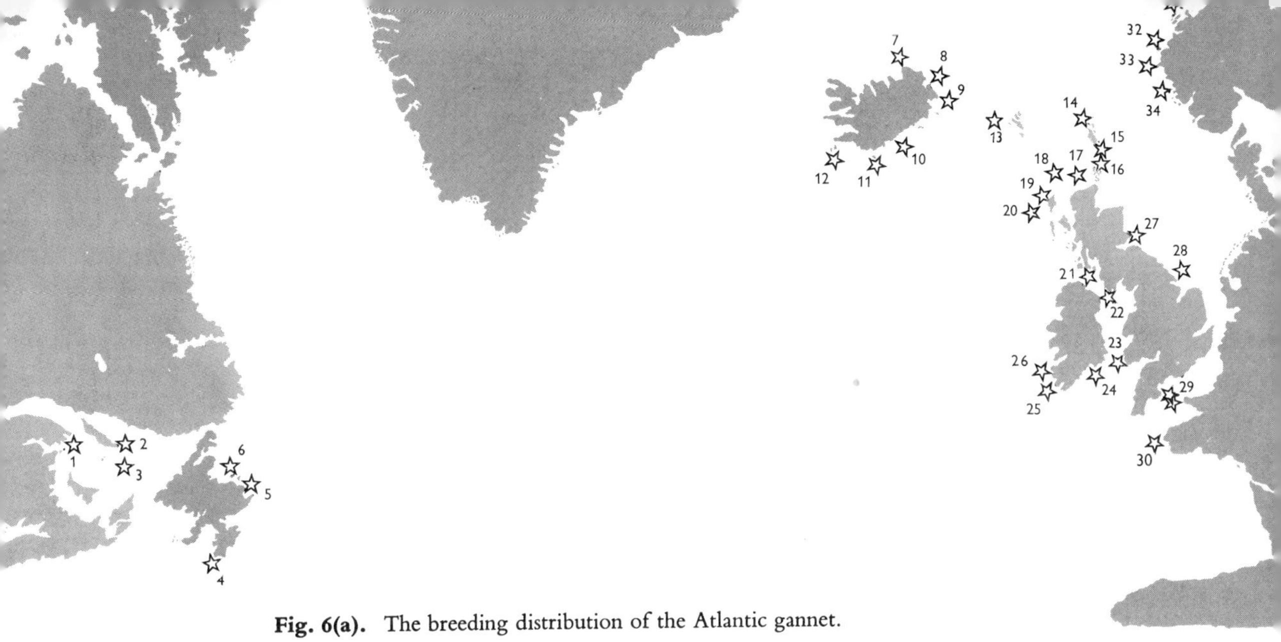

Fig. 6(a). The breeding distribution of the Atlantic gannet.

1. Bonaventure
2. Gullcliff Bay, Anticosti
3. Bird Rocks
4. Cape St. Mary's
5. Baccalieu Island
6. Funk Island
7. Raudinupur
8. Stori-Karl
9. Skrûdur
10. Mávadrangur
11. Westmann Islands
12. Eldey
13. Myggenaes
14. Hermaness
15. Noss
16. Fair Isle
17. Sule Stack
18. Sula Sgeir
19. Flannans
20. St. Kilda
21. Ailsa Craig
22. Scar Rocks
23. Grassholm
24. Saltee
25. Bull Rock
26. Little Skellig
27. Bass Rock
28. Bempton
29. Ortac and Les Etacs
30. Rouzic
31. Runde
32. Mosken
33. Nordmjele
34. Syltefjord

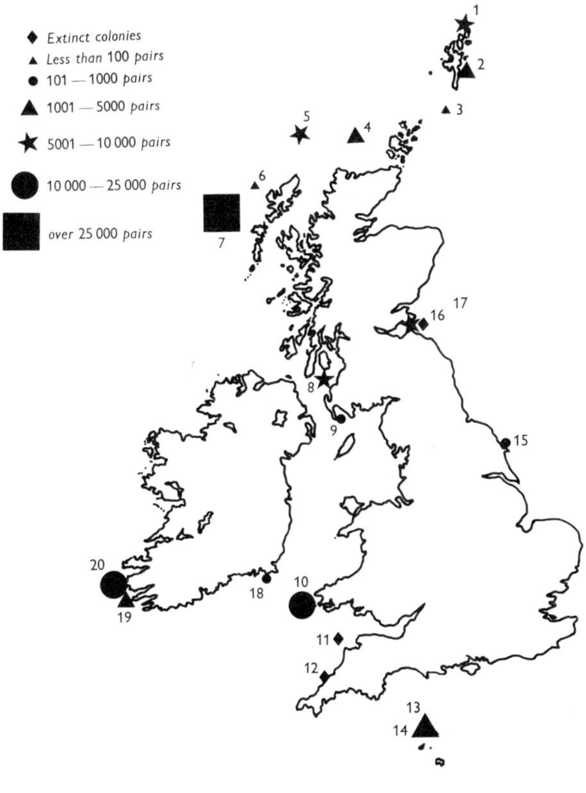

Fig. 6(b)

The distribution of gannetries in Britain.

1. Hermaness
2. Noss
3. Fair Isle
4. Sule Stack
5. Sula Sgeir
6. Flannans
7. St. Kilda
8. Ailsa Craig
9. Scar Rocks
10. Grassholm
11. Lundy
12. Gulland Rock
13. {Les Etacs and
14. {Ortac
15. Bempton
16. Bass Rock
17. Isle of May
18. Saltee
19. Bull Rock
20. Little Skellig

but is itself outnumbered by all three pantropical boobies and by the Peruvian. It thus stands fifth in the world league of nine.

In terms of British seabirds gannets far outnumber the other pelecaniforms (cormorant and shag) but are outnumbered by all other species except the terns, gulls (herring gull excepted) skuas and black guillemot.

Large gannetries certainly are thrilling. Like all seabird colonies they are intensely active, but the power and grandeur of the gannet sets it above lesser fry. Regrettably, space forbids the inclusion of much fascinating but peripheral detail about individual colonies. The gannet's breeding places are wild and often awesome. It is an overwhelming experience to stand on a ledge with gannets on their nests above, below and on each side, the air vibrant with strident calls, alive with the great sailing white birds and pungent with the ammoniacal stench of decaying fish and seaweed, whilst far below the sea swells against the base of precipitous cliffs upon which one is reduced to small and apprehensive stature.

GENERAL FEATURES OF DISTRIBUTION

The North Atlantic gannet inhabits cold, rich waters overlying continental shelves and fishing banks. Reinsch (1969) has shown that the gannet's breeding distribution (Fig. 6) is closely correlated with that of the herring and birds from most if not all British colonies can depend on large numbers of inshore mackerel from June to September. Brun (1972) has postulated a link between the new Norwegian colonies and good fishing areas particularly for herring and capelin and all the St. Lawrence colonies are situated near rich fisheries. As I have repeatedly stressed, every aspect of the gannet's breeding regime is geared to abundant and seasonally dependable food.

The northerly limits of herring in fact go beyond those of gannets, to the Barents Sea and to seas north of the gannet's Norwegian colonies, but other factors, perhaps principally the shortness of the available breeding season, prevent the gannet from extending northwards. The south-westerly limits of the herring are reached at about the entrance to Biscay and the French gannetry, Rouzic, may be about as far south as the species can go. Reinsch (1969) propounds a more detailed hypothesis linking gannets and herring distribution and shows that in both eastern and western Atlantic areas, gannets always breed within easy foraging distance of major herring concentrations. The timing of breeding, too, appears to be adapted to herring movements, particularly to spawning, which make them more accessible.

Around Britain, herring shoals occur mainly in summer. Off the Shetlands, commercial fishing begins in May–June; off northern Scotland in June and off western Britain it continues all year. The biggest catches are made in August. In the North Sea, herrings usually become plentiful in early summer and their zones of abundance move south. Between June and August the most important fisheries are Dogger Bank, Gat and Fladengrund and the first named becomes especially important in September–October. Thus, all west and east coast gannetries are within easy foraging distance of major herring grounds and the fledging season for gannets produces young that may be helped by the September–October southward spread of herring.

In Icelandic waters, herring fishing takes place between June and September off the north coast and moves eastwards during summer. Later, shoals occur off the east coast before migrating to the Faroes, to winter spawning grounds off southern and mid-Norway. The northern Iceland gannetries (Drangey, Raudinupur and Stori-Karl) are thus well sited for herring, whilst off south-west Iceland Eldey and the Westmann Islands are on the doorstep of herring concentrations, spring to autumn, in Faxa Bay.

There is summer herring fishing north of the Faroes of stocks situated in the boundary zone between polar waters and the Atlantic.

Mackerel (see Fig. 7) are similarly within foraging range of all west Atlantic gannetries between June and October. The presence of these two extremely nutritious fish, both of which have for centuries been known to form a staple part of the gannet's diet, at the time of maximum requirement, is undoubtedly a main factor in the gannet's breeding biology and a complex system of adaptations hinges on this (p. 78).

The Gulf of St. Lawrence, the gannet's west Atlantic breeding area, almost half the size of the North Sea, is an Arctic (boreal) sea covered with sea ice in February and early March.

There is a good correlation between areas of the Gulf with high mineral concentrations and with seabird stations. Bird Rocks and Bonaventure, the two principal colonies, lie in an area fed by currents coming from zones of high primary productivity and rich in spawning fish.

Whereas in February and March herrings occur mainly well south of the gannet's breeding area, they move in spring to George's Bank off the southern tip of Novia Scotia and from May to October (the gannet's breeding season) are found, and caught commercially, in the Labrador Current and in coastal waters around the Gulf of St. Lawrence and around Newfoundland. Massive shoals of spawners and pre-spawners are found in September and October north of George's Bank. At this time they ascend to surface waters not only at night, but even on sunny days and are thus highly accessible to gannets. They may thus provide a further 'reason' for young gannets fledging in September.

Besides good fishing, rocky islands, often with towering cliffs, are a feature of the gannet's breeding areas. The combination of remote (and therefore safe) and windy, cliff-girt islands and dependable concentrations of fish occur notably off the north and west coasts of the British Isles and here, in the eastern North Atlantic, the world's major gannetries are located. The British and Irish colonies together contain more than 70 per cent of the world population. The offshore waters to the north and west of Scotland could be considered the focal point of the world population. The St. Kilda complex holds the largest gannetry, some 50 000 pairs (though this is less than half the population of Bird Rocks in the St. Lawrence, early last century) and this sector includes Myggenaes, Hermaness, Noss, Sule Stack and Sula Sgeir, altogether some 80 000 pairs or nearly 40 per cent of the world's total. North of this concentration lie the Icelandic colonies, altogether some 21 000 pairs. Grimsey used to be the gannet's most northerly breeding station but that distinction now belongs to the Norwegian colony of Syltefjord at 70°35′N. well within the Arctic circle. The colonies in Faroes and Shetlands link Iceland with the cluster of gannetries off north-west Scotland, south of which the predominance of the west coast of Britain continues, with large colonies at Ailsa, Grassholm and Little Skellig. With the establishment of colonies in the Channel Islands and Brittany, the gannet has extended its East Atlantic range further south than ever before, to (at Rouzic) 48° 53′N. It thus spans 22° of latitude. It is debatable whether its considerable food requirements during the breeding season will allow it to go much further south, for it needs large numbers of sizeable and nutritious fish and it is not clear that the Bay of Biscay could provide these.

The east coast of Britain lacks suitable islands except for the Bass Rock, which so far as gannets are concerned, has dominated this seaboard for centuries and indeed may have done so ever since man inhabited the coastal regions and could ransack low-lying islands a few miles offshore. The western seaboard of Europe is little favoured and until the recent establishment of Rouzic in the south and the Norwegian colonies in the north, entirely lacked gannetries. Again this may be due to the relative lack of suitably high and cliff girt islands. It may be noted that the present-day Norwegian colonies are, on the whole, situated on low islands and suffer severely from interference.

In the western North Atlantic there are some 33 000 pairs, over 70 per cent of which breed in the Gulf of St. Lawrence and the rest on the Atlantic coast of Newfoundland (Fig. 26). Until the eighteenth century, this population was able to utilise the flat tops of some islands in vast numbers but spectacular destruction terminated this habit and several of the colonies founded this century would appear to be in sub-optimal breeding habitat.

At present (1976)[1] there are 16 colonies in Britain (counting Orkneys and Shetland and counting Channel Isles as one) and Ireland (155,500), 7 in Iceland and the Faroes (22 000 pairs), 6 in Canada (33 000 pairs), 4 in Norway (some 600 pairs) and 1 in France (2500 pairs). The eastern Atlantic has probably always held more colonies than the west, but last century the enormous colony on Bird Rocks, estimated at some 125 000 pairs (Fisher & Vevers 1943–44), tipped the balance of actual numbers in favour of the west.

As mentioned, this pattern of distribution is dominated by the presence of suitable nesting islands within foraging distance of rich feeding areas. It cannot be too strongly emphasised however, that the actual *numbers* of gannets are not limited by shortage of nesting sites. At most gannetries there is still considerable room for expansion. Sule Stack, Little Skellig and Eldey come nearest to full capacity. The northern limits of distribution may be fixed by the length of the gannet's breeding cycle. This amounts to some 26–30 weeks and thus, although many

[1] Although I say 1976 I have 1976 figures for only some colonies and I take the latest counts for the remainder.

islands off Greenland, Spitzbergen, Novaya Zemlya and Franz Josef Land could undoubtedly support gannets, the Arctic summer would be too short. Even as it is, the gannet has compressed its growth period compared with the boobies (see p. 898). The factors limiting its southern extension are not understood but may be a combination of lack of suitable islands and sub-optimal food supply during the period of maximum growth of young. At present the gannet is increasing its range and numbers on both sides of the Atlantic. This trend is discussed after the section on individual gannetries.

THE WORLD'S NORTH ATLANTIC GANNETRIES

1. Definition of terms and comments on the validity of census figures

There is a good deal of confusion in the literature when it comes to deciding exactly what gannet-counters actually count. Early counts were sometimes expressed in terms of individuals, but Fisher & Vevers (1943–44) used 'pairs' and virtually all subsequent estimates have done so. The above authors, however, frequently refer to their estimates in terms of 'breeding pairs' which is incorrect. Actually, they are *site-owning individuals*, many of which *are breeding*, most of which *have nests*, and the great majority of which (but not all) *have mates* and therefore do represent pairs. This becomes clear when one considers the categories of birds that constitute a gannetry. These are: (1) *Breeding pairs* (2) *Non-breeding nest owners* (3) *Non-breeding site owners* (4) *'Casuals'* at the fringes or on spare ledges, which are not strongly attached and may spend only a small amount of time there (5) 'Club' birds (see also p. 151) which may gather in large dense groups beyond the colony. Category (1) should be defined as any pair which attempts to breed that season. Thus, depending on the timing of the count, the figure obtained will be below the true one because, in the case of a count in April or May, some pairs will not have laid, or in June and particularly July, some will have lost their egg or chick. In practice the only way to obtain a figure for *breeding* pairs in a large colony is to count the pairs with nests and allow a percentage for those that have yet to lay or have laid and lost. In category (2) the non-breeding nest owners may be, (a) new pairs that build but do not lay, (b) possibly experienced pairs taking a rest-year, (c) pairs about to lay or, (d) pairs that have lost egg or chick. It is certain that all counts purporting to estimate pairs include *at least* all these four, and probably others (see below). Normally, at least one bird in each pair in all those categories will be on guard. Category (3) introduces difficulties for without any doubt, many such pairs are included in estimates of breeding pairs, gained either by direct count or from photographs,

KEY

•		No fish
○	●	10 — 49 fish
△	▲	50 — 99 ,,
□	■	100 — 199 ,,
◇		200 — 499 ,,
◖	●	500 — 999 ,,
▲		1000 — 4999 ,,
///		Breeding area

Winter — Spring spawners

Summer — Autumn spawners

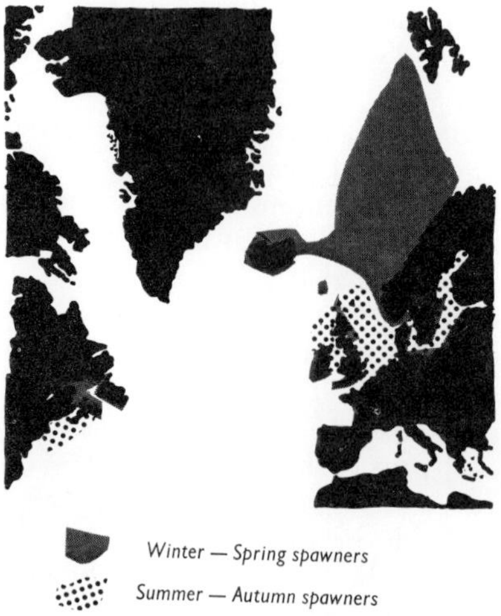

Fig. 7(a). Distribution of mackerel *Scomber scomber* in the North Sea, July 1960. (After Sarhage 1964 in Reinsch 1969.)

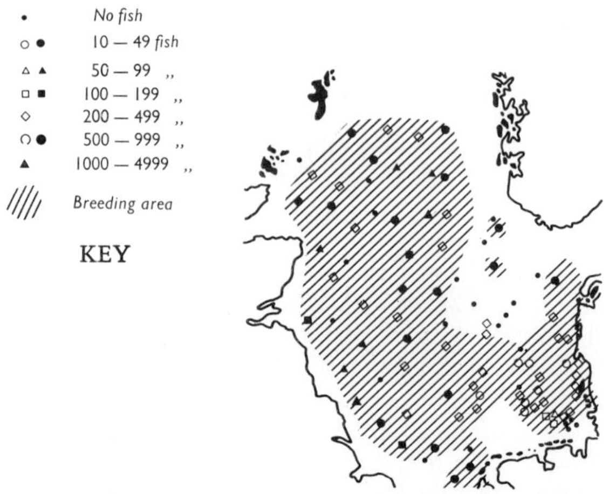

Fig. 7(b). Distribution of sprats *Sprattus sprattus* in the North Sea, July 1960. (After Sarhage 1964 in Reinsch 1969.)

since it is often impossible to see whether the bird has a nest or not. Also, such birds may sit, as though incubating. This might not matter were it not for the fact, widely unappreciated, that a proportion of such sites are completely unoccupied at any one time. The differences between counts in successive years could be substantially affected, for the proportion of unoccupied sites varies both with time of day and with season (see Appendix 2). Also, site owners are warier and a large number could be absent as a result of a recent scare by a passing boat or an aeroplane. This is an imponderable which one can do little or nothing to evaluate, but it could make nonsense of counts which claim high accuracy. In my opinion, the potential error in most gannet counts is considerably greater than is commonly allowed; often, 20–30 per cent inaccuracy would not surprise me. Category (4), the casuals, grade into (3) and are probably included in most counts on cliffs but may be excluded from some counts on flatter ground since they are sometimes fairly distinct, being rather raggedly and widely spaced, lacking any nest, and looking more like category (5), the Club birds. These latter are often recognised correctly by census takers and excluded from totals of pairs or individuals. However, they *can* cause trouble in interpreting photographs. For example Dixon (1971) mentions their propensity for gathering near nesting ledges, and implies that they could contribute substantially to the huge variation which has been noted in counts of the same sections of St. Kilda in different years (up to 215 per cent in one section, Dixon 1971) whilst at Bempton, Club birds occupy ledges among breeders.

Thus, when counts are given in *nests*, the criterion is clear enough but does not justify any assumption that they are breeding pairs; when the total is in *pairs* it includes several categories (above) and is a minimum because an unknown proportion will be absent. Estimates are usually straight counts of individuals, which correspond to occupied sites so long as allowance is made for the proportion of sites at which both members of the pair were present at the time of the count. When it is given in *breeding pairs* it implies that corrections have been made for non-breeders but this, in fact, is almost never done. Although Fisher & Vevers said, in their opening paragraph, that 'observers were asked to make accurate counts of the number of breeding pairs' and treated the results as though this had been done, in fact it had not. In terms of comparison between different colonies and years, this does not matter. It is, however, relevant to any interpretation of the rate of increase that can be expected in a colony as a result of its own output. Finally, when counts are given as numbers of *individuals* it is presumably a straight count and the remarks made under 'pairs' apply, with the additional rider that some sites are occupied by unmated males. When considering rates of increase, it should be remembered that anything above 5 per cent per annum means that immigration is occurring (see p. 64); in fact 3 per cent is nearer the true rate of intrinsic increase.

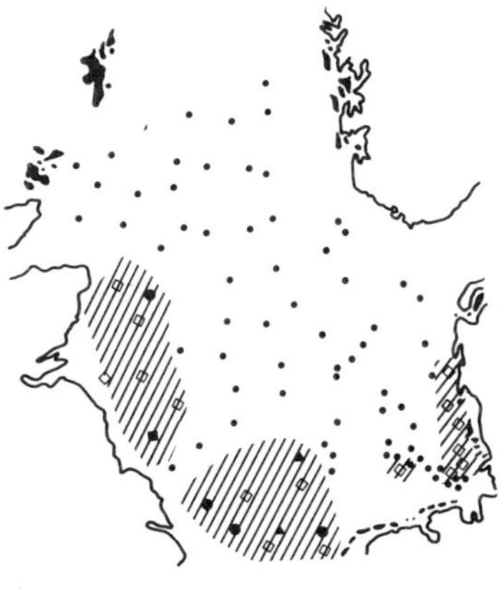

Fig. 7(c). Distribution of herring *Clupea harengus* in the North Sea, July 1960. (After Sarhage 1964 in Reinsch 1969.)

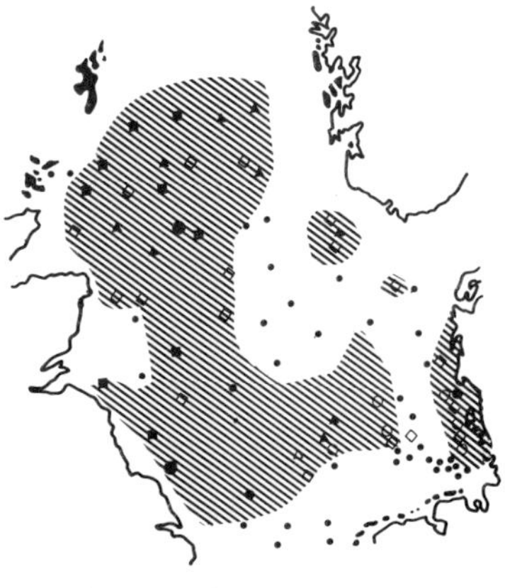

Fig. 7(d). General distribution of herring in the north-west and north-east Atlantic. (After Parrish & Saville 1965.)

In the account which follows, I have tried to include enough information for each gannetry to make its past history clear but space forbids inclusion of *all* the known details which, prior to 1939 and 1910 respectively, are to be found in Fisher & Vevers (1943, 44 and references) and Gurney (1913). The latter's historical treatment is admirable and nothing can substitute for the long and enthralling quotations which Gurney gives.

The treatment of gannetries is by regions, which largely but far from entirely correspond with those used by Fisher & Vevers, and which form the basis for the subsequent discussion of general trends. A list of gannetries is given in Table 6, p. 71.

2. *South-west Britain group*

(*a*) *Grassholm, Pembrokeshire, Wales* (Latest count 20 370 nests, 1975)

This low, basalt rock of some 9 hectares lies 17·7km north of Milford Haven, Pembrokeshire. It is more than half bare with large areas of outcropping rock. Its history seems obscure but aerial photographs reveal the outlines of possibly Bronze age settlements, which presumably could have caused the extinction of gannets at that time, for there are no high cliffs to act as reservoirs, as there are on some other relatively accessible gannetries, such as the Bass or Ailsa Craig. The present gannetry was founded certainly by 1860 and possibly by 1820. The long period during which Grassholm stood empty of gannets embraces that in which Irish and Scottish gannetries were being heavily exploited and presumably there were too few pioneers and 'floaters' (see p. 68) to re-colonise old gannetries or establish new ones. Between 1886 and 1913 there were probably never more than about 300 pairs (Salmon & Lockley 1933) and in most years disturbance and exploitation by fishermen ensured that fairly few young were reared—probably less than 100 per year. In 1922 there were 800–1000 nesting pairs and in 1924 nearly 2000. The 1933 count by Salmon and Lockley is particularly valid because each carried it out independently from both sea and land photographs. Their totals tallied well (5045 and 5181 adults) which allowing 7 per cent of sites occupied by pairs meant 4750 occupied sites. In addition there was a Club of some 1500 birds, mostly immature. At that time the colony extended from West Tump almost to the extreme northerly point, an area of about one hectare, the greatest extension having travelled north-east. They calculated that the annual increase between 1914 and 1922 was about 16 per cent but between 1922 and 1924, 42 per cent per annum. The increase of 2750 from 2000 pairs in 1924 to 4750 in 1933, however, they claimed could have been achieved by an increase of 10 per cent per annum. However, on the fairly generous assumption that, in any one year 80 per cent of the pairs occupying sites actually breed, of which 80 per cent do so successfully, and that of the young fledged, 30 per cent survive to breed for the first time in their fifth year and 10 per cent of adults die each year, the increase produced by the 2000 pairs of 1924 would by 1933 have been 1167. This works out at an annual increase of 6·4 per cent per annum. Thus, less than half of Salmon & Lockley's increase of 2750 between 1924 and 1933 is likely to have come from Grassholm's own output. So even in this period of relatively slow increase (and of course much more so between 1914 and 1922), there must have been considerable immigration—a conclusion opposite to that drawn by the above authors, who considered that the increase could reasonably have come from within. They did of course recognise that the more substantial increases, particularly between 1922 and 1924, must have resulted from immigration and suggested Skellig and Bull Rock as probable sources. Subsequently, Grassholm continued its rapid increase; 5875 in 1939, 9200 in 1949 (the annual increase between 1939 and 1949 works out at 4·6 per cent), 15 528 in 1964 and 16 128 in 1969. But the increase was tailing off rapidly and between 1964 and 1969 averaged only 0·8 per cent each year, which means that Grassholm was either exporting or, much less likely, that from at least 1960 onwards, had suffered a very low breeding success. Counts from aerial photographs taken in 1970 and 1972 indicate that the 1969 figure may have been a slight over-estimate, for they yielded 15 400 ± 500 pairs and 15 100 ± 500 pairs respectively. On the other hand, despite the closeness of the 1964 and 1972 counts, it seems clear from photographs taken in both years that the colony did increase in extent during that period, the probable answer being that the 1964 estimate was slightly too high. The 1973 photographs (D. C. Emerson, pers. comm.) show that the colony had crossed the ridge that bisects the island and which, until that year, hid the gannets from the south-east. Emerson's

Fig. 8(a). Grassholm, May 1973. Note the avoidance of the splash-zone and the regular spacing where topography permits.

Fig. 8(b). Grassholm from the summit, August 1975. Note the clean outer edge of the colony.

comments on the situation in 1974 are that there are far more breeding birds near the summit and on the north-east side than in 1972 and 1973 while areas to the south-west that were occupied in 1971 and 1972 were deserted except by Club birds. Cullen & Pratt (1976) made a count from aerial photographs taken on May 7th and August 5th 1975 and arrived at a total of 20 370 occupied nests. This indicates that the rate of increase again accelerated sharply (between 1972 when there were 15 100, and 1975), after having slowed right down for a period of several years. As in the previous periods of massive increase cited above, immigration must have occurred, for at an increase of three per cent per annum, the figure would have been under 17 000. By 1975 the breeding birds had extended beyond the steep ridge from which one used to be able to scan the huge snowfield of nesting gannets sloping down to the south-west rock.

The Club at Grassholm is now very large (c. 3000 + in August 1975 and June 1976). It was noted to be large in 1933 (mainly immature) though absent or small in the 1920s. Probably a large Club is present when a gannetry is thriving; certainly, in some cases, it increases markedly just at the time the colony is growing quickly.

(*b*) *Little Skellig, Kerry, Ireland* (Latest count 20 000 pairs 1970 but reduced in 1974).

'Seen from Puffin Island the Little Skellig stands out grandly pyramidal rearing its tall head 136m into the blue vault of heaven' (Gurney 1913). It lies 12km off the rocky coast of Kerry and is now bare rock with hardly a flat patch on it. It is an old gannetry. Birds bred there in large numbers as early as 1700 but exploitation reduced it to about 1000 in 1850 and some 30 pairs by 1880. Astonishingly the 150–200 pairs of 1882 had increased to several thousands by 1890 and an estimated 15–20 000 birds by 1906. The 1913 figure was 8000 pairs and in 1930, 10 000 pairs, at which total it was said that almost every available ledge was occupied. Estimates in 1938, 1939 and 1941 also gave 9000–10 000 pairs (west 1000, north 5000–6000, south 3000) but in 1949 there were an estimated 12 000 pairs and in 1966, 17 700. A count from photographs gave 18–20 000 pairs in 1969 and 20 000 in 1970 (Evans, pers. comm.), a figure which proves yet again that even when a gannetry looks full, there is often a great deal of available space. A hasty survey by Evans in 1974 showed a substantial decline, with some bare areas which in 1970 were covered with gannets. These recovered in 1975.

Skellig is of outstanding interest first in having climbed from 200 to several thousand pairs in eight years, an increase which, even allowing a massive potential error in estimating, must have depended on large-scale immigration, and second in having continued to increase until, at twice the numbers it appeared capable of holding, it is probably now exporting large numbers, and may well have been doing so for several years. The immigrants in the early days must have come from the Scottish colonies to the north (the implications of this are discussed later), and the emigrants from Skellig probably supplied Grassholm, Rouzic, the Channel Islands and perhaps interchanged with some Scottish birds (see p. 67).

(*c*) *Bull Rock, Cork, Ireland* (Latest count 1500, 1969)

Until the founding of the Saltee colony in 1929 the Bull Rock was the only Irish gannetry, besides Skellig, from which it is 27km south-south-east. Founded, apparently, about 1856 it had grown to many hundreds by 1868 (immigration being responsible) and to about 2000 by 1884. By 1891 the population was down to about 200, a decrease plausibly attributable to blasting operations and interference by workmen, and by 1908 was still only about 600. Subsequent acceptable counts are 442–500 pairs (1938), 295 pairs (1949), 550 pairs (1955) and c. 1500 pairs from a direct count in 1969 (Evans, pers. comm.). The latest count thus takes it beyond any former strength and together with the increase in the Skellig with which the Bull probably exchanges birds, suggests that both may be now near the limits of their respective capacities, and the source of recruits to other colonies.

(*d*) *Great Saltee, Wexford, Ireland* (Latest count 193 nests, 1975)

I owe most of the details in this account to R. F. Ruttledge and from 1972 onwards, to Cabot (1976). The gannetry is at the southernmost tip of the island, which has a cliff about 30–40m high. Apparently, suitable cliff nesting space is limited on Saltee; Cabot estimates a capacity of about 1000 pairs; there is, however, space at the top of the cliff. The gannets first nested only on the main cliff faces, but later expanded and are now somewhat diffuse. The year in which birds were first known to breed (1929) is not in doubt, but there have been conflicting reports about whether there were two pairs or only one. Kennedy (1961), who was probably the discoverer, gave one pair, but elsewhere gave two. Ruttledge thinks there probably was only one but most of the general accounts (including Witherby 1940) and the original entry in the Saltee log book, give two. The point is of theoretical interest because it is not known for certain that a single, completely isolated pair of gannets could breed. Coulson believes that such a pair of kitti-

Fig. 9. Little Skellig, 1964. Note that there is some unoccupied, but suitable space. *Photo:* A. W. Diamond.

Fig. 10. Bull Rock. The birds at mid-base are probably Club birds.

wakes could not. In any case, the egg, or eggs, was lost and the colony teetered along for the next 20 years never more than three pairs strong and not known to rear more than a total of three young between 1929 and 1944. The colony started to increase more rapidly from about 1954, in which year it still numbered only about four pairs, though these bred successfully. In 1955 at least eight pairs bred and some 50 birds were present. According to the Saltee Observatory log, 1956 saw 17 nests (Kennedy 1961 gives 14) but only seven were known to hold eggs or young. In 1957 12 young were reared; 1958 at least 15 young hatched; 1959 at least 24 young reared; 1960 about 60 nests were built and at least 28 young reared; 1961 at least 65 nests built and at least 48 young hatched; 1962 the maximum nest count was 10 fewer than in 1961

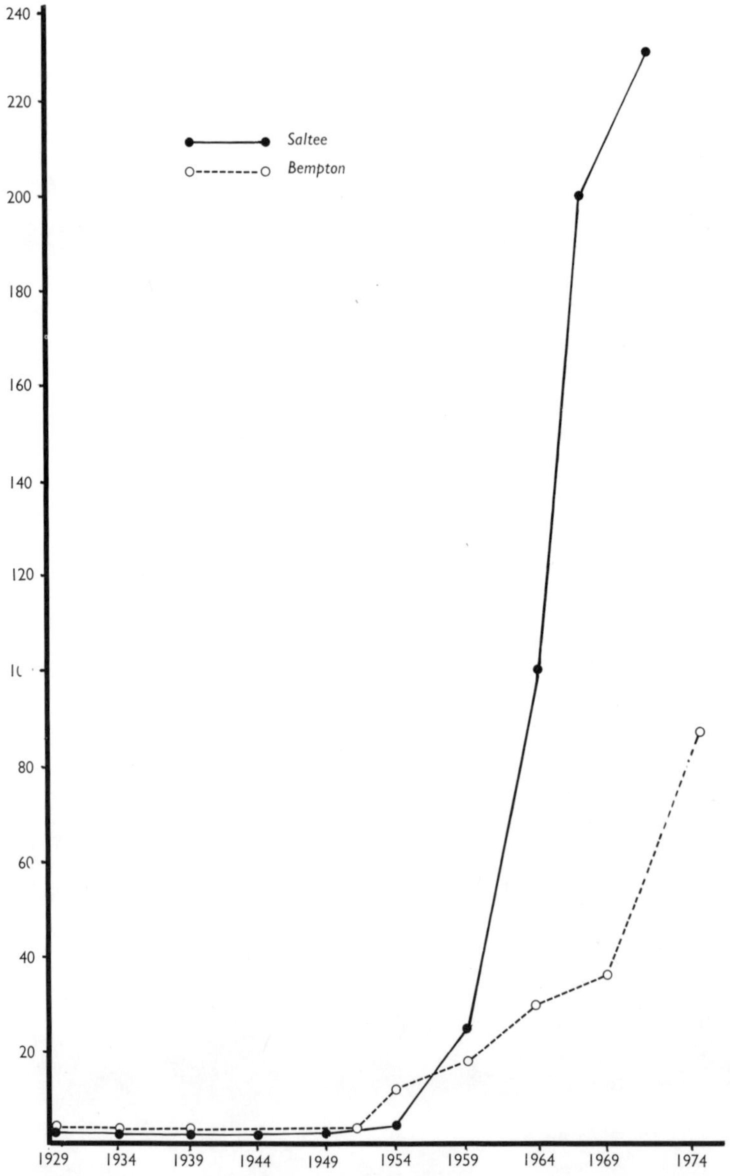

Fig. 11. The growth of two gannetries, both founded at about the same time but one of which (Saltee) is open to immigrants from a range of west coast colonies and the other (Bempton) open mainly (perhaps only) to immigrants from the Bass. Note the apparent 'take-off point' in both.

(though owing to the difficulty of seeing all nests this does not necessarily mean a decline); 1964 at least 150 young hatched and up to 500 gannets seen on the cliffs; 1966 about 114 occupied nests; 1967 at least 200 nests and 150 young hatched; in 1971 at least 175 pairs nested (this figure seems surprisingly low and in view of the difficulty of checking the entire colony, may be a considerable underestimate) and in 1972 there were 225–250 occupied nests, though Cabot gives 175. Cabot's figures for 1973, 74 and 75 are c. 200, 200 and 193 nests.

The rapid growth since 1954 has certainly depended on immigration and it is interesting to see (Fig. 11) that Saltee has grown so much more rapidly than Bempton which was founded at almost exactly the same time and like Saltee struggled along ineffectually for many years. As discussed on p. 67 I suggest that great numbers of young recruits from most or all the gannetries off the west coast of Britain move around investigating different colonies before settling in one. Saltee is thus likely to receive more immigrants than is Bempton, on the east, where the only other colony is the Bass. Once Saltee passed a numerical threshold, it apparently became highly attractive to recruits, a phenomenon for which there is some evidence (p. 135).

(*e, f*) *Ortac and Les Etacs, Channel Islands* (Latest count 1000 pairs and 2000 pairs respectively, 1969).

The bare rock of Ortac is about 1350 sq. m, 24m high and composed of ancient sandstone. Gannets started nesting there probably in 1940 (one nest) and in 1946 Dobson & Lockley visited the islands and photographed them from the sea and air, estimating c. 250 pairs on Ortac and c. 200 on Les Etacs. Ortac's most suitable nesting areas are on the crown and eastern face. The above authors predicted that there would not be room for more than about 500 nesting pairs but the population in 1950 was 570 pairs and in 1969 about 1000 pairs.

Les Etacs (Garden Rocks) are two groups of igneous rock about 600 sq. m and 39m high. The gannets colonised mainly the largest, most westerly islet, which had some soil and vegetation. In 1946 there were 190 nests on the two sides of the summit ridge, about 130 on the northern slopes and 60 on the southern. A further 10 pairs occupied a pinnacle in the eastern

(*a*)

(*b*)

Fig 12(a). The increase in the gannetry on Rouzic
(b). (Brittany) 1953–63. (From Milon 1966.)

Fig. 13. Ailsa Craig, showing mainly the west side. Note the very limited extent of the spread onto the slopes above the cliff top. (*Photo:* Aerofilms.)

group of rocks, some 100m from the main colony. The population in 1960 was 1010 pairs and in 1969 c. 2000 pairs (counts from land and sea).

The increase in the Channel Island gannets has certainly depended on immigration probably from the Irish colonies, which are about 600km away. Grassholm is 312km distant and was itself expanding rapidly at the same time as the Channel Island gannetries. The problem of interchange between gannetries is discussed on p. 65.

(*g*) *Rouzic, Brittany, France* (Latest count 2500 pairs, 1967)

Rouzic, a Nature Reserve in Les Sept Isles, is the gannet's most southerly breeding station

in Europe, as it is also for the fulmar, which was first noted there in 1960. It was established around 1939, when the two Channel Island colonies were also established. In 1939 there were 30 nests but by 1947 the number apparently still remained much the same, though this was probably an artefact due to disturbance, since the following year 92 eggs were counted. Milon (1966) counted the number of nests for the years 1950–65, with an estimated potential error of around 10 per cent: 1950 (100); 1955 (550); 1956 (690); 1959 (1000); 1960 (1150); 1961 (1350); 1962 (1650); 1963 (2000); 1964 (2400); 1965 (2600); 1967 (2500).

3. *West and north Britain group*

For reasons discussed on p. 65 I feel unable to follow Fisher & Vevers in separating a western and a northern region; indeed, the interchange between the south-west region and the combined west and north area makes even the present division purely a matter of convenience.

(*a*) *Ailsa Craig, Ayrshire, Scotland* (Latest count c. 16 000 occupied sites, 1976)

'Elsay, . . . quherin is ane grate high hill, round and roughe, and ane heavin (haven) and als aboundance of Soland Geise.' The Craig stands in the Clyde as the Bass in the Forth, but more massively; its vast hump beautifully symmetrical, towers 340m and the Barestacks fall more than 183m sheer. Besides the Bass, it is the only easily accessible Scottish gannetry, lying 15km west of Girvan. Sheer cliffs rise from the rocky foreshore on the north, west and south sides whilst to the east the silver boulders of Foreland Point, a spit of some 12 hectares on which sits the lighthouse, give way to close cropped sward and then precipitous bracken and heath-covered slopes on which the grey scree lies prominently. Ailsa covers some 90 hectares and is 4km around the base, negotiable at low tide. It is composed of a fine granite (syenite) which stands in many-sided columns, on the broken tops of which the gannets nest. The grey-green granite, in places rusty with ferric compounds, is intersected by ridges of dolerite. There are three main gulleys, two of which meet at a small loch near the summit. Rats and rabbits are common, but the sheep and goats which used to inhabit the slopes (the latter providing delicious milk which I remember from a stay in 1953) are gone. Gibson (1951a) gives a general account of this famous Craig, 'Paddy's milestone', and Gurney deals with its early history so far as gannets are concerned.

Ailsa's gannets are much more inaccessible than those of the Bass. A far higher proportion nest on cliffs and have always done so; they spread just beyond the cliff top in a very few places but nowhere up onto the slopes. This, and its size, deny one the immediate impression of

Fig. 14. The main gannet cliffs arranged in linear spread. Beneath these cliffs, several hundreds of young of all stages, and adults come to grief by falling or being knocked off their nests. *Photo:* S. Wanless.

numbers that the Bass provides, and indeed, for all its huge population, Ailsa cannot equal it in roar and bustle. Perhaps for these reasons there are fewer useful early estimates of size. Nevertheless it is an ancient colony, first referred to in 1583 and subsequently described in phrases indicating vast numbers. It was exploited for birds from at least the early seventeenth century to about 1880 but never to the same extent as the Bass, probably because it was much more difficult to work. The maximum harvest of young between 1853 and 1860 was only 500. Later (until 1929 or beyond) eggs were harvested. Just before the mid nineteenth century, at the time when the Bass also began to suffer from firearms, shooting afflicted Ailsa, and does so to this day. Nevertheless, by 1871 one observer thought that the ledges were about full. Fisher & Vevers (1943) quote, with justifiable mistrust, estimates of 5000–10 000 pairs in 1868 and 6000 pairs in 1869. Gurney's visit in 1905 resulted in an estimate of 6500 *individuals* which Vevers & Fisher (1936) considered too low. Wynne-Edwards *et al.* (1936) point out that the basis for the figure (some 725 visible nests on a photograph said to comprise a sixth of the total colony) in fact suggests at least 4300 *pairs* so Gurney's deduction is faulty even if his facts are roughly correct. Figures for the numbers of gannets on the various parts of the Craig in the years 1922–42 inclusive are given by Fisher & Vevers (1943, p. 184). The 1922, '24, '29 and '35 figures (c. 4900, 8000, 7000 and 7500 pairs respectively) are undivided totals. The 1935 estimate of 7500 pairs is based on little more than an informed guess. Possibly the only real population change which these figures indicate is that which occurred between 1922 and 1924. Between 1936 and 1940 inclusive (4800, c. 5945, 5387, 5419 and 6232 pairs respectively) the apparent changes are potentially explicable in terms of counting errors together with inadequate allowance for some of the variables described on p. 24. Thus far there is nothing much to suggest any significant change in over 70 years (1868–1940). However, Barestacks was first occupied in 1924 and Main Crags (or East), in 1936, so an increase *may* have been afoot during this period. It would certainly be inadmissible to claim any steady trend one way or another, or any considerable fluctuations.

However, the decrease in 1941 was undoubtedly real and drastic (from 6232 in 1940 to 3518 in 1941). With one trivial exception every one of the 20 areas counted, showed a decrease, usually to half or less of its 1940 strength. In discussing this Fisher & Vevers probably make too little allowance for the fact that it was early April when (despite their emphatic assertion to the contrary) not all potential breeders are back and, more importantly, birds are still very wary. The naval gunnery practice in the Clyde was probably responsible for scaring off large numbers for (at least) the period of the count and probably one need look no further for the cause of the decrease.

Since 1936, yearly counts made by J. A. Gibson have yielded evidence of remarkable fluctuations. Since nothing comparable exists for any other large gannetry, I enclose full details (Appendix 2). Even if the potential counting error is reckoned at 20 per cent (which is twice as high as most authors allow) it is still evident that real and substantial fluctuations occur each way. Over the last 20 years, however, the population has mostly been around 8000 pairs: the huge increases have not been maintained. Ailsa is not at present a vigorously expanding colony, but a fluctuating one. Indeed, in some ways it seems in slight decay compared with some sections of the Bass; it holds remarkably few three- and four-year-olds among the breeding ranks.

Fisher & Vevers (1943) suggested that Ailsa could accommodate 8000 pairs before the cliffs would be full. Yet the population has reputedly been as high as 13 000 pairs (1969) without causing birds to spread above the cliffs. When one looks critically at Ailsa, it is quite clear that there is a great deal of spare capacity on the cliffs. I paid particular attention to this in 1974 and climbed to a mid-cliff area in the region of Ashydoo. Gannets nest around here in large numbers but there was a vast amount of unused ledge space which was in every way ideal. (I refer readers who doubt the validity of such statements to p. 28). The same was true in a number of other places on the west side and I have no doubt that in this year Ailsa could have held at least three times its then population on the cliffs, even without resorting to cliff areas elsewhere on the Craig, which have apparently never been popular, if used at all. In addition, the upper slopes are completely unused and, judging by the Bass, are ideal. If *they* are taken into account, the Craig's capacity is more than 90 per cent unused. I labour this point because it is relevant to the topic of interchange between colonies.

In 1974, 75 and 76, Sarah Wanless has counted the gannets each month using photographs of each section of the cliffs with appropriate direct-visual checks of some. The detailed figures are not yet available but in 1974 the maximum count gave 11 500 occupied sites, whilst by 1976 it had risen to c. 16 000. These are not all breeding pairs, nor even all *pairs*, but are simply occupied nests or sites, the great majority of which will in fact hold a pair. These figures indicate substantial immigration during this period and it is interesting that, simultaneously, the Club has increased.

We know from ringing that one Ailsa-born bird emigrated to Norway to breed; also, the increases in population in several west coast gannetries have undoubtedly depended on immigrants, From their rates of increase, it is beyond doubt that at one time, gannetries in the south-west region of Britain also received many recruits from outside. All this suggests that Ailsa could be supplying immigrants to other colonies, both to north and south. From Appendix 3 it is also clear that in many years Ailsa exports recruits, but that in others, it *receives* immigrants. *Why* Ailsa-born birds should desert their under-populated colony in favour of another (possibly with less spare nesting space) is part of the larger topic of interchange between colonies (p. 65), the adaptive significance of which is not clear, but that they do so seems clear. A few 'pioneers' can be expected from every large colony and are obviously useful to the species, but if the *large* decreases seen in Appendix 3 are real, they must imply a failure of the expected recruits from five years previous and inexplicably massive mortality or emigration of adults of the previous year. The latter can be dismissed, and 'failure' of the crop of five years ago is far more likely to be due to their emigration than to their death.[1]

In some years gains outweigh losses and Ailsa shows a massive increase. These must indicate the receipt of immigrants from other colonies. If interchange occurs on a large scale between colonies, there is no reason why this should not be so. Nevertheless, the scale of some of the increases is astonishing. Why, in some years, should two or three thousand young adults converge on Ailsa whilst in others there is an equally large net loss? If one views all the gannetries on the west and north of Britain as a vast network, with complex interchange, the phenomenon may be explicable in terms of good and bad survival years for the year class as a whole, combined with complex social dynamics regulating the inflow to any particular colony (see p. 69). It must be stressed that there is nothing to indicate that adults, having once bred, will *ever* change their breeding place, and much to suggest the contrary.

I cannot leave Ailsa without commenting on the many dead adult gannets, mostly males, to be found beneath the cliffs on the west side. Indeed, Gurney's account (p. 105) is uncannily descriptive of my own most recent visit (June 1974). Sarah Wanless, who is doing an intensive study on Ailsa, has picked up scores of adults, mostly broken-winged. Presumably, some fall locked in combat and separate too late, others may make bad landings whilst a few may be knocked down by falling fragments which are common on Ailsa due to the rottenness of the rock, perhaps partly as a result of the blasting which used to occur when granite was quarried for curling stones. The occasional depredations of vandals with guns add further victims.

(*b*) *Scar Rocks, Wigtownshire, Scotland* (Latest count 432 nests, 1976)

The Scar or Scare Rocks (gaelic 'sgeir', old Norse 'sker') lie in Luce Bay, midway between Burrow Head and the Mull of Galloway about 10km from the nearest land and south of Ailsa Craig. They are bare, composed of a hard, blue-grey schist with some quartz and 'have weathered to a shattered, angular, ledgy surface attractive to breeding seabirds' (Young 1968). Gannets nest solely on the Big Scar 18–21m high and 92m long. The early counts, documented by Young, show a tiny colony of 2–6 pairs in 1939 rising to c. 450 pairs by 1969. The figures obtained by various visitors between these dates are: 1941 (about 10 pairs); 1942 (at least 20–25 nests, probably over 30); 1943 (140–150 pairs); 1945 (35–45 nests); 1946 (at least 28 nests); 1948 (90 nests); 1949 (100 nests); 1953 (134 nests); 1954 (137 nests); 1957 (158 nests); 1960 (167 nests); 1962 (about 200 pairs); 1965 (at least 240 breeding pairs with a probable maximum of 300 nests); 1968 (437 nests); 1969 (450 nests); 1970 (500 nests); 1971 (480 nests); 1972 (430

[1] This in itself would not be enough to account for the big decreases and I suspect these may be artefacts.

nests); 1973 (471 nests); 1974 (482 nests); 1975 (410 nests); 1976 (432 nests). I am much indebted to J. G. Young for the 1969–76 figures. See also Young (1973).

These figures show that the Scar colony has undoubtedly been built up partly by immigration. The rate of growth has been considerably faster than that of Bempton on the east, which started at roughly the same time. This may be because Scar Rocks are considerably nearer to Ailsa than Bempton is to the Bass, lies athwart the movement up and down the west coast which obviously affects many colonies (see p. 68) and is also a more attractive breeding place. An attempt at establishment was made as early as 1883 but between then and 1939 there are no details. Perhaps the 1939–45 war helped the first pairs to become established and their presence then drew in a steady trickle of recruits which helped to build up the colony.

(*c*) *St. Kilda, Outer Hebrides, Scotland* (Latest count 59 258 pairs, 1973)

Situated on the edge of the Continental shelf, 72km west of North Uist, these volcanic islands are the visible remnants of a broken ring of granite and gabbro, deeply sculptured. St. Kilda possesses the greatest cliffs in Britain. Boreray's western wall is a sheer 380m, a fitting setting for the gannets. It is attended by Stac An Armin (191m) and Stac Lee (166m), which are also gannetries. As a group, the only words to describe them hackneyed though they be, are 'awe inspiring'.

The difficulties of counting gannets in such a place are formidable and estimates prior to Boyd's count from photographs (Boyd 1961) probably have a potential error of at least 30 per cent. The first reasonable estimate is that (quoted and accepted by Gurney) of Wiglesworth in 1902 (3500–4000 nests on Stac Lee; 3000 on Stac An Armin and 8000 on Boreray, totalling some 15 000 nests). This is considerably less than would be calculated from the number of gugas and adults reputedly taken during the seventeenth century (Martin Martin's account), a matter fully discussed by Gurney. All that need be said is that these guga figures were almost certainly highly exaggerated. The next estimate was 21 300 *birds* (10 000 on Stac Lee, 7000 on Armin and 4300 on Boreray) from a count in 1931 by Harrison which he himself said had an extremely wide margin of error. This figure was transmuted to at least 16 500 breeding *pairs* (Wynne-Edwards *et al.* 1936) by assuming that 20 per cent or less of the population were non-breeders and virtually all the remainder single representatives of breeding pairs. No allowance was made for nests occupied by pairs at the time of the count. It is interesting that, on this count, Boreray apparently held thousands *less* than either of the others whereas in 1902 it held thousands *more*. Later, the original proportions were restored. This sort of fluctuation is reminiscent of Ailsa (p. 35) and in the most recent counts (1974) perhaps of Skellig and Grassholm, and may support my generalisations (p. 73) on interchange between colonies. In 1939, a partial count given by Fisher gave almost the same figure (16 900 pairs) and the 1949 count, again by Fisher, was virtually identical (17 035 pairs). If those figures are correct, there was

Fig. 15. Scar Rocks, Luce Bay, a relatively new gannetry. *Photo:* B. S. Turner.

no significant increase during the first half of this century—a time when many colonies were burgeoning. Gannet raids virtually ceased by 1902 and excess productivity of the colony (assuming there was some) must have gone elsewhere.

This steady state of affairs had altered by 1959 in which year Boyd's careful count from photographs produced a figure of 44 526 pairs (not breeding pairs it is to be noted). This represents an average annual increase of 10·1 per cent since the last count, which means that St. Kilda must have been receiving immigrants. Ten years later again, and the 1969 'Seafarer's' count gave 52 099 pairs. This was from photographs taken in three different months (May, August and September) and giving only partial coverage. Dixon counted the best sections and compared them with Boyd's of 1959. Since the latter gave each section as a percentage of the whole colony, Dixon was able to calculate a total even without full coverage. But since he had figures for only 21 sections out of Boyd's 116 the deduced total is very unreliable; any large changes in sections unrepresented in the 1969 coverage would completely invalidate it. The fact that the 1969 count was made from photographs taken in three different months further complicates matters for, whilst the sections counted from the photographs taken in May showed no difference when compared with their 1959 counterpart (12 463 against 12 439) both the August and September counts were well down.

From photographs taken in May 1973, Dixon derived a total St. Kilda population of 59 258 pairs occupying sites. Both his 1969 and 1973 totals assume that 16 per cent of nests were occupied by both pair-members at the time of the count (Boyd used a figure of 22 per cent). Bearing in mind that, in a vast gannetry like St. Kilda, errors of several thousand pairs are far from impossible, due to the variables mentioned earlier, these figures for 1973 represent a 37 per cent increase over 1959 which is a 2·7 per cent increase per annum. Whether, in fact, the trend has been a fairly steady increase over a long period, say since the 1930s or 1940s, masked by errors in successive counts due to different methods and the large errors inherent in the task, or whether in fact the increase has been in the nature of some large increments, meaning immigration, it is perhaps difficult to tell. It must be acknowledged that the evidence for massive increments is at best inconclusive. The first grounds for suspecting it came from the large difference between the 1949 and 1959 counts, but Boyd, in my view rightly, refused to conclude that it necessarily reflected a real increment of that magnitude. Since 1959, right up to 1973 the increase has been compatible with intrinsic output *averaged* over these years, although if the difference between the 1969 and the 1973 figures is real, it indicates immigration in this period.

Elaborating briefly on the probability of error, Boyd concluded that, though the gannetry had increased between 1939 and 1959 the errors in previous methods could have been so great that sound comparison is precluded. However, a significant comparison was possible in the case of one locality in which an isolated colony numbered 61 pairs in 1939 and some 273 in 1959. But we now know that local increases can occur by 'drawing in' a disproportionate number of young birds, so that one cannot extrapolate to the gannetry as a whole. So far as the reliability of his own count is concerned there is the sheer difficulty of counting from a photograph, the percentage of nests containing pairs to be allowed for and third, there is the strong possibility that a significant number of site owners could have been absent from the photograph, perhaps scared off by the approach of the 'plane. These points in no way detract from the counts, but suggest that even with such care, the final figure cannot be more than an approximation. The same points apply to the 1969 and 1973 counts.

It would be of the greatest interest to know what actually has happened at St. Kilda but the figures available do not permit a firm conclusion. Possibly this huge gannetry has been exporting a considerable number of recruits as well as increasing itself.

(*d*) *Flannans* (*Roareim*) (Latest count c. 17 nests in 1975)

There are seven main islands in this group, which lies some 27km west north west of Gallan Head, Lewis. Like the others, Roareim is cliff bound (about 50m high) and difficult to land on. The gannets were first noticed in June 1969 and about 16 pairs and 35 birds were counted from the sea; nest contents could not be determined. In June 1975 Hopkins (pers. comm.) counted 29 birds on 17 nests. They were surrounded by guillemots and fulmars. He reports, also, that at least two birds have been seen on the island of Bearasay off Little Bernera, 1973–75.

(*e*) *Sula Sgeir, Outer Hebrides* (Latest count c. 9000 pairs, 1972)

This remote gannetry well west of Sule Stack, 64km north-north-east of the Butt of Lewis and a great haunt of grey seals and Leach's petrels, is known by repute to every ornithologist but trodden by few. Gannets now nest not only on the cliffs but on the summit flats (70m high) having increased their area within living memory. The Westmann Islands, Myggenaes and Sula Sgeir are the only gannetries where gugas are still harvested, a practice which on Sula Sgeir has gone on since at least 1549 and perhaps since the twelfth century or earlier. Fisher cites the following early estimates of population: c. 7000 pairs (1884); over 5000 pairs (1887); 'perhaps twice as many as Sulė Stack' (meaning about 7000 pairs) (1891); c. 5000 pairs (1932); c. 4400 pairs (1937) occupying a smaller area than in 1932; c. 4000 pairs (1939) in a breeding area still smaller; c. 62000 nests (1949). The 'Seafarer' count in 1969 gave 8964 pairs (say 9000) whilst a direct count and one from photographs both in July 1972, gave 9940 and 9000 occupied sites respectively (Evans, pers. comm.). Visible evidence of the increase is the extension of occupied ground to (in 1958) some 6m beyond a 'limits' marker cairn erected by McGeoch in 1954.

If the average *breeding* population between 1919 and 1958[1] is taken as 6000 pairs (probably a generous estimate), then on reasonable assumptions of breeding success and mortality, Sula Sgeir gannets produced 180 000 young of which the Noss men took at least 44 840 (assuming only 19 raids) leaving 33 750 to return as adults. Since 27 800 adults would have died in this period (assuming an adult annual mortality rate of 6 per cent) the colony could have increased by its own output. However, the figure of 180 000 young is probably much too high since the population is unlikely to have averaged 6000 pairs. At 4000 breeding pairs the increment over the 40 years would be 5000 birds. As the population increased, the absolute number of adults dying each year would be more than 480 (6 per cent of 8000), so allowing for this an increment

[1] Years chosen because the number of gannets taken by man is roughly known.

Fig. 16. St. Kilda, the world's largest 'gannetry' (actually three separate stacks). *Photographs:* J. M. Boyd.

of somewhere around 2000 pairs could have accrued between 1919 and 1958. It might thus appear that Sula Sgeir, despite the guga harvests, has increased in numbers as a result of its own output. However, the gannet raiders have traditionally taken both young and adults in large numbers. Fisher describes Noss men as killing 'usually several thousand annually' up to 1869; an average 2000–2500 (max. 3000) taken annually by 1883; 2300 birds killed in three days in 1884; 2500 killed in 1898; 2200 in 1912; 1100 young in 1915; 2000 birds killed in 1931 and again in 1933; 1400 in 1934; 2060 in 1936; 1800–2000 in 1937, c. 2000 in 1938. The effect on the population of taking adults is far more serious than taking young and very probably rules out any possibility of Sula Sgeir's increase stemming from its own output. Indeed, it is almost certain that immigration has been required to maintain the numbers (the annual increase between 1939 and 1969 was 2·7 per cent, which is close to the intrinsic output of an unexploited colony). Probably many have come from Sule Stack.

The only modern ornithologist who has stayed for periods with the Noss men during their 'business' which, with the best will in the world and an acceptance of the justification for such 'harvesting' I can only describe as grim, was the late James McGeoch from whose account I have taken the following description. They normally cross in a seine-netter and/or an open boat capable of beaching. Two such crews total 18 men. The average kill on 19 raids between 1919 and 1958 was 2360 young gannets. In 1958 McGeoch remarked on the tendency to kill larger numbers but noted also that the market seemed easily glutted and almost half the 1958 catch was not sold on arrival at Noss. The birds are taken from the cliff ledges when fully feathered (in the black, juvenile plumage) by spring-loaded jaws attached to a bamboo pole. They are then clubbed, passed to the top of the island and plucked and singed over a peat fire, gutted, salted and stacked for loading.

Fig. 17. Sula Sgeir. The thinly scattered birds, extreme right, are gulls. The cluster of gannets, far edge, top left, is probably of Club birds. *Photo:* 'Operation Seafarer' (1969).

(*f*) *Sule Stack or Stack Skerry* (Latest estimate 4018 pairs, 1969)

This eroded stack of hornblende gneiss about 40m high covering about 2·4 hectares and quite bare, lies over 64km north of Sutherland and west of Orkney mainland. There is a small south rock, separated by a narrow channel from the main hump, which in turn is almost split in two by a deep cleft. The north hump is covered with gannets and Sule Stack, indeed, is the rock which in James Fisher's view gave the strongest impression of being 'full-up'. The south hump is much frequented by non-breeding (probably mainly young) gannets. It has held nesting birds (6 pairs in 1914 and 100 pairs in 1939) but in 1967 there were no nesting birds on it (Stark 1967) though some 3500 'non-breeders'. Sule Stack is an ancient gannetry, established at least as early as 1710 but so inaccessible that only a small handful of naturalists have visited it this last half century. Until about 1932 it was regularly exploited for gannets, up to 1200 birds being taken in some years. Despite this, the population evidently remained fairly stable. In 1887 the entire summit was densely populated. Estimates were: 3500 pairs in 1890 (this was merely a guess); 4000 pairs in 1904 (another guess); 3418 pairs in 1937; 3490 nests in 1939 (probably the most accurate count that had been made); 2010 pairs in 1949; 3500 nests in 1967 (2000 on the summit and sides other than the east; 1500 on the east face) and finally (the mots recent estimate) 4018 pairs in 1969. This means that Sule Stack exports almost all its recruits (the annual increase between 1939 and 1969 has been less than 0·5 per cent). A notable

feature of Sule Stack, evidently, is the large population of non-breeding birds on the south hump, including (as several people mention) many immature birds; Stark (1967) estimated 3500 which, in proportion to breeding birds, is the highest number ever recorded at any gannetry. There are two possible explanations for this. They could be the produce of Sule Stack itself, precluded from breeding by lack of space (one of the very few gannetries where it seems this could happen at present) or they could include many 'floaters' from the western population as a whole. Since it seems clear that there is considerable interchange between western colonies the latter must be judged the more likely.

(*g*) *Fair Isle* (Latest count 34 occupied sites, 1977)

In the summer of 1973 up to 300 gannets, mostly immatures, spent time along the west coast of the island. A few adults were noted high up on the cliffs of the main island. In 1974, birds came back to the same ledge from April 26th (or earlier) and by early June up to 100 were on the main island at Dronger, though usually there were 25–35 birds. Five nests were built on a ledge at Glimpster but no eggs were noted. In 1975, five eggs and four chicks came from 17 nests; in 1976, 17 or 18 eggs and probably 14 chicks from 27 nests; and in 1977, 20 eggs and 15 chicks from 34 occupied sites.

(*h*) *Noss, Shetlands* (Latest count 4300 pairs, 1969)

A small island lying on the east side of the Shetlands, Noss, the nose or rocky point, was early inhabited, as its brochs show. The gannetry lies on the south-east cliffs from the Noup of Noss, a 184m cliff with faces to the north and south, to about 1·6km south of the Noup. All the gannets nest on inaccessible ledges well down the cliff face. From Rumblewick, a cliff between the Noup and Geordies Holes, one gets an excellent view of part of the gannetry, whilst the whole of the north and south faces of the Noup and Rumblewick can be viewed from a distance, and the north face of the Noup from the Point of Heogatoug (Fisher & Venables 1938). Fisher summarises its early history: no birds present, 1909; birds first showed interest, 1911 or 1912; one pair bred, 1914; four pairs bred, 1915; three young reared, 1918; five pairs bred 1919; 10 pairs 1920; c. 200, 1930 or 1931; c. 800, 1924 or 5 (but this was an extremely rough estimate); c. 900, 1937 (but estimated by a totally unreliable 'alighting' method which Fisher and Venables dreamt up but later abandoned): 1518, 1938 (probably much more accurate than the 1937 figure) and 1830 nests, 1939. In 1946 Perry reckoned it was beyond an accurate count but roughly estimated the 1946 population at 2600–3775 pairs. The 'Seafarer' count yielded about 4300 pairs in 1969. This represents an annual increase of 2·8 per cent between 1939 and 1969. Most of the nesting sites now cannot be seen from the land. There are still substantial uncolonised areas of cliff and Kinnear (pers. comm. 1973) notes that non-breeding birds gather in several areas. There is also a fringe or tier of newly established pairs along the edge of the breeding groups and one or two groups of non-breeders on wave-cut platforms at the foot of the Noup. Noss' explosive growth in its early days is evidence of considerable immigration but since about 1939 it has grown at a rate consistent with no immigration. Together with Hermaness it represents a major aspect of the gannet's extension of breeding range this century.

(*i*) *Hermaness, Shetland* (Latest count 6012 nests, 1976)

Hermaness is a peninsula in the extreme north-west of Unst, the most northerly island in the Shetlands. The strata slope to the east and the high cliffs and stacks are on the west. The gannets breed on the offshore skerry to the north and on the western cliffs of the Hermaness nature reserve. The colony was established on Vesta Skerry by 1917 from whence it spread to Burra Stack (109 pairs by 1920), Humla Houl, the Neap and Neapna Stack by 1932 (possibly over 600 pairs in 1934 and c. 1000 pairs in 1935) and to Humla Stack by 1938 (a count gave 2045 pairs). Subsequent counts for the entire colony gave 2611 nests (1939); nearly 4000 (1945); at least 3150 nests—estimate—(1949); 3450 ± 900 sites (1965) and 5894 pairs (1969). The 1965 count (Dott 1967) excluded the western faces of the large stacks on the west coast of part of the area; part of the Neap facing north-west was visible as were many small sections of rock

Fig. 18. Sule Stack (Stack Skerry). The separate rock on the left is often the site of a large Club. *Photo:* 'Operation Seafarer' (1969).

face though none of them were suitable for, or showing any signs of, occupation by gannets. The pattern of increase depends, as so often, on which part of the curve is examined. Between 1935 and 1938 immigration was definitely continuing, from the early days of the colony's establishment. Between 1939 and 1969 the average rate of increase (2·6 per cent) was slightly below the intrinsic rate of increase but between 1965 and 1969 (10·8 per cent) well above it. Immigration must therefore be taking place at an uneven rate. Since writing this, counts (in terms of *nests*) by Sage (pers. comm.) have confirmed that substantial fluctuations are occurring. Taking counts for Humla, Burra and Clingra stacks:

1965	*1969*	*Decrease since previous count*	*1974*	*Decrease*	*1975*	*Decrease*	*1976*	*Increase*
1200	1148	52	892	256	618	274	988	370

The overall decrease from 1965 to 1976 is 212 (17·6 per cent).

By contrast, the population in the area from Neap to Saito Point has been:

1965	*1969*	*Increase*	*1974*	*Increase*	*1975*	*Decrease*	*1976*	*Increase*
2250	2470	220	4333	1863	3692	641	3799	107

Fig. 19(a)

The Burra Stack, Hermaness (Shetland).

Photo: B. L. Sage.

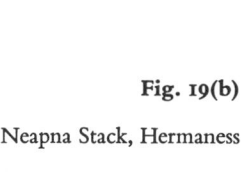

Fig. 19(b)

Neapna Stack, Hermaness

Photo: B. L. Sage.

Here, the increase between 1965 and 1974 was 2083 nests, and overall, from 1965 to 1976, was 1549 (68·8 per cent).

Comparing, in detail, 1975 and 1976, Sage's figures are:

	Rumb-lings	*Vesta Skerry*	*Humla Stack*	*Burra Stack*	*Clingra Stack*	*Neapna Stack*	*Soorie Geo.*	*Neap area*	*Saito Point to the Neap*	*Grand total*
1975 (July)	275	770	352	126	140	328	24	1640	1700	5355
1976 (July)	295	930	533	335	120	346	32	1762	1659	6102
Increase	20	160	181	209	—	18	8	122	—	657
Decrease	—	—	—	—	20	—	—	—	41	—

There are apparently large fluctuations in the numbers of Club birds (up to c. 1800) around the colony, which could indicate that 'floaters' are constantly swelling and depleting the reserves from which transitory site-holders could come.

Clearly, and allowing even a substantial margin for potential error in the counts, certain areas (notably Burra and Humla Stacks) are funnelling in a disproportionately large share of the immigrants whilst others are remaining fairly stable or even decreasing slightly. This seems in accord with the general picture, now building up for many colonies, of substantial variation in social attractiveness of groups within a colony.

4. *East Britain group*

Until the foundation of Bempton in the 1920s or 1930s the only colony on the east coast of Britain was the Bass Rock. The situation is thus very different from that on the west, where a string of gannetries extends along the entire seaboard.

(*a*) *Bass Rock, East Lothian, Scotland* (Latest estimate c. 13 500 occupied sites, 1977)

I can hardly treat the 'Solangoosifera bassa' dispassionately, having visited it for seventeen years and lived on it for three. Also, it is the *locus classicus* for the gannet, the most famous British gannetry and perhaps the one for which the earliest mention may be traced. It lies in the Forth, just over 3km from Tantallon, whose castle faces the forbidding battlements of the Bass' great fortress. Up the Forth lie several lesser islands and 15km to the north is the Isle of May, which once held breeding gannets. The Fife coast and the rich sand-eel fishing grounds of St. Andrew's Bay and the Tay estuary are about the same distance to the north, whilst well to the south lie the rich fishing grounds around the Farne Islands, where Bass gannets often feed. The Bass is one of a series of volcanic plugs stretching across the Scottish Lowlands, matched on the mainland by North Berwick Law and Arthur's Seat in Edinburgh. It is made of a trap or clinkstone basalt, black and sombre rust in hue, where not whitened by the excreta of its seabirds. It looms massively, though in fact it is not really large, being only some 1600m round the base, and 103m high and with a planar area of some 2·5 hectares. The sheerest cliffs, approaching 92m in height, are on the north-west side; the west and south-west are more round-shouldered with larger ledges. The east is also towering, in parts virtually smooth faced, denying a foothold even to kittiwakes and descending to gloomy caverns alive, in season, with the gargling of guillemots. Miller (1847) describes it evocatively:

> '. . . the angles stand out as sharp and unworn as if they had been first exposed to the atmosphere but yesterday, and to this indestructibility, possessed in a high degree by all the harder clinkstones, does the entire island owe its preservation in its imposing proportions and singular boldness of outline. Had it been originally composed of such a yielding tuff as that on which the fortress of Tantallon is erected we would now in vain seek its place amid the waters or would find it indicated merely as some low skerry'.

Its surface is well vegetated and even boasts of a small walled garden near the summit. Its civil and ecclesiastical history has filled a fascinating volume, for it was the site of St. Baldred's cell in the seventh century and an impregnable fortress from the twelfth to the seventeenth centuries. Its dungeons held devout covenanters whilst its caves knew smugglers and French allies against the 'auld enemy'. The Buccleuch's family treasure was stored there and King James VI was impressed enough by his visit to exact special protection for the gannet from 1592 onwards. Nothing remotely comparable to all this, and much else, attends any other gannetry, for first and foremost the Bass is a gannetry. In 1535 its rent was 400 gold pieces a year, such was the value of its gannets for eating, grease and feathers.

The early records of gannets are admirably and extensively chronicled by Gurney but space forbids excerpts here. Bass gannets are first mentioned in *The Scotichronicon* (Fordun 1447), but Beowulf, in the sixth century mentions North Sea gannets which were probably Bass birds. Hector Boece's oft-quoted account (*History of Scotland*, 1526, Hollinshead's translation) 'Certes there is nothing in this rock which is not full of admiration and wonder; therein also is great store of Soland geese . . . and, nowhere else but in Ailsaie and this rocke', probably drew at least in part on Major's *History of Great Britain* (1521) in which Bass gannets are described as a 'marvellous multitude'. Other sixteenth-century descriptions, probably derivative, are equally lyrical and imprecise. Harvey (1651) accompanied Charles I to the Bass in 1641 and remarked that the surface of the island was almost completely covered with nests 'so that you can scarce find free footing anywhere'. This is consistent with other early chroniclers such as Slezer (1693) 'the surface of it being almost covered with their nests, eggs and young birds'. Sibbald (1710) and Mackay (1723) also refer to the whole surface being covered. Into the nineteenth century they still, by report, nested on the summit (Jardine 1816) and whilst MacGillivray's estimate of 20 000 birds in 1831 may be too high, his remark that the nests 'are placed on all parts of the rocks where a convenient spot occurs but are much more numerous towards the summit' is of interest. He also mentions 300 nests on a gravelly slope near the landing place, which must refer to the slope beneath the battlements, a most unlikely

Fig. 20(a). Bass Rock, showing the west side and immediately below the deep shadow left of the centre, group 5 which has increased some ten-fold in the last 15 years and is the group which has provided most of the information on breeding biology. The spread up the western slopes has been held back by disturbance from visitors but is nevertheless continuing. Note the walled garden (top right) and 14th-century chapel (immediately in front of lighthouse). *Photo:* Aerofilms Ltd.

place for gannets. Fleming's (1847) estimate of 5000 pairs, based on an extrapolation from the 1800 juveniles taken annually, seems likely to be the most accurate up to that time.

The sharp decrease from around this time until, probably, the end of the nineteenth century, was due to the wanton shooting of nesting birds, made possible by cheaper firearms. In Gurney's words:

> '. . . evil days came upon the gannets when their principal value was thought to be only as a mark of sportsmen. Colquhoun says that there was one year when the whole west front of the rock was depopulated. This sort of treatment must have gone on for a good many years for when I was at the Bass in 1876 the lessee still bitterly resented the numbers shot after the 1st August (when at that time the close season ended) many of them even while flying with fish to their young ones'

adding that he had seen the sea strewn with dead gannets which the shooters did not take the trouble to pick up. Nevertheless, Robert Gray claimed that they had not yet abandoned the upper slopes (1859) and Gurney quotes Cunningham as evidence that there were still some on the slopes as late as 1862. This, however, need not mean more than that a few were to be found just above the cliff edge.

Actual estimates in the second half of the nineteenth century were c. 6000 pairs (1869) and c. 10 000 pairs (1871). These are almost certainly unreliable as at that time shooting was rife

Fig. 20(b). Part of the west side, Bass Rock. The birds in the group on the upper left are establishing themselves but have not yet bred. *Photo:* Aerofilms Ltd.

and the rate at which young were being taken (see Appendix 3) dropped, indicating a falling population. At any rate the first critical estimate in the twentieth century, that of W. Evans from photographs in 1904, was of 7000–8000 individuals which Gurney considered much too high, (he suggested 4800 birds actually on the rock at the time of the photographs and 1500 away). If we may take Evan's lower figure of 7000 birds, a total of 3000 pairs is probably a generous estimate for the 1904 population. After this, protection and the cessation of culling after 1885 began to take effect and numbers slowly began to rise. The 1913 estimate was c. 3250 pairs; the 1929 count 4147 nests; the 1936 estimate 4150 pairs; the nest counts of 1939 and 1949 respectively, 4374 and 4820. My own count in June 1962 gave a maximum of 7126 occupied sites (minimum 6690) which, allowing for a potential error of at least 10 per cent gives a figure of between 6021 and 7839 or, in round figures, 6000–8000. For general purposes, I took the figure to be 7000 occupied sites. Another estimate in July 1968 gave 8977 (say 9000) pairs which on the same potential errors gives 8000–10 000 pairs. In 1974 it was clear that some 1500–2000 sites, extra to 1968, were occupied, extensions having occurred chiefly on the north-west and west slopes and to a lesser extent along the cliff-top margin above the north face. I would therefore estimate the 1974 population as 9500–11 500 site-holding 'pairs' and consider that it is unlikely to be more than the higher figure of this range. This figure excludes only Club birds and is *not* the breeding (i.e. laying) population.

The increase in some of the colonies described so far has undoubtedly been due in part or

Fig. 20(c). The east cliffs of the Bass, extending round to the north fog horn; note the topographical differences between east and west of the Bass. Extension up the eastern slopes (which were once occupied) is prevented by the path. *Photo:* Aerofilms Ltd.

often mainly, to immigration. The main question about the Bass population is whether the same applies. From the figures of: 3000 pairs, 1904; 4000, 1936; 5000, 1949; 7000, 1962; 9000, 1968 and 10 000, 1974 it appears that over 70 years, the increase per annum has been very

Fig. 21(a). The north-west slope, Bass Rock (group 5)—an open-ended, rapidly expanding group. Photo taken 1971, from the side.

Fig. 21(b). Same group, 1975, from above. Asterisk marks same nest in both. Line marks 1961 limits.

steady at about 3 per cent fluctuating between less than one per cent and 5·5 per cent in successive periods. Between 1939 and 1969 the annual increase was 2·4 per cent. The periodic large increases and decreases which have been recorded on Ailsa are completely missing from the Bass' progress. Thus, on the reasonable assumptions used previously (p. 25) the Bass increase fits extremely well with that which would be predicted (Nelson 1966b) were it an autonomous colony, experiencing no significant loss or gain through emigration and immigration. The observed increase is also perfectly consistent with Brun's (1972) more sophisticated analysis of the population dynamics of an increasing colony (see p. 57). It is known that the Bass loses some recruits to Bempton, but so far the number has been negligible. The interesting contrast between the situations in east and west coast gannetries respectively is discussed further on p. 67.

Finally, some points about the past and present distribution of gannets on the Bass should be mentioned. At present, Bass gannets (indeed the species as a whole) may still be climbing back to their former strength, though it takes a good deal of faith in earlier accounts to convince me that on a rock garrisoned by soldiers, with upwards of 1500 young gannets and some adults taken each year, and disturbance of pairs with eggs and small young, the colony could have been thriving! Certainly, however, they reached their lowest ebb early this century entirely as a result of persecution and have since climbed steadily upwards. There seems no reason why they should not continue their advance up the north-west and west slopes, which are particularly suitable (steep and windy). On the east they find it impossible to cross the concrete path and handrail and I think it highly unlikely that they will ever occupy the entire summit, which in places denies take-off on too many days to suit a gannet's requirements. The growth on the north-west slope has been particularly dramatic in the last 15 years. My study group which in 1960 occupied a small patch just above the cliff edge is now a vast snowfield of gannets. This disproportionate growth is because it has been specially protected and has drawn in recruits from other parts of the Bass, whilst losing very few of its own to other areas. Further round to the west there are now considerably more than 1000 pairs above the cliff edge though the 'edge' is difficult to define. For almost 50 years, there has been little increase on the west side. This has undoubtedly been due to the effects of human disturbance, particularly in opening the nests to predation from herring gulls. Now they are making real progress partly due to reduced (though still very considerable) disturbance. Since the ledge sites are about full, recruits have had little alternative but to use the slopes. Whilst, as mentioned, this has led to a vast influx on the protected north-west it may also have meant that a higher proportion of young adults than would normally have done so, joined the Club rather than take up a site in such a disturbed area. Frequent disturbance unsettles young adults and delays, sometimes (I suspect) for several years, their eventual breeding. If this has been so, it would help to explain (a) why the Bass Club was (and is) so large; (b) why it contained such a high proportion of adults and (c) why (see p. 153) the proportion of adults is *now* declining, the assumption being that the increase, well under way on the north-west and seriously beginning on the west,[1] has drawn some adults from the Clubs. At other (western) gannetries Clubs tend to be smaller and to contain a lower proportion of adults than on the Bass, perhaps partly because of colony-interchange on the west.

Further round to the south the island loses its impregnable cliffs and presents a terraced slope, the lower reaches of which hold the battlements and lighthouse. There is a small discrete group above the south cliffs, west of the garrison, which has trebled since 1960, and another on a level with the top of the light. This group grew from less than 10 pairs in 1960 to above 80 in 1974, again as a result of protection. The mighty east cliffs are, at the south end, too smooth to hold gannets, though there is a group on a low spur just above the splash zone. Further round to the north they present broader ledges and are densely occupied right to the top, where further spread is prevented by the path. The northern rim, west of the foghorn, is now attracting some growth but suffers from the attentions of visitors, who (necessarily) swing west after following the concrete path to the end.

The present distribution of Bass gannets is thus entirely explicable in terms of man's

[1] Mainly due to the conservation efforts of Fred Marr who always briefs visitors when they board his boat, the *Sula II*, to be taken out to the Bass.

influence. Slopes are wholly acceptable to gannets and there yet remains enough suitable ground to accommodate at least as many as already exist on the entire rock, even without crossing the path and without having to colonise 'downhill', a procedure which they avoid, preferring to prospect by landing at least level with, or preferably above, existing nests.

(*b*) *Bempton, Yorkshire, England* (Latest count 169 pairs, 1977)

The sheer limestone cliffs of Bempton (Fig. 22) are an ancient haunt of seabirds, but gannets first gained a toehold in the 1920s or 1930s. The growth of the colony is described on p. 133 in relation to its ecology and behaviour. Here it may merely be said that it grew from one or two pairs, to less than 10 occupied sites throughout the 1950s and to 21 by 1969 after which it began to increase more rapidly; 24–30 (1970); 33 (1971); 44 or more (1972); c. 80 (1973); c. 100 (1974) and at least 120 (1975). The recent increase (some 25 per cent per year between 1970 and 1974), like the earlier, has undoubtedly been due largely to immigration.

Iceland, Faroes and Norway group

This is merely a grouping of convenience. Whilst it may turn out that all these gannetries interchange with my 'West and North Britain' group, there is a good chance that the Icelandic gannetries at least may not do so and it seemed preferable to include Faroes with Iceland rather than with the North Britain cluster, members of which are nearer together than any of them is to the Faroes. Norway is somewhat out on its own and included on the grounds that it obviously is receiving immigrants and falls more naturally in this group than any other.

Gannets have long bred in *Iceland*, but there are apparently no records (except the name) in early Icelandic literature (Fisher & Vevers 1943). The current extension in range and increase in numbers of gannets has led to the establishment of new colonies in addition to the ancient ones, namely the Westmann Islands (Súlnasker, Hellisey, Geldungur and Brandur), Eldey and Grimsey. The new colonies are Skrúour (or Skrúdur), founded 1943; Ravoinúpur (or

Fig. 22(a). The limestone cliffs at Bempton produce relatively few ledges suitable for gannets

Fig. 22(b). Part of one of the Bempton groups (1968) from the south. *Photo:* R. Vaughan.

Raudinupur) founded 1944 or 45; Drangey (founded 1949 but since extinct); Stori-Karl (founded 1955) and Máfadrang (or Mávadrangur) founded sometime prior to 1962.

In the last 20 years Th. Einarsson has carried out most of the surveys of Icelandic gannetries and writes (pers. comm.) that, with the probable exception of Raudinupur, all colonies are currently increasing. The results of his visits and enquiries since 1962 are not precise enough to embody in actual figures. However, the 1962 total of 22 086 pairs cannot be far wrong, or increases in specific colonies which have been visited since 1962, would have been noticed.

TABLE 3

ICELANDIC GANNETRIES (UP TO 1974)

	1939–41			1949–52			1959–62		
1. Eldey									
cliffs	628	9328		1177	10877		2400	16300	
top	8700			9700			13900		
2. Westmann Isles									
(a) Súlnasker									
cliffs	814	1600		1002	1918		772	1682	
top	786			916			910		
(b) Stori-Geldungur									
cliffs and				652	802		820	1020	
top	589			150			200		
Little Geldungur						913			1122
cliffs			4359	111	111	5534	102	102	5315
and top				0			0		
(c) Hellisey									
cliffs	1703			2216			1960	2075	
top							115		
(d) Brandur									
cliffs	456	467		479	487		432	436	
top	11			8			4		
3. Máfadrang									
cliffs							100		
(Mávadrangur)								100	
top	0			0			0		
4. Skrúdur									
cliffs				134	134		304	314	
top	0			0			10		
5. Stori-Karl									
cliffs							0		
(Stori-Karlinn, Skoranhurb-Jarg)								23	
top	0			0			23		
6 Raudinupur									
(a) Sölvanöf									
cliffs				8			33	33	
top	0			0			0		
(b) Karlinn					8				34
cliffs							1	1	
top	0			0			0		
7. Drangey									
cliffs				1	1				
top	0			0			0		
8. Grimsey									
cliffs	45	45		0			0		
top	0								
Grand totals	13732			16554			22086		

It is also an ancient inhabitant of the *Faroes*, culled for centuries, but a very recent addition to *Norway's* breeding birds, though a visitor of longstanding to her rich fishing grounds. Gannets first nested in Scandinavia on Runde off Ålesund in South Norway in 1947, the period in which they were colonising, or rapidly increasing in, several other places (Rouzic in Brittany, Ortacs and Les Etacs in the Channel Isles, Scar Rocks in s.w. Scotland and others). Since then, three new colonies have been established in Norway (Skittenskarvholmen, Skarvlakken and Innerstauren). It is of great interest to note that at least some of the pioneers came from the west, if the chick colour-ringed on Ailsa Craig in 1966 and breeding on Skarvlakken in 1970 and 1971 is representative. This is consistent with the view that there is considerable interchange between the western British colonies. The Bass, though it supplies Bempton (which lies on one of its main flyways) may be less likely to be the source of birds which move far afield. However, Bass birds fish off Norway, so their involvement in the Norwegian colonies cannot be ruled out. A good account of Norwegian colonies and their growth is in Brun (1972).

(*a*) *Westmann Islands* (Latest count 5315 pairs, 1960)

The Vestmannæyjar or Westmann Islands are of unequal size and importance so far as gannets are concerned. The largest, Súlnasker, is about 92m high and gannets nest on the cliffs and summit. Geldungur split into two stacks in 1896 (Stori and Litli) and gannets nest on both.

The nineteenth-century population was probably in the order of several thousand pairs. The record of 400–500 gannets taken annually from Súlnasker alone (Fisher & Vevers 1943–4) means that this colony probably held well over 2000 pairs; it was the largest of the four Westmann colonies. Gurney thought there were probably more than 4000 breeding individuals and Nielsen (1919) considerably more than 5000 pairs in the Westmanns, but Robert's count, in 1932, of 3900 'breeding' pairs was nevertheless considered too high by Lockley & Salmon (1934) and modified by them to 3514 pairs. In 1935 Lockley counted 317 nests on Brandur and c. 2600 on Hellisey, but the first accurate count of all four rocks was that of Vevers, Evans

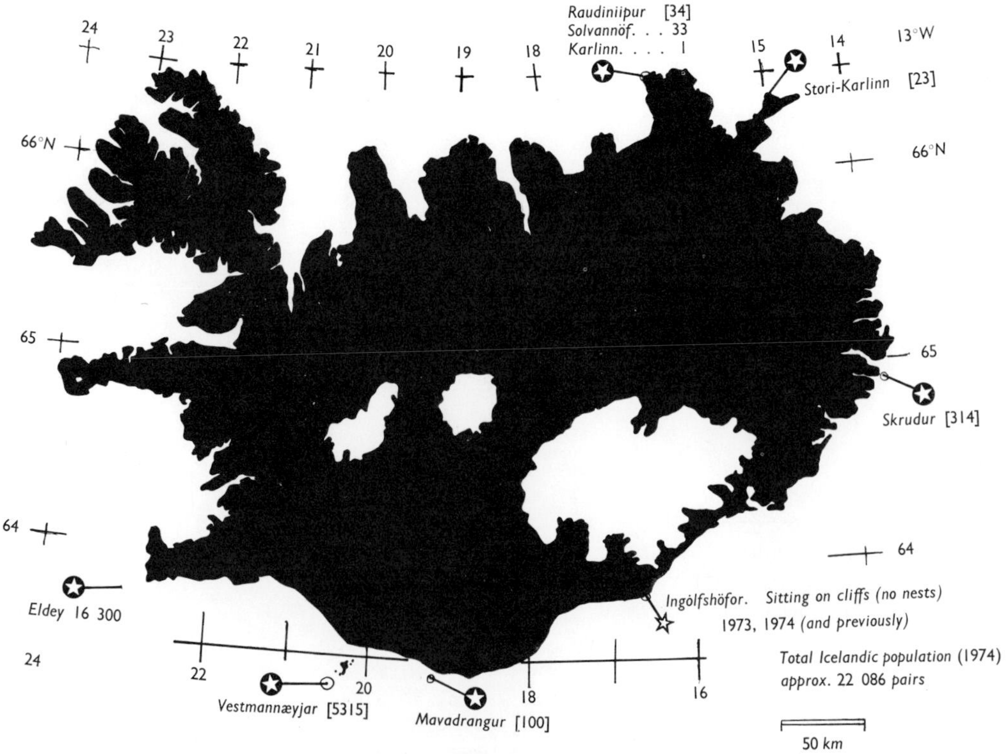

Fig. 23. Icelandic gannetries 1974. (From information supplied by Th. Einarsson.)

and Alexander in July 1939, which in terms of nests gave: Brandur (467); Hellisey (1703); Geldungur (589) and Súlnasker (1600)—a grand total of 4359. In 1949 the comparable figures were 487, 2216, 913 and 1918, total 5534 pairs. In 1960 the figures were very similar (Brandur 436, Hellisey 2057, Geldungur 1122 and Súlnasker 1682, total 5315) but the items counted were probably not strictly comparable since (presumably) birds owning sites but not nests were excluded from the 1939 totals.

The relative stability of this group depends on the fact that a substantial but *variable* proportion of its members is killed each year. Thus it has not increased markedly though probably it does receive immigrants, perhaps particularly from Eldey which for many years has been apparently nearly full up.

(*b*) *Eldey* (Latest count 16 300 pairs, 1962)

Eldey, 77m high, is one of four volcanic rocks south-west of Cape Reykjanes. Eldey itself, 'the mealsack', is the most northerly, the only gannetry of the four and an ancient one, the first references under the generic term 'Fuglasker', the bird skerries, going back to at least 1772 (Gudmundsson 1953). Its table-like top is crowded. Around 1908 about 4100 birds a year were being taken from Eldey and the population must presumably have been well over 6000 site-owning pairs (it can be put so low only because the 4100 represents a far larger proportion than can be taken from most other gannetries; the population may indeed have been as high as 10 000 pairs). Robert's estimate of the 1934 population was about 14 500 birds. His subsequent interpretation of this figure as representing about 9000 breeding pairs is however unjustified. Not only did he *add* 30 per cent of the 14 500 to allow for individuals away from nests (by which he meant leaving them unoccupied when in fact this does not happen) but he failed to *subtract* a percentage for the proportion of nests occupied by pairs. The 14 500 birds (assuming it to be a correct figure) probably represented no more than 6000 site-owning pairs (not breeding pairs) whilst if it was merely 10 per cent overestimated the figure could have been as low as 5000 pairs in 1934, which is not much more than half Robert's figure! In view of this, it is remarkable that in the following year an actual count of nests by Gisli Gudmundsson gave 8700 on top of the rock and 628 on other parts, a total of 9328. The accuracy of this count was verified by one from a photograph taken in June 1941 which gave a total on top of at least 7832 'breeding' pairs. A July 1942 aerial photograph yielded a count of 8840 'breeding' pairs. In July 1953 a count from an aerial photograph yielded 11 634 pairs on the plateau and 3544 on the cliff faces, a total of 15 178 pairs. The 1962 total was 16 300 which gives an annual increase of 3·1 per cent between 1939 and 1962. This might appear to conflict with earlier reports that the rock was overcrowded on top, at a density of a little less than 1 pair/sq. m, and taking the planar area as one hectare. But the surface is fissured and the available area substantially more than a hectare. Also, a density of at least 2·0 pairs/sq. m is not excessive. Thus there seems no reason why Eldey could not hold at least 18 000 pairs.

It has been protected since 1940 which means that it is probably now producing more young than can easily be accommodated, notwithstanding the above remarks, and may well provide recruits for the Westmann Islands.

(*c*) *Grimsey* (Extinct since 1946)

Grimsey lies well within the Arctic circle and until the founding of the Norwegian colony of Syltefjord, was the most northerly gannetry. It is of interest also, because it is subject to disruption by earth tremors. Fisher & Vevers claim that it has always been a small colony though possibly an ancient one. In 1819 there were three pairs on Grimsey and 10–12 on nearby Hafsulastapi, which subsequently grew to 50–70 pairs by 1903 but collapsed, probably in the 1920s so that by 1933 all the nests (21) were on Grimsey. The next year a tremor shook Grimsey and disrupted the year's breeding attempt; between 40 and 50 birds were present in the area. In 1939 there were 45 occupied sites and the colony thus seemed to be recovering. However it was deserted by 1946, the period when new Icelandic colonies were springing up.

(*d, e, f, g, h*) *Skrúdur, Raudinupur, Stori-Karl, Máfadrang and Drangey*

These five small colonies were founded between 1940 and 1960, but none have grown much. The earliest and largest, Skrúdur, numbered 134–150 pairs in 1949 and 314 in 1961. By then 10 pairs had moved onto the top of the island; previously all had nested on the cliffs. Raudinupur consists of the main colony on Sölvanöf and since 1959 a pair or two on Karlinn. In 1949 and 1952 there were only eight pairs on the cliffs (50m high) and none on top. Since then, part of the cliff has collapsed (Einarrson, pers. comm.). Nevertheless, in 1959 and 1962 there were still 33 pairs on the cliffs and none on top. Stori-Karl held 23 pairs in 1959–62 and Máfadrang 100 pairs in 1959 and 1962, all of them on cliffs. The fifth 'colony' Drangey consisted of one pair in 1949 but did not persist. The Skrúdur increase probably could have taken place by virtue of the colony's own output.

The Icelandic gannet population, in common with those of all other 'areas' of the species' range, is at present increasing. The increase is within the population's own capacity for production (assuming that the Icelandic gannets indeed form a closed population, which is by no means certain). Within Iceland, there is certainly interchange, most probably a flow from Eldey to the Westmann Islands, where there is spare space and artificially created vacancies. Possibly, some birds born in Icelandic colonies breed in the Faroes or Norway.

(*i*) *Myggenaes* (*Mykines*) *Holm, Faroes* (Latest count 1500–2550 occupied nests, 1972)

The Holm lies westwards of Myggenaes and is a stack of basaltic columns. An ancient colony, probably much older than its first record (1673) and long culled for food. Vevers & Evans (1938) describe the colony. On the Holm itself, most nests were on a broad ledge on the north face about 30m above sea-level, with small groups of nests above and below. Then, as now, the gannets nested on the small neighbouring stacks of Pikarsdrangus and Flatidrangur, almost exclusively on the summits, 31·7m and 24·7m respectively. Myggenaes has never been a huge colony and figures are therefore more accurate. The 1892 estimate of 750 pairs was made at a time when perhaps 300 adults and twice that number of young were being taken each year. It is not surprising that it was still only around 750 pairs in 1928. By 1935 it was c. 900 rising to 1615 pairs in 1937, about the same in 1938 and 1473 in 1939. The 1966 count gave 1801 pairs and 1972 gave 2982 birds counted from photographs and representing 1500–2550 occupied nests, depending on correction factors used (Olsen & Permin 1972). This colony is thus by no means full and is probably being kept down by culling. Nevertheless, in the first few decades of the twentieth century, the colony annually yielded more young than before this, probably because at this time gannets were much on the increase and Myggenaes was receiving many immigrants. Between 1909 and 1939 it grew at 2·3 per cent per annum despite culling. This colony is one of the only three (the others are Sula Sgeir and the Westmanns) which is still culled and the number taken is adjusted to that which the islanders

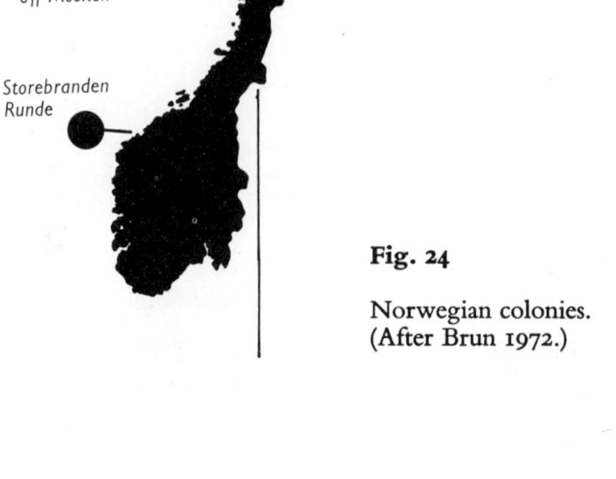

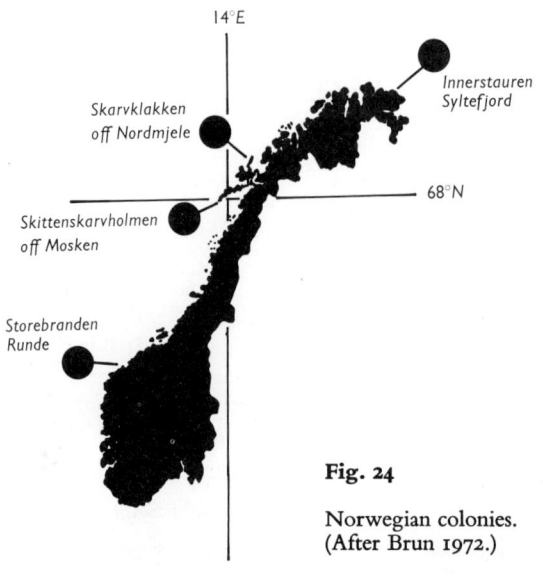

Fig. 24

Norwegian colonies. (After Brun 1972.)

consider it can lose without damage. Apparently about 1000 birds per year were still being taken in 1969 (Seabird Report 1969).

(*k*) *Storebranden, Runde, Norway* (Latest count 494 nests, 1974)

Norway's largest gannetry is on a rock of granitic gneiss, with steep cliffs in the N.W. (on which they first bred) rising to more than 152m. The gannets established themselves in 1946 on a ledge about 80m above sea-level and later spread up and down to 150m and 30m forming a straggling line some 400m long. The increase between 1947 and 1956 was slight (14 individuals (1947); 48 (1954); 60 (1955); 80 (1956)) but then began to rise more steeply. The population just about doubled between 1959 and 1960 though it is difficult to judge how much of this apparent increase was an artefact. The population (individuals) in 1962 was 325. Counts subsequent to 1960 in terms of occupied sites were: 13 July 1963 (196); 31 May 1966 (214); 8 June 1968 (326); 27 May 1970 (331); 30 June 1971 (383); 10 June 1972 (422) and 12 July 1974 (494 pairs) (Brun, pers. comm). Although the different methods used to arrive at the number of pairs make it impossible to ascertain the exact rate of increase, particularly in the early days when small absolute numbers mean large percentage increases, the growth was certainly due largely to immigration.

(*l*) *Skittenskarvholmen, Mosken, Outer Lofoten Islands, Norway* (Latest count 65 nests, 1974)

This is a group of bare granite islets some 2 km north-west of Mosken. The largest 125m long, 50m wide and only 5m high, holds the gannetry though it is a highly atypical site. The nests are a mere 5–12m above sea-level on the eastern part and intermixed with about 70 pairs of cormorants. The colony may have been established in 1960 but breeding was first confirmed in 1968. The first count, 19 June, 1969, revealed 50 nests with eggs or chicks, which indicates at least 60 established pairs. On 21 June, 1970, there were 83 nests with eggs or chicks. Although this would seem to be a greater increase than could occur intrinsically, especially since the loss of eggs and chicks is so high at this accessible colony (over 40 per cent in 1970 and over 66 per cent in 1971). In June 1971 the count was only 77 nests with eggs and in June 1972 and July 1974 it was down to 60 and 65 pairs respectively (latter figure, Brun, pers. comm.), so it is clear that, despite its increase overall, the growth rate is being grossly distorted as a result of disturbance.

(*m*) *Skarvlakken, Nordmjele, Norway* (Latest count 145 pairs, 1974)

This is another small granite rock, 150m long, 50m wide and 8m high. The nests are only 4–7m above sea-level and the rock is shared with 150–200 pairs of cormorants and about 30 pairs of shags. Nordmjele, too, (like Skittenskarvholmen) is really far too low for a gannetry, but the Outer Lofotens and islands off Vesterålen do not possess many cliffs. The Røst group of islands and the seabird cliffs off Nykvag and Bleiksøya have no broad ledges but the island of Vaerøy provides a site similar to Runde (above) and is equally near to good fishing areas. Yet the gannets chose the small, low islet of Skittenskarvholmen. Brun (1972) makes the interesting suggestion that the cormorants on Skittenskarvholmen and Skarvlakken attracted the gannets. Since social stimulation plays such a major role in the gannet's life this seems by no means impossible, even though it implies considerable unselectivity in the gannet's response to external stimuli. The colony (4 pairs) was established in 1967. It held a high proportion of non-breeders in 1968 and 1969 and then, in 1970 and 1971, the number of breeding birds increased rapidly. As with Skittenskarvholmen, human interference has obviously had a marked influence (the colony has been protected by law since 1969 but this is no guarantee of immunity) and in August 1969 there were 77 birds but only 7 young. Then, in two successive years (1970 and 1971) visits in June and July of each year revealed substantial drops in the number of occupied nests (from 36 to 29 in 1970 and from 65 to 35 in 1971), the number of young present being 22 and 30 respectively. Rather earlier in 1972 (June) there were 103 occupied nests but only 64 chicks on 3 August, whilst in 1973 and 1974 the June counts were 127 and 145 pairs, yielding a mere 35 and 39 young respectively by August (Brun 1974). Despite this remarkably poor success, Brun claims that the island has been very efficiently protected and almost totally spared from human disturbance. In this case, there is something odd here!

Again, it is clear that the colony is receiving immigrants but the pattern of increase is being masked.

It is at Nordmjele that the chick, colour-ringed on Ailsa in 1966 was found breeding in 1970 and again in 1971, in which year it was caught and its metal ring number checked.

(*n*) *Innerstauren, Syltefjord, Norway* (Latest count 55 nests, 1974)

This is a 40m tall stack attached to the mainland towards the western end of the seabird cliff on the north side of Syltefjorden, East Finmark. The gannets have chosen the edge of the flat top and some broad ledges on the side facing the sea. The colony was established in 1961 (2 pairs) and subsequent figures for occupied nests are: 1962 (3); 1964 (6); 1966 (9); 1967 (13); 1968 (23); 1969 (28); 1970 (29); 1971 (44) and 1974 (55). There has been a particularly high proportion of non-breeding birds here. In 1966 there were only 9 occupied nests but 51 birds present.

General comments on the Norwegian gannet population

Brun has been the principal investigator of Norwegian gannetries and makes some interesting comments on the correlation between their distribution and that of food fish

Fig. 25. Skarvlakken (off Nordmjele). An unusually low-lying gannetry. Note the cormorants, which may have attracted gannets. *Photo:* E. Brun.

(Brun 1972). He remarks that Runde was a natural choice for the first Norwegian colony, being the only sizeable seabird cliff in Norway and lying near to a rich herring spawning ground. Skarvlakken and particularly Skittenskarvholmen are also near to herring grounds. Early in the 1960s there were rich herring fisheries in Vestfjorden and the other Lofotens. Brun (1972) considers this to have been the main factor in the establishment of the latter colony and one must agree that topographically the site is far from ideal. The Syltefjord colony is near the northern limit of the herring's distribution but is particularly well placed in relation to the distribution of capelin. This fish spawns in great numbers off East Finmark and in 1970 and 1971 massive spawning as far south as Andøya is suggested to have caused the immigration of new gannets to Nordmjele and Syltefjord in those years. This seems likely, for the spawning falls in the gannet's pre-breeding period and young adults remaining long in the area will be likely to stay there, particularly if at least a few are already established.

Brun's analysis of the increase in Norwegian gannets assumes (1) that the probability of an individual aged 0, surviving to one year (P_0) = 0·6; (2) that the analogous factor between the age of 1 and 2 years (P_1) = 0·8; (3) P_2 = 0·85; (4) adult survival (P_x) = 0·94; (5) that birds breed first at five years of age.

Various figures for annual breeding success are built into his equations to investigate the range of potential increases. He concludes, as I have argued elsewhere, that the increase of 12 per cent per annum proposed by Fisher & Venables (1938) and Salmon & Lockley (1933) as reasonable for an intrinsic rate, is far too high and that given 75 per cent breeding success, an increase of 5 per cent per annum or less would be more realistic (my own calculation for the increase on the Bass between 1949 and 1962 indicated a yearly increase of some 3 per cent and I suggested that this resulted entirely from the colony's own output, it is therefore highly significant that the *world* increase between 1939 and 1974 (for which period the figures are the most reliable) is 2·9 per cent per annum (see Table 5). With only 60 per cent breeding success the Norwegian population's doubling time would be about 22 years. Brun's conclusion that, therefore, the Norwegian increase has depended on immigration is thus uncontestable and supports my own suggestion that *all* new gannetries depend for their increase on immigration. Brun concludes that even at Runde where the rate of increase in the first eight years was relatively slow, there must have been immigration. The recruits probably came from Scottish colonies. Hermaness and Noss are the nearest, at 430 km and St. Kilda is also an attractive candidate, but the only proof of source concerns the Ailsa bird that bred on Skarvlakken in its 4th year, laying its first egg when 3 years 10 or 11 months old. The bulk of recoveries of ringed gannets from Norwegian waters are of Bass Rock birds but this may be because Bass gannets perhaps feed off Norway more than do birds from western or even northern colonies. Also, and more importantly, a much higher proportion of them are ringed (indeed virtually all ringed gannets are marked on Ailsa and the Bass, with some from Grassholm). However, it remains possible that recruits stem also, or even mainly, from the Bass or from Iceland.

6. *Canadian* (*St. Lawrence*) *group*

Bleak though the cliffs of British gannetries may be in late winter, when most birds return, they cannot match the severity of the icy Gulf of St. Lawrence and Newfoundland colonies where birds may become largely buried in snow as they sit on their nests. Yet, though summer comes later, there is enough time for the gannet's relatively compressed breeding cycle, and the rich waters of the Canadian fishing banks lie within easy foraging distance of all colonies. The largest colony of the North Atlantic gannet ever recorded was on Bird Rocks, Quebec, and before it was devastated by what Fisher & Vevers aptly describe as wanton savagery, the North American population dominated the world figures, comprising over 60 per cent of the species' total numbers. For details of present numbers and recent changes in Canadian colonies and for colony descriptions including Figs. 27 to 29 I am deeply indebted to Dr. David Nettleship.

(*a*) *Bird Rocks, Magdalen Islands* (Latest count Great Bird 4527, Little Bird 804 pairs, 1973)

Bird Rocks lie in the twelve islands of the Magdalen Archipelago, Gulf of St. Lawrence. Great Bird's (Fig. 27) limestone cliffs are 30m high but North or Little Bird, now two stacks

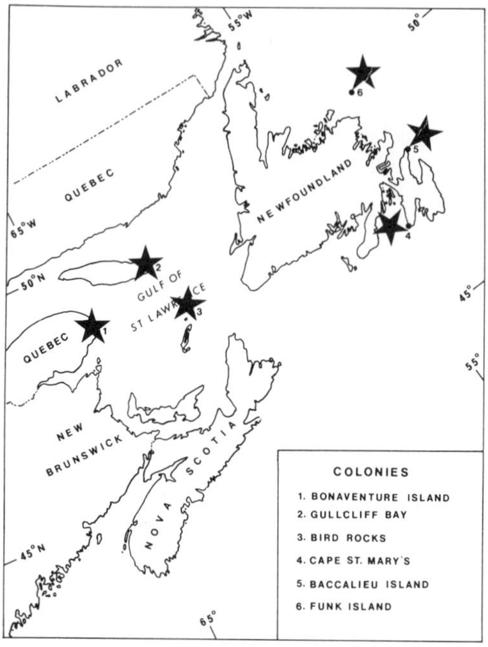

Fig. 26

Canadian gannetries. From Nettleship (1975a).

Fig. 27

Bird Rocks (Magdalen Islands). Great Bird (A) was once covered on top with gannets and was the largest colony ever known. *Photo:* Nettleship (1975a).

immediately north-west of Great Bird, is being rapidly eroded. The earliest account, quoted by Gurney, is that contained in Hakluyt's story of Cartier's voyage of 1534, in which the three islands in the group were 'as full of birds as any medow is of grasse, which there do make their nestes; and in the greatest of them there was a great and infinite number of those that we call Margaulx, that are white and bigger than any geese'. Although this vast colony continued undiminished until the nineteenth century, there is no estimate of numbers until Bryant's visit of 1860 by which time the slaughter wreaked by the fishermen since (at least) the 1820s, had taken effect. Even so, he estimated about 50 000 nests on half the summit of Great Bird Rock and about half that number on the sides of Great and Little Bird. From this, Fisher & Vevers calculate that at a density of a little under 1 pair/sq. m the top of the rock held in the neighbourhood of 100 000 pairs and the whole colony 125 000 pairs. The density figure used by these authors is in fact minimal and the population may have been considerably higher. On the other hand the figure of 50 000 is subject to possibly, 50 per cent error. In any case it was probably by far the greatest in the world, including Cape and Australasian gannetries, though still as nothing compared with the piqueros of Guañape. The decrease within the next four years, if accurately judged, was to say the least, remarkable. Fisher puts the 1864 population on the plateau at 40 000 pairs (plus 25 000 on the sides) which means that 30 000 adults, and presumably many young, were killed *annually* in those four years. Assuming that 10 000 young were taken and that the period during which the gannets were approachable lasted four months, this means 2500 birds each week. The slide continued at the same terrific pace. Following the building of the lighthouse in 1869 the 1872 plateau population was put at 2500 whilst by 1881 the summit, which well within a man's lifetime had held 100 000 pairs, was nearly deserted. A paltry 50 nests were there, all recently robbed! However, the cliff sites were as full as ever and Little Bird was probably full to capacity. Even this situation apparently did not endure. Chapman's visit (1900) suggested only about 600–700 pairs for the entire rock. Little Bird (by 1900 eroded into three stacks) was evidently fairly well occupied in 1900 (it was shot-up and robbed the same year). An estimate in 1932 gave about 700 birds on Great Bird and 300 on Little Bird.

Nettleship's (1975a) report gives three recent photographic counts, in terms of nest-site holders (which is the best expression). For Great Bird those are 27 June 1967 (3750); 25 July 1969 (4397); 7 July 1973 (4527) and for Little Bird on the same dates, 1250; 807 and 804, in total 5000; 5204 and 5331 respectively. Assuming the 1932 estimate was correct and converting to pairs gives a total of 500 at that time. At an increase of 5 per cent per annum the 1967 total would have been 2762 whereas it was 5000. The discrepancy is not so great when one considers that the 1932 figure, which was not a count, may have been substantially wrong and there seems no firm justification for concluding that the increase depended on immigration, though it may well have done so. Similarly, the increase between 1967 and 1973 was extremely slight—less than 2 per cent per annum—though again the potential error in the assessment could mean that a steady increase of the order to be expected from intrinsic production is occurring. The shift of birds from Little Bird to Great Bird between 1967 and 1969 was perhaps due to cliff erosion.

(*b*) *Bonaventure Island, Quebec* (Latest count 17 281 pairs, 1973)

Bonaventure is roughly circular, about 2·7 km by 2·5 at the widest points and with an area of some 730 hectares. The cliffs, 76m high on the south-east where the gannets nest, are a mixture of conglomerate and red sandstone. Its early history is unknown. The first record was about 1860 (no numbers given) and the first 'estimate' (1887) was a rough guess at 15 000 pairs, though in 1898 Chapman guessed at 7000 birds. Much the same estimate (4000 pairs) was made in 1914, 1915 and 1918. Then there seems to have been an increase; 1932 gave an estimate of 6000 pairs, 1938 7000 pairs and 1940 6600–7000 pairs. By 1934 the birds had spread onto grassy slopes above the cliffs (Poulin & Moisan 1968) and continued to increase there, nesting even under trees. A combined count from the ground and photographs taken from a boat, July 1961, gave 13 250 pairs (Peakall 1962) whilst a detailed count from boat, ground and aerial photographs in 1966 gave 8967 pairs on the cliffs and 12 248 on top (total 21 215). This could have been produced by an increase of less than 5 per cent per annum on the 1938 figure of 7000 pairs (which I select because it was the count by Wynne-Edwards and likely to be as accurate as possible). The increase on Bonaventure between 1938 and 1966 may thus be considered to have occurred as a result of the colony's own output rather than from immigration (see also Nettleship 1975b).

Oddly enough, the colony decreased between 1969 and 1973. Nettleship's data, using two strictly comparable counts from aerial photographs, yielded 20 511 in July 1969 and 17 281 in July 1973, a decline of about 16 per cent. Whilst such a discrepancy could result from the potential errors of the count, it seems likely to represent a real decrease, much of which seems to have occurred among the cliff breeders. In 1969 there were 8657 cliff-top pairs and 11 584 ledge nesters but in 1973 the equivalent figures were 8007 and 9274 pairs. This could be due partly to colony interchange or to mortality. Alternatively, it is possible that toxic chemicals may be involved (see pp. 63 and 108). Nettleship (1975b) in fact concludes that the decline has resulted from reduced fertility due to contamination by toxics and to disturbance by tourist boats and visitors on land. The decline continues (1976).

(*c*) *Gullcliff Bay, Anticosti Island* (Latest count 135 pairs, 1972)

This gannetry lies on the south-east tip of Anticosti, an island 225 by 48km situated in the western entrance of the St. Lawrence. The birds are scattered in small groups of between 2 and 37 pairs along 1·6km of highly fractured and crumbly limestone cliffs 45–60m high. It is relatively new, formed before 1920 and perhaps as early as 1913. In 1923 there were reputedly hundreds in at least two distinct groups, a small one south-east of Table Head and the main one at Gullcliff Bay. The latter group numbered about 500 nests in 1928 and the same in 1940, at which latter time there was thought to be little or no room for increase. In fact the colony has since decreased from 200 pairs in August 1963 to 167 pairs in July 1969 and 135 in June 1972 (Nettleship 1975a). If this decrease is natural, by which I mean not caused by man's agency, it is of great interest. The site is obviously not ideal and may have been colonised as a result of the terrible disturbance at traditional colonies, which continued into the twentieth century. Now, young birds may be attracted to these traditional sites, currently underpopulated, and Anticosti may be slowly running down. This, however, is pure guesswork.

(*d*) *Cape St. Mary's, Newfoundland* (Latest count 5260 pairs, 1972)

Slightly separated from the south-west extremity of the Avalon Peninsula lies a 152m

Fig. 28. Gullcliff Bay, Anticosti Island: a good example of a relatively unsuitable nesting area, colonised probably because other major ones were disrupted by man. *Photo:* Nettleship (1975a).

stack, Bird Rock (Fig. 27) now densely covered with gannets on the steep, seaward face. The year in which the colony was founded has been accurately judged as either 1878 or 1879 at which time there were three pairs or less. This had grown to about 8–10 pairs by 1883 but by 1890 there must have been hundreds (said to be 'literally covered with birds' and 'thick' with gannets and murres). In 1934 Wynne-Edwards found about 4000 nests covering the whole of the steep, sea-facing slope and the upper-cliff. This situation was reckoned to represent an increase of one-quarter over the population of ten years earlier and perhaps twice as many as were present in 1913. In about 1926 gannets first crossed the narrow gap to the mainland but did not actually attempt to breed until 1931 and apparently still do not nest there successfully. Up until 1939, at least, mainland nests were destroyed by fishermen but presumably this no longer happens. Bird Rock, however, may have been filled nearly to capacity by 1934, for later counts show little increase: 4294 ± 350 pairs, (1939); c. 3000 (July 1969) by ground count; 5260 (1972) by aerial photography. The difference between 1969 and 1972 probably reflects the different methods used (1969 counts too low) for on the basis of the extent of the colony it was considered that it had not fluctuated significantly between 1959 and 1969, so there is no reason to think it would suddenly shoot up between 1969 and 1972.

Cape St. Mary's would seem to be another colony established as a result of the persecution at traditional sites. It may well have been producing immigrants for some time, since a spread to the mainland has been frustrated. As early as 1934, Wynne-Edwards noted 500–700 adult-plumaged birds standing on the mainland slope! Probably at least some of these were young adults unable to acquire a site on Bird Rock.

(*e*) *Baccalieu Island, Newfoundland* (Latest count 673 pairs, 1973)

Baccalieu is a rocky island situated off the north-east tip of the Avalon Peninsula, about 2·5km east of Split Point. It is about 6·5km long but less than 1·6km wide. The gannets nest on precipitous cliffs near the middle of the east coast facing the sea. The colony was not discovered until 1941 by which time it was already about 2000 pairs strong and by local repute some 40 years old. The cliffs are not ideal; most of the horizontal faces are undercuts rather than ledges and again it looks as though its colonisation was enforced by the persecution at Bird Rocks and Bonaventure. The first proper census was in July 1960 when some 900 occupied nests were counted from land and sea. In 1969 the population was estimated to be 351 pairs but it seems

Fig. 29. Cape St. Mary's, Newfoundland. Note the dense evenly-spaced birds. *Photo:* Nettleship (1975a).

quite likely that two of the three occupied cliff areas that comprise the colonies were not examined. In 1973, counts from aerial photographs yielded 673 nests. The difference could be a result of the two different census methods and it may probably be concluded that the colony is more or less stable or possibly declining.

(*f*) *Funk Island, Newfoundland* (Latest count 4051 pairs, 1972)

Funk Island is a slab of granite a mere 14m high, 0·8km long and 400m wide, lying some 56km north-north-east of Cape Freels. Mentioned by Cartier in 1534 this colony has had an eventful history. It became extinct sometime between 1857 and 1873 and was re-established probably in 1935 (there were none in 1934 and about 7 pairs breeding in 1936). Subsequent counts were about 200 pairs (1945), 1204 occupied nests (1956); 2760 pairs (July 1959); 2900 pairs (July 1967); 2786 pairs (July 1969); 2987 pairs (1971) and 4051 pairs (June 1972). All were ground counts except for 1972, which was from photographs. The ground counts were probably underestimates but it is still likely that a real increase did occur between then and 1972.

7. *Summary of Canadian gannetries*

Surveys in 1972–73 indicate a total North American gannet population of about 32 800 pairs (six colonies) of which 22 700 (69·2 per cent) nest in the Gulf of St. Lawrence and 10 100 (30·8 per cent) on the Atlantic coast of Newfoundland. A summary of changes in the six colonies from 1959 to 1973 is given in Table 4.

The numbers in the St. Lawrence peaked around 1966 and have since slightly declined mostly due to the drop in numbers at Bonaventure (q.v.). The Anticosti colony, also, appears to have declined by perhaps 19 per cent between 1969 and 1973. The reasons are unknown but may involve low recruitment due to toxic chemicals. Both Bonaventure and Anticosti are

TABLE 4

ESTIMATED NUMBERS OF PAIRS OF GANNETS* AT NORTH AMERICAN COLONIES BETWEEN 1959 and 1973.† ONLY 1972, 1973, AND THREE 1969 COLONY ESTIMATES ARE BASED ON STANDARDISED CENSUS PROCEDURES; FOR DETAILS SEE INDIVIDUAL COLONY TABLES AND THE TEXT (NETTLESHIP 1975a)

	Previous counts using various methods									Present numbers from aerial photography	
Colony	1959	1960	1961	1963	1966	1967	1969	1970	1971	1972	1973
Bonaventure Island	—	—	13 250	—	21 215	—	20 511	—	—	—	17 281
Anticosti Island	—	—	—	200	—	—	167	—	—	135	—
Bird Rocks	—	—	—	—	—	5000	5204	—	—	—	5331
Cape St. Mary's	—	—	—	—	—	—	(*c.* 3000)††	—	—	5260	—
Baccalieu Island	—	*c.* 900	—	—	—	—	(351)††	—	—	—	673
Funk Island	2768	—	—	—	—	2900	2786	2760	2987	4051	—

* Represents the number of 'nest-site holders'.
† Years with no census data are omitted.
†† Count based on incomplete survey.

situated in the most contaminated part of the Gulf (towards the St. Lawrence estuary) and the concentration of chlorinated hydrocarbons and heavy metals is greater in the Gulf than along the Atlantic coast of Newfoundland. The levels of toxic chemicals in gannet tissues are significantly higher at Bonaventure than at Funk (Pearce *et al.* 1973) and egg shells are thinner (17 per cent thinner than pre-1915 eggs). Correspondingly breeding success is lower. Due to incomplete counts, changes in the Newfoundland colonies are difficult to interpret, but Funk Island increased rapidly in the early 1950s and apparently further since 1971, which again suggests that the St. Lawrence decline is local and not due to factors operating generally on the Canadian population.

Between 1909–39 and 1963–69 the west Atlantic population has increased at a rate of 2·6 and 3·2 per cent per year respectively. Thus, the overall rate of increase for the whole of the present century has been near to that which would be predicted from the gannet's known recruitment and mortality rates. It probably differs slightly from the pattern of increase shown by the east Atlantic population in that the latter increased significantly more slowly in the first of these 30-year periods, perhaps due to the number of east Atlantic colonies which were still being exploited. In the second of the 30-year periods the annual percentage rates of increase were highly comparable on the two sides of the Atlantic (3·2 on the west, 2·9 on the east).

Defunct colonies

Gannets are usually faithful to their breeding localities but, usually because of interference by man, several colonies have become defunct. They are of interest because they complete any account of its distribution and supplement an understanding of what constitutes a topographically acceptable locale. The following list comprises all stations at which gannets have been known or suspected to breed but no longer do so; it is derived mainly from Fisher & Vevers (1943).

South-west Britain group

1. *Gulland Rock*, Cornwall. An ancient (1468) unconfirmed record.

2. *Gannet Stone*, Lundy, Devon. An ancient (1274) colony. Still plentiful in 1871, but rapidly decreasing, about 70 nests in 1890; extinct by 1909, or possibly 1906. An attempted re-introduction via cormorant-fostered eggs (1938 and 1939), failed.

3. *Stags of Broadhaven*, Mayo. There is considerable reason to doubt that gannets ever bred here. Knox's young 'on the wing' were probably from Skellig and nobody claims to have actually seen nests there. In any event, 1836 is the last claim that they nested here.

4. *Calf of Man*, Isle of Man. It seems that gannets bred here, possibly in considerable numbers, in the sixteenth and seventeenth centuries. There is no record of their demise.

West and north Britain group

Oddly enough in this region of cliff-girt islands galore, there is not one sure or even probable record of a defunct gannetry. The following have extremely tenuous claims to be so considered:

5. *Islay*; 6. *Eig*; 7. *Rum*; 8. *Haskeir*; 9. *North Rona*. A pair made an unsuccessful attempt to breed on 10. *Copinsay* (1915 or 1916), (Aplin 1915). On Holy Island, Arran, up to 25 birds frequented the east cliffs and carried nest material (1950) after appearing there in 1946, but in 1951 there were only six, and in 1952, none (Gibson 1952).

East Britain group

11. *Isle of May*, Fife. Bred here (but no record of numbers) before 1850 and a pair tried to nest in 1922. It is so near to the Bass that future colonisation is not unlikely.

Iceland, Faroes and Norway group

No records to add.

St. Lawrence group

12. *Gannet Rock*, Grand Manan, New Brunswick. Possibly some numbers breeding before the lighthouse was built (1830) but probably extinct before 1870.

13. *Gannet Rock*, Yarmouth, Nova Scotia. Hundreds of gannets and at least 150 nests in 1856. Probably extinct soon afterwards, as a result of persecution by local fishermen.

14. *Perroquet Islands*, Mingans, Quebec. At one time, gannets bred on the north-western island of the group, apparently in considerable if not great numbers, up to 1857–59. In 1881 it contained only robbed nests and by 1887, though a few birds were still around, none were breeding, nor have they done so since.

From this it is clear that very few erstwhile major gannetries have become extinct within historical times. It seems that, for at least many hundreds of years, the gannet has stuck fairly closely to a few traditional breeding places, most of them supporting great colonies which have managed to persist, despite man. On the other hand, the growth of several gannetries to a size of several thousand pairs, this century, tends to belie the attractive proposition that the 'few but great colonies' trait means that there are but that number of suitable stations available. This raises the intriguing matter of the adaptive significance of colony size, which is discussed on p. 80.

World population

The 1976 world statistics for the gannet (see also Tables 5 and 6) are: 34 colonies holding a grand total of some 213 000 site-holding pairs, divided among countries (though these do not correspond to any biologically meaningful boundaries) as follows: Britain and Ireland 16 colonies (over 70 per cent of total numbers); Canada 6 (17 per cent); Iceland, the Faroes and Norway 11 (12 per cent) and France 1 (2 per cent). The eastern North Atlantic holds 28 of the 34 colonies, with 180 000 pairs or 84 per cent of the world population, and Canada holds 32 800 pairs or 16 per cent. The most densely populated 'area' is that to the west and north of Scotland. Since (at least) 1939, the population has been increasing at approximately 3 per cent per annum, which is an almost exact fit with the figure which would be predicted from known breeding success, mortality rates, etc.

GENERAL ASPECTS OF POPULATIONS

The basic facts are quite clear, namely that on both sides of the Atlantic the gannet population was drastically reduced from its earlier numbers by man's persecution for food, bait and 'sport' mainly in the nineteenth century. Subsequently, due to protection, it began a spirited recovery in the early twentieth century and this still continues. These facts, firmly established by Fisher & Vevers (1943, 44) and since brought up to date in a remarkable series of counts unparalleled for any other seabird in the world, have been reviewed in the preceding section. The counts, however, make it feasible to discuss several topics besides straight numbers. Among these are 1. Regional trends and interchange between colonies; 2. The founding and growth of new colonies; 3. Pioneering and philopatry; 4. The nature of man's effect on gannet numbers.

1. *Regional trends and interchange between colonies*

Information about the population trends in individual colonies, regions and the world is given in Tables 5 and 6 and Figs. 30 and 31 (see also Appendices 2 and 3). Gurney's estimate of the number of gannets in 1910 was 16 colonies and 101 000 individuals, excluding Club birds and immatures; Fisher & Vevers' equivalent figure is about 67 000 pairs (134 000 individuals of the categories included by Gurney). The increase in the 30 years between 1909 and 1939 is about 22 per cent whereas that between 1939 and 1969 is 140 per cent. This great recovery has occurred as a result of increases throughout the gannet's range, though by no means equally, and the faster rate of increase in the second 30 years is perhaps mainly due to reduced persecution during this period.

The rate of increase which one would expect from a gannet population enjoying the breeding success typical of the Bass colony, and the mortality rate and age of first breeding of its birds and (most importantly) neither suppressing its own reproductive rate nor limited by density-dependent external factors, is about 3 per cent per annum (see p. 131). However, different 'populations' (and a 'population' is often impossible to define, for the gannet, in terms that satisfy requirements for demographic prediction) could have different breeding success and/or adult mortality. This may be true even excluding man's direct interference, whilst if man *is* taken into account, extremely potent variables are introduced. Nevertheless, an increase of around 5 per cent per annum is the most that can reasonably be expected from a colony's own output, and 3–4 per cent is nearer to the correct figure for most colonies, whilst anything from an annual decrease to stability or slight increase could, depending on degree, result from man's interference in a colony receiving no immigrants.

The obvious cross-check on this figure of 3 per cent is by direct observation of the increase actually attained. This, however, depends heavily on there being no (or a known amount of) emigration or immigration—usually difficult or impossible to gauge—no 'unnatural' killing of adults (and to a lesser extent young) and on accurate counts (with a potential error of at least 20 per cent in counts of a large gannetry the interpretation of trends can be hazardous). Thus the increase of any one colony is rarely dependable as a cross check; that of a region might seem more trustworthy, but it is very difficult to be reasonably sure that they are self-contained. Probably east and west Atlantic populations *are* discrete but within these limits one can merely attempt to balance the evidence and probabilities and demarcate 'regions' accordingly. Usually it is quite clear when a particular colony *is* receiving immigrants because the rate of increase is obviously far too high. The trouble arises in deciding that a colony (or region) is not receiving immigrants or losing emigrants. In fact, the only acceptable direct cross check on prediction is the Bass Rock, which probably *is* autonomous and whose observed rate of increase over the last 30 years fits extremely well with prediction based on its breeding success and mortality rate. More importantly, using these figures, the rate of increase of the *total populations* in the east and west Atlantic respectively also fits.[1] The following discussion of interchange therefore employs the figure of approximately 3–5 per cent per annum as the intrinsic rate of increase. It is worth noting that a similar figure (5·3 per cent between 1945 and 1964) applied to the increase of the Australasian gannet on Cape Kidnappers (Wodzicki 1967).

It is worth emphasising that large-scale interchange between widely separated colonies, over a distance of hundreds of miles, as here postulated for the gannet, is a new and important idea. Formerly it had been assumed, albeit tacitly, that, except for a few pioneers, geographically discrete colonies were virtually autonomous. It is therefore interesting to note that recent evidence reveals that kittiwake and herring gull populations are subject to the same phenomenon. Kittiwakes that are ready to establish a site visit several colonies, up to 100 miles (160km) or more apart, before joining one, to which thereafter they are faithful. But less than 35 per cent of the newcomers to Coulson's South Shields colony were birds that had been born there. Similarly, herring gulls ringed on the Isle of May are breeding in considerable numbers at gulleries up to 100 miles (160km) away. The implications are that at the beginning of each breeding season, large numbers of young gannets and gulls (to stick merely to these species) travel between colonies, assessing local conditions. Among the factors likely to influence their choice I would include the number of topographically suitable sites, the degree of social (behavioural) stimulation in the whole area, the age structure of the colony or sub-colony and local feeding conditions. Coulson has evidence that, in the kittiwake, the density of the colony or sub-colony, is an important determinant, birds preferring neither the densest nor the least dense. Thus colonies with the right sort of 'gaps' are more attractive than much emptier or fuller ones. In gannetries, density varies so little that it cannot be important.

The regions into which Fisher & Vevers divided the world's population of gannets are not equivalent to each other either in number and size of colonies, total population, 'spare' nesting places or anything else. Indeed these authors used them merely as arbitrary devices to divide up the world's colonies into convenient units. It is particularly difficult to draw lines separating colonies or groups of colonies to the west and north of Britain. A superficial glance at the distribution map (Fig. 6(b)) suggests grouping the Irish colonies, Grassholm, the Channel Isles and Brittany (equivalent to Fisher & Vevers' south-west Britain group) and then the St. Kilda-Shetland axis group. But this leaves Ailsa (and less importantly Scar Rocks) high and dry, in an isolation which almost certainly they do not experience. It therefore seems advisable to include them with the north Britain group. The east Britain 'group', as remarked, is a natural

[1] This eliminates the emigration problem and allows a valid cross-check on pre-breeding mortality, since all other factors in the equation are known.

unit. The Iceland gannetries, also, *may* be fairly discrete, but the Faroes and Norwegian colonies certainly are not and, though there is no direct evidence linking them, I have grouped these three together. The alternative, linking Faroes to the west and north Britain group, is perhaps equally valid, but would mean leaving Iceland on its own (or linking it with the west and north Britain group). As emphasised, the whole procedure is largely one of convenience. Without it, one would either have to discuss each colony in isolation, or leave

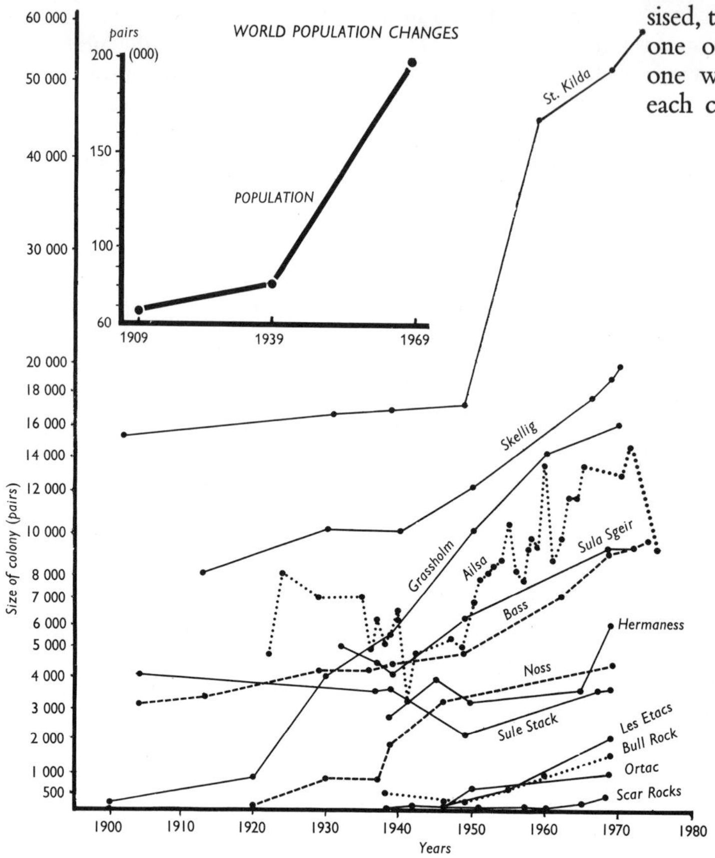

Fig. 30(a)

Population trends in British gannetries, 1900–1970.

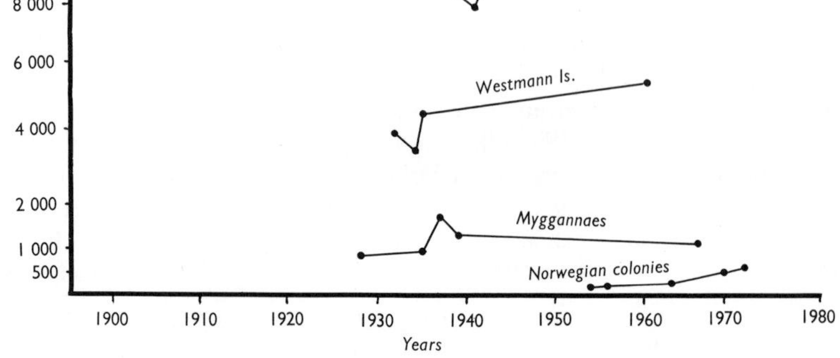

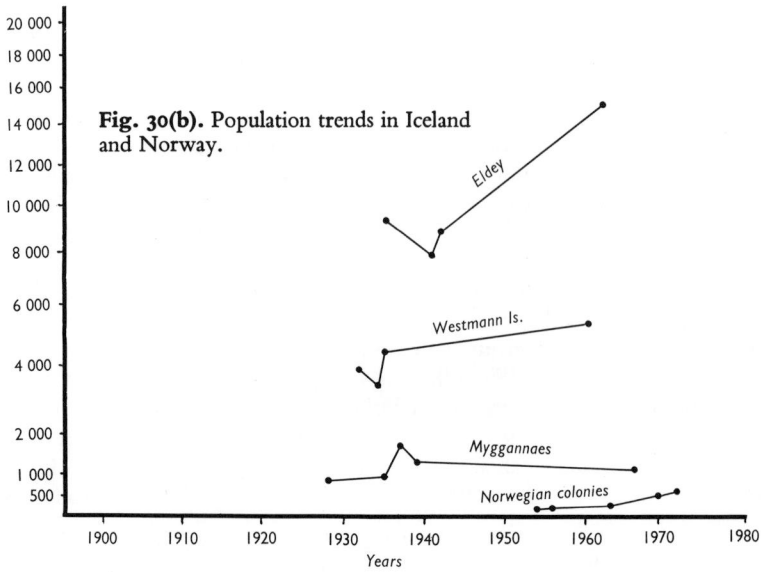

Fig. 30(b). Population trends in Iceland and Norway.

the entire east Atlantic population undivided. The west Atlantic population probably is a 'unit'. The rates of increase associated with various hypothetical groupings are shown in Table 5.

(*a*) *South-west Britain group*

Gannets have steadily increased in this region, starting from the low point of about 1859. Between 1859 and 1909 the population rose from at most 300 pairs to almost 16 000 pairs, which unarguably requires immigration, though in the last 30 years or so, the increase probably could have been generated from within the group (between 1939 and 1969 it increased at the rate of 3·4 per cent per annum). This situation means *either* that gannets from outside (probably from the west and north of Scotland) colonised the south-west group, noticeably Skellig and particularly during the latter half of the nineteenth century, but later stopped doing so, *or* that they still do so. In the latter case, extensive *interchange* must necessarily be occurring between the south-west region and the west and north Scotland region, for we have seen that the production of the former, alone, would give the increase which *has* occurred and therefore, if the south-west is receiving immigrants in addition, it must be exporting to redress the balance and stay within the observed rate of increase. Both alternatives have important implications. The former (import without export) means that, as the south-west colonies grew, young birds from other colonies stopped coming in. But why should that happen? On the contrary, a growing colony with spare space is a powerful attractant to young adults or near-adults. Possibly the influx is still occurring but the only colony within the south-west group to be receiving large numbers is Grassholm, Skellig and Bull Rock being nearly full. Even this, however, is not supported by the Grassholm figures for the last 10 years, which show no significant increase. The interchange hypothesis, on the other hand, means that birds are still coming in, whilst some recruits from south-west colonies are themselves going elsewhere, presumably north. This seems far more likely than that young birds should suddenly stop investigating strange colonies as potential breeding areas.

Fig. 30(c). Population trends in Norway 1940–1973.

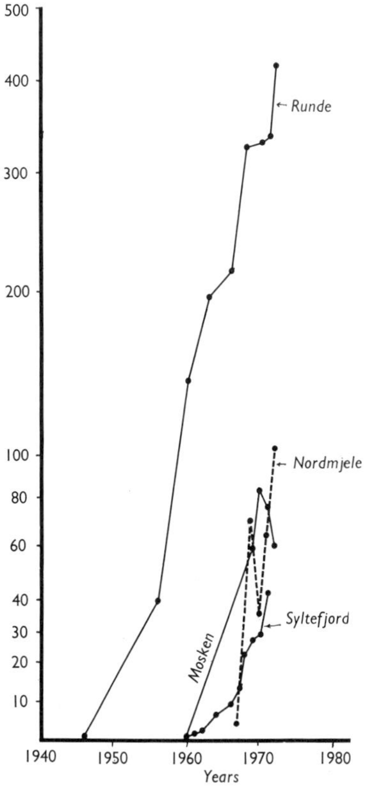

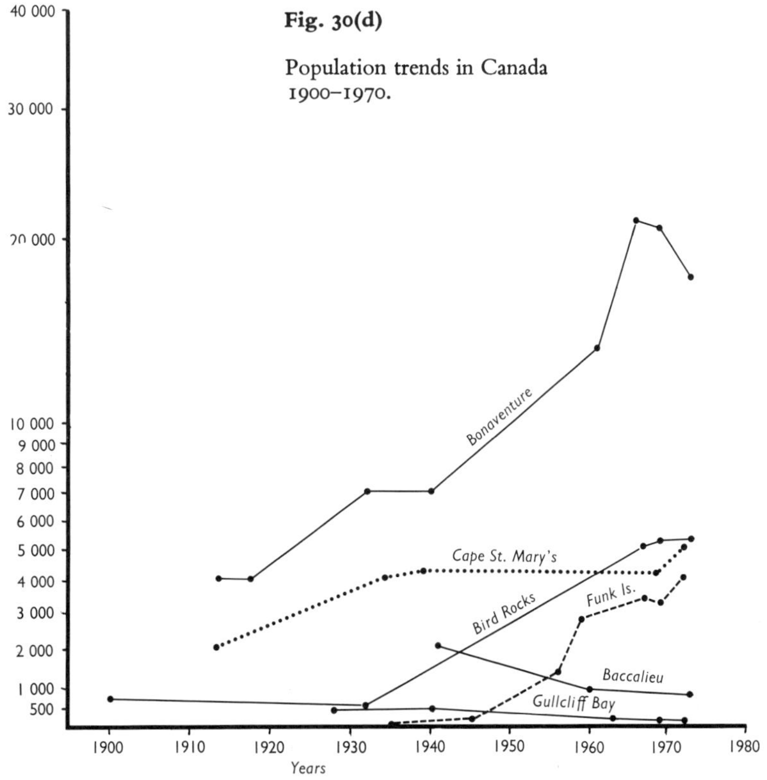

Fig. 30(d)

Population trends in Canada 1900–1970.

Such 'floating' (a term which distinguishes between actually founding a new colony, or pioneering, and joining a colony other than the one of birth) implies considerable fortuitousness in the choice of breeding colony. Thus, for example, some Grassholm and Ailsa birds would (on the interchange hypothesis) be 'floating to' or joining, other colonies even though their own are not full, while Skellig and Sule Stack birds would be 'floating' to other colonies, their own being apparently fairly full. The other event, namely birds floating from a full natal colony to a full 'other' presumably, on this hypothesis, also occurs. It would of course be attractive to suppose that 'floating' occurs only from full natal to roomy 'other' colonies, but the Grassholm and Ailsa figures indicate otherwise (see pp. 26 and 34). Nevertheless, this type may well be the commonest and most important. In any event, it would become necessary (if continuous interchange operates) to consider the south-west region and the west and north Scotland region as one huge population and indeed, since the rate of increase in both these areas has been exactly comparable (Table 5) it is impossible to separate the alternative hypotheses (that they are operating as one 'group' or two groups). The only way to quantify the situation would be to gain dependable figures for each colony for the proportion of young birds returning to breed at their colony of birth. This is an impossible task, but it might be attempted for a selected few.

A second factor, besides interchange, that greatly affects the population dynamics of a colony is human exploitation. During the period under review, this has not been important in the south-west region. The relaxation of human pressure on Skellig, from at least 1880 onwards, undoubtedly allowed the colony to increase, as it did so markedly (from about 30 pairs in 1880 to perhaps 17 500 in 1906), and this increase was due to immigration from outside the south-west region, there being no source of recruits within the south-west at that time.

With this background, we may discuss individual colonies, within the region. For, almost all this century, the main producer of 'spare' recruits has been Little Skellig. It has seemed fairly full ever since 1906. In fact 10 000 pairs has seemed, to some observers, a full house, though we now know that Skellig managed to hold twice this number by 1969. Several authors have speculated that Grassholm has been a beneficiary of the Skellig output and this seems very likely. As a slight disgression, here, it may be worth stating the implications of the view that a full colony causes young birds to go elsewhere, for it is not as simple as it

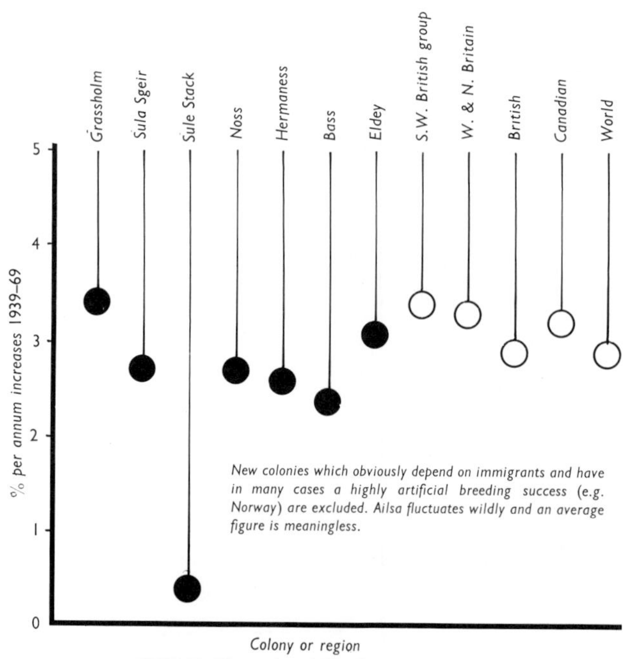

Fig. 31. The rates of growth (per cent per annum) in some gannetries, 1939–1969.

sounds. One necessarily implies *either* that young adults return, try to find a site but experience difficulty and so move elsewhere *or* that they assess the situation before they actually attempt site acquisition and some move elsewhere. Alternatively, some may 'float' without even returning to Skellig (or at least without having been influenced as free-flying individuals, by crowding there). There is no evidence for any of these; my own hunch is that a combination of the second and third occurs. The likelihood of a gannet leaving a colony in which it has actually got as far as attempting site-acquisition seems remote. The actual mechanism which operates may have to do with the behavioural 'look' of a colony (or part of a colony) which has a high proportion of young site-establishing birds already there, for I am convinced that this attracts others. The possibility that some young birds simply 'tack on', fortuitously, to another colony (though perhaps also being influenced by its behavioural look) is of course enhanced by the mere presence of other gannetries within the general area. The *extent* of the inflow of recruits at any particular colony doubtless depends partly on the suitability of the locality, on whether there is a large and crowded gannetry nearby and on how many other gannetries are growing in the neighbourhood, but once the pioneers have established it, the

TABLE 5

POPULATION OF THE ATLANTIC GANNET, 1909–69

Region (in order of size of population) (see Table 6)	Year	No. of colonies	No. of site occupying pairs (to nearest 500)	Per cent increase 1909 to 1939	Per cent increase 1939 to 1969	Per cent per annum increase 1909 to 1939	Per cent per annum increase 1939 to 1969	Per cent (in 1969) of: east Atlantic population	Per cent (in 1969) of: World population
1. West and north Britain	1909	4	28 500						
	1939	7	34 000						
	1969	8	89 000	19	162	0·6	3·3	54	45
2. South-west Britain	1909	3	15 500						
	1939	5	16 000						
	1969	7	43 000	3	169	0·1	3·4	26	22
3. Canada (west Atlantic population)	1909	4	6000						
	1939	6	13 000						
	1969	6	33 000	117	154	2·6	3·2	—	16
4. Faroes, Iceland, Norway	1909	4 {3I, 1F}	14 000						
	1939	4 {3I, 1F}	15 000						
	1969	11 {6I, 1F, 4N}	22 500	7	50			14	11
5. East Britain	1909	1	3000						
	1939	2	4500						
	1969	2	9000	50	100	1·3	2·4	6	5
Total east Atlantic population	1909	12	61 000						
	1939	18	69 500						
	1969	28	163 000	14	134	0·4	2·9	100	84
World population	1909	16	67 000						
	1939	24	82 500						
	1969	33	196 500	23	98	0·7	2·9		
	1976	34	213 000						

'floater' hypothesis would ensure some growth. And this indeed usually seems to happen, even where localities are distinctly unfavourable (as in some Norwegian gannetries and to a slight extent, at Bempton q.v.). Grassholm was evidently in an ideal situation for growth, once founded, for it was fairly near to crowded Skellig and was itself an excellent site with great capacity for increase of gathering momentum. As we have seen, it evidently did draw in large numbers of 'floaters'. Now, it is perhaps nearing saturation and maybe stable or even somewhat fluctuating.

(*b*) *West and north Britain group*

This massive and complex group, including St. Kilda, the world's largest gannetry, has increased at an annual rate of about 3·3 per cent between 1939 and 1969, which is about the predictable intrinsic rate. As we have seen, the region must at one time have supplied recruits to the south-west and if the interchange hypothesis discussed above is correct, it is still exchanging some with it. Within the west and north Britain group the colonies most likely to be producing potential emigrants to other colonies within the area (and perhaps outside it) are St. Kilda and Sule Stack. St. Kilda may not have grown nearly as much as has been supposed (see p. 37) which could mean that over the past decades it has produced far more recruits than have found places there, whilst Sule Stack has appeared to be full up for half a century or more. On the other hand Sula Sgeir has been receiving immigrants in compensation for the losses due to exploitation whilst the dramatic growth of Noss and Hermaness has probably been built up from Kilda and Sule Stack. The most puzzling colony within the entire group is Ailsa. Its extraordinary fluctuations are difficult to understand. As suggested on p. 35 the occasional massive decreases must reflect a failure of the recruits from year class of five years previous, which are far more likely to have emigrated than died. The unique position of Ailsa, midway between two clusters of gannetries to north and south, may make it particularly prone to lose and gain recruits on a mainly fortuitous basis.

(*c*) *East Britain group*

There is little to add to what I have already said about the Bass' autonomy and the equivalence between observed and 'expected' rate of increase on the basis of known breeding success and mortality. The provision of immigrants to Bempton is proven, and it is probable that the Norwegian colonies also receive some Bass birds but at their present size, neither constitutes much of a drain. The mechanism by which the Bass retains autonomy is presumably simply that there are no other gannetries in the course of foraging trips on the east, so young birds are not caught up in their activity spheres. West coast birds, on the other hand, must frequently pass near to other gannetries and susceptible age classes must stand a chance of becoming involved with them. It is probably significant (p. 135) that, as soon as Bempton became of a 'reasonable' size, it began to attract more recruits and accelerated its rate of increase.

(*d*) *Iceland, Faroes and Norway group*

The Icelandic gannetries have been much affected by exploitation. Between 1910 and 1939 the mean annual catch on Eldey was recorded as 3257 (it became protected in 1940) whilst on the Westmanns, gannets are still taken, as they have been for centuries, the catch varying between 500 and 1000 birds a year. It is therefore interesting to find that the increase per annum of the Icelandic population between 1939 and 1959 was about 2·6 per cent. The interest lies partly in the fact that Icelandic gannets apparently increased (from 4800 pairs in 1910 to 13 732 in 1939) whilst *still* providing in the region of 4000 victims per year, and also that they increased about as much during that period as subsequently, when exploitation was reduced. However, the figures leave room for error, since Eldey is huge and difficult to count, and there may in fact be no real difference between the two periods. As for the increase between 1910 and 1939, this could have occurred intrinsically if the cull in that period was almost entirely of young birds. Otherwise it would become necessary to postulate immigration from other regions. Nowadays emigration from the crowded Eldey (at least) to the Faroes cannot be ruled out. There, too, culling occurs and could partly offset any immigration (Myggenaes has not grown much this century).

TABLE 6

NORTH ATLANTIC GANNETRIES

(numbers before braces refer to regions treated in Table 5)

Region	Colony	Founded	Year of latest estimate	Approximate number (pairs)*	Comment
	1. Grassholm	1820–60	1975	20370	Increase at times due to immigration; considerable emigration in recent years.
	2. Little Skellig	Before 1700	1974	18 000?	Massive initial emigration after colony founded; considerable emigration most of this century.
2	3. Bull Rock	1850s	1969	1500	Initial immigration; possible emigration in recent years.
	4. Great Saltee	1929	1975	193	Increase to date due largely to immigration.
	5. Ortac	1940	1969	1000	Initial increase due to immigration. Possibly exporting by now.
	Les Etacs	c. 1940	1969	2000	
	6. Rouzic	1937	1965	2600±10%	Initial increase due to immigration.
	7. Ailsa Craig	Before 1400	1976	c. 16 000†	Curious apparent fluctuations from year to year more marked than in any other gannetry.
	8. Scar Rocks	1939	1974	482	Established and initially augmented by immigration which is now tailing off or has ceased.
	9. St. Kilda	Before 800	1973	59 000	Ancient and huge gannetry which may or may not have been receiving immigrants since 1949, depending on accuracy of estimates. Prior to that, no need to postulate immigration and probable that some emigration. Now the largest Atlantic gannetry.
1	10. Fair Isle	1974	1975	? 5+chicks	
	11. Roareim (Flannans)	1969	1975	17	
	12. Sula Sgeir	Before 1400	1972	9000	An exploited colony which maintains its numbers by recruiting immigrants.
	13. Sule Stack	Before 1600	1969	4000	A 'full' colony (?) which exports most of its recruits, probably many to Sula Sgeir.
	14. Noss	1914	1969	4300	For 20–30 years after establishment, increased rapidly by immigration. Since, Hermaness at least has had periods of substantial immigration even though the per annum increase, 1939–69, was low enough to have stemmed from the colony's own output.
	15. Hermaness	1917	1976	6012	
	16. Bass Rock	Before 500	1976	11 000±10%	Rate of increase at all times consistent with intrinsic production. Is exporting small numbers.
5	17. Bempton	1920s	1976	c. 133	Accelerated growth in late 'sixties and during the 'seventies due largely to continuing immigration, probably all from Bass (some certainly are).

	Colony	Founded	Year of latest estimate	Approximate number (pairs)*	Comment
4	18. Westmanns	Before 1600	1962	5300	A relatively stable, exploited colony dependent for the maintenance of its numbers on immigrants.
	19. Eldey	Before 1700	1962	16 300	A large and ancient colony which increased by some 2 per cent per annum between 1939–62 but is probably nearly full and likely to have been exporting for several years.
	20. Skrúdur	1940s	1962	314	New Icelandic colonies, all of which have depended on immigration and are currently increasing, except possibly Raudinupur where some cliff has collapsed.
	21. Raudinupur	1940s	1962	34	
	22. Stori-Karl	1950s	1962	23	
	23. Máfadrang	1950s	1962	100	
	24. Myggenaes	Before 1600	1966	1801	An ancient, exploited colony which depends partly on immigration to maintain its numbers.
	25. Storebranden, Runde	1946	1972	422	Recent Norwegian colonies all of which have grown by recruiting immigrants. which they are probably still doing. One breeding adult on Skarvlakken was ringed as a juvenile on Ailsa Craig.
	26. Skittenskarvholmen, Mosken	1960s	1972	60	
	27. Skarvlakken, Nordmjele	1967	1972	103	
	28. Innerstauren, Syltefjord	1961	1976	44	
3	29. Bird Rocks	Before 1500	1973	5300	Formerly the world's largest gannetry. Increase since 1932 possibly partly dependent on immigration but could have occurred intrinsically.
	30. Bonaventure	Before 1800	1973	17 300	The largest west Atlantic gannetry. Recently has begun to decrease (1969–1973).
	31. Anti Costi Island	1913–20	1972	135	A decreasing colony; somewhat unsuitable terrain. Possibly founded by birds debarred from traditional colonies by persecution.
	32. Cape St. Mary's	c. 1878	1972	5300	Initially grew by massive immigration but little increase since 1934. The Bird Rock section is probably full.
	33. Baccalieu Island	c. 1900–10	1973	673	A decreasing colony; also probably unsuitable terrain. Initial increase by immigration.
	34. Funk Island	Before 1500	1972	4100	An increasing colony, receiving immigrants.

World total 213 800 pairs

Note: Potential error in world total in my opinion could be 30 000. World total more likely to be an overestimate than an underestimate.

* This figure is NOT breeding pairs and is NOT calculable directly from photographs. For accuracy it requires several corrections to be applied.

† This is a provisional figure only; see full account of Ailsa (p. 33).

(e) Canadian (St. Lawrence) group

The trend in the west Atlantic has been one of steady increase since the cessation of the incredible slaughter which reduced over 100 000 pairs on Bird Rocks to a handful and exterminated the Perroquet Islands colony. Between 1939 and around 1969 the annual increase in the western North Atlantic gannet population has been around 3·2 per cent, which is a good fit with expectation. There may be interchange between the St. Lawrence colonies (indeed this seems likely) but there certainly is no reason to suspect trans-Atlantic interchange. At no time have the Canadian colonies as a whole grown so fast that they must have received immigrants from outside the group. The founding of Canadian gannetries at sub-optimal sites such as Gullcliff Bay, Anticosti Island and Baccalieu Island may probably be attributed to disturbance at traditional sites in the nineteenth and early twentieth centuries.

Summing up this part of the general discussion, the main points are:

1. The rate of increase which a largely undisturbed colony may expect from its own output is about three per cent per annum, NOT the much higher figure used by earlier authors.
2. Both the western and eastern Atlantic populations have (independently) increased at the above rate for most of this century, due mainly to much less persecution by man. Thus the increase in the gannet population, dramatic though it may seem, is NOT explosive, (as claimed by Cramp *et al.* 1974) but a gradual recovery at the normal rate, over the species' entire range.
3. There has been (and presumably is) interchange between colonies, at least in the eastern Atlantic. This takes the form of young birds attaching themselves to colonies other than the one of their birth, but probably NEVER of adults breeding in one colony and then changing to another.
4. There is probably some degree of interchange between *all* the west and north British colonies, from Brittany to the Shetlands, though depending on available space and perhaps other factors, some colonies will export far more than they import, and vice-versa. But it may be impossible to draw lines demarcating autonomous regions within this vast complex. Thus, rates of increase show that the south-west region must have received immigrants at certain stages, and probably these came from the north. However, the increase in the south-west in the recent past has been low enough to show that it can no longer be receiving immigrants unless it is also exporting recruits. It seems more likely that it is doing so than that it has stopped receiving immigrants.
5. The east coast colonies (Bass and Bempton) are probably autonomous but the Bass and some west coast colonies may be providing recruits for Norway.
6. The Icelandic colonies may be autonomous or interchange with the Faroes. The evidence is difficult to interpret.

2. *Factors affecting the founding and growth of new colonies*

In 1910 Gurney listed 16 colonies, counting St. Kilda as one and the Westmann Islands as one, 3 in Canada (there were actually 5 but he did not know about Cape St. Mary's and Baccalieu); 3 in Iceland; one in the Faroes and 8 in Britain. By 1939 this number had grown to 24. Now, in 1974, the number has increased to 34 (Table 5; see also p. 64). The gannetries involved in this increase, in chronological order of founding, are:

1. Anticosti Island	(1913)	135 pairs by 1972
2. Noss	(1914)	4300 pairs by 1969
3. Hermaness	(1917)	6012 pairs by 1976
4. Funk Island	(1935 Re-established)	4051 pairs by 1972
5. Bempton	(1920s or 30s)	c. 133 nests by 1976
6. Scar Rocks	(1939)	482 pairs by 1974
7. Rouzic	(1939)	2600 pairs by 1965
8. Ortacs	(1940)	1000 pairs by 1969
9. Les Etacs	(1940)	2000 pairs by 1969

10. Skrúdur	(1943)	314 pairs by 1962
11. Raudinupur	(1944)	34 pairs by 1962
12. Storebranden	(1946)	422 pairs by 1972
13. Great Saltee	(1949 Re-established)	193 pairs by 1975
14. Stori-Karl	(1955)	23 pairs by 1962
15. Innerstauren	(1961)	44 pairs by 1971
16. Máfadrang	(1962)	100 pairs by 1962
17. Skittenskarvholmen	(1965)	60 pairs by 1972
18. Skarvlakken	(1967)	103 pairs by 1972
19. Flannans	(1969)	17 pairs in 1975
20. Fair Isle	(1974)	c. 20 pairs in 1974 (5 nests, no eggs); 5 + chicks 1975

As already mentioned, this spread has come about as a result of normal, *relatively* undisturbed breeding and is in no way comparable to the dramatic fulmar explosion in which the species raced from one new station to another at unprecedented speed. Increased output has resulted in more 'pioneers' and 'floaters' (see p. 68). The pioneers establish new colonies and the 'floaters', evidently relatively weakly 'imprinted' onto their natal colony, are attracted to other gannetries, among them the new ones, into whose neighbourhood they wander. The actual rate of increase at a new colony probably depends on several factors, including degree of proximity to a major colony and/or a main fishing ground; the physical attractiveness of the new station; the amount of disturbance by man and the degree of social 'excitement' at the colony (itself dependent on fortuitous circumstances, such as the number of floaters that happen to be around in any year and therefore available to form a strong growth-nucleus, and on some of the other factors just listed, such as the amount of suitable space). The role of social stimulation in the growth of a colony is in my view important and is discussed on p. 140 in connection with Bempton.

A perusal of the list of colonies just given reveals that:

1. New colonies may be founded whilst there is still room at major ones nearby.
2. They may be founded at stations which could never become major gannetries.
3. A new colony may receive immigrants from more than one old colony.
4. The new colonies which have attained rapid and substantial growth (Shetlands, Channel Islands, Rouzic, Funk Island and the same applies to Grassholm) are either fairly near to a major colony or colonies or athwart major sea-paths used by birds returning from the juvenile migration to North African waters. They are thus favourably placed to intercept 'floaters', just as Bempton is favourably placed to intercept Bass birds.

3. *Pioneering and philopatry*

Point 1 above is not surprising if one accepts the view that colonies are not founded as a result of young adults being frustrated in an attempt to gain a site in their natal colony, or the nearest one to it, but stem from 'pioneers', whose numbers naturally increase as the population does. The evidence too, is against the 'crowded out' hypothesis. Neither the Bass (which gave rise to Bempton) nor Ailsa (which presumably contributed to Scar Rocks) are even remotely full, whilst the birds that founded the Channel Island colonies could have gone instead to a half-empty but thriving gannetry (Grassholm). The pioneer principle has long been regarded as an important adaptive mechanism in maintaining the success of a species. Equally, however, 'philopatry', the return to one's own group, confers several advantages and is extremely marked in seabirds. Indeed it has usually been regarded as of prime importance though the nature of its survival value has been (and is) in dispute. The importance of 'interchange' is that, if there is much of it, we may have to readjust our estimate of the relative survival value of 'philopatry' as against 'pioneering' and 'floating'. We may also have to review opinions on the nature of the advantage conferred by philopatry.

'Floating', as defined here, is an attenuated form of pioneering and, like it, means that a bird opts out of the gene-pool from which it drew its genome. One might think this would be a relatively rare phenomenon, on the grounds that populations are likely to be genetically adapted to their locality. However, if there *is* much interchange, one must greatly increase the size of one's local unit, and perhaps allocate a larger role to learned adaptation. If one rejects group selection in the sense of a genetically co-adapted local population, the (breeding) interests of whose *individual* members must be overridden in the interests of the group, there remains the matter of local adaptations. Some of these are certainly learned rather than innate (knowledge of wind conditions in the breeding locality, fishing lore at different seasons and weathers) and can be as well acquired by an outsider as an insider. The former can also acquire a suitable site as easily as the latter. About the possibility of physiological adaptations to locality, nothing can yet be said.

Even if the above is true, probably most birds *do* return to their natal colony, and moreover near to the precise spot on which they were reared. This may, perhaps, be explained in the following terms (taking, first, the tendency to return to nest-locality). Chicks become visually fixed on their birth area, which under some circumstances can be an advantage (see p. 214), and certainly cannot be a disadvantage. This leads them back to the locality of their old nest, once they have returned to the colony. It may also be possible that genetic membership of a *small* group (rather than of the colony) could lead to the formation of adaptive gene-pools, though I can cite no actual cases of this phenomenon. As for the return to the colony as a whole, it may be largely (as Lack has frequently postulated) a matter of 'proven safety', this, however, being unimportant enough to be fairly readily overridden (as 'floating' would require).

The fact (point 2 above) that new colonies may be founded in unsuitable localities, in the sense that they could never support large gannetries (which are presumably adaptive) probably merely reflects the flexibility of 'pioneers' with regard to habitat-selection—a necessary trait in such individuals.

Points 3 and 4 require no further comment.

4. *The effects of man on gannet numbers*

The gannet's habit of congregating in large colonies, often on slopes or flatter ground, exposed it to heavy predation by man, whilst its edibility and the value of its fat, feathers and carcase (bait) made exploitation worthwhile and man's predatory nature ensured that, even where killing was not worthwhile on practical grounds, vulnerability alone condemned it. And its low reproductive rate meant that loss of breeding adults was a serious matter. The facts and figures concerning gannet culls have been well worked by Gurney and Fisher and I have merely summarised them in Appendix 4. So far as gannet numbers are concerned, the main points are that, by economic exploitation, heedless destruction and vandalism, the world population was drastically reduced in the nineteenth century and the recovery in the twentieth has been largely if not entirely due to the relaxation of that pressure. The reduction included the extinction of five colonies (Gannet Rock, Grand Manan (1871); Gannet Rock, Yarmouth (1883); The Perroquets (1887); Funk Island (1857–73) and Lundy Island (1909)) and the slashing of Bird Rocks from over 100 000 to 1000 pairs, of Skellig from several thousands to 30 pairs and of the Bass, possibly from more than 10 000 pairs to 3000. At other colonies, notably Ailsa until 1880, the Bass until 1805, St. Kilda until 1910, Sule Stack until 1932, Eldey until 1940 and Sula Sgeir, Myggenaes and the Westmanns until now, man managed to maintain an acceptable level of exploitation, though in some cases probably only because the colonies received recruits from elsewhere. Much earlier, Vikings ate gannets in Shetland and prehistoric man may have had a notable effect on numbers and distribution.

Nowadays there are several other ways in which man affects gannet numbers. Some of them are discussed briefly under 'mortality' (p. 130) but all may be listed here:

1. *Fishing activities*. Direct and appreciable mortality results at sea from drowning in nets and on hooks and shooting or otherwise killing deliberately. Man may compete significantly with gannets for certain fish, though this is unlikely, but his increased fishing activity may on the other hand have contributed a significant amount of fish-offal, which gannets take avidly. Again, however, it is unlikely to have been important.

   Indirectly, the ever increasing amounts of indestructible synthetic fish lines and nets floating around in the sea and being incorporated into gannets' nests, where they entangle adults and young, constitute a significant hazard.

2. *Pollution.* Oil kills some gannets and the forthcoming developments in the North and Celtic Seas, and particularly off Shetland, carry with them a menace on a greater scale then anything hitherto.

Toxic chemicals, accumulated in fish, may be, or become great killers. There is now evidence of considerable concentrations of PCB's and breakdown products of DDT, in the Irish Sea, Bristol Channel, Firth of Clyde and Gulf of St. Lawrence, and methyl mercury in Norwegian waters, to name only a few places, and evidence of residues in gannet tissues and eggs (Appendix 15). At present, no one can say how important this may be, but potentially it is a great threat. In 1974 Skellig apparently showed gaps, and some St. Lawrence gannetries may be declining. Ailsa has decreased in several recent years. All these events may be totally unconnected with toxic chemicals, but certainly warrant attention with these in mind, especially since lethal levels have been found in an Ailsa bird.

3. *Indirect interference.* The increase in large gulls has been a factor at several gannetries. Combined with disturbance by visitors (however innocuous in intention) and low-flying 'planes, which frighten off adults and expose eggs and small chicks, gulls take probably several thousand eggs and young each year. Nevertheless, in view of the high mortality among juvenile gannets this is certainly not an important check on reproductive success.

Now that direct massacre has largely ceased, the gannet suffers comparatively little at the hands of man. Its colonies and nests are largely inaccessible to disturbance and it can easily foil unaided gull-forays or encroachments. Man-introduced rats are not a menace, as they have reputedly been to puffins, and up to now, oiling has affected it much less than it has auks. Toxics perhaps pose the greatest threat in the future.

SUMMARY

1. The population of North Atlantic gannets in 1976 numbered roughly 213 000 pairs (i.e. excluding all Club and immature birds) of which 33 000 were on the western side of the Atlantic and 180 000 on the east. These were distributed in 34 gannetries (6 western, 28 eastern). In addition, Foula (Scotland) and Ingolfshöf(or) (Iceland) are likely to be new breeding colonies in the immediate future.

2. On both sides of the Atlantic the increase this century has been consistent with that which known reproductive and mortality rates would predict (almost 3 per cent per annum).

3. On this basis, most of the colonies which have increased this century have at one period or another received substantial influxes of immigrants.

4. A vast system of interchange operates between most or all of the British west coast gannetries. The Bass/Bempton pair may be autonomous.

5. Many estimates of numbers at gannetries fail to take account of all the factors which could affect them (p. 24). Correction factors are given in Appendix 1.

6. Since 1939, 10 new colonies have been founded especially in Iceland and Norway. Thus, although the increase has largely been a process of recuperation from human predation, it may also have coincided, at least latterly, with changes in the distribution of some food fish, or even in a change in the proportions of age-classes within some species, due to overfishing.

3. BREEDING ECOLOGY

INTRODUCTION

The North Atlantic gannet inhabits cold, food-rich waters in a highly seasonal climate, with a seasonal surge of highly nutritious fish, principally mackerel and herring, has a considerable foraging range and is without competitors in its offshore feeding niche (plunge diving with great penetration and the ability to handle large prey) which secures for it monopoly of a rich food source. Its morphological specialisations, evolved primarily in connection with feeding, impose certain requirements in relation to breeding habitat which relatively few localities can fully meet.

This combination of characteristics is of the greatest value in understanding gannet breeding ecology, and through ecology, breeding behaviour, and is in most respects in direct contrast with the environmental factors which have shaped the adaptive syndrome of the pan-tropical boobies (p. 347). The timing of the gannet's breeding season, the nature of its reproductive success, the fact that it breeds in colonies, the nature of its dispersion within them, the size and distribution of these colonies and its social behaviour are all directly or indirectly related to its environmental factors in a consistent and causally related manner. Several of the links in this adaptive web are treated in detail in the sections on morphology and behaviour; here, it is the ecological aspects which are under review.

These characteristics of the Atlantic gannet contrast, too, with their equivalents in the other two gannets and thanks to recent work on the Australasian and Cape gannets it is now possible, for the first time, to develop a coherent picture of these differences.

BREEDING HABITAT

1. *Islands*

Thirty-two out of the 34 existing gannetries are on islands, and almost all these are rocks, or stacks. The only two mainland gannetries (Bempton and Gullcliff Bay, Anticosti, if the latter can be called a 'mainland'), are both on cliffs. There are three main advantages to offshore islands. They are safe from large mammalian predators among which wolves, bears and tigers could have been important in the past. At the present time, foxes could possibly tackle gannets, though I doubt it. They are windy, which is of great importance to a heavy seabird with long narrow wings and they are surrounded by potential food-giving areas, whereas a mainland colony is dead ground on all save the seaward side. Mainland cliffs provide the first two of these advantages and wherever gannets nest on the mainland, they use cliffs.

The islands used by gannets are almost always small and precipitous. Whilst this is partly because they prefer cliffs, and offshore islands with high cliffs are often small, there are, on the British coast, several large islands, or peninsulas with towering cliffs (Horn Head, Donegal, Mull, Arran, Rum, Skye, and many more) yet without gannets. Land masses repel them; they are afraid of them and, as specialised seabirds, with good cause. They are least afraid on small islands, with vertical cliffs and the sea all round. Only the motivation produced by reproductive hormones drives them to land at all and when they return after the period at sea, they are extremely wary. Later in the season, as their ties loosen, they again become highly suspicious and wary.

2. *Cliffs*

The gannet prefers precipitous faces (Fig. 32) so long as these have ledges wide enough to allow the accretion of nest material, aided by the cementing action of the gannet's excreta. At the majority of its breeding stations it occupies mainly cliffs. There is not a single gannetry which utilises flat ground or slopes and ignores cliffs where these are present, but many solely on cliffs where slopes and flat ground also occur. At least 18 gannetries are on cliffs more than 30m high and only eight on cliffs lower than this. About 80 per cent are on non-sedimentary rock. Gannets have several cliff adapted features (Table 7). On the other hand, slopes are important nesting habitats and on Eldey (Iceland) and Bird Rock (Canada) they utilise even flat ground on a large scale. On Bonaventure some nest among dead trees (Fig. 33), a very odd situation for a gannet and interesting in that (counting the three gannets as one) it leaves only the Peruvian booby, among sulids, that never nests under or among trees.

It is impossible to determine whether the gannet has always been able to use both cliffs and flat ground or (if it has not) which came first. The ancestral sulid is perhaps more likely to have nested mainly on slopes and flatter ground than on cliffs, particularly if it originated in the central Pacific, as has been suggested. Undoubtedly, however, the gannet is now primarily a cliff nester. Its colonies spill over from cliffs onto slopes, rather than vice versa; where both are present but only one used, it is always cliffs. Of the 19 colonies founded this century, all except two somewhat atypical Norwegian colonies (Skarvlakken and Innerstauren) have been on cliffs. The gannet's adaptations to cliffs do not debar it from flat ground; rather, flat ground poses no problems which cliff adapted gannets cannot overcome. The reverse could not apply, for cliffs hold special dangers with regard to windiness and safety. Cliffs intensify the advantages of islands. Atlantic gannets weigh up to 3600g, almost twice as much as the white booby of equal size and they find it difficult to take off from flat surfaces in calm conditions. Furthermore, they do a great deal of 'social reconnoitring' from the air (p. 160) and during the early stages of breeding land and take off very frequently. In such long-lived birds, landing hazards become an important consideration and strong winds remove much of the danger. High islands mean more wind and they mean cliffs, which often provide up-draughts even in moderate to slight winds. Even cliff colonies suffer significant mortality from landing accidents (p. 132). Especially the Cape, but also Australasian gannets are much more committed to flat ground and are considerably lighter.

Even on islands, the extra safety of cliffs may also be important. Some low islands (such as Tiree) are extremely windy, and free from large mammalian predators, but man is a major predator and may have exerted an influence in the past, especially on islands easily accessible from the mainland, thus pushing the gannet further towards cliff nesting, which anyway suits its anatomy (heavy, with high aspect-ratio wings and small pectoral muscles). Large congregations of seabirds are enormously vulnerable if they cannot take off easily and man is heedlessly destructive. In many tropical regions, the predominance of the arboreal red-foot over the brown, and especially the larger white booby, can probably be ascribed to this factor.

Gannets prefer broad horizontal ledges upon which nest material easily accumulates, in mid-cliff, of fair to great height, but they will use extremely narrow ledges (Poulin (1968b)

TABLE 7

INDICATIONS THAT GANNETS ARE PRIMARILY ADAPTED TO CLIFF NESTING

Behaviour or characteristic	Significance
Fighting	Intensity maladaptive on flat ground; method leads to displacement of cliff opponent; diving onto opponent effective only on ledges.
Cementing of nest with excreta	Enables utilisation of ledges which would otherwise not accumulate material. However, does not bring mud as cliff-adapted kittiwakes do.
Lacks ability to retrieve egg	Useless on cliff ledge; but some ground nesting species also lack this ability.
Does not discriminate its own from strange young	Young cannot usually wander on cliffs so discrimination superfluous; but this trait could have evolved on flat ground as result of adult aggression to young.
Extreme clinging ability of young	Anti-falling behaviour.
Passive begging of young	Anti-falling behaviour, particularly cogent compared with boobies.
Black plumage of young	The most different-from-adult plumage in entire family, possibly to eliminate features which could elicit attack from the male (see p. 209) with displacement of young—fatal if cliff nester.

gives 10cm as the absolute minimum used by gannets on Bonaventure), badly sloping ones and low cliffs. They will nest within about three metres of the splash line, as on the east face of the Bass and on Sule Stack. The tendency to return to the natal group often causes males to attempt to establish sites in ridiculously unsuitable spots (see Fig. 36).

Prospecting gannets do not reconnoitre an entire colony and then try to establish a site on the topographically most suitable slope. Rather the area(s) of the colony that are growing most rapidly attract recruits. On the other hand, the choice of a particular area in a broader sense often does have a topographical basis. Thus the west slope of the Bass is much more suitable than the east, being steeper and windier. Completely flat patches are generally avoided, though in cases such as those mentioned above they may be over-run. But in fact the topography of a slope when gannets have been on it for a few years may differ substantially from its original condition. Turf and other vegetation is removed, soil loosened and eroded, boulders dislodged and surface irregularities increased.

Grassholm is the flattest British colony and exemplifies the species' ability to blanket gentle slopes in a dense, evenly spaced mass of birds (Fig. 8). One wonders how individuals locate their nests, but compared with the problem facing a guanay cormorant, in a colony perhaps 100 times as large and 4 times as dense, the task is trivial.

COLONY SIZE, DENSITY AND STRUCTURE

1. *Size*

Typically gannets breed in large colonies. Their 34 colonies now break down as follows: 1–100 pairs (6), 100–1000 (10), 1000–5000 (5), 5000–10 000 (9), 10 000–20 000 (3), 20 000–50 000 (0), more than 50 000 (1).

The mean 'natural' (unexploited) size of old-established gannetries is very roughly around 10 000 pairs, for of the 30 colonies which fall below this figure, 20 have been established this century and a further 6 have been or are exploited. However, precise averages are meaningless in view of all the variables. The main points are that well established colonies are generally large (several thousand pairs), sometimes huge (over 50 000 or even 100 000 pairs) but that there is an enormous *range* of sizes, all about equally viable in terms of reproductive success.

Fig. 32(a). Extreme cliff habitat (north-west face, Bass). Virtually no linear spread (nests on individual ledges) and never enough width for nests to be more than one deep.

Fig. 32(b). Ledges mainly narrow but considerable linear spread and occasionally groups of nests two or more deep. Extension onto flatter ground above cliff edge.

In total contrast to the situation with regard to *density*, it is evident that there is no strong selection pressure favouring any particular colony *size*. It is simply that large colonies are brought about because: (a) gannets require types of nesting localities which are somewhat limited and therefore enforce a degree of coloniality, (b) their wide foraging, communal hunting and deep diving, and their distribution in rich waters combine to remove any penalty (through inter- or intra-specific competition) resulting from large colonies, (c) large colonies offer important social benefits (p. 123). The limits to any particular colony are probably not called until available nesting space runs out, hence the massive size of St. Kilda and Bird Rock. However, the practice of interchange between colonies introduces a levelling factor. There is no evidence that its function is to limit local density, though this is always a theoretical possibility. Rather, perhaps, it results from the application of the 'pioneer' principle and a susceptibility to social attraction (see p. 135). At the other end of the scale, small colonies probably do need to reach a certain threshold size (though this is low) before becoming fully viable. The social benefits mentioned above stem, of course, from membership of a large (and dense) group, but in this context, large means a few hundred pairs, since any individual is stimulated only by those gannets within range of its vision and hearing. From this point of view there is probably no significant social difference between a colony of 5000 and one of 50 000. This is consistent with the observation that gannetries tend to be large but extremely variable in size.

2. *Density*

Gannets almost invariably nest about 80cm apart, nest centre to nest centre. Actual figures were: Bass 58–120cm; mean 76cm; 72 per cent of nests 61–76cm apart. Bonaventure 61–99cm;

Fig. 32(c). Ledges sloping and difficult to build on. This face (south-west Bass) holds a high proportion of non-breeders.

mean 80·2 mode 74cm; 233 measured; 95 per cent of nests between 64·3 and 96·3cm apart. Where the terrain is even, the nests in the colony achieve a quite remarkably regular spacing and even irregular ground does not much disrupt this pattern. On ledges too, the distance between nests remains fairly constant, though there is often less room for manoeuvre if a newcomer pushes in. Very occasionally a pair nests several metres from their nearest neighbour. The density is about the minimum space required by a site that must at times accommodate two large adults and a chick larger than either of them and the regular spacing results from everybody crowding as near as possible but coming up against the limitations imposed by these minimal space requirements. Poulin makes the interesting point that gannet's nests being spaced, as it were, within hexagons (Fig. 34) there is 'dead' space between nests, and axis A is shorter than B. Gannets tend to sit with their beak–tail axis along B rather than A. Of course, this pattern can be overridden by other factors, such as a strong wind, in which case all gannets face the same way. The reason why gannets crowd together at this density rather than half, or a quarter or a tenth of it has been explained in quite different ways. Some have attributed it to sheer shortage of nest sites, an explanation which is only a contributory factor and is not responsible for the degree and the uniformity of the density, as anybody with half an eye can see. It has been suggested to be an anti-predator device, but islands and cliffs are safe from mammalian predators whilst the gannet's size and strength protect it against all avian ones, except possibly sea-eagles, which in any case would take it in flight (and gannets have no communal flight reaction such as gulls have) and can never have caused the crowding. As for man, dense nesting helps rather than hinders him. There remains only one valid answer, which is that dense nesting provides behavioural or social stimulation, which in turn has effects important enough to justify the considerable energy expended in the effort to nest as close as possible to other breeders. This process is halted only when other factors (here accommodation and landing requirements) intervene. Hence one ends up with the observed minimal and regular spacing. It is interesting to note that the Cape gannet nests more densely than the Atlantic, but also much more variably. Here, too, there is considerable competition for sites (p. 253) but presumably a different balance of selective forces (nesting space is more limited, especially space in highly exposed areas, suitable for take-off on flat ground). The nature and role of social stimulation will be discussed when dealing with the timing of breeding: here it may merely be stated that timing is extremely important in the gannet, probably especially the Atlantic, and that social stimulation is one of the mechanisms by which optimal timing is achieved. So it is that, whether the colony be large or small, on slope, cliff or flat ground, the nesting density remains about the same, at 2·3 pairs sq. m.

The social stimulation theory accounts for the otherwise puzzling observation that in an expanding group on fairly even terrain the fringe creeps outward at the standard density and

Fig. 33. Nesting beneath trees on Bonaventure. *Photo:* J. M. Poulin.

that in the process of achieving this degree of proximity, the young, site-establishing males often become involved in severe fights, which they would avoid if they accepted wider spacing. Together with site (rather than merely group) philopatry, it also explains the great attraction of sites *within* groups rather than at the fringe. This is a topic that, it seems to me, has been much misunderstood and will be discussed below under the heading of 'Colony Structure'.

3. *Structure*

A gannet colony is like an organism, the complexities of which we are only just beginning to grasp. One's understanding of the vascular system of a mammal is greatly helped by injecting a specimen with coloured latex so that veins and arteries stand out in blue and red. If one could suddenly give different colours to the many categories of gannets that comprise any large group, it would be transformed from a homogeneous mass of white birds to a complex pattern of colours. Colony structure depends partly on topography and partly on social factors (position effects) and the main questions to be asked, are:

1. Given comparable topographic conditions is there a difference between fringe and central sites with regard to breeding effort and success?
2. Is there a difference, too, between topographically different sites and
3. Are these differences a function of age-structure or something else?

These questions will be considered under the appropriate headings, such as 'breeding success', but the relevant general remarks are brought together here.

At its simplest, any 'group' within a colony (the latter being the discrete unit) exists in one of six states and these apply to cliff as well as flat groups. Either it is part of a uniform mass, in which case its limits are impossible to define on anything but an arbitrary numerical basis, or it is a semi-discrete unit (like that in Fig. 35(b)). In either case it may be stable, expanding, or shrinking. A *colony* (such as the Bass) may be stable whilst certain *parts* of it are not, but probably usually, a stable colony is stable in its parts (groups) as well. A semi-discrete group in a stable condition (often on cliffs, imposed by topography) will, by definition, remain the same size and density. Young adults will come in and take over sites vacated by those which die. There will be minor re-adjustments in the distribution of nests within the group, but unless the edge suffers a higher mortality rate than the centre, or edge birds systematically vacate their sites to move towards the centre, the age structure of the group will be the same throughout and the fringe will NOT consist of younger birds than does the centre. The evidence is that mortality of adults at the edge is NOT higher and that once they have established a site, edge or fringe birds usually do not move, or if they do, they move only one or two metres. Therefore the oft-repeated generalisation that fringes consist of young birds on physically inferior sites is often invalid. This occurs only where a group is *expanding*, in which case the fringe does consist almost entirely, or entirely, of young birds, usually in their fourth or fifth year, but even then not on *physically* inferior sites. As an aside, it may be noted that in the first season in which a fringe area is colonised, pairs are spaced a bit more irregularly and wider

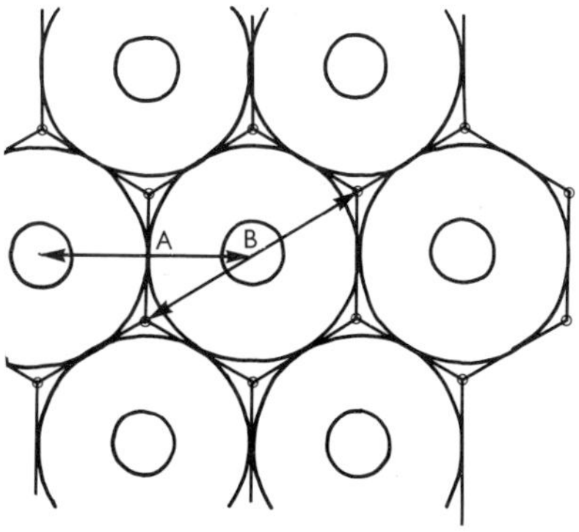

Fig. 34

Characteristics of the spacing of gannets' nests. (From Poulin 1968b.)

apart than subsequently (Fig. 35). In an expanding situation, a number of differences in breeding regime may be expected between the fringe and the centre, but these will depend partly on the age difference between the two areas. Thus young females lay later, and have a lower breeding success. In such a case it is generally impossible to decide how much is due to age and inexperience and how much to fringe position (see p. 110). Any conclusions depend heavily on fringes being undisturbed, for human disturbance delays laying, exacerbates site disputes and causes loss of nest material and eggs (even if gulls are not present). On the other hand, fringe sites are subject to less social stimulation than central ones and if it were practicable to compare mean laying dates and breeding success between inexperienced fringe females and inexperienced central (replacement) females, the effects due to position could be disentangled. A final adjustment would then have to be made to take account of the effects of partnering an experienced male for most central females are so partnered, whereas virtually all fringe females are partnered by inexperienced males. Unfortunately, direct analysis of this sophistication has yet to be undertaken for the gannet, and depending as it does on known-age birds, full time observation and complete immunity from disturbance, is unlikely to be so. Furthermore, there is the complicating factor of topography to take into account. Cliffs and flat ground, compared in terms of breeding effort (proportions of non-breeders) and breeding success, may show distinct differences, and these have been detailed for the Bass (p. 111) and similarly for

Fig. 35(b) *on facing page*

Group 6, an open-ended semi-isolated group (Bass Rock) often referred to in the text. It grew from the ledge, bottom left and held about 8 pairs in 1960. The concrete cones are markers.

Fig. 35(a)

Typical spacing in a gannetry (Bass Rock group 5). Even on irregular ground, standard distance between nests is maintained. At the fringe, nests are more widely spaced but belong mostly to pairs establishing themselves. By intercalation of new pairs and minor readjustments of existing ones, compaction will occur.

Bonaventure (p. 111). But the cliffs, in the two cases mentioned, are largely full up ('closed') and cannot be divided into 'centre' and 'fringe' as can a flat ground ('open-ended') group. Therefore the age structure of such a cliff-group is not the same as that of an expanding flat-ground group (usually it contains a higher proportion of old birds). And so one cannot treat a cliff group simply as a vertical flat group. Thus if one is looking for position effect, one must take account of topography, for this affects age structure which affects interpretation of position effect. Conversely, when comparing cliff and flat ground groups in terms of breeding success etc., one must remember that they *are* different in age-structure.

Despite these complications, some issues involved in the analysis can be approached. They are the effects of age and inexperience on breeding; the effects of social stimulation and the predation aspects of nesting in the fringe.

As just mentioned, youth and inexperience are often correlated with a fringe position. Social stimulation and predation are the two major, if not the only factors which affect breeding success in the fringe as against the centre. All these aspects are discussed elsewhere but so far as their relevance to colony structure is concerned it may be said that:

1. Youth and inexperience correlate with later breeding and lower success;
2. Social stimulation hastens ovulation, so that the onset is earlier and synchronization of laying greater in birds subject to much behavioural stimulation than in equivalent birds subject to less (p. 122);
3. Natural (non-human) predation is totally insignificant.

Thus, (2) means that fringe birds are likely to be later than central birds partly as a result of position (receiving less social stimulation), though partly or mainly as a result of (1), and (3) means that edge-predation cannot be invoked as a mechanism favouring a move towards the centre of a group. As mentioned, there is anyway no evidence that birds systematically move towards the centre, but if such a trend *were* detected, its survival value could not be postulated to lie in decreased predation. This is worth emphasis, for throughout his writings, Lack consistently forbore to discuss social aspects of colonial breeding, preferring to confine his brief remarks on this subject to predation and feeding aspects of coloniality. This, perhaps one of his few major omissions, may partly reflect a disinclination to get involved with behavioural aspects of ecology.

A later section deals with productivity in relation to colony structure.

NEST SITES AND NESTS

The types of sites used by gannets can be seen from Figs. 32–35. Two aspects are particularly noteworthy; the tendency to occupy 'impossible' sites and the role of 'cementing' the nest. The first has been graphically illustrated by the events on a minor pinnacle of the Bass (the Needle, Fig. 36) where, since I first looked at it in 1961,

Fig. 36

The Needle, a precipitous stack very difficult to nest on. It attracts a steady flow of recruits (Needle offspring?) which fail to establish themselves.

almost exactly the same number of 'impossible' sites have been occupied annually, without ever developing into nests. Almost undoubtedly, the birds concerned are descendants of Needle pairs, returning to their home locality, but unable to find good sites. Some (possibly most) eventually give up and move elsewhere. The use of excreta to stick nest material to ledges or sloping faces is crucial to success and sometimes enables massive structures to be built up on incredibly difficult sites. The number of such nests loosening and falling is almost nil, whereas in the kittiwake (which uses even more microscopic projections) it is one of the main causes of mortality among young (Cullen 1957).

The gannet builds a substantial nest of seaweed, other vegetation and general flotsam. The structure begins as a ring of nest material, which becomes a hollowed mound and later forms a pedestal which over years of compressing and adding material, becomes an extremely solid base to which a new 'cup' is added each year. Most nests are about 30cm in diameter and 20cm high, but pedestals with a sloping side measurement of about 1000cm do occur, and specimens almost half that height are common, at least on the Bass.

The seaweeds commonly used are *Fucus vesiculosus*, *F. serrator*, *Pelvetia canalicula* and *Laminaria digitata* and no doubt any other seaweed the gannet can get hold of. The gelatinous nature of seaweed often causes it to stick to the rock and allows the accretion of further nest material. Growing seaweed is rarely pulled, though occasionally a bird swimming close to the cliff base at an appropriate stage of the tide will detach some. Grass and other vegetation, however, is actively pulled from the vegetated parts of the nesting island, or even from one nearby. The St. Kildans of Hirta complained of the activities of the gannets, which denuded parts of the island. A great variety of flotsam may be found decorating gannets' nests; straw, moulted feathers, bits of wood, plastic articles, synthetic nets and lines (a significant hazard, see p. 132) etc. Among the more unusual items recorded have been false teeth, a gold watch, a catheter, roses, a sandal, fountain pen, spade and golf balls (Gibson 1951b and pers. obs.).

Gannets building on slopes and island tops soon remove not only vegetation but also the top soil which they add to the sides of the pedestal. Erosion continues the removal process and soon exposes rock between nests. A deep litter then builds up, which after rain becomes a quagmire of sulphurous, black ooze. Under such conditions a high pedestal is indeed adaptive in keeping the chick above the level of mud and water.

THE EGG AND CLUTCH

1. *Characteristics of the egg*

The egg varies in shape from long, sub-eliptical to oval. It is pale blue and translucent when newly laid but quickly becomes white and opaque, with a thick chalky outer layer (which may help to protect the egg against the penetration of hard fragments in the nest when the adult's considerable weight is applied in incubation). The chalk layer soon becomes rough and chipped and helps the adult's webs to grip the egg in incubation (donated pot eggs sometimes shot out from beneath webs). The shell is about 0·6mm thick, which is more than the average for this size of egg. It soon becomes deeply stained, occasionally even blackish and shiny, when mud is transferred from the webs and polished during incubation. Such a covering, though it must adversely affect gaseous interchange, apparently does not affect the development of the embryo though transferred oil in one case retarded hatching by some six days. The egg loses 9–13 per cent of its weight during incubation (Fig. 37).

The average measurements of 100 British eggs were 78·06 × 49·1mm (max. 78·6 × 53·7 and 87·5 × 49·0, min. 62·5 × 43·1); of 20 from Canada 82·27 × 49·66 (Palmer 1962) and of 44, also from Canada, 77·6 × 47·0mm (Bent 1922) which is not significantly larger than those of the other two gannets. The average weight of 393 fresh eggs (Bass Rock) was 104·5g (range 81–130g; Fig. 38) and of 57 partly incubated Bonaventure eggs 98·1g (range 70–118g). Poulin calculates the loss due to incubation and concludes that the fresh weight was 103·2g which is almost identical with the Bass weights. The average shell weight of 100 eggs was 11·59g (range 10·8–12·9g) which is 11·1 per cent of the fresh weight, an unusually high proportion due to its thickness (see above). The considerable range in fresh weight may be correlated with an unusually low selection pressure against underweight newly hatched chicks, due to the high probability that adults will immediately be able to feed them adequately (the opposite situation occurs in, for example, the red-foot and eggs are less variable in weight). The same interpretation may apply, also, to the low weight of the egg as a proportion of the female's weight (3·4 per cent on the Bass and 3·2 per cent on Bonaventure). Thus, it is significantly less than the equivalent figures in the Cape and Australasian gannets (3·9 per cent) and their foraging trips are significantly longer. Their chicks therefore presumably benefit from being born with more food reserves.

2. *Egg weight in relation to time of laying*

Earlier eggs tend to be heavier than later ones (Fig. 39) probably because they come mainly from older females, which are known to lay heavier eggs. There is as yet no study relating breeding success to egg weight.

3. *Clutch size*

The clutch size is invariably one; where two eggs occurred naturally in the same nest in the observation colony, there had been two females involved, so, although I have twice seen natural 'twins', once on a sheer cliff, it seems likely that the same explanation applied. Lloyd (1926) recorded many nests on Grassholm containing two eggs or chicks; no explanation was obvious and he concluded that 'a considerable percentage of the Grassholm gannets must either lay two eggs at one brood or indulge a very marked proclivity for a dual sharing of nests'. Thomas Bewick (1816) goes further: 'she lays three eggs although ornithologists assert that she will lay only one eggs if left to herself undisturbed'. However, he was probably referring to *replacement* laying. On Bonaventure Poulin examined 1112 nests without finding a two-egg clutch and Robertson has never known an authentic two-egg clutch in the Australasian gannet. Although Jarvis concluded that some genuine cases *do* occur in the Cape bird, he was not able unequivocally to exclude alternative explanations (p. 239). The single-egg clutch thus appears to be extremely invariable in the gannets, although it seems probable that natural variation will occasionally produce a two-egg clutch, this being the normal condition in the Sulidae. However it certainly seems unlikely that, in the gannets, the proportion could be high enough to stand much chance of establishing a polymorphism with respect to clutch size. *Why* it should be so invariable it is difficult to imagine, particularly in the Atlantic gannet, which seems readily able to rear twins (p. 99).

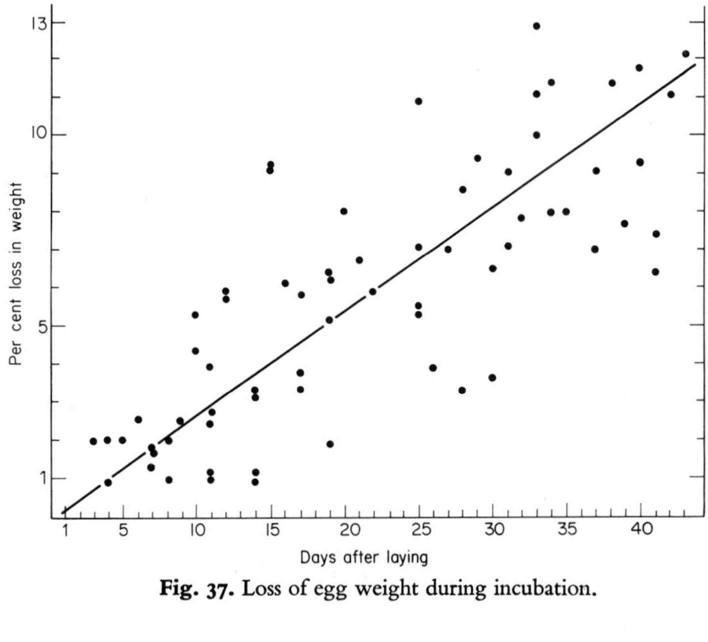

Fig. 37. Loss of egg weight during incubation.

4. *Replacement laying*

On the Bass lost eggs are replaced in 6–32 days, usually in about three weeks unless lost more than about 25 days after laying. Four females re-laid a second time. Experienced females showed a greater tendency to re-lay than did birds breeding for the first time (26/34 compared with 2/16) perhaps partly because first-time breeders lay later in the season and the tendency to re-lay wanes as the season advances. There is little natural egg loss to justify this strong tendency to re-lay which may perhaps be a relic of the family tendency to lay larger clutches. A significantly lower proportion of re-lays than of first eggs gave rise to fledged young (10/27 or 37 per cent against 152/192 or 79 per cent in 1962 in the same group of birds), apparently partly because a higher proportion of re-lays were infertile (37 per cent against 10 per cent). On Bonaventure 27·3 per cent of lost eggs were replaced (1966 21 per cent; 1967 32·3 per cent). In 52·8 per cent the first egg had survived < 4 days; in 75·5 per cent < 7;

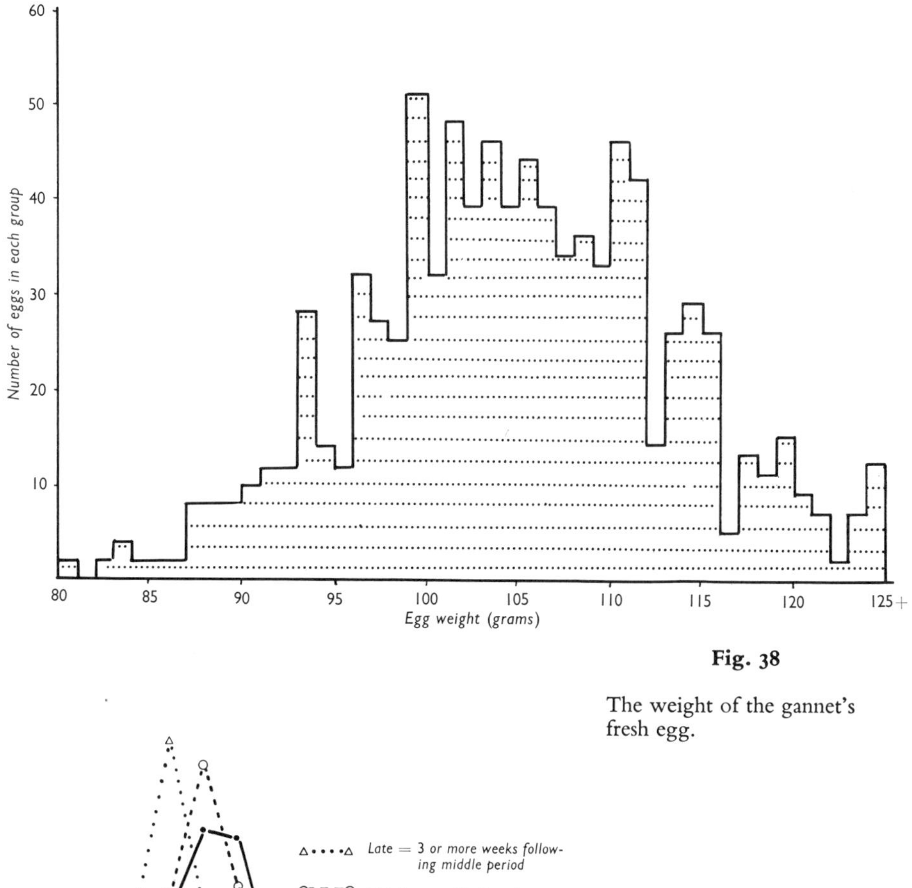

Fig. 38

The weight of the gannet's fresh egg.

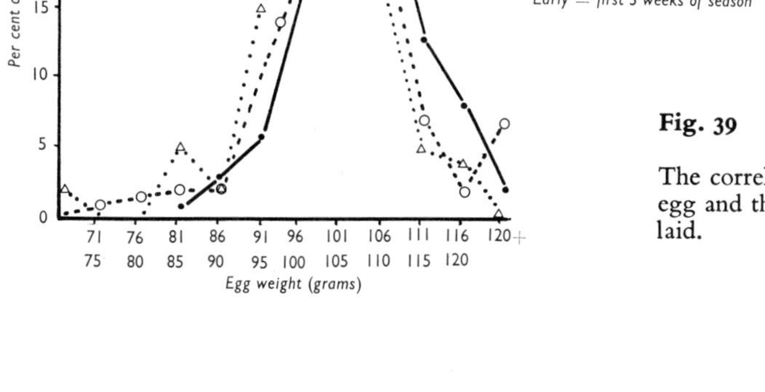

Fig. 39

The correlation between the weight of the egg and the time (seasonal) at which it was laid.

in 87·4 < 14 and in 95 < 28 days. The interval between loss and replacement varied from 1–39 days (mean 14); 17 per cent re-laid in 5 days or less; 61·6 per cent 15 or less; 74·8 per cent 20 or less; 89·9 per cent 25 or less and 96·2 per cent 30 or less. The longer incubation had proceeded, the longer the replacement time and after 43 days incubation replacement did not occur. This is understandable since the time involved in incubating the first egg, waiting for the second, and completing the cycle would be 204–224 days and there is not enough time in the breeding season. A higher proportion of centre birds (29·2 per cent) than of fringe (21·2 per cent) replaced lost eggs. Poulin recorded 160 cases of second eggs; 15 of thirds and two of fourth eggs, never before recorded; 16·9 per cent replacement eggs hatched, which, as on the Bass, is much lower than the figure for first eggs.

5. *Incubation period*

On the Bass, the average incubation period in 83 cases, 75 accurate to ± 24 hours and 8 to ± 6 hours, was 43·6 days distributed as follows: 42 days (9 cases); 43 (25); 44 (38); 45 (9) and 46 (2). Incubation of infertile eggs persisted for up to 102 days but Poulin recorded birds incubating for 148 days! He gives 43·9 days as the mean incubation period of 220 eggs on Bonaventure, a parallel interestingly exact in view of the vastly lower ambient temperature there. Gannet incubation must be extremely efficient. The egg temperature achieved by incubation underfoot (the webs of breeding birds are highly vascularised and hot during incubation though non-breeders have cool webs) compares favourably with that of brood-spot incubation.

6. *Incubation regime*

Both sexes incubate. During the first half of the incubation period the average stint on the Bass lasted 37·2 hours (range 7 to 84) in the male and 30·8 (4 to 70) in the female. During the second half, these shortened to 33·2 (6 to 62) in the male and 29·1 (10 to 46) in the female. Foraging absences (assuming the absent partner is not merely resting elsewhere in the breeding station) are thus both very flexible (which is consistent with the wide range of feeding areas and techniques) but usually of considerable length. A few days before hatching, the duration of incubation stints decreases sharply, probably as a result of cues emitted by the chick which begins to vocalise within the egg once it has penetrated the air space (Vince, pers. comm.). This response ensures the minimum length of parental absences when the chick is newly hatched and a high proportion of nests with chicks a day old or less, have the pair in attendance.

THE CHICK

1. *Morphology and plumage development*

The newly hatched chick typically weighs around 70–80g and is about 11cm long. Its skin is loose especially in the gular area. The eyes (dark bluish) are partly or entirely closed until the second or third day. The bill is dull and darkish, paler towards the tip and with a whitish egg tooth. The legs and feet are deep grey. The chick is blackish; it looks almost naked but is very sparsely covered with the first generation of white down, with hair-like tips (neossoptiles) distributed as in Fig. 40(a). This is replaced by fluffy down varying in length and density according to location. It is very long and dense on the sides and underparts but often short and sparse on the forehead, around the eyes, on the throat and chin. This second generation of down is shed as the juvenile feathers grow but is not replaced by them nor is it replaced directly, in continuous growth, by the under-down of the feathered stage, though the under-down may succeed it (Witherby *et al.* 1940). The chronology of development is as follows (see also Fig. 40):

Week 1 By the end of week 1 the chick has become noticeably white though down (neossoptiles) is still sparse and tracts of blackish, bare skin, are still very evident. Movements still wobbly.

Week 2 Down thickens over the body and by the end chicks look considerably larger than their parents' webs. The head and neck are often barish and the radio-ulna and 'hand wing' are still blackish. Down still looks scrubby. Chicks now vigorous and well co-ordinated.

Week 3 Down becomes longer; chick fully covered in white fluff and head down usually well grown; wings covered; beak black and shiny (when clean!). Becoming too big to be effectively brooded but still can be partly covered.

Week 4 Down notably long and fluffy and chick large and fat (now about 1800g). Takes up most of nest and looks perhaps two-thirds as large as the adult. No sign of wing or tail feathers.

Week 5 By the end of week 5, in early birds, the primaries and rectrices have erupted and begin to show a peep of black through the down. The chick looks very large, approaching adult body size.

Week 6 Down extremely long and scapulars, wing and tail feathers becoming conspicuously black. Chick looks bigger than parent. Retarded chicks may be at same stage as advanced five-week-olds.

Week 7 Black on wings, back and tail steadily expanding and chick now covered in long white down beneath and on head and neck and mixed black (feathers) and white (down) on back.

Week 8 Advanced chicks are beginning to lose down from feathered forehead, back and tail and black areas winning rapidly over down on dorsal surface.

Week 9 Process continues and down beginning to thin, also, on parts of ventral surface, though still thick on flanks, belly and parts of neck.

Week 10 Rapid clearance of down, but some remains on nape, flanks and back. Chick now mainly black.

Week 11 Early in week 11 advanced chicks retain only wisps on nape and flank. By the end of the week they may be clear. Retarded birds may not reach this stage until 93 days old.

2. *Feeding*

(*a*) *Feeding frequency*

Continuous observation of 27 Bass Rock chicks throughout the day-light hours of a two-day period (July 14–15) revealed (Tables 8 and 9) that chicks were fed on average 2·7 times each day, counting *all* the times a chick entered its parent's mouth during a bout of feeding as merely one feed. The large number of feeds delivered between 04·00–08·00 hrs was due to the return of parents after a night at sea and there was a further influx between 14·00–18·00 hrs, many of them being adults relieved from guard duty in the early morning. Table 9 shows the number of feeds given to chicks of different ages and to twins as against singles. Whilst the weight of food delivered was not known, the number of times food transfer actually occurred was impressive. Thus one pair of twins between them received nine bouts of feeding containing at least 37 and possibly 45 transfers of food, whilst the maximum delivered to a single chick—only three weeks old—was five bouts and possibly 21 food transfers. The commonest food fish were mackerel and sand-eels, with herring and small cod also recorded (see p. 155). Booth remarks that, in captivity, Bass gannets would take only mackerel, herrings and sprats, whereas my birds readily accept saithe and flatfish (*Pleuronectes*). He also graphically describes the many parcels of fish (herring and mackerel) that are spilled during feeding and lie in stinking heaps between the nests. I have **never** found this, despite numerous extensive forays into the heart of nesting masses when ringing chicks, and can only surmise that times have changed, or (more likely) that his observations followed on the heels of those careless and destructive incursions by visitors which were the hall mark of his day (and are still not unknown). Similar observations have been made on Grassholm (again, mackerel were the principal fish) and are probably subject to the same explanation.

(*b*) *Duration of fishing trips*

Over the entire period the chick is in the nest, the sexes take about equal shares of guard spells and foraging, though the males' guard spells are longer than the females' during the second half of the chick's growth (the average length of male guard spells was 18·5 and 23·7 hours during the first and second halves of the chick's growth respectively, whilst those of the female were 18·8 during both halves). The lengths of foraging trips during the 48 hour check were between 2–26 hours, distributed as follows: 1–4 hours (10 cases); 4–7 (11); 7–10 (28); 10–13 (31); 13–16 (6); 16–19 (1); 19–21 (3) and 26 (1). Thus 64·8 per cent fell between seven and thirteen hours. This may well reflect a tendency to visit specific fishing grounds, which is not unlikely in view of the known attractiveness to gannets (which must be Bass birds) of, for example, the Farne Island area. The journey there and back would take about five hours, which would leave between two and eight hours for actual fishing and associated activities. In view of the species' 'social signalling' of the whereabouts of shoals, this is a realistic division of time. Nevertheless, the observed absences allow for considerable individual variation in the distance travelled, which indeed could easily amount to a maximum fishing range of well over 400km. It would be fascinating to know more about the gannet's foraging techniques. Conceivably, they may merely hunt wherever they strike prey on the outward journey and rest on the sea for a variable time; alternatively (and more likely) individuals learn several fishing grounds and use them according to season and weather and (perhaps) a tendency to specialise

Fig. 40. Stages in the development of the chick.

(b)

(a)

(c)

(d)

(e)

(a) 5-day-old
(b) 10-day-old
(c) month-old
(d) 5-week-old
(e) 9-week-old chick, now at its heaviest and up to half again as heavy as the parent.

on certain prey species. Where the feeding areas of several colonies overlap, as they do on the west of Britain, the situation could be exceedingly complex and adaptive.

Bass parents spent about 15 per cent of daylight hours together at the nest (Table 10). This applied even to parents of large chicks; indeed parents with chicks 1–17 days old spent less time together than those with chicks 26–43 days old, possibly because small chicks demand more frequent feeding, though little at a time, and parents are unable to hold up their own assimilation of the food in their stomach. It seems, from the observed deployment of time, that gannets are not forced to work to the limits of their capacity to feed their chick, or even to feed twins. In the context of breeding success, there were two remarkable cases at Bempton in which the female of the pair disappeared when the chick was part grown (9 and 5 weeks respectively). In both, the chick fledged. In the first case it undoubtedly received far less than the normal amount of food, begged constantly, frequently elicited unsuccessful regurgitation attempts from the male and must have fledged severely underweight. The male's absences were usually less than 20 minutes. A three-year-old intruder persistently invaded the site and several other prospectors did so more desultorily. In the second case the chick fledged when 12–13 weeks old. It, too, was rarely left for more than an hour and its main persecutors, launching frequent and severe attacks, were neighbours from the same ledge. The male parent fished mainly between 10.00–11.00 hrs and 16.00–17.00 hrs and seemed to provide for the chick more adequately than in the other case. These two instances of a single parent coping successfully are the only recorded ones. On the Bass, whenever a parent went missing, the chick died.

These points are significant when interpreting the gannet's relationship with its food supply. During three seasons' intensive study, I had no reason to suspect that a gannet chick

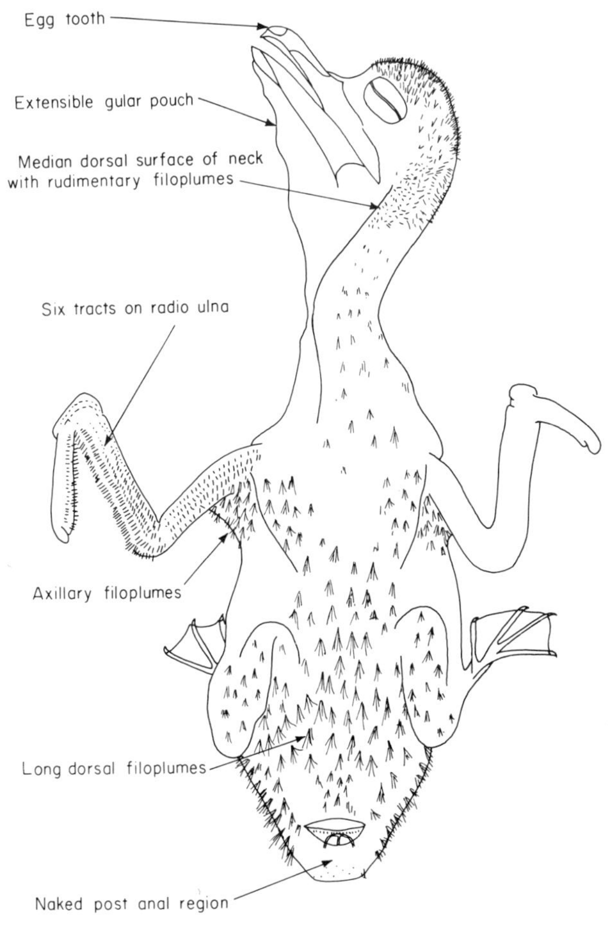

Fig. 40(f)

Distribution of down on gannet chick.

TABLE 8

THE FREQUENCY WITH WHICH GANNET CHICKS ARE FED
(40 HOUR WATCH, 27 CHICKS)

	Number of feeding bouts in two-hour periods									
	2–4*	4–6	6–8	8–10	10–12	12–14	14–16	16–18	18–20	20–22
Day 1	4	8	7	8	10	11	12	16	11	3
Day 2	1	9	15	5	5	6	9	8	9	6
Totals	5	17	22	13	15	17	21	24	20	9

* First feed 02·45 G.M.T.
Average number of feeding bouts per chick per day = 2·7.

TABLE 9

NUMBER OF FEEDS IN 40 HOURS, ARRANGED ACCORDING TO THE AGE OF THE GANNET CHICK

Age (days)	Number of feeding bouts	Number of entries	
		Fed	Probably fed
1	7	15	–(4)*
1	6	8	–
2	7	6	1
4	4	4	2
4	5	8	–
17	3	10	–
23	5	19	2
24	4	9	3
25	4	17	–
25	4	14	4
26	6	10	5
Twins 26/27	9	37	8
Twins 27/28	6	26	11
28	7	20	2
29	6	16	5
31	5	13	7
35	5	24	1
35	5	11	1
Twins 35/37	8	22	3
37	5	12	3
37	5	12	3
40	4	9	–
42	4	6	1
42	4	15	2
42	3	10	–
43	6	15	3
43	4	16	16

* Figures in brackets represent unsuccessful entries.

died of starvation. A greater contrast with the situation in some of the boobies could not be imagined.

3. *Growth*

(*a*) *By weight*

An outstanding feature of the Atlantic gannet's ecology compared with that of all other sulids, is the extremely rapid growth of its chick (Fig. 41). Not only is the chick (at a maximum weight in some cases of 4500g) some 1000–1500g heavier than other sulids of similar size but it takes a shorter time to achieve this weight. From about two to eight weeks the rate of growth is fastest, but after about the 53rd day (at about 3800g), the curve flattens and the difference between consecutive mean weights is no longer significant (this does not mean that less food is needed; feather growth and greater activity maintain requirements at a high level). Detailed comparison between successive years (Poulin 1968a) failed to reveal any difference in the rate of growth—a fact which accords with a situation in which food is abundant.

All three gannets are rapid growers compared with most other sulids (the Peruvian booby beats them in terms of biomass reared and the blue foot does so on the occasions when it rears two chicks) but the Atlantic gannet exceeds the other two in this respect (Table 11). It fledges with fat deposits of some 1000–1200g whereas the other two have recessed considerably further from their maximum weight (reached earlier) by the time they fledge. This is because the Cape and Australasian gannets spend more time exercising away from the nest before fledging, and grow their wing feathers further. Thus when they fledge they are both proportionately lighter and have a greater wing area and so immediately can fly much further. Nevertheless, in all three the fat deposits emphasise this trio's complete departure from the normal sulid regime of post-fledging feeding of young by their parents. The Atlantic gannet has merely gone further in this respect.

The variation in weight at all ages is considerable but much of it is due to temporarily retarded growth, which quickly accelerates again. Individuals sometimes jump from a far-below average weight to above average in a week or two. The recessions are never comparable to those attending the growth of the pan-tropical boobies of some areas (q.v.). Although it was not possible to obtain growth curves of late chicks it is likely that they were retarded and fledged at lower weights and with smaller bills and wings than those growing in the optimal period. Recently, S. Wanless (pers. comm.) has shown that late juveniles on Ailsa Craig weigh and measure less than those fledging in the main period. Whilst this *may* indicate a falling off in the food supply, it could alternatively result from the adults' increasing reluctance to spend time at the colony late in the season.

(*b*) *By other measurements*

Poulin measured the growth rate of bill, wing, tail, tarsus and toe (Fig. 42) which grow

TABLE 10

TIME SPENT BY GANNET PAIRS TOGETHER AT THE NEST DURING A CONTINUOUS 48 HOUR WATCH

Number of hours pair present	Age of chick (days)			
	1–14	15–24	25–34	35–44
0–3	4	2	1	2(1)
3–6	0	1	1	1
6–9	0	0	2(1)	2
9–12	0	0	1	3
overnight	1	0	3(1)	3

Figures in brackets represent nests with twins.
Mean number of hours pairs present in daylight = 6 or 15 per cent.

at different rates and some of which show much more variability than others. The relatively invariable parameters (bill and total wing length) can safely be used to age chicks. Between 10 and 26 measurements of each parameter for each age were made at four-day intervals from 1 to 77 days of age.

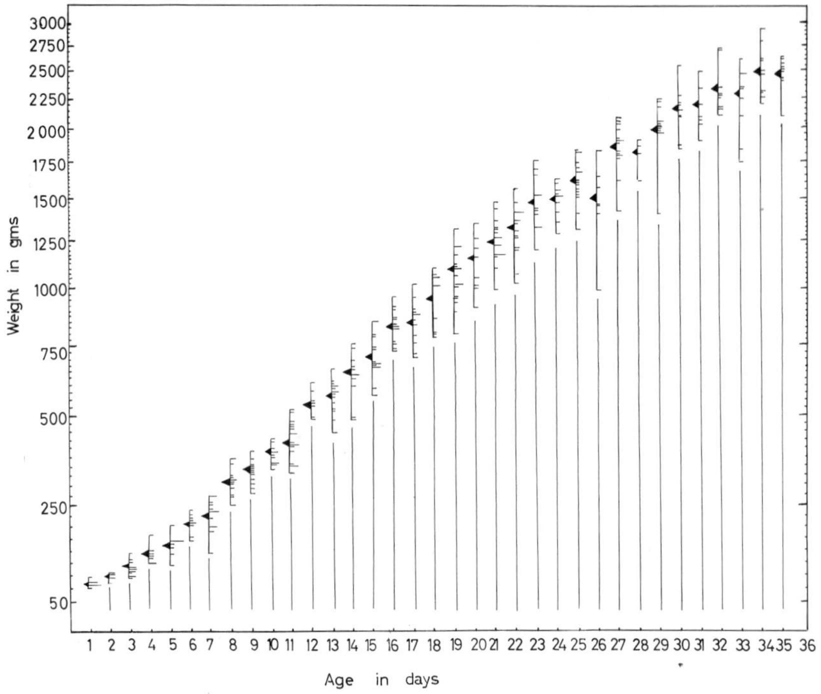

Fig. 41(a)

Growth curve from hatching to 35 days. Bass Rock.

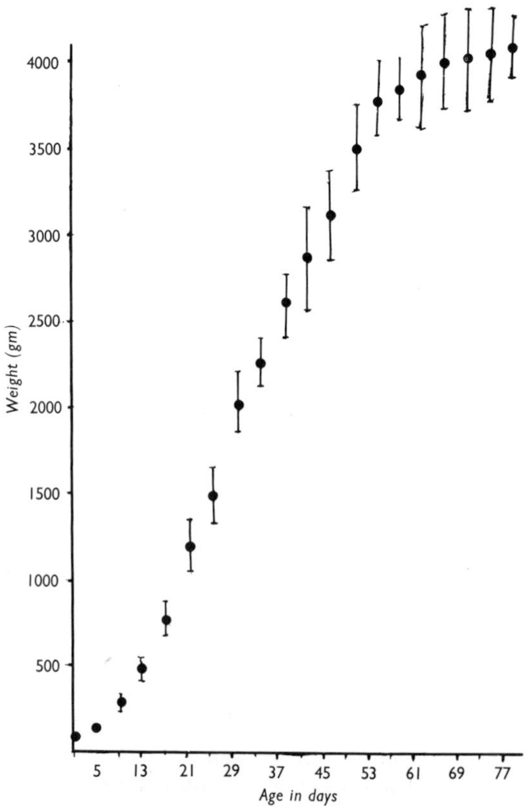

Fig. 41(b)

Growth curve from hatching to 11 weeks, Bonaventure. (From Poulin 1968a.)

(i) *Culmen*. The maximum growth rate occurs between nine and 33 days, over which period it averages 2·7mm per day, but after the 49th day the difference between consecutive mean measurements is no longer significant. Then the curve flattens, and becomes asymptotic at 96 mm. There is little variation around the mean culmen length for any age and the mean coefficient of variation (that is taken over the whole period of culmen growth) is only 3·7 per cent compared with 9·2 per cent for weight. Thus bill length is a sound indicator of age up to about seven weeks. Comparing years, 1967 birds grew slightly better than 1966, showing at four ages significantly longer bills.

(ii) *Tenth primary*. By the 29th day, wing and tail feathers appear and thereafter grow very rapidly (5·5mm per day during the period of quickest growth). The coefficient of variation is large (mean 15·7 per cent; minimum 5·3 per cent at 73 days; maximum 47·2 per cent at 33 days). This means that, of two chicks about 33 days old, one may have a tenth primary half as long again as the other. Mean growth in 1966 and 1967 was similar up to 57 days. After that, 1966 birds grew slightly faster. This is opposite to the culmen findings and if meaningful would seem to indicate relatively faster wing growth under poorer conditions. The tenth primary measures 228mm at 77 days, whereas in the adult it averages 296mm. Since it will grow relatively little between 77 days and fledging, the remainder of the growth must occur after fledging, probably whilst the juvenile is swimming southwards.

(iii) *Wing*. The length of the entire wing and of the wing from carpal joint to tip, given in Fig. 42, enables one to deduce the growth of the various components of the wing. If, from each mean, the length of the tenth primary is subtracted, the growth curve is asymptotic, having its point of inflexion between 33 and 49 days. Feather growth continues beyond 77 days.

Total wing length is a good indicator of age. Between day one and 77, each mean point is statistically different from the preceding or following one. Moreover, there is no difference between years. The growth of the wing from wrist to tip (tenth primary excepted) is also a good indicator of age, though slightly more variable. Between 49 and 57 days the difference between successive lengths is not significant. The coefficient of variation for the whole wing is 5·2 per cent; for the hand 5·6 per cent and for the tenth primary 15·7 per cent.

(iv) *Toe*. Immediately after hatching, the middle tow grows rapidly from 18mm at one day to 97mm at 33 days.

TABLE II

RATES OF GROWTH IN THE GANNET SUPERSPECIES

		Weight (mean)		
		Atlantic	Cape	Australasian
Age (weeks)	3	1243	*c*. 950	900
	6	3125	*c*. 2200	2100
	9	3980	—	—
	12	*c*. 4000	*c*. 3100	*c*. 3200
Mean maximum weight achieved	Absolute	*c*. 4100	3200	3200
	Weight as percentage of adult	132%	123%	139%*
Mean weight at fledging		*c*. 3900	2920	*c*. 2900
Age at which peak weight reached		65–75 days	*c*. 80 days	*c*. 80 days?

* N.B. This figure is possibly much less accurate than the other two because there is little published material from which to judge weights.

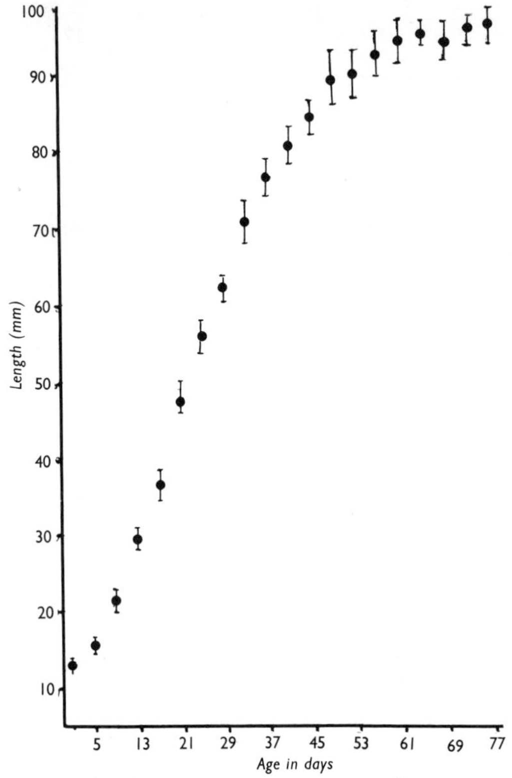

Fig. 42(a). Growth of culmen, Bonaventure. (From Poulin 1968a.)

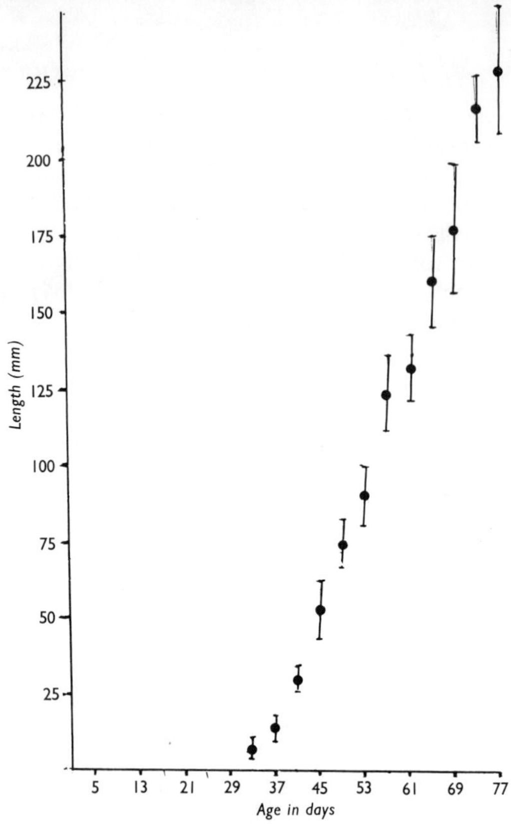

Fig. 42(b). Growth of tenth (outermost) primary, Bonaventure. (From Poulin 1968a.)

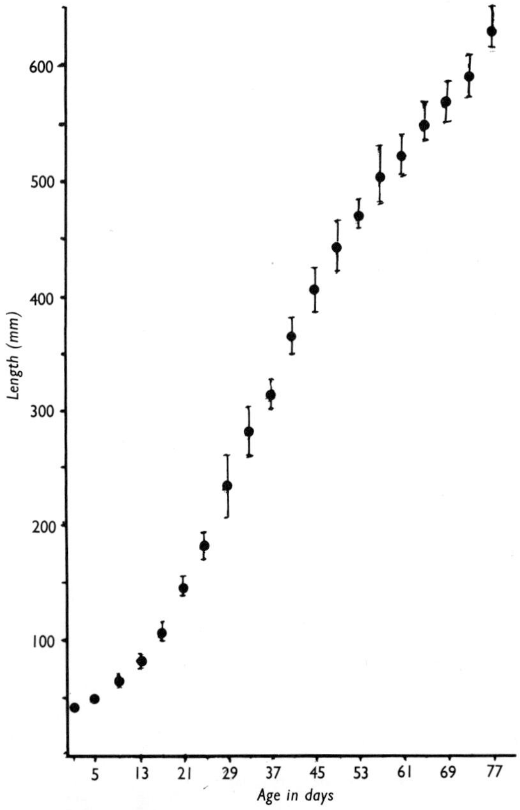

Fig. 42(c). Growth of wing, Bonaventure. (From Poulin 1968a.)

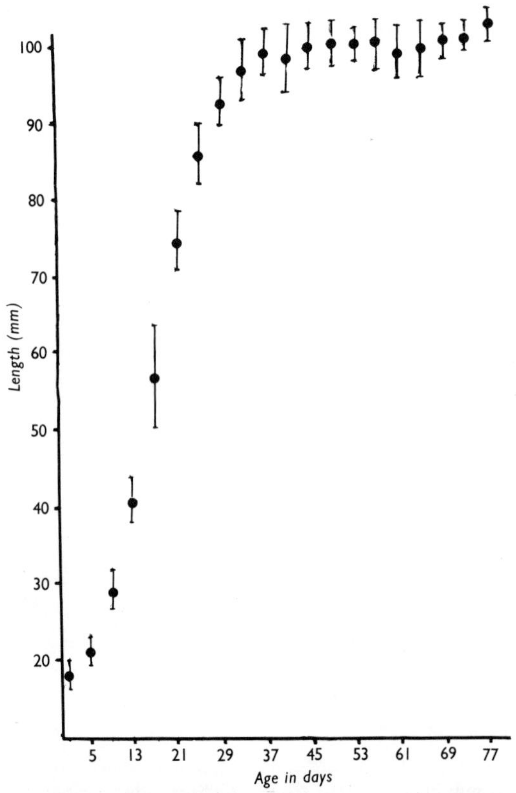

Fig. 42(d). Growth of middle toe, Bonaventure. (From Poulin 1968a.)

During this period each mean differs significantly from that on either side whereas later they do not: it should thus be used as an indicator of age from one to 33 days. Its length is proportional to the size of the whole foot and its rapid growth in the first month means that just when the chick has become too large to be covered by its parent, its own equipment for losing body heat, of which the webs are an important part, has largely been acquired.

(v) *Tarsus*. Tarsi show considerable variation in rate of growth and are not good indicators of age. This makes the relatively invariable web growth even more significant, for if one part of the limb grows so irregularly, the fact that another does not implies adaptive significance.

(*c*) *Effect on adult*

It is interesting to note that the effort of feeding the chick does not cause the adults to lose weight (Table 12). This evidence agrees with that for other sulids, even those in which food is often scarce and presumably indicates the great value of the adult in a slowly maturing seabird. Chicks are expendable but harmful stress on adults is to be avoided.

4. *Twinning experiments*

In 1964 I reported the results of donating an extra egg to several pairs of gannets and comparing the growth rate and fledging success of the twins against normal singletons. The conclusion, that Atlantic gannets can rear twins sufficiently well to give them substantial reproductive advantage over pairs with but a single chick and yet never do so naturally, aroused interest because it provided (and still does) an apparently clear exception to the widely accepted view due mainly to Lack that birds rear as many young as they can adequately feed (adequately meaning with unimpaired chances of survival). Fig. 43 shows the growth of twins compared with singles. Provided the twins were of the same age, they grew up together about equally but slightly behind normal singletons. At fledging, the twins may have weighed as much as 10 per cent[1] less than the singles, though this is unlikely. Thus, at 72 days two twins averaged 3500g against 3930g for two singles, and at 74 days two twins averaged 3900 whilst two singles averaged about 3800g. Twins fledged at an average of 94 (84–103) days against 90 (84–97) for singles and thus had extra time to make up any deficiency. Furthermore, at ages 7, 21, 26, 33, 39, 55 and 60 days, in larger samples (at least seven pairs in each case) the average weight of twins actually *exceeded* that of singletons whilst at the ages of 26, 28, 33, 39 and 59 days the

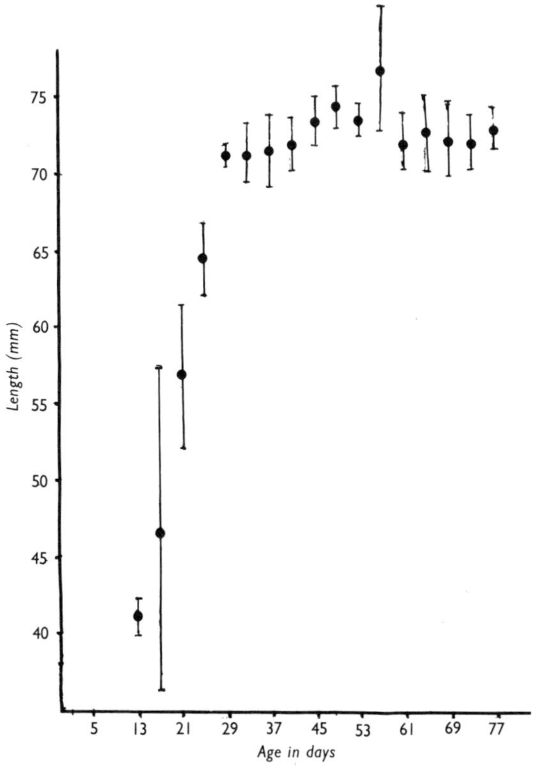

Fig. 42(e). Growth of tarsus, Bonaventure. (From Poulin 1968a.)

[1] Of course, 10 per cent less weight overall *could* mean that they had considerably more than 10 per cent less fat, depending on the relative contributions of fat versus other tissues, to the weight difference.

TABLE 12

WEIGHT VARIATION IN THE GANNET IN RELATION TO THE STAGE OF THE BREEDING CYCLE

	Incubating (Bass)	Guarding young (Bass)	Status unknown—probably incubating (Ailsa)
Males	2954 (2470–3470) 14 cases	2908 (2520–3360) 13 cases	3120 (2400–3600) 17 cases
Females	3122 (2760–3610) 20 cases	2910 (2570–3070) 7 cases	2941 (2300–3600) 18 cases

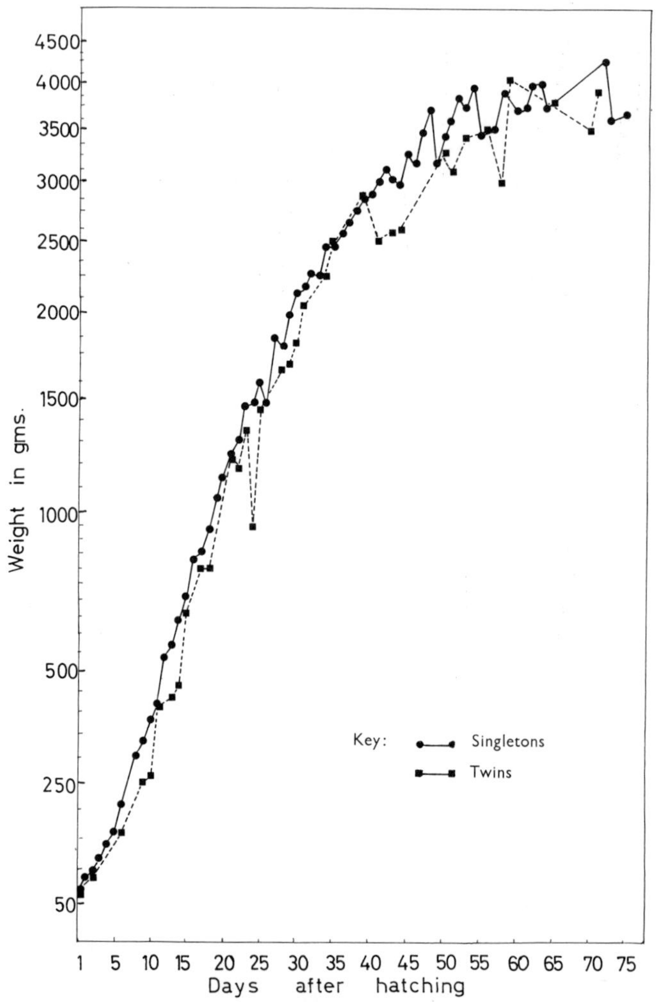

Fig. 43. The normal growth of single chicks compared with that of twins in pairs given an extra egg or chick.

heaviest twin outweighed the heaviest single from a sample of at least ten birds. Thus although the lack of an adequate sample of weights of twins and singletons between the ages of 75 days and fledging age precludes absolute certainty, the fact that the twins came through the main period of demand without falling significantly behind, and had an earlier history of repeatedly catching up and at times exceeding singletons, strongly suggests that they would not have fallen behind in the final stages. I noted (Nelson 1964) that parents of twins began to work harder during the period of maximum or near maximum size of the twins (they spent less time together on the site and occasionally foraged simultaneously). Of course, the important question is not whether the twins were marginally lighter than singletons at fledging, but whether the parents of these twins contributed more or less progeny to the future breeding stock. Even if there was a small difference in fat reserves I think one can hardly doubt that they did. Indeed, such was the fledging success of twins (Table 13) that their parents produced on average 76 per cent more young than parents of singletons. Since over 70 per cent of normal single chicks die anyway, the mortality of the twins would have had to be fantastically high to contribute even fewer survivors, despite starting off with 76 per cent more fledglings. That this could happen often enough seems practically impossible when one considers that the twins fledged with very considerable fat reserves; that *normal* variation in fledging weight among singletons is always enormous (far greater than any possible difference between twins and singletons which implies that getting away on time is more important than reaching a certain weight) and that survival anyway depends to a large extent on highly fortuitous circumstances (the timing of autumn gales which varies considerably from year to year). Twins were only four days later than singletons. Under all these circumstances it is straining credulity too far to suggest that, every 2·5 years (which would be the required frequency) so many twins would perish, compared with singletons, that the average selection pressure would favour the latter. Where weather is so critical, the lack of a few grams of fat could easily be more than offset by a few days' calm, and with only four days between singles and twins, the chances are almost 50:50 that the latter would hit as favourable or more favourable weather. These points should be strongly made because it has recently been suggested (Jarvis 1974) that the experiments just described may well not indicate that the parents of these twins gained a reproductive advantage; the evidence suggests that they did so. Similar experiments conducted by Jarvis on the Cape gannet yielded equivocal results, but in a different ecological situation (p. 242).

Further points emerging from the twinning work were:

1. Twins had to be within a day or two of the same age, otherwise the larger chick persecuted the smaller and prevented it from begging adequately and thus from being fed. 2. The twins did not differ much in weight. Cape gannet twins by contrast, were markedly unequal. 3. Oddly enough, the average twin weight was slightly less than that of the singleton from the very first day after hatching, when the amount of food required was negligible.

TABLE 13

FLEDGING SUCCESS OF TWINNED GANNETS

	Age difference (in days)	Number in sample	Fledging success		
			Both	One	None
Twinned as eggs	0	4 (2)	2	1 (1)	1 (1)
	1	5	0	4	1
	2	5 (2)	1	4 (2)	0
	3	3 (1)	0	3 (1)	0
Twinned as chicks	0	13	9	3	1

Figures in brackets represent nests in which only one of the eggs hatched.
Number of chicks reared = 39 from 30 nests, of which only 25 hatched both eggs.

Possibly (to put it crudely) adults have a programmed 'amount' of feeding tendency (rather than, at this stage, depending *wholly* on the external stimulus of the chick's begging behaviour, which is almost non-existent)[1] and naturally it is geared to one chick rather than two. After the initial lag, the mean curve for twin growth runs parallel to singleton, showing that at any given weight the twins are receiving as much food as the singles did at that weight but lag a little behind in time (i.e. they should have reached this weight earlier). The inference is that the adult's response is being regulated adequately by the chick's begging. In fact, a 48 hour watch revealed that twins were fed (in total) twice as often as singletons (twins received 66 feeds: singles 36). 4. The variation in weight at any age was on the whole greater for singles than twins. 5. The lightest chicks, both twins and singles, tended to vary more from day to day than the heaviest. 6. Compared with the growth of natural shag siblings (Nelson 1964) the gannet twin was less behind its singleton counterpart than the younger shag was behind its brother. Whilst the habits of shag and gannet differ, they are comparable in many respects and yet the two shag chicks survive well.

Finally, it may be pointed out that greater danger of falling from cliff ledges could not sufficiently select against twins (usually, only one would fall; usually, there is room for two; also, a sizeable proportion of gannets nest on flattish ground). Neither does rearing twins have a deleterious effect on adults (see pp. 93 and 243).

If the results are valid, there are three possible explanations:

1. The clutch size of one evolved in conditions under which gannets could not adequately feed more, and, though conditions have changed, the hereditary mechanism determining clutch size has not. In a bird with such a low reproductive rate as the gannet, a change in clutch size could take a long time to come about.
2. The low clutch size is a way of keeping reproductive rate low and so of allowing more individuals to breed without boosting the population too high for the carrying capacity of the environment.
3. The low clutch size is inescapably tied in with the importance of the site in gannet breeding biology (p. 123) by virtue of the following circumstances. Twins are incompatible with the degree of site competition and site attendance required. By guarding the chick and site less, the parents would greatly increase their food gathering powers. Instead, they show enormous site tenacity, guard their chicks unremittingly, and even attack unoffending chicks of absent neighbours, thus discouraging such absence. This strongly developed aggression is presumably essential for successful site establishment and maintenance, and the socially adequate site is important for reasons already discussed. In other words, it may well have been advantageous to restrict the clutch to one, in order to develop to the full the present site system with its important advantages. I see this third possibility as consistent with the all powerful mechanism of co-adapted evolution and it fits persuasively into the whole system of gannet ecology and behaviour.

5. *Fledging period*

Bass birds fledged at a mean age of 90 days (range 84–97) which, incidentally is virtually the same age (94 days) at which Booth's (1887) captive gannets, with unlimited food, stopped receiving food from their parents, Actual records were 84 days (3% of 111 cases); 85 (5%); 86 (4%); 87 (5%); 88 (12%); 89 (17%); 90 (13%); 91 (12%); 92 (6%); 93 (12%); 94 (5%); 95 (3%); 96 (2%); 97 (1%). Chicks from cliff-edge nests (16 cases) fledged at 88·8 days (84–95); from inland fringes (20 cases) at 88·9 (83–96); first time breeders (20 cases) at 90·1 (83–96); experienced breeders (50 cases) at 90·1 (85–97); twinned chicks (24 cases) at 94 (89–103). The equal fledging periods of chicks from experienced and inexperienced parents is another indication of the thorough hunting competence achieved by gannets before ever they breed (which may be one reason for the greatly deferred maturity) and of the good food supply. The difficulty of passing through the colony to the cliff-edge obviously did not delay fledging. There

[1] Cf. the situation in passerines where feeding response is entirely controlled by external stimuli.

was, however, a relationship between the length of the fledging period and the time of year. Chicks fledging in August and October took significantly less time than those fledging in September. The figures were August, 87·8 (83–90; 11 cases); first half September 91·5 (86–97, 42 cases); second half September 90·0 (83–96; 39 cases); October 86·4 (85–88; 7 cases). This probably means that early chicks grew best, and late ones fledged prematurely due to the general desertion of the colony by adults (for a discussion of timing of breeding see p. 117).

Bonaventure birds fledged at 90·6 days (82–99) and different parts of the colony did not differ in this. Thus their food supply must be equally as good as that of Bass birds and indicates that this decisive environmental factor is typical of the Atlantic gannet on both sides of the Atlantic—which has important implications for population dynamics (both populations seem to have a rate of increase of three per cent per annum). Chicks from replacement eggs (like chicks from late Bass eggs) took less time to fledge (mean 87·4, 12 cases). Poulin attributed this to the rapidly deteriorating weather conditions of late September; the late young were not underweight.

Gannets fledge at a weight of about 3800–4000g. The mean weight of 26 Ailsa juveniles that fell short of the sea was 3659g (range 3000–4320g). They are unlikely to have been very much lighter than successful birds.

6. *Fledging season*

Fig. 44 shows that, on the Bass, 1961–63, two-thirds fledged in the first half of September, almost a fifth fledged in August or very early September and a sixth in late September or early October. In fact, the real mean fledging date is at least 2 weeks earlier than these dates indicate.[1] Therefore, the optimal fledging season for Bass gannets (and Bempton is similar)

[1] Though at the time I did not realise it, in 1961 and 1962 the mean laying date of the group of birds from which the bulk of these figures came was still unnaturally late. Due to excessive disturbance in the 1950s birds were very wary and returning late. Also, the group was fairly small. In the 1960s, complete protection engendered notable confidence in the birds; they returned earlier, social stimulation was high, the group increased in size and the mean laying date advanced (p. 121). It has now stabilised.

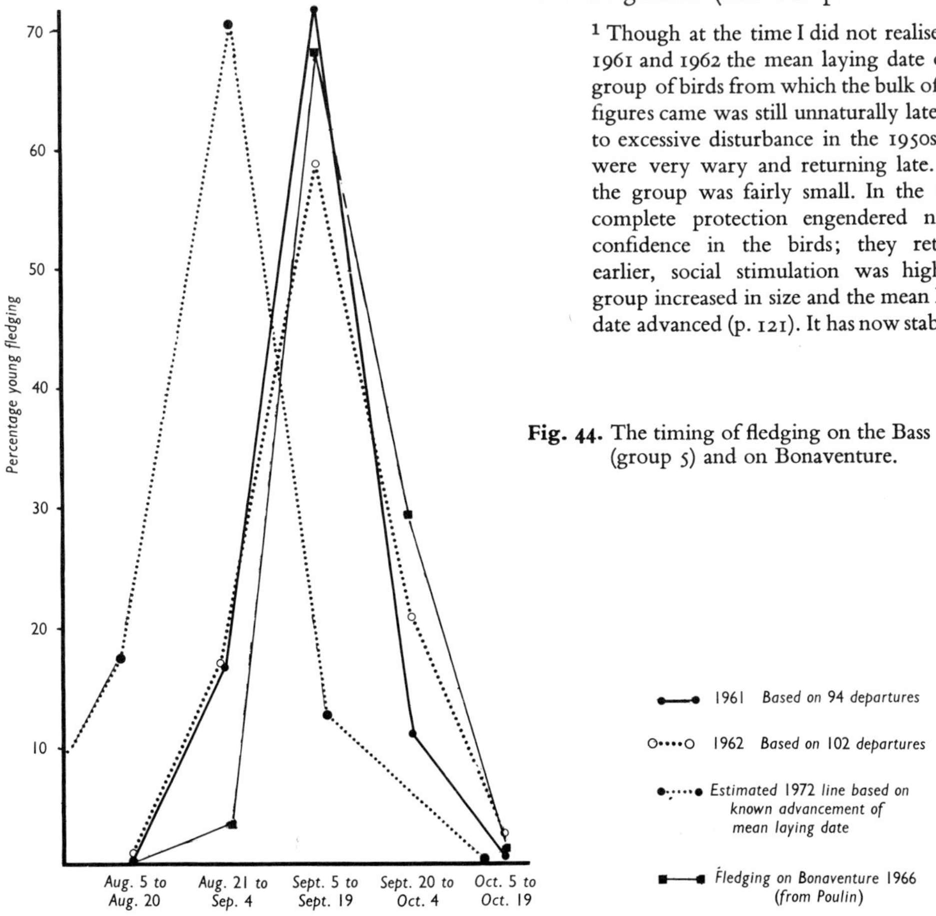

Fig. 44. The timing of fledging on the Bass (group 5) and on Bonaventure.

is the end of August, but a sizeable proportion fall on either side of this period. This correlates extremely well with the most nicely judged avoidance of gales that can be achieved under the variable weather regime of the North Sea. Thus, early September gales are relatively rare (though they occurred in 1974); by mid-September the probability increases sharply whilst from late September onwards they are highly probable. By laying from late March onwards, with a marked and annually consistent peak around mid-April but also considerable spread (assuming they cannot lay much earlier (see p. 119)) gannets are clearly hitting the most favourable time for fledging but are also allowing for the unpredictable variation in weather (both with regard to vulnerable young in the nest and to fledglings). There may be other factors affecting the timing of breeding, but (apart from seasonally abundant food for young in the nest) we know nothing about them. An indication of the effect of the time of year at which the young fledge, on survival, may be sought from ringing returns. If one excludes artificial recoveries (shooting, drowning in fishing nets and oiling) on the grounds that these are unlikely to bear any relationship to seasonal time of fledging there remain a few recoveries (Table 14), from which it appears that early fledgers survive better than late ones. It must be stressed that the comparison, here, is not between early fledgers and abnormally late (October) ones, but by birds differing in their hatching dates by three or four weeks and all of them well within the normal spread of laying. To detect any difference under these circumstances is highly suggestive.

Ailsa Craig gannets fledge about two to three weeks later than those on the east. If their mean laying date is fixed by pre-breeding availability of food (and we do not know this), their late fledging is simply an inevitable concomitant. It is possible, though, that migrating west coast fledglings face a different weather pattern and different availability of food (for example, spawning stocks of herring) than their North Sea counterparts. A critical evaluation of this suggestion would be useful. Grassholm gannets fledged mainly in the latter half of August 1975 (a visit on the 8th showed a huge proportion almost or completely clear of down and very well synchronised). On June 5th 1976 the mean age of chicks was about two weeks, which again would produce fledglings in the second half of August, though a substantial number of nests contained eggs. Probably the colony was slightly later than the Bass but earlier than Ailsa.

On Bonaventure, 75 per cent of young fledged between September 2nd and 20th with a peak between September 18th and 22nd (39 per cent in 1966; 26 per cent in 1967). By September 30th only 3 per cent had yet to fledge in 1966 and 2 per cent in 1967. This was achieved despite a much later start to the season than that made by east Atlantic gannets. The season is shortened at both ends in the Canadian colonies, and it says much for the efficacy of the Atlantic gannet's adaptations (morphological and social) to the cold-water regime that it can squeeze a reproductive cycle into this period.

Perhaps comparable factors affect the timing of fledging in the other two gannets; their high post-fledging mortality suggests so, but there is also reason to believe that they are not quite so seriously affected by weather as are North Atlantic gannets. Unfortunately, in both cases, we lack comparable data on the shape of the graph for fledging.

TABLE 14

DIFFERENTIAL MORTALITY ACCORDING TO EARLY OR LATE FLEDGING

	Age (weeks) when ringed (usually between June 26 and July 7)		
	0–2	4–6	6+
Number ringed	156	1775	253
Number recovered (natural causes only) up to December of year of ringing	4	27	2
Per cent recovered	2·6	1·52	0·8

BREEDING SUCCESS

1. *Hatching success*

In 1961, 62 and 63, gannets in my Bass Rock observation group hatched 87 per cent, 85 per cent and 74 per cent (average 82 per cent) of 148, 163 and 189 eggs respectively. Of these 500 eggs, 7·3 per cent were infertile and 11 per cent were lost. Between 1964 and 1976 hatching success was never lower than about 85 per cent, in group 6 (Fig. 35(b)). In 1963, 20 per cent of eggs were lost overall (43 per cent in the case of first- and second-time breeders), an unusually high proportion, but the cause was obscure. This was the highest egg loss ever recorded. There was no egg loss due to predation. Herring gulls nest in large numbers close to Bass gannets but we repeatedly confirmed that they could take eggs or small chicks only if these were first exposed by human interference or freak behaviour of the gannets. Egg loss was proportional to the extent of human interference in the areas we did not specially protect; fringe nests, in particular, suffered and authors commenting on the inferiority of fringe sites have not taken full account of artefacts introduced by human disturbance. Freak weather can cause egg loss on cliff sites. A severe north-westerly gale in May 1962 completely cleared a broad flat ledge on top of the north-west face and also emptied nests on ledges part way down the sheer face, due to terrific updraught sweeping the birds off their nests. On Bonaventure only 38 per cent of eggs hatched (39·9 per cent in 1966 and 36·5 per cent in 1967). Most of this low success was due to egg loss, but, in addition, 16·5 per cent failed to hatch after a normal period of incubation compared with only 7·3 per cent on the Bass. Probably, a combination of chilling and a high concentration of toxic chemicals was responsible.

Snow (1960) has shown for shags that the ratio of yolk to albumen varies according to the availability of food prior to laying, but this seems unlikely to be important in gannets. Wodzicki & McMeekan (1947) recorded a particularly low breeding success (16 per cent or less) in the Australasian gannets at Cape Kidnappers in 1945–46, due mainly to infertility, but the cause remained obscure.

Fig. 45. Gannet eggs, even at the edge of a colony, are immune from predation by herring gulls unless gannets are disturbed.

Poulin obtained information in 537 cases on the times at which egg loss occurred. Eighty-one were lost around hatching (I suspect that the chick was killed by inadequate parental response): when lost, 312 had been incubated for less than 40 days and 144 for more than 50 days. A proportion of the latter were presumably chilled, a distinct hazard under the extraordinarily severe climatic conditions, with mean temperatures of 6·7°C. in April and 4·4°C. in May, high rainfall and in some cases snow soaked nests. In addition Poulin noticed that some inexperienced (fringe) birds, where loss was high, incubated abnormally and were prone to leave the egg when alarmed. A nice illustration of the effect of weather lay in the observation that in the very severe (snowy) spring of 1967 the nests protected by trees (see Fig. 33) hatched more than unprotected groups.

There was a clear correlation between low hatching success and inexperience. Inexperienced Bass pairs hatched 62·5 per cent of eggs laid, compared with 86 per cent by birds breeding for at least the third time, the difference being due almost entirely to egg loss, but also to ineffective incubation. Three females breeding for the first time ignored and soon lost their new laid egg, whilst one bird incubated the egg on top of her webs and later lost it. Inexperienced females were also less successful in coping with newly hatched young (p. 203).

2. *Fledging success*

Gannets have an exceptionally high fledging (and thus breeding) success; 89 per cent of all Bass eggs hatched gave fledged young in 1961, 94 per cent in 1962 and 94 per cent in 1963 (average 92·3 per cent based on 500 nests) where fledging is defined as irrevocably leaving the nest when fully feathered. Since then in the years 1965, 1966, 1968, 1970–76 inclusive, my records have been less exhaustive and visits too few to gain figures for fledging success, but sample groups in the main observation colony have yielded records of large young in July in, on average, 85 per cent of nests which held eggs in April or May. Allowing 10 per cent egg loss and assuming 95 per cent of these large young would eventually fledge (and there is no reason to suppose otherwise), gives an average breeding success (fledged from laid) over these ten years of 80 per cent. In no year was success significantly poorer, despite variations in weather, which provides further proof of the highly dependable food supply. Thus, in 13 years, starvation was never a cause of chick mortality. On Bonaventure, fledging success (not breeding success) was 78·3 per cent and there was no difference between different groups or between 1966 and 1967. This significantly lower success was due to loss of small chicks as a result of disturbance by man. On Ailsa, fledging success, from eggs hatched, was 93 and 91 per cent in 1974 and 1975 and similar in 1976 (S. Wanless); on Grassholm, in 1975 and 1976, I judged it to have been at least 90 per cent and on Bempton in 1973, 1974 and 1975 it was 93, 92 and 92 per cent (J. Fairhurst). On the Bass the following factors were involved in chick loss:

Weather. High wind with prolonged rain and low temperatures caused death in some three- to five-week-old chicks. Very considerable mortality has been noted among Australasian gannets for the same reason; Wodzicki & Robertson (1953) say 10 per cent of Kidnappers chicks may die in bad weather and very much greater mortality was recorded in one year at White Island and Horuhoru where more than 80 per cent of young died, but here, apparently, starvation was a major cause of death. If all chicks were at the vulnerable age simultaneously the colony could suffer heavy loss, which is presumably one reason why natural selection has favoured a considerable spread of laying (another is the similarly unpredictable weather attending the peak fledging period). This argument is rejected by Perrins (1970) who thereby apparently ignores the importance of selection pressure for variability. Variability in the temporal aspects of laying is presumably subject to selection pressure acting on individuals (or pairs), just as is variability in clutch size.

Attack by neighbours. Five recorded deaths were caused by the attacks of neighbours on unguarded chicks (due in three cases to the death of a parent). However, these records are mainly of interest in showing that it is disadvantageous to leave chicks unguarded rather than as a demonstration that such attacks constitute a significant cause of mortality.

Falling. Several chicks were knocked off their nests by departing adults (not their parents) and four fell off whilst wing-exercising. On the Needle and south-west face of the Bass—both extreme cliff areas—breeding success averaged 77 per cent, and 84 per cent[1] over 4 and 3 years respectively, so it seems that cliff sites are not significantly prone to loss of chicks compared with flatter ground. Similarly, fledging success at Bempton was as high as in the flatter Bass groups. Booth (1887) gives the impression that a lot of young are dislodged from the nest, by neighbouring young or by their own parents fighting! All this was almost certainly due to disturbance by visitors; the last two events at any rate rarely occur in undisturbed groups. He describes the great number of young of all stages, from newly hatched to fully feathered, along with several adults, on the rocky platform at the base of the west cliffs, and it is on the west that disturbance has always been a considerable menace to the nesting gannets. On Ailsa Craig a considerable number of young birds do fall from their cliff ledge onto the extensive rocky foreshore (Table 15). In this connection S. Wanless has discovered that, whilst the young which fall before they are six weeks old are of normal weight, those which fall after that age are significantly lighter than normal, indicating that they might have been fed less adequately and perhaps that unusually vigorous begging behaviour led to their fall.

Inadequate parental care. A minor source of chick loss, mainly among inexperienced females, due to inadequate brooding and feeding of tiny young.

Fledging descent. The percentage of juveniles that crashed during fledging was extremely low on the Bass. I saw two crashes out of 50 departures. In 1961–62, a total of only 10–20 injured or excessively fouled young were seen beneath a stretch of cliffs which held 1000–1500 pairs. On the other hand, Ailsa claims many more victims. Here in addition to the chicks mentioned above, about 250 fully feathered short-fall, injured or dead young were found beneath cliffs mainly on the west side (S. Wanless, pers. comm.). Most gannetries are not as dangerous as Ailsa; either the cliffs fall sheer, or are much lower, or are broken by slopes and terraces which provide checks on an out-of-control descent. Heavy fat reserves obviously endanger fledging but in most places the resulting mortality is too slight to matter much. The cliff ledges generally provide a much safer departure platform than a site far back on flat ground. In fact it is doubtful whether young could travel far through aggressive adults on really flat ground and one wonders how Eldey juveniles fare.

Nest falling. No nests were known to become detached from the cliff face, as apparently not infrequently happens to kittiwakes (Cullen 1957). Usually (but not always), there is enough of a supporting ledge to rule out this possibility. But six nests disappeared from the Needle (Fig. 36) during winters.

Predation. Unaided predation by gulls is totally insignificant. The great skua in Shetland often takes young kittiwakes from the nest, but is unable to take gannets.

Man. Man is undoubtedly the main cause of chick mortality either directly or indirectly through disturbance (low-flying planes, ships' sirens, careless visitors (particularly the odd rogue photographers) and occasional deliberate vandalism).

[1] Young alive in July were counted as 'fledged'. Less than 5 per cent are likely to have fallen between July and their fledging date.

TABLE 15

GANNET CHICKS FOUND AT THE FOOT OF AILSA CRAIG IN 1974
(Data from S. Wanless)

Age (weeks)	June 1	June 2	July 1	July 2	August 1	August 2	September 1	September 2	October 1	October 2	Total
0– 2	1	2	2	2	1	0	0	0	0	0	8
2– 4	1	8	11	24	3	7	4	0	0	0	58
4– 6		1	1	20	18	9	7	1	1	0	58
6– 8				3	15	32	7	3	0	2	62
8–10				1	15	16	2	4	6	1	45
10+					9	83	91	43	5	6	237
											468

Number of chicks found in each half-month period.

3. *Overall breeding success*

Overall breeding success in terms of young fledged from eggs laid (excluding replacement eggs) is extremely high (Table 16). Incomplete observations for several parts of the Bass since 1963 have given an overall minimum breeding success figure of about 73 per cent[1] (total of c. 1800 nests over 8 years), with little variation from year to year. The success of *replacement eggs* is much lower (37 per cent on the Bass and 7·5 per cent on Bonaventure). This may be partly because these birds have already shown themselves to be loss-prone and are also predominantly inexperienced. Breeding success, one of the major parameters in the species' breeding biology, can be considered under many headings.

(*a*) *Regional variation*

The high success shown by Bass gannets is in no way exceptional, but many other gannetries may, for several reasons, do less well. Human disturbance exerts a marked effect but presents no biological problems and need not be documented further than has already been done in the section on populations and elsewhere; it should always be considered as a potentially important factor in the interpretation of gannet breeding success and population dynamics. Poulin (1968b) recorded only 29·6 per cent breeding success at Bonaventure; this was due to extremely low hatching success, perhaps mainly due to climatic factors (chilling) and a high level of toxic chemicals in the eggs, possibly compounded by disturbance. Extremely small gannetries have a lower breeding success but this is a social effect (discussed below) rather than a regional one.

Brun (1974) has analysed the success of the Skarvlakken (Nordmjele) colony in Norway. Assuming that large chicks present in August would fledge, breeding success between 1970 and 1974 was 61, 46, 62, 35 and 39 per cent respectively. Sub-groups of the colony, taking only those numbering 19 pairs or more, had success varying between 3 and 84 per cent. Overall, this is significantly lower than the Bass, Ailsa or Bempton. Although Brun points out that (a) the colony is growing and has a high proportion of young breeders whose success is, as a group, lower than that of experienced pairs and (b) eggs of the Nordmjele colony taken in 1972 had high levels of methyl mercury and may have had significant levels of PCB and DDT (analyses awaited), the low success may have been at least partly due to predation by gulls in concert with disturbance by man. Brun appears to imply that herring and greater black-backed gulls are natural predators (unaided by man) but there is no evidence that this is so. He suggests, also, that the difference in breeding success between different years is primarily due to short but extreme periods of bad weather (storm, heavy rain or frost).

Grassholm, judging from my own single visits in 1975 and 1976, had a success at least as high as 80 per cent, and Ailsa (1974–76) well over 70 per cent.

Table 17 compares breeding success, not only between the three gannetries for which details are available, but also for Bass groups with different characteristics and for a gannetry (Bempton) which was rapidly increasing during the period concerned.

The Atlantic gannet's high breeding success throughout its range, due largely to its dependable food supply, contrasts with some of the boobies, whose breeding success varies with region.

[1] This is slightly lower than real, due to disturbance, though the great bulk of my sample nests were not disturbed.

TABLE 16

BREEDING SUCCESS IN THE GANNET ON THE BASS ROCK

Year	Number of nests	Per cent hatched of eggs laid	Per cent fledged of chicks hatched	Per cent chicks fledged from eggs laid in: April	May	June
1961	145	87	89	85	67	0
1962	159	85	94	91	90	75
1963	186	74	94	84	60	—

TABLE 17

A COMPARISON OF BREEDING SUCCESS (PER CENT CHICKS FLEDGED FROM EGGS LAID) IN GANNETS FROM DIFFERENT GROUPS

	Approx. no. of nests (if the group is growing, nos. are given between two dates)	1961	1962	1963	1964	1965	1966	1967	1968	1969	1970	1971	1972	1973	1974	1975	1976
Bass group 5 (sample only)	250–500 (1961–74)	77 (145)	77 (159)	69 (186)	NR	NR	87 (150)	NR		NR	78	80	72	83	70	74	78
Bass group 6 (almost entire)	10–70 (1961–75)	61 (18)	61 (18)	83 (25)	NR	NR	69 (36)	NR	78 (35)	NR	86 (45)	70 (52)	75 (66)	75 (67)	OD —	88 (58)	81 (72)
Bass Needle (entire)	c. 35	68 (35)	68 (27)		NR	NR		NR		NR	NR	72 (32)	72 (31)	79 (24)	68 (34)	40 (28)	83 (34)
Bempton (entire)	2–104 (1950–75)	75 (8)	60 (10)	42 (12)	46 (15)	64 (14)	69 (13)	77 (13)	78 (14)	67 (18)	75 (24)	70 (30)	75 (40)	81 (52)	77 (71)	73 (104)	82 (109)
Ailsa Craig (mean of 3 groups)	? 150	NR	NR	NR	NR	NR	NR	NR	NR	NR	NR	NR	NR	NR	73	72	76(?)

Notes:
1. Figures in brackets are the number of eggs laid.
2. NR = no record.
3. OD = Records spoiled by obvious disturbance.
4. Where full records not available, breeding success calculated from number of chicks in July, stemming from known eggs in April, assuming 95% such chicks would fledge (they are mostly well grown by July and few fail).

(*b*) *Breeding success in relation to colony (and group) size and colony structure*

(i) *Size.* As Bempton grew from a very few pairs to a sizeable group, breeding success rose until it equalled the Bass (p. 136). This is the only case known in which we can be sure that disturbance played no part and for which detailed records are available. It seems very likely that the basic cause of the increased success was the rise in social stimulation and thus in the motivation upon which adequate site maintenance and pair relations depend (p. 140). Comparisons between semi-isolated groups of different size *within* a 'colony' are less clear-cut since it is impossible to allow for social stimulation gained in the immediate vicinity, or for local disturbance, for example by air traffic and ships' sirens. All the figures available are given in Table 17. The main points are that all the Bass groups except group 6 did about equally well. Group 6 was initially slightly less successful but improved as it grew. All Bass groups were significantly more successful than Bempton, when the latter was very small.

(ii) *Structure.* Breeding success in relation to colony structure is a complex phenomenon, really to be considered not merely as 'straight' success but also as breeding effort (the proportion that 'bother' to breed). These two measures are themselves related to age, position within colony (fringe or central) and topography (cliffs or flatter ground). Topography works by affecting age structure, as I hope to show below.

(*c*) *Effect of age on breeding success*

Young, inexperienced birds are less successful than experienced ones, because they incubate and care for small young less adequately (p. 203). Table 18 compares breeding success in pairs in which male, female or both were inexperienced. Consistently, inexperienced pairs reared fewer chicks. Those parts of a group that contain the highest proportion of young breeders will therefore show the lowest breeding success.

(*d*) *Effect of position on breeding success*

Despite frequent assertions to the contrary, there is absolutely no evidence to suggest that, *when undisturbed*, fringe pairs are less successful than centre pairs of the same age. The undoubted lower success of fringe pairs is due to disturbance and to the fact that the fringes of *expanding* groups hold a higher proportion of young breeders than do central areas. If the breeding success of experienced birds near the edge is compared with that of central ones, there is no significant difference. Poulin's work on Bonaventure indeed showed, in both 1966 and 1967, a conspicuous difference between the hatching success of fringe plateau birds (21·5 per cent) and central birds (42 per cent) but the fringe was expanding rapidly and contained a high

TABLE 18

THE EFFECT OF AGE (EXPERIENCE) ON BREEDING SUCCESS (PER CENT CHICKS FLEDGED FROM EGGS LAID) IN THE GANNET

	Number of previous breeding attempts								
	None			One		Two	Three or more		
	1961	1962	1963	1962	1963	1963	1961	1962	1963
Chicks fledged	59	54	35	81	48	77	78	88	79
Chicks died*	11	14	13	4	9	8	12	1	1
Eggs infertile	15	14	9	11	0	8	6	6	7
Eggs lost	15	18	43	4	43	8	4	5	13
Total eggs laid	27	22	23	26	23	26	121	115	117

* In the cases of birds breeding for the first time and losing chicks, 89 per cent died when less than two weeks old.

In subsequent years, observations were inadequate to apportion causes of failure, but the approx. overall figures for breeding success for first-time versus experienced breeders, taking only groups 5 and 6, were 54 and 86 per cent respectively.

proportion of young birds. He mentioned, also, the greater exposure of fringe birds to predation, but this strongly suggests human interference since, unaided, gulls cannot take eggs from a gannet. Thus his findings do not give any reason to suppose that position *as such* exerts an effect on breeding success. Coulson's work on the kittiwake shows that central nests are preferred and are more successful irrespective of age, but they are owned by 'superior' (heavier) birds. The situation differs from that of the gannet in that kittiwake density is far more variable and central nests are denser.

(e) Effect of position on 'breeding effort'

Apart from the **success** of eggs laid, there is the matter of **attempted** breeding. A far higher proportion of 'central' than of 'fringe' pairs actually lay. Poulin's figures were that 95 per cent of central nests received an egg compared with 60 per cent of edge nests, and whilst the former group did not vary in this respect in 1966 and 1967, the edge group did; 32·7 per cent of nests remained eggless in 1966 but 44·3 per cent in 1967, a significant difference. Again, this is easily explicable in terms of age structure, since the fringe contains more 'establishing' pairs, which often hold a site for a year (and build on it) without breeding. Finally, of those pairs which lost their egg, a higher proportion of centre birds re-laid (29·2 per cent compared with 21·2 per cent in the fringe). The greater tendency of central birds to re-lay is probably because they laid earlier in the first place and because first-time breeders are less prone to re-lay. Again, these are age, and not position, effects.

(f) Effect of topography on breeding effort and success

We come now to a comparison of breeding effort and success in relation to cliff as against flat ground nesting. This is really a matter of comparing groups which, *because of their different topographical features, subtend different age and social structures.* The comparison stemmed from the observation that one of the cliff faces on the Bass contained more empty nests (and sites) than did group 5 which was on flatter ground.[1] The counts were made in July, when no chicks had fledged and no eggs remained to be laid, and the results are given in Fig. 46. In sum, averaging counts totalling over 2000 entities for each area over nine years, 37·2 per cent of occupied sites on the south-west face contained a visible chick in July, and 35·3 per cent of sites were empty and without nest material. The corresponding figures for group 5 were 68·8 per cent and 9·0 per cent. The possible explanations were that cliff sites lost more chicks through falling, or that a higher proportion of cliff pairs withheld breeding. The first suggestion can be discounted immediately, since observations showed that samples of the cliff nests produced as many fledged young, from eggs laid, as did the flatter ground nests. Of 60 nests that held eggs or young in April/May 1973, 93·6 per cent held young or eggs in July when the counts were made. In 1974 the equivalent figure was 89·8 per cent.

The second suggestion is more difficult to evaluate. In July, about half the sites on the south-west face hold adults but no chicks, whereas in the group on flatter ground the figure is less than a quarter. This huge difference requires an explanation. In a nutshell, and to anticipate the argument, I suggest that proportionately more of the birds in the flat group breed, because this group is expanding rapidly, and social stimulation is high. The skeleton, however, needs a little flesh. Any reasonably large section (say 50 pairs or more) of a gannetry consists of four major categories of birds: (1) experienced pairs, (2) pairs in which at least one member is breeding for the first time, (3) new pairs which are strengthening their ownership and pair-bond prior to breeding for the first time (which they will do next season) and (4) single males

[1] The reason why the percentage of empty nests and sites in group 5 apparently decreases each year from 1963 to 1974, even though the group grows at an accelerating pace, is that the counts were made from a standard location which, in 1963 and 1965 commanded an adequate view of the inland fringe area, where the majority of site establishing pairs are found. In later years, the outer ranks were obscured by the inner, and an increasing proportion were omitted from the July count because their contents could not be seen properly. The 1963 and 1965 counts may therefore be taken as directly comparable with the cliff-face counts, but the later group 5 counts require adjustment. This can only be crude, depending on an estimate of the number of empty-handed fringe pairs that were excluded from the sample count.

with a variably firm attachment to a site. If the three large groups (south-west face, north-west face, group 5) were all stable, the *proportions* of these four categories would probably be about the same in each, since the same proportion of adults would die and provide the necessary vacancies. In fact, however, group 5 differs strongly from the other two in being an open-ended, rapidly expanding group. The cliff groups offer to would-be colonisers only the sites of deceased birds, together with any spaces which have been left empty either because they are marginally acceptable or because previous demand had been low. Group 5 offers, in addition to these, an inland fringe which can accommodate as many birds as find it acceptable. The fact that group 5 has, in the last ten years, increased about five-fold whilst the other two have remained substantially stationary, means that the population structure of group 5 has been (and is) different from that of the south-west and north-west faces. The question therefore is can these socio-structural differences explain the remarkably low productivity of the cliff groups—or conversely, the high productivity of group 5? Taking the low productivity first, one can observe that among the empty-handed July pairs on the south-west are:

(a) birds with excellent nests
(b) birds with mere weathered pads
(c) others with a handful of unstructured loose material and
(d) site-owners on bare ledges.

Most of the empty-handed pairs are in category (d). These site-owners must belong to one of the following three classes:

(i) old pairs whose nest has disintegrated and not been rebuilt. This never, in my experience, happens.
(ii) Pairs with only one new member (which could also account for some of category (b) and (c))
(iii) new pairs or single males, which must form the bulk of the site-owners.

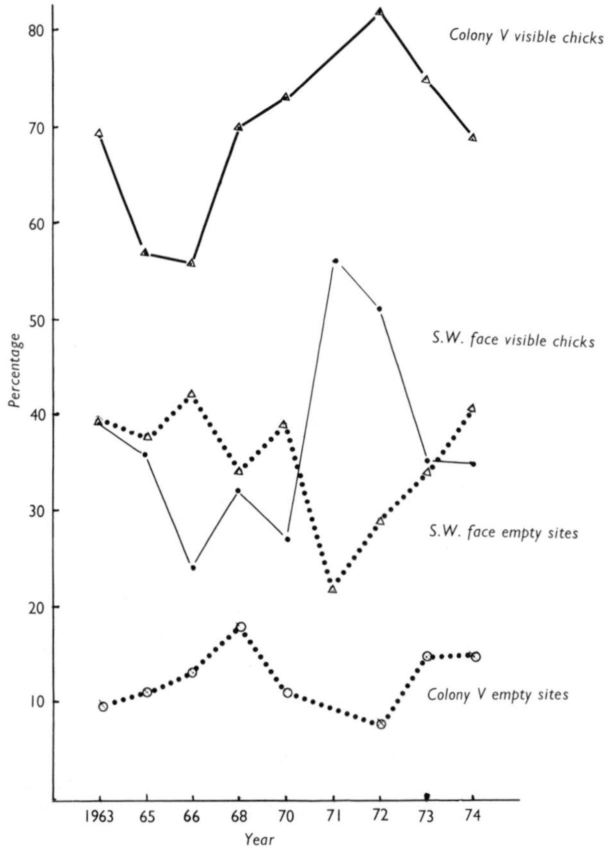

Fig. 46

A comparison between two parts of the Bass Rock (a cliff face and a group on flatter ground) showing the higher proportion of non-breeding pairs in the former.

This leaves new pairs as the likeliest source of these empty-handed site-owners. The number of (b), (c) and (d) together, however, is far too high to represent merely the influx of new pairs, or individuals replacing a deceased partner, *in any one year*. It seems possible that, on the south-west face, many new or part-new pairs are holding a site, without breeding, *for more than the single season* which is normal in some other areas of the Bass. This tendency (which I will try to explain below), may well be increased by the sheer difficulty of forming a nest on some of the sea-ward sloping ledges of the south-west face, but this is certainly not the main factor involved. For the moment, however, the main points to note are that among the empty-handed population of the south-west face, there are many pairs with good nests or good broad ledges, as well as those with medium or marginal sites, and that the empty-handedness is *not* due to loss of eggs or young.

Turning now to the high productivity area, group 5, the notable feature is the relatively *low* proportion of empty nests and sites. Striking as this is at first sight, it becomes even more so when one realises that group 5 is drawing in many recruits from outside its own area; its rate of increase shows this beyond doubt. This means that it contains each year a *higher* proportion of young males establishing a site, and young females prospecting for partners, than if it merely absorbed its own output. Since those young birds rarely lay in their site-establishing and pair-forming year, group 5 would be expected to show a substantially *higher* proportion of empty sites than does the south-west face, yet the opposite is the case; the real difference is thus even greater than appears.[1] Finally, group 5 is vulnerable to disturbance by man whereas the cliff faces are not, and this should also increase its proportion of empty July nests.

The 1963, 1965 comparison (Fig. 46) shows that group 5 averaged about 10 per cent empty sites, and the south-west face 39 per cent. Adding a generously estimated number of empty fringe sites to the actual group 5 figures (overall 15 per cent) for the remaining years increases the *overall* percentage averaged over these years, to about 25 per cent against 35 per cent for the south-west face. So, even after this correction, the difference between the two areas remains substantial, with the cliffs holding more non-breeding pairs (especially on sites only) than the flatter ground.

The probable explanation is that group 5 is a rapidly expanding group and the higher tempo of reproductive activities associated with this precipitates breeding in many pairs that, were they in the behavioural environment of the south-west face, would not breed. Secondarily, there are topographical difficulties associated with the cliff faces. This is easy to say, but difficult to prove, and I would like to adduce some circumstantial evidence, discuss some implications and make and test some predictions. First, however, I will quote, *verbatim*, from my field notebook of 4 July 1973, warts and all, because although it is not hard evidence it is, nevertheless, a valid contribution to the point at issue: 'Unless one has sat near the colony (5) most of a day at this time of year, one can have no idea of the fantastic activity that goes on virtually continuously. The colony is in a more or less continuous ferment of excitement, vast crescendos of noise and waves of Mutual Fencing and Bowing, one after the other. Nobody could have a true idea of the level of this social stimulation unless they had really watched and listened to it for a day. A one-hour period might be thought to be exceptional but when it goes on non-stop the effect is tremendous. And this is not in edge areas with new birds, but in the heart of group 5. It is certainly much more active than the south-west face, socially.'

(g) *The effect of age-structure on the level of behaviour and on breeding*

The entry of many young birds into a group for site establishment and pair formation, involves considerable trafficking. New males trespass on temporarily unguarded sites, fly repeatedly over the colony, land on the fringe near to newly established males, and perhaps crash in the colony on one of their numerous take-offs. Every time they land, they perform the site ownership display. This sparks off similar display in lone neighbouring males, or mutual display in pairs. There is a high level of noise, since incoming and landing, and display, are all accompanied by strident calling. Similarly, prospecting females cause endless disturbance. A group such as 5 is therefore subjected to a considerably higher level of behavioural excitement than is one like the south-west face. This is doubly the case in this particular instance,

[1] A precise figure cannot be given, because a few were so intermittently attended that it became difficult to decide whether they represented sites or not.

since cliff ledges, by their nature, preclude long fights and rampaging departures and are, moreover, linear rather than planar, so that a bird has two neighbours instead of four, five or six. Quantitative evidence, which I need not present, simply bears all this out by showing that the incidence of Bowing, Menacing, arriving, departing and Mutual Fencing even among established pairs, is considerably higher in an expanding group than in a stable or less rapidly expanding one.

Though real, the link between the level of behaviour and breeding is less easily discerned. The observational approach is unable to indicate whether an experienced pair that *fail* to lay on the south-west face *would* have laid in group 5, but, as mentioned, the vast majority of empty nests and sites do not belong to such pairs. They belong to those with one or more 'new' birds, and two suggestive trends of recent years in group 5 have been an increase in the proportion of such pairs that lay *in the same year in which they obtain a site* and an increase in the number of three- and four-year-olds establishing sites and forming pairs. Precise comparative figures for the first of these traits for the period in question are not available, since new pairs in the fringe are particularly vulnerable to disturbance and therefore, without living at the colony, it is impossible to know how many held eggs and lost them. However, when living on the Bass in 1961–63, we never recorded a pair acquiring a site and breeding in the same year whereas in 1971 and 1972, we recorded several cases. Similarly, the proportion of birds establishing sites at the age of three and four years, in the fringes of two closely observed groups (5 and 6) was considerably higher in 1970–74 than in 1961–63. In the outer four ranks of the fringe of group 5 in 1974 no fewer than 55 per cent of pairs had one or both partners in (usually slightly) immature plumage. In 12 per cent, at least one partner was markedly immature. Comparably, in the smaller group 6 in 1974, about 40 per cent of the fringe pairs were immature (one or both). In 1961–63, the corresponding figure for groups 5 and 6 was less than 4 per cent.

Why, then, have such a large number of three-, four- and five-year-old birds recently chosen to settle in group 5 rather than elsewhere on the rock? The above evidence strongly suggests that it is the high level of reproductive behaviour associated with the expansion and protection, which is both encouraging young birds to come in and then speeding up the establishment of sites, pair formation and laying. The history of group 5's growth in the context of the overall growth of the Bass colony, indicates that it was initially more successful (in 1961) than other topographically open ended areas, such as the west slopes and the top of the east cliff, because we strictly protected it from all interference. Whilst, in the *short* term, this could not result in a high number of returning group 5 offspring, it meant that site-attachment could quickly harden, and pairs form, without constant interruption. Clearly (and this has since been confirmed by colour-ringing) young birds from other areas were being drawn in, and the process snowballed. By contrast, the west slopes and east cliff-tops have scarcely expanded in this time. The effect of behaviour on the maturation of gonads is well proven and I have shown (p. 122) that exposure to a higher level of such behaviour causes earlier laying. It seems a reasonable deduction that the extremely high stimulus level in group 5 as against the south-west face quickens breeding and causes more new pairs (including those in which only one member has been replaced) to breed in the year of pair-formation.

Further evidence suggesting that the south-west and north-west faces hold a number of pairs which remain there without breeding, for two or more seasons after gaining the site, comes from an investigation of the effect of topography. I have followed the fortunes of a precipitous stack, the Needle (Fig. 36), since 1961 and discovered that more than 70 per ecnt of the 30 or so sites (without nest material) that were occupied in that year, never in fact developed into nests, because the site could not accumulate nest material. I do not know for how long such pairs, or single males, remained there before abandoning the hopeless venture, but it makes no difference to its application here, for whether there is a succession of males and pairs, staying a year or two on the south-west face without breeding, or a 'population' of such males and pairs that remain there indefinitely without breeding, the net result in terms of empty sites is the same. However, I am here arguing by analogy with the Needle, and on the south-west face the ledges are broader.

In sum, it is therefore suggested that the south-west and north-west faces hold many more empty nests and sites than group 5, mainly because whilst the former are full up and therefore stationary, the latter is open-ended and expanding rapidly. In group 5 the high stimulus level associated with expansion causes more pairs to breed in the year in which they are formed than is the case on the cliff face. Further, the topographical difficulties of the latter lead to either a succession of pairs that try to form a nest, fail and move elsewhere after a year or two, or stay on but cannot breed. The combination of these factors leads to a large difference in the annual productivity of the two 'sub-colonies'. The suggestion that the difference is due simply to loss of young or eggs from the cliff ledges must be rejected.

The situation just described has several implications:

1. The marked difference in social structure and associated growth rate between group 5 and other open-ended areas on the Bass is primarily an artefact, brought about by differential protection. Possibly, the growth of gannetries and perhaps colonies of other species could be to some extent 'guided' in this way.
2. Behavioural (social) factors can be very influential in deciding whether or not a pair breed in a particular year.
3. There is a strong tendency for young birds to join local groups which already have a high proportion of young pairs, probably through the mechanism of attraction to areas with the highest level of displays and vocalisation associated with breeding and particularly with the early stages of breeding. I believe that the seeking of behavioural parity, leading to a marked degree of local synchronisation of breeding, is strong in many colonial seabirds. However, it is not the only factor in determining where a young bird settles down, for the tendency to return to the precise area of birth is also very strong in the gannet. Hence many young birds from the Needle and south-west face at least try to settle in these areas, even though it may in the end prove impossible to breed there.

On Bonaventure, too, the cliff areas are largely full, and parts of the plateau expanding rapidly. Correspondingly, Poulin found that 79·4 per cent of cliff nests received an egg in 1966 and 78 per cent in 1967, whereas the figures for the plateau were significantly higher at 90 per cent in 1966 and 82·4 per cent in 1967. He concluded that there were more non-breeders on the cliffs and that many of them hold a sub-optimal site there for a period and then move up to the plateau. This is exactly what happens on the Needle and probably, also, on the south-west face of the Bass. He thus showed that, overall, Bonaventure contained in the region of 15 per cent of pairs that possessed sites or nests, but did not breed. This figure is likely to vary between gannetries (see p. 126); one cannot expect a neat and tidy picture in such a complex matter, for the proportion of empty nests or sites in any one year is a function of many variables. For example, in the most rapidly growing part of Poulin's colony the percentage of site-owners without an egg rose from 7·4 per cent in 1966 to 24·6 per cent in 1967, whilst in all other groups the proportion did not differ in these two years.

Two of the predictions which appear to follow from the facts and interpretations given above are that the success of pairs which lay in groups such as 5 and 6 should be greater than that of pairs from the south-west face and the Needle and, ipso facto, the success of large and expanding colonies should be greater than that of small, stable ones, by the same mechanism. The differences may, however, be fairly small when comparing (say) the south-west face and group 5, since the difference in level of social stimulation may be expected to act mainly or entirely on inexperienced birds and the number of such breeders is small on the south-west face. Furthermore, the lower success to be expected from inexperienced birds will lower the relative success of group 5 (which contains more) and thus work against the hypothesis. Possible mechanisms for these predictions are discussed below.

On the Bass, failure in breeding is rarely, if ever, due to the gannet's inability to catch enough food for the chick. It is due, among other things, to imperfect maturation of the behavioural components of breeding (p. 203). This is in exact agreement with Coulson's much better-documented findings on the kittiwake. If appropriately timed breeding (laying) is partly effected by behavioural stimuli (the level of intensity of certain behaviour patterns) and these are in turn affected by the nature and level of the activities of neighbours, then there is a clear link between social structure of the breeding group and its breeding success. Where there is a high level of excitement (measurable in terms of the frequency of agonistic and sexual behaviour) the reproductive physiology of young breeders is probably stimulated, and the tendency to spend time at the nest site increased. Two consequences of the former could be that young breeders would be adequately motivated to incubate the egg as soon as it was laid (this is by no means always the case with a new pair) and when appropriate, to switch to chick care behaviour. A consequence of spending more time at the site would be shorter foraging trips and hence more frequent feeds for the chick in the early stages of its development. Also, pairs would by virtue of their stronger site attachment engendered by the repeated expulsion of intruders, remain longer on it during long absences of the partner. All these things could make the difference between breeding success and failure and groups like 5 clearly provide the behavioural conditions for the greater success. So apart from the proportion that *lay* in the two types of group, the proportion that is *successful* should differ; large thriving groups should be more successful than small, more stable ones. The best available test of this is the breeding success of four groups, the Needle and groups 5 and 6 from the Bass and Bempton colony at different stages in its growth (Table 17). The Needle is inaccessible and stable at about 35 breeding pairs; group 6 is small but growing vigorously at about 70 pairs and Bempton is a young colony, now beginning to grow rapidly after a long period of slow growth. We would predict that:

1. Group 6 should be more successful than the Needle.
2. Group 6 should be more successful than Bempton during the latter's period of slow growth.
3. Bempton should now be more successful than it used to be.
4. Group 5 should be as successful or more successful than any other.

It should be noted that group 6 alone is open to human disturbance, which works against our prediction. Also, the fact that many of the members of the groups which are growing (group 6 and Bempton) are themselves increasing in experience is irrelevant in contributing to the success of these groups, since, as they grow, they take in an increasing proportion of inexperienced birds each year. Table 17 broadly supports these predictions.

However, groups cannot indefinitely remain open-ended and expanding and so presumably the greater success is a transient phenomenon of no significance in the long-term demography of the population.

(*h*) *Breeding success in relation to replacement laying*

On the Bass, a significantly lower proportion of re-layings (10 out of 27, 37 per cent) than of first eggs (152 out of 192, 79 per cent), resulted in fledged young mainly because a higher proportion failed to hatch (37 per cent against 10 per cent) either because they were infertile or had been inadequately incubated. On Bonaventure, only 16·9 per cent of replacement eggs hatched (centre 20·3 per cent, fringe 3·1 per cent). This was probably due to disturbance, especially affecting the fringe.

BREEDING REGIMES

1. *General features of attendance at colony*

The Atlantic gannet's unusually long period of active site attendance *before* the egg is laid and *after* the chick has fledged has already been emphasised (p. 173). In this respect it differs markedly from all other sulids, including the other two gannets. The stress involved (particularly for the male) during the pre-laying period is greater than that imposed by feeding the chick despite the latter's great appetite. Early records show that gannets return fat to the colony after their winter at sea, but are lean later in the season. However, no weight is lost as a result of feeding the young (as Jarvis found also for the Cape gannet); it is lost as a result of strenuous and prolonged sessions guarding the empty site or nest. The attendance, which begins about mid-January, is presumably adaptive and (by reducing fishing time) may be one reason why gannets cannot achieve an earlier mean laying date (there may be others, such as the timing of the inshore movement of mackerel on which they feed their young and the advantage to the fledgling of coinciding on its southward migration, with spawning herring stocks (p. 104).

Attendance in January–February–March is possible only because (despite the shortness of the winter daylight, which is only 66 per cent as long as the shortest Cape gannet's day) fish are abundant. Even off Iceland and Norway, coalfish and other species are plentiful in January, February and March (Reinsch 1971).

The return of breeding adults to the Bass bears no obvious relation to weather; newly returned birds in January and February sit on their nests throughout gales and appalling storms of sleet. Return is correlated with the age and previous breeding experience and sex of the bird, experienced males arriving first and birds that have bred only once, or not at all, about 2–4 and 4–6 weeks later, respectively. Old adults usually return in some force (2000 +) in the early second half of January and at this time the continuous procession of birds to the Bass has been specially remarked by Fred Marr as being astonishingly sudden. In some winters there may be at least a few hundred adults on the rock throughout, except perhaps for a few days here and there, particularly late November and early December, whilst on 20th December 1974 Fred Marr estimated 4000–5000 birds on the Bass. Apparently, they used to return significantly later. Booth (1887) who, prior to Gurney was by far the most knowledgeable about gannets, mentions early March as the return date.

There appears to be some variation between colonies in the attendance period. At small colonies adults return later and leave earlier. Birds from large colonies probably have a stronger motivation to return, and this can only be a result of 'conditioning' by the greater social stimulation previously experienced there. During the period of site attendance before laying, territorial and pair display, copulation and nest building all reach their greatest height. These highly stimulating activities help to bring the female to the point of ovulation and so affect the timing of egg-laying (see below). However, British west coast colonies may return later than the Bass or Bempton (which, since 1974, has had birds back in December and been occupied in force before mid-January). Ailsa held about a third of its population in mid-February 1975 but few in January. The birds were dense in some areas whilst others were empty (this again hints at locality differences in social attractiveness perhaps due to age structure). Judging from the dates of first eggs in 1975 and 1976, Grassholm birds must be back in force in January. Icelandic colonies, also, are attended in January. St. Lawrence colonies do not return until April. The reasons for the later return of west coast colonies is obscure. Canadian cliffs are, however, not free enough from snow and ice until April/May. The temperature at Bonaventure when the birds return is lower than that of Bass in mid-winter (Fig. 47). In autumn, British gannets may leave precipitately, the colony virtually emptying in a day or a few days, though the time varies from October to mid-November. Occasionally, even the Bass may be very thinly attended in late September. Canadian birds leave in late September or October.

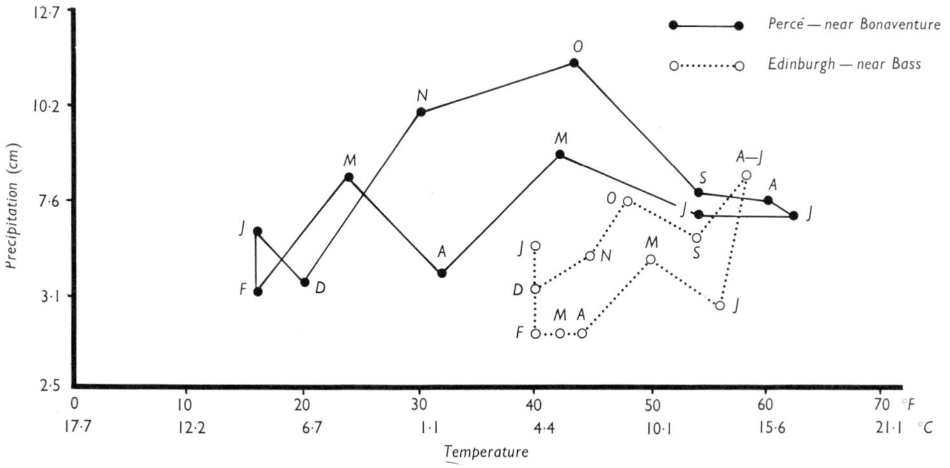

Fig. 47. The contrast, in weather conditions, between east and west Atlantic gannetries. (From Poulin 1968b.)

2. *Aspects of seasonal and synchronised breeding*

In general, synchronised laying can be seasonal or a-seasonal. Gannets and kittiwakes are seasonal, annual breeders with fairly rigidly fixed onset and termination to laying, and with an annually consistent mean laying date which, in the gannet's case, has evolved to synchronise the feeding of young with the massive availability of the principal food-fish, and the fledging period with favourable weather. On the Bass the gannet lays between mid-March and early July, but mainly in late April and early May (on Ailsa, two weeks or more later). The earliest recorded date is 2 March 1975 (Bass) and in most years the first egg appears before the end of the month. That this has been so for a very long time is indicated by Booth's record of a first egg on 27 March 1867 and his comments showing that peak laying was in late April. However, there seems to be a slight tendency for laying to be earlier now than it used to be. First Bass eggs, 1961–74, have been: 1961 March 31; 1962 April 5; 1963 April 3; 1965 March 28; 1966 March 26; 1968 March 29; 1970 March 19; 1971 March 10; 1972 March 23; 1973 March 13; 1974 March 20; 1975 March 2 and 1976 probably March 2 or earlier. First eggs on Ailsa, 1974–76, were April 13, 11 and 7 (although in 1976, back-calculation from a fledgling gave March 27) and on Grassholm, 1975 and 1976, March 29 or earlier, and March 18 or earlier, respectively. On Bempton they have progressed from late April, up until the mid-sixties, to April 4; March 29; March 24; March 25 and March 24 in 1971, 1972, 1973, 1974 and 1975 respectively.

The last egg on the Bass is definitely now later than it used to be, perhaps due to the greater

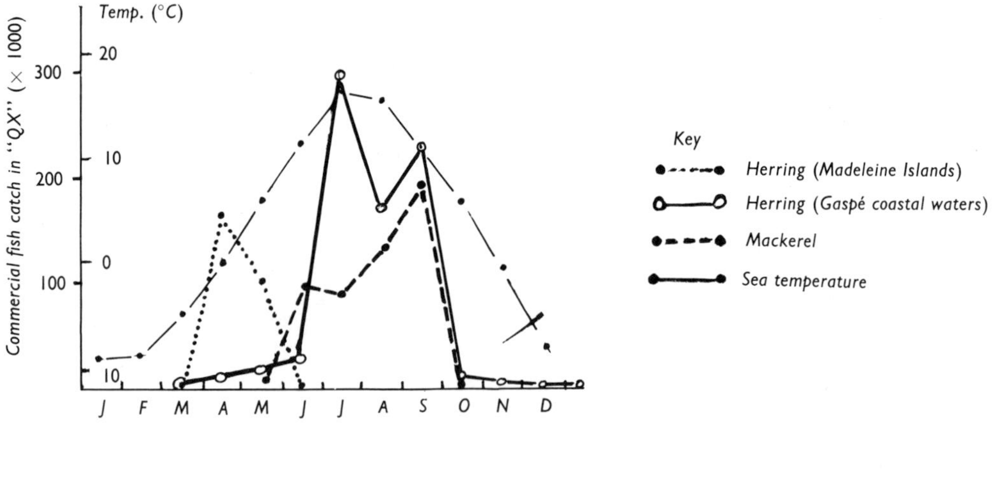

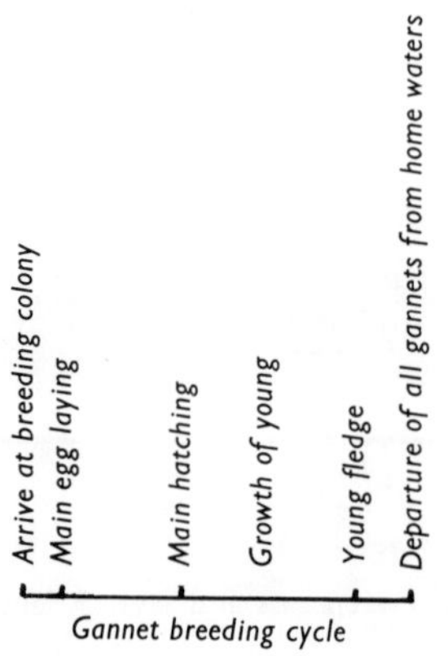

Fig. 48

The relationship between the timing of breeding and the abundance of fish at Bonaventure. (After Moisan & Scherrer 1973.)

proportion of young birds now breeding (though it is clear from old records that, even then, some birds bred whilst still in immature plumage). Every year, a few late young remain on the rock until early November. The latest fledging occurred on 25 November 1963 which means that the egg was laid around 17 July.

The facts just given mean that the population, made up of birds which are physiologically variable and of different ages, has arrived at an adaptive state in which the *distribution* of laying, taken over a long run of years, is optimally effective in countering the various destructive forces which are pitted against survival of eggs and young. On the other hand, we know that, by and large, *early* breeding gannets and kittiwakes have a higher success, and we know also that as birds get older they lay earlier, and that social stimulation brings on egg-laying. Thus, whilst a spread of laying of certain proportions is certainly adaptive (p. 106), it is still true that, in any year, there is a proportion of the population which could benefit from laying nearer to the mean laying date than in fact it does. In some cases, age is the restraining factor, in others, position within the colony, adequacy of partner, etc. Thus no population can ever achieve in any single year the theoretically perfect distribution of laying if this is defined purely in terms of that which would have produced most young, but is always striving towards it within the constraints imposed by the heterogeneity of the group.

The mechanisms involved in the timing of laying are physiological, through photoperiodicity and the maturation of gonads, and behavioural, through the effects of social excitement. Theoretically, it may be possible that if all Bass gannets simply remained at sea until two weeks before the female's laying date, and the nest sites of late-comers were left intact for their arrival, all would lay on precisely the date which in fact they achieve after a long but variable period in the colony. This, however, is hardly conceivable in practice. The period in the colony has a physiological effect; social stimulation makes breeding earlier than would otherwise have been possible (p. 123). Many factors affect the pattern of laying, some of which are discussed below.

(a) Regional variation in the timing of laying

Gannets inhabit a range of climatic and associated feeding conditions and the timing of breeding must also vary. On the eastern side of the Atlantic, however, gannets do not show the clear north–south variation that one might expect. In *Iceland* gannets begin laying at the end of March (Gudmundsson 1953) with a peak in April and many birds laying in May. This sounds almost identical with the situation on the Bass, some 800 miles (1280 km) south, and Bempton further south still. In fact the major axis along which laying becomes later is east to west, not south to north. Thus Ailsa, at the same latitude as the Bass, shows peak laying early in May, against mid-April for the Bass, and Grassholm is roughly the same as the Bass, or possibly a little later. Although data are lacking, I suspect all the west coast colonies off Scotland have fairly similar peaks of laying despite their considerable latitudinal range.

A possible explanation for the relatively early laying dates in Iceland and on the Bass may be their specially favourable location with regard to feeding. Around Iceland, saithe and herring are abundant in winter and the gannets begin to visit their breeding stations in February or possibly January. In terms of the adaptive value of early breeding, Icelandic young fledge at a better time (see p. 104 and above). The Bass and Bempton gannets may have special feeding areas available early in the year. One possibility is that sand-eels are abundant and accessible in St. Andrew's Bay, the Tay Estuary and areas off Tentsmuir, to name but a few localities to the north; there are also suitable sand-eel areas south to the Farnes. These are probably not matched in the topographically different west. Certainly regurgitations of Bass gannets early in the season contain many sand-eels. By contrast, S. Wanless found that sand-eels were rare in the stomachs of Ailsa gannets which had died (by falling) in the pre-laying period.

In the Canadian colonies, laying is about a month behind the Bass but roughly the same as at western British gannetries. On Bonaventure (Poulin 1968) the first egg is laid in the last week of April or the first week of May and the last egg by about the third week in June, a spread about two-thirds as long as that on the Bass. However, laying proceeds so rapidly that much of the late start is made up. Thus, peak laying is in the second week of May, merely two to three weeks behind the Bass, despite a start six weeks later, and by mid-May more than 50 per cent of eggs have been laid (Fig. 49). Poulin's actual figures for 1966 and 1967 were that, by May 15th 1967, 71 per cent of eggs had been laid and by May 30th, 95 per cent. The equivalent percentages were attained by May 28th and June 4th in 1966. This difference between years is larger than occurs on the Bass. Taken together, the modal laying point occurs a mere *five days* after the beginning of laying. Thus, by the end of the second or third week of May, about as many birds had laid as on the Bass. This impressive phenomenon is probably due to more rapid maturation of gonads at Bonaventure, following a return 'en masse' and a resultant high intensity of social simulation from the moment of return. If so, social stimulation here plays a major role in mitigating the effects of a late return enforced by the climate. The system is made possible because (presumably) conditions are so severe that early return by a few birds is precluded; hence site-usurpation is prevented. On the Bass this does not apply and a similar system therefore could not work. Similar compression of the breeding cycle at higher latitudes has been recorded for the kittiwake (Coulson & White 1965).

Poulin attributes the adaptiveness of this timing partly to the fact that, commonly, between May 15–25, weather is exceptionally bad with sleet and high winds. This, and the need to complete the cycle before the end of September when weather deteriorates rapidly and young would be severely handicapped, could help to explain why laying is not *later*, but the fact that it is not *earlier* probably depends more on feeding than on the effect of weather at the colony. Icelandic weather is presumably also severe but laying begins in March. Pre-breeding feeding is very important (gannets lay down most fat at this time in all three allo-species) and in conjunction with other factors such as best availability of food for the young and selection pressures on newly fledged young, will determine the timing of laying.

(b) Seasonal and synchronised laying in relation to group size and structure

In big groups the first egg is earlier and the last egg later than in small ones, and the *mean* laying date is earlier. Also, large groups are more synchronised in that proportionately more eggs are laid within a given time of the mean.

(i) *Seasonal aspects of laying, in relation to group size.* The earlier first and later last egg is partly because a large group is more likely to include a physiologically precocious and also a retarded individual. But once groups attain a reasonable number (say 50 pairs or more) their spread is very similar, rather than proportionate to group size. In big groups, variability is reduced and the 'telescoping' factor is social stimulation.

The earlier mean laying date of large groups is shown by the following data:

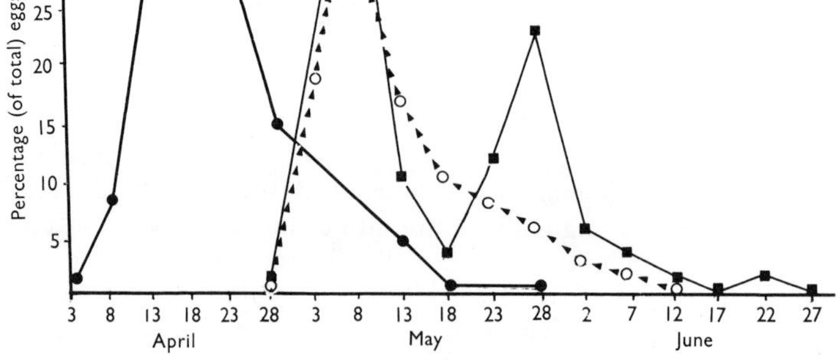

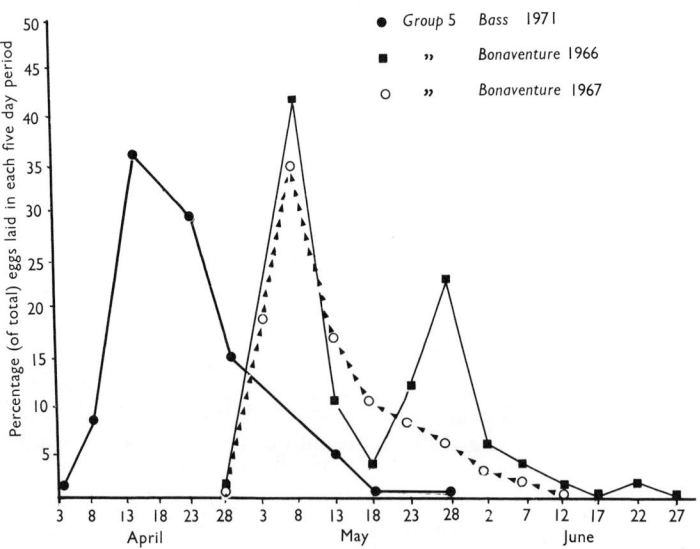

Fig. 49. Rate of laying in an early British colony (Bass Rock) and a Canadian colony (Bonaventure). (Canadian data from Poulin 1968b.)

1. A small group (group 6, Fig. 43(b)) grew from about 20 pairs in 1960 to 100 in 1975. The date of its first egg advanced from April 17th to 1st and its mean laying date from May 1st to April 21st (see also Table 27). This was not due to increasing average age within the group for it was continually receiving new recruits.
2. As my main observation colony has grown in size, the mean laying date has advanced (Fig. 50). The date of the first egg has moved from April 20th to March 18th and the approximate mean laying date from April 27th to 15th. Again, the effect cannot have been due to age, since large numbers of young birds flooded into the area during this period. If anything, the mean age of breeders in 1974 was less than in 1961. In this group, as in group 6, however, the change in laying dates was not due simply to increased group size, but also to protection. They had previously been much disturbed and this had retarded their return and the early stages of the breeding cycle.
3. When one compares group 5 (large) with group 6 (small) it is clear that, in 1971 (by which time *both* groups had expanded and become earlier) group 5 laid earlier than group 6. In 1961 the difference was hardly detectable because (as events proved) group 5 was so abnormally late.
4. In 1962 (the only year in which I obtained dates for the first and median eggs in several groups) the correlation with group size was as follows:

First egg	*median egg*	*group size* (nests)
April 4	April 27	200
6	28	150
8	May 1	135
10	1	125
19	2	20
16	5	59

It is not possible to say anything about the relationship between *density* and laying, because density is remarkably standard. Although fringe areas of expanding groups *are* less dense, they are also composed of younger birds, which invalidates straight comparison. In this respect the gannet differs importantly from the kittiwake, in which density as such is variable and is correlated with the date of laying (Coulson & White 1959).

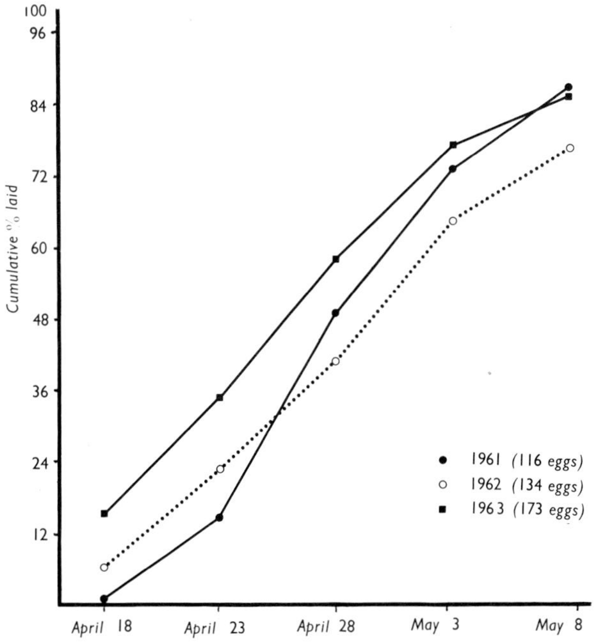

Fig. 50

Rate of laying in the same group in three successive years during which the group (on the Bass) was increasing in size and in the amount of social stimulation to which its members were exposed.

(ii) *Synchronisation of laying in relation to group size*. Fig. 51a and b shows the rate of laying in groups 5 (large) and 6 (smaller) in 1961 and 1971, from which it appears that (a) there is proportionately greater spread of laying in group 6 than in group 5, both in 1961 and 1971 and (b) in both groups the spread was less in 1971 (when both were larger) than in 1961. One may conclude that not only do large groups lay earlier than small, but they also show greater spread.

Several groups, of different sizes, were found to show different degrees of synchronisation in the same year (1962). Thus, in a group of 20 nests, egg-laying was spread over 41 days, whilst in larger groups the spread decreased (47 nests, 46 days; 78 nests, 46 days; 53 nests, 58 days; 13 nests, 62 days; 136 nests, 59 days). Whilst this comparison takes no account of age composition (which, however, probably was comparable), or degree of isolation, it is enough to show that synchronisation increases markedly with increase in group size. Large groups thus push potentially late-layers forwards.

(iii) *Social facilitation of egg-laying*. Since Darling's (1938) suggestion that synchronised laying increased breeding success in gulls, social (behavioural) stimulation has generally been invoked as the cause of synchronisation. Direct evidence has always been difficult to obtain because the factors associated with social stimulation (mainly group size and density) are correlated, also, with age and/or other aspects of 'fitness' and these, too, affect breeding success.

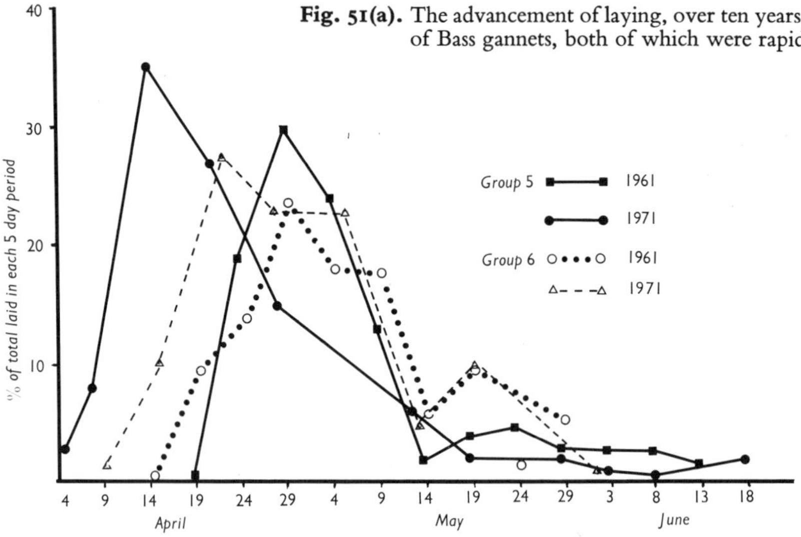

Fig. 51(a). The advancement of laying, over ten years, in a large and small group of Bass gannets, both of which were rapidly expanding.

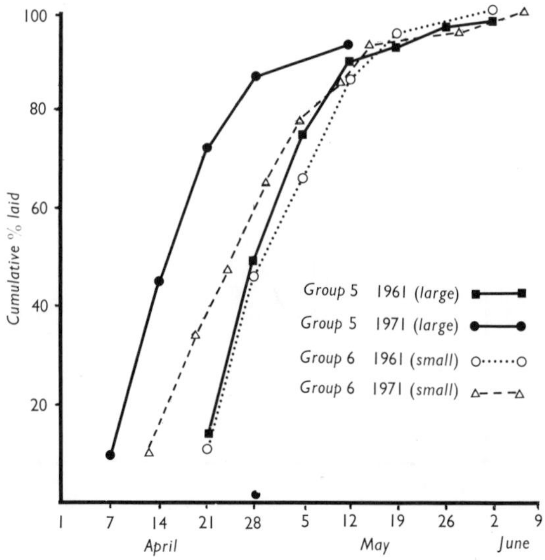

Fig. 51(b)

As above,
showing cumulative totals.

In 1962 we compared the pattern of laying in three groups of 20, mainly experienced pairs; one group was almost isolated but the other two were each in the midst of a large mass. The density of all three groups was about the same and they differed only in that two groups received much social stimulation whilst the third received less. The birds in the two latter groups began laying earlier and were more closely synchronised; the two non-isolated groups began laying on April 16th, whilst the isolated began on April 19th; by April 29th group 1 (non-isolated) had laid 66 per cent of its eggs, group 2 (non-isolated) 61 per cent and the isolated group only 22 per cent. Groups 1 and 2 finished laying by June 19th and May 14th respectively, whilst the isolated group finished on July 3rd. This appears to show that exposure to more behavioural stimulation made laying earlier and more synchronised. A similar mechanism probably explains the phenomenon that younger birds, returning later than older ones, compress the pre-laying period spent at the colony (Table 19).

The survival value of these traits lies in the production of young at the optimal time (p. 104) and if this is materially assisted by social stimulation, a direct selection pressure is provided for the acquisition of a site which exposes its owner to the maximum amount.

This mechanism confers great advantage on the habit of nesting in large colonies and also on nesting densely—in fact as densely as other requirements will permit. As already described, I see the severe competition for a site, which dominates gannet behaviour, partly as competition for a *socially* adequate site. Similar, though perhaps milder, selection pressures probably operate on the other two gannets. In some sulids, however, totally different environmental circumstances obtain and laying may not be geared to a season. Nevertheless, regardless of the time of year at which they lay, *there is no sulid in which local synchronisation* (that is, of small groups within the colony as a whole) *does not occur*. Thus behavioural facilitation always operates to reduce variability in laying dates within a group. The advantages, if indeed there always are some, must be decided for each species on merit.

(c) Breeding in relation to age and experience

In general in birds, females lay progressively earlier as they get older. This precession of laying stops after a time which varies with species. Age thus contributes to the spread of laying. The female must be expected to affect laying date more than the male, since there is no courtship feeding in the gannet and therefore no direct nutritional effect exercised by him; the male red-billed gull feeds the female and so has a marked effect on her laying date (Mills 1973). Fig. 52 shows that gannets lay progressively earlier up to the fourth time of breeding. Some examples of laying dates of individual females are given in Appendix 5. It emerges that, once stabilised, the same female tends to lay at the same time each year.

One cannot distinguish between maturation of the female, and other effects. However, an indication that there is more involved than simply the female's age, is that an inexperienced female partnered by an experienced male tends to lay earlier than such a female with an inexperienced male (Table 20). In those cases in which an old male acquired a young female, their egg was later than the mean date for the group concerned but earlier than that of pairs in which both partners were inexperienced. This agrees with similar evidence for other seabirds and, I suspect, has to do with the greater security and 'assurance' of an old male which reduces the tension to which the new females are subjected and so affects them physiologically.

The effect of an experienced male is shown, also, by the fact that a female showing slightly

TABLE 19

THE TIME ELAPSING BETWEEN RETURNING TO THE COLONY AND LAYING IN THE GANNET

Minimum number of times bird known to have bred	Number of days between return and egg laying					
	51 or more	41–50	31–40	21–30	11–20	10 or less
3 or more	34	45	15	—	—	—
2	10	7	7	2	—	—
1	—	1	6	16	7	—

immature plumage, may breed in her first year in the colony if partnered by an experienced male (eight cases) whereas when joining a newly established male, such a female never, in my experience, breeds until the year after. Also, we recorded three cases in which an immature male, partnering an experienced female, bred in his first year in the colony, but none in which an immature *pair* did so, though this has been known on Bempton. Evidently, it is harder for a young male to be influenced by his mate than vice-versa, probably because he stimulates her (nape-biting, leaving and returning etc.) more than vice-versa, and dictates the tenor of the pair relationship and the security of site tenure.

Several cases of mature-plumaged but newly established pairs breeding in the year of establishment have occurred in recent years in group 5 on the Bass, whereas in 1961–63 none did so. I attribute this change to the rapid expansion of group 5, which has led to an increase in social stimulation (see p. 140).

The death of a partner, or divorce, retards laying in the year after, mainly because the replacement is usually young. We had insufficient cases of experienced birds mating with new but experienced partners, to assess the effects of divorce as such, though Coulson has demonstrated that it retards laying in the kittiwake. Thus, the age of the female, the experience of her mate and the social attributes of the group are the main external determinants of laying date. They act on a genome which inclines females to individually-specific laying dates, which

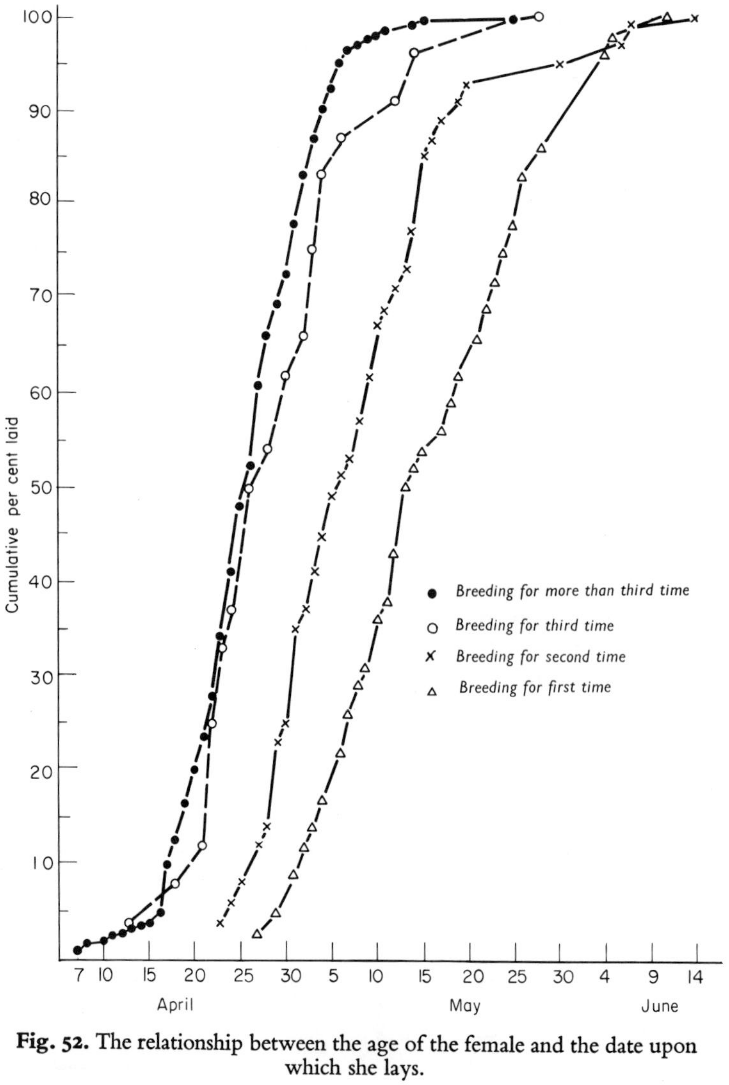

Fig. 52. The relationship between the age of the female and the date upon which she lays.

(presumably) are heritable. Since pairs usually remain together for several years and the tendency to lay earlier with age levels out, and the pair remain in the same group and usually on the same site, it is to be expected that a given pair will tend to lay each year in the same

TABLE 20

EFFECT OF EXPERIENCED MALE GANNET ON DATE OF LAYING OF INEXPERIENCED FEMALE

	1962		1963	
	Old male partnering new female	New male partnering new female	Old male partnering new female	New male partnering new female
Number in sample	7	23	15	25
Spread	22 April to 16 May	27 April to 14 June	18 April to 24 May	3 May to 24 June
Mean	7 May	15 May	2 May	12 May
Average number of days later than mean for group 5	10	18	9	19

Since not all birds involved in this sample were colour ringed, it is possible that some of the records of old males partnering new females involved females that had simply changed partners i.e. were in fact experienced. However, I have tried to exclude such possibilities from knowledge of the local situation, and it is unlikely that this will significantly affect the comparison.
The differences between the categories with respect to the mean laying date is significant in both years.

TABLE 21

THE RELATIONSHIP OF THE LAYING DATES OF INDIVIDUAL FEMALE GANNETS IN DIFFERENT YEARS TO THE MEAN LAYING DATE OF THE GROUP IN THOSE YEARS

	Experienced marked females	Experienced unmarked* females	Marked females first bred 1961	Unmarked* females first bred 1961
Laying date within 3 days of same departure from mean in 3 successive years	7	9	1	0
Within 3 days of same departure from the mean in 2 out of 3 years	18	27	8	3
Within 3 days of same departure in mean in 2 out of 2 years	3	2	1	1
More than 3 days' difference in departure from mean in 2 or more years out of 3	6	14	3	4
Totals	34	52	13	8

* The status (experienced or otherwise) of these females was known in 1961, but as they were unmarked we could not be sure that the same individuals were involved in all three years, though they probably were.

position with respect to others. Table 21 shows that most experienced females consistently lay the same number of days away from the mean for the group, whether this moves forwards or backwards.

In sum, the gannet lays mainly in April or May, with a consistent peak which varies little from year to year in a given locality. It also shows a considerable spread of laying. The peak is timed partly through social stimulation and ensures that a high proportion of young fledge, on *average*, at the most favourable time consistent with a fairly rigidly fixed onset of laying. The spread persists because, in certain years, the vagaries of weather (during chick growth and, particularly, at fledging time) would heavily penalise many pairs if it were too closely synchronised. Laying dates are affected, also, by the age and experience of the female and the male, the genome of the female, and the social attributes of the group.

3. *Frequency of breeding*

(*a*) *Apparent non-breeding years*

The gannet is basically an annual breeder. Accidental loss of egg or chick, and change of partner, mean that very few pairs rear a chick every year of their breeding life. Apart from these inevitable 'rest' years, on average one in four (Table 22), there is no evidence for non-breeding years, although pairs with a nest or site but lacking egg or chick are often numerous. Thus, on Grassholm in mid-season 1934, about 20 per cent of nests were empty but attended (Wynne-Edwards, Lockley & Salmon 1936), in 1975 and 1976 the figures were about 22 and 30 per cent respectively; on Ailsa (1974, 75 and 76) the comparable figures were 41, 38 and 44 (22–65 per cent depending on group) (S. Wanless, pers. comm.) though these figures are for empty sites as well as nests; on Bonaventure, overall, some 15 per cent were empty in 1966 and 1967 (Poulin 1968b) and on the Bass 7–37 per cent (more, if sites are included), depending on locality, are empty each year. I believe, however, that the great majority of such pairs are failed breeders, or contain at least one partner who is young (even though adult-plumaged), and are still establishing themselves. We have no unequivocal case of an old pair failing to refurbish their nest and lay.

Despite annual breeding, and assuming an undisturbed situation, the proportion of sites that contain a nest, or a nest and egg, will vary from group to group in a gannetry, from gannetry to gannetry and even from year to year. All will be affected by the proportion of site-establishing birds. Poulin's figures for Bonaventure were that 84·9 per cent of site-owning birds built nests; in 1966 88·5 per cent of nests held eggs and in 1967 82·1 per cent.

(*b*) *Breeding frequency in relation to previous success*

There is a significant difference in the proportion of pairs that lay the year after successful, compared with failed, breeding. This is mainly due to a greater tendency for failed breeders

TABLE 22

BREEDING FREQUENCY IN STABLE GANNET PAIRS

Number of years known (ringed) pair stayed together	Number in sample	Number of breeding attempts made by each pair
10	1	10
9	4	9
8	3	8
7	1	7
6	2	6
5	4	5
4	2	4
3	39	3 (38 pairs) 2 (1 pair)
2	9	2

Note: The sample number for most years is small because many pairs break up through death etc. and only a small proportion of the nests observed have both birds colour ringed. It nevertheless shows conclusively that gannets attempt to breed every year.

to dissolve the partnership (see 'mate fidelity', p. 129). Pairs that remain together after failure breed in the following year in as many cases as do successful pairs. Thus, 23·3 per cent of nests that failed in one year were, the year after, occupied by a pair which did not rear a chick. This is significantly higher than the equivalent figure for successful nests. And if I confine myself to records for which it is known that the unsuccessful nests did not even 'lay', the figure is 6·9 per cent compared with 0·5 per cent for successful ones.

4. *Age of first breeding*

Deferred maturity, widespread in birds, has more than one cause and function. Atlantic gannets mature later than any other sulid (except, perhaps, Abbott's). Generally, males acquire a site during April or May of their fourth or fifth year. Whether they breed in that year depends on circumstances (see below). Between 1956 and 1974, a high proportion of site-establishing birds in *expanding groups* were immature, in their third to fifth year. Earlier (1961–63) all site-establishers had been in adult plumage, but protection had helped the groups to expand, and expansion drew in younger birds (p. 114). In 1965 there were about 20 three-year-old birds on territories in the fringe of group 5 and about 25 four-year-olds. A high proportion of both these age classes bred the following year. Subsequently, the numbers of third- and fourth-year birds increased even more and by 1974 a broad belt, some three or four birds 'deep', on the outer fringe consisted predominantly of birds in immature plumage, some of them in their second year (approximate proportions of different age classes were: adults 45 per cent; 5th and 4th year 35 per cent; 3rd year 15 per cent and 2nd year 5 per cent). A similar sequence of events occurred, for the same reasons, in the much smaller group 6. In 1961–63 there were no birds with immature plumage and in 1974 at least 28 sites contained one or both birds with immature plumage, including six markedly immature (3rd year) birds.

From direct observation of birds of known age it is now clear that both sexes can breed successfully in their fourth year (that is, they are exactly four years old in June and so are in their fourth year when they begin breeding, but in their fifth year when rearing their chick). They may still possess one or two black tail feathers and secondaries. Also, such birds can lay without having spent more than a small part of the previous season in attendance.

In view of this, one wonders why so many three- and four-year-olds remain outside the breeding population. One pointer may be the fact that there is a higher proportion of immature females than males among birds becoming established. Where the exact ages of pair members were known from colour rings, and were unequal, males were one year older than females in six cases whilst there was no instance of the reverse. Furthermore, where one partner had more immature plumage than the other, the female was the immature one in 49 per cent of 153 cases; the male in 19 per cent and the sexes looked equally mature in 32 per cent. Whilst these are highly significant differences, the position is slightly complicated by the (unexpected) finding that in five cases where the pair members were known to be of equal age (four years) and were compared on the same day, the female nevertheless *looked* more immature. To this unequivocal evidence may be added a further 16 cases in which both members were somewhat immature, but only estimated to be equivalently aged. Of these, four were three-year-old pairs, in which the female looked more immature than the male in two, less immature in one and equal in one, and 12 were four-year-old pairs in which the female looked more immature in five, equal in four and less immature in three.

Finally, there are the cases of sexed individuals (as against pairs) of known age. Of 20 colour ringed three-year-olds, 10 females, but only 3 males, fell in the category 'several to many black secondaries and tail feathers' and of these, 3 females but only 1 male, also had black scapulars. Of 43 known four-year-olds, 4 females but only 1 male fell in the category 'two or more black secondaries' and 11 males as against 1 female were apparently fully adult. These records, however, are less unequivocal than comparisons within pairs, because the sexes are not equally represented in the sample and there has been no allowance made for the time of year when the records were obtained.

The conclusion must be that females actually take longer to gain adult plumage, in addition to breeding at a chronologically earlier age than males. I suggest that this chronological disparity is partly because the stresses involved in site establishment, which devolve mainly upon the male, are greater than those experienced by the female and presumably it requires higher motivation for a male to fight for a site than for a female merely to respond to a male's 'advertising'. It seems very probable that the actual extent of the deferred maturity is in fact determined largely by these factors. Protracted site attendance requires the ability to find enough food in relatively little time which in turn may require extensive local knowledge. If the first two or three years are spent south of home waters (p. 144) and a further year acquiring local fishing lore, the observed pre-breeding period is fully accounted for. This is not to suggest that the acquisition of the physical skills of diving take so long; I believe these can be acquired in a year or two, at most. The typical sequence of events from hatching to breeding is shown in Fig. 53.

The non-breeding, adult-plumaged birds within the breeding ranks of a gannetry fall into several categories:

1. Bereaved or divorced birds, with or without a new partner. Often the new partner is an adult-plumaged fifth-year bird and such a pair commonly spend the first season together without breeding.
2. Newly-established pairs with both partners in their fifth or sixth year.
3. Failed breeders.
4. Adults with topographically difficult sites (as on the Needle, p. 86).

At many, if not most, gannetries there is no question of a shortage of sites precluding breeding in young birds. Nevertheless, even where there is physical space, birds may be unable to use more than a part of it, for at least two reasons. First, and taking for simplicity an open-ended group on flat ground, there may be a social limit to the number of rows of sites that can be established in any year. As it happens, group 5 has crept outwards by between two and five rows each year. Such areas are less dense and regular than areas populated by breeding pairs and have a different tempo of activity. Also, they are contagiously wary and lack the strong ties provided by eggs or young. It could be that the further away one gets from the outermost breeding rank, the weaker the attraction of such a site regardless of its physical characters and that this limits the attractive ground each year and so excludes some individuals. Second (and this operates on the Bass), human disturbance may effectively bar many physically adequate areas. Instead of expanding evenly around the fringes of the entire colony the recruits will then be channelled into preferred (protected) areas, like groups 5 and 6, and may then run into the rank number limitation just postulated. So, as far as the Bass is concerned, it cannot be automatically assumed that the relatively large number of three-, four- and five-year-olds in the Club could in fact have found *socially* suitable and physically adequate sites. The noticeable increase in the number of immature birds establishing themselves in groups 5 and 6 could be partly due to protection, such birds being particularly wary and liable to desert disturbed areas. Alternatively, it is possible that adult-plumaged or slightly immature but apparently non-breeding birds are slightly retarded or marginally unfit. Of course, if such birds are in fact off-duty breeders the problem is resolved, but this is almost certainly not the case (p. 154).

The tendency to hold a site for a year before laying lengthens the entire pre-breeding period but it may well be that, usually, there is insufficient time to rear a chick in the site-establishing year. It is adaptive for young males to return considerably later than older birds (see p. 161) and this makes breeding impracticable. It cannot be plausibly suggested (though the point has often been made) that fourth-year birds refrain from breeding because their success

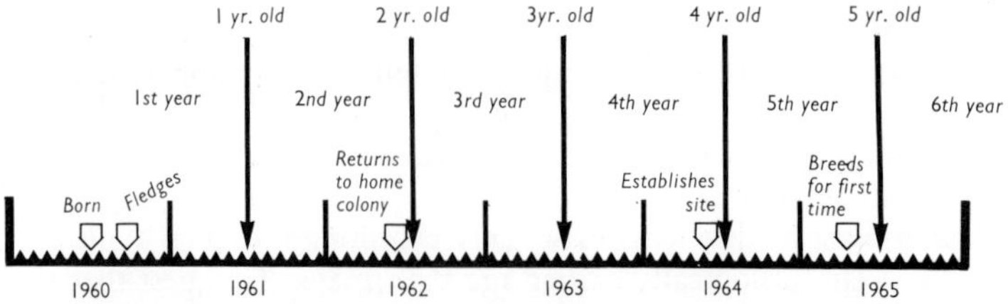

Fig. 53. The typical sequence of events from birth to first breeding.

would be too low and the strain too high, for (a) lower success is associated with inexperience rather than age, though the maturation of certain innate behaviour patterns may be important and these probably are age-linked, and (b) the ease with which inexperienced fifth-year birds feed their young belies any suggestion of stress. Lack and Ashmole emphasised the general idea that in young birds food gathering capability is too poorly developed to warrant a breeding attempt but this almost certainly does not apply to a fourth-year gannet.

In sum, deferred maturity in the gannet is not due to lack of physical sites, nor to inadequate fishing ability as such, nor, I think, is it primarily a homeostatic device regulating recruitment and hence reproductive output. It is largely an indirect result of the gannet's social (site competitive) system which makes such demands that they usually cannot cope any earlier. It requires males, in particular, to catch enough food in a fraction of the daylight hours available, early in the year. This interpretation is not wholly satisfactory, however, for it does not account for the way in which stimulating social conditions (expansion of the group) apparently can 'persuade' many birds to breed a year earlier than they would have done (but see caveat on p. 119).

5. *Fidelity to group, site and mate*

Gannets usually return to the group, not merely the colony, in which they were born and remain faithful to their first site. Fidelity to their mate is also strong. The exceptions to all three tendencies are, however, also important.

On the Bass over 95 per cent of colour-ringed young that eventually returned to breed, came back to their group of origin; only 3 cases out of more than 150 sightings came from an area other than the one adjacent to the group of their birth. In a few cases we were able to tell that individuals returned to the actual ledge on which they were born, though usually we were able to recognise only the group and year (incidentally, we had three instances of chicks reared on flat ground later establishing their sites on cliffs). On the other hand, group 5 drew in large numbers of birds that must have been born elsewhere on the rock (they were too numerous to have come exclusively from group 5). It was probably a case of group 5 attracting outsiders but not losing its own recruits.

Site fidelity is very strong (Table 23) particularly in males; about 95 per cent return to their site of the previous year. Since mate fidelity also is strong it is usually not possible to tell whether a bird is returning to site or mate or both. Taking site/mate attachment as theoretically indivisible where both partners remain alive, the males were faithful in 94 per cent of cases and

TABLE 23

FIDELITY TO SITE/MATE, GROUP 6

		Per cent of sample in which, in year (n + 1):						
Year (n)	No. in sample	Male and female return to same site	Male returns to site, female moves elsewhere	Male returns to site, female disappears	Female returns to site, male moves elsewhere	Female returns to site, male disappears	Male disappears, female moves	Female disappears, male moves
1961	8	87·5	—	—	—	—	12·5	—
1962	12	58	25	17	—	—	—	—
1965	14	43	7	14	22	—	7	7
1970	23	78	13	—	—	9	—	—
1971	19	74	—	10·5	—	10·5	5	—
1972	21	67	—	—	9·5	9·5	—	14
1973	17	65	6	17	—	6	6	—
1974	15	73	13	7	—	7	—	—
1975	12	42	16·5	25	—	16·5	—	—
1976	8	38	24	38	—	—	—	—
Total	149	64·4	9·4	10·7	3·4	6·7	2·6	2·6

Male returns or dies in 94 per cent of cases and moves in 6·0 per cent
Female returns or dies in 88 per cent of cases and moves in 12·0 per cent

females in 88 per cent. The female's weaker site attachment is adaptive since, after bereavement, she has to respond to advertising males (see p. 176) whereas he can simply remain where he is. On the other hand, as the behaviour account clearly shows, it is essential that her site attachment be firm. So it usually chances that a bereaved female stays on her site until a prospecting male (probably recognising her status from aerial reconnaisance) alights nearby, when she may then be accepted as a mate. Because of her virtually complete inhibition against attacking a male, she does not attempt to reject a new male, though conversely she may herself be rejected. Thus of 13 instances in which the male disappeared during the winter the female acquired a new male on her old site in 10 cases; one moved to another site within two metres; one tried unsuccessfully to pair with a neighbouring male and one remained alone on the site but was displaced by a pair formed in her absence. Of 16 males that lost their females, 15 acquired a new female on the same site and one moved to a bereaved female next door. It seems common for bereaved individuals to gain their new partner from among close neighbours and this is in fact how threesomes are often caused.

All site changes by males were to sites next door, or next but one or two. Even the few fringe birds whose changes we were able to follow usually did not move more than this distance towards the centre. I must again emphasise that a progressive shift centrewards does not occur. Apart from the one or two ranks on the outer fringe of a gannetry, whose members are undoubtedly less relaxed than birds surrounded by neighbours, it is of no consequence to a gannet whether it is six ranks within the colony, or sixty. The strength of the tie to the site is one reason why birds often hang on to second-class sites, once established within their natal group.

The exceptions to the tendency to return to natal colony, group and mate means that 'floating' and 'pioneering' can occur (p. 174), that there is a certain amount of outbreeding and that incompatible mates can change.

6. *Mortality rates and causes of mortality*

(*a*) *Mortality rates*

From direct observation of ringed birds it may be calculated that the annual adult mor-

TABLE 24

ADULT MORTALITY RATES

Year (n)	Number alive		Number alive year (n + 1)		Maximum mortality (per cent)	
	♂	♀	♂	♀	♂	♀
1960	27	31	27	30	0·0	3·2
1961	46	50	43	49	6·5	2·0
1962	46	47	40	43	13·1	8·5
1963	5	3	4	3	20·0	0·0
1964	4	3	4	3	0·0	0·0
1965	4	3	4	3	0·0	0·0
1966	12	13	10	12	16·7	7·7
1967	10	12	9	10	10·0	16·7
1968	9	10	8	10	11·2	0·0
1969	8	10	7	10	12·5	0·0
1970	18	22	14	18	22·3	18·2
1971	24	22	22	22	8·3	0·0
1972	26	26	24	20	7·7	23·1
1973	24	19	21	16	12·5	15·8
1974	21	15	17	11	19·1	26·7
1975	17	11	14	9	17·1	18·1

Mean annual mortality (max.) ♂ 11·1 per cent
♀ 8·7 per cent

Notes: 1. From 1963 onwards, records are for colony 6 only, hence smaller numbers.
2. It must be stressed that these figures are *maxima*, due to ring loss and birds moving site; 4–6 per cent is probably nearer the true figure for mean annual adult mortality.

tality rate is about 5 per cent (Table 24). This is probably a maximum figure and implies an average life expectancy of about 20 years.

The mortality of gannets in their first two or three years is difficult to ascertain because it bears no directly calculable relation to recovery rate, which depends on many imponderables. However, pre-breeding mortality can be calculated from known adult mortality and breeding success on the Bass. With a life expectancy of 20 years from the third year onwards (mortality being independent of age from this point)[1] and an annual breeding success of 75 per cent, each pair rears on average $20 \times 0{\cdot}75 = 15$ chicks. If the population were stable, only two would be required to replace the parents and therefore 13 or 86 per cent must die. But the Bass, and world, population is expanding at about 3 per cent per year, so the pre-breeding mortality must be about 75–80 per cent.

Undoubtedly, most of this falls in the first year of life (Tables 25 and 26). Thus, of 1600 recoveries of birds ringed as chicks 54·2 per cent fell in the first year. Thereafter (correcting for recoveries already taken into account) they are proportionately the same (second year 34·8 per cent; third year 34·6 per cent; fourth year 33·5 per cent and fifth year 33·1 per cent) and this pattern is not found in adults (Table 26). This of course does not imply actual mortality at these rates, but merely that the levels are the same.

Most recoveries are made in October:

Jan.		Feb.		Mar.		Apr.		May		June	
1	2	1	2	1	2	1	2	1	2	1	2
28	17	15	14	13	16	16	19	9	13	24	6
July		**Aug.**		**Sept.**		**Oct.**		**Nov.**		**Dec.**	
1	2	1	2	1	2	1	2	1	2	1	2
19	44	36	43	42	55	**84**	**86**	49	25	27	22

October deaths are mainly juveniles and are caused by their failure to become self-sufficient. In the Australasian gannet, a *direct* check of the proportion of birds ringed as chicks and returning to the breeding colony as adults gave a figure for pre-breeding mortality of about 70 per cent. The recoveries of gannets on the west side of the Atlantic (Moisan & Scherrer 1973) have

[1] It is assumed that mortality remains independent of age even in old birds; however, 20 years can hardly be regarded as old so this factor should not affect the calculation.

TABLE 25

AGE AT RECOVERY OF 1600 GANNETS RINGED AS NESTLINGS
(From Landsborough Thomson 1974)

Year of life from 1st May	1st	2nd	3rd	4th	5th	6th	7th	8th	9th
Number recovered	867	255	165	105	69	44	42	27	9
Year of life from 1st May	10th	11th	12th	13th	14th	15th	16th	17th	18th
Number recovered	9	2	3	2	—	—	—	1	—

TABLE 26

YEARS FROM RINGING TO RECOVERY OF 161 GANNETS RINGED AS ADULTS AT UNKNOWN AGE (From Landsborough Thomson 1974)

Year from 1st May	1st	2nd	3rd	4th	5th	6th	7th	8th	9th
Number recovered	31	34	21	15	10	16	12	7	6
Year from 1st May	10th	11th	12th	13th	14th	15th	16th	17th	18th
Number recovered	3	3	2	—	1	—	—	—	—

Four birds recovered twice are counted at the older age.

added little to the above picture. Arranged by age they were: 1st year (54), 2nd (17); 3rd (8); 4th (5); 5th (12); 6th (13); 7th (8); 8th (2); 9th (2); 10th (2); 11th (3); 17th (1); 21st (1).

(b) Causes of adult mortality

In apparent order of importance are: death at sea due to man; accidents at the breeding colony; presumed starvation (though little evidence) and (probably unimportant) disease. At sea, natural predators are insignificant, though a gannet occasionally falls victim to a large fish, whilst at the breeding colony there are no predators powerful enough to tackle them. On Bonaventure there are red foxes, but they do not trouble the gannets (Poulin 1968b).

Death at sea is usually by drowning in nets or on baited hooks or by shooting. Forty-seven per cent of recoveries of adults were specifically linked to these causes and many more undoubtedly went unremarked. If the line is paid out near feeding gannets they take the bait just beneath the surface and cannot then be removed until the line is hauled. I have been given a first-hand account of a line fishing boat from Peterhead (134 hooks per line and c. 34 lines per boat) recovering baited line with hook after hook holding a dead gannet, about 200 being hauled on deck at one time. The boats concerned fished up to 160 miles (256km) offshore, April–September, using herring bait. Nowadays, however, this method of fishing is much rarer than it used to be. Deaths in nets are due to the excited birds diving into the struggling mass of fish being drawn to the surface and becoming entangled. Probably many are alive when landed, but despatched in the mistaken view that gannets are significant competitors to fishermen. Many are shot at sea, probably because they are annoying fishermen. Other hazards encountered at sea and originating in man are oiling and fish containing toxic chemicals. Gannets suffer relatively slightly from oil. For example, in the west coast and Irish Sea oil disaster of autumn 1969, 35 gannets were collected from a total kill estimated at 15 000–30 000 seabirds, mainly auks, and in the east coast oil kill of winter 1970, 45 oiled gannets were picked up compared with 7757 auks out of a total kill conservatively estimated at 50 000. Gannets comprised 5·5 per cent of seabird corpses collected in Merioneth, 1966–69, and only two were oiled (Seabird Report 1969). The toll due to toxics is impossible to estimate, for in many cases birds die only when stressed, at which time mobilisation of fat containing high levels of toxics releases lethal amounts into the blood. It is then impossible to disentangle natural from induced mortality. However, there is disturbing evidence that some Ailsa birds contain extremely high levels of P.C.B.'s and other toxics (see Appendix 15) and it may be that there is growing cause for concern.

Accidental death at the breeding colony stems from bad landings (broken wings), fighting (falling and becoming jammed in a crevice or damaging a wing). Between March and October 1974 S. Wanless collected 120 dead or injured adults at the foot of Ailsa's cliffs, whilst in 1975 the total was even higher (78 up to mid-June compared with 35 in 1974). This is roughly one per cent of the adult gannet population per year, or almost one-third of the total annual mortality. This is such a high figure that Ailsa may well be abnormal. It certainly is so in the presence of a rocky foreshore onto which birds can fall after landing badly or being dislodged by falling stones or other birds; Bass birds would fall into the sea.

The injury rate was particularly high at the time when the gannets were re-establishing sites and performing many 'leave-and-return' flights (see p. 161), thus increasing the probability of a bad landing. Nowadays, becoming entangled in synthetic cordage from nets and lines gathered as nest material is a grisly hazard probably universal in gannetries. Sample counts at different colonies have given the following percentages of nests containing such materials: Bass c. 50 per cent; Bempton c. 75 per cent; Ailsa less than one per cent. (S. Wanless—an interesting and inexplicably low figure); Grassholm 49 per cent of nests. Birds become anchored to their nest or to each other or to irregularities and I have several records of adults dangling by one leg until they died. Mandibles may become bound together or the remorseless stuff jammed in the beak serrations or gape angle. Unfortunately there is no complete solution since we can hardly prevent loss of nets, lobster pots and lines, but there is much casual disposal of unwanted stuff at sea and this could be reduced. But since it is so difficult to persuade people to refrain from littering the land, how should they cease to treat the sea as a convenient refuse tip?

Occasionally gannets are driven onshore and inland by gales. It seemed hardly worth collating all the records of birds picked up inland. They reach the centre of England, occasionally in amusing circumstances as when well intentioned but ornithologically naïve onlookers attempt to pick up this white duck, unaware that it possesses one of the most lethal beaks in the bird world. The continent, too, has been peppered with inland records. These incidents, however, never involve more than a few birds. The 'wrecks' which sometimes occur in petrels or auks are unknown in gannets, presumably because they are too powerful to be driven onto a lee shore or, if large numbers were, could easily cross Britain.

It seems highly unlikely that significant numbers ever starve as a result of sustained stormy weather. They can feed in almost gale force winds and can go without food for at least two weeks. Furthermore, after a period at sea in winter they are fat rather than lean.

Disease seems to play a minor role. No epizootic diseases have been recorded among gannets, though a Salmonella infection has been isolated from two wild females and the same virus *S. typhimurium* has been isolated from herring meal. Newcastle disease has been isolated from a gannet carcase (Wilson 1950); bone marrow from a gannet found at Rousay (Orkney) and injected into fowl caused the disease in one. This was the first time it had been discovered in a wild bird in Britain. Domestic fowl which used to be kept on the Bass suddenly acquired fowl pest and seabirds (possibly herring gulls) were suspected as carriers though nothing was proved.

(*c*) *Juvenile mortality*

Starvation is the main cause of death in the immediate post-fledging period. Once away from the nest they are at the mercy of the weather. Occasionally wind from an unfavourable quarter may catch fledglings at the peak of the fledging period and cast a number ashore (Bass birds have sometimes been caught by north easterly winds in September) but the main hazard is the difficulty of acquiring fishing skill (see p. 218). When found, carcasses are often too old to show the cause of death but many are emaciated and those recovered alive are almost always weak and underweight. Analysis of 460 recoveries mainly in the first year of life gives the following causes of death: recovered dead on beaches 303; shot or netted 103; oiled 54.

OTHER ASPECTS OF BREEDING ECOLOGY

1. *Case history of the growth of a new gannetry*

Bempton is the only gannetry in the world for which there are records, even though incomplete, of the growth in numbers and of gradual changes in the social structure, breeding regime and breeding success which accompanied this increase. The following section is based almost entirely on the remarkably persistent work, under difficult conditions, of Henry Bunce and particularly, latterly, of Joan Fairhurst. Some of the behavioural data was gathered by Sarah Wanless.

(*a*) *The colony*

A spectacular stretch of limestone cliffs runs north from Flamborough Head to beyond Bempton on the Yorkshire coast. Rich fishing grounds lie close inshore to north and south, much used by seabirds from the Farne Islands (Pearson 1968) and gannets from the Bass. Although gannets strongly prefer igneous rock, such as basalt, or granite, presumably avoiding sedimentary limestone and sandstone because the ledges tend to be narrow, Bempton was clearly in a strong position to attract passing birds, not only from fishing trips but from the northward movement of two- and three-year-olds from Biscay and North African waters.

Nobody knows exactly when gannets first came to Bempton. One or possibly two pairs tucked themselves away far down the cliffs, invisible from above and for some years may have escaped the notice of all save the 'climmers' (egg collectors). However, between the 1920s and 1950 (after which records became progressively fuller) the colony was at best a struggling nucleus, fluctuating between one and about three pairs and rearing on average considerably less than one chick per year.

The present colony (Fig. 22) is in two separate parts, north and south. The south colony centres around the original main ledge. For many years this was the only known breeding area on the cliff, though it gave few possibilities for expansion. In 1965 two pairs successfully used a ledge on the north side and three more site-owners ranged along the same ledge. In

1974 there were 11 nests with eggs on a north face beyond the original one and a new spread to the south. It appears that the colony is beginning to establish pockets which are necessarily, by topography, separated from the original ones, thus entering a phase of development which could result in a linear spread along a very considerable stretch of cliff. It is worth noting that the usual spacing was maintained even when there were so few pairs and plenty of extra ledges. These were not used until birds were forced onto them.

(*b*) *Immigration*

Bempton has grown and continues to grow from immigrants and its own production of young. The figures for the number of young reared each year prior to 1951 involve so few (usually one or more) that their potential contribution to the population of 1951 and beyond is negligible. The year 1951 saw two pairs occupying sites and, starting from this point, Fig. 54 shows the actual rate of increase compared with that which could have occurred given only the input from surviving young produced in earlier years.[1] The theoretical number which would be expected from the colony's intrinsic growth diverges increasingly from the observed number of site occupiers. This difference is even greater than it seems, for it must be remembered that the breeding population is *itself* partly made up of immigrants. Without these there probably would have been insufficient young produced to allow any growth whatsoever.

[1] Assuming that 10 per cent of site occupiers die each year and 70 per cent of fledged young die before they reach breeding age (fifth year).

Fig. 54. The actual increase in the Bempton gannetry compared with the increase to be expected solely on the basis of Bempton's own output.

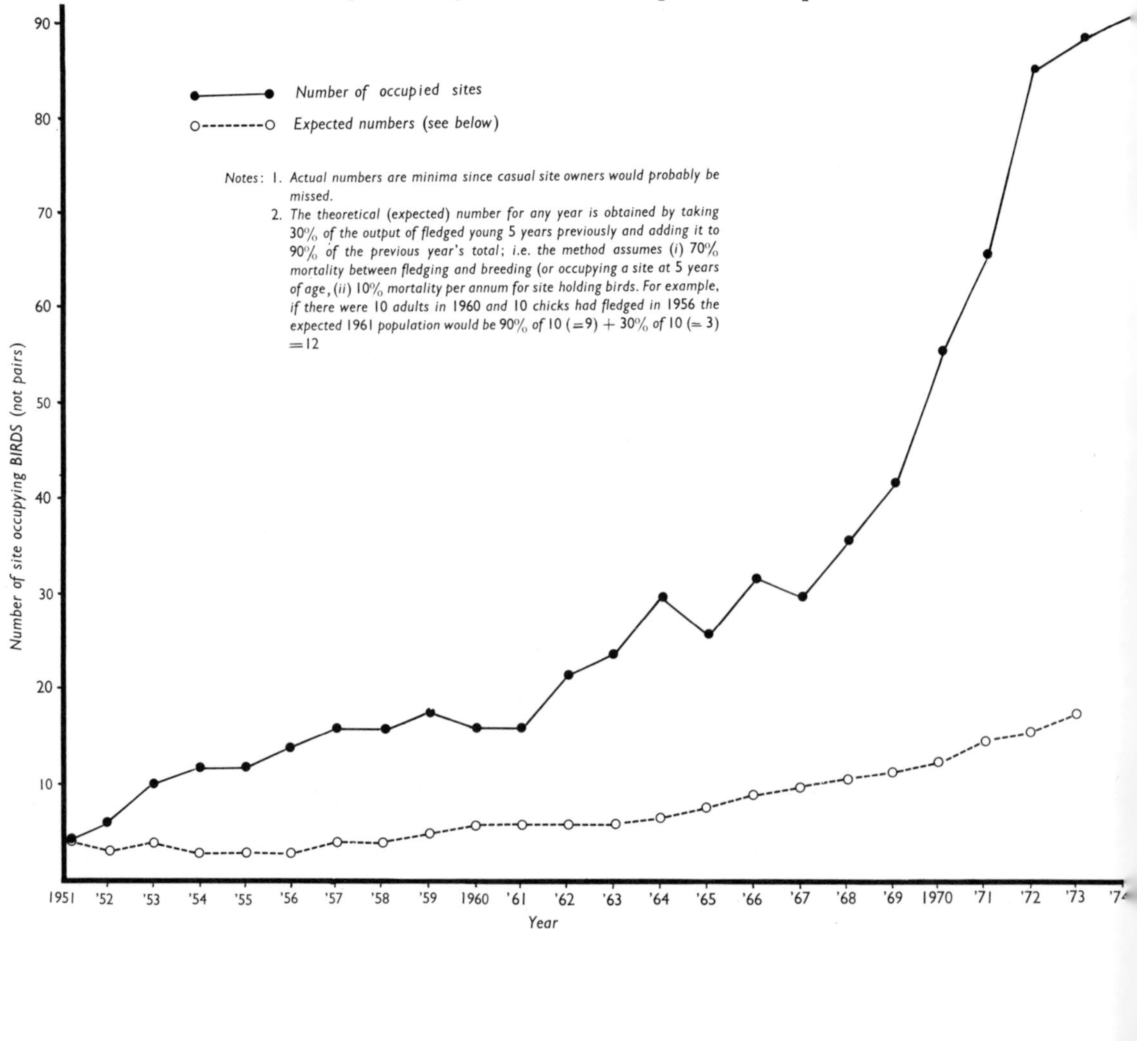
Number of occupied sites
Expected numbers (see below)
Notes: 1. Actual numbers are minima since casual site owners would probably be missed.
2. The theoretical (expected) number for any year is obtained by taking 30% of the output of fledged young 5 years previously and adding it to 90% of the previous year's total; i.e. the method assumes (i) 70% mortality between fledging and breeding (or occupying a site at 5 years of age, (ii) 10% mortality per annum for site holding birds. For example, if there were 10 adults in 1960 and 10 chicks had fledged in 1956 the expected 1961 population would be 90% of 10 (=9) + 30% of 10 (= 3) =12
Number of site occupying BIRDS (not pairs)
90
80
70
60
50
40
30
20
10
1951 '52 '53 '54 '55 '56 '57 '58 '59 1960 '61 '62 '63 '64 '65 '66 '67 '68 '69 1970 '71 '72 '73
Year

Throughout the first 20 years or more of its existence the Bempton gannetry must have attracted one or two passing birds from time to time. Concrete proof lies in the Bass colour-ringed birds, three of which have now turned up at Bempton, the latest in 1974, in its fourth year. The colony tottered precariously along without anything but the odd bird until the 1960s, when numbers began to rise, and the 1970s, when the influx increased dramatically. The rise in numbers between 1969 and 1972 was about equal to all the previous growth of the colony.

The implication seems to be that as the colony grew, so did its social attractiveness, so that, after reaching a threshold, the group began increasingly to attract immigrants. Since its own output was also rising, the two factors worked together. This phenomenon (p. 114) can be responsible for rapid growth in one section of a large colony, in which case the immigrants may be mainly from other parts of that same colony. An expanding group, whether a whole colony or a section, has a 'behavioural badge'. Its members do not do anything which cannot be seen elsewhere in the colony, but spend more time in certain activities (see p. 113), come and go much more and are dispersed more irregularly. And Bempton is well placed for attracting recruits from the hundreds of immature birds streaming past to and from the Bass.

(*c*) *Structure of the colony*

Gannetries are 'structured' (p. 83) in terms of the status of their constituents; Bempton could hardly attain a social structure when it consisted of two or three pairs, but as it grew larger it could be expected to become more complex and to acquire a Club and a few site-owning non-breeders.

Bempton gannets never settle on the cliff tops as they do on islands; presumably they are afraid of feeling virtually land-locked and, also, are liable to be disturbed. Because of the nature of the cliffs, the immature birds and those adults without permanent sites either had to settle on a grassy area about 30m below the nesting birds or gather on large ledges with room for about a dozen birds on each, or distribute themselves on the ledges occupied by breeding birds. At first they chose the two latter, probably feeling more secure there, but later began to gather in a more conventional Club (p. 151) on the large ledges well below the nesters. Topography was thus partly responsible for thwarting the formation of the usual dense Club but, as numbers grew, they did begin to gather more normally.

The Bempton Club grew by attracting immigrants. There were about 25 three- and four-year-olds, mid-season average, in 1972, increasing to about 40 in 1973 (on August 22nd 45 were present on the Club ledges) and, with normal mortality, the output of the gannetry three or four years previously would have produced only 20 per cent of that number. The social nature of Bempton Clubs seemed normal; as on the Bass there was a constant state of flux, with different birds holding the same site in quick succession, pairs quickly forming and dissolving and individuals (recognised by particular plumage patterns) ranging widely throughout the group.

An interesting result of the Bempton situation was that the large ledges which attracted Club birds eventually 'hardened' into breeding ledges. In effect Clubs spear-headed the gannetry's spread. In 1973 they appeared on the far north face where they had not previously settled and in 1974 birds began to nest there. Clubs do not play this role quite so obviously on the Bass, tending to move from place to place dictated by wind direction; it is the case that the areas now expanding most rapidly (the north-west and west cliff tops) are also most favoured by Clubs, but also they face the prevailing wind.

The tendency for Bempton Club birds to disperse among nesters, and the lack of individually marked birds, often made it difficult to recognise the status of individuals, but continuous watching for several hours (an exacting task) showed that some breeding birds possessed resting ledges in addition to their nesting ledge. Thus, an individual on a ledge, but without a nest, might be a Club bird or an off-duty breeder. Finally, in addition to the breeding birds, some young birds settled determinedly on particular sites which they occupied for part of a season without breeding, though some built nests.

The two noteworthy differences between this colony structure and any part of the Bass are the tendency of immatures to settle among breeders and that of off-duty breeders of both sexes to seek an alternative ledge. Birds from at least 7 out of 20 breeding pairs used extra ledges, in some cases near the nesting ledge, in others as far away as possible. In all cases, the nesting ledge was large enough to accommodate both partners and a large chick. Typically birds spent several hours on a resting ledge, mainly preening and sleeping though one male accepted an immature female and displayed with her before rejoining his mate and others performed the site ownership display on it. In those cases the ledge was treated as a second territory. However it was clearly not always a case of holding an alternative territory, for some of the ledges were used, though not simultaneously, by several birds.

In sum, Bempton, once it began to flourish, showed the structure typical of a large gannetry with a relatively substantial Club performing the normal function of low intensity social intercourse, leading to prospecting and the eventual establishment of its individuals within the breeding colony.

(d) Breeding success

Species which typically form large colonies do so either because space is limited or more usually because it enhances their breeding success in a variety of ways (p. 82). The question arises: is there a minimum size for a colony, below which its breeding success suffers? If so, what are the mechanisms? Bempton happens to be ideal for studying the effect of colony size on breeding success because it cannot be disturbed by man and so the major source of misleading results is eliminated, and it can be compared with groups of similar size in similar or different habitats, or likewise compared with larger groups. For these purposes, fortunately, figures for breeding success on the Bass are available (see Table 17) for some of the same years. This eliminates biases which might have arisen if west and east coasts or different years had been compared.

Between 1950 and 1960 the information is too incomplete to allow much interpretation. In terms of young fledged from eggs known to have been laid, the gannetry, though tiny (between two and eight properly established sites) did unbelievably well. Thus in 1951–60 inclusive the eggs seen each year numbered 2, 3, 3, 4, 3, 2, 2, 4, 5 and 7 (total 35) whilst the young thought to have fledged numbered 2, 3, 3, 4, 3, 2, 2, 4, 5 and 6 (total 34). But visits were so few—merely one or two per season—that eggs could have been laid and lost as eggs or chicks without ever being noticed. To assume a breeding success of almost 100 per cent would be unjustifiable. In the 1960s records gradually became fuller, but there is much room for error because in each year several nests were built but it was never discovered whether eggs were laid. When dealing with such small numbers the percentage figure for breeding success is heavily influenced by these nests. I have assumed that if a good nest was built an egg would be laid. Where no nest was seen I have assumed that no egg was laid, although one could easily have been lost and the nest material pilfered. On balance it seems likely that the adopted figure for eggs laid will not err on the high side. Chicks are assumed to have fledged even if they were only half grown when last seen. Thus the figure for breeding success is likely to err on the high side.

On these terms, the breeding success for Bempton from 1961–75 works out at: 6/8 (75%) 1961; 6/10 (60%) 1962; 5/12 (42%) 1963; 7/15 (46%) 1964; 9/14 (64%) 1965; 9/13 (69%) 1966; 10/13 (77%) 1967; 11/14 (78%) 1968; 12/18 (67%) 1969; 18/24 (75%) 1970; 21/30 (70%) 1971; 30/40 (75%) 1972; 42/52 (81%) 1973; 55/71 (77%) 1974 and 76/104 (73%) 1975. In view of the imponderables it would be foolish to attempt sophisticated analyses of these figures, but there is a strong indication that in the first half of the 1960s breeding success was consistently lower than thereafter. The more frequent observations make the latter figures more accurate, but the infrequent observations of earlier years undoubtedly greatly overestimate the real breeding success. If the mid-1960s' 'break point' means anything, it is interesting to note that it corresponds with a shift from a lower success rate than the Bass to one about equal (Fig. 55). Further, it is about the period when the total number of birds at Bempton began to increase more sharply.

I suggest that increasing social stimulation increases breeding success by enhancing site attachment and strengthening the pair bond, thus facilitating co-operation between mates. This has a direct effect on the efficiency of incubation and chick care. Also, it attracts more newcomers.

But of equal importance is the clear demonstration that a *tiny* colony can produce chicks and that, once having reached a score or so pairs, it can become about as efficient in this as a large colony. Its efficiency in producing the next generation depends, also, on post-fledging survival and thus on the timing of breeding (to be discussed below). The causes of death in chicks (21 cases) in 1971, 1972, 1973 and 1974 were as follows: falling 11; tangled in synthetic fibres 3; oiled 1; inadequate parental care of newly hatched young 2; unknown 4. The heavy toll taken by falling (see also p. 107) emphasises that ideally gannets need broad ledges; Bempton's are narrow and particularly dangerous. On the other hand, few Bempton chicks are in danger of being dislodged by departing adults, a far from negligible danger on some steep Bass slopes.

(*e*) *Immature breeders*

A further interesting change in the Bempton gannetry, as it has grown, has been the increase in the proportionate number of breeding birds in immature plumage. This is typical of a rapidly growing colony (or group) probably because of the increased social stimulation.

The increase in the numbers of markedly immature birds at Bempton over the last few years has not been recorded in detail but is undoubtedly real. In 1972 there were two nest-occupying pairs in which both partners had some dark wing and tail feathers and eight in which one partner was immature. Thus, in 10 out of about 50 occupied sites (20 per cent) the pair was at least partly immature and (almost certainly) inexperienced. As a percentage of breeding pairs the figure is even higher (25 per cent). In 1973, again, 10 nests involved immature birds, out of 52 breeding pairs; 9 partnering an adult (sexes not noted) and one in which both were immature.. This is considerably more than in a similar-sized but not expanding cliff group (the Needle) on the Bass (4 per cent of site holders, 3 per cent of breeding birds).

Of the 10 immature pairs at Bempton in 1972, five had an immature female and an adult male, one an immature male and an adult female, two had both sexes immature and in two the sex of the immature bird was unknown. The tendency for females to breed earlier than males, already mentioned for the Bass (p. 127) is thus confirmed here.

Presumably the significant increase in the proportion of young birds breeding at Bempton in the early 1970s reflects increased immigration and increased social stimulation. A comparable situation developed on the Bass in my observation group and in group 6 (pp. 114, 127) where rapid growth was followed by an especially strong inflow of young birds and subsequently by the incorporation of young breeding pairs, to the extent that the proportion of experienced to inexperienced pairs in the groups altered significantly.

Immature birds tend to have a lower breeding success than experienced ones, for the reasons already mentioned (p. 203) and could significantly depress the overall breeding success of such a small colony as Bempton. Here, as on the Bass, inexperienced birds tend to lose eggs

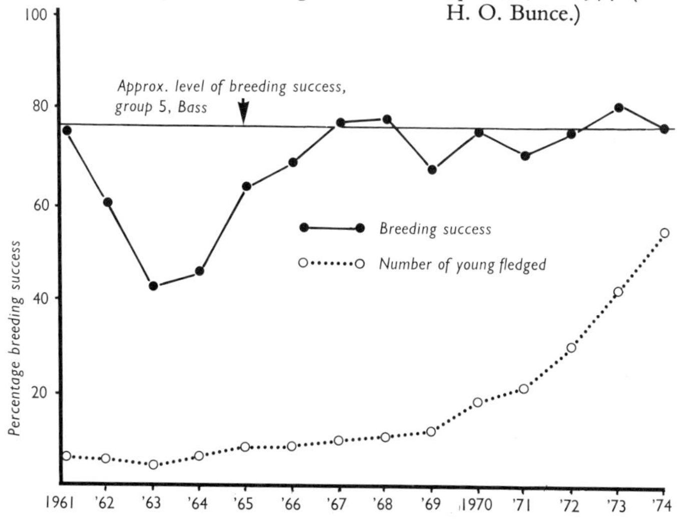

Fig. 55. Breeding success at Bempton, 1961–1974. (Data from J. Fairhurst and H. O. Bunce.)

or very small rather than large young. In the ten 1972 cases mentioned above, five chicks were lost and five fledged. Of the failures two were lost soon after hatching, two in a way which could not possibly reflect on the competence of the parents (one by oiling and one by falling) and one died from unknown causes. The 20 per cent loss due to inadequate parental care, though admittedly from a tiny sample, is about typical of inexperienced pairs. Both cases involved the pairs in which both partners were immature. Nevertheless had it not been for the rare misfortunes of falling and being oiled, 70 per cent of the pairs containing one or more immature partners would have bred successfully. This would have been near to the adult success rate. In 1973 nine out of the ten pairs containing at least one immature bird bred successfully; the unsuccessful pair was that in which both birds were immature.

(f) Breeding regime

As Bempton has grown, the length of the season spent there by site owners has increased; the first egg comes earlier and the mean laying date has advanced. Since about 1970 birds have started returning to the cliffs by late January or early February and leaving around late September or mid-October. Old-established pairs are nearly all back before mid-February and newly-established pairs in March.

The exact laying dates are often not known but the fledging dates are known to within a fortnight. From this the laying dates can be calculated (Table 27). In 1973, the first egg

TABLE 27

THE TIMING OF LAYING AT

	Date of first egg:			Approx. date of median egg:		
Year	Bempton	Bass Group 6	Bass Needle	Bempton	Bass Group 6	Bass Needle
1961	? Mid-April	April 17	March 31	Roughly early May	May 1	April 25
1966	? Mid-April	April 11	March 31	Roughly late April/ early May	April 25	NR
1971	April 4	April 6	April 4	April 17	April 18	April 14
1975	March 24	April 1	March 4	April 22	April 21	April 14

COMMENT: These are interpretations; others may be possible.)

In all groups, the first egg becomes earlier. It looks as though this is a general phenomenon as well as a social effect.

Steady progression of median egg at Bempton and group 6 until reversed, in both cases, by effect of late-laying young breeders. Closely similar actual dates. Not closely matched by Needle.

Notes:
1. Bempton grew from about 8 to 83 eggs laid, between 1961 and 1975. It is an entire colony (open ended). Group 6 grew from about 20 to 74 eggs laid, between 1961 and 1975; it is almost a discrete group (open ended). Needle remained almost constant, growing from 35 to about 40, 1961–75; it is almost a discrete group (closed).
2. The figures in brackets are the percentages of eggs laid in April as a whole.

appeared on March 24th, the earliest date so far. Whilst it would be misplaced effort to try and calculate an accurate mean laying date in these years, it is clear that it has become considerably earlier since the 1960s. It is now earlier than that of a similar sized group on the Bass but later than group 5 (Fig. 56).

Thus, the mean fledging date at Bempton has become progressively earlier. As late as 1970, 61 per cent of chicks fledged in September or October. In 1971 this became 34 per cent, in 1972 37 per cent and in 1973 36 per cent, the majority fledging in the second half of August (Table 27). However, even in some of the 1950s all chicks had fledged by the end of August. At this stage the colony consisted of a few, probably very old, pairs and old birds tend to lay early. In other words, the colony then had an unusual age structure. After 1973 the proportion of young fledging after the end of August rose significantly. This was due to a sharp increase in the number of young breeders and therefore of later eggs. Exactly the same thing happened in group 6 on the Bass. So long as rapid expansion goes on, there will always be a substantial proportion of late fledgers. Since early fledging probably confers survival value, the progressively earlier mean laying date may be seen as an important effect of increased colony size and the resulting social stimulation. It is interesting that such a small colony as Bempton has achieved a mean laying date as early as that of the Bass. There may be a threshold level of social activity which, at around 50 pairs, Bempton has now passed. The more southerly position of Bempton may also have a slight effect in advancing its mean laying date.

BASS AND BEMPTON, 1961–75

Percentage of Total Laid During:

First half April (fledge second half August)			*Second half April (fledge first half September)*			*May or June (fledge second half September or later)*		
Bempton	Bass Group 6	Bass Needle	Bempton	Bass Group 6	Bass Needle	Bempton	Bass Group 6	Bass Needle
Small	0	7	Medium	40 (40)	52 (59)	Large	60	41
Small	12	NR	Medium	45 (57)	NR	Large	43	NR
66	14	35	14 (80)	71 (85)	61 (96)	20	15	4
38	23	52	29 (67)	46 (69)	30 (82)	33	31	18
)ramatic increase in percentage of 3empton eggs laid first half April lue to rapid growth 1969–71 of rstwhile tiny colony. Not fully natched by group 6 which experinced slower growth. Reversed nost markedly in Bempton beause of late new breeders.			Greater proportion late layers in Bempton and group 6, than in Needle			Effect of late-laying new breeders evident in Bempton and group 6, reversing earlier trend, which was to reduce proportion of birds laying in May.		

(g) Breeding behaviour

Much of the foregoing has concerned ecological comparisons between Bempton and Bass gannets and social stimulation has been invoked. But social stimulation, of course, does not exist as a specific type of behaviour. It is the sum of certain kinds of behaviour each of which has its own particular function. The function of fighting is to evict, but fighting birds powerfully excite neighbours and so contribute to the social stimulation which the group experiences. On the other hand self-preening does not excite neighbours and does not count as social stimulation. Social stimulation is an important aspect of colonial breeding and to assess it one must compare the frequency of relevant behaviour patterns in groups with different characteristics.

Aggressive and sexual behaviour are the two categories which are obviously socially stimulating. Of these, there is most information for the former. Because displays normally occur at a typical intensity it is impracticable to compare their intensities, but their frequency can readily be compared. The prediction would be that a colony which was small and not growing, in addition to having its numbers scattered rather than in a dense Club, would show a lower frequency of aggressive behaviour than would an equivalent number of birds in a dense and thriving group. One might also expect that the Bempton colony, after a period of rapid growth, would reach a level of socially 'exciting' behaviour higher than before and perhaps as high as an equivalent sized group in a large colony.

Two territorial displays, Bowing and Menacing, may be compared for Bempton and two Bass groups (large and small). From this (Fig. 57) it appears that in 1972 the Bempton birds showed as much aggressive territorial behaviour as Bass birds. The figures for an earlier stage in Bempton's development are unfortunately few but counts made in June 1966 indicated a considerably lower level of activity than at present.

There is thus some objective evidence in support of the predictions just mentioned. It is

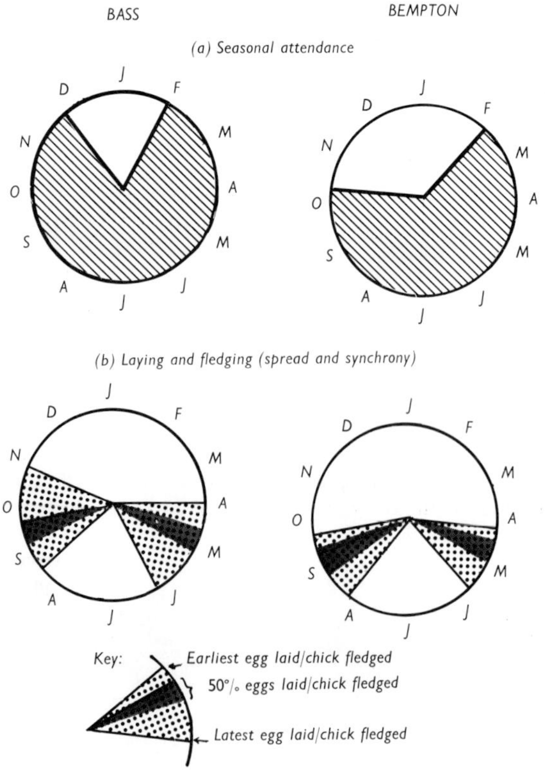

Fig. 56. A comparison between Bempton and Bass Rock (group 5) in some aspects of breeding biology in 1972. (From S. Wanless, unpubl.)

particularly noteworthy that, by 1972, Bempton was such a hive of activity that the frequency of threat and site ownership behaviour even slightly exceeded that of a large, dense Bass group. The impact of young, prospecting birds was evidently considerable.

(*h*) *Bass–Bempton comparison summarised*

1. Bempton, the only mainland gannetry in Britain, was almost certainly founded by immigrants from the Bass.

2. It was sustained in its early days and built up in later years by immigrants, and still receives more, several of which are birds colour-ringed as chicks on the Bass.

3. It remained tiny for many years during which, compared with the Bass, it was occupied for a shorter season each year, later in its main laying date and less successful.

4. The frequency of aggressive (territorial) behaviour was less than on the Bass.

5. The organisation of time (particularly the length of incubation and guard stints) differs between the two colonies, probably reflecting local differences in fishing grounds, etc. (see p. 119).

6. After slow growth, possibly to around a rough threshold, rate of colony growth accelerated; attendance lengthened; mean laying date advanced; breeding success rose and the frequency of socially stimulating behaviour increased markedly. The rate of immigration also rose.

7. Thus one of the main points of theoretical interest to be drawn from Bempton is that the success of the colony was closely related to its size, the link probably being through increased social stimulation enhancing territorial behaviour and pair co-ordination.

8. Also, the importance of sustained immigration in the early years, when output from the colony was insufficient to maintain it, is revealed.

9. The nature and role of the Club at Bempton is in many respects similar to that on the Bass, but with the important differences that, owing to topography it is more diffuse and, at Bempton, off-duty breeders sometimes 'loaf' on the Club ledges whereas on the Bass such birds probably do not join the Club.

2. *Movements*

The Atlantic gannet's movements, excluding the foraging trips of breeding birds, are best considered in relation to age, since the most extensive migration is undertaken by juveniles. In the eastern Atlantic the great majority of juveniles leave their natal colony and migrate southwards as far as West African waters, north of the equator (they have never been recovered in the southern hemisphere). Once having returned (which they do at a variable age) few will go back so far south again. Thus their movements subsequent to their re-association with their natal colony are more of a dispersal than a true migration. There are, however, exceptions and complications to this over-simplified picture.

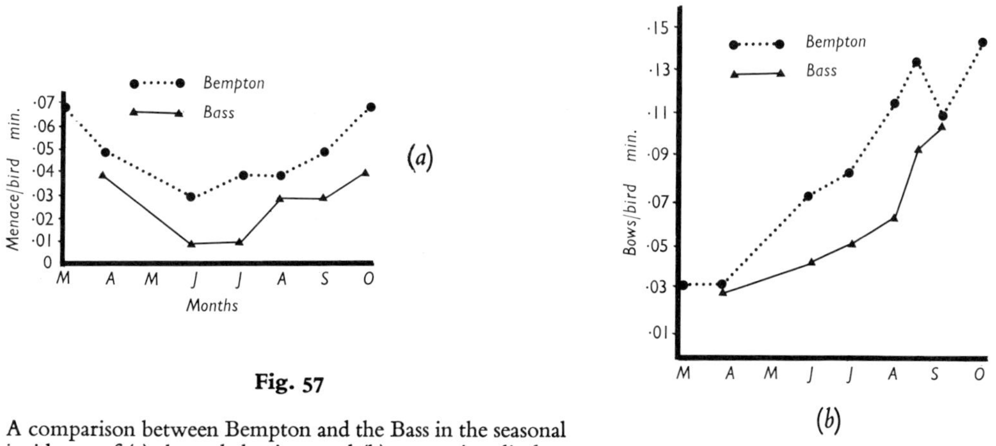

Fig. 57

A comparison between Bempton and the Bass in the seasonal incidence of (a) threat behaviour and (b) aggressive display.

(*a*) *Migration*

(i) *Direction and distance of movement.* Up to 1968, on the east side of the Atlantic, 32 681 gannet chicks had been ringed and 1761 or 5·4 per cent recovered (Thomson 1974).[1] This is considerably higher than for the other two gannet species, largely because (compared with the Cape gannet) a greater proportion fall into, or at, European hands and are thus more likely to be reported and (compared with the Australasian) more are killed by fishermen and more end up on inhabited areas of coast. Almost all the chicks were ringed on the Bass Rock, Ailsa Craig and Grassholm, but mainly on the Bass, where in 1904 Gurney started the process by marking nearly 100 gannets with private rings. The recovery rate of birds ringed up to 1937 was only 3·2 per cent and the present figure of 5·6 per cent is probably mainly due to the far higher proportion of birds ringed on the Bass (as against Ailsa and Grassholm) since 1937, these being more likely to be recovered; the North Sea is a very favourable catchment area.

Birds in their first year. Fig. 58 shows recoveries of all Bass birds ringed[2] as chicks in July and recovered, mainly in the northern zone, in August to December of the same year. A substantial proportion had moved north, including one to the Shetlands, before migrating down the western side of Britain, mainly west of Ireland. September and October were the main recovery months and several birds were blown (or possibly in the case of birds west of the Forth, flew) inland.

[1] The grand total ringed and recovered up to 1973 was 37 297 and 2106 (5·65 per cent) (Spencer & Hudson 1975).

[2] Includes all British Trust for Ornithology records up to 31st December 1970 and all my records up to 8th May 1973.

Fig. 58. Recoveries, between August and December of their first year, of birds ringed as chicks on the Bass.

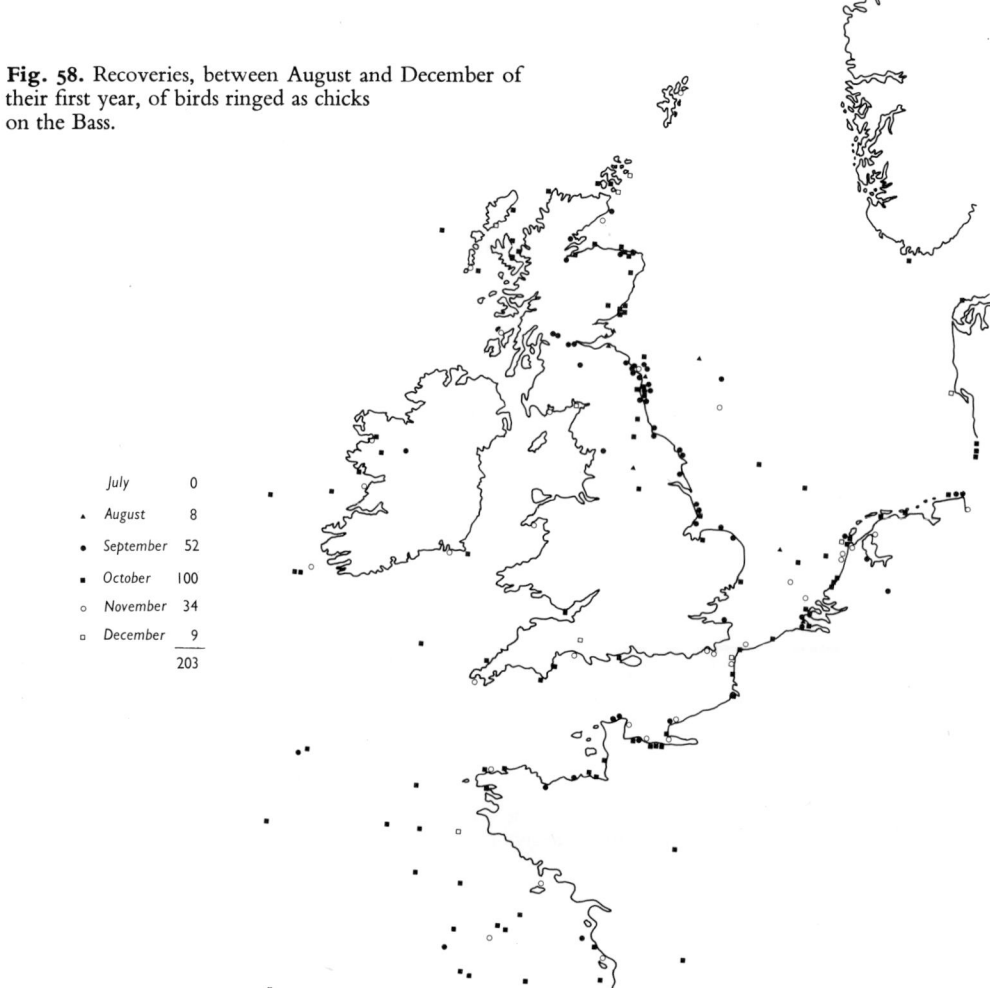

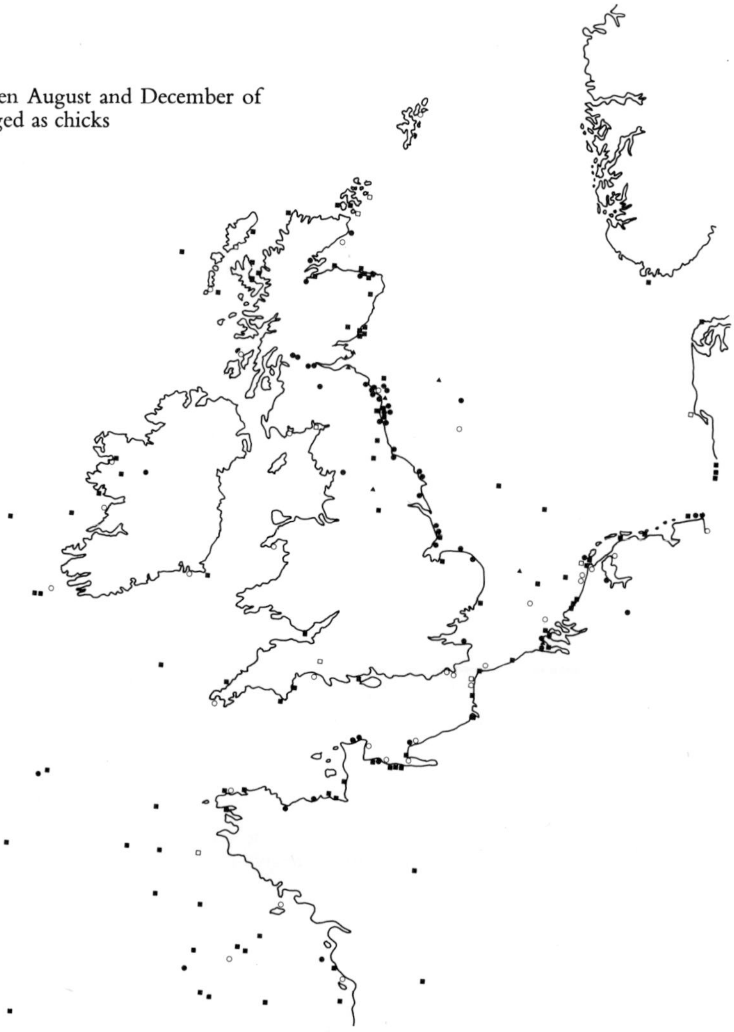

	July	0
▲	August	8
●	September	52
■	October	100
○	November	34
□	December	9
		203

Fig. 59 shows the places of recovery of 157 chicks ringed on the Bass and recovered during their first year. Of these, all except three were recovered before October 31st—i.e. during the first three months after fledging. The general southward movement along Europe's western seaboard is well shown, though many birds first move north and through the Pentland Firth before turning south, whilst some move eastwards across the North Sea into the Baltic. Presumably these would later have turned south. Most, however, leave the North Sea via the English Channel. Most birds by-pass the Straits of Gibraltar without entering the Mediterranean, but a few penetrate and move eastwards and there is a recovery at 36° 40′N.; 36° 00′E. off Turkey (the avoidance of the Mediterranean may reflect its relative poverty as a feeding area). They continue south as far as Senegal, where, incidentally, they overlap with Cape gannets. Thomson (1939, 1974) divides this recovery range into four belts, comprising the home waters (N) and successively more distant zones (W, A and T). Recoveries in these zones, arranged by months and according to the year of life in which they occurred, are given in Table 28, which shows a similar picture; the 11 recoveries in December and 6 in January represent that fraction of the juvenile population that stays in home waters. The February, March and April recoveries probably also belong in this category rather than to first-year birds which had returned to the north.

The southward trek is shown by the increase in recoveries, successively, in zones W, A and T, the maximum rate for the latter falling in December, by which time probably the bulk of first-year birds have penetrated as far south as they will go. They have covered over 3000 miles (4800km), though the rate of progress of the fastest is not known because their fledging date is unknown. Probably few birds reach their southern limit in as little as two months after fledging; more likely most move quickly into west European waters and then go further south

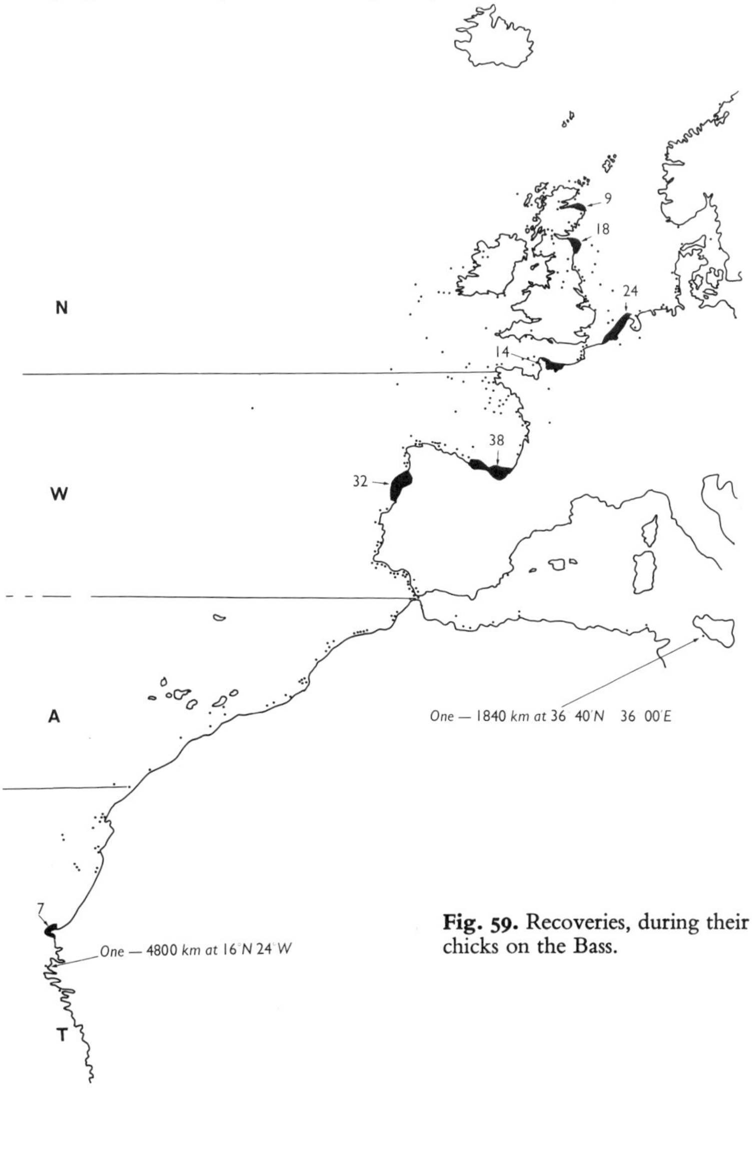

Fig. 59. Recoveries, during their first year, of birds ringed as chicks on the Bass.

from November onwards. However, a juvenile ringed on Ailsa in August 1974 was recovered in Morocco 14 days later, the fastest journey yet recorded.

Birds in their second year. From Table 28 it may be seen that good numbers of second-year birds are recovered in home waters in July to November. Fig. 60 shows the distribution of recoveries of Bass ringed birds and from this and Table 28 it may be seen that many are recovered also in zone W and some remain in zones A and T. Thus, in July of their second year, when just over a year old, some birds move north to home waters, though many remain further south. Insofar as sight records at the Bass are concerned, relatively few such two-year-olds are seen; most (appearing in May) are late second-year birds, which have presumably spent a second winter in southern waters. Several Bass birds were recovered west of Britain in their second year, thus making it perhaps unlikely that *all* Bass birds return to east coast colonies to breed (but west-born birds are probably less likely to go to the east, since the 'traffic' is west and this, combined with an inborn tendency to return to the coast of birth, should favour a west coast return). Of the 98 recoveries of Bass ringed birds in their second year in the N zone 88 (90 per cent) were to the east of Britain; 62 (63 per cent) were on or near the coasts of Belgium, Holland and Denmark, particularly the latter.

Birds in their third year, many of them three years old to the month, are mainly recovered in home waters from June to October (59 out of a total 165 third-year recoveries in all zones). These are birds that have moved north, probably mainly from west European waters or perhaps further south still, where they may have remained during their third winter. Alternatively they may include birds which have already been north and have returned part of the way south prior to moving north for the second time. Fig. 61 shows that the distribution of recoveries is similar to that of second-year birds, but as a result of fairly heavy mortality in their second

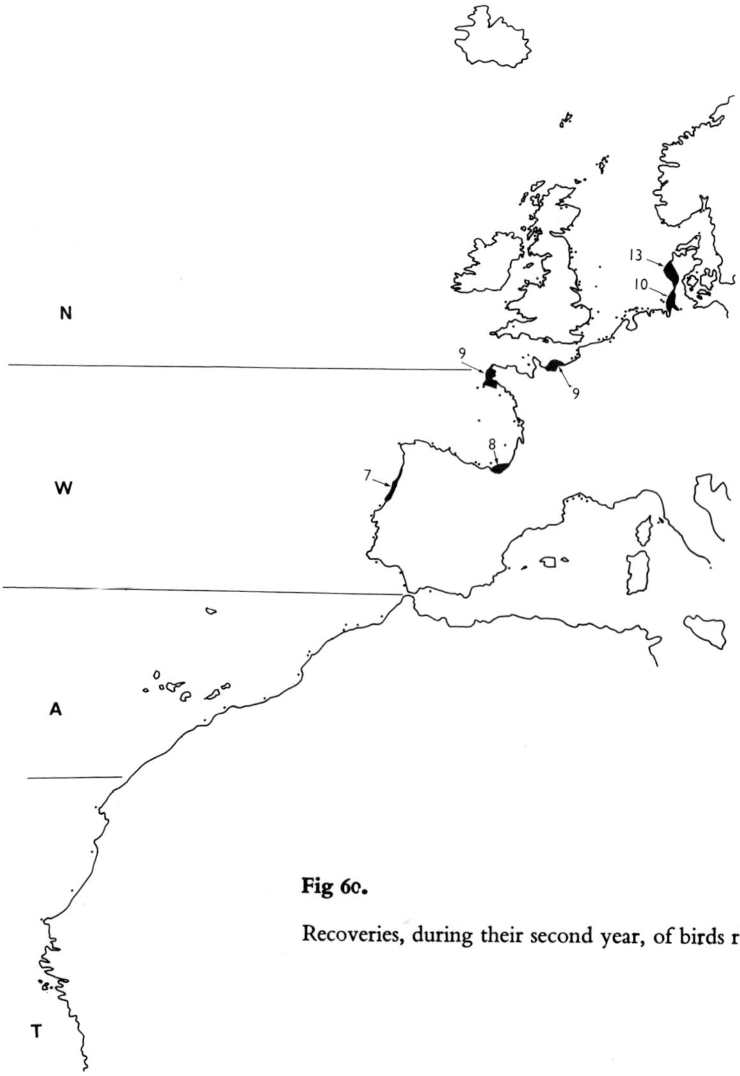

Fig 60.

Recoveries, during their second year, of birds ringed as chicks on the Bass.

year, there are fewer of them. As seen in Table 28 more third- than second-year birds stay in northern waters between December and March (17 as against 14, despite their being fewer third- than second-year birds remaining alive). However, after October, there seems a tendency for a few birds to return some distance south, as reflected in the increased recoveries in zone W.

Birds in their fourth year. Fig. 62 shows 157 fourth-year, or later, recoveries of Bass ringed birds, which is 90 more than comparable third year recoveries. Many of them are clustered on the east coast of Britain and at similar latitudes on the other side of the North Sea, and all except three of the British recoveries on land are on the south and (overwhelmingly) east coasts of Britain. The exceptions were Wexford (1), Pembrokeshire (1) and Galloway (1). Table 28 shows 105 fourth-year recoveries, all but two of which were in zones N and W, and of the

Fig. 61

Recoveries, during their third year, of birds ringed as chicks on the Bass.

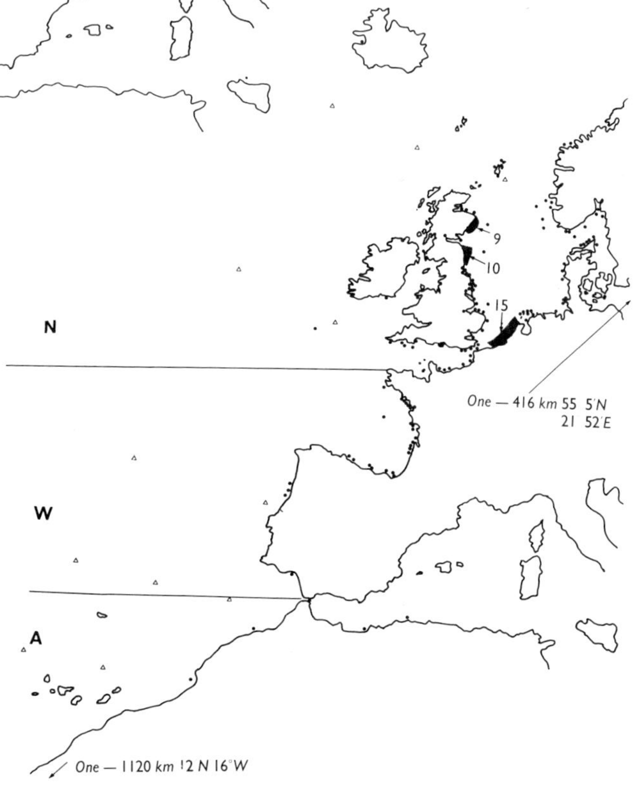

Fig. 62

Recoveries, during their fourth year, of birds ringed as chicks on the Bass.

77 in home waters, 63 were recovered between April and October. Practically all the survivors of the cohort of any year are thus back in home waters by the time they are four years old. There is every possibility that even those birds recovered in zone A had already been back in home waters.

Birds in their fifth year and later. The recoveries in Table 28 are mainly of birds at their breeding colony. An interesting one was of a colour-ringed male in my observation colony that had bred at least once before being killed by natives in Senegal at 12° 34′N in April. It

TABLE 28

DISTRIBUTION BY MONTH AND ZONE OF RECOVERIES OF GANNETS

(From Landsborough Thomson 1974)

	Zone	May	June	July	Aug.	Sept.	Oct.	Nov.	Dec.	Jan.	Feb.	Mar.	April	Totals
a														
recovered	N	—	—	8	67	143	132	36	11	6	2	2	2	409
in 1st	W	—	—	—	9	83	155	63	18	4	4	11	1	348
year of	A	—	—	—	—	—	13	25	12	9	8	1	1	69
life	T	—	—	—	—	—	1	7	13	11	7	1	1	41
	Totals	—	—	8	76	226	301	131	54	30	21	15	5	867
b														
recovered	N	1	4	25	22	15	24	16	7	4	2	1	1	122
in 2nd	W	1	8	12	11	6	9	17	15	11	5	7	2	104
year of	A	2	—	2	1	1	3	4	—	1	2	1	2	19
life	T	2	2	—	2	—	—	—	1	2	1	—	—	10
	Totals	6	14	39	36	22	36	37	23	18	10	9	5	255
c														
recovered	N	5	20	11	12	5	11	7	5	4	5	3	6	94
in 3rd	W	8	2	1	1	3	7	5	6	12	8	3	6	62
year of	A	1	—	1	—	—	—	—	2	2	—	2	—	8
life	T	—	—	—	1	—	—	—	—	—	—	—	—	1
	Totals	14	22	13	14	8	18	12	13	18	13	8	12	165
d														
recovered	N	8	10	7	12	6	12	3	2	4	3	2	8	77
in 4th	W	1	—	—	2	1	—	5	2	2	7	3	3	26
year of	A	—	—	—	—	—	—	—	—	1	1	—	—	2
life	T	—	—	—	—	—	—	—	—	—	—	—	—	—
	Totals	9	10	7	14	7	12	8	4	7	11	5	11	105
e														
recovered	N	17	20	37	18	6	11	5	3	11	10	10	24	172
in 5th	W	3	—	2	—	—	3	3	5	3	6	4	2	31
year of	A	—	—	—	—	—	1	—	—	1	—	1	—	3
life	T	—	—	—	—	—	—	—	—	1	—	—	1	2
	Totals	20	20	39	18	6	15	8	8	16	16	15	27	208
f														
ringed as	N	18	16	16	18	6	5	5	9	11	6	13	17	140
adults	W	2	1	1	—	—	2	—	3	6	2	1	1	19
	A	—	—	—	—	—	—	—	—	1	1	—	—	2
	T	—	—	—	—	—	—	—	—	—	—	—	—	—
	Totals	20	17	17	18	6	7	5	12	18	9	14	18	161

would probably be unwise to trust the recovery date too closely, but even so it proves that even experienced breeders may penetrate to zone T in winter. The recoveries of birds ringed as adults (and therefore almost certainly breeding when caught) also show the same thing (two winter records from zone A). The recoveries of Bass birds ringed as adults are given in Fig. 63. Clearly, they do not usually move far south, though many of the Bass birds move out of the North Sea and many of the west coast Scottish birds probably move south at least to the Channel. An adult male from one of my Bass study groups was recovered in January two kilometres inland on the west coast of Ireland (at Cork), released and eventually returned and bred again at its old site. Thus a proportion, at least, of Bass birds range into the same winter feeding areas as birds from west coast gannetries.

(ii) *Movement into the Mediterranean, Baltic and extreme northern waters.* Fifty-one recoveries in the Mediterranean are now available, but these are nevertheless a mere 6 per cent of the recoveries south of Ushant (Thomson 1974) and indicate simply a trickle from the main southward flow. Numbers fall off rapidly with distance and the spread occurs on both the north and south coasts. There are highly exceptional records from the Levant; a Bass bird recovered in March of its first year in the Gulf of Iskenderun, Turkey (36° 48′N, 36° 00′E) and an Ailsa bird in March of its fifth year at Ashdod, Israel (31° 48′N, 34° 38′E). Of the recoveries in the Mediterranean, all, except one, came from birds ringed as chicks. The ratio of birds recovered in their second year, rather than their first, was about twice as high as for all birds recovered south of Ushant, which suggests that many of the first-year birds that penetrate

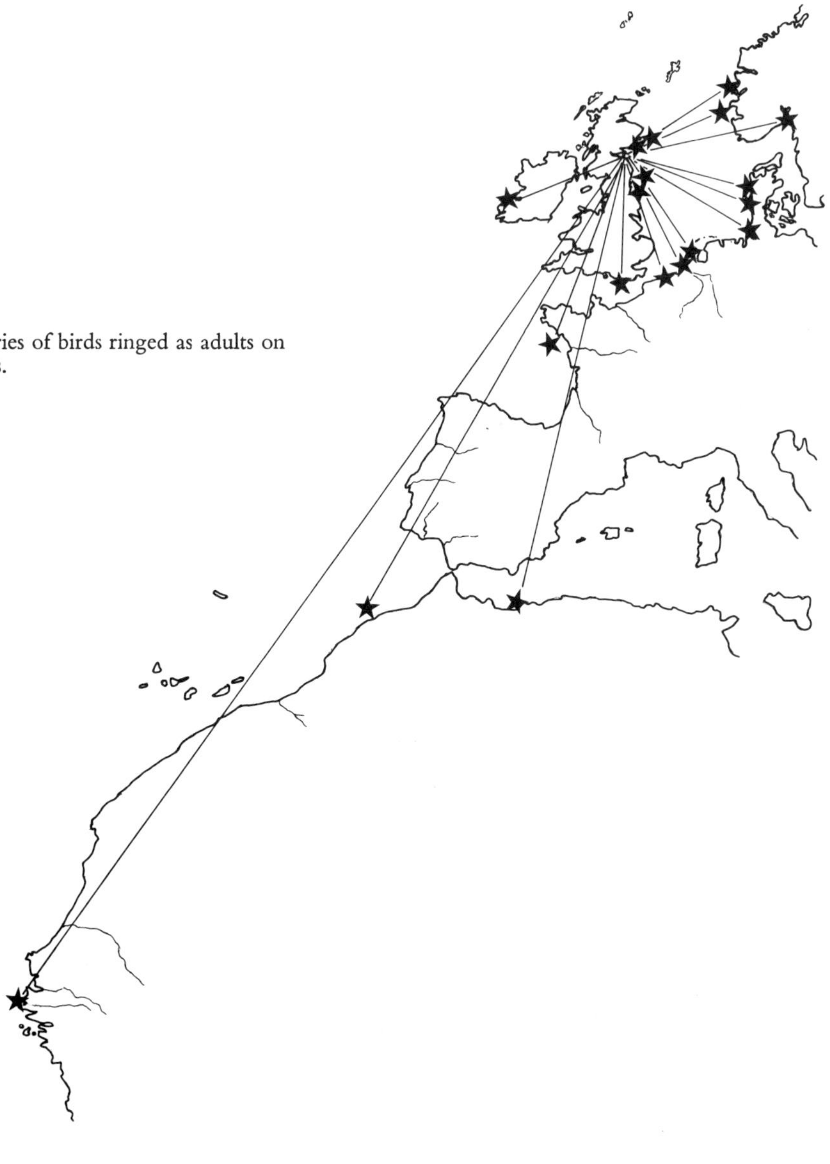

Fig. 63

Recoveries of birds ringed as adults on the Bass.

the Mediterranean remain there into their second year. Some such birds move northwards in summer, into the Gulf of Lions.

Gannets are uncommon in the Baltic Sea in winter and most recoveries are in the approaches to the Baltic. However, a Bass bird was recovered in June of its fifth year in Lithuania at 55° 5′N, 21° 52′E.

Recoveries north of the most northerly British breeding station (Hermaness) where birds from both east and west of Britain (Bass, Skellig, Grassholm, Ailsa and Hermaness) have been recovered, are almost all within the ambit of the gannetries of Iceland, Norway and the Faroes. All except one of the recoveries were in summer and most of the birds were less than, or about, three years old; a few, however, were adults. The young birds, or indeed all of them, may have been on foraging trips, but since we know from the Bass ringed bird recovered breeding on Skarvlakken, Norway, that a visiting bird may attach itself to such a colony, the possibility that Icelandic, Faeroese and Norwegian colonies may receive significant numbers of immigrants from British colonies cannot be ruled out (see p. 57). I suspect, however, that most of the recoveries in these northern regions are birds which have already attached themselves to a British colony or are actually breeding and which forage in these waters. There are no indications that gannets from different colonies migrate to different areas; the recoveries from Skellig (Fig. 64), for example, correspond closely to those from the Bass.

(b) Age distribution of recoveries

As we have seen, first-year birds show a very strong southwards movement; very few stay in northern waters beyond November and few stay even in west European waters. A much smaller percentage of second-year than of first-year birds remain in the far south, or return there in winter (Table 29) whilst even fewer third and fourth winter birds do so. Instead, and increasingly with age, more over-winter in western Europe and northern waters. Roughly equal proportions of second, third and fourth winter birds over-winter in western European waters, but fewer adults do so.

The major differences between age classes in the degree of southward movement (or duration of stay in the south) is between first- and second-year birds. It rather appears that a fair number of birds remain in zone T or A (particularly A) for two winters; many third-year birds,

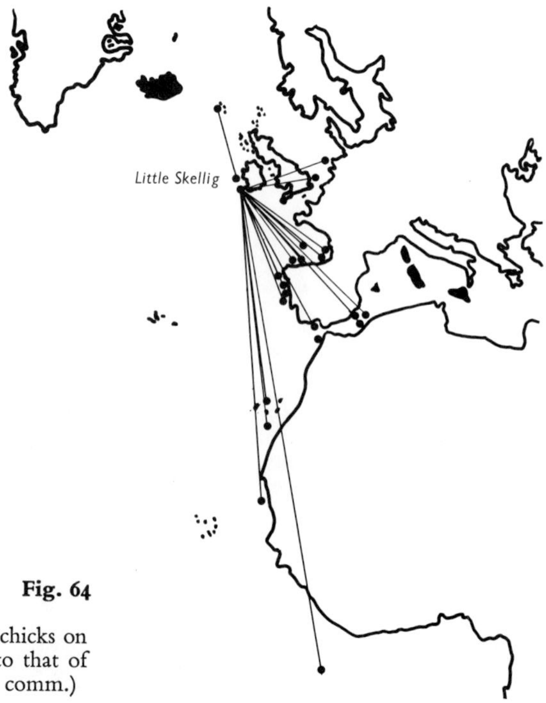

Fig. 64

Recoveries of birds ringed as chicks on Little Skellig; pattern similar to that of the Bass. After P. Evans (pers. comm.)

in winter, move up to zone W (from T) or back to W from N and older birds remain mainly in N though some go to W.

(*c*) *Other aspects of gannet migration and movement*

The strength of the innate tendency of the fully grown young gannet to move south is shown by an incident recorded by G. T. Kay (pers. comm.). A young bird swam ashore at the head of a long voe facing north (near Lerwick) and though put back into the water persistently came out again. Early one morning it was picked up on a main road a few hundred metres south of the voe head. Kay then took the bird to a bay facing south and released it on the beach. Immediately the bird took to the sea and despite a heavy swell, ducked beneath the breakers and made off strongly south to the open sea. On the other hand, Sarah Wanless reports that several stranded but uninjured juveniles on the grass slopes at the base of Ailsa's cliffs made no attempt to gain the sea and after several days had to be taken there and released. Perhaps these, too, could not see the southern horizon.

The gannet has an aversion to flying over land, however narrow. Kay quotes the example of the Noss gannets, some of which feed on the west side of Shetland but never cross overland, preferring to round Sumburgh Head despite the considerable detour entailed. It is therefore of particular interest that adult and juvenile gannets frequently penetrate the Firth of Forth to a point beyond Kincardine Bridge (J. Potter; I. Taylor, D. Fleming, pers. comm.) especially in September and these observers speculate that a Forth-Clyde passage might occur. Details are given in Appendix 7.

The common tendency of juveniles to attach themselves to adults at sea has led to some controversy. These adults are not the parents, but may release food begging from the juveniles. Thus MacIntyre's account (in Kay 1948) of young gannets pursuing adults and screeching for food is not fanciful and he claims to have seen them fed. It is extremely likely that, on its journey south, the juvenile will encounter groups of feeding adults and, if it can by then fly, it will probably dive itself (response to white adults and to diving will probably be innate and a hungry juvenile will be highly susceptible to such triggering). Birds of the year may be seen flying and diving anywhere off the east coast of Scotland in September and October, with or without adults.

A unique recovery of a bird ringed as a fit juvenile on Ailsa Craig in August and picked up, on Grassholm, some two or three weeks dead, in October of the same year (1974) probably arose from this tendency of juveniles to follow adults. This Ailsa chick must have picked up a Grassholm adult and followed it back to the colony; it was recovered on the fringes of the breeding area.

TABLE 29

AGE DISTRIBUTION OF WINTER RECOVERIES OF GANNETS EXPRESSED AS PERCENTAGE OF ANNUAL TOTALS (From Landsborough Thomson 1974)

	Year of life					Ringed as
Zone	1st	2nd	3rd	4th	5th	adults
N	23	31	38	40	62	76
W	40	57	53	54	33	21
A	22	8	9	6	3	3
T	15	4	—	—	2	—
N+W	63	88	91	94	95	97
A+T	37	12	9	6	5	3
W+A+T	77	69	62	60	38	24

Winter is taken from November to February inclusive.

(d) Canadian gannet migration

The main account of the movements of the gannets from Canadian colonies is that of Moisan & Scherrer (1973), from which the following details have been taken. Ringing on Bonaventure began in 1922 and yielded 417 recoveries and sightings (3·8 per cent) up to October 1971. The movement of juveniles (south-west for up to 5300 km) is very comparable to that of their conspecifics from the eastern Atlantic. It takes them (Fig. 65) to about 26°N (Mexican border). The general 'target area' seems to be off Florida, and it is there and in the area immediately south of the colony that most recoveries have been made. The southward movement gets under way in late September and is very marked by the second quarter of October. By November, most juveniles are in the region of Massachusetts, Long Island and New Jersey, and Florida is reached by December. In January, juveniles have been seen in the Gulf of Mexico. As in the other two gannet species, the initial direction of travel differs from the main direction; Canadian gannets set off south-east but their main travel is to the south-west.

Sub-adults and adults also move up to 4000km south each autumn. This is a greater movement (at least in the case of adults) than in eastern Atlantic birds. Just before the main movement south there is a greater tendency for adults and immatures, than for juveniles, to be recovered to the north-east of Bonaventure, presumably due to feeding trips. The complete desertion of home waters by Canadian gannets in autumn contrasts with the situation in the eastern Atlantic and reflects the arctic conditions of the Canadian winter. Some of both age classes reach Texas.

The pace of the southward migration and return is shown by the progressive shift, with time, of the main areas from which recoveries are made, as shown on the next page (from Moisan & Scherrer 1972).

Clearly first-year birds remain further south than older, but still immature birds, whilst adults go less far (recoveries in the Gulf of Mexico were only 8 per cent of the total for adults, compared with 13 per cent for immatures and 40 per cent for first-year birds; a highly significant difference) and return to northern waters ahead of immatures, just as in the eastern Atlantic.

In February, all ages are in the Gulf of Mexico but by then adults are on their way north, reaching home waters by April, the first birds arriving at Bonaventure in mid-April. Immatures leave in March, travel more slowly and arrive in May, and by June first-year birds are spread out along the coast from Gaspé to the Gulf. Whereas adults arrive back at the breeding area when the weather is still severe and fishing may be difficult, younger birds arrive when conditions are mild and fish plentiful.

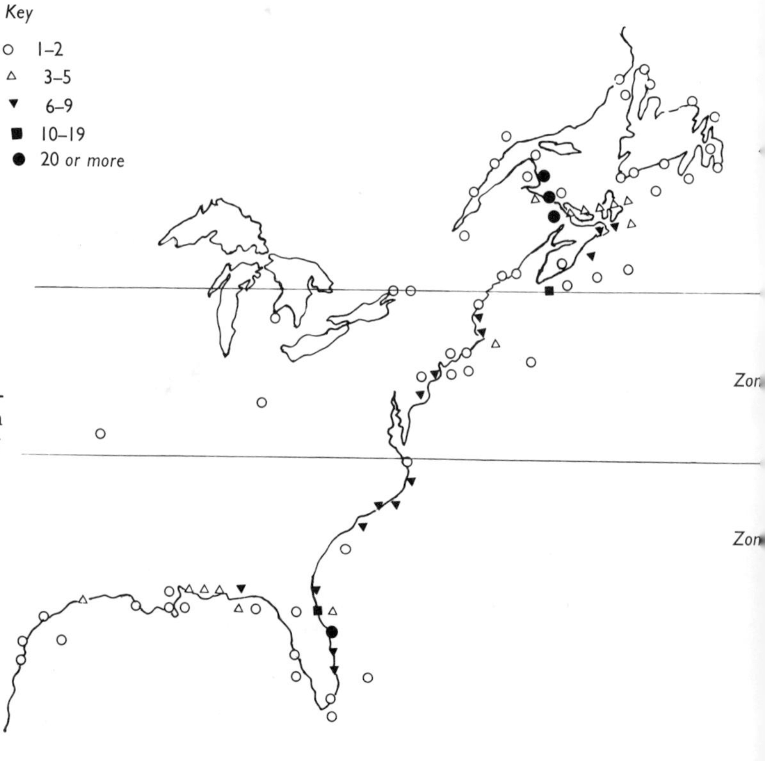

Fig. 65(a)

Recoveries of gannets as juveniles, of birds ringed as chicks on Bonaventure. (After Moisan & Scherrer 1973.)

The return journey is considerably faster than the southward movement (estimated 40–100 compared with 25–35km per day). Once back in the region of the breeding colony, over 93 per cent of adult recoveries (15 cases) were made within 60km of Bonaventure (approximately the fishing range). The immatures wander more widely and only 27 per cent of 11 cases were recovered at less than 60km. First-year birds are rarely found within this distance of the breeding area (only 6 per cent of 16 recoveries).

	Recoveries of first-year birds			Recoveries of immatures			Recoveries of adults		
	Zone* 1	Zone 2	Zone 3	Zone 1	Zone 2	Zone 3	Zone 1	Zone 2	Zone 3
Mid-September to October	39	10	1	12	1	2	16	1	0
November	4	11	0	3	5	0	3	3	1
December	1	1	4	0	3	4	0	—	—
January	0	2	11	0	1	0	0	—	—
February	1	1	9	0	2	7	0	2	3
March	0	0	17	1	1	5	0	3	3
April	0	0	22	0	3	4	6	2	1
May	8	6	8	12	3	2	2	0	0
June	16	2	4	12	2	1	3	0	0
July	9	2	2	8	1	1	3	0	0
August to mid-September	11	2	0	1	0	0	11	0	0

* See Fig. 65.

3. *'Clubs' and immature birds*

Every gannetry contains some immature and adult plumaged birds that are not breeding, though the number varies considerably in different colonies. They fall into two categories: those within or on the fringes of the nesting ranks, and, far more conspicuously, Clubs or gatherings outside. The consistently high attendance of those birds, either central or fringe, which are seriously attached to their sites rules out any possibility of their spending much, if any, time in Clubs, but it is possible that late and desultory fringe birds spend time there. The

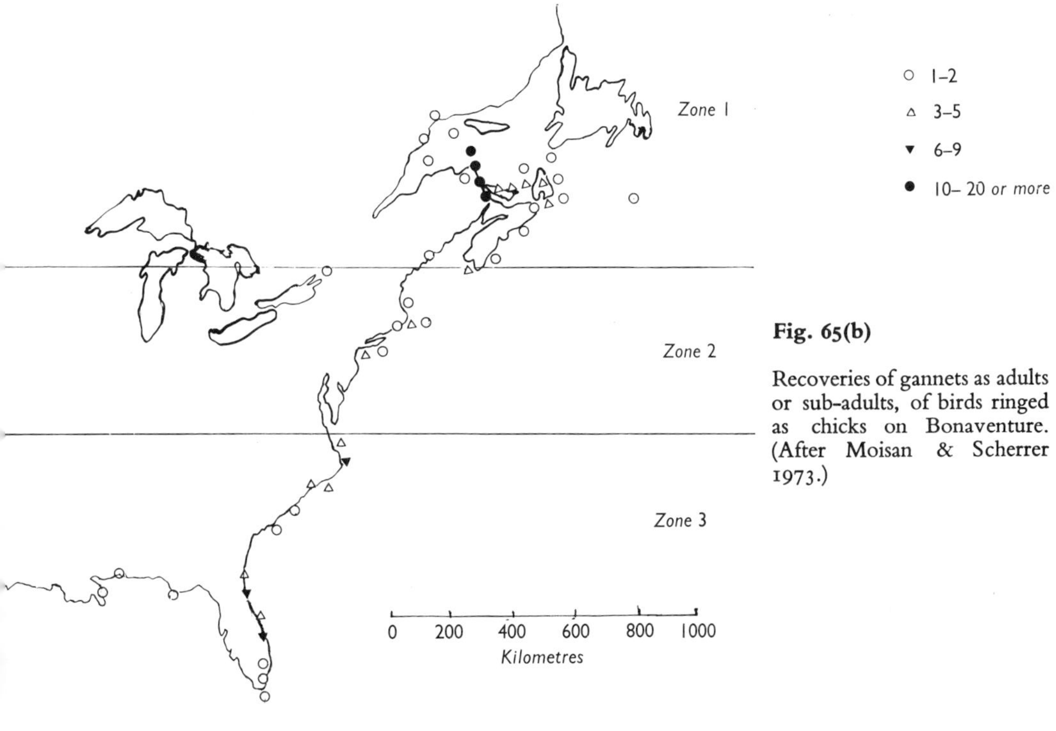

Fig. 65(b)

Recoveries of gannets as adults or sub-adults, of birds ringed as chicks on Bonaventure. (After Moisan & Scherrer 1973.)

first category has already been discussed in other contexts (p. 127) and it is with Clubs that I deal now.

Gannet Clubs congregate in three sorts of places. Probably most typically, at large gannetries, they gather in windy localities on the fringes of the nesters. This usually means favoured patches on top of the island or rock, as on Grassholm and the Bass (Fig. 66), where they are easily recognisable by their great density and lack of the regular spacing so typical of nesting pairs. Clubs of this nature are usually large. A second Club locale is on large ledges or mid-cliff slopes which are free from nesters. The ledges may be too low for breeders (occasionally

Fig. 66(a). A gannet Club, on the north slope of the Bass Rock. Birds congregate more densely and irregularly than in a nesting group.

Fig. 66(b). A portion of this Club, containing a high proportion of second- and third-year birds; birds of a similar age tend to gather together.

swept with spray) as at the foot of the cliffs on the south-west sector of the Bass. Ailsa furnishes examples of grassy slopes partway down the cliffs, favoured by Clubs. At Bempton, Clubs now gather on two large ledges below the nesters. Whilst still very small, Bempton also provides an illuminating example of Club birds dispersing among nesters (see p. 135). This has not been reported elsewhere but in a large gannetry it would be difficult to detect. Any such birds would be distinguishable from desultory site owners only by virtue of plumage (if very immature) or attendance pattern. It seems likely that the Bempton birds are a special case. Finally, on Sule Stack a large Club gathers on the southern hump, which contains few or no nesting birds; the other part of Sule Stack is full of breeding pairs. It is difficult to make much sense of the size of Clubs at different gannetries. The Bass Club population is between 2000 and 3000 birds, often almost all of them congregated in one extended group on the north-west segment of the rock. Grassholm Club is also large (probably in the region of 2000) whilst Ailsa's musters, at most, some 500 and even these are never to be found in one congregation. Among other gannetries at which sizeable Clubs have been noted, are Sule Stack (over 3000), St. Kilda (Martin Martin's 'barren tribe of solan geese that never mix among the rest that build and hatch') and Cape St. Mary. Factors affecting the size of a Club may be: the amount of suitable ground; the state of growth of the colony (rapidly growing ones attract 'floaters', see p. 68); whether the colony is well placed with regard to feeding grounds and the number of colonies in the vicinity. With regard to the second, Salmon & Lockley (1933) noted a great increase in immatures on Grassholm from 1928 to 1930 (from less than 500 to about 1500) which was presumably due, in part, to the great increase in the colony's output in the late 1920s and early 30s. I suspect that considerable fluctuations are caused within and between seasons, by immatures 'visiting' colonies other than their own.

Only the Bass Club has been watched closely over a long period and most of the following account refers to it.

Composition. Probably all reasonably large Clubs contain every age group from first year to adult. On the Bass, two-year-olds are prominent but three- and four-year-olds constitute the bulk of immature birds (Fig. 66). Club birds spend a shorter season at the colony than breeders. They are never in evidence at the Bass until April (and even then are small, up to 200), and have gone by late September or earlier. They reach full strength in May and are conspicuous throughout June, July and August. Third-, fourth-year and older birds arrive first and leave last.

First-year birds are usually at least 11 months, but the few that appear in April are only 10 months. They increase throughout summer and by August (when they are into their second year) constitute about 5 per cent whereas in May and June they comprise merely 1–2 per cent. One assumes that they are *all* birds which have migrated south but returned unusually early, though it is very possible that a few juveniles *never* migrate beyond home waters and it may be these birds that return first. Certainly, gannets difficult to distinguish from birds-of-the-year are seen in the North Sea in December. They are of varied plumage: some have white napes and collars whilst others are completely dark above.

Second-year birds appear from the end of February onwards, but the main influx is in early May, increasing from two or three in late April to at least 100–200 in early May. The exact proportion which they contribute to the population is difficult to determine because plumage is so variable and the birds are moulting all the time. Chronologically they change from second- to third-year birds midway through the summer, but there is no precisely corresponding plumage change. Within this loose framework, however, late second year grading into early third comprise 20–30 per cent of the Bass Clubs, from May onwards.

Third-year birds, to which the complications mentioned above apply, may be seen from February but arrive in numbers in late March or early April, sometimes late April. The late third- to early fourth-year birds taken as a class comprise 30–35 per cent of the Club. By this time, probably, all the survivors of their cohort have returned from southern waters. Although merely the roughest of estimates it may be noted that about a third of about 3000 Club birds (2000–2500 often to be seen and a proportion absent) would represent a thousand individuals from the output of three years previous (probably about 4000 + chicks). This gives an order of magnitude mortality of at least 75 per cent which is approximately the figure calculated by other methods.

The remainder of the Club consists of sub-adults, with variable traces of immaturity, and adult plumaged birds. The latter, who may be late four- or early five-year-olds (or older), sometimes comprise around 30 per cent of a particular Club gathering.

Nature, activities, function and significance of Clubs. There is a marked tendency for birds in Clubs to congregate with their own age group, which often gives a false impression of their composition, one section perhaps containing 50 or 60 per cent of two- to three-year-olds.

The dense packing and often patchy appearance of Clubs differs markedly from the regular ranks of breeding birds and reflects two important facets of their nature: their intense sociableness and their lack of rigidly territorial behaviour. They are extremely active gatherings with much overflying and coming and going. Besides resting and preening, Club birds engage in all the displays and behaviour characteristic of breeders, though at a lower intensity. Thus one sees fighting, threatening, Bowing, Fencing and even copulation.

The functions of the Club, apart from providing a safe resting place, are clearly mainly social—otherwise gannets could easily rest on remote and empty rocks and islets rather than gather in large numbers, as they invariably do, at breeding colonies. Clubs provide an opportunity:

(i) to learn local topography and air currents and the skills of landing under different wind conditions;
(ii) to interact socially and so 'polish' the appropriate responses (a conditioning process akin to 'perceptual sharpening');
(iii) to acquire the necessary timing abilities with regard to foraging trips from that particular base, in different weathers.

These functions would be useful whatever were the relationships of Clubs to the breeding population. For instance, if Clubs were reservoirs of potential breeders, to be fed into the breeding population at the dictate of the current balance between food and population strength, or simply (and more likely) congregations of birds too young or in other ways unfit to breed or unable to acquire socially adequate sites (p. 82), they would in any case need these skills. The relationship between adult Club birds and the breeding population is in fact the central puzzle. Are they non-breeders (and if so, for what reasons) or are some of them, at least, off duty breeders? The following facts strongly support the first alternative. (i) They behave like adult non-breeders, establishing temporary sites and showing incipient sexual behaviour in a way which breeding birds would not. For example, whereas a breeding male is at this time hostile to females other than his mate, Club males accept wandering females. (ii) They are much warier than breeding birds, showing panic at a ship's hooter which breeders ignore. (iii) All the evidence shows that nesting birds, or firm site holders, spend their non-foraging time at the nest. Thus if a pair loses its egg or chick attendance at the nest *increases* rather than decreases, whilst when incubating or caring for young they still spend 15 per cent or more of daylight hours together on the nest in addition to their solo stints. With foraging time added, this leaves little or no time for loafing in a Club. Indeed, given the evidence for the extraordinary pre-eminence of the site in the gannet's deployment of time and energy, it would be highly inconsistent were it to spend time elsewhere. (iv) Clubs do not build up until long after breeding birds are back at the colony. (v) At Ailsa, the total size of the Club is so small that, even if *all* of it comprised off-duty birds, the habit could apply to less than two per cent of the population. Even on the Bass, the proportion would be small.

One could *never* prove that there are no off-duty birds in Clubs, but it seems virtually certain that the great majority, or all, are non-breeders. They are certainly *not* excluded from the fringes by established birds, so they must 'choose' to stay out. One possibility is that the socially acceptable depth of the 'fringe' is a finite, and fairly small, number of 'ranks' (see p. 128) and that this limits socially acceptable sites whatever the abundance of physically adequate ones, or they may be young adults, marginally unfit.

The situation at a west coast gannetry, with considerable interchange, may differ from the Bass. For instance, Ailsa's small Club may result from the greater attractiveness of some other gannetry for Club birds, perhaps because the quarrying operations until recently kept them away.

4. *Food*

In the east Atlantic, recorded prey species are: coalfish or saithe *Gadus virens*; cod *Gadus morrhua*; codling *Trisopterus minutus*; haddock *Melanogrammus aeglefinus*; whiting *Merlangus merlangus*; herring *Clupea harengus*; sprat *Sprattus sprattus*; pilchard *Clupea pilcharda*; mackerel *Scomber scomber*; hake *Merluccius* spp.; gurnard *Trigla* spp.; sand-eels *Ammodytes ammodytes*; garfish *Belone belone*; capelin *Mellotus villosus*; pollack *Pollachius pollachius*; anchovy *Engraulis encrasicolus*; and salmonids *Salmo* spp. (Witherby *et al.* 1948; pers. obs.). Reinsch saw gannets taking the following: *Arengus minor*; *Engraulis encrasicolus*; *Alosa* spp.; *Osmerus eperlanus*; *Belone belone*; *Gadus morrhua*; *Melanogrammus aeglefinus*; *Pollachius virens*; *P. pollachius*; *Trisopterus luscus*; *T. minutus*; *Gadus merlangus*; *Boreogadus esmarki*; *Trachurus trachurus*; *Mullus* spp.; *Pagellus* spp.; *Mugil* spp.; *Ammodytes* spp.; *Micromesisteus pontassou*; *Coryphaena* spp.; *Molva byrkelange*; *Lycodes* spp.; *Anarhichas* spp.; *Microstomus kitt*; *Limanda limanda*; *Hippoglossoides platesoides* and *Pleuronectes platessa*. Perry (1946) records them gorged with eels off Lindisfarne (in October up to 60 vomited). Palmer (1962) adds capelin *Mellotus villosus*; menhaden *Brevoortia* spp. and squid *Loligo* spp. from the Western Atlantic. Dogfish *Squalus* spp. apparently are not eaten but probably all other fish will be accepted. Reinsch states that gannets will not take 'free' crustacea or echinoderms but ingest them with fish. Offal from fishing boats is greedily devoured and even bread and other waste food has reportedly been taken.

Observation on captive gannets (Booth 1887; pers. obs.) show that up to 1000g may be taken in one meal; at least four medium sized mackerel can be accommodated and Reinsch relates that up to seven large herrings per day were eaten by a captive gannet on board his fishing vessel. My birds, reared from chicks to 18 months at the time of writing, take rather less (three or four medium herring or saithe at a time) and readily accept whole or cut-up flatfish (*Pleuronectes* spp.). Periodically they refuse food for a day or two. Booth's birds, which he reared to maturity and which bred successfully in captivity, swallowed many unusual items including sparrows, complete with bird-lime and seed-cup, a water-rail and an adult guillemot. An attempt to rear an incubator-hatched gannet was made in Cambridge by Margaret Vince who reported that small pieces of whole fish slimed with egg yolk were probably best; enzyme-treated fish was difficult to administer and lodged in the oesophagus. The chick died on the eighth day, from an infection.

Herring and mackerel are the gannets' main food fish; every colony from which there is a mention of the identity of regurgitations names one or both of these species. Sprats, saithe and sand-eels are also important. There are productive coalfish grounds off Norway, Iceland and the Faroes and they contain a high proportion of suitably sized fish (up to 50cm). Recent work (Reinsch 1971) shows that there are rich young year classes in all the north-east Atlantic fishing grounds, perhaps especially off Iceland and Norway. It is also possible that overfishing of the North Sea herring has changed the spectrum of fish sizes to the gannet's advantage. On Bonaventure herring was the most important food fish until June, after which mackerel predominated, with a squid (*Loligo* spp.) second most important.

5. *Relationships with other species*

Gannets effectively lack any opposition for nesting space. Although they sometimes come into competition with kittiwakes, fulmars, herring and lesser black-backed gulls, guillemots, shags and cormorants, they are successful against them all. On flatter ground the blanket-like advance of a gannetry pushes other ground nesting species in front of it whilst on ledges only the fulmar resists. It can repel a gannet on most occasions but is eventually ousted by the gannet's greater persistence and its less frequent absences; the fulmar's pre-laying exodus is a handicap in this context. On Bempton long and vigorous disputes between these two species have been recorded, lasting more than an entire breeding season, the ledge changing hands back and forth and the current occupier usually dominant. Auks are usually remarkably well tolerated and sometimes nest within beak range, but (as at Bempton) if the gannet wants the ledge it simply displaces the guillemot and tosses its egg away. Despite this, massed guillemots, or kittiwakes for that matter, probably do cause gannets not to bother appropriating ledges which, had they been empty, they would have taken over. Considering their superior strength and equipment gannets, off-site, are remarkably unaggressive to other species and to their own. They stand irresolute on a herring gull's territory, ducking in discomfiture and shouting in alarm as the gull swoops, when one swift lunge would effectively dispel, if not despatch it (Morris 1848 records a doughty gannet attacked by two male mute swans in concert and after an exhausting battle 'beating them both off, and laying them prostrate, totally disabled, helpless and seemingly seriously injured'). On their nest, however, woe betide a gull that approaches within beak range. Even fluffy gull chicks send gannets berserk and if they are unfortunate enough to stumble amongst them, they are stabbed and shaken to death.

An interesting phenomenon has been recorded by Joan Fairhurst, who has now on four occasions followed in detail, attempts by Bempton gannets to foster guillemot chicks. The situation can arise either by parent guillemots being forced off a ledge and separated from their chick or by a chick falling onto a gannet ledge. Oddly, even a chick that was later able to rejoin its parents returned of its own accord to the gannet. The guillemot chicks were treated in normal gannet fashion, tucked on top of its webs and offered food by 'engulfing' in widely opened beak. This alien feeding method meant that they received very little food (perhaps a few spilt fragments) though they did try to take food from the gannet's throat. Two adoptions lasted 17 days during which time, in one case, the parent guillemot managed, on occasions, to feed it. The guillemot chick elicited food-giving by pecking at the base of the gannets bill. It would appear that the white underparts of the guillemot was a sufficient 'releaser' to elicit parental behaviour (note the difference in reaction to a small brown gull chick).

A somewhat comparable case (behaviourally) was the attempt by a black-browed albatross, which visited the Bass in 1967 and 1968, to display to gannets (Waterston 1968). The albatross approached gannets and performed a low intensity version of its own display without eliciting any response from the gannet. Clearly, whilst the latter possessed enough features to release display in the albatross (which presumably had an extremely low threshold), the gannet, in the presence of the real thing, had too high a threshold for response. The attraction which gannets, as large, white, colonial seabirds, have for stray albatrosses is shown, too, by the well-known case of the black-browed which lived among gannets on Myggenaes from 1860 to 1894. More recently (July 1966) one turned up among the Westmann Islands gannets (Waterston 1968).

At sea, gannets face little if any competition for most of their food, there being no other deep plunge divers in the North Atlantic and no large, offshore divers of any kind except a few northern, black-throated and red-throated divers (cormorants and shags usually feed near the shore). All the auks, gulls, skuas, terns, shearwaters and petrels take much smaller prey than do gannets. When scavenging for offal, gannets usually dominate other species, fulmars and skuas included (Reinsch 1968). On the other hand, Arctic and, particularly, great skuas frequently victimise gannets. Off Hermaness great skuas were successful in causing regurgitation on 11 out of 93 chases. Chased gannets usually did not alight on the sea, where presumably they could have countered an attack, for it is their relative lack of manoeuvrability compared with the lighter, broader-winged skua, that disadvantages them in the air However, on 10 out of 36 occasions on which the skua actually touched them, they did alight (Andersson 1976). They have been seen to dive repeatedly when harassed by bonxies. When single bonxies chased gannets (85 cases) they regurgitated in only 7, but where several (up to 10) skuas combined, in 4 out of 4. They harass fishing gannets, particularly emerging or taking off after a dive. The skuas often grasped the gannet's wing or tail or used its feet on the gannet's back. On the water, Andersson saw a skua land on the gannet's back and push its head beneath the surface. Gannets did lunge at skuas, but apparently rather ineffectually compared with the way they tackle other gannets.

A. M. Edwards (pers. comm.) tells me that, on several occasions, he has seen great skuas attack and damage gannets in the air, apparently twisting a wing and leaving the gannet disabled on the water. This is the only record of bonxies actually damaging them. Overall, bonxies are obviously totally insignificant as food-robbers, but it is conceivable that, where they are common, some gannets may lose a measurable amount.

Gannets, it would appear, have no natural predators. Their inaccessible breeding haunts safeguard them from 'large' mammals of which, in any case, there are now few in Britain (fox, wild cat, otter). Rats are abundant on Ailsa but there is no evidence that they can get at eggs or young and they have not acquired the habit of eating into the body cavity of brooding adults as *Rattus exulans* does to albatrosses on some Pacific Islands. Potential avian predators must always have been few, though the sea-eagle could have been one. Predation can be ruled out as a possible factor limiting populations.

Man has killed more gannets than any other predator (see Appendix 4) and his activities in collecting adults for food, bait and feathers, and gugas for oil and food have certainly in the past reduced the world population very considerably and almost wiped out certain vast colonies. It is largely relaxation of this pressure in this century that has enabled the current welcome expansion of the gannet population to occur.

SUMMARY

1. The correlation between the gannet's size and feeding behaviour, and the seasonal abundance of food, are postulated as basic factors determining the timing of breeding.

2. Island cliffs are the preferred habitat, but flatter ground is often used. Windiness and safety are two major advantages.

3. Colonies are typically large, around 10 000 pairs is a characteristic size, but colonies larger than 100 000 and less than 10 occur.

4. Density (just over two nests per sq. m) is highly constant and is NOT mainly due to physical shortage of sites, but is a social phenomenon.

5. Colonies and sub-colonies are complex in structure (physical, social and experiential) and these affect breeding success, etc.

6. The nest (seaweed and other vegetation) is important for protection of egg and chick.

7. The egg is small relative to the gannet's size (3·4 per cent). It loses 9–13 per cent of its weight during incubation. The shell is unusually thick.

8. Natural clutches of more than one are unknown, but sometimes two females lay in the same nest.

9. Lost eggs are replaced sometimes twice and rarely three times. The interval between loss and replacement is usually two to three weeks.

10. The incubation period is just less than 44 days. Incubation stints on the Bass were 35 hours (male) and 30 hours (female). Probably they vary with area.

11. Bass chicks were fed about 2·7 times per day.

12. Foraging trips vary according to the age of the chick but average around 20 hours. The fishing range is at least 250km. The chick is never left unguarded during its entire time in the nest, and on the Bass the pair spent about 15 per cent of daylight hours together at the nest.

13. Chicks grow rapidly, particularly between weeks three and eight (maximum weight about 4500g) and acquire large fat deposits. Variation in weight is considerable but starvation is virtually unknown at any colony.

14. Other parameters are not equally good indicators of age; culmen is reliable up to about seven weeks and total wing length up to about 11 weeks.

15. Bass gannets coped well with the burden of an extra (artificially donated) chick. Almost certainly, twins fledged at little less weight than singletons and pairs rearing twins apparently gained substantial reproductive advantage.

16. Chicks fledge at about 90 days. The myth that adults desert their young before these fledge continues to be propagated (e.g. Dementiev *et al.* 1966). In fact, they attend and feed them until the day or even hour of departure.

17. Fledging season varies with area; and the egg-laying period upon which it depends is geared (a) probably to the pre-laying feeding situation, (b) to the seasonal abundance of mackerel and herring for feeding the young and (c) to the seasonal onset of bad weather which greatly affects newly fledged juveniles.

18. Hatching success is usually over 80 per cent and fledging (from hatched) over 90 per cent, giving an overall breeding success of between 70 and 80 per cent or more. The major causes of failure are inexperience and human disturbance. There is no evidence that, unaided, gulls can take eggs or small chicks but a single human incursion into the colony can cause heavy loss. This greatly affects interpretation of low success, where this occurs.

19. Different areas of the Bass apparently held different proportions of site-holding, adult-plumaged non-breeders. The possible reasons for this are discussed at length.

20. Inexperienced pairs do less well than experienced and the (common) statement that fringe birds are less successful than centre is largely (or entirely) to be explained in these terms.

21. Colonies vary in the annual pattern of attendance. For example, the Bass (well populated as early as December in some years) is consistently several weeks earlier than Ailsa. Canadian birds return in mid-April. The explanation probably lies in the nature of the early feeding available, rather than inclement weather as such. The pre-laying period is the most demanding time in the whole breeding cycle, probably especially for the male.

22. The timing of egg laying is affected by social stimulation among other things. This confers direct survival value on behavioural facilitation and hence on dense nesting, probably mainly via survival of newly fledged young (earlier ones survive better). Site competition is geared to this, rather than simply to physical site shortage.

23. Deliberate non-breeding years in experienced pairs that remain together apparently do not occur.

24. Gannets can breed successfully in their fourth year but most do so for the first time in their sixth.

25. Females breed at a younger age than do males; they also take longer to acquire adult plumage. Deferred maturity in the gannet is probably partly explicable in terms of the time spent in southern waters, time required to learn local fishing areas and time acquiring a site.

26. Gannets tend to return to the part of the colony in which they were born. Usually site owners return yearly to the same site, but many move slightly at least once in their life.

27. Mates usually remain together in successive years but there are some divorces.

28. Annual adult mortality is less than six per cent and may be as low as three per cent. Life expectancy after the second year is at least 20 years. Probably the main causes of death are accidents at the breeding colony and killing by man at sea.

29. 75–80 per cent of fledglings die before reaching breeding age, mostly in their first year. The main cause of death is starvation.

30. The main events in the growth of the Bempton colony are described—the first time such information has been gathered. It grew by immigration; as numbers increased, breeding success rose, laying became earlier and the proportion of immature birds increased. The incidence of certain behaviour patterns increased and it may be deduced that the concomitant increase in the level of social stimulation was responsible for some of the changes just mentioned.

31. Migration is discussed, both for east and west Atlantic birds. Both populations of juveniles move over 5000km southwards, as do some adults, particularly of west Atlantic birds.

32. Clubs vary from gannetry to gannetry but typically comprise birds from one year old to adult-plumaged. Probably almost all adults are non-breeders, rather than off-duty birds.

33. Recorded food fish are listed.

34. Gannets do not face competition for sites from any seabirds except, occasionally, fulmars.

35. At sea they are sole occupiers of an important feeding niche.

4. BREEDING BEHAVIOUR

INTRODUCTION

A gannetry in full cry is a memorable spectacle. Once the language is understood it becomes possible to gain some inkling of what it must mean to a gannet. The indescribable hubbub and the often frenzied and bizarre activities, the constant traffic of inquisitive birds are all part of the complex organisation of the colony. To describe what goes on is not enough. We must try to interpret it. If the often tedious details are read with that in view, I hope they will be seen to be relevant.

Gannets occupy their breeding colonies from about January to November, mainly at their nest site. Most of a Bass gannet's life is spent, not at sea, but on a cliff ledge or a small patch of muddy or stony ground. The establishment of this nest site is of great importance to a gannet and its retention occupies much time and energy.

ESTABLISHMENT AND MAINTENANCE OF TERRITORY

It is the unpaired male, sometimes three years old, but usually at least four or five, who first establishes the site, usually quite near the nest in which he was born; a female joins him later. He usually has to stake his serious claim in the colony once only during his life, thereafter simply returning year after year to the same nest remnants, or in many cases moving only a few feet. The details in this section were gathered mainly from a large, expanding group (Fig. 35(a)) spilling over the cliff edge on to sloping ground, with an inland fringe to which most prospecting males were attracted. Site establishment slides imperceptibly into site maintenance, but I have arbitrarily divided the two after 'fighting', when, as a result, the winner can be said to have vindicated his claim in the most unequivocal manner.

1. *Aerial and ground reconnaissance*

One of the lasting impressions from a great gannetry is the constant traffic of birds sailing endlessly past, often almost stalling, with depressed tail and lowered head, only to lift away once more. If one can locate an individually recognisable bird it becomes clear that it is constantly passing and re-passing the same area, often quite obviously peering down at a particular spot. I saw a pink-dyed male do this over 50 times in just over an hour and it is unlikely that he had just commenced or would thereafter stop. Similar records of colour-ringed birds prove that young males fly past the area in which they later settle many hundreds, probably thousands of times. It is also the case, however, that a male may investigate more than one area of the colony; a known individual with a fringe site was seen to investigate a different area.

This aerial reconnaissance is followed by ground reconnaissance in the fringe of a group or from a vacant vantage point or a temporarily unoccupied nest in the colony. In less than an hour I recorded five different males successively occupying a vacant nest whose owner had joined a widowed female nearby. Every time, he drove away the site-prospecting male and then returned to the female. This incident, and many scores of comparable ones, occurred in April in a rapidly expanding group and shows the considerable pressure on attractive and unoccupied sites. Such prospecting males are easily displaced, which means that an owner who returns from foraging to find his site usurped has no difficulty in reclaiming it. A male may become attached to two sites, dividing his time between them and driving intruders from both. If two females are also involved, this, incidentally, is probably the underlying cause of some of the occasional two-egg clutches. On the other hand, he may persistently drive away the owning female if there is one.

A prospecting intruder is usually sleek and long-necked (a posture correlated with anxiety and the tendency to flee) and even if he ventures to display it is recognisably different from that of an established bird. He peers around and frequently headshakes (q.v.). After a few minutes he may suddenly leave, without any obvious external stimulus and without the posturing (described later) which normally precedes departure. On the other hand much depends on the status of his immediate neighbours. Young birds (three or four years old) wandering in the fringe, may stay for a while in any vacant spot, Bow and actually menace newly-settled neighbours, but such males chancing across an empty site in a well-established group are very unlikely either to Bow or menace.

The spatial disposition of sites in such a fringe is constantly changing, the boundaries still fluid. Changes occur with bewildering speed and unless an observer has kept his eye fixed on a site he cannot be sure that the male he sees now is the same individual as two minutes ago. The situation is further complicated by equally fickle females prospecting for mates (see Pair Formation, p. 175).

It is difficult to discover for how long a new male must be allowed to remain on a site before his attachment hardens sufficiently to compel him to fight in its defence, but it is certainly at least a few hours and probably two or three days or more. Early in the season an established site is rarely unattended for more than about a day. Even if the female is not yet back, the male can subsist on relatively short foraging trips unless the weather is very stormy, in which case virtually all the gannets leave. Strife is further mitigated by the tendency of young males to return to the breeding colony only after most of the old males are back in residence.

It is probably extremely rare for a young male to return to the colony and eventually build on the first site he acquires. Commonly, males wander in the fringe, or among the ledges on a cliff face, and settle, for short periods—a few days or even weeks—in several places, late in the season prior to the one in which they form a firm attachment to a single site. This is in effect a gradual transition from the behaviour shown by young males in the Clubs (q.v.) where extremely temporary sites are held wherever the Club happens to be located, depending on wind direction. Although it is impossible to show that a four- or five-year-old *never* comes back for the first time and straightaway acquires a definitive site, since one can never know what he did the year before, one may safely assume that a male who apparently suddenly develops an interest in a site, remains on it and begins to defend it, has gone through all the motions elsewhere before, probably several times, though with less motivation.

2. *Flight-circuiting*

Having chosen a site, the male gannet proceeds to establish himself. Flight-circuiting, a pattern invariably associated with this phase, is by no means obvious, yet very important. The bird takes off, flies round once or twice and lands again. Each time he comes in to land he begins calling loudly on the approach run. The strident calls, given about four times per second, accelerate and become louder just before landing, which is followed by a display Bowing (see below). He does this repeatedly, not just when returning from foraging or bathing, etc.

Since gannets certainly recognise each other's voices (White 1971) Flight-circuiting must obviously result in a bird becoming known to neighbours (an important aspect of establishment) but this is not its sole function. It is also an alternative method of maintaining vigilance and may be adaptive in providing a new male with easy opportunities for dislodging intruders. I recorded many instances of males leaving their sites, only to descend from the air the moment an intruder stepped onto the site. Such behaviour helps to harden the owner's site attachment. Flight-circuiting therefore must be considered as a discrete and adaptive piece of behaviour and not just a matter of stretching a limb now and again.

Finally, it may be compulsorily associated with being a lone, site-owning male. An old male who in April lost a mate of long standing, began Flight-circuiting repeatedly, all day and every day. In effect having become a single male he was re-establishing his site prior to forming a partnership. This same situation was observed on other occasions, though less dramatically because the males concerned gained new mates more quickly. This suggests that it may advertise the male's condition to prospecting females, for, although gannets have a close-range advertising display (p. 176) a lone male in the middle of a nesting mass would be very inconspicuous. Circuiting and landing could thus be highly functional in pair-formation as well as site advertising.

Site establishment involves other readily recognisable behaviour which, together with the length of time spent on the site, shows whether birds are in earnest or mere casual visitors. A male laying claim to a spot, which in the early stages may be simply a patch of grass without distinguishing features, calls as he flies in and makes a characteristic nest-biting movement after landing there. If there is no nest material he bites the ground or makes intention movements of doing so, still calling loudly, and this biting has also given rise to a more elaborate display Bowing (p. 166). Males bent on establishing a site threaten other males wandering nearby, Bow frequently and when relatively idle stand in a relaxed manner with retracted neck, preen or sleep. By contrast, an intruder or casual visitor lands without calling or nest-biting and stands in the anxiety posture, scanning the neighbourhood. He does not Bow or show marked aggression towards birds nearby but is, on the contrary, easily displaced by challengers. Since individuals later establishing themselves first come to sites as casual visitors it follows that the transitional stages are difficult to recognise.

3. *Fighting behaviour*

In defence of their sites gannets commonly fight with almost incredible ferocity. It will later become apparent that site competition and its associated aggression have been very important factors in the shaping of gannet pair and social behaviour and it is therefore appropriate to stress the unusually high premium which natural selection has evidently placed on fighting. Serious fighting is very much the exception among animals. Yet of 53 sites whose establishment was followed in detail, 34 were known to involve at least one fight and a total of 57 fights were recorded—and this was only an unknown proportion of the true figure.

Gannets are highly gregarious when fishing, gathering nest material or resting on the sea. Yet, although they may snatch grass or food from each other there is virtually never even mild fighting. When breeding birds meet on the fringe of the colony, perhaps en route to a take-off point, they are not aggressive. Yet on their sites they become fiercely hostile. The following account refers to fights on flatter ground rather than cliff ledges.

Fighting often begins after high intensity threat behaviour but often one bird lands and dashes straight against the other. The combatants interlock bills and attempt to drive each other from the nest or site; strong pushing movements of the legs, with feet curved for better grip, are transmitted to the opponent through straining body and extended neck. The wings thresh the ground and the tail is spread and depressed for increased leverage. Although the beak is the focal point for attack, other parts of the face, head and neck are also seized; the birds shift grip with amazing speed and intersperse slashes, stabs and worrying or shaking movements (exactly like those used to subdue large fish) with the main, tense pushing. On flat ground fights may continue without respite for two hours or so, but most last between 5 and 20 minutes. The extreme length of some fights is partly due to the surroundings (they would fall off a cliff ledge) but also to a strong tendency shown by dominant rivals to deny escape to the opponent. Even when the latter tries to pull loose and flee the other hangs on or pursues him and renews the struggle. This may be to inflict a sound defeat and lessen the chance of further challenge from that rival. This behaviour is carried to its extreme when both birds fall over the cliff and one renews the attack on the sea or, if the rival takes to flight, in mid-air. There may be determined and lengthy aerial pursuit, with attempts to grapple, following fights on the sea.

During fights damage is inflicted on both combatants by surrounding birds, particularly where the head of one is held as it were on the chopping block of the opponent's beak. But it should not be inferred that the extended neck enables one to thrust away the opponent whilst

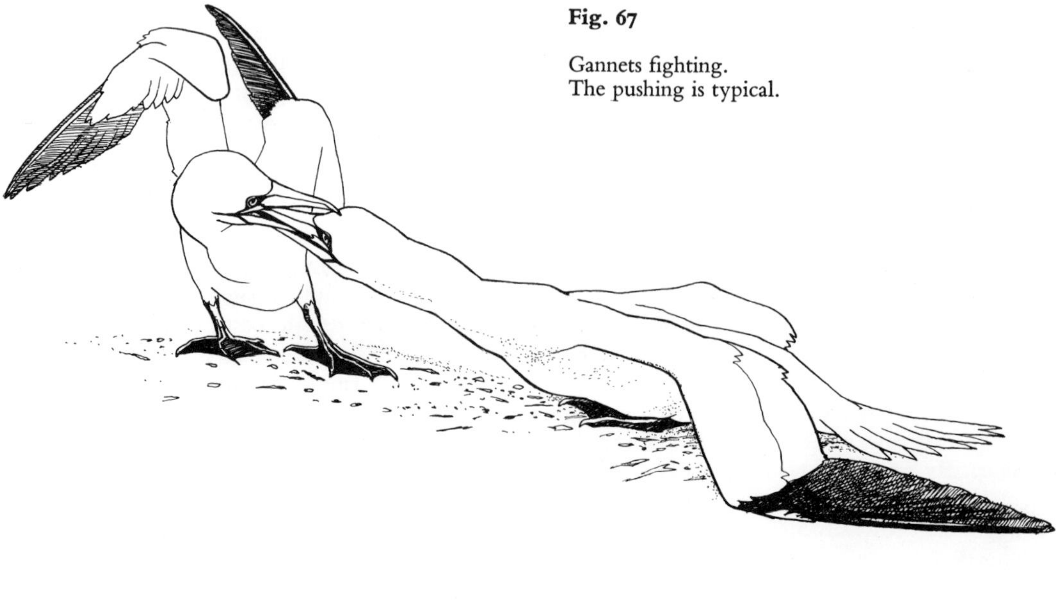

Fig. 67

Gannets fighting.
The pushing is typical.

itself remaining on the site, for the winning bird makes no attempt to do so, on the contrary, he drives his opponent before him, ignoring the bites of enraged neighbours.

This method of fighting is well suited for displacing an opponent from a cliff ledge, and probably evolved in the context of cliff-nesting (like the kittiwake's comparable method of 'twisting' an opponent off the ledge (Cullen 1957)). The apparently dysgenic severity of fights on flatter parts of the colony may be because the fighting method evolved in a different context in which an important factor was the tendency to fall or be pushed off the ledge, so ending the struggle. Gannets sometimes attempt to displace opponents by diving on to them in a typical shallow fish-hunting dive. Whereas this is effective against a ledge opponent it is of course futile on flat ground.

The eyelids do not protect the eyes during fighting but the semi-transparent nictitating membrane is drawn across as a reflex response to any anticipated contact. The lens can withstand fierce jabs. Gannets certainly do not avoid each other's eyes when fighting, or for that matter when mutual preening. Birds caught whilst sleeping off the effects of a severe fight (which they sometimes do for three days) often bore nasty wounds; in one most of the eye tissue was hanging out of the socket (Fig. 69) another had the eye socket filled with blood and a third had an opaque eye. Many others had deep cuts in the facial soft parts and one had a deep peck wound near the oil gland. The head is often pock-marked and bleeding where neighbours have stabbed it hard. One bird died from a peck wound in the abdomen. Extreme exhaustion and filthy, tattered wing and tail feathers caused by the wild threshing are further consequences underlining the severity of these titanic struggles. Yet it should also be said that adult mortality due to fighting is totally insignificant; a male which spiralled 300 feet into the sea, with its plumage glued together with mud after a fight, returned immaculate after two days!

On only one occasion did a serious fight end in a draw. An established male who had lost his mate returned, in April, after an unduly long absence, to find a pair on his nest. They had been there for some considerable time, and therefore fought vigorously, but the original owner would not succumb and eventually the conflict ended with the two parties crouching at opposite sides of the nest drum. Neither male left the site at all during the ensuing three days, after which they began to 'split' it into two. The original owner acquired a mate on his 'new' site.

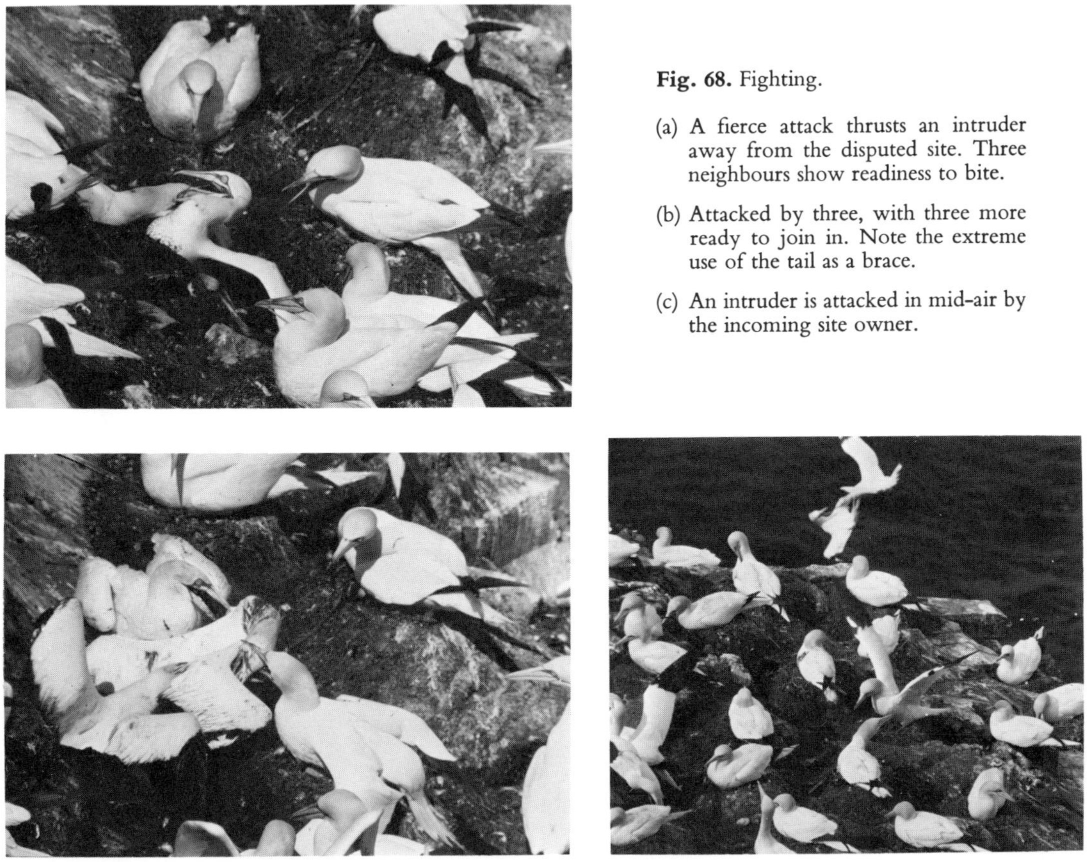

Fig. 68. Fighting.

(a) A fierce attack thrusts an intruder away from the disputed site. Three neighbours show readiness to bite.

(b) Attacked by three, with three more ready to join in. Note the extreme use of the tail as a brace.

(c) An intruder is attacked in mid-air by the incoming site owner.

Most of the foregoing applies equally to fights between females. Although the majority of female fights occurred in the presence of the male, females will certainly defend the site against other females. Although they were occasionally observed to drive away males, a serious male: female fight was never seen; either the male withdrew upon the initial attack or the female accepted an intruding male (see Pair Formation, p. 175). Females fighting in the presence of a male (but not vice versa) were unwilling to carry the fight off the site. Usually they pushed up against the male and would endure tremendous attack from the rival so long as they could remain in this position. Here it was apparently the male rather than the site for which they were contesting. In his absence, females showed the male pattern of fighting, pursuing the opponent some distance from the site.

In fights between females the one willing to accept the greatest punishment usually won, though not necessarily the rightful owner or the most aggressive (by vigour of attack). The same quality helps such a female to form a pair with an aggressive male and is thus doubly valuable. The male tends to switch his attack to whichever female is losing at the time. He is obviously puzzled and shows conflict behaviour throughout (nest building movements, comfort movements and so on). Occasionally, in the heat of the struggle, both females mistake the male for the opponent and by the fury of their combined attack drive him ignominiously from the site.

Fig. 69

Adult gannet (alive) with left eye badly damaged through fighting.

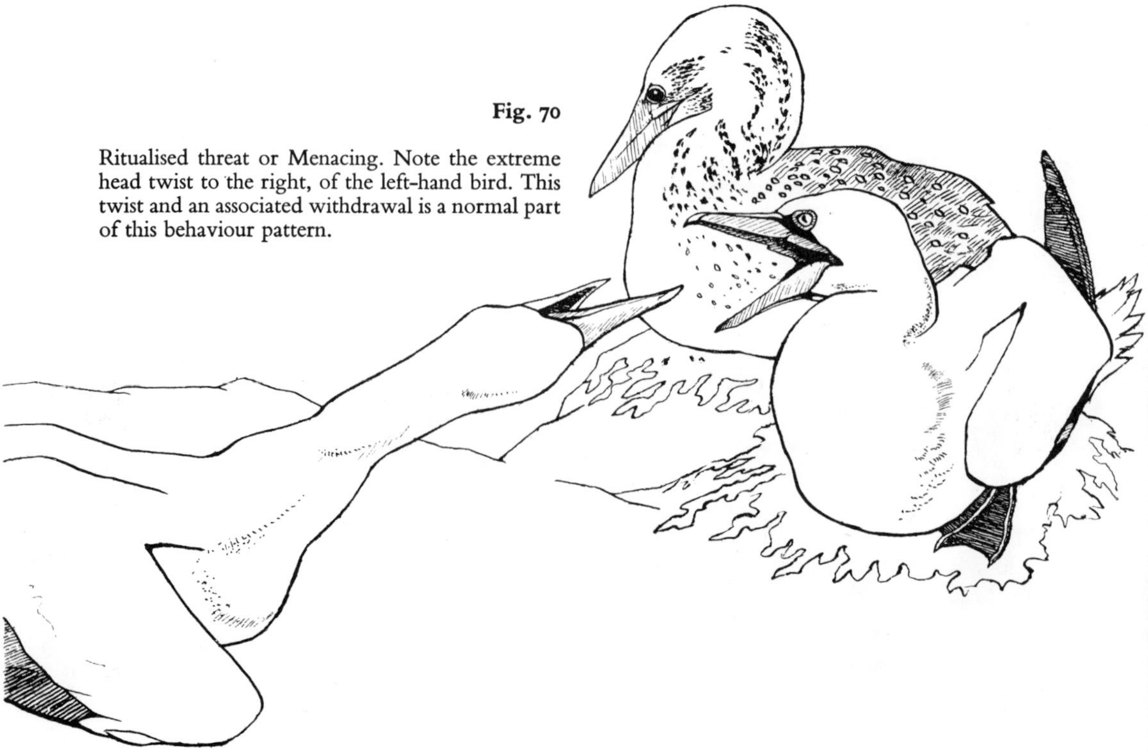

Fig. 70

Ritualised threat or Menacing. Note the extreme head twist to the right, of the left-hand bird. This twist and an associated withdrawal is a normal part of this behaviour pattern.

In sum, fighting in the gannet is uncommonly severe; it is an effective method of settling site disputes and is probably adapted to cliff nesting, which would explain some of the features, including biologically undesirable severity on flat ground. There are sex differences in fighting procedure.

4. *Threat behaviour* (*Menacing*)

Fighting is the final arbiter, not infrequently called during those first critical weeks, but it is the crudest, most damaging and costly method of retaining territory. Threatening behaviour between neighbours consists of incipient overt aggression—as though a real fight were imminent—and a stylised form of Menacing (Fig. 70).

Incipient aggression is intermediate between fighting and stylised Menacing and mostly occurs as high intensity antagonistic behaviour between newly-established pairs or strong rivals. The rival is threatening by thrusting towards him a widely opened bill whose lower mandible may twitch spasmodically. Often there is actual jabbing or gripping. This behaviour is accompanied by strident calling which, from its occurrence in other situations, one can recognise as aggressive/fearful. This behaviour is not really suitable for quantitative analysis because it is relatively infrequent and unstereotyped.

Stylised Menacing is highly stereotyped. Gannets Menace from standing, sitting and incubating positions. In encounters between equals the beak is opened and thrust with a marked sideways twist of the head towards the opponent and then withdrawn. The withdrawal is clearly a 'pre-set' part of the behaviour and does not depend on aggressive reaction from the opponent. The sideways twist and withdrawal are ritualised exaggerations of Menacing and probably enhance its signal value. Although one bird initiates the Menacing bout, the movements of the participants often synchronise. Although near enough to bite, established birds rarely do so in these encounters—hardly surprising when one realises that during the nesting season each bird Menaces and is Menaced thousands of times. Every bird, during the daylight hours spent singly on the nest throughout the season, Menaces a neighbour on average more than once per hour. The value of ritualisation is evident here, since it would be extremely wasteful if even a small proportion led to real fighting.

Pairs Menaced pairs about half as frequently, but when they did so both birds Menaced their own sex most, as one would expect from the nature of the pair relationship. Singles were more likely to be Menaced by pairs (if adjacent) than by other singles and were also more likely to be seized. High-intensity Menacing between hostile birds is associated with head-shaking, frequent touching of nest material, repeated Pelican Postures (see later) and Bowing.

The form of Menacing, the situations which elicit it and the actual attack to which it may lead show that it is at least partly aggressively motivated. Although clearly hostile (all stages between ritualised Menacing and fierce fighting occur), it acquires certain overtones during the course of co-existence with neighbours. Whilst even slight intrusion immediately elicits full threat behaviour, perfunctory Menacing occurs on countless occasions, sometimes without visible cause, at very low intensity and without calling. Indeed, during quiet periods when birds are incubating peacefully, it is not uncommon for one to tweak another's tail, eliciting in reply a slow, gentle-looking Menace. In such cases its ritualised nature is clearly evident, for there is never any chance of real aggression. Fig. 72 shows the seasonal incidence of Menacing. The higher incidence towards the beginning and end of the season corresponds with a similar trend in Bowing partly due to internal factors and to the relatively high level of external stimuli eliciting aggression at these times (wandering birds, prospectors and so on).

Menacing helps to ensure the characteristically regular spacing-out within the colony. The most intense and prolonged (half an hour or more) bouts occur when site boundaries are least well-defined, soon after establishment. Such behaviour may even prevent successful breeding by squeezed-in pairs and, though rarely, hostility by neighbours may drive away a nearby pair. Although in breeding groups on flatter ground each nest is normally just beyond practicable jabbing distance of the neighbours, inserted pairs once accepted may be tolerated even when the wing tip or tail actually touches a neighbour. Again, even stereotyped reaction shows modifications which could lead to important changes in habit (here, denser nesting).

5. *Bowing*

As in most birds and despite the fighting and Menacing, gannet aggression on the site mainly takes the form of displays. The commonest and most conspicuous of these may be descriptively termed Bowing (the 'wing bow' of Perry 1948, and the 'curtsy' of Fisher & Lockley 1954, and Warham 1958). This movement plays an important part in the gannet's social behaviour and also well illustrates several general points concerning displays. The following account covers the form, frequency (including diurnal and seasonal variation), motivation, function and derivation of Bowing.

A full male Bow (Fig. 73) is a stereotyped movement taking four to twelve seconds and performed from a standing position with neck slightly elongated but not stretched as in the 'anxious' long-necked position. The first movement is usually a sideways headshake, starting slowly and increasing in speed and amplitude. The bill is inclined slightly downwards or sometimes held horizontally. After one to five headshakes the head and thorax sweep smoothly forwards and downwards alongside either wing or foot[1] (occasionally between the feet), usually with the bill in the median line, but sometimes pointing a little to one side. This 'bow' gives the movement its distinctive character, the whole forepart of the body moving, not just the head. Often the tail is raised or even cocked vertically, possibly for balance. Between each downward movement, of which there are three or four (termed 'dips' to distinguish them from the entire performance or 'bow'), the head is raised and shaken rapidly from side to side.

During the Bow the wings are held away from the body, either widely spread or merely hanging loosely. Commonly, the wing tips are crossed and the carpal joints held well away from the body, the bird, from behind, resembling an equilateral triangle. As the Bow proceeds the wings often open more widely.

After the final dip the wings are folded and the bill tip pressed tightly against the upper breast in a Pelican Position (Fig. 74(c)) (65 per cent were followed by this posture). Usually the bill tip lies to the same side of the median line as the dips and sometimes even points to the wing-bow. The Pelican Posture is held for two to four seconds, then gradually relaxed. Finally the tail may be shaken from side to side (24 per cent of 372 cases). Often several Bows are given in quick succession (27 in 27 minutes was the maximum recorded for one individual). During the Bow the gannet calls *urrah* loudly 10 to 30 times.

Certain individuals showed consistent and permanent peculiarities in their Bows from year to year. One male had a high-flinging, rapid head-shake. Another bowed lazily with the wings only a little open and with never more than two dips. Others were distinguished by stance, speed, direction and extent of dip, movement of wings and silent Bowing. Thus, even within a stylised display one finds individual differences, possibly heritable, which could form material for selective modification comparable to that which has produced the Bow in its present form.

The intensity of Bowing may be gauged by counting the number of dips, classifying the extent of the wing-opening, timing the duration of the Pelican Posture and, somewhat arbitrarily, dividing performances into 'co-ordinated' and 'unco-ordinated' (a measure of muscular control in terms of jerkiness or smoothness, hesitancy or assurance which is useful in distinguishing between the Bows of males varying in status). Finally, it is usually possible to

[1] Out of 669 recorded, 44 per cent dipped to the right and 56 per cent to the left. This difference is statistically highly significant but puzzling. Warham (1958) also noticed this tendency.

Fig. 71(a). Two adults begin low-intensity territorial hostilities. The left-hand bird is averting its bill most.

(b). Ritualised threat.

(c). The rivals simultaneously thrust their beaks at each other and twist them sideways, indicating both aggression and avoidance.

(*a*) (*b*) (*c*)

classify Bows as 'stimulated' when evoked by some external stimulus, such as threat or a neighbour's Bow, or 'endogenous' when performed without any obvious external stimuli. Circumstantial evidence suggests that gannets Bow in the complete absence of external social stimuli. Subliminal stimuli may nearly always be suspected, but seem highly unlikely when isolated males Bow for no obvious reason. Admittedly distant flying birds are always in view, but are hardly likely to influence nesters in this context. I even saw sleeping birds awake, Bow and go back to sleep!

The measures of intensity given above were clearly linked in both sexes and Bows with most dips also showed greater opening of the wings, longer Pelican Postures and more co-ordination. These well-marked differences were measured in many hundreds of Bows from both sexes, though it seems unnecessary here to give a full analysis of the results.

Besides the above correlations, a marked sex difference was found. Male Bows were more intense by all measures (more dips, wings further out, longer Pelican Posture and more co-ordinated) and also three and a half times as frequent in a sample of 1068 Bows. Such sex differences in the same display provide a further measurement of differences between the sexes in site attachment. Males establish the site, spend more time on it and are more faithful to it from year to year. Correspondingly, their site ownership display shows measurably higher intensity. Similarly, the analysis of Bowing components and the measure of its frequency are quantitative assessments of intensity and with enough refinements could enable things like the strength of Bowing tendency in different categories of site owners (new, old, fringe, central, cliff nesting, flat ground nesting) to be more accurately assessed. For example, newly-established males Bowed more frequently than old ones; experienced birds with no egg Bowed more frequently than the same class of bird with egg and the presence of the female reduced Bowing frequency in all categories of males to almost zero (this is mainly because Mutual Fencing took over from Bowing). Also Club males showed only a female-type Bow of low intensity; since the sexual and territorial behaviour of these males is highly transitory it is not surprising to find a territorial display less intense than in established birds.

Bowing shows clear-cut diurnal variation which is partly a result of greater coming and going with attendant territorial stimulation, early and late in the day, but probably also due to a circadian rhythm in general activity.

There is also a marked seasonal pattern to Bowing. Fig. 75 shows that the frequency of Bowing gradually wanes after first return to the site, even before the main egg-laying period, though it continues to decline during incubation. By comparing the incidence of Bowing among birds with and without egg, though otherwise similar, it was shown that broodiness inhibits Bowing. After hatching Bowing increases, but only gradually, probably due to the difficulty of Bowing whilst brooding a small chick. However, birds with infertile eggs show a rise in Bowing as the season progresses, indicating an internal (hormonal) change despite the continuous presence of the egg.

The gradual increase in Bowing frequency following the incubation-low corresponds with a comparable increase in threat behaviour and the length of Mutual Fencing bouts. These latter measures suggest a rise in aggression which, towards the end of the season, could be correlated with both a change in the external stimulus situation (the presence of large chicks or increased trespassing by some adults) and also with a rise in the internal contribution to aggressive behaviour. Oddly enough, however, towards the end of the season, Bowing becomes even *more* frequent than it was in the early days. A gannetry in September, with many young

Fig. 71(d). The thrust-twist often stops short of contact but here beaks are actually gripped, though the right-hand bird is attempting to disengage

(e). Beaks are now averted. Typically displacement nest-touching or building movements follow such an encounter.

(*d*) (*e*)

already departed, is a hive of activity, full of shouting, fighting, displaying and even copulating adults, whilst all the other seabirds have deserted the island. This later flowering of territorial behaviour seems an unusual reversal of the tendency in most seabirds to show a rapid decline even before the culmination of breeding and certainly soon after. On the other hand, many passerines show an autumnal resumption of song, connected with a recrudescence of gonad activity. In the gannet the prolonged and active post-breeding stay at the site must have survival value.

The form of a movement may indicate its motivation, as when obviously related to attack, fleeing and so on. Other criteria include the kind of behaviour with which it is associated in time, either long- or short-term. The circumstantial evidence indicating Bowing to be a mainly aggressive display is as follows. Although Bowing is not obviously a hostile act, it closely resembles nest-biting, which is re-directed aggression. It is elicited by all acts of territorial infringement or the threat of such. The frequency of Bowing increases about tenfold when non-breeding birds fly time and again over a nesting group. A veritable frenzy of Bowing sweeps the group if an over-flying bird crashes among the nesters after catching a down-draught. Even birds landing legitimately on their own site cause increased Bowing locally. The approach of an unmated female to a receptive male elicits an inhibited form of Bowing, which is in fact his advertising display, whilst in established pairs the arrival of the mate immediately gives rise to a prolonged meeting ceremony which is also a modified form of Bowing. In all these different circumstances, therefore, the approach of another individual elicits Bowing or related behaviour.

There is a long-term association between the frequency of Bowing and other manifestations of aggression. First, the seasonal pattern of Bowing follows that for Menacing and where two (or more) behaviour patterns vary in the same way throughout a season parallel long-term changes in motivation are probably involved. Second, when Bowing is most frequent (seasonally) Mutual Fencing bouts are longest (see p. 186) and the length of these depends on the amount of aggression between the sexes, though it may also be correlated with differences in sexual tendency. So again, aggression and increased Bowing are apparently correlated. Cross checks like these are some test of the accuracy of interpretations about any single behaviour pattern. Thus the frequency of Bowing, Menacing and Mutual Fencing all rise together, but independently of, say, comfort behaviour, a phenomenon which can be relatively simply explained if these three behaviour patterns share aggression as a common causal factor.

One cannot necessarily conclude that when the frequency of Bowing is low (as during incubation) aggression has declined. The actual expression of hunger, fear, aggression, and so on reflects both the strength of the readiness to respond and the external stimulus situation (perhaps further complicated by whatever other drive systems happen to be interacting with these at the time). For example, the aggression of a male stickleback *Gasterosteus aculeatus* to other *males* may remain high or even rise, at the same time as his aggression towards a *female* declines. These points may make it unnecessary to invoke complicated seasonal fluctuations in the internal motivation contributing to Bowing.

Bowing and aggression are also linked during short periods of time, since Bowing is highly predictable in certain situations associated closely with overt aggression which it accompanies or follows rather than precedes. After intense fights the winner Bows frequently; Bowing is interspersed between bouts of jabbing and also in Menacing matches; it often

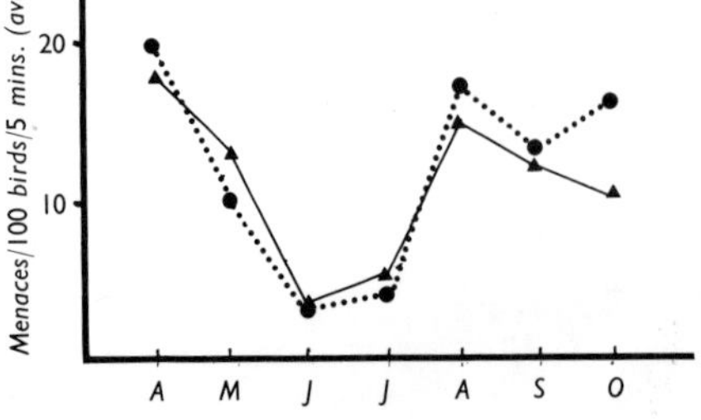

Fig. 72

The seasonal pattern of Menacing in two groups of gannets.

accompanies attacks on chicks; it is often performed by males alighting on their unguarded nest sites, a situation in which they commonly first show aggressive nest-biting. Also, if the female is on guard the male bites her fiercely before taking part in the meeting ceremony which, as noted above, is a modified form of Bowing. In all the above cases aggression and Bowing are closely linked.

After a fight only the winner, now occupying the site, Bows, but if the contestants are neighbours, both owning sites and ready to continue the fight (i.e. still aggressive), *both* Bow. Occasionally two males fight to exhaustion and both leave the disputed site, in which case *neither* Bows. Thus without aggression and the nest site with which it is associated gannets do not Bow. The increased frequency of Bowing after fighting does not merely reflect a *general* arousal of all behaviour. Other behaviour patterns (except nest-touching and aggressive nest-biting from which Bowing is probably derived) are then absent and re-appear only as Bowing wanes.

In many animals aggressive displays are also thought necessarily to involve some element of fear or escape motivation. In the gannet, matched antagonists consistently Bow away from each other which probably indicates some avoidance of a potentially dangerous opponent. Many fights are started or renewed in response to the challenge of disputed ownership, signalled by Bowing, and it would be hardly surprising if, in that situation, a fear element should form part of the motivation of Bowing. We might therefore look for a component most exaggerated when occurring in response to some fear and perhaps reflecting escape or appeasement behaviour in some form.

The Pelican Posture is just such a regular and conspicuous component of Bowing. Often when a Pelican Posture occurs by itself it does so most intensively in frightened birds. Its position at the end of Bowing fits with expectation, since at that point the Bowing bird might be attacked. This view accords with the observation that 'stimulated' bows incorporate Pelican Postures more often than do 'endogenous' Bows (70 per cent as against 57 per cent in males, 34 per cent as against 21 per cent in females) and stimulated Bows were more likely to be unco-ordinated—a feature which might be expected from behaviour performed under some stress, here probably fearful rather than anything else. Further, the Pelican Postures were of longer duration when following stimulated Bows (however, see p. 173).

Direct proof of the function of complex displays is seldom possible and few authors attempt to demonstrate the accuracy of their functional interpretations of bird displays. Some

Fig. 73. Gannet neighbours Bowing. This display indicates ownership of a site.

(e.g. obviously aggressive but nonetheless ritualised behaviour such as Menacing) hardly need demonstration. Bowing in the gannet is a predictable response to certain recurrent situations already mentioned, and all the evidence suggests that it functions as an ownership display of the 'distance evoking' type to repel potential intruders. Indeed (apart from obvious exceptions) Bowing is the only behaviour pattern entirely restricted to the site. The chance observation of an unusual incident strikingly confirmed site and Bowing relationship. An adult alighted on a piece of floating driftwood and Bowed several times. Two or three others attempted to displace it; one succeeded and immediately Bowed. He, in turn, was deposed and the new 'owner' Bowed. Yet the usual behaviour after alighting at sea is a comfort movement, never Bowing. The piece of wood was clearly treated as a temporary territory. Similarly, at feeding time the male of my pair of captive one-year-old birds often Bows where the fish is.

Bowing is most marked when there are strong ownership ties plus the need to display ownership. Males do it more than females, and especially males establishing a site, when there is more likelihood of challenge. Thus males newly-establishing themselves Bow more than males re-establishing themselves on sites held previously. Also those periods when most trespassing occurs, early and late in the season (e.g. during periods of increased 'site interest' when birds are taking advantage of absentees to steal nest material), are precisely when Bowing is most frequent.

Turning to the effect of Bowing on other individuals, we find that the necessary choice situations cannot be observed except by rare chance; the simple question, 'which of two birds, one Bowing and the other not, is avoided by a third?', is meaningless in practice. All birds within the breeding colony, Bowing or otherwise, are avoided by all others except their mate and rivals. In the case of the latter Bowing elicits attack rather than avoidance. Yet we would not say that Bowing functions in attracting rivals. Rather it is because the rival recog-

Fig. 74

(a) High-intensity Bowing (found only in males). The headshake takes the bill almost to the vertical and the wings are held far out.

(b) The beginning of the downward dip; the bird is calling loudly.

(c) The Bow terminates with this bill-tucking or Pelican Posture.

nises the display that he attacks and disputes the other's claim. In much the same way some song birds will permit a rival on their territory so long as he does not make some provocative gesture like singing. This attack-eliciting property of Bowing in a balanced aggressive situation is very striking and leaves no doubt that the Bowing has effected a response, of a kind entirely to be expected where both are 'rightful' owners. Only in unequal situations should one expect to find that Bowing repels the inferior bird.

The above evidence supports the view that Bowing is connected with establishment and defence of territory. In this respect it is equivalent to the agonistic displays of many passerines, gulls, waders and so on. A difference of note, however, is that in many passerines and gulls (the kittiwake is particularly comparable because of its colonial and cliff nesting habits) the 'song' or ownership display is also the advertising display by which females are attracted, whereas in the gannet the two displays are quite distinct although the advertising display is a modified form of Bowing.

To sum up, the situations in which Bowing occurs, the conditions which increase its frequency and the effect on other birds may be consistently interpreted to show that it functions in signifying site ownership and preventing site usurpation.

As to derivation, Daanje (1950) in a well known paper, showed how locomotion intention movements can give rise to displays and Tinbergen (1952) has discussed in detail the ways in which displays may (or possibly *must*) be derived from simple behaviour patterns (such as intention movements and displacement activities) which may then be so greatly exaggerated or changed that their origin becomes difficult to trace (see also p. 224).

Two parts of the Bow may be traced back to such simple behaviour. First, the actual dip or curtsy, which is the most conspicuous element and has given the display its name, is actually modified ground or nest-biting which in turn is re-directed aggression akin to the grass pulling of the herring gull. Many of the dips performed during Bowing do in fact terminate in actual biting of the ground or, in some cases biting movements just clear of the rock surface. This type of Bowing is typical of a site owner immediately after landing, particularly early in the season. One knows from other evidence that an incoming male is aggressive, particularly early in the season. Other typical contexts are after a fight or high intensity aggressive interaction or after regaining the nest when knocked off it by accident (due to a fracas or a departing bird). In these situations the bird is aggressive and his Bow loses its fully ritualised nature and becomes more like overt aggression, though directed onto a substitute object. This seems good reason to suggest that it is from such 'primary' behaviour, in the very situations chiefly eliciting aggressive site-ownership signals, that the more polished Bowing has been derived. Now, in less stressful contexts, the dip no longer touches the ground and the bill no longer makes biting movements, the whole performance looking smooth and more relaxed. By watching a series of Bows in suitable contexts, one can actually see, in the same individual, the Bows gradually change in character from the ground-biting and jerky type to the smoother, more stylised version.

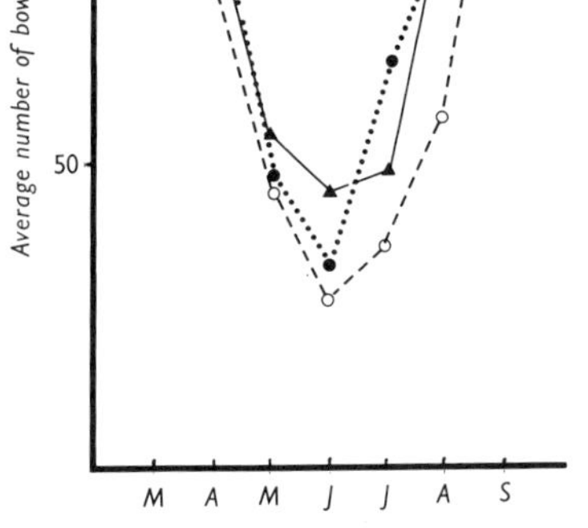

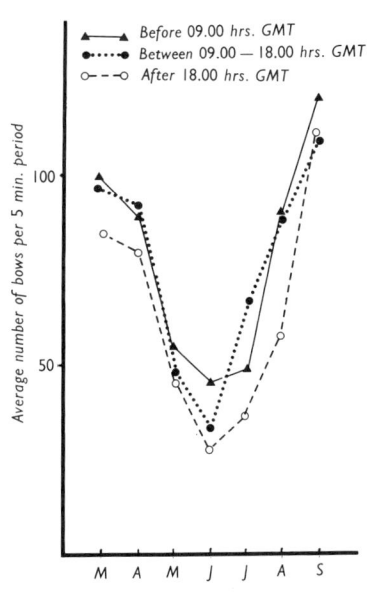

Fig. 75

The seasonal and daily pattern of Bowing.

Further, it is always the male who is in the throes of establishing his site, often in the teeth of opposition from neighbours, who performs the ground-biting type and the securely established male who performs the polished Bows, not the other way round. It is important that the nature of the dip should be clearly established because it occurs in modified form in other displays, the correct interpretation of which hangs on the nature of this simple little movement.

The second part of the Bow, which has also arisen from a simple, originally non-signal movement, is the headshake. Gannets shake their heads from side to side to dispel water or dirt and biting the muddy ground or nest is the appropriate stimulus to elicit headshaking. A ground-biting type of dip would thus be followed by a vigorous, cleansing headshake. Now, the headshake has been retained—or even exaggerated—even where the dip no longer dirties the bill. In this way two simple acts, neither of which were originally ritualised, have been welded together into a single ritualised display. If shaking the foot had happened to be the way to deal with the external stimulus of getting dirt on the bill, then 'dip and footshake' would have formed the raw material for the Bow.

The third part of the Bow, the Pelican Posture, resembles the way in which a chick hides its beak during appeasement behaviour, for example when attacked by an adult. However, the chick tucks its bill medianally beneath its body, whilst crouching or lying, whilst the adult's Pelican Posture is much less extreme—a mere tucking of the bill whilst in an upright posture. Nevertheless, it has probably been derived from infantile beak hiding.

Summarising this complex display: Bowing is a highly stereotyped, largely aggressively motivated display which signifies ownership of a site and so repels potential intruders. It consists of several components which occur, discretely, in other contexts and have been welded together to give Bowing.

This concludes the analysis of discrete behaviour patterns which are specifically concerned with establishing and maintaining a site; reconnaissance (aerial and ground), Flight Circuiting, fighting, stylised threat behaviour and Bowing. Many other behaviour patterns are performed on it and help to form the attachment to it, but are more suitably considered under Pair Formation (p. 175). Before this, however, the Pelican Posture is best described here, because of its connection with Bowing and the subject of attendance at the site is also most relevant to this section.

6. *Pelican Posture*

The posture which terminates the Bow may be described as bill tucking or the Pelican Posture. The bill tip is pressed into the upper breast centrally or to one side in a semblance of the pelican's resting posture (Fig. 74(c)). It also occurs alone in many contexts. It may be held for as long as 20 seconds or expressed fleetingly. After the intense version the bill is lifted slowly and may be quickly returned to the 'tucked' position if the bird is threatened. Sometimes, the slow bill raising accompanies an equally slow turning away from an opponent, often with the same droopy, slow foot movement used in Skypointing. Birds moving in the Pelican Posture usually do so slowly and with wings busked—never with wings held out sideways. Nor do birds ever run in the Pelican Posture. In all these ways it seems to provoke attack as little as possible.

The context of the Pelican Posture may best be described as any situation involving markedly ambivalent fear/aggression motivation. The main difficulty in understanding it is that it occurs both in situations where aggression is clearly the dominant emotion, right across to the opposite end of the spectrum, where fear dominates. Thus, Pelican Postures may occur in the male during and after redirected attack on the female; after notably aggressive copulation; after the eviction of an unwanted female; after a strong attack on a chick or after an attack on say a herring gull which comes too near. On the other hand, intense Pelican Postures are likely to ensue in a bird which has been subjected to violent threat or attack from neighbours; one which has made a bad landing and been roughly handled; or is simply fearful. An example of the latter, a bird landed in the fringe, where he was probably not well established and assumed a deep Pelican Posture, was startled by another gannet flying over, flinched and assumed an even deeper and more protracted Posture, was menaced just as he emerged from this one and immediately assumed yet another. The context indicates so unequivocally that the birds in the first series of examples are almost 'purely' aggressive, whilst those in the second example are equally clearly predominantly fearful, that it becomes difficult to decide just what the motivation is. Nor is this all, since, while the above situations probably involve slight ambivalence, even though fear or aggression as the case may be, is dominant, there are many situations in which these two components are more or less evenly matched and in which Pelican Postures characteristically occur. Thus it frequently occurs in evenly matched aggressive encounters between site establishing birds; in birds trespassing to attack a chick, or in males approaching a threatening female; in males landing on their empty sites where they are liable to attack if another male has acquired an attachment, and the neighbour-scanning eye movements of such males, conducted from a deep Pelican Posture, show that they are very much aware of this possibility. In all such cases there is an obvious source of both fear and aggression.

Finally, it may be added that neither site, mate, the near presence of any other gannet nor the performance of any specific behaviour pattern are necessary to evoke a Pelican Posture.

Without much more detailed evidence it is impossible to understand this obviously complex motivational situation; about all that may safely be said is that the Pelican Posture seems to occur chiefly at times of considerable fluctuation in motivation. It could be produced by the rate at which contributory tendencies are changing, rather than the dominance of any one of them. A male that I happened to see at such a juncture, immediately after the female had laid an egg and moved off it to allow him his first incubation stint, moved onto the egg in a deep Pelican Posture and tucked it beneath his webs. Again the situation was hardly likely to elicit fear or aggression but probably was one of rapid changes in motivation. In other sulids too, there are one or two ritualised postures or movements that occur over a particularly wide range of conditions.

For the same reasons, the function of the Pelican Posture must remain obscure. Nevertheless, it clearly removes the weapon of offence from a potentially attacking position and makes it almost impossible for an opponent to grip and occurs in many situations that could easily degenerate into actual hostilities. So, despite the fact that it occurs in many situations where the bird seems much more likely to be the aggressor than the aggressed, perhaps the most fitting interpretation of function is that it tends to reduce the likelihood of attack or retaliation and is therefore an appeasement posture.

It is difficult to measure its efficacy. It often fails to prevent attack or retaliation and certainly does not stop attacks already launched, nor does it necessarily inhibit the performer from attacking, though it clearly removes the bill away from an antagonist whilst at the same time maintaining full readiness to retaliate. It seems unlikely to function in protecting the eyes and visual field of the bird performing the Pelican Posture.

It is, however, restricted to the above situations. Appeasement postures elicited in other situations (e.g. male aggression to a female) are different in form. It may be significant that these situations mainly lack the aggressive motivation which may be necessary to evoke the Pelican Posture.

It may be noted that of the four possible ways of averting the bill (tucking it, pointing it upwards, turning it to one side and retracting it by drawing the head backwards) the gannet has evolved the first three, though only one (Facing-away) is clearly appeasing and one (Sky-pointing) certainly is not.

7. *Attendance at the nest site*

Gannets spend a phenomenal amount of time at the nest site. It is probably true to say that no other seabird devotes so much time just to being there, regardless of whether they have an egg or chick. In fact, for almost half of the many months during which Bass birds, at any rate, guard their sites, they have neither egg nor young. At this point discussion will be restricted to attendance in relation to site maintenance, leaving details of incubation patterns, chick-guard spells and comparative seasonal attendance at different gannetries to other sections.

(*a*) *Seasonal pattern*

Usually, the first eggs are not laid in Britain until late March or early April, but gannets are back and highly active in January (see Appendix 1).

At this early time in the season gannets are relatively wary and easily scared, often staying on their sites for a few hours only and interspersing these appearances with long absences. Although they are clearly uneasy on the breeding area, they do not show 'rafting' behaviour like that of Manx shearwaters or kittiwakes, which congregate in dense offshore gatherings for some time before the desire to be on the breeding ledges gains ascendancy. Often there are gannets sitting on the sea around the breeding island, maybe in thousands, but they are not in rafts. However, their unease is nevertheless detectable in three ways; first, they show periodic panics, which are probably extensions of their wariness so that even one individual taking fright for some minor reason or perhaps simply through the build-up of tension, triggers a mass departure, the birds flying out to sea with every sign of alarm, including fear calls. Usually most of them return within minutes, but if it happens late in the day, they all stay away till another day. The same tendencies gradually reappear towards the end of the season. Thus they well illustrate the importance of seasonal, internal factors in affecting responses to relatively unvarying external stimuli.

Secondly, there is a notable tendency to occupy cliff sites and particularly mid-cliff sites, before those on flatter ground. This is presumably because the former are easy to get away from and therefore less scaring.

Thirdly, areas (flat ground or cliff) which allow large numbers of birds to nest close to each other are usually re-occupied before those which support merely a small, fairly isolated group, even though this may consist of old and experienced birds at much the standard density. This may be one reason why small gannetries such as Bempton tend to be re-occupied later and deserted earlier than large ones like the Bass, even though climatic conditions are very similar. In the same way, kittiwakes return, first, to the densest parts of their colonies.

Some possible factors controlling the date of return and the pattern of build-up will be discussed when comparing colonies in different areas, but it may be said here that whilst weather in general is doubtless important, it probably exerts its effect by influencing fishing conditions. Certainly all the evidence indicates that even the most severe winter weather does not inconvenience birds at the breeding colony. This makes it difficult to see any obvious and immediate cause and effect relationship between return (and tendency to remain) and weather. Birds returned in January 1963, when severe weather was at its worst and in any winter many remain on their ledges regardless of conditions; gales with sleet and snow do not worry them. Then they may leave for a variable period when the weather may or may not seem bad, returning again and so gradually building up periods of attendance until, by late February, many nests are rarely unattended. Yet, even as late as the second week in April, areas occupied even by old and experienced birds may suddenly become three-quarters empty. At each stage, the precise reasons governing the situation may differ. Thus, absences so late in the year perhaps reflect the need for males to feed heavily after a long and arduous period of attendance—much longer than that of the female—whilst she may be feeding hard in preparation for laying and increased attendance during incubation.

(*b*) *Status and sex differences*

The salient details of site attendance in males and females of different status are given in Fig. 76 and Appendix 1. Experienced males return first and are present most often before egg laying during which period they take considerably longer guard stints than females. The same two differences also hold good for inexperienced males and females. Indeed, for the male, this period is probably the most exhausting part of the entire breeding cycle and could be an important factor in setting the limits for the onset of breeding (on the assumption that the lengthy spells of attendance would not be possible earlier in winter). The experienced or well-established male spends so much time at the site at this stage that it seems impossible he could maintain his body weight and the few figures I have for males weighed early in incubation indicate that they have lost weight (p. 100). This is a more testing time than the period during which they feed the chick, voracious though this is. Some males seem hardly to leave their sites and their absences are often extremely short. In this way they ensure that their ownership of the site remains unchallenged. If a mated male guards his site in this way during April, he will almost certainly breed that year. Conversely, a male who is often away is unlikely to do so.

(*c*) *Diurnal variation in attendance*

During the period when full attendance is building up, morning and evening attendance (Appendix 1) is considerably greater than midday. Evening is the time when the pair is most likely to be in attendance early in the season.

This completes the account of site establishment and maintenance. The unusual importance which the gannet obviously attaches to his site is attested not only by his strenuous defence of it, but by these extra months of attendance before the egg is laid and after the young have flown. When they could be feeding or resting at sea, they are instead fighting or displaying with increased vigour at their empty sites. One must conclude that this enhances their chances of retaining it and that this is a considerable advantage.

FORMATION AND MAINTENANCE OF PAIR

In gannets, pair formation is closely linked with site establishment for, at the same time that males are site-prospecting by aerial and ground reconnaissance, females are looking for males in the same way. One never sees a female attach herself to an unoccupied nest or site, except as a vantage point from which to scan the neighbourhood for receptive males, whose behaviour is easily recognisable (p. 176). Like the male establishing his site, the mate-hunting female may be casual or highly motivated. If the former, she will travel from one male to another. We have recorded a female responding to and accepted by five different males in half an hour. If the latter, she will passively accept prolonged harsh treatment in order to remain close to the male (the ways in which an apparently receptive male may yet attack a responsive female will become clear later). Females prospect right up to the end of a breeding season and

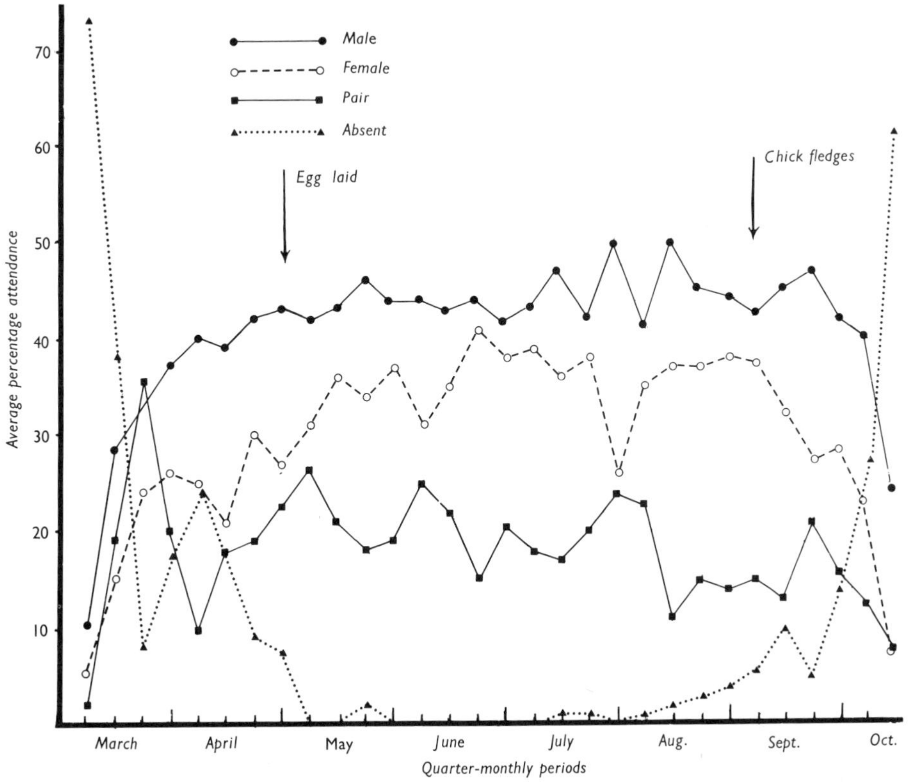

Fig. 76. The seasonal pattern of attendance of established pairs at the nest site (Bass 1962). Note (a) the high level of attendance before the egg is laid and after the chick has fledged; (b) greater attendance of male than female; (c) peak in pair attendance two or three weeks prior to egg laying.

many bonds formed late in the season do not endure the winter separation. Before a pair will breed they must be together a considerable time, which usually means part or all of a season prior to the one in which they first breed, although a few pairs form and breed in the one season.

Pair formation involves a special advertising display by the male, prospecting by a female and a series of interactions which occur after the two have come together. Pair-formation and pair-maintenance are not really separable but are parts of the one ongoing process.

1. *Headshake and Reach*

It might be supposed that for such a vital matter as obtaining a mate, natural selection would have produced a really dramatic display. In fact, it is highly inconspicuous. It consists merely of a side-to-side headshake and a slight reaching movement of the head towards the female (Fig. 77). Since headshaking is one of the commonest things a gannet does, the advertising display scarcely stands out, and one has to be able to recognise a slightly emphatic form of the ordinary headshake, plus the hint of a 'reach'. There is no doubt, however, that it is a specific signal, which the ordinary headshake is not. It is not performed solely by unmated males, but also by males temporarily alone on their sites and by males whose mates happen to be nearby but not within their territory (for example, on their way out of the group or having landed off site), and sometimes by females.

The context of the display and associated behaviour indicates that it is sexually motivated but there is good reason to believe that aggressive motivation is also involved. Its function is to attract the female on to the site, or in the case of female's headshaking, to attract the male.

A natural choice situation is often presented to the female, who has the chance to respond either to an advertising male or a male, equally near, who is not advertising. In 74 cases in which females elicited advertising from fringe males 32 per cent approached the advertising male rather than a passive male near-by, a further 41 per cent displayed interest in the advertising male but did not approach and 27 per cent ignored the advertising male. *None* approached a passive male. These figures show that male advertising has a real effect in attracting females.

A major point of interest is the relationship between this display and the site ownership display, Bowing, of which the Headshake and Reach appears to be a modified form. Thus, the downward dip has been greatly reduced and is, in this interpretation, the slight forward

Fig. 77(a). Sexual advertising (Headshake and Reach) has been derived from Bowing (a territorial display). Low-intensity Bowing (shown immediately to the right) resembles the Headshake and Reach but in the latter the wings are opened even less, the forward dip is reduced (to give the Reach) and the side-to-side headshake accentuated.

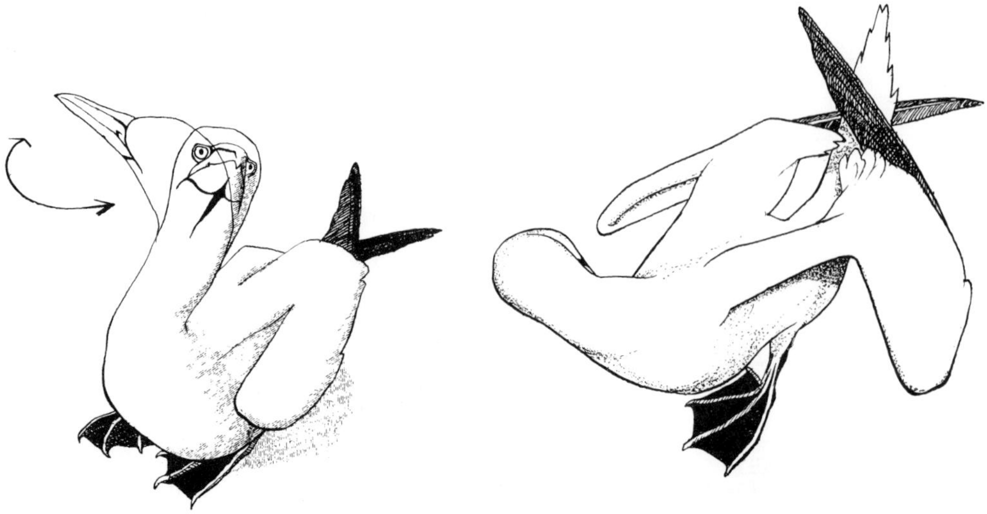

and downward reaching movement. The wings remain folded instead of held out: the display is silent, whereas Bowing is accompanied by strident calling and the headshake is exaggerated in amplitude. Thus Headshake and Reach is Bowing with the aggressive elements eliminated or reduced and the non-aggressive component exaggerated. The dip, here reduced, is the nest-biting movement, clearly aggressive; the strident calling, here omitted, is like that of the overtly aggressive bird (accompanying fighting, jabbing and flying in to the site). The wings-out position in Bowing is not in itself associable directly with aggressive behaviour being perhaps derived from post-landing balance-recovery, but the newly-landed bird is aggressive and the degree to which wings are held out is positively correlated with a direct measure of the intensity of Bowing, namely the number of dips in one Bow. Thus the abolition of a raised wings position in Headshake and Reach is in essence the elimination of a posture with a further aggressive connotation. Only the headshake remains and this is clearly neutral being a dirt-dispelling movement and this it is which has been exaggerated in Headshake and Reach.

This interpretation of observed differences between the two displays fits exactly with reasonable prediction, both on general and specific grounds. In many species the same display functions as male ownership display, repelling rivals, and male advertising, to attract females. Passerine song is an example. Thanks to Tinbergen it has now become common knowledge that much animal display is in fact the result of actions prompted by fear, aggression and sexual motivation in different balance according to the sum of the external and internal stimuli at the precise moment in question. Several complex sequences have been analysed using this concept and found to be explicable in terms of it. So it would not be in the least surprising if the aggressive site ownership display and the sexual, advertising one were linked in the gannet. In particular in a species proved to be exceptionally aggressive in defence of its territory and in which the female looks almost indistinguishable from a male, it is to be expected that an approaching, or potentially approaching, female would elicit site ownership, repelling display from the male. Since the 'message' conveyed by the Bow is incompatible with the close proximity necessary for pair formation, the Bow has become modified by the suppression of the distance-evoking components and the exaggeration of the neutral one and the net result is a display which looks like greatly inhibited Bowing. The implication that sex motivation has partially inhibited aggression fits with much of ethological observation and accords also with many details of gannet interactions, to be discussed.

2. *Female prospecting*

Female gannets must perform the initial searching to obtain a mate since the male cannot, except fortuitously, contact her away from the site. This is a quite different situation from that in, for example, the black-headed gull, which has special pairing territories, or some auks (puffins, razorbills and guillemots) and terns which perform aerial flights together; these may well forge the initial link, the birds subsequently going to a nesting area and acquiring a site. Male shags may lead the female to the nest site after contacting her away from it and shelducks pair-off on the mudflats and then house-hunt. In the gannet, the male remains on his definitive site and the female must come to him.

Fig. 77(b). Bird 1 is Reaching and bird 2 Headshaking, both of them to the same female (out of the picture).

Fig. 77(c). Male advertising (right foreground) eliciting movement towards him from the neighbouring female, who is Sky-pointing (a posture which precedes movement).

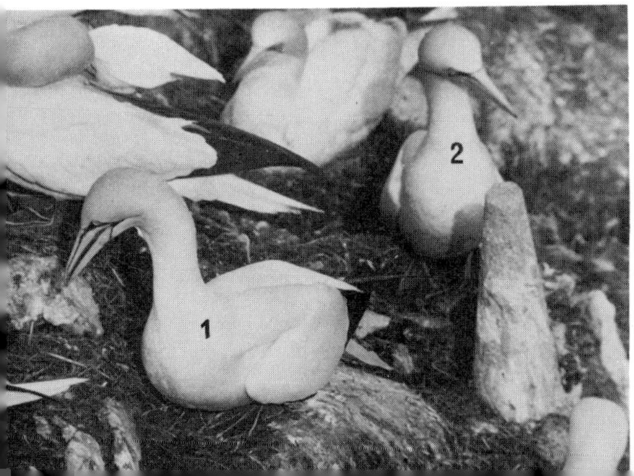

Prospecting females, mainly four or five years old are not present at the colony in large numbers until April (females return later than males); in February and March bereaved, established males may wait more than two weeks before acquiring a new female.

Before landing in or near a breeding group they often fly over and probably land and take-off repeatedly before approaching a male. Like site-searching males they know the layout of a small area intimately as shown by the certainty with which they return to a site, once acquired, even in the absence of the male (the alternative, that females almost instantly acquire a 'photographic' imprint of the area at pair formation, is much less probable). This ability is necessary in areas which forbid exploration on foot to correct a wrong landing. Prospecting females land anywhere, not necessarily near an advertising male, then peer around in the typical long-necked anxiety posture, which often releases full advertising from nearby unmated males. The male's advertising is by no means exclusively directed to unmated females and males probably cannot distinguish mated from unmated.

An advertising male stimulates the female to approach, which she does often hesitantly and with small-amplitude head shakes (a sign of conflicting emotions) before finally rushing up in the Facing-away (appeasement) position. Sometimes she merely cranes forward and delicately touches his bill before gradually increasing this to the full meeting ceremony with no prior Facing-away.

Two characteristics of prospecting females are particularly noticeable. First, they are initially ready to accept almost any male, so that should the site change hands (which new sites often do) the female is prepared to stay with the new male; one female began the meeting ceremony with a new male whilst her first mate was still at grips with a challenger! Their extreme responsiveness also facilitates pair formation, since males are usually strictly confined to their sites and have only an inconspicuous behaviour pattern to attract females. Initially, prospecting females show little preference for a particular male and may copulate with five in less than two hours. This promiscuous behaviour resembles that shown by Club females. In the colony proper it has obvious disadvantages and leads to the formation of both kinds of triangular and multilateral associations. Also the female's tendency to break the first few pair-bonds she forms requires the male to continue advertising *after* he has obtained a mate. This often leads to the male acquiring two females and hence to severe female conflicts (out of 57 fights concerned with establishing new pairs, 31 were between females for the above reason). However, the advantages of female opportunism and high responsiveness must presumably favour these traits despite attendant disadvantages.

Second, prospecting females show astonishingly high tolerance of punishment from males and extreme reluctance to retaliate—characteristics which sometimes win acceptance from a hostile male. Clearly, the most aggressive males could only breed and perpetuate this trait to the extent that females were prepared to accept the results of such aggression. The two characteristics, male aggression and female tolerance, must therefore have evolved in linkage.

Although the female approaches, she is clearly afraid, even though the male does not usually threaten her. Her appeasement posture (Facing-away) is mainly a response to an aggressive male and indicates some fear, as does the flurried, flinching nature of her behaviour in the meeting ceremony in which she may also Face-away repeatedly. Occasionally females show slight aggression, though this is rarely detectable. Correspondingly, I could not recognise male fear in the new pair situation.

At this point it is appropriate to describe three behaviour patterns intimately connected with the interactions of male and female during the formation of the pair bond, and indeed afterwards, and already mentioned in passing; male Nape-biting, female Facing-away and the meeting ceremony (Mutual Fencing).

3. *Nape-biting*

The most stereotyped way in which a male gannet 'attacks' his mate is to grip her at the back of the head Fig. 78(a). Whilst this Nape-biting is not far removed from 'ordinary' biting that just happens to find the head, it is nevertheless a ritual in so far as it has become an invariable part of the meeting behaviour, even between old and fully compatible mates. An inexperienced observer would perhaps not, at first, classify it as ritualised because it is not highly stylised (the male may bite high or low, take one jab or two or three and so on) but ritualised it has undoubtedly become, as later discussion will verify. Nevertheless, it remains extremely forceful and anyone who has been properly bitten by a gannet can imagine that it must hurt the female; but perhaps she has protective fat or other device here. He does not intersperse headshaking with this apparently aggressive behaviour and in some cases his biting gradually becomes less vigorous, though even after long periods (up to 30 minutes or more) he may still break out into new attacks with all the initial force. He calls stridently during the most intense phases.

Whilst one readily interprets aggression by a male towards his new mate as territorial behaviour elicited by a relatively strange individual, it does seem remarkable that male gannets should continue to show this aggression towards their mates throughout their period of attachment, which might last a life-time. Thus, in 98 per cent of 294 cases, incoming males bit their females and in 75 per cent of 253 cases incoming females were bitten by their males (the difference may be due to the greater difficulty in biting in the latter situation). Among these hundreds of observations, there was but one record of a male being bitten by his female, who was greatly startled by his arrival. Some authors have implied that the incoming bird bites the bird on the site, but this is not so; only males bite. Further remarks on Nape-biting are made below in the context of the ensuing female appeasement behaviour.

However one may interpret the function of this behaviour (I suggest that it is sexually stimulating because it is linked with actual copulation), Nape-biting is undoubtedly aggressive and shows the same seasonal trends as other aggressively motivated behaviour, namely a greater intensity early and late in the season.

4. *Facing-away*

Females respond to incoming males by rapid headshaking and averting the beak, sometimes lying almost prone in the infantile beak hiding position. When males arrive with nest material females are much less prone to Face-away (only 13 per cent of cases compared with 90 per cent when males arrive without nest material) showing that it is to the prospect of being bitten and not merely to the inflying male that they react.

Facing-away is often only a highly exaggerated flinching, rather than a stylised movement and looks as though the female is merely taking evasive action. At other times, however, it is very pronounced and prolonged and looks as though the female is actually presenting her nape to the male. In such cases she may also push up against him. Established females Face-away, often extremely briefly, when their mate bites them as part of the re-union behaviour, after a fairly long separation (hours or days, rather than minutes). However, when female Facing-away occurs in the context of a delicately balanced relationship, as in some new pairs or would-be pairs, it is extreme in form and is accompanied by pushing-up to the male and by repeated and often violent headshaking. For his part, in such cases, the male prods, bites and seems to exert every ounce of strength to force her away by gripping the skin on her nape and pushing so hard that when she relaxes he leaves the marks of his grip and feathers are dislodged.

Facing-away is clearly partly fear-induced, as shown by its form (avoidance) and context (response to actual attack by the male) but since it occurs only in the heterosexual situation, sex motivation is probably involved also and may even be the dominant motivation. This appears more likely when one realises that Nape-biting and the associated Facing-away are invariably part of the meeting ceremony and of copulation. At first sight, when one sees an aggressive male vigorously attacking a female for 20 or 30 minutes almost without respite and the female merely 'absorbing' this and Facing-away deeply, it may appear to be mainly a fearful reaction, but merely by remaining near to the male and absorbing the punishment, the female clearly shows that she is not merely fearful; she could flee, but she persists in staying.

Her vigorous headshaking is also significant; pronounced sideways headshaking is associated with sexual behaviour—as when females solicit copulation and males Headshake-and-reach to attract females. The idea that it is simply a response to the painful stabs of the male can be dismissed, since headshaking is not seen during fights with other females.

Its form immediately suggests that Facing-away is appeasing behaviour, which would explain why it is not shown to another female. Particularly in the early stages of pair formation, the female is so severely attacked, that any new observer would assume that he was watching a one-sided fight or the eviction of an intruder. Actually, however he would be witnessing the ambivalent response of a male, simultaneously reacting to the intruder qualities of the female and to her sexual status. In such a situation, the motivational conflict is clear to see and indeed the impression that the outcome, acceptance or rejection hangs in the balance, is not fanciful for sometimes the female is evicted despite strenuous Facing-away and sometimes with many a relapse on the part of the male, she gradually wins acceptance. So Facing-away is not dramatically successful in switching off the male's attack and its value as an appeasement posture may thus seem suspect. However, it is often eventually effective in borderline cases which probably means that it has considerable value. Its probable function is to reduce the intensity of male attack in the critical stages of pair formation, rather than to be an automatic switch-off of male attack and it should be emphasised that it is effective only when the male is not too strongly hostile.

In new pairs Facing-away was followed by cessation of male attack in 12 out of 41 cases and failed to stop it in the remainder. These figures cannot be compared with cases in which the female did not Face-away, since these are so rare. If it helped these 12 females to form a pair, it may be considered highly adaptive. Females intruding on to a male's territory (as when two males independently acquire the same site and different females, one of which returns to the 'wrong' male or is present when he returns) are usually displaced (78 per cent of cases) despite conspicuous Facing-away and acceptance of male aggression. So in this situation Facing-away is less effective as appeasement behaviour.

One can easily see that with the male gannet so primed for attack and the female an equally capable fighter, natural selection has necessarily had to ensure that females evolved powerful inhibitions against retaliation, otherwise pair-bonds would snap like gossamer threads. It is in fact extraordinarily impressive to watch an established female Facing-away from an intruding male—because the inhibition against attacking a male on site is so powerful—but immediately striking at him once he has moved off the site, and even more impressive when one knows that females can fight as well as males (they are often slightly heavier and during temporary mix-ups can drive males before them). Comparably, in triangular situations where two females are fighting in the presence of the male, who in obvious bewilderment may attack both with equal vigour, the females usually manage, despite the wild scrimmage, to alternate lightning changes of response—violently counter-attacking the other female but Facing-away from the male. Occasionally mistakes are made and the fight becomes, momentarily, female against male, but soon the appropriate response re-asserts itself in the female and the battle goes its proper way.

Fig. 78(a). Nape-biting; ritualised aggression from male to female (never vice-versa) accompanied by female appeasement (Facing-away).

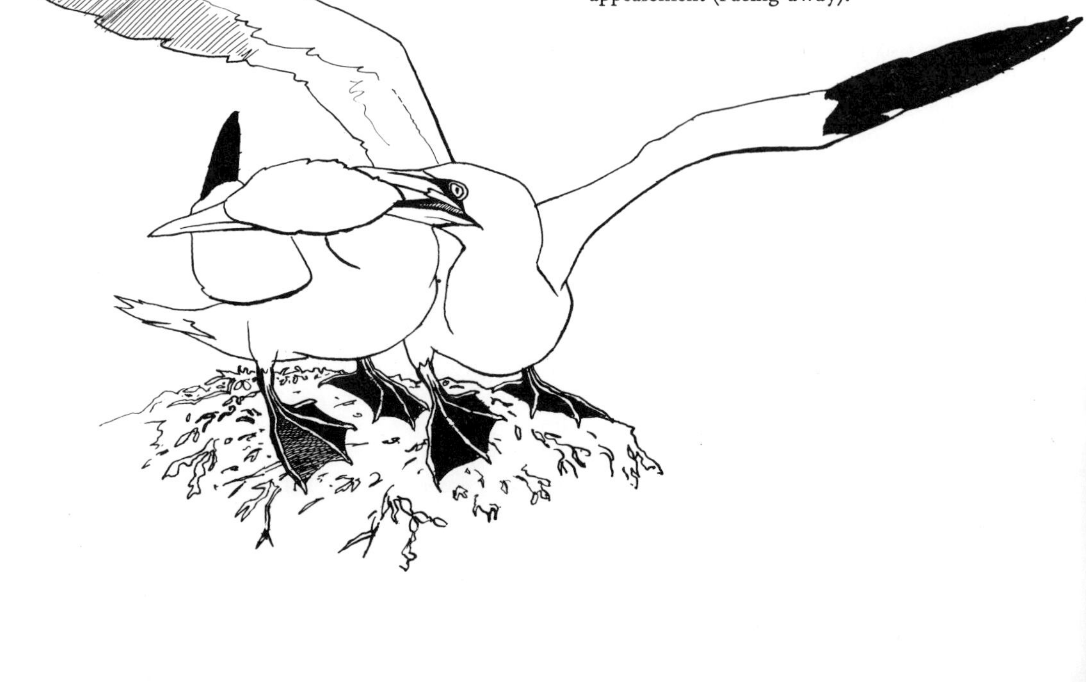

The prolongation of male Nape-biting and female Facing-away throughout the duration of the normal pair bond thus suggests that the simple releasing mechanism—'attack any gannet that comes onto the nest'—has not been susceptible to the drastic modification 'except your partner'! The attack and the appeasing response have remained, but the interaction may have gained additional adaptive value by becoming sexually rewarding to the female (and possibly the male), thus reinforcing the pair bond.

Finally, it should be added that mates do recognise each other, so there can be no question of all females being treated as intruders until, by an appropriate behavioural response, they reveal their true identity as 'the mate'. Thus, as has been proved experimentally, males recognise the voice of their mate as she calls when flying in and Headshake to her before she lands.

5. *Leave and return*

This is an accurate, if inelegant description of a behaviour pattern which is extremely common and in my view important in the early stages of pair formation. At this time, it quickly dawns on the observer that the male is constantly leaving his site, only to disappear for a minute or two and then return, with the usual in-flight calling and biting the female. A colour-dyed male, conspicuous at long range, made nine such aerial excursions in less than half an hour. If the site is on the fringe of the colony, he often goes a few feet away, with all the necessary posturing, and then turns, rushes back, bites the female and participates in another bout of the meeting ceremony. These trips often have nothing to do with fetching nest material, although he may make many gathering trips as well. They are typical of the early stages of pair formation and I became convinced that they effectively strengthened both the female's attachment to the site and the pair bond. They quickly accustomed the female to the male's departure but, before she could lose interest in the site or become too intimidated by hostile neighbours, she was rewarded by his return and the ensuing greeting. In this way, she could quickly become strongly attached to the site and capable of guarding it during her partner's absences. Indeed, one can easily see that new females are at first easily scared, and lose interest when the male has gone. She flinches at every landing nearby and is much on the defensive when menaced by neighbours. Yet is is vital that when left alone for the first long stint, and regularly thereafter, she will remain on the site, for it is precisely at this stage that most site usurpation and triangular associations occur, with the inevitable conflicts. Her participation in guarding is also necessary to prevent neighbours pilfering nest material, which is important in ensuring successful breeding (see p. 87). The male's pattern of repeated short absences and returns quickly reinforces her attachment, and builds up rapport. Thus, after the initial phase of interest centred solely on the male, she acquires strong attachment to the site and begins to perform all the displays associated with site ownership. Her importance as an almost equal partner in site defence cannot be over-estimated and it is presumably because of this role that she has evolved plumage almost identical to that of the male.

Fig. 78(b and c). Male returns to female with nest material and performs the ritual attack.

Fig. 78(d)

In new pairs, Nape-biting sometimes grades into actual eviction of the female, as here. She does not retaliate. In this instance, the male is a four-year-old intruder but, nevertheless, the female is not attacking him.

6. *Further aspects of intra-pair aggression*

As already mentioned, males continue to show aggression to their mates throughout the season. One need only instance the case of a male who, in September, strongly attacked his mate for two minutes although this pair had bred together successfully for at least two years. This, and the general observation that males are more aggressive to females at the beginning and end of the season than in the middle, shows that the changes in internal motivation override the

A B C D E F G H

Fig. 79. A, Leave-and-return, ritual behaviour involved in establishing the pair bond. Here the male leaves in the Sky-pointing position. B, he returns and Nape-bites. C, he leaves again in identical posture. D, he returns and Nape-bites again; she Faces-away. E, they perform the greeting ceremony. F to H, the male Sky-points preparatory to leaving for the third time. All this occurs in less than five minutes.

effects of past experience, of 'knowing' the female, and of having had a satisfactory relationship with her for a long period. One might have supposed that old pairs would have overcome violent aggression between themselves or even developed 'affection'. Instead, and whether or not the latter is true, males respond to rising aggression by more severe attacks. This is not to say that personal factors such as the state of the pair bond exert no effect, but certainly they do not eliminate male agression. Aggression late in the season cannot be due to the male becoming less familiar with his mate (as one might argue happens in winter) and proves again how directly and automatically birds may react to internal changes.

The adaptive value of female tolerance may lie on two levels. At its simplest, the female's ability to accept protracted, violent treatment without being provoked to retaliation, enhances her chances of forming the pair in the first place and of avoiding open conflict and pair disruption later on. She provides an object for re-directed attack and is often used as such, though one cannot imagine that this has much survival value.

Secondly, however, there is evidence that male attacks stimulate the female sexually, for it would be difficult to interpret otherwise a behaviour pattern so intimately and completely linked with copulation. If this is so, late season attacks may reinforce the female's attachment and increase her tendency to return early in the following year. If this seems unlikely, remember Coulson's kittiwakes that return, first, to the densest areas; his explanation, that there is a 'carry-over' of the effect of social stimulation from one year to the next, is in principle the same as the one I have just put forward for the gannet pair. Again, the memory of the site location evidently persists, so why should not memory traces produced by other types of experience? Later, I will show how a tendency for pairs to re-unite early in a new season would be highly adaptive. This is obviously an attempt to read adaptive significance into the observations; it may be argued that there is none and that a male's attacks on his mate are an inevitable outcome of aggressive tendencies whose adaptive value lies in territorial defence. Yet this would leave much unexplained and it would be strange had the all-pervasive effects of natural selection not turned this trait to double advantage. At any rate, the gannet is, so far as I know, the only bird in the world in which male aggression to female is sustained at this level throughout a long life.

The tendency of the male to attack and of the female to accept or retaliate, is affected by their position relative to the nest-site. Females are more likely to be attacked when off the site. One male alternated between two sites, each occupied by a female, and consistently attacked whichever happened to be *off* the site he was occupying. Yet he Mutual Fenced with the other. Thus, he was attacking a female one minute and Mutual Fencing with her the next and behaving in both ways to both females, all within the span of a few minutes. This 'site effect' probably partly explains the female's usual hesitant approach to an advertising male, followed by a quick rush to get close. Similarly, the female is powerfully inhibited from attacking an intruder male if he gets onto the site and, conversely, less inhibited from attacking him, or even her mate, once he is off the site. One frequently sees females menace or jab at their mates once these have left the site on their way to a take-off point. The probable explanation is that a male off-site has weaker sexual and fear-evoking valence, and since these inhibit aggression their partial removal releases at least low intensity aggression.

7. *Sexual receptivity*

Despite the permanence of the pair-bond, and the strong reaction against intruders, partners remain remarkably receptive to strangers of the opposite sex. First, a site owning male without a partner advertises a great deal and this is obviously necessary, since females often join such males, only to move on soon afterwards. Even mated males must also retain a fairly strong readiness to advertise so that the loss of a partner need not result in a wasted season and the danger of site usurpation during his absences. On the other hand, such a tendency aided and abetted by the equivalent tendency of females inevitably leads to a large number of triangular situations. Several season's documentation revealed how commonplace and complicated were changes in relationships within a small group, due to changes of site or mate. This leads to many fights. Secondly, in almost all cases where eggs simply disappeared and all obvious possibilities could be discounted, at least one owner was known to be interested in a third party. Indeed, this factor is perhaps the most important single cause of egg loss. Receptiveness is, therefore, a matter of balance; in the gannet it remains very high presumably because competitiveness leads to many abortive pairings and the disadvantages of remaining mateless long, if bereaved, are greater than those of losing an egg or precipitating a conflict.

Another intriguing aspect is that of personal recognition and preference. In the gannet, the receptiveness of one sex for the other is not entirely predictable. Males are markedly receptive early in the season, become highly selective later and then go through a second receptive phase towards the end. After a pair bond has been properly forged, both are obviously selective but even in long established pairs, male or female may remain highly receptive to individuals with whom they had previously associated and who are clearly still recognised. One male not only accepted back his previous mate after a year in which both had bred successfully with new partners, but even drove away his new mate of one year's standing in favour of his original one. Thus personal factors *can* play a strong role, despite being readily overridden by 'non-personal' reaction to internal changes. This case was the more outstanding because his original mate, in her 'come-back', had been decisively beaten by the newer one in an epic struggle. Nevertheless, and notwithstanding the latter's strenuous efforts to remain with him, accepting his attacks and Facing-away for long periods, he drove her violently from the site. On the other hand, another male completely rejected his original mate after an estrangement of less than two months. In some cases the male simply accepted the winner and if the beaten female did return (she usually did not) he forcibly ejected her. Again, however, the precise opposite occurred in other cases—the loser returned, was accepted and had to be displaced again by the victorious female. This sort of thing is a clear warning against the dangers of a simplistic mechanistic approach to behaviour.

In several instances, males retained relationships with two females and vice versa, on two sites. In one case a female changed mate and site, but, when the male was there alone, continued to 'stop-off' at her old site on her way to take off and was allowed to do so. Where male or female are attached to two sites, they show normal pair relationships with mates on both. Even when one site has an egg, the other is visited from time to time and intruders repelled. In one case, where the two-site triangle involved one male and two females, both produced eggs and the male incubated both, but favoured the first laid, even though it was not on the site where he had bred the two previous years. Even when the other female lost her egg he continued to visit the site and repelled many site establishing males with great determination. His dual attachment caused at least ten fights in one season, though he eventually lost the site.

8. *Mutual Fencing*

Pair formation is an on-going process; all the behaviour seen during the initial coming together of the pair continues during their later relationships, but with modifications in form and emphasis. An established female does not cease to Face-away as a response to the arrival

Fig. 80(a). High intensity Mutual Fencing (the greeting ceremony). The birds are calling loudly.

Fig. 80(b). Low intensity Mutual Fencing in a pair of young, transient site holders.

and Nape-biting of her mate, but the gesture is often perfunctory. In the same way, Mutual Fencing occurs from the first meeting onwards, however hesitant it may be initially.

Mutual Fencing has also been called 'sparring' or 'bill fencing' and is the gannet's most conspicuous behaviour. A detailed analysis of it can lead to several interesting conclusions. It occurs most commonly as a meeting ceremony following the re-union of the pair at the nest site. Usually, the incoming bird flies in, calling, but Mutual Fencing follows arrival even if the mate merely moves in from the fringe, on foot. It is also extremely common as a reaction to aggression-evoking stimuli, such as an attack or menace from a neighbour, the intrusion of a departing bird failing to take-off properly or the fracas of a nearby fight. Thirdly it is usually followed immediately by copulation in the stages prior to egg-laying and often resumes again afterwards. It rarely or never occurs apparently endogenously, as Bowing does, but may flare up and die down many times after the initial bout, before finally ceasing.

The interaction of which it is the main component begins with the strident approach-calling of the incoming bird, of either sex, at about four syllables per second. The bird on-site Headshakes rapidly and if a female may begin Facing-away in anticipation of the male's Nape-biting. The male lands with a final 'urrah' call, bites the female more or less fiercely depending on circumstances, and then the partners stand breast to breast and, with wings widely spread and bills inclined upwards, perform a rapid fencing or 'scissoring' movement with their bills, calling throughout—loudly when displaying vigorously and more softly as display dies down (this display and Bowing are the main sources of the constant background of noise at a gannet colony). Interspersed with bill-fencing are downward movements of the head (dips) perhaps as far as the nest or only a little to one side, which often results in one bird reaching over the neck of the other in a sinuous 'neck-smoothing' movement. As a vigorous bout of Mutual Fencing dies down the wings are held closer to the body, heads more horizontal and head movements become slower and less extensive. In Mutual Fencing between birds new to each other the partners may stand rather far apart, their movements may be nervous and jerky, and the male may intersperse slight biting of the female.

A pair of gannets Mutual Fencing look extraordinarily like two individuals Bowing, or trying to but getting in each other's way. The wings are out, the birds call, there is the dipping movement and the headshake. However, there are differences. First, the birds co-ordinate their positions relative to each other very precisely. The way in which they keep their bills apposed is clearly more than the accidental clashing of two birds Headshaking in close proximity. Second, the time-relationship of the components are different; the bill fencing takes up most of the time rather than being a quick shake between successive dips. There is no regular dip—headshake rhythm as in the Bow and, finally, the whole display is both much more variable in total length and at its longest, some 20 times as long as the Bow. There are other minor differences. For example, the bill position in Mutual Fencing is usually upwards, but downwards in Bowing, whilst the headshaking, even when not resulting in contact with the partner's bill, is different in form, sometimes becoming the 'soliciting headshake' (p. 188) in the female, which it never does in Bowing. Nevertheless, the resemblance between the two displays is so marked that it is probably correct to consider that Mutual Fencing is modified Bowing (the reasons for putting it that way round will become apparent).

When analysing the display, one may time the duration of the whole interaction, count

Fig. 80(c). After the initial greeting ceremony, both partners may indicate (by Sky-pointing) a tendency to leave the site.

Fig. 80(d). This stimulates the partner on the left to resume low intensity Mutual Fencing to 'keep' its mate on the site.

the frequency of various acts (for example the 'dip') and estimate the amplitude of some components (for example, how far the wings are held out). By quantifying these and similar factors for both sexes in different contexts, one can attempt a relatively objective assessment of motivation and function. The aim, in such an analysis, would be to understand what can be *seen* to happen in all the many, slightly different instances of Mutual Fencing, first in terms of a particular model of behaviour and second, in terms which are fully consistent with the interpretation of *related* gannet behaviour. The relevant material may be presented, here, as seasonal differences and status (including sex) differences.

(*a*) *Seasonal differences*

Mutual Fencing continues throughout the whole season, January to October, but the bout-length and the frequency of some components varies at different times. To understand these it is important to take into account the status of the pair (new or experienced) and the length of the absence preceding the bout, because short absences are usually followed by short bouts of Mutual Fencing, regardless of season. This severely restricts the amount of data one can gather since it is very difficult to know how long a bird has been away! However, taking 'long absences' as anything over six hours, we collected 88 cases in one season. Dividing the season into three 'blocks' (March through to mid-April; mid-June to the end of July and September to mid-October) Mutual Fencing bouts averaged 208 seconds (39 cases) in the early one, 30 seconds (38 cases) in the middle one and 88 seconds (11 cases) in the late one. Thus there was a clear tendency for Mutual Fencing to be longer early in the season and shortest in mid-season. This seasonal difference is also present in new pairs. The effect was diluted but by no means eliminated if one took *all* cases of Mutual Fencing regardless of length of preceding absence, when the figures were 180 (55 cases), 29 (56 cases) and 87 (13 cases). In fact, bouts became shorter soon after egg laying and during part of the period when the chick is present they may be very short (10 seconds or so). If a pair lose their egg, bouts suddenly become much longer again.

The duration of a bout of Mutual Fencing is one measure of the strength of the motivation involved; another is the vigour of the display as gauged by wing position and the amplitude of dip and headshake; duration and vigour are positively correlated.

(*b*) *Status differences*

There are sex differences in the *form* of Mutual Fencing; males tend to dip more, 11·6 times per bout (range 3–27) females 4·6 (range 2–21) and females hold their wings further out and are most prone to continue the display.

Furthermore, comparing relatively new and experienced pairs and taking mid-seasonal bouts only, ignoring the length of the preceding absence, new pairs averaged 97 seconds per bout (range 10–180; 9 cases) and established pairs 45 seconds (range 5–150; 31 cases).

From the description given previously, and these measurements, it is possible to suggest something about the motivation and function of Mutual Fencing.

First, aggression is intimately involved, at least in the male. This is indicated directly by the close association between Nape-biting and Mutual Fencing and indirectly by:

(a) the seasonal trends
(b) the form of the display and the sex differences
(c) the contexts of the display.

The corollary is that some 'fear' is probably involved as the other side of the aggression/fear coin; certainly, in the female's case, the Facing-away is fear-motivated behaviour.

Second, sexual motivation may also be involved, as indicated by the association with copulation (prior to egg laying in at least 90 per cent of cases, copulation immediately follows prolonged Mutual Fencing) and indirectly by the form of Mutual Fencing and its seasonal trends.

The facts given above may be further interpreted as follows. The seasonal trend of Mutual Fencing is much the same as that for aggressive behaviour such as Menacing (p. 165) and Bowing (p. 166), but quite different from non-aggressive behaviour such as Rotary Headshaking (p. 221). This is at least consistent with the hypothesis of aggression as an underlying causal factor common to both.

The tendency of males to dip more is fully consistent with the interpretation of this act (as in Bowing) as derived from biting (i.e. aggression) re-directed to the ground (p. 171). Just as males dip more than females in their Bowing, so they dip more in Mutual Fencing. In both cases, this is in accord with the fact that males are the more aggressive sex.

The above interpretation of the 'dip' in Mutual Fencing assumes that this movement is homologous with the dip in Bowing (q.v.); the formal resemblance between Bowing and Mutual Fencing has already been remarked and this, together with the contextual similarity (see below) is probably adequate ground for the assumption. The site ownership display, Bowing, would be a predictable response to the 'intrusion' of the partner but, as in Nape-biting, its effect has necessarily been modified in the pair context.

The contexts (which shed light on motivation) may be in large part summed by saying that aggression-eliciting stimuli elicit Mutual Fencing *when the pair are present* together. In other words, when one or both members may be judged from other behaviour to be aggressive they Mutual Fence intensively. Two protocols illustrate this perfectly:

(i) A male attacked his mate for 15 minutes and tried to drive her off the egg. The female Faced-away most of the time, but also retaliated three times and almost drove the male away. After the third retaliation they began high intensity Mutual Fencing which lasted for 4 minutes 25 seconds. The new outlet for the aggression which both had previously shown completely prevented any further attack.

(ii) The male of a new pair returned, Mutual Fenced, copulated and was then Menaced by a neighbour and turned on the female in violent re-directed attack. At the first pause this passed into intense Mutual Fencing lasting several minutes.

Thus it seems clear that, for the males at least, Mutual Fencing is called forth when stimuli—external, internal or both—make him 'feel' aggressive. The same is probably true for females, though the relative contributions of aggression and fear and sexual motivation are different, with fear or at least non-hostile motivation of some kind, playing a larger role than in the male. Here, the females tendency to be more persistent in the display may be mentioned. Whilst its motivational significance is obscure, it may reflect her greater need for 'reassurance' and hence be another facet of the greater part played by fear.

Turning now to the sexual motivation which may be involved, there is first the strong short term correlation with copulation early in the season and to a lesser extent towards the end. But it is dangerous to place much reliance on this, since it is usually only the first copulation following re-union that is preceded by Mutual Fencing; subsequent ones may occur without. Similarly, although females may briefly attempt to Mutual Fence after copulation, this is by no means invariable. Also, whereas Nape-biting and Mutual Fencing tend to remain inextricably mixed—outbreaks of biting occurring in the midst of Mutual Fencing—this is never true of sexual activity and Mutual Fencing. Thus aggression and Mutual Fencing seem more closely linked than sex and Mutual Fencing. The seasonal trend is similar in both Mutual Fencing and copulation, but sexual and aggressive activity are often positively correlated anyway. Whilst one can be sure that the aggression/fear duplet are causally strong in eliciting Mutual Fencing—when a pair are aggressive they Mutual Fence—it is much less certain that a sexually motivated pair will Mutual Fence. The involvement of sexual motivation in Mutual Fencing must therefore be considered not yet proven.

This sets the stage for a discussion of the function of this important display. The discussion of context has shown that, so far as its effect is concerned, it is friendly, reassuring, greeting, non-hostile behaviour. It is the 'ecstatic' display of long separated mates, the 'reassuring' display to which they turn after threat or intrusion, the interaction to which the prolonged endurance of the harassed and bitten female eventually leads, the prelude to copulation and so on. Clearly then Mutual Fencing is an essential part of the pair relationship; its complexity, vigour, protractedness and continuation throughout every season leave no doubt about that. Clearly, too, it is closely linked with aggression and aggression-eliciting stimuli. Certainly it is not (as are some displays in birds) chiefly a means of achieving short-term behavioural co-operation in copulation. The seasonal and status differences already described show that Mutual Fencing bouts are longest and most vigorous when there is a strong tendency to act aggressively. Early and late in the season, when aggression is high, early in the pair relationship, when the same applies, during short-term 'emergencies' when one or both members of the pair are made to 'feel' aggressive by external circumstances—in all these situations intense Mutual Fencing occurs between pair members. Thus Mutual Fencing expresses aggressive motivation and yet reinforces the pair bond. The more aggressive the male (as judged by context) the more the female needs 'reassurance' and, in terms of this simple motivation model, the more intensively both will perform the Mutual Fencing; and this is precisely what happens. The beauty of this arrangement lies in its neat economy. The same two major motivational systems—fear/aggression and sex—operate in both male and female. Yet, via a different balance of fear and aggression in the two sexes, the male is presented with a virtually open-ended motor-outlet for his aggression, which in turn acts positively on the female (the more aggressive he is and the more he Fences, the more she is 'reassured'). The net result is a strengthened pair bond.

Like the Triumph Ceremony of the grey-lag goose, to which it is in many ways very similar, Mutual Fencing continues to play an important part in pair-relations throughout life and perhaps acquires subtle motivational determinants, and subtle functions, as a result of reinforcement from past experience. We know nothing about these, but there is, for instance, the observation that old pairs often perform extremely long bouts of Mutual Fencing and it would be contrary to all the circumstantial evidence to suggest that this is because the male is more aggressive and the female more in need of reassurance than in new pairs. Possibly their long personal relationship with its continuing positive feed-back from shared rewarding behaviour has made Mutual Fencing itself rewarding. This is sheer speculation, but the basic facts given above leave no doubt that Mutual Fencing is motivationally complex, is variable and gives great scope for expressing subtle differences in mood and may well maintain and increase the strength of the pair bond. Nevertheless, even after a full year's relationship including successful breeding, the male may still under special circumstances revert to outright hostility and drive away his partner (see p. 182). This illustrates the perplexing element of unpredictability in animal behaviour.

Whilst I think most of the above case is sound, it remains difficult to 'pigeon-hole' the function of Mutual Fencing more precisely. Those who seem to think that 'drives' do not exist may deride the idea that such a display could serve to express aggressive motivation (= drive). Nevertheless, it obviously does so. The strength of the aggressive tendency does vary and the objectively measured display, Mutual Fencing, does co-vary in positive correlation. But what term is best applied to this function? Is Mutual Fencing 'reassuring' behaviour, appeasing, pair bonding, aggression-accommodating or what? Whatever else it does, it certainly provides a partly aggressive, protracted and intimate pair-interaction which gives every appearance of creating and strengthening the bond between the partners, much as does the Triumph Ceremony in the grey-lag goose. It may be recalled that this, too, is an aggressive display, not a sexual one.

Summary. Females elicit aggression when the sexes meet on the site; they are themselves afraid. Their initial appeasement behaviour is followed by a mutual display which expresses sexual attraction mixed with aggression in the male and fear in the female. Variations in form, intensity and seasonal incident, together with status differences, agree with the suggestion that Mutual Fencing reduces tension between members of a new pair, strengthens the pair bond and is the ownership display when both members are present.

9. *Copulation*

Before egg laying, copulation commonly occurs within ten minutes of the pair coming together on the site (never elsewhere) after a long separation and therefore it is usually preceded by the meeting ceremony, Mutual Fencing. It is solicited by the squatting female (though she sometimes solicits whilst standing) with violent and rapid sideways headshakes, which sometimes become vigorous flinging movements of such amplitude that the bill tip points over her back to her tail, and this continues to some extent during actual copulation. Soliciting is extremely stimulating to the male and almost forces him to mount even if he is aggressive. Before mounting, usually from the side, the male tends to adopt an arched-neck posture, with head kept still, patters his feet and then grips the female's head or nape and mounts (Fig. 81). He maintains a fierce grip (particularly aggressive males intersperse it, at the beginning and end, with stabs) throughout copulation, which takes 15–35 seconds (average 24 seconds, 180 measured) from placing one foot on the female's back to dismounting. During copulation the female headshakes repeatedly and may arrange nest material (the behaviour associated with copulation will be described later). The male waves his outspread wings and patters noisily with his feet, which move alternately. Occasionally he rests back on his tarsi and moves both feet in unison. These foot movements may be a powerful tactile stimulus to the female and may serve to synchronise the act. Occasionally the female tries to touch the male's bill. After he has dismounted, she usually rises and almost always headshakes. (Other post-copulatory behaviour is discussed below.)

I strongly suspect that, far from merely tolerating nape biting, the female is sexually stimulated by it, particularly as a prelude to copulation. A neat evolutionary method of accommodating the male's aggression, so necessary in territorial behaviour, but potentially a disadvantage in pair relations, would be for natural selection to make it sexually stimulating to the female and its strong association with copulation adds circumstantial evidence. That a genuine double mechanism is here involved (that is, the male really is aggressive and his attacks are not mere sexual stimulation to the female) is indicated by the fact that they not infrequently drive her off the site and break up the pair. If biting is sexually stimulating, aggressive males are able to benefit both territorially and in their pair relations, and females are handed the sugar-coating which enables them to swallow the bitter pill of male attack. Incidentally, the absence of nape biting as a method in female: female fights would also be explicable in these terms; the rightful site and mate owner would not be acting appropriately if, instead of a punishing attack, she delivered a sexual stimulus!

An element of individual recognition is involved in copulation; females that are receptive to their mates may refuse other males even when these actually mount. This is probably because in such cases the motivational balance is wrong, the element of fear being probably too strong.

Reverse copulations are rare in gannets, though fairly common in the Phalacrocoracidae. I have seen only one, out of many hundreds of normal copulations and in this case the female gripped the male's head and pattered, though without achieving cloacal contact. Later, the same pair copulated normally.

Copulation (male role) with chicks is not uncommon. I recorded 15 male cases in three of which the female was present, so that this behaviour obviously occurs even when the normal releasing, orienting stimuli are there. In 11 of these cases the chicks were about fully feathered and had by then adopted the typical adult posture (which smaller chicks do not) but were, of course, about as different in plumage as could be. In the remaining four, the chicks were younger and still fluffy; hence they were the 'right' colour but the wrong, size, shape and posture.

Although females so rarely adopt the male role with their partners, they more often do so with their offspring. Of 15 such cases, 13 involved chicks of 9–11 weeks, one of eight weeks and one of about seven weeks. The male was present on two occasions. The females gripped their chicks in the usual male manner and in three cases preened their heads afterwards. On one occasion the male attacked the chick after the female dismounted and on another the female

Fig. 81(a). During copulation the male bites the female vigorously on the nape. It is possibly through this link that male aggression towards the female has become 'acceptable'.

Fig. 81(b). After copulation, often, the female attempts to initiate Mutual Fencing.

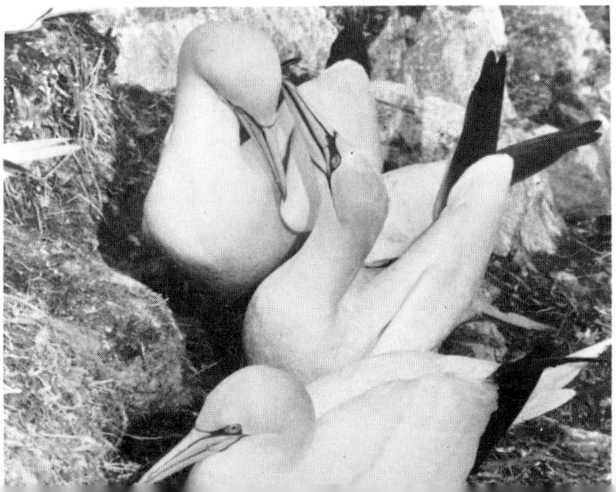

did so very strongly. The chick usually made little response but on occasions faced-away, begged for food or briefly and excitedly attacked the adult.

Gannets copulate from early February to the end of September an exceptionally protracted period. Semen is certainly produced on both these extreme dates; it is not simply that pseudo-copulation extends the apparent period. This direct proof of the prolonged activity of the gonads, is in full accord with other, circumstantial, evidence, such as the equally prolonged territorial behaviour and partly sex-motivated pair behaviour (Mutual Fencing) which are presumably partly dependent on active secretion of sex hormones. Thus, a gannet pair begins full sexual behaviour at least six to eight weeks before egg laying and shows a resurgence late in the season (Fig. 82).

Individual pairs copulate probably at least 100 times in the period before egg laying—perhaps more. The highest frequency during a short period was four times in 40 minutes (twice in five minutes is common) though this is perhaps not unusually high for a seabird. The frequency of copulation increases in the 10–14 days before the egg is laid. Thus the copulation peak in the third week of April reflects the immediate pre-egg laying period (counting from the mean egg) of the colony as a whole.

A further speculative point about the relation between copulation frequency and egg laying is that replacement eggs are usually produced in 12–14 days. This roughly corresponds with the peak in copulation 10–14 days before the main egg laying period and suggests that females may be particularly prone to solicit copulation at the time of ovulation.

Between egg laying and the chick leaving the nest copulation is suspended and there is a very sharp drop in copulation rate (Fig. 82) which comes just after the mean egg laying date. Whilst I have several records of copulation in the presence of an egg, the overwhelming majority of pairs cease copulation immediately the egg is laid. Indeed, one gains the firm impression that an inhibitory switch-mechanism operates, such that a male about to mount, catching his first glimpse of the egg, immediately desists. Thus, males returning to the nest soon after the egg has been laid made copulation intention movements but did not mount, though almost certainly they would have done had there been no egg. The advantage could be to prevent damage to the egg. A further indication that the egg inhibits the male came from a triangular association in which a female with two males laid an egg to one, who then stopped copulations, whereas the other male, on another and empty nest, copulated with her 13 days afterwards. A third and most convincing piece of evidence is that copulation restarts within 24 hours of egg loss irrespective of the degree of incubation achieved (in one case this was 32 days). Unless one were to postulate an improbably rapid recrudescence of partially regressed gonads, one must assume that the male had remained capable of full copulation during the days following the appearance of the egg, but had been inhibited by its presence.

Later in the season, when the chick is well grown or fledged, copulations, though common, never reach the pre-laying peak. They are often successful and do not differ in any noticeable way from earlier ones, except that females do not show the intense soliciting behaviour found before egg laying.

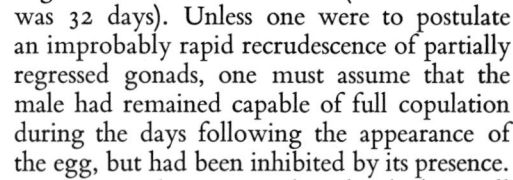

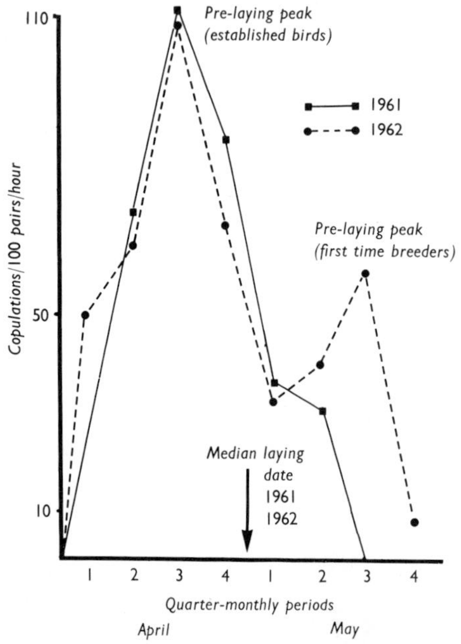

Fig. 82

The seasonal pattern of copulation in group 5 on the Bass.

(a) Behaviour associated with copulation

Gannets never, as it were, start up from cold, copulate and return to complete inactivity; this of course is simply a specific example of a general phenomenon. Activities tend to occur in groups or associations. Females most commonly perform a nest building movement immediately after copulation, often merely reaching down to the ground or nest rim and touching it. This happened in 60 per cent of all cases in which behaviour was recorded up to ten seconds after the male dismounted (the male touched nest material on only 20 per cent of occasions). On the other hand males tend to Sky-point more often (35 per cent in the same sample, females none). The other common post-copulatory activity is Mutual Fencing (40 per cent of cases). Nest touching may be partly due to postural facilitation; the female sitting in the nest cup is in the normal position for arranging nest material. Nevertheless she tends to nest touch more predictably at this time than at others. The link between copulation and subsequent Sky-pointing in the male is readily understandable, since at this point he very often leaves the site to gather nest material and departure is typically preceded by Sky-pointing. Post-copulation trips for nest material vary from a few inches to over a mile. Often the male doesn't even move from the site, but simply reaches for nest material.

Mutual Fencing commonly precedes copulation and its occurrence after it may indicate an association with a certain level of sexual motivation, in association with the changing intensities of fear and aggression which, as a general phenomenon, certainly accompany sexual activity. It is known, for example, that the consummatory act of copulation disinhibits aggression and this could well account for the occurrence of the post-copulatory Mutual Fencing situation.

In this connection, female Facing-away follows aggressive copulation in some cases and the male (rarely the female) often assumes the Pelican Posture, which is probably an ambivalent fear/aggression posture. Thus even in the most overt form of sexual activity there are clear signs that other motivational systems, which are such a feature of pair formation displays prior to copulation, are also involved. These complex behavioural situations cannot always be 'understood' in these somewhat cut-and-dried terms, however. Males are quite likely to do nothing at all immediately after copulation, except stand and gaze around.

10. *Mutual Preening*

Members of a pair, particularly a well established one, often follow Mutual Fencing or copulation by Mutual Preening (Fig. 83), in which each delicately nibbles the head, throat and neck feathers, or occasionally the wings and back of its partner. The eyes are often closed, though this is certainly not as a protective measure. The head is heavily infested with *Mallophaga*, but Mutual Preening does not appear to remove them and may perhaps persist because it is pleasurable. It may possibly be appeasement behaviour, though it usually occurs after Mutual Fencing has removed tension between the participants, often after long quiet periods. However, its connection with aggression is clearly indicated in unstable pairs when a vigorous and 'irritable' form may alternate with overt hostility from the male. Once an intruding male preened the female and then showed intention movements of copulation. Copulation in this situation is often aggressive and, as mounting approached, his preening became rougher and finally graded into biting prior to copulation. The reverse also often happened—a male starting with attack often ended by preening. This may be in part an expression of postural facilitation, the biting grading into nibbling and preening due to the bill being brought into the 'correct' position but the fact remains that there is sometimes a marked short-term correlation between aggressive behaviour and preening of the female by the male. Similarly, adults often alternate attack on strange chicks with rough preening of them. There is a tendency for females to preen males more frequently than vice versa.

11. *Sky-pointing*

All the ritualised behaviour described so far is important in expressing mood and tendency to other gannets—potential mate, potential rival, mate, neighbour and so on. There remains another very spectacular and highly ritualised display, Sky-pointing, which may be discussed at this juncture because it is very much concerned with regulating the coming and going of the partners.

In Sky-pointing the neck is stretched vertically to its fullest extent and held stiffly, whilst the bill points skywards (sometimes even backwards of vertical) and the eyes look binocularly forwards. The closed wings are raised upwards, not outwards, by rotating the arm at the shoulder joint and lifting the wing-tips. This 'wing busking' is a movement performed to some extent during ordinary walking and as part of the wing movement involved in taking flight. The first of these features prompted the descriptive name used here, but it should be made clear that in the following discussion the associated movements (not merely the frozen posture) are included. This is important when interpreting the effects on neighbours; in fact one cannot dissociate the two and demonstrate the effect merely of Sky-pointing.

In this extremely conspicuous, somewhat comical posture, the bird begins slow, 'on the spot' foot raising before turning and walking, or flying, away from the nest. Usually, just as it moves, it utters a soft groan, somewhat disyllabic ('oo-ah') and often high pitched, particularly when the gannet is taking off from a cliff. By drooping the feet, so that the upper surfaces are the visible ones, the striking digital lines are conspicuously displayed. When in the full Sky-pointing posture, a gannet moves slowly, with a characteristic rolling gait, raising and lowering

Fig. 83

Mutual Preening (like Mutual Fencing) is a ritualised form of aggressive behaviour.

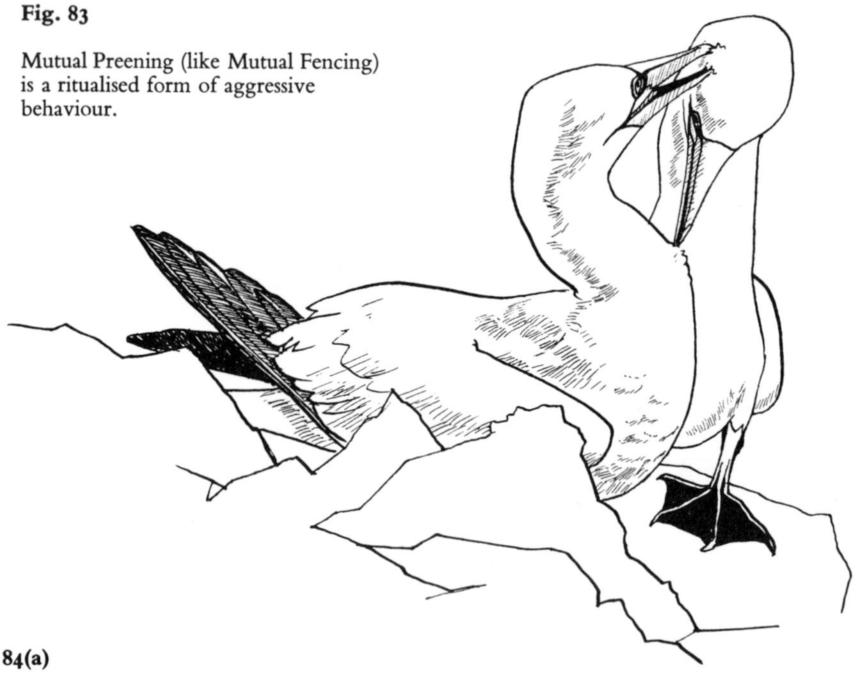

Fig. 84(a)

Typical intensity Sky-pointing with on-the-spot foot raising displaying the green lines on the upper surface of the web. The wings are loosened but hardly raised at the tips. This may continue for several minutes.

Fig. 84(b). A partner about to leave, begins to turn and to Sky-point.

each foot with great deliberation. It seems oblivious to the activities of birds nearby, apparently ignoring threats and jabs, though if one looks closely, one sees that its eyes are swivelling in all directions, evidently taking all in. Space permitting, the bird may run a few paces in this posture, or even hop—a ludicrous sight. After the first careful steps the gannet sheds caution and, if surrounded by neighbours, makes a dash for the fringe or some convenient stopping place. It may have to 'row' its way through the hostile ranks, enduring harassment, and on occasion shows stress by gaping and swallowing once it has reached a safe point. Often, it then rearranges its plumage by vigorous Wing-flapping and the Rotary Headshake.

The most comprehensive description of the context of Sky-pointing is that it precedes and accompanies movement, usually on foot, away from the nest or site. Occasionally, a bird returns to its site on foot, in which case it may Sky-point; fringe birds returning with nest material, or pilfering birds with their booty, are common instances of this. Basically, however, Sky-pointing is a pre-leaving posture, usually begun on the nest site, typically by the partner which has just been relieved. Sometimes it continues for two minutes without a break, before the Sky-pointing bird actually leaves. Occasionally the incomer Sky-points, either because it is about to leave again (perhaps for nest material) or perhaps because it has not yet taken over the nest-centre, and the necessary locomotion involved in this in turn elicits Sky-pointing. One may even have the bizarre spectacle of *both* birds Sky-pointing simultaneously, though one always 'wins' and is the one to leave.

Usually, at least on flattish ground, a Sky-pointing bird is surrounded by others, but this is not necessary to elicit the posture; completely isolated birds Sky-point, both on cliffs and flat ground, when leaving their nest. Sky-pointing *may* occur in birds which are moving about in the fringe, but almost always these are en route from the nest to a take-off point, or are returning to a site; birds without sites moving around in the fringe do not Sky-point. All these points are relevant to an understanding of its function.

As a posture preceding flight, Sky-pointing typically occurs in a sequence of behaviour patterns which runs as follows: Sky-pointing with wings busked; wings flicked (intention movement of flight), crouch (intention movement of jump), actual take-off, with tail depressed to increase lift, still in Sky-pointing position. Even when taking off from a cliff edge, a gannet may jump upwards in the Sky-pointing posture (Fig. 84(d)).

Birds taking off with the Sky-pointing posture usually groan (60 per cent of cases) whereas those taking off without, groan in about 20 per cent of cases.

Turning to the function of Sky-pointing, one can readily understand why it has been so widely, but in the case of the North Atlantic gannet wrongly, interpreted as 'appeasing' behaviour. First, there is the form of the movement, in which the bill is lifted out of any possible attacking position. Second, one can readily see that gannets do not Sky-point merely in the pair context but also in what seems to be a wider social context, as when moving through the nesting ranks of the colony. This has led several authors to assign an appeasing function to it. Some, indeed, have inverted the evidence of their own eyes in asserting that a gannet thus posturing is guaranteed a safe passage to a take-off point. Nothing could be further from the

Fig. 84(c)

The turning movement continues.

Fig. 84(d). The bird departs in the Sky-pointing posture. Typically it 'groans'.

truth. Admittedly a gannet would be well served with such an efficacious piece of behaviour, and this no doubt influenced previous interpretations, but it does not possess one (not even gannets are *perfectly* 'designed'!).

Short of experiments with models, the only way to gather evidence on the point seemed to be to observe precisely *when* it occurred and what effect it had on other individuals. Systematic notes were therefore made of about 500 occasions on which it occurred, where there were no additional complications of attack, stealing nest material, disturbance and so on. These fell into seven classes:

(1) Birds leaving their nests to move through the colony Sky-pointed and then dashed in 60 out of 83 cases (72 per cent) and merely dashed in the remainder.
(2) Birds moving some distance from their nests but without having to pass through others Sky-pointed in 69 out of 76 cases (91 per cent). The differences between categories (1) and (2) suggests that the prospect of passing between hostile neighbours decreases, rather than increases, the tendency to Sky-point.
(3) Birds moving only slightly off their sites—a metre or less—Sky-pointed in all of 19 cases.
(4) The few records of birds approaching their sites on foot indicate that where they have to pass through others they do not Sky-point (no cases out of 14), but where they can approach without they may do so (four cases out of 11 = 36 per cent).
(5) Prior to flying from their nests after changeover, birds Sky-pointed in all cases but, taking into account departure after short visits only, in 47 out of 130 cases (36 per cent).
(6) Although Sky-pointing never occurs prior to take-off with nest material, birds occasionally walk in this position holding nest material. Birds taking off without nest material other than from their nests Sky-pointed in 16 out of 132 cases (12 per cent). Many of these had left the nest on foot and were taking off from some vantage point. In a literal sense, therefore, they are still 'leaving the nest'.
(7) Movement on foot along the fringe of the colony involved Sky-pointing in 58 out of 118 cases (49 per cent). Many of the Sky-pointing birds had just left the colony, but precise proportions cannot be given, since a bird's behaviour prior to its arrival in the fringe was often missed.

The preceding analysis reveals a posture which, though highly predictable in a few situations, is far from an invariable response to the pre-movement situation. Further it does *not* effectively prevent attack (see below) and is *not* adopted when attack is likely; instead the bird dashes. Sky-pointing usually occurs *before* the bird has been attacked. When attack appears imminent, a bird may 'freeze' in a non-Sky-pointing position for over five minutes before dashing.

To see whether Sky-pointing reduced the probability of attack, counts were made of its effect on the behaviour of neighbours. In 78 cases of Sky-pointing, 60 per cent elicited a Menace from previously quiescent neighbours. This should be compared with the effect on neighbours of other movements of roughly similar magnitude. Thus 33 out of 432 Rotary Headshakes (8 per cent) and none of 56 Bows drew Menaces. It appears that Sky-pointing is more likely than these other behaviour patterns (both of which involve vigorous movement) to elicit hostile behaviour.

Whilst this may well be due to conditioning, the neighbours recognising Sky-pointing as an intention movement of departure probably involving blundering past their nest, it strongly suggests that the performer is not thereby any more immune to attack, but rather less so. In fact the Sky-pointing bird actually makes his departure by dashing through the nesting ranks, a procedure he could equally well carry out without the preliminary posturing, since neighbours attempt to bite him in either case. (However, see p. 259.)

If an appeasing function seems unlikely on the above evidence, some other must be found for such a striking display. Successful site maintenance and breeding is highly dependent, in the gannet, on efficient change-over. Unattended nests are liable to lose egg or small chick, through predation by gulls, or (particularly) neighbours pilfering nest material, and gannets cannot return sufficiently quickly to prevent mishaps. It is therefore important that a conspicuous pre-leaving signal should be given to remove the danger of both adults leaving together.

The elaborate and prolonged posturing of Sky-pointing could clearly perform this signal function; it is certainly recognised and responded to by the mate. Its function in ensuring proper collaboration at change-over is often very convincingly demonstrated in cases where both partners obviously want to leave and both Sky-point in a prolonged and intense manner, but one gradually gains ascendancy and continues or even intensifies its Sky-pointing, whilst the other gradually winds down. Here, the strong impression is that neither leaves until there is no question about which one it is to be! Never do they both Sky-point and leave together or one after the other. One leaves and the other stays and the leaver is always the victor in the Sky-pointing contest. This interpretation makes more sense of Sky-pointing on cliff ledges where it is usually possible to leave without approaching any neighbour—a particularly cogent point since there is evidence that gannets are primarily cliff-nesters. It may be doubted whether this explanation could account for Sky-pointing in situations away from the nest. It may, however, have become 'frozen' into the pre-moving situation, which in this species usually means departure from the nest, and now occurs even when the movement is not actually from the nest.

Although Sky-pointing sometimes occurs in sexual and hostile situations, it also occurs much more widely, as the preceding examples have shown, and it is not a particular balance of fear, aggression or sexual tendencies which forms the common denominator on these occasions. Rather, it is the situation 'about to move', particularly from the site. The motivation of Sky-pointing is therefore much less obvious than that of the gannet's agonistic displays.

So far as derivation is concerned, Sky-pointing is probably a ritualised flight intention movement. Whilst many geese show neck lengthening before flying up, some have incorporated chin lifting movements and lateral head shakes. It is not difficult to see how progressive elaboration of a simple neck lengthening could produce the Sky-pointing posture. The peculiar rotation of humeri now associated with Sky-pointing could be an intention movement of flight adapted to a restricted take-off position. Whilst the gannet appears to have retained and elaborated Sky-pointing in this phylogenetically primitive context, *all other Sulidae* have transferred it to an entirely different one, that of male advertising. In this functionally emancipated context it has undergone great elaboration different in each species.

To sum up, the observations show that Sky-pointing does not have a marked appeasing function, but is, if anything, more likely to provoke attack than are other movements. It is very probable that Sky-pointing functions as an intra-pair signal movement facilitating change-over at the nest.

OTHER BEHAVIOUR INVOLVED IN BREEDING

1. *Nest building and associated behaviour*

The spacing, siting and functions of the gannet's nest are discussed on pp. 81 and 87. Here, only nest building and associated behaviour and the nest itself are considered.

(*a*) *Gathering nest material*

Nest building in the gannet goes on from January to October. Indeed, there is no month in the year when a gannet may never be seen flying around the Bass with nest material. They are obsessed with nest material; they pilfer shamelessly, gather seaweed by the hour, rob each other in mid air and pull grass with a vigour that earned the gannets of Boreray the castigation of the St. Kildans for denuding Hirta of its vegetation.

Gannets often gather nest material communally, sometimes in groups numbering some scores. They always choose areas onto which the wind is blowing, so they can take off easily. As a result, the Bass and doubtless other vegetated gannetries, are prone to patchwork denudation.

They do not fight over their spoils, but may try to rob each other, eliciting rapid 'qua-qua-quas' quite different from the strident anger calls. Kittiwakes gather communally too and in both cases, no doubt, the habit helps allay their distinct unease at landing on empty ground so far away from established parts of the colony. Fear notwithstanding however, they may become so engrossed as to be oblivious to all else and can be cut off from their escape route. They pull grass with quick, vigorous sideways shakes as well as mighty backward tugs. At the height of the nest building period, individual males bring several lots per hour, one such record was ten lots of grass in 55 minutes, which period included two copulations and attendant Mutual Fencing.

As a result of these labours, they accumulate large, compacted nests of seaweed, grass, moulted feathers and flotsam and add to it any earth they can reach around the nest. Nowadays, synthetic fibres used for nets and lobster creels are much used and constitute a serious danger. Anything from 1 to 50 per cent of nests in a gannetry (see p. 132) may contain such material and at large gannetries many scores of birds, adults and chicks may die each year as a result of entanglement. The drum or pedestal occasionally measures almost two metres from rim to base, the product of many annual increments, though in most cases a well-established nest is much smaller (varying with locality). It has a firm, shallow cup lined with grass or sometimes seaweed, and often containing feathers. The finer material in the cup results from removal of larger items rather than a deliberate choice of fine material. However, there is enormous variation not only in the size but also in the quality of the nest. Some females lay and incubate on large well-lined nests, others on a patch of muddy ground with a few scraps of material. The sides of the pedestal are heightened by a continuous 'gardening', the birds reaching down and drawing loose earth and debris up the slope to the rim.

Although nests are not systematically added to by the bird's own excrement, which is usually voided well clear by both adults and well-grown young, adults sometimes lower their tails and excrete onto the side of the nest. It is usually the more viscous residue from the alimentary tract which is 'directed' in this way, the liquid faeces being squirted clear. On small, sloping ledges where nest material sticks with difficulty, the cementing action of excreta is unquestionably valuable in providing a base for subsequent accretions. Indeed, were it not for this and the use of earth and humus (often pulled up with grass) nests would never stick onto some of the sites used, a measure of the potential value of this habit to the species (Fig. 36). Shag nests, which lack this 'cement', could not accumulate on some sites used by gannets, whose adaptability compared with some cliff-nesters is worth special mention, and could be significant in permitting extension of range. However, quite apart from ability to stick nests, the gannet could never use certain kinds of sites open to the agile kittiwake, and its choice may often be limited by its manoeuvrability. Nevertheless, Gurney was quite wrong to deny, so emphatically, the value to gannets of cementing. No doubt he was reacting to the fanciful accounts of gannets 'soldering' their eggs to the ledge.

Gannets collect nest material (273 Bass records of grass and 131 of seaweed) mainly from the end of February to October. Systematic counts showed that the frequency with which nest material was brought rose steadily in April, was lower in mid-season and rose again in August. The rise before egg laying is associated with the increased rate of copulation, since this is usually followed by nest material gathering. Some days before egg laying, females spend longer on the nest with the male, thereby facilitating copulation and the attendant nest material gathering, a chain of events producing a well-built nest just prior to laying. Before laying, nest material is brought mainly by the male only (231 visits by males recorded, five by females), but subsequently though still less frequently than the male, by the female also. Males, but rarely females, bring nest material to their sites even in the absence of a mate to guard it between collecting trips.

For the remainder of the year gathering is scattered, although sudden rain elicits a dramatic outburst of nest building. In five minutes during rainy weather in August 1962, for example, 28 birds arrived with nest material at the group of 250 nests, only about 40 of which were attended by pairs. Since gannets do not normally leave their nests unattended, three-quarters of the possible total were gathering nest material at the time of the count. This activity continued for hours. Kittiwakes react to a similar extent. The function in the gannet may be to elevate the nest and keep the egg or chick drier, though even pairs without egg or chick respond in this way.

(b) *Nest building movements*

Gannets spend much time touching and arranging nest material (Fig. 85) throughout the season; the nest, in addition to eliciting a great deal of maintenance behaviour which is presumably necessary to keep it in good order (at least until the chick is large) provides an object to which displacement activities can be directed. Since the actual movements of bending the head and touching the nest are very common as functional behaviour in the straightforward sense they are particularly likely to be used as the 'irrelevant' response in a conflict situation. Thus, touching the nest has become common in both contexts. There are numerous comparable examples, of which a good one in the gannet is the incorporation of headshaking into displays (see p. 172).

Taking first the behaviour patterns directly concerned with forming or maintaining the nest, actual building is crude. Gannets have no complicated method of interweaving the material; they merely place it in front or to one side whilst standing or sitting and with rhythmic, small amplitude, sideways head movements and trembling of the mandibles, push it into place. In the early stages material is merely dropped onto the site and perhaps handled briefly. There is obviously no appreciation of the practicalities; for example, gannets continue to bring grass to excruciatingly difficult cliff face sites from which it inevitably drops away, when the adaptive procedure would be to gather gelatinous material (seaweed) and stand on it until it had become slightly stuck to the rock, thus forming a base for accretion. When, as they not infrequently do, gannets succeed in building on such sites, it is apparently by sheer luck and incredible persistence.

A cup is formed in the accumulating material by turning movements, applying the webs and lower breast. Once there is enough material to do this, gannets spend prolonged periods arranging and re-arranging new additions and forming the cup. Usually, as already described, pronounced nest building coincides with the period immediately before egg laying and, probably via positive feed-back stimuli from the developing cup, results in an adequate hollow for the egg, which is very important for its safety. Gannet nests quickly become flattened if the birds just stand on them, so the prolonged attention to nest building and cup-forming and the tendency to sit in the cup for some time prior to egg laying is adaptive.

(*c*) *Mandible vibration*

After depositing material, the mandibles are characteristically opened and vibrated to dislodge adhering material such as mud followed by a quick sideways headshake, sometimes a violent flinging movement. The same combination is also used extremely vigorously after picking up regurgitated and therefore messy fish fragments, after feeding the young. Mandible vibration, however, is often shown after handling clean, dry material and is in fact not even

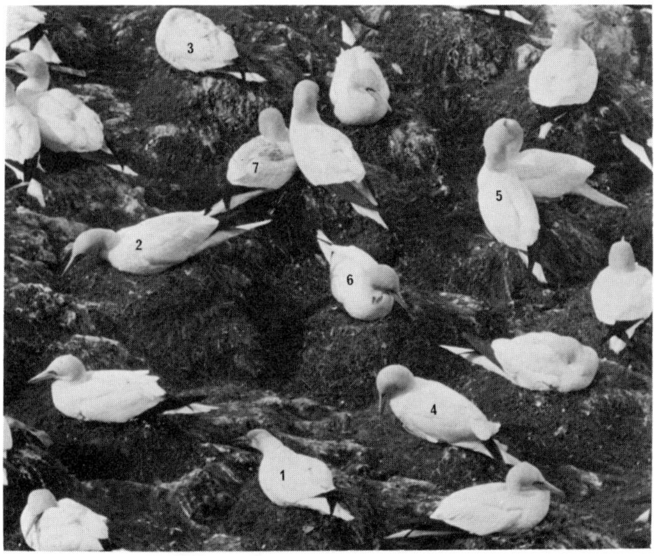

1, 2 'Gardening'—reaching for scraps of nest material and adding them to the side of the nest drum.
3. Sleeping, head in scapulars.
4, 6 'Nest settling' movements; form cup and (if egg present) adjust position of webs on egg.
5. Preening partner.
7. Female with 'copulation marks' (mud transferred from male's webs). Note that at this stage in the season, the nests are constructed almost entirely from seaweed.

Fig. 85. Nest building activities. Early in the laying period much time is spent drawing up material from the sides of the nest pedestal and tucking it into the nest rim. This may be an important adjunct to the gannet's method of incubation (underfoot) by helping to seal in heat.

confined to the context of handling any 'material'. Sometimes it occurs in high intensity conflict situations. For example a male attempting to rape a female preened her roughly and followed this by mandible vibration; normal preening of the partner does not elicit it. Again, on a new fringe site, the male attempted copulation after which the female attacked him—a most unusual event and doubtless involving intense conflict—menacing him with the same vibratory mandible movements seen when depositing nest material.

2. *Nest digging*

Around hatching time and whilst the chick is small, gannets become especially prone to nest digging, thrusting the mandibles, slightly parted, forcefully into the floor and probing for hard lumps which are lifted out and flung away with the same sideways head movements used to dispose of split fish. Digging is often performed with concentration and vigour and is adaptive in removing hard, sharp objects which could injure the egg or small chick, especially given the gannet's not infrequent habit of standing on its young! A 3000g bird concentrating its weight on a small area applies considerable pressure. I actually saw a bird move the egg to one side and remove an object from the spot where the egg had been.

3. *Nest-oriented displacement*

Turning to the nest-oriented behaviour in conflict situations, one finds that nest-touching or nest-handling is extremely common in aggressive interactions (menacing, post-fighting, hostile pair interactions). However, it is found both in the dominant and in the inferior individual. A male under intense jabbing and menacing from a neighbouring pair, and therefore outgunned, will intersperse agitated-looking nest-touching. On the other hand, the winner of a severe fight usually mixes nest-touching with his Bowing. No doubt the nuances are different in the two situations, but nest-touching is the main element in both. As in all complex interactions, the entire context is relevant; for example, a single bird engaged in menacing will almost certainly also touch nest material; a member of a pair, similarly engaged, will do so less frequently, but will Mutual Fence.

Touching nest material during Bowing and Mutual Fencing is hardly surprising since the dip in these displays is in fact a modified nest biting movement. Its common occurrence in the female after copulation has already been discussed (p. 189).

Nest-biting has already received mention as the re-directed aggressive act from which Bowing has been derived. It is genuine, very vigorous, occasionally frenzied, grasping of earth or rock, with accompanying calling and it occurs most commonly after males land on their unoccupied nests or sites, fairly early or late in the season, when aggression is more evident than in the middle period. Of 91 such landings recorded early in the season, 29 per cent were immediately followed by full intensity nest biting and a further 64 per cent either by touching nest material or Bowing. Frightened birds showed much less tendency to behave in this way. In early February, when gannets are still extremely wary of land and liable to sudden panics, landing was mainly followed by the anxiety posture and only three out of 27 birds touched nest material; none Bowed. Site owners landing away from their sites and birds without sites landing in the fringe, do not show nest biting or touching movements. The other contexts in which the aggressive-looking nest biting occurs are after birds have been knocked off their nest or otherwise disturbed during a fracas or by a departing bird; following a fight and during aggressive (but non-fighting) encounters.

Finally, it is interesting that, in the sort of situations described above, both nest building movements and nest biting sometimes occur in the complete absence of any nest material. For example, a male accidentally slid down the smooth wet slab of rock on which his nest was situated and was attacked, whereupon he started nest building, bringing 'material' from his side and putting it beneath him, though there was absolutely nothing there to handle.

In all the situations just described, nest touching and nest building movements are obviously not improving the structure of the nest, so they may be considered functionally 'irrelevant', though they are certainly relevant in as much as they provide some motor activity which can 'employ' the current state of arousal. From the viewpoint of causation it may be asked why nest touching, rather than anything else should be the 'irrelevant' behaviour performed. It has already been suggested that their very commonness renders them likely to be taken up in the 'conflict' context. Also, nest material is an effective directing stimulus. On this assumption, if the conflict occurred at sea, for example, bathing or 'false' drinking could become the irrelevant act. In fact fights ending on the sea are invariably followed by excited bathing, but this could possibly be true bathing, elicited by soiled and disarranged feathers. However, successful diving (capture of prey) is typically followed by displacement bathing. Thirdly, most of these conflict situations involve the site, which has close ties with nest building. The assumption here is that this link renders birds more likely to slide over into nest touching than say preening, scratching or other actions. Some slight circumstantial evidence in support of the first and third suggestions (and none of the three are mutually exclusive) is the observation mentioned above, that nest material need not be present in order for the nest touching movements to be shown. It is the movement, not merely the directing stimulus of the nest material, that is tied to the conflict situation.

These interpretations make sense of the wide variety of stimulus situations that can give rise to nest touching or building movements, since the important parameters are 'conflict, on site'.

4. *Taking over the nest centre*

Gannets spend a great deal of time on the nest site together, standing or sitting. Early in the season, males spend far longer than females in attendance, and usually stand, rather than sit, right in the centre of the site, but some time before egg laying the females tend to take over the centre when the pair are present together and also begin to sit more than the males and more than they themselves did earlier. Only very occasionally do the pair sit side by side on the nest; usually one stands nearby. Later still, the chick takes over the nest centre.

The female's taking over and sitting in the nest centre is, again, just part of the sexes' subtly different behaviour complexes; females build more than males, who in turn do almost all the gathering of nest material and so females are usually positioned centrally. Females spend longer at the site and copulate and build more frequently as egg laying approaches and so are more often sitting in the centre at this time. Additionally, no doubt, there is an increasing tendency to sit as laying approaches and the brooding tendency becomes stronger. Presumably, for the same reason, the foot movements associated with incubation (p. 200) become more frequent at this time. It is, in fact, then very difficult to determine whether a bird has an egg or not, since females may sit tightly on empty nests, from time to time making the foot movements which one sees in incubating birds. This is a practical point to be borne in mind when determining, by observation, which nests hold eggs!

5. *Laying*

The act of deposition was partly or fully seen on many occasions. The one accurately timed egg laying took two minutes. The tail is depressed at the last instant and appears to guide the egg into the nest. This may well be an important adaptation in the gannet, which can rarely retrieve an egg laid outside the nest. Often the female tipped forward or slightly to one side, sometimes awkwardly. Eggs were laid at any time of day and also during the night. Immediately after laying the female makes nest building movements, headshakes and tucks the egg. She may tuck it on top of her webs before putting it beneath them. The act of tucking the egg, at this time, is usually followed by mandible vibrations. Incubation begins immediately.

6. *Incubation*

One of the few gannet habits that received early and accurate mention was that of incubating the egg underfoot—'On my first visit to the Bass Rock, which was in 1876, one of the men surprised me by saying that the gannet incubated her single egg by covering it with her large webbed feet. I was not then aware that this singular habit had been placed on record in the sixteenth century by Conrad Gesner though subsequently it was discredited by less informed writers and disbelieved. By good fortune I was destined to have my incredulity removed' (Gurney 1913). It seems incredible that such an easily verified habit should have given rise to any contradictions, particularly in view of the attention paid to the more accessible gannetries as sources of food.

The gannet's webs together cover an area of about 63 sq. cm. The egg is relatively small (total surface area about 40–50 sq. cm) so that its exposed surface can easily be entirely covered by the webs, which fit snugly round it overlapping where they join (Fig. 86). The shell is relatively thick. The egg is most frequently incubated lengthwise, long axis aligned along the bird's head-tail axis, but also crosswise. The webs are placed one after the other on the egg, their positions adjusted by means of small shifting movements and the bird then lowers itself and settles into an incubating position with slight rocking or 'settling in the nest' movements (called nest settling for purposes of behaviour counts). It makes major shifts in position several times an hour and 'nest settles' much more frequently than that. After major shifts the egg is tucked beneath the webs, using the closed bill, and with the head bent far under the body. During hot weather the egg is sometimes transferred to the upper side of the webs or the bird stands with the uncovered egg between its webs, presumably to cool it by exposing it, under shade.

Gannets can easily incubate two eggs. I donated a second egg to many nests and the hatching success was equal to that of singles. Similar experiments carried out with the South African gannet (q.v.) showed the same thing. The incubation period, however, was two days longer, due to inefficient covering (a control transfer of single eggs did not lead to any difference in incubation period). The two eggs were incubated in a variety of positions and the additional stimulus led to a large increase in the frequency of rising and shifting, tucking and nest settling movements. During incubation, gannets are constantly touching and arranging material and seem particularly prone to arrange nest material around their breast and flanks, tucking small pieces, often moulted body feathers, delicately between themselves and the nest. It is possible that this has significance; conceivably it 'seals in' part of the warmth. Booth (1887) noticed that his tame breeding gannets plucked feathers from their backs and used them in this way.

Pairs breeding for the first time do not take any longer to hatch their eggs, implying that their incubation behaviour, once properly begun is just as efficient as that of experienced birds. On the other hand, they lose a significantly higher proportion of eggs due to an inadequate initial response (precisely the same applies with respect to their chick, p. 203). Thus, several such females were seen to ignore the newly laid egg, which was dislodged from the nest. This is probably an example of a behaviour pattern maturing slightly out of step. Thus, in one case, such a female re-laid and incubated properly. She had not practised or performed the behaviour imperfectly, thereby learning, but had merely had the experience of laying. By the second time, the appropriate innately programmed behaviour came into action. Again, there is a precise parallel in the first-time breeder's response to a new chick.

Fig. 86

Rocking movements adjusting the position of the webs before placing them over the egg for incubation. Similar movements are used to perfect the nest cup before laying.

This raises the question of the nature of the response to stimuli, though here merely with reference to the gannet's response to the egg as an external stimulus.

The following experiments were on only a small scale and inconclusive since, unfortunately, the full previous history of the birds involved was not known. Two questions which they answer, however, are: Does a female gannet require to have laid in the current season before she will incubate properly (in other words are laying and incubation independent of each other)? If not, is there a clear-cut point, prior to laying, at which the bird suddenly becomes incubation-minded?

The answer to the first question is that a female gannet will sometimes accept an egg without having laid one. Apparently, however, if she has already ovulated she will reject the donated egg. Thus, of five birds which only temporarily accepted a foster egg, four laid themselves 4, 5, 9 and 9 days later (the other either did not lay or laid and lost).

However, of 12 immediate rejections, 11 subsequently laid 6, 9 (four cases), 10 (two cases), 14–19, 20, 21 and 27 days later. Since the period between ovulation and laying is probably not more than 14 days at the most four of these cases had not ovulated and yet refused a donated egg. The only birds to fully accept, incubate and hatch a foster egg (four cases) were those which failed to lay their own.

The position is therefore unclear; some birds rejected, but had not ovulated and later did so, some accepted and had not ovulated and did not do so and some rejected but had probably already ovulated. Only those birds which had not ovulated and were able to repress doing so, fully accepted the donated eggs. All the others either rejected it outright or accepted it temporarily and then (perhaps because they ovulated) rejected it. This was borne out by an unusual case, in which a female rejected a donated egg nine days before laying, lost her own, rejected another donated egg and re-laid; both rejected eggs having been donated either after she had ovulated (the first time) or before she was about to do so (the second time).

This is not the expected picture, since Beer (1963) found that the closer a black-headed gull was to laying, the readier it was to accept donated eggs and this is certainly what one would predict.

7. *Behaviour during incubation*

(*a*) *Patterns of activity*

Except when sleeping, gannets rarely incubate for more than two successive minutes without also performing numerous other behaviour patterns. Spells of activity alternate with periods of rest. Certain activities, such as Menacing, touching nest material and Bowing are linked and when one occurs at much higher frequency so do the others. Other activities, such as nest digging, occur in concentrated spells in contrast to Rotary Headshaking which occurs at a fairly uniform level. The commonest activity is touching nest material since this occurs as a displacement activity in conflict situations as well as 'normally'. Preening and ordinary headshaking are the two other commonest behaviour patterns.

During incubation, quiet spells are usually ended by a sudden stimulus such as the arrival or departure of a neighbour. The activity resulting—perhaps Menacing—then leads to another,

Fig. 87(a). Incubating the egg underfoot (Australasian gannet). (*Photo:* C. J. Robertson.)

Fig. 87b. Small chicks are incubated on top of the webs. The appropriate change in the adult's behaviour (from incubating underfoot) is critical.

such as egg shifting as a result of changed position. However, some activities occur without any such observable stimulus.

(*b*) *Egg-shifting and nest-settling movements*

The position of the egg beneath the webs is altered, on average, almost twice an hour, using the lower edge of the closed or slightly open bill pointing backwards between the webs (Fig. 86). Settling movements, altering the position of the webs on the egg, are common and invariably follow egg-shifting. Only rarely are they followed by leg or wing stretching, so that they seem to concern incubation rather than the relief of muscle cramp. Nest-settling movements occur even before there is an egg in the nest and become commoner just before laying. The gannet's settling movements do not seem to alter the position of the egg.

(*c*) *Egg-retrieval*

The ability to retrieve eggs might be expected in most ground nesting birds liable to displace them and indeed, after a detailed study, Poulsen (1963) reached this conclusion. Gannets, however, show little retrieving ability. They successfully roll eggs into the cup from the rim and will attempt, usually without success, those just within reach though a little below the rim. However, the egg usually rolls away from the gannet's beak, for the bird lacks any ability to steer it. Nevertheless, on flat ground it is reasonably successful and there can be no doubt that, where nest rims are very low, this behaviour could lead to doubling-up if a neighbouring egg were to be left unattended. I have one such record and it probably happens more often in the South African gannet (q.v.), which builds nests of excreta on flat ground and in which, probably for this reason, 'clutches' of two are more commonly observed.

From the adaptive point of view, retrieving behaviour would be useless on cliff ledges and equally so were an egg to be displaced from the steep-sided pedestal nest characteristic of flatter habitats. Unlike some birds, gannets will not incubate an egg outside the nest. Again, such a response would rarely be useful.

(*d*) *Role of the sexes in incubation*

When the female first vacates the egg, which, if the male is present, she usually does soon after laying, he immediately begins his first incubation spell, the sight of the egg apparently releasing the appropriate behaviour. The early change-over may be partly due to the female having already spent a long pre-laying spell on the nest. A similar procedure occurs in many other species which habitually take long incubation stints.

Two-hourly checks over several days and once or twice daily checks over several weeks established that the number of incubation stints was roughly equal in the sexes, though the male's were longer (average 35·6 hours against 30·2 hours). Incubation stints are probably related to the foraging behaviour of the off-duty partner and so may be expected to vary with locality. At Bempton, they are shorter than on the Bass (see p. 93). In both sexes the spells became slightly shorter as hatching approached, then dropped suddenly after hatching.

8. *Change-over*

Arrival of the partner during incubation is followed by Mutual Fencing and change-over. An odd fact is that before the incoming bird relieves its mate it usually Sky-points (see p. 195) and moves slightly *away* from the nest before returning and taking over. Departing birds very often elicit Mutual Fencing intention movements from the partner, as though the latter is trying to influence it to remain on the site. Once the incubating bird rises, the incomer pushes directly on to the egg and settles down, usually ignoring the mate, who repeatedly Sky-points before leaving. Females are significantly less willing than males to vacate the egg, which may possibly indicate a stronger incubation tendency or reflect the fact that males have usually been on duty longer. Calculating from time of arrival at the nest, to stepping onto the egg, males took 8 minutes (longest time 22 minutes) and the females 3 minutes (longest time 11 minutes).

Although change-over times are scattered throughout daylight hours, there is a tendency for most arrivals to occur between dawn and mid-day (probably representing birds which departed late the previous day, fished in the early hours and then quickly returned), and there is a second influx in the early evening.

After change-over, some time usually elapses before the outgoing partner leaves the vicinity of the nest, but once away it does not usually return until the next relief, though I recorded birds flying over and inspecting their nests several times from the air before finally departing. Significantly, these were usually birds which had been involved in competition for mate or site. Occasionally a relieved bird brings nest material and may then spend further time sleeping beside the nest. I had reason to believe that off duty birds did not usually congregate in Clubs, which were composed of immature birds and non-breeding adults (but see p. 154).

9. *Brooding and care of young*

(*a*) *Transference to top of web*

When the egg begins to chip it is transferred to the top of the webs, although I have observed pipped eggs to be incubated underfoot. The stimulus to which the adult responds in performing this highly adaptive behaviour is probably in the first instance auditory. Experimental work on artificially incubated gannet eggs (Vince, pers. comm) detected movements 13 days before the egg hatched and the chick started breathing from the air space 2½ days before hatching. It started cheeping eight hours after beginning to breathe. The shell pipped at 20.30 hours on June 15th and hatched at 15.20 on June 17th. The chick responded to bill stroking by gaping for about three seconds, which fits with my suggestion (p. 204) that the adult is initially responsible for eliciting the feeding reaction from the chick. The head was tucked almost in the adult (scapular) position, with appropriate raising of the wing, from three days onwards.

The newly-hatched chick also is brooded on top of the webs and in four observed cases aberrant behaviour resulted in its death, the adult continuing to incubate the hatching egg or new chick underfoot. Of 13 other cases in which egg or small chick were lost, eight eggs disappeared around their due hatching date and five chicks disappeared at less than five days, possibly also due to trampling underfoot or perhaps to faulty feeding; Snow (1960) mentions that shags sometimes experience great difficulty in feeding small young and Coulson makes the same observation for the kittiwake. Of the 17 cases referred to above, seven were first time breeders, a disproportionately high number. In a further case, the small chick almost died during a spell of female attendance during which she trod on it; it then subsequently recovered, but at three weeks died during bad weather. This is probably another case of death due to parental inadequacy. Still, even experienced adults sometimes stand on their newly-hatched chicks, which must be highly resistant to rough treatment. The presence of more feathers than usual in the nest at this stage may help to protect the chick. When the chick is trampled to death, the adult may respond either (presumably) to the different 'feel' of the object or to its configuration, and prise the flattened chick from the bottom of the nest, placing it in the correct position on top of its webs.

When moving a very young chick the parent often opens its bill widely and tremors each mandible, one on either side of the chick, nudging it along in a series of fine movements. Gannets moving eggs usually keep their mandibles closed or only slightly open and they sometimes move the chick in the same way. As long as it is able, the chick pushes its head and foreparts beneath its parent for shelter. Its increasing fat layer and thickening down subsequently protect it from almost all weathers; the only deaths due to climatic conditions occur during heavy, prolonged rain with wind and low temperatures, which happen not infrequently in late June. A minor advantage, considering the population as a whole, of the gannet's habit of producing its eggs over a period of several weeks rather than within a week or two, is that it thereby avoids the possibility of mass mortality among young chicks as a result of climatic factors and the same applies later, after they fledge. The onset of rain stimulates parents to try to tuck even large young beneath their breasts.

(*b*) *Treatment of eggshell*

One female was seen to prise half an eggshell off the hatching chick in a precisely performed action which was not merely due to accidentally mandibulating the eggshell with the chick inside. However it is apparently not necessary and chicks are certainly capable of freeing themselves, though they may take over 36 hours to emerge after chipping.

Gannets leave the eggshell lying around the nest for some time after hatching (up to four days noted) and may eventually drop it over the side or place it on the rim, though sometimes it is merely trampled into the nest. Occasionally it is mandibulated like nest material and pieces are flung away with a quick sideways headshake. This disposal is not practised systematically. Non-removal may be connected with lack of predators which could be guided to the nest by the shell. The possible reasons for eggshell removal discussed by several authors (such as lacerating the young and nest hygiene) could, of course, account for the gannet's eventual disposal, though in view of the time lag this seems unlikely.

(*c*) *Change of attendance rhythm*

The pre-hatching vocalisations of the young gannet are very probably the cue to which adults respond by shortening their incubation and foraging stints, for change-overs become remarkably more frequent just before hatching. This is probably adaptive in ensuring that the newly-hatched chick will be brooded by a parent capable of feeding it. Chicks may certainly be fed in much less than 24 hours after hatching.

Guard spells then lengthen again and over the first six weeks of the chick's growth average about 18·5 hours in both male and female. During the second half of the chick's period in the nest the male's spells become longer (male 23·7; female 18·8 hours) and this trend continues after fledging when, as happens early in the season, they become very much longer reflecting the male's stronger site attachment. However, it should be noted that the duration of the attendance spells and the foraging trips varies considerably with area. This doubtless reflects the nearness of the main feeding areas. The foraging trips of the Bempton gannets were much shorter (see p. 141).

Throughout the entire period spent on the nest (90 days on average) the chick is constantly attended by a parent and for some 15 per cent of daylight hours by both parents. At first this obviously protects vulnerable young from such predators as herring gulls; gannets with eggs or young watch hovering gulls intently, with head retracted and bill vertical, and lunge at them if they approach. Even man is liable to be attacked at this stage. Later the guarding of the chick is necessary to protect it from attack by neighbours or from intruders looking for a site within the colony.

10. *Feeding of young*

Feeding rates, amounts and types of food and so on are best discussed in the account of ecology. Here, only behaviour concerned with the transference of food will be considered.

During the first few days little is seen of the constantly brooded chick except wobbly head movements beneath the adult. These and the chick's cheeping may stimulate the adult to offer food; it is hard to settle this point. Such behaviour is certainly not necessary to orientate feeding by the adult and we saw adults bend their heads and offer food in a variety of unusual postures without the slightest sign of prior activity from the chick. In one variant the head was bent over so that the upper surface of the upper mandible lay on the floor of the nest and the chick fed from the trough. Chicks may be fed even before they are clear of the shell.

Some evidence bearing on the nature of the stimuli evoking the adult's feeding response came from twinning experiments which I carried out on the Bass in 1962. I discovered that the newly hatched twins immediately fell behind normal singletons in putting on weight, which was unexpected because at that stage they require a negligible amount of food in relation to the contents of the parent's crop. This could suggest that the parent is programmed to feed one chick endogenously, that is without specifically eliciting stimuli (begging) from the chick, though the mere fact of its presence is of course a necessary external stimulus which also directs the adult's presentation of food. In this case, the pre-set quota, as it were, would be split two ways and each would get less than it should. Alternatively, the adult might have a feeding response to the feeble and unco-ordinated movements of its chick. In this case, and particularly if such movements were not directly proportional to the chick's hunger, two chicks would not provide twice the feeding stimulus. In general, the performance of an innate behaviour pattern like feeding the chick lowers the readiness to perform it again for some time, this refractory period presumably resulting from some negative feed-back consequence of performing the act. Such refractoriness would result in each twin getting less than would a normal singleton. Later, the chicks perform persistent and well-oriented begging and certainly manage to elicit twice the normal response from the parents (see p. 91). The likely answer, then, is that adults at first feed chicks endogenously, but later respond in proportion to the intensity (frequency and duration) of the chick's begging behaviour.

11. *Other aspects of parent/young relationship*

The young gannet, growing up within the strict confines of its nest, surrounded by aggressive adults and other chicks, develops in an atmosphere of feverish noise and activity and soon begins to interact with its parents and to a limited extent with other adults and young. The relationship between parents and young, no less than that between mates or neighbours, reflects the nature of the species' social organisation. Just as the evolution of highly aggressive territorial behaviour has influenced the nature of the pair relationship, so it has influenced that between parent and chick.

(*a*) *Parent/young recognition*

Do adults reject all except their own chick? Adult rejection of strange young is widespread in the animal kingdom and often has obvious advantages. Many colonial species attack strange young and one may instance Arctic terns, black-headed gulls and herring gulls, guillemots, king penguins, yellow-eyed penguins and albatrosses. Even when the young of adelie penguins have formed creches, the adults find and feed only their own (Sladen 1953). In most species this recognising ability gradually matures; substitutes are accepted when chicks are small, but not later. Young shags gather on the sea-rocks after fledging and are fed by their parents, although after becoming active and until about a month old chicks 'often go to neighbouring nests and

Fig. 88. Eleven- to 13-week-old gannet chick begging and being fed. Note the persistent following of the adult's evasive movements, the gentle grasping of the adult's bill, the restrained begging (an anti-falling mechanism; cf. the frenzied begging of ground-nesting boobies) and the gulping back of the adult.

are accepted' (Snow 1963), something one certainly would not expect. In fact, the red-footed booby develops strong powers of discrimination between its own and other young precisely at this stage in their development; at least it quickly drives away strange young that attempt to 'poach' and even the young themselves suddenly begin to attack intruding young, which they formerly did not. Coots will adopt young if they are less than 14 days old and resemble their own in size; otherwise these may be killed (Alley & Boyd 1950). Similarly, female seals and sea-lions reject strange young in the rookeries. It is seldom possible to known how the distinction between young is achieved, though calls and, in some mammals, scent, appear to play some part.

In the above species it is clearly advantageous to reject strange chicks, since many chicks approach and beg from strange adults. To accept them could result in the inadequate feeding of all. On the other hand, in the gannet, as also in the kittiwake, because chicks normally stay on the nest there is usually no danger of feeding strange ones. Consequently there is no advantage in discrimination, and one might expect, as indeed one finds, that in the correct context—on the nest—strange young are accepted either in place of or in addition to their own. I have proved this many times by donation and substitution experiments (see below). On the other hand, any youngster, their own included, will usually be attacked if it approaches from 'outside'—that is, off the nest. This can be observed when young ones are dislodged and have to regain their nests in the face of attack, sometimes severe, from their parents. Whilst, for the reasons given above, the acceptance of strange young is not surprising, it is perhaps more so that the breeding adult will often accept young that, in age, differ greatly from their own and may even accept an egg and revert to incubation.

Substitution of eggs which hatched as long as 32 days before the recipient's own would have done, showed that the ensuing chick was cared for normally right up to fledging. Similarly, so were chicks that hatched as much as 19 days 'late'. Similarly, when, instead of an egg that hatched earlier than it should have done we donated chicks for eggs, these too were accepted. All six chicks, ranging from 3–23 days or 50–1250 gm and 'hatching' (i.e. appearing in the nest) 0–16 days early, were accepted in lieu of eggs. This showed that adults did not require, each year, the external stimulus of hatching an egg to enable them to switch over to the appropriate chick care behaviour. Probably, though we were unable to test this, even birds that had never experienced a hatching egg would also switch satisfactorily. Of course, their method of feeding, in contrast with that of pigeons, probably does not require any particular physiological state to accompany hatching.

In four out of five cases the adults accepted eggs in place of chicks varying from three to 17 days old. In the fifth case the chick was 23 days old and the adult treated the egg as nest material.

Six exchanges were made involving pairs of chicks differing in age by nought to seven days and covering an age range of two to 36 days. All substituted chicks were accepted, showing that up to this age of chick at least a gannet will accept young differing considerably in age from its own. In fact, occasionally, chicks ten to eleven weeks old wandered on to a nest during the adults' absence as a result of human disturbance, and were accepted in lieu of or in addition to the rightful chick. In one case the rightful chick was smaller and died competing with the intruder, but usually, if both chicks were large, both survived. Also, in at least 20 cases, adults whose own chicks had fledged accepted and even fed chicks which paused at their nest en route to the cliff edge. For example, a juvenile fledged on September 3rd 1961, and on September 7th another arrived at the nest from one further inland, was accepted and remained for 24 hours. Another juvenile fledged on September 4th and a stranger was accepted from September 8th to 12th. Further, in one case a strange chick was preened by the chick at whose nest it stopped, though the usual reaction of owning chick to intruder is attack.

To balance this picture it is necessary to add that in the presence of their own young adults usually discriminate against a strange chick *if they see it arrive*. Under such conditions it is, of course, a wandering chick and as such fiercely attacked. This may well be because in such circumstances an intruding chick shows evident signs of fear which a rightful offspring would not. In most of the cases given above, circumstances were different in that the rightful chick had left the nest when the intruder arrived. Even when an intruding chick gains the nest it is by no means automatically accepted. Having seen it arrive, the adult usually continues to attack, though occasionally it will eventually desist. It seems that short-term 'recognition' is involved here since, where rightful and intruder young are together on the nest, adult attack is directed solely to the latter, even when the chicks exchange position. But such 'recognition' need involve only spatial discrimination of two movable objects, neither of which has been lost to sight. If the rightful chick is then removed the adult will accept the other, though in such a situation the adult has left the nest, due to the disturbance, and returns as to a 'normal' chick.

Yet observations revealed puzzling variation in parent reaction to their own chick off the site; sometimes they attacked and other times they accepted them. In one instance a female who was attached to two nests, one empty, attacked her own chick fiercely when it tried to join her on the second nest, but accepted it when it, and later she, returned to the proper nest. However, adults also tend and defend their chicks slightly off the nest. Therefore one cannot say that parents accept a chick, their own or another, only and precisely at their own nest; but chicks are certainly more likely to be attacked away from it. Similarly, females are powerfully inhibited from attacking an intruding male on the nest, but aggression may be released as soon as either bird moves off the nest. Of course, adult gannets attack intruders of their own sex without such inhibition. Sometimes an adult whose chick had moved on to an empty nest near-by and been threatened or attacked by a neighbour jumped across to engage the attacker. This naturally gave the strong impression of parent defending its chick even though the latter was 'off' its rightful nest. Yet on other occasions an adult ignored serious attacks on its off-site chick. The great variability in the reaction of the adult to its own and other young remains a puzzling feature of its behaviour.

Gannet chicks definitely recognise their parents. We twice noticed that fringe chicks which had wandered some yards off the nest (a rare event possible only from nests on the extreme fringe) recognised their parent and rushed to beg, even though it landed not on their own nest but on an empty nest near-by. Yet the chicks had not responded to other adults landing similarly near to their nest. It also seemed, though I could not prove the point conclusively, that recognition could be either visual or auditory. Auditory recognition is certainly within their ability (p. 19) and it seemed, in two cases where parents landed with relatively little calling, that the chicks (which were some feet away in the fringe) ignored this, but after a few seconds turned their heads, saw the adult and immediately went to beg for food. Despite this, chicks displaced either naturally or experimentally, will remain with foster parents if allowed to do so. If the chick can regain its nest it does so; otherwise it makes the best of any haven that offers.

It would be a disadvantageous division of labour if some pairs reared their own and a neighbour's chick. The aggression of the adults towards wandering chicks and the cliff position of many sites, to which the young respond innately by staying strictly on the nest, make it unlikely that a gannet chick will normally find its way on to a strange nest.

In sum, gannets accept chicks of widely differing ages in place of their own egg. They do not require either the experience of the full incubation period (or even half of it) or of hatching to respond appropriately to the chick. Their reaction is reversible for some time and they can change from chick care to incubation and back again. They also accept substituted chicks widely different in age from their own and over the entire range of the chick's growth. However, they fiercely attack wandering chicks and chicks outside the strictly de-limited area of their nest. This, together with the chick's innate tendency to remain strictly on the nest means that parents are rarely called upon to discriminate. The biologically desirable goal of feeding only their own offspring is usually achieved without discrimination on the nest; whether there is ability to distinguish their own young from others remains unshown but probable, even though unexpressed behaviourally. On the other hand, chicks appear to recognise their parents and, as shown below, their sites.

(b) *Adult aggression towards chicks*

There has been occasion already to mention the fact that gannets will attack young, their own included, that approach the nest. The whole phenomenon, however, is worth more notice.

Adults, even non-breeders on the fringe, are conspicuously aggressive towards unattended or wandering chicks of any age (Fig. 92), and after the colony had been disturbed several females attacked unattended chicks indiscriminately. I also have many records of adults leaving their own nests to attack unattended young near-by. Even a small, downy chick releases violent attack. One such chick, already almost dead from previous attacks, crept up to a nest with a chick of similar age and lay there. The adult on duty attacked it violently and killed it. When change-over took place the incomer did not apparently notice the dead chick for some time, but later launched a beserk attack for several minutes, calling stridently and striking repeatedly at the chick. Similar adult attacks were recorded on dead, feathered young. This frenzied reaction to a chick outside the nest was never seen in any of the boobies.

In two cases at Bempton, chicks which lost one parent were attacked by neighbours when the surviving adult went off to feed. There can be no doubt that an unguarded gannet chick, on or off its nest, powerfully incites attack from adults and gannets rarely leave their chicks unguarded, even for a moment, unless a spell of bad weather occurs during the later stages of chick growth or it is very late in the season. I have five records of unguarded chicks killed by neighbouring adults, even though the chicks remained quietly on their nest and performed the usual appeasing behaviour. Boobies terminate their chick guard period when the young are about a month old and able to withstand temperature changes. Although unoccupied white boobies, particularly males, occasionally attack unguarded young they very rarely kill them.

In the gannet, adult hostility is an effective and presumably advantageous method of discouraging chicks from wandering but the habit of attacking non-trespassing chicks seems to be a dysgenic extension of a functional behaviour pattern. Non-selective and apparently of no advantage to the performer, it has persisted perhaps because there has been no selection pressure capable of eliminating it without incurring other disadvantages. If adults did not attack unattended chicks in this way, members of a pair could fish simultaneously, thus increasing their food gathering capacity, which could be important in a less constant environment, but seems relatively unimportant for the gannet. One may say that the favourable feeding environment of the gannet (see p. 78) has permitted the evolution of adult aggression even with such side results, whereas the relatively unfavourable feeding environment of most boobies would, quite apart from its other effects, prevent the evolution of aggression which involved curtailment of the pair's hunting activities.

On the rare occasions when a number of gannet chicks in a group on flat ground were simultaneously left unattended they wandered about and indulged in playful behaviour, showing that it is apparently adult aggression which chains them to their nests. Also, the chicks of the closely related South African and Australasian gannet show far more tendency to wander, especially in the later stages and, correspondingly, there is evidence (p. 255) that the adults are less aggressive than adult Atlantic gannets.

In sum, wandering chicks, are strongly attacked by adults even though the chicks, as individuals, would be accepted as substitutes for their own. The tendency to attack off-site or unguarded chicks effectively discourages wandering or the absence of both parents together.

Whilst the extreme nature of adult hostility to young may seem dysgenic enough in the colony, it seems a thousand times more so on the sea. Nevertheless, newly-fledged young, unable to rise from the water, are often attacked on the sea around the colony from which they so recently flew. Gurney could have filled a page with the imagined dismay of the young gannet, sole object of parental care and attention for three unremitting months, only to find, on the very instant of its foray into the outer world, a throng of adults waiting to initiate a cruel baptism.

The attack may be prolonged and concerted, involving up to 20 or 30 attacking adults for an hour or more. They peck and hold tenaciously to the juvenile, forcing it below the surface and hanging on as it flaps and threshes in its efforts to win clear. As one attacker tires of the activity another flies in, attracted by the commotion and takes its place. The first young birds of the season seem much more likely to be attacked than the later ones, as though the novelty of flight-incapable youngsters attract attention and attack but the response rather quickly wanes (a similar tendency in the black-headed gull has been noticed, although their attacks are much milder). Occasionally the juvenile becomes thoroughly waterlogged and returns to the base of the cliffs, where it lands, if it can, and may remain for several days. Almost certainly a very few young birds die as a result, but the number is totally negligible. Senseless, in adaptive terms, though these attacks may seem, natural selection could not be expected to eliminate them unless there was enough disadvantage to the attackers. Since the matter is out of the hands of the parents the moment the youngster fledges, no trait of theirs could affect the survival of their youngster in this particular trial. Thus, there is no obvious way in which the tendency for any particular adult not to attack young at sea would benefit its own progeny. My interpretation is that these attacks are part and parcel of the gannet's well developed intra-specific aggression; they are not sufficiently harmful to the species for natural selection to have produced a mechanism by which adults differentiated between young-off-the-nest in the colony (to be attacked as a trespasser) and young-off-the-nest at sea (to be left alone). The risk of diluting intra-specific aggression and hence handicapping an adult when it is vital to be fully aggressive would seem too great to justify adding refinements of this inessential nature.

(*c*) *The behavioural significance of black plumage in the juvenile*

This seems the most appropriate point at which to advance a possible—in my opinion a very probable—interpretation of the juvenile gannet's black plumage, for the reader should by now be convinced that adult gannets, and males in particular, are prone to attack other adults and also young ones. Basically, in this view, the adaptive value of the black plumage lies in its attack-inhibiting, or perhaps better, the absence of attack-eliciting, properties. By putting on black plumage the juvenile, though now as big as an adult and standing like one, manages to look about as different as possible. Earlier, admittedly, it was white like an adult, but at this time it was quite different in size, posture and (being fluffy) texture. Since it is indisputable that a chick which looked like an adult could readily become the object of re-directed attack from the male—as the female is—and since even one episode in which the male pushed the chick away from the nest (as he may do the female) would be fatal on cliffs, anything that reduces this likelihood would confer strong and direct survival value. The role of key releasers in eliciting behaviour suggests that by looking totally different—i.e. lacking the releasers for attack—the juvenile will indeed reduce attack. Tinbergen long ago suggested that the general significance of juvenile plumage and special postures is in fact just this, and the gannet seems a prime example, since not only are adults extraordinarily aggressive, but the nesting situation is extremely dangerous and, as if that were not enough, the period over which one attack could be fatal, is a very long one. The point bears labouring, because there are significant disadvantages in a plunge diver having black underparts. Yet the juvenile gannet, at the one stage in its life when it needs all the advantages it can get as it struggles to acquire the difficult art of catching fish by plunge diving, is handicapped by black underparts. This surely means that they have a function valuable enough to override associated disadvantages and the one suggested above is of an appropriate magnitude.

BEHAVIOUR OF YOUNG

Much of the chick's behaviour is adaptive in relation to two important aspects of its life—its interactions with aggressive adults and its tendency to nest on cliffs. Some chick behaviour, for example that with which parents are directly involved, has been described. This section completes the account up to the moment of fledging and the behaviour immediately afterwards. Migration occupies a separate section.

1. *General*

Gannet chicks are not very active. When they are small they need warmth and shelter and are therefore comfortably ensconced beneath their parent. As they become larger, they are debarred from much activity by the habitat (if cliffs) or by the hostility of neighbouring adults. Mostly they lie around sleeping. During hot weather large chicks seem obviously uncomfortable, and mildly heat-stressed. They sprawl listlessly on the nest or, panting heavily, stand with drooping wings, hitching them up only to let them sag again; the wings, from about six weeks onwards, are heavy with blood-filled quills and in any case a loosened position probably aids heat loss. Often chicks support themselves on their tarsi, exposing the under surface of the webs, or they may thrust one foot stiffly out from the body, with web spread, thus aiding heat loss. Unlike the red-foot, they do not elevate their posteriors to facilitate heat loss from the cloaca or conserve energy by using their beak as a prop, by spiking it into the nest to form a tripod between beak and legs. Gular fluttering is common in warm weather and may be the main heat-losing mechanism. It can occur in very young chicks.

2. *Feeding*

The cheeping calls and more unco-ordinated movements carried out by the chick from its first day may stimulate the adult to offer food. Clearly recognisable food begging behaviour was first seen at about ten days, the chick reaching up and nibbling at the underside of the adult's lower mandible.

In fully developed begging, the chick pesters the adult by pointing its bill upwards, swaying its head from side to side and aiming mild lunges at the parent's beak. High intensity begging includes a repeated 'yipping' note, which is itself highly stimulating to the adult and may elicit regurgitation movements before the chick touches the adult's bill. In contrast to most boobies, gannets do not pester wildly, nor do they use violent wing movements. This restraint is probably a valuable adaptation to cliff nesting, by reducing the danger of the chick falling.

3. *Comfort movements and body care*

During the first few days the chick does little except make wobbly head movements, feed and distend its gape. Comfort movements other than gaping appear when it is about a week old, when it makes its first attempts at wing flapping, sideways headshaking (these may emerge sooner, but are difficult to distinguish from involuntary head movements) and Rotary Headshaking. Sideways wing stretching and wing arching, with neck forwards and downwards and head horizontal, occur within the first fortnight.

Wing-exercising, as sustained bouts of wing-flapping, occurs from three weeks onwards, but does not become regular until the flight feathers have erupted, at which stage it is also unfailingly stimulated by rain. Wing-exercising bouts usually last about 30–60 seconds. At

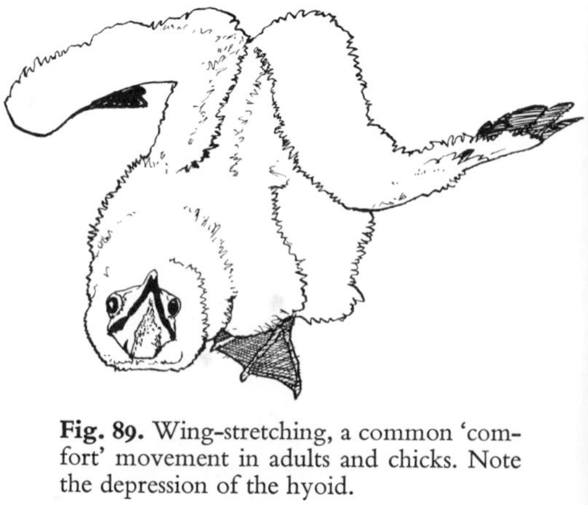

Fig. 89. Wing-stretching, a common 'comfort' movement in adults and chicks. Note the depression of the hyoid.

Fig. 90. Chicks sleep in prone positions, often with wing(s) drooping over the side of the nest and one web thrust out. They appear to be dead! Adults sleep with their head in their scapulars.

first the whole wing is flapped, but gradually the action of the proximal part decelerates until only the wing tip moves. It is usually performed facing the wind, except on narrow ledges where the young mainly face inwards, and it is not accompanied by walking or jumping, as it is in herring gulls, for example. This would usually be dangerous. Young kittiwakes, too, jump much less than other gulls (E. Cullen 1957), probably for the same reason. Nevertheless, many gannet chicks fall to their death as a result of wing-exercising and this is almost certainly the main source of mortality (p. 107).

Rotary Headshaking remains relatively infrequent and even the period when down is shed produces nothing comparable to the spectacular increase which accompanies the adult moult of body feathers. Nevertheless, the full adult pattern, in which the hyoid is depressed, the head thrust forwards and the wings are opened and flapped (Fig. 89) is recognisable.

Chicks begin preening, nibbling their down, at about two weeks, though until the feathers grow it is relatively perfunctory behaviour. Adults preen their chicks from about one week and chicks begin preening their parents and mutual preening with them from about ten weeks; the latter seems relatively rare in birds. Often chicks preen their parents on the wings and back, which allo-preening adults hardly ever do; the preoccupation which adults show with the others' head and neck apparently develops later.

'Oiling', the movement by which birds with an oil gland distribute the secretion over their plumage, including rolling the crown on the oil gland at the base of the tail before rubbing the wings and back, was seen from about eight weeks onwards. By this time the feathers are well grown, though still thickly covered with down in many places.

Yawning, that is mouth-opening involving only the lower mandible and not using the naso-frontal hinge as adults occasionally do to raise the upper mandible, occurs within the first ten days. Gross distension of the inter-ramal skin to dilate the pharynx and accommodate fish occurs early in development, certainly by seven to ten days, probably much earlier. Gular-fluttering, so characteristic of the Pelecaniformes, also appears in this period and is seen (Fig. 101(a)) during hot weather or intense food begging. The exposure of a spread web to the air (Fig. 101(c)) is also a commonly used temperature-regulating device.

Chicks sleep with their heads hanging over the nest rim (Fig. 90), or curled round like a dog, until they are six to eight weeks old, when they begin to adopt the adult posture, standing or sitting with head in scapulars. Even fully grown chicks, however, occasionally sleep prone, with head lying on the ground, a habit never found among adults. The persistence of juvenile or pre-juvenile habits is an interesting topic; young herring gulls, perfectly able to fly, will often crouch instead, though healthy adults never do so. One often finds that behaviour patterns occurring in young birds and later giving rise to adult behaviour patterns, are, in their new adult form, at first more like the original chick behaviour than in their later, fully differentiated form.

Although tiny chicks cannot void clear of the nest they do not produce faecal sacs, and merely soil the nest. The adults occasionally dig in the nest bottom and fling away bits, but it is usually not possible to see whether soiled material is specially selected. Later, the chick voids clear of the nest cup. Direction of faeces downwards on to the side of the nest, as sometimes seen in adults, was not observed in chicks.

4. *Interactive behaviour*

As the chick becomes stronger and its motor co-ordination improves, it begins to respond in a more adult-like fashion to its environment, including surrounding birds. It begins to show a marked interest in nest material. From the age of about two weeks it picks up straws, feathers, etc. and mandibulates them. Later it snatches seaweed from an incoming parent and places it on the nest rim with nest building movements and vibrations of the mandibles.

Chicks menace each other when about a month old, but only perfunctorily. Later they develop adult-type (ritualised) Menacing, darting their beaks towards each other, with the final sideways twist. They fiercely attack trespassing chicks, irrespective of size difference, and sometime maintain attacks, accompanied by yapping, for long periods. This hostility doubtless helps to deter chicks from wandering and strengthens the effect of adult aggression in maintaining the one chick per nest system.

Chicks occasionally menace neighbouring adults, who usually ignore them, and from about seven weeks frequently menace and attack their parents (Fig. 91) so severely that the adult female often faces-away and both sexes, but particularly the male, occasionally retaliate strongly. Chick attacks are delivered with the unco-ordinated movements typical of young animals; violent and mistimed jabs, excited yapping, contortions and perfunctory self-preening are all mixed up. The stimulus received by an adult when the chick grabs its beak in an attacking manner never causes regurgitation, whereas the touch of the chick's bill in food soliciting does. It is unusual for young birds to threaten and attack their parents as much as young gannets do. Even as youngsters they are aggressive and from the earliest age become conditioned to some of the inter-actions which are important to them later. It may seem surprising that the young of such an aggressive species 'risk' eliciting attack from their parents, but presumably the physical characteristics and appeasement behaviour of the young are enough to inhibit or switch off parental attack.

The gannet chick is guarded unremittingly for its entire life in the nest. Nevertheless, one might expect the development of appeasement behaviour if only to cope with the occasional aggression (sometimes re-directed after a fracas) of the male parent. Bill hiding (Fig. 92) is, in fact, extremely pronounced and is the chick's response to attack. It is clearly a fear response and appears during the first month of life. The bill is tucked either centrally or to one side beneath the body and the chick lies flat on its ventral surface. The arched nape is thus, as it were, presented to the attacker. In the rare cases where a strange adult gains access to an unguarded chick it may peck all the down off its nape. The muscle layer seems extremely thick, however, and the gannet chick can survive severe attacks that would kill most other birds of a similar size. Adults may attack and sometime rough-preen chicks for long periods

(*a*)

(*b*)

Fig. 91

(a) Chicks often 'threaten' or 'attack' a parent in play. This may release threat (or rarely attack) from the parent.

(b) Often, adults face-away from importunate young.

(up to 30 minutes). The chick's appeasement posture is not, therefore, immediately effective. Indeed, as already mentioned, the appeasement behaviour of the chick may be insufficient even to save its life. It seems desirable, where possible, to have some measure of the effectiveness of appeasement behaviour to avoid creating a false impression of its efficacy. Bill-hiding and adult Facing-away are two relatively straightforward examples, compared for instance with the complications of the black-headed gull's head-flagging and, as one would expect, both have limited effect. Nevertheless, they are effective enough to confer survival value on their possessors. The stimulus eliciting bill-hiding is perhaps mainly tactile and quite independent of the presence of another gannet. It may readily be induced by tapping the chick on the nape.

From nine weeks chicks show Facing-away in the form used by adult females, which also results in the beak being hidden but is different from bill-hiding as defined. They still continue the infantile bill-hiding. Chicks frequently and fleetingly Face-away from each other, but bill-hide only when severely attacked by a much larger chick or an adult.

The adult Pelican Posture, in which the bill tip is pressed against the upper breast (Fig. 74(c)), could be considered a reduced form of beak-hiding, but is rarely seen in chicks, although occasionally a brief form, passing into Facing-away, can be detected. It is interesting that this posture, which is probably partly aggressively motivated should be lacking in the chick. It becomes more frequent in fully feathered young just before their departure.

Chicks are noticeably less prone to beak-hide from their own parents, even if these attack them. During the excessively boisterous attacks which large young make on their parents, Facing-away sometimes occurs spontaneously without the parent having retaliated, the chick apparently associating its own aggressive behaviour with parental retribution.

Probably the chick's tendency to drive other chicks away from the nest (and perhaps even its tendency to attack its parents) represents emerging territorial behaviour. It would not be surprising if ritualised territorial behaviour were also to develop and in fact Bowing, though extremely rare, does occur in chicks of eleven weeks or more.

The Bows observed were ill-defined, but clearly incorporated the headshake and an incipient dip, with wings partly open and were accompanied by shrill yapping (cf. adult calling). Equivalent aggressive territorial behaviour occurs in young boobies and in other groups; I have seen long-calling in herring gulls no more than eight weeks old.

I also several times saw fully grown chicks performing a short bout of low-tensity Mutual Fencing with the female parent, following aggressive action by a neighbouring pair. This is exactly the situation in which the female would have fenced with the male had he been present.

By the time the chick fledges it may have shown all adult behaviour patterns (though it is unlikely to have Bowed or Mutual Fenced) except copulation, aggressive nest biting, nest-digging, gathering nest material, Sky-pointing and behaviour associated with incubation and care of the chick. It is striking that even when chicks leave the nest they never Sky-point, though adults almost invariably do so. This only develops in later social behaviour, in the Clubs of immatures and young adult birds which gather on the fringes of the breeding groups and perform incipient sexual and territorial behaviour.

Fig. 92

An adult attacks a displaced chick which adopts a prone position, turning its bill away or hiding it beneath its body. Displaced young are killed unless they can struggle onto a nest, in which case they are eventually accepted.

5. *Fledging behaviour*

(*a*) *Site fixation and philopatry*

An interesting topic closely associated with leaving the nest is the chick's ability to learn the visual features of its immediate surroundings. This may seem a useless accomplishment and during all its life in the nest it usually is, but it serves at least two useful functions (see below). Clearly if it is to develop it must do so either instantaneously or more gradually and at (or over) some particular period during its development. In a nidicolous sedentary chick such as the gannet, one would hardly expect immediate (post-hatching) visual imprinting akin to that by which a gosling becomes fixed on its parents. In fact, young gannets probably learn their immediate surroundings gradually, during the first months or so of life. By then they are capable of effective locomotion. Whilst displaced younger chicks will crawl back into a nest or towards an adult, they cannot regain their own nest from a distance—say of several yards. After a month, however, some chicks if displaced show a marked ability and astonishing persistence in returning to their nest. Chicks that wander as a result of disturbance by man often regain their nest, even if it takes them two days and at the cost of terrible punishment by neighbouring adults, from which they may subsequently die. During such returns they will even travel downhill, an action which understandably they normally rigorously avoid since chicks displaced from their nests are almost always displaced downwards and the adaptive behaviour is obviously to climb upwards; also their centre of gravity is all wrong for downhill travel. In fact they are well equipped to climb. Their toes are flexible and furnished with sharp claws and their beaks make good levers and props (they are never used for grasping). By using claws and beak they can lever their awkward and heavy bodies up steep and difficult inclines and even up the sides of the nest pedestal. They are obviously strongly inhibited from moving in directions which threaten a fall and cling grimly until they can manoeuvre into a better position.

When fledging, the young gannet from flatter areas sometimes receives such a hot reception en route to the cliff edge that it is unable to continue, and in such cases may, by a devious route which, of course, it has never traversed before, regain its own nest and recover there, for a few hours or a day. This is one of the two functions served by the ability to recognise the pattern of visual features in the area around the nest and it can, though rarely, save the chick's life.

This ability must reside in a gestalt-perception mechanism enabling object-transposition in such a way as to enable recognition of features never before seen in that particular perspective. The implications of this perceptual ability and the powerful site fixation are interesting, for they are probably the behavioural basis of the young bird's tendency to return to breed at or near the birthplace. A full consideration of this 'philopatry' would lead too far afield here; it is commonly found in colonial birds although individuals of any species may break the rule. In gannets it is very precise, usually leading individuals to return at least to the small group in which they were born and often to within a few feet, as one might expect from the site-fixation already mentioned. One occasionally notices dogged attempts by a four or five-year-old male to establish a site in the middle of a small group where there happens to be a slight gap, but one which nobody has attempted to use for years. Probably such birds were born in that immediate area and are trying to establish themselves there. This tendency would also explain why, every year some birds try to establish sites on the Needle (Fig. 36)—an extraordinarily difficult pinnacle upon which almost all attempts to build further nests prove in vain.

It would be interesting to know whether birds from cliff ledges differ from those of flatter ground in their degree of philopatry. The former are certainly much less prone to move from the nest when disturbed, but this may be a non-genetic trait. Emlen showed that a similar tendency in herring gulls was due to conditioning and was not innate; eggs transferred from flat ground to cliff nests produced young that behaved like normal cliff ledge chicks. On the other hand, young kittiwakes have inborn adaptations to cliff nesting and retain them in experimentally flat conditions. Young gannets normally do remain on the nest even on flat ground, but probably due to the restraining influence of hostile neighbours, for after about mid-September many adults tend to desert the flatter parts of the colony during gale-force winds with rain. With fewer adults present, the 10–13 week-old young wander, exercise vigorously, toss nest material about, tussle with other chicks and attack smaller ones.

(b) *Fledging*

After about 13 weeks in the nest the young gannet, fully feathered, all traces of down having disappeared, is ready to leave. It has exercised its developing wings for two months or more, at first perfunctorily, then ponderously as the heavy, blood-filled quills were sprouting and finally in sustained and vigorous bouts with competent fully-feathered wings. The young gannet can just fly when about ten weeks old, but probably would not survive if it left at this age. They tend to exercise facing the wind from whatever quarter. Rain induces a great outburst of wing exercising; the mass of white birds suddenly and startlingly sprout myriads of rhythmically beating black wings—an extraordinary effect. In adults rain induces wing-flapping and Rotary Headshaking, but never simply wing-beating. Rain continued to elicit prolonged wing-beating from my captive young gannets for at least a year after fledging, but not usually from my captive adult.

From one to four days before departure, the chick shows distinctive patterns of behaviour associated with leaving, but one cannot predict when this will be, for it goes through all the motions several times before taking the plunge. Between each abortive attempt it turns its back on the abyss and resumes normal life as though it had never stood a hair's breadth from that irrevocable step. The posture of a chick contemplating departure—I nearly wrote disaster—is that of any anxious gannet; sleeked, long-necked, slightly forward, and peering, with beak slightly downwards (Fig. 93). It has, however, a fixed air of concentration, gazing intently out to sea. It may remain in this attitude for many minutes before relaxing and preening or playing with a bit of nest material. Certain individuals, watched continuously for 13 hours, repeated this process 20–30 times. After facing the sea for some time the chick may begin to flap its wings and will then almost certainly not leave on that occasion, but will terminate the wing flapping with a Rotary Headshake (p. 221). In the last few minutes before leaving, the chick shows rather more specific behaviour though even now it is not always possible to predict departure. The following account is generalised from many pre-departure observations.

The chick takes up the long-necked position, facing the sea. It is then practically oblivious to happenings immediately round about which would normally have attracted its attention. It peers down at the sea, often thrusting its neck forward as though to get a better view. It half lifts its wings from its back in the flight-intention movement which adults often show when about to take off from a tricky position. If the young bird has lifted its wings like this but not flown, it often starts a bout of wing flapping, probably brought on by the act of opening the wings. This transition from a tense, pre-flight attitude in which the wings are suddenly jerked open, to a more relaxed wing flapping position is conspicuous. After the flapping it then rapidly shakes its tail from side to side. After an interval of seconds or minutes, the chick resumes its sea-gazing, often suddenly stopping to toss nest material about or preen, usually half-heartedly for a short time, but occasionally earnestly for two or three minutes. The brief, perfunctory preening was characteristic of behaviour immediately before leaving; longer and more functional preening occurred when the chick was not due to leave immediately. In the final few minutes it may turn inland several times, but always jerks back to face the sea. Convulsive swallowing movements characterise the moments prior to a real or abortive take-off, and often the chick patters its feet and shakes its head (sideways headshaking).

Take-off occurs after two or three preparatory wing flicks and the chick then simply jumps into the air. If, however, it is denied all these preparatory movements, as when knocked over the edge by an adult, it can still make a successful recovery.

Chicks from nests on the edge of the cliff are quickly airborne, but those from flatter parts of the colony may be unable to clear the nesting birds and crash among them; they then flounder to the edge (Fig. 94), violently attacked by adults and other chicks. In a worse predicament, however, are those chicks from inland nests without any jumping-off place. They are forced either to work their way gradually to a more favourable spot or blunder blindly through. They often make two or three abortive runs and may return to their nest from a considerable distance. Occasionally they get stuck in a difficult place and may lie still for hours. Some unfortunate individuals are so hounded that they seem unable to force their way through even when an opportunity arises. One chick treated in this way for five days became so exhausted that it had very little chance of fledging. Yet others were accepted by strange adults, preened and even fed on their way to the edge. One is constantly amazed at the amount of variability in what one might expect to be fairly straightforward responses to a given external stimulus.

The parents do not take any part in the chicks' departure and as Perry (1948) noted, do not appear even to notice its take-off. If it goes they show no visible sign of registering the event and if it returns to the nest after an abortive attempt they accept it back again without demur. Both adults continue to frequent the nest for weeks after the main chick departure period and in the vast majority of cases there could be no question of them feeding their chick at sea. Both parents are often at the site for up to two days after the chick leaves and clearly could not then fly out and find their chick on the open sea. After chick departure, they spend more time on the site, not less, which they could hardly do if they were having to fly ever further to feed their chick.

Once in the air, the chick usually flies strongly after a shaky start. It often falls 15 or more metres before levelling out, but if the wind is fresh and onshore, it may rise from the second it jumps off the nest. Its wing movements are at first wobbly and it yaws and side-slips erratically, making too-vigorous compensating strokes. Then its wing beats, though shallow, become more regular, and it flies strongly in a wide curve, for at least a quarter of a mile, often soaring much higher than the cliffs it left, banking and gliding in an accomplished manner. The chick can fly a long way and we have watched several still going strong at least two miles from the Bass. It must be stressed that the juvenile does *not* leave because it is starved; on the contrary, it is fat and heavy and fed right up to fledging. The 'starvation theory' persistently gets into popular accounts about gannets.

Although the process of launching a fat-laden body from precipitous cliffs, on untried wings, may sound hazardous, on the Bass (and probably at most other gannetries) the mortality directly due to this method of fledging is in fact slight indeed. This loss was estimated in two ways. The first was to count how many 'crashes' were seen out of the total number of departures witnessed. Two crashes were seen out of 50 departures, and these two chicks suffered attacks from neighbouring adults before they managed to struggle clear; as a result they fell over the edge whilst facing in to the cliff face. They were then unable to right themselves and could not face into the wind to get the necessary lift. Consequently they fell like stones for 100 metres on to the rocky cliff base. One bird, which landed breast downward on bare rock, survived this terrible fall for two or three hours before dying; there can be no doubt that gannets are extraordinarily robust and able to withstand falls which would kill most heavy birds.

A second way was to count the number of injured birds at the base of a cliff section and roughly estimate the number of nests in the section. Several of these injured young probably got away eventually and only injured or very fouled young, standing in places where excreta fell on them, were counted. By this method about 10–20 young were seen below a sheer section of the north-west face, which held a nesting mass of some 1000–1500 pairs, but some injured birds could have fallen into the sea. Mortality due to fledging is probably less than four per cent but on Ailsa it is more. In 1974 S. Wanless collected 250 fully-feathered juveniles from

Fig. 93. A fully grown youngster (middle one) about to depart. It has triggered site ownership display from the left-hand adult and Mutual Fencing from the right-hand pair. The two adults between which it must pass are both in the Pelican Posture (fear/aggression).

the rocky base, which may represent at least 10 per cent of the young fledging. Mortality due to attacks by adults on fledged chicks could not be estimated but is likely to be insignificant compared with the main mortality factors. This figure is very low compared with certain other cliff-nesting seabirds, such as the guillemot whose chicks suffer a 25 per cent mortality during descent and departure. Gull predation causes some loss of newly-descended guillemot chicks—a factor which does not affect young gannets.

Departure times were spread over much of the day, though there were significantly fewer in roughly the last third. Sixty-six left between 06·00 and 09·00, 85 from 09·00 to 15·00 and 16 between 15·00 and 21·00. There was not a massive post-dawn or pre-dusk exodus, as in the guillemot, where most of the chicks appear to leave around dusk.

The direction of the initial flight merely reflects the direction faced by that part of the colony from which the chick flew and the wind direction at the time. East-facing chicks flew roughly south-east, east or north-east and west-facing ones south-west, west or north-west. Even the birds facing west-south-west flew roughly towards Edinburgh initially. The flight often curved widely and several birds ended by flying at an acute angle to their original line of flight. However, as shown from ringing recoveries, orientation must occur soon after the gannets begin swimming away from the Rock.

Weather has little effect on departure. Gale-force winds inhibit it, but strong winds do not, nor does calm, settled weather. Visibility is relatively unimportant and young birds left in very misty and overcast weather, with visibility of a few hundred yards. They also leave in rain. Rough water does not appear to affect them, nor does the state of the tide.

(c) *Post-fledging behaviour*

Once on the water the newly fledged gannet cannot rise again. I have watched scores of youngsters land and then try to rise again, but however much they thrashed along, even with a strong wind, none ever succeeded in becoming airborne, nor has this ever been recorded. However, occasionally, they almost succeeded and under ideal conditions slightly lighter birds may just manage it. Almost invariably the fledgling (or juvenile as it now is) ducks, bathes and wing flaps vigorously. Bathing may be extensive and sometimes even waterlogs the plumage—especially the tail, which trails in the water (adults swim with tail slightly elevated). This evokes vigorous preening in which the bird rolls, exposing the ventral surface. Very soggy birds may return to the Rock and remain there until they dry out.

In the vast majority of cases, however, the young gannet, once on the sea, begins swimming, usually in a southerly direction. The ensuing migration merits a separate section, but it remains to comment on the transition from a water bound juvenile, living on its fat, to a free-flying juvenile capable of performing the highly skilled plunge diving which is essential to its survival. One can merely attempt to imagine what must happen, for this episode is virtually impossible to observe. The juvenile is far out at sea, a grey speck amidst grey waters and even if observed, one cannot know what has gone before and will ensue.

Its fat reserves of 1000g or more (Fig. 95) should keep it going for about a fortnight (see p. 241) during which period it must learn to fish. Even in species which care for their young after

Fig. 94(a). Actual fledging, once and for all. The young bird dashes to the edge, attacked en route. Note that it has its eyes closed.

Fig. 94(b)

Over the edge. The next few seconds are often dramatically difficult as the juvenile struggles to cope with the wind.

fledging, the acquisition of adult skills is a testing process and of course the more highly skilled the hunting method the more difficult the acquisition of this ability. An extreme example may be taken from the Pelecaniformes. The great frigate bird subsidises its free-flying offspring for more than six months (up to 14 months has been recorded by Schreiber). Yet, even after all that time, some young fail to acquire feeding skills and starve when their parents stop feeding them. On Tower Island, in the Galapagos, we recorded juveniles which had dropped to 650g and this in a bird with an eight-foot wing span. The gannet's feeding method is no less skilful, yet the juvenile has absolutely no subsidy—no time during which, as a free flying individual, it can depend on at least some food from its parents. This puts into perspective the magnitude of the task facing the young gannet.

The necessary ability to recognise free-swimming fish as food poses little problem; even if it were not innate, recognition of fish shape would have been acquired during the period in the nest, when the chick sees fish spilt or protruding from the adult's mouth during unsuccessful regurgitation. Soon after landing on the sea, juveniles bathe excitedly and thrust their heads under water. This causes the nictitating membrane to pass by reflex action across the eye and so improves underwater vision. Eventually they will see a fish and perhaps attempt to snatch it, but will almost certainly fail. At first they are buoyant and unable to drive themselves beneath the water. As they become lighter and can more easily raise themselves a little, their ability to penetrate will increase until they can fly properly and plunge in the normal way. A comparable phylogenetic diversification probably led to the evolution of plunge diving within the Pelecaniformes in the first place. Thus, American white pelicans fish from the surface; brown pelicans plunge clumsily but do not usually submerge fully, whilst all sulids have become fully adapted plunge divers.

Adult gannets can dive from the surface and propel themselves under water in search of fish and it is possible that the non-flying juvenile can do the same, but we lack evidence on this point. Except in unusually favourable circumstances, however, one suspects that young gannets will not succeed in catching fish in the first, water-bound stage and will, therefore, be left with a reduced period, during which they can fly and continue to metabolise reserves, in which to learn to fish adequately. Once on the wing it seems, from several scattered records of juveniles fishing in association with adults, that the dazzling plumage of the latter may well attract young birds, as it attracts other adults, to areas in which gannets are diving. This could provide an important marker enabling young birds to locate shoals in the critical transition stages.

Reports by Macintyre (1950), later supported by Perry (1950), of adult gannets feeding young at sea probably stem, as Perry realised, from the juvenile habit once capable of flight, of pestering passing adults. I have often seen single juveniles, or even pairs, pursuing adults at sea and making the chick yapping call, and in general it is by no means rare for young animals to beg indiscriminately from passing adults. However, even if an adult responds to such importuning it cannot be regarded as anything but an interesting aberration and its main significance is that it supports the surmise that such juveniles will be desperately hungry.

Fig. 95

Large deposits of fat beneath the skin and around the gut fuel the young gannet during the two critical weeks after it has left and before it can fish adequately.

Macintyre's supposition that records of fighting between young and adults at sea really refer to adult feeding young is quite wrong. These observations almost certainly refer to the adult gannet's habit of attacking newly-fledged young on the water (page 208). Such young do not fight back. His assertion that adult gannets disable fish and leave them for the less skilful young birds to pick up is fascinating but probably fanciful.

It needs little imagination to realise that during this critical stage in the gannet's life history, a spell of stormy weather can spell disaster and when interpreting the adaptive aspects of the gannet's breeding regime, particularly its timing, considerable weight will be laid on the importance of producing young at the optimal time for this post-fledging transition to independence (see p. 104). The very considerable post-fledging mortality is largely due to starvation and in a situation so fraught with difficulty the additional handicap of gales, which increase from mid-September onwards could hardly be other than fatal. Yet in some years, early youngsters could run into worse weather than later ones, which is presumably one reason why natural selection has not produced gannets all of which lay early in April and fledge their young early in August, but has opted in favour of a consistently early mean laying date and rapid chick growth (so far as the large biomass to be produced allows).

The way, unique in the Sulidae, in which the gannet produces its independent juvenile raises several questions, but these are discussed in the context of the entire family on p. 913. It is a pity that, in the gannet, it is so difficult to learn more about the exact processes involved but painstaking observations of young at sea in the week or two after they have fledged may eventually provide a fuller picture.

MAINTENANCE BEHAVIOUR

1. *Stance and movement*

The normal stance of the gannet may best be judged from photographs. It is fairly horizontal when fully relaxed, but more vertical during periods of agonistic behaviour. Movement on flat ground is a heavy waddle, increasing to a run or (exceptionally) a series of hops. During locomotion, the wing tips are often lifted and tail depressed, whilst the neck is somewhat elongated and the head carried with bill pointing either upwards or downwards. Under stress, the wings are used with a rowing motion to aid progress. The tail is never cocked as it so typically is in some boobies; for flight see pp. 17 and 225.

2. *Preening and associated behaviour*

(*a*) *Preening*

Gannets preen thoroughly for much of their long periods of site attendance. After bathing, the complete preening procedure, including oiling, is performed on the water. Gannets also occasionally preen in flight. They do not wing-dry like shags, cormorants and pelicans, nor adopt marked sunning positions like other members of the family, though they often loosen their wings.

Whilst a detailed study might reveal a pattern of preening different parts of the body, it is not readily apparent. Gannets switch abruptly from one part of the body to another. The remiges and rectrices are drawn separately between the mandibles and the tail is sometimes bent sideways at right angles to the body to help this. The thick quilt-like body plumage is nibbled with the points of the mandibles, and the lower breast and flanks are 'stropped' with a sideways motion of the bill. In a thorough preening session, which may last for 2 or 3 hours, the bird also 'oils' (see below). Preening is occasionally followed by direct head scratching in which the pectinated middle claw is mainly used.

Perfunctory preening often follows other activities. The area preened is often decided by postural facilitation. Following Bowing, the bill tip rests on the upper breast and this region is most frequently preened then. Also preening occurs at a specific point in the behaviour sequence following a fight or a bout of menacing. As the tension gradually relaxes the first non-hostile behaviour, apart from headshaking is invariably a Rotary Headshake and then short preening bouts. The preening can be seen to arrange the plumage which is often soiled and disordered. The frequency of preening rises sharply with the onset of moult.

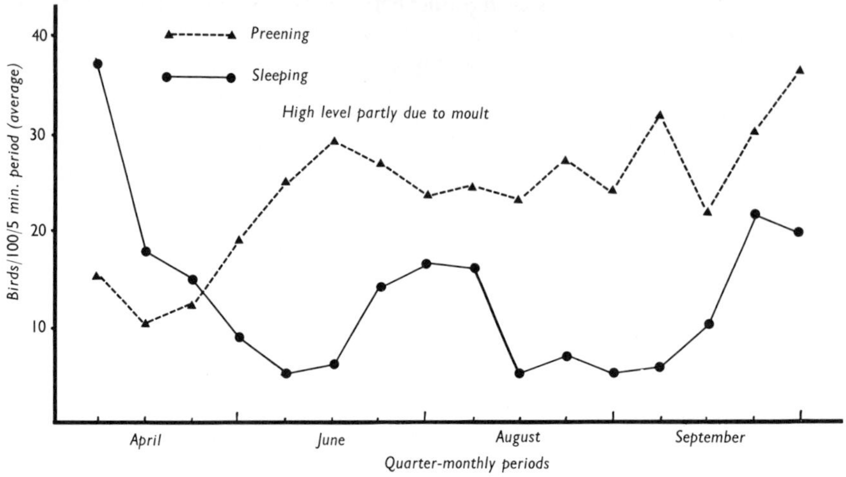

Fig. 96. Seasonal pattern of preening and sleeping.

(b) Oiling

All truly pelagic birds require waterproof plumage and few species are more at home on and below the ocean than the gannet, which in winter probably spends unbroken weeks at sea. The plumage is kept waterproof by rubbing oil on to it from the oil gland at the base of the tail (Fig. 97) (it has, however, been claimed that waterproofing depends on the maintenance of the correct physical structure of the feathers rather than on oil). The back of the head is rolled to and fro in the gland and then rubbed onto the body, particularly the back and wings. Gannets often oil and preen diligently after taking over the egg or chick, at which time they have just returned from foraging. They often preen and oil on the sea around the colony even during the breeding season.

(c) Bathing

Gannets almost always enter the sea head first. The fishing dive is quite distinct from the shallow slant dive (Fig. 98) with which they alight for floating or slightly submerged seaweed or simply in order to come down on the sea. Gannets rarely alight feet first like a duck. Bathing consists of threshing the water with loosened wings and dipping head and bill. Roll-bathing—exposing the ventral surface by rolling onto one side—definitely occurs, but is relatively uncommon in my experience, though I have not paid much attention to it. A curious difference within the family is that whereas the white booby does not roll in this fashion when bathing, both the blue-footed and Peruvian boobies invariably do so.

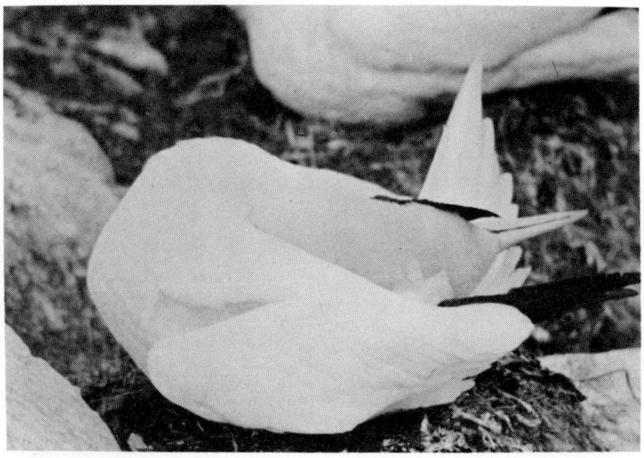

Fig. 97

Oiling; rubbing the head on the oil (preen) gland before rubbing it on to the back and wings.

(d) Other comfort behaviour

Scratching, yawning and stretching are relatively minor behaviour patterns which play a part in maintaining the gannet's physical condition. Scratching is always direct, that is the leg is brought forward under the wing, and employs mainly the middle toe, which has a pectinated claw. Gurney remarks on the apparent uselessness of this feature and it is indeed difficult to see that it could significantly enhance the effectiveness of scratching. As a comb with which to filter out mallophaga from the fine head feathers it might fulfil a real function, but it certainly does not prevent heavy infestation. Scratching is probably more to relieve itching than anything else! Still, the fact that toothed claws are a feature of many birds, strongly suggests that they have a use.

Yawning covers three different ways of opening the mouth and distending the buccal cavity. The gannet, unlike most birds, can lift its upper mandible by means of the naso-frontal hinge. Secondly, it can enormously distend the buccal cavity sideways by separating the rami of the lower mandible; combined with a deepening of the pharynx this creates a truly cavernous aperture which is obviously useful in accommodating large fish and in feeding large chicks, whose own beaks are inserted and their mandibles 'worked' inside the parent's mouth and gullet. It also occurs as a comfort movement in resting birds. Finally, there is ordinary yawning, without lifting the upper mandible or distending the mouth sideways.

Stretching or wing limbering is common to most birds and the gannet is no exception, though in fact it is not a common movement. Wing Flapping and Rotary Headshake seem to achieve all that is necessary as an accompaniment to preening, etc.

4. *Headshaking and Wing Flapping*

(a) Rotary Headshake

This is a useful bit of behaviour; to the bird no doubt, but also to the ethologist who wants a discrete, quantifiable unit that is manifestly not related to sexual or aggressive behaviour and can be used as a natural 'control'. It is also a useful index of 'alarm' or general apprehension in a group of gannets.

There are three distinguishable forms of this movement, each with their characteristic connotation. In the most conspicuous and longest one, the bird stretches its neck forwards and upwards at about 45° (Fig. 99), may depress the tongue bone, thus imparting a peculiar facial expression, flaps its wings powerfully and at increasing speed, ruffs its head and neck feathers and then vigorously and rapidly rotates its head partway around the horizontal axis and back, turning it until the crown almost faces the ground. It may finish off with a tail waggle and a wing shuffle. Form two is a short version; the wings are not flapped, but the head and neck movement is just the same. Form three is well described as a 'dogshake'. The wings are loosened, the contour feathers all over the body ruffed and the whole plumage shaken either as the head is rotated or just before. The wings are not flapped.

They are all so similar, apart from the presence or absence of the wing flap, that it may seem pointless distinguishing them. Why not lump them all as simply a general method of loosening, shaking and re-settling the plumage? Actually, however, two of the three at least differ in context and motivation.

Most birds shake and settle their plumage after bathing, dust bathing, preening or other disturbance of the feathers, such as through being soiled or handled. The third form, described above, is the gannet's usual response to obvious plumage soiling—say from a neighbour's excreta. In fact, it will Dogshake if just its web is soiled in this way, or even if it merely sees the excreta fall nearby (the association between seeing excretion and the threat of soiled plumage perhaps eliciting the Dogshake as a conditioned reflex). The first and second forms and particularly the first, however, are more than this. They are certainly mainly associated with plumage care, sometimes with soiling and particularly with moult. They occur all season, with a noticeable rise in frequency when body feathers are being shed (Fig. 100) and indeed, the wing flapping and Rotary Headshake can be seen to dislodge loose feathers. This form also occurs after plumage disarrangement; in the female after copulation, after fighting and so on.

But the Wing Flap and Rotary Headshake are equally certainly associated with tension or

Fig. 98

The shallow slant-dive which is the gannet's normal method of landing on water. *Photo:* R. Reinsch.

alarm. In other words, although a gannet will Wing Flap and Rotary Headshake in response to a stimulus mediated through its skin (the 'feel' of its plumage at that moment) it will also Wing Flap with or without the Rotary Headshake, in response to fear. This becomes obvious when one looks at the seasonal incidence and finds it is extraordinarily high at the beginning and end of the season which are not times of moult, but are times of great unease and scariness for gannets (see p. 174) when they are very much afraid of being on land at all and prone to sudden panics. Much more demonstrably, however, Wing Flap and Rotary Headshake are responses to suddenly-induced fear. If a man appears at a distance the frequency of this behaviour shoots up; if gulls rise with alarm calls, a dramatic outbreak of Wing Flap and Rotary Headshake ensues.

It is noteworthy that in the alarm situation, the Wing Flap is usually accompanied by the Rotary Headshake. Wing Flapping is understandable as incipient flight movements induced by a rising tendency to fly, but the Rotary Headshake 'ought' to be dispensable here, particularly since birds sometimes do Wing Flap without the Rotary Headshake, just as they Rotary Headshake without the Wing Flap. It is also interesting that in the alarm situation, the response is never the Dogshake, but in the soiled plumage situation the response may be either Dogshake or Wing Flap and Rotary Headshake.

The way in which fear has come to be expressed via what is mainly a plumage arranging behaviour pattern is perhaps understandable if one assumes that the basic stimulus eliciting

Fig. 99(a). Wing Flap prior to Rotary Headshake; this is a common form of plumage settling behaviour. Note that the head feathers have been erected before the actual headshake begins.

Fig. 99(b). Now the wing, body and head feathers have all been raised and will be shaken violently.

Fig. 99(c). A typical reaction to t stimulation is simply feather raising shaking (the Dogshake) without Wing Flap. When alarmed (but in ted from flying) it is always the V Flap, with or without the r shake of the head, that is formed.

Wing Flap and Rotary Headshake is excitation of nerve-endings in the feather follicles. Tactile stimuli will produce this, as, also, may automatic tightening of the plumage through 'sleeking' due to fear. This might explain why gannets in this situation Wing Flap and Rotary Headshake instead of performing merely the intention movements of flight. However, many boobies with rising flight motivation simply shake and 'loosen' the wings rather than bothering with the head and body plumage.

Though it certainly is not a display, Rotary Headshake does possess communication value, since other individuals certainly recognise its import. An outbreak of Rotary Headshaking is highly contagious. Thus, it serves to transmit alertness and may therefore be adaptive, though against what, if not man himself, it is difficult to imagine.

Gannets frequently Rotary Headshake in flight and Wing Flap and Rotary Headshake on the sea after diving or bathing. In both these cases its function is very probably simply to re-arrange and settle the plumage.

Finally, since Rotary Headshaking is correlated with the tendency to fly, it is not surprising to find that it is also strongly correlated with Sky-pointing, which itself precedes movement. Sky-pointing birds tend to flatten their plumage, which could provide peripheral stimulation and thereby cause Rotary Headshaking in the way proposed above. Since Sky-pointing is so strongly linked with flight preparation, the correlation between flight and Rotary Headshake will generally occur through the link.

It seems justifiable to regard Rotary Headshaking in all cases (except perhaps its occurrence as a possible displacement reaction to alarm) as a response to some form of peripheral stimulation probably acting via the feather follicles. Thus, whether it occurs in response to rain, excreta, soiled or disarranged plumage or simply feather tightening, it may be referred to the same general causal situation. It *need* not be functional in the alarm situation in the sense of preparing the feathers for flight.

(*b*) *Sideways Headshake*

The ordinary side to side headshake, one of the commonest movements the gannet performs, is of interest because it has been incorporated into several functionally distinct displays. Unlike the Rotary Headshake, the head is held normally and not aligned with the neck, so that the movement seems to be between the base of the skull and the articulating neck vertebra; in the Sideways Headshake only the head moves, whereas in the Rotary Headshake the head and neck seem to move as a single unit.

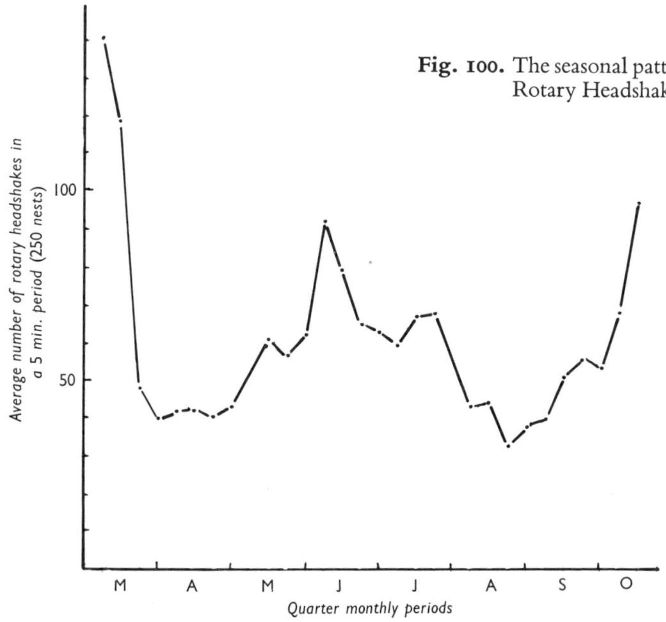

Fig. 100. The seasonal pattern of Rotary Headshaking.

A similar headshake occurs in herring gulls, kittiwakes, guillemots and shags, and doubtless many other birds. It displaces water from the head, the secretion of the salt gland from the bill and so on. In the gannet it is much commoner than in the above species and occurs in several social situations, alone, or as part of more complex behaviour such as the Bow.

The following summary shows the occurrence of the headshake in all its modified forms:

(1) Violent head-flinging is used to dispel strongly-adhering matter from the beak. With mandibles widely parted, it is also used to dislodge fish bones and similar objects from the throat. Spilt fish, egg-shell remains and stones from the nest cup are all dispelled with this movement.

(2) Probably as a non-signal part of threat behaviour, vigorous headshakes are interspersed throughout menacing matches, together with Pelican Postures and nest touching movements.

(3) The sideways headshake is 'locked' in the Bow and occurs after each dip. In the male's advertising display (resembling an inhibited Bow), the headshake component is very conspicuous whilst the dip is suppressed. Headshaking is one of the main components of Mutual Fencing, but differs in form from ordinary headshaking and resembles rather more an attempt to maintain contact with the other's bill during irregular side to side movements, though its resemblance to headshaking can be seen when the partner's bill is momentarily out of reach.

(4) Females use a very inhibited headshake when reacting to the presence of a male near-by which they want to attract. Both sexes also react to the voice of their incoming mate by rapid headshaking. An exaggerated form of headshaking is also used by the female as a ritualised signal in soliciting copulation. The head is held loosely and flung violently from side to side. The female usually squats, with head held low, and continues the movement intermittently during copulation.

By contrast to the wide occurrence of ordinary headshaking, Rotary Headshaking is confined entirely to a few situations. In none of the situations described above, with the possible exception of the first, does the gannet use a Rotary Headshake.

Clearly one can say little about the function of the headshake in its emancipated form, since it usually occurs as part of a complex behaviour pattern. I have the strong impression, however, that it has non-hostile overtones in many situations. A headshaking bird is very likely to be slightly afraid or friendly, rather than aggressive.

In summary, the sideways headshake in the gannet is a good example of a simple basic movement which nevertheless shows wide variation in form, context and function in its incorporation into complex displays.

5. *Heat regulation*

Panting and gular fluttering are concerned with heat balance. During warm weather, sunny or overcast, gannets pant, with bills inclined slightly upwards. They may also flutter the strip of skin in the gular region and often half close the eyes. The function of this behaviour is to produce a flow of air over the bare skin, which radiates heat. The face may be pointed skywards (Fig. 101) to help this process, radiating it to the sky, which is usually thermodynamically cooler than the ambient air.

Fig. 101(a)

Temperature regulation in the adult: upward orientation and fluttering (resonating) of the gular skin; mouth open; eyes closed, exposing the eyelids which radiate heat; wings loosened.

6. *Sleeping*

Adult gannets, including incubating birds, sleep with heads tucked in scapulars which tend to stand up a little from the rest of the plumage and snugly embrace the head. The bill is dexterously inserted between the feathers and the head is almost entirely covered. Usually gannets sleep whilst standing, except just prior to egg laying, when they tend to sit. Much of the time on the site is spent sleeping, particularly during wind and rain. They occasionally doze with bill forwards, but never sleep properly in this way. They tend to sleep much more in the last hour of daylight (and presumably also at night) but otherwise show no periodicity. Unlike shags, gannets do not usually rest side by side on the nest; if one sits the other stands. There is no precise point in time at which the female takes over the centre of the nest, though she does so before egg laying.

After an exhausting fight gannets invariably fall into a deep and prolonged sleep, no doubt part of the necessary recuperative process and possibly comparable to battle fatigue in soldiers. I have several times caught by hand gannets sleeping on the fringe of the colony following a fight and have records of such birds sleeping almost continuously for three days.

FISHING

When flying to cover distance rather than searching an area intently gannets fly low over the surface with almost continuous wing beats, at between 170 and 190/minute, gliding and banking at a speed estimated to reach more than 50 knots (*Sea Swallow 11*). When flying like this, they may make occasional opportunistic dives. In the presence of a shoal they beat upwind with downward-pointing beak, diving or circling to repeat the process. Often, they check their flight, or occasionally even hover or rise slightly, before diving. When really among fish they dive from various heights (as little as half a metre) and angles. If height permits, they manoeuvre on the way down, even rotating as they fall, to enter the water steeply or obliquely. Immediately before entry, the wings are folded back so that their tips project beyond the tail (Fig. 103). Probably, when fishing a shoal in a group, they often dive at random and then strike or follow fish when under water. Kay (pers. comm.) mentions that it is extraordinarily easy to fool several birds into diving simultaneously, simply by raising a splash with a stone. The full dive is a thrilling sight. Gannets are the heaviest sulids and dive from as much as 45 metres though 10–15 metres is probably the usual range. Occasionally they begin a plunge under power, with wing beats, but usually plunge by gravity alone. Barlee analysed cine film and showed that the bird is travelling at more than 60 m.p.h. when it hits the water, often with a leaden thump that resounds for hundreds of metres on a calm day. Its passage through the water churns up masses of milky wake through which the bird is seen as a pale green blob fizzing into the depths. They probably do not penetrate much more than three metres as a result of the unaided dive and perhaps 5–15 metres by swimming. Reports of gannets diving to more than 30 metres are probably due to mistaken interpretation of the evidence (gannets brought up from big depths in nets have probably been trapped on the way up), most

Fig. 101(b). Temperature regulation in the chick (same mechanisms as in the adult). The wing-loosening is probably the origin of the adult sunning posture.

Fig. 101(c)

A further device used by chicks is to expose the spread web, which then loses more heat.

submergences last between 5 and 7 seconds, more rarely up to 10 seconds; Reinsch gives 5–20 seconds and the latter figure, though considerably more than most authors', rests upon many observations at sea. The bird often emerges facing in a direction different from the one in which it entered and may rise immediately from the surface, gaining a mere three or four metres before diving again, the whole making a perfect arc (the wings are not used to swim to the surface). Almost always, it emerges facing into the wind.

If the dive has been successful the fish is usually swallowed under water but large ones may be brought to the surface (Fig. 103(c)) and shaken vigorously before being swallowed. Often, such fish are tossed or juggled and swallowed head first, but tail-first swallowing has been recorded and is common in captive birds. It seems likely that fish are seized as the gannet comes up from below them. Birds do not enter the water with mandibles parted but may open them as the impetus of the dive weakens, and so take the fish on the descent. There are reports of exceptionally large fish being speared and this must occasionally happen, for a gannet has been recovered alive with the carcase of a puffin around its neck. The oft-repeated account of fishermen killing gannets by luring them to dive onto herring nailed to floating boards is probably basically true and there are many stories of gannets diving onto fish in holds, on decks, in nets, and even into a fish-curing shed in Penzance. Barlee has suggested that the terrific

Fig. 102. A group of gannets showing (even when they have well-grown young) a high frequency of display. In the instant captured by this typical picture, at least 11 birds or pairs are Bowing or Mutual Fencing. Most gannet behaviour patterns can be seen in this one photograph, which gives an idea of the sharp tempo of activity in a gannetry. Note, also, the high proportion of pairs with chicks and the marked synchrony in the development of these.

impact of the dive stuns fish just below the surface and has himself stunned and caught a 5kg pike by hitting the water above it with an oar. After a successful dive gannets usually remain momentarily on the surface, making excited bathing movements (shufflings) of the wings, touching the water with the bill (drinking or false-drinking) and headshaking. When a bird rises straight from the surface it may probably be assumed to have been unsuccessful.

Helped, no doubt, by their considerable weight they continue diving in extremely strong winds, when sheets of spray are being blown from the surface. They may well exceed the other two gannets in this capability (the Cape gannet stops 'mass' fishing when winds reach force 4 but has been seen diving in force 6), but Reinsch reports that they are not seen fishing, or even on the wing, in winds beyond Beaufort force 8. Clarke (1902) noted that gannets successfully caught pollack in rough seas off Eddystone but not in calm waters. Possibly they are helped by some wind, since a disturbed surface may well, by refraction, obscure the fishes' view whilst still allowing the bird to discern enough to plunge accurately. It is possible that plunge-divers may have polarising lenses. The Navy were at one time interested in this, for obvious reasons, and I understand that the Russians, in particular, are putting a lot of research effort into the investigation of natural systems for their potential in applied fields.

Although gannets do not land in the breeding colony after dark they have been recorded diving in the darkening evening and (judging by the splashes) continuing to do so after they could no longer be seen. But Reinsch mentions that they are not to be seen on the wing at night. Harris (pers. comm.) has seen them diving in the thousand around fishing boats anchored off St. Kilda, by floodlight, and saw one or two shear off a wing on hawsers.

Besides plunging properly they have been recorded swimming among fry, scooping up beakfuls, fishing on foot in shallow sandy bays, presumably for sand-eels, diving from the surface for coal-fish in winter in Lerwick harbour and pursuing them by swimming with strokes of the half-opened wings. About 500 birds fed there daily for about a month in 1945/46. An underwater film of the brown booby shows in detail how the birds swim underwater with wonderful verve and agility, using wings, webs, and tail to bank and turn, and extending their necks to grab. No doubt gannets do the same. Whilst swimming, Booth's captive birds dived in a manner 'closely resembling the plunge made by the coot'. The wings were used below the surface, like a guillemot's. Gale-driven birds have been recorded diving into fresh water inland, as, also, have two species of boobies. A highly unusual incident was recorded by Major Thatcher, near Lochgilphead in April 1976. He saw an adult gannet above and amongst a flock of gulls following a plough! I suspect that the sight of the cloud of gulls and the noise of the diesel engine triggered off trawler-scavenging behaviour in the gannet.

Clouds of gannets commonly attend fishing boats to take netted or hooked fish and to scavenge for offal, where they dominate gulls, skuas and fulmars. They do not follow boats for long periods as do gulls, but rather stream out to boats operating nearby or near to their colony. Some have become conditioned to the noise of lifting gear and will join a boat in response to this even before there are any fish to be seen. In their excitement they venture close enough to be caught or killed. Some fishermen tie the gannet's head to one of its legs, presumably to reduce its powers of interference with the catch. Not infrequently these unfortunate birds either escape overboard or, unimaginable as it may seem, are deliberately released to starve to death in this state.

During the breeding season their fishing range is at least 200 miles (320km) from the colony and may be much more (see p. 92). Adults (probably breeders) fish off the Dogger, 200 miles (320km) from the Bass, in summer, and go far south of the Farnes and to the northern tip of Scotland (though it is not certain that the latter are Bass birds). In winter they range up and down the entire British coast, up to 50 miles (80 km) offshore (some go much further south; p. 147). There are many records of adults and immature gannets attending the North Sea herring fleets in October and November and wherever they find large shoals of sprats, from the English Channel to beyond the Moray Firth, feeding flocks several hundreds strong may be seen throughout winter. A similar situation occurs off the western coast. They enter harbours but usually (or always) retreat to roost on the open sea. Winter life is thus nomadic and is probably not usually a hard time for gannets.

Gannets often dive solitarily but commonly fish in flocks of scores, hundreds or occasionally a thousand or more. The dazzling white plumage is undoubtedly a social signal, marking the presence of diving birds and helping a group to form (the benefits to *individuals* of diving communally is discussed on p. 821). Many observers from Darwin onwards have remarked on the way in which birds stream to join diving gannets. Barlee (1947) once saw over 1000 birds leave Skellig en masse and fly north-west to where a shoal of mackerel were breaking the surface and about two dozen gannets were already diving. Nor is the stimulus visual only, for diving gannets make a great commotion, a raucous gabble. Except when gathered at a shoal, it is rare to see gannets flying at sea in groups of more than 10–30 birds. Usually, they return to the colony in skeins of up to 70–80 individuals (extremely rarely, if ever, more), most commonly in skeins of 16–20 birds, some containing immatures but none consisting solely of these. Scattered observations at sea indicate that gannets can readily home directly to their breeding colony. Several observers have seen groups of gannets, at sea, flying steadily in one direction and by extrapolation have found that they were heading straight for 'a' (presumably 'their') gannetry. Grassholm gannets fishing off South Bishop moved north-east in files of up to 20 birds, from 90 minutes before sunset, 2000–3000 leaving the area in this way. This was not seen before mid-July and persisted until mid-September (McCauch, in MS.).

Finally, a marvellous excerpt about gannets and Clyde fishermen, from Angus Martin (in prep.):

> That imperial fish-hunter, the gannet, unwittingly led many fishermen to great catches. His presence was always investigated if his behaviour suggested that he might be working on herring. Indeed, summer daylight fisheries were periodically based on the presence of great concentrations of the birds. The warm summer sun would bring to the surface banks of *Calanus*, to which the herring, too, rose and 'fed in the sun'. Over the shoals ranged the gannets, and constantly watchful of these industrious birds the fishermen ranged, too, on the bright sea. Daylight fishing was uncertain work, however, as the herring were able to see the nets set around them, and might evade capture by 'dooking' below the soles before the net was closed. 'Ye missed them of'ner than ye got them,' John McWhirter remarked ruefully.
>
> A gannet prowling in the sky with a peculiar persistence was an almost sure indication that a shoal of herring was below it. 'When ye see them hingin' yon wey, cockin' their nebs,' said Donald McIntosh, 'that's when the herrin' wir right thick.' Explanations of the phenomenon of the uncertain bird were offered by Robert MacGowan and James Reid. The former remarked: 'We always knew when a gannet circles round and round (that) it's on a spot. It must just be waiting' to get the

Fig. 103(a). Gravity plunge at a shallow angle. *Photo:* A. and E. Bomford.

Fig. 103(b). Extreme extension of the wings upon entering the water. *Photo:* A. and E. Bomford.

edge o' the herrin.' The latter remembered: 'We used tae say about a gannet comin' along an' seein' herrin'—if he made a dive an' then turned back: "Oh, they're too thick." And we'd ring on that sign.' A high vertical plummet was an almost infallible indication. If the bird was working on *Sile* close to the surface, his dive was shallow and angled, though I have heard of gannets fishing, with that technique, on herring feeding close to the surface; but it was evidently not a frequent phenomenon.

The winter 'spawny herring' on the Ballantrae Banks attracted tens of thousands of gannets from the nearby colony of Ailsa Craig. John McWhirter recalled the spectacle: 'I could safely say that (there) wis a solid mass o' herrin' on these banks for aboot five miles. Ye could hardly see the sky wi' gannets. Ye wir almost afraid tae sail on it. No' an odd gannet hittin' here an' there—they wir comin' pourin' oot the sky lik' shrapnel the whole blessed day frae mornin' until night. A skyfu' o' gannets pourin' down . . .' The Ayrshire fishermen called the formations of fishing gannets *rallies*. 'They'd gather, just a few,' said John Turner McCrindle, 'an' they'd go round an' round till the sky wis white. Ye could hear the noise a mile away, them goin' down plop, an' the odd time ye saw the unfortunate one that had been het by some o' the others.'

Fig. 103(c). Gannets do not usually surface with fish unless they need to disable them. *Photo:* A. and E. Bomford.

When fishermen came into an area where gannets were resting full-bellied on the surface after intensive feeding, they would prod one with an oar or otherwise alarm it, so that it regurgitated the content of its stomach to lighten itself and take off. In that way, the fishermen discovered whether or not the birds had been feeding on herring. Eight or nine herrings were frequently 'bouked' up by a disturbed bird.

There was a belief among some of the fishermen that gannets were prone to blindness. 'The lenses o' his eyes, wi' so much divin' intae the waater, get hardened, an' he loses his sight,' said John Turner McCrindle. Fishermen occasionally saw blind birds, flapping unseeingly away from the boats. This is unlikely to be the correct interpretation. Natural selection would hardly produce a specialist plunge-diver with such a weakness and it is certain that gannets can endure at least 40 years of diving. Few live beyond that!

Fig. 103(d). Competing for trawler spoils. *Photo:* R. Reinsch.

2

Sula [bassana] capensis

AFRICAN OR CAPE GANNET

1. NOMENCLATURE; EXTERNAL FEATURES; MORPHOLOGY; MOULT AND VOICE

NOMENCLATURE

1. *Common*

South African, African or Cape gannet; Malgas; Malagash or Margout; Kolonjane

2. *Scientific*

The comparative taxonomy of the gannets is discussed on p. 307. In this work, the gannets are treated as a superspecies (in the genus *Sula*), containing three allospecies. Most frequently, the Cape gannet has in the past been treated as a full species, *Morus capensis*. *Sula [bassana] capensis* (Lichtenstein), previously used as a trinomial without the square brackets; *Sula capensis* Licht; *Dysporus capensis* Lichtenstein; *Morus capensis* Licht.; and *Morus [bassana] capensis* are synonyms.

GENERAL FEATURES

1. *Adult*

The Cape gannet has a wing span of about 171–185cm and an overall length of about 84–94cm. It is said to flap more often between glides which imparts a distinctive character to its flight. Like the other two gannets, its body plumage is snow white, but it has more extensive black than them. The primaries, primary coverts and secondaries are black, giving a black trailing edge to the wing (Fig. 104) though the black stops several cm short of the body. Unlike the white booby the humerals are white. The tail is usually all black (but see below) whereas in the Australasian gannet usually only the four central tail features are dark (but see p. 266). The

Fig. 104

The Cape gannet, showing the black tail and the extent of the black on the wings.

Photo: M. F. Jarvis.

shafts of the central tail feathers are often conspicuously bleached. The head is a deep golden buff, probably slightly darker than that of the Atlantic gannet and the strip of black skin on the throat is 13–19mm long, three or four times as long as in the Atlantic and may be more heavily pigmented (it probably helps regulate body temperature). It is longer in males than females (Jarvis 1971). The black facial skin pattern and the lines on the bill are the same as in the Atlantic gannet. The eyelids are bright blue but the irises are typically darker than the light grey-blue of the Atlantic bird. The bill is light blue and the legs and feet blackish (sometimes greyer) with light greenish-yellow lines. Broekhuysen & Liversidge (1954) found that about 11 per cent of birds which were more than a year old had varying amounts of white in the tail, the commonest variant being birds with two white outer feathers on each side. Some had tails indistinguishable from the typical Australasian gannet. In all, 114 different combinations of white and black tail feathers were recorded in a sample of 3682 birds.

2. *Juvenile and immature*

The newly feathered juvenile (Fig. 105) appears identical with that of some Atlantic gannets and in areas of overlap (chiefly the Gulf of Guinea) is not separable. Care should be taken in distinguishing the advanced one-year-old from the juvenile white booby (q.v.) in north-west African waters. An albino juvenile has been recorded, as it has for the Atlantic gannet.

We lack information on the full series of intermediate plumages, but it may be assumed that the changes, though quicker, are like those in the Atlantic gannet (p. 12) and, especially in view of the variability in the tail of the Cape birds, some immatures of the two species are not separable in the field by plumage, though they probably are by flight. A second-year bird (Fig. 106) may show the plumage characteristics of a three-year-old Atlantic gannet or it may look adult. The bill may retain traces of darker colour at this age. Adult plumage is attained during the third or fourth year. Of 28 known two-year-olds, many were adult-plumaged though some had black feathers on the wing coverts and rump. Twelve of these, captured again a year later, when three years old, had adult plumage in all but two cases (Jarvis 1972).

Fig. 105

Juvenile Cape gannet. *Photo:* M. F. Jarvis.

Fig. 106 (*below*)

Cape gannet (second year). Note that it is much whiter on the back than an Atlantic gannet of this age. It could be distinguished from a third or fourth year Atlantic bird by its solid black secondaries. *Photo:* M. F. Jarvis.

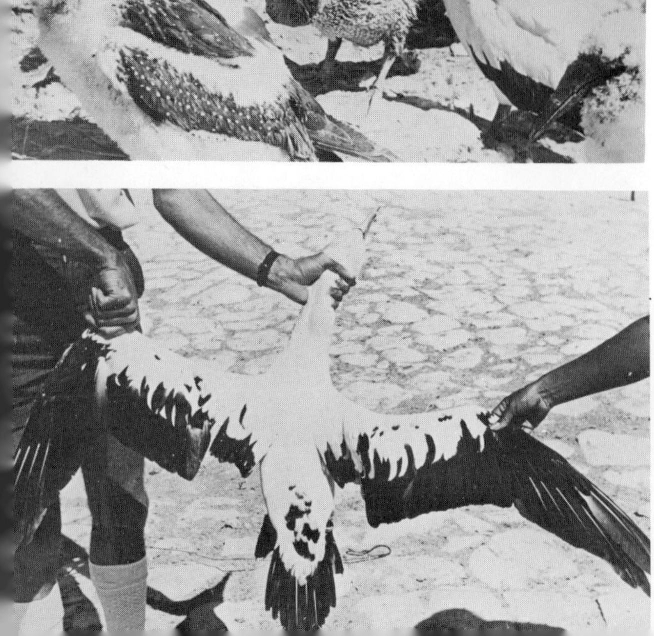

MEASUREMENTS AND WEIGHT

Rand (1959a) and Jarvis (1971) give the measurements shown in Tables 30 and 31. The Cape gannet is larger and heavier than the Australasian and a little smaller but considerably lighter

TABLE 30

MEASUREMENTS OF THE CAPE GANNET

	Culmen length (mm)		Total wing span (mm)		Body length (mm)		Weight (g)		Wing (mm)		Tail (mm)		Source
	Male	Female	Male	Female	Male	Female	Male	Female	Male	Female	Male	Female	
1	94(10)	91(10)	1800(11)	1778(10)	888(11)	875(10)	2618(61)	2669(53)					Jarvis
2	(90–100)	(85–100)*	(1770–1847)	(1712–1823)	(835–916)	(852–907)*	(2296–2920)	(2381–3118)					(1971)
1	92(43)	91(51)			885(4)	930(5)	2665(55)	2608(61)	480(20)	477*(16)	189(16)	191(30)*	Rand
2	(88–97)	(91–97)			(860–910)	(930–945)	(2523–3005)	(2240–3291)	(450–510)	(477–510)	(180–205)	(191–206)	(1959a)

1 Mean, with number of cases in brackets.
2 Range.
* Presumably some error here; mean and minimum are given the same value.

TABLE 31

WEIGHTS OF CAPE GANNETS CAUGHT AT SEA (from Rand 1959a)

Month	Mean		Maximum		Minimum		Number in Sample	
	Males	Females	Males	Females	Males	Females	Males	Females
April	2722	2693	2948	2693	2437	2693	2	1
May	2778	—	2977	—	2608	—	2	0
June	2665	2353	3005	3288	2040	2211	17	29
July	2523	2722	2722	3316	2097	2550	7	7
August	2608	2485	2892	2863	2352	2155	6	4
September	2665	2552	2948	2608	2465	2485	4	2
October	2523	2523	2863	2920	2465	2140	10	9
November	2722	2920	2863	3033	2409	2750	5	7
December	2722	—	2722	—	2722	—	1	—

than the Atlantic gannet. As in the latter, males are slightly larger than females (probably for the same reasons (p. 17)) except in weight, which is about the same. Females showed greater variation in weight than did males (Rand 1959a). The lighter weight is correlated with its nesting and feeding habits (p. 253) and its warmer environment.

MOULT

Adults moult in summer, extending into June–July by which time all new feathers are fully grown. Birds may replace feathers whilst incubating (Rand 1959a). The nature of the moult is likely to resemble that in the Atlantic bird (p. 18).

VOICE

The voice is similar to that of the Atlantic gannet (p. 19). As in the Australasian which in most respects the Cape gannet closely resembles, males have slightly higher pitched voices than females. The repetitive 'urrah' call is delivered by incoming birds in the usual way and accompanies Bowing, Mutual Fencing, Menacing and fighting. The groaning 'oo-ah' call accompanies Sky-pointing. Birds recognise the voice of their mate and chicks of their parents.

2. BREEDING DISTRIBUTION, NUMBERS AND OTHER ASPECTS OF POPULATION

INTRODUCTION

The Cape gannet has an extremely limited breeding range (Fig. 107) between 25° 43′ and 33° 50′S and 14° 50′ and 26° 17′E. This is considerably less than that of the Atlantic gannet and less even than of the Australasian. In fact, Abbot's booby excepted, it has the most restricted breeding range of any sulid. However, some of its few colonies are large and its total numbers (some 362 000 individuals in 1956, since when there has been no further census) far exceed

Table 32

THE NUMBERS AND DISTRIBUTION OF CAPE GANNETS IN 1956

(Original figures from Rand 1959a, 1963a & b, amended by me)

Breeding island	Mean count of individuals from aerial photographs	Corrected total (pairs)	Comments
Mercury	5 797	5 040	
Ichaboe	144 000	125 217 minus non-breeders say 100 000	No means of estimating number of roosting birds on outlying rocks, included in count
Possession	19 464	16 924	
Malagas	24 194	21 038	In 1958 the count was 40 000 or 34 782 pairs
Bird (Lambert's Bay)	6 152	5 349	
Bird (Algoa Bay)	20 567	17 884	
		166 235	

those of the Australasian gannet. Three sulids are rarer than it; five are commoner. Except for the piquero, it is the only sulid important for its guano and this is probably the chief reason why it still survives in such good numbers, for there have been requests from the fishing lobby for the destruction of South African seabirds.

The principal feature of its breeding distribution is the proximity of the Benguela Current, with its associated food fish, particularly pilchards, maasbankers, anchovies, mackerel and many other species, and also squid. Thus, it resembles the other two gannets in breeding in relatively food-rich areas, to which its breeding biology is geared (a trait developed even further in the Atlantic gannet). The vast numbers of cormorants, and penguins with which it shares the 30 or so South African bird and seal islands may limit the space available for Cape gannets. If so, this is a factor which, in most colonies, does not operate on Atlantic gannets.

Rand (1959a, 1963a and b), from whom most of the following information derives, gives the only account of numbers and distribution. On the basis (in most cases) of his counts from aerial photographs, and assuming 15 per cent of sites were at that time occupied by pairs (he allows 25 per cent but this seems high), the adult population of the Cape gannet in 1956 (Table 32) was about 166 000 pairs in the breeding areas of the six colonies together with perhaps 30 000 to 40 000 individuals which were roosting on outlying parts of the islands (some of these may, however, be the mates of birds counted in the colony and therefore already included in the estimate of pairs); a total of 362 472 individuals. The counts are almost certainly accurate to at least 25 per cent so that the 1956 figure for pairs in colonies, mostly breeding, may be taken as between (to the nearest thousand) 125 000 to 208 000. A major variable is the unknown proportion of birds included in the counts but actually roosting and therefore not representing a pair as most of the others were. Rand's conclusion was that the counts revealed a total of 352 000 individual adult gannets in 1956 (approximately 270 000 on the three more northern islands off south-west Africa and 82 000 on the more southerly ones off Cape Province). Elsewhere (1959b) he gives a figure of some 350 000 individuals spread over all the northern islands and some 100 000 on the three southern islands. He states, also, that about 200 000 young birds are reared each year.

Whilst the Atlantic and Australasian gannets have been increasing in the last 20 or 30 years it seems that the Cape gannet has been declining. This emerges from Jarvis' (1970) study of guano, which has shown a downward trend since the 1940s, and from undocumented but nonetheless distinct impressions of several people. Also, there is circumstantial evidence linking the gannet decline with the development of the inshore fishing industry. There are reports of fishermen killing gannets and of attempts by the fishing lobby to legalise mass destruction of seabirds, including gannets. There is a parallel, here, with the Peruvian anchovy fishery v. seabird controversy (p. 605).

COLONIES

Cape gannets breed on six islands (Fig. 107); MERCURY, ICHABOE, and POSSESSION ISLANDS off south-west Africa, PENGUIN ISLET of BIRD ISLAND, Lambert's Bay (sometimes called Lambert's Bay Island), MALAGAS ISLAND off the western Cape Province (where most of the ringing has been done) and BIRD ISLAND, Algoa Bay, off the east coast. They used to breed on Hollamsbird Island. The largest colony is that on Ichaboe (more than 100 000 pairs in 1956). The smallest sub-groups (isolated groups within a colony) are about 25 pairs but some, at least, have been isolated by man.

MERCURY ISLAND is a small, precipitous island 3 hectares in extent and 42m high in Spencer Bay only ½km offshore and 35 miles (56km) from Ichaboe. The gannets share the island with cormorants and penguins and nest in eight groups on the eastern (lee) side. Counts from aerial photographs in November 1956 gave 5797 individuals. Assuming that 15 per cent of nests were occupied by pairs gives a population of 5040 (say 5000) pairs. Rand remarks that the island is full and (most interestingly) that some birds are nesting on precipitous cliffs and suggests that the provision of wooden ledges would doubtless enable more birds to nest there.

ICHABOE ISLAND is a low (7m high) flattish island, some 6·5 hectares almost 1 mile (1½km) offshore in Douglas Bay, 30 miles (48km) north of Luderitz. Ichaboe supports a huge gannet colony distributed over most of the flat, sandy surface and also on the rocky hill in the centre.

Some even nested on iron platforms near the jetty. Counts from aerial photographs gave 144 000 individuals but this included birds roosting on outlying rocks (proportion not specified). Assuming 15 per cent of sites held pairs at the time of the count gives 125 217 pairs. An arbitrary number must be subtracted for roosting birds but even assuming 25 000 (improbably many) the population would appear to have numbered more than 100 000 pairs. This seems an astonishingly high figure and would in fact make Ichaboe the largest gannetry in the world, including all three species. Rand remarks that it is doubtful whether Ichaboe could accommodate any more gannets. The most densely occupied part held 430 nests/1000sq.ft which is about 4·2 nests/sq.m, but less than half this on rocky areas and only 0·8/sq.m on the uneven ground. Rand does not say how the nests were distributed in the areas concerned, but assuming that in the low density areas they were not clumped, Ichaboe shows the considerable variability in density found in the Cape bird and certainly not paralleled in the Atlantic. It also casts slight doubt on the suggestion that Ichaboe is full up.

POSSESSION ISLAND is a large island of 90 hectares, only 26m high and just over a mile offshore in Elizabeth Bay. It has a few bushes. All the guano species nest here, together with some gulls and terns. The gannets occupy an enclosed, partly cemented area. Counts from photographs gave 19 464 individuals in November 1956 or 16 924 pairs assuming 15 per cent of nests held pairs at the time of the count. The density within the enclosed area was between 3 and 4 pairs/sq.m.

MALAGAS ISLAND is a rocky island of 8·3 hectares, fairly flat, lying about 400–800m offshore at the northern entrance of Saldanha Bay. Broekhuysen & Rudebeck (1951) estimated that the gannets occupied an area of some 17 400sq.m and that there were about 4 nest/sq.m. This makes 34 800 pairs, in addition to which there were an estimated 9000 non-nesting birds outside the main area. Elsewhere, they remarked that the average density of nests in the main rookery was $2\frac{1}{2}$/sq.m and compute a total figure on this premiss. However, Rand (1963a) points out that the main colony is in fact not more than 7900sq.m of which roughly 2600 were unsuitable for nesting. Clearly, therefore, the 1951 figure is totally unreliable.

In November 1956 Rand counted a maximum number of 24 194 individuals from aerial photographs (the mean count is not given) which gives 21 038 pairs. However, in 1958 similar counts gave 40 000 birds which represents 34 782 pairs. This large discrepancy is not explained. Also, Rand elsewhere (1963a, p. 15) comments that 'the largest gannet colony of 15 500 nests is at Malagas'.

Gannets now nest in four groups on Malagas (Main Colony, East Colony, Die Dam Colony and Skulpies). There may have been a decrease this century, for Sclater (1904) noted that they covered the whole of the interior of the island.

BIRD ISLAND (Lambert's Bay) is a small rocky island about 8m high, joined to the shore by a breakwater and frequented by cormorants, penguins, and gulls as well as gannets. Gannets were first noted around 1912 and numbered only one or two pairs (Jarvis 1971). In 1956 they

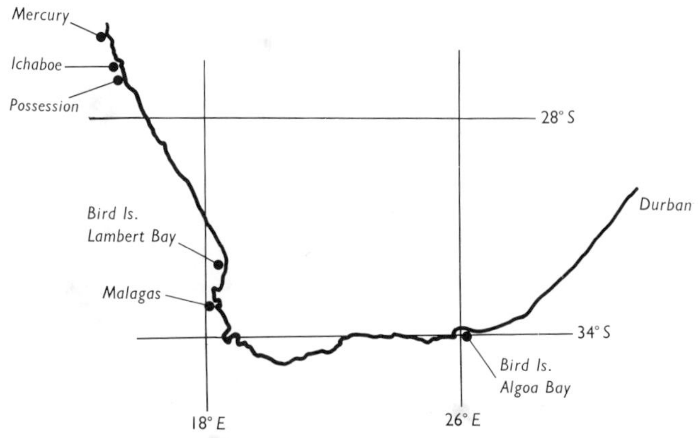

Fig. 107. The breeding distribution of the Cape gannet.

formed a single colony in the middle of the island; 6152 individuals, representing perhaps some 5250 pairs, were counted. This rate of increase means that immigration must have occurred. Now, however, the population is slightly less. Jarvis & Cram (1971) estimate 5000 pairs and Jarvis (1971) says that comparison with old photographs indicates that it is slowly declining. In 1956 the estimated number of nests (4920) were concentrated in 2400sq.m which gives an average density of 2·05 nests/sq. m. Jarvis gives the maximum average density as 8·6 nests/sq.m and the minimum as 3·76.

Bird Island (Algoa Bay) is about 19 hectares, 10m high and 4½ miles (7km) from the nearest land (Woody Cape). It is the largest of four outcrops forming a group of islands. Gannets are far more abundant than penguins and there are no cormorants. Aerial photographs in 1956 gave 150 birds in July, 13 418 in October and 20 567 in November. Correcting for an assumed 15 per cent of nests occupied by pairs gives 17 884 pairs. In November 1956, 40 per cent of the island's surface was inhabited by gannets and some 16 500 pairs nested in the main area of 9057sq.m, which is a density of 1·9 pairs/sq.m. Even this is greater than the density calculated by Gibson-Hill (1948), but it is far less than the minimum density on Bird Island (Lambert's Bay). The main gannet nesting places have been inhabited for at least 150 years, though some areas have been cleared by persecution and as a result of harvesting guano.

All the other South African seabird islands—Seal (Algoa Bay), Stag, St. Croix, Seal (Moseel Bay), Quoin Rock, Dyer, Geyser, Seal (False Bay), Duikerlip, Dassen, Vondeling, Jutten, Marcus, Schaapen, Meevw, Paternoster, Sinclair, Plumpudding, Pomona, Albatross Rock, Long Island, Halifax and Hollamsbird—are devoid of gannets, though many hold vast colonies of cormorants and penguins and Hollamsbird once held gannets and was their most northerly breeding station. Penguins, at least, can hold their own against encroachment by gannets, and it may be sheer competition for physical space which has limited the numbers of Cape gannets. There is insufficient evidence to encourage any attempt to trace trends in the population of Cape gannets but it may be noted that they are likely to show interchange between colonies (as Atlantic birds do) and that the rate at which a colony can grow from its own output (and of course the rate at which the entire population can increase) is very probably around 3 per cent per annum (see p. 64).

3. BREEDING ECOLOGY

INTRODUCTION

In morphology and ecology, the Cape gannet differs from the Atlantic gannet more than it does from the Australasian and it has been studied (Jarvis 1971, 1974) with the specific intention of comparing the two former. Until very recently, there has been little information on the breeding biology of the Cape gannet; now that this has been remedied, it becomes possible to compare the three gannets in considerable detail. Taking the three together (each with areas investigated particularly thoroughly) one gains an exceptionally complete picture of breeding biology and each species should be read with constant reference to the other two. The account of the Atlantic gannet is fullest and much of it applies to all three. The most important features of the Cape gannet's ecology are its restriction to a relatively few highly crowded bird islands mainly in the vicinity of the Benguela Current and the generally hot, dry and flat nature of its breeding environment. Unless otherwise attributed, all quantitative information on general breeding biology comes from Jarvis (1971).

BREEDING HABITAT

The Cape gannet is a bird of fairly flat, open areas (Fig. 108) on low-lying islands of the Continental Shelf of the south-west of Africa, which it shares, particularly, with cormorants, just as the piquero shares the Peruvian islands with the guanay cormorant. Colonies usually possess runways to which departing birds make their way for take-off (Fig. 125). This sometimes precludes colonisation of parts of the periphery. Nevertheless, Cape gannets are capable of breeding on precipitous cliffs, as on Mercury Island (Rand 1963b) though this habit is clearly exceptional.

The climate is hot, dry and windy. The more northerly islands, which hold most of the gannets, are barren and windswept, in contrast to the southern ones, but suffer sea fog, high seas and excessive spray. Piled boulders, which Cape gannets dislike, are conspicuously absent from northern islands.

COLONY DENSITY

There are conflicting reports of the density at which Cape gannets typically nest. Clearly, however, they nest at variable densities even on the same island and are sometimes (probably typically) much denser than either of the other two gannets. Normal spacing on Malagas is said by Rand (1963a) to be 2·3 nests per square metre (nests mainly 56–58cm apart) and 'occasionally' more congested than is allowed by lunging distance. Broekhuysen & Rudebeck (1951) earlier gave the average density in the main areas of Malagas as 2·5 nests/sq.m (see p. 236). On Ichaboe density is said to be 4·2 nests/sq.m in the densest area but less than half this on rocky areas. On Bird Island (Algoa Bay) Rand (1963a) gives 2·0 nests/sq.m and on Bird Island (Lambert's Bay) 2·2/sq.m. However, Jarvis, also for Bird Island (Lambert's Bay) gives the maximum density as 6·8 nests/sq.m and the minimum as 3·76/sq.m, the

Fig. 108

A nesting group of Cape gannets showing the flat habitat. *Photo:* M. F. Jarvis.

densest nesting being in the most exposed portion of the colony. On this figure, the area with the lowest density in the Cape gannet was still more densely populated than the densest area recorded for the Atlantic gannet, whilst the densest Cape gannets were denser than any Australasian gannets. As in the case of the piquero, it may be a case of a restricted supply of suitable islands; indeed, in 1957 man-levelled ground on Malagas was occupied almost immediately. At the present time, however, Cape gannets may be declining and there is probably no serious lack of space.

NEST SITES AND NESTS

Cape gannets nest mainly on flat ground, on sand, bare rock, cement surfaces or even platforms made of iron. Artificially provided platforms have attracted cormorants to breed, but so far, not gannets. Despite their liking for flat ground, the ability to use cliff ledges deserves special note. They make their nests entirely from excreta (guano) and detritus such as feathers and nest material dropped by other species. The size of the nest depends on the amount of guano available (on Malagas the average nest weight was 1770g) and if it is nearly all removed by man there may be so little remaining that birds lay on bare rock. This is of interest since, as Jarvis (1970) showed, the onset of laying is earlier and breeding success is probably highest (egg loss reduced) when ample nest material is present. The effect on laying was checked by artificially providing one area out of four comparable ones with much guano. As a result, by October 20th 1967, this area held three times as many nests with eggs as the next most laid-in area. If this positive correlation between the amount of nest material and the onset of laying is indeed valid, it is significant, since early fledged chicks tend to be heavier than later ones and therefore may be expected to survive better. Abundant nest material could facilitate laying by intensifying interactions, with concomitant effects on maturation of gonads. The habit of using guano for the nest depends on a dry climate, otherwise it becomes wet and sticky and would coat the egg or chick. The advantage is obscure; it eliminates the take-offs and landings entailed in fetching seaweed (which is not scarce and is indeed used by cormorants). It may have resulted from the Cape gannet's habit of regulating its body temperature by excreting on its feet (p. 263).

THE EGG AND CLUTCH

1. *Characteristics of the egg*

Broekhuysen & Rudebeck (1951) give the mean of 100 egg measurements as 76·13mm × 48·22mm (range in length 64·8–85·2 and in breadth 42·6–?48·2). Other series were 80 × 51·3 and 78–85 × 48–50. These are very similar to the figures for 100 Atlantic gannet eggs (76·06 × 49·1), indicating that the mean volume and therefore weight of the Cape gannet's egg is about the same. This means that its weight as a proportion of female weight is about 3·9 per cent which is significantly more than the 3·4 per cent of the Atlantic gannet. The egg of the Australasian gannet (77·57 × 46·07) is about the same as that of the Cape birds.

2. *Clutch size*

Jarvis (1974) found that 1·05 per cent of 1337 nests contained two eggs, the incidence of two-egg clutches being highest in the areas of greatest density of nests. He was of the opinion that of the seven cases in which both eggs hatched (and their laying dates could thus be calculated) it was likely that at least some of the two-egg clutches had been laid by the same female. This, however, remains uncertain since (a) he showed that some of his two-egg clutches were due to inclusion of neighbouring eggs, (b) he based his conclusion on the relative ages of the two eggs (five days apart) but was unable fully to evaluate the possible role of local synchronisation of laying in producing this effect and (c) under these circumstances the sample is too small to be statistically significant. In view of the corresponding lack of evidence for the Atlantic and Australasian gannets laying two-egg clutches, for neither of which is there a single authenticated instance, the point is of considerable theoretical interest and it should not yet be concluded that some Cape gannets do so. The point is also relevant to the interpretation of Jarvis' twinning experiments (p. 242).

3. *Replacement laying*

Of 41 pairs that lost their egg before the end of November (mid-December is about the latest a bird can lose its egg and still have a chance of re-laying) 18 re-laid and a further 18 probably did so but the females concerned were not individually recognisable and it is just possible that some may have been new mates. Sixteen pairs had their egg removed on December 14th and only one re-laid. Of the 18 cases just mentioned, six lost their egg when it was one day old and re-laid in 12 (2), 15 (2), 16 and 24 days, two lost when two days old were replaced two and 25 days later; the remainder were replaced as follows (age when lost given first): 6 (20); 7 (20); 11 (30); 18 (24); 22 (27); 23 (26); 23 (27); 27 (27); 28 (20–55). The two-day interval is interesting because it is so short. Three females laid two replacement eggs, taking 22, 18–23 and 21–26 days respectively to replace their egg for the second time (replacing it for the first time they had taken 24, 14–15 and 16 days respectively). Replacement laying in the Cape gannet is thus extremely similar to that in the Atlantic bird (p. 89).

4. *Incubation period*

The egg takes about 44 days to hatch (42–46). Three birds with infertile eggs incubated them for 61, 63 and 64 days respectively. Chicks take on average about 30 hours between pipping the shell and full emergence.

THE CHICK

1. *Morphology and plumage development*

Development is apparently as in the Atlantic bird. Although this has not been critically examined, it seems likely that Cape juveniles have paler underparts than Atlantic juveniles. In terms of my interpretation of the adaptive significance of the latter's dark plumage this may correlate with the Cape juvenile's flatter (safer) habitat and its less aggressive parents, factors reducing both the likelihood of a fatal accident due to displacement and also the premium on appeasing plumage. The earlier achievement of pale underparts in the juvenile in fact foreshadows an earlier achievement of adult plumage. However, judging from photographs, many Cape juveniles are quite as dark as dark Atlantic ones (Fig. 3).

2. *Growth*

The growth curve (Fig. 109) shows that peak weight was reached about 80 days after hatching and then weight decreased slightly, as it does in all sulids. A comparison of weights of Cape and Atlantic gannets at various ages shows the slower growth of the former. They achieve maximum weight later and reach a lower percentage of the adult's weight. Peak weight, about 3190g (some 109 per cent of adult weight) is reached at 80–90 days whilst in the Atlantic gannet 4000g or more, representing up to 140 per cent adult weight, is reached at 56–70 days. Cape chicks fledged at 2920g taking 451 weighed in one season only but at 2894g taking 1004 weighed over two seasons (Fig. 110). Atlantic gannets fledge at about 3800g. Growth is apparently slightly better early and late in the season than in the middle, but it is not clear that the differences are significant; for example, birds fledging in the first half of April (the period of lowest weights) were in 1968 only 74g lighter than those fledging in the first half of March (the period of highest weights), though in 1967 the difference was 200g which is significant. A longer run of years is needed to settle the point.

3. *Fledging period*

The average of 15 cases was 97·2 days (range 93–105). This is significantly longer than in the Atlantic gannet, despite the Cape gannet's smaller size but it is shorter than the fledging period (102–107 days) of the Australasian.

4. *Post-fledging loss of weight*

The interesting habit of juvenile Cape gannets of hanging around the edge of the colony for some days after leaving the nest (and many are not fed during this period) indicates that it is important to exercise and practise flight; it is also important to use their limited fuel reserves to acquire the art of flying; some swim away with more fat whilst others spend longer at the colony and fly away with less. Jarvis investigated the rate at which these fringe juveniles lost weight (Fig. 111). Of 74 birds weighed at intervals, 38 showed consistent decreases in weight and were assumed to have remained unfed (however, see below). The results showed that a bird could lose up to 425g in six days (the maximum time recorded) but the minimum figures are of little value because the birds concerned may have been fed. Thus one lost only 85g in six days, which is impossible if unfed, and yet it (and similar cases) are included in the calculations of mean weight loss per day. At least twice as much weight would be lost in a bird flying and diving at sea and since the average fledgling weighs only 2900g on leaving the nest (the average adult weighs around 2650g), it is highly unlikely that a juvenile can afford to drop to a weight below around 2000, bearing in mind that it lacks an adult's experience and has therefore shorter grace. In fact Jarvis records that even at a weight of 2050–2250g juveniles appear relatively inactive. Thus, a Cape juvenile is unlikely to possess fuel reserves for much more than a week's flying at sea, even if it departs when weighing about 2900. Most juveniles depart after losing much less than the 425g quoted above, and probably have around a week's fuel in reserve. Jarvis concludes that they have, at most, about 12 days, but for the reasons just mentioned, this figure may be too high. Although the probable correlation between weight at

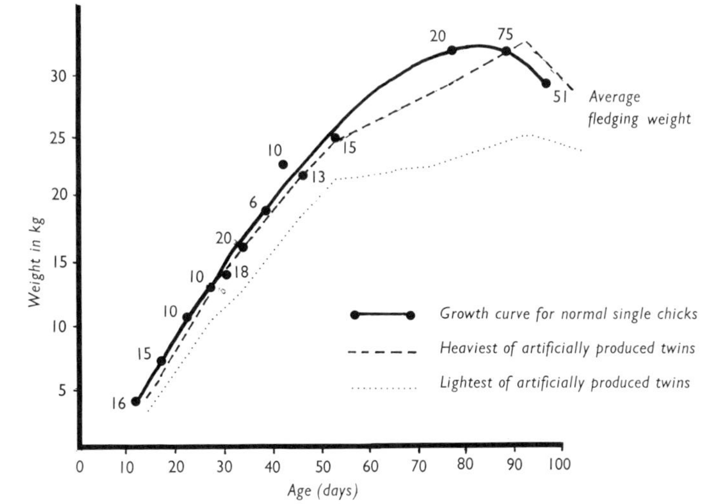

Fig. 109

The growth of normal (single) chicks and of artificially produced twins. (From Jarvis 1971.)

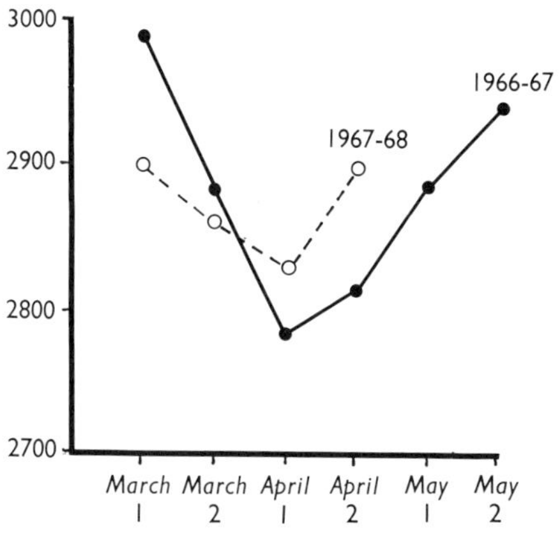

Fig. 110

Variation in the average fledging weights in two seasons. (From Jarvis 1971.)

fledging and subsequent survival has been mentioned, it must be added that this is far from critical; fledglings covering a considerable range of weights survived to breeding age. Fifteen young gannets shot and weighed soon after they had left the island (April, May and June) weighed on average 2977g (Rand 1959a). This is higher than Jarvis' figure for *fledging* weight (2894g) and indicates either that they had already learned to fish (Rand estimates they were only a few days away from the island) or that in that year and place they fledged at a considerably greater weight than Jarvis' birds.

5. *Twinning experiments*

At this point it is appropriate to discuss Jarvis' duplication, with the Cape gannet, of my twinning experiments (Jarvis 1974). My original experiments gave surprising results, in that twins were reared with remarkably little effort. In the Cape gannet, donation of extra eggs showed that in 1966–67 (allowing for the normal failure rate in single egg clutches) about 46 per cent more fledglings were reared from the 21 artificially doubled clutches than would have been reared from 21 single egg clutches. In 1967–68 the equivalent figure was, at most, only 19 per cent more, due mainly to high egg loss during incubation.

The twinned chicks grew markedly more slowly than normals and in each pair, one grew faster than the other, thus leading to the production of one essentially normal and one underweight sibling; this is important in interpreting these results. Yet the fledging period was apparently not significantly different (97·2 range 93–105, in singles; 99 in twins).

The average fledging weight of twins was virtually the same in both years of the experiment (2506g 1966/67 and 2583g 1967/68) so one is justified in lumping them for comparison with the average weight of single chicks (2895g), than which they are significantly lower, but it must be remembered that the average of twins comes from light and heavy birds and not from two equally underweight individuals. The important question is whether they survive sufficiently poorer than normal singletons, not only to offset any advantages of rearing two but actually to incur a *disadvantage*. In the absence of direct evidence, a relevant pointer was the survival of low weight singletons compared with higher weight individuals. It was found that, of 24 recoveries (13 only a few miles from the colony and 11 much further) the 13 chicks which died near to the colony had weighed, on average 2604g at fledging (which is underweight) whilst the more distant recoveries had weighed the normal 2930g. A difference of 10 per cent in body weight at fledging had apparently had a significantly adverse effect on survival for although both lots had died, the heaviest birds had got further. So probably (though not necessarily) twins would survive less well than normal young (late young, irrespective of weight, survive less well than early young and the fledging dates for the two categories

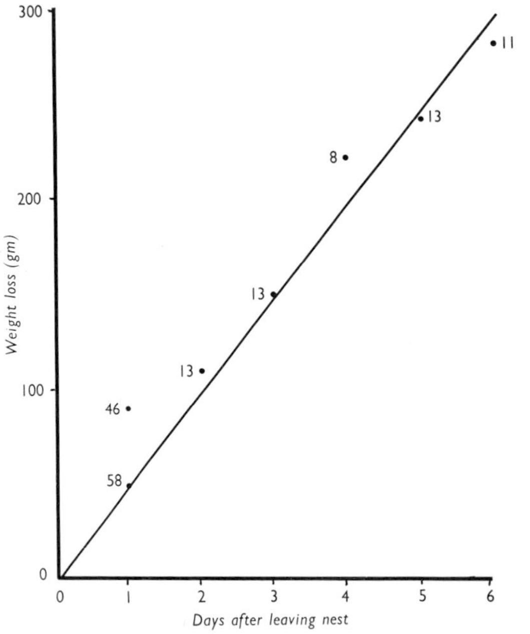

Fig. 111

Weight loss per day after fledging. (From Jarvis 1971.)

compared above were not given). It remains to be demonstrated whether the additional mortality would offset the reproductive advantage gained by producing twins. However, twins grew less well than singles and probably survived less well. This is of particular interest because the conclusion reached differs from that drawn from the Atlantic gannet twinning experiment (Nelson 1964). There, I concluded that twins grew almost as well as singles and would not survive significantly less well; certainly not enough to offset the reproductive advantage (85 per cent) gained by rearing twins. It is therefore worth emphasising that, for the following reasons, the Cape results in no way invalidate the Atlantic gannet conclusion:

1. Cape young fledge with little or no fat stores whereas Atlantic birds are not only larger, but have far greater fat deposits. The effect of a 10 per cent deficit on the Cape bird would therefore be considerably greater than such a deficit would be in the Atlantic bird.
2. The observed average weight deficit in the Cape birds stemmed mainly from the *lighter* of the twins, and these individuals would therefore be more than 10 per cent in arrears and would be the likely victims of the enhanced mortality. In the Atlantic gannet, twins were mostly equal to each other.
3. The Atlantic twins were in any case unlikely to have fledged at a weight 10 per cent below normal. Although last weighed when 70–75 days old, they had by then passed their maximum weight and on many occasions up to 60 days, the *average* of the twins' weights was actually greater than the average weight of singletons of comparable age. Furthermore, on five days (including the 59th day) the heaviest twin outweighed the heaviest single. There was thus no question of the persistently inferior weight shown by Cape twins (Fig. 109) and even *they* ended up only 10 per cent lighter.

This is of course entirely consistent with all the other evidence showing that the Atlantic gannet feeds its young with considerably greater ease than does the Cape gannet.

Finally it may be added that the selection pressures operating on the newly fledged Cape gannet may be different from those acting on Atlantic birds; in fact the different fledging procedures makes this likely. Chance bad weather almost certainly plays a major rôle in the Atlantic bird and could easily swamp a marginal advantage conferred by a slightly greater fat deposit. In fact, the variability in weight between normal *singletons* is far greater than the small difference that may have existed between singles and twins; rather than make this up by a variable fledging period (as many sulids do) the Atlantic gannet simply retains the short fledging period despite the lightness of some individuals and so gets its young off as early as possible. Cape birds may not experience such climatic uncertainties and may in any case fly relatively quickly to their fishing grounds, where survival may then depend more straightforwardly on fuel reserves in relation to the acquisition of fishing skills. It seems that many of them reach their target area in an exhausted condition (and are caught for food), but whether this is due to a fast journey (much as in the Australasian) or to bad weather en route, is unknown.

Rearing twins did not have a deleterious effect on adult weight (12 birds that reared two chicks afterwards averaged 2591·2g against 42 weighed after rearing one chick, averaging 2588·4g). Nor, apparently, did it prejudice their chances of laying in the subsequent season.

BREEDING SUCCESS

1. *Hatching success*

About 85 per cent of a sample of 55 eggs hatched in 1966–67 but in 1967–68 hatching success was only 60 per cent (from 40 nests). In the two years therefore, hatching success averaged 76·8 per cent. Hatching success was low in 1967–68 because human activity had removed much of the nest material Otherwise it is similar to that of the Atlantic gannet.

2. *Fledging success*

In 129 nests whose chicks hatched during the first half of the 1966–67 season, 125 (96·9 per cent fledged. There are no figures available which take the other half of the season or other year into account, but if the sample just quoted is representative, this figure is similar to that of the Atlantic gannet and clearly indicates that food is relatively plentiful and predictable.

3. *Overall breeding success*

On the above figures, overall breeding success was about 74 per cent; probably hatching success is generally higher than the figure used here and fledging success lower, so the overall average is probably about right. Rand (1959a) makes a curious and unsubstantiated statement to the effect that 'unless food is obtained near a nesting island, eggs or young may be deserted'.

BREEDING REGIMES

1. *General features of attendance at colony*

Cape gannets are annual breeders. They occupy the colony mainly between late August and late May, most adults dispersing as soon as their chick has fledged. On Bird Island (Lambert's Bay) there were always a few hundred adults (no immatures) roosting at night throughout the year. These were mainly males (ratio of males to females probably 3:1). The situation, however, varies with locality and year. For example, in some years nearly all adults disappear during May, June and July. In June 1956 there were 15 gannets on Malagas but in June 1957 there were almost as many as in summer. As in the Atlantic gannet (and doubtless the Australasian also) adults return fat to the island. Rand (1959a) records large amounts of yellow fat around the stomach and beneath the skin in winter and early spring. A male in August, weighing 2752g, had 106g of perivisceral fat and another, weighing 2892g, had 114g of fat.

2. *Seasonal aspects of breeding*

Unfortunately there is little information on the timing of laying, but it appears that they lay from early October until late December with peak laying around the first half of November, a total laying period of around 90 days. But eggs have been laid considerably outside these dates; Rand (1963a) gives April as the latest month, which has no counterpart in the Atlantic gannet. Peak fledging is around March, but many fledge in April and May.

Jarvis makes the general statement that the timing of laying is important in the Cape gannet since 'there appears to be a relatively short optimal breeding period'. Although he does not describe the seasonal aspects of laying, he presumably infers from the apparently poorer survival of late chicks, that eggs laid around late October/early November survive best. Little is known about the adaptive significance of the timing of laying in the Cape gannet. Moreau (1950) mentions a flush of small fry, including the mackerel *Scomber colias*, about midsummer (December/January) which would fall at a convenient time for the feeding of gannet chicks and Rand's (1959a) graph of the seasonal abundance of pilchards, maasbankers and squid (Fig. 114) shows that June to August are the poorest months. The post-fledging mortality (which is heavy) is presumably also an important aspect. Broekhuysen & Rudebeck (1951) mention that due to heavy seas, considerable mortality may occur after the young have left the nest but before they have got away from the island. This presumably refers to birds that tried to swim. It may partly explain why most Cape juveniles *fly* from the colony and why they hang around for up to a week before leaving. Jarvis gives evidence that most of the birds recaptured at the breeding colony two years after fledging had fledged early in the season. Also, the recoveries of birds in their first year showed that late fledgers fared worst.

3. *Synchronisation*

So far as synchronisation is concerned, in a group of 120 nests checked each day from the onset of laying in mid-October until November 23rd, it took five weeks from the onset of laying until 82·5 per cent of the nests contained eggs. This is a less rapid rate of laying than occurs in the Atlantic gannet (Fig. 112). The three weeks when most laying occurred was between October 25th and November 15th (62·5 per cent of the total were laid in this period).

Jarvis makes the point that, though the Cape gannet nests even more densely than the

Atlantic, its egg laying seems less synchronised and goes on to question the relationship between dense nesting and the synchronisation of laying in the Atlantic gannet. However, the point is that synchronisation is enhanced by social stimulation which, other things being equal, is greater in densely nesting species. *Both* the Cape and the Atlantic birds nest extremely densely, actually within biting distance, and since the incidence of socially stimulating behaviour (e.g. Bowing) is demonstrably higher in the Atlantic bird, the latter probably is exposed to greater behavioural facilitation of laying. The fact that it nests slightly less densely than the Cape bird is irrelevant to this issue and probably depends partly on its greater size and weight which in turn requires more space, particularly when the chick is present. It is in fact particularly interesting that, despite suffering a greater shortage of physical sites, and nesting more densely, the Cape gannet is *less* aggressive than the Atlantic (see p. 255). The Atlantic must be competing for something, and if this is a social property, which facilitates laying, we could expect (as we find) greater synchrony in Atlantic gannets. It is also consistent that the Cape bird nests at more *variable* densities than the Atlantic, for if there is less survival value in synchrony, greater variability in the mechanism producing it is to be expected.

4. *Length and composition of the breeding cycle*

The incubation and fledging periods together require about twenty weeks, which is about the same as in the Atlantic gannet. The period of attendance at the colony before laying seems to be about four weeks, for Jarvis notes that the number of gannets begins to rise about late August or early September, whilst the first eggs appear about early October. Most adults leave the colony immediately their chick fledges. Thus, their pre-laying attendance is less than half that of the Atlantic gannet and they entirely lack the period of post-breeding attendance which in the Atlantic bird averages at least two months. The total length of the Cape gannet's breeding cycle is only about 24 weeks compared with some 35–38 weeks for the Atlantic. This interesting difference may be related to the Cape gannet's obviously lower premium on defence of the nest site and perhaps, too, the reduced role of social stimulation in breeding (which in my view is a major reason for the Atlantic gannet's 'obsession' with its site (see p. 254).

5. *Frequency of breeding*

There is no information on the subject of possible 'rest years' in the Cape gannet. Presumably

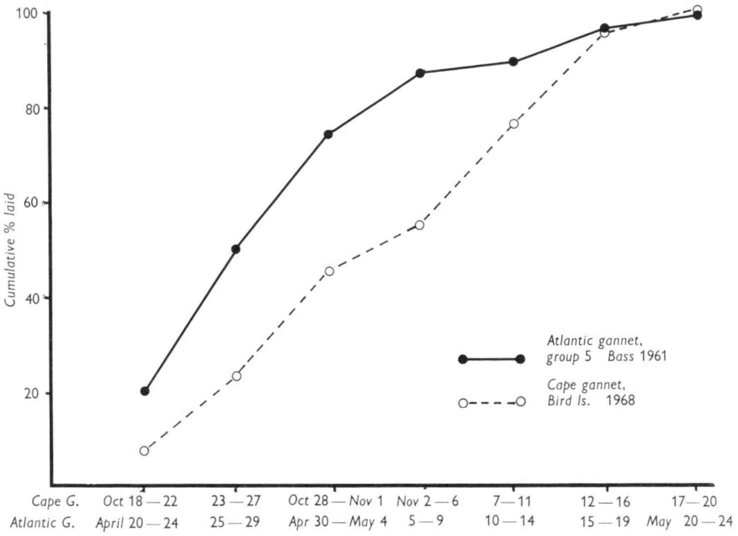

Fig. 112. Synchronisation of laying compared in the Atlantic and Cape gannets. Note that the first point on the graph is difficult to equate but is approximately the same period after laying began in both groups. (Data on the Cape gannet from Jarvis 1971.)

it attempts to nest each year but any individual is periodically relieved of the duty by loss of egg too late for replacement, or by death of chick, or divorce or loss of partner. Thus periodic rest years are obtained.

OTHER ASPECTS OF BREEDING ECOLOGY

1. *Food*

Thanks to the work of R. W. Rand, more is known about the food of the Cape gannet than of any other sulid. Between 1954 and 1956 Rand (1959a) shot 257 gannets up to 15km offshore between Lambert's Bay and Quoin Point and examined their stomach contents. The main aspects of this work concern (a) prey species and the proportions taken of each, (b) the weight and size of meals and associated data and (c) the seasonal pattern of abundance of prey (to which one can attempt to relate the gannet's breeding regime). They fish in areas which are also important commercial fisheries, as, mostly, does the Atlantic gannet and to some extent the Australasian, too.

(*a*) *Prey species*

Cape gannets preyed on at least 20 different species of fish, an unidentified range of cephalopods, crustaceans and one species of polychaete.[1] Fig. 113 shows the main prey species and the contribution each makes to the gannet's diet in each month. Table 33 gives further details of the characteristics of the prey species.

It appears, not unnaturally, that where a few species were abundant shoalers, gannets concentrated mainly on them; elsewhere they made up in variety of prey. Thus, in St. Helena Bay, they took five fish all of which were rather small, shoaling species. Fish recorded were: French madam *Boopsoidea inornata*; mullet *Trachystoma euronotus*; silverfish *Rhabdsoargus fasciatus*; rat tail *Coelorhynchus fasciatus*; sand cord *Gonorhynchus gonorhynchus*; pilchard *Sardinops ocellata*; maasbanker *Trachurus trachurus*; mackerel *Scomber japonicus*; anchovy *Engraulis japonicus*; mullet *Riza ramada*; skipper *Scomberesox*; sand-eel *Ammodytes capensis*; round herring *Etrumeus micropus*; needle-fish *Hyporhamphis knysnaensis* and *Hemirhamphis far*; gurnards *Trigla* spp.; leer fish *Hypacanthus amia*; snoek *Thyrsites atun*; stock fish *Merlucius capensis*; flying fish *Cypsilurus furcatus*; squid *Loligo reynaudi*. Also unidentified squid, cuttlefish, crustacea and polychaetes. Around the Cape Peninsula they took 17 species.

[1] Davies' (1955) comparable figures for 98 stomachs were 50 per cent pilchards, 16 per cent maasbankers, 11 per cent anchovies and 16 per cent mackerel.

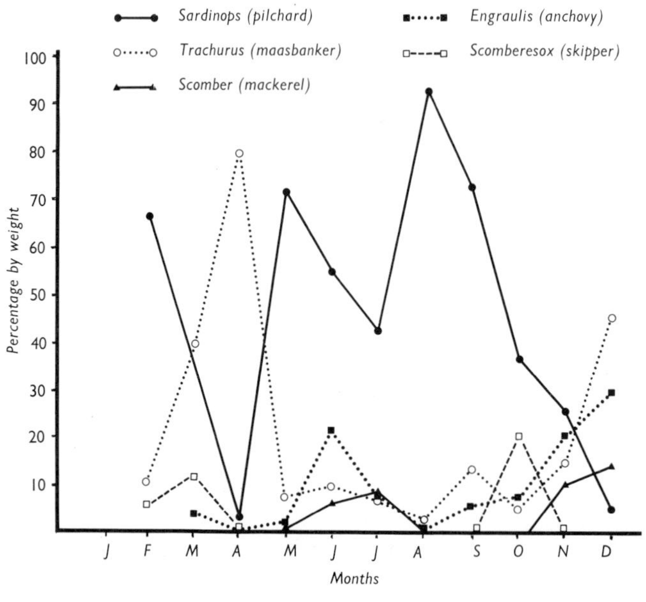

Fig. 113

The main food fishes (by percentage weight) of the Cape gannet in different months of the year. Note the peak reliance on *Sardinops* in the very early stages of the gannet's breeding cycle. (From Rand 1959a.)

The main food fish was pilchard, rising to 94 per cent of the diet by weight in August. They were the chief prey for nine months of the year, including the winter months of June and July. The small sizes were taken in April, May and July. Pilchards were taken with cephalopods and maasbankers more often than with anchovies, sand-eels or skippers.

The second most important prey was the maasbanker. They were taken more in 1955 than at other times and in that year were more important than pilchards. They were taken more often alone than with pilchards or cephalopods and were found even less in association with anchovies and sand-eels.

The third most important food species, but far behind the other two, was the anchovy. Anchovies appeared most often in association with cephalopods. The smallest were taken in April and May and most (51 per cent) were caught between Table Bay and Saldanha Bay.

Mackerel were recovered from stomachs both in mid-winter and mid-summer, skippers in February, March, September and October. Sand-eels occurred in June, July, September (spawning) through to December and in November formed 13 per cent by weight of all food for that month.

The crustacea (isopods, euphasiids, mysids, copepods and stomatopods) were said to 'come mostly' from fish stomachs; why they could not all have done so is not stated. Four nereids (polychaetes) were found in the stomach of a young gannet and were thought to have been caught by the bird. They were recorded, also, from an adult.

(*b*) *Meal size, etc.*

Fifty birds shot when considered to have just finished feeding all contained more than 200g of food. By the state of digestion it was possible to tell what fish constituted past or present meals. The mean weight of the last meal was 342·7g. All birds that locate enough fish to feed

TABLE 33

CHARACTERISTICS OF THE PREY-SPECTRUM OF THE CAPE GANNET
(data from Rand 1959a)

Species	Per cent of stomachs in which it occurred	Per cent of total diet (by weight)	Number in one stomach (a) largest (b) mean	Greatest weight in one stomach (g)	Size spectrum (per cent (in cm) of each size)	Weight (g)
Pilchard	35	51	(a) 23 (8cm) (b) 4	652 (6 fish)	5–10 (30%) 11–15 (6%) 16–20 (33%) 21–25 (22%) 26–30 (9%)	Mean 39 (357) (in 1955 69·4)
Maasbanker	17	20	(a) 54 (5cm) (b) 12	NR	1– 5 (18%) 6–10 (62%) 11–15 (17%) 16–20 (1·5%) 21–25 (1·5%)	Mean 22 (85)
Anchovy	13	12	(a) 54 (5cm) 52 (12cm) (b) NR	186 (12 fish)	5–13	NR
Mackerel	7	5	(a) 33 (10cm) (b) 4	NR	8–36	NR
Skipper (Garfish)	3	3	(a) NR (b) 3	NR	16–35	Av. 52·69
Sand-eels	5	3	(a) 21 (12 cm) (b) 9	NR	8–15	NR
Cephalopods	19	2	(a) 32 (beaks) (b) 3	NR	Largest 17cm along mantle edge	452 (3 squid)

NR= Not recorded

to repletion in a fairly short time will not feed again that same day. Davies' earlier estimates that gannets consume three pounds of fish on each 'successful' fishing day (later he amended it to four pounds) are extremely inaccurate. The daily intake is not over two pounds and is normally well below this. Rand gives the theoretical maximum intake (derived from his actual figures by allowing six times the standard deviation as giving the range of the sample) as 839g (1lb. 14oz.) and says gannets rarely eat so much. Probably the average daily intake is about 368·5g (13oz.). From stomach contents meals exceeded 600g on only two occasions and one of these involved fish stolen from a net. From this Rand computes that Cape gannets eat about 4375 tons of commercial fish each year out of 6250 tons of marine food. Jarvis found that in November, regurgitations from adults freshly back from foraging weighed on average 147·5g and in February, when most birds had chicks, averaged 301g. He found that a hungry captive gannet, given unlimited food, took on average 752g of pilchards at a meal. An average daily meal of 349g represents about 13 per cent of adult body weight, which is slightly lower than many raptors take.

(*c*) *Seasonal pattern*

The gannet's diet reflects the relative abundance of the various species taken commercially (Figs. 113d and 114b).

2. *Annual mortality*

(*a*) *Adult*

Whilst this has not yet been adequately calculated, there are good pointers. The oldest adult known was fourteen years three months, but extensive loss of the early (soft) rings

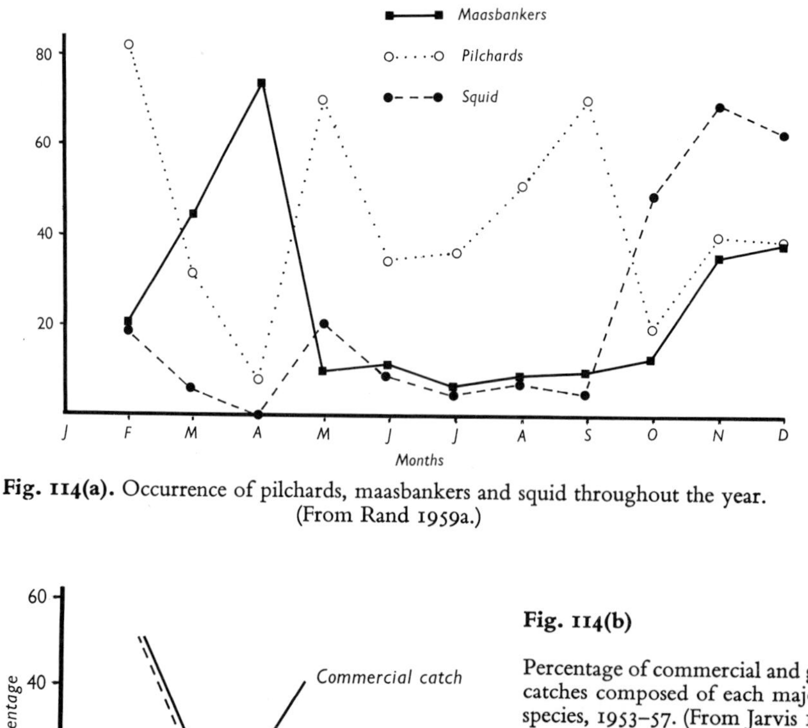

Fig. 114(a). Occurrence of pilchards, maasbankers and squid throughout the year. (From Rand 1959a.)

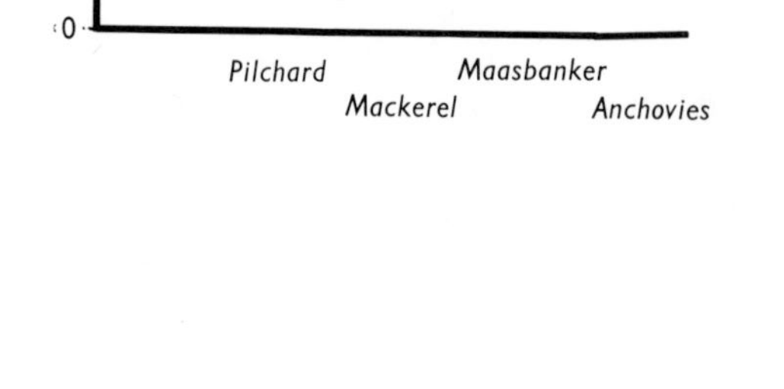

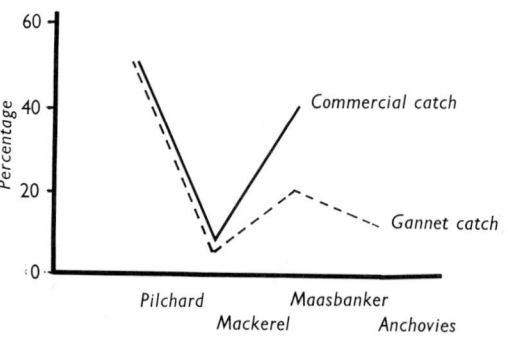

Fig. 114(b)

Percentage of commercial and gannet catches composed of each major fish species, 1953–57. (From Jarvis 1970.)

occurred. Many were recaptured twelve years after ringing. Of 129 adults ringed in 1951 64 per cent had been recaught at least once by 1955, and that was achieved merely by sporadic observations. Almost half (47 per cent) of all adults ringed on Malagas were seen again at least once and there was extremely little drop-off in the proportions re-observed in the first three years after ringing. Thus 1044 ringed birds were seen in the first year after ringing, 595 in the second and 981 in the third. (The figures for the fourth, fifth and sixth years were 576, 176 and 18.) On Bird Island a high proportion of birds roosting in winter bore rings put on ten years or more previously.

Broekhuysen, Liversidge & Rand deduce an annual mortality of 12½–15 per cent, but this figure depends on the number of ringed birds recorded and is certain to be too high. Of 11 birds which reared twins and were deliberately sought out the year after, 10 were found, showing 91 per cent survival in that small sample. In fact an annual adult mortality rate of 5–8 per cent, probably nearer the former, is probably about right (6 per cent would give a life expectancy of 17·2 years).

(*b*) *Juvenile and immature*

Juvenile mortality is undoubtedly extremely high, as it is in the Atlantic gannet. Three per cent of 10 145 ringed juveniles were later recovered at the colony, though this represents only an unknown proportion of the survivors. One would probably not be far out in assuming that pre-breeding mortality of the same order as that which the Atlantic gannet experiences (70–80 per cent) applies, also, to the Cape. But it may not be correct to assume that the *pattern* of this mortality is the same in the two species. There may well be more mortality in the first few weeks after fledging in the Atlantic bird, but proportionately less in the remainder of the first two-year period. Certainly the difference in the pattern of fledging in the Cape and Atlantic gannets may be expected to be adapted to different post-fledging circumstances and to subtend a different pattern of post-fledging mortality. Further speculation would, however, be useless at this stage.

As mentioned, Jarvis suggests that heavier fledglings from the earlier part of the breeding season survive best. Besides recoveries of dead birds whose weight at fledging had been known, it was found that 31 two-year-olds recaptured at the breeding colony, had fledged at a mean weight of 2937g, which is a trifle higher than the mean weight of all fledglings. Furthermore, nearly all the birds recaptured alive at the colony had fledged relatively early in their season whilst the dead birds recovered in Angola and Natal had nearly all fledged later in the season. This suggests that some factor(s) operates against birds which reach their target area relatively late, quite apart from a probable differential mortality en route.

(*c*) *Causes of mortality*

Cape gannets, like the other two, die mainly at sea, probably mostly at the hands of native fishermen. Young birds are killed in large numbers when they arrive in a weak condition off Angola and French Equatorial Africa after their migration. A number of adults damage their wings in landing at the colony.

So far as disease is concerned, Rand (1959a) reports nematode infection (*Anisakis* and *Contracaecum*). Fifty-eight per cent of stomachs were heavily infected in October, 29 per cent in July and none in April and June. *Aspergillosus fumigatus*, a saprophytic mould, is a well-known disease of poultry and its occurrence in a male Cape gannet, showing emaciation and heavy infestation with mites, was the first record of the disease in a wild bird in South Africa (Uys *et al.* 1966). Since this fungus does not occur on fish, it must have been picked up whilst roosting in company with birds, such as gulls, that have contact with sources of infection.

3. *Age of first breeding*

Some birds return to the colony during their second year, whilst still in immature plumage; of 31 such birds recaptured at the breeding colony 28 had been ringed two seasons previously and the other three were three-year-olds.

Two-year-olds may already possess adult plumage, though on the other hand even three-year-olds may still show traces of immature plumage. Breeding, however, does not occur until the third or fourth year (no details available). Broekhuysen & Rudebeck saw incubating birds on Malagas which still had a few dark axillars and which were probably in their third year whilst Jarvis (1972) reports that two out of 12 known three-year-olds (i.e. three years after ringing, so therefore late in their third or early in their fourth year) were 'almost certainly breeding'. It seems, therefore, that Cape gannets acquire adult plumage and breed when younger than the Australasian gannet and Atlantic birds. This is the reverse of its tendency to develop more slowly as a chick whereas, generally, slow developers are also slow maturers. One would have predicted that the Cape gannet's age of first breeding would be greater not less than that of the Atlantic gannet. However, the Cape (and to a lesser extent Australasian gannets) are in this respect in line with the boobies and it is the Atlantic gannet that is out of step and has undergone selection pressure for excessively deferred maturity (see p. 128).

4. *Movements*

Cape gannets have been reported off the coast of Africa nearly everywhere south of the equator. On the east they reach the Gulf of Zanzibar and occasionally Mombasa and on the west throughout the Gulf of Guinea (Rand 1959b). It has been known for almost a hundred years that Cape gannet young move far to the north of the breeding colonies and in such waters greatly outnumber adults.

(*a*) *Adult*

Of 5362 adults ringed on Malagas, only 99 (2 per cent) were recovered away from the island. This low recovery rate (lower than that of the Atlantic gannet) may be explained by a combination of ring loss, the high proportion of areas uninhabited by man (or those from which recoveries are unlikely to be reported), low adult mortality and (possibly) relatively high predation by marine animals. The birds which were recovered (Fig. 115) were mainly (71 per cent) less than 540km away from Malagas; however many adults did travel further and 17 per cent

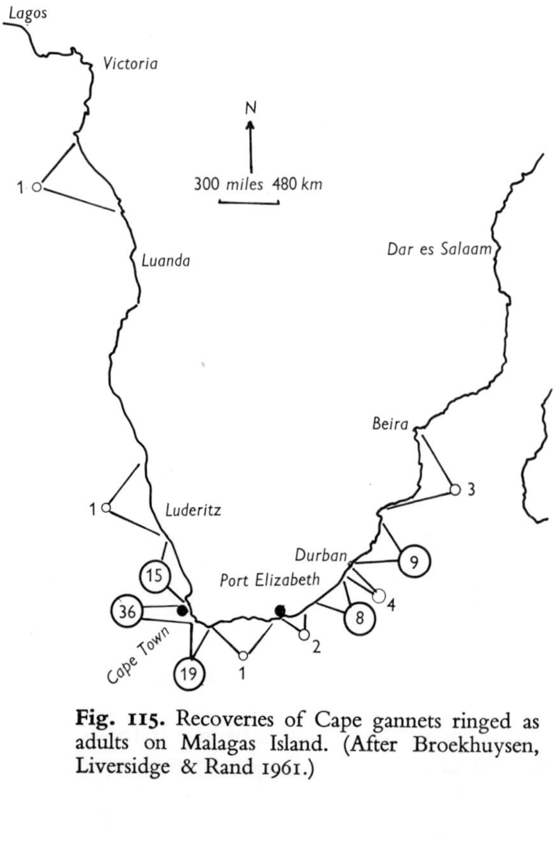

Fig. 115. Recoveries of Cape gannets ringed as adults on Malagas Island. (After Broekhuysen, Liversidge & Rand 1961.)

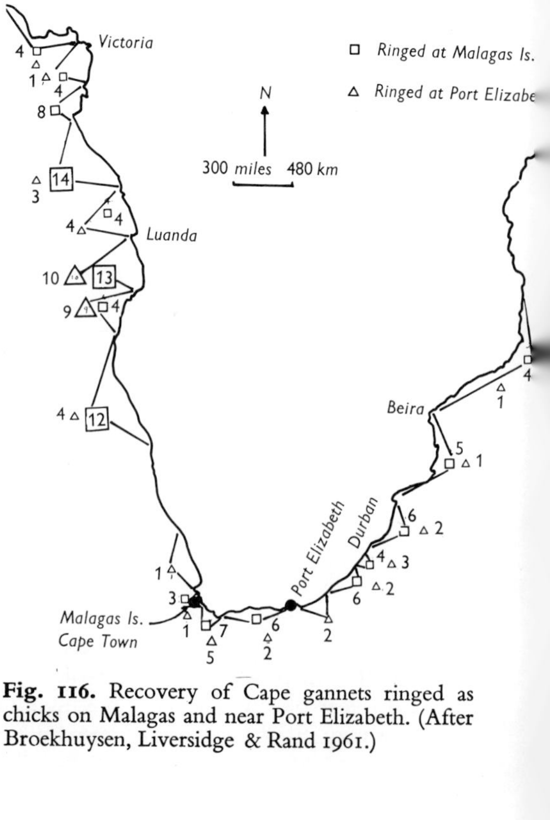

Fig. 116. Recovery of Cape gannets ringed as chicks on Malagas and near Port Elizabeth. (After Broekhuysen, Liversidge & Rand 1961.)

were recovered more than 1460km away. The two greatest distances recorded were 2700km and 3380km. Adult gannets leave the breeding colonies during May, June and July and mainly move along the west coast of Africa, some as far as Ghana though (as just mentioned) the majority remain within about 500km of their breeding place. Occasionally, adults are seen in the first half of July on the east coast (for example around Delagoa Bay and Inhambane) where reputedly they are taken for food. Thus adult Cape gannets may be seen in tropical coastal waters off Africa mainly or entirely in the non-breeding season, arriving in June and departing in August, and even then, in vastly smaller numbers than immatures. At Point Gentil the arrival of the gannets coincides with a decrease in water temperature and their departure with an increase. In general, Cape gannets (and possibly Australasian for that matter) may tend to follow the movements of cold water. Davies (1956) has correlated the restricted movements of the Cape gannets on the east with the migration of the pilchard *Sardinops ocellata*. He mentions that both adults and juveniles move with these fish shoals along the south-eastern and eastern shores of the Union. At Cape Lopez and Port Gentil, in 1945, the first gannets appeared on June 18th (nearly all juvenile or later immature stages) and a few adults appeared about a month later. A month later still, adults outnumbered juveniles by 15–20 to 1 but it was suspected that many may have just acquired adult plumage. Numbers dropped in late September. It appears from the above that the adult Cape gannet behaves much as do the other two with regard to post-breeding dispersal; most stay fairly close inshore within about 60km and within a few hundred kilometres of 'home' whilst a few move much further, to warmer waters.

(b) Juvenile and immature

The juvenile Cape gannet mainly migrates northwards along the west coast of Africa as far as the equator. It thus parallels the equivalent southward migration of the juvenile Atlantic gannet, also to equatorial waters off northern Africa, where juvenile and immature birds of the two species mingle, and the northward migration of the Australasian gannet. Details of the Cape gannet's migration have largely resulted from the recoveries of birds ringed mainly as chicks between 1951–57 on Malagas Island. The following information is largely from Broekhuysen, Liversidge & Rand (1961).

By April and May most newly fledged birds have left Union waters. In March 1952 Rand's sea counts showed nearly 30 per cent of juveniles, but this dropped to 1·2 per cent by June and for the rest of the year did not exceed 1 per cent. Of 10 145 birds ringed as juveniles on Malagas, 104 or 1 per cent were recovered at localities away from the island. Comparably, by March 1960, only 56 out of 4000 chicks (1.4 per cent) ringed on Bird Island, Algoa Bay, in 1954 had been recovered. These are even lower percentages than for adults, probably for much the same reasons and compare with a 2·6 per cent recovery rate for the Australasian gannet and around 5 per cent for the Atlantic. In the case of Cape juveniles, however, the recovery figures may be exceptionally heavily depressed due to human predation. Large numbers are killed with canoe paddles and the rings are often kept (Rand 1959b).

The recoveries (Fig. 116) show that Malagas juveniles mainly migrate at least between 2000 and 4000km north, whilst 15 per cent of recoveries were more than 4000km distant. The main trend is towards the Angolan and west African equatorial coastal waters and it is possible that the proportions recovered on the west as against the east is artificially high due to the greater number of Europeans on the west. The furthest recovery point was Porto Amelia 3780km distant on the east coast, and Calabar 4610km on the west. The tendency to move up the west coast applies even to birds ringed on the east (for example at Bird Island). From the relative proportions of birds ringed at Bird Island and Malagas and recovered at various western and eastern localities, given in the above paper, it appears there is no significant difference in the distribution of the two sets of recoveries. This shows (and the same applies to the equivalent movement in the Atlantic gannet) that the migration is not just a matter of moving north; many Bird Island juveniles first move west or south-west before north, and when rounding the Cape have moved 120km south of their point of origin. It seems, rather, as though it is largely 'directed' towards certain areas (mainly west) which are presumably good fishing grounds. One wonders why a proportion nevertheless move up the east coast if the species as a whole has an innate tendency to seek a specific area but there seems no reason why there should not be intraspecific differences in this, as in most other traits. Alternatively, the birds may (as has been observed) follow shoals of pilchards on the east, which they eventually 'lose', but continue moving northwards (Liversidge 1959). Juveniles which leave the colonies about April reach northern regions by June. Most, apparently, remain there (or at least away from their natal colonies) for at least a year, returning mainly in their second or third years. However, they are mainly to be seen in tropical inshore waters between June and August, and possibly move further out to sea during the summer, perhaps due to lack of food close inshore. Thus at Cape Lopez and Port Gentil, almost all the gannets which arrived in June were juveniles, though sub-adults followed later.

The juvenile Cape gannet thus behaves very much as do the Australasian and (especially) the Atlantic, in exposing itself to a long and dangerous migration, with all the attendant risk of bad weather and exhaustion en route. Presumably they would all find it more difficult to survive in the more immediate vicinity of the colonies in winter, and on balance benefit by seeking warmer, perhaps calmer, and (presumably) areas rich in suitable food. The precise nature of the advantages gained in all these cases are at the moment unknown. Perhaps it is a combination of calmer seas (presumably less difficult to fish in), warmer seas (though this does not apply to the Cape gannet) in which it costs less energy to keep warm and a higher probability of encountering suitably sized prey in any one day as against less frequent location of larger and possibly deeper and more abundant prey, which may suit an experienced adult with adequate reserves but not an inexperienced immature bird with less reserves. It may thus well be that the areas in which juvenile and immature gannets of all three species spend their first months or years of independence are not *richer* than the breeding areas at the same time of year (they might even be poorer), but that prey is more readily obtainable for birds which can spend their whole time foraging, than it would be around the breeding areas.

5. *Fidelity to group, site and mate*

Little has been published on these aspects but recoveries of birds ringed as adults were overwhelmingly (80 per cent) in the areas where they were originally marked (Broekhuysen *et al.* 1961). By 'areas' is meant discrete groups on the Malagas Island. They usually retain their site from year to year and Jarvis (pers. comm.) describes the pair-bond as 'strong'.

DISCUSSION OF THE CAPE GANNET'S ECOLOGY COMPARED WITH THAT OF THE ATLANTIC GANNET

The foregoing sections have revealed several aspects of the Cape gannet's breeding biology which deserve special interpretative comment, particularly in the light of equivalent aspects in the Atlantic bird.

The most important points are:

1. Cape gannets nest on flat ground in hot dry areas and very densely.
2. The adults are smaller and lighter than Atlantic birds.
3. The laying season is protracted; the peak laying period is only fairly constant from year to year (compared with very constant in the Atlantic) and the great majority of eggs are laid within three or four weeks.
4. The breeding success is high, but the young grow more slowly than Atlantic birds, deposit much less fat and fledge at a lower weight (as a proportion of adult weight).
5. Post-dispersal mortality is evidently heavy.
6. Cape gannets mature earlier than Atlantic ones and breed a year or two earlier.

Looking at these characteristics as an interrelated set, one sees that most of them bear on the nature of available nesting sites and of the food supply, just as do those of the Atlantic gannet, but the selection pressures are different in the two cases.

The hot and flat ground nesting reflects the nature of available islands. Whether sulids were ancestrally cliff, or (more likely) slope-cum-flat ground nesters is a moot point (p. 79), but either way, the flat, hot habitat now correlates well with the Cape gannet's low weight (as against the high one of the predominantly cliff nesting Atlantic gannet) and its habit of using guano, which can better accumulate in sufficient quantities and moreover is only usable under dry conditions; under wet ones it becomes foul and sticky.

The density at which they nest could have at least two causes: the need to share with other species relatively limited nesting sites in a favourable area for food (similar to the Peruvian situation) and the presence of other advantages to dense nesting, of which one could be the timing of breeding. Social facilitation of laying must undoubtedly occur to some extent in such a densely packed, noisy and active bird and whilst on present evidence it *seems* that this effect is likely to be less important than in the Atlantic bird, considerable synchrony nevertheless does occur (which means in effect that birds which would have laid later are brought forward) and earlier fledged young apparently survive best, there being considerable post-fledging mortality to act as a severely discriminating force. The indications are that *immediate* post-fledging mortality may well be less than in the Atlantic bird (there is less likelihood of storms in the vicinity of the breeding area) which, as mentioned, may imply a greater role for socially mediated timing in the Atlantic bird. This would be consistent with the Atlantic bird's greater site competitiveness and its strong tendency to nest at a remarkably constant density (in which respect the Cape bird is more variable) the point being (p. 82) that competition for a socially adequate site may well engender the fiercest fighting. Here, as elsewhere, the interpretation of the density and degree of site competition in the two species must take each species on its merits rather than attempting to fit them both into a general premiss (such as, that more densely nesting species are more aggressive) which, whilst it *may* be true in general, is not universally valid.

All the evidence is consistent in showing that the Cape gannet has a less abundant food supply than the Atlantic. With this one may again associate the smaller and lighter adults (the absence of insulating fat fits, also with the hotter environment), the slower growth of young and the behavioural evidence, such as long foraging absences and the adults' practice of leaving their young unattended. This is by no means to suggest that the Cape gannet experiences difficulty in feeding its young—quite the reverse, for when compared with all other sulids except the Atlantic gannet it rears young very quickly, has a high breeding success and even manages to cope with twins—but nevertheless it seems to illustrate the extremely favourable situation enjoyed by its northern relative. It also illustrates the extreme subtlety of the web of adaptations related to food, for the difference in availability (and probably, if we knew more about it, particularly of large prey items) has evidently helped to tip the balance against adults labouring to give their young large fat deposits, which in turn means significant difference in the latters' fledging and post-fledging dispersal regimes (p. 241). Of course, other factors may have co-operated in this; for example the young need less insulation than Atlantic birds and may be less likely to encounter prolonged periods when fishing is impossible and vast fuel reserves of critical importance. The fact that their lightness enables them to fly rather than swim away from the island may (though I would rate this marginally important) reduce the risk of predation by large fish.

The earlier maturation of Cape than Atlantic gannets is not the puzzling fact, for it fits perfectly well with the situation in the sulids as a whole. Rather, it is the late maturation of the Atlantic gannet that must be interpreted (see p. 127).

4. BREEDING BEHAVIOUR

INTRODUCTION

The three gannets are extremely similar in their behaviour and the most useful approach is to identify the differences which have arisen during the period for which they have been separated. If these can be related to differences in the habitats and associated breeding strategies of the three allo-species so much the better. This (and the Australasian account) follows the main lines of the Atlantic gannet but most behaviour is described much more briefly; a great deal of the material given under the Atlantic gannet applies here, too. Most of the information on the behaviour of the Cape gannet stems from Jarvis (1972) whose account is particularly useful for comparison, since he followed, fairly closely, my methods and areas of investigation.

Among the most obvious differences between the Cape and Atlantic gannets, which affect behaviour, are that the former inhabits much hotter areas and typically nests on low flat islands in contrast to the cliffs of the latter. It also nests more densely and at more variable density than flat-ground nesting Atlantic gannets. Nest material is scarce and Cape birds use their own guano.

ESTABLISHMENT AND MAINTENANCE OF TERRITORY

In general, and despite nesting more densely, Cape gannets are less aggressive than Atlantic gannets.

1. *Fighting*

There appear to be no significant differences in the form of fighting behaviour (Fig. 117), nor in the distribution of fighting between the sexes (birds fight only their own sex). However, Cape gannet fights are usually shorter (average duration of 19 fights—5 between females, 8 between males and 6 unknown—was 5·4 minutes, longest 15 minutes) and probably somewhat less damaging. They are probably also less frequent.

2. *Re-directed aggression*

Cape gannets almost never bite their vacant nest or site after landing on it (one case in several hundreds) whereas Atlantic gannets frequently do so, particularly early in the season.

3. *Menacing*

Menacing (thrust-threat or threat) is very similar in form to that of the Atlantic gannet and includes the head-twist (Fig. 118). When threat results in beak gripping Jarvis calls it a pull-fight. I did not measure the frequency of this event, but he gives a frequency of once during 21 daylight hours. The frequency of Menacing (presumably over the entire season) worked out at one threat per 0·008 bird/minute, compared with 0·13 in the Atlantic bird, or over 15 times as frequent in the latter. Its maximum frequency was also considerably higher than in the Cape gannet.

4. *Bowing*

Bowing (Fig. 119) is similar in form in the two species, but in the Cape gannet the wings are held in a less extreme position and the mean number of dips (the repetitive downward movement in the display) is slightly less. Also, the Cape gannet's Bow contains less of the aggressive component (nest biting). In addition, the average frequency throughout the season is probably three times higher in the Atlantic gannet and the maximum frequency at least six times higher, from many five minute counts of 250 birds. So by all these measures, Bowing in the Cape gannet may be considered a lower intensity version of the Atlantic gannet's display.

Thus in these three manifestations of territorial aggressiveness—fighting, threat behaviour and ritualised site ownership display, the Cape gannet is consistently less intense than the Atlantic. Furthermore, its Mutual Fencing (to be discussed under pair relations), which has a marked aggressive component, is of shorter duration and lower intensity than that of its northern counterpart. Nor is there anything to suggest that, by any other measures, the Cape gannet is as territorially aggressive as the Atlantic. Why should this be so? It might be suggested that the Atlantic gannet has to compete for space more than does the Cape gannet. Yet in fact the latter nests considerably more densely. Once again, therefore (see p. 82), any simple theory that available

Fig. 117

Fighting in the Cape gannet; less frequent and prolonged than in the Atlantic. (After Jarvis 1971.)

Fig. 118. Ritualised threat in the Cape gannet; note the sideways twist of the head, as in the Atlantic gannet. *Photo:* M. F. Jarvis.

Fig. 119. Bowing in the Cape gannet; less frequent and intense then in the Atlantic gannet. *Photo:* M. F. Jarvis.

space dictates the degree of site competition is facile and the 'social' explanation preferred to explain the unusual competitiveness of Atlantic gannets (p. 119) is again better. The Cape gannet, like the Peruvian booby, is probably constrained by space limitations to nest densely and in both, this engenders considerable competition, but the important fact that Atlantic gannets are even *more* competitive must be explained in quite different terms. To pursue this theme entails a comparison of the selection pressures acting on the two gannets. In the Cape gannet the main function of site competition may be the acquisition of a share of the limited physical space. Thus spacing as such is rather variable. In the Atlantic gannet, space is often superabundant, but 'nearness' is all important and engenders fiercer competition than does mere squabbling for space (see p. 123). Consequently spacing is very constant. Are, then, socially mediated factors more important in Atlantic gannets than in Cape gannets? If synchronised and seasonal laying have more survival value in the former (as they seem to have, see p. 104) this may well be so.

In all other, more minor details of territorial behaviour, the Cape and Atlantic gannets seem identical. Thus, landing on the site is preceded by one or more circuits over the nesting area and, on the run in, by loud and repetitive calling; site prospecting is similar in both; territorial aggression is often re-directed to the female (but less so in the Cape). There are no territorial traits peculiar to the Cape gannet. An interesting point, though only indirectly related to the degree of territorialism in the two species, is that Cape birds often land in the dark whereas Atlantic birds do not, probably because there is less danger to the lighter Cape bird, landing on flat ground, than to the heavy Atlantic gannet touching down on a cliff ledge. An indication of the male's greater site attachment was that it had a greater tendency to land on the actual nest than had the female (over the whole season males landed on it on 86 per cent of occasions whilst females did so on only 61 per cent). In the northern bird both sexes normally land on the nest.

5. *Pelican Posture*

The form and context of this posture is apparently much the same as in the Atlantic gannet (p. 172) and, as in that species, typically terminates the Bow. In the Cape gannet Jarvis noticed that birds approaching their nests on foot began the Pelican Posture when within about 30–50cm of the nest and on reaching it either threatened any close neighbour or the nest itself. This, and also an observed close association of Pelican Posture with threat, is consistent with the situation in the Atlantic gannet.

FORMATION AND MAINTENANCE OF PAIR

Pair formation seems similar or identical to that of the Atlantic gannet. Females prospect around or in the colony, often moving in the Sky-pointing posture and males advertise by reaching towards them headshaking, with intention movements of Bowing. Often the female is bitten when she joins the male, frequently in a low intensity Sky-pointing position, whereupon she may present her nape or Face-away (p. 179) before the two begin a bout of Mutual Fencing (p. 185). Once pair formation has occurred the partners co-operate in constant guarding of the site and one may assume that conditioning of the female to remain on guard (p. 181) takes place as in the Atlantic bird. In the Cape gannet the pair relationship is characterised by significantly less overt aggression from male to female than in the Atlantic gannet, as may be traced in the following descriptions.

1. *Nape-biting*

The incoming male Cape gannet bit the female (Fig. 120) on 96·6 per cent of 319 cases (a figure almost identical to that of 98 per cent in the Atlantic gannet), but the incoming female attracted bites on 60 per cent of 130 cases, which is significantly less than the comparable 75 per cent in the northern bird. In both cases, the nape-biting occurs throughout the breeding season. Moreover, the Cape male rarely if ever attacks his mate vigorously, whereas the Atlantic gannet not infrequently does so. This reduced aggression may imply that appeasement will be less strongly marked in the Cape.

2. *Facing-away*

The female Cape gannet does Face-away, usually in anticipation of the male's attack but, it seems, less invariably than the Atlantic female. Sometimes she may, instead, grip the male's beak (which virtually never happens in the Atlantic gannet). This could indicate a lower threshold for reciprocal aggression in the female Cape gannet, more akin to the situation in boobies. If the male is not likely to respond with full attack, as the Atlantic male would, there is less need for females to evolve extreme mechanisms to inhibit this.

3. *Mutual Fencing*

Another key display which, on the basis of its motivation as proposed on p. 186, would be expected to reflect the difference in the two species, is Mutual Fencing (Fig. 121a and b), the gannets' greeting ceremony. This display varies in length and intensity throughout the season but in the Cape gannet, even when its bouts were longest (during courtship, average duration 57·8 seconds) it was less than a third as long as that of the Atlantic gannet, whilst the latter's longest bouts were far longer than the comparable ones of the Cape gannet. Furthermore, the Cape bird's Mutual Fencing was less intense in that the wings were not held as high or as far out. Jarvis found that during the courtship period Mutual Fencing was most commonly followed by Sky-pointing and the soliciting headshake. This may be partly explained by the tendency (fully discussed in the Atlantic gannet) for the male to leave for nest material or Flight Circuiting and to Sky-point before doing so. The soliciting headshake is typically the partner's reaction to Sky-pointing, probably reflecting the tendency to try to 'attract' the partner (i.e. prevent it from departing).

The case for interpreting Mutual Fencing as behaviour which serves both to 'express' aggression and in direct ratio to reinforce the pair bond has been fully argued for the Atlantic gannet (p. 187). If aggression from male to female is weaker in the Cape bird, Mutual Fencing may be expected to be less intense and, possibly, the pair bond weaker. The former seems to be

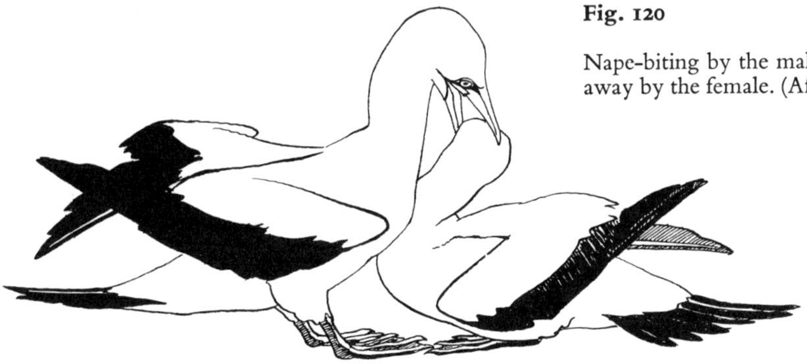

Fig. 120

Nape-biting by the male and Facing-away by the female. (After Jarvis 1971.)

Fig. 121

Mutual Fencing in the Cape gannet, less prolonged and intense than in the Atlantic gannet. (After Jarvis 1971.)

the case. However, the link between sex and aggression (which constitutes the basis of the 'double mechanism' by which aggression becomes of positive value in the pair relationship) might be weaker in the Cape gannet. It is difficult to adduce concrete evidence for this but as a pointer it may be mentioned that copulation in the Cape gannet is shorter, thus providing less prolonged sexual stimulation. Unfortunately there is no published information on mate fidelity, which one might expect to be lower than in the Atlantic gannet. I would predict also a lower incidence of Mutual Preening in the Cape gannet. Jarvis remarks that Mutual Allo-preening does not often closely follow Mutual Fencing, whereas it does so in the Atlantic bird. There may thus be tenuous grounds for believing that the pair relationship is slightly weaker in the Cape gannet but a more adequate evaluation is needed.

4. *Copulation*

Copulation seems identical with that of the Atlantic gannet; the male bites the female's nape, treads and waves his wings (Fig. 122). However, if Jarvis' observations encompass the onset of copulation it appears that Cape birds do not copulate for as long a period prior to egg laying. Copulation began about October 1st and the first egg was laid on the 22nd, whereas Atlantic gannets may begin in late January but the first egg is not laid until late March. Also, the duration of each copulation may be significantly shorter (it lasts about 20 secs compared with 24 secs in the Atlantic). If so the behaviour may be slightly less important as pair bonding activity, which would be consistent with other indications.

5. *Nest building*

Although this is functionally mainly concerned with the protection of egg and chick rather than the pair relationship, it may nevertheless be mentioned here, since it is an important interaction between mates. In the Atlantic gannet it involves the male in hundreds of excursions and returns. The Cape gannet, however, does not fly to the nest with material but simply scrapes together any guano that happens to be present immediately around the nest or lays its eggs on the bare ground. Material is then deposited (Fig. 123) with vibrations of the mandibles followed by vigorous sideways shaking of the head. If space permits, local foraging for nest material takes place on foot. Whether this involves the Cape gannet in more or fewer interactions at the nest than its northern relative has not been determined. Very occasionally males flew in with nest material which had been picked up on land. As in the Atlantic gannet, nest building continues (though not at uniform frequency) throughout the breeding season and is a common displacement activity (prior to copulation; when the partner is Sky-pointing; during bouts of Menacing, etc.). Cape gannets may lack the habit of flying in with nest material as a result of the abundant guano that would naturally accumulate in flat localities with low rainfall, the use of which absolves them from the effort (and dangers) attending landing and taking-off.

Fig. 122. Copulation with Nape-biting. (After Jarvis 1971.)

Fig. 123. Mutual nest building. (After Jarvis 1971.)

6. *Sky-pointing*

The Cape gannet's version (Fig. 124) of this interesting behaviour pattern is quite distinct from that of the Atlantic gannet. In context it agrees closely, occurring before movement (walking, a short run or a hop) towards or away from the nest. In addition to the posture of head and wings, Sky-pointing performed in conjunction with forward movement involves raising and lowering of the feet with strongly drooped webs, frequent dipping movements of the head and groans (ooo-ah). Birds may expand the long and conspicuous strip of black skin which runs down the throat, to two or three times its normal width. The *low* intensity form of Sky-pointing is closely similar to the *high* intensity form in the Atlantic gannet, but the head movements impart a characteristic look and at progressively higher intensities the Cape gannet assumes postures which are quite different from those of the northern bird. Thus, the wing movement continues beyond the tip-lifting stage until, in the extreme position, they are lifted high. At about the middle point in this range of wing positions (Fig. 124b), the posture looks as though a slight rotation of the humerus would produce the wing-swivelled position of the blue-foot (see Fig. 234) with the backs of the wings facing forwards, but in fact the Cape gannet continues to lift the wings upwards and slightly outwards (Fig. 124c). At the same time the upward pointing of the bill becomes extreme, taking the head well behind the vertical line. This posture may be compared with the extreme wings-out position preceding take-off run (Fig. 125).

Thus, starting from a common beginning (the slight lifting of wing tips) the wing lifting movement (which is in all cases associated with Sky-pointing) has in some sulids remained slight, in others gone further by a swivelling action, whilst in the Cape gannet alone it has gone further by a continuation of the straight lift, which is a quite different movement from the swivel. Thus the *initial* movement of the wings by which a sulid prepares (1) for flight by spreading its wings out (2) for Cape gannet-type Sky-pointing by raising them high with little spread and (3) for booby-type Sky-pointing by swivelling them, is the same in all cases. If the Sky-pointing display in fact derives from movements preparing for flight this is only to be expected, but until the situation in the Cape gannet was described, type (2) above was not on record as a stereotyped Sky-pointing display and one might conceivably have supposed that the swivelling and spreading wing movements in fact had different origins.

My analysis of Sky-pointing in the Atlantic gannet showed that this behaviour does not save the displaying bird from attack by the neighbours between which it must often pass, but indeed increases the likelihood of attack. Thus it is not effective appeasement behaviour if this term be given its logical functional interpretation. It is therefore of interest that Jarvis

Fig. 124(a, b, c). Sky-pointing in the Cape gannet at increasing intensity. This posture differs from its homologue in the Atlantic and Australasian gannets by much greater upward extension of the wings. (After Jarvis 1971.)

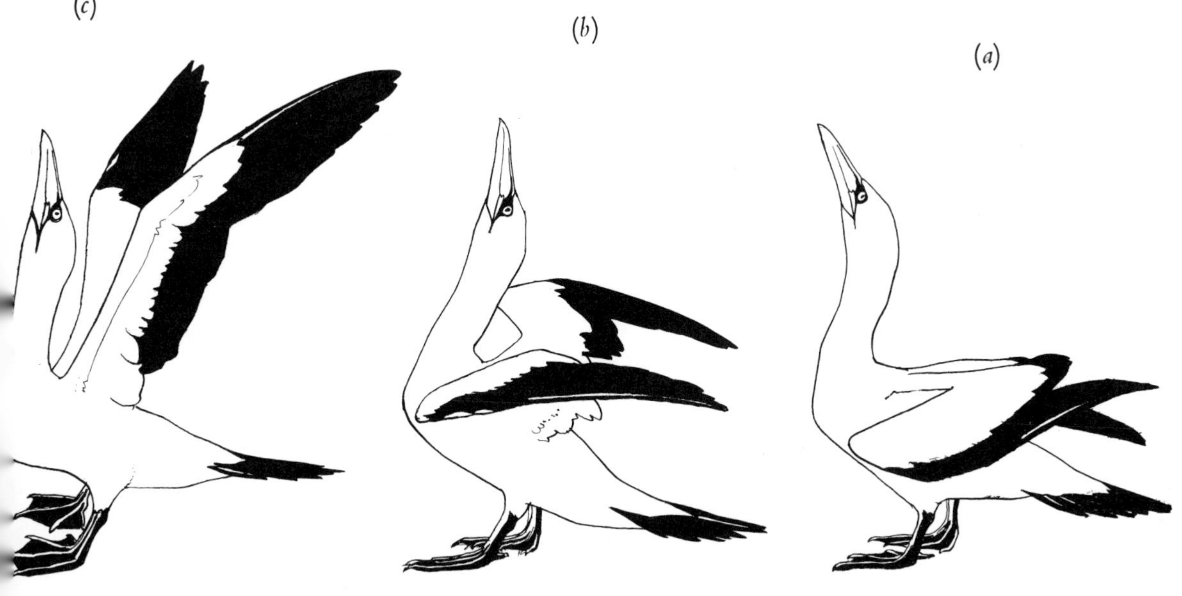

follows an earlier interpretation by Tinbergen and claims that in the Cape gannet it *is* appeasing. Whilst Sky-pointing is more conspicuous in the Cape bird, Jarvis' observations seem to me to provide circumstantial evidence that, as in the Atlantic gannet, it has in fact no appeasing function. The Cape gannet is not merely unable to rely on Sky-pointing to achieve an uninterrupted passage to a take-off point in even a small proportion of instances (it abandons Sky-pointing and resorts to dashing or 'running the gauntlet') but is actually more prone to elicit attack as a result of Sky-pointing than by performing other displays. Neighbours reacted aggressively (by threat or pecks) to Sky-pointing birds on 35 per cent of occasions compared with 26 per cent to Bowing birds, 25 per cent to copulating pairs, 20 per cent to Mutual Fencing pairs and only 1·5 per cent to birds wing-flapping with Rotary Headshaking (a comfort activity). Jarvis' contrary interpretation, however, is based on the following: (a) Sky-pointing often occurs off the site whereas these other activities do not and birds off site are more prone to elicit attack, (b) only 9 per cent of the aggressive responses of neighbours were actual pecks, (c) the duration of Sky-pointing was generally longer than the other acts and therefore gave more time for aggressive responses. These boil down to the simple but invalid thesis that although Sky-pointing elicits attacks or threat, it does so less than one might expect compared with other behaviour patterns and is therefore appeasing. Even *on* site and when corrected for duration, Sky-pointing elicits more threat than does, for example, Rotary Headshaking and its comparable relation to the other behaviours listed above is at best debatable. Strictly, one should compare Sky-pointing with non-Sky-pointing instances within equivalent contexts. Since, however, birds do not usually depart without prior Sky-pointing this is impracticable and one is denied the natural control. In the face of the evidence that it is specifically Sky-pointing (the other behaviour patterns which drew attack are of course not postulated to be appeasing), and not merely any movement, which elicits aggression from neighbours, it is not justifiable to assume that a bird which simply *walked* off site prior to dashing would be attacked more than a bird which Sky-pointed prior to dashing. On this criterion it therefore cannot be concluded that Sky-pointing has appeasement value in the Cape gannet and there seems no good reason to believe that the situation differs substantially from that in the Atlantic gannet.

Having said this, it must be admitted that the Cape gannet's flat nesting environment and great density may conceivably have given its Sky-pointing an appeasing function, though this remains to be demonstrated. It seems, moreover, theoretically possible that Sky-pointing can fail to prevent aggressive responses, or can even elicit them, and still be an appeasement posture in a more subtle sense. Birds receive feed-back as a consequence of behaving and it may be that Sky-pointing birds lower their *own* readiness to retaliate (their bill position certainly makes this difficult). Also attacks by neighbours may be of lower intensity than they would have been had the message (that the Sky-pointing bird is harmlessly leaving) not been signalled. Unfortunately these speculations are virtually untestable.

Jarvis records some further observations on Sky-pointing in the Cape gannet, which I deferred so as to maintain the thread of the main discussion. It was shown much more fre-

Fig. 125

Cape gannets take off along runways relatively clear of boulders; high weight would be a big disadvantage. (After Jarvis 1971.)

quently by males than by females (the same holds for the Atlantic gannet) which is consistent with the fact that males leave the nest more often than do females; Sky-pointing was often preceded by Mutual Fencing (again consistent with the tendency for greeting to be followed by the departure of one partner); copulation was usually preceded by Sky-pointing, which is not the case in the Atlantic gannet. This seems a real difference between the two species, of particular interest in that it is Sky-pointing which, in the boobies, has become the sexual (advertising) display. The sequence for the functional change may have been: Sky-pointing precedes movement for nest-material; mutual nest-building precedes copulation; Sky-pointing comes directly to precede copulation and so becomes linked with sexual activity and becomes the sexual advertising. Commonly, a Sky-pointing female seemed to elicit Sky-pointing from the male (this occurred in the northern bird and in most cases circumstantial evidence suggested that both birds wanted to leave and were signalling this; the eventual leaver was the one whose Sky-pointing gradually gained ascendancy).

OTHER BEHAVIOUR INVOLVED IN BREEDING

1. *Egg laying*

Of 44 cases determined to within one hour, 34 were laid between midday and 07.00 hours; 19 were laid between 12.00 and 15.00 which thus appears to be the favoured period.

2. *Incubation*

During the first half of incubation, male incubation spells averaged 45 hours and female 38 hours; during the second half the figures were not significantly different (43 and 40 hours respectively). After hatching the spells shortened (1–20 days, males 28 hours, females 31 hours; 21–40 days, 18 and 19·5; 41–60 days, 18 and 16; 61–80 days, 13 and 11; 81–100 days, 10 and 10). The incubation spells (overall average 41·25 hours) were longer than in the Atlantic gannet (32·9) which seems consistent with other information, particularly slower growth, indicating less abundant food for the Cape gannet.

3. *Aspects of parent/young relationship*

All behaviour concerned with tending and feeding the chick is apparently identical with that in the Atlantic gannet.

In the Cape gannet practically all the chicks were left unattended for considerable periods after they were about 45 days old. Some were even unattended for periods soon after they were 30 days old, which is about the age at which sulid chicks are capable of regulating their body temperature (see p. 948), whilst at 45 days 18 out of 20 chicks were left alone for irregular periods of several hours, especially around midday (the main fishing time). This stands in absolute contrast to the situation in the Atlantic gannet, whose chicks are normally guarded throughout their entire period in the nest. The length of the spells for which Cape chicks were unguarded averaged between 7 and 12 hours and very often involved overnight absences. Again, this reflects the Cape bird's need to spend more time foraging. It appears from superficial observation that adult Cape gannets guarding their own young tended also to protect nearby unattended chicks by threatening intruders that attacked them. If this is correct, it implies an interesting adaptive trait which could relate to the Cape birds' foraging needs.

BEHAVIOUR OF YOUNG

Begging, feeding, appeasing, sleeping, play and comfort behaviour is apparently identical with that described for the Atlantic gannet. The most important difference between the two species is partly a direct result of the Cape gannet's habit of leaving its young unattended. These (like ground nesting boobies) are then much more prone to wander from their nests before they leave the island as newly-fledged juveniles. They may begin to stray a few feet at about seven weeks and by the time they are fully feathered, chicks may congregate on the fringes and even return to the nest to be fed. It is obviously easier to do this on flat ground but the habit may depend, too, on a reduced tendency of Cape adults to attack chicks. The Atlantic gannet is the odd bird out in its strict adherence to its site. The wandering habit is important in the life history of the Cape gannet, for it modifies the dangers of fledging (p. 24).

Cape gannet chicks, unlike those of the Atlantic gannet, rarely menace or attack their parents. Also, unattended young usually accept intruder chicks without retaliation. Older chicks form small groups and play together or mildly threaten each other. Grouping may reduce the chances of an adult attacking any member. However, groups are confined to chicks that were close neighbours and form only when there are few adults nearby. Australasian gannets behave similarly.

1. *Fledging*

When chicks leave the colony for the first time they generally make their way to the fringe and form loose groups in more open areas. Several days may elapse before they actually leave the island and during this time they perform long bouts of wing flapping, jump a few paces and try to take off. Some fledglings periodically return to their nests and may be fed, but at least half do not. This procedure subtends the possibility of fledging with full powers of flight, a capability denied to the heavy, unpractised and often cliff-dwelling fledgling of the Atlantic gannet. Most Cape fledglings actually flew from the island; a few jumped off and swam away. Twice, fledglings were seen to fly back to the island.

MAINTENANCE BEHAVIOUR

1. *Stance and movement*

The Atlantic gannet usually takes off without first holding out its wings, though occasionally it extends them a little or flicks them open once or twice. The Cape bird, however, holds its wings far out before starting its take-off run or before lifting off into the wind. The difference is probably correlated with the generally steeper sites of the Atlantic gannet and the ability of the lighter Cape bird to gain more benefit from light winds. Nevertheless, it is usually necessary for the Cape bird to run the gauntlet of hostile neighbours in order to reach a take-off point.

2. *Headshaking and wing flapping*

The Cape bird wing flaps, rotates its head and ruffles its feathers', or merely 'dogshakes', just as does the Atlantic gannet. As in the latter, soiling (as from a neighbour's excreta) mainly elicits the dogshake. Jarvis found, also, that the dogshake (Rotary Feather Shake) was elicited by noises, such as hand clapping. This may still be due to tactile stimuli (feather tightening as an alarm response to noise). He states, however, that noise and direct tactile stimuli did not elicit Rotary Headshake with wing flap (his Rotary Wing Flap). In the Atlantic gannet, however, auditory stimuli associated with alarm (e.g. gull calls) elicited large numbers of Rotary Wing Flaps and direct tactile stimuli elicited some, though they elicited more Rotary Feather Shakes. In both species Rotary Wing Flap is correlated with Sky-pointing.

Sleeping, yawning, preening, oiling and wing-stretching seem identical in the two and need not be further described. Jarvis found that 94 wing stretches involved stretching one wing backwards and in the remainder, both wings were stretched above the back. Wing stretching occurred mainly between 08.00 and 10.00 hours, which was probably due to the toilet activities of birds which had returned from foraging that morning. Head-flinging, often with 'coughing' and 'retching' to bring up fragments of hard material often accompanied by viscous droplets, occurs as in the Atlantic bird. Jarvis recorded an increase in exaggerated swallowing movements and 'coughing' towards the end of incubation, coinciding with the peak moult of breast feathers, suggesting that some of these small feathers may lodge in the throat.

3. *Heat regulation*

The Cape gannet inhabits much hotter areas than the Atlantic gannet and its heat regulating mechanisms may have to be more efficient. At 68°F. about half the birds gular-fluttered and at 78° or above nearly all birds did so. The lowest air temperature at which any adult was seen to perform this behaviour was 64°F.

4. *Defaecation*

The two types of defaecation (squirting clear and directing downwards onto the nest) described for the Atlantic gannet, occur also in the Cape. The second type occurred mainly during incubation and with small chicks in the nest and was more likely to be followed by a tail wag. There is no mention of deliberate defaecation onto the webs (possibly a cooling device) as apparently occurs in the Australasian gannet. Cooper & Siegfried (in press 1976) record that a young Cape gannet in captivity responded to high ambient temperatures by standing, gular fluttering with raised head and open bill, wing drooping, defaecating at a fast rate close to the feet, paddling in the excreta and increased breathing rate. They monitored body temperature by inducing the bird to swallow a radio which emitted clicks at a rate corresponding to temperature, and found that gular fluttering and wing drooping assisted the bird to tolerate heat stress. Standing on the excreta-wetted substrate also reduced the heat load, presumably due to evaporative heat loss and an enhanced conduction of heat to the substrate. Warham (1958) noticed that the Australasian gannet deliberately excreted onto its feet, though he did not know why. The Atlantic gannet's method of defaecating onto the nest rim, rather than squirting clear, could conceivably serve to regulate body heat though I have interpreted it as a mechanism by which the nest is cemented to the rock. This behaviour should be looked for in other sulids; it has been reported for storks and turkey-vultures (references in Cooper & Siegfried).

This concludes the account of behaviour in the Cape gannet. It remains to summarise and interpret the main features. First, it must be stressed that there is no behaviour, with the possible exception of Sky-pointing, that is very different in form in the Cape gannet compared with the other two. Nor is anything missing. It is simply a question of slight differences in amplitude and differences in the frequency of several behaviour patterns. These differences are, however, consistent with each other. All behaviour which is mainly aggressive (fighting, threatening, re-directed nest biting, Bowing and Mutual Fencing) occurs at lower intensity and less frequently in the Cape gannet than in the Atlantic. This is probably the most important difference between the two. It implies that the Cape birds are subject to less intense selection pressure with respect to site competition. The fact that they nevertheless nest more densely is irrelevant; some penguins, guanay cormorants, guillemots, some terns and others nest more densely than any gannet, yet are nevertheless not markedly aggressive. The highly invariable nesting density of the Atlantic gannet is the result of conflict between an intensely strong tendency to nest close to neighbours for *social* reasons (p. 123) and a comparably strong tendency to defend the space necessary for optimally efficient nesting. Cape gannet density may be greater because (for whatever reasons, of which size is one) the optimal space required is less. The Cape gannet may be less aggressive because there is less competition for socially acceptable sites and the greater variability in density shown by this species tends to support this view, since it implies that birds which do not 'bother' to compete for a site at precisely the regulation distance from neighbours are less penalised than in the Atlantic gannet. In turn there may be less competition for sites with these social (stimulating) qualities because the stimulation which they confer has less survival value. This could be because the timing of breeding (to which social stimulation contributes) is slightly less important in the Cape bird (see p. 244). If this chain of reasoning is correct and aggression is in some sense 'unitary', it follows that all aggressively motivated behaviour will be less intense. The reduced premium on site competition fits beautifully into the ecological circumstances of the Cape gannet, which require both parents to leave the site and the chick unguarded. An Atlantic gannet, with its strong site attachment, does not leave either unguarded, but then its food circumstances allow it not to. Further, the absence of Cape adults allows the young to wander and exercise more freely, which again is highly adaptive in their circumstances and with their particular fledging behaviour (p. 262) and fits well with the flat ground habitat.

Differences between the two species with regard to the remainder of their behaviour are listed in Table 42.

FISHING

There is little information relating specifically to the fishing behaviour of the Cape gannet. Apparently it remains within about 45km of land and most fish within 10km, though it has been seen 100km east of Algoa Bay and Rand (1959a) notes that observations from the cruises of R.S. *Africana II* between 1951 and 1953 showed that adults moved 100km offshore, the maximum distance at which birds were sighted throughout every month of these years seldom dropping below 38km and was usually between 52 and 90km. Thus even during the breeding season they moved far offshore. In fact Rand characterises them as essentially offshore feeders, seldom entering bays or moving close to land as do, for example, Cape cormorants. Nevertheless, the numbers at sea do drop off in October and are highest between June and September. Feeding gannets were seen south west of Cape Point under circumstance suggesting that the continental shelf in this area is an attractive feeding zone. Gannets were often seen west of Cape Point or south of Cape Hangklip. The general impression gained during these cruises was that when the gannets move rapidly southwards from Lambert's Bay or Saldanha Bay, they keep 10km or more from the land to disperse off the southern part of the Cape Peninsula, turning towards Danger Point and elsewhere further east. Also, near Algoa Bay gannets tend to disperse to the Continental shelf rather than closer inshore. Often they feed on migrating pilchards, but they do not always manage to find them; apparently the pilchards veer out to sea and return westwards with the Agulhas Current (Davies 1956) but do not follow a predictable route and timetable. At any rate the adult gannet movements are subject to wide variation in time and place. Usually the gannets move at a very low density over a wide area and no concentrations were regularly found in any specific area.

Since average foraging periods are long, the Cape gannet probably also covers considerable distances up and down the coast (possibly over 200km from the colony) much as does the North Atlantic gannet. Concentrations have been seen in known fish-spawning areas—for example north of St. Helena Bay—but they occurred in all the search areas covered by Rand's numerous voyages (p. 246). Table Bay was long ago described as a great haunt of gannets in pursuit of fish shoals in April and May, and streams of gannets have been described as following mackerel shoals as these moved eastwards off East London.

Almost certainly the Cape gannet penetrates the water much less deeply than the heavier Atlantic gannet, but there is no recorded information on the height from which it dives or any other aspect of this behaviour.

Like the other two gannets, Cape birds rarely land at the colony after dark and do not leave before sunrise. No birds were encountered at sea after sunset. They are said to return to islands or sheltered coves in stormy weather, but single birds were seen diving in force 6 winds. Mass feeding was not seen in winds above force 4. However, because gales are very short-lived around the Cape and wind force drops off out to sea, Rand believes that hunting gannets are probably never seriously affected by bad weather (he probably refers, here, to adults).

Cape gannets move in small groups, usually 2–8, but flocks and rafts of 50 or more were seen, often so heavy with fish that they could hardly rise. Large feeding flocks (over 500) were rarely encountered. Foraging birds fly about 10m above the sea, but constantly skim the waves or soar high. Rand asserts that they *spear* many fish from above. Occasionally they feed whilst swimming among a shoal. Once they locate a shoal, they can catch fish rapidly. Rand spotted pilchards at 16.000 S.A.S.T. when no gannets were in attendance, but in three-quarters of an hour birds were diving repeatedly into the shoal. The first two shot had empty stomachs but 10 minutes later eight others had taken up to five pilchards each. An interesting finding was that birds feeding singly averaged only 32·4g in their stomachs, but those feeding in a flock averaged 171·6g. However, this need not imply an advantage in flock feeding but merely a difference in the abundance of food; flocks mean shoals.

As would be expected, gannets do not follow any definite daily trend in feeding; if they encounter plentiful food early in the day they feed to repletion and either return to the islands or cease feeding. Otherwise they feed steadily and slowly over a long period, foraging all the time. Rand states that at least 85 per cent of the stomach contents disappear before feeding is resumed. The rate of digestion varies with the amount of food and the rapidity with which it was taken. Of five captive gannets each given a meal of mullets and killed at hourly intervals, one had digested 35 per cent of its food in two hours but another, given twice as much, had digested 41 per cent in two hours.

3

Sula [bassana] serrator

AUSTRALASIAN GANNET

1. NOMENCLATURE; EXTERNAL FEATURES; MORPHOLOGY; MOULT AND VOICE

1. *Common*

Australian or Australasian gannet; Pacific gannet; Maori name, Takapu ('we shall see the watchful Takapu searching for food in tidal waters').

2. *Scientific*

The comparative taxonomy of the three gannets is discussed on p. 307. Here, I merely list the names which have been used for this species, starting with the one which is accepted in the present work. *Sula [bassana] serrator* (Grey 1843); without the square brackets (thus allocating ordinary sub-specific status), the N.Z.O.S. Checklist (1953) used *Sula bassana serrator*; *Sula serrator* (R.A.O.U. checklist and amendments); *Morus serrator*; *Morus [bassana] serrator*; *Morus serrator*; *Sulita serrator serrator* (Tasmanian Sea) and *S.s. rex* (new sub-species from New Zealand) were split by Mathew and Iredale (1921) but invalidly.

GENERAL FEATURES

1. *Adult*

The Australasian gannet has a wingspan of about 170–180cm and an overall length of about 84–91cm. Like the Cape gannet its flight is lighter than that of the Atlantic gannet. It is mainly white with black wing tips (primaries) and all but the proximal three secondaries, giving a black trailing edge (Fig. 126). The three innermost secondaries and the tertials are white giving a white 'gap' of about 12cm on each side of the body. The alula is black and the primary coverts black or white or both. The tail, generally 10 or 12 feathers, is white except for (usually) the four centre feathers which are blackish (Fig. 127). However, there is considerable variation in this feature; the black feathers may number anything between three and 10. The outer two are always white. Often there are variegated feathers, one or two each side, separating the whites from the blacks. The four white, four black, four white pattern does not indicate a more mature bird than one with variegated feathers, for some birds showing the 4, 4, 4 pattern one year, showed 10 feathers of all three types the next. The head and neck are golden buff, varying with season, but usually deepish (deeper than the Atlantic gannet), the bill blue-grey with black lines and the facial and gular skin are blackish (the gular strip is about as long as that of the Atlantic gannet and much shorter than that of the Cape; indeed, due to the variability of the tail in the Cape gannet, some individuals differ from Australasians only in the length of the gular strip). The orbital ring is bright blue and the eyelid blue, particularly deep on the upper half and the iris is grey-blue, like the Cape gannet's, noticeably darker than that

Fig. 126

Australasian gannet about to land; note the parted and emarginated primaries, raised alulae, depressed tail (using the feet) and the downward oriented binocular vision. *Photo:* J. Warham.

of the Atlantic gannet. In the Australasian, there is often a distinct narrow band of dark pigment encircling the pupil, rather than a uniformly dark iris. The legs and feet are blackish grey with conspicuous greenish lines (varying between bluish and yellowish) along the tops of the toes and up the tarsus.

2. *Juvenile and immature*

The fully feathered juvenile (Fig. 128) is similar to the Atlantic and Cape juveniles (q.v.) but very noticeably paler on the underparts and head and neck. The white spots on the wings and back are often distinctly larger than in the other two species.

The juvenile plumage gives way to the adult via a series of intermediates which, though nowhere described in detail, appear to differ from those of the Atlantic gannet in that the immature Australasian never acquires the bold, 'large-scale' black and white pattern of Atlantic birds but is more finely variegated brownish-black and white above. It is said (Serventy *et al.* 1971) to attain adult plumage in two years, but this seems unlikely to apply to all individuals. An approximately nine-month-old bird had head, neck and underparts as adult; dorsal surface blackish brown variegated with white (Buller 1888) which is considerably in advance of an Atlantic bird at that age. A bird known to be almost a year old had acquired white head, neck and underparts. The upper surface was blackish brown irregularly marked with new white feathers. This moult began in mid-July which is equivalent to the Atlantic gannet

Fig. 127

Tail feathers from a four-year-old (sub-adult) bird. (From Stein 1971.)

beginning to moult about March of its first year. Stein says that the black on body and wings is nearly gone by the end of the first year though a pattern of small black feathers remains on the crown. Two known two-year-olds (ringed March 1956, observed March 1958) had lost all dark body plumage but retained many dark feathers (these, however, are variable even in adults). Thus they must have closely resembled adults. On the other hand, Robertson states categorically that, from evidence supplied by ringed birds, adult plumage is generally not attained until the fifth year (birds first breed between four and seven years). I suspect that normally, adult plumage is attained sometime during the third or fourth year.

MEASUREMENTS AND WEIGHT

The relatively little data on the weights and measurements of the Australasian gannet is given in Table 34.

TABLE 34

MEASUREMENTS OF THE AUSTRALASIAN GANNET

Weight (g)	Culmen length (mm)	Wing (mm)	Tail (mm)	Tarsus (mm)	Middle toe (mm)
2350 (2000–2800) 44 cases	89 (85–93) 14 cases	463 (443–482) 14 cases	212 (206–218) 14 cases	54 (51–57) 14 cases	107 (105–110) 14 cases

Fig. 128(a). Australasian gannets (Cat Island 1957) showing juvenile plumage. Note that their underparts are much paler than those of Atlantic juveniles and that their pectoral bands are more marked. *Photo:* J. Warham.

(*b*)

(*c*)

(*d*)

(*e*)

(*f*)

Fig. 128(b) Juvenile male.

(c) Male eight months old.

(d) Male one year old.

(e) Female one year old. Note that, as in the Atlantic gannet, she is behind the male in developing adult plumage.

(f) Two years old.

[**Fig. 128(g)** on following page.]

Photos: (b–g) by C. J. Robertson.

Fig. 128(g)

Three years old.

VOICE

The main note is the generically distinctive 'urrah urrah', used in all the contexts described for the Atlantic gannet. A snoring 'yorr' accompanies Sky-pointing and flying birds are described as 'quacking' and 'snorting'. There are individual variations distinguishable even by the human ear and (interestingly) a distinct sex difference, the male's call being clearly higher pitched. This parallels the situation in the Cape gannet and forms yet another resemblance between these two (and between them and the boobies). In the Atlantic gannet there is no sex difference in the voice detectable by the human ear. The chick 'yips' when small and later supplicates using a repetitive 'ugh ugh' at about three calls per second. The intense alarm note of the chick is a loud quacking call.

2. BREEDING DISTRIBUTION, NUMBERS AND OTHER ASPECTS OF POPULATION

INTRODUCTION

With the exception of Abbott's booby, the Australasian gannet (some 25 colonies and perhaps 35 000–36 000 site occupying pairs) is the rarest sulid in the world. It is difficult to understand its low numbers and restricted distribution; almost 90 per cent of the world population breeds within a narrow band of 4° of latitude. Fairly recently its total population has been estimated and population changes carefully studied at the Hawke's Bay gannetry and at Horuhoru. This enables some interesting comparisons between the Australasian and the Atlantic gannets to be drawn. Most of the caveats concerning problems of counting, discussed on p. 24 apply here, too (though there are no huge colonies) and a particularly striking example of seasonal variation in numbers concerns Horuhoru which in early October was counted as 1228 breeding pairs but in December of the same year totalled 316! This was almost certainly due to disturbance.

DISTRIBUTION AND GENERAL TRENDS

The Australasian gannet breeds mainly on rocks and islands up to 60km off the east coast of the North Island of New Zealand (Table 35, Fig. 129) although it has one mainland colony, at Cape Kidnappers.

TABLE 35

POPULATION OF THE AUSTRALASIAN GANNET

	Area and island		Number of site-occupying pairs: 1946/47 census figure	1970/71 census figure	Latest figure
	NEW ZEALAND				
	Three Kings (total)		4134	5000	
1	South West Island	824			
2	Hinemoa Rock	1520			
3	Hole in the Wall	490			
4	Tutanekai Rock	300			
5	Arbutus Rock	1000			
	Poor Knights Islands		1650	c. 3150	
6	Gannet Stack	150			
7	Sugar Loaf	c. 1500			
	Great Barrier Island				
8	Mahuki		325	1900	
	Colville (Coromandel) area		1806	3500	4000+
9	Bush Island or Motukaramarama		1513		3000 (1974)
10	Double Island		5		
11	Motutakapu		288		1000 (1964)
12	Horuhoru		1228	1600	1800+(1974)
	Muriwai area				
13	Oaia Islet		338	350	
14	White Island		5227	5900	
15	Kawhia (Gannet Island or Karewa)		3715	5800	
16	Hawke's Bay complex		2760	4750	
17	Otago (The Nuggets)		40	20	
	Foveaux Straits				
18	Little Solander		20	20	
19	Marlborough Sounds		—	5	
20	Gisborne locality		—	500	
21	Mokohinau		—	30	
22	North Auckland locality		30	10	
	AUSTRALIA AND TASMANIA				
	Bass Straits				
1	Cat Island		c. 400	c. 12	
	South of Tasmania				
2	Pedra Branca		c. 1000	c. 1000	
3	Eddystone			c. 500	
	Portland, Victoria				
4	Lawrence Rocks				c. 640 (1961)
	Black Pyramid				c. 450 (1961)
5	Port Philip Bay				
6	Wedge Light				c. 6 (1972)
			2 2763		

Total 35 843 (taking the latest counts)

The breeding range of the Australasian gannet extends over more than 14° of latitude (between 32° 12′ and 46° 36′S.) but over 99 per cent breed between 34° and 40°S. and 86 per cent between even narrower limits, 34° and 38°S. The 7° of latitude, from 40°S. to almost 47°S. is occupied by less than 100 pairs. Almost the entire population breeds in the cold waters of the sub-tropical zone, which are nevertheless somewhat warmer than those around most Atlantic gannetries. Thus, since the Cape gannet's waters are cooled by the Benguela, all three species breed in cool waters.

Altogether, there are 28 gannetries, six (four small or very small) are in Tasmanian waters and the rest in New Zealand. This counts each gannet 'complex' as one gannetry. If one reckons each occupied island as a separate group, the exercise becomes more arbitrary but the general picture is similar. According to the census figures (1946–47) together with some later ones for a few minor gannetries, there were some 23 000–24 000 pairs of which some 21 000 or 88 per cent were in New Zealand. However, since then, visits to ten of the breeding colonies have revealed substantial increases and Stein (pers. comm.) puts the 1971 population at around 30 000 pairs.

It appears from the records that the Australasian gannet population has followed a similar pattern to that of the Atlantic, decreasing markedly due to human persecution and now increasing substantially (though probably not as rapidly as the Atlantic). The timing has been slightly different, for the Australasian decrease seems to have continued for a good part of the present century before being reversed, and the present population may still be smaller now than at the beginning of the century. Fleming & Wodzicki (1952) take a different view and summarise population trends as follows:

> 'Historical data on the past status of New Zealand gannetries are so scanty that it has seldom been possible to determine population changes during the past century. Of the 32 gannet stations[1] listed in Table 1, two (Bird Rock and Sugarloaf, Aldermen Islands) were formerly gannetries but are not now used for nesting. Possibly Matapia is also an abandoned gannetry. At at least nine stations there is evidence of increase, in some cases by colonisation. Cape Karikari Stacks and two of the Mokohinau Islands were colonised recently but their status is still uncertain. One of the Colville gannetries (Bush Island) has certainly increased during the past twenty years and

[1] All dealt with on pp. 274–81

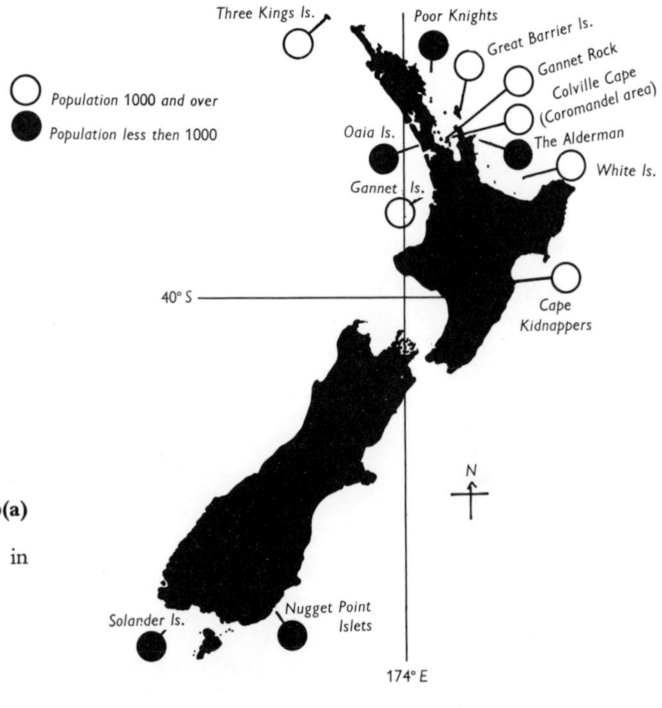

Fig. 129(a)

The distribution of gannet colonies in New Zealand.

another (Double Island) has been established recently. Finally, the oldest of the Hawke's Bay gannetries was evidently established about a century ago, and two subsidiary gannetries have since been colonised so that the Hawke's Bay complex now ranks as the fourth largest in New Zealand. Other gannetries may also have increased but we judge the early estimates of their strength too uncertain to be considered in this discussion. The gannetries that have decreased or that were abandoned were all small and were perhaps never firmly established; some of the newly established stations are also small and may only be temporary. However, the clear increase at the Colville and Hawke's Bay gannetries is far greater than the known decrease at other gannetries' (this statement seems unlikely to be accurate, see p. 277), 'we conclude, therefore, that the general trend of the New Zealand Gannet population has been one of increase during the past century.'

However, the relatively small-scale increases (Kidnappers excepted) seem unlikely to balance the loss of many thousands in the cases mentioned above. Cat Island alone has probably lost as many as the whole of the present-day Cape Kidnapper colony whilst South West Island, losing 'vast numbers' and Matapia 'countless numbers' of seabirds which were probably gannets, surely outweigh the increases reported in those gannetries which have recently grown. The apparent increase from a total New Zealand population of 11 000–12 000 pairs based on censuses up to 1946, to 21 033 pairs in 1947, is an artefact due to the improved accuracy of the 1946/47 census (Fleming & Wodzicki 1952). However, the increase since has been fairly considerable. Stein (pers. comm.) found that in the four Hauraki Gulf colonies and Sugar Loaf alone, the 1946/47 census figure of 4645 had jumped to 8421 by 1961. Between 1961 and 1971 Stein believes there has been a further increase of some 800 pairs in this group and reports indications of slight increases in some other areas. The latest counts indicate a total population of some 35 000–36 000 pairs (33 085 in New Zealand and 2608 pairs in Australia), which is an increase of 14 660 pairs or 2·8 per cent per annum between 1946 and 1974. Since most of the 'most recent' figures are 1971/72 rather than later, the true 1974 figure is probably slightly more than 36 000 and the per annum increase fractionally greater than 2·8 per cent. This is almost exactly the same as the figure for the Atlantic gannet's increase in recent decades (2·9 per cent per annum).

The decline earlier this century can be attributed to human slaughter, as in the case of Cat Island, and frequent and severe disturbances of breeding colonies causing wholesale loss of eggs and young. Time and again, observers record masses of empty nests, or a very low breeding success, or successive visits to the same colony show heavy loss of eggs and chicks.

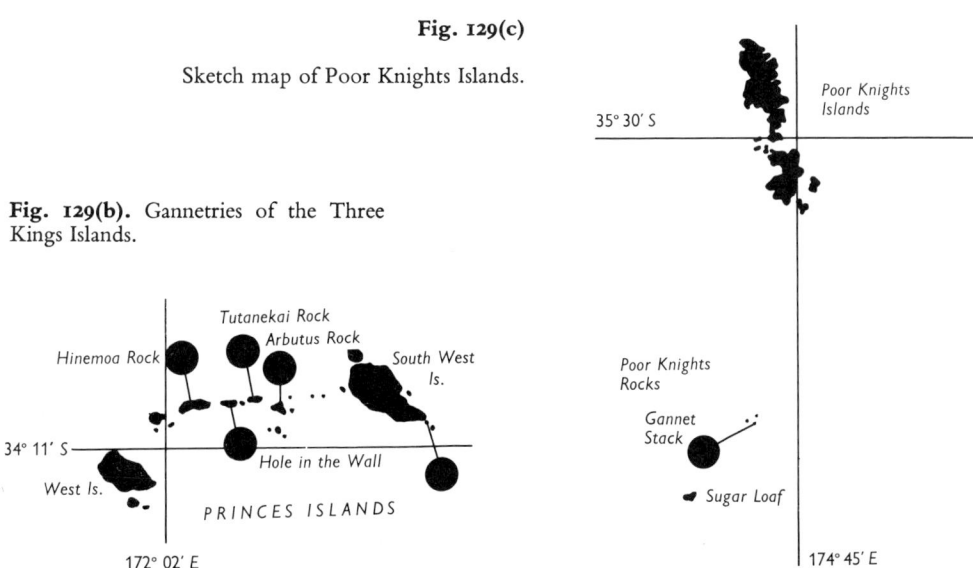

Fig. 129(c)

Sketch map of Poor Knights Islands.

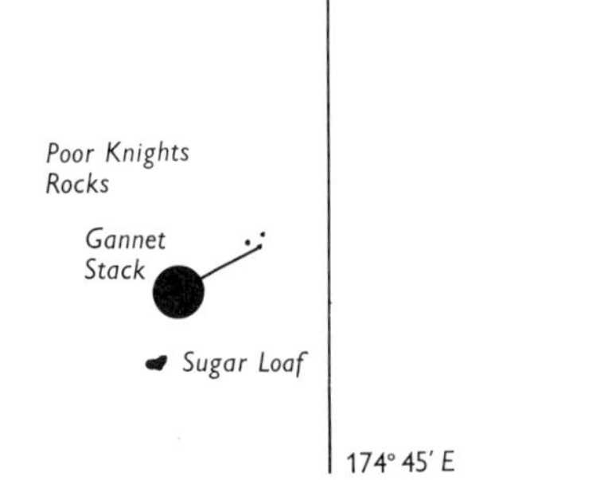

Fig. 129(b). Gannetries of the Three Kings Islands.

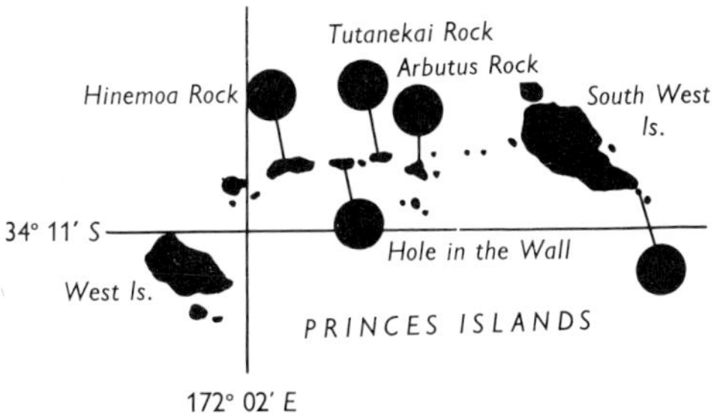

The early estimates, from which any subsequent decline or increase must be judged are almost always vague, and the details of persecution or careless visitation are rarely recorded or distinguished from natural disasters. A densely colonial species like the gannet can be catastrophically affected by vandals, visitors or exploiters and it seems far more likely that these factors have severely depressed recruitment for the first half of this century than that climate, food or any other physical change in the environment has done so. The killing of adults together with a low recruitment rate could thus have resulted in a decline.

Now the Australasian gannet is increasing. This, too, is explicable in terms of recently improved conservation and recruitment, whereas the thesis of a *general* upward trend for the *whole* of this century would pose considerable problems in view of the known deprèdations by man.

1. *New Zealand gannetries*

Most of the information in this section comes from Fleming & Wodzicki's (1952) account of the 1946/47 census, supplemented by C. J. R. Robertson (pers. comm.), Stein (pers. comm.), and miscellaneous observations from a few recent papers.

Three Kings Islands (c. 5000 pairs in 1970/71). The ancient gannetries which spread over five of the Prince's Islands (part of the Three Kings group, Fig. 129b) about 53km west-north-west of Cape Maria van Diemen, have been depleted, probably by Maoris and subsequently by Europeans. The Princes are spread over roughly 3km from east to west and, almost certainly, there will be interchange between them.

1. SOUTH WEST ISLAND (824 pairs in 1947). In 1889 there were 'vast numbers' (Cheeseman 1888); in 1934 Falla estimated 2000 pairs as the total population. Aerial photographs in mid-January 1947 gave 1030 birds which Fleming & Wodzicki transmute to 824 pairs. They were on the cliff edge, on a bare strip of sloping rock, 5–20m wide and split into 12 sections by the intrusion of scrub. Ten days earlier, a count on the ground yielded only 220 nests, but many may have been hidden behind scrub.

2. HINEMOA ROCK (1520 pairs in 1947). This island falls steeply on all sides from a broken summit ridge around 50m high. Gannets nest on the eastern and western crests and extensively on the central saddle and the south slope, which is least steep. Disturbance by man is apparently a feature of this colony and destroys large numbers of eggs and chicks. Buddle in 1947 estimated around 1000 birds (probably equal to the same number of pairs) and in 1948 revised this to around 1500. A count from an aerial photograph in January 1947 gave 1520 pairs.

3. HOLE-IN-THE-WALL (490 nests in 1947). Gannets occupy the bulk of the narrow summit plateau. Two large ledges on the north-east held birds (probably Clubs) in 1947. A count from aerial photographs yielded 490 nests in January 1947.

4. TUTANEKAI ROCK (300 nests in 1947). A small, steep-sided pyramid on which gannets are confined to the narrow, sloping summit ridge. Two separate estimates in January 1947 gave 300 nests and 500 birds.

5. ARBUTUS ROCK (1000 pairs in 1947). This rock slopes steeply to the north and gently to the south, the upper two-thirds of which are occupied by gannets, nesting on bare ground among irregular clumps of *Coprosma*. A photographic count in January 1947 indicated about 1000 birds but a 1948 estimate suggested around 1500. Fleming & Wodzicki estimate that these figures are equivalent to 1000 pairs.

Poor Knights Islands (c. 3000 1970/71). A few kilometres south of the Poor Knights (Fig. 129c), lie three rocks (Poor Knights Rocks).

6. GANNET STACK (150 pairs in 1948). One of the Poor Knights Rocks, Gannet Stack is a pinnacle of columnar rock 25m high with vertical walls and a fairly flat summit, a mere 25m in diameter, upon which about 100–150 pairs of gannets have long nested, secure from interference. In 1934 there were considerably fewer than 200 birds; in 1948 there were around 150 nesting birds, closely packed.

7. SUGAR LOAF (1327–1629 pairs in 1948). About 1km south of Poor Knights Rocks lies Sugar Loaf, an irregular, conical mass around 100m in diameter and 50m high, almost vertical. Gannets nest on the tops of the broken columns. It is a long established group which probably has changed little. The only reasonably accurate figure is from photographs in 1947 on which

1237–1629 birds were counted; even this, however, could be considerably wrong. The western ridge held 44–62 birds; the south face 430–480; the east face 432–572 and the north face 329–515. Presumably a percentage of these birds represented the second bird of a pair. An old inhabitant of the mainland opposite considered that in 1892 there were as many gannets as in 1948. However, Stein visited the colony in December 1955 and counted 2400 pairs or virtually twice the lowest 1947 estimate, whilst the 1970/71 estimate was 3000, with a number on gannet stack (presumably c. 150).

Great Barrier Island (c. 1900 1970/71). There are five gannetries which Stein groups as the Hauraki Gulf gannetries (Fig. 130) (Mahuki, Motukaramarama or Bush Island, Motuwi Stack or Double Island, Motutakapu and Horuhoru), the middle three of which Fleming & Wodzicki refer to as the Motukawao group, off Coromandel.

8. MAHUKI (Gannet Island) (300–350 pairs in 1947). This is the most south-westerly of the Pig Islands off the west coast of Great Barrier Island. Although quite large (about 73 hectares) and around 50m high, gannets nest only on the narrow north-west promontory. It is probably a very old gannetry which may well have decreased between 1920 and 1947 due to visitors and persecution. Also, a low wall built about 1934 around the south-east margins, might have interfered with the gannets' take-off. In 1928 there were about 600 pairs; in 1934 and 1935–36 probably around 400 and in 19464–7 a very rough estimate gave 300–350 pairs. Only one chick and 50 eggs were seen, and the colony was thought to have been raided the week before. Stein visited Mahuki ten times between 1954 and 1964, six of them in the height of the season. Only once was the count less than 900 pairs and twice it was over 1000.

Colville (Coromandel Peninsula) (3500 pairs in 1970/71). There are gannetries on three of the islands called the Motukawao group, 3–5km off the west side of Coromandel Peninsula, south-west of Colville, in the Hauraki Gulf.

9. BUSH ISLAND (c. 3000 pairs 1974). Of the three Motukawao islands, Bush or Motukaramarama, relatively large and flat, with scrub on top, holds the most gannets. It is apparently ancient, though the first record (roughly 800 pairs) is 1928. It seemed to increase between 1938 and 1948. The south promontory was first used about 1938–39 and the central group expanded down towards the sea, onto ledges. Estimates in 1940, 1942 and 1946 gave about 1000, 1100 and 1513 pairs respectively. A low figure of 360 young in February 1948 was probably caused by heavy rain earlier in the season, but it was suggested that the breeding population in 1947–48 was at least as high as that of 1946–47. Stein's subsequent figures are: 1954, 2543 pairs; 1974, 3000 or more. The recent increase has involved colonising a completely new area and also adding some 200 pairs to the lower ledges of the central group (Stein, pers. comm.). As on Sugar Loaf, the 1946/47 population has now about doubled.

10. DOUBLE ISLAND (20 pairs in 1948). This island, one of the largest of the Motukawao group, has a small colony on a semi-detached stack off the north west point. It was probably

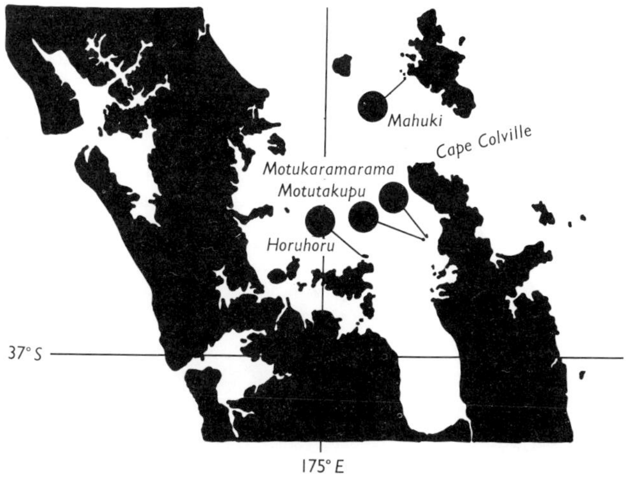

Fig. 130

Gannetries in the Hauraki Gulf.

established around 1942–43. In 1946 there were 6–10 birds, some of which appeared to have nests and in 1948 roughly 20 young were seen.

11. MOTUTAKAPU (c. 1000 pairs in 1964). This is the westernmost of the Kawao group and probably an ancient (pre-European) colony, though now not a large one; Stein (1971) considers it the oldest of the Hauraki Gulf gannetries. In 1928 there were around 200 pairs; in 1942 400–500; in 1946 288 nest in September and in 1948 around 100 young estimated to have come from 400 pairs. In 1954 Stein (pers. comm.) estimated 650 pairs; in 1956, 960 pairs and thereafter about the same. Room for further expansion is limited.

Waihake Island. 12. HORUHORU (1800 pairs in 1974). About a mile north of Waihake, Horuhoru is a small, irregular and steep-sided islet about 25m high and cliff bound except in the centre of the west side. There are five groups of gannets, four on top of the island separated by belts of scrub and a fifth on the semi-detached North Stack, where they nest within reach of sea-spray in north-east gales. Stein (1971) gives details of the topography of Horuhoru. It is probably an ancient gannetry (but early records are lacking) and its name has perhaps been derived phonetically from the gannet's cry, 'urrah urrah'. In 1928 it was guessed at 1000 pairs, at which it apparently remained between 1930 and 1946. In October 1946 there were an estimated 1228 occupied nests. Since then, Stein has made several counts: November 5th 1949, 1503 pairs; November 22nd 1958, 1575 pairs; December 2nd 1974, over 1800 pairs.

Muriwai. 13. OAIA ISLET (338 pairs in 1947). This small, dome-shaped and extremely inaccessible islet lies 1½km off Muriwai Beach, Aukland. The gannetry was established some time before 1914 and around 100–200 pairs were estimated on several occasions up to 1946 (minimum of 160 pairs in 1940; 150–225 nests in September 1942). Photographs taken in January 1947 show the main (perhaps the only) strip of nests, along the summit ridge. North and south of this are patches of what may have been Club birds. The number of site holding pairs was assessed at 338 and the total population of individuals at least 800.

14. WHITE ISLAND (5900 in 1970/71).[1] This spectacular volcanic island is the site of a large and ancient colony; 'thousands of young' before 1882 and 'vast colony, thousands upon thousands'. The groups (sub-colonies) occur on:

WEST POINT (1254 pairs in 1947 and 1367 in 1949). This is a promontory at the end of the narrow western ridge of White Island and its alternative name is Te Matawiwi.

ROCKY POINT (1408 pairs in 1947 and 1359 in 1949). This point lies on the south coast of the island and is called Ohauora.

GANNET POINT (2565 pairs in 1947 and 2650 in 1949). Gannet Point is the first headland west of Crater Bay and has the largest group of gannets on White Island (alternative name Otaketake).

The first estimate of the population of the whole of White Island was 1200 pairs in 1926 and the first detailed one in January 1947 (actual counts supplemented by aerial photographs) produced the following results (though it should be noted that, before this visit, the gannetry had been heavily disturbed):

On West Point seven areas held 1254 nest sites in addition to which 400 'idle' (Club?) birds were counted.

On Rocky Point three areas held 607 pairs but a further 801 empty mounds presumably belonged to birds which, it was known, had been disturbed before the photograph was taken.

Gannet Point is a headland divided by a ravine into two unequal areas (eastern A and western B) both of which have held gannets for a long time. The group on A held between 1500–1800 nests in February 1935. In 1947 the ground count gave 1280 pairs in A and 465 in B but there were, in addition, some unoccupied mounds. Counts from aerial photographs gave the following mean figures for A: occupied nest sites 1660 (10 per cent of which held pairs) and 790 'idle' birds outside the nesting area. Allowing for empty nests the total population was assessed at 2100 pairs. For B the aerial count was, at 446, very near to the ground count. The total population of Gannet Point in 1947 was thus about 2600 pairs and of White Island as a whole, 5227 pairs. In 1949 it was 5376 (estimated) and in 1970/71 5900.

The Club Rocks off the south coast is said to have been a breeding site in 1912 but is now only a roost and may possibly always have been so.

[1] 1970/71 population figures for some gannetries are from C. J. R. Robertson (pers. comm.).

It seems clear that White Island is periodically subject to catastrophic disturbance by man. In January 1947 Wodzicki found that 64 per cent of nests were empty and only 3 per cent held chicks. It is clear from his comments on the regurgitated fish lying about and their panicky readiness to vomit, that they had been grossly disturbed. Any interpretation of the timing of egg laying here, or apparent breeding success, should bear this in mind.

Kawhia 15. GANNET ISLAND OR KAREWA (5800 pairs in 1970/71). Fleming & Wodzicki (1952) suggest that the common name 'Gannet Island' be reserved for this, New Zealand's largest gannetry and the first to be seen by Europeans, though the name has been applied, also, to Horuhoru and Motutakapu. This ancient colony dates back at least to 1500. The island lies in a rich fishing area and has thus been visited both by Maoris, who took young gannets for food and by European fishermen, who have probably been responsible for a substantial if not massive reduction in numbers this century. The gannets nest on a rough tableland of about 1·6 hectares, only 10–25m above sea level. Severe storms have reputedly 'driven huge rollers completely over the island and swept thousands of the fledgling gannets into the surging sea'. Last century their numbers were obviously very great ('incredible numbers' and 'tens of thousands') but there are no actual estimates. The mean of three counts from photographs taken on January 14th 1947 showed 3715 birds in the nesting area and 360 which appeared to be outside it.

Hawke's Bay (4750 pairs in 1970/71). The famous Cape Kidnappers gannetry (Fig. 131 a–d) is situated on a peninsula, at Hawke's Bay on North Island, and is one of the most visited in the world. Its mainland position opens it to occasional intrusion by cattle and goats but these do no damage. Nor are the rats (probably *norvegicus*), established on the beach at the bottom of the Cape, harmful.

The Cape Kidnappers complex now contains three groups—Cape Kidnappers, Kidnappers Plateau and Black Reef, but since the two first named are only about 500m apart they are hardly to be designated as separate gannetries though I have followed Wodzicki in treating all three separately. They have been well studied in recent years, providing most of the available information on the Australasian gannet.

16. CAPE KIDNAPPERS (2060 pairs in 1965). This, the largest and oldest of the Hawke's Bay group, probably was established in the mid-nineteenth century (Fleming & Wodzicki 1952). It consists of a central saddle and an eastern and western slope. In 1878 it held only about 50 gannets (pairs?) but this rests on recollection long after the event. In 1888 there were perhaps 500 nests; in 1896 probably over 600 nests; in 1900–3 about 1211 nests; in 1913–14 roughly 1300 and in 1920 perhaps 1800. By then, the area covered by gannets, as shown from photographs, had increased to almost twice that of 1903 and extended almost to the southern edge of the saddle and up the west slope to the crest (Fig. 132). On the eastern slope the level of occupation was the same as in 1903. By 1923 the outermost stack had been reduced to a reef (Kidnappers consists of a soft sandstone) and since then the general appearance of the Cape has remained substantially unaltered. Subsequent counts were around 2000 nests in 1923 and 1930; less than 2000 in 1931; 2265 nests in December 1945 distributed as follows: 1590 pairs on the central saddle; 200 on the eastern slope and 475 on the western slope. Counts from aerial photographs taken in November 1946 show nearly 3000 nests of which 2337 were occupied and this figure was taken as the strength of the colony. In 1957/58 it was 2425 pairs and in 1964/65 2060 pairs. Thus in half a century no significant increase in this group had occurred, though its spatial distribution (and possibly its numbers) had changed within this period. This is not to say that the Hawke's Bay population had not increased (see below).

KIDNAPPERS PLATEAU (487 pairs in 1965). This new group, named by Wodzicki, was established in 1945[1] in an old Club area (initially it consisted of one cluster of nests but has since become two). As a whole, it grew from 196 pairs in 1945 to 487 in 1964/65 an average annual increase of 5·3 per cent. The growth of this group is discussed further on p. 298.

BLACK REEF (1038 pairs in 1965). These offshore stacks lie about one km west of Kidnappers. The colony was first known in 1938/39 but was probably established slightly before this. In 1945/46 there were 376 pairs on five of the higher stacks and on ledges of the mainland cliffs, an additional rock being used as a roost (the mainland ledges were unoccupied in 1946/47). Clearly there had been great immigration in this period. In 1957/58 the population was 883

[1] The summary in Wodzicki 1967 is presumably mistaken in giving 1938.

pairs and in 1964/65 1038 on eight rocks, one of which, however, held only one pair. This increase clearly shows that Black Reef continued to receive immigrants from the main Kidnapper group.

The total population of the three Hawke's Bay gannetries is shown in Table 36.

The rate of increase (less than 2 per cent per annum) is theoretically well within the intrinsic production capacity of the colony and whilst, as mentioned, there is obvious interchange between the three Hawke's Bay groups, there seems nothing to suggest immigration from other gannetries during this period. Earlier, however, it must certainly have received many immigrants. Thus, between 1879 and 1888, it increased from 50 to 500 pairs or about 30 per cent per annum, and between 1878 and 1903 it increased at over 20 per cent per annum. The rate of increase then slowed down between 1903 and 1945 to a rate well within the colony's productive capacity and has remained so since. Thus, after reaching some particular size (which is probably not critical and is anyway unknown) it seems that the flow of immigrants ceased and the gannetry subsequently grew by means of its own production. Why immigration

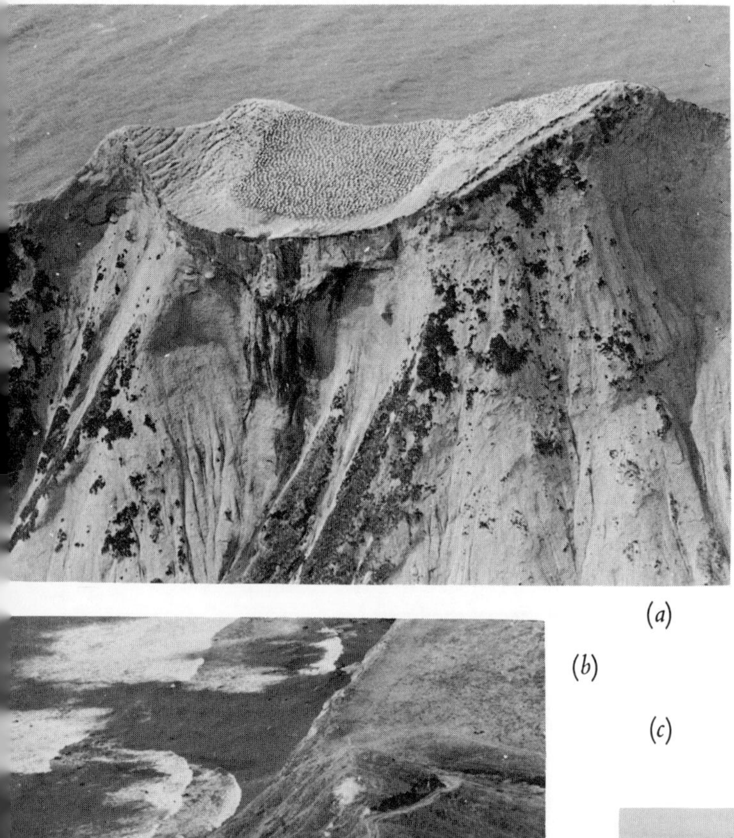

Fig. 131. Cape Kidnappers gannet colony.

(a) Looking south; western slope to the right and eastern to the left, of the central saddle (December 1964).

(b) Plateau gannetry (groups A and B), looking south, showing the groups discussed on p. 298.

(c) Black Reef group, looking north-west from the sea, showing stacks 1–6 (centre), 7–8 (right) and roosting areas on the mainland (9).

(a)

(b)

Photos: S. N. Beatus.

(c)

ceased (if it did) and whether Hawke's Bay now contributes to other gannetries is unknown, though on the evidence of its low productivity the latter may seem unlikely.

The failure to increase at all between 1958/65 is itself puzzling in view of the availability of nesting areas and the conservation efforts, which largely offset the erstwhile disastrous effects of visitors. Prior to that, between 1945/57 there had been an overall increase of some 27 per cent. The fact that the two new groups flourished between 1955/65 does not alter the failure of the gannetry as a whole to do so. I would myself ascribe this failure to a diluted version of the same general phenomenon which has prevented the Australasian gannet from even maintaining its numbers[1] for most of this century—artificially depressed breeding success due to human interference. Wodzicki, on the other hand, ascribes this relative failure of the Hawke's Bay complex to adverse environmental change in the main breeding area (the Saddle group). He suggests erosion, but does not hint at the effects of this. Destruction of vegetation

[1] This is merely my own view; better qualified local observers suggest that the trend this century has been upwards.

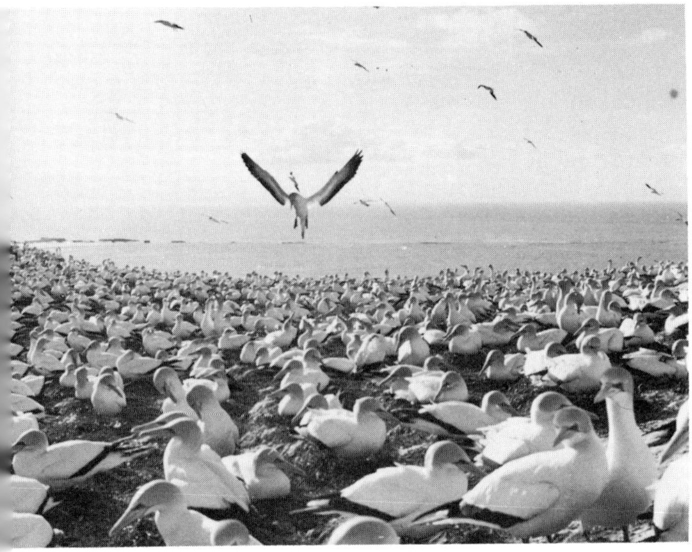

Fig. 131(d)

A dense nesting mass early in the season at Cape Kidnappers (September 1950), looking towards Black Rock, from the southern cliff. *Photo:* Ecology Division, D.S.I.R., New Zealand.

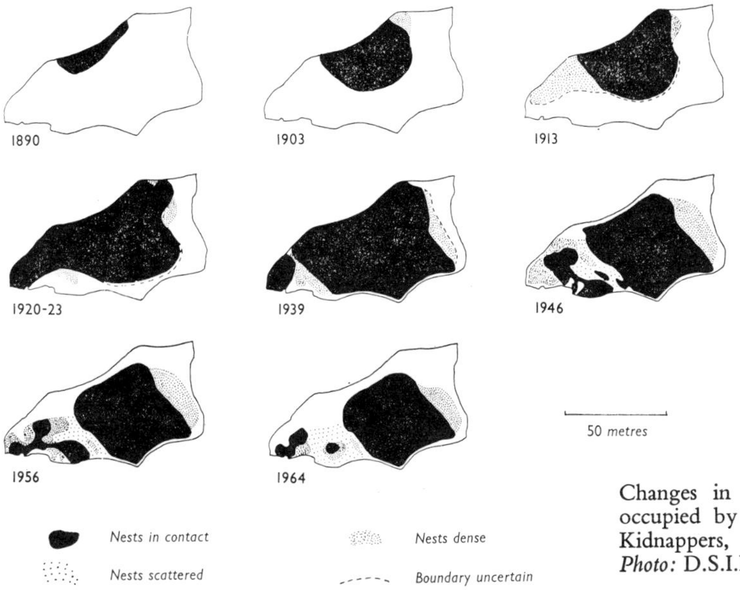

Fig. 132

Changes in the distribution of areas occupied by nesting gannets on Cape Kidnappers, between 1890 and 1964. *Photo:* D.S.I.R., New Zealand.

and subsoil certainly occurs in Atlantic gannet colonies too, but such areas are then, if anything, more suitable because drainage channels have been created and the drums raised further above the general morass. Take-off may also be assisted.

Otago. 17. The Nuggets (40 pairs in 1948). This colony was occupied before 1923 but first recorded in 1936, when about 30 pairs were building on the far islet and three on the flat island nearby. In January 1940 there were about 12. In 1946–47 and 1947–48 40 nesting pairs were estimated. The 1970/71 figure was 20 pairs.

Foveaux Straits. 18. Little Solander Island (20 nests in 1947). Although long reported by fishermen to be a gannetry, it was confirmed only in December 1947 (probably fewer than 20 nests) and again in July 1948 at which early date Falla found 14 birds occupying sites.

Summary of defunct New Zealand gannetries

In addition to the gannetries listed in Table 35 there are nine sites which used to support nesting gannets or might have done so:

1. Matapia Islet. This used to be the main gannetry in the North Aukland region. It holds no gannets at present, but an old (1843) record of 'countless numbers of seabirds' nesting on this small rock, 17km from Cape Maria van Diemen, probably referred to gannets.

2. Cape Karikari Stacks. Two small rocks about one km off Karakora Point in North Aukland, this is very dubiously a nesting place. Suspected nesting occurred in January 1947 but in December 1947 there were no birds and in February 1948 only one.

3. Bird Rock. This rock in the Bay of Islands has held only roosting birds since at least 1933, though gannets may have nested there earlier this century.

4. Groper Rock. Gannets first bred on this rock, in the Mokohinhau Islands, in 1945–46, but have not been known to do so since.

5. Cathedral Rocks. These rocks, which are also in the Mokohinhau Islands, may have been a breeding place in 1948, when 16 adults but no eggs or young were seen.

6. Arid Island Stack. This is a roost of doubtful status off Great Barrier Island.

7. The Sisters. Two small stacks on the south-west coast of Great Mercury Island, these were a roost of doubtful status in 1946–47, but definite verbal accounts of nesting on them have been given.

8. Sugarloaf. On the taller of the two Sugarloaf Rocks, in the Alderman Islands, five or six gannet nests occupied a small plateau for some years prior to 1921 and up to 1927. In December 1947 and February 1948 there were no gannets on the rock.

Two sections of White Island (Dam Site and Club Rocks) used to be breeding places but have not been so since at least 1946–47.

2. *Tasmanian and Australian gannetries*

Although the New Zealand gannetries contain some 92 per cent of the population of the Australasian gannet, there are six colonies in Tasmania and Australia.

Bass Straits, Tasmania. 1. Cat Island (around 12 nest mounds in 1971). The granite Cat Island, about 40 hectares and 35m high, lies a few km off the eastern coast of Flinders. Much of

Table 36

HAWKE'S BAY GANNET POPULATION 1945–65
(after Wodzicki 1967)

Group	1945–46	1957–58	1964–65
Cape Kidnappers	2307	2425	2060
Kidnappers Plateau	196	278	487
Black Reef	376	883	1038
Totals	2879	3586	3585

its surface is covered in sand and it is a great haunt of short-tailed shearwaters. The gannets nested mainly on flat ground about 25m above sea level and (in 1957) 150m from the sea. This old and once thriving gannetry, the most famous in Australia, is now virtually extinct, its demise another telling commentary on man's impressive capacity for stupid destruction. It was first recorded in 1799 but no doubt existed long before that.

When John Warham made the first study of the behaviour of the Australasian gannet in 1957–58 there were only 20 pairs on Cat Island (about 50 years previously there had been some 2500) and he made a strong plea for simple conservation which has apparently been largely ignored. The estimates available show that a massive decline occurred in the first 50 years of this century (1938 around 2500 pairs; 1939 around 1000 pairs; 1945 600–900 birds; 1948 around 400 pairs; 1951 around 140 pairs). This was due principally to the activities of fishermen who, the world over, have wreaked havoc on sulids, whether on ground nesting white boobies on tropical Pacific islands; piqueros in Peru; Atlantic gannets on the Canadian Bird Island; brown boobies on the Malasian Pulau Perak or, by attempted legislation, intended on the Cape gannet. During the war years (1939–45) the gannetry suffered heavily but well after this in 1953 when there were only about 50 pairs, every chick was slaughtered. The decline continued (1953 around 50 pairs; 1957 around 20 pairs) and seems now (1971 around 12 nest mounds) to have approached near to extinction. Nothing but consistent wardening could safeguard such a remnant. It is shameful that Australian crayfishers continue such destruction and that the Tasmanian government allows them to do so.

South of Tasmania. 2. PEDRA BRANCA (around 1000 pairs in 1971). Now the largest Australian gannetry, this island is so inaccessible that, at least until 1972, no ornithologist had recorded landing on it and an estimate of around 1000 in 1939 was from an aerial photograph.

3. EDDYSTONE (around 500 pairs in 1972). This island lies two or three km to the east of Pedra Branca and is likely to interchange recruits with it. It holds perhaps 500 pairs, though this is a guess rather than an estimate, nesting on ledges. In April 1947 there were only about 20 adults present.

Portland, Victoria. 4. LAWRENCE ROCKS (around 640 pairs in 1961). These are two small basalt islands off Cape Danger and the gannets, nesting only on the larger of the two (McKean 1966), have increased from an estimated 200 nests in 1900, 1907 and 1943 to around 406 in 1952; 605 in 1960 and 639 in 1961. Between 1943 and 1961 the growth (just over 5 per cent per annum) is slightly unlikely to have occurred as a result of the colony's own output. In December 1962 and 1963 observation from the mainland indicated that the colony had continued to grow. Breeding success seems high (332 chicks ringed in December 1961). It may be another case of a fairly small but vigorous colony attracting recruits.

5. BLACK PYRAMID (about 450 nests in 1961). This highly inaccessible island, probably a long established gannetry, was landed on in November 1961 (Green & MacDonald 1963). It is dome-shaped, largely cliff girt, with a steep north face above the 15m cliffs and a precipitous wall on the south-west side. Gannets nest on the north side, beginning about 50m above sea level; about 200 nested on a sloping ledge here and another 200 scattered on the north-east face in fairly well separated groups. A tight group of 50 nests were found on the south summit but the three other summit groups shown on photographs in 1939 and 1943 were empty. No immature birds were seen.

Port Philip Bay. 6. WEDGE LIGHT (about 6 pairs in 1972). This is the newest Australian gannetry, started in 1966 on the man-made light and about six pairs strong in 1972. About 200 birds have been seen in the vicinity (Serventy pers. comm.).

Due to the nature of the migration of the Australasian gannet (p. 293) Australian gannetries are in a position to receive recruits from New Zealand and are unlikely to be as autonomous as, by contrast, are the Canadian gannetries and those on the eastern side of the Atlantic.

SUMMARY

1. The Australasian gannet is, in world numbers, the second rarest sulid and has a very restricted breeding distribution.

2. In 1974 it occupied some 28 stations (22 in New Zealand and 6 in Tasmania and Australia) and numbered very approximately 35 000–36 000 pairs (probably slightly more).

3. It is currently increasing after a decline in numbers between (about) 1880 and 1950, due to human persecution (certain colonies are still heavily disturbed and/or persecuted) and the per annum increase between 1946/47 and 1974 has been about 2·8 per cent compared with about 3 per cent for the Atlantic gannet.

3. BREEDING ECOLOGY

INTRODUCTION

I would like to show how the Australasian and Atlantic gannets differ in ecology. As in behaviour, these two species and the Cape gannet have much in common and the fuller accounts given under the Atlantic gannet should be used to supplement the other two. Perhaps the most fruitful areas of comparison concern habitat, the timing and general strategy of breeding and breeding success. The Australasian gannet (like the Cape, to which it is most closely related) is not simply a North Atlantic gannet that happens to breed in the other hemisphere and therefore at opposite times of year. It is a 'species' which has been isolated from the ancestral gannet stock long enough to evolve significantly different size and breeding habits. Fortunately the Kidnappers colony and Horuhoru have been extensively studied, and for the first time it is now possible to compare it with the other two gannets in considerable detail. Details attributed to C. J. R. Robertson are mainly from personal communications or from cyclostyled reports.

BREEDING HABITAT

Australasian gannets, like Atlantic, prefer sea-girt rocks. They appear to choose mainly small ones but this may be a false impression caused by the abandonment or destruction of colonies on larger and probably more accessible islands.

They nest mainly on flat or flattish ground rather than ledges. In this respect they resemble the Cape gannet and differ from the Atlantic. They will use ledges, as on Poor Knights, but this is rare and even then they are usually broad and flat rather than the narrow, sloping and precipitous sites so frequently used by Atlantic gannets. Even slopes seem less favoured than flatter ground. One may ask why the Atlantic gannet chooses cliffs, rather than why the Australasian and Cape gannets prefer flatter ground. The answer is almost certainly safety, easier take-off for a heavier bird with hostile and close packed neighbours and greatly facilitated fledging for the exceptionally heavy young, which would have an often impossible task to get through dense and aggressive adults on flat ground. The lighter Australasian gannet can get away with flat ground nesting more easily and since such sites are probably most numerous and are safer (except from man) they are preferred.

COLONY DENSITY

The inter-nest distance (Fig. 133) presumably centre to centre, is given by Wodzicki & McMeekan (1947) as 79cm (max. 87cm; min. 70cm). This compares with a mean value of 80cm for the Atlantic gannet on Bonaventure, 76cm on the Bass and 48cm for the Cape gannet. Thus the Australasian and Atlantic gannets nest at the same density and considerably less than the Cape. Robertson gives a maximum density for the Australasian of 2·59 nest/sq.m (minimum 1·68/sq.m) although, he says, newly established groups are rarely denser than about 1 pair/sq.m.

Robertson distinguishes four stages by which a new group attains its density: a group may form, first, as a loose aggregation (perhaps in a roosting area) taking several years to cohere into a breeding group at a density rarely higher than one site per sq.m. Compaction then occurs with the centre of the group reaching a maximum density of 2·5 nests per sq.m. Mortality in the centre of the group means that some nests are deserted (if the female dies the male remains and re-mates but if the male dies the female usually goes to a male on another site) which allows neighbours to enlarge their sites by 'gardening' away the sides of adjacent nests, sometimes transforming them into concave-sided pedestals. Eventually when the age-structure is about the same throughout, relatively even density is reached. This did not happen on the Bass, probably because vacated sites were taken over by new males before they had been reduced in size.

All three gannets show the same tendency to form nesting groups with clean edges rather than to thin out gradually into widely dispersed clusters or pairs; as a result of this and of the regular spacing within them gannetries have a distinctive appearance quite different from a group of any of the ground nesting boobies, the Peruvian excepted. I cannot believe that physical shortage of sites is the sole arbiter of this tendency, although the explanation suggested for the Atlantic gannet (p. 82) may not apply in full force to the Australasian (see p. 290). Nests may move position by about ½m from year to year (details in Stein 1971).

Fig. 133. Flat ground nesting in the Australasian gannet (Cat Island). Although so few, the pairs nevertheless nest at the standard density. *Photo:* J. Warham.

NEST SITES AND NESTS

The nest is substantial, containing several hundred items in some cases, but although various plants form an important part, the bulk of the nest is built up from guano (Moore & Wodzicki 1950). Thus the Australasian gannet is midway between the Atlantic (almost all plant material) and the Cape (almost all guano). The materials used are seaweeds and flowering plants gathered in the vicinity of the colony. The most favoured seaweeds are *Carpophyllum plumosum* and *C. maschalocarpum*, which are the most abundant seaweeds about low tide level and in drift. Other seaweeds recorded are *C. flexuosum*, *Cystophora retroflexa*, *Sargassum sinclairii*, *Glossophora kunthii* and *Plocarmium* sp. and *Pterodadia lucida*. Flotsam is used (for example the skin and plumage of a cock pheasant). During the winter, gannetries become green due to the growth of lichens and algae and many nesting mounds are reduced or destroyed. There are no records of nests approaching the size of the largest Atlantic gannet's and possibly the average size of the latter is also slightly greater, but in both cases an important function is to protect the egg and chick from the effects of heavy rain, which can cause significant losses. The Cape gannet, the only one of the three which does not use nest material other than guano, and consequently builds a relatively slight structure, is not subject to this danger.

THE EGG AND CLUTCH

1. *Characteristics of the egg*

Two hundred eggs measured (average) 77·57 × 46·97mm; max. and min. length 88mm and 67mm; max. and min. breadth 50mm and 43mm (Wodzicki & McMeekan 1947). Robertson gives the weight as 80–90g which, considering that the dimensions of the egg are almost the same as those of the Atlantic gannet (which weighs 104g), is rather little. Newly hatched chicks weigh about the same as those of Atlantic gannets, and Robertson's weights were probably of part-incubated eggs. Assuming for these reasons, an average weight of at least 90g and given an adult female weight of about 2300g, the egg is 3·9 per cent of the female's weight, compared with 3·9 per cent for the Cape gannet and 3·4 per cent for the Atlantic gannet. The Cape and Australasian birds are thus alike in this, as in many other aspects of their breeding biology and differ significantly from the Atlantic. The larger egg accords with the slower growth of the two first-named.

2. *Clutch size*

There are no unequivocal records of females laying clutches of two, although two eggs are very occasionally found in the same nest (about one per 1000 nests according to Robertson, pers. comm. and 7·5 per 1000 according to Wodzicki & McMeekan 1947). As also in the Atlantic gannet, nests with two eggs thus occur much less frequently than in the Cape gannet, doubtless due to the latter's habit of nesting closer together than the other two and having a lower nest or none at all and so increasing the chances of rolling in a neighbour's egg (see p. 239). Even in this species authentic two-egg clutches remain to be proved.

3. *Replacement laying*

Details are lacking, but general statements and Robertson (pers. comm.) show that some, or perhaps most, birds replace eggs which are lost before late December. On Horuhoru lost eggs are replaced in about four weeks (Stein), though I suspect usually less, and a third egg is sometimes laid if the replacement is lost.

4. *Incubation period*

The incubation period of 43–44 days, is probably identical with that of the Atlantic gannet (43·6), which means the egg is likely to be about the same size.

5. *Incubation regime*

Warham gives the incubation stints of Cat Island birds as 27 hours 17 minutes; three accurate determinations were 24h 57m; 26h 32m and 30h 40m. This is slightly less than the Atlantic gannet (32·9 hours) and the Cape (38·75 hours) but still implies a considerable foraging range and the sample is too small for the difference to be significant.

THE CHICK

1. *Morphology and plumage development*

The general appearance of the chick (Fig. 134a–c) is closely similar, if not identical, to that of the Atlantic gannet. It weighs 60–70g on hatching and is black and naked. It becomes covered by down just over 1cm long by the age of about two weeks, at which stage it can still be completely brooded by the parent. A week later it has become obvious beneath the adult, the down is much longer and the chick spends considerable periods fully exposed (this is about the age at which young sulids become able to regulate their body temperature). At a month old the chick is large, white and fluffy and too big to be covered by the parent; it becomes matted and soiled during heavy rain. At six weeks the chick looks bigger than its parent, has reached adult weight and has become venturesome, often moving from its nest. Primaries and rectrices first appear shortly afterwards (43–47 days) and grow rapidly until, at nine weeks, the chick is half covered with feathers. Chicks are by then increasingly prone to leave the nest for periods. Down persists most on flanks, belly and particularly head and nape, and is not completely cleared until about 13 weeks (80–90 days) after which the fully feathered young may remain at the colony a further 18 days. This schedule of development is slower than that of the Atlantic gannet, despite the latter's greater size and the final stages of growth increase the difference, for the Australasian gannet's wing feathers are not fully grown until it is about 15½ weeks. At 14 weeks Stein's chicks on Horuhoru had wings about 10cm shorter than those of the adult. Warham's birds fledged at 102 days (93–109) but Robertson gives 105–111 days.

2. *Guard spells*

Although the Australasian gannet guards its chick constantly for at least the first six to eight weeks, a fairly large proportion of adults then begin to leave chicks unattended, just as do adult Cape gannets. This is a significant difference from the state of affairs in the Atlantic gannet and is consistent with slower growth indicating a poorer food supply. Warham (1958) showed that the average brooding spell lasted 12 hours 43 minutes (range 9h 12m–18h 20m). Later in the growth of the chick it averaged 5 hours 4 minutes. This progressive fall in the length of the attendance spells was correlated with more frequent returns and is similar to the situation in the Cape gannet (attendance spells 29 hours when the chick is 1-20 days old, falling to 19 hours at 21–40 days, 17 hours at 41–60, 21 hours at 61–80 and 10 hours at 81–100 days). It presents some points of difference from the Atlantic gannet, whose attendance spells averaged 31 hours during the first half of the fledging period and 26 hours during the second half and which never left its young unattended. The unremitting guarding by at least one adult is an indication of the northern bird's favourable food situation.

3. *Feeding*

Warham's observations showed that, in the daylight hours of one day, chicks (ages unspecified) received between one and four 'bouts' or 'rounds' of feeding. On average each was fed twice, receiving 2·8 fish. He notes that there was no correlation between the size of the chick and the number of fish obtained, though bigger chicks may have received bigger fish. I found, for the Atlantic gannet, that each chick received 2·7 feeding bouts per day.

4. *Growth*

(*a*) *By weight*

In absolute terms the Australasian gannet chick, at a maximum weight of about 3250g equals the Cape but falls far short of the Atlantic gannet's maxima (4220 for a 60-day-old chick; 4260 for a fully feathered young). However, in terms of its weight relative to the mean weight of the adult, it grows at almost the same rate as the Atlantic gannet and to a similar extent. Both reach a maximum weight of about 130–140 per cent of the adult's weight. There is a strong indication that the Atlantic gannet reaches adult weight sooner than either the Australasian or the Cape, despite the Atlantic gannet's greater weight (a small bird generally reaches adult weight faster than a large one). Also, the Australasian is behind in plumage development and takes 10–20 days longer to fledge. On these grounds, the Atlantic gannet grows faster. But the Australasian gannet's extra days are spent completing the growth of the flight feathers rather than increasing in weight, a procedure which in all probability (though this has not been measured) the Atlantic bird carries out whilst in the swimming phase of its southward migration—a period which also lasts about two weeks. This difference is correlated with the Australasian (and Cape) juvenile gannet's habit of flying away from the nesting island rather than swimming. Over the first 13 weeks (at which point the Atlantic gannet fledges) the three species show fairly similar growth curves. All lay down fat deposits but the Atlantic gannet far more than the other two. The growth of the Australasian bird (as of the Cape) suggests that food is generally plentiful, though two indications (slower growth and the tendency for both adults to fish simultaneously) indicate that the superabundance available to the Atlantic bird is not equalled. Several pairs were given an extra young, but none succeeded in rearing twins (Robertson, pers. comm.). Cape gannets did so, but one twin was underweight, whereas Atlantic gannets did so and twins were less underweight and may indeed not have been significantly lighter (see p. 101).

(*b*) *By other measurements*

There are no details of wing or culmen growth but an interesting remark by Stein, to the effect that the rate of growth of tail feathers was so constant that tail length gave age dependable to within three days.

5. *Fledging period*

Well feathered young may wander to the fringes of the colony, but once they fly out to sea they do not return. Some, at least, are fed right up to the day they leave, but once having left the nesting mound, they may be fed by adults other than their parents (Wodzicki & Robertson 1953). As with the other gannets, they are certainly not accompanied to sea by their parents, nor fed at sea by them. Warham (1958) provides 12 fairly accurate fledging periods which range from 95 days precisely to 109 ± 3, defining fledging as the day of departure from the nesting island. (Jarvis, on the other hand, defined fledging as 'leaving the nest' and since his birds hung around for up to a week his fledging periods were probably the same as those of the Australasian gannet.) The shortest possible individual fledging period from these figures was 91 and the longest 112 days. The overall mean works out at 102 days, which is 12 days longer than in the Atlantic gannet. Stein (1971) gives the commonest fledging period on Horuhoru as 107–109 days.

The Australasian gannet, like the Cape, normally leaves the gannetry in sustained flight

Fig. 134(a). Chick about five days old; note the egg tooth. *Photo:* Ecology Division, D.S.I.R. New Zealand.

Fig. 134(b). Chick about two weeks old. The bare forehead is common in all gannets at this age. *Photo:* Ecology Division, D.S.I.R., New Zealand.

rather than, as in the Atlantic gannet, merely flying down to the sea or a few miles out to sea. If the Australasian (and Cape) bird typically undertakes its migration more or less from the outset on the wing, instead of swimming for a week or two first, it has important implications. First, it 'explains' the longer fledging period—the Australasian bird waiting until its flight feathers are fully grown; second, it means that the post-fledging selection pressures are different from those operating on the Atlantic gannet. It reaches its wintering area (the seas south of Australia) sooner after fledging. Presumably it has been less fat in proportion to its size that the Atlantic fledgling otherwise it, too, would be unable to rise from the surface of the sea (as a few, in fact, seem to be). Since at one point before fledging it has put on nearly as much fat as the northern bird, it must lose some of it during the final week or two at the colony instead of losing it whilst swimming at sea. The Atlantic gannet has no choice. It must rely on fat deposits, whereas a species which may or may not spend time practising flight (thus using stored energy) opens up more alternatives. It may leave with much stored fat and unable to fly; or become a proficient flier at the expense of stored fat, or practise flying and return periodically to be fed right up to the time of leaving. The relative merits of these two methods are quite obscure, but one can see that they are correlated with habitat differences; the cliff nesting Atlantic gannet could not undertake the pre-fledging exercising away from the nest, as the flat-ground nesting Australasian and Cape gannets do. Being tied to the nest it continues to be fed and does not use up so much of its fat. When it fledges, it is too heavy for long-sustained flight.

Fig. 134(e)

Chick about nine weeks old.

Fig. 134(c)

Chick about four weeks old. *Photo:* Ecology Division, D.S.I.R., New Zealand.

Fig. 134(d). Chick about five weeks old. The web exposure is a device for regulating body temperature. *Photo:* J. Warham.

BREEDING SUCCESS

1. *Hatching success*

Hatching success can be extremely high; 17 out of 18 eggs hatched even in the small Cat Island gannetry (small groups of Atlantic gannets tend to have a lower hatching success than large ones). Stein gives a hatching success of 98 per cent for 1350 eggs at Horuhoru. There are few published figures for hatching success at the large Kidnappers colony, but any figures are worthless unless it can be guaranteed that eggs have not been lost as a direct or indirect result of human interference. Wodzicki & Robertson (1953) note that prolonged rain produces ankle-deep mud in the Plateau gannetry at Cape Kidnappers and besides killing chicks is likely to cause heavy loss of eggs. Robertson gives the following figures for hatching success in six different groups: 459 pairs (45·7%); 208 (31·2%); 150 (60%); 100 (65%); 35 (0); 31 (6·5%). There is no evidence for the Australasian gannet, any more than for the Atlantic, that gulls can steal eggs by their own unaided efforts, and these low figures must surely reflect interference. In sum, there is no firm reason to believe that Australasian gannets fall short of the high hatching success found in the Atlantic and Cape gannets.

2. *Fledging success*

Warham's Cat Island birds successfully reared 16 out of 17 (94 per cent) chicks hatched. Wodzicki & Stein (1958) record that out of 4001 chicks ringed at Kidnappers and Horuhoru over a period of six years, almost all fledged. Thus, between about six weeks (the youngest chicks ringed) and fledging, there was virtually no loss. Robertson says that in established groups, for example on a Black Reef filled to capacity, more than 85 per cent produce chicks. He suggests that fledging success (from chicks hatched) is normally extremely high, but no figures are given (see overall breeding success) and it may be assumed that at Cape Kidnappers normally 90 per cent or more of chicks hatched are reared to fledging. This is the same as in the Atlantic gannet and indicates a plentiful food supply. Nevertheless there may be very important exceptions to this high figure. In December 1948 nearly 10 per cent of the chicks on Cape Kidnappers Plateau died through rain and Wodzicki & Stein (1958) report that on Horuhoru in 1952 the weather was so wild and wet that by Christmas 80 per cent of the 1500 chicks on the island had died; Stein referring to the same incident says 'up to 86 per cent of the chicks died'. He amplified this (pers. comm.), writing that starvation of small young, caused by rough weather preventing adults from feeding adequately, was an important cause of death (140 dead chicks in 1949, all between three and six weeks old, many of them clearly emaciated). This wholesale mortality is by far the most dramatic case of weather-induced mortality that has been recorded for any sulid (except the piquero with respect to El Niño) and adds strong point to the remarks (p. 126) on the factors influencing the spread of laying. It is particularly important in view of the high success of larger chicks (from ringing age onwards) described above. Nor, apparently, is it exceptional on Horuhoru for Stein (1971) reports that in 1949/50 55·6 per cent of 840 chicks died before fledging; in 1950/51, c. 250 chicks fledged out of the entire colony of about 1500 breeding pairs, whilst in 1951/52 only 208 chicks fledged. Again, older chicks fared best, for of these 208, 197 were from the 198 that had been old enough to be ringed. In 1953/54, 1954/55, 1955/56 and 1956/57, 900–1000 chicks fledged each year from Horuhoru. This breeding success apparently fluctuates fairly widely between stations and (at least on Horuhoru) between years. Even in good years, there, it is less than 60 per cent, whilst in a bad year it may be as low as 10 per cent.

3. *Overall breeding success*

As the figures for hatching and fledging success show, overall breeding success in an established group of undisturbed birds can be extremely high—probably 80–90 per cent. New groups have a lower success; thus Robertson cites two new groups, one of 35 and the other 31 nests, which between them hatched two chicks. The number of eggs laid is not stated, but assuming that most of these 66 nests held eggs the failure rate is far too high to be ascribable to inexperience and must be due to interference. Young and inexperienced birds do have a lower breeding success than old and experienced ones, but there is no evidence that fringe birds, regardless of age, fare worse than centre ones, except insofar as they are more likely to be disturbed by man and therefore robbed by gulls. Thus, several pairs occupied a new area at Kidnappers (Plateau colony 8) in 1946–47 but not until the fourth year after the first egg was laid were the first fledged chicks produced. In 1949–50 about 50 pairs built nests, but nesting success remained low, and from 21 nests occupied during the 1951–52 nesting season only 4 chicks fledged, which represents 20 per cent breeding success. But again, one does not know how much of this failure was due to disturbance. Stein's (1971) account of a visit to Horuhoru, November 9th 1968, seems to me to tell its own tale of man's hand: 'The spring had been mild and gales few . . . we expected to count nearly 1600 (nests). Instead, strewn around in irregular groups, there were some 300 occupied nests. Every egg, laid before the first week in September, and every (chick) had vanished in some catastrophe. There were lots of well made nests lying empty.' The Australasian gannet, overall, probably enjoys breeding success similar to that of the other two, and like them, usually suffers its heaviest losses in the period immediately after fledging. However the heavy weather-induced mortality among young in the nest, in some years, has no counterpart in the other two gannets.

BREEDING REGIMES

1. *General features of attendance at colony*

Adult attendance varies with time of season and of day, though the latter has not been adequately studied (in general, as in the Atlantic gannet, attendance is highest in the late afternoon and evening, next highest in the early morning and lowest around mid-day). This variability imposes correction factors upon counts or estimates, since the proportion of the total population which these represent depends on the time of year and of day at which they were made. That part of the adult population which could be 'missed' by estimates taken too early or too late in the season consists largely of young birds just establishing sites, but in the Australasian and Cape birds there is an added complication since the habit of leaving young unattended means that a proportion of the adults will be absent but this proportion will depend first on the time of year (when chicks are large) and second, on the timing of laying in that particular season (which varies from year to year). At Kidnappers, it was found that peak numbers of adults occurred between the last week of October and the first of November. The proportion of the total (peak) population present at the beginning of the nesting season (i.e. end of August to end of September) varied from about 50 to over 88 per cent. The decline was gradual and in the latter part of December between 10 and 20 per cent of 'peak' numbers were present. Variation between seasons was considerable. Wodzicki & Robertson (1953) comment on interseasonal variation in the population of the Plateau group. They derive a figure for the mean peak population between 1945 and 1951 and then compare years in terms of what proportion of this peak was reached in mid-December of each year. They produce figures of between 70 per cent (1946) and 112 per cent (1951) but since the group was growing it is difficult to understand the significance of these figures. Nevertheless they conclude that in some years New Zealand gannetries contain a smaller proportion of their population than in others. This is tantamount to saying that in certain years part of the adult population (and that part variable) stays away from the colonies. However this may be, the variation in the composition of the group at the same time in successive seasons was certainly very marked (see Table 37).

2. *Length and composition of the breeding cycle*

Australasian gannets spend six to eight months at their breeding colonies; they return to northern Australasian gannetries about a month earlier than to southern ones. At Colville they return in July and in some years as many as a third of the nests contain eggs by the end of August (Fleming & Wodzicki 1952), whereas further south at Cape Kidnappers it may be August before birds are attending their nests and the end of October before the first eggs are laid. On the other hand, birds may be present at the end of the third week of June. Kidnappers may be deserted before mid-March, although in some years there may be chicks right up to the end of April (Wodzicki & Robertson 1953).

As usual in long lived, seasonally breeding seabirds males return first, and return progressively earlier with age. At Cape Kidnappers old birds (ten years or more) probably usually return at the end of July, five-year-olds about the end of October, four-year-olds early December, three-year-olds mid-December and two-year-olds early January. Working back up the scale, one-year-olds stay for about 3–4 weeks; three-year-olds about 7–8 weeks and four-year-olds about 9–10 weeks. The departure dates for older birds are not given but if one assumes that the oldest birds may be around until April, their stay is some eight calendar months, a period nearly comparable to the longest stay of the Atlantic gannet[1] and significantly longer than the Cape. The Cape gannet typically shows no post-breeding attendance and if the Australasian resembles it in this its cycle length would be about the same. It seems clear that the pattern of attendance (and eventually of laying) is considerably less seasonally consistent in the Australasian than the Atlantic gannet.

The period at the colony thus exceeds that required merely for incubation (six weeks) and chick rearing (15–16 weeks) by several weeks—a length of time which may be in excess of that needed for pair formation, mating and nest building (given as 'upwards of a month' by Stein). If so, as in the Atlantic gannet, there is considerable selection pressure favouring prolonged attendance at the site, though it is far from clear why this should be necessary.

3. *Timing of breeding*

Over its range as a whole, the first eggs are laid in August and the last in December, a five-month span equalling that found in the Atlantic gannet and exceeding the Cape gannet's. The earliest egg on record was laid on July 12th 1959, Horuhoru (Stein 1971), which appears to be 4 or 5 weeks ahead of Kidnappers—a difference about the same as that between the east and west coasts of Britain, in the case of the Atlantic gannet. Possibly, replacement laying may occur as late as January. At White Island 'a few weeks later' (than December 27th 1946) there were 35 eggs 'in various stages up to hatching' in every 100 nests (Fleming & Wodzicki 1952). At any one gannetry the span is usually less than this. Robertson reports that at Cape Kidnappers the first eggs usually appear in the last two weeks of September (though they may be as late as the end of October) and the last at the end of December. This spread of around 107 days is very near that of the Atlantic gannet on the Bass (113 days). Again, at Cape Kidnappers

[1] The picture is, however, less clear cut than this. Fleming & Wodzicki (1952) mention that at several gannetries, for example Oaia, Colville and Horuhoru, gannets may roost during the winter, whilst others are vacated in autumn and reoccupied in late winter. Much the same variation is found in the Atlantic and Cape gannets.

TABLE 37

THE SIZE AND COMPOSITION OF THE PLATEAU GROUP IN SUCCESSIVE DECEMBERS, 1945–51
(from Wodzicki & Robertson 1953)

Date in December	Year	No. of breeding pairs*	Percentage of: Empty nests	Eggs	Chicks
18th	1945	196	18·4	18·1	0·5
16th	1946	155	36·8	25·8	37·4
16th	1947	230	16·5	47·0	36·5
16th	1948	210	45·2		54·8
19th	1949	220	9·5	15·0	75·5
22nd	1950	230	28·2	9·7	62·1
22nd	1951	237	19·3	54·3	26·4

* Not defined but presumably those holding good nests?

peak laying occurs in the middle two weeks of October. However, from Wodzicki & McMeekan (1947), who say that on February 4th 1946, 97 per cent of chicks were feathered, and virtually all had gone by early March, it is clear that the main fledging period was the second half of February, or the main laying period the second half of September. The authors' own conclusion, which is clearly inconsistent, is that peak laying was early or middle December. They base this on the claim that in the third week of December more than half the breeding pairs laid eggs, which is impossible if their March fledging is also correct; eggs in late December could not fledge by March 11th. This raises the interesting point, however, that, apparently, the mean laying date may vary by three weeks in different years for Robertson say that 'the *average* ages of chicks at the end of December has varied from season to season by up to three weeks'. He amplified this (pers. comm.) by saying that in 1970/71, 1971/72 and 1972/73 laying was three weeks later than the previous mean date, due he thought to offshore winds affecting either food or possibly nest material (the nests were poorer in these years). Many chicks died and there were extensive wrecks of other species. Later, laying reverted to its earlier mean. Equally significant evidence of fluctuation between seasons (Table 37) is given by Wodzicki & Robertson (1953). This shows that the percentage of nests with eggs or chicks varies enormously from year to year. Again, however, much of this could be due to human interference, causing egg loss, chick loss and replacement laying. Otherwise it is an important phenomenon, with far-reaching implications. It is even suggested that early this century, peak laying at the Cape was up to a month earlier than now. It would be rewarding to have figures for a *completely* undisturbed breeding cycle at Cape Kidnappers; only thus could the imponderable factor of the direct and indirect effect of disturbance be eliminated. Egg loss is only part of the story; behavioural effects, even though subtle, can be significant.

So far as individual groups are concerned, though, a smaller group (35 pairs) had a peak laying around November 20th 1967 compared with October 26th for bigger groups. But the former held more young birds, and these lay later. Clearly, however, the Australasian gannet has a well marked peak of laying coupled with a wide spread. Little is known about the advantages of the former. Is it linked with seasonal abundance of food, or with the production of fledged young at a propitious time? The spread presumably takes care of climatic fluctuations from year to year, so that bad weather never catches an entire crop of chicks at the most vulnerable age (see also p. 288).

It is clear from ringing returns that, like the Atlantic gannet, the Australasian suffers heavy mortality soon after leaving the gannetry. Between 1950 and 1968, some 3252 chicks were ringed at the Plateau groups, Cape Kidnappers; 637 (19·6 per cent) were subsequently sighted or recaptured, back at the gannetry (none at any other gannetries). If all the ringed birds that returned were sighted and none emigrated, around 75 per cent die between fledging and about 4 years of age. It is not possible to say what proportion of these die in their first year, but probably most do so. Stein (pers. comm.) comments that attempts to assess the proportion of fledglings which eventually return to Horuhoru gave figures as low as three per cent and that probably at least 80–85 per cent do not return.

Assuming an adult rate of mortality (c. 5 per cent) in the fourth and third years of life and 10 per cent mortality in the second year, 61 per cent of all fledglings would have to die in their first year on Robertson's figure (derived from ringing returns) of 76 per cent that fledge but never return to the gannetry. Elsewhere, however, Robertson gives some 70 per cent as the mortality between fledging and reaching the age of 5 years; an assumption of a 5 per cent annual adult mortality, and mortality independent of age after 2 years (but twice adult mortality during the second year), would make mortality in the first year 56 per cent. This estimate is probably too low (see above) and the real figure is likely to approach that of the Atlantic gannet. Probably most of these die during their migration (p. 293).

OTHER ASPECTS OF BREEDING ECOLOGY

1. *Food*

The Australasian gannet's food is very similar in nature (range of species and size of individual items) to that of the Cape gannet, though there has been no detailed investigation. Wodzicki & Moreland (1966) give 13 species from 18 vomits, which ranged from 100 to 400g in weight;

the biggest item (squid) was 300mm. Anchovy *Engraulis australis* numbered 23 in nine White Island vomits and 53 in eight from Cape Kidnappers; in size they ranged from 60–135mm. Barracouta *Thyrsites atun* numbered 17 in the White Island sample (150–200mm). Garfish *Reporhamphus ihi* numbered one at White Island and 10 at Cape Kidnappers (240mm). Sardines or pilchards *Sardinops neopilchardus* three at White Island and six at Kidnappers (20–150mm). Flying fish *Cypselurus* spp. seven at White Island. Horse mackerel *Trachurus novaezelandiae* four at White Island and one at Cape Kidnappers (150–280mm). Yellow-eyed mullet *Aldrichetta forsteri* three at White Island. Piper or needle fish *Scomberesox forsteri* three at Kidnappers 120mm). Squid *Notodaurus sloanii* and another unidentified species one at White Island and eight at Cape Kidnappers (150–300mm). The remains of a perch-like fish (Serranidae?) and a puffer (*Spheroides* spp.) were also identified. A vomit from Little Solander contained five *Mendosoma lineatum* around 120mm long. All these species occur within a few kilometres of the coast and probably the Australasian gannet forages mainly within 30 or 40km offshore.

2. *Annual mortality*

The massive ringing programme at Cape Kidnappers and Horuhoru has produced valuable information about mortality and also the age structure of the groups concerned. On the basis of direct observation of ringed birds, it has been calculated that the annual adult mortality rate is 4–5 per cent. This is highly comparable to the 5–6 per cent of the Atlantic gannet and gives a life expectation of some 20 years. Robertson has birds up to 21 years old at Kidnappers and Stein has now recorded birds at least 20 years old on Horuhoru. However, on the basis of the proportion of unringed to ringed birds recaptured in a specified area of Horuhoru, and by making certain assumptions, Stein (1971) shows that of 180 unringed birds 96 could be 18–24 years old, 48 25–30, 24 31–36 and 12 37–42. This calculation is, however, merely speculative.

At 75 per cent breeding success (at Kidnappers) and prebreeding mortality of 85 per cent (65 per cent in the first year, 10 per cent in the second year and 5 per cent in third and fourth years) one pair breeding for 20 years would produce 15 young of which 12·75 would die before breeding, leaving 2·25 young produced per lifetime per pair. These (approximate) figures fit the present increase quite well.

There is little information on the causes of adult mortality. Some (and immature birds also) are hooked by anglers' spinners and presumably are also netted and shot at sea and taken by predatory fish. Others injure themselves landing badly. Most first-year birds die of starvation (see below).

3. *Age of first breeding*

Australasian gannets reputedly first return to the gannetry in their second year of life (this, presumably, is meant by 'birds start returning to the colony from two years onwards'; literally, they would be in their third year). It would be strange, however, if no first-year birds ever did so and in fact one bird was recovered back at Horuhoru at an age of one year four months. At Kidnappers, Wodzicki (1967) made efforts to record ringed birds each year and found that he saw most, for the first time, when four years old (57 out of a total 276 sightings) and five years old (101 out of 276). Two-year-olds were exceptional in marked contrast to the situation in the Atlantic gannet. They do not breed until they are in their fourth to seventh year; the youngest breeding records that I can find are of birds in their fourth year. One laid when almost exactly four years old (conceivably a week before its fourth birthday) and another probably laid before its fourth birthday (ringed on February 2nd 1953 and therefore born in November 1952, it laid in October or November 1956). In six cases birds bred for the first time when about four years 10 or 11 months old. Of a further 23 birds recovered in their fifth or sixth years of life, nine were breeding, though not necessarily for the first time. Of these, six fifth-year birds (mostly just approaching their fifth birthday) were breeding (that is, had laid) and eight were in Clubs, whilst three birds in their sixth year were breeding as against six in Clubs (Wodzicki & Stein 1958). From the above it would seem that most birds first lay in the sixth year (but see below). A bird fledging in March 1960 would lay in October 1965 when 5½ years old calculated from fledging or nearly six calculating from hatching. Wodzicki & Stein (1958), however, state that 'at the age of 6–7 years only about half the birds are breeding' and Stein (pers. comm.) says they breed for the first time at 'often six to eight years'. Robertson states that in young pairs the female is generally at least one year older than the male which is the reverse of the tendency in the Atlantic. It appears from this that Australasian gannets certainly do not begin breeding as early as Cape birds (p. 249). Consistently, they are also older by the time they attain adult plumage (usually in the fifth year against third or fourth in the Cape gannet). Is it possible, however, that most females in fact lay in their fifth or sixth years and that the large number of birds known to be older than this and yet not breeding could be either failed breeders or temporary non-breeders?

4. *Movements*

The juvenile Atlantic and Cape gannets migrate towards the equator, covering a maximum distance of 4000–6000km, but the Australasian juveniles migrate westwards from New Zealand, covering up to 5000km. In all cases the movement takes the birds from cool to warmer or even tropical waters. Between 1951 and 1965, 3616 chicks were ringed at Horuhoru (4·6 per cent recovery rate) and 2513 at Cape Kidnappers (4·7 per cent recovery rate). Wodzicki & Stein (1958) forms the basis of the following discussion and Wodzicki (1967) has further analysed the results.

The recoveries (Fig. 135a) show that young gannets from New Zealand travel across the Tasman Sea, mainly towards the east coast of Australia. Before this they swim or fly either north, clearing North Cape and then proceeding westwards, or they go south to Cook Strait and thence west. There is a strong indication that whilst birds from Cape Kidnappers migrate both north and south along the east coast of North Island, birds from Horuhoru almost all migrate north, a procedure which presumably sets them on their main course most quickly. Even the Kidnapper birds probably move north more than south. All birds seen to leave Cape Kidnappers flew north-east, whilst those leaving Horuhoru flew north-west or north-north-west and all southerly records of Horuhoru birds are gale-driven or drifted. There are no records of birds south or south-west of Coromandel Peninsula, though there are some in the Hauraki Gulf south of the gannetry itself. Perhaps Cook Strait is a hazard for a swimming juvenile. At least some of the north moving birds move south once they have cleared North Cape. Thus several have been recovered on the west coast of North Island, well south of North Cape. Very occasionally birds turn up on South Island. One such, a Kidnappers bird, was recovered near Otago eleven weeks after leaving the gannetry and a Horuhoru juvenile was recovered at Port Nicholson. The picture provided by recoveries is supported by observation, which shows a heavy northward passage of juvenile gannets in the coastal waters to the east of North Island.

In all three gannets some individuals initially move in the direction opposite to the eventual path of migration. Thus some Bass and Ailsa Atlantic gannets move north and then south, whilst some Cape gannets move south and then north.

Probably the great majority of young Australasian gannets are on the wing by the time they begin to cross the Tasman Sea. Several recoveries show that they can on occasions cover considerable distances at an average speed of over 200km a day. Thus, one bird covered 1700 miles (2720km) in seven days, another 1800 miles (2880km) in eight days and two 1650 miles (2640km) in seven days and so on. These are minimum speeds, since the bird may have been lying where it was recovered for some time. If, in addition, it had spent a day or two swimming, the distance covered by flight could be more than 500 miles (800km) a day in some cases. This suggests that juvenile gannets do not dally in mid-ocean but head rapidly for more coastal waters off Australia. This would make sense if coastal waters gave them the best chance of catching fish, for at this stage they have to surmount the considerable hurdle of achieving fishing skill whilst living on dwindling fat reserves. Considering recoveries from all gannetries up to 1965 (Wodzicki 1967), 203 were recovered in Australia, and 62 in New Zealand, before they were a year old. The comparable figures were 20 and 5 for birds in their second year and 9 and 2 for third-year birds. After that, the proportions reverse as the bulk of the survivors are back in home waters.

The dispersal of young gannets over the coastal waters of east Australia is extremely widespread, extending to 19° 14'S., north of Capricorn, to 41° 19'S. off northern Tasmania a span of nearly 22° of latitude and 1550 miles (2480km). Most recoveries occur between 25° and 37° but this may partly reflect the distribution of centres of human population.

By no means all New Zealand gannets concentrate off eastern Australia. There is a significant and possibly considerable movement along the southern coast, extending part way up the west coast as far as 32° 01′S.; 115° 29′E. and 28° 45′S.; 114° 42′E. 4500 miles (5200km) and 4800 miles (7680km) respectively from Horuhoru. So far as the recoveries go, it appears to be only Horuhoru birds that are involved. Furthermore, Horuhoru birds appear to fall short of the northerly limits reached in eastern waters by Kidnappers birds. Thus, there is at least a hint that young birds from these two gannetries may have overlapping but significantly different ranges during the period in which they are absent from home waters.

It appears that immature gannets remain in Australian waters usually for two or three years (Fig. 135b). Whilst recoveries of birds in their second year are common there, third-year birds are much rarer and fourth-year ones extremely rare. Since the heaviest mortality occurs in the first year and there is probably not much difference between mortality in the second and third years, Wodzicki & Stein (1958) suggest that there is a significant mortality in the late spring and summer of the second year (but there is no good evidence for this). The large difference in recovery rates for these two age groups suggests an exodus of birds from Australian waters in their third year. Correspondingly, birds in their third year, unlike those in their second, are common in the gannetries whilst birds in their first year are hardly ever seen there. Some of the first-year birds that are to be seen around New Zealand may have remained there since fledging rather than returned early from Australian waters but it is now known that a few stay in New Zealand waters, just as some first-year Atlantic gannets stay in home waters. Heavy mortality attends the migration of the juvenile gannet, especially during the first few

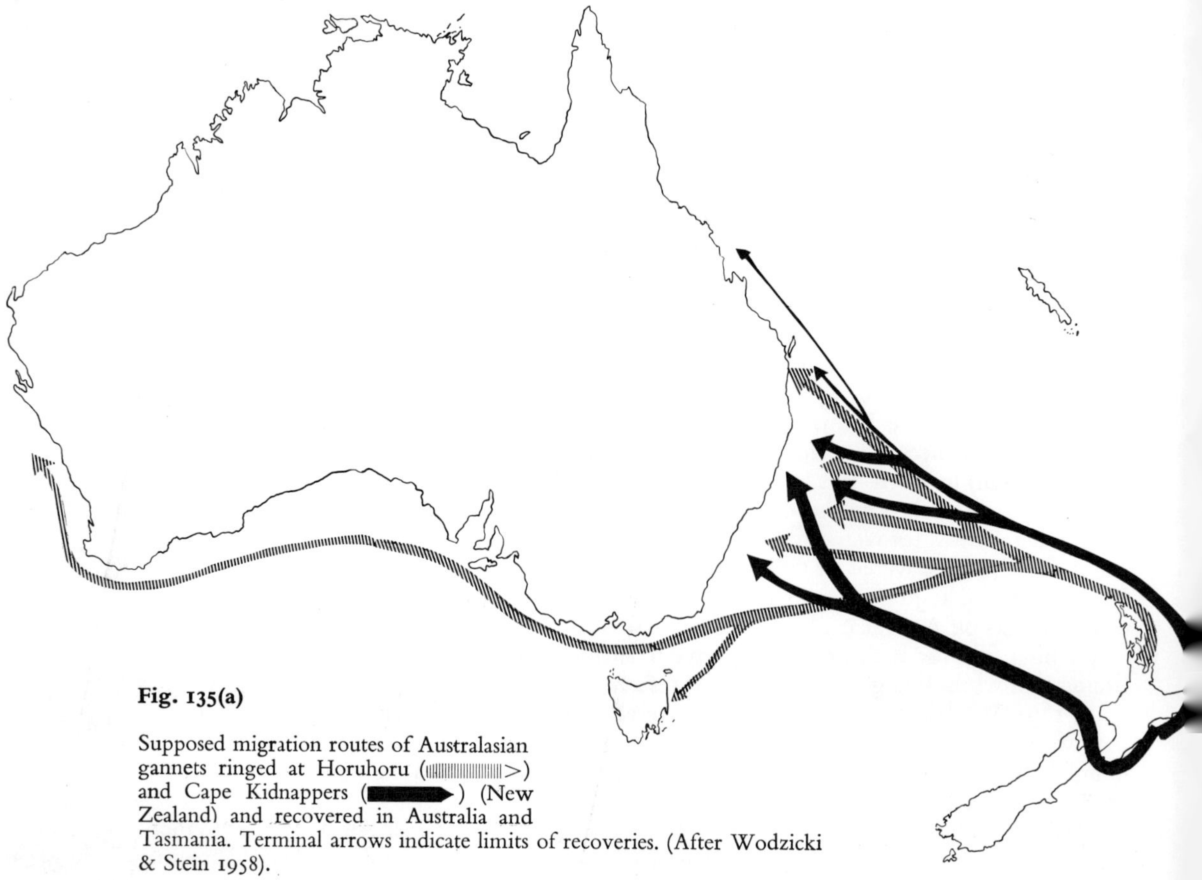

Fig. 135(a)

Supposed migration routes of Australasian gannets ringed at Horuhoru (|||||||||||||||>) and Cape Kidnappers (▬▬►) (New Zealand) and recovered in Australia and Tasmania. Terminal arrows indicate limits of recoveries. (After Wodzicki & Stein 1958).

weeks. Out of 45 recoveries in the first year of life, 51 per cent were of birds that had fledged between two and six weeks previously and 88 per cent were within nine weeks of fledging. Out of 28 recoveries for which the cause of death was ascertained, 14 occurred after storms, indicating the importance of weather at this time. Of the others, 10 became entangled in net or line. The rest were shot or oiled. The observations reported in Stein (1971) of first-year birds being killed by coming ashore in Australia in heavy surf are of interest in indicating that such birds are weak, probably through starvation. Whilst there probably are factors mildly distorting the recovery picture, such as a greater likelihood of recovery in the period during which they are in New Zealand coastal waters as against the Tasman Sea, which might favour the chances of recovery in the first two to four weeks, the general picture of a heavy initial mortality is certainly correct. This may indicate selection pressure favouring early fledging, in which case a situation similar to that of the Atlantic gannet would obtain, with the spread also maintained in the same way (see p. 291). However, given an average breeding success of 0·75 young per pair per year and an annual mortality of 4 per cent every year after the first, the young cannot die at more than 75 per cent in their first year if adults are to replace themselves, let alone increase.

5. *Fidelity to site and group*

The Atlantic gannet tends to keep its site, having once bred there. If a young bird joins a stable group—in this context one that is changing neither its spatial disposition nor its numbers—its chance of acquiring an edge site or one further in is simply a function of the size and shape of the group assuming that birds are equally at risk whatever their position within the group.

Fig. 135 (b). Australian recoveries of gannets ringed as chicks at Horuhoru and Cape Kidnappers. (After Wodzicki & Stein 1958.)

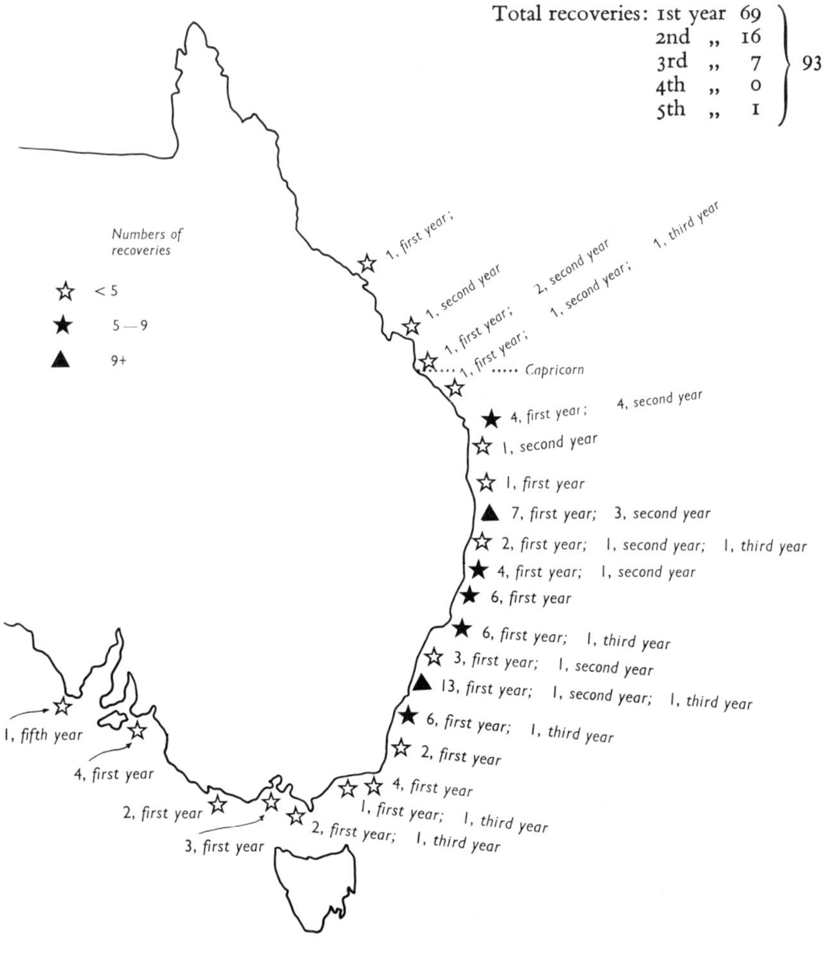

Prospectors will take over vacant sites whether these are central or otherwise. However, this simple situation is probably hardly ever realised. Groups often shrink, expand or change their disposition and a variable amount of site changing goes on. Robertson & Williams (1968) say that in the Australasian gannet young males occupy a territory, generally on the outside of the breeding colony, for one season, but that the older the bird the closer to the centre it nests. This implies that the bird gradually moves there or that the group expands and envelops the erstwhile fringe nester. No evidence is given for the first possibility and there seems unlikely to be survival value in so doing. Breeding success is better in the centre only because of man's interference at the fringe and, in some cases, because fringe birds are young. Furthermore, Robertson elsewhere states that there is strong site tenacity in breeding birds and Stein that 'they endeavour to use the same nest each year'.

At Cape Kidnappers many birds reared in the Saddle group established their sites in the Reef or Plateau group (p. 298). Of birds reared in the Plateau group, however, less than 0·5 per cent have been recovered in other groups. There was thus a marked tendency to return to the group in which they were born (two five-year-old birds were recovered at Horuhoru breeding within a few feet of their birthplaces) but there is also immigration into rapidly expanding groups. This demonstrates the potential fluidity in the shape of a gannetry, with unequal growth causing bulges and retraction. The initiation of new nuclei or a new bulge depends on circumstances which are usually unknown but in the Kidnappers case may be linked with the pattern of human disturbance. But 'pioneers' are produced from time to time.

6. *Fidelity to mate*

Although figures are not yet available, it appears that there is a strong tendency to remain faithful to the same mate. Stein's study of Horuhoru birds 'suggests that a gannet pair mate for life'. But in such a long lived bird there could be high mate fidelity in successive years and yet, over the entire life of the bird, a good chance of divorce. And of course, due to the death of their partner, most birds will be forced to remate at least once.

7. *Colony structure*

A detailed study of the growth of part of the Plateau colony at Kidnappers (see p. 279) has provided information on the formation and structure of colonies (see Fleming & Wodzicki 1952; Wodzicki & Robertson 1953).

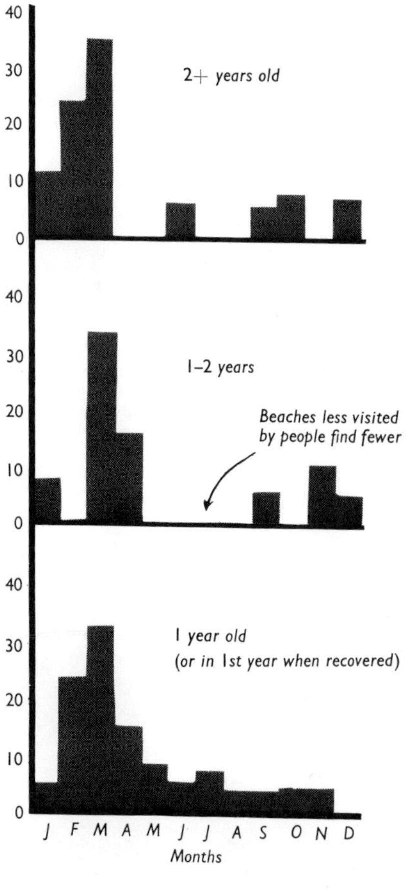

Fig. 136

Proportions of different age classes recovered.

From figures given by Robertson, the proportion of different age classes within this particular group can be calculated (Fig. 137). The commonest class was six- and seven-year-olds. Nevertheless, 35 per cent of the group were ten or more years old. However, these proportions are not to be treated quite at face value, since they must have depended (for chances of identification) on the number ringed in the year from which they derive, and these numbers vary (see also Stein's calculation for Horuhoru (p. 292).

From the distribution of ringed and unringed birds within this group, derives information about the growth of the colony between 1961 and 1966. Of the 204 birds involved in establishing sites in this period 78 per cent were unringed and were therefore immigrants (virtually all the group's *own* chicks had been ringed). From the distribution of ringed and unringed birds there is no clear tendency for ringed birds (the produce of the Plateau group) to clump together.

The Hawke's Bay gannetry is now made up of three parts, the main Cape Kidnappers or Saddle group (Fig. 131a), the Plateau group, divided into two (Fig. 131b) and the Black Reef colony (Fig. 131c). The Saddle group, established in the 1870s, held about 2000 nesting pairs in 1964, which represented a decline of 17 per cent (nearly 400 pairs) since 1957. The Reef colony (eight small rocks) founded about 1937, grew from 320 to 883 pairs between 1945 and 1957, an increase of 176 per cent and by a further 155 pairs or 18 per cent between 1957 and 1964. The Plateau groups, founded about 1938, grew from 178 to 278 pairs or 56 per cent between 1945 and 1957 and by 209 pairs or 75 per cent between 1957 and 1964. The complex as a whole increased by some 27 per cent between 1945 and 1957 but remained steady between 1957 and 1964.

Thus, between 1945 and 1964, (a) two new groups were founded, substantially away from the main (Saddle) group, and one of these (the Plateau) grew as two fairly discrete sub-groups, and (b) the main group declined slightly during the period when the others were increasing. These changes are well documented and raise several points of general interest, discussed below.

The Reef group attracted 662 pairs in 19 years, an increase which was far in excess of that attainable from its own output. Probably most of its immigrants came from the Saddle, though a few were shown to originate in the Plateau group. The details in Wodzicki (1967, Table IV) indicate considerable swapping and changing between some of the eight rocks. Rock 4 (see Fig. 131c) dropped from 300 to 216 pairs in two successive seasons, a 28 per cent change highly unlikely to be due to mortality, but changed by only one pair between 1957 and 1964, and that stability was maintained when it held a much higher population than the 300. Between one season and the next, Rock 8 lost its seven breeding pairs and reverted to a mere roost. Both changes imply that birds tried nesting on a particular rock but then moved to another. Presumably the distinction between properly established pairs and mere Club birds was adequately made; otherwise a movement of Club birds could explain the observations.

The Plateau group (A and B), like the Reef, was initially a roosting area. Its growth (Fig.

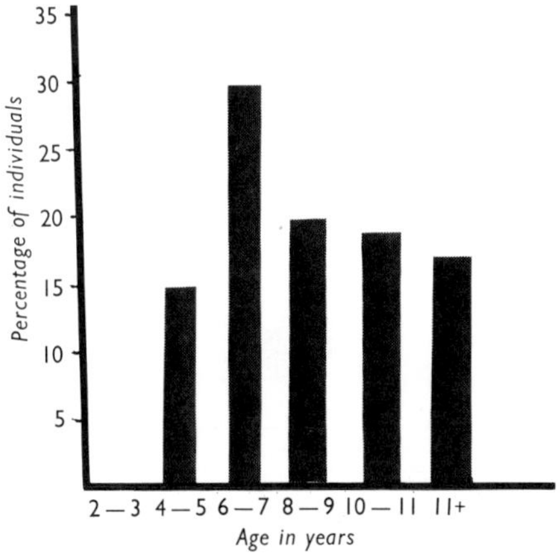

Fig. 137

The age structure of a breeding group of Australasian gannets, Cape Kidnappers. (After C. J. R. Robertson.)

131b) from 1945 to 1964 worked out at a steady 5·3 per cent per year, which is potentially obtainable from the group's own output, and is very nearly a straight line geometric increase. However, a considerable number of its recruits in fact came from the Saddle. Thus, 60 per cent of birds establishing sites in the main group between 1961 and 1967 were unringed and therefore, since virtually all Plateau chicks had been ringed, must have come from outside. Conversely, a few chicks ringed on the Plateau went to Black Reef and the Saddle to breed. Nevertheless, 99·5 per cent of 637 birds ringed in the Plateau and subsequently seen or recovered at Cape Kidnappers were back in the Plateau colony. Thus it lost hardly any of its own output.

The second Plateau group a mere ten metres from the first (Fig. 131b) cannot be considered in any way a separate entity, for there was considerable interchange between them. Thus 46 per cent of 122 chicks ringed in group A bred in group B, and vice versa (Robertson 1969). Nevertheless, the formation of a second nucleus so near to an existing group is interesting, and so are its growth characteristics. In 1946 when group A already numbered 159 pairs, several pairs attempted to build nests several metres away, and a solitary pair laid. From then onwards the new group grew faster, proportionately, than group A (Table 38).

Clearly, although both groups were obviously taking recruits from outside (for example both showed a massive increase between 1957 and 1958) they did so unequally. The more rapid growth overall of group B and its occasional enormous increases (it doubled between 1957 and 1958) could indicate that at some point it began to exercise a greater attraction to incomers (Saddle birds) and probably, also, drew more birds born in group A than it gave to group A of its own. Without much more detailed information than is available, a more sophisticated analysis is impossible, but even the one given above is consistent with my own experience, which is that the most rapidly growing points in a gannetry attract more than their fair share of recruits. This is undoubtedly a behavioural phenomenon by which prospecting birds are attracted to areas containing a high proportion of newly established birds.

It is interesting, however, that 'B' ever formed in the first place, for thre was in 'A', so nearby, a rapidly growing nucleus to which immigrants from the Saddle or elsewhere in the Hawkes' Bay complex, could go. Perhaps 'B' began as a nucleus of particularly young birds and achieved momentum by an influx of fortuitously available birds of similar age. If 'B' began as a satellite Club on the fringe of 'A', this would amount to much the same thing

The decline in the main (Saddle) group (Fig. 131a) deserves comment. Counts in 1945, '46, '57 and '64 gave respectively 2307, 2337, 2425 and 2060 pairs. The loss of some 365 pairs between 1957 and 1964 is not large and theoretically could easily be accommodated by the

TABLE 38

GROWTH IN TWO SLIGHTLY SEPARATE PARTS OF A GROUP OF AUSTRALASIAN GANNETS

Year	Number of occupied sites		Year	Number of occupied sites	
	Group A	Group B		Group A	Group B
1945	196	0	1955	251	41
1946	159	1*	1956	240	64
1947	228	3	1957	222	56
1948	210	1	1958	335	111
1949	220	50	1959	314	85
1950	258	18	1960	257	95
1951	228	15	1961	325	103
1952	197	14	1962	331	112
1953	202	19	1963	360	106
1954	234	20	1964	359	128

* There is some discrepancy here between Wodzicki & Robertson (1953) and Wodzicki (1967) for the former says several pairs occupied B in 1946 though only one laid.

adult mortality rate (around 5 per cent per year) together with a loss of recruits to the Reef and Plateau groups. Robertson points out that although 80 per cent of the young raised in the Plateau groups between 1950 and 1967 were ringed, the percentage of ringed adults there in 1966/67 was a mere 22 per cent, showing that the Plateau was receiving unringed immigrants, doubtless from the Saddle. This is consistent with the observation that some nests, particularly on the landward and seaward slopes, were not taken over when they became vacant, suggesting that once young Saddle birds began to be attracted to the focal points of 'growing' areas they continued to go there even when there was room at the Saddle. Thus, although initially, saturation of the Saddle may have led to the formation of new groups, the drain continued even when the Saddle was no longer full. It is interesting that the nests in the flatter part of the area did not suffer proportionate neglect (the Australasian gannet has a strong preference for flat ground).

The entire Hawke's Bay gannetry is an extremely interesting case, considered from its inception, probably in the 1870s. Between 1879 and 1903 it increased so rapidly that it must have received immigrants. Between 1903 and 1945 the average rate of increase slowed down considerably—a common pattern of events in gannetries.

As already mentioned, the structure and density of a group changes with age until stability is attained. Young birds take over central sites as these fall vacant, and on occasions, as shown by observations on the Plateau group, the central part of a group may come to consist of quite a high proportion of young birds.

8. *Clubs*

At Cape Kidnappers there are many Club or roosting birds apparently comparable to Atlantic gannet Clubs. They used certain rocks at Black Reef, mainland ledges, the fringes of the main gannetry, the pinnacles to the east of this, a steep bare slope between the main Kidnappers and Plateau groups and bare ground along the cliff edge north and south of the Plateau group. As with the Atlantic gannets of the Bass, they build up until, in November or December, some hundreds are present. They show mainly low intensity territorial and sexual behaviours including copulation. Almost all of them must wear adult plumage, since otherwise observers would certainly have commented on the fact. However, they could still be young, sexually immature birds.

4. BREEDING BEHAVIOUR

INTRODUCTION

In appearance the Australasian gannet resembles the Cape more than it does the Atlantic. In behaviour, however, it seems at least as similar to the latter. Warham's (1958) account is the only detailed one, though there is further useful information in the script to Robertson's excellent film strip.[1] Ideally, a comparative study at this level, where behaviour differences

[1] 'Life History of the Australasian Gannet.' Dept. of Education, New Zealand (undated).

are so slight, should be carried out by the same worker but this has not been done, nor have measurements of the frequency of any stereotyped behaviour patterns of the Australasian gannet been made. Thus some of the interesting differences between the Cape and Atlantic gannets (p. 310) cannot be checked for the Australasian. Nevertheless, there is now enough information to establish the extremely close behavioural relationships of all three gannets. It will be found helpful to refer constantly to the account of behaviour in the Atlantic gannet for background information.[1]

ESTABLISHMENT AND MAINTENANCE OF TERRITORY

1. *Fighting*

The Australasian gannet nests at a maximum density of 2·59 nests per sq.m compared with a maximum density of 3·53 per sq.m for the Atlantic gannet and more than 6·0 per sq.m for the Cape. Like the other two species it sometimes fights (Fig. 138) to establish or maintain this territory. Warham records a probable casualty of such a fight in the Cat Island colony, but whether fights are frequent and typically intense is not recorded. Robertson notes that fights may continue for hours and that occasionally birds die from the punishment received. He attributes these fights to inadvertently landing on the wrong site but, though trespassers undoubtedly are vigorously attacked, this seems highly unlikely to be the main cause. Typically, such mistakes are likely to result in a brief struggle, the erring individual attempting to break away. They are more likely, I think, to result from genuine attempts to contest a site, or a mate. In the former case, they could provide evidence for notably strenuous site competition, a phenomenon which would need interpreting bearing in mind the apparent abundance of nesting sites in most cases. Low intensity fighting, in which a bird rushes at and displaces another, is seen among young birds holding temporary or new sites, much as in the extreme fringe of an expanding group of Atlantic gannets. It is impossible to decide whether the Australasian fights more than the Cape or less. There are indications that it is less aggressive, but these are by no means conclusive.

[1] It has not proved practicable to organise the material in exactly the same way for all three gannets, though the main sequence is similar.

Fig. 138. Fighting is sometimes severe, but shorter lived than in the Atlantic gannet. *Photo:* C. J. R. Robertson.

2. *Threat behaviour*

Birds threaten or Menace rivals and neighbours (Fig. 139). So far as may be judged, low intensity threat is identical with that in the Atlantic gannet, but high intensity may differ from it by lacking the twist and withdrawal component and by making more use of an apparently balancing movement, the wing tips and tail flicking up behind the head more than in the Atlantic gannet. Robertson suggests that the tail flick is in fact not balancing, but a ritualised

Fig. 139

High intensity threat from a site owner (right) and fear response from a potential intruder. *Photo:* J. Warham.

Fig. 140

Bowing; apparently occurs at lower intensity than in the Atlantic gannet. *Photo:* J. Warham.

display of the black and white tail, which is presented to the rival, very conspicuously, between the white wings. He rates the incidence of threat as 'extremely high' and Warham as 'frequent'. Obviously, it spaces out, as in the other gannets. Sometimes it results in actual gripping, often prolonged and is followed by the Pelican Posture (ambivalent aggression/fear).

3. *Bowing*

Warham called this the 'curtsey' and there seems no significant difference between Australasian and Atlantic gannets in its form (Fig. 140). The extent and number of the 'dips' are similar, also wing position, the tendency to dip slightly left of centre rather than right, the accompanying call and the termination of the Bow with the Pelican Posture. It was the most frequent display and was particularly common among males with a site but no egg or chick, exactly as in the Atlantic gannet. The motivational context was identical and the function (site ownership) obviously the same. Males Bow with greater frequency and intensity than females.

4. *Attendance at nest site*

Males return first and spend some time at the site before breeding. Their actual attendance periods have not been specified but it seems clear that the procedure described for the Atlantic gannet occurs here, too (protracted attendance the year before breeding; flight circuiting; lengthy periods of site guarding with a high frequency of Bowing and threat behaviour). The main period of nest relief is 15.00–17.00 hours and display is most frequent at this time. Incidentally, gannets at the Bass and to a lesser extent at Ailsa, very frequently use 'standing waves' generated by wind flowing over the island and hitting the sea on the lee side, in which to circle and gain height. Australasian birds apparently do not do this.

FORMATION AND MAINTENANCE OF PAIR

The general sequence of activities leading to pair formation is apparently identical to that of the Atlantic gannet. Young birds (three, four or perhaps five years old) attend the colony for a season or more before breeding. Males with sites advertise to females, who in many cases actively prospect for receptive males. The male advertising display (Headshake and Reach p. 176) is typically followed by the approach of the female and the usual sequence of events which initiate and then consolidate the pair bond. The headshaking of the advertising male may be matched by similar head flagging movements from the female as she leans towards and then moves (often in the Sky-pointing posture) to the male. Such females are not usually bitten on the nape (presented by a Facing-away movement) as are Atlantic gannets. Presumably, the difference stems from the latter's greater aggressiveness evolved in connection with site competition, but manifesting itself, also, in pair relations. Subsequently the pair perform the meeting ceremony (Mutual Fencing) and probably, though this is nowhere stated, the male of such a newly formed pair soon begins to leave his site and mate, fly round and return, thus conditioning her to remain, increasing her attachment to the site and strengthening the pair bond. The nuances at this stage in pair relations are fully discussed on p. 179.

1. *Nape-biting*

Interestingly, Warham hardly mentions this behaviour, which is so striking in the Atlantic gannet when the pair meet on the site and one must conclude that male Australasian gannets are considerable less prone to bite their mates. Robertson (pers. comm.) informs me that in fact they do so on less than 10 per cent of occasions on which males fly in to join females on the site. Male Cape gannets bite on more than 90 per cent of such occasions and Atlantic gannets on 98 per cent; females do not bite males. Warham notes it particularly in pairs that had lost or had not laid their egg. This is exactly what one would predict from a knowledge of the Atlantic gannet, in which male aggression tends to be higher in new pairs and in pairs prior to egg laying.

2. *Mutual Fencing*

Again, from Warham's account, the meeting ceremony (Fig. 141) is identical with that of the Atlantic gannet in form, context and vocalisation but its duration is shorter. He says 'it may continue for a minute or more, but is usually shorter especially towards the end of the season' On the other hand, Robertson claims that 'early in the breeding season . . . the display may continue, interspersed with Mutual Preening, for up to 15 or 20 minutes'. Wodzicki & McMeekan (1947) give 10–12 seconds. From this it is difficult to judge the typical length of a Mutual Fencing bout at different stages in the cycle, but from Warham's statement it seems clear that it is characteristically shorter than that of the Atlantic gannet. It is probably also less intense (in amplitude and speed of components). It follows a similar seasonal pattern, becoming shorter during chick care. Presumably it lengthens again towards the end of the season. Certainly it continues throughout the season.

3. *Mutual Preening (reciprocal allo-preening)*

This typically follows a bout of Mutual Fencing and as with Mutual Fencing bouts may be shorter than in the Atlantic gannet. Warham gives 'from a few seconds to as long as a minute', a length which is often greatly exceeded by the northern bird. If this straw in the wind is also real, it is consistent with the relative lack of nape-biting and shorter Mutual Fencing, in indicating less aggression in the pair context.

4. *Copulation*

This is preceded by violent soliciting headshaking from the female and accompanied by nape-biting from the male. Wing waving, foot pattering at gathering speed and a final immobile stage occurs as in the Atlantic gannet.

5. *Nest building*

Australasian gannets build substantial nests. The male (principally) gathers seaweed, grasses and other material and flies or walks back with it. Pilfering is common and birds with nest material must guard it constantly. Several trips may be made in quick succession and, before egg laying, may be interspersed with copulation. One nest taken apart by Stein contained 542 items, 376 of them from the three commonest species of seaweed (*Carpophyllum*). Nest-building movements are like those described for the Atlantic gannet and nest digging occurs. As in the Atlantic gannet, the large nest is undoubtedly important in protecting large young during heavy rain.

Fig. 142

Mutual preening. *Photo:* J. Warham.

Fig. 141. Mutual Fencing; apparently typically occurs at lower intensity than in the Atlantic gannet. *Photo:* C. J. R. Robertson.

Even so, they may become bedraggled. At Cape Kidnappers Wodzicki & Robertson reported considerable mortality among chicks as a result of persistently cold and wet weather. Without a nest drum few chicks of the critical size (too large for brooding, yet not feathered) could survive in the quagmire which results. The Cape gannet, by contrast, manages perfectly well with no nest material except guano because its nesting environment is dry.

6. *Sky-pointing*

Warham called this the 'flying up ceremony' (Fig. 143). He noted its connection with departure from a nest or site and return to it by a male on foot, and described it thus: 'the bird first pivots around, deliberately marking time with its feet. Then, with the neck up stretched and head erect, it peers at the ground before bringing both eyes to bear binocularly from under the bill. The head is slowly moved up and down through a shallow arc during this inspection and the folded wings are raised somewhat from the back. Eventually the bird faces the direction least crowded with other birds, still staring and tilting its head. After further deliberation the gannet suddenly shakes out its wings and bounds upwards, not necessarily into the wind, alighting one or two yards away. The statuesque posture is maintained for a short time after alighting. As the bird leaps up it emits a wheezing note and on calm days the alighting birds may be heard to inhale like (a pair of) bellows as they touch down. This ceremony does not precede flight out to sea but only seems to carry the departing bird clear of its neighbours.' Robertson's description concurs. Neither say whether the feet are drooped during the pivoting with foot raising, but the whole procedure is so like that of the Atlantic gannet that they probably are. There is no reason to believe that it has a different function from that suggested for the Atlantic gannet (p. 193), namely that of co-ordinating change-over at the nest, through which it has become 'frozen' into the premovement situation where this involves the nest, and no evidence that it has an appeasing function (however see p. 260). The only hint of a difference is the suggestion that the Australasian bird uses rather more emphatic wing movement when bounding clear of the site; the Cape bird (p. 259) has taken this much further (see Fig. 124).

Before change-over, the pair Mutual Fence, may preen each other and then Sky-point. Often both birds do so, but the one which is to leave postures most while the other ceases to do so.

Actual take-off under windless conditions is preceded by an accelerating series of hops, as in the Cape gannet but never in the Atlantic.

Fig. 143

Sky-pointing; apparently does not show the high wing lifting of the Cape gannet. *Photo:* J. Warham.

OTHER BEHAVIOUR INVOLVED IN BREEDING

Whilst details comparable to those given for the Atlantic gannet with respect to other aspects of breeding behaviour are not available, the following general statements are basically correct. Incubation is shared about equally (possibly males take slightly longer stints) and uses the same behaviour patterns. The ability to retrieve eggs is very limited; there is no systematic disposal of egg shells. New young are transferred to the top of the webs from the incubating position and attendance spells shorten around the time that the eggs hatch and thus visits with food become more frequent. There are no special features to the care of the young.

1. *Aspects of parent/young relationship*

Warham's account indicates some differences in the parent/young relationships of the Atlantic and Australasian gannets, from which one may possibly infer that the adults of the latter are less aggressive. First, young Australasian gannets seem more prone to attack their parents. Whilst it is difficult to assess the degree of this difference, since Atlantic gannet chicks can also be boisterous, the protracted vigour of the Australasian chicks' attacks, jabbing at bill and nape, seems greater. Also, during food begging, feathered chicks often poke their parent, sometimes so persistently that it leaves the nest. Young Atlantic gannets do not behave in this way. Second, young Australasians may visit neighbouring nests even when the owner is there, and usually the adult shows no hostility to the visitor. This tendency to wander, evinced as early as six weeks, becomes marked in the late stages of growth, providing an important contrast with the case in the Atlantic gannet but resembling that in the Cape. Third, Cat Island adults tended to leave their large young unattended—an event which, because of the danger of unattended young being attacked by adults is rare in Atlantic gannets but normal in Cape gannets. These are mere straws in the wind, but are consistent with others already mentioned which support the suggestion made above. They are consistent also with the lighter coloured plumage of the young Australasian gannet (see p. 267).

BEHAVIOUR OF YOUNG

Young Australasian gannets show appeasement bill hiding (Fig. 144) as extreme as anything seen in the Atlantic gannet. It is apparently about as partially effective in reducing attack from adults but has no such effect on other young birds. Chicks strongly resist intrusion by other young birds. At the age of about 40 days by the time wandering starts, the chicks have a good

Fig. 144

Bill-hiding (appeasement) in a young Australasian gannet when attacked by an intruder (or possibly, though unlikely, by the parent). *Photo:* J. Warham.

visual 'fix' of the area around the nest and (if allowed by adults) can return through intervening nests from a distance of several metres. Thus doubling up will rarely occur, even if some adults would accept strange young.

1. *Fledging*

Before actually leaving the colony, fully feathered young wander (at least where they are not massively hemmed in) visiting, sparring with and even preening other young, wing exercising and taking short leaps and flights into the air when the wind is brisk and returning to their nests towards nightfall or when their parents alight there. There is no information about the proportion of young from a large colony that manage such practice (Robertson says most birds do *not* make practice flights) but many do so and Wodzicki & Robertson say that at about eight to nine weeks the chick moves from the nesting mound and with the acquisition of juvenile plumage wanders throughout the gannetry and exercises its wings. Later still it goes to the cliff edge and engages in frequent wing flapping and short wind borne flights. As in the Cape bird, which behaves similarly, an important new factor is introduced into the whole equation of fledging when compared with their northern counterparts. Thus, firstly, they gain flight practice and may be capable of prolonged flight and of rising from the surface of the sea and secondly, they may lose considerable weight before fledging, thus significantly altering the balance of selective forces acting on fledglings (see p. 217). Of the four departures seen by Warham, three chicks flew away from the island (two north and one south), two of them climbing and going well. One was watched flying for 13 minutes before it disappeared into the haze. The fourth bird swam away and seemed too heavy to rise (it was a calm day) although it flapped. Of five other departures from Cat Island four were by flight and one by swimming. These records thus confirm the suggestion that the Australasian gannet's mode of fledging differs from that of the Atlantic gannet. Wodzicki & Stein (1958) say that fully fledged chicks 'suddenly take flight. Most . . . continue to fly in a straight line until they are out of sight, . . . Other birds fly a mile or less, and after "crash-landing" in the water, they continue to proceed in the same direction by paddling.' Elsewhere, Wodzicki & Robertson (1953) say that all the fledglings they saw 'dived over the cliff into the air and . . . flew to the north-east as long as they could be kept in sight with binoculars'. At Cape Island the direction of the initial flight was north-east, between north-west and north-north-west at Horuhoru and to the north-east, at Montara. Nevertheless, it seems to be generally assumed that young Australasian gannets are, for an undetermined period after their first flight, incapable of rising from the surface. Stein writes 'on the 108–110th day, they flew off to the north-west, continued flying for upwards of a mile and finally crash landed on the sea. Although they were unable to take off again they flapped along and paddled in the original direction until they disappeared.' At present one can merely suggest that the Australasian gannet seems far less wedded to the strategy of producing fat-laden, non-flying young than does the Atlantic gannet; the same undoubtedly applies also to the Cape gannet. Actual fledging may be delayed in places such as Cat Island, where tussocks form a barrier to departing chicks, which must walk and scramble downhill before reaching the sea. Weather seems relatively unimportant.

MAINTENANCE BEHAVIOUR

Sideways headshaking, Rotary Headshaking, preening, oiling, scratching, stretching, gular fluttering, yawning, bathing and regurgitating fish bones, seem identical with these behaviour patterns in the Cape and Atlantic gannets. Robertson gives an account of Rotary Headshaking which in form and association with moult agrees closely with my own. Warham timed preening and found that birds with chicks spent about half their time on the nest preening themselves. Oddly, some birds, both young and adult, defaecated onto their own feet. I suggest that this behaviour may help to regulate body temperature by evaporative cooling (see p. 263). They also expose webs to radiate heat (Fig. 134 (d)). Hot sun is much more of a problem for Australasian, and even more for Cape, gannets than for Atlantic gannets, which do not deliberately behave in this way. Adults were never seen sunbathing, though they loosen their wings to help dissipate heat and extreme wing loosening in fact resembles the sunbathing posture. An interesting observation on the heat-regulating properties of the juvenile's black plumage, compared with the adult's white, is made by Probine & Wodzicki (1955). They placed a copper shell inside a gannet skin, heated it and measured the energy necessary to keep the skin at life temperature. They had to provide more energy (heat) to keep the young gannet's skin at the right temperature than the adults. The youngster's black feathers thus provided poorer insulation than the adult's white ones (the actual differences were: adult 0·12 cal./sec./°C; young 0·15 cal./sec./°C).

FISHING BEHAVIOUR

There are no detailed observations on the height and duration of plunges, but these are probably similar to those of other gannets (p. 225) and 10–15m has been quoted (Wodzicki & Robertson 1955). From attendance spells Warham calculated that during incubation, off-duty birds would be able to range up to 752km from their nests and whilst caring for chicks up to 360km, but this of course need not imply that distance offshore. During stormy weather they fed close to Cat Island, sometimes harrying surface shoals in company with gulls, pelicans and crested terns. They fish in small groups, often of two to six birds, but at least 500 have been seen diving together and no doubt, like the other two gannets, even bigger concentrations will occur. Sometimes, when following a shoal, the birds on the front edge of the group dive continually whilst behind them, previous divers emerge to the surface, rest on the water or take off to fly forwards and rejoin the diving birds. It probably has a wide range of subtly different techniques (see Atlantic gannet p. 227) but obviously cannot penetrate as deeply as the heavier bird.

This completes the behaviour account. A summary of the differences between the three species, in terms of the form, context, motivation, function, frequency and ecological correlates of the behaviour patterns is given in Table 43.

THE THREE GANNETS COMPARED

The specially close relationship between the three gannets gives point to a separate summary and interpretation of the differences which do occur, rather than submerging these in the general comparative account.

1. *Taxonomy*

Historically, the gannets have been included together with the boobies in the genus *Sula* after Brisson (1760), but Leach (1816) chose *Moris* (= *Morus*) to distinguish the gannets from the boobies (*Sula*). Since then, both names have been in common use, and even (e.g. Broekhuysen & Rudebeck 1951) the terms *Morus capensis* and *Sula bassana* have appeared on the same page without comment. The anatomical grounds for distinguishing two genera (see p. 812) seem inadequate. There is as much variation in wing length (and the lengths of the humerus and radius/ulna relative to each other) within the boobies as there is between boobies and gannets, whilst the bicarotid or monocarotid condition is of dubious taxonomic importance. Sibley's (1972) studies on the structure of egg white proteins indicate close similarity between gannets and boobies. In general, including ecological and behavioural features, there is probably as much difference between some of the boobies as between any booby and the gannets, which suggests that if one puts gannets in a separate genus, one should also split the boobies into at least two and possibly three genera (removing *abbotti*, at least from the genus *Sula*). This seems undesirable; it seems better to use one genus (*Sula*) for all the sulids. On the other hand, one can easily see why the boobies appear to belong together and separate from the gannets and the fossil evidence indicates an early divergence of some magnitude between booby and gannet 'types' (p. 810). The main reason for choosing one or other system is for future consistency.

The three gannets have in the past been treated as conspecific in the genus *Sula* (Winterbottom 1969), conspecific as *Morus* (Palmer 1962) or given specific status in *Sula* (Witherby *et al.* 1940) or *Morus*. Whilst there can be no hard and fast rule determining whether they are races, allo-species, or full species, they seem best accommodated as allo-species of one superspecies (sensu Amadon 1966b). This is because there are substantial differences, particularly between the Atlantic gannet and the other two, but also very close resemblances. Sub-specific status seems totally inadequate but the special nature of their relationship seems best expressed by grouping within one superspecies (*Sula* [*bassana*] *bassana*: *S.* [*b*] *capensis*: *S.* [*b*] *serrator*).

2. *Morphology*

The main differences are that the Cape and Australasian gannets have retained dark secondaries and tail feathers whereas the adult Atlantic gannet loses these; that the Cape has increased the size of the bare throat skin and that the Atlantic has become unusually heavy. The evolutionary and functional significance of the dark tail and secondaries is obscure. Possibly it implies that the Atlantic has moved furthest from the ancestral gannet stock (see Fig. 359). Perhaps the dark tail is more resistant to abrasion in the flat habitats used by the Cape and Australasian birds. The strikingly pale underparts of the Australasian juvenile are also noteworthy. The possible thermo-regulatory role of the throat skin and the significance of weight are discussed on pp. 232 and 915. Table 39 shows that weight and to a lesser extent bill length vary more between the three species than does wing length. Presumably this reflects the fact that all forage widely (and so find long wings useful) but take different sizes of prey (hence different weights and bill sizes.)

The very close resemblance between Cape and Australasian gannets, which in some cases are indistinguishable but for the darker iris and shorter throat skin of the Australasian, possibly implies relatively recent divergence, for the two habitats are far from identical. It seems more likely that the ancestral gannet arose in the general area of the (now) south-west Pacific and spread west and north to give the other two gannets, than that it spread north and east from an origin in the (now) south Atlantic.

3. *Numbers and distribution*

Compared with other sulids the gannets, especially the Cape and Australasian have relatively restricted distribution and low numbers. The latitudinal ranges of the three species are: Atlantic (14°), Cape (8°) and Australasian (14° but effectively merely 4°; see p. 270). In terms of numbers, they compare as shown in Table 40.

TABLE 39

RELATIONSHIP BETWEEN THE THREE GANNETS IN CULMEN, WING-LENGTH AND WEIGHT. THE ATLANTIC GANNET'S MEASUREMENTS ARE TAKEN AS 100 PER CENT

Allospecies	Culmen (mm)	Wing (mm)	Weight (g)
Atlantic gannet	100 (100%)	510 (100%)	3110 (100%)
Cape gannet	92 (92%)	479 (94%)	2643 (85%)
Australasian gannet	89 (89%)	463 (91%)	2350 (75%)

TABLE 40

SOME CHARACTERISTICS OF THE WORLD POPULATIONS OF ATLANTIC, CAPE AND AUSTRALASIAN GANNETS

Allospecies	No. of colonies	No. of pairs*	Colony size max.	Colony size min.	Colony size mean†
Atlantic gannet	34	197 000	59 000	<10	5000
Cape gannet	6	150 000	100 000	6000	28 000
Australasian gannet	28	36 000	5000	<10	1000

* Not equally up-to-date for all species.
† These figures are merely orders of magnitude.

Crude though these figures are, they do reflect significant differences; Cape gannet colonies are few but large, Australasian gannetries much smaller and Atlantic colonies in-between. The greater number of Atlantic colonies compared with Cape gannetries probably reflects the abundance of suitable nesting islands and the Cape gannet's situation is simply forced on it.

At present Atlantic gannets are increasing more rapidly than the other two (in fact the Cape is probably decreasing). Superficially it appears that the difference is due to less disturbance of the Atlantic population but an advantageous change in the distribution or availability of food fish, lacking a counterpart in the Cape and Australasian gannets, cannot be ruled out. The lower breeding success of the Australasian gannet, due to climatic factors, combined with a mortality rate (adult and pre-breeding) similar to that of the Atlantic gannet, would also give the population a slower growth rate.

4. *Ecology*

The principal differences concern habitat (the Atlantic gannet prefers cliffs, the Cape flat ground and the Australasian somewhat inbetween but mainly flat) nesting density (the Cape has much the highest maximum density but is also more variable in this; the Atlantic is the most stereotyped), timing of breeding (the Atlantic gannet has much the most consistent mean laying date each year) the growth of young (the Atlantic grows fastest) and age of maturity and first breeding.

Habitat differences need little comment except, perhaps, that the flat ground preferences of the Cape and Australasian gannets could strengthen the case for interpreting the Atlantic gannet's cliff nesting adaptations as derived rather than original (see p. 79).

The suggestion (p. 82) that *uniformly* high nesting density correlates with the use of social

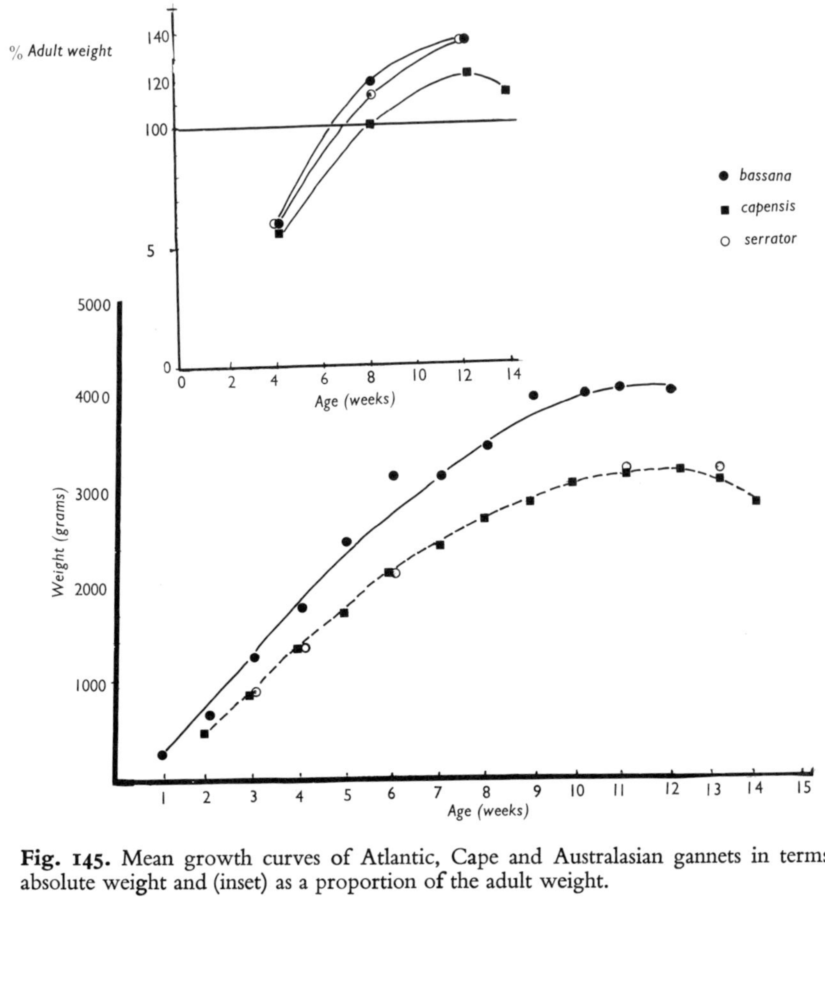

Fig. 145. Mean growth curves of Atlantic, Cape and Australasian gannets in terms of absolute weight and (inset) as a proportion of the adult weight.

stimulation as a mechanism helping to time breeding adaptively seems plausible. There is increasing evidence (p. 104) that the very precise mean laying date of the Atlantic gannet is adaptive in that late layers produce chicks which grow (and probably survive) less well. By contrast, the mean laying dates of the Cape and Australasian are *far* less consistent from year to year. This difference cannot yet be convincingly correlated with definable differences in climate acting on food and/or conditions at the colony, or with a different type or balance of post-fledging selection pressures in the three forms, but there seem in principle likely to be such connections. At any rate, variability in nesting density is likely to affect the timing of laying; variable density is positively correlated with variable mean laying date in the Cape and Atlantic birds.

The slower growth of young Cape and Australasian gannets (Fig. 145 and Table 41) is consistent with their larger egg weight and habit of leaving their young unguarded and relative inability to rear artificially contrived twins, in indicating less easily available food than that of the Atlantic gannet. Nevertheless breeding success is probably equally high in the Cape and Atlantic and there is uniformly high mortality in the first year of life in all three. At least at Horuhoru, Australasian gannets have a notably lower breeding success than the other two species, but it is not yet clear that this is an important characteristic of the Australasian gannet as a whole. One must bracket all three gannets as the fastest growers in the family (possibly excepting the Peruvian) which only serves to emphasise the unique position of the Atlantic gannet.

There is some difference of opinion as to when Australasian gannets lay for the first time but it seems to be usually in their sixth or seventh year (p. 292). It is in any case significantly later than in the Cape gannet (third or perhaps fourth year) and may be later than the Atlantic, which usually lays in its fifth or sixth year. One may speculate that the Cape birds need less time, certainly than the Atlantic, to acquire local fishing lore (p. 128) since the Benguela is on their doorstep. The Cape gannet, at least, resembles the boobies in the relative shortness of its deferred maturity. In fact, of all three, the Cape seems to show the most points of similarity to the ground nesting boobies.

5. *Behaviour*

I think the most heuristically useful differences are undoubtedly those concerned with territorial behaviour and (associated) pair interactions. It would be totally misleading to depict the Cape and Australasian gannets as other than fiercely territorial (more so than any of the boobies except perhaps, the piquero). Yet the salient point is that even *they* show measurably less aggression in the contexts of site defence, pair interactions and behaviour towards young, than does the Atlantic; this competition for a socially adequate site, in which context aggression is particularly adaptive in the Atlantic gannet, has already been laboured more than enough. It is, however, interesting that the Cape is apparently more aggressive than the Australasian, for this is at least consistent with its obvious shortage of sites. If (relatively speaking) the Australasian lacks incentive on both counts (physical and social) it is not surprising that it shows less aggression (Table 42).

Some of the differences mentioned above can be speculatively drawn together in relation to certain key 'shaping factors' (Table 43).

TABLE 41

THE THREE GANNETS COMPARED FOR GROWTH AND FLEDGING PERIOD

	Age of maximum weight (days)	Maximum weight and as per cent of adult	Mean fledging period (days)
Atlantic gannet	55–65	4250 (137%)	91
Cape gannet	80	3200 (121%)	97
Australasian gannet	70–80	3250 (138%)	102

TABLE 42

COMPARISON OF BEHAVIOUR* IN THE GANNET SUPERSPECIES (FOR FULLEST ACCOUNT OF EACH BEHAVIOUR PATTERN SEE ATLANTIC GANNET BEHAVIOUR SECTION)

	Differences between the three allospecies in					
Behaviour pattern	Form	Context	Motivation	Function	Frequency	Suggested ecological correlates
Aerial and ground reconnaissance	none?	none? (territorial)	none	none	*bassana* uses aerial more	windy cliff sites
Fighting	none	none (territorial)	none (aggressive)	none (territorial)	*bassana* most	more site competition (social?)
Threat	none	none (territorial)	none (aggressive)	none (territorial)	*bassana* most	more aggressive in site competition
Bowing	slight; wing position possibly more extreme in *bassana*	none (territorial	none (aggressive)	none (territorial)	*bassana* more than *capensis* and prob. than *serrator*	greater site attachment
Pelican Posture	none	none (conflict?)	none? (aggression/ fear?)	none? (appeasement?)	?	—
Attendance at site	—	—	—	—	*bassana* most	more site competition and attachment
Headshake-and-reach	none	none (sexual)	none (sexual)	none (to attract male or female)	?	—
Female prospecting	none	none	none (sexual)	none (to locate potential partner)	?	—
Nape-biting	none	none (reunion on territory)	none (aggression/ sex)?	none?	*bassana* most *serrator* least	more aggression in *bassana*
Mutual Fencing	none except amplitude	none (reunion on territory)	none (aggression/ sex)	none (appeasement and pair-bonding)	*bassana* longest	pair bond more important in site maintenance
Mutual Preening	none	none (following meeting or sexual activity)	none (aggression/ sex?)	none (appeasement and pair-bonding?)	?	—

	Differences between the three allospecies in					
Behaviour pattern	Form	Context	Motivation	Function	Frequency	Suggested ecologieal correlates
Copulation	none	none (sexual)	none (sexual)	none (fertilisation and pair-bonding)	*bassana* possibly longer	?
Sky-pointing	similar but wing movement most in *capensis*; least in *bassana*	mainly pre-movement; male *capensis* uses it before copulation; *bassana* does not; position in *serrator* not clear	probably none	possibly appeasing function in *capensis*	*capensis* most; *bassana* probably least; *serrator* not known	possibly most frequent and prominent in *capensis* due to greater density
Nest building, etc.	*capensis* does not fly in with nest material	none (mainly pre-laying in *capensis*)	none?	nest important in *bassana* and *serrator* in raising young above ground	?	*capensis* in dry habitat uses guano and smaller nest
Nest digging	none	none (presence of egg and small young)	none	none? (removes hard or sharp lumps)	?	—
Incubation	none	none	none	none	none	none
Egg retrieval	none	none	none	none	none?	?
Treatment of eggshell	none	none	none	none	none	none
Transference of young to top of webs	none	none (immediate post-hatching)	none	none (to brood young without putting too much pressure on them)	none	none
Change of attendance rhythm	—	none (pre-hatching period)	none	none (shorter foraging trips)	—	—
Feeding young	none	none	none	none	possibly *bassana* most	more abundant food; faster growth
Parent/young recognition and adult aggression to young	—	—	—	*bassana* more likely to attack intruding young; consequently young do not leave nest	—	*bassana* more aggressive; different fledging technique in *capensis* and *serrator* q.v.

	Differences between the three allospecies in					
Behaviour pattern	Form	Context	Motivation	Function	Frequency	Suggested ecological correlates
Behaviour of young	all actual behaviour patterns are the same	—	—	more wandering and wing exercising in *capensis* and *serrator*. Also less restrained (beg more strongly, attack adults, etc.) and less aggressive to each other	—	Different fledging technique (correlated with different feeding situation) young *capensis* and *serrator* fly away; young *bassana* swim away
Post-fledging behaviour	*bassana* swim more; *capensis* and *serrator* fly more initially	none	none	none; all go to seas where presumably inexperienced birds find a more available prey spectrum	—	—
Stance and movement	*capensis* and *serrator*, 'hop take off' *bassana* does not	?	?	—	—	flat habitat in *capensis* and *serrator*, cliffs in *bassana*
Preening and associated behaviour	none	none	none	none	none	none
Headshaking and wing flapping	none	possible differences in situations eliciting Rotary Headshake in *capensis* and *bassana*. Not ritualised in *serrator*	?	?	?	?
Heat regulation (gular fluttering; wing-drooping; eye-lid exposure, etc.)	excreting on feet noted only for *serrator* and (mainly) *capensis*	none	none	none	?	greater heat on *capensis* web. Bigger throat strip; probably stronger tendency to use all heat-losing mechanisms

* The headings are not always perfectly applicable but the sense is clear. Similarly, the items listed under Behaviour Pattern are not all strictly equivalent as categories (some are discrete behaviour patterns, others are not) but the comparison between the three species remains valid.

TABLE 43

ATLANTIC AND CAPE GANNETS COMPARED FOR THE EFFECTS OF CERTAIN ENVIRONMENTAL FACTORS ON BEHAVIOUR AND ECOLOGY

ATLANTIC GANNET		
large shoaling fish irregularly found	→	extensive foraging, deep penetration, powerful bill, resistance to starvation, high growth rate, etc.
cold climate	→	fat advantageous (penetration, resistance to starvation) heat loss no problem
cliff-girt islands	→	permits heaviness and high aspect ratio wings
seasonal environment, predictable autumnal deterioration	→	selectively encourages optimally timed breeding; uses social facilitation, which favours evolution of aggression; largeness favoured
CAPE GANNET (AND PERHAPS TO A LESSER EXTENT, AUSTRALASIAN)		
smaller prey items	→	smaller size and weight, slower growth
warmer climate	→	less fat, more bare skin
fewer (and flatter) islands	→	greater density, larger colonies (does not apply to Australasian); lightness aids take off
autumnal deterioration less predictable and marked	→	breeding more seasonally variable; less social competition; less aggression

4

Sula dactylatra

WHITE, MASKED, OR BLUE-FACED BOOBY

1. NOMENCLATURE; EXTERNAL FEATURES; MORPHOLOGY; MOULT AND VOICE

NOMENCLATURE

1. *Common*

White booby; masked booby; blue-faced booby; whistling booby; lark; piquero blanco; boba de cara azul.

Fou generau (Seychelles); Burong gangsa (Malaya); Mouakena (Gilbert Islands); Lellap (Marshall Islands). This booby is the only member of the family in which three vernacular names have been widely used. Unfortunately, I used 'white booby' in my earlier work and, by habit, in this book also. I now consider that, because this name is confusable with the adjective used as a non-specific term (where it would be applicable to a white morph red-footed booby), is the least distinctive of the three, has the worst pedigree and is least used, it would have been better to have used the name masked booby. The decision came too late to be implemented in the book.

2. *Scientific*

Sula dactylatra Leson 1831, Traite d'orn livr. 8, p. 601 (Ascension Island).

Sula personata, Gould, Proc. Zool. Soc. London, 1846, p. 21 (Raine Island).

Sula cyanops, Finsch, Ibis 1880, p. 219 (Taluit).

Binomial synonyms have included:

Sula cyanops, S. elegans, S. melanops, S. nigrodactyla, S. personata, S. bassana, Parasula dactylatra, P. dactylatra, Dysporus cyanops, Pelecanus piscator, P. bassanus.

Wood-Jones (1912) mistakenly called *Sula dactylatra* on Cocos-Keeling *Sula abbotti*, thus leading to some subsequent confusion. Rothschild & Hartert (1899), Snodgrass & Heller (1904), Gifford (1913) and Fisher & Wetmore (1931) all erroneously recorded as *S. variegata* what was in fact the Galapagos form of *S. dactylatra*. Rothschild & Wetmore later corrected this mistake (Murphy 1936).

The trinomial nomenclature distinguishes the following races:

Sula dactylatra dactylatra Lesson
of the Caribbean and Atlantic is certainly distinct, being decidedly smaller (see Table 44) than the Pacific races and apparently alone possessing (in males in early breeding condition) bright orange legs.

Sula dactylatra personata Gould
of the vast central Pacific area, extending an undetermined distance to the west.

Sula dactylatra melanops Heughlin
of the west Indian Ocean.

Sula dactylatra bedouti Mathews
from Cocos-Keeling, the Banda Sea and north-west Australia.

Sula dactylatra granti Rothschild
of the Galapagos and possibly other eastern tropical Pacific islands.

Sula dactylatra californica Rothschild
off western Mexico.

The four latter are probably not all valid. *Bedouti* and *personata* are said to differ (Mathews 1913)[1] by the former having a smaller bill and blue feet but no measurements are given and the colour of so-called soft parts was certainly not critically assessed. Mathews was a notorious splitter and earned strict censure on account of his 'pretty nonsense' with respect to *Sula leucogaster* (Gibson-Hill 1950a). Similarly, Murphy (1936, p. 848) concluded so far as eastern Pacific 'races' were concerned, that Rothschild's use of soft-part colours to separate *S. d. granti* and *californica* was unjustified and that sub-specific division within the eastern Pacific had not been adequately proven. He decided that white boobies from the Revillagigedos, Galapagos, Ecuador, northern Peru and Chile are all the same and should be called *S. d. granti*.

At the present time there seems no real justification for accepting more than *S. d. granti* and *S. d. personata* for the whole of the Pacific and it is possible that even these two may not be usefully separable.

If, indeed, *personata* were to swallow up *granti* and *bedouti* this would then leave merely three well defined races: *dactylatra* of the Caribbean and Atlantic; *melanops* of the western Indian Ocean and *personata* of the eastern Indian Ocean and Pacific. This may well be too extreme, but the eventual separation of more races should take account of sexual and seasonal variation in soft parts and must not rely on the interpretation of these colours from dried skins. For the moment, *dactylatra*, *granti*, *personata* and *melanops* are probably acceptable with a query against *granti*. For the differences in colour and size, see p. 321 and Table 44.

GENERAL FEATURES

1. *Adult*

The white, masked or blue-faced booby is the largest and most robust booby, with less difference in size between the sexes than in any booby except Abbott's. It is about 76–84 cm long with a wing spread of about 160–170 cm (over five feet). Notable features are the dazzling white plumage and the black primaries, distal half of the secondaries, humerals and tail. It thus appears brilliantly all white, with black trailing half of the wing and black tail. The only possible confusion, at a distance too great to see the colour of bill and feet, would be with the white morph of the red-footed booby or the Cape and Australasian gannets. It differs from the red-foot in its black tail (the red-foot's is usually white[2]) and in the way the black secondaries run right up to the body, whereas in the red-foot there is usually more white showing between the proximal part of the wing and the side of the body. The Australasian gannet has a yellowish, not pure white head and there is some white on the outer edge of the tail. The Cape gannet usually has an all black tail and (like the Australasian) dark primaries, secondaries and primary coverts, thus bearing an even closer resemblance to the white booby. Its

[1] Austr. Av. Rec. i, 1913, p. 189. Bedout Island, N.W. Australia.

[2] Morphs vary in this respect (see p. 662).

Fig. 146(a). Underwing and tail pattern. Note conspicuous mask.

head, however, is deepish yellow and it lacks the black humerals. Also, the white booby's dark facial skin 'mask' gives it a characteristic 'look' which can be recognised at a fair distance.

There is regional variation in the colour of the bill and feet; usually the bill is deepish orange or more pinkish and the feet a darkish grey with a hint of green (olive-drab). The iris is piercing yellow.

The flight is powerful and steady, usually fairly high above the water (7 metres or more) rather than shearing it as the red-foot often does, and can achieve more than 70km per hour. It is said to be attracted to ships but to depart after circling once or twice. It is usually seen singly or in pairs and may be encountered far out to sea, being the most pelagic booby, with the possible exception of the red-foot. When swimming, it floats high on the water.

2. *Juvenile and immature*

The juvenile can cause considerable trouble and has been responsible for mistaken records of brown and Peruvian boobies in Galapagos waters and has been confused with juvenile Atlantic gannets (see Fig. 4) off West Africa.

The juvenile is predominantly brown above and whitish below, the white running up onto the throat and variably onto the sides and back of the neck. At the base of the back of the neck there may be a patch of whitish feathers somewhat like that of the blue-foot. The underside of the wing is whitish, ending vaguely rather than in the clear cut manner of the brown booby.

Fig. 146(b)

Adult white booby. Note the black humerals as well as primaries and secondaries.

The bill is an indefinite lightish colour (horn or yellowish, variably tinged or suffused bluish), and the iris at first brown, becoming paler.

For the details distinguishing it from the many other sulids with which it may be confused see the Comparative Section. Here it may merely be mentioned that good distinguishing features are the pale collar, slightly barred back, irregular merging of colours on flank and untidy finish to the white bar on the under wing.

In the immature, post-juvenile, stages, the head is the first area to become white and the rump retains brown flecks longest; the back is variably mottled depending on age. Heads may be virtually white by 13 months and rumps virtually clear (at least so far as a view of a flying bird is concerned) by 20 months.

DETAILED DESCRIPTION

The races of the white booby are nothing like so distinctive as those of the brown, or as the morphs of the red-foot, depending almost entirely on differences in the colour of bill and feet. Thus there is no need for the detailed racial treatment given to these others.

1. *Adult male and female*

Pure, brilliant white all over except for the primaries and secondaries (blackish brown, with the inner webs of the primaries tending to become greyish and the secondaries white at their bases), black humerals and tail. The latter is largely (sometimes entirely) black or blackish but the centre is often conspicuously white. The base of the tail is also white. The shafts of the flight feathers bleach with age.

The underwing is white except for the parts of the primaries and secondaries not covered by the wing coverts. Thus, it has a broad black tip and a blackish trailing edge which is almost half the width of the wing where the outer secondaries begin, narrowing to about a quarter

Fig. 147(a). Plumage of juvenile (Galapagos) just after its first flight. Note the brown thigh patch, typical of most immature sulids.

(b). Plumage pattern on back, wings and tail.

(c). Underwing pattern.

or so on the proximal half of the wing. This is quite a different underwing pattern from that of the brown booby (q.v.) and since the juveniles of these two species show dull versions of the adult pattern, this helps to separate them.

The bill colour varies with region and with season. In the Atlantic, on Ascension, the bill of both sexes was straw coloured, in some cases bright straw (deepish yellow). On Los Hermanos, Lowe (1909) gives it as greenish yellow. In the west Indian Ocean, on Mait Island (Gulf of Aden) the bill was orange-yellow to yellow-green. In the Chagos Archipelago the bills of adults with young were greyish or greenish yellow (Hirons, pers. comm.). In the eastern Indian Ocean, on North Cocos, it is yellow with a hint of greenish grey at the base in the male and yellowish grey, with the base greyer in the female. In the Coral Sea it is given as bright yellow in the male and dull yellowish green in the femalc. In the Galapagos it is rosy pink in the female and more orange in the male. On Clipperton it is given as yellow with a slight red tinge. On La Plata it is bright orange-yellow at the base in males and pink or light red in females. Similarly on San Ambrosio and San Felix some had yellow bills and some pink—these were probably male and female respectively as Chapin had earlier found (he described the male's bill as ochreous lemon-yellow (dull) and the female's as dull yellow with a pink base.

The commonest colour is thus some shade of yellow, with more or less orange or pink in some areas (the pink characteristic of the female) and sometimes with greenish at the base. The variations with state of breeding condition, though undoubtedly real and potentially useful, have not been worked out for any population.

The iris is invariably yellow. Observers append slightly different qualifying adjectives ('piercing', 'yellowish grey', 'orange-yellow', 'golden yellow', 'deep yellow', etc.).

The bare skin around and on the face, which gives this booby its typical 'masked' appearance comprises the orbital ring, eyelids, facial skin running onto the beak and gular skin. It is black, more or less 'inky'. The mask does not have clear-cut edges, but seems much the same shape in birds from different areas although the extent of the black gular skin varies with individuals and possibly with season. It is certainly more intense, if not larger, early in the breeding season.

The legs and feet vary. Atlantic birds (Ascension) have 'dull orange' or in some females 'dull olive'. Some males have rich orange legs. Extreme western Pacific (Australian) birds have lead grey feet frequently with a dull purplish tinge. The eastern Pacific birds have olive or khaki legs in the male and lead coloured or olive in the female. An Indian Ocean (Chagos) bird had lead-grey feet with a hint of purple. Thus, there is more variation than in bill or eye colour, but drab olive or grey seem the basic shades more or less brightened with yellow pigment (see Comparative Section).

2. *Juvenile*

a) *Plumage*

The crown, forehead, back of the neck, sides of the neck, nape and ear coverts are mainly brown, in some cases entirely so, but in others flecked with white. The scapulars, lesser and median wing coverts are warm brown with lighter edgings to some feathers. The back and rump are brown, the former again with light edgings giving a variably, though faintly, barred appearance (the light (sometimes white) edges to mantle feathers distinguish it from the juvenile brown booby, which is plain brown). The primaries, secondaries and tail feathers are dark brown, sometimes appearing blackish. The underparts are white, the white extending in some cases round on to the bottom of the neck and in an inverted V, up on to the throat. It is this plumage which much resembles some late first year gannets. The underwing is mainly white, with a line and patch of brown, whereas the juvenile brown booby has a regular white bar on the underwing.

(b) *Bill, feet, etc.*

The bill is yellowish horn, often suffused with blue-grey in patches. The facial skin is blue or blackish, having gradually darkened from the grey-blue or light blue of the chick. The iris, dark brown in the chick, lightens to lead grey in the juvenile, though it does not become yellow until the immature bird is more than a year old (see below).

The legs and feet, greyish in the chick, remain so in the juvenile, beginning to show signs of colouring only after the first year. Caribbean juveniles have drab greenish tarsi, dirty yellowish webs.

3. *Immature*

There is no systematic account of the stages between the juvenile and adult plumages, but details given in Dorward (1962b) and scattered remarks elsewhere provide a reasonable picture.

Replacement of juvenile feathers begins at about 5½–7 months of age, so that before it is six months old (or some two months after it can fly) it may already be shedding the innermost primaries and, from seven months onwards, some body feathers also. The mechanism thus exists for appreciable changes to occur well within the first year.

The head is first to go white; by the age of nine months it is only slightly speckled with

TABLE 44

MEASUREMENTS OF THE WHITE

Area	Race	Overall length male	Overall length female	Wing male	Wing female	Tail male	Tail female
Atlantic Ocean	*dactylatra*	800–820 9	760–840 7	424 406–433 9	429 417–440 7	166 153–173 9	164·6 151–180 7
Arabian Sea	*melanops*			421 407–430 6		176 169–180 6	
Cocos Eastern Indian Ocean	*bedouti*	800 784–814 4	861 1	428 424–434 4	446 1	189 184–193 4	201 1
Kure Atoll Central Pacific	*personata*			440 427–462 27	456 435–476 27	188 170–215 27	192 173–205 27
Vostok Central Pacific	*personata*						
Eastern Pacific Galapagos (1)	*granti*			429 413–443 5	450 427–468 6	178 172–181 5	183 176–189 6
Galapagos (2)	*granti*			451 445–457 6	484 457–495 5	198 192–205 5	201 185–212 5
Ecuador and Peru	*granti*			451 439–457 3	470 465–474 2	186 180–196 3	191 188–193 2
San Felix Chile	*granti*				471 453–486 4		192 188–196 4
Immature birds Cocos	*bedouti*	773 741–802 4	802 750–836 3	412 351–452 4	440 437–444 3	177 165–184 4	169 165–177 3

brown; by 13 months the brown specks are detectable only at close range and by 14–15 months the head is pure white.

The back and wing coverts become increasingly speckled with white from about seven months onwards, until by 14 months they are only slightly flecked brown and by 17 months are almost pure white. The rump remains brown until 13 months, thereafter whitening until by 20 months, it retains but a few brown specks.

The bill turns from greyish horn to dull yellow by about 20 months; the facial skin darkens and the iris is nearly pure yellow by the age of 20 months. The legs and feet acquire a dull version of adult colour by 20 months.

The last traces of immaturity to disappear are brown flecks on the rump. Full adult plumage is reached by 32–33 months, though the male still retains the juvenile (female-type) voice. Breeding is probably first attempted at three years or later.

BOOBY FROM DIFFERENT REGIONS

Tarsus		Culmen		Weight		Source
male	female	male	female	male	female	
54 53–56 9	53·4 52–54·6 7	95·6 92·6–97·2 9	95·7 91·6–99 7			Murphy (1936)
56 51–58 6		100·7 97–104 6		1565 1480–1660 6		Bailey (1966)
51 48–53 4	53 1	100·9 97·5–104 4	102 1			Gibson-Hill (1950a)
63·6 60–67 27	65·2 60–70 27	102·7 97–107 27	105 98–109 27	1880 1503–2211 27	2095 1616–2353 27	Kepler (1969)
					1684 1373–2020 3	
55 52–58 5	57 54–59 6	102·7 102–104·4 5	106·5 102–114·5 6			Murphy (1936)
		106·8 88–113 47	109·3 105–115 36	1627 1220–1970 48	1881 1470–2350 37	Nelson (unpublished)
54 54 3	55·5 55–56 2	102 101–103 3	110 109–111 2	2155 1		Murphy (1936)
	58·7 57–61 4		104·1 100·5–108·4 4			Murphy (1936)
52·3 51–54 4	52 51–53 3	100·4 90·5–106 4	103·7 102–106 3			Gibson-Hill (1950a)

4. *Measurements and weight*

Some samples of the measurements and weights of white boobies from different regions are given in Table 44.

MOULT

1. *The pattern of moult*

The most detailed observations are Dorward's (1962b) from which the following account has been constructed (for general remarks see gannet p. 18).

Primary moult began when the juvenile was about seven months old or in some birds earlier (at 5½ months one had shed the innermost primary from each wing). Thereafter, primaries were replaced, working towards the outermost, at the rate of a little less than one per month. At about 15 months when primaries 6 and 7 were growing, the innermost were shed again and a second cycle commenced, although the first cycle of replacement did not reach the outermost until the bird was about 18 months old, when juvenile primary 10 was shed (the first generation of primaries can easily be distinguished by their abraded tips and light colour). Once the second generation of replacements began the rate appeared to slow down to about one feather in almost two months (3 feathers in 5 months was an actual case). There is every reason to suppose, however, that moult continues steadily, the wing thus containing, at one time, two or even three generations of primaries, though the first replacement generation and subsequent ones are not distinguishable.

An example of the wing of a 29-month old bird is given below, showing three generations of primaries. At this stage the bird was in adult plumage (it had been captured six months earlier and calculated to be about 23 months old). Fig. 148b shows actual moult sequences in four birds caught several times in two successive years.

The moult of body feathers began at the same time as the replacement of juvenile primaries. Tail feathers were moulted irregularly and asymmetrically. These sequences brought the young bird to adult appearance at about 30 months. Adults in the breeding colony may continue to moult primaries whilst occupying a site and possessing a mate, but it is probable that moult is suspended for a period prior to egg laying and during incubation. The rate at which moult occurred in adults apparently left enough time for such a pause in moult of perhaps two months each year. For example, an unmated bird which Dorward captured five times between August 12th, 1958 and July 15th, 1959 paused in August 1958 (or perhaps longer) and July 1959 (or perhaps longer) whilst in between it grew some primaries belonging to three different generations. In fact, since at any one time, three generations are in the process of replacement, the primary in each position (1–10) would be replaced annually. In other words, primaries are replaced in three spaced cycles, moving outwards, each cycle proceeding at the rate of about one primary in two months and a generation of primaries taking more than a year to be replaced. The pause in the moult does not depend upon the point which has been reached; the process can halt anywhere and, as mentioned, probably does so prior to egg laying. This should mean that an individual would be at about the same stage in moult at roughly the same time each year and Dorward obtained six records which substantiated this. However, if moult suspension is in fact linked with the pre-laying period (rather than the point reached in the moult) and laying varies (as it does) from year to year, probably partly in accord with environmental conditions, it is not to be expected that birds could reach exactly the same position in the moult sequence for many years in succession. Successive cycles in adults were about two or three feathers apart (e.g. eight adults checked in March 1959 were growing primaries 1 or 2, 5 or 6 and 8–10) whereas in juveniles successive cycles were more spaced, the seventh primary usually growing before the next cycle began with the shedding of primary number 1.

The pattern just described is not always followed strictly. Dorward recorded a bird which grew the same primary twice within four months, possibly due to injury. Also there is likely to be some individual variation in the rate of moult.

2. *Synchrony in moult*

Analysis of the moult records of Ascension, examined month by month, showed that there was no marked synchrony, birds apparently moulting largely without relation to each other. Thus, the wing score (showing which primaries were growing and at what stage) of, say, ten adults caught in the breeding colony on the same date, would not resemble each other significantly more than could be accounted for by chance. Examined in certain arbitrary

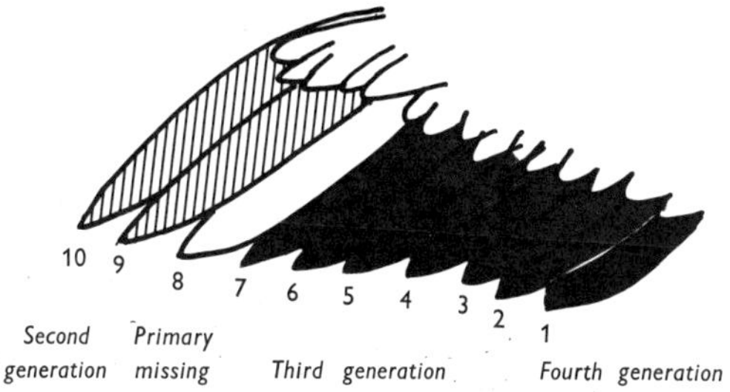

Fig. 148(a)

Wing, showing three generations of primaries in a bird calculated to be 29 months old (from data in Dorward 1962)b.

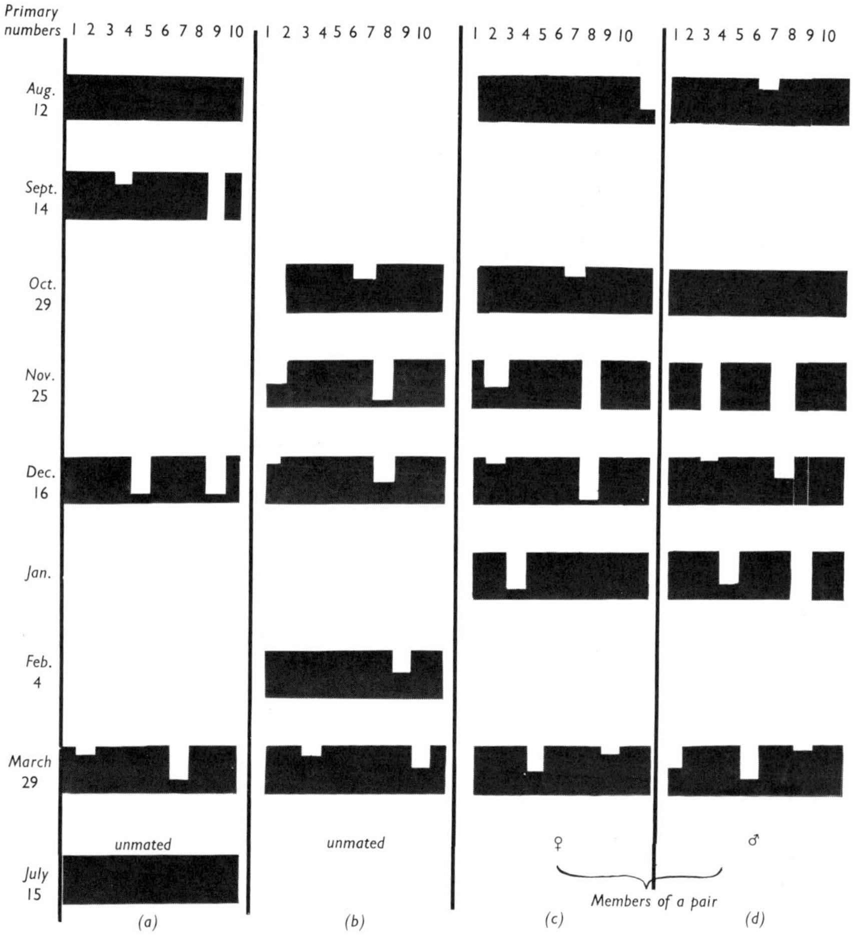

Fig. 148(b). Moult sequence in four white boobies examined five or six times in a year (from data in Dorward 1962b).

NOTE: Birds (*a*) and (*b*) were probably seeking a first mate but may have been adults whose mates had died. The mated pair, (*c*) and (*d*), were not known to lay in the period of observation, but could have done so, losing eggs soon afterwards.

KEY: Primaries numbered 1–10 (inner to outer) along top; gap means feather missing; growing feathers represented proportionately (vertically). Moult score averaged over both wings.

groupings of months, however, there was some indication that the pattern of moult was not entirely uniform from month to month and that 'not all birds were moulting in an entirely unrelated manner' (Dorward 1962b). This situation could well reflect the probability that each breeding season produces a crop of young that are roughly of an age and should subsequently tend to moult in step, this, however, being subject to gross distortion by many factors (failed breeding; individual variability; etc.) leaving a barely detectable synchrony in a moderately small sample.

3. *The pause in moult*

Dorward recorded a highly significant tendency for birds not to be moulting in August–September 1958, which was just after the main peak of laying on Ascension. In fact this was probably true, also, of the pre-laying period, but the number of birds examined was too small and the chances of including non-breeders too great, to show this. In birds caught at this time, it was difficult to distinguish between old and new primaries, which means that there had been a period of suspended moult long enough for the newest feathers to become well 'weathered'. On evidence from a bird caught six times between August and March, this no-moult period is likely to have been about two months. Many authors have suggested that the most stressful period for adults is whilst feeding young, but this may well not be so. There is good evidence (p. 116) that the pre-laying period, during which adults attend the site a great deal and are often active territorially and in courtship, is a highly demanding time. Incubation, also, is metabolically costly (long stints, high temperatures) so that suspended moult at this time, rather than later would be more adaptive than might superficially appear. Dorward, on the other hand, suggests that a pause in moult would be most advantageous if timed to coincide with the presence of young chicks when, he suggests (though erroneously), the need to obtain sufficient food would be greatest and maximum flight efficiency an advantage. In my opinion, the fact that *all* boobies moult whilst feeding large young, in their most demanding stages, means that flight efficiency is not materially impaired by moult. If so, the energy involved in feather replacement would seem to be the main factor and as suggested above, the time when extra energy is least available (excluding the non-breeding season) is the pre-laying and incubation period. On the evidence available, this is as likely to coincide with the pause as is the young-chick phase and would seem to be more adaptive.

Data from the Galapagos bears on some of the points made above. Like Ascension, it is a fairly aseasonal area in which, nevertheless, white boobies breed at approximately annual intervals. Moult data was collected from six categories of birds—pre-breeding territory owners; incubating birds; birds with relatively young chicks (0·1500g); those with larger young; failed breeders and birds without egg or chick which have failed or may not have been breeding that season. Six out of eight birds which were attending territories at the beginning of a breeding cycle had paused in moult. The two exceptions were halfway or more towards replacing primaries 6 and 10 (one bird) and 9 (the other) and both had been back on the island only a short time. Of three incubating birds examined, none were moulting. This strongly supports the suggestion that moult is suspended in the pre-laying and incubation periods. Of six birds caring for relatively small chicks, four were not moulting but two were; these had primaries 1 and 5 half grown. By contrast, of 14 birds caring for larger young, all were moulting. This shows that the suspended period often carries on into the first stages of chick rearing, and that moult recommences partway through chick growth. The failed breeders (5) were all moulting. Finally, all but one of 16 birds caught in the colony but without egg or chick and of unknown status, were moulting. The exception, a bird caught in February, could well have been in the pre-laying period.

Of the total 38 moulting birds examined, one had 4 primaries growing (1·5; 2·5; 4·1 and 10·3); three had 3 growing; 16 had 2 and 18 only 1.

Tail feathers numbered 13 (5 cases); 14 (9); 15 (15); 16 (16); 17 (5) and 18 (1) and the pattern of replacement seemed irregular.

VOICE

The white booby is a noisy bird. During the early and late parts of the breeding season it often perches on vantage points and the male shouts or whistles. The female has a loud, shouting or honking voice, variable in pitch and amplitude. Usually the syllables are short and often in descending pitch. Occasionally there is a break in the voice. During intense interactions the shouts are frenzied but they lack the pleasant sonorous quality of the blue-foot and are not deep and resonant like Abbott's. On the site she may produce short, soft, talkative notes.

The male produces a thin whistle, which sounds ludicrous coming from such a robust bird. Sometimes it is forced out with extreme vigour but succeeds only in becoming even harder and thinner. The calls are delivered singly or in small groups. The male white booby does not produce such a 'chuff chuff' whistle as the brown, and his voice is most flute-like when relaxed and during advertising. The advertising whistle descends in pitch at the end—'whee-ee-$\overline{\text{oo}}$' and lasts about two to three seconds.

The sexual dimorphism in the voice, as in the blue-foot, Peruvian and brown boobies, depends on structural differences in the syrynx.

Juveniles of both sexes possess a female-type voice, which the male retains for almost three years. This seems an inordinately long time when he has by then acquired full adult plumage and brightly coloured bill, etc. It may be a device to prevent pairing and breeding during the stage at which he appears mature, but physiologically is probably not (for a discussion of breeding in immature plumage see p. 333).

2. BREEDING DISTRIBUTION, NUMBERS AND OTHER ASPECTS OF POPULATIONS

INTRODUCTION

The white (breeding between about 25°N. and 29° 50′S.), red-footed and brown boobies are the three commonest and most widely distributed members of the Sulidae, occupying oceanic and offshore islands and islets throughout much of the pan-tropical blue water belt. Flying fish, its principal food, tend to avoid continental coastal waters. The white booby contends with the red-foot as the most oceanic of sulids, foraging far from land and avoiding inshore, estuarine or bight islands, but sometimes nesting on even the most rugged and barren of tiny, oceanic rocks. Where there are many suitable islands, as in the central Pacific, white boobies tend to form numerous, fairly small colonies and where there is a dearth of islands in a vast expanse of blue water, the colonies may be large, as on Ascension (Boatswain Bird Island) and Clipperton.

The elucidation of the present-day distribution and numbers of white, brown and red-footed boobies is a formidable task. There are hundreds or even thousands of colonies that have never been mentioned in the literature and many more for which there is no estimate of population and little or no recent information of any kind.

For all three pan-tropical boobies, I have arranged the information under the headings of oceans or ocean segments in the order: Atlantic and Caribbean; Indian Ocean; South China and neighbouring seas; Western Pacific; Central Pacific; Eastern Pacific.

Within this broad framework, island groups find their place and within these the island or island-locality concerned. I have sometimes included a few remarks on the nature of the island, particularly to provide representative material for cross-reference with the remarks on habitat, in the ecology section but space has restricted this.

Ideally, it should be possible to correlate the distribution of seabirds with that of suitable feeding zones and breeding habitat, but in an area as vast as, for example, the central Pacific, with seasonally changing boundaries to surface water zones, a detailed correlation of breeding distribution with feeding is enormously difficult to obtain.

Whilst certain groups of islands—notably the Hawaiian Islands, the Leeward chain, Johnson Atoll and some other central Pacific atolls—have been closely investigated in connection with military activities and latterly as part of the Pacific Ocean Biological Survey Programme, many enormous tracts of the world's oceans are seldom if ever visited by ornithologists. Literally thousands of island groups in the central Pacific, Polynesia, Melanesia, Micronesia and Indonesia and many islands in the western Indian Ocean, are virtually unknown so far as their seabird populations are concerned. Any account of the distribution of the three boobies concerned is thus bound to be grossly uneven, which is why some groups receive island by island treatment whilst others are dismissed with the merest of generalities. Whilst

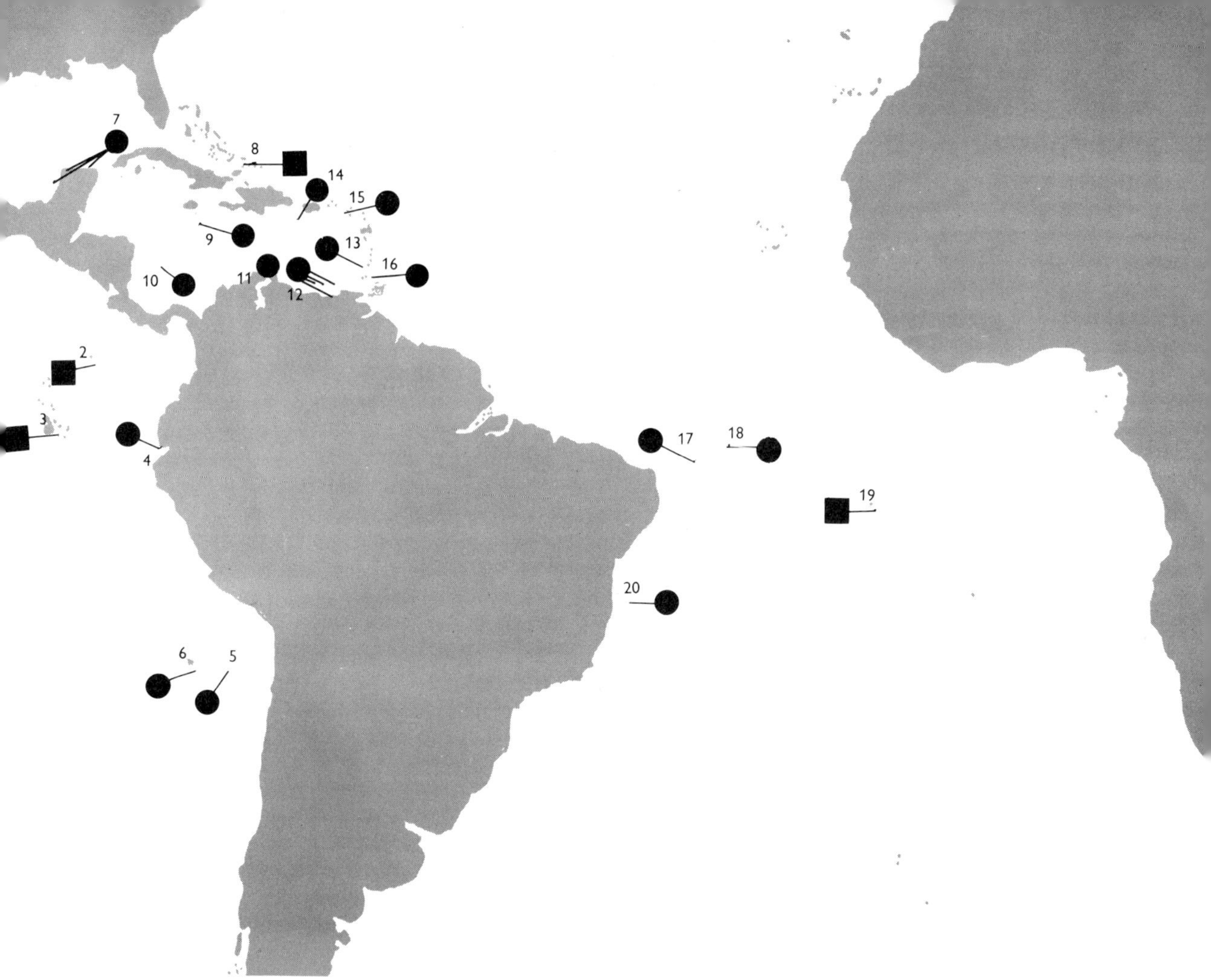

Fig. 149. The breeding distribution of the white booby in the Atlantic and eastern Pacific. Square symbols indicate the largest concentrations.

1. Clipperton.
2. Malpelo.
3. Galapagos Archipelago.
4. La Plata.
5. San Ambrosio.
6. San Felix.
7. Cayos Arcas, Cayo Arenas, Alacrán Reef.
8. Bahamas (Santo Domingo Cay).
9. Pedro Cays (Middle Cay).
10. Serranilla Cays (Bank).
11. Los Monjes.
12. Venezuelan Islands (Los Hermanos, La Orchila, Archipel los Roques; Margarita).
13. Isla de Aves.
14. Monito (4·7km N.W. of Mona).
15. British Virgin Islands (Cockroach Cay).
16. Grenadine Islands (Battowia, Bullet, All-awash, Diamond Islands and Kick-em-Jenny).
17. Rocas Reef.
18. Fernando Noronha (Rata).
19. Ascension (Boatswain Bird Island).
20. Abrolhos Islands.

this probably does not much matter in terms of the global picture of any species' breeding ecology, it would be interesting to have more details of differences between populations, in terms of breeding regimes and behaviour. It would be most useful if ornithologists visiting remote islands would make full notes on the numbers and state of breeding of the seabirds they find there and deposit these with an ornithological library, after inserting a note to that effect in one of the international ornithological journals.

DISTRIBUTION AND NUMBERS IN THE MAJOR OCEANS

1. *Caribbean and Atlantic*

The islands of the Caribbean and off Brazil are famous for seabirds among which boobies are abundant, but of the 'big three' the white booby is undoubtedly the rarest and most local.

The race occupying the tropical Atlantic and the Caribbean is *Sula dactylatra dactylatra*. It has very few breeding stations within the area enclosed by the West Indies, Lesser Antilles and the Central American Isthmus, preferring, or having been driven, to the more outlying positions, a characteristic which it shares with the red-billed tropic bird. It also occurs on cays in the Gulf of Mexico.

There are three colonies on low sand islands about 144km north of the Yucatán Peninsula (Mexico) on CAYOS ARCAS, CAYOS ARENAS and ALACRÁN REEF (Murphy 1967). Details are lacking, but Lowe (1909) remarked that white boobies on Arcas and Arenas were much more abundant than on Los Hermanos (q.v.) so these must have been fair-sized to large colonies. Kennedy (1917) reported white boobies on CHICA and PAJAROS islands of the Alacrán Reef. In the **Bahamas**, SANTO DOMINGO CAY holds a colony and the Santo Domingo area was, last century, a significant source of guano (Hutchinson 1950), some of which might have come from booby colonies. South of Jamaica, on the **Pedro Cays,** a group of four low islets, there are white and brown boobies on MIDDLE CAY. However the former number only 50–100 pairs, whilst the brown numbers several thousand pairs. It breeds, also, on the **Serranilla Cays**. Since the area is used as a source of seabirds' eggs and as a fisheries centre it is possible that the boobies fare badly and the present state of the colonies is not on record. In the **British Virgin Islands** (COCKROACH CAY) there is a colony and other cays in this group may hold white boobies. An isolated coral island, referred to as BIRD ISLAND to the west of the Lesser Antillean arc, provided enormous numbers of seabirds and their eggs last century (eight men living on the island from January to April reputedly killed 5000 birds between January and February 17th 1857 and reckoned to obtain 1000 eggs per day (mainly terns and boobies) for three months, or say 90–100 000 eggs. If only a quarter were boobies (and almost certainly mainly ground nesting boobies) the numbers must have been extremely high. There is no information on the present status of birds on this island, but they are likely to be a mere fraction of the numbers indicated above. Kepler (pers. comm.) reports that MONITO ISLAND (4·5km north-west of Mona, Puerto Rico) has 50–60 nesting pairs, on the cliffs and the edge of the plateau on the east.

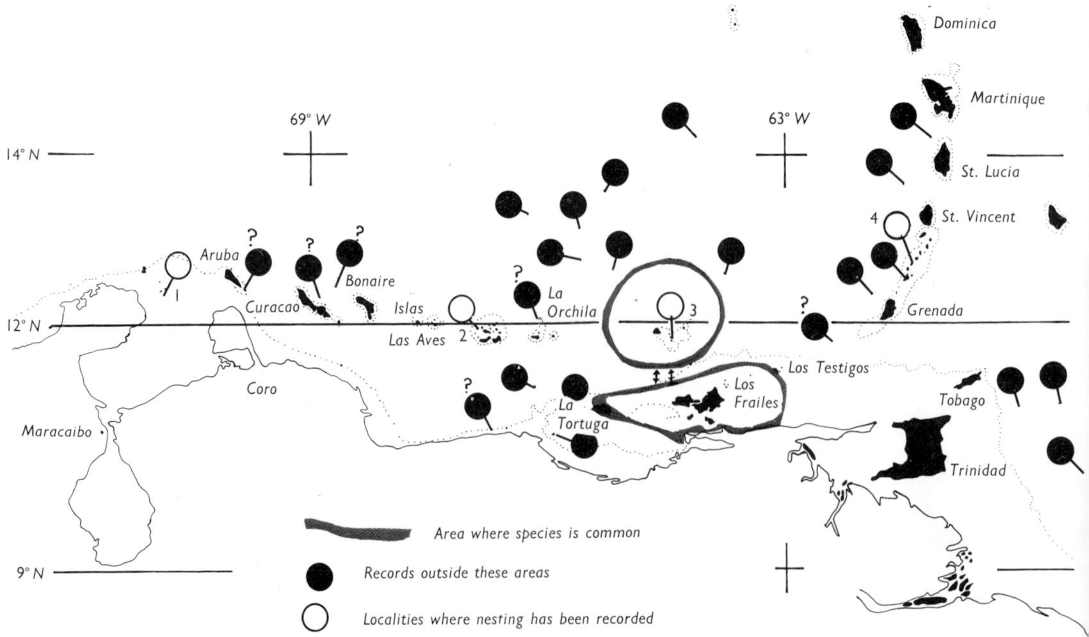

Fig. 150. The breeding distribution in the south-east Caribbean (from R. van Halewijn, pers. comm.).

1. Los Monjes.
2. Archipel Los Roques.
3. Bahia Blanquilla and Los Hermanos.
4. Grenadines.

Southwards again, islands off the **Grenadines** (BATTOWIA, BULLET, ALL-AWASH, DIAMOND ISLANDS and KICK-EM-JENNY) are reputedly white booby colonies.

The islands off Venezuela are notable seabird stations. Many of them originally bore phosphatic guano and the names of some (ISLAS DE AVES) testify to the dominant impression which they conveyed to the visitor. They are the driest islands on the fringe of the Caribbean (mean annual precipitation less than 380mm along the central part of the Venezuelan coast; most rain falls June to December) and as such should appeal to the white booby.

LOS TESTIGOS hold brown and red-footed, but apparently not white boobies. LOS HERMANOS is one of the few Venezuelan island groups which holds white boobies and even there the other two species far outnumbered it early this century. Halewijn (pers. comm.) found evidence that considerable numbers bred here in 1972. He was unable to confirm fishermen's reports that white boobies breed on LOS FRAILES, though his observations suggested that it does so. He saw many white boobies around LAS ISLAS MARGARITAS and believes that it nests in the vicinity. He saw large numbers returning from their feeding grounds south of Margarita and suggests that there is an important breeding station within this area (maybe Los Frailes). He mentions LOS MONJES as a possible breeding place. ORCHILA is included in Lowe's (1911) account and in Murphy's list of white booby colonies, and the main island once produced guano. In this area the most useful guano booby is the white. However, the guano was an old deposit rather than current produce.

If one regards guano as an indicator of fairly recent booby populations and accepts the white booby as the most highly regarded guano booby in this area, the following conclusions of Hutchinson (1950) are of interest here. He says the localities that appear to have had colonies of birds actually producing guano in the last 150 years are the Serrana Cays, Pedro Cays, Monito, Bird Island and five or six of the Venezuelan islands. The much greater deposits on Cayman, Swan Island, Desecheo, Sombrero, Navassa, Bonaire, Curacao and Aruba may all be Pleistocene in age.

In sum, in this area the white booby is not, and probably within historic times has not been anything like as numerous as the red-footed and brown boobies. At present its population may number a very few thousand pairs or less.

There is a gap in the breeding distribution of the white booby between the southern end of the Antillean arc and the latitude of the Abrolhos region at about 17°s. This is perhaps largely due to a dearth of offshore islands, the inshore ones lying off the vast stretch of Brazilian coast with its shallow and often muddy waters. These sharply limit the southward spread from the Gulf of Paria, even of pelicans, let alone boobies.

The **Abrolhos Islands,** only 65km from the mainland, are a great seabird station. Murphy was unable to say what species occurred there, but he suggested at least two booby species, of which one is likely to be the white. There could also be brown and red-footed, though there are only cacti and small shrubs on the islands. Flying fish are abundant in the area and in fact the Abrolhos were the seat of an extensive fishing industry, 'Everywhere about the islets the water is shallow, warm and clear and coral reefs of both the fringing and the barrier types harbour multitudes of rock dwelling and bottom fishes, beside which flying fish and other surface species come close inshore from the Brazil Current' (Murphy 1936).

Rocas Reef is far enough offshore (over 200km) to count as oceanic and is apparently a large white booby breeding station (1500 pairs in April 1926). It is an atoll, consisting of two small cays on a coral reef, supporting little vegetation.

Fernando Noronha was originally heavily forested. The group as a whole supports all three tropical boobies (mainly on the outlying islands) together with two tropic birds (*Phaethon aethereus* and *P. lepturus*), a frigate (*Fregata magnificens*) and four terns (*Sterna fuscata*, *Anous stolidus*; *A. minutus* and *Gygis alba*). The northernmost island, RATA, reputedly holds white boobies (Murphy 1936).

BOATSWAIN BIRD ISLAND, off Ascension, is one of the largest white booby colonies in the world (see Clipperton, Latham and Malpelo). Dorward (1962b) estimated 1200–1300 breeding pairs, 3000–4000 unemployed adults and 3000–4000 immatures and juveniles—a total population (if they were all there together, which they never are) of 8400–10 600 individuals. Ascension itself held white boobies in the past, as fossil remains show (Ashmole 1963) but no longer does so.

South Trinidad, though included in Murphy's (1936) list of Atlantic breeding stations, does not, in fact, support the white booby. Red-footed boobies were once abundant there, but the two other tropical boobies were absent. Now, even the red-foot is virtually extinct due to the death and decay of all the trees on the island.

Thus on the Atlantic side of Central and South America the white booby is a bird of the tropical and sub-tropical zones of surface water, breeding mainly on oceanic islands and on several, once numerous, stations in the Caribbean. Its most northerly station in this sector is about 22°N. in the Gulf of Mexico and its most southerly at Ascension, though of course it penetrates to much higher southern latitudes in the Pacific and Indian Oceans.

Its absence from the Cape Verdes and islands off Africa and in the Gulf of Guinea, where there are brown boobies, may be attributed to human persecution, for this booby rarely utilises steep and inaccessible nesting places. Its present inferior position in the trio of pan-tropical boobies may be due to this very factor. Certainly there is no evidence that its reproductive success is lower than others.

2. *Indian Ocean (including Red Sea, Arabian Sea, etc.)*

The form usually ascribed to this area is *Sula dactylatra melanops*. It is not to be seen in the Red Sea north of Port Sudan or in the Persian Gulf.

White boobies breed on HASIKIYA ISLAND in the **Kuria Murias** (Khorya Morya) Arabian Sea; the islet of JAZIRAT SABUNIYA off Socotra (Suqutra); KAL FARUN off Abd-al-Kuri in the Gulf of Aden, off the point of Somalia; MAIT ISLAND further into the Gulf of Aden, again off Somalia; AIBAT off the Somali coast and probably also on islands off the Mekram coast. There are few available details. Ripley & Bond (1966) found 'possibly 100 pairs altogether' on KAL FARUN and JAZIRAT SABUNIYA in March 1964 in all stages of breeding. About 20 per cent of the birds flying near the islets were in immature plumage. There is a small colony on NORTH-EAST HAYCOCK, one of a group of three small islands south of the Hanish Islands in the southern Red Sea, supporting mainly brown boobies (Morris 1962). They had young at all stages on November 4th 1961. In May 1962, however, there were no breeding boobies at all.

On HASIKIYA (Haski in the guano accounts of the mid-nineteenth century) Bailey (1966) reported 2000–3000 adults on March 10th 1964. Only some 50 nests held eggs, but there were many empty. This colony is an old one (breeding was reported by Von Heughlin 1873). Breeding (500 pairs with eggs and young) has also been reported from QIBLIYA ISLAND (April 1954) in this group (*Sea Swallow* 9). There are large numbers of white boobies to be seen all the year round in the region of the Kuria Murias.

The white booby is the only representative of its genus in the Arabian Sea, which suggests that conditions are somewhat exceptional for blue-water boobies. Temperatures on the islands are very high and there is no cover. This is likely to be more acceptable to the white than the brown booby or certainly the red-footed. Yet brown boobies occur in equally arid conditions on some Red Sea islands. The characteristics of the area, hydroclimatic and marine upwellings, are mentioned in the Comparative Section.

MAIT ISLAND or Bur-da-Rebschi holds white boobies in small groups along both sides of the rock, mainly on the tops of the cliffs and on sloping rocks at their bases. It appears to be an ancient colony (records exist for 1857) and the numbers in 1942 were estimated to be about 240 adults. At least some birds roost on the island throughout the year. However, it is said to have been reduced by rats and the size of the present population is unknown.

LATHAM ISLAND, a low coralline island about 200m × 80m, about 50km south-east of Zanzibar, is the most important seabird island off East Africa. Moreau (1940) quotes an early account of the 'numerous sea-fowl' as follows: 'Some were of the sooty petterel kind, but by far the greater number resembled the gannet. . . . The steep rocky wall of madrepore that bounded the surface of the island was covered with a complete phalanx of them, offering a most motley variety of shades, from the snow white coats of the young to the dark tint of the old ones. . . . The surface of the island was literally covered with them; some of the hens sitting on their eggs, others tenderly watching their young in their first sally from the nest or awkward efforts to fly. . . . The surface [of the island] is perfectly smooth and composed entirely of [their] excrement.' Latham is of considerable interest as the site of a large colony of white

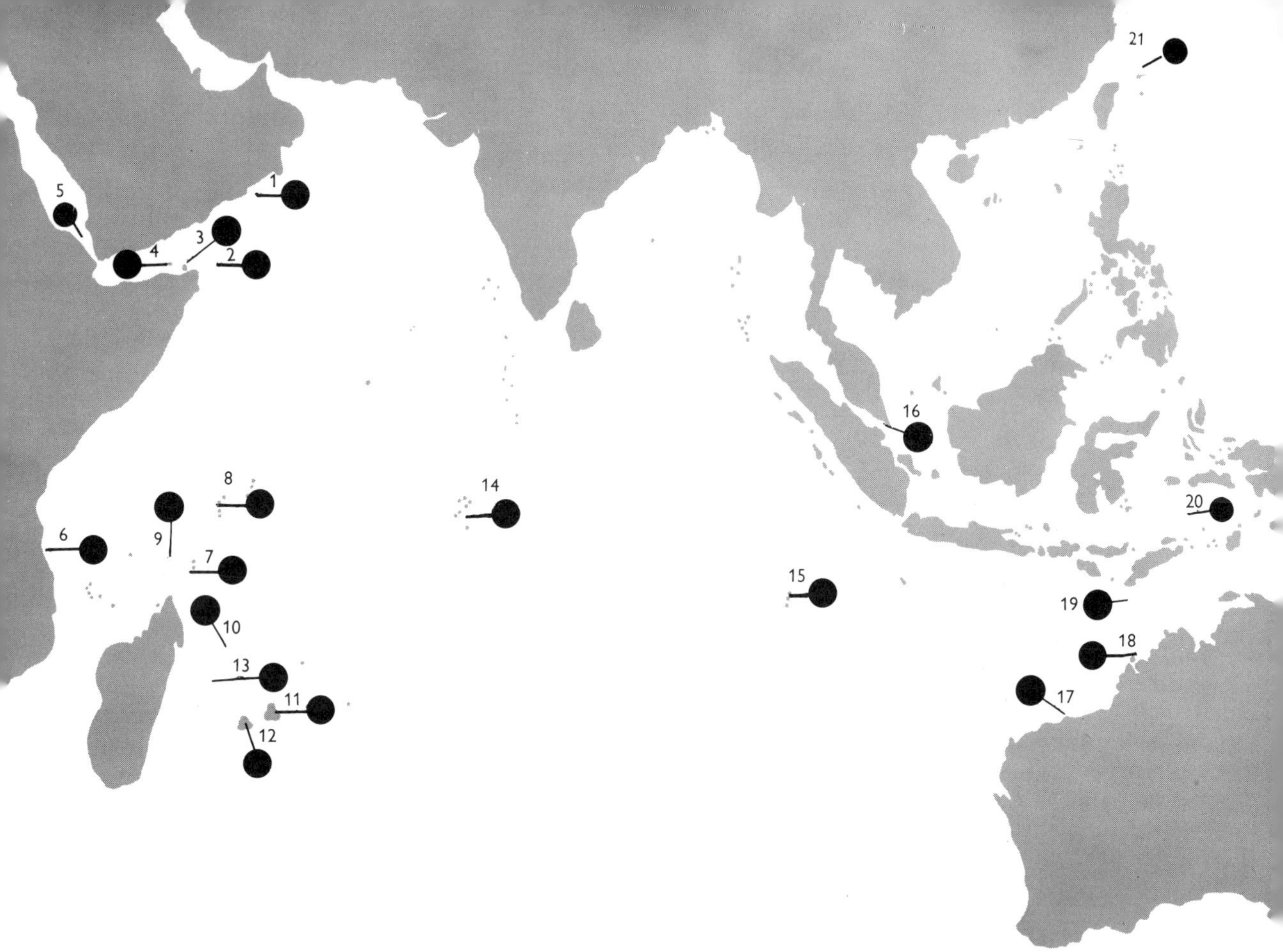

Fig. 151. The breeding distribution in the Indian Ocean.

1. Kuria Murias (Hasikiya Island).
2. Jazirat Sabuniya.
3. Kal Farun.
4. Mait Island and islands off point of Somalia.
5. North-east Haycock.
6. Latham Island.
7. Farquhar Atoll (Goelette Island, Desnoefs).
8. Amirantes (Etoile and Boudeuse Island).
9. Cosmoledo Atoll (West North, East North, Polyte and South Islands, Wizard Island, Pagoda Island).
10. Cargados Carajos Archipelago (St. Brandons).
11. Mauritius (Serpent Island).
12. Réunion.
13. Tromelin.
14. Chagos Archipelago.
15. Cocos Keeling Atoll (North Keeling).
16. Pulau Perak.
17. Bedout Island.
18. Adelie Island.
19. Ashmore Reef.
20. Manoek.
21. Sekibo Sho (near Sento Shosho group).

boobies many of which were said to breed whilst still in brown, immature plumage. This report originated from Lt. Cmd. Cole, who said he found, in November 1936 'thousands of gannets breeding, some white and some brown'. The white were assumed to be Cape gannets but Moreau (1940) rightly cast doubt on this and asked Cole to bring back a wing. This was done in 1938 and it turned out to be of the white booby. Since Cole had stated quite definitely that the brown birds were 'actually on eggs and young' at the time of his visit it seemed clear that they must be breeding and as such this record has stood. A complication had arisen from a Major Pearce's collection, in 1918, of a Latham booby which had been identified as *S. leucogaster* but on re-examination later, turned out to be an immature *S. dactylatra.* At this stage things seemed fairly straight; there was only one species *S. dactylatra*, some of which were breeding whilst still in immature plumage. However, Parker (1970) visited Latham in September–October 1967 and found white boobies very numerous, but did not record breeding in immature plumage. On the other hand, he claimed that there *were* numerous *S. leucogaster* there and a small number nesting, with young in all stages. He collected two, both said to be females in non-breeding condition, (could they have been immature *S. dactylatra*?). Parker thus claims to have disproved the suggestion that only one species breeds there. Finally

M. Gillham (in litt.) visited the island in January 1970 and found that although there were plenty of juvenile *S. dactylatra* none were engaging in anything other than normal juvenile activity and there were no *S. leucogaster*. It *looks* as though the immature *S. dactylatra* are not breeding birds, that Cole's observations were incorrect and that there are some *S. leucogaster*, (if one accepts Parker's claim unreservedly, which there are slight reasons for not doing).

Unfortunately neither of the recent visitors provides an estimate of numbers; the colony is an ancient one, reported at least 150 years ago and reputedly thousands strong.

In the Seychelles region, white boobies are more numerous than brown, but there are few large colonies. Vesey-Fitzgerald (1941) lists GOELETTE ISLAND of **Farquhar Atoll**; ETOILE and BOUDEUSE of the **Amirantes** and WEST-NORTH, EAST-NORTH, POLYTE and SOUTH ISLANDS of **Cosmoledo Atoll** as breeding sites of white boobies, but gives no numbers. On WIZARD ISLAND off Cosmoledo Atoll about 200 pairs were occupying clearings in long grass on the western side and on the dune ridge to the east, on March 6th 1968. Most were displaying, but five nests held eggs; thus the main laying period was about to begin. In 1969–70 Gillham (in litt.) reported that a feral cat or cats were killing white boobies (presumably chicks). Gillham reports white boobies and red-foots breeding on PAGODA ISLAND. Earlier, Farquhar (1900) had reported white boobies on Goelette in 1897 and Betts (1940) reported them from FARQUHAR and BIRD ISLAND, breeding in clearings among scrubby *Veloutier*. In August 1964, a landing party from H.M.S. *Owen* found some 200 nesting on an island at the south end of Farquhar Atoll. Ridley & Percy (1958) record that on Boudeuse (King Ross) Island in May–September 1955, over 5000 boobies were nesting, chiefly white. They remark that BIRD ISLAND and BOOBY ISLET must both now be considered defunct, despite earlier reports (e.g. Betts 1940) that boobies breed there annually. On DESNOEUFS (Amirantes) Ridley & Percy recorded several small colonies near the western edge, the total in June 1955 amounting to 228 pairs and by August 453 pairs. The remaining 13 islands or islets in the group held few or no boobies in that year. In 1963 there were around 200 pairs breeding on Desnoeufs (Bailey 1968) and in 1964 around 100 pairs with 70 young on the west side (Sea Swallow *18*). Apparently the white booby used to nest on Glorioso (Ile du Lys) but the relevant references are merely to 'fous blanco et gris' (Frappers 1820), 'gannets' (Coppinger 1883) and *Sula cyanops* (Ridgway 1895).

Forbes-Watson (1969) notes that although few seabirds have been recorded from the **Comoros,** they 'could be' breeding stations for boobies, among other species. CHACO ISLET, off Moheli, was very white-washed. White boobies do not breed on Assumption, though they did early this century; they were destroyed by guano operations. White boobies are also absent from **Aldabra Atoll,** though they occasionally visit.

From the Seychelles we move south as far as Reunion and then back north to the Laccadives and south again, taking in the Maldives and Chagos Archipelago, before continuing eastwards to Cocos Keeling and thence through into the western Pacific.

On the **Cargados Carajos** (St. Brandon's), an archipelago of reefs, shoals and low lying islands, extending over 500km of sea and hardly ever visited by ornithologists, there was a colony of about 200 pairs on ILE DU NORD in 1955 and this was unchanged in 1963 and 1964 (Staub & Gueho 1968). Red-footed boobies also breed in the archipelago (but see p. 672) and brown boobies may do so. SERPENT ISLAND, Mauritius, a few miles north of Round Island (which has no boobies) supports a colony of white boobies (Gill, Jouanin & Storer, 1970). REUNION is said 'possibly' to hold breeding white boobies as the only (possible) representative of its genus (Watson *et al.* 1963). On RODRIGUEZ, of the **Mascarenes,** white boobies are not known to breed and probably have not done so. At any rate the only boobies recognisable from the early (eighteenth century) accounts are red-footed, Abbott's and *possibly* brown boobies. Gill (1967) does not include any sulids in his list of breeding birds. TROMELIN ISLAND 390km east of Madagascar, supports a modest colony of white boobies—some 50 pairs scattered along either side of the air strip (Staub 1970).

The white booby has not been recorded as a breeding species in the **Laccadives** and its status in the **Maldives** (see brown booby p. 435) is uncertain. It has been recorded on CASSANFARU MARDOONIE (Watson *et al.* 1963). It does not breed in the **Andaman** or **Nicobar Islands.**

The **Chagos Archipelago** (five island groups and one small outlier) is mainly a red-foot colony but white boobies breed on some islets. Details are lacking. In March 1975 M. J. D.

Hirons (pers. comm.) found a breeding colony of *c.* 200 pairs on Resurgent, a small island lying between Middle Brother and South Brother, east-north-east of Eagle Island. He visited, also, all the islands in the Chagos except Diego Garcia and Peros Banhos and remarks that, unless they breed off the latter, Resurgent is the only colony in the Chagos.

By the time one has moved eastwards to the island of NORTH KEELING, of **Cocos Keeling Atoll,** the white booby is represented by *Sula dactylatra bedouti* (type locality Bedout Island, north-west Australia) rather than the *melanops* of the western Indian Ocean. However, *bedouti* is doubtfully distinct from *personata* of the central and western Pacific and north-east Australia (see p. 318). On Cocos, it reaches its most westerly breeding point. The colony is situated on open ground at the south-east corner of the island and is but a small one (in 1941, some 40–50 breeding pairs). The birds are resident throughout the year and seldom visit the main atoll to the south.

White boobies do not figure in the list of breeding birds of Malaya (Gibson-Hill 1949), the brown booby being the only sulid to do so. Nevertheless, two white boobies were seen by Gibson-Hill, on PULAU PERAK (Malacca Straits) in 1949. They are absent from CHRISTMAS ISLAND, which is somewhat surprising, since there is a great deal of suitable ground, almost identical to that on part of Tower Island, Galapagos, which holds large colonies.

3. *South China, Sulu, Celebes, Java, Flores, Banda and Coral Seas*

The white booby is abundant off northern, north-western and western Australia, sharing the distribution limits of the brown booby almost exactly. Information on breeding localities in the Banda and China Seas is scanty, but white boobies were identified along with brown and red-footed on Manoek Island in the Banda Sea (see p. 438) in June 1973, though the number was not estimated. 'Many hundreds' of white boobies were identified also standing or sitting on the cliff tops of Sekibo Sho Islet, 80km east of the Sento Shosho group in the eastern China Sea, in May 1972 (Simpson 1973).

In the principal investigation of the Coral Sea (Hindwood, Keith & Serventy 1963) the white booby was recorded breeding on 26 and resting on 10 of the islets investigated (Fig. 152). The only extensive colony was on RAINE ISLAND where about 1000 pairs were nesting compared with 400–500 birds in February 1959 (Warham 1961). Early this century it used to be covered from end to end with brown boobies and white boobies were the next most abundant species (Macgillivray 1910). Since then there would seem to have been a substantial reduction in numbers, although Warham (1961) says 'there appears to have been little change in the birds frequenting this cay and their numbers in the last 120 years'. However, in the 1960 and 1961 visits referred to above, there were only about 2000 pairs of brown boobies and the main booby nesting area was in the bare, central depression. The other islands or cays on which white boobies were nesting were: **Flinders Group** (LARGE SAND CAY A); **Moore Reef** (SOUTH EAST CAY); **Diana Bank** (SAND CAY); **Marion Reef** (PAGET and CAROLA CAYS); **Kenn Reef** (SOUTH WEST OBSERVATORY CAY); **Willis Group** (MID ISLET); **Lihou Reef** (NUMBER 1, 8 and 9 CAY, TURTLE ISLET); **Mellish Reef** (HERALD'S BEACON ISLET); **Saumarez Reef** (SOUTH WEST CAY); **Wreck Reef** (PORPOISE CAY, BIRD ISLET); CATO ISLAND; **Herald Group** (SOUTH WEST CAY, NORTH EAST CAY); **Coringa Group** (SOUTH WEST ISLET, NORTH EAST ISLET, CHILCOTT); **Magdelaine** (SOUTH EAST CAY); **Diamond Island** (WEST, MID, EAST and SOUTH WEST ISLETS).

Of these 26, no fewer than 24 breeding places were shared with brown boobies; only the South East Cay of Moore Reef and Observatory Cay of Kenn Reef held white boobies but no brown. Similarly, of 26 brown booby breeding places noted, only two lacked white (North Cay of Frederick Reef and South West Projection Cay of Kenn Reef).

Thus both white and brown boobies are widely distributed on the outer cays. On the inner ones white (and brown) boobies nest on GILLET CAY and perhaps others of the **Swain Reef**. This is in strong contrast to the situation in the red-foot (q.v.) which does not breed on the inner cays and is much less numerous and widely distributed on the outer ones.

White and brown boobies do not come into much direct competition, despite their almost total overlap on often tiny islands. The white breeds mainly on the fringing beaches

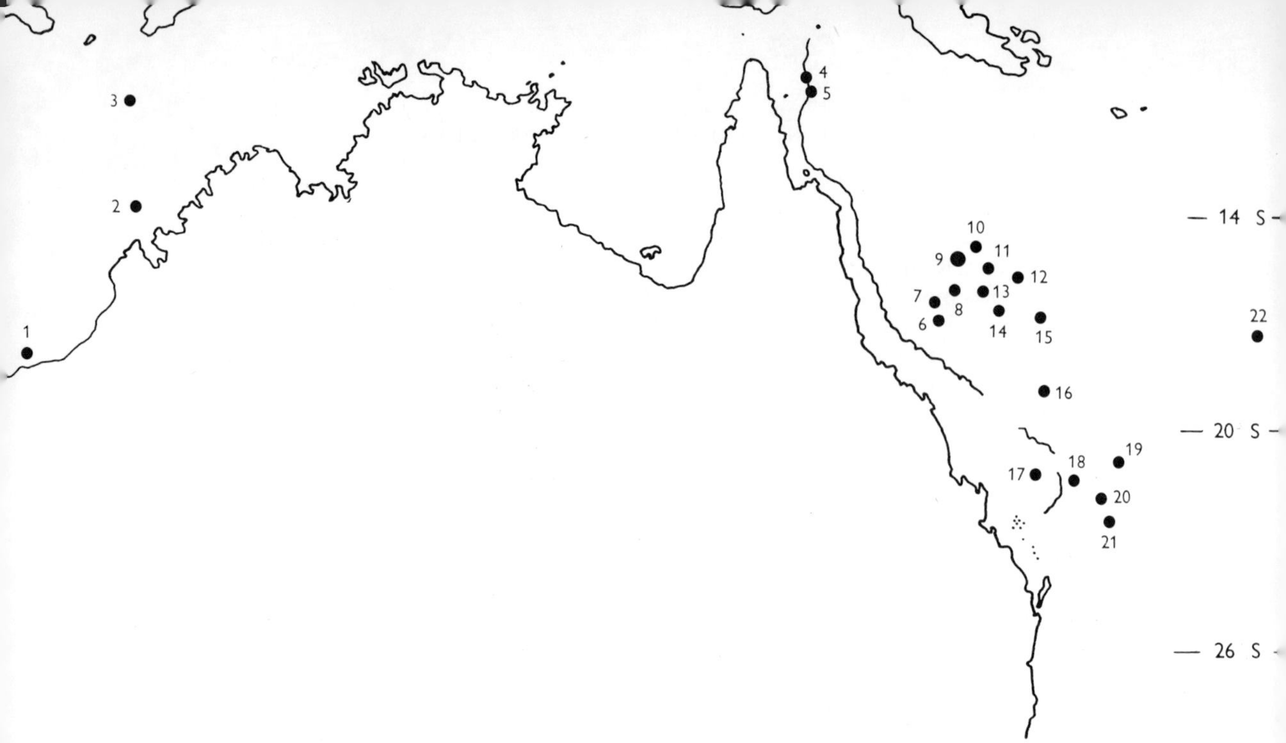

Fig. 152. The breeding distribution off Australia.

1. Bedout Island.
2. Adèlie Island.
3. Ashmore Reef (?).
4. Pandora Cay.
5. Raine Island.
6. Flinders Reefs.
7, 8. Herald Group.
9. Moore Reef.
10. Diana Bank, Sand Cay.
11. Willis Islets.
12. Magdelaine Cays.
13. Coringa Islets.
14. Diamond Islets.
15. Lihou Reef.
16. Marion Reef.
17. Swain Reef.
18. Saumarez Reef.
19. Kenn Reef.
20. Wreck Reef.
21. Calo Island.
22. Mellish Reef.

and the brown in small clearings among the herbage. This reflects the overall habitat preferences of the two species (see p. 452) but may also indicate a considerable degree of reciprocal exclusion, for there are areas elsewhere in the world, where brown boobies nest completely out in the open on flat ground and where white boobies nest among and even under vegetation. Indeed, even on these Australian cays, the division of habitat is not complete.

Other Australian breeding stations of the white booby are: Pandora Cay (Queensland); Bedout Island and Adèlie Island (western Australia). Bedout Island, the type locality of *Sula dactylatra bedouti*, held about 300 birds when visited by Serventy in 1949. There were two nesting groups on bare, guano covered patches. Brown boobies outnumbered them. Adèlie Island, 50 miles north-north-east of Cape Lévêque, is an elongated heart-shaped sand cay. Serventy's 1949 visit disclosed 40–50 young birds on the beach; again, brown boobies outnumbered them. Although many other little known islands in this area were visited by Serventy, white boobies were seen only on **Ashmore Reef** (one adult, East Island and one or two Middle Island).

4. *Western Pacific*

The Pacific Ocean covers some 165 246 000 sq. km (63 800 000 sq. miles) which is twice the area of the Atlantic (Wiens 1962). It stretches from the Bering Straits to the shore of Antarctica —15 500km—and is 17 200km wide between Panama and Mindanao in the Philippines.

The western Pacific is not a homogeneous hydroclimatic area comparable to the central Pacific. There is nothing equivalent to the vast meridional separation that lies between central Pacific islands and those—notably Cocos, Malpelo and the Galapagos—far to the east. In the absence of a clear cut hydroclimatic divide one could include the western Pacific islands with the central, but this would be virtually tantamount to treating the entire, vast area of the Pacific as one entity. To follow the geophysical western boundary of the central Pacific would virtually exclude the white booby from the resulting western sector. For convenience, here, the line is drawn east of Fiji, which leaves the Ellice and Gilbert Islands, the Marshalls, Wake, Mariana, the Carolines and Norfolk and Lord Howe Islands to represent the population and breeding regimes of the western and south-western Pacific.

Whilst the white booby breeds on most island groups in the tropical Pacific where it is not too severely disturbed, it becomes rare in the extreme south-west and north-west (New Caledonia, New Hebrides, Solomons, Bismarcks, Carolines, Palaus, Bonins and Volcanos). In these areas it occurs mainly as a visitor (King 1967) though it may nest in small numbers on some of them.

In the extreme north-west, however (MARCUS ISLAND or Minami-Tori-Shima), there used to be a colony of white boobies, though much outnumbered by brown. King (1967) now lists it as a mere visitor and it may have been destroyed by wartime activities and Japanese occupation.

There are details for several atolls in the **Marshall Islands** in Amerson (1969). In October 1964 and April 1967 respectively there were 400 and 200–300 white boobies on SIBYLLA (**Taongi Atoll**) nesting on the upper sand beaches and among *Scaevola* and *Messerschmidia.* KAMOME held 50 and BREJE 'some'. Two ringed white boobies were recovered on **Makin Atoll,** but they are not known to breed there. Two white boobies were seen on BIKAR ISLAND (**Bikar Atoll**); on JABWELO they were breeding and on ALMANI some 300 were seen in October 1964, though only 32 nests were found, but there were fewer in May 1967. A ringed bird was recovered on NIKUNAU ISLAND in October 1964, the first record of white boobies on this island, and it may possibly now breed here. It probably does not breed in the Gilbert and Ellice Islands.

LORD HOWE ISLAND used to hold 'prodigious' numbers but these have long since largely disappeared as a result of destruction by man. In June 1963 it held a paltry 100 pairs or so on ROACH ISLET and about 50 birds on Mutton Point. The breeding season was mainly finished so the population could be a few hundred more, but it remains a shadow of its former self. McKean (McKean & Hindwood 1965) visited Lord Howe four times between 1956 and 1963 and ringed 501 white boobies.

White boobies also occur on islets adjoining NORFOLK ISLAND (NEPEAN and PHILIP ISLANDS) but not on Norfolk itself.

5. *Central Pacific*

The central area of the Pacific in which there are only islands so small that they are lost in the immensity of water is reputedly one of the largest and most stable structural units on earth. The 'natural' boundary between the western margin and the central Pacific is not close to the adjacent continent but runs hundreds of miles seaward, following southwards the line of a series of volcanic islands (the Andesitic line)—Aleutian, Kurile, Bonin, Mariana and Palau Islands—then running south-eastwards to the Fiji Islands and south-west to New Zealand.

Many of the central Pacific islands lie on submarine ridges. Thus the Hawaiian Islands are the peaks of a 2575km long ridge; the Gilberts and Marshalls stand on a ridge and the atolls of Palmyra, Fanning, Christmas and Washington stand on the Fanning ridge (Wiens loc. cit.). Most of these volcanic islands are fringed by coral reefs, whose fragments form the beaches often used as nesting places by white boobies.

Climatically, the central Pacific is extremely stable. The air temperature ranges over 6–8° daily and a mere 2° or less annually, with a greater range as one approaches 15–20°N. and S. On the islands, mean temperatures are around the high 70s and low 80s, with maximum temperatures reaching the high 90s on some islands. Winds are mostly those of the trades and associated cyclonic depressions. Gales are infrequent and in many atoll areas, winds rarely rise above force 6, though there is considerable regional variability. Tropical storms are unknown in the north. The air is humid. Rainfall varies considerably between different atolls and may conceivably influence the distribution of the white booby, which prefers dry areas.

The idealised Pacific Ocean water zones and convergences, which are not static but shift with the seasons, each have their associated seabird fauna. Thus the tropical and sub-tropical convergences (10° and 42°N.: 38°S. respectively) with wind and current mainly from the

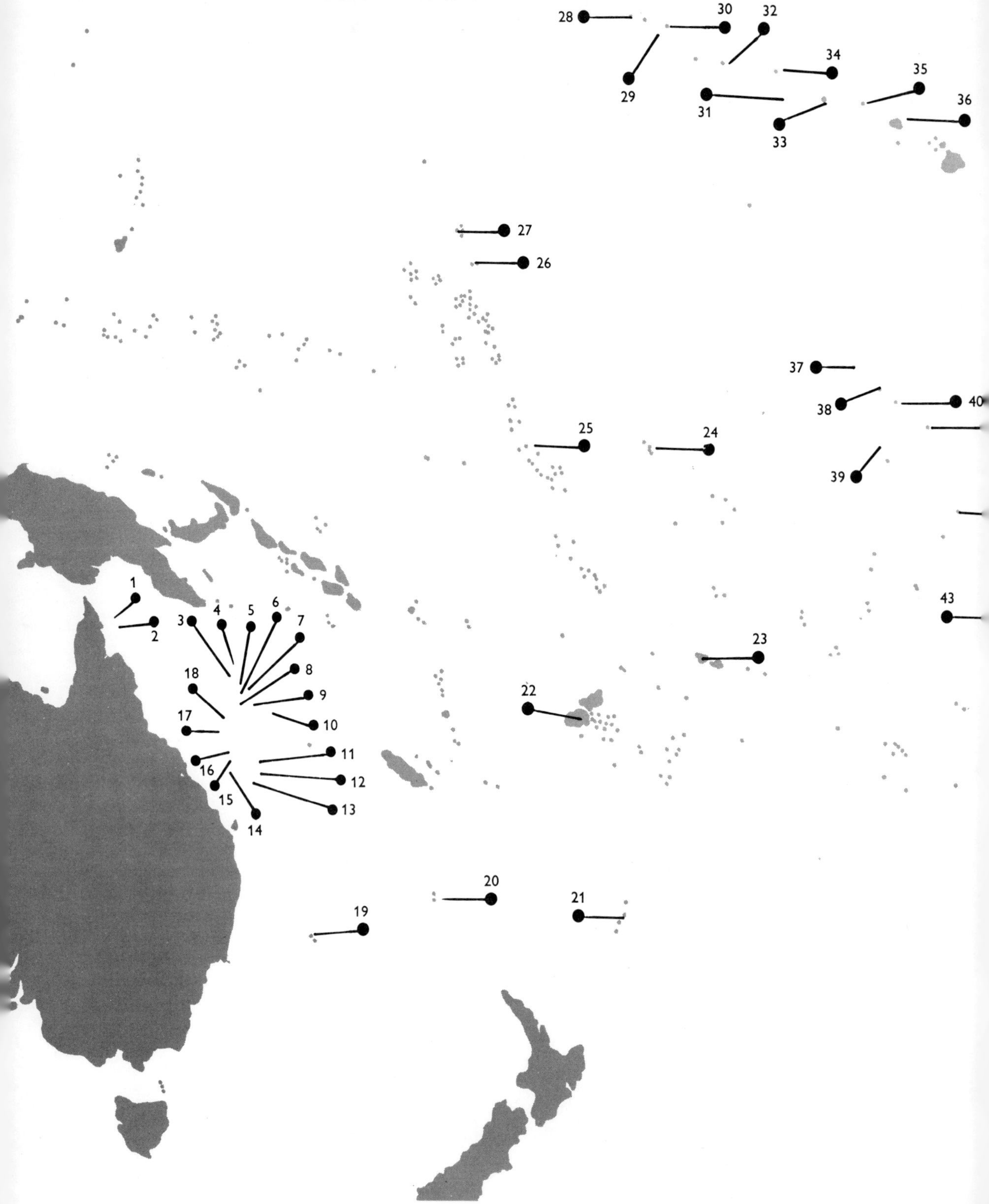

Fig. 153. Breeding distribution in the Pacific Ocean
(see also Figs. 152 and 154).

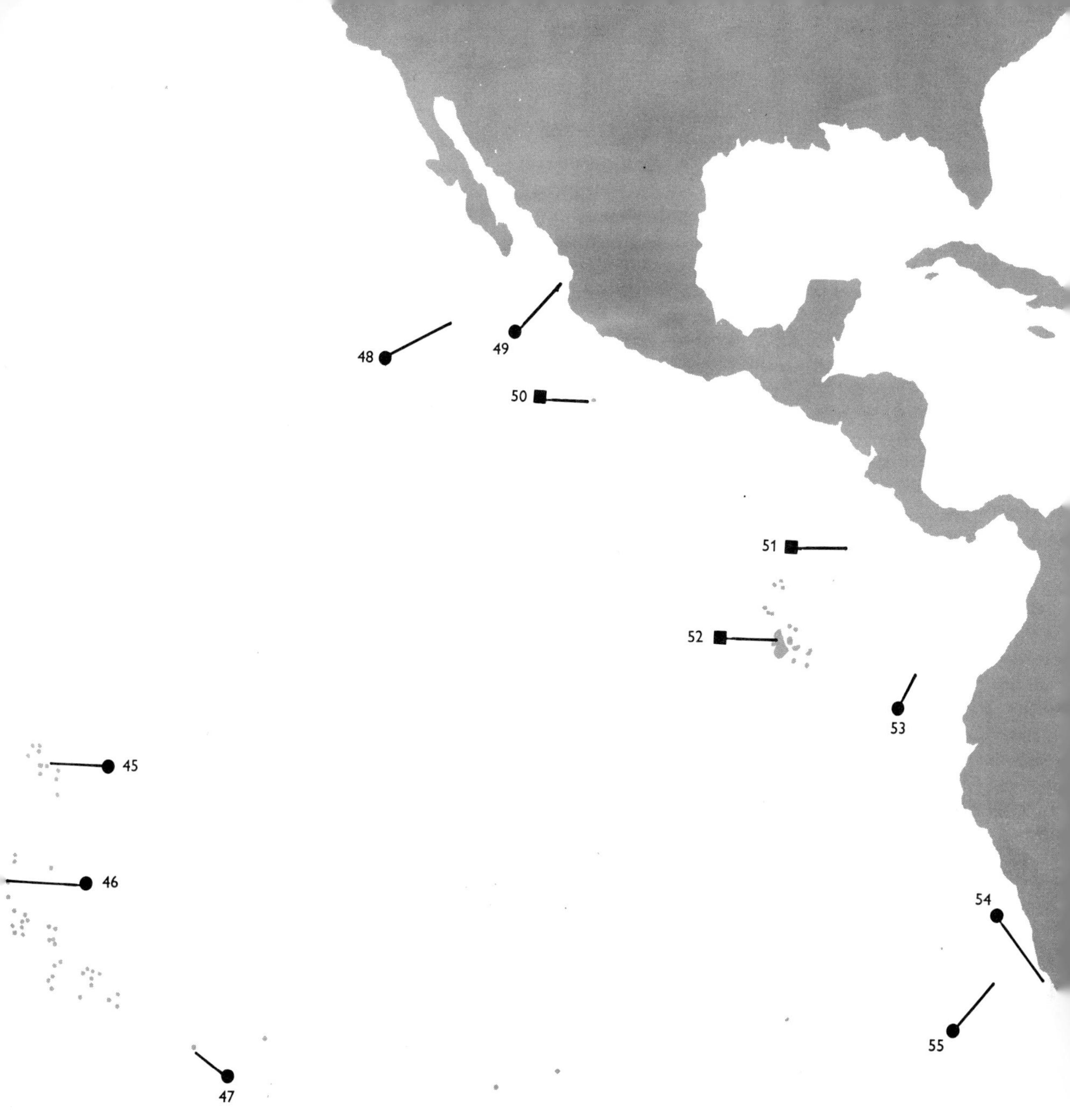

NOTE: Key to the colonies located in this Fig. is on next page.
Square symbols indicate the largest concentrations.

east, subtend warm water (15·5–25°C.) of high salinity (35–36·5 per cent) but poor in nutrient salts, and support, among other seabirds, the brown, white and red-footed boobies.

Starting with the Hawaiian Leewards, on **Kure Atoll**, the northernmost coral atoll in the world, about 54 pairs of white boobies breed annually on GREEN ISLAND. Many of the following figures are from Roger Clapp (pers. comm.) and the maximum populations referred to are of flying birds, including non-breeders and (usually) juveniles, seen on a single visit. They often err on the low side.

Midway, Pearl and Hermes Reef, Lisianski and Laysan all possess colonies of white boobies, though none of them large. Estimates of size are not available in every case, but the average population of these atolls is unlikely to exceed a few hundred pairs. MIDWAY (EASTERN and SAND ISLANDS) was virtually defunct and held only one nest on Sand Island in 1945, thanks to war-time activities. During seven visits between 1961 and 1963 it never held more than nine adults and only once as many as four nests. Maximum population estimates on **Pearl and Hermes** (1963–8) indicate a total of 600–700 'flying' birds on 8 islands of which the main appear to be SOUTH EAST, NORTH and SEAL (Clapp, pers. comm.). The highest estimate for breeding population on LISIANSKI was 450 birds, though a maximum of 1200 (including non-breeding individuals) has been recorded.

On LAYSAN, early this century (1902), they nested on the north-east, east and south sides, on sedgy slopes, though even then the colony was not large enough to excite comment (Fisher 1903). Now, Laysan probably holds about 400 pairs at most. The highest breeding population estimate between 1963 and 1968 was 800 (Clapp, pers. comm.).

GARDNER PINNACLES, two very small and barren volcanic rocks around 30 and 50m high, have white boobies breeding mainly on the upper third. The population appears to have declined from an estimated 800 breeding individuals in 1923 to something less than 100 in 1969 (150 in 1963, 80 in 1966, 250 in 1967 and 75 in 1969). This may be due partly to the blasting off of the larger pinnacle; the white boobies used to breed mainly on the upper third (Clapp, 1972).

French Frigate Shoals, a crescent-shaped reef almost in the middle of the 2575km long Hawaiian Archipelago, comprise 13 sand islands of which some are vegetated. The islands enclose a lagoon of 363 sq. km. As an indication of the climate, at this mid point, that of the French Frigate Shoals may be cited briefly. They have a marine tropical climate (temperatures 16–27°C. mostly) with predominantly easterly trade winds; storms are common in winter and most rain falls between December and March (average 114cm per year). White boobies nest on EAST, GIN, LITTLE GIN, ROUND, TRIG and WHALE-SKATE ISLANDS and used to breed on TERN ISLAND. They roost and may have nested on LA PEROUSSE PINNACLE. With an

Key to colonies located in Fig. 153.

1. Pandora Cay.
2. Raine Island.
3. Moore Reef.
4. Diana Bank.
5. Willis Islets.
6. Coringa Group.
7. Magdelaine Cays.
8. Diamond Islets.
9. Lihou Reef.
10. Mellish Reef.
11. Kenn Reef.
12. Wreck Reef.
13. Cato Island.
14. Swain Reef.
15. Saumarez Reef.
16. Marion Reef.
17. Flinders Group.
18. Herald Group.
19. Lord Howe.
20. Norfolk Island.
21. Kermadec Islands (Meyer Island, Curtis and Haszard Islands, South Chanter, North Chanter, Dayrell).
22. Fiji Islands (Vatu Ira).
23. Samoa.
24. Phoenix Islands (Enderbury, Birnie, Phoenix, McKean, Howland, Baker).
25. Gilbert Islands.
26. Marshall Islands (Jabwelo, Almani).
27. Marshall Islands (Taongi Atoll—Sibylla, Kamome, Breje).
28. Kure Atoll (Green Island).
29. Lisianski.
30. Pearl and Hermes.
31. French Frigate Shoals.
32. Laysan.
33. Necker.
34. Gardner Pinnacles.
35. Nihoa.
36. Moku Manu.
37. Palmyra.
38. Washington.
39. Jarvis.
40. Fanning.
41. Christmas Island.
42. Malden.
43. Vostok.
44. Caroline Atoll.
45. Marquesas.
46. Tuamotus (Oeno, Henderson, Ducie).
47. Pitcairn.
48. Revillagigedos (Clarion, San Benedicto (?), Aljos Rocks).
49. Isabela.
50. Clipperton.
51. Malpelo.
52. Galapagos Islands (approximately 24 stations, counting islands or well-separated headlands as one each).
53. La Plata.
54. San Ambrosio.
55. San Felix.

estimated maximum population of 1190 individuals on the entire atoll in June 1969 it is a significant even if not a large breeding aggregation. It is not a single colony in the true sense of the word.

NECKER, a 100m high volcanic island of terraced lava, used to hold a large colony, on top of the island and out on the bare rocks around. The highest 1963–68 estimate of the breeding population was 460. NIHOA apparently used to hold a big colony. Hutchinson (1950) interprets earlier records as indicating that it was very large, but the maximum 1963–68 estimate was 300. On the small rocky island of MOKU MANU, off Mokapu Peninsula, Oahu Island, there were about 40 pairs of white boobies and 25 pairs of brown in 1967 (Schreiber pers. comm.) together with some apparent hybrids (see p. 814) and some red-footed boobies. Berger (1972) says it nests on all the Hawaiian Islands from Kaula to Kure, except La Perousse, and earlier Caum (1936) said it was 'rather common' on Kaula, near the East Horn and towards the northern end.

White boobies breed, also, on the scattered islands of the Line and Phoenix Groups, with which may be included Johnston and Caroline Atolls of the Southern Lines (not to be confused with the Caroline Islands several thousand km to the west), and Howland which may be lumped with the Phoenix Islands. However, the numbers are small.

On JOHNSTON, some 200 nested in 1923 but in 1957 there were only about a dozen, mostly adults, resting on the shore near the colony of brown boobies. One–30 birds used SAND ISLAND throughout the year (1963–69) but did not breed (Amerson, pers. comm.). **Caroline Atoll** consists of three large islands (Nake and Long in the north and South Island in the south) and about 15 small islets. Like many islands in the central Pacific it has a long history of occupation, which is probably why boobies are relatively few on many apparently suitable islands. Tuamotus were there before Europeans. Guano has been gathered (10 000 tons between 1873 and 1895). The population of free-flying white boobies in June 1965, however, was a mere 10 (4 nests) on NAKE ISLAND, along the ocean beach (Clapp & Sibley 1971b).

The main Line islands are Palmyra, Washington, Fanning, Christmas and Jarvis. The **Fanning** group now holds very few white boobies. They used to support many more seabirds and almost 50 years ago Kirby (1925) suggested that even then the population was much less than it had been. Nowadays the white booby nests in a single remote part of the island, on the extreme southern edge and there may well be only 20 pairs on the entire atoll. Ground nesting seabirds in general are few on Fanning. They have been and are, much affected by man and also by pigs (now thought to be exterminated, Bakus 1967). There are also hordes of land crabs which are capable of destroying eggs and small young, though this cannot be a serious factor since birds and crabs co-exist on many islands. On PALMYRA and WASHINGTON the white booby was rare even in 1924; Palmyra has a tiny 'remnant' colony and Washington no breeding birds. On JARVIS there is on occasions an enormous club—9000 birds on one spring visit, and also between 1250 and 4800 breeding individuals (including flying young).

A total of not more than 500 pairs breed on CHRISTMAS ISLAND. However, the maximum number of nests recorded at any one time in recent years has been about 175, mostly on the *Lepturus–Sida* plain along the perimeter of the south-east peninsula, in loose groups separated by a few kilometres (Schreiber & Ashmole 1970). Up to 500–600 individuals roost on the island each night for most of the year. MALDEN has a breeding population of 1000–1500 birds at most and up to 3000 individuals have been seen there.

On VOSTOK, a low-lying coral island of some 24 hectares in the southern Lines, the white booby nested solely on coral rubble at the east of the island in mid-June 1965 (Clapp & Sibley 1971a). A complete count of nests gave 111 with eggs or young and 'many' pre-nesting pairs, which suggests that the breeding population in that year would be at least 200 pairs. As on Christmas Island, there were many extra individuals present; the estimated total was 475 ± 50, including immatures, and no doubt there would have been more at sea.

The **Phoenix Islands** are a low-lying coral group. Gardner, Hull, Sydney and Canton (the largest) are typical atolls, whilst Enderbury, Phoenix, Birnie and McKean have hardly any lagoon. One needs only to mention that at one time during the 1939–45 war, there were some 30 000 American troops on the islands and it will be appreciated what happened to the bird life. The white booby was once, possibly, the commonest bird on CANTON. In 1949 there were barely a dozen pairs, beginning to nest on open parts of the lagoon beach. At present, it is a non-breeding visitor. The breeding population on ENDERBURY apparently fluctuates considerably from year to year. Typical July estimates have indicated breeding populations of 800–850 individuals, but the maximum population estimate is 2000. BIRNIE had in 1973 at least 350–400 breeding birds (R. Clapp, pers. comm.) and 800–900 have been seen there. PHOENIX's maximum breeding population is 850 and maximum population 1800. The equivalent figures for McKEAN are 600–700 and 1500. HOWLAND has a maximum population of 3000 against its name, but the breeding population is unknown. BAKER has merely 10–20 breeding pairs, or less, but 400 individuals have been counted there, in a Club. One pair now breeds on SYDNEY (1973), but none on Gardner or Hull.

Moving eastwards, from more tropical latitudes, the **Marquesas** attract white boobies as visitors (King 1967) but it seems likely, in fact, that they breed there; both the brown and red-footed boobies nest and the white breeds to north, south, east and west of the Marquesas.

South and slightly east, they breed in the **Tuamotus** and on **Pitcairn**. On OENO it is common; eggs and young were found everywhere in mid-October and there were large congregations of unoccupied birds under the *Pisonia* and *Messerschmidia*. It was common too on HENDERSON, breeding in clearings among thick vegetation near the shore in January 1957. It also breeds on DUCIE. These three islands are uninhabited, but apparently it also bred previously on PITCAIRN itself and part of the crater rim is still called Gannet Ridge (Williams 1960).

Much further south-east, well south of the tropics, on EASTER ISLAND the white booby is seen probably more often than has been suspected. King (1967) lists one record only, but Johnson *et al.* (1970) says that it was 'scarce' and not nesting between December 10th and 30th 1968 on MOTU-NUI, an islet off Easter Island. The islanders assured them that no seabirds nested on the main island.

The **Society** and **Cook Islands** ought to hold white boobies, but are classed by King as merely 'visited'.

It breeds on the islands of **Samoa** and **Fiji**. In the latter group, though it is rarely seen, Smart (pers. comm.) suggests that the most likely breeding localities would be in northern LAU and the YANUCAS (outer islets). However, Shorthouse (1967) found white boobies breeding, along with brown and red-footed, on VATU IRA, at the southern end of Bligh Waters. It is not recorded from **New Caledonia, Loyalty Islands** and the **New Hebrides,** though this may be due to insufficient observation. It strays to the **Bismarck Archipelago** but apparently does not breed in the **Solomons.**

Far to the south, at the northern limit of several antarctic petrels and albatrosses, the white booby breeds in the **Kermadec Islands** its most southerly breeding locality (further south than San Ambrosio and San Felix off Chile). It nests on out-lying islands, but not on RAOUL itself. On MEYER ISLAND, for example, in 1944 Sorensen (1964) found two birds nesting and saw others and in November 1966 there was a large chick on a stack off North Meyer. It has been recorded, also, from CURTIS and HASZARD ISLANDS. In August 1966 there were about 30 pairs breeding on MACAULEY, laying having just begun. On December 26th 1966 there were two occupied nests on DAYRELL, 12 on SOUTH CHANTER and 20 on NORTH CHANTER, covering a range of young from newly hatched to fully fledged (Merton 1970). Nests were scattered singly in small clearings. Thus there are several scores of breeding pairs in the Kermadecs. The brown booby straggles this far but does not breed.

6. *Eastern Pacific*

The enormous stretch of tropical Pacific Ocean east of the 150° meridian and between latitudes 30°N. and 20°S. is virtually empty of islands. Compared with the central Pacific to westward, it is a waste of undivided water. Arbitrarily moving eastwards within the tropics, I have taken the oceanic islands of Clipperton, Malpelo and Cocos, then south westwards to the Galapagos Archipelago, straddling the equator, before taking in the whole sweep of breeding stations off the western seaboard of the Americas, from the Gulf of California in the north to the Chilean Islands of San Felix and San Ambrosio in the south—a range of no less than 52° of latitude.

CLIPPERTON is yet another locality in which the white booby has been brought low by man and his agents. Snodgrass & Heller (1902) said 'immense numbers' nested and at this time Clipperton may have been the world's largest colony. Beck, in 1907, reported 'thousands' but Stager (1964), who spent most of August 1958 on the island records that there were no more than 150 individuals in scattered pairs and showing no signs of breeding—an almost incredible destruction wrought apparently by wild pigs, introduced to the island. Even more astonishing, however, was the increase subsequent to the eminently laudable destruction of the pigs by Stager. Thus, Ehrhardt (1971) records that no fewer than 4239 white boobies were present in 1968, inhabiting mainly the most northerly and westerly sides. It is patently obvious that these birds must have been, in the main, immigrants, but from where did they come and why in such vast numbers?

The most obvious suggestion, which may well be wrong, is that they came from other breeding stations in the area. The nearest breeding colony is at least 1200km away, in the Revillagigedos to the north. There is evidence that white boobies which breed on isolated oceanic islands tend to use these as their permanent base, whereas those from an island in, say, the Hawaiian Leeward Island chain, move freely between the islands. It is hard to believe that there were thousands of white boobies from islands several thousands of kilometres away, waiting to colonise Clipperton. It seems more likely that the colonisation was by Clipperton birds, the survivors of the larger population, and young birds, many of whom had probably been adult for several years without having bred successfully, if at all. At first sight Stager's 1958 figure of 150 birds would suggest that by then the Clipperton population was virtually extinct, but of course an unknown number could have been at sea and if events on the island had regularly wrecked all breeding attempts for years, one would expect this proportion to be abnormally high. Furthermore, white boobies are long-lived birds and from a population as vast as Clipperton's evidently had been, a fair number of adults from the 1940s and 1950s would be still alive in the 1960s. On balance, it seems to me more probable that the astonishing increase from virtually no breeders in 1958 to over 4239 in 1968 resulted from an influx of surviving Clipperton birds whose breeding cycles had been totally disrupted for years by pigs, rather than an influx of birds from other breeding stations, mostly several thousands of kilometres distant.

MALPELO is another colony with something of a mystery attached to it. Hutchinson (1950) refers to 'perhaps 15 000 pairs', which is a colossal size for a white booby colony. A new appraisal would be extremely welcome. Whatever the outcome, it remains true that the eastern Pacific is notable for the enormous size of its booby colonies, which is doubtless directly attributable to the dearth of islands in a vast expanse of tropical seas.

The **Galapagos Archipelago** straddles the equator. It is notable for the number of endemic species, including seabirds, but it is less commonly appreciated that in sheer numbers of other, commoner seabirds, it ranks extremely high in the world. This is somewhat obscured by the large number of islands, their often inhospitable terrain and the fact that many 'colonies' are either highly dispersed (like the red-footed boobies on Tower which nevertheless probably number over 100 000 pairs) or on seldom visited stretches of coast on which it is often impossible to land. Fig. 154 shows the main white booby breeding stations.

TOWER ISLAND holds at least 2500 pairs, though this would not be evident from a casual visit. A small colony at the head of Darwin Bay consists of pairs scattered in clearings among the *Cryptocarpus* shrubs, often completely hidden except when they mount a lava outcrop. A colony on the south-east horn of Darwin Bay is mainly on lava cinders and ash on the fringes of scattered *Cordia* and other trees, which, for almost the whole year, are dry and leafless. A colony on the south-west horn is large, widely dispersed and may well number more than 1000 pairs; many are hidden by undulations and hollows in the ground and since there is also scanty growth in that area, a comprehensive overview of the colony cannot be obtained from the ground. The substrate is solidified lava flow, somewhat smoothed.

In addition, there are small groups at points on the cliffs around Darwin Bay and all along the northern coast, in places forming sizeable groups, but mainly just a few pairs or a single pair here and there. In none of these places do white boobies nest densely; on average the distance between nests is many times greater than on Ascension (q.v.).

On DAPHNE MAJOR white boobies nest in widely scattered groups and single pairs mainly around the top of the island (there are none among the blue-footed boobies in the crater bottoms). The total population is around 300–500 pairs. Most of these are in extremely exposed sites, often on sloping ground, but none are in any sense on ledges or precipitous ground.

On Hood there are two main breeding areas. On Punta Suarez, white boobies occupy the exposed extremity of the peninsula on the broken outcrop-strewn edge to the west. Here they nest largely to seaward of the blue-footed boobies, on bare sites among the outcrops. The group numbers perhaps 100–200 pairs. On Punta Cevallos, at the other end of the island, there is a huge colony, many thousands of pairs (Harris pers. comm.) and probably the largest in the Galapagos.

There are white booby colonies also on Tortuga Island; Gardner-by-Floreana; Enderbury; Champion; Culpepper; Wenman; an island in Sullivan Bay on James Island; Punta Pitt on San Cristobal; Plaza (new nesting 1971, Harris pers. comm.); Isabela (Cape Berkeley and north, east, south and south-east coasts); southern Narborough; southern James; Seymour; Jervis; Barrington; all round the north and east of Charles and doubtless others (Harris 1973).

On Culpepper, almost never visited, there are thousands of white boobies. So little is on record about this magnificent seabird station, and the equally remote Wenman, that Fosberg's account of his visit, by helicopter, in January 1964 is well worth quoting. 'Culpepper, from the air, is a small, cliff-girt plateau, the top made up of two low, gently sloping hills separated by a shallow, hanging valley and ravine. The surface is wooded with low trees. Several green, meadow-like openings are scattered here and there, mostly around the periphery, as well as a bare area with only sparse vegetation. The helicopter landed in the largest of these meadow-like areas, amid a cloud of astonished boobies and sooty terns.' The low green plants were *Alternathera helleri*, a compact, densely branched dwarf shrub, but the principal vegetation, a scrub, is a practically pure strand of *Croton scouleri*, slender trees which produce either a completely closed canopy, or open scattered growth. Fosberg, in 1964, found in an area of

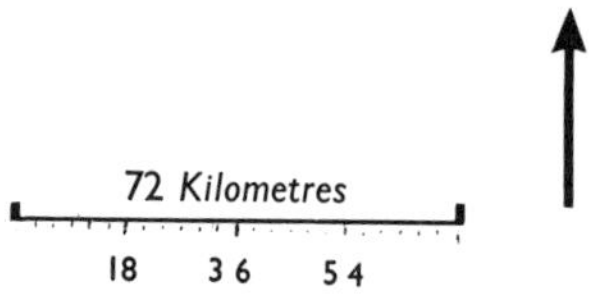

Fig. 154

The breeding distribution in the Galapagos.

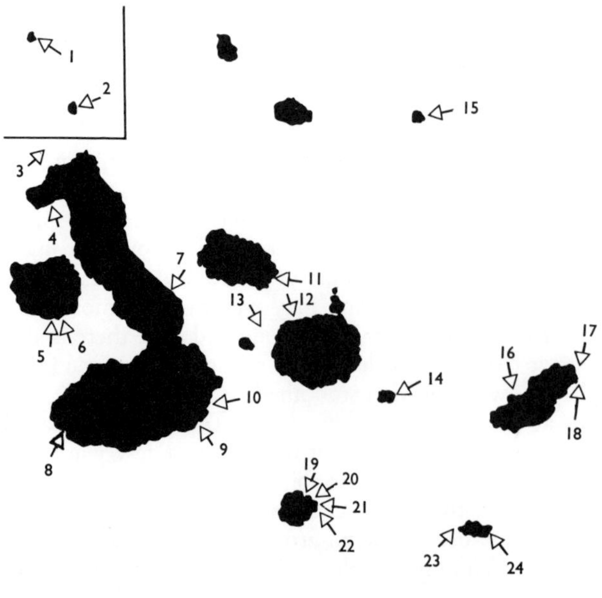

1. Culpepper.
2. Wenman.
3. Roca Redonda.
4. Banks Bay.
5. }
6. } S. coast Fernandina (Narborough).
7. Cowley Island. }
8. Iguana Cove. }
9. Tortuga Island. } (Isabela).
10. Crossman Islands. }
11. Bainbridge Rocks (James).
12. Daphne.
13. Guy Fawkes.
14. Barrington.
15. Tower.
16. Kicker Rock.
17. Punta and Isla Pitt (San Cristobal).
18. Punta and Isla Pitt.
19. Champion. }
20. Enderbury. }
21. Caldwell. } (Charles).
22. Gardner-near-Floreana. }
23. Punta Suarez (Hood).
24. Punta Cevallos (Hood).

about one hectare high on the island, hundreds of nesting pairs of white boobies and reports that they were nesting in large numbers on the bare strip between the edge of the scrub and the cliffs round much of the island's periphery. He then describes a small, oven-hot canyon in which boobies, frigates and swallow-tailed gulls were nesting, from the mouth of which could be seen a guano-stained stack of lava 'resembling the leaning tower of Piza'. Some boobies were nesting on its ledges, a relatively rare site for this species.

Fosberg also mentions an off-lying rock, arched and with a flat top, bearing some resemblance to the Arc de Triomphe, packed with seabirds among which were 'untold thousands' of red-footed and white boobies. Thus, Culpepper must rank as a major white booby colony; perhaps 5000 pairs would be a very conservative guess.

The equally remote Wenman, at which we occasionally gazed from Tower Island is also evocatively described by Fosberg. He landed in an opening, a large terrace from 100m above the sea, on the north-west of the island. The ground was thickly covered by jagged lava boulders. A sharp ridge rose at least 200m to a peak, separated by a practically impassable knife-edge from the main part of the island, which was a sloping plateau several times as big as Culpepper. *Croton* scrub, much of it dead, dominated the island. On a strip of open ground at the top of the cliffs there were great numbers of white boobies. On the cliffs of the west side, the entire cliff edge, for great stretches, and a knife-edged isthmus connecting with a peninsula, held an 'enormous population' of white boobies. Again, could these descriptions refer to less than 5000 pairs?

The total population of the Galapagos is probably not less than 25 000 pairs and may well be considerably more; a figure of twice that population being easily possible. Such numbers contrast markedly with the small colonies so common on the central Pacific atolls, but the almost unimaginable numbers of these tiny islets must also be remembered.

There remain now a number of islands down the western seaboard of the Americas from the Gulf of California south to Chile.

The high temperatures in the Gulf of California favour boobies rather than cormorants, but the brown and blue-footed (p. 518) seem to outnumber the white. It is by no means certain that white boobies are absent from the Gulf islands, but available records refer only to the other two species.

Las Tres Marias are occupied only by the brown and blue-footed boobies (Grant & Cowan 1964) and the early accounts (Bailey 1906) refer mainly to the brown. White boobies do not breed on the Tres Marietas (Grant 1964).

ISABELA, south of the Gulf of California, is reputedly a breeding station of the white booby (Hutchinson 1950). Anderson (pers. comm. 1974) writes 'blue-faced boobies have been seen in the Gulf but we have never identified them'.

The uninhabited **Revillagigedos** 338km south-west of the tip of Baja California and over 645km off the shores of Mexico, are a famous haunt of seabirds. SAN BENEDICTO is famous, also, for the massive eruption on August 1st 1952, of the volcano El Buquerón, which killed many nesting seabirds. In 1953 the white booby was common on CLARION, especially on the south and east sides, groups of 18–20 birds, paired and unpaired, were sitting in the low grass, 7–10m apart, each group some 100m from the next. The total population in March was about 150 birds. About 20 were on or near Roca Partida and by November 1953 many were again roosting on San Benedicto, the largest group consisting of about 500 birds, including juveniles and immatures (Brattstrom & Howell 1956). There were some, also, on Socorro.

This nevertheless represents a vast decrease since the days of Hanna's visit in 1923, when, on Clarion, white boobies nested 'from beach to summit'. The population may increase, however, for, according to Brattstom & Howell (1956) this group of islands is seldom molested and is, thankfully, still free from introduced pests such as goats and cats, which have had such disastrous consequences on other islands.

The ALJOS ROCKS two volcanic pinnacles 30 and 25m high and 12 and 8m in diameter respectively, are said to hold nesting white boobies, together with sooty terns and red-billed tropic birds, but no numbers are given.

Further south, in the Gulf of Panama the brown and blue-footed boobies are much more in evidence than the white, for which I know of no breeding records.

The island of LA PLATA in the Gulf of Guayaquil was first recorded as a breeding place by Murphy, who visited it in 1925 and found white boobies breeding in the lush rain vegetation above the cliffs at the south end. This, he suggests, is the closest colony to the Pacific coast of South America, for this species avoids islands close to the shore or in bights. In May 1955, Marchant saw many immatures flying off the south point of the island and adults nesting on the pampa at the cliff-tops. He states his belief that no boobies breed between La Plata and Santa Clara Island. Owre (pers. comm.) counted the 'several hundred birds of the breeding colonies of masked boobies' in 1976 and says (pers. comm.) that there are 150–300 (pairs?) nesting there at any time.

A fairly recent visit to the species' most southerly breeding outposts, San Ambrosio and San Felix (Millie 1963), revealed that white boobies were common on both and had a protracted breeding season. Fresh eggs were taken from San Felix in late August 1960. Jehl (1973) visited both islands in June 1972 and found hundreds or thousands roosting on San Ambrosio, though no evidence of nests (but he was unable to climb to the main area). On San Felix there were 400 pairs on the flat north-east side, with nests some 30–100m apart and about 15 per cent with eggs.

It is not found on the Chilean coast (Johnson 1956).

3. BREEDING ECOLOGY

INTRODUCTION

The features of the white booby's tropical environment dominate its breeding ecology. Although there are significant differences in the breeding strategies of different populations, the most influential characteristics are the nature of the principal food (squid and flying fish) and the aseasonal environment. The white booby's adaptive response to its widely scattered and relatively scarce prey is to forage widely. This entails long absences which in turn are best accommodated by low brood size and slow growth of young. The aseasonal environment means the absence of severe selection pressure on the precise timing of laying. Small colonies on innumerable tiny islands are viable since there is no need for intense social stimulation to act as a fine-timing mechanism. Since vast numbers of small atoll islands are dotted all over the central Pacific—this species' main region—the ability to use them is obviously adaptive.

Thus, the white booby's breeding ecology is characterised by small colonies, relatively a seasonal breeding, a single, slow-growing chick and in areas, such as the Galapagos, where food is highly unpredictable, exposure to the risk of heavy breeding failure.

Dorward, on Ascension (Atlantic Ocean) was the first to study this species, then we looked at Galapagos birds and Kepler worked on Kure Atoll (Pacific). Much valuable longer-term information on breeding biology is contained in the reports of the Pacific Ocean Biological Survey Programme (Amerson 1971, Woodward 1972) and further material awaits analysis.

BREEDING HABITAT

In general, the white booby, although catholic, is a species of barren slopes or flatter ground. Most of the tropical oceanic islands upon which it breeds are either low lying, sandy, and fairly barren or the areas chosen by the booby are peripheral and therefore usually low and bare, or xerophilous and scrubby with patches of open ground. Perhaps the smallest islets known to be inhabited by white boobies are the Aljos Rocks in the Revillagigedos, one of which (South Rock) is a 40m pinnacle a mere 12m in diameter and the other (North Rock) only 24m high and 8m in diameter. At least in eastern Australia, headlands are also used. The decisive factor is proximity to clear blue water.

White boobies rarely breed on cliff ledges (but see below). Where, as on Boatswain Bird Island, Ascension (Dorward 1962b) they spread from the flatter top and gentle slopes onto cliffs, it is on to level places part way down the cliffs and even this is a rare contingency. On Tower (Galapagos) they avoid the steep slopes near cliff edges but frequent flat cliff-top margins,

(*b*)

(*a*)

Fig. 155

Some nesting habitats:

(a) On mat of vegation, Kure (dyed birds). *Photo:* C. Kepler.

(b) Beneath xerophytic scrub, Galapagos.

(c) Bare slope, Ascension. *Photo:* D. F. Dorward.

raised beaches and gently sloping ground on the north-west coast. On Daphne Major, steep slopes are everywhere available but they choose the flatter rims around the summit volcano (the flat crater floor is occupied entirely by blue-footed boobies). Formidable slopes may be awkward for this species to move around on and much of its ritualised behaviour involves locomotion. Many nesting areas are extremely flat (Clipperton, Latham, most Pacific atolls and Australian cays, etc.) and the largest colonies are in fact on this type of terrain. Nevertheless, I did record several individuals on gannet-type ledges on a sheer cliff face and Fosberg noted white boobies nesting on ledges on stacks off Wenman. Comparably, on Mait Island, in the Gulf of Aden, white boobies nest in small colonies and prefer ledges either on the summits of precipices or on sloping rocks at their bases.

The bare surface of most islands on which this species breeds is either particulate (often coral fragments) or variably crusted bedrock, often of igneous origin, with or without outcrops. One of the world's largest colonies (Latham) is on coral sand. In the French Frigate Shoals it prefers the sand of the upper beaches, but also uses open, sandy areas inland. On Boatswain Bird Island large areas are devoid of anything except fragments of rock and detritus and a few boulders. On north-west Tower (Galapagos) an unevenly solidified lava flow has produced mounds and hollows much used by white boobies, whereas dense, sharply fragmented lava is understandably avoided. On Punta Suarez, Hood (Galapagos) rough, heavily outcropped and weathered rock with large irregular boulders is densely colonised, the boobies nesting on the bare interstitial patches but avoiding the dense boulder litters so characteristic of this peninsula. On Green Island (Kure Atoll) they ignore the wide beaches and brush-covered dunes and choose the inland plain, which is flat but vegetated.

The white booby is not averse to nesting among or beneath scrub or small trees. The colony at the head of Darwin Bay (Tower) is among low but dense *Cryptocarpus pyriformis* and elsewhere on this island the boobies nest beneath shrubby trees, often choosing to make the scrape in their shade even when there are open areas nearby. On Kure they nest on a central plain ringed by a formidable hedge of the bush *Scaevola taccada* and sustaining seven angiospermous plants which form a thick green mat at the time of year when the boobies breed. The courting birds thus have to walk over this dense vegetation and tear some of it away to make their scrapes. Woodward records that a female breeding for the first time actually laid her egg on top of the vegetation (*Tribulus*). A good example of the effect of vegetation on the distribution of this bare-ground loving booby is the spread of *Verbesina* on the central plain of Kure, which eventually restricted them to a small area, at increased density, whereas formerly they were widely distributed.

Other records of white boobies nesting among vegetation include: La Plata, where Murphy recorded it nesting in a knee-deep, tangled bed of greenery, but with easy passage to a nearby cliff; Christmas Island (Pacific), *Lepturus–Sida* plain; Clarion Island (Revillagigedos) *Euphorbia* scrub and cacti.

COLONY DENSITY

White boobies are certainly colonial, choosing to congregate even where space does not enforce this, but they tend to form small, fairly loose groups often separated by large distances (maybe miles) rather than one larger colony. The spacing of breeding seabirds has many functions. We tend to assume that it is most important in those species which show a highly stereotyped pattern. If it is very variable it seems less likely to have strong survival value and more likely to reflect fortuitous circumstances. The white booby is in fact highly variable and nobody has suggested any ways in which a particular pattern or density confers advantage. Nevertheless there probably is an optimal density, even if it is not very important and Kepler suggests that Green Island birds might show it, since they congregate by choice, even where there is plenty of space and suitable habitat. About 44 pairs occupied 8780 sq. m—a density of about one pair in 201 sq. m. This may be compared with an estimated density of one pair per 125 sq. m and one pair per 84sq.m on Tower and Hood respectively; 'at least 92m separating most nests and several kilometres between colonies' (i.e. groups) on the Pacific Christmas Island; 1–2m between nests on Hasikiya (Arabian Sea) and roughly one pair per 3·3 sq. m on Boatswain Bird Island, which is by far the densest white booby colony recorded. They are probably forced to breed so densely here because of the lack of alternative safe sites. At the other extreme, a single pair of boobies may breed in complete isolation on their own small island, as on Baker Island, Pacific, October 1965 (Kepler 1969).

Whatever the density, white boobies do not disperse evenly, but tend to clump leaving large gaps. Kepler's determination of territory sizes on Green Island showed that the distance between a nest and its nearest neighbours varied between 2m and 30m, with an average of 8m. Thus the actual density, averaged over the occupied areas within the total perimeter of the colony was about one pair per 42 sq. m, or some four times as great as the figure calculated from the pairs within the total area.

Kepler further investigated exactly how much ground a given individual and pair actually traversed or defended. This was far less than would have been predicted by simply measuring the number of birds per unit area in the colony. On average a pair 'used' only 50 sq. m. In terms of the colony as a whole, this means that less than 25 per cent of the area covered is actually used. Bachelor males used less ground than a mated pair (this is not surprising since mated males wander around collecting fragments of nest material). Furthermore, the territories of all mated pairs shrank by at least 75 per cent after the laying of the first egg. Courting pairs defend at least four times as much territory as they will use when actually nesting though in the very late stages the feathered chick may wander a considerable distance from the nest site. Thus a superficial estimate of territory size, obtained by measuring a colony's area and dividing by the number of pairs, would be somewhat meaningless. Not only must clumping be taken into account when considering a pair's true spatial relationships, but even within the clump, only a proportion of a pair's theoretical area is actually defended and even this shrinks drastically after the egg has been laid.

The massive variability in breeding density shown by this species may be interpreted in the light of the observations that it has no ground or aerial predators against which a mass attack could be important; that there are no reasons for thinking that mass synchronisation of laying would be advantageous (in fact the reverse is more likely to be true) and that there is usually no shortage of acceptable terrain. Thus there are no pressures which could be expected to favour the evolution of dense (or conversely, widely spaced) nesting.

NEST SITES AND NESTS

White boobies do not construct a proper nest, nor even scrape out a decent hollow, although they 'garden' in the area which they can reach whilst sitting and so produce a conspicuous circle of cleared ground (Fig. 156).

Fig. 156. Nest clearing and eggs. The small twigs around the clearing have been accumulated during symbolic nest building.

The material used has no structural significance; males, in particular, gather nest material from the immediate vicinity and may accumulate several hundreds of fragments, including twigs up to a few centimetres long, guano scraps, pebbles, feathers, bones and general flotsam. They may tear living twigs from bushes, but the highly vestigial nature of the nest in most areas shows that nest material has merely symbolic value.

THE EGG AND CLUTCH

1. *Characteristics of the egg*

When laid the egg is chalky white over a hard blue surface. The deposit rapidly scratches and chips away and the egg becomes discoloured. Fresh weights and measurements from various localities are given below (Table 45). The egg is 3·6 per cent of the female's weight.

Second eggs are significantly lighter than firsts, but their incubation periods and hatching success are the same (for a discussion of the significance of clutch size see Comparative Ecology section).

2. *Clutch size*

The proportion of white boobies laying clutches of two eggs[1] varies slightly with range. Mean clutch sizes were as follows: Ascension 1·3 (96); Desnoeufs mostly 2; Kure Atoll, series 1, 1·9 (105); Kure Atoll, series 2, 1·8 (229); Vostok 1·8 (97); Galapagos, series 1, 1·6 (209); Galapagos, series 2, 1·4 (163); Revillagigedos usually 2. [Figures in brackets = number of nests in sample.] The differences may not be significant because existing records usually do not distinguish between completed clutches of one and clutches in which only the first egg had been laid. There are insufficient records to demonstrate any correlation between clutch size and latitude, but this may exist.

Woodward (1972) gives records of clutch size for six consecutive years on Kure (Table 46). The significant difference between the average clutch size in 1966 and that in other years is interesting in that it suggests that clutch size is influenced by prevailing economic conditions;

[1] Very occasionally clutches of three occur and Dorward recorded up to seven in one nest, as a result of eggs rolling or being rolled from neighbouring nests.

TABLE 45

CHARACTERISTICS OF THE EGG OF THE WHITE BOOBY

Area	No. of cases	Length (mm)	Diameter (mm)	Volume (cc)	Weight (g) Egg 1	Egg 2	Egg 1 or 2	Source
Ascension	12	57·4–70·6 (60·4)	40·6–46·6 (44·4)	50·1–78·5 (65·2)			52–82·5 (67·3)	Dorward 1962b
Mait Is.	1	60·8	43					North 1946
N. Keeling	10	66·5–69	43–45					Gibson-Hill 1950a
Coral Sea	7	61–64 (64)	43–49 (46)					
Willis Is.	8	62·8–73·5 (68·5)	44·4–47·8 (46·1)		(80)	(75)	70–85 (77·5)	
Kermadecs		64·5–70 (67)	46–49·3 (47)					Merton 1970
Pacific localities	67	60–77 (67)	40–48·5 (46)					Bent 1922
Galapagos	3						65–70 (68·3)	
Galapagos	3				69	70	65	
San Felix	1	67·7	47·7					

1966 was an exceptionally poor year and breeding was very late. The clutch size of re-nesting pairs, at 1·67 (24 cases) is significantly less than that of first clutches.

However, whatever the validity of regional variation, the typical clutch in all races is two. Eggs on Kure were laid five or six days apart (range 3–15, mean 5·6; 85 cases). The mean interval between eggs in two successive seasons was the same (Kepler 1969). Woodward, presumably including Kepler's data, gives 2–12 days, mean 5·3; 99 clutches. The interval on Tower was five to eight days.

3. *Replacement laying*

Pairs that fail to hatch their eggs or rear their young may re-nest, but the tendency to do so is probably subject to regional and seasonal variation. Thus, even on Kure (which is in a good feeding area) there were proportionately more re-nesters in 1965 than in 1964 (Kepler 1969). In 1965 21 out of 40 first clutches failed, 18 of them due to egg loss; 10 clutches were abandoned early in incubation (after a mean period of 28·25 days) and in total 9 pairs out of the 21 failures re-nested. The magnitude of the loss in 1964 was less; 19 failed out of 51 (13 losing clutches) and only 2 re-nested. However, there is no difference between the two seasons in the proportion of early failures that re-nested (the figures are in any case very small; 4 out of 10

TABLE 46

CLUTCH SIZE OF THE WHITE BOOBY ON KURE ATOLL, 1964–69 (from Woodward 1972)

Year	One egg	Two eggs	Three eggs	Mean	Number of cases
1964	4	53	0	1·93	57
1965	5	34	0	1·88	39
1966	6	8	0	1·57	14
1967	2	3	0	1·60	5
1968	3	20	0	1·86	23
1969	4	49	1	1·94	54
Totals	24	167	1	1·88	192

TABLE 47

RE-NESTING IN THE WHITE BOOBY ON KURE ATOLL (after Kepler 1969)

Nest number	Days first egg incubated	Days after loss first egg replaced	Date of replacement
1	26	30	April 16th, 1964
2	49	17	May 11th, 1964
3	50 (c2)	27	April 6th, 1965
4	21	23	March 25th, 1965
5	106	30	July 2nd, 1965
6	68 (c23)	26	May 24th, 1965
7	8	28	February 28th, 1965
8	76	59	July 13th, 1965
9	58 (c1)	30	May 28th, 1965
10	7	33	April 17th, 1965
11	5	32	May 28th, 1965

Average = 30·45 c = number of days chick attended

in 1965 and 2 out of 4 in 1964). Therefore, the proportionally greater replacement in 1965 stems from the re-nesting of late failures, which did not occur in 1964.

Kepler stressed the adaptive significance of re-nesting on Kure and although he had a total of only 11 cases (9 in 1965 and 2 in 1964) these deserve close attention. First, there is the important fact that re-nesting occurs after the loss of a chick as well as that of a clutch (Table 47). This could happen only in a species with a relatively non-seasonal regime (cf. the gannet). Second, Kepler emphasises that the productivity of the replacement clutches may contribute substantially to the output of the colony (see p. 336).

In all cases re-nesting birds retained the same mates and the average time between the loss of nest contents and re-laying was 30·45 days. The spread in the length of this intervening period, though fairly considerable (see Table 47) is remarkably slight considering the great range in time spent on the nest prior to the loss of nest contents. One pair had been incubating five days, whilst another had remained on eggs for 106 days; three pairs had successfully hatched a chick and one pair had attended their chick for 23 days. The relatively uniform re-nesting time has interesting implications for the underlying reproductive physiology.

There is no information on replacement laying in other areas; it did not occur in our Darwin Bay (Galapagos) colony in 1963–64 nor on Ascension (Dorward 1962b). This probably indicated, not surprisingly, that in impoverished conditions re-nesting is rare or absent. More detailed observations might well show that if a high proportion of initial attempts fail early, due to adverse economic conditions, and a marked improvement quickly follows, re-nesting would occur on a large scale. On the whole, however, re-nesting seems likely to be more useful on Kure than in a highly impoverished environment.

4. *Incubation period*

Incubation begins with the first egg, though it may be somewhat desultory and the egg is sometimes left unattended in the Galapagos. Since clutch size and the subsequent fate of the chick is an important aspect of breeding biology, it is interesting to know whether the first and second eggs require equal incubation or whether the advantage of the early egg is wholly or partly lost through differential development. On Kure 58 first eggs required a mean incubation period of 43·78 days (range 40–49; 13 taking less and 45 taking more than 43 days). Forty-eight second eggs took 42·76 (range 38–47, 20 taking less and 28 more than 43 days) (Kepler 1969). Woodward's (1972) figures are 43·6 for the first egg and 42·7 for the second. The actual interval between the hatching of two eggs in the same clutch was 2–9 days (mean 4·7). Incubation periods on Ascension were 42–46 days and the two eggs hatched about five days apart (Dorward 1962b). Thus, although first eggs take slightly longer to hatch, the gap remains largely unclosed, giving the older chick a distinct advantage (see below).

5. *Incubation regime*

Incubation stints, as the opposite side of the coin to absence periods, are valuable indicators of the species' foraging habits, provided that the absent partner really is foraging and not just resting somewhere else. However, if they are directly related to the time required to find food,

TABLE 48

INCUBATION STINTS IN THREE DIFFERENT POPULATIONS OF WHITE BOOBIES

Area	Sex	No. of cases	Length of incubation bouts (in hours)							
			0–10	11–20	21–30	31–40	41–50	51–60	61–78	Mean
Kure (Kepler)	Male	24	9	12	3					11
	Female	23	13	9	1					8
Galapagos (Nelson)	Male	68	3	11	33	5	9	3	4	30
	Female	64	5	10	40	4	3	2	—	25
Ascension (Dorward)	Male & Female	27	—	4	12	2	7	1	1	27

rather than merely a fixed species' characteristic, one might expect regional differences. The alternative, namely that incubation stints are related to food only in as much that all white boobies are far foragers, and in that way adapted to relatively scarce food, is less likely than that this basic adaptation is strongly influenced by regional differences in food. The incubation stints recorded for three different populations of white boobies (Table 48) support the latter, since they are longer in food-poor areas than in relatively rich ones.

Incubation is by both sexes. The length of individual stints varies considerably both within and between regions, but a round figure is just over 24 hours in some areas, down to less than 12 hours in others.

THE CHICK

1. *Morphology and plumage development*

The **newly-hatched** white booby chick measures about 10cm and weighs from 40 to about 60g and is very sparsely covered with white down over a grey, sometimes slightly pinkish skin. The eyes are often fully open (rounded) upon hatching, whilst the chick is still damp. The bill and feet are grey (the former bearing a white egg tooth and a broad band of pinkish on upper mandible) and the eyes dark blue-brown. During the **second week** down covers the back and flanks but remains thin and fairly short. By the age of **three weeks** the chick is more or less down covered, though not thickly and often with bare patches on head and neck. Exceptionally it may be left unguarded at this stage but only if the parents are under considerable stress. The gular skin is often creamy, but sometimes pinkish. Between 26 and 35 days (on average by the 31st day) the egg tooth is lost (Kepler 1969). By **one month** the chick is normally thickly down covered and looks perhaps a third as big as an adult (but culmen length is a better guide to age, see Fig. 162). The neck may still be barish in places and often the forehead too. In the **fifth and sixth weeks** (between the ages of 28 and 42 days) the chick is fluffy and, latterly, large, but without any primaries or tail feathers showing. On Kure, which may be taken as fairly typical, primaries began erupting after the 44th day and by 50 days most birds showed primary development, shortly after which the tail feathers began to sprout. However, in the Galapagos, which is perhaps typical of impoverished areas, primaries do not erupt until the chick is about **eight weeks** old and even then do not show on the closed wing. By then, the gular and facial skin may still be pink or it may have gone grey or bluish. The orbital ring may be grey. At about **nine weeks** in the Galapagos, primaries showed on the closed wing.

Once the black wing and tail feathers are through they quickly become conspicuous, but until about **10 weeks**, the chick still looks essentially downy. By about 10 weeks on Kure, and a few days later in the Galapagos, the scapulars begin growing and then the wing and tail coverts, so that by just over **11 weeks**, when these have united in the mid line, the bird begins to look properly feathered on the back. Then it is a matter of the down disappearing from the rest of the body. It always lingers longest on head, neck, flanks, belly and lower back. In the Galapagos a great deal of thick down persists until the chick is **12–13 weeks** old and this gradually thins, but clings on in some cases until the chick is **16 weeks** old, though some are clear by the time they reach 15 weeks.

At about **12 weeks**, the Galapagos birds had a pale blue gular pouch, forehead and face and lead grey iris. The bill was yellowish horn, with darker blotches. Later it becomes lighter in colour.

On Kure the juvenile plumage was complete (clear of down) by about 100–105 days, just a little sooner than the earliest Galapagos birds. The wing feathers, however, are not fully grown until about 114–120 days by which time the juvenile first becomes capable of sustained flight. Interestingly, the Galapagos birds are not behind those from Kure in first flying; their wing feathers grow as rapidly, even if their body weight remains slightly behind. To illustrate how tardily some individuals may acquire full juvenile plumage, I cite the survivor from a pair of chicks which we forced to live together for longer than normal. It eventually killed the sibling, but itself then took 142 days to fledge and was not clear of down until 126 days old, three weeks later than normal. This shows, incidentally, what a massive effect the sharing of food with a sibling would have on an individual's development. In the case cited, the two were together for a mere month, and that in their least demanding stage of growth.

The gular, facial and forehead skin becomes pale blue, at the age of about nine weeks, after first passing through grey. A few days after fledging the plumage becomes dramatically improved. It looks much glossier, no doubt due to water-induced oiling and preening. The feet become clean and provide an easy means of telling that a juvenile has been to sea.

The following main stages could help determine the age of chicks during a quick visit to a breeding station, when there may be little time for weighing or measuring:

1 week: tiny and with little down.
2 weeks: small and with thin down.
3 weeks: medium downy.
4 and 5 weeks: large downy, no wing visible.
6 to 9 weeks: large downy, wing and tail visible or conspicuous.
10 to 12 weeks: well feathered on wings and back, but thick down on the neck, flanks, belly and lower back.
12 to 14 weeks: thin or wispy down, especially on radio-ulna and neck and flanks.
15 to 16 weeks: Clear of down.

Fig. 157(a). A 4-week-old chick, Galapagos. Normally they are never left unattended until at least this size (they cannot regulate their body temperature).

Fig. 157(b). 6–7-week-old chick, Galapagos. No wing or tail feathers visible. Note denudation of down by attacks of non-breeding adult.

Fig. 157(c). Approx. 8-week-old chick, Raine Island. Wing feathers just visible.
Photo: J. Warham.

Fig. 157(d). 9½-week-old chick, Galapagos. Wing and tail well grown but predominantly downy.

The stages between 6 and 14 weeks are the most difficult to subdivide and any attempt to do so should take account of the locality.

2. *Feeding*

As in all sulids, the chick is guarded continuously at first and usually until it is about three to four weeks old. After that both parents forage simultaneously and mostly return to the colony in the late afternoon and evening. Chicks are fed in the normal sulid manner, by incomplete regurgitation. On Ascension the white booby's brooding stints averaged 11·6 hours (20 cases) which represented a substantial drop compared with incubation stints (32 hours). Thus the adults were returning more frequently to chicks than to eggs. Some change-overs occurred at night. Probably the chick received something less than two feeds per day. The brown boobies on Ascension averaged slightly shorter brooding stints (9·3 hours).

Feeds on Tower averaged 1·4 per day, a 'feed' being the total number of entries into the parent's beak in one 'bout' of feeding. Almost always young boobies beg so importunately that they obtain all the available food in a few entries, within a few minutes.

In a continuous watch during daylight in 48 hours on four nests the feeds were distributed as in Table 49.

A most important point in connection with the timing of feeds is that, due to the irregular nature of the food supply, parents cannot achieve an adaptive pattern of return. Thus, not infrequently, *both* adults return within an hour and a small chick, though it may be nearly dead of starvation, cannot take advantage of both parents. In the Galapagos, some chicks died because of this.

3. *Growth*

(*a*) *By Weight*

Growth curves by weight (like egg weight and clutch size) are valuable indicators of ecological circumstance, varying from population to population within a species and, of course, dramatically between species. This section is concerned with the actual data, whose significance is discussed in the Comparative Ecology Section.

The only existing growth curves for the white booby are for Ascension, Galapagos and Kure Atoll. These are given in Figs. 158 to 160. The Ascension figures are unfortunately largely unsuitable for detailed comparison with those from the other two localities, but are included in the smoothed-out, comparative graph (Fig. 158).

The most instructive features of the white booby's growth can be appreciated only by comparison with other sulids but even within the species it is clear that young grow very differently in different localities. Fig. 158 shows that the chicks on Kure gain weight considerably faster than those on the Galapagos. This difference emerges even more clearly from a comparison of maximum and minimum weights at arbitrary three-weekly intervals (Fig. 160). Kure chicks fare considerably better than the others. Until the chicks are just about fully feathered, the minimum Kure weight is about as high as the maximum Galapagos for the same age of chick. The conclusion that food is less erratic around Kure is supported by a number of related observations.

There is enormous variation in weight at any given age. Ability to withstand prolonged

TABLE 49

FREQUENCY WITH WHICH YOUNG WERE FED, GALAPAGOS

Total feeding bouts given by:	Nest 1	Nest 2	Nest 3	Nest 4
Male	3 (3)	1 (4)	2 (15)	1 (1)
Female	1 (3)	2 (2)	0	1 (4)

Figures in brackets = number of entries

starvation, with arrested growth and massive utilisation of tissues, is well developed and of great survival value in the white booby. The mean maximum weight achieved varies with locality, Kure birds reaching, at about 80 days, approximately 114 per cent of the mean adult weight whereas Galapagos birds reach only about adult weight. However, by the time they fledge, both are approximately adult weight. After fledging, Galapagos birds show a sharp drop in weight (Fig. 161) before climbing slowly back. This is probably due to the energy used in flight rather than to a sudden decline in the amount of food delivered by the adults, though it is likely that the free-flying juveniles miss some feeds and are unable, at first, to catch much for themselves.

(b) Growth by other measurements

On Kure, chick growth (Figs. 162a–d) shows that the various parts reach near adult dimensions at very different points during development; tarsus and middle toe at 45 days, culmen 70–80 days and primaries and tail feathers not until about 120 days (chicks started flying between 115 and 124 days). The rapid growth of the feet may be connected with need for increased ability to thermo-regulate once the parents stop shading the chick, at around five weeks. The slow growth of wings doubtless reflects the slow overall development; the production of wings takes a great deal of energy and in a species liable to suffer irregular food shortages, a commitment to concentrated energy requirements over a short term would presumably be highly maladaptive.

In keeping with the growth by weight the culmens of Kure chicks grow faster than Galapagos ones, which in turn do better than those from Ascension (Figs. 163 and 164). But the wings of Ascension birds grow faster than Kure (there are no figures for Galapagos birds). This difference implies strong advantage in flying as soon as possible on Ascension. Thus, despite a dramatically slower growth by weight, Ascension birds take no longer to fledge than do those from Kure. In fact, on the figures for wing growth one might expect them to take a significantly shorter period, because not only are their wings longer, age for age, up to 100 days at least, but their weights are much less. Flying should thus be easier. The advantage presumably lies in advancing the age at which the chicks can begin to contribute to their keep, consistent with a slow growth for the reasons mentioned.

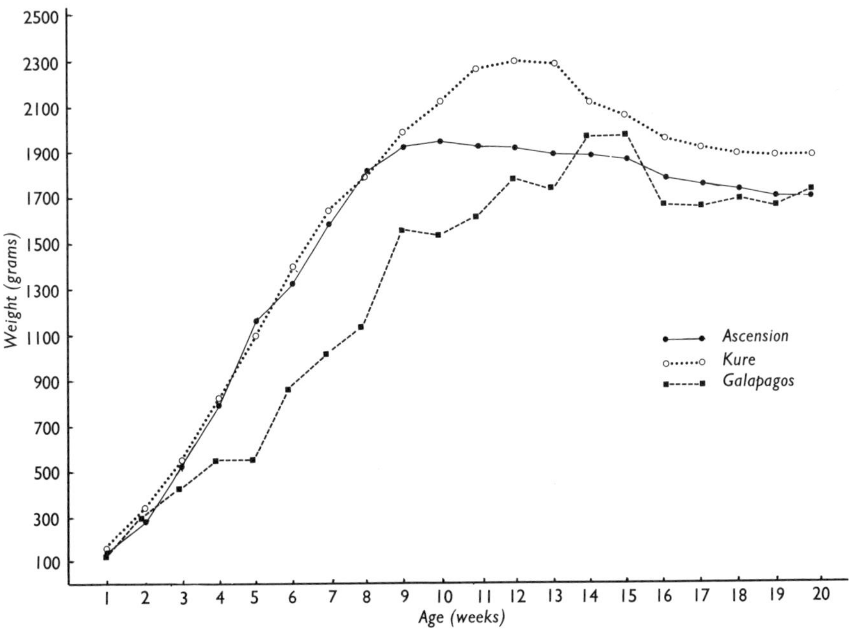

Fig. 158. The growth of the white booby chick in three different areas showing marked differences in growth rate.

Expressing culmen, wing and weight as a percentage of the equivalent adult characters in the same area shows that culmens grow much faster than wings, reaching adult size at about the same time as maximum weight is attained. Kure chicks grow better than those from the Galapagos, though in both areas (and doubtless everywhere else, too) the different parts grow in the same order relative to each other.

4. *Fledging period*

Since the rate of growth varies with locality, the time taken to reach the free-flying stage could be expected to do the same, but in fact does not. The slight Ascension data indicates a long fledging period (c. 120 days given for one chick and more than 141 for another, the latter having suffered severe stunting of growth during a period of extreme food shortage in August 1958). However, 120 days is indicated as 'normal fledging age'.

On Tower Island, in 1963–4, fledging periods ranged from at least 113 to about 120 days (7 cases) the mean probably lying around 120 days since some of these figures were probably under-estimates. The actual estimates were: 113+, c. 115, 116 (2), c. 120 (2), c. 121. The one precisely known case was 116 days. This excludes a case in which twins were artificially kept alive for some time, the eventual survivor taking 140 days to fledge. It seems that Tower and Ascension, both of which are known to suffer periods of extreme food shortage, are fairly comparable in their regimes and impose similar fledging periods on their white boobies.

On Kure, the precise age at which five juveniles first flew ranged from 115–124 (mean

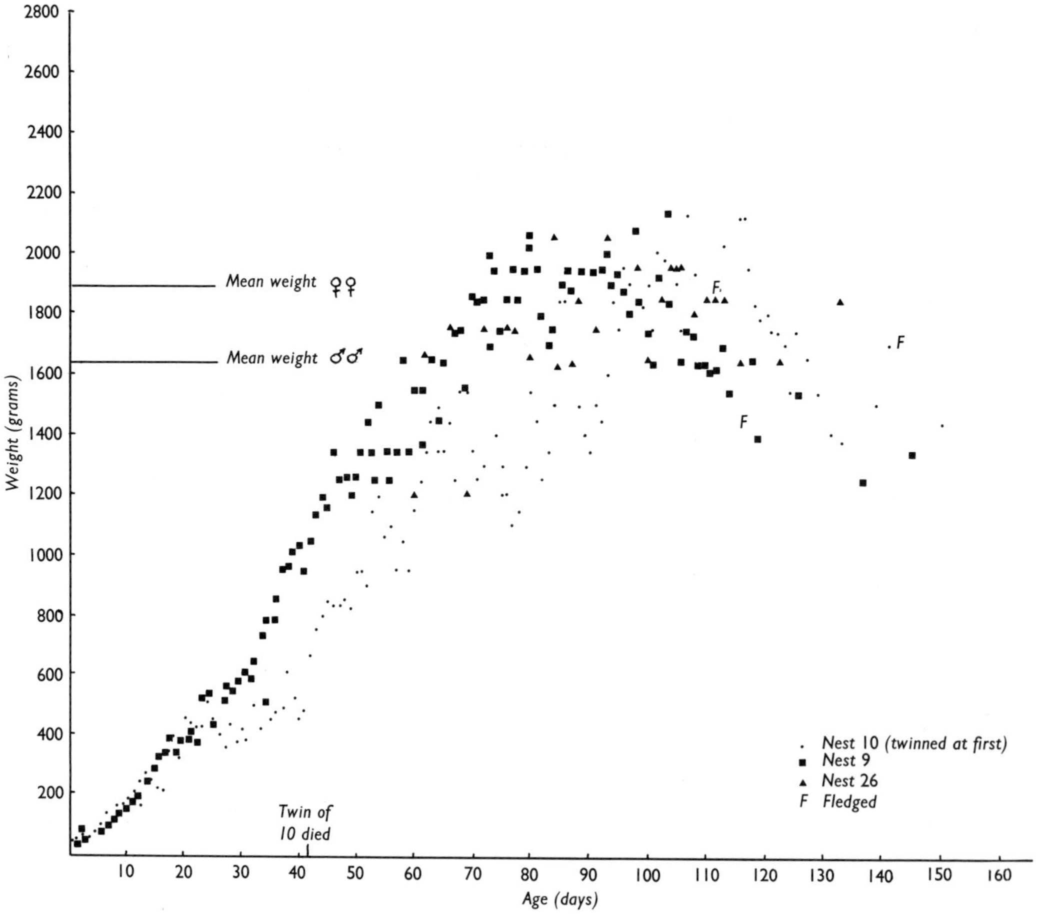

Fig. 159. Individual growth curves for white booby chicks, Tower Island, Galapagos. Note the marked depression in the chick which started life with a sibling.

117·6) (Kepler 1969), which is not significantly less than the Galapagos and Ascension figures. Woodward reports that they began flying from 109 to 151 days (average 123 days, 44 cases).

Thus, despite the considerably poorer feeding, the Galapagos and Ascension chicks managed to grow their wings as fast as (or faster than) the Kure birds and so were able to fledge at the same age. It is apparently necessary for the juveniles' wings to reach adult size before sustained flight becomes possible—a state of affairs which, of course, is by no means universal among birds.

5. *Post-fledging feeding*

White boobies feed their free-flying juveniles for a variable period. The young birds spend much of their time on the fringes of the colony or on inshore waters, returning to their parents' territory in the afternoon or evening to be fed.

On Ascension, fledged chicks returned to the nest site, and probably were fed, for at least a further three or four weeks. In the Galapagos this period was 30–62 days; six juveniles were seen to be fed 30, 33, 49, 50, 59 and 62 days respectively after fledging. Since all of these represent minimum periods, the mean is probably somewhat greater than 47 days and may be 50–60. They then abruptly disappeared completely, presumably having begun a nomadic period, wandering at sea and roosting wherever they could.

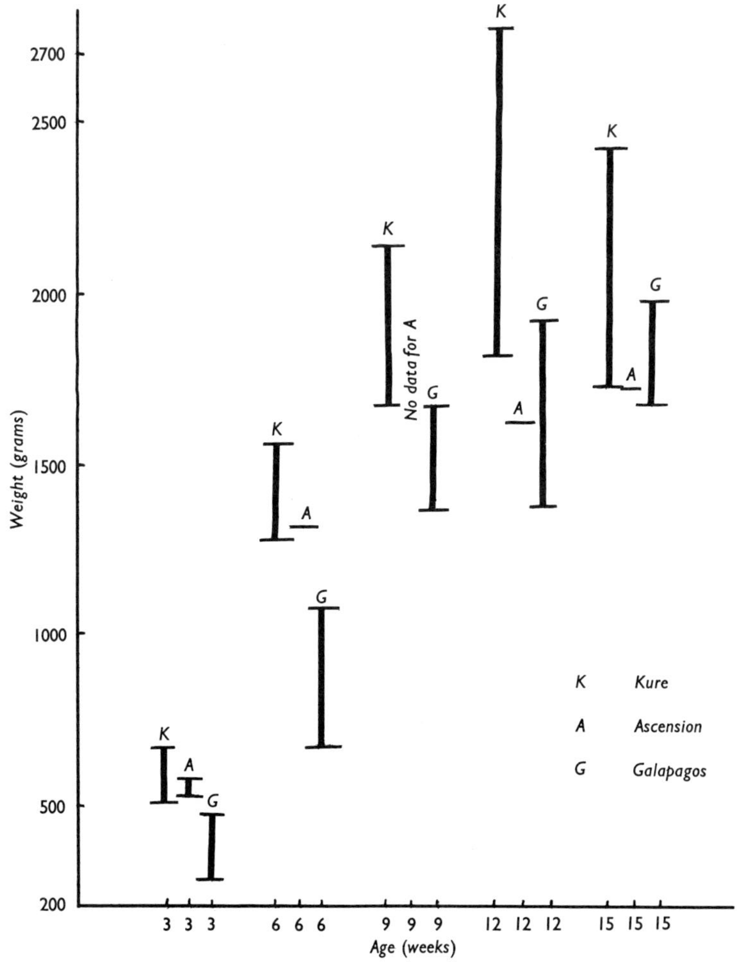

Fig. 160. Maximum and minimum weights at ages 3, 6, 9, 12 and 15 weeks, of white booby chicks on Kure, Ascension and Tower Island.

On Kure, flying juveniles remained in the colony for one or two months before leaving entirely. They were probably fed during this period, which is thus similar to that on Tower.

In sum, white boobies, even from geographically and ecologically distinct areas require about 120 days to grow to the flying stage. They then remain in or around the colony, being fed more or less regularly for a further 30–60 days, probably nearer the latter.

BREEDING SUCCESS

1. *Hatching success*

Kepler's investigation on Kure showed that, taking his two years together, 59·6 per cent of first eggs hatched and 55·1 per cent of second eggs—a statistically insignificant difference. Woodward presents his findings in a slightly different way; 43·1 per cent of two-egg clutches hatched both eggs, 33·3 per cent hatched one egg and 23·6 per cent failed to hatch any. Thus the hatching success in practical terms was 76·4 per cent which is very close to the figure obtained for other sulids, though this does not explain the low hatching success in absolute terms. Dorward's figures from Ascension were lower. In the two areas studied ('A' and 'B') 37 per cent of 631 clutches in area A gave rise to a chick and 56 per cent of 68 in area B; an average of 46·5 per cent. On Tower, 79·6 per cent of 49 eggs laid in the small colony at the head of Darwin Bay, hatched. However, by the time observations began on Tower, many young had hatched and most remaining eggs probably represented those whose owners had survived conditions leading others to desert, giving an unfairly high figure for hatching success.

The nature and extent of egg and chick loss must differ in accord with different environmental pressures and therefore, like development, act as ecological barometers.

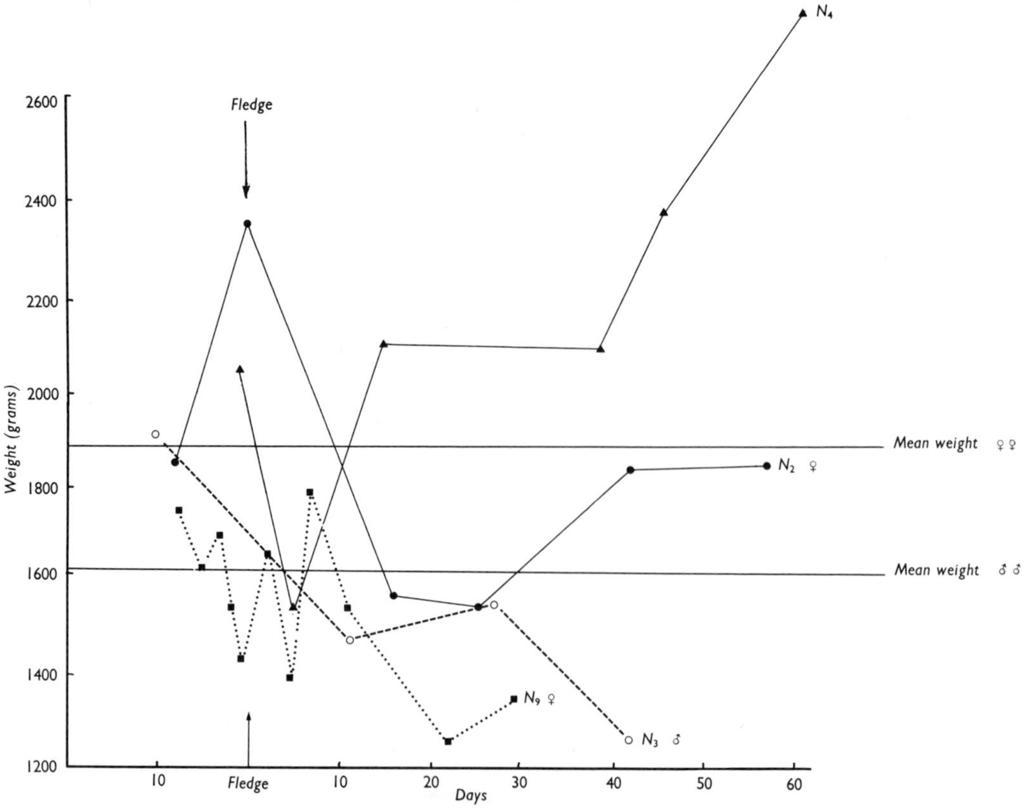

Fig. 161. Post-fledging fluctuation in weight, Tower Island. Note the marked drop in weight followed by a rise.

The failures on Kure were due to infertility, reasonably assumed if the eggs were incubated for more than the normal period (average age on desertion 93 days) in 8/178 cases (4·5 per cent) or to behavioural inadequacy (assumed if eggs were abandoned before 43 days). In 1965 there were two and a half times as many early abandonments as in 1964 (6 of the 1965 eggs were abandoned before the eighth day of incubation) strongly suggesting an environmental influence, in this case a particularly stormy period early in the season. The average age of abandonment in the two years was 28 in 1964 (4 cases) and 14 in 1965 (10 cases).

On Ascension, apparently, the situation was somewhat abnormal, perhaps due to crowding. Large numbers of eggs were found abandoned and there was interchange of eggs between neighbouring nests due to eggs being displaced and rolled in by a neighbour.

The detailed pattern of egg loss on Ascension was as follows. In area A 631 clutches were started between May and October 1958, 27 per cent of them in May or June. In area B 57 per cent of 68 clutches were started in May or June. Area B was thus markedly earlier than A. The figures for egg loss due to desertion in the two areas were 457 (72·4 per cent) in A but only 33 (48·5 per cent) in B. The difference was largely due to a drastic food shortage in August. which led to the desertion of a high proportion of existing clutches (275 in A and 13 in B) but by then, proportionately more eggs had already hatched and the chicks become well grown and better able to survive in area B. Thus, as it chanced in 1958, the earlier laying birds did better. The inference is that undue difficulty in finding food meant that incubating birds—perhaps already hungrier than normal—had to sit much longer than normal awaiting the return of their partner and many simply deserted. Similarly, on Tower, several clutches were abandoned in February 1964 (which as later events showed, was to be followed by a period of severe food shortage) though these were all fairly new eggs, which are particularly prone to desertion in times of stress.

Set against this major fact, predation is of very minor importance. In fact, few islands contain predators capable of robbing eggs from this powerful bird.

Amerson recorded two nests destroyed by green turtles digging their own nests! The same author declares that weather and seas have a big effect on breeding success on Gin Island (French Frigate Shoals) and the same holds for other very low lying islands, such as Little Gin and Round Island; the latter is a mere two metres high.

2. *Fledging success*

In a species losing many eggs through prolonged absences of parents in search of food, it is hardly to be expected that chicks will always thrive. Kepler has compared overall fledging success (number of young which fly as a proportion of those hatched, but ignoring the second chick where two hatch, since one always dies) on Kure and Ascension. On Kure fledging success was 79 per cent of 43 chicks hatched in 1964 and 83 per cent of 30 chicks hatched in 1965, compared with 25 per cent of 272 chicks hatched on Ascension in 1958. The Kure figure agrees almost exactly with that from one colony in the Galapagos for 1964 (79·5 per cent) but differs markedly from another. In the latter there was extremely heavy loss of eggs and small chicks in February–March; of 14 nests with eggs or small chicks in January–February only 3 (21 per cent) had chicks by March–April. The actual fledging success of this small group was 25 per cent.

Almost all chick loss in the white booby is due directly or indirectly to difficulties in finding enough food. It is hardly to be expected that the white booby will show a marked correlation between the month in which the eggs are laid and their success in producing fledged young, since in many cases breeding is only broadly seasonal and it is obvious that the factors which affect it most operate on the availability of its food in a markedly irregular fashion. Even on Kure, where it is perhaps as seasonal as anywhere, Kepler's figures for the percentage of nests started in a given month which produced fledged young, show that in 1964 early nesters were more successful, while in 1965 the reverse was true. Probably white boobies are not anywhere subject to selection pressures which would favour laying in a particular month, but in some areas a moderate degree of seasonal laying is probably advantageous over a long time span.

On Ascension the pattern of chick mortality reflected the situation already described for egg loss. In area A, no chicks were found dead in May, June and July, but 38, 96 and 5 were found dead in August, September and October respectively. The corresponding figures for B were none in May and June and 1, 18 and 5 in July, August and September.

August and September were thus the critical months and the most susceptible young were, apparently, three to four weeks old, at which age they not only require a lot of food, being within the period of maximum growth, but are first left alone, with the corresponding energy cost of thermo-regulation or even, if adults were forced to leave them unattended before they were properly covered with down, with attendant dehydration and possibly death. Even a relatively short period of drastic food shortage could, by this mechanism, lead to appreciable chick mortality. Chicks from any eggs laid in early May would, by mid-August, be eight

Fig. 162(a–d). Growth of wing, tail, culmen, tarsus and middle toe on Kure Atoll (all from Kepler 1969). Note the usefulness of these parameters, in combination, for determining the age of a chick.

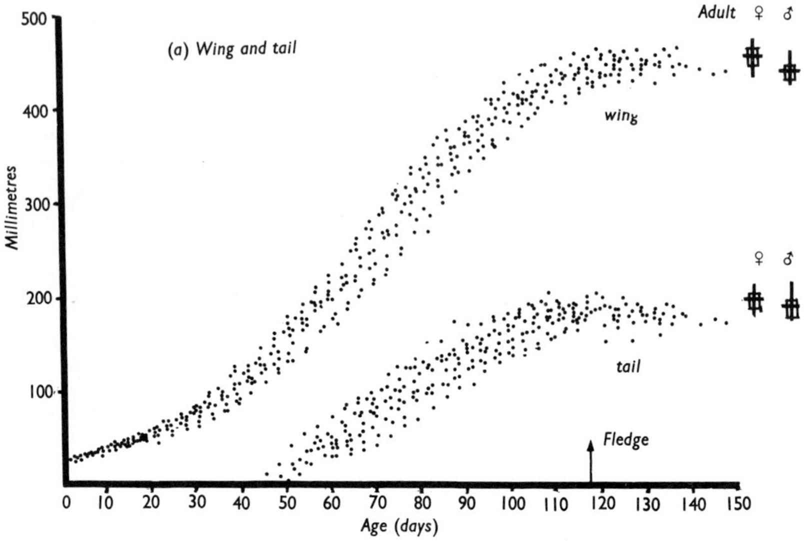

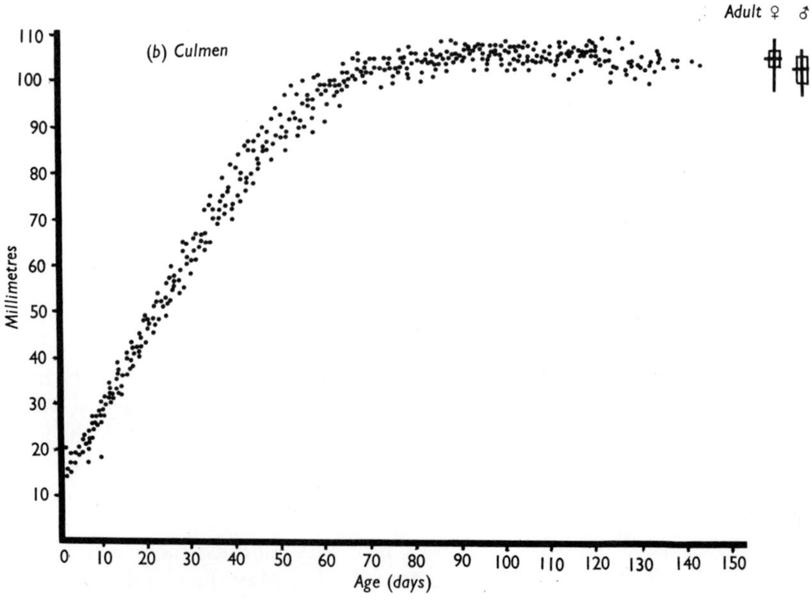

weeks old and even those laid in early June would be about a month old. The six to eight week-old young would stand a much better chance of survival.

There were indications that 1958 was an abnormally severe year on Ascension and it would be unwise to assume either that chick mortality is usually so high or that eggs laid earlier in the year always survive better. However Dorward had no figures for 1959 and merely deduced from the number of chicks present in December, that 1957 had been more successful than 1958.

Chick loss on the sub-temperate Kure Atoll was completely different. The figures for success presented earlier, show that nothing remotely similar to the mass starvation on Ascension occurred there and most of the losses were in the egg stage.

In the Galapagos there was definite evidence of food shortage and a few cases of chick starvation. However, the sample was small (four chicks died between March 11th and 31st,

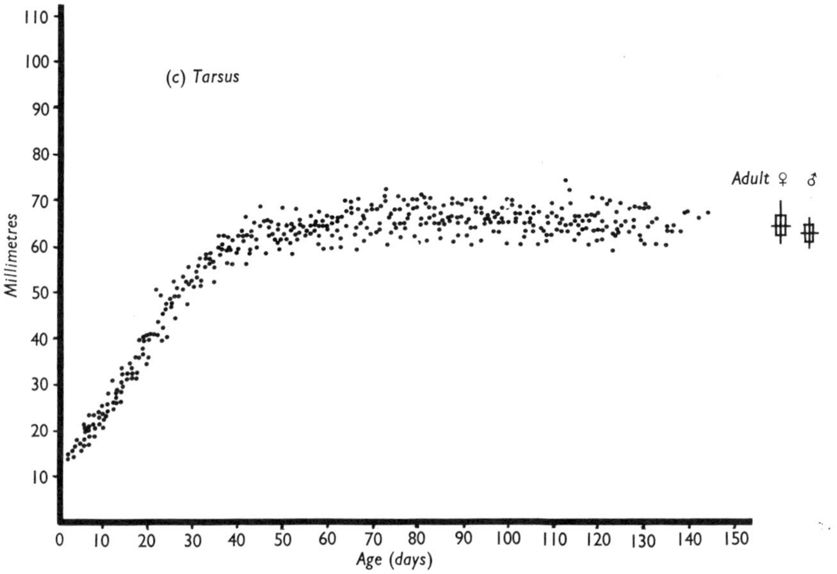

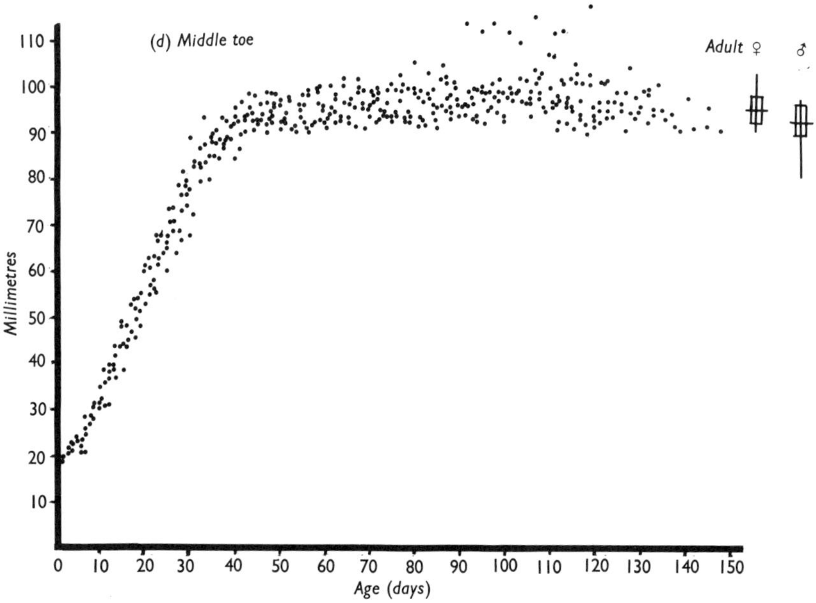

aged between 18 and 54 days) and most of the young on the island were considerably more than a month old when food shortage was most acute (March–April) and were therefore better able to survive.

Little is known about mortality in the period between fledging and achieving independence.

3. *Overall breeding success*

(*a*) *Regional differences*

In terms of actual production of fledged young from clutches laid (again ignoring one egg of the two-egg clutches) the figures were 9·7 per cent on Ascension in 1958 and 63 per cent from Camp Colony in the Galapagos in 1964. From Kure the figures are 71·5, 68·3, 69·2, 69·6, 57·4 and 86·4 per cent, 1964–69 respectively, based on an average of 55 nests each year

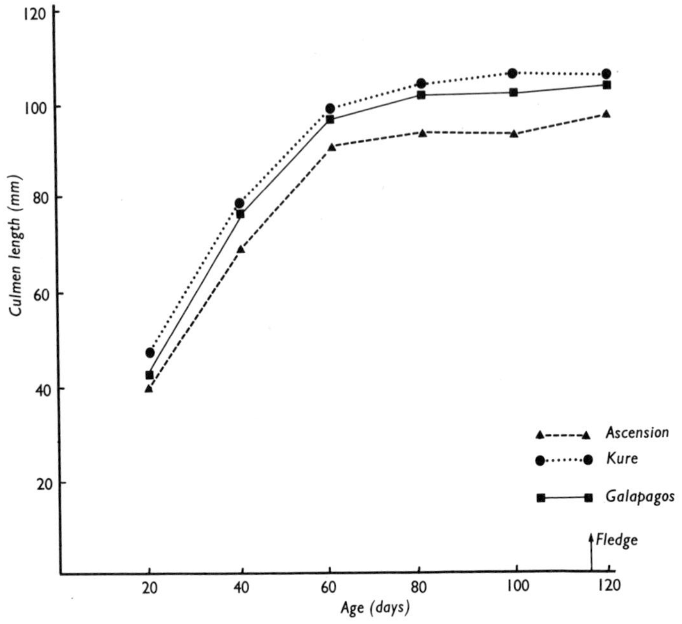

Fig. 163

Chicks from Ascension, Kure and Tower (Galapagos) compared for growth of culmen.

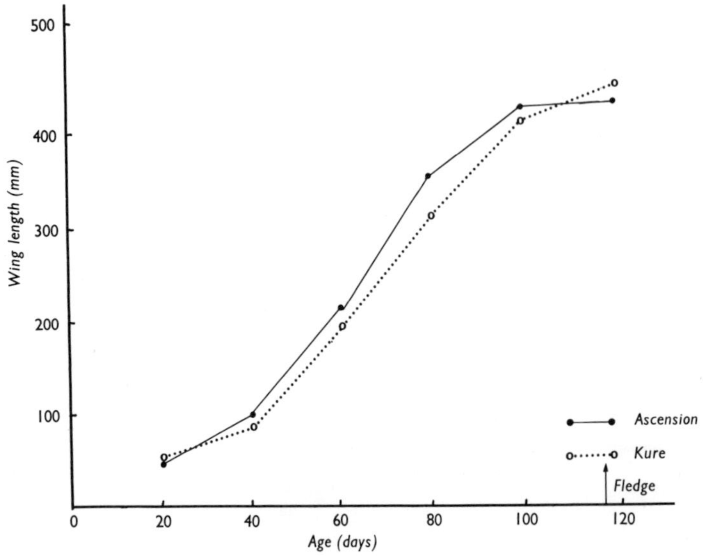

Fig. 164

Chicks from Ascension and Kure compared for growth of wings. Note that whilst, on Kure, culmens grow faster than on Ascension, wings grow more slowly.

(Woodward 1972). Kepler's figures for two of these years (1964 and 1965) were 63·5 and 52 per cent, presumably from a different sample of nests. Woodward gives full details for nests on North Antenna Field, Kure, and these are reproduced in Table 50. These are the only published figures for this species. They show that breeding success can fall phenomenally in the white booby, but also that it can compare favourably with most other seabirds. This is so even under the difficult conditions prevailing around the Galapagos.

(b) Breeding success in relation to the two-egg clutch

Clutch size within the Sulidae is fully discussed in the Comparative Section, but the facts for the white booby are set out below.

All the information on the advantages of laying two eggs we owe to Kepler and Woodward who have made a careful study of the contribution of one-egg versus two-egg clutches, to the young produced. Earlier, Dorward pointed out that several authors refer to the white booby's curious habit of laying two eggs but raising only one chick and he suggested persecution of the smaller chick by the larger (they hatch 3–7 days apart) rather than direct parental neglect of one as the mechanism causing death. He describes attacks on the smaller chick by its sibling, and later I extended observations on this (see Behaviour Section, p. 411). Certainly there is no case known in which two white booby chicks grew up together and fledged under the care of one set of parents. Dorward mentions a case of two chicks surviving for at least 34 days before the smaller died, but even there, adds that there may have been two sets of parents involved. There is a record of a nest on Tromelin, Indian Ocean, with two young aged 30–40 days, though nothing is known of their history. My records include only one pair of young in which the smaller was as much as a week old. In the vast majority of cases, the death of the smaller chick occurs within the first few days of life and it may be found trampled in the nest or dead or dying just outside.

Returning to the Kure data, Kepler reports that in 37 clutches of two, the mean hatching interval between first and second eggs was 4·8 days, though the interval between laying first and second was 5·6. In no case did less than 3 or more than 7 days elapse between first and second hatching. The average survival time of the second chick was 3·3 days, if one excludes cases in which, due to accidental death of the first, only the second hatched survived. The detailed figures were that, out of 31 nests containing two small chicks, the second chick disappeared in 8 cases, was found dead in 22 and fledged in 1, the older chick having died in infancy. Out of the 30 that died, 2 lasted less than one day, 5 two days, 7 three days, 3 four days, 2 five days, 2 seven days, 1 eleven days and 1 fifteen days. The Kure chicks which vanished were probably displaced in the usual way and then taken by frigates or rats. Frigates may, similarly, have taken displaced young on Ascension.

TABLE 50

BREEDING SUCCESS OF THE WHITE BOOBY (EXCLUDING REPLACEMENT EGGS) ON KURE ATOLL 1964–69 (Woodward 1972)

	Number of:				Percentage of:			
Year	Nests	Eggs	Young hatched	Young fledged	Young hatched	Young fledged from eggs laid	Young fledged from eggs hatched	Young fledged from nests laid in
1964	57	110	67	36	60·9	32·7	53·7	63·0
1965	40	74	35	19	47·3	25·7	54·3	47·5
1966	25	38	22	16	57·6	42·1	72·7	64·0
1967	38	63	31	28	49·2	44·4	90·3	73·7
1968	35	59	20	12	33·9	20·3	60·0	34·3
1969	34	66	45	c 23	68·1	34·8	51·1	69·7

The first point to be established is whether two-egg clutches produce more young than one-egg clutches. If they do, one then wants to know how the second egg contributes. Woodward's figures are quite conclusive on the first point. The success of two-egg clutches in producing a fledged chick, in 1964, 65 and 66 was 65·3 per cent, 61 and 84·6 (average 68 per cent) and of one-egg clutches 50 per cent, 0 and 41·6 (average 31·8 per cent). The actual numbers of chicks were 68 produced from 103 two-egg clutches and 7 produced from 22 one-egg clutches.

With regard to the contribution of the second egg, the first chick may die before the second egg hatches, may fail to hatch through being cracked during incubation or may even be lost. Woodward's figures on the contribution of the second egg are:

TABLE 51

FIRST- AND SECOND-EGGS OF CLUTCH COMPARED (YOUNG PRODUCED)

	Number of young produced	
Year	Egg 1	Egg 2
1964	29 (85·3%)	5 (14·7%)
1965	17 (68%)	8 (32%)
1966	14 (100%)	0
Totals	60 (82·3%)	13 (17·7%)

Kepler analyses the contribution of the second egg on Kure as follows:

Yields fledged young because 1st egg fails	10
Yields fledged young because 1st chick dies before 2nd egg hatches	2
Yields fledged young because 1st chick dies after 2nd chick hatches	1

22 per cent of second eggs produced fledged young.

In sum, therefore, it would be completely invalid to assume that the advantage of two-egg clutches lies in the occasional production of two young or that just because two-egg clutches virtually never give rise to two fledged young they are of no advantage. They contribute to the production of young by taking over from the first egg in certain circumstances. This, indeed, may well explain their prevalence in white booby populations and the main question is why so many females should lay only one. Could they be females breeding for the first time?

(c) Breeding success in relation to replacement laying

The significant contribution to recruitment which a replacement clutch may make, has already been mentioned. On Kure, in 1965 the six young produced by re-nesters represented 24 per cent of the young of the year. Kepler interprets late re-nesting as an adaptation enabling boobies to combat adverse years and points out that 1965, on several counts, was such a year. It is thus interesting that re-nesting was actually proportionately more successful than initial nesting in 1965 (67 per cent as against 48 per cent) indicating that indeed conditions did get better as the season advanced. Woodward reports that in 1966, an unusual year, no fledged young were produced from re-nesting pairs, but in 1968 the figure was 22·5 per cent. Thus in some years almost a quarter of the young raised came from replacement eggs—a much higher figure than has been established for any other seabird.

(d) The effect of breeding on the adult

The possibility that breeding may stress the adult has to be taken into account when interpreting breeding frequency, clutch size, etc. The little information we collected strongly suggested that, if anything, adults in the Galapagos gain rather than lose weight whilst feeding their chick. Even the pair that fed twins for over three weeks apparently did not lose weight; the male weighed the same after a $5\frac{1}{2}$ week interval and the female weighed 620g more on the second occasion. Table 52 shows that rearing young apparently has no adverse effect on adult weight.

This finding, though perhaps superficially surprising in view of the obvious difficulty experienced by Galapagos birds in feeding their young, is consistent with the breeding strategy of a long-lived seabird, particularly in an impoverished environment. Thus, in such circumstances, breeding failure can probably happen even with the best parents, who would be doubly penalised if their fruitless efforts damaged their own condition. It is far more productive in the long term, to prolong one's breeding life and thus attain the maximum chances of hitting favourable years.

BREEDING REGIMES

The timing of breeding and its duration and frequency must be determined by natural selection, the selection pressure being applied through the better survival of young, taken over a period of many years, which (a) are born strictly seasonally, loosely seasonally or a-seasonally, (b) which come from eggs that are relatively large or small (the latter placing the minimal burden on the egg-producing female), (c) which grow quickly or slowly thus determining, in conjunction with seasonality, the breeding frequency which is possible (a species which 'must' lay in April, for example, and yet takes 14 months to breed successfully, can lay only every second year). These aspects of breeding may be called the breeding regime of the species, and the tropical boobies present special complications. Synchronisation (which is usually an extreme form of seasonal breeding such that individual variation is reduced to a very small factor—perhaps a few days only) may also be considered part of the breeding regime. The adaptive aspects must be deferred for comparative treatment.

1. *General features of attendance at colony*

For approximately nine months of each year white boobies are in some way bound up with their breeding colony, but for the remaining three months may rarely visit it. Yet there appear to be regional differences in the ways in which the breeding colonies are used. On Ascension, in an area where there are very few islets suitable for resting and roosting, birds may use their breeding colonies for a much greater proportion of the year—perhaps even for all of it. (This factor, incidentally, may exert an appreciable effect on the pattern of events within the colony, particularly since areas which are short of roosting sites are, ipso facto, short of breeding areas and the density may thus be greater than normal.) However, Vesey-Fitzgerald (1941) says that white boobies in the Seychelles roost at their breeding grounds throughout the year, yet there are many other islets in the neighbourhood.

Taking, first, the pattern within the Galapagos archipelago, where roosting sites are plentiful, there is a clear separation between breeding and non-breeding seasons. During the latter, there are usually no birds at the colony during the day and few if any at night. Whilst there are no positive records to substantiate the suggestion, it may be assumed that the Galapagos white boobies are semi-nomadic during much of this period, probably coming ashore to roost in many places where they do not breed. If they return to the colony during this period they are territorially inactive.

TABLE 52
THE EFFECT OF REARING YOUNG ON ADULT WEIGHT (IN G.) OF THE WHITE BOOBY

State of birds	No. in sample	Male Av.	No. in sample	Female Av.
Not breeding	7	1516	3	1900
With eggs	7	1646	8	1869
With young age 0–1 month	5	1746	5	1750
With young, age 1–2 months	4	1630	3	1940
With young age 2+ months	15	1603	12	1962

During the breeding season the individuals attending the colony fall into several categories:

(i) The experienced breeders return to the general or precise area in which they nested before and gradually increase their attendance spells and territorial and courtship activities. During this pre-laying period the males attend more than the females; they are almost always present from late afternoon, during the night and for one to three hours after dawn.

Once the chick is able to regulate its body temperature and defend itself against petty predators, it is left unguarded. From this time onwards, parents usually return once each day to feed it, although this pattern may be severely disrupted during (presumed) food shortages. Returns are usually in the late afternoon or evening, sometimes during darkness and the parents may stay in their territory for several hours or leave it almost immediately. In the latter case (and increasingly as the chick grows older and more importunate) they may retire to a 'neutral' area at the fringe of the colony (not a Club) to rest and preen.

When the chick is fully feathered and particularly during the latter stages of its dependence as a free-flying juvenile, the parents increase their attendance in the territory and show a noticeable recrudescence of territorial and sexual activity. This continues for a brief period after the juvenile has disappeared and could easily mislead a casual observer on a single visit, into believing that he was seeing the beginnings of a cycle whereas the opposite is the case. Then the attendance becomes sporadic and finally ceases.

(ii) The failed breeders are a significant part of a white booby colony and after losing egg or chick continue regular attendance throughout the remainder of the breeding season, showing the typical late-season increase in attendance.

(iii) The pre-breeders. Without marked birds of known age it is impossible to discover whether white boobies typically spend a season or part of one attending the colony but not attempting to breed. In Camp Colony on Tower there were certainly a number of individuals frequently to be seen within the colony, often somewhat footloose and who gave no indication of having lost egg or chick. These birds were more sporadic in attendance than others. Fig. 165 compares seasonal attendance in different categories of white boobies on Tower.

The pattern of attendance at Kure seems comparable in that there is a period of about 2–3 months during which the colony may be devoid of birds. As the breeding season progresses attendance increases, both in terms of numbers present and the length of time for which each bird remains. Early in the season there are few birds present between 09.00 and 14.00 hours, but as birds begin to lay, so the numbers present all day rise, to reach a peak in April. Clearly the number of individuals that a casual visitor would see depends heavily on the time of day and the stage of the breeding cycle and a census which ignores these contingencies is relatively worthless. The most useful type of single-visit census would be a dawn count of all occupied territories together with a statement of the proportions of empty (occupied) territories, one and two-egg clutches and young classified by broad categories (see p. 354).

Kure birds without eggs or young (largely in the period before laying) tended to leave the colony for fairly short feeding trips, mainly 1–10 hours. A large proportion, particularly of male feeding trips at this time, were a mere 1–2 hours long. A very few lasted more than 24 hours. The mean length of feeding trips was significantly different in males (4·91 hours) and females (5·91 hours). The males thus tend to spend more time at the colony and less at sea, which is in accord with their greater territorial behaviour.

Once the eggs are being incubated the pattern changes, but only slightly. Male absences are a trifle longer (mean 6·5 hours) and incubation stints are 11·16 hours. Female absences are a trifle shorter (4·47) and incubation stints average 8·41 hours. It is of course not possible to know whether birds absent for merely an hour or two have in fact fed.

The general pattern of attendance and renewed sexual and territorial activity towards the end of the season is similar to that in the Galapagos.

On Ascension it seems from Dorward's account that the colony was occupied throughout the year and that there were always some birds engaged in territorial behaviour. He remarks 'territories were strictly defended even outside the breeding season' (though this was not clearly defined). Elsewhere, he notes that unmated adults (ringed) and adults (dyed) with an incubating partner, were seen in Clubs (q.v.) on the fringes of the breeding colony. It is most unlikely that any pair would breed and then continue to behave territorially until the beginning of and then throughout the next cycle, but it seems very possible that they might continue to attend the island. In this case, and with a prolonged period during which some laying occurs, another pair might then establish itself in the general area, thus creating the impression of continuous territorial defence from one pair. Were it otherwise, the Ascension white booby would become the only seabird known to retain and defend its territory continuously throughout its breeding life (but see brown booby p. 475). The tendency of breeding birds to visit Clubs indicates that Club and site attendance are not mutually exclusive (as they almost certainly are in the gannet). Thus there is no reason why the Ascension birds, having bred, should not spend their time at the colony, in the Club.

Summarising these general remarks on the pattern of attendance:

> in those parts of its range where breeding is relatively seasonal and roosting islands are not too few, the white booby attends the colony for some nine months. Unless incubating or guarding chicks, it is mainly present in the early mornings and late afternoons and evenings (remaining throughout the night). The males spend longer in their territories than the females. After a late-season renewal of attendance and associated activities it visits the colony much less frequently, if at all, until the beginning

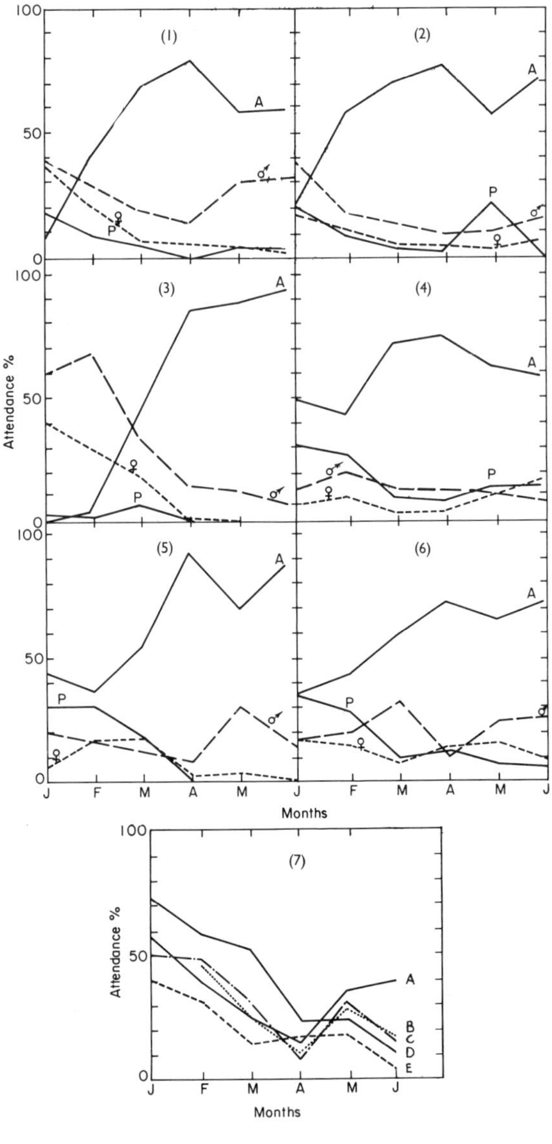

Fig. 165

Seasonal attendance at the nest site in different categories; Galapagos 1964.

Pair (1) Chick from January to May 28.
(2) Chick from January to April 27.
(3) Egg hatched Feb. 7. Chick died April 1st.
(4) Egg lost in December.
(5) } No egg or chick; status unknown.
(6) }
(7) Male solo attendance only.

In graphs (1)–(6) male and female attendance-lines exclude times when pair in attendance (shown separately). Attendance expressed as percentage of checks, morning, afternoon and evening, on which ♂, ♀ or pair were present. The numbers of checks involved were: (1) 613; (2) 631; (3) 641; (4) 615; (5) 501; (6) 503.

In (7) male A = (1), B is not included in (1) to (6), C = (5), D and E are not included in (1) to (6).

♂ ♂ B and E had no mates.

A = Absent

P = Pair

of the next cycle. On Ascension, however, it appears that non-breeding boobies continue to frequent the island (though perhaps not their territories) to such an extent that it is always well-populated.

2. *Seasonal aspects of breeding*

As a species widely distributed in the tropics, the white booby must be expected to lay in most months and in fact there are none in which its fresh eggs may not be found. Nevertheless, one might expect to find meaningful differences in the timing of breeding in the different regions of its world range, for these must subtend significant differences in the seasonal pattern of availability of food and other important environmental factors such as temperature and rainfall. On the other hand, even within restricted localities, there is marked variability between and within islands and between years.

The following clock-diagrams (Fig. 166) summarise the records—mostly sketchy—for the major ocean segments and, within this framework, for some island groups and individual islands.

Fig. 166. The timing of breeding in different parts of the white booby's range.

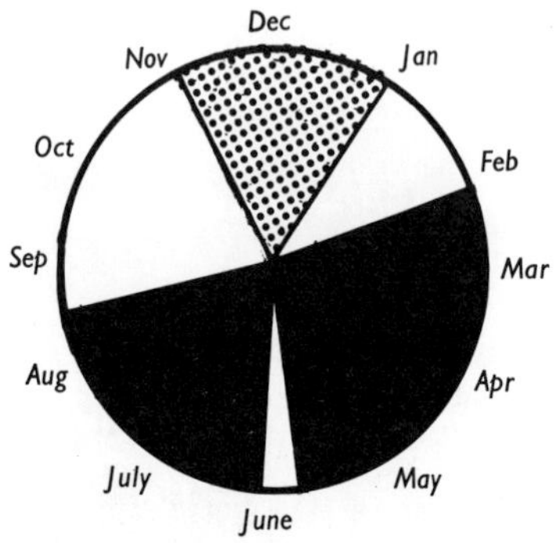

Fig. 166(a)

Caribbean and Atlantic

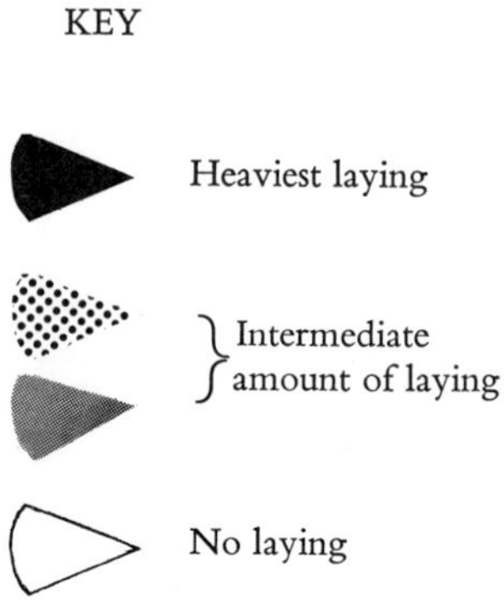

1. Alacran Reefs	Kennedy (1917)	Laying apparently Feb.–May.
2. Bird Island		Laying Feb.–April.
3. Monito (near Mona)	Kepler (in prep.)	Laying peaks in March and April, 1969, 1973 and 1974, but also major laying periods late 1972 and 1973; laying normally Sept.–June, probably with two peaks (Kepler, in prep.).
4. Ascension		Laying June–Aug., peak Aug. 1957, 58, 59. Some laying Nov. and Dec. 1957.

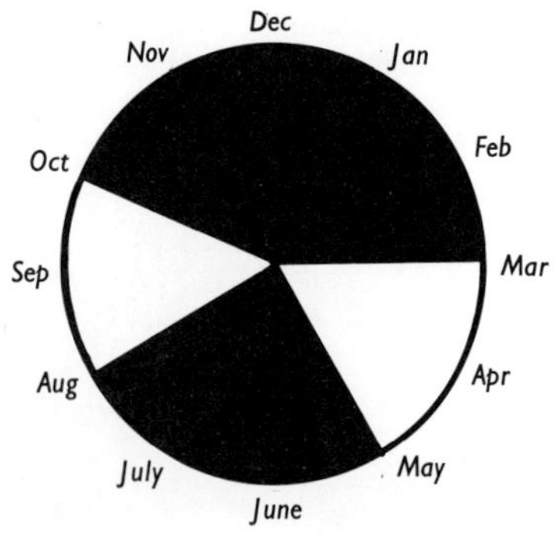

Fig. 166(b)

Indian Ocean (western)

KEY: as in Fig. 166(a)

1. Hasikiya	Bailey (1966)	Laying Nov.–March.
2. Kal Farun Jazirat Sabuniya	Ripley & Bond (1966)	Laying Nov.–March.
3. Mait Island	North (1946)	Laying May–July. Most chicks fully feathered and flying in late Nov.

4. Serpent Island	Gill *et al.* (1970)	Laying mainly Oct.–Nov.
5. Latham Island		Laying in all months, Jan. and March least favoured.
6. Desnoeufs	Ridley & Percy (1958)	Laying at least in May.
7. Tromelin	Staub (1970)	Laying June–July, also Nov.

Fig. 166(c)

Indian Ocean (eastern)

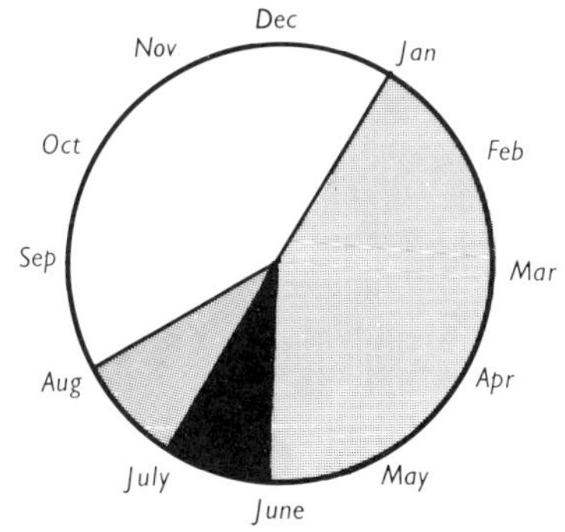

KEY: as in Fig. 166(a)

1. North Keeling	Gibson-Hill (1950a)	Laying Jan.–July. June peak.

Fig. 166(d)

Seas north of Australia

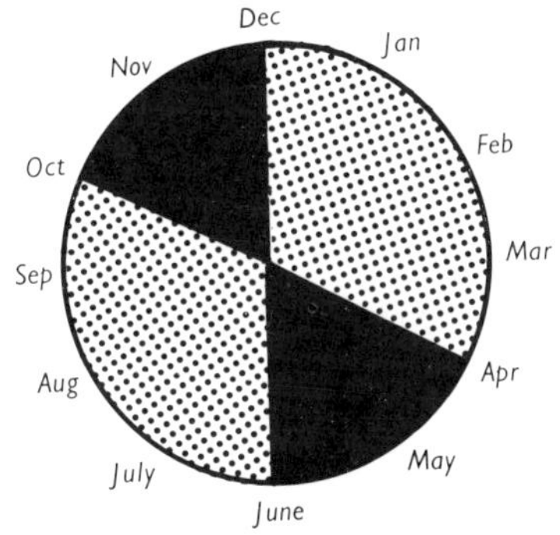

KEY: as in Fig. 166(a)

1. Coral Sea Islands	Serventy *et al.* (1971)	Continuous breeding, autumn and spring laying peaks.
2. Raine Island	Hutchinson (1950)	Laying peak April and May.
3. Lord Howe Island	McKean & Hindwood (1965)	Dec. laying peak.

Fig. 166(e)

Western Pacific

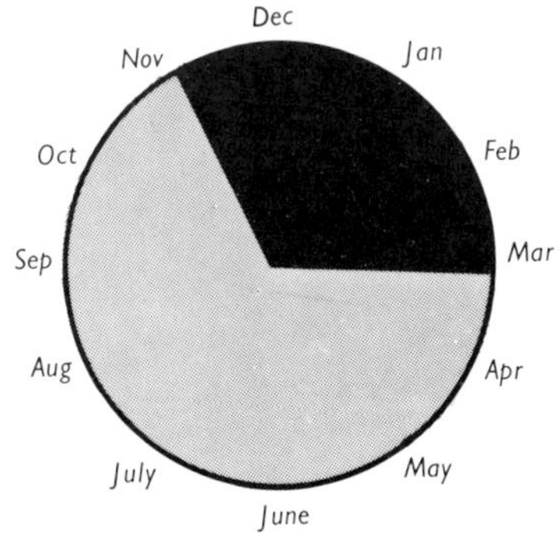

KEY: as in Fig. 166(a)

1. Marshall and Gilbert Islands.	Amerson (1969)	Laying concentrated between Nov. and Feb.; eggs may be laid in other months.

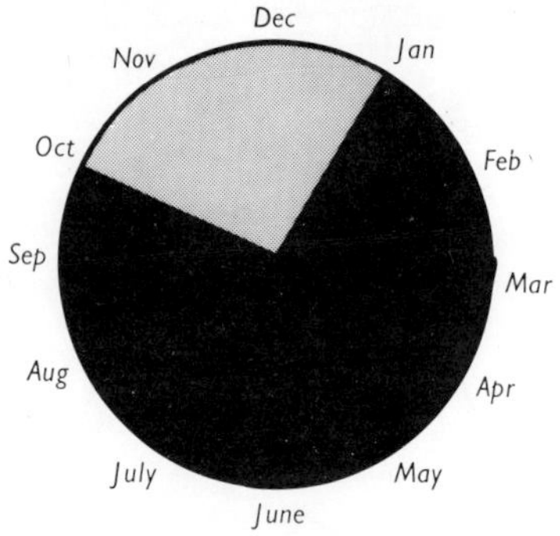

Fig. 166(f)

Central Pacific

KEY: as in Fig. 166(a)

1. Hawaiian Leewards		
(a) Kure	Kepler (1969)	Laying Jan.–July, peaks in Feb. and early March 1964.
(b) Gardner Pinnacles	Clapp (1972)	Eggs mainly laid Jan.–April.
(c) Laysan	Fisher (1903)	Laying March–April.
2. Line Islands		
(a) Christmas Island	Schreiber & Ashmole (1970)	Laying in every month of the year, main period April–Oct.
	Gallagher (1960)	
(b) Fanning	Kirby (1925)	Aug. 1924. All stages from eggs to full-grown young.
(c) Vostok	Clapp & Sibley (1971a)	Laying March–June.
(d) Caroline Atoll	Clapp & Sibley (1971b)	Eggs present in June.
3. Phoenix Island	Various	Laying probably in all months, mainly June/July.
4. Pitcairn Islands	Williams (1960)	Eggs and young of all ages present in mid-Oct.

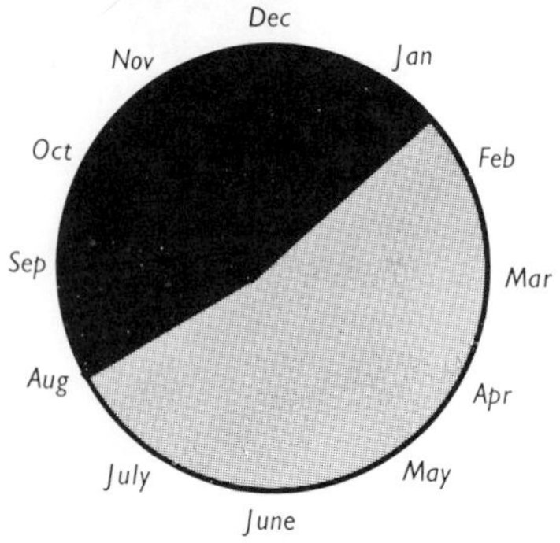

Fig. 166(g)

Eastern Pacific

KEY: as in Fig. 166(a)

1. Galapagos	Nelson (1968) and Charles Darwin Research Station records	Laying mainly Aug.–Oct. 1962, 63, 64, 65, 66, 69, 70, 72.
(a) Tower	Harris, pers. comm.	Laying mainly Sept.–Nov.
(b) Daphne	Harris, pers. comm.	Laying mainly around Dec. 1957, 61, 62, 63, 64, 65.
(c) Hood	See Appendix 10.	Laying mainly Nov.-February.
2. Gardner by Floreana	C.D.R.S. records and various.	Dec.–Jan. laying peak.
3. Enderbury		
4. Champion		
5. Wenman		
6. Fernandina		Laying in May.

7. Revillagigedos	Brattstrom and Howell (1956)	Laying probably from Jan.–April. March 1953 laying beginning; mid-May 1897 fresh eggs and young (Clarion).
8. La Plata	Murphy (1936)	Very little data, eggs present in Feb. 1925.
9. San Ambrosio and San Felix	Millie (1963)	Nesting all year round, laying peaks unknown.

3. *Synchronisation*

Seasonal breeding and synchronised breeding are closely related phenomena. The latter is an important aspect of breeding biology, but often badly defined partly because a broad, grey field lies between the two extremes of marked synchrony in a discrete and compact colony and little or none in a diffuse one. Also, synchronisation of a whole colony may be lacking, but sub-group synchrony may nevertheless be clearly evident. This, in turn, raises the definition of 'colony' (see p. 860). This section simply arranges the facts, to be discussed in the Comparative Section, p. 911. Sub-group synchrony may (and probably usually does) have survival value independent from that of overall synchronisation within a large colony.

The large Ascension colony, divisible into several sub-groups, was mildly seasonal but only loosely synchronised, though it appears that there was marked synchrony within sub-groups. Ascension birds thus did not fall neatly into any of the three categories mainly typical of the sulids—seasonal and fairly well synchronised (gannets); fairly seasonal with little overall, but considerable local, synchronisation (boobies in many loosely seasonal environments) and aseasonal, but with local synchronisation (boobies in substantially aseasonal environments).

In the Arabian Sea, breeding is clearly non-synchronous on Hasikiya, though it is probably loosely seasonal (p. 370) and the matter of sub-group synchrony has not received attention. On Latham, laying is clearly spread over a very long period and in the western Indian Ocean there is nowhere a suggestion that any population lays in a closely synchronised manner.

One could cite many more scattered observations which indicate that the white booby lays in a non-synchronised manner, but few of these give details or consider sub-group synchrony. Kepler's Kure work is the most detailed and indicates that in some years at least there is a marked peak of laying. In 1964, 60 per cent of clutches were laid within one month, but in other years the peak is flatter or even non-existent.

The situation on Christmas Island (Line Islands) was interesting because here the colony consisted of loose groups, widely separated. Within the sub-groups there was closer synchronisation than one might have expected in view of the scatter for the island as a whole. On Kure, the spread and timing of laying over several years is shown in Fig. 167.

Of 111 nests on Vostok in June 1965, 97 held eggs and 5 small young, showing that laying had been fairly closely synchronised in that year; nests were scattered uniformly rather than clumped.

In the eastern Pacific, the Galapagos Islands clearly show that colonies on different islands and on different parts of the same island, are often considerably out of step with each other (Fig. 168) (see App. 10). However, even the colonies on different parts of an island experience two or more loose 'waves' of laying rather than a homogeneous scatter throughout the entire period. These waves can be closely synchronised, particularly in small, fairly isolated sub-groups. The two Tower colonies in which both overall and sub-group synchrony were most obvious were in relatively open habitat, quite large and fairly dense. A third colony, by contrast, was in a shrubby area, small and well-spaced. These combinations were very probably correlated with the degree of synchrony of the colonies as wholes and of their sub-groups, and indeed with the time of laying, colonies 1 and 2 being earlier and more synchronised than 3.

In sum, it seems clear that, nowhere in its world wide range, is highly synchronised laying (whether seasonal or not) a marked phenomenon in the white booby. This is clearly but a reflection of the non-seasonal environment and possibly, even, indicates an advantage in avoiding a large number of dependent young at any one time, though this seems unlikely. On the other hand, sub-group synchrony undoubtedly occurs and may be advantageous in ways quite unconnected with food or season.

4. *Length and composition of the breeding cycle*

The breeding cycle of all sulids may be divided into four main stages (pre-laying, incubation, chick care and post-breeding) the absolute and relative lengths of which reflect several adaptations linked to the environment of the species concerned. The term 'post-breeding' is perhaps a misnomer, for it refers to an active period of renewed territorial and sexual behaviour before the recuperative (often largely nomadic) non-breeding period. All four stages are necessary for breeding and should be included in the calculation of the length of the breeding cycle. The breeding cycle is the time a species *must* normally spend in a successful breeding effort, where success is defined as the production of independent offspring. Both Dorward and Kepler err by ignoring the pre-laying period and so their estimates (six and seven months respectively) of the length of a successful breeding season are too low.

(*a*) *Pre-laying period*

Although the time required for a pair of boobies to assert or re-assert their ownership of a territory, establish or re-establish adequate relationships with each other and produce the egg(s), is highly variable, it is probably always at least three weeks and often much longer.

Attendance builds up gradually. Males tend to return to the colony before females and are particularly evident in the late afternoon and evening and early the following morning. (Seasonal attendance patterns for several categories of individuals are given in Fig. 165.) At this stage, pairs spend more time together, actually on the territory, than at any other time. Later they must incubate, guard or feed young, all time consuming activities. Even after the young became independent, several adults on Tower spent much time away from each other, on rocks at the edge of the colony.

(*b*) *Incubation and care of young*

Incubation and care of the young take 43 and about 150–180 days respectively. The latter comprises the 120 days which the young take to grow and the 30–60 days post-fledging feeding. Taking 170 days as a reasonably accurate figure for fledging and post-fledging gives a total of 213 days or 30–31 weeks involved in incubation and the rearing of the chick.

(*c*) *Post-rearing period*

On Tower the white booby continues to attend its territory for some three or more weeks after the juvenile has left the area. During this time the pair may become extremely active,

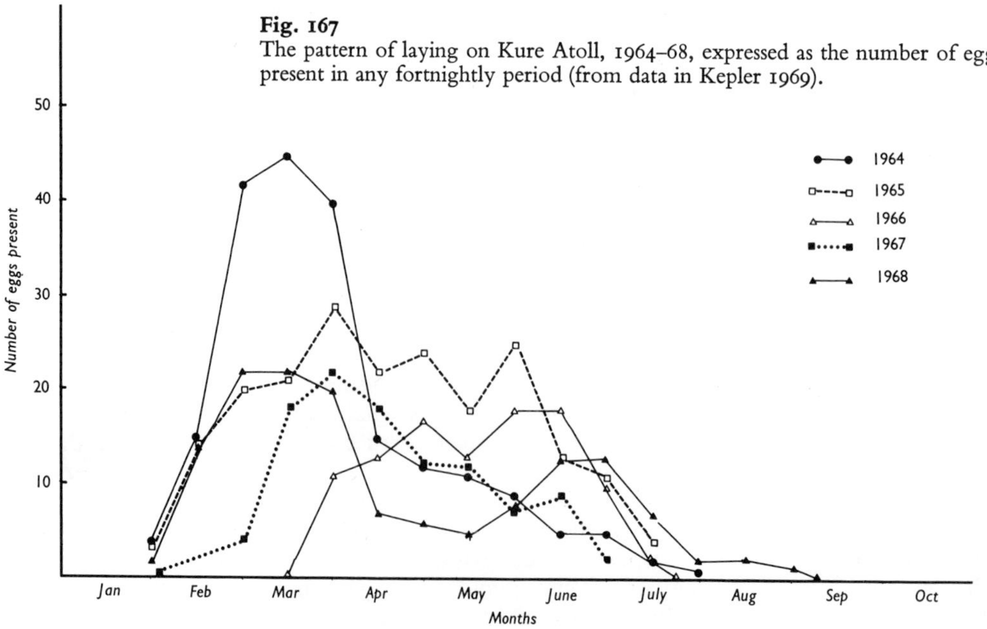

Fig. 167
The pattern of laying on Kure Atoll, 1964–68, expressed as the number of eggs present in any fortnightly period (from data in Kepler 1969).

engaging in all the early season breeding behaviour, a recrudescence of sexual activity which is probably correlated with the post-breeding increase in activity of the gonads. My observations ended before the adults which had bred successfully finally dispersed (see Attendance p. 368) and neither Dorward nor Kepler mentions the phenomenon. However, if one allows three weeks, plus three to six for the pre-breeding period, the total time required for successful breeding is 33–40 weeks. Even if (as may well happen) it stretches to 40 weeks, this still leaves three months for recuperation if the cycle is annual (see below).

5. *Frequency of breeding attempts*

This is one of the main factors affecting recruitment to the population and also throws light on the nature of the species' adaptive responses to environmental conditions. With respect to the latter, even within a species and far more between them, there will be environmentally imposed differences in breeding frequency. Thus, two populations of the same sulid species in different areas may differ in cycle length and breeding frequency. Also different species may differ markedly in cycle length, such that in one annual breeding may be imposed, whereas less than annual is possible in another. Or they may possess similar breeding cycles, but nevertheless differ in breeding frequency, even on the same island.

The white booby has an almost exactly annual breeding frequency. One year elapses between the laying of a clutch which gives rise to fledged young and the next clutch. There are, however, minor complications.

(*a*) *Frequency in relation to successful breeding cycles*

On Tower Island I obtained dates of laying by the same two pairs in two successive seasons, after successful breeding in the first. Both intervals were almost exactly one year. In addition, in one case a male bred successfully, lost or changed his female and the new female had not

Fig. 168. The state of breeding as observed on spot-checks of Tower Island and Daphne (Galapagos) in different months (1963–67).

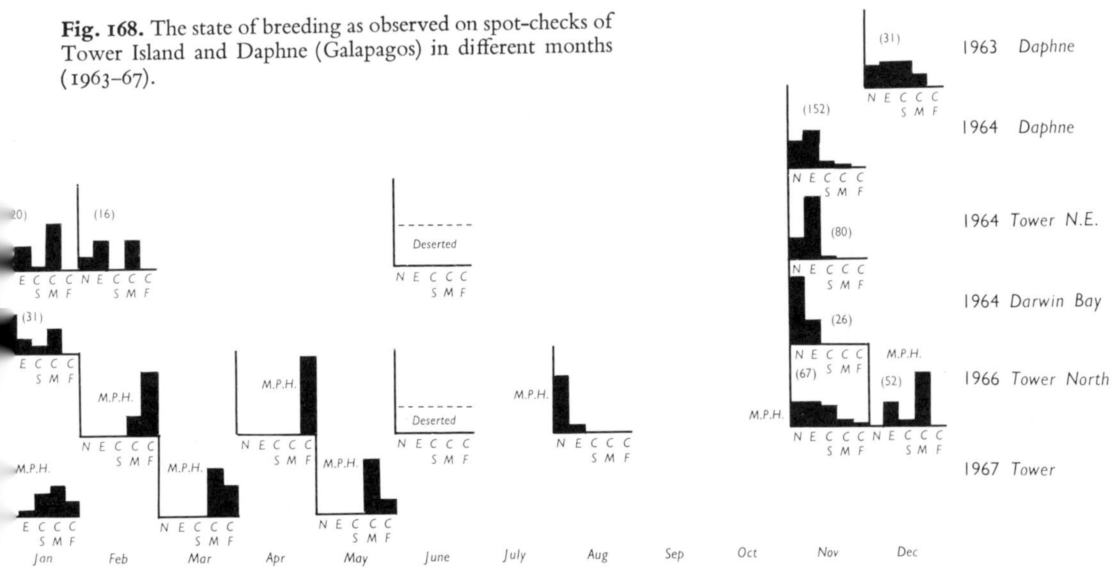

N — No breeding
E — Eggs
CS — Chick (small)
CM — Chick (medium)
CF — Chick (feathered and fledged)

NOTE: All entries on same horizontal line refer to region and year depicted in extreme right-hand column. Differences in seasonal laying between islands in same year, and on same island in different years, can thus be obtained.

[Data for 1966–67 from M. P. Harris.]

laid 13 months after the date of the previous clutch, though from the behaviour of the pair, she was close to doing so. In another the interval was 328 days, but I lacked firm evidence that the previous breeding had been successful. Finally, a pair which laid on November 30th 1963 and bred successfully, seemed, from behaviour, about to lay on November 25th 1964. In five out of a further seven cases of successful breeding in 1963–4, the egg had been laid before the end of November, yet by November 25th 1964 there was no egg at that site, but in only one of these was the same pair known to be involved. This female seemed about to lay and if she did so, would have taken some 57–8 weeks between layings. These records show that when the same pair breed in two successive seasons, on Tower, they space their efforts one year apart if the first has been successful.

Kepler provides excellent data on breeding frequency at Kure. Of 19 pairs which bred successfully in 1964 and came together again in 1965, no less than 14 (73·6 per cent) took between 50 and 56 weeks between successive clutches and of these, eight (57·1 per cent) laid within a week of exactly a year. The remainder of the sample varied from 47 weeks (1 case) to 62 weeks (2). The mean interval worked out at 54 weeks for this category of breeding pairs.

The Ascension figures are fewer and less accurate because Dorward regarded the pairs as permanent and therefore in year 2 (1958) interpreted a sighting of one known member to indicate the same pair as in year 1 (1957). This may have been an erroneous assumption and therefore the intervals between layings are not strictly comparable with those given for other areas. Further, the date of laying of the egg in year 1 was back calculated from measurements of large young, which gives only fairly approximate data. Dorward's Fig. 1 contains information on three pairs that bred successfully in one of his three seasons and whose laying date was known in one or more subsequent seasons (the three unbroken lines denoting 'successful laying to fledging' in one season):

Pair 1 (B on his Fig.) laid in late March 1958 and late March 1959 (losing its egg in 1959).
Pair 2 (H on his Fig.) laid about the end of December 1957, is not recorded as laying in 1958, but laid in April 1959.
Pair 3 laid in late November 1957 and again in late July 1958, losing its fairly new chick around late September. It then laid again that same season, in latish November.

Dorward concluded from his study that, although the species as a whole showed annual peaks, individual pairs having bred successfully and laying again the next season, did not necessarily do so a year after the first laying. He suggested that late birds one season may shorten their recuperative period and come into breeding 'in phase' (i.e. within the major peak) the next season. On the few figures available, however, it is at least equally possible that the interval between layings in successive seasons, given successful breeding in the first and retention of mate, is a year as it is in the Galapagos and on Kure.

(*b*) *Frequency in relation to unsuccessful breeding attempts*

It seems reasonable to ask whether pairs which lose their egg or small chick tend to reduce the period for recuperation and lay again before a year has elapsed since the unsuccessful laying. Kepler's data are again the best and show that of four pairs which failed in 1964 but kept the same partnership in 1965, the intervals were 52, 53, 56 and 58 weeks (54·75). Thus losing egg or chick had no effect on the timing of the subsequent breeding in pairs which bred the following season, when compared with successful pairs.

The bulk of Dorward's data refers to this category of birds. Bearing in mind the caveat with respect to the validity of assuming the continuance of the same partnerships, and the inevitable approximation of data resulting from intermittent visits, the information on 32 cases in his Table 1 is as follows:

Two pairs took one year between successive layings (mid-July to mid-July), although a further two were, within the limits of accuracy of the observations, near enough to count as a year (mid-August to end July), another one within a month (early May to early April) and three possibly within six weeks (mid May to early April), (mid or end September to end July) (mid-August to end June). Of the remaining 24 cases, two took approximately 10 months between successive layings; four took 9 months; seven took 8–9 or c8 months; seven took 7–8 or c7 months; one took 6–7 months; two lost both their first and replacement clutches and if one ignores the latter, laid 10–11 and c10 months apart and one laid in August 1957 but was not known to lay again until late May 1959.

This situation seems clearly different from that on Kure and probably also the Galapagos, where a clear circannual rhythm seems to prevail. On Ascension by contrast, failed breeders were obviously highly variable in the interval which they allowed to elapse between successive layings (ignoring replacements). The effect in many cases was to cause pairs which had laid late in one year and been unsuccessful, to lay much earlier in the next. Since successful pairs laying early in one year (where 'early' might be July–August) would tend to lay again a year after (if they laid at all) and unsuccessful pairs laying late one year would tend to lay earlier the next, the bulk of the population would tend to breed 'in phase' and 'early', leaving only successful 'late' breeders and very early breeders to breed late or early again, out of phase. The implications of this would seem to be that an a-seasonal environment confers advantage, on average, on pairs laying at a certain time of year, but this (to be discussed later) bristles with difficulties. The Ascension situation is thus far from clear.

(c) Non-breeding years

It is by no means certain that all pairs breeding successfully one year (or season where this extends over parts of two years) and both partners remaining alive, attempt to breed the next. Dorward states that of 75 pairs marked while breeding, only 35 were known to attempt to breed the following season, although most of the others were seen in the colony and these apparent non-breeders included birds which had been successful in their last effort. While some of these may have laid and lost eggs or chicks unknown to the observer, it is probable that this did not apply to all. Kepler remarks that, in 1965, there were no unemployed birds on the island, all pairs either breeding or attempting to do so. Woodward (1972) quotes the following interesting figures for Kure: 84 birds bred in both 1967 and 1968 but 11 bred in 1967 and failed to do so in 1968, though they were present in the colony. Similarly, 86 bred in 1968 and 1969 but 9 bred only in 1968 though present in 1969. 14 'went missing' between 1967 and 1968 and 12 between 1968 and 1969.

My information from the Galapagos was inconclusive, although it very strongly suggested that some pairs hung around the colony for most of the breeding season without attempting to breed. However, in no case did I know the previous history of such birds, which could conceivably have been young birds spending a pre-breeding year in the colony. Another important pointer was that, on Tower, out of 17 pairs in the Camp Colony known to attempt breeding in 1963–64, only four had eggs or young in late November 1964 (by which time most pairs which were going to breed in 1964–65 should have had eggs), although in a further four cases, copulation and nest building activities indicated (though by no means conclusively) that egg-laying would follow. If these are accepted and about half the remainder assumed to be potential breeders, whose indicator-activities were missed simply because my November visit was so short, it still leaves 5 out of 17 or some 30 per cent of pairs that attempted to breed in 1963–64 but very probably would not attempt to do so in 1964–65.

It may thus be taken that, at least in some parts of its range (and very possibly in all) the white booby takes 'rest years' even though having bred successfully in the previous season and in cases where both partners are still alive (and presumably still together, for otherwise it would not count as a 'rest' year). The selection pressures behind this phenomenon are a matter for discussion (see Comparative Section).

OTHER ASPECTS OF BREEDING ECOLOGY

1. *Food*

As a warm (blue) water species, the white booby feeds to a large extent on flying fish and the correlation between the distribution of boobies and fish was long since pointed out by Murphy (1936) in relation to this species' distribution in South American waters.

On La Plata (Ecuador) the main, indeed almost the sole food, were flying fish, 15–20cm long, though a specimen of 28cm, together with some squid remains, were taken from a bird at sea off southern Peru. This is completely eclipsed by a flying fish 41·3cm long, regurgitated in the Kermadecs. In the Seychelles (Vesey-Fitzgerald 1941) and Hawaiian Islands (Munro 1944) squid and flying fish (*Exocoetus* spp.) were the main food items. On Lord Howe Island (McKean & Hindwood 1965) samples of food were identified as flying fish (*Cypselurus* spp.), mullet (*Mugil* spp.), kingfish *Regificola grandis* and cephalopods. On Bedout Island (western Australia) boobies, white and brown, appeared to have been feeding on *Rastrelliger kanagurta*. Off Latham, a mature male was shot and found to have 20 cephalopods in its stomach.

Dorward examined 28 food samples from Ascension white boobies—incubating or guarding adults and chicks (23 per cent from chicks). The fish taken were mainly small (under 10cm) 390/430, but large fish (mainly 15–25cm) accounted for 38/430. One of the remaining two was no less than 37cm long. Of the small fish, *Ophioblennius* was the commonest. Where a food sample consisted entirely of small fish there were on average 50 in the sample and where large 1·6. The samples were composed of the fish species shown in Table 53.

Dorward suggests that since the white boobies rarely took the young (and therefore small individuals) of the larger species (whereas terns did) but took small adults of other species in abundance, the deciding factor may have been the dispersion pattern of the fish. Where small fish were abundant (as presumably in shoals of small adults) the boobies took them, but where they were not, they didn't bother. Doubtless there is an optimal economical ratio between time and energy (number of dives) and amount of food gained (size of prey) which it is usually maladaptive to transgress.

Twenty of Dorward's 28 samples were taken between January and March (1958) and whereas *Ophioblennius* was common in them, it was absent from samples taken at other times. *Engraulis* appeared on the menu in September and had their stomachs full of the red copepod *Eucheta marina*. At this time Dorward noticed that the faeces of both white and brown boobies all over the colony were red. There was very considerable overlap in the prey spectra

TABLE 53

PREY FOUND IN FOOD SAMPLES FROM WHITE BOOBIES, ASCENSION
(from Dorward 1962)

	(A) Food Species	No. of fish	No. of samples	(B) Prey Size	
Large	*Exocoetus volitans*	39	20	up to 4cm	3
	Scomberesox saurus	1	1	5–7	355
	Selar crumenopthalmus	3	1	8–10	32
	Fistularia spp.	1	1	15–20	
				21–25	35
Small	*Oxyporhamphus micropterus*	15	6	26–30	3
	Ophioblennius webbi	300	6	37	1
	Engraulis spp.	26	2		1
	Benthodesmus simonyi	38	1		
	Holocentrus ascensionis	2	1		
	Centrolophus niger	1	1		
	Cephalopods (*Hyaloteuthis spp*?)	5	3		

Note: Columns (A) and (B) are independent.

from both these boobies and other seabirds (the various terns) were also feeding on several of the species taken by the boobies. Dorward remarks that squids formed an unexpectedly small part of the diet of Ascension boobies and suggests that previous accounts may have overestimated its importance as a result of the accumulation in booby stomachs of the indigestible squid mandibles.

The important possibilities indicated by this study are that white (and other) boobies may well be somewhat selective in feeding, with implications (a) for resource-sharing in sympatric species and (b) indicating caution in interpreting isolated food samples which may fail to reveal even the major food prey.

2. *Annual mortality*

The Pacific Ocean Biological Survey Programme produced much information about survival rates of white boobies ringed as chicks on Kure and either seen or handled in subsequent years. The data presented by Woodward (1972) is in the form of percentages of a given cohort (that is, the produce of one year) seen alive in succeeding years. This may be transformed into percentage annual mortality (Table 54). Assuming that from the second year of life onwards, mortality is independent of age, the figures average out to an annual mortality of 8·6 per cent. This errs, of course on the high side since some surviving birds may have been missed by the observer and a few may even have emigrated to other islands. Probably 5 to 7 per cent would be a more accurate figure and at that very much in line with the mortality rate of the gannet. 6 per cent would give an expectation of life of 16·2 years.

The figure for mortality during the first two years of life, again erring on the high side, averaged 67·5 per cent over six years' figures involving 206 ringed chicks. The true figure may be well under 60 per cent, which is consistent with other boobies but less than that of the gannet—hardly surprising when one remembers that the figure for the latter is heavily boosted by starvation, exacerbated by the species' lack of post-fledging parental feeding of the juvenile.

Adult mortality calculated from birds ringed as adults on Kure and seen or re-caught in subsequent years (Woodward 1972) works out at 18·69 per cent (Tables 55 and 56). However, recapture or even sight-records of ringed adults from year to year does not give an acceptable picture of survival because many are likely to escape observation and if all these are treated as deaths, the mortality will err on the high side. Adult 'mortality' ranged from 3·7 per cent to 64 per cent. However, the high figures are certainly not due to mortality, since in fact many of the birds failed to show up one year, but returned the next. Neither do the low figures (around 4 per cent) unequivocally demonstrate that mortality can be so low, since they may be produced by birds that had been missing for a year. On the whole, however, the figures probably indicate a real adult annual mortality of less than 10 per cent, and at any

TABLE 54

SURVIVAL OF WHITE BOOBIES ON KURE ATOLL (from Woodward 1972)

Year	Number ringed as chicks	Number back on Kure aged 2	Number alive at age: 3	4	5	6	7*
1962	32	13 (40·6%)	11	11	10	10	8 (1969)
1963	43	15 (34·8%)	13	12	10	9 (1969)	—
1964	50	21 (42·0%)	21	19	19 (1969)	—	—
1965	38	7 (18·5%)	6	6 (1969)	—	—	—
1966	27	11 (40·7%)	9 (1969)	—	—	—	—

Average mortality (plus emigration?) between independence and return to colony during third year of life = 64·7%.

Maximum average annual mortality between return to colony at 2 years of age, and x years afterwards = 8·6% per annum.

* Records run up to 1969 only.

point after the second year, a further expectation of life of some 17 years. Some birds must reach an age of more than 30 years.

3. *Age of first breeding*

The information gathered by the P.O.B.S.P. shows that, when in their third year, some white boobies began to spend more time on their native island and a few even bred, though most did not breed until their fourth year. It was thought, on the basis of limited data, that very few if any bred for the first time after their fifth year. Thus a bird fledging in June 1963, say on Tower, could breed for the first time in October or November 1965, by which time it would be about 34 months old, calculating from hatching date. A chick (male) ringed on Roach Islet in November 1959 was retrapped on the same islet as a breeding adult in September 1963 and was thought not to have bred previously. Thus the bird was four years old, just entering its fifth year. Doubtless there will be considerable variability.

TABLE 55

SURVIVAL FROM YEAR TO YEAR OF ADULT WHITE BOOBIES ON KURE (from Woodward 1972)

1959	1960	1961	1962	1963	1964	1965	1966	1967	1968	1969
25	9	9	8	8	8	6	4	3	2	2
	10	5	5	4	3	3	2	1	1	1
		75	66	64	59	49	40	40	33	27
			59	56	55	45	31	31	27	21
				35	30	26	21	21	20	19
					9	7	6	4	4	4
						1	1	1	1	0
							2	2	2	1
								1	1	1

The bold figures are the number of adults ringed in that year.

TABLE 56

PERCENTAGE ANNUAL ADULT MORTALITY OF WHITE BOOBIES ON KURE (from Woodward 1972)

Year A	No. of adults alive in year A	No. of these adults alive in year A+1	Percentage mortality
1959	25	9	64
1960	19	14	26·3
1961	89	79	11·3
1962	138	132	4·4
1963	167	155	7·2
1964	164	136	17·1
1965	137	105	23·4
1966	107	103	3·7
1967	104	91	12·5
1968	91	76	16·5

Overall average 18·69%

This introduces the interesting matter of breeding in immature plumage, a phenomenon which has been reported for birds on Latham Island (p. 332) but which has not been fully proved. Beck (1907) recorded a juvenile (which he mistakenly identified as a Peruvian booby) paired with a white booby on Clipperton, but again it is not clear that it was indeed a partner, rather than the offspring. Since, by the age of two years, white boobies are almost like adults, birds breeding in brown, juvenile plumage would either be less than two or would have retained juvenile plumage longer than usual. In fact, breeding in substantially immature plumage is a very rare phenomenon among sulids. The red-foot, which in some areas breeds in brown plumage, is not (as sometimes stated) an example of the phenomenon, for the brown plumage in question is not, in that sense, immature; it lasts for the life of the individual.

4. *Movements*

Both adult and young white boobies, especially the latter, move about between islands. Five adults ringed on Kure were recaptured elsewhere (four on Eastern Island, Midway Atoll and one on Laysan) but none were known to breed on more than one island. Eight chicks ringed on Kure were recaptured as juveniles or immatures elsewhere—one on Midway, one on Pearl and Hermes Reef, three on Lisianski, one on French Frigate Shoals and two on Johnston Atoll. Two of these subsequently returned to Kure. Similarly, birds ringed as chicks on French Frigate Shoals have been recaptured from Johnston (14), Kure (5), Laysan (3), Pearl and Hermes (2), Lisianski (1), Kauai (1) and Nihoa (1).

One bird, reared on Kure, bred on Midway. This is especially interesting, since the bird in question travelled to Midway, returned to Kure, but went back to Midway to breed. Thus it had actually, as it were, obeyed its philopatric promptings before settling to breed elsewhere.

Movement to Kure from other islands was less in evidence (13 cases). Woodward attributes this to the lack, on Kure, of permanent aggregations of non-breeders. Apparently, such aggregations do occur on other islands in the north west of the Hawaiian chain and birds moving between islands are thought to roost in them. In the Line Islands, movement was recorded between Vostok and Jarvis, Enderbury, Birnie and Phoenix Island, the longest distance being 1908km, but none of this involved breeding on two different islands.

White boobies ringed on Phoenix, Howland and Birnie were recovered in the Marshall and Gilberts, on Makin Atoll and Nikunau. Two nestlings ringed on Lord Howe Island were recovered 1287km away in New Caledonia in their first and second year respectively.

5. *Fidelity to group*

To understand the population dynamics of any colonial seabird it is essential to know whether or to what extent it returns to its natal colony to breed and stays there throughout its breeding life.

No study has yet continued long enough to show to what extent young white boobies return to their colony of birth although, on comparative grounds, there can be no doubt that their tendency to do so will be strong. The P.O.B.S.P. has provided several records of young birds moving between different islands in the Central Pacific and one of a bird reared on Kure breeding on Midway (see above).

On the other aspect—the tendency of an individual to remain faithful to its locality having once established itself, there is good evidence. Kepler found that the Kure colony was divided into two discrete sub-colonies of unequal size, containing roughly three-quarters and a quarter of the breeding population respectively, and divided from each other by a dense growth of *Scaevola*. Although less than 90 metres apart, there was almost no interchange of members between them. In four months (October to February) which included the pre-breeding period when sites are established and re-established and pairs formed, only one bird, a female, switched from one group to the other. On Tower, all the birds colour ringed in January 1964 and seen again in November, were back in the original area, which was surrounded by large tracts of booby-free ground. On Ascension, Dorward's colour-ringed individuals obviously returned to the same general area in two successive years, judging from the very high proportion which he was able to see in season two.

One may conclude that not only do adult white boobies remain faithful to their island having bred there, but that they stick very much to their own group, at least where this has a convenient topographic definition as on Kure.

6. *Fidelity to site*

Whilst attachment to a particular site is simply the extreme expression of attachment to an area, site fidelity is probably not subject to the same selection pressures as group fidelity. In any case, it cannot be taken for granted that just because a pair return to the same sub-group, they will necessarily nest in exactly the same spot as before. Nevertheless, Kepler's finding that very *few* white booby pairs returned to their old territory is somewhat unexpected. Out of 22 pairs that remained together in two successive years, only two renested within six metres of their old site. The rest moved anything up to 65 metres, the mean distance moved being 19·8. The tendency to move was even stronger in pairs consisting of new but experienced mates (re-mated pairs). Out of 22 such pairs, the female partner moved on average 28·4 metres from her previous site and the male 23·8 metres. Altogether 90 per cent of the population moved from their territory of the previous year. At least in the cases of successful pairs that moved, one must assume that there is some advantage in doing so, since one would obviously expect a 'proved' site to be re-used. Perhaps the move reduces the degree of re-infestation with parasites, particularly on Kure, where boobies nest on a mat of vegetation.

My own limited data showed that a much higher percentage of marked birds used the same territory in two successive years. Out of (coincidentally) 22 pairs colour-ringed in 1963–64 and seen in late 1964, no less than eight pairs were back in the same territory and a further nine males and two females were seen (though alone) on their old sites. This makes a total of 19/22 (86 per cent) in which one or both pair members were back on their old site the following season. Of the remaining three cases, one pair and two females were seen in areas some considerable distance from their previous sites.

Whilst this situation clearly differs from that on Kure, it may do so less than appears. On my brief November visit, I did not have chance to compare the actual nest sites in the two seasons, but only whether or not the pair, or one of them, was present in the same territory. Since territories were often quite large, a number of my pairs could have remained within it and still nested a few metres away from the previous site, thus qualifying as 'having moved' on Kepler's scale. Nevertheless, the mean distance moved could not possibly have equalled his figure of 19·8 metres.

It seems perhaps more likely that the Tower situation of some 80–90 per cent site fidelity is representative of the species and the Kure Island pattern of 90 per cent site infidelity exceptional, than the reverse. Nevertheless it is of interest to know that different populations of the same species can differ in this way, even though the predisposing factors remain obscure.

Woodward makes the interesting observation that sub-adult birds on Kure occasionally roosted among breeders and generally near the site on which they were born.

7. *Fidelity to mate*

Kepler found that of 42 pairs which attempted to breed in 1964, 23 remained together in 1965 and 19 (45 per cent) split up. Of the 42 pairs, 32 were successful in 1964 and nevertheless 13 of them (41 per cent) split up the following year. Although the percentage 'splits' in failed 1964 breeders was slightly higher (6 out of 10) the difference is too slight to show that successful pairs tend to remain together more than do unsuccessful pairs, though this may be suspected from the figures.

The Galapagos figures agree closely with those from Kure. Thus, of 22 pairs colour ringed in 1963–64, 8 were seen, still together, in our short November visit and a further 10 individuals (6 males and 4 females) were alone on their appropriate sites. Only four colour ringed birds were definitely with new unringed mates, assuming that these were not birds which had lost colour rings. Taking the known cases, therefore, 8–12 pairs (66 per cent) remained faithful. Due to the smallness of the sample, one cannot safely assume that the other 10 individuals would be faithful in the same proportion and therefore the actual fidelity rate for the whole sample could be as low as 50 per cent or as high as 80 per cent. One may thus conclude that white boobies have a fairly strong tendency to change mates, irrespective of the pair's success or otherwise in the previous season.

From what is known of other species it might be suspected that pairs remaining together would enjoy more success than pairs comprised of new, even though experienced, partners. Kepler's results confirm this. Twenty-three pairs that attempted to breed in 1964 and remained together in 1965 then produced 17 chicks, representing 74 per cent breeding success. Seventeen pairs comprised of re-mated individuals (from 19 pairs that split up after 1964) produced 8 chicks, representing 47 per cent breeding success. This difference, statistically highly significant, poses the difficult question, why do so many pairs break up? At present there is no answer.

Although Kepler's data could not show that success in breeding caused mates to be retained the next year (or rather could not reject the null hypothesis that success in one year does not cause mates to be retained) nor the null hypothesis that breeding success in one year did not predispose to breeding success in the next, his figures nevertheless accord precisely with expectation in that the most successful breeders in 1965 were the pairs that not only were successful in 1964 but remained together in 1965 and the least successful were the failed breeders of 1964 that, in addition, changed mates for 1965. Thus, of 32 successful 1964 pairs, 19 remained mated and produced 15 chicks (79 per cent success) and 13 split up and produced 6 chicks (46 per cent success) whilst of 10 failed 1964 pairs, 4 remained mated and produced 2 chicks (50 per cent success) whilst 6 split up and produced 2 chicks (33 per cent success). Thus, overall, the 1964 successes enjoyed 66 per cent success in 1965, whilst the 1964 failures only 40 per cent. Taking mate retention as the criteria, as we have seen 23 'faithful' pairs enjoyed 74 per cent success in 1965 whilst 19 'broken' pairs only 42 per cent.

In sum, pairs that remain mated have a higher breeding success than pairs that break up, but, paradoxically, success does not seem to predispose towards mate retention. The other point, that there is no correlation between breeding success, as such, from year to year, is perhaps less surprising when one considers the often fortuitous nature of egg or chick loss.

From the behavioural viewpoint, it was clear, on Tower Island, that very many triangular and quadrangular relationships were afoot, involving birds without egg or chick and also, sometimes, birds that were actually breeding. This situation may not be typical of the species, perhaps resulting from the tendency of Galapagos birds to spend long periods away from their colony outside the breeding season.

8. *Population structure*

The only population of boobies in the world for which there is published information on structure, is that of white boobies on Kure (Woodward 1972). In 1968, 90 of the 118 individuals in the colony were known to have bred before, 17 were first time breeders and 11 non-breeders. In 1969 these figures were 94, 9 and 9. Thus around 11 per cent of the population were breeding for the first time, and 9 per cent were non-breeders, leaving 80 per cent of the colony composed of experienced breeders (cf. Australasian gannet, p. 296).

A small proportion of the population was sub-adult (which probably means around two years old), ranging from three to 16 per cent between 1966 and 1969 (averages over variable periods of time rather than absolute maxima). The highest figure represented 12·5 per cent of the population of the island, but this figure means little in view of the fact that many of the sub-adults may have been visitors from other islands.

9. *Clubs*

Many seabirds form gatherings in the general area of breeding groups during the breeding season, but composed of immature and/or non-breeding adults which use them for resting, preening, roosting, etc. Thus 'Clubs', as they are called, are a phenomenon of general interest, not least because of their potential role in population regulation.

Dorward considered that the Clubs on Ascension were sited in traditional areas around the perimeter of the plateau and on the steep edges. He observed six discrete gatherings (though there is no suggestion that they avoid interchange) each of which tended to consist of birds of roughly comparable age; two of adults and sub-adults; one of adults with some immatures, usually segregated; one of juveniles and two of juveniles and immatures. The total numbers involved were obviously considerable. In March–April of 1959 Dorward roughly estimated that the island accommodated, in addition to the 1200–1300 territory holding pairs, 3000–4000 unemployed (i.e. non-breeding) adults and the same number of immatures and juveniles. In addition, he states, from evidence of dyed birds, that individuals which are incubating may spend some of their off-duty time in Clubs, thus further increasing the number of birds using them. The behaviour of birds in Clubs of course differs markedly from that of birds on their territories (see Behaviour Section, p. 387).

Kepler reports similar Clubs from the Phoenix Islands (Howland and Enderbury Islands) noting that on the former they occurred on the windward beaches, which were unsuitable for breeding. Enderbury contained about 550 boobies on October 2nd 1965, of which approximately 100 were in the two Clubs. On Kure, however, there were no 'unemployed' birds permanently on the island, in 1965. All birds were breeding or attempting to do so. In later years, however, there were quite a number of such individuals. On Green Island, in 1968, 11 birds out of 118 individuals were 'unemployed' (did not attempt to breed) and in 1969 the figure was 9 out of 112. These, however, were not Club birds but merely non-breeders. But on one occasion a group of six birds roosted together on the north point of Green Island and might have counted as a Club. Kepler associated the absence of Clubs with the large territories of Kure birds. In this situation there is no need to seek aggression-free areas for resting, etc. Ascension, on the other hand, is unusually densely populated and also very bare, so that there is constant visual contact between neighbours. However, this applies only to Clubs of off-duty birds; there remain the non-breeders and immatures. On Vostok, in mid-June 1965 there was a Club of about 75 birds, containing several which had been ringed on other islands in the Lines. Many breeding stations support birds all year round (Mait Island, Hasikiya, Latham, Seychelles and no doubt hundreds of others).

There were no Clubs around the Camp colony on Tower. All the non-breeding adult birds held territories or wandered more or less extensively and there were no immatures in the area. It may be that, where there are many islands in a small area, or a small population of boobies, there is little tendency for immatures to gather in or near breeding colonies. The reverse applies to Ascension.

10. *Relationships with other species*

The role of interspecific competition, of whatever kind (direct predation is not included here) in a species' ecology is comparatively rarely investigated and usually tacitly assumed to be unimportant. It would most likely operate, if at all, in feeding and the acquisition of a nest site. About the former there is no direct evidence, though the extent to which differences in prey-species or size, or proportions of size groups are found when looked for, indicates that interspecific competition is reduced as much as possible.

So far as competition for nesting space is concerned, Kepler provides a nice example of interspecific territoriality between white boobies and Laysan albatrosses. He recorded 29 booby threats or aggressive acts directed against albatrosses, 11 involving an actual attack, 10 of which caused them to flee. In the 11th the albatross reciprocated with an aggressive display, the Head-up-and-whine. In 10 interactions the booby displayed at the albatross, which responded by altering direction and moving away. On one occasion a booby returned to his site and found it occupied by an albatross, whereupon he bit it severely and drove it away. Kepler concludes that the boobies and albatrosses are in competition for broadly the same nesting habitat and that the boobies' interspecific territorialism is important and enables them to compete successfully against albatrosses. He also recorded two instances of white boobies vigorously dispelling brown boobies and several instances of white boobies calling aggressively at overflying red-footed boobies. Brown and white boobies often do nest extremely close together and without doubt the latter is dominant. In the Seychelles, Ridley & Percy (1958) recorded several instances of sooty terns, killed by boobies near to which the terns had tried to nest.

Another important type of interaction is that between boobies and food-robbers—principally frigate-birds, with one or another species of which they are often sympatric. Frigates are said to persecute white boobies less than red-foots; the former are credited with an 'avoidance technique'—coming in high and then descending at speed to the site. I did not myself notice this on Tower. Simmons (1967b) credits the white booby with robbing the brown, but gives no details.

An unusual form of exploitation of white boobies by another species is found in the Galapagos, on Wenman, where a finch *Geospiza difficilis* drinks the booby's blood by pecking at the wing in the carpal joint area, until it bleeds (Bowman & Belleb 1965). Possibly they puncture the quill bases. They also attack the bases of tail feathers in red-footed boobies (Fosberg 1965). It is suggested that the habit arose as a consequence of accidental blood-letting during pecks aimed at the parasitic hippoboscid flies which infest boobies. The attacks may then have become concentrated on the wing bow and tail base because it is easiest to draw blood there. However, the Wenman finches seem extraordinarily versatile and bold and have been observed to congregate at a booby's nest upon hearing the young begging and eat spilt fish and to pick ecto-parasites from boobies. They have been seen to examine the cloaca of a nestling booby (similarly I recorded mocking birds pecking at the cloaca of a blue-footed booby) and to attack eggs of frigates and gulls—and no doubt boobies are not exempt.

11. *Predators*

Predation other than by man is an unimportant factor in the white booby's breeding success. Adults are immune, but chicks occasionally fall prey to birds (for example, short-eared owls in the Galapagos) mammals (rats, cats and on Clipperton wild pigs) and perhaps land crabs. Some chick deaths are certainly due to the interference of unemployed adults, perhaps failed or non-breeding birds. On Tower we saw many such attacks. At sea, some birds of all ages may be taken by large fish, especially sharks.

SUMMARY

1. The white booby's typical breeding habitat is a small, bare, flattish, oceanic island, preferably the fringes. However, it shows considerable versatility and can use cliff ledges, steep slopes, littered and vegetated terrain and even the edge of a land mass.
2. Colony size and density vary enormously, from many thousands of pairs a metre or so apart, to tiny groups of widely scattered pairs or isolated pairs.
3. However ill-defined, there is nevertheless a tendency to clump, leaving gaps between groups varying considerably in size.
4. No real nest is constructed but a distinctive bare circle is cleared around the sitting bird and symbolic nest building activities are important.
5. Clutch size is one or two eggs (mean varies with locality from around 1·5 to 1·8, though there are as yet insufficient figures to correlate clutch size with geographical location).
6. Eggs are laid $5\frac{1}{2}$ days apart.
7. The length of incubation stints varies with locality from (on average) about 24 hours to less than 12 hours. It probably reflects availability of food.
8. The incubation period is 44 days for the first egg of a clutch and 43 for the second. Thus the gap created by the laying interval persists, but is slightly diminished.
9. The second-hatched chick is always killed by the first, if this is still alive. Usually ejection occurs within four days.
10. The stages in development of the chick are described.
11. Chicks are fed between once and twice per day (actual figure for Tower 1·4), largely on flying fish and in some areas, squid.
12. Growth, by weight is slow compared with most other boobies and shows dramatic regional differences, Ascension and Galapagos being much worse than Kure. In food poor areas, fluctuations in growth can be enormous and the ability to withstand prolonged starvation is a well-developed adaptation.
13. Juveniles fledge at approximately adult weight.
14. After fledging Galapagos birds show a sharp drop in weight, before climbing back up.

15. Growth is allometric; the various parts reach adult size at very different points during development. The feet grow most rapidly (perhaps because used in thermo-regulation) and the beak most slowly.

16. The nature of these differential growth patterns is subject to regional variation. Though bills grow more slowly on Ascension than Kure, wings grow as fast or faster. Thus flight is attained as soon as possible, which is very probably highly adaptive.

17. The fledging period is about 118–120 days.

18. Free-flying juveniles are fed for about 50–60 days.

19. Hatching success seems highly variable, from 37 per cent to 80 per cent. Kepler's figures of around 60 per cent may be near the representative figure for the species. If so, the white booby has a relatively low hatching success.

20. Egg desertion and chick loss are largely due to scarcity of food.

21. Fledging success varies with region. Ignoring the second chick, where two hatch, it was about 80 per cent on Kure, 25 per cent on Ascension and 80 per cent in one colony on Tower, though only 21 per cent in another.

22. Kepler conclusively showed that the two-egg clutch is adaptive; 22 per cent of second eggs produced fledged young, though in no case did any adults rear two young.

23. Breeding regimes are discussed. Attendance at colonies show regional differences. In some cases adults return regularly throughout the year; in others, outside the breeding period most birds may be absent for most of the time.

24. Different parts of the breeding cycle each have their own pattern of attendance, for which some details are given.

25. Failed breeders, non-breeders and pre-breeders are part of most or all colonies and have some importance in interfering with breeding pairs and creating triangular and quadrangular relationships, though this aspect has not been adequately studied.

26. In different regions, white boobies breed at different seasons or are aseasonal in some and less so in others. This is discussed for each of the world's major ocean segments and the general pattern given.

27. The breeding cycle takes about 33–40 weeks (3–6 weeks or more pre-laying attendance; 6 weeks incubation; 17 weeks fledging period; 4–8 weeks post-fledging feeding and 3 weeks or more post-breeding attendance).

28. The breeding cycle is basically annual, so far as is known.

29. On Kure, 74 per cent of pairs which remained together took from 50 to 56 weeks between successive clutches.

30. On Kure, failure did not affect the timing of the subsequent breeding attempt; laying still occurs about a year after the laying of the clutch that failed. On Ascension, however, some failed pairs laid again as little as 6–7 months after the laying of the clutch that failed.

31. However, non-breeding years probably occur.

32. Around Ascension, the fish taken were mainly under 10cm long but large fish (15–25cm) accounted for 9 per cent of Dorward's food samples. Other aspects of the food spectrum are discussed.

33. Annual adult mortality is less than 10 per cent and may be considerably lower. Mortality in the first year is probably 50–60 per cent. Adult life expectancy is at least 17 years.

34. Probably the commonest age for the first breeding attempt is three, perhaps sometimes four, but probably very rarely two.

35. Juveniles travel long distances from their birth place and may breed on islands other than their own.

36. Fidelity to group is very strong but not absolute.

37. Fidelity to exact site was very weak on Kure; 90 per cent of the population moved from their territory of the previous year. In the Galapagos it was much stronger.

38. Fidelity to mate from one year to the next is not much more than about 50 per cent. Seemingly paradoxically, pairs that remain mated have a higher breeding success than pairs that break up, but success seems not to predispose to mate retention.

39. On Kure, in any one year, some 80 per cent of the population are experienced breeders, 10 per cent are first time breeders and 10 per cent non-breeders.

40. Clubs of immature and/or non-breeding adults occur. They may number but a few, or several thousands. Adult non-breeders may roost in a Club separate from breeders; or among breeders.

41. Predators are unimportant in white booby breeding biology except in a very few exceptional cases involving introduced pests. The main causes of adult mortality are not really known.

4. BREEDING BEHAVIOUR

INTRODUCTION

There are three behaviour studies of this interesting booby: Dorward's (1962a) on Ascension (south Atlantic), my own on the Galapagos (eastern equatorial Pacific) and Kepler's (1969) on [Green Island] Kure Atoll (central equatorial Pacific). These three studies refer to three races, namely *S.d.dactylatra*, *S.d.granti* and *S.d.personata* respectively.

To make the behaviour account more meaningful it may be mentioned that the Ascension birds nested on the bare rocky slopes and top of Bosun Bird Island, the Galapagos birds in clearings among shrubs (Tower Island) or litters of boulders (Hood Island) and the Green Island birds often among considerable vegetation on flat ground.

As before, the behaviour is grouped mainly under functional headings, arranged chronologically.

ESTABLISHMENT AND MAINTENANCE OF TERRITORY

After a post-breeding period of virtual absence, or intermittent visitation for resting and preening, the white booby returns to its colony and takes up a territory. It begins to show certain behaviour patterns which are the outward signs of rising territorialism and which were quite absent whenever it happened to be present in the 'quiet' period.

Males, probably solely, choose and establish the site and as will later appear, show a much higher incidence of territorial display. Kepler and I both noted that unmated males sometimes established and maintained territories, but females did not.

1. *Aerial and ground reconnaissance*

Aerial reconnaissance is probably not important in most situations, where these boobies are thin on the ground and therefore minute and prolonged inspection for vacant sites is unnecessary. However, they probably do fly over the general area and inspect it before choosing a site and, later, aerial behaviour certainly plays a part in establishing it.

White boobies reconnoitre on foot, usually, it seems, to determine the boundaries of their territories and, in females, to investigate potential mates. We had several instances of non-breeding but colour ringed birds of both sexes, turning up in slightly different parts of the (small) colony and behaving in this way.

2. *Flight circuiting and outposting*

Male white boobies in the early stages of the breeding cycle frequently take off and make brief aerial excursions, returning with the landing call and 'V-flighting' (Fig. 169), wings held almost motionless in a steep 'V'. This repetitive and stylised behaviour signifies ownership by providing repeated demonstrations to neighbouring birds, an interpretation supported by the fact that it continues to occur long after it could serve any useful reconnoitring function.

In the Galapagos, these flights often started from certain conspicuous vantage points on which the boobies, particularly males, posted themselves. 'Outposting' was very noticeable in the mornings and particularly the evenings, of the early season. At these times, birds fresh from foraging stationed themselves on top of outcrops, boulders or even on suitable branches and with much calling and often in an alert posture, watched the activities of their fellows. On Hood Island, after a three-month quiet period, the breeding season (1964–65) started in mid-October and for the first three weeks territorial activity was mainly confined to aggressive calling delivered, whilst outposted, from a characteristic long-necked forward-leaning posture and often directed at birds flying over. Outposting also occurred in response to outbreaks of activity within the colony, when both sexes would quickly seek their vantage points. Thus, all the birds of a small area tended to be outposted simultaneously. If there was no direct route from the actual site to the vantage point, the bird would fly out in a detour and land on it.

3. *Fighting*

It is rarely necessary for the white booby to fight to establish or reclaim his site. Kepler records that out of 754 agonistic encounters he never once saw interlocking of bills. The two longest fights which I saw in the Galapagos lasted six and four minutes and the remainder (some half-dozen) were merely fleeting border encounters. When fighting, white boobies interlock beaks and push with extended neck (Fig. 170).

Despite this relative lack of serious fighting white boobies are highly territorial. The postures

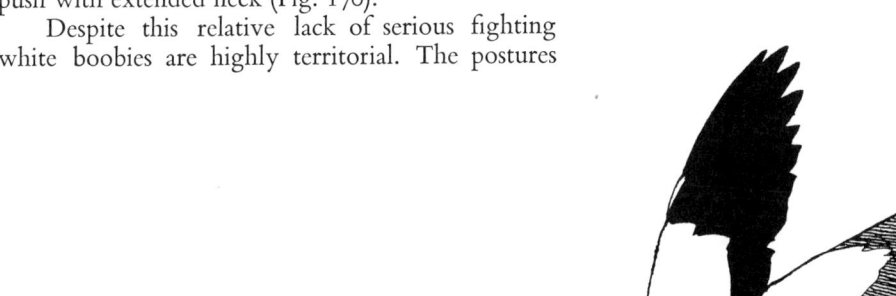

Fig. 169

'V' flighting; a ritualised form of flying into the territory in the early stages of the breeding cycle. Accompanied by repetitive calling.

and movements used in territorial behaviour do not occur in discrete blocks or in any obvious order but form a mosaic. Nor do the external stimuli which elicit them emanate solely from territorial rivals in the literal sense, for much of this behaviour may be seen in the pair context. Nevertheless it is primarily territorial in function. If one begins with behaviour most commonly associated with the most intense territorial disputes and works down to behaviour patterns typically associated with low intensity territorial interactions, the order is from Wing-flailing through Jabbing and the main site ownership display Yes/No Headshaking to simply touching nest material.

4. *Wing-flailing*

In high intensity hostilities against a territorial rival, an intruder of another species or a mate or potential mate which temporarily elicits aggression, white boobies make prominent use of a wing-flailing action (Fig. 171), combined with jabbing or biting, in a sudden opening and lifting of the wings which are spread and brought smartly downwards, though not to strike the opponent. It seems to be an intention movement of flying at the reactor and is performed from a forward crouching position with bill inclined slightly upwards. Wing-flailing is often a single swift movement, but may be violently repeated. It greatly resembles the wing-flailing of high intensity food begging behaviour in young.

Wing-flailing occurs in conjunction with high intensity Mutual Jabbing and Yes/No Headshaking (q.v.) but not usually with low intensity forms of these behaviour patterns. Here, as generally in displays, high intensity may be defined as involving not only increase in frequency, amplitude and emphasis, but also incorporation of additional elements; conversely, low intensity displays are often incomplete. Wing-flailing is almost always accompanied by calling and jabbing, even where the antagonists are far too distant to reach each other except by leaving their territories. It is not usually mixed with Pelican Postures (q.v.).

5. *Jabbing*

Jabbing between territorial rivals and Jabbing between members of a pair (Fig. 172) is very common behaviour. In both contexts it is usually highly stylised and does not result in an actual peck or jab but only (at most) in a clash of beaks. It is debatable whether there are real differences in the form of Jabbing between rivals or mates. However, the contextual and functional differences between the two situations justify considering it under both heads. One may reserve Jabbing for rivals and Mutual Jabbing (Sparring) for pairs, but even the former usually involves reciprocal action.

Jabbing between neighbours is commonly delivered from a forward leaning posture,

Fig. 170. Fighting; rare and usually brief.

often with partly raised wings and tail, the latter perhaps widely spread. The actual jab has a flinging motion and may have a twist to the head such that the bills clash, side to side, often very loudly. The head feathers may be sleek or ruffed and the difference is partly one of sex (females ruff more) and the balance of fear and aggression (fearful birds are more ruffed). Kepler notes that opposing birds stand up to a metre apart and so rarely reach beyond each other's bill even when leaning forwards, and often the whole frenzied affair of Wing-flailing, Jabbing and Yes/No display takes place in thin air, the birds never once coming into contact.

Males are involved in Jabbing encounters much more than females. Most bouts are between males of pairs confronting each other at territorial boundaries. Jabbing between different sexes (non-mates) or between females alone is uncommon. One expects this on the assumption that males more than females are concerned with establishing the territory. The observation is, however, interesting when one recalls that in the *pair* context, Jabbing between sexes is very common. In other words, a female facing a pair across an invisible territorial boundary rarely elicits Jabbing from the male, whereas a female in his territory does so. This is because Jabbing is basically aggressive and in the boundary context the rival male is a stronger external stimulus and so releases and directs almost all the Jabbing. In his territory the female releases it because there is no alternative aggression-releasing stimulus. Kepler's work clearly showed that this form of Jabbing was elicited by intrusion or a neighbour's approach to a territorial boundary. This context, and the form of the behaviour, together with its association with Wing-flailing and occasionally actual fighting, show that it is aggressively motivated.

It prevents trespass and by its close-range nature, demarcates more precisely than could long-range display, the boundaries of the territory. In 30 out of 33 Jabbing encounters between territory owners and intruders, which ended simply by cessation of Jabbing without driving the other(s) away, it was the territorial bird(s) who eventually walked away. Yet 'in all cases the intruders failed to move into the territory after the bout was terminated'. Thus the display inhibits further approach so effectively that the territorial border is 'safe' without the presence of the territorial birds. Having delineated the boundaries by a series of such encounters, they can be maintained by mere presence or display from within the territory.

Kepler names Chasing as a special case of Jabbing in which one bird so dominates the situation that it actually chases the other, Jabbing as it goes. White boobies will also Wing-flail when actually moving towards or after an opponent. Neither is more than a high intensity form of the behaviour in question, for it is the case that most such behaviour, though it may occur in a 'typical intensity' form, does so over a more or less narrow range, and not precisely alike in all instances.

Fig. 171

Wing-flailing; high intensity aggressive behaviour at the boundaries of territories.

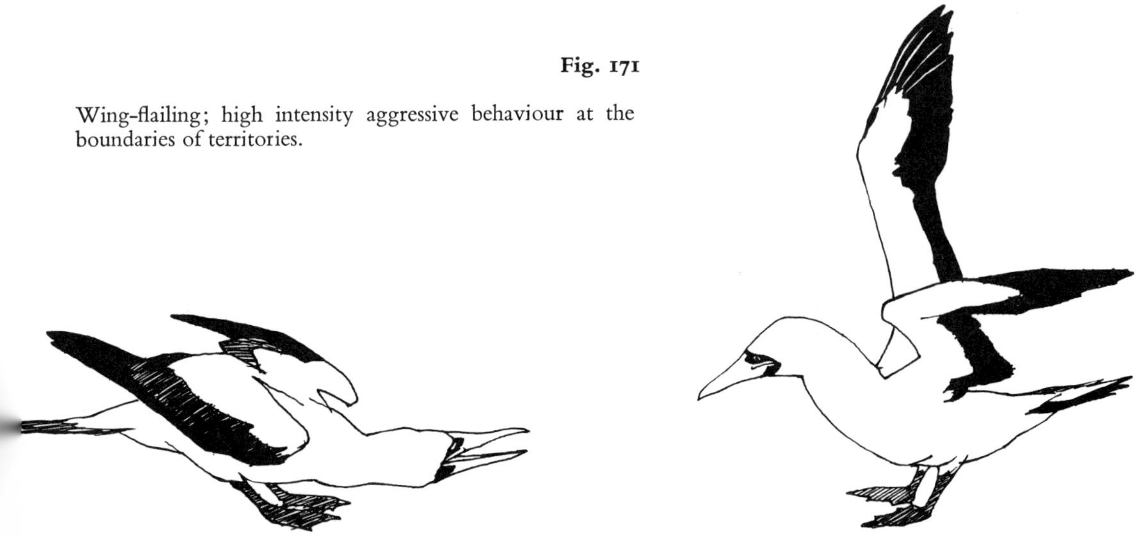

6. *Yes/No Headshaking*

This useful term stems from Dorward (though he called the display Head-wagging). It is a bizarre performance, sometimes frenzied, at others restrained, and looks as though the bird were nodding a violent Yes superimposed on a slow No (Fig. 173). It is typically given from a low forward position, head retracted and bill inclined slightly upwards and the head feathers are often ruffed, enlarging the face and enhancing the contrast between black facial mask and white background. The tail may be slightly cocked and the wings held loosely, partly raised or even widely spread. At low intensity the retracted head is simply nodded up and down with slight indications of the sideways movement, whilst in the typical form the head traverses a semi-circle, simultaneously moving rapidly up and down. At the highest intensity the Yes movement becomes extremely violent and the No component takes the head so far back that the bill points towards the tail and the whole movement is inclined forwards and downwards. During the Yes movement the bill is horizontal or inclined upwards, but is lowered during lunges at a rival or in the touching of nest material and also in Yes/No Headshaking accompanying the lunges. In fact, in high intensity Yes/No Headshaking, even without lunges or wing action, the bill tends to be pointed downwards and nest touching movements are incorporated. It is not a symmetrical movement; normally the Yeses are concentrated in the mid point, bill straight ahead. In the near presence of a rival, however, most Yeses occur in the half of the No arc which is directed at the rival. Thus the display is strongly oriented to the opponent.

Further movements enter the display as its intensity increases, depending on the external situation. The presence of a rival elicits jabs and intention movements of jabs and, at the very highest intensity, sudden and high wing lifting (Wing-flailing) as the bird simultaneously jabs and headshakes. At low intensity the display is silent, but throughout medium and high intensity display the bird calls, a 'whee-o' whistle in the male and a harsh shout in the female, usually at the end of each swing of the No movement, not during the Yes nodding. Where Yes/No Headshaking occurs without the aggression-evoking stimulus of an intruder it is typically interspersed, as the bird parades around its territory, with repeated touching of nest material. Yes/No Headshaking is thus an involved movement, clear enough in its typical form but merging, at low intensity, into an undifferentiated forward leaning with some head waving and on the high intensity side to a complex mosaic of Jabbing, nest touching, Wing-flailing and Yes/No Headshaking of the more usual form.

Yes/No Headshaking most commonly occurs as a display following landing on the territory and in other territorial contexts, as when outposted and responding to potential intrusion from neighbours moving around, birds flying over and so on. These and other situations in which it typically occurs but space forbids describing, show absolutely clearly that it is basically an aggressive display.

Fig. 172. Jabbing; this looks like straightforward aggression, but is in fact ritualised. It is particularly common between mates, before egg laying.

In balanced territorial encounters each bird is to some extent afraid of its rival, yet both perform high intensity Yes/No Headshaking; in actual fights, a dominant bird shows more Yes/No Headshaking than its rival. In the most intense fight recorded, between two females, the less aggressive bird alternated Yes/No Headshaking with frequent Pelican Postures (q.v.) whereas the dominant one merely performed high intensity Yes/No Headshaking. In the above situations and in pair relationships (where it also occurs) one can discern mixed fear and aggression in the circumstances eliciting Yes/No Headshaking.

Kepler's analysis of the context of this display supports the conclusion that it is mainly aggressive behaviour. He reduced the eliciting circumstances in 650 cases to 14 categories, five of which involved actual or threatened territorial intrusion by another bird and six of which involved a nearby bird performing Yes/No Headshaking or aggressive behaviour such as Wing-flailing or Jabbing, and found that between them these categories elicited almost all the observed Yes/No Headshaking bouts. He records, as I did, that Yes/No Headshaking may occur apparently without any external stimulus and also as a post-landing display. He concludes 'it is clear that the display is an agonistic one, occurring in hostile situations' and makes the interesting point that the fixed stare which these boobies often direct at other individuals frequently elicited Yes/No Headshaking very obviously oriented towards the peering bird.

Clearly it signifies ownership of the territory and so tends to keep rivals at a distance thus subserving a spacing-out function. Although it is particularly intense on the vantage points and boundaries of the territory where trespass is most likely, it also occurs apparently *in vacuo*. In the early mornings and late evenings in areas where the nesting sites are in hollows or clearings among vegetation, male white boobies mount their vantage points and perform Yes/No Headshaking without any apparent threat of intrusion. Like the song of passerines, it is timed to fit in with a relatively concerted outburst of the same territorial activity from neighbours. It is the more obvious in situations in which for most of the day the boobies are hidden amongst boulders or vegetation and appear with exaggerated conspicuousness when all take up their vantage points. As with Bowing in the gannet and song in passerines, so here the Yes/No Headshaking seems to advertise the presence of site-owning males.

Fig. 173(a). A complex, aggressively-motivated territorial display (site-ownership) called 'Yes/No' headshake to indicate the form of the head movement.

(*a*)

Fig. 173(b). A male facing a rival and 'Yes/No' Headshaking. Note the conspicuousness of the face when seen from the front. The bird is calling (the site-ownership display in all sulids involves calling).

(*b*)

Kepler collected 375 cases of what he presumed were reactions to Yes/No Headshaking and used them to buttress a similar conclusion about its function. He found that about 55 per cent of Yes/No Headshaking bouts elicited agonistic behaviour; 14 per cent were followed by the antagonist walking away and in only 4 per cent did the recipient actually move nearer. In the rest of the sample there was either redirected behaviour, displacement behaviour, reaction by peering or flying away or no action. Since it is very common for territorial behaviour to elicit a like reply—one thinks immediately of song in passerines—this and the positive repelling effects of Yes/No Headshaking are consistent with the above interpretation of its function.

Easy though it may be to understand the motivation and function of the display, it is difficult to reach a sound conclusion about its evolution. From what is it derived and under what forms of selection pressure? The choice of source seems to lie between food begging or touching nest material. Yes/No Headshaking very strongly resembles food begging behaviour of the young (see Figs. 173, 181). Low intensity food begging is the Yes movement performed rapidly, without the No component. High intensity begging develops in the latter half of the chick's growth and includes both Yes and No components and also Wing-flailing. Yes/No Headshaking shows less use of wings, a more forward head position and a less vertically oriented bill than does food begging. Both movements are accompanied by calling. In ontogeny, the begging behaviour of the young bird grades insensibly into the Yes/No Headshaking display, which then contains more Wing-flailing than does the adult form. Thus, when still using the Wing-flailing component in its begging behaviour, the young bird is also more likely to incorporate it in the display which food begging so strongly resembles. This is a temporary phenomenon; later the Yes/No Headshaking normally lacks the Wing-flailing. Sometimes an intruding adult landing in the territory elicits from the chick food begging behaviour which then changes into Yes/No Headshaking. Once, a chick performing high intensity food begging to its parent simply changed the note from the food call to the aggressive call associated with Yes/No Headshaking every time an intruding male flew over.

Thus, in form there can be no doubting the resemblance between food begging behaviour and Yes/No Headshaking. On the other hand, it is more consistent with the situations in most other sulids to derive Yes/No Headshaking from a nest touching or biting movement. Since both sources could conceivably have given rise to a movement with the characteristics of Yes/No Headshaking it seems impossible to draw a firm conclusion. Whichever is the derivation, the fact remains that post-landing behaviour in the white booby involves a nest touching movement, either modified to form Yes/No Headshaking or interspersed with it.

Before moving on to pair formation behaviour, it is worth mentioning that the tendency of birds to express aggression and fear in the pair situation, means that some behaviour occurs both as territorial and as part of pair interactions. Their position within a functional scheme such as this one is therefore not axiomatic, but I have tried to place them where they most typically occur.

FORMATION AND MAINTENANCE OF PAIR

Early in the season male boobies station themselves in their territories and scan the area, calling and Yes/No Headshaking. Females fly over the area 'prospecting' and receive sexual display from males on the ground. Prospecting females land somewhere near such males, looking alert, leaning forward with long neck (in Darwin Bay, Tower Island, they used the broken cliffs overlooking the colony). Their presence then elicits display from the male, which tends to attract them to close range. If they approach, several interactions occur and this may mark the beginning of an actual partnership.

1. *Sky-pointing or Advertising*

At the outset readers are referred to the Comparative Section, for this display is a particularly interesting ethological 'specimen' and the species accounts are better read against the comparative background.

A Sky-pointing male (Fig. 174) first stretches his neck from the normal relaxed position, points his bill upwards, often at about 45° but sometimes vertically, lifts his wings and whistles through slightly opened bill. Between repetitions of the posture the male, neck elongated but bill horizontal, peers alertly towards the female. 'Catching her eye' stimulates him to Sky-point again, although he will do so even when the female cannot see him. Her movement either away from or towards him, frequently elicits further Sky-pointing until she goes beyond a certain distance or approaches to within a metre or so.

When viewed from the front and due to the upward pointing of the bill, the conspicuousness of the blackish inter-ramal skin is enhanced by a slight bulging caused by depression of the hyoid. Slight ruffing of the head and neck feathers provides a fringe of white against which the black face stands out boldly. Kepler notes that as the humeri extend upwards, lifting the folded wings, the upper secondary coverts and primaries present a pattern of black and white behind the head and neck. A further stimulating quality is added by the thin whistle 'wheeo'. It appears that there may be slight regional (that is racial) variation in form and that Kure birds, for instance, elevate the bill less, but the tail more than Galapagos birds.

The display does not usually occur as a single event (unless to overflying females) but is

Fig. 174(a and b). Front and side views of a dyed male Sky-pointing (the sexually motivated display by which males advertise their presence and receptiveness to females). *Photo:* C. Kepler.

(*a*) (*b*)

Fig. 174(c and d). Sky-pointing attracts the female but as she leaves the site, the male's aggression is disinhibited and he bites her.

(*c*) (*d*)

repeated several times in quick succession. Kepler's birds averaged five per bout, but he counted 52 in one prolonged encounter. He measured the average interval between bouts at 7·4 seconds.

Males rarely Sky-point to distant females or to females actually beside them; they advertise mainly to females a few metres away or flying over fairly low. Of 144 encounters, 140 were directed to females on average 5·6m away and in only four were they 9 or more metres distant. Cullen saw Ascension males Sky-point in flight, but this must be very rare. He even noted Sky-pointing twice from a female (probably the same bird) though neither Kepler nor I saw females Sky-point at all and our observations together total over 1200 instances. However Dorward recorded 12 instances of females Sky-pointing on Ascension.

Unmated males Sky-point about equally to both unmated and mated females. Mated males concentrate their Sky-pointing almost exclusively on their own females (55 cases to one where the recipient female's status was unknown). Occasionally males Sky-point to other males, but the circumstances indicate that these are cases of momentarily mistaken identity.

When males Sky-point to birds flying over, however, the situation is very different, for out of 215 such displays, 93 per cent were given by bachelor males, who advertised indiscriminately to male and female alike. This apparent lack of recognition of the sex of overflying birds is probably an artefact produced by the situation, for if such an advertiser waited until a bird flying over was near enough for its sex to be recognised, it would probably be too late to display with any chance of eliciting a response.

Since Sky-pointing occurs mainly when there is a female nearby, it is a fair assumption that it is a sexually motivated display. However, females eliciting it evoke other behaviour patterns closely associated in time and these indicate that other motivation is involved. Counts of 253 instances of 'behavioural events' immediately following male Sky-pointing showed that in most cases males touched nest material or the ground, peered at the female or the ground, or performed the Head-fling. If the female actually approaches, the male often Sky-points and then touches the nest in front or to one side, often that furthest away from the female. When the male Sky-points from one of his vantage points and the female approaches, he 'touches nest material', though there is none, and Head-flings. Males who followed Sky-pointing by Head-flinging and touching nest material seemed more aggressive to the female than were others.

Kepler noted what females were doing immediately *before* a male advertised to them and found that in 84·9 per cent of 264 instances they were looking at or walking towards the male. Looking, or peering, in particular, elicited Sky-pointing. It is, in fact, very noticeable that in between Sky-pointing the male peers at the female and immediately responds when she happens to gaze towards him and he undoubtedly times his display in this way.

Although not included in the figures quoted above, my observations showed that in the early stages of pair formation Sky-pointing may be interspersed with aggressive behaviour (Yes/No Headshaking and, when the pair meet, Mutual Jabbing). Also, late in the season (when aggression rises) males responded to prospecting females by Sky-pointing, but mixed with a great deal of Yes/No Headshaking. The fact that the activity most frequently associated with Sky-pointing is touching nest material could also indicate slight aggressive motivation; such touching, biting or handling nest material or the ground is usually redirected aggressive behaviour. Less likely, in my view, is a causal link between Sky-pointing as sexual behaviour and touching nest material as nest building, even though in many birds copulation and nest building do tend to occur in close temporal association. Yes/No Headshaking is undoubtedly aggressive and its occurrence early in pair formation and directed at prospecting females late in the season fits well with the tendency for aggression to be disinhibited at such times. Indeed, late in the season, males may strongly attack either their own or other chicks and mix this overt aggression with Sky-pointing.

The tendency to touch the ground on the side farther from an approaching female could indicate slight avoidance. No doubt the precise manner in which nest material is touched—quickly or emphatically or more deliberately—betrays subtle states or shifts of 'feeling'. It is fine differences such as these that enable interactions to express nuances.

The 'peering' is low intensity sexual behaviour. When the female returns his gaze, the 'typical intensity' display is released from the male. The Pelican Posture is associated with movement (p. 402) and it occurs as the female moves away from, rather than towards, the male, perhaps indicating a tendency to move after her.

So, Sky-pointing is sexually motivated but aggression is clearly involved and there is probably very slight avoidance too. Thus, at this crude level of analysis, the fear, aggression and sex model 'explains' the situation adequately.

The function of Sky-pointing in divulging the status of the male to a prospecting female and attracting her to close quarters, is the main but not the only one. Mated males Sky-point repeatedly to their mates and their continued 'advertising' is clearly pair bonding and perhaps sexual co-ordinating behaviour. Even in mated pairs the display serves to bring pair members closer together, for Kepler observes that in 79 per cent of cases mates were standing or moving apart before the display, but in 86 per cent they moved closer after it and mostly the female moved to the male. But one can hardly assume that in the mated pair Sky-pointing is merely a device for reducing distance so that contact interactions can occur. It has become one of the pair interactions, although the female has not evolved a reciprocal display (see Comparative Section). In fact it may occur even when the pair have a large chick.

Sky-pointing has the further function of enabling the male, after choosing the precise nest site (for it is he who selects it) to draw the female to it.

A related function is to guarantee receptivity before the pair members come into close contact. Thus, males do not fly directly in to their females but to some other point in the territory from which they then advertise. If the female is receptive she joins the male. Thus both are then sure to be receptive, which would not necessarily be so if he flew to her directly.

The question of the derivation of Sky-pointing is best discussed in the Comparative Section, where the various forms taken by the display in the entire family can be compared. It is sufficient, here, to suggest that it is homologous to the gannet's Sky-pointing (q.v.) but has acquired new motivation and function. In other words, it has evolved, by a process of change, from a posture which in the ancestral form was like Sky-pointing, but which, according to this hypothesis, was not sex motivated nor functioned as advertising.

It has been mentioned that the male's Sky-pointing display must be regarded as something more than just pair-forming in function. However, the distinction is somewhat artificial, since the pair relationship is a dynamic process and there is no instant of formation. Rather, a pair interact from the beginning and the interactions change and fluctuate as the relationship progresses, but no single behaviour is rigidly confined to any part of the relationship.

In the white booby, there are several distinctive behaviour patterns which occur as the pair come together and remain together in the territory. They are certain to occur, frequently, in the early stages, before the egg is laid and desultorily thereafter, flaring up again towards the end of the breeding season. Into this category may be placed one possibly ritualised behaviour pattern, Gazing and eight ritualised ones—Mutual Jabbing, Head-flinging, Parading, Pelican Posturing, assuming a Bill-up-face-away position, symbolic nest building and Wing Rattling. These activities, together on occasions with Sky-pointing, are therefore those which, were one adopting different headings or categories, could be considered under 'Behaviour of the Pair upon Meeting' and 'Behaviour of the Pair on their Territory'.

2. *Gazing*

This would hardly warrant special notice were it not such a well marked and common precursor to so much interaction between pair members. It is simply an intent stare, obviously oriented towards the other bird and often maintained until it is reciprocated, when a further response may then occur—perhaps Sky-pointing or Parading for nest material or Mutual Jabbing or Mutual Preening.

3. *Mutual Jabbing*

Jabbing has already been described as a territorial display. In the pair context it is common and unmistakably ritualised.

In extreme meeting behaviour the pair rush together, long necked, and thrust their wide open beak literally into the other's. The term Mutual Jabbing is apt and implies comparison with the gannet's equivalent Mutual Fencing. It is a vigorous, unco-ordinated flinging movement in which the partners, necks lengthened and forward leaning, appose their beaks, usually slightly open, and by rapidly and erratically shaking their heads from side to side audibly and briefly clash their mandibles against each other's. It often grows out of a formalised bill-touching (Fig. 175) in which the tips of the closed bills are delicately though tensely apposed, as though the birds were cautiously reaching out to investigate a strange object. Sometimes the mandibles are widely parted, the neck stretched and head feathers ruffed (a sign of fear). As the bills are thrust at each other they are opened and closed so that the birds sometimes appear to be biting each other. Usually, however, both shake and withdraw their bills without being seized by the other and the behaviour is clearly not an attempt to grip the other's break. It is accompanied by calling, particularly in the female, who makes a loud and abrupt shouting 'aaah-aah-a-yah' which cannot be distinguished from the aggressive calling in territorial disputes.

I could not predict whether bill-touching would lead to Mutual Jabbing. Often, on meeting, established pairs simply touch bills with calling and then stand parallel (Fig. 175c) with beaks slightly averted from each other, or perhaps in the Bill-up-face-away position (q.v.). The parallel standing was a regular part of their behaviour after meeting. They may however touch bills and then Mutual Jab violently. Occasionally pair members go through the motions

Fig. 175

The context and nature of Jabbing illustrated by actual incidents:

(a) An established pair (possibly failed breeders) calling and Jabbing within their territory. Note the ruffed head feathers (indicating the tension, due to fear, engendered by close proximity).

of Mutual Jabbing even though their bills are not in contact. The behaviour does not depend on prior tactile stimulation.

Turning now to its motivation, Mutual Jabbing looks hostile and can hardly be distinguished from that between rivals, though a really close study might show that the latter gripped more and used less of the flinging movement. Even in territorial disputes between male and female, I noted that Mutual Jabbing was very fierce and seemed to involve more gripping than

Fig. 175(b)

Jabbing between members of a pair, preceded by fixed orientation (staring) and apposition of bills (bill-touching). Note the upward and away movement of the female (left) to avoid actual gripping.

between mated birds. Certainly the formal difference between functionally aggressive Mutual Jabbing and that between members of a pair is only one of degree. Other evidence, too, points unequivocally to the aggressive nature of Mutual Jabbing. Thus, if one member of a pair fights an intruder, the pair subsequently perform Mutual Jabbing of the highest intensity. Similarly, a mated pair dispelling an intruder intersperse the action with high intensity Mutual Jabbing and disturbances usually elicit Mutual Jabbing from pairs nearby. Adults were seen to intersperse violent attacks on their own food-begging juvenile, with Mutual Jabbing. In all these cases, Mutual Jabbing closely accompanied more obvious aggression. It is thus not surprising that the most prolonged and intense Mutual Jabbing occurs between new pair members and indeed between any pair members early in the season, when it may occur on average almost once every ten seconds for up to ten minutes on end. The male, particularly, may bite, Jab or Wing-flail at the female if she turns her back, even though he has just been advertising to her. This is similar to the situation in the gannet, except that in the white booby females give almost as good as they get, whereas this is most certainly not the case in the gannet. However, it is a further example of the tendency of aggression to outcrop in pair relations.

The behaviour pattern most frequently associated with Mutual Jabbing in both sexes, is the Oblique Headshake (q.v.) and this is particularly likely to occur after a vigorous clash of beaks—perhaps as a response to the strong tactile stimulus entailed.

Mutual Jabbing in the white booby, though much cruder, may well bear similar functional interpretation to that advanced for the analogous Mutual Fencing in gannets. Mates obviously are aggressive when together on the site and Mutual Jabbing is the behaviour which expresses this, but in a 'harmless' (that is, non-injurious and non-dispelling) way. It pre-empts attack. One gains the strong impression that, in white boobies, to point the bill at the partner elicits Jabbing. Even pairs which have been standing together for over 12 hours may flare up into Mutual Jabbing immediately they find themselves facing each other. My own interpretation is that to point bills is attack-eliciting (a threat) and the 'attack' takes the form of Mutual Jabbing. Indeed, it is very obvious that pairs often take pains to stand parallel in a very striking way. This, of course, takes the bill out of the aggressive 'pointing at the partner' position. Interestingly, Kepler's birds, on coming together, seemed to perform Mutual Jabbing more rarely than mine, although they often did so as the second or third event in interactions beginning with Gazing.

I once saw a known pair of white boobies meet on the sea and noted that they Mutual Jabbed in the usual way. This observation is interesting in that it showed that it is not necessary for the female to be on the male's territory before she will elicit Mutual Jabbing.

The interpretation of the derivation of a behaviour pattern is often a matter of opinion. I believe Mutual Jabbing to be a modified form of aggression, derived from movements of

Fig. 175(c). Jabbing preceded by deliberate and relatively prolonged avoidance of pointing the bill at each other, the simultaneous forward orientation giving rise to 'parallel standing'.

attack, particularly biting and shaking, but it strongly resembles food begging behaviour in which the chick jabs at the parent's beak. Commonly parents respond to intensive chick begging, particularly from large young or juveniles, by Mutual Jabbing with them. Could not Yes/No Headshaking and Mutual Jabbing be derived from food begging behaviour; the former from the movements preceding actual contact and the latter from the jabbing itself? Begging and Yes/No Headshaking grade imperceptibly into each other and likewise jabbing for food and Mutual Jabbing with the parent. Thus, in the order in which they appear in an individual, food begging precedes Mutual Jabbing and Yes/No Headshaking, which may be in that sense derivative, but it is quite possible that the resemblance between Mutual Jabbing and feeding movements is fortuitous and that one grades into the other through postural facilitation. Bill-touching is probably a low intensity form of Mutual Jabbing.

In sum, Mutual Jabbing is mixed fear/aggression motivated behaviour between the pair at the nest site. It is ritualised but less so than the equivalent Mutual Fencing in the gannet. It occurs mainly and most vigorously in new or disturbed pairs.

4. *Reciprocal allo-preening*

This occurs frequently (Fig. 176). Non-reciprocal allo-preening is usually preening of the male's head by the female.

5. *Oblique Headshake*

The headshaking closely associated with Mutual Jabbing and fighting is a vigorous flinging movement, with the head held ordinarily or obliquely. The Oblique Headshake is associated with aggressive behaviour, not only Mutual Jabbing but also Yes/No Headshaking. Although it is such a simple quick movement, it probably has considerable signal value. It was noticeable that females, in particular, gave the vigorous Oblique Headshake after the male had simply peered at her. She did not even need bill contact, though vigorous contact was almost sure to produce Oblique Headshake from both.

The upward orientation of the Oblique Headshake is perhaps due to its occurrence after Mutual Jabbing (tactile stimulation) when the bill is often inclined upwards in the Bill-up-face-away posture (appeasement). Females, who more often than males follow Mutual Jabbing by Oblique Headshake, also more often follow it by Bill-up-face-away. The occurrence of Oblique Headshake in a 'head up' position has become normal and now, even when no partner is present to elicit Mutual Jabbing or Bill-up-face-away, it still occurs with bill held upwards.

This brief, rapid head flinging with bill inclined upwards and often tilted sideways is very common in most booby species.

6. *Parading*

After meeting on their site, white boobies often Parade around their relatively large and often bare territory. The male, in particular, often wanders some distance away, usually returning

Fig. 176

Reciprocal allo-preening. Its function is social rather than body care.

with a fragment of nest material. The foot movements are unmistakably exaggerated; the feet are lifted higher than necessary and flaunted a little to the side (Fig. 177). When walking in this way, the bill is usually tucked repeatedly, regaining the normal position between tuckings. As one partner leaves the other, prior to Parading into some corner of its territory, it assumes a distinctive Bill-up-face-away posture (q.v.). Reference to the Comparative Section will show that, with differences, this ritualised locomotion occurs in other sulids.

The pair spend much time Parading around the territory, rejoining each other, touching nest material, Mutual Jabbing and moving away again. For example, in one minute, a pair Paraded off the site eight times, commencing with the Bill-up-face-away posture and returning with repeated Pelican Postures and performing seven bouts of Mutual Jabbing with associated headshaking. This amounts to a very concentrated and complicated series of ritualised movements and postures. Difficult—indeed impossible—though it is to assess the 'reasons' behind all these interactions, the individual patterns must each have their signal value. No doubt the movement away from the partner and the subsequent return help to perfect the pair's rapport —they reinforce the tendency to re-unite and encourage the 'on site' partner to remain there until the mate returns. No doubt this would happen were the territorial wandering to be conducted in an ordinary walk. But its exaggeration perhaps enhances the 'excitement' engendered by the whole procedure. Most Parading occurs in the period before egg laying and is largely associated with the male bringing nest material for symbolic nest building (q.v.).

7. *Pelican Posture*

When moving around its territory, the white booby repeatedly tucks its bill tip against its upper breast (Fig. 179), often holding the position so briefly that it seems merely to glance down before lifting the bill again. Often the head is held slightly backwards. There is often definite lateral displacement of the bill tip, away from the reactor, during Pelican Postures which occur as part of an interaction and this is particularly noticeable in birds which have been the subject of attack. Occasionally a bird Pelican Postures repeatedly on the spot. As mentioned above, the Pelican Posture is closely linked with exaggerated foot movements (Parading). On Kure, the boobies often cocked their tails almost vertically when Parading and Pelican Posturing and this characteristic seems to be peculiar to the population (or race) concerned.

The Pelican Posture occurs in both agonistic and epigamic interactions. Predominantly aggressive individuals, for example, running to attack, or having dispelled an intruder or having attacked and displaced intruders of another species, Pelican Posture frequently. Yet individuals moving 'peacefully' about their territories also Pelican Posture. In the epigamic context, males often Pelican Posture after advertising, or when approaching a female with an offering of nest material. In all these situations ambivalent aggression/fear are present, but obviously at different 'levels' and in different proportions. Kepler attempted to analyse this

Fig. 177. 'Parading' is merely an exaggerated walk, used in movement around the territory. It is further developed in the blue-foot.

situation by noting, for each sex and for agonistic and epigamic contexts respectively, whether birds Pelican Posture most when moving towards or away from the bird with which they are reacting. He found that in the agonistic situation, out of 71 encounters involving a Pelican Posturing male and a territorial rival, in 33 the male moved towards and in 38 away from the rival. The corresponding figures for females were 7 and 3. In a further 12 (male) and 2 (female) cases the birds Pelican Posturing were just moving about, neither towards nor away from a rival. In the courtship situation, Pelican Posturing males were in 48 cases moving towards, in 25 away from and in 62 around the female. The corresponding figures for females were 27, 9 and 6. Thus, in both contexts males Pelican Postured much more than females, but whilst they did so equally when moving towards or away from a rival, they tended to do so more when moving towards than away from a female. Females, too, Pelican Postured more when moving towards than away from a male.

These figures may be interpreted to mean that Pelican Posturing does indeed characterise birds which are in several different states of motivational balance, mainly between aggression (Aa) and fear (Ff), thus Af, AF, af or possibly aF. This would be in fair accord with the situation in the gannet (q.v.).

The function of the Pelican Posture may be to remove the bill from the 'pointing' position (a situation which often leads to jabbing). It is noteworthy that it is quite common *both* between rivals and between mates, though this is not the case in all sulids. The possible derivation of the Pelican Posture is best discussed in the Comparative Section.

8. *Bill-up-face-away*

The incipient form of this very frequent but easily overlooked movement, is a mere cocking of the head slightly to one side as though squinting at the sky, but its marked expression is an unmistakable and exaggerated upward, backward and sideways movement (Fig. 178). It

Fig. 178(a)

Bill-up-face-away (low intensity) with partner in relaxed stance. Bill-up-face-away is used by birds moving away from the partner. It may be appeasing.

(b) Bill-up-face-away, extreme position.

(c)

A posture, resembling extreme Bill-up-face-away more than anything else, but performed infrequently and context and function not clear.

characteristically occurs in birds turning and moving away from their mate. Rarely, a bird threw its head right back (Fig. 178c) but this happened too infrequently for me to recognise the nature and meaning of the movement.

Thus of 109 recorded instances 61 were in males moving away from their mates and 43 in females doing likewise, whereas only 5 cases (all female) were recorded in birds moving towards their mates. Most of the useful information about the possible motivation of this very highly ritualised posture is implicit in the suggestions which may be made about its function.

Bill-up-face-away is probably an appeasement posture, as the situation in which it occurs indicates; precisely those individuals turning and moving off the site tend to elicit attack from the partner and particularly from the male. Males of new pairs in particular not infrequently bite, jab or Wing-flail at the female when she turns her back. This is probably partly explicable on the hypothesis that sexually inhibited aggression is released when the inhibiting factor (near presence of the partner) is removed and finds expression when the partner is near enough to be an intruder but too far to be a 'mate'—i.e. just off the nest site.

Bill-up-face-away, however, is certainly not an appeasement posture comparable to Facing Away in the gannet or to bill-hiding in the white booby chick. More often than not it does not occur as a response to aggression from the partner; whereas a female gannet jabbed by her mate immediately Faces Away, a female booby turns and jabs her partner, then, when moving away, briefly shows the Bill-up-face-away.

Unlike the Pelican Posture which single birds perform when walking about their territory, the Bill-up-face-away occurs mainly in the presence of the partner. Thus a single bird fetching nest material frequently assumes the Pelican Posture, but usually not the Bill-up-face-away, although even solitary individuals sometimes show it when moving off the site. In long interactions birds may perform this movement prior to each of many scores of short trips for nest material.

The connection between performing the Bill-up-face-away and then moving off the site is so marked that unless one saw the stages of pair formation in which there is recognisable aggression between the partners, one would interpret the posture simply as a ritualised intention movement of locomotion comparable to Sky-pointing in the gannet. Although the pre-movement posture Sky-pointing has become the white booby's advertising display, another pre-movement posture, derived from the same basic intention movements (of locomotion) as Sky-pointing, has taken its place. Instead of stretching the neck and pointing the bill vertically upwards as in Sky-pointing (advertising) the white booby about to move off the site turns its head slightly over its shoulder in the direction it is about to take, with the bill at about 45°. This is the Bill-up-face-away. Two entirely distinct movements have thus been derived from the same intention movements of locomotion (probably the 'look' phase) but presumably at different periods in the species' evolution. The first apparently was further modified and became advertising, whereupon a second movement developed and here became Bill-up-face-away.

9. *Symbolic nest building*

Although the white booby makes no nest of structural significance the gathering, presentation and building in of nest material is a common part of courtship. Some pairs gather thousands of pebbles, tiny twigs, clumps of vegetation or fragments of coral, etc., feathers, dung and other detritus and arrange them around the centre of the nest site. A cleared, circular patch results. As mentioned, the most intensive courtship activity takes place in the evenings in the prelaying phase of the breeding cycle, but is maintained throughout the cycle and flowers again after the juvenile has left. Even late season building may add over 200 pieces of nest material in one bout and in one case the male of a pair which was still feeding a juvenile fetched 30, 60, 110, and 23 pieces of nest material on four successive evenings. Since the male spends more time on the territory early in the season and returns earlier each day, he is usually on the site when the female arrives. He may carry out desultory gathering of nest material when alone, but becomes more active following her arrival and is largely responsible for gathering the fragments. Occasionally males fly right away from the territory and return with nest material; usually they pick up an absurdly tiny fragment a metre or so from the nest, hold it between the tips of their mandibles and peer, long-necked, towards the female before advancing and 'offering' the particle in a symbolic manner by pointing it towards or actually touching the female's bill. There is no elaborate presentation in a sweeping arc as there is in the blue-footed booby. The female either takes the fragment or the male deposits it on the nest site and the female joins in by simultaneously reaching down to the same spot with her bill (Fig. 179). This may be accompanied by soft, sharp whistling by the male and calling by the female. Dorward called this bending down to the nest site Bowing, but to give it a special name implies a distinctive movement or posture and this seems simply an ordinary reaching down to the ground. Nevertheless, the pair do make a ritual of placing the particle by keeping their heads down, close together, much longer than would be necessary merely to put the fragments on the ground. In so doing they may come into physical contact, or Gaze at each other, following this by Mutual Preening. Kepler noticed that whereas males placed 89 per cent of the items they brought in front of the female (136 out of 209) and only 23 in front of themselves, females placed 34 out of the 42 items (81 per cent) in front of themselves and only 8 in front of the male.

Often the mere apposing of bills triggers off Mutual Jabbing and the nest material is dropped—sometimes down the partner's throat! Although males usually 'present' nest material to a female actually on the site they will, as a normal part of pair formation behaviour, leave

Fig. 179. Stance and head positions in pair interactions:

(a). ♀ (left) Pelican posturing; ♂ (right) low-intensity Sky-pointing.

(b). Intent 'gazing' characteristic during pairing interactions.

Fig. 179(c). Both birds in variants of low-intensity Bill-up-face-away (the left-hand bird is walking away from the site and the right-hand bird is probably about to move off the (symbolic) nest.

Fig. 179(d)

Symbolic nest building.

their site and go to a female specifically to offer the nest material. Females also wander around the territory picking up pieces of nest material or even attempting to break off twigs and returning with them. Often the deposition of nest material is followed by headshaking, even though the bill remains clean (headshaking was originally a response to a soiled bill) so it is to some extent ritualised here.

Clearly the white booby's nesting activity, though in a sense only a relic of the habit, has acquired a transferred functional importance as an activity which strengthens and maintains the pair bond. It may also co-ordinate sexual condition and activity in the medium and short term, for it is closely associated with copulation, as in all sulids. The white booby has retained the frequency of leaving and returning with the individual pieces of nest material, but reduced the size of these, lost the habit of selecting 'useful' material (it often gathers stones) and mainly lost the movements necessary to build a real nest. It seems an interesting example of a behaviour pattern in transmutation during the process of functional emancipation.

At close range, through binoculars, one could see that the bill was opened for longer than necessary in depositing material and detect traces of the lateral tremoring or sideways nest building movements by which those members of the family building more substantial nests—for example, the red-foot and the gannet—work the material into the nest structure, but for all practical purposes the building movements have been lost in the white booby. So, too, have the rapid up and down vibrating of the lower mandible by which gannets disengage sticky material (seaweed or humus) and red-footed boobies, cormorants and shags deal with twigs, stipes, detritus and other material. Instead white boobies use headshaking. Sometimes, solitary males which had gathered many pieces of nest material repeatedly picked them up, put them down with an imprecise, jerky and 'impatient' headshaking movement on the far rim and then drew them into the centre. The incompleteness of the movements, which achieved nothing, gave a strong impression of the rudimentary nature of the white booby's nest building behaviour. Or the items may be placed with exaggerated care, opening the bill widely and slowly retracting the head.

As mentioned under Yes/No Headshaking and landing behaviour, nest touching or mandibulating is ambivalent, mainly aggressive behaviour in the white booby. A male who wants to dispel an intruder but cannot get at it will perform Wing-flailing mixed with rapid nest touching movements and so dispel it. Nest touching occurs in other aggression-arousing situations, notably after landing at the nest site; of 24 cases in which birds landed (with the partner absent) 21 showed nest touching movements as the after-landing behaviour, often quickly followed by aggressive Yes/No Headshaking. In addition males may touch or mandibulate nest material in agonistic situations even when they are off the actual nest site. When nest touching occurs as a displacement reaction in ambivalent situations as, for example, when new females with aggressive males touch nest material, the movement is oriented away from the male.

Nest digging, or probing into the bottom of the 'nest' is rare in this species. The mandibles are opened and shut spasmodically, but in the instances I observed, nothing was dug out or picked up.

10. *Copulation and associated activities*

The female's exaggerated forward bending whilst arranging nest material may be particularly prone to elicit mounting from the male, but there is no conspicuous female soliciting behaviour. Males mount standing or sitting females from the side and hold their wings fairly close to the body, laying their bill alongside the female's head and perhaps changing it from side to side. Kepler noted that the male sometimes places his bill firmly alongside the female's head, which is interesting from the comparative viewpoint (q.v.). Prior to copulation, the male approaches the female in a conspicuously alert, forward leaning posture, with exaggeratedly high steps (Parading?). The alert gaze has already been mentioned in connection with other pair activity, but in combination with this particular form of walking, it was seen only prior to mounting. During copulation the male treads, and moves his tail from side to side. The female's wings are loosened and her tail raised. She may gape slightly, with head forward and down. Any attempt to Mutual Jab breaks up the copulation attempt. It is possible that the female 'controls' copulation as in the brown booby (p. 496).

Copulation is followed by further excursions for nest material which is jointly arranged or mandibulated. Sometimes the pair touch bills or perform low intensity Mutual Jabbing, probably due to disinhibition of mild aggression.

11. *Wing Rattle*

The only reason for including this behaviour here is that it occurs mainly during pair interactions. It is a conspicuous and common movement in which the loosened wings, held slightly out from the body, are shaken vigorously and rapidly in a small amplitude horizontal movement. The bill is usually inclined upwards, sometimes obliquely. In about 14 per cent of cases the Wing Rattle was followed by a brief Rotary Headshake in which the head and neck are incompletely rotated once, twice or three times around the horizontal axis; and in a further 15 per cent the Wing Rattle was followed by an ordinary upward head fling. A similar rotary movement (see below) is extremely widespread in birds and usually follows preening, bathing, dust-bathing or some form of tactile stimulation such as dirt on the plumage.

The interest of the Wing Rattle here lies partly in its strong correlation with flight or movement on foot, which it frequently precedes and through this in its value as a signal behaviour pattern, mainly to the partner. When alarmed, white boobies perform the Wing Rattle as a violent shake of the wings as though loosening and preparing them for action. Here the nature of the motivation (tendency to fly) and the function of the Wing Rattle in preparing the feathers for flight seem obvious. Its performance evokes similar action from the mate. In these circumstances it completely lacks the Rotary Headshake component. Comparably, even chicks less than three months old, still in down and unable even to flutter, will Wing Rattle as an alarm response, for instance when approached by man.

The Wing Rattle, however, often occurs in a non-alarm situation, though it nevertheless still indicates a tendency to fly or move away from the site; for example, during the male's frequent flight excursions typical of the early stages of pair formation, one or several Wing Rattles usually precede take-off. A Wing Rattle is sometimes sufficient to dispel an intruder at some distance; it is recognised as a signal preceding actual movement towards him and he flees.

The link between Wing Rattle and impending movement leads us to expect (correctly) a correlation between Wing Rattle and Bill-up-face-away, since the latter typically occurs just as the bird moves or is about to move away from its partner; Bill-up-face-away follows Wing Rattle in a higher proportion of cases than it follows any other behaviour pattern.

OTHER BEHAVIOUR INVOLVED IN BREEDING

1. *Incubation*

The one or two eggs are incubated in the usual sulid way, beneath or on top of the webs according to the ambient temperature. Sometimes the bird stands right off the eggs, presumably to cool them. The eggs are laid about five days apart and partial incubation begins with the first egg, though it is not infrequently unattended. The development of the embryo does not suffer, for the eggs hatch about five days apart.

Incubation stints (Table 58) are just part of the overall pattern of attendance (Fig. 165), which starts long before egg laying and varies with the different phases of the breeding cycle. White boobies may leave their sites completely unattended at all points in the cycle except when there are eggs or small young; males attend more than females; both sexes show high attendance early in the season when they spend relatively much time together, followed by a decline after egg laying and particularly when feeding young, with a late season upswing in attendance once the juveniles have departed; and finally the pattern of attendance differs in pairs or single birds of different status (that is, whether single, having lost egg or chick, having failed to breed or having a chick). The diurnal pattern of attendance before egg laying and again after the chick can be left unguarded shows that sites are attended mainly in the morning and evening.

Eggs are retrieved if within beak-reach but otherwise ignored. Dorward showed that white boobies do not have a mechanism which inhibits them from retrieving and/or attempting to incubate more than the normal clutch, for one female rolled in eggs until she was sitting on seven! Substitute objects are readily accepted.

2. *Change-over*

Change-over occurred mainly in the evening. Details for three different areas are:

TABLE 57

TIMES AT WHICH NEST-RELIEF OCCURRED IN THE WHITE BOOBY

	Kure	Ascension	Galapagos
Dawn		11	
06·00—09·00			20
07·00—11·30		3	
06·00—12·00	38		
09·00—17·00			54
12·00—17·00	63	17	
After 17·00	42	25	67

There is no standard greeting ceremony comparable to that in the gannet. The incoming booby calls loudly in the usual manner as it lands in the territory, usually some distance from the nest. Often the situation does not allow them to land right at the nest, so there is time for the sitting bird to move away without coming into contact with its partner. Interaction between pair members varies from brief Mutual Jabbing to no contact whatsoever, although usually both call. When the male is on duty he sometimes reacts to the landing of the female by the aggressive display Yes/No Headshaking. After an average length incubation spell the relieved bird normally leaves the eggs between three and 15 seconds after the partner's arrival. Frequently, relieved birds fly from their territory to one of their regular preening stations (they may have two or three) and remain there for some time (even overnight) before going to sea. When walking off the site the leaving bird normally performs the Pelican Posture and the Wing Rattle with its associated Oblique Headshake, but not usually the Bill-up-face-away; this is mainly confined to the earlier stages of the breeding cycle.

Two significant features of nest relief in the white booby are first the lack of any stereotyped meeting behaviour and second, the tendency of the leaving bird to move right away from the partner—either to a far point in the territory or to an entirely different area. This behaviour contrasts strongly with that shown early and late in the season, when the pair spend long periods close together on the actual site. It seems that during incubation and chick rearing sexual interest in the partner is relatively weak.

3. *Brooding of young*

The helpless young require constant brooding for protection against predators and also against the fierce sun and cold nights. It is adaptive to shorten the *absences* from the nest at this time so that the new young can be fed and in fact the corresponding attendance spells during the first fortnight of the chick's growth are significantly shorter than during incubation (Table 58), and they gradually decrease in length.

TABLE 58

AVERAGE LENGTH OF STINTS (IN HOURS) DURING INCUBATION AND CHICK GUARDING IN THE WHITE BOOBY IN THE GALAPAGOS

	Incubation	Chick guarding						
		Stint prior to hatching	Age of chick in weeks					
	Av.		0–1	1–3	3–5	5–7	7–9	9+
Male	30 (68)	23 (4)	18 (19)	20 (23)	18 (14)	17 (30)	15 (30)	14 (13)
Female	25 (66)	21 (4)	18 (22)	14 (24)	20 (10)	9 (31)	10 (28)	12 (14)

The number of stints are given in brackets

The age at which young are first left unattended seems very variable in the white booby. In the Galapagos where it was between 22 and 62 days this was partly a seasonal effect (Table 59); the late hatchers were left unattended sooner than the early ones had been. On Kure, the guard stage is 29–84 days, average 60 days (Woodward 1972). This is significantly longer than in the Galapagos, where food was scarcer. In general, guarding may stop because of a seasonal waning in the underlying physiology or a direct effect of food shortage or the absence of neighbours (which tend to stimulate site owners to attend). In the later stages of chick development the adults merely stay with the chick long enough to feed it (since this is usually in the evening, they often stay in the territory overnight). By this time the young clearly discomfit their parents.

4. *Feeding of young*

Food is taken directly from the adult's crop (Fig. 180). Nothing is known in detail about the way in which the tiny young elicit feeding. They were fed, on average, about 1·4 times a day

TABLE 59

SEASONAL EFFECT ON THE AGE AT WHICH THE WHITE BOOBY CHICK IS FIRST LEFT UNGUARDED, IN THE GALAPAGOS

	Date first unattended													
	January									Feb.		March		
	12	14	15	17	20	21	21	21	24	3	29	7	7	11
Age first unattended	60	62	45	48	43	54	51	44	47	32	22	25	22	30
Age unattended more than 50% of the time	107	103	76	80	83	86	66	83	83	53	—	49	48	—

Fig. 180(a–c)

Begging, insertion and feeding from a six-week-old chick.

in the Galapagos (there are no comparable figures from other localities). As they become older and often extremely short of food, their begging behaviour becomes increasingly importunate—indeed, so vigorous that it not only discomfits the adults, which show every sign of ill-ease, but may elicit vigorous jabbing or even overt attack from the male—a response which in no way quells the youngster. But the adult may return, feed its off-spring and depart, all in less than 20 seconds! On the other hand it may ignore the chick for over an hour before feeding it. Some moonlight feeds were observed.

We noticed that young white boobies were much more prone to pick up spilt food than are young gannets. No doubt there is much heavier selection pressure against waste.

The Galapagos young were fed for a total of about 150±20 days, of which some 30–60 were as free-flying young. (Details of feeding frequency, etc. are given in the Ecology Section).

5. *Other aspects of parent/young relationship*

The adult white booby does not interfere in any way with the older chick's attacks on and eventual displacement of the younger (p. 365). The age at which the chick is first left unguarded varies (Table 59). As the season advances, the adults show less tendency to remain on the site.

As the chick grows it begins to defend its parents' territory and often to behave aggressively towards its parents. Commonly, the vigorous pestering of the chick becomes actual jabbing. Indeed, when fully feathered, the juvenile frequently evokes the aggressive territorial display Yes/No Headshaking, jabbing and in some cases prolonged, overt attack from both male and female. Then, as the attack subsides into jabbing and Yes/No Headshaking and the chick resumes normal food begging, feeding may follow. In one case, a female was still feeding a free-flying juvenile three weeks after behaving aggressively to it. It seems, in this case, that a combination of the aggressive jabbing from the young and the adult's waning attachment produces actual attack. The young bird possesses mild appeasement behaviour—Bill-hiding—but nothing like so extreme as that of the attacked gannet juvenile.

BEHAVIOUR OF YOUNG

1. *General*

At the age of about three weeks white booby chicks invariably move away from the actual nest site, and not merely to seek shade. They usually move about 10–30 yards and tend to choose one spot within the territory as their own resting area. Unlike the densely massed gannet chicks, which do not wander from the nest, young boobies wander extensively from the age of about 10 weeks and exercise their wings in short flights from about 90–100 days old, before their first real flight out over water.

2. *Begging*

The first movements of newly-hatched white boobies are unco-ordinated wobblings of the head, movements of the wing stumps and strongly developed crawling by which they actively seek the shelter of the adults. To beg for food the tiny young poke out their heads from beneath the parent's breast and reach upwards to nudge its lower mandible. These pesterings become stronger as the chick grows and grade eventually into high intensity begging behaviour in which the head is laid back, often with upward pointing bill, and moved rapidly from side to side whilst nodding up and down and making occasional bobbing and feinting movements in an irregular fashion during which the bill may point downwards (Fig. 181). The accompanying food call is a rapid 'aa-aa-aa' varying in pace and loudness. Vigorous lunges are aimed at the parent's bill, usually about half way along its length or nearer the base, whilst the wings are held out and threshed violently. In hungry chicks, low intensity but protracted begging occurs completely *in vacuo*. Young which we kept temporarily but did not feed, often awoke and begged, showing the side-to-side head waving, beak pointing upwards and uttering the begging note, even though they certainly could not see an adult. Of course, the parent is necessary to release full and oriented begging. Fingers held in the form of a beak and placed over the chick's mandibles evoked intense feeding (pumping) movements.

It is strikingly obvious that young white boobies beg far more vigorously than young gannets; the latter 'pester' the adult's bill tip but do not lunge and never show the mad, frenzied wing flailing that most booby chicks perform, nor the passionate calling. This is doubtless related to the different degree of hunger attained by booby and gannet young; also it must be highly adaptive for booby young to have evolved the most potently stimulating food begging behaviour. They sometimes reach such straits that success or failure to stimulate feeding on even a single occasion could be decisive for their survival.

3. *Interactive behaviour*

Aggression between nest-mates starts early; a chick six days old attacked its newly-hatched companion. These attacks are persistent and, within the limited capabilities of the chicks, fierce. They are undoubtedly responsible for the death of the smaller bird and are, therefore, an important factor in regulating reproductive rate. There does not need to be a large discrepancy in size to elicit attack—one chick attacked another only 50g (10 per cent) lighter. By experimentally regulating the growth of the nest-mates by withholding food from the heavier, one can prevent either chick from gaining a significant weight advantage but even in matched young, aggression persists and results in the eventual death of one through eviction and subsequent starvation, chilling or overheating.

In response to attacks from sibling or adult, young white boobies show marked Bill-hiding. They Bill-hide from their own parents and from any alarming stimulus without necessarily being touched or pecked; even a slight movement of a strange adult will elicit a Pelican Posture or Bill-hiding (the two grade into each other) from the chick. The gradual transition between chick Bill-hiding and the adult Pelican Posture tends to support the derivation of the latter from a fear motivated behaviour pattern (Bill-hiding). As soon as they begin to move around the territory, chicks show repeated Pelican Postures when walking, even when alone.

The importance of Bill-hiding in reducing the severity of adult attack was graphically demonstrated by red-footed booby chicks, when attacked by adult white boobies. Red-foots entirely lacked the appropriate Bill-hiding behaviour—they retaliated instead of appeasing—and in consequence were severely mauled or killed. Such a fate never befell white booby chicks even though they were sometimes vigorously attacked.

It was usually sexual interest in the young, with whom males attempted to copulate, that led to these attacks. As in gannets, only young approaching maximum size (though not necessarily feathered) elicited copulation behaviour. White booby young, four to eight weeks old, performed Yes/No Headshaking against intruding adults, but reverted to appeasing behaviour—Bill-hiding—when the adults approached closely.

Fig. 181

Part of the begging behaviour of the juvenile, using vigorous wing movements.

From the age of about eight weeks white boobies actively defend their territory against intruding adults (they evict other young long before this). Defence involves vigorous Yes/No Headshaking (first shown at six to seven weeks) with Jabbing and Wing-flailing. Nearly full-grown chicks also actually attack and invariably manage to dispel intruders. Even chicks no more than 12 weeks can drive off intruders, illustrating the real difference in aggression between adult white boobies and gannets. Young gannets do not defend their nests against adults, since this would elicit violent retaliation; they often receive severe punishment even though they Bill-hide deeply. In keeping with their relative lack of site defence behaviour, young gannets do not perform the site ownership display (Bowing) whereas young white boobies perform the analogous pattern Yes/No Headshaking.

Sexual advertising—Sky-pointing—directed to both males and females, was seen from a 38-day old chick. The full movement, including lifting the wings, was performed, accompanied by a 'cow-call' version of the male's whistle. The same precocious chick Wing Rattled (q.v.) when I approached, signifying the tendency to fly, in this case clearly fear-induced.

From their first flight onwards, juveniles, like adults, characteristically show incoming calling followed by the post-landing behaviour of touching nest material and Yes/No Headshaking. They also show the flights around the territory characteristic of site-establishing males, though in this case it may be simply exploratory behaviour. Thus from the first moment of independence they exhibit full territorial behaviour in all forms.

After fledging they revert to the precise nest site of their parents, from which they had wandered during development. For a time, they land very near to the site and spend their time on it.

Away from their territory juveniles react to others with more hostile Mutual Jabbing than that used between adult mated birds. Also, when highly aggressive and frightened (e.g. after handling) juveniles redirected attack to the ground (stabbing and biting) or to their parents. In this case the Jabbing is 'straight' hostile jabbing, without the head flinging movement and open mandibles shown in Jabbing by mated pairs.

When they go to sea, their very first alighting is a splash-landing, feet first, but by the second day (or perhaps before) they are executing shallow dives. It is interesting that diving is not fully automatic from the first, nor is it in the juvenile gannet. They are extremely boisterous and clumsy at this stage, chasing each other and other species with many shouts, and diving fussily near the breeding island.

MAINTENANCE BEHAVIOUR

There remain a number of aspects of white booby behaviour which have not found a place in the functional scheme used here.

1. *Stance and movement*

The normal relaxed stance contrasts strongly with the 'alert' one (Fig. 179) which is long-necked and curiously forward-leaning. The normal walk is somewhat nautical, but quite agile and clearly different from the ritualised Parading. The conspicuous part played in courtship by locomotion and its various behavioural precursors and follow-up behaviour has already been remarked.

2. *Headshake and wing flapping*

The white booby shows an ordinary sideways headshake, a casual side to side movement of the head. This is about the commonest thing gannets do and has become part of several of their more complicated, ritualised behaviour patterns, but white boobies rarely just 'headshake'. They do so frequently when secreting copiously from the salt gland or, with swallowing movements, when settling fish in a full crop, but not, as gannets do, just interspersed with everything else—such as nest building or reacting with another individual. They do, however, employ a brisk version of the sideways headshake in conjunction with the ritualised Bill-up-face-away. No doubt the effectiveness of any signal movement is enhanced—indeed depends on—its difference from non-signal behaviour, which may be why the white booby has little tendency to use the sideways headshake as behavioural 'small change' the way the gannet does.

Wing flapping is a normal part of feather maintenance behaviour, interspersed with preening. It is simply a synchronous beating of widely spread wings usually cambered and turned forwards, with the head, body and tail performing the necessary compensating movements. Sometimes, as a concluding movement, the head is shaken briskly in the Rotary Headshake (rotating from side to side). The whole movement serves to re-settle the plumage and to dislodge loose feathers. It has nothing to do with alarm and is not performed in conflict situations or as a pre-flight movement—that is, it has not acquired signal value.

Another shaking movement used when preening is well described as a 'Dogshake'. This is a form of the Wing Rattle which more often incorporates the Rotary Headshake. All the body feathers are loosened and vigorously shaken (rather than, as in the Wing Rattle, merely the wings) just as a wet dog shakes itself. It would be a mistake to lump the Dogshake and Wing Rattle together even though they are so similar in form (partly due to the fact that both may involve the Rotary Headshake) because the function of the Wing Rattle is essentially a signal, whereas that of the Dogshake is to shake the plumage. Thus the Wing Rattle is a highly specific behaviour pattern occurring in a different motivational context from the Dogshake and acting as a communication in a way that the Dogshake does not. Dogshakes are extremely widespread in birds, as a response to tactile stimulation. Perhaps the Wing Rattle is a ritualised form of the Dogshake.

3. *Heat regulation*

In the sunning posture the wings hang loosely, tips crossed and backs to the sun (Fig. 182). The feathers are ruffed and the bird may pant. Other boobies do it and the function is obscure. Panting, gular fluttering and wing-hanging are used as heat-dissipating behaviour. Cloacal exposure was not seen in adults.

4. *Sleeping and roosting*

Adults usually sleep with head in scapulars or back feathers or (rarely) if they are sitting, with the head on the ground. Booby chicks often sleep in this supine way, lying more like a mammal than a bird, but it is rare in adults. In very hot conditions it may save energy and is probably

Fig. 182. Panting, gular fluttering and wing hanging as heat dissipating mechanisms. Wing-hanging grades into the sunning posture.

equivalent to 'head hanging' in the adult red-foot, which one sees only during the hot part of the day.

Breeding adults usually roost in their territories, at least in the early stages of breeding, but later may roost away from them, on the beach or sea-rocks. Similarly, non-breeding but territory-holding or even immature birds, may roost among breeders, though often they roost on beaches, etc., away from them. White boobies commonly roost on islets and rocks which are totally unsuitable for nesting—for example, they may be washed by seas on occasions only, or too small and steep for nesting. Thus, records of roosting birds need not indicate a breeding colony. They commonly roost on the sea.

5. *Fishing*

Anderson (1954) claims that white boobies do not fish in flocks, but in pairs and they tend to avoid fishing with other species. The tendency to fish as individuals, if true, is interesting. Whilst it accords with the species' known tendency to forage far, it seems odd that such dazzling white plumage would have evolved unless as a marker, attracting conspecifics to a diving bird. Simmons recorded up to 80–90 white boobies fishing on inshore shoals together with even larger flocks of brown boobies, off Ascension. Anderson mentions a tendency to fish in 'family parties' but this is probably not strictly true and is more likely to refer to adults which have been joined by any juvenile, not merely their offspring.

White boobies will dive into water as shallow as 1½m but cannot begin to equal blue-footed or brown boobies in inshore fishing. They plunge rather more heavily than other boobies, and have been observed, in clear water, to penetrate deeply (perhaps 2–3m). Submersion has been timed at about six seconds and was followed by floating with head partly submerged, perhaps whilst swallowing prey. Dives have been recorded from about 12m and Anderson has seen them hover over the sea at a height of between 25 and 100m and then dive headlong. A dive from this height could lead to a penetration far beyond 3m and may be connected with this species' ability to take very large prey (p. 378). With deep penetration may be associated this species' tendency to swallow a higher proportion of its prey under water. They do not take as many flying fish on the wing as do brown and red-footed boobies, though they have been known to do so. Simmons, also, emphasises that white boobies plunge steeply from 15–35m. He considers them to be more stereotyped plungers than the versatile brown booby. Typically they fly fairly high, bill pointing directly downwards, searching below rather than in front. Before diving they often fan their tail, with feet held down and spread sideways and wings moving at the tips. Then they plunge, with a half twist, in a gravity dive, though occasionally they power dive with rapid beats of the primaries. They rarely perform shallow slant dives. He describes a peculiar cry, given just as the dive commences; a bugle-like double honk, ringing and high pitched, quite unlike the calls of either sex in the breeding colony. Even brown boobies responded by leaving the stacks and flying out to it.

Juvenile white boobies plunge dive near to the colony, whilst still partly dependent on their parents. They use shallow dives to alight on the sea, but also simply alight on the surface.

SUMMARY

1. After a period of absence (usually following previous breeding) male white boobies establish their site by aerial and ground reconnaissance followed by flighting over the area, flying in with a special wing movement and fighting (rarely).

2. They maintain the site against neighbours by somewhat ritualised Jabbing and, long range, by a mainly aggressive display (Yes/No Headshaking).

3. Pair formation is achieved by male advertising (a sexual display called Sky-pointing) which attracts prospecting females to close quarters where contact behaviour (Mutual Jabbing) occurs. Over a period, pair interactions increase and include Parading in the territory (with associated ritualised behaviour, such as the Oblique Headshake, Pelican Posture and Bill-up-face-away), symbolic nest building and copulation.

4. Incubation is shared, the average stints being about 28 hours in the Galapagos but

shorter (10 hours) on Kure. These indicate that white boobies generally forage at a good distance from the breeding colony.

5. After guarding the young for at least 4–5 weeks, both parents feed it equally (over once per day) until it fledges (about 17 weeks) and after that for another 5–10 weeks.

6. The young soon begin to defend their parents' territory and show most adult behaviour patterns. They possess an appeasement posture which can mitigate adult attack.

7. Some body-care behaviour, and fishing, are described.

5

Sula leucogaster

BROWN BOOBY

1. NOMENCLATURE; EXTERNAL FEATURES; MORPHOLOGY; MOULT AND VOICE

NOMENCLATURE

1. *Common*

Brown booby; brown gannet; black gannet or fou noir (probably refers to *S. leucogaster* in some cases at least; used in Pacific Islands Pilot); common booby; Colombian booby; white-bellied booby or gannet; Atlantic booby; Gorgona booby; Brewster's booby; booby gannet; le fou de Cayenne; le fou commun; le petit fou. Many of these common names show that this species and the red-footed booby have often been confused, not surprisingly in view of the latter's brown morphs and the smallness of the males of both species.

Pájaro bobo; Alcatráz murgulhão (Brazil); Fou capucin, (Seychelles); Burong bebek (Malaya); Kaló; Tol (Marshall Islands); Kiburi (Gilbert Islands); Kariga (Tuamotus); Keni (Manihiki); Boba prieta (Spanish); Bubi chaleco (Spanish).

2. *Scientific*

Sula (= *Pelecanus*) *leucogaster* Boddaert, 1783, Table Planches Enlum., p. 57, based on plate 973 of Daubenton 'Le Fou de Cayenne', no locality but equals Cayenne.

Sula sula Brisson 1760.

Binomial synonyms for *Sula leucogaster* (sometimes *leucogastra*) have included: *Sula brewsteri*, *S. etesiaca*, *S. fiber*, *S. australis*, *S. furca*, *S. fusca*, *S. fulca*, *S. fulica*, *S. leucogastris*, *S. sinicadvena*, *S. nesiotes*, *S. brasiliensis*, *S. parva*, *Pelecanus parvus*, *P. plotus*, *P. sula*, *Dysporus sula*, *D. fiber*, *D. leucogaster*, *D. brasiliensis*. The tendency to use *Sula sula* for this booby, as Andrews (1900), Wood-Jones (1912), Robinson & Kloso (1921) and Williamson (1916 and 1918), following the Brit. Mus. Catalogue 1898: 436–40, was particularly confusing, since the red-footed booby *Sula sula* often nests on the same island as the brown.

The trinomial nomenclature distinguishes the following races:

Sula leucogaster leucogaster Boddaert, 1783, Table Planches Enlum., p. 57, from the Caribbean and tropical Atlantic.

Sula leucogaster plotus Forster, 1844, Descriptiones animalium, ed. Licht, p. 278 (near New Caledonia), with a vast range from the central Pacific westwards into the Indian Ocean and possibly as far as the east coast of Africa, taking in the Red Sea.

Sula leucogaster brewsteri Goss, 1888, Auk 5, p. 242 (San Pedro Martir), characteristic of arid areas of the extreme eastern Pacific (Gulf of California).

Sula leugocaster etesiaca Thayer & Bangs, 1905, Bull. Mus. Comp. Zool., 46, p. 92 (Gorgona Island), was given specific status by the above authors because it is quite different from *leucogaster* and *brewsteri* and they were 'not quite prepared' to consider *leucogaster*, *brewsteri*, another 'form' *nesiotes* (see below) and *etesiaca* all to be nothing more than sub-species. It inhabits the humid zone from western Panama southwards to northern Ecuador (it is the form often called Colombian booby) and the wet Cocos Island.

Sula leucogaster nesiotes Heller & Snodgrass, 1901, Condor, 3, p. 75 (Clipperton Island), synonymous with *S. leucogaster albiceps* Van Rossem (Wetmore 1939) and both of them seem to me to be the same as *S.l.brewsteri*. The so-called *nesiotes* is found on Las Tres Marias and also on Clipperton. Wetmore (1939) considered the Clipperton birds to be distinct from *brewsteri* but identical with the Tres Marias birds. This means that the latter must be distinct from the *brewsteri* of the Gulf of California and this seems by no means proved. Climatically, the Tres Marias birds would be expected to be *brewsteri* and Murphy thought that the Clipperton birds would also turn out to be *brewsteri*. Thus *nesiotes* seems not yet proven as a 'good' race distinct from *brewsteri*.

Sula leucogaster rogersi Mathews, 1913, Avian Record, 1, p. 189, Bedout Island, Western Australia. This is doubtfully distinct from *Sula leucogaster plotus*.

GENERAL FEATURES

1. *Adult*

The female brown booby is a medium-large sulid, about 80cm long with a wing spread of about 150cm. The male is much smaller (75cm with a wing span of 140cm) and has a longer tail relative to the length of his body, and a smaller more delicate bill.

The best identification features are the darkish brown upperparts (wings, back and tail), head, neck and upper breast (a brown cowl), the brown ending in a sharp line across the breast where the white lower breast begins. The white of the ventral surface extends onto the abdomen, back to the tail. The undersurface of the wing has a conspicuous, clearly outlined white bar running out from the white of the lower body towards the wing tip and ending, after tapering, at about the carpal joint. The adult brown booby is thus exceptionally clean-cut, lacking the indefinite areas and the patches that mark most other boobies (see Comparative Section).

The colour of the bill, face and feet varies with sex, region and breeding condition (see below) but is typically lime green to chrome yellow, sometimes pale.

The flight is powerful, alternating glides with steady wing beats; it has been described as 'workaday' and 'gull-like'. Members of a group often flap in unison and rise at an angle of 20°–30° before gently descending. Brown boobies are less likely to be encountered far from land than are either the red-foot or the white. They may occur singly or in groups, but rarely more than 40–50. They (and white boobies) have been seen in full control of flight in cyclonic winds (force 9–12+) in the Caribbean.

2. *Juveniles and immature*

The juvenile is an extremely drab version of the adult with the pale brownish underparts and

(b) Wing positions in the brown booby.

Fig. 183(a)

Shape and pattern of the ventral surface in the brown booby.

Photo: J. Warham

under-wing bar often scarcely visibly demarcated from the darker areas, though much more obviously in some. The primaries are distinctly blackish.

The immatures have a variable amount of dark mottling on the lower breast and belly, the last traces of immaturity being a few dark flecks on the lower breast, in which condition breeding may occur. Immature stages are less conspicuous and variable than in other sulids, because there are no areas of white to be acquired on the upper parts. The coloured parts remain relatively drab and pale.

DETAILED DESCRIPTION

The brown booby is one of the two sulids (the other is the red-foot) which exists in several distinct forms. These are not all of comparable status or validity. In the following account the descriptions which exist for each of the sub-species accepted here are quoted in detail. The full description is given for the nominate race *Sula leucogaster leucogaster* and other races are treated merely with respect to the features in which they differ from the nominate and from each other.

Sula leucogaster leucogaster (Boddaert)

This race is common to the whole of the tropical Atlantic, the Caribbean and the Gulf of Mexico and little different from the form *S.l.plotus* which occurs in the Indian and Pacific Oceans.

1. *Adult male and female*

(*a*) *Upperparts*

Head, neck and upper breast clove-brown; upper surface of wings, tail and back a paler brown (Murphy 1936), but according to Palmer (1962) head, neck and upper breast blackish-brown, remaining upperparts fuscous. The primaries are blackish on their outer webs and the brown secondaries whitish at their bases and on the inner webs. The shafts of the remiges are blackish when new, paling distally to horn colour when old. The rectrices are brownish-black at their bases.

(*b*) *Underparts*

The ventral surface, backwards of the demarcation line on the upper breast, is white.

There is a conspicuous white under-wing bar running from the body to the carpal joint, formed from axillars, median and greater under wing coverts; the lesser under wing coverts are fuscous.

(*c*) *Bill, feet, etc.*

Male. (*i*) *Bill.* Early in the breeding cycle, the bill is yellow, shading to bluish horn towards the tip; later it becomes greenish-grey with a lighter tip. On Ascension the bill was yellow with a pale flesh tip. (*ii*) *Face.* In early breeding condition, the facial skin and gular area become deep chrome yellow which fades during incubation until in the parental phase it is merely whitish, perhaps with a faint blue tinge. Some birds (or all?) have bright blue eyelids and orbital ring and grey skin around the eye. In non-breeding condition the facial skin is yellow or greenish and eyelids and orbital ring bluish. This always serves to distinguish it from the female, in which the eyelid and orbital ring are yellow. There is a bluish patch in front of the eye, but paler and less clear cut than in the female. (*iii*) *Eyes.* The iris is dark in Atlantic (Ascension) birds, but pale greyish or whitish in South American birds. (*iv*) *Feet.* The feet are chrome yellow in the early stages of breeding regressing to green in the parental phase and paler in the non-breeding phase.

Female. (*i*) *Bill.* The bill is yellow, shading to bluish-horn towards the tip in the early breeding stages and later becomes greenish and paler. (*ii*) *Face.* There is less seasonal variation than in the male. The female has mainly pale yellow facial skin, though the yellow is stronger during the nuptial period, with a conspicuous inky patch in front of the eye. The eyelids are bright blue or, maybe, yellowish. (*iii*) *Eyes.* As in the male. (*iv*) *Feet.* Pale yellow, showing little seasonal variation.

Sula leucogaster plotus (Forster)

This is the race found in the western and central tropical Pacific, the whole of the Indian Ocean and its extensions (the Red Sea and Gulf of Aden), Malasian waters and the minor seas in the Australasian–Indonesian area (Celebes, Coral Sea, Banda Sea, etc.). As such, it occurs on Cocos Keeling and Christmas Island, Indian Ocean, among others and the most detailed information comes from these two islands. It has been 'split', but unsatisfactorily (for example the attempt to isolate the birds from Western Australia as *rogersi*, type locality Bedout Island, was rightly decried by Gibson-Hill as 'pretty nonsense' because it relied on colours of eyes and feet).

Fig. 184

Plumage of juvenile (Christmas Island, Indian Ocean).

The Christmas Island and Cocos Keeling birds have the following characteristics.

(*a*) *Plumage*

Head and neck very slightly darker than the rest of the upper parts.

(*b*) *Bill, feet, etc.*

Male. (*i*) *Bill.* Greenish-grey; light greenish-blue, nearly white at tip. Coral Sea birds had a creamy or grey bill, sometimes tinged yellowish or greenish, and rich blue at the base. (*ii*) *Face.* Facial, ramal and gular skin dull purple or purplish-grey; eyelids blue. Coral Sea birds had facial skin and orbital ring rich blue. (*iii*) *Eyes.* Iris grey or yellowish-grey, or putty colour. Coral Sea birds from yellow to deep brown. (*iv*) *Feet.* Pale arsenic green; green to bluish green. Coral Sea birds greenish yellow.

Female. (*i*) *Bill.* Light greenish-yellow, almost white at the tip; or greyish-green. Much the same in Coral Sea birds. (*ii*) *Face.* Lighter coloured than that of the male. Facial and ramal skin greenish-yellow, with bluish patch in front of the eye. Eyelids blue. Coral Sea females had chrome yellow facial skin and orbital ring and they also had a blue patch in front of the eye. (*iii*) *Eyes.* The iris is grey or yellowish-grey; Voous records red in two specimens from Christmas Island, where I saw a female with brown irises. Coral Sea birds had yellow to deep brown irises. (*iv*) *Feet.* Pale green or yellowish-green. Coral Sea birds almost chrome yellow.

Red Sea birds, presumably the same sub-species, are described by Al-Husaini as having bill, face and feet variable, either bluish-yellow to greenish-yellow or light yellow throughout but these descriptions are potentially conformable to those given above.

Sula leucogaster brewsteri,[1] Goss

This form occurs in arid areas. It is the brown booby of the Gulf of California and Mexico and possibly some of the eastern Pacific islands (Clipperton). Its range abutts that of *S.l.etesiaca*, a bird of humid zones of central America and western South America (see below) and these two forms (*brewsteri* and *etesiaca*) inhabit the western side of the Isthmus of Panama, being sharply and effectively divided by this narrow land barrier from the nominate race of the Caribbean side.

(*a*) *Plumage*

Male. Murphy describes the male *brewsteri* as having a hoary grey head and throat. In Palmer (1962), it is similar to the nominate, but differs in having forehead and forecrown, the area behind the eye and the chin white, shading into pale brownish grey on the neck and greyish brown on the upper breast and upper back.

Female. In the female these areas are fuscous and a slightly different colour from the rest of the upperparts (Palmer states that they are the same, but Thayer & Bangs 1905, who originally described *etesiaca*, make a special point of the difference between the female *brewsteri* and *etesiaca*, the former having head and neck distinctly lighter than the back whereas the latter does not).

There are no published details of bill, face and feet colours for this form.

Sula leucogaster etesiaca (Thayer & Bangs)

This is the brown booby of the humid zones, west of the Panamanian Isthmus, off central America and western South America; the type locality is the wet Gorgona Island, Colombia, but it occurs as far north as Cocos Island. It is a smaller, darker form than *brewsteri* or *leucogaster*.

(*a*) *Adult plumage*

Male. The male is grey headed. The forehead is very pale, almost white, becoming grey and then brownish-grey on the sides of the head and hind neck and passing into dark sooty brown at the nape, cheeks, throat below the gular sac and on the back, upper wings, tail and

[1] *brewsteri* probably = *nesiotes* = *albiceps*.

upper breast, the brown darkest on the under surface of the primaries. The lateral tail coverts are brown, the rest white. Originally, Thayer & Bangs described it as intermediate in colour between *brewsteri* and *leucogaster*.

Female. The female lacks the grey head. Its head is the same colour as the upperparts, thus differing from the female of the nominate race in which the head and back are of different shades of brown.

(*b*) *Bill, feet, etc.*

Male. (*i*) *Bill.* Dusky, slightly yellowish. (*ii*) *Face.* Gular areas and around the eye are dusky, sometimes tinged greenish-yellow. (*iii*) *Eyes.* Grey. (*iv*) *Feet.* Light pea green.

Female. (*i*) *Bill.* Sulphur yellow. (*ii*) *Face.* Gular sac and base of bill are pea green or sulphur yellow with a slate blue smudge in front of the eye. (*iii*) *Eyes.* Grey. (*iv*) *Feet.* Light yellowish or sulphur yellow.

Brewsteri and *etesiaca* are thus fairly similar and were indeed regarded as a single form. Thayer & Bangs state that the male *brewsteri* differs from male *etesiaca* by having the head entirely whitish and the neck ashy grey and that the female *brewsteri* has the head and neck distinctly lighter than the back, whilst in female *etesiaca* head and back are concolour. However, this last point is in distinct disagreement with Palmer, who may be confusing or amalgamating the two forms.

The above differences in plumage, particularly the colour of bill and face in the various races, may be the result of selectively neutral variation.

2. *Juvenile and immatures*

The following details of juvenile plumage concern mainly the nominate form with, where appropriate, notes on any sub-specific differences. Stages in the development of the chick are described under Breeding Ecology (p. 457).

(*a*) *Plumage*

The head and neck are fuscous, slightly darker than the back and scapulars. The upper breast is fuscous, more or less obviously demarcated from the lower breast, belly and under tail coverts, which are grey-brown; the feathers being grey with a broad sub-terminal ashy brown bar, succeeded by a whitish tip. The tail is fuscous, paler at the tip; the primaries blackish brown and the secondaries like the back. The juvenile *plotus* has the areas which will be brown in the adult a uniform, dark, greyish-brown, with head, neck, back and dorsal surface all the same colour. The underparts that will be white are a pale, dirty grey, the demarcation line being clearly marked but a bit irregular. In all, the bar on the undersurface of the wing is a dull replica of the adult's, formed by greyish-brown, pale-tipped median and greater under wing coverts and axillars, the lesser under wing coverts being brownish. Even in juvenile plumage the neck is distinctly darker than the back in *S.l.leucogaster*, thus differentiating this race from *etesiaca*.

This plumage is worn for almost a year, during which time the underparts may become darker due to abrasion of the pale tips. Slight spangling on the belly, from week 33, becomes barring or crescentic marks by weeks 39–41 and 50 weeks after fledging the lower underparts are more pale than brown. Traces of brown may remain on the lower breast and belly until the bird is just into its third year, in which dress breeding may very rarely occur.

(*b*) *Bill, feet, etc.*

(*i*) *Bill.* At first dark (in *l. leucogaster* until week 35 post-fledging), mauve to purple-flesh by week 40 but may remain greyish much longer. Later becomes pale bluish, turning dull greenish-yellow probably in second year. Grey-blue in *plotus*, becoming greenish-grey. (*ii*) *Face.* Gular and facial skin dark grey-blue in *plotus*, becoming dull purplish in the male and greenish-grey in the young female. In *leucogaster* the face becomes flesh-coloured from week 5 after fledging, then yellow from week 11. (*iii*) *Eyes.* Iris pale (whitish or pale grey, sometimes flecked). (*iv*) *Feet.* Pale yellowish; light orange-pink in *plotus* and *leucogaster*, sometimes almost whitish; becoming lemon-yellow in second year.

3. *Measurements and weight*

Table 60 gives measurements of brown boobies of different races. Since they were measured by different investigators and come from a mixture of living birds and museum specimens, it is unwise to read much into regional differences. However, the difference between the sexes emerges clearly and some of these are summarised in Table 61.

MOULT

On Ascension one brown booby chick returned when nine months old; apparently it had not shed any feathers and looked exactly as at fledging. Five weeks later, however, primaries number 2 were growing (score 2·8), which means that it had already lost and replaced primaries number 1. Another three weeks later, primaries 2 were full grown and primaries 3 were just growing (Dorward 1962b). Thus replacement had started at about the same age as in the white booby. A bird judged to be 16 months old had a primary score of 1·5 and 9·1, thus having started the second cycle of replacement (bringing in the third generation of wing feathers) when the first replacement cycle had reached the 7th feather.

On Christmas Island I examined 32 adults for moult (Table 62) and found that only one bird out of 14 with eggs and one out of 12 with small chicks were in wing moult. However, on Pulau Perak, 11 out of 12 incubating adults were moulting wing and tail feathers in March 1973 (Langham & Wells 1974). Most adults with fully fledged young had moulted primaries and tail feathers lying on their sites on another occasion (Gibson-Hill 1950c). The pause in moult therefore seems, as in other boobies, to come during the pre-laying period and probably often during incubation, even extending into the first part of chick rearing. There is no information on the speed of moult, but no *a priori* reason why it should differ much from the white or red-footed boobies, despite the less frequent breeding of the latter two species.

VOICE

The brown booby is in my experience less vocal than the white and blue-footed boobies. This may be related to its tendency to nest in relatively small groups or even isolated, for vocalisation is certainly stimulated by neighbours.

The voice has much the same degree of sexual dimorphism as that of the white and blue-footed boobies. The female utters a harsh quacking or honking noise 'kaak-kaak-kaak' or 'ar-k, ar-k' almost indistinguishable from that of the blue-foot and the male a much quieter, sibilant, whistling call, sometimes almost a hiss. When he is aggressively motivated (landing in the territory to dispel an intruder in the early stages of breeding) the whistle becomes a violent 'chuff, chuff', which I used to call the 'steam-engine' whistle. During Sky-pointing, the male may utter a soft call which has been rendered 'iruk, iruk, iruk'. The calls of both sexes probably resemble those of the blue-foot more than any other sulid. In intimate pair interactions there are soft and abbreviated versions of these calls.

The young grunt more (agk, agk) and rattle their mandibles at intruders. Both sexes have the female-type call, and if one may judge from the one recorded instance of an immature male breeding and retaining the female-type voice, they retain it for at least two years.

The alarm call is an agonised 'karrk', very like that of any booby, though the timbre varies.

TABLE 60

MEASUREMENTS OF THE BROWN

Area	Probable sub-species	Overall length Male	Female	Wing Male	Female	Tail Male	Female
Fernando Noronha;	Mainly	710–760	—	372–391	384–415	169–198	162–198
Ascension;	*S.l.leucogaster*	—	760	381	400	186	180·5
Dry Tortugas;		13	10	13	10	13	10
Bahamas;							
Brazil							
				383–415	389–413	181–203	183–200
Brazil				395	401·8	193·7	191·4
				9	10	9	10
				378–411	395–412	173–208	177–200
Cape Verdes	*S.l.leucogaster*			392·2	404·3	190	191·5
				10	10	10	10
				370–410	390–420		
Ascension	*S.l.leucogaster*			—	—		
				14	26		
		780–784	755–830	379–400	385–418	196–209	190–200
Cocos-Keeling	*S.l.plotus*	782	805	390	405	203	194
(Indian Ocean)		4	3	4	3	4	3
Christmas Island		—	—	—	—	—	—
(Indian Ocean)	*S.l.plotus*	781	811	389	413	202	201
		6	6	6	6	6	6
		731–804	800–828	392–398	406–426	198–210	204–227
		764	815·7	395	417·5	206·8	216
		5	4	5	4	5	4
				384–428	418–440	204–236	207–223
				405·5	429	221	214
				10	8	8	6
				386–398	410–415	195–196	193–206
Clipperton	*S.l.brewsteri*			389	413	196	200
				4	2	4	2
				365–378	390–403	172–183	182–183
Tres Marias				372	397	176	182·5
				—	—	—	—
Gorgona;	*S.l.etesiaca*			374–380	398–405	168–187	192–198
Saboga;				377·7	401	180·3	195·6
San Miguel				3	3	3	3
Pearl Islands;	*S.l.etesiaca*			365–382	360–412	170–182	174–191
Cocos (Pacific);				374·3	390	178	186
Gorgona				3	8	2	8

Key: 710–760mm (range)
740 (mean)
13 (number of cases)

BOOBY FROM DIFFRENT REGIONS

Tarsus		Culmen		Weight		Source
Male	Female	Male	Female	Male	Female	
42–48·4	45–48	87·8–101	91·8–102			
44·3	46·8	92·7	93·3			Murphy 1936
13	10	13	10			
44–49	45–49	90–99	90–100			
45·6	46·9	93·5	94·2			Palmer 1962
9	10	9	10			
45–51	47–51	90–100	97–102			
47·9	48·8	94·7	100·1			Murphy 1924
10	10	10	10			
		87–91	91–99	850–1200	1100–1550	
		—	—	—	—	Dorward 1962b
		14	26	14	26	
40–44	44–47	97–99	100–110			
42	45	97·7	104·6			Chasen 1933
4	3	4	3			
—	—	—	—			
42	44·5	98	104			Gibson-Hill 1947
6	6	6	6			
41–43	44–45·5	96–101	102–107			
42·1	44·9	98·6	104			Gibson-Hill 1950c
5	4	5	4			
		88·2–99·5	95–107·1	850–1190	970–1480	
		96·2	102	962	1260	Nelson unpubl.
		15	22	20	29	
		93·5–97·4	97·9–110·2			
		95·9	104			Stager 1964
		4	2			
		84–91·4	92·6–96·5			
		89	94·6			Stager 1964
		—	—			
45–47	47–50	94–95	97–100			
45·6	48·3	94·7	99			Thayer & Bangs 1905
3	3	3	3			
43–50	44–48·5	87–95	93–102			
44·2	—	90·3	97·8			Murphy 1936
3	8	3	8			

TABLE 61

COMPARATIVE MEASUREMENTS OF THE RACES OF THE BROWN BOOBY

Race	Wing M av.	Wing F av.	Wing M as % of F	Tail M av.	Tail F av.	Tail M as % of F	Culmen M av.	Culmen F av.	Culmen M as % of F	Weight M av.	Weight F av.	Weight M as % of F
S.l.leucogaster	388	401	96·7	190	186	102	93·1	95·3	97·7	850 to 1200	1100 to 1550	77·3
S.l.plotus	397	418	95	208	206	101	97·2	103	94·4	962	1260	76·4
S.l.etesiaca	376	393	95·7	179	188	95·2	92·5	98·1	94·3			
S.l.brewsteri	381	405	94	186	191	97·2	92·5	99·3	93·1			

TABLE 62

CORRELATION BETWEEN MOULT AND THE STAGE OF THE BREEDING CYCLE IN THE BROWN BOOBY ON CHRISTMAS ISLAND, INDIAN OCEAN

Stage	Number of primaries growing: None	1	2	3	4	% of sample in moult
Incubating	13	—	1	—	—	7
Relatively small chick	11	—	1	—	—	9
Relatively large chick	3	1	1	—	—	40
Unknown status but no egg or chick	—	1	—	—	—	
Totals	27	2	3	—	—	19

2. BREEDING DISTRIBUTION, NUMBERS AND OTHER ASPECTS OF POPULATIONS

INTRODUCTION

The brown booby is 'the' common booby, occurring between the tropics right across the world although in one major belt of ocean—part of the Indian Ocean east of the Seychelles—it is very thin or absent in archipelagos where it might be expected to breed. Brown boobies nest amidst the sodden vegetation and daily downpours on Gorgona off Colombia, on blindingly arid islands in the Gulf of California, the Red Sea and the Gulf of Aden, on the precipitous ledges of La Perousse in the Pacific, Pulau Perak in the Malacca Straits and St Paul's Rocks in the Atlantic, and on countless tiny coral islands in the atolls of the southern seas. It rarely forms vast gatherings, though colonies numbering several thousands of pairs do occur, and the tendency to nest in small colonies of a few to a few hundred pairs, tucked away on tiny islets, together with its wide and oceanic distribution, pose virtually insoluble problems when it comes to estimating world, or even regional, populations.

The brown booby is often found on the same islands as the white and red-footed boobies; these three tropical, blue-water species all depend heavily on flying fish and squid and are sympatric over much of their range. The brown booby can also claim the distinction of sharing part of its range with the blue-footed booby (in the Gulf of California and the eastern Pacific) and with Abbott's booby (on Christmas Island) a record of congeneric fraternising which only the red-foot can equal, and that barely. In general, brown boobies are less tied to the clear, blue-water tropics than are the white and red-footed and are more likely than these species to be found on islands near to land masses and in the vicinity of coastal waters, harbours and estuaries, which are more turbid. They do not forage as far from land.

Like all sulids, and perhaps more than others, it has suffered substantially at man's hands and many islands have lost much or all of their populations through direct depredation for food, by military activity or the introduction of pests. This should be borne in mind when evaluating relative abundance in the different parts of its range. In the more accessible and man-colonised areas, its numbers are enormously fewer than they were, which is hardly to be wondered at when one recalls that slaughter has been going on for hundreds of years. Over 300 years ago Dampier records that the numbers of brown boobies in the Dutch Indies had been 'much lessened by the French fleet' and in the southern oceans sea birds have for thousands of years been part of man's food.

Many of the remarks made in the section on Numbers and Distribution of the white booby apply equally to the brown and the same divisions of the oceans into segments is followed here. Starting in the north Atlantic with the Bahamas, we explore the Caribbean, with its great centres of booby populations in the West Indies and off the Venezuelan coast. Next we take in the islands off the northern shoulder of South America, south to the São Paulo coast, encompassing the famous Brazilian stations and going out as far as Fernando Noronha and Rocas Reef and the ill-fated South Trinidad. Then via the great and remote oceanic stations—St. Paul's Rocks and Ascension—we move to the eastern stations in the tropical Atlantic, the Cape Verdes and the booby islands off the bulge of Africa and in the Gulf of Guinea.

The Indian Ocean survey takes us south from the Arabian Sea to the western Indian Ocean atolls and islands—the Seychelles, Aldabra, the Amirantes and lesser known groups, eastwards via the Chagos archipelago to Cocos-Keeling and Christmas Island, thence through the Coral Sea to the western Pacific and across that vast expanse of tropical sea to the eastern Pacific, to the Galapagos, Cocos Island, the islands off southern California and Mexico and south to the Gulf of Panama, separated by the narrow but astonishingly effective Isthmus from the islands of the Caribbean with which we began. What a trip it would be. Given a suitable boat and five years one could go a long way towards establishing the present position of seabirds on island groups for which there are few if any records and towards documenting the drastic changes that have undoubtedly occurred on many more.

DISTRIBUTION AND NUMBERS IN THE MAJOR OCEANS

1. *Caribbean and Atlantic*

In this area the brown booby is represented by the nominate race, though there are probably regional differences, especially in the colour of bill, face and feet.

The brown booby reaches its most northerly Atlantic breeding station in the southern Bahamas. The Atlantic is ill-supplied with islands between the bulge of Africa and South America; west of the Cape Verde Islands there is nothing until the string of islands which form the eastern boundary of the Caribbean, sweeping round from the Bahamas to Trinidad. This area is, or has been, one of the greatest strongholds of the brown booby and today it is the commonest of the three booby species (brown, white and red-footed) which occur there. Without doubt it used to flourish there in hundreds of thousands. Colonies, huge by brown booby standards, occurred on several islands. Indeed, the Cape Verdes, once also a notable stronghold, probably acquired its great numbers by virtue of the same circumstances; namely a vast belt of tropical sea, suitable for blue-water boobies but, except near its western and eastern boundaries, devoid of islands. The West Indies and the Cape Verdes thus had to support a population commensurate with that which the adjacent seas could feed. As we shall see, not only the size, but also the density, of these colonies is, or was, exceptionally great. Also, the southern equatorial current flows along the whole of the coast of north-eastern South America and may lead to enrichment by upwelling there, so that the area is good for food as well as nesting sites.

The brown booby, alone among the three species found in the Caribbean, occurs all along the mainland coast of Venezuela but does not nest on it. Van Halewijn's (1975) voyages indicated that there were few between La Vela and San Juan de los Cayos but many between Puerto La Cruz and Carúpano.

Murphy (1967) lists 18 breeding stations in this area (see Fig. 186) and recent work by Van Halewijn (pers. comm.) has provided the most up-to-date information on colonies in the south-eastern part of the Caribbean Sea (Fig. 185).

The Bahaman colony on CAY VERDE ISLAND was one of the seabird colonies studied by Frank M. Chapman (1908). Over half a century later it was owing to the generosity of the F. M. Chapman Foundation that my wife and I were able to visit the Galapagos and so begin the work which led to this book. The colony on Cay Verde used to number some 1500 pairs distributed in several groups and there are colonies also on GREAT RAGGED, LITTLE RAGGED, SAN (SANTO) DOMINGO CAY, SAMANA CAY and MIRAPORVOS ISLAND.

In the West Indies there is a very large colony (several thousand pairs) on MIDDLE CAY of the **Pedro** group (south of Jamaica) (C. Bernard Lewis, in litt. to Hutchinson, 1950).

The Puerto Rican colony on the nature reserve of DESECHEO, little more than a rock about 2km by 1km, and 150m high rising from the restless waters of Mona Passage, reportedly held 8–10 000 birds (Wetmore 1927) mainly in groups within one or two hundred metres of the beach but also over the entire island. The population has certainly declined since then. Other Puerto Rican colonies are reputedly to be found on ISLA MONA, BLANQUILLO and ISLA CAJA DE MUERTOS. The Mona colony may have been large, principally on the small off-lying island of Monito. Red-foots were common too, but there is no mention of white boobies, though these do occur. Recent work by Kepler (in press) shows that this is the most widely distributed breeding bird on Monito, in a wide range of habitats. The population varies from about 150 pairs in the non-breeding 'season' (mainly summer) to about 500 pairs during main laying periods.

Off the Venezuelan coast the two **Islas de Aves**, AVE DE SOTAVENTO and AVE DE BARLOVENTO (not to be confused with the Isla de Aves or Bird Island west of Dominica, which also holds brown boobies) used to be the sites of substantial colonies (Cory 1909). One islet off Ave de Barloventa held deposits of guano for which boobies were probably responsible, though whether the boobies were white or brown one does not know (the former seems perhaps more likely. Van Halewijn estimates at least 1000 pairs on the two islands. A few kilometres east of the Islas de Aves lies the circle of islands **Islas Los Rogues** (or Los Roques) still holding at least several hundreds of pairs (Van Halewijn) and east again LA ORCHILA upon which brown, white and red-footed boobies, frigates and tropic birds were nesting in great numbers in the early years of this century and still nest today, though their numbers are not on record; Van Halewijn estimates many hundreds to thousands of pairs. On Orchila the brown boobies use cliff sites. Both brown and red-footed boobies occur all along the Venezuelan coast from La Guaira to Trinidad, doubtless nesting on scores of small islands. The island groups of **Los Hermanos** and **Los Testigos** held substantial numbers of brown boobies. They used to be present in great numbers on Los Hermanos though even the brown booby was outnumbered by red-foots (there were also a few white boobies). Van Halewijn estimates that at 'probably several hundreds of pairs' brown boobies are still outnumbered by red-foots. The Testigos, some 69km offshore, are seven islets and several smaller rocks and most or all held small colonies of brown boobies (Lowe 1909). Van Halewijn recorded several hundred pairs breeding there in 1973. At least several dozen pairs nest on **Los Frailes** (Van Halewijn pers. comm.). Perhaps the most important nesting islands in this area are Los Aves, Los Roques, La Orchila, Los Hermanos, Los Frailes, and Los Testigos.

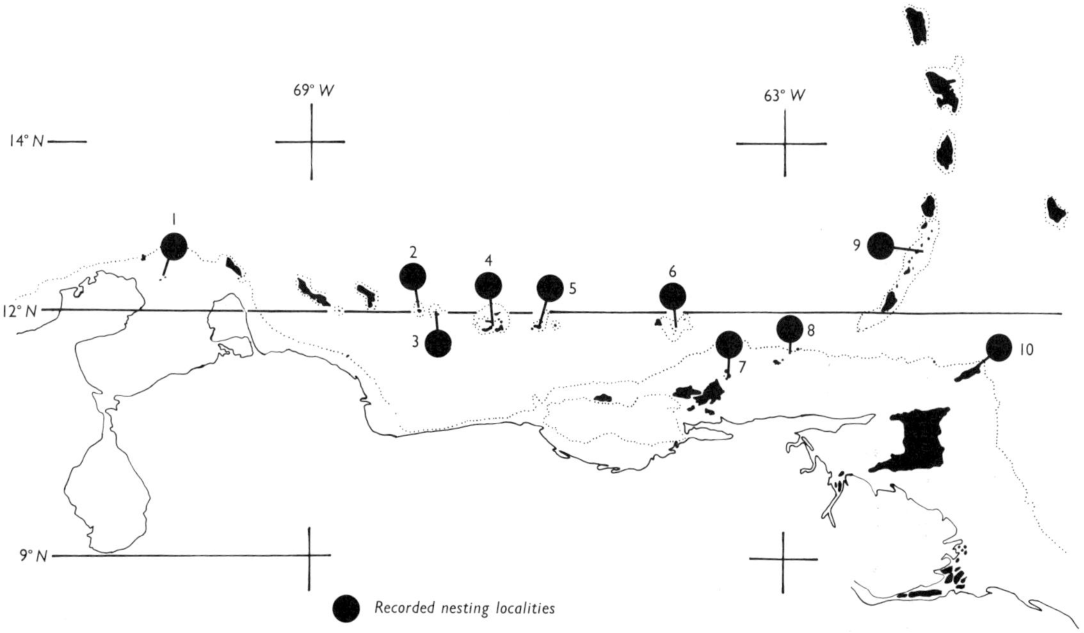

Fig. 185. The breeding distribution of the brown booby in the Caribbean (data partly from Van Halewijn, pers. comm.).

1 Los Monjes
2, 3 } Islas Las Aves
4. Archipel Los Rogues
5. La Orchila
6. Between Blanquilla and Los Hermanos
7. Los Frailes
8. Los Testigos
9. Grenadines
10. Tobago

In the **Virgin Islands** it breeds on Cockroach Cay, Cricket Rock, Dutch Cap, Sula Cay, Kalkun Cay (Leopold 1963) and French Cap.

The islets off Trinidad and Tobago hold brown boobies. There are colonies on St. Giles and probably on El Soldada Rock in the Gulf of Paria, 29km south-west of Trinidad. Tobago itself used to support brown boobies but probably does not today. Little Tobago has a breeding population of something over 300 pairs. Dinsmore (1972) located 220 nests in 1965–66. No other boobies nest there.

Moving westwards and then northwards, there are the boobies of the **Swan Islands,** between Great Cayman and Honduras. Cayman Brac held good numbers early this century and C. Bernard Lewis (*loc. cit.*) said that it still nested on the east side, largely on cliff-type (cave-entrance) sites. Van Halewijn notes that there are three breeding localities in the **Grenadines**, possibly containing several hundreds of pairs, but details are lacking, and that breeding has been recorded from a rock off Martinique.

There is no doubt that scores of small islands in the Caribbean, in addition to those mentioned above, hold some brown boobies. For example Nichols (1943) reports that it breeds on several cays north and west of St. Thomas, but apparently not on the islets near St. John. Unfortunately we lack up-to-date estimates of the major colonies, let alone the scores or hundreds of small ones, and so are in no position to assess the pattern of the decline which has occurred this century. Nor do we know the current trend, though with the increased range of many motor fishing vessels it would indeed be surprising if it were not downwards. The two south-west Caribbean atolls of Roncador Cay and Serrana Bank are both reputed to be 'covered with boobies and terns' (Milliman 1969). The latter held an estimated 100 000 birds on South West Cay in 1966. Milliman quotes Parsons (1956) to the effect that 300 000 eggs are collected annually from Serrana and 25 000 from Roncador, but I was unable to locate these details in the paper concerned.

Off north-eastern and eastern South America the brown booby occurs on many islands as far south as Rio de Janeiro (probably it once bred in the harbour there), although there are long stretches of coastline, muddied by the fantastic volume of silt-bearing river water which pours down from Brazil, which are largely unsuitable for boobies. Offshore from Cayenne lie the **Salut** group (Devil's Island, The Battures, The Connétables, etc.). Great Connétable is called, also, Bird Island, and is (or was) occupied by boobies, almost certainly brown. Somewhat oddly, less is known about the seabirds which frequent the coastal islands of Brazil than about those to be found on remote oceanic islands. Mitchell (1957) describes the brown booby as one of the commonest birds of the littoral of the state of Rio de Janeiro. It breeds on islands in Guanabora Bay and on larger islands 'down the coast'. Ilha do Francês, a small wooded island loosely in the Cabo Frio Archipelago, holds a 'large' nesting colony of brown boobies (Sick 1965).

Between latitudes 12° and 23°s. there is reputedly a region of somewhat greater plankton production than further south or north and there is evidence of an extensive bird population in this 'Abrolhos region' (banks and islands). The **Abrolhos Islands** lie on an extensive submarine plateau which begins at about 17°s. They are composed of reef limestone and comprise four principal and two smaller islets in an irregular ring, some 65km from the nearest point of the mainland (Santa Barbara, Redonda, Siriba, Southeast, Guarita and one un-named). All the islets are reputedly the haunts of innumerable seabirds, which certainly include the white booby and almost certainly the brown, though it is not known in what numbers. Darwin's *Beagle* visited them and, using guns, sticks and stones, indulged in such wholesale slaughter of the sea birds that their landing boats could not hold the corpses. One can imagine the hundreds of broken birds, many of which must have jumped into the sea and then died of their injuries or starvation, the chaos and the panic, followed by the slow starvation of the orphaned young.

Rocas Reef (Atol das Rocas) is the oceanic island closest to the South American mainland (222km) and the only true atoll in the south Atlantic. Simmons (1927) reported a vast seabird colony, mainly of sooty and noddy terns (many hundreds of thousands) but one cay which he happened to investigate held an estimated 1500 white booby nests and there were some 350 brown boobies and a few red-foots to be seen in the air around the island, and at least the brown boobies were probably nesting.

The **Fernando Noronha** group of islets (besides the main island there are PLATFORM, EGG, ST. MICHAEL'S MOUNT, BOOBY and RATA) lies about 134km east of Rocas Reef and 356km from the Brazilian coast. Murphy records that most of the sea birds, which include brown, red-footed and white boobies, nest on the lesser islets of the group. An interesting association was noted by Moseley, Naturalist to the Challenger Expedition, who found a South American ground dove *Zenaida auriculata noronha* nesting on ledges among brown boobies and noddies on Booby Islet', 'the eggs of all three species being closely intermingled' (Murphy 1936).

From Rio southwards the coast becomes rugged and there are many large islands; fragments of the mainland which have split off. A little further offshore are much lower, smaller and considerably drier islands—such as Alcatrezes, Castilho, Figuira and Queimada Grande. Probably all these and many more are breeding sites for brown boobies. At one time, they probably bred on an island in the harbour of Rio de Janeiro.

The brown booby is reputed to breed off the São Paulo coast, though not so the white nor the red-footed. Murphy suggests that these two tropical boobies do not penetrate southwards of the clear, warm ocean that ends near Cape São Tomé, not far from the Tropic of Capricorn. Beyond this point the tropical sea birds give way to those of more temperate latitudes where the tubenoses, terns, penguins and cormorants reign supreme.

Out in the tropical Atlantic there are the famous bird islands of St. Paul's Rocks, Ascension and St. Helena and South Trinidad. The two latter were once luxuriously forested and the home of a rich and abundant avifauna. Both are now barren, destroyed by a combination of forces of which goats were probably the most lethal. Neither are, nor probably were, important brown booby colonies, but St. Paul's and Ascension are great stations.

St. Paul's Rocks are composed of igneous rock, the summit of a mountain 4000m high. They are actually a group of one large rock and several small ones, no more than 20m at the highest, lying in a part of the Atlantic which may be enriched by upwelling—the equatorial counter-current—and are also very isolated. This is a recipe for seabird abundance and the brown booby has for long been a notable inhabitant of St. Paul's precipitous ledges and the only sulid present. On BOOBY HILL, the second rock from the north, Darwin noted the white brilliance, due partly to 'the dung of a vast multitude of sea-fowl and partly to a coating of a hard glossy substance with a pearly lustre, which is intimately united to the surface of the rocks'. Nicoll (1904) called the brown booby the most abundant bird there, nesting on the bare rock and so dense that 'it was impossible to walk without touching the birds, everywhere surrounded by dead and decomposing flying fish'. Remoteness surely protects this lonely rock from systematic despoliation and the colony is presumably as great today. However, on November 25, 1960 a landing party (Sea Swallow 15) found only few boobies. Altogether, less than 200 individuals were counted and only about 50 nests. This was presumably the non-breeding season.

The principal Atlantic breeding station south of the equator is BOATSWAIN BIRD ISLAND, off Ascension. Boatswain Bird Island is a very steep-sided rock, over 91m high, some 200m off the eastern corner of Ascension. It is devoid of vegetation and covered in guano.

The brown boobies nest mainly on ledges, promontories and steep slopes around the sides of the island, utilising, also, the path to the top and ledges and walls cut by guano workers. A few nested on top of the island at the edges of the white booby colonies. Dorward estimated 400–450 breeding pairs on the island and another 200–250 on the minor stacks. This was thought to be a minimal estimate and, including immature and non-breeding birds, the total could possibly have been almost 3000 individuals.

ASCENSION is one of the *loci classici* of seabirds, for it was here that the highly productive British Ornithological Union centenary expedition of 1959 conducted its studies, including those on the brown and white boobies, which at that time had attracted extremely little serious attention. The island (some 98 sq. km) is a volcanic peak lying on the mid Atlantic ridge and is mainly arid lava and cinder plains, though the high part (it rises to 860m) is well vegetated. It used to support large (probably enormous) colonies of sea birds but now the only species breeding on the main island are wideawake terns, a few red-billed and yellow-billed tropic birds and some black noddies. However, in the past, the colonies, probably mainly of boobies, were large enough to encrust the rocks on large areas of the lowland with white phosphatic deposits and one of the hills is named South Gannet Hill.

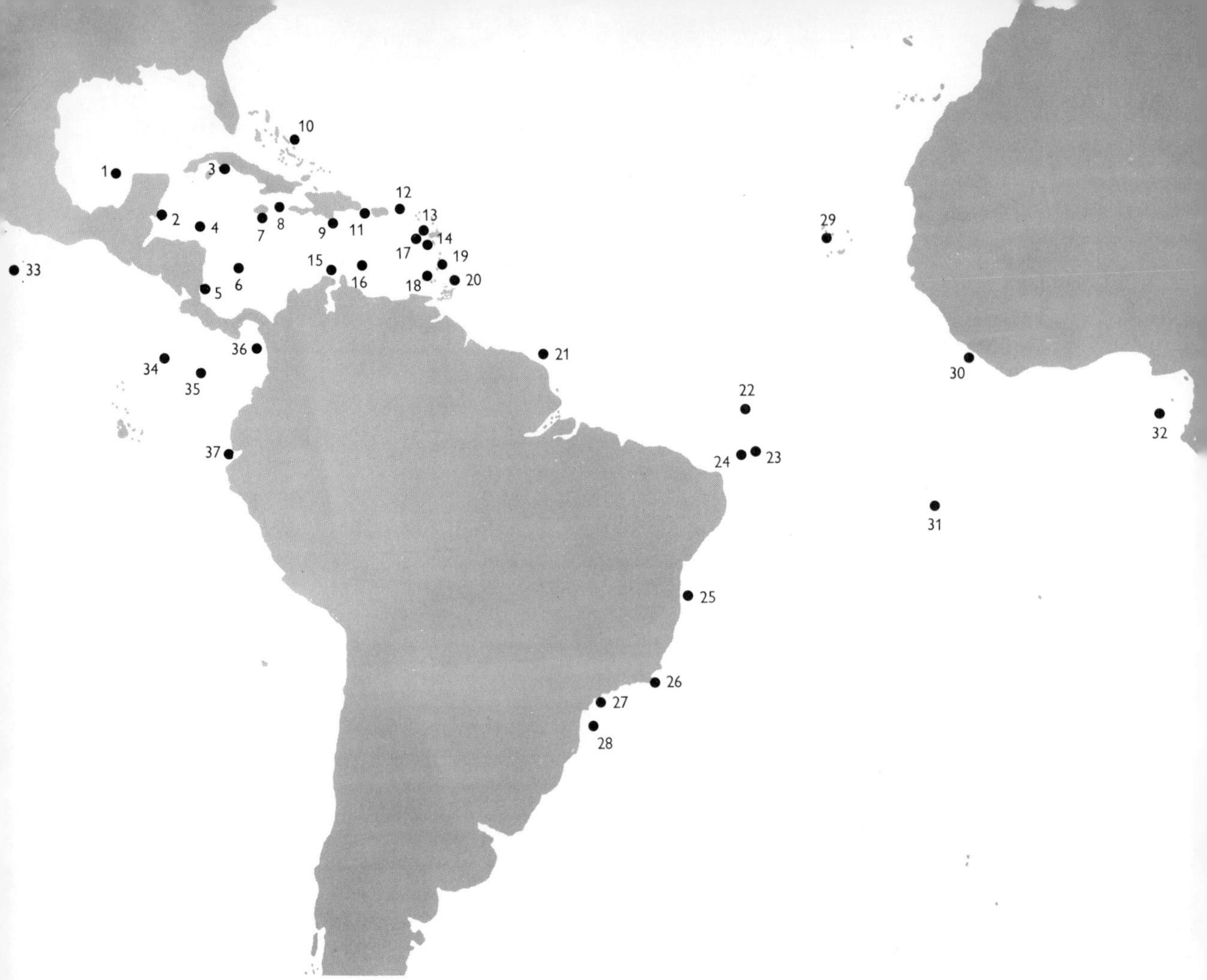

Fig. 186. Breeding distribution in the Caribbean, Atlantic and eastern Pacific.

1. Yucatan (Cayos Arcas).
2. British Honduras (Mauger Cay).
3. Cuba (Cayo Piedras).
4. Little Swan (Swan Islands, Cayman Brac).
5. Costa Rica (Isla de Uva, islets off Rio Moin).
6. Rocando Bank and Serrana Bank.
7. Pedro Group.
8. Navassa Island.
9. Dominican Republic (Isla Alta Vela).
10. Bahama Islands (Cay Verde, Great Ragged, Little Ragged, San Domingo Cay, Samana Cay, Miraporvos Island).
11. Puerto Rico (Isla Mona, Monito, Desecheo, Blanquillo, Isla Caja de Muertos).
12. Virgin Islands (Cockroach Cay, Cricket Rock, Dutch Cap, Sula Cay, Kalcun Cay).
13. Redonda.
14. Dominica.
15. Los Monjes.
16. Islas Las Aves, Los Roques, La Orchil(l)a (Venezuela).
17. Isla de Aves.
18. Los Tostigos, Los Hermanos, Los Frailes (Venezuela).
19. The Grenadines (Carriacon Islands, Les Tantes).
20. Tobago (Giles Islet, Little Tobago, El Soldada Rock).
21. Salut group.
22. St. Paul's Rocks.
23. Fernando de Noronha.
24. Rocas Reef.
25. Abrolhos Islands (Santa Barbara, Redonda, Siriba, Southeast, Guarita).
26. Cabo Frio Archipelago (Ilha do Frances).
27. São Paulo Coast and Guanoboro Bay.
28. Alcatrezes.
29. Cape Verde Islands (São Vincente, Razo, Balnark, Curral Velho, São Tiago, Rombos Islands, Fogo, Brava).
30. Guinea (Alcatraz and other islets).
31. Ascension (Bosun Island).
32. Principe, Sate Pedras, São Tome, Tortuga Islet, Annobon.
33. Clipperton.
34. Cocos Islands.
35. Malpelo.
36. Pearl Islands.
37. Gulf of Guayaquil.

Most of the fossil bones collected on Ascension (Ashmole 1963) were of boobies, many of them white. One tarsus of the red-footed booby was also found and it was concluded on this and other evidence that Ascension once supported a colony of red-footed as well as white and, probably, brown boobies. Now, however, all the boobies are confined to the off-lying Boatswain Bird Island and some minor stacks. St. Helena probably does not support any breeding brown boobies. Local people have said that it breeds on cliffs on the south side, but they probably misidentified either red-foots or juvenile white boobies.

On the eastern side of the north Atlantic lie the Cape Verde colonies, the Guinea colonies (Alcatraz and other islets) and those in the Gulf of Guinea.

The **Cape Verde Islands,** many of them cliff-girt, used to hold great colonies. Bannerman (1968) quotes Bolle to show that some of the place names stem from the booby (Alcatraz). Obviously it nested on islands where today it does not occur. Bannerman's text account shows that, today, there are colonies in the following localities within the Cape Verdes:

São Vincente (a small colony on precipitous cliffs on the south west coast).
Razo (the west part is occupied, but depredations by man continue to deplete it).
The islets of Balnarte and Curral Velho, off Boa Vista.
Sao Tiago (some 250 pairs on inaccessible cliffs near Santa Clara Bay).
Rombos Islands (once a stronghold, now very few, the decline due to human predation).
Fogo (one or two colonies).
Brava (many hundreds on the north and south sides).

There are now none on Maio, Sal, Branco, Santo Antao or Cima. The last named was the island upon which, according to an early account, the colony was so dense that there were 'hardly two feet between nests'.

The total population of the Cape Verde Islands today may be substantially less than 3000 pairs and is the most northerly breeding station in the east Atlantic (the Canaries are not even visited).

Alcatraz, a small island in a group of reefs off the coast of French Guinea, held a flourishing colony of brown boobies as late as 1938 and is worked for guano, so presumably the birds are partially protected. Other islets in the vicinity are said to hold boobies also. In the Gulf of Guinea the islands of Principe, Sate Pedras, São Tomé (St. Thomas), Tortuga Islet and Annobon hold colonies. The colony on the west coat of Principe (Prince's) Island, used to be considerable but its present status is unknown.

The entire coastal area, including off-lying islands, from Cap Barbas to the boundary of Guinea, was thoroughly searched for seabirds (Naurois 1969). They saw only one (roosting) group of brown boobies, adults and immatures, on a sand bank near Ile Lomo, obviously from Alcatraz. I cannot find anything factual on the supposed colony of brown boobies in the Bissagos Islands off West Africa.

2. *Indian Ocean*

The brown booby is represented in this vast stretch by the form *Sula leucogaster plotus*, stretching, so far as we know, from the Red Sea to Christmas Island and then into the Coral Sea and perhaps the western Pacific (Fig. 187).

The Red Sea, Gulf of Aden and Arabian Sea are not outstandingly good areas for boobies. In general, the southern reaches of the Red Sea would be expected to hold the most seabirds, because most upwelling occurs along the western shore and at the southern end and the general productivity is in fact said to be higher there (Hutchinson 1950). Guano deposits do occur in the area, indicating that large seabird populations have existed and there are old references to colonies of boobies, terns and gulls, traceable to two groups of islands, the **Dahlak Archipelago** off Massawa and the **Hanish** and **Mohabbakah Islands**. The Dahlaks are a group of several hundred islands covering 207 sq. km and extremely hot and humid (the temperature is almost at 37°C. day and night in August and September). There is apparently a high plankton concentration in the area. Clapham (1964) reports over 100 pairs breeding on Isratu and around 20 pairs on an islet off Wusta. Rats, which were present, seemed to be having little effect on the nesting boobies. No brown boobies were found on the remaining 16 islands visited. A recent (November 1961) visit to the Hanish Islands—actually to the Haycocks, a group of three rocky islets south of the main Hanish Islands—revealed large numbers of brown (and a few white) boobies (Morris 1962). The former were breeding 'in

Fig. 187. The breeding distribution in the Indian Ocean. Square symbols indicate major colonies

1. Dahlak Archipelago (Isratu, Wusta).
2. Hanish, Mohabbakan Island, Haycocks, Zubain Group (Quoin Island).
3. Ghardaga or Hurghada Group (Om Qam'r).
4. Fassan Islands.
5. Kuria Murias.
6. Brothers Island.
7. Mait Island.
8. Latham Island.
9. Amirantes (Boudeuse, Desnoeufs, St. Joseph Atoll).
10. Gloriosa.
11. Cosmoledo.
12. Cargados Carajos Archipelago.
13. Chagos Archipelago (Coin du Mine, Nelson Island).
14. Cocos-Keeling (North Keeling).
15. Christmas Island.
16. Pulau Perak.
17. Sin Cowe Reefs (Spratly Island).
18. Tub Bataha Reef.
19. Kakabia.
20. Paracel group (Triton Island).
21. Sento Shoso.
22. Sekibo Sho.
23. Bedout Island.
24. Manoek.
25. Adelie Island.
26. Ashmore Reef.

large numbers' on North-east and Middle Haycocks and in smaller numbers on South-west Haycock, with young in all stages. On a second visit in May 1962, there were no breeding boobies. Investigations in the Zubair group, southern Red Sea, in April 1964 indicated some 6–10 000 birds, with individuals on or around all the islands and some 250 pairs on Quoin Island with well-feathered young (Sea Swallow 18).

The islet of Om Qama'r (part of the Ghardaqa or Hurghada group) holds some brown boobies on its precipitous flanks (Al-Hussaini 1939) and brown boobies are said to breed on the **Fassan Islands** in the Gulf of Suez.

The bird islands of the Arabian Sea are, at least today, somewhat disappointing though the fact that last century, 37 707 tons of guano were recovered from the Kuria Muria Islands, off the south coast of Arabia, in two years, indicates that there must have been considerable deposits.

In the Gulf of Aden the **Brothers Islands** (Jabel Jeir) held brown boobies on the southern end of two of the islands (12 pairs on one and an unstated number on the other) in August 1944. However, they were not breeding at the time, on one of them, and may not have been on either (Jones 1946). Mait Island (Bur-da-Rebschi), off the Somali coast, is in a region of considerable vertical mixing in the fast-flowing Somali current and holds vast colonies of seabirds. The white booby is the main one on Mait, but apparently some brown boobies nest there, too.

Further south, off the African coast (17½km south-east of Zanzibar) lies the now-famous LATHAM ISLAND, discussed more fully in relation to its supposed breeding colony of immature white boobies. It has long been believed that the only boobies on Latham were the white, but Parker (1970) has recently claimed to have shown that the brown booby also nests there. He says 'Moreau (1940) was of the opinion that *S. leucogaster* did not occur on Latham Island and that *S. dactylatra* was the only species present there. The current data prove conclusively that both species inhabit and breed on Latham Island.' Since he took a specimen (a female in non-breeding condition) his claim would seem indisputable except on the unlikely hypothesis of mistaken identification. That this hypothesis is not to be rejected completely out of hand is shown by a previous mistake made in this connection (not by Parker) when a bird labelled '*leucogaster*' from Kenya Museum was identified by the British Museum as an immature *dactylatra*. It is of interest that Parker (1970) reports taking another specimen, also a female in non-breeding condition, on Cosmoledo, where white boobies breed but, so far as we know, brown boobies do not.

The western Indian Ocean contains a wealth of islands within the tropical belt south of the equator and many of them have been great seabird metropolises in the past. The **Seychelles** have long been famous as the breeding station of huge congregations of sooty terns. They lie 483km south of the equator and some 1046km north-east of Madagascar, occupying some 194 sq. km of a shallow bank 41 440 sq. km in total area (Baker & Miller 1963) and are the only granitic oceanic islands in the world. Two of their outliers (Bird Island and Dennis Island), at the edge of the bank, are of coral. The brown booby is now uncommon in the Seychelles (Vesey-Fitzgerald 1941). Formerly it nested annually on BIRD ISLAND, but there were none in 1955 (Ridley & Percy 1958).

South of the Seychelles lie the coralline **Amirantes**. Brown boobies occur on BOUDEUSE (King Ross) ISLAND, among a huge colony of white boobies, and also on DESNOEUFS, where in 1955 there were about 20 pairs nesting among sooty terns in isolated pairs or groups of two or three nests (they must have been crowded out in the days when Desnoeufs reputedly held 5 000 000 terns!). In March 1964 there were some 15 pairs at the south-western end. One pair was recorded nesting on ST. JOSEPH ATOLL (Vesey-Fitzgerald 1941).

Further south still, GLORIOSO was said to have a colony in the 1920s though earlier, in 1906, Nicoll found only one or two pairs, nesting on an islet, little more than a large rock, near Glorioso. The record of the great colony supposedly on Aldabra really refers to red-footed boobies.

The brown booby is seen on **Cosmoledo** and was collected there by Parker in 1967, but there are no details of its numbers. Even if it breeds, and that is by no means certain, it is obviously scarce. Diamond visited WIZARD and MENAI ISLANDS in March 1968 and saw white and red-footed boobies on the former and red-footed on the latter, but no brown boobies. Gillham (pers. comm.) visited Wizard and PAGODA in 1971 and found white and red-footed boobies but no brown. Parker (1970) reported small numbers at sea off Farquhar, Cosmoledo, Aldabra and Astove, and small numbers are commonly seen from Aldabra itself.

To the east lies RODRIGUEZ, the smallest of the **Mascarene Islands**. Bourne (1968) in a summary of the early information on this remote group recounts Francois Leguat's record of vast seabird colonies on all the outlying islands and reasonably interprets one of the old records as referring to red-footed boobies. However there was also a reference to 'fou with pale yellow legs'. These were very probably brown boobies which are thus indicated as having nested in very large numbers in the Mascarenes. Gill (1967) in a visit to two offshore seabird colonies (SANDY and COCOA ISLANDS) saw only three species of terns (*Anous stolidus*, *A. tenuirostris*, *Gygis alba*) and no boobies. Gill was informed that these were the only two islets with seabirds Thus it seems that Rodriguez must be added to the sad list of once-thriving seabird stations that, due to ignorant and excessive exploitation, have been reduced to complete insignificance.

In the **Cargados Carajos** archipelago (St. Brandons) to the north west, it may breed but there are no records.

The **Laccadives, Maldives** and the **Chagos** archipelago between them span some 21°

of latitude in the central Indian Ocean. Our knowledge of their bird life is extremely thin; the brown booby has been recorded once from the Laccadives, on PITTI, but the record is in doubt. Its status in the Maldives is uncertain; it may breed for example on MARDOONIE.

The Chagos archipelago (see also p. 672) consists of three groups, Peros Banhos and Salomon in the north, Nelson 34km south and Diego Garcia. Loustau-Lalanne (1962) saw brown boobies on all three and reported breeding on COIN DU MIRE of the Peros Banhos group and NELSON ISLAND, in both cases between December and March. Hirons (pers. comm.) reports breeding on NORTH BROTHER (300 pairs) and DANGER ISLAND (25 pairs).

Brown boobies do occur in the Bay of Bengal but relatively uncommonly and perhaps not as breeding birds. However, Phillips (1963) suggests that it breeds in the more remote islands of the Maldives a group of 2500 small islands of which less than 250 are inhabited.

Thus, the western half of the Indian Ocean is almost an empty belt for the brown booby and probably this cannot be ascribed solely to human factors. How far, if at all, it may be related to the lack of suitable nesting islands is not clear, but this too seems highly unlikely to be the sole cause. The number of seabird species diminishes as one goes north-east from the Seychelles area, until on the Maldives and Laccadives respectively, only 11 and 5 species are known to breed. This is the area most affected by the monsoons (Bailey 1974).

It seems that there are no boobies of any kind breeding in the Andaman Islands. Abdulali (1971) visited them and recorded none. Earlier the same author (1964) records in his *Birds of the Andaman and Nicobar Islands* that only one red-footed booby has been recorded from the area (Bay of Bengal, collected 1929); no other species are known and there is no evidence that any nest.

In the eastern Indian Ocean the brown booby breeds on COCOS-KEELING and has, perhaps surprisingly, one of its major strongholds in the world, on CHRISTMAS ISLAND. The Cocos-Keeling colony is on North Keeling, an island some 24km north of the main atoll. On the east and south sides there were some 75–100 breeding pairs in 1941 (Gibson-Hill 1950a).

On Christmas Island, however, there were an estimated 5000–6500 pairs in 1938–40 (Gibson-Hill 1950a). This, if the estimate is accurate and if the major Caribbean colonies are now in decline, could be one of the world's biggest colonies of brown boobies, although some of the little known but obviously substantial colonies, such as St. Paul's Rocks or Malpelo Island, might easily exceed it. The Christmas Island brown boobies would never impress the casual visitor with their abundance, for there are no large congregations. Instead, on the shore terraces around most of the long coastline and on the edge of the inland cliffs there are medium and small groups and hundreds of tiny nucleii of two or three pairs. There is a colony of 200–300 pairs on the mid-west coast; one that used to number at least 200 pairs near Steep Point on the north-east, but has been exploited by Malays; many groups of 30–100 pairs along the north coast and so on. Much of the coast is virtually impenetrable and in 1967 only one man, Roy Bishop, had circumambulated the entire perimeter on foot and it took him over 14 years! Since one can stumble on brown boobies almost anywhere, it will be readily apparent that an accurate estimate is impossible to obtain, but my own conservative extrapolation from areas known to me produced a figure in the region of that given earlier by Gibson-Hill and I believe that it errs on the low side. Since the red-foot is abundant and there are over 1000 pairs of Abbott's boobies, to say nothing of the world's only colonies of Andrew's frigatebirds, a population of endemic golden bosun birds, colonies of great frigatebirds, red-tailed tropic birds and common noddies, Christmas Island is indisputably one of the world's great seabird islands.

Moving next into Malaysian waters, the Banda and Coral Seas and then through into the western Pacific, one is in an area which has been under heavy human pressure for centuries. The seas around Malaya are not favoured by boobies. This may be because they are extremely shallow and also extensively muddied by the silt-laden rivers which empty into them and by the extensive vertical mixing facilitated by the shallowness. They are not the sort of seas favoured by the tropicopolitan boobies' chief prey, although there is presumably no reason why they could not subsist equally well on other species (individuals which stray inland survive well enough for months in fresh water) and the waters are certainly not impoverished.

The doyen of ornithological research, perhaps especially seabirds, in this area was undoubtedly the late Gibson-Hill. He wrote (1950c) that the only breeding station of the brown booby in Malayan waters, PULAU PERAK near the middle of the northern entrance to the Malacca Straits, held 4500–5000 pairs. Pulau Perak is a barren, steep-sided rock, 115m high and about 457 by 366m. When Gibson-Hill visited it on April 9th 1949 there were about 5000–6000 adults on the island and several hundred more feeding or resting on the water. The entire surface of the island appeared to be dotted with nests spaced 3·5–6·1m apart. Similar numbers were seen in January 1954 and February 1956, but in 1973 a catastrophic decline had evidently taken place. Langham & Wells (1974) report that there were a mere 450 occupied nests and though they consider this to be an underestimate, the real total could not have been more than about 700 pairs. There were never more than 1500 birds on and around the island. This decline, which is certainly still going on, and has had a noticeable effect even since 1971, is due to predation by man. Every night during Well's visit, at least two Malay fishing boats tied up and sent parties ashore in search of nests (eggs and young birds). There can have been little if any recruitment at all during the last few years and if adults too are being taken (which Langham does not suggest, but which from my experience on Christmas Island seems very likely) the virtual demise of the colony and that within a short time, seems assured. As he points out, the only answer would be effective wardening of the island during the nesting period. Even if the long-term source of food be the only consideration, it is simply stupid to over-exploit in this way.

There used to be another colony on Pulau Tokong in the Aroa group first reported by Robinson in 1906, who, though he was unable to land, saw 'some hundreds' nesting there. Madoc (1956) in two later visits in January and June (no dates given, but the article received for publication in 1952, says 'a few years ago') saw not a single brown booby and this colony is apparently now defunct. The only other breeding colony almost in Malaysian waters, is SPRATLY ISLAND in the Sin Cowe Reefs, which held brown boobies in 1964 (Haile 1964).

No breeding colony is known to the north of Pulau Perak. The brown booby is known from the Gulf of Siam, though records are few and Gibson-Hill, discussing these, cites Williamson to the effect that the brown booby was found on two small islets on the eastern side of the inner Gulf of Siam in 1916 and an adult male in 'full plumage' was collected. However, Madoc did not encounter the species when examining the islands in this area in 1949. It seems that there must be a colony hereabouts, since the birds are unlikely to hail from the Malacca Straits and the nearest breeding stations to the east are in the Sulu Sea and the Paracel group.

3. *Seas north of Australia*

The South China, Sulu, Celebes, Java, Flores, Banda and Coral Seas are climatically and oceanographically complex areas, with seasonal reversals of the monsoons (from the north-east in the northern summer and the south-west in the northern winter). The rainy season is correlated with the latter and is from May to October in most areas and rain in general increases from north-west to south-east (Hutchinson 1950). There is thought to be upwelling off Saigon and high productivity in the Sulu Sea and in the southern China Sea.

Bird information is scarce and out-dated. Worcester (1911) recorded numerous nesting brown boobies on the TUB BATAHA REEF in the Sulu Sea. BUTU KAPAL off the north-eastern end of Celebes is a guano island and boobies have been seen there, but the record is old, the birds may have been roosting and there is no indication of species. KAKABIA (Baar's Island) in the middle of the Flores Sea, apparently supported both brown and red-footed boobies at the beginning of this century, but there are no recent records. TRITON ISLAND and the neighbouring islets of the **Paracel** group in the centre of the South China Sea is said to contain a breeding colony of brown boobies (Delacour & Jabouille in Gibson-Hill 1950c). Further north, the rocky islands of the **Sento Shosho** group and 80km further east SEKIBO SHO ISLET (also known as Raleigh Rock) are probably the most important seabird colonies in the eastern China Sea (Simpson 1973). Sekibo Sho was visited on July 4, 1972 when some 200 brown boobies were flying around the island whilst 'many hundreds' of white boobies were present on the cliff tops. It would be interesting to have fuller details. One has the impression that this area should be, and has been, well colonised by boobies, but perhaps subjected to heavy human pressure. The south-east Asian conflicts of the last ten years can hardly have helped matters.

Fig. 188. The breeding distribution off Australia.

1. Bedout Island.
2. Lacepede.
3. Adele Island.
4. Ashmore Reef.
5. Wellsley Islands.
6. Booby Island.
7. Bramble Cay.
8. Ashmore Banks.
9. Pandora Cay.
10. Raine Island.
11. Flinders Reefs.
12, 13. Herald Group.
14. Willis Islands.
15. Diana Bank, Sand Cay.
16. Coringa Islets.
17. Diamond Islets.
18. Magdelaine Cays.
19. Lihou Reefs.
20. Marion Reef.
21. Swain Reefs.
22. Frederic Reef.
23. Kenn Reef.
24. Saumarez Reef.
25. Wreck Reef.
26. Cato Island.
27. Bunker Group (Hoskyn, Fairfax, Lady Musgrave).
28. Mellish Reef.

An important seabird colony, MANOEK or Manuk Island, in the Banda Sea, has recently been described (Sea Swallow 21 & 23). It is a steep cone with almost vertical sides about half a kilometre wide densely covered with scrub and stunted trees. Apparently it was 'swarming with boobies and frigatebirds like so many insects' on October 23rd, 1969. In such circumstances estimations of numbers are quite unreliable except as broad indicators. However, the observers concerned guessed that there could well have been 80 000 birds, 90 per cent of which were boobies (equal numbers of brown and red-footed) and the remainder frigates. In February 1970, Simpson again estimated 90 000 birds, including 40 000 each of brown and red-footed boobies. In June 1973 Guy Mountfort landed and thought about 20 000 seabirds were present, mainly frigates, but including some brown, red-footed and white boobies. The real breeding population of boobies is thus still unclear but is obviously substantial.

There are many notable bird islands in the Coral Sea and some, for example, Raine Island and a group of islands forming the southern extension of the Great Barrier Reef, are guano islands. The area is one of markedly seasonal rainfall, the wet season culminating in January or February.

The islets in the Coral Sea, beyond the outer Great Barrier Reef are of three distinct types—sand cays, grass cays and tree cays (Hindwood *et al.* 1963). The sand cays are formed of sand and shingle, more or less without vegetation. They are constantly being reshaped by the sea and some of them never become fully stable, though they are used by nesting seabirds. Cays of the second type are covered with grass, creepers and succulents, though seldom to more than a foot. They attract terns, brown and white boobies and frigatebirds. The tree cays are the richest in birds and attract frigates (*Fregata minor* and *F. ariel*), red-tailed tropicbirds, sooty terns, common noddies, white-capped noddies, wedge-tailed shearwaters and three booby species (brown, white and red-footed). Altogether they support great numbers of seabirds and are probably relatively undisturbed, except possibly by Japanese fishermen, this nation having a traditional record of systematic exploitation of seabirds and other animals. There are no animal predators except on South West Cay of the Coringas, where rats *Rattus rattus* are common.

The brown booby is widely distributed throughout the south west Coral Sea, though probably the least numerous of the three boobies. It is more widely distributed than the red-foot, but does not form such large colonies. Hindwood, Keith & Serventy (1963) whose group, in 1960 and 1961, explored most of these remote cays, seldom or even never before visited, were responsible for bringing our knowledge of their seabird colonies more or less up to date. All the boobies but especially the red-foot, breed mainly on the outer cays. They found brown boobies nesting on 26 of the 47 islands and cays investigated, preferring the vegetated islets though nesting also on bare cays. About 30 pairs were nesting on the sand and shingle of SOUTH WEST PROJECTION CAY of KENN REEF, without nesting material; some 50 pairs were breeding on PAGET CAY of MARION REEF and 7 pairs on nearby CAROLA CAY. Brown boobies were found breeding, or had bred, also on CAY A, FLINDERS GROUP; DIANA BANK; NORTH CAY, FREDERICK REEF; islets in the BUNKER group and the cays of the SWAIN REEFS; islets 1, 8 and 9 of LIHOU REEF; TURTLE ISLET; HERALD'S BEACON ISLET of MELLISH REEF; SOUTH WEST CAY of SAUMAREZ REEF; PORPOISE CAY and BIRD ISLET of WRECK REEF; CATO ISLAND; SOUTH WEST CAY and NORTH EAST CAY of the HERALD GROUP; South WEST ISLET and NORTH EAST ISLET (Chilcott) of the CORINGA GROUP; SOUTH EAST CAY of MAGDELAINE; WEST, MID, EAST and SOUTH WEST ISLETS of DIAMOND ISLAND.

In the north, in the entrance to the Torres Strait, BRAMBLE CAY, a sandy island with some vegetation, apparently once held a very dense colony of brown boobies among prodigious numbers of other seabirds, notably sooty and noddy terns. Apparently the booby nests were so thick on the ground that it was difficult to walk without treading on them. However, the island was leased for guano work last century and no doubt the birds suffered accordingly. Nevertheless, the unusual density is particularly interesting, combining with similar records from, for example, the Cape Verdes and St. Paul's Rocks to show that this normally rather dispersed colonial breeder sometimes tolerates densities almost as great as those shown by the most highly colonial sulids.

RAINE ISLAND, a vegetated sandbank between the Barrier Reef and the Great Detached Reef, though only some 600m long and 450m wide is also a notable seabird island, perhaps the most important for tropical seabirds in Australian waters. Once, it was covered from end to end with seabirds of which nine-tenths were brown boobies (North 1912) though there were also white and red-footed boobies. Since there were prodigious numbers of terns, as well as some frigates, Raine must have been a thrilling island. Warham, who visited the island in February 1959 estimated 7000–9000 brown boobies, these including all free-flying birds and those coming to the island to roost. In addition, there were some 400–500 white boobies, 300 red-footed, 2000 lesser frigates, 2000 common noddies some sooty terns, an uncounted number of wedge-tailed shearwater burrows and a few red-tailed tropic birds and silver gulls. In 1961 Hindwood, *et. al.* estimated that at least 2000 pairs of brown boobies were nesting, mainly in the bare central depression, though some nests were on the beach fringe.

Lawry (1926) recorded all three sulids on WILLIS ISLAND and Reithmuller's (1931) remarks indicate good numbers, but Serventy (1959) found 141 occupied nests in June 1954 and even at that they were the commonest boobies (an earlier record had suggested that they were less numerous than the white). Most nests were in the grassy area of this Coral Cay, though a few were on the shingle, with sooty terns. There is a weather station on the island, which is one of several known collectively as Willis Islets.

The BUNKER ISLETS of the Great Barrier Reef held brown boobies and Cooper (1948) reported that it still nested freely there, though not in the Capricorn Group (see below). FAIRFAX, at least, has a colony and HOSKYN ISLETS are similar. At this latitude, and further south, the brown booby yields to the white, as on NORFOLK and LORD HOWE ISLANDS.

However the CAPRICORN ISLETS rather similar to the Bunkers, were also once worked for guano and Domm (1971) says that they hold brown boobies on some of the uninhabited cays, but gives no details.

BIRD ISLET, of WRECK REEF was also once a productive guano island and may well have supported a large booby colony. There are no details on its present seabird population.

WALPOLE ISLAND is an elevated coral island, with cliffs and marine terraces which sound highly suitable for brown boobies. It is apparently a good seabird island and Hutchinson interprets a reference to 'black gannets' as referring to the brown booby. No numbers are given.

In the western part of northern Australia, the brown booby breeds on BEDOUT ISLAND, LACAPEDE ISLANDS (Middle Island), ADELIE ISLAND and ASHMORE REEF (East, West and Middle Islands) (Serventy *et. al.* 1971). On EAST ISLAND it has suffered considerable persecution. Serventy (1952) records that Indonesian fishermen use the islands as a temporary base and 'make heavy inroads on the nesting sea birds'. In 1949 there were a few adults but no flightless young on the island. Quantities of the remains of boobies were present. On WEST ISLAND the situation was similar. MIDDLE ISLAND held most brown boobies, adults and immatures were congregated on the sandspit, which was 'black with birds', with hundreds more on a nearby sand-bank. As on East and West Islands, bird remains were found.

WHITE ISLAND appears to be an important roosting place for brown boobies; 4–5000 birds have been seen there, although they are not known to nest.

On ADELIE ISLAND the brown booby is common and outnumbers the white by some 15 to 1 (Serventy 1952). In 1949, there were many with downy young on the beach and a group of 600–700 birds (adults and young) on a bare flat in the grass.

Bedout Island, though the type locality for a race of the white booby, supports a very large colony of browns. Serventy estimated that (in 1949) there were about 3000 birds nesting on the beaches and inland, between clumps of *Spinifex*.

So the seas of north-west Australia emerge as a major area for the three tropical boobies. The population is so widely scattered that it is difficult to estimate, but each species probably numbers tens or scores of thousands and possibly more.

4. *The western Pacific*

This area has been divided off from the central Pacific not along the natural boundary proposed by the nature of the underlying strata and the emergent islands, but arbitrarily so as to split up the vastness of the Pacific (Fig. 189) into western, central and eastern zones (see the white booby account for further remarks on this, p. 336). A convenient treatment is to move south-east from the Marianas through the Marshalls and Gilberts.

MARCUS has been a superb seabird island, ruthlessly desecrated by the Japanese who killed, for example 50 000 adult sooty terns each year for feathers. Thousands of brown boobies used to nest beneath trees beyond the beach crest (Bryan 1903) and were the commonest breeding booby. Now it visits but probably does not breed.

The brown booby is listed as a breeding species in the **Bonin** and **Volcano Islands**, and also in the **Palau Islands** (King 1967) but no details are known. Ripley (1951) took a male within the reef off BABELTHUAP ISLAND and remarked that it had not previously been recorded in the Palaus, so it seems unlikely to be abundant. According to King, brown boobies breed on WAKE ISLAND and on OCEAN ISLAND near the **Gilberts,** but Pearson (1962) found no nests on the latter, between July and October 1961. It 'visits' islands in the **Bismarcks** and **Solomons** and there is one record from the **Kermadecs,** but it does not breed there.

There appear to be some notable bird islands in the region of the **Marianas** and **Carolines**. The Marianas, being north of the equatorial rain belt, are somewhat drier than the predominantly wet islands of the equatorial western Pacific and thus may suit boobies. The brown booby nests there, but details are lacking. Early this century there were reportedly 'incredible numbers of seabirds' on WEST FAYN, GASPAR RICO and MAGUR, but details are lacking. EAST FAYN is also a breeding site; doubtless there are many other such islets inhabited by boobies.

Many of the atolls in the Marshall and Gilbert Islands have recently been visited and reported on by Amerson (1969) whose work is the basis of the following account.

On **Taongi Atoll** about 150 brown boobies were resting on the windward side of SIBYLLA in October 1964; pairs were forming but no nests were seen at that time. In April 1967 immature birds were on the wing and it was thought that breeding had occurred on Sibylla.

Brown boobies nest on all three islands of **Bikar Atoll** (BIKAR, JABWELO and ALMANI); in May 1967 there were half grown young and fledglings on all three. Populations are small, probably no more than 200 pairs on any island (Jabwelo held an estimated 300 birds in May 1967, Almani 200 and Bikar 100). On **Taka Atoll** (TAKA, ELUK, BWOKWEN) many are killed by man (bones and skulls have been found around fire pits). An immature from Sand Island (Hawaiian Leewards) was seen here in October 1964. In May 1967 on Eluk there was no evidence of breeding, but it is possible that a few breed when allowed to do so. A very few brown boobies nest on JEMO ISLAND on the north-east (windward) side at the edge of the vegetation. In May 1967 one large downy young was found and constituted a new breeding record.

Brown boobies are thought to breed on **Likiep Atoll**. A ringed bird was recovered here, but may have been merely visiting. They also nest on open ground beneath *Pisonia* and coconut palm on **Erikub Atoll** and around 75 nests were present in October 1964, half with eggs, a quarter with chicks and a quarter in the pre-laying stages, on **Aradojairik**. Some 200 individuals were estimated (it is not clear whether these included the chicks, but probably not).

The brown booby breeds on **Mili Atoll** but no estimate of the population is available.

On the 42 islands of **Eniwetok Atoll** the brown booby seems to be the only sulid. It probably breeds and the population may be as many as 300 individuals. However, Pearson & Knudsen (1967) had only four records between early February and early May 1965 and found no evidence of even a roosting colony, so its status is seriously in question. It should have been breeding at this time of year.

In May 1967 four islands of **Ailinginae Atoll** were visited and adults, sub-adults and immatures were seen. It was thought to breed, but no direct evidence was found.

Large numbers were seen on LIJERON of **Jaluit Atoll** in April–May 1958, but there is no direct evidence of breeding.

In addition, the brown booby may breed on the following atolls: Majuro; Bikini; Wotho; Ujal; Kwajalein; Makin; Nonouti and Tabitenea.

The brown booby probably nests in the **Fiji Islands,** but in small numbers. Morgan (1965) saw it at Ba and Suva Point, but not nesting. Templeton, in a written report, records brown boobies nesting at YANYUA ISLAND (ONO-I-LAU), where there is a large colony of red-foots. It nests on the more isolated of the limestone pinnacles and 15 nests (9 with contents) were found in June 1971. Smart (pers. comm.) says 'small numbers commonly seen' but has no breeding records. Shorthouse (1967) recorded brown boobies, along with red-foots and white boobies, breeding on VATU IRA, a small isolated island at the southern end of the Bligh waters, in September 1966.

5. *The central Pacific*

We may conveniently begin a survey of this vast area of tropical ocean with the Hawaiian Leeward Islands, a chain of small islands and reefs stretching north-west from the Hawaiian Islands. From the north-west to the south-east Kure, Midway, Pearl and Hermes Reef are atolls with very little land surface; Lisianski and Laysan are elevated atolls and Gardner Pinnacles, La Perousse, Necker, Nihoa and Kaula are volcanic rocks. Some of these are famous names in seabird annals, noted for their great populations of albatrosses as well as the usual populations of tropical seabirds. They have suffered disastrously at the hands of 'the military', that great expropriator and destroyer of the earth's surface.

Kure Atoll (GREEN ISLAND) has recently been the site of intensive studies by the Pacific Ocean Biological Survey Programme. Its brown booby population is slight—only about 30–40 nesting pairs (90 individuals is given as the maximum population, but this includes immature birds). They nest mainly along the edges of the central plain and have apparently been little affected by man this century.

On **Midway Atoll** (EASTERN and SAND ISLANDS) the brown booby was, in 1941, the commonest of the three species (the others were, of course, white and red-footed) although, even so, its numbers were probably never great. Military occupation and infestation by rats (Fisher & Baldwin 1946) wiped them out and in May 1945 none were to be seen on either island. Since then a few birds have been visiting Sand Island and on March 29th 1957 there were four

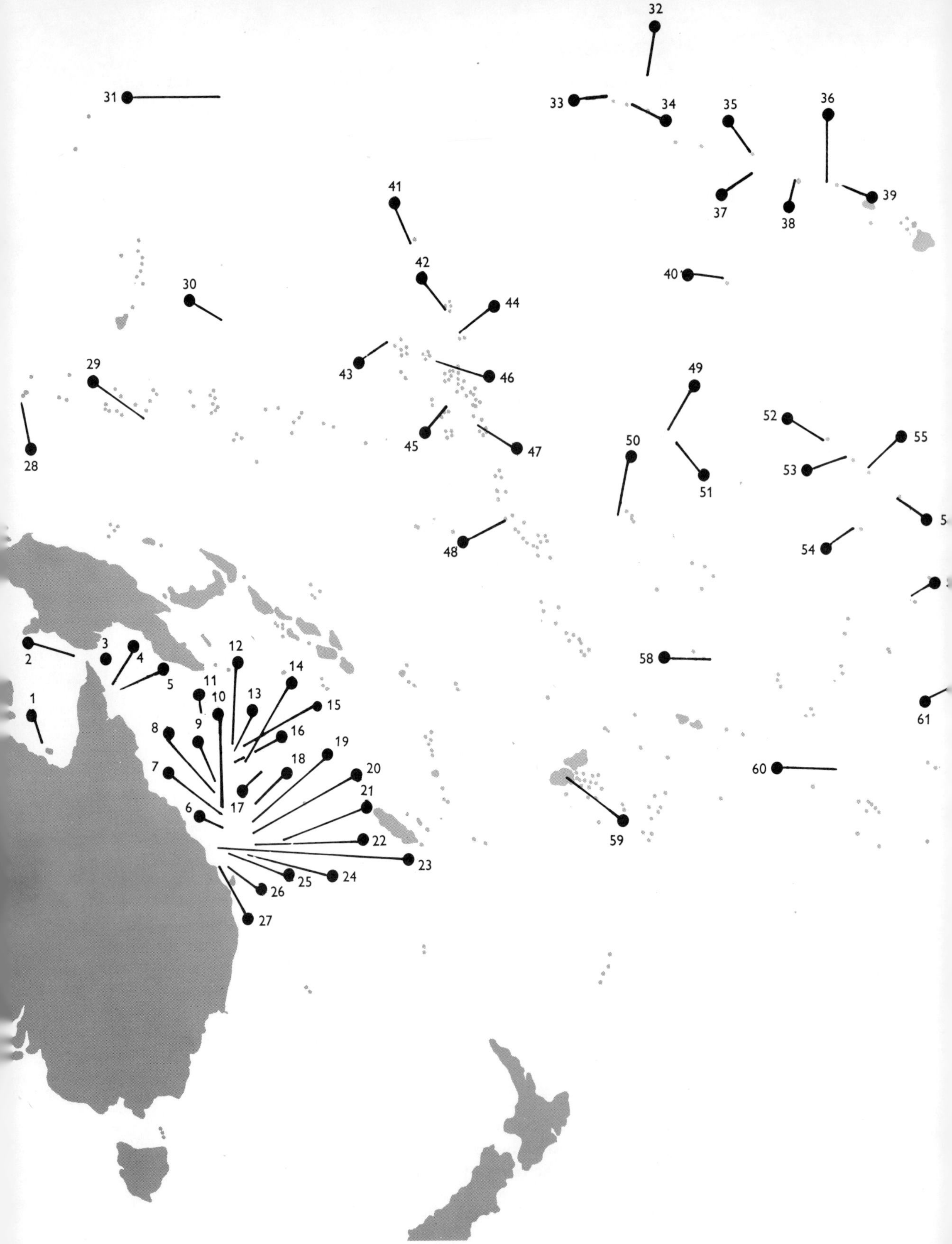

Fig. 189. Breeding distribution in the Pacific.

NOTE: Key to the colonies is on next page.
Square symbols indicate the largest concentrations.

pairs nesting on Eastern Island and at least two more pairs present, whilst on Sand Island there were 18 nests in July 1963 (young flying by August), so the colony may gradually increase, though this atoll is not as favoured as the rocky islands of the chain. On PEARL and HERMES REEF, SOUTH EAST ISLAND is again the most favoured (maximum breeding population over 195 birds). On the others there are only roosting birds.

LAYSAN is not favoured and Fisher looked carefully but in vain in 1902 for nesting brown boobies. Dill's (1912) list does not include it, though both the white and red-footed are included as breeders, but recent P.O.B.S.P. records (Clapp, pers. comm.) reveal that at most 50 birds breed there. LISIANSKI's maximum breeding population has been estimated at 40 birds.

GARDNER PINNACLES have probably never held many, though a few pairs breed probably every year. 20 adults, mostly with young, were recorded on June 1st 1969 (Clapp 1972). They are austere crags and that brown boobies choose to nest there at all speaks volumes for their habitat predilections—further underlined by their occupancy of the precipitous LA PEROUSSE, upon which they are the only boobies to breed (Amerson 1971), along with Hawaiian noddies and white terns. This choice of nesting place is particularly interesting in view of the proximity of 'ordinary' flat islands.

La Perousse Pinnacle lies partly encircled by the FRENCH FRIGATE SHOALS, a sandy atoll of several islands. Brown boobies regularly frequent them but apparently do not breed. Richardson recorded them on Skate Island, but none nesting anywhere in the group during three visits 1953–54, whilst Amerson (1971) says they occur but do not breed on East Island.

Off the windward (east) coast of the large Hawaiian Island of Oahu there are some 17 small islands of which MOKU MANU (Bird Island or Nihoa) and MANANA are the main seabird islands. Both are bird sanctuaries. The cliff-girt Moku Manu is separated from Ulupau Head of Mokapu Peninsula by a narrow channel. It is part of a volcanic cone and has a fairly flat top, about 277m high. W. K. Fisher's (1903) account depicts an island alive with breeding boobies, the brown boobies preferring the brink of the south escarpment. However, another Fisher, 45 years later, counted a mere 75 nests on February 23rd 1947—hardly a teeming multitude. The nests were generally scattered over the lower, south-facing slopes, just above

Key to colonies located on Fig. 189.

1. Rock north-west of Mornington Island.
2. Booby Island.
3. Bramble Cay.
4. Pandora Cay.
5. Raine Island.
6. Swain Reefs.
7. Saumarez Reef.
8. Flinders Group.
9. Herald Group.
10. Marion Reef.
11. Diana Bank.
12. Willis Islet.
13. Coringa Group.
14. Lihou Reef.
15. Magdelaine Cays.
16. Diamond Islets.
17. Mellish Reef.
18. Frederic's Reef.
19. Kenn Reef.
20. Wreck Reef.
21. Walpole Island.
22. Cato Island.
23. Capricorn Islets.
24. Bunker Group.
25. Hoskyn Island.
26. Fairfax Island.
27. Lady Musgrave Island.
28. Palau Islands.
29. Caroline Islands.
30. Marianas (West Fayn, East Fayn, Gaspar Rico, Magur).
31. Bonin and Volcano Islands.
32. Pearl and Hermes Reef.
33. Kure Atoll (Green Island).
34. Midway Atoll (Eastern and Sand Islands.
35. Gardner Pinnacles.
36. Kaula Island.
37. French Frigate Shoals.
38. Necker.
39. Moku Manu.
40. Johnson Atoll (Sand Island, Western Islet).
41. Wake Island.
42. Taongi Atoll, Ratak Chain.
43. Eniwetok Atoll, Ratak Chain.
44. Bikar Atoll (Bikar, Jabwelo, Almani), Ratak Chain.
45. Jaluit Atoll (Ligeron), Ralik Chain.
46. Likiep Atoll.
47. Mili Atoll, Ratak Chain.
48. Gilbert Islands (Ocean Island).
49. Jemo Island.
50. Howland.
51. Taka Atoll (Taka, Eluk, Bwoken).
52. Palmyra.
53. Washington.
54. Jarvis Island.
55. Fanning.
56. Christmas Island.
57. Malden.
58. Phoenix Islands (Enderbury, McKean, Birnie, Phoenix).
59. Fiji Islands (Yanyua Island, Vatu Ira).
60. Tonga.
61. Vostok.
62. Caroline Atoll (Nake Island).
63. Austral Islands.
64. Tuamotus.
65. Marquesas.
66. Pitcairns.
67. Consag Rock.
68. Georges Island.
69. San Pedro Martir.
70. Ildefonso.
71. Revillagigedos (Clarion, San Benedicto, Socorro, Roca Partida).
72. Cayo Island.
73. Farallon de San Ignacio.
74. Clipperton.
75. Isabela.
76. Las Tres Marietas.
77. Tres Marias (White Rock, Juanito).
78. Cocos.
79. Malpelo.
80. Gorgona and Pearl Islands.
81. Gulf of Guayaquil (La Plata).

high tide, but one gulley on the north top slope held about 20 nests. In April 1948 there were even fewer, but breeding had been upset by January storms. Most nests were on fairly level rocky ground but some were 'on' (among?) very low vegetation. There seems little doubt that extensive slaughter has occurred this century, despite the island's reputation for being extremely difficult to land on. More recent maximum estimates of breeding birds have ranged between 110 and 200.

There are no boobies breeding on Manana but NECKER held breeding brown boobies in 1902 although, even then they were not abundant. Nowadays there are some 40 birds, or, according to the P.O.B.S.P. maybe more. Berger (1972) lists KAULA ISLAND, also, as a brown booby breeding place.

At the present time the Hawaiian Leewards are far from the stronghold they once were for boobies and now hold a few pairs, here and there, but no colonies that are even sizeable. It is a familiar story.

The Line and Phoenix Islands are scattered, elevated atolls, with which may be included **Johnston** and **Caroline Atolls**.

Johnston, an isolated atoll lying between the Hawaiian and the northernmost Line Islands, supports a small breeding colony of brown boobies on SAND ISLAND, among low grass and shrubs, on the southern tip of WESTERN ISLET. There were 18 nests in July 1963 but much of the time the population of adults fluctuates around 75. This group nevertheless holds the interesting distinction of having provided the only record of a brown booby breeding whilst in immature plumage; a male of a pair with a small chick had the mottled belly of an individual in its second year and still retained the honking voice of the juvenile (April 6–10 1957). The islands were an air base during the 1939–45 war and were greatly modified—which means a lot of seabirds were killed, but there are no records of past numbers except for a general reference to 'hundreds of individuals of a dozen species' (Bryan 1942).

In the **Line Islands** proper, boobies used to be extremely numerous. The following recent estimates are from P.O.B.S.P. records (Clapp, pers. comm.). From early accounts it seems that PALMYRA supported all three species, though chiefly the red-foot (the account of '*Sula sula*, with brownish plumage and a black bill' roosting in *Tournefortia* branches, must refer to juvenile red-footed boobies, even though the name *Sula sula*, at that time and place, usually meant the brown booby). At present it holds a maximum estimated breeding population of c. 4000 birds. JARVIS supports around 225 birds though maximum estimates have been much higher (up to c. 1000 birds). MALDEN comes next (150–200) but numbers are trivial on WASHINGTON (20). It does not breed on STARBUCK but last century this island held boobies among other seabirds, including frigates. Brown boobies used to be fairly abundant on FANNING, especially on the south and south-east shores above the beach crest (Kirby 1925) but even then they had already become much less common. Now there are about 10 birds. On CHRISTMAS ISLAND, better known but, even with an estimated and incredible 14 million sooty terns in 1967, less distinguished than its Indian Ocean counterpart, there are large numbers of red-footed boobies, but very few brown. From Gallagher's (1960) account there obviously were not many in 1958–59 and in 1967 there were no more than 35–40 nests altogether and 25 at any one time, at the extreme south-east point and on islets in Manulu lagoon. It was reputedly 'abundant' at the southern end earlier this century.

VOSTOK lies in the south of the Line Islands and supports a tiny colony (some 7–10 pairs) at the eastern end, beneath *Pisonia* canopy. NAKE ISLAND of Caroline Atoll has a very small breeding colony of about 5–7 pairs.

On HOWLAND, to the west of the Line Islands, Hutchinson (1950) thinks it possible that the brown booby was the most important guano bird and it used to be the commonest booby. At present there are about 54 breeding individuals.

The **Phoenix Islands** are another central Pacific group, comparable in many ways to the Line Islands. ENDERBURY and MCKEAN ISLANDS were the most important sources of guano in the Phoenix group and both held boobies; the most recent maximum breeding population on the former was 200 and on the latter about 50. BIRNIE now holds about 50–60 and PHOENIX 24. The brown booby visits, but is not known to breed, on HULL, GARDNER, SYDNEY and BAKER (where it used to breed). It seems never to have been common on CANTON. However, it did breed there in 1937 though it was not doing so in 1949 or 1952 though a dozen or more were over the lagoon. It bred in 1954. Its present status is about 20–40. It occurs in the **Tokelau Islands** to the south of the Phoenix group, on FAKAOFO, NUKUNONU and ATAFU, but uncommonly and not, so far as is known, as a breeder (Thompson & Hackman 1968). It visits the **Samoan Islands** and **Cook Islands**, and in 1938 was nesting on ROSE ATOLL, the easternmost Samoan island, 'enormous numbers of white and brown boobies with young'. It breeds on the **Tonga Islands**, and the **Australs** (King 1967).

Far to the east, the **Marquesas** hold (King 1967), or have held, large numbers of seabirds and some—notably two of the HERGEST ROCKS—have guano deposits, but there are no details of their bird populations.

The **Tuamotus** are reputedly poor in seabirds and little is known of their booby populations; King lists all three tropicopolitan boobies as nesters and Morrison (1954) cites small numbers at Raroia but no proof of nesting.

Southwards again, the **Pitcairn Islands** support all three boobies, but the brown is rare there. Williams (1960) reports that the islanders were not familiar with it. He saw a pair roosting on a cliff edge on PITCAIRN itself.

6. *The eastern Pacific*

From the immense stretches of central Pacific one moves to even greater wastes of water in the east, with many fewer islands. From Tahiti to Panama is over 7200km and for most of the way, the water rolls unbroken by an island.

CLIPPERTON ISLAND is reputedly the only atoll in the eastern Pacific and a remarkable bird island. The atoll is elliptical, about 3·6km along the north-west south-east rims and about 2·6km wide, with a fringing reef. It is composed largely of coral fragments and is at most 2·4m high, except for a great rock 29m high in the south east corner. The rainfall is markedly seasonal, from June to August, but even in the dry season there is some rain. There is very little vegetation, due, it has been suggested, to the vast numbers of birds and land crabs.

Clipperton has experienced remarkable fluctuations in fortune. In the first years of this century there were vast numbers of white boobies (see p. 342), the most numerous seabird on the island, nesting in the coral fragments, whilst the brown booby was much less abundant. Later pigs were introduced to the island and eventually wrought havoc among the nesting seabirds, eating eggs and young. Some brown boobies were still nesting there in 1938 (though the white booby was not mentioned in the report concerned—Wetmore 1939). In August 1958 Stager visited the island and found no more than 500 brown boobies, with eggs and young of all ages. To evade the pigs they were nesting all over the rusting hulk of a wrecked ship and on small pinnacles surrounded by water. Not a single white booby was nesting there, the world's largest recorded colony having been completely destroyed in a few years, by wild pigs, an enemy as deadly as the cats of Ascension. Stager deserves a medal for exterminating the pigs and as a result the most phenomenal increase in the history of a tropical seabird took place. In just ten years the brown boobies climbed from less than 500 individuals to 15 300 (of course, excluding chicks). This latter figure is uniquely accurate because it was obtained by the co-ordinated counts of a team of 16 people (Ehrhardt 1971). Such an increase could not possibly occur as a result of the output of the colony. Thus, assuming the most outrageously generous terms (5 per cent annual adult mortality, 80 per cent of pairs rearing one chick each year, 50 per cent first year mortality and recruitment to the breeding population in the third year) the population would have increased during that period, from an initial 200 pairs to 1415 birds. Even more remarkable, the white booby, which in 1958 was not even breeding, totalled 4059 individuals. It will be most interesting in years to come to see if the balance between these two sulids reverts to its former situation, with the white predominating.

Eastwards again lie two more notable seabird islands, Malpelo and Cocos. MALPELO 'the black iceberg', a volcanic island some 2km long and 258m high, is largely protected from human despoliation by the violent currents which surround it. Despite its somewhat rainy climate it is reputedly the site of an immense colony of white boobies. Hutchinson mentions the figure of perhaps 15 000 pairs, evidently without quite realising that this would make it the largest colony in the world. Brown boobies are not mentioned, but seem likely to occur.

Cocos evidently supports brown boobies in fair numbers. Gifford reported that they nested abundantly on small islets off Cocos and later records (particularly Slud 1967) confirm that very few nest on Cocos itself but that it is common or even abundant around the island. The main group may be on a small islet between Nuez and Cascara.

The Galapagos must be mentioned in order to stress the absence of the brown booby from the archipelago. This is a curious phenomenon which we do not understand, for the other two blue water boobies are common enough and there is plenty of the rocky, precipitous terrain preferred by the brown booby. Added to this, it is common to the north and east (the only directions in which there are any islands). Yet it has certainly never been known to breed, though recently an authentic record of its occurrence in Galapagos waters has been obtained.

There remains a considerable booby stronghold in the eastern Pacific, off Mexico and in the Gulf of California. This is a very interesting area because in some ways it parallels the situation in the Humboldt Current off Peru, and is the only region in which the brown and blue-foot breed together on the same islands, in any numbers.

The **Revillagigedos** lie some 670km offshore (off Colima State, Mexico). They are widely scattered, Isla Clarion lying well to the west, followed by Roca Partida and Isla Socorro, with Isla San Benedicto some 50km north of Socorro. They are in an actively volcanic area and an eruption in 1952 killed many of the seabirds nesting on San Benedicto described by Kaeding (1905) as 'a vast heap of broken lava, pumice, tufa, ashes and obsidian'. Brown boobies are here sympatric with white, blue-footed and red-footed, though less at home than the former. On San Benedicto brown boobies were 'abundant' (Hanna 1926) though Kaeding listed them as breeding sparingly; in 1940 they were nesting in scattered groups all over the island and on the sides of a ravine in the centre of the island, whilst in 1956 they comprised about five per cent of the total booby population and were also nesting on Roca Partida, though in small numbers (Brattstrom & Howell 1956). These authors do not mention the status of the brown booby on Clarion and Socorro; however, Hanna (1926) found them (together with red-footed and white boobies) in 'large numbers' on Clarion and though he nowhere refers to them by name, his general remarks indicate that they were common on Socorro, also. At one time, though perhaps not now, San Benedicto and perhaps Clarion seem to have been the only islands in the world upon which four species of boobies nested (white, brown, red-footed and blue-footed).

North-eastwards lie the Islas Tres Marias, actually four islands (from north to south, Isla San Juanito, Maria Madre, Maria Magdalena and Maria Cleofas, with a rock, White Rock (Piedra Blanca) about 61m high, lying between the two latter). Nelson (1899) and Bailey (1906) found a fine colony of brown boobies nesting on top of White Rock and the latter described them as 'this countless flock of birds which had probably been breeding there for centuries' and elsewhere' 'the whole island surface was literally covered with birds'. The birds were suffering drastic disturbance as a result of guano operations and early this century it was believed that they were removing to another island (Isabela) between the Tres Marias and the mainland. It is uncertain whether the brown booby was breeding on any others of the Tres Marias, but evidently White Rock was the only important colony and the only real guano island. Nelson described an islet which was probably White Rock (off the north-west shore of Cleofas) on which many thousands of boobies were nesting (laying eggs on the bare rock) spaced a mere 1·5m apart. Tafall (1944) also noted brown boobies in great numbers on Piedra Blanca. A recent assessment of the Tres Marias (Grant & Cowan 1964) lists the brown booby as breeding on Juanito and Cleofas, on the authority of Stager's (1957) statement that 'thousands' nest on a precipitous offshore islet (White Rock) on the north-west side of Cleofas and approximately 50 pairs on the cliffs at the north end of Juanito. Between the Tres Marias and Nayarit (35km due east) lies the small low island, Isla Isabela. The most recent survey (March 1975) by Howell (in press) confirms that it is a major seabird resort, free of terrestrial predators. The brown booby far outnumbers the blue-foot; there may be many thousands, perhaps tens of thousands. In March, most pairs were still courting and there promised to be a considerable degree of synchrony. However, the fishermen and their families, semi-resident, wreaked enormous destruction, and in a particularly barbarous manner, and Howell doubted if more than a small percentage of brown boobies nested successfully. Disturbance by visitors from pleasure craft is also increasing and it seems clear that Isabela needs properly wardening if its large and varied seabird population is to be conserved.

Not to be confused with Las Tres Marias are **Las Tres Marietas,** small islands lying a mere 4–6km offshore. These islands are or were a considerable stronghold of brown boobies, which they share with the blue-foot. The most recent account is that of Grant & Cowan (1964) who counted 3000 birds in May 1961, c. 800 in May 1962 and c. 500 in April 1963. Earlier, Lamb (1910) had recorded 'immense' numbers of brown and blue-footed boobies, the former greatly predominating. The islands are presumably at considerable risk from man.

Within the Gulf of California there are a number of important seabird islands (see Fig. 219) for it contains several areas of extremely rich primary productivity and high densities of fish particularly around Magdalena Bay, the sea off Punta Abreojos and Sebastian Vizcainó Bay. Whereas the lower temperature of the water off the Pacific coast of lower California attracts vast numbers of cormorants, the warmer water within the Gulf favours boobies; the race of brown booby is said to be *brewsteri* which likes hot and arid areas. The majority of the bird colonies lie on the eastern side of the bay. The bird population used to be so great that the potential of the area for commercial guano operations was seriously investigated on behalf of Mexico, by Peruvian experts, who declared that they were indeed worth working. Unfortunately there is rather little information about the bird populations of most of the islands at the present day, but Anderson (pers. comm.) has kindly extracted recent data from Gulf investigations carried out by the United States Fish and Wildlife Service. He stresses the considerable effects of human disturbance and characterises the brown booby as a generally widespread nester in the Gulf, particularly in the north, breeding in pockets on steep slopes or in caves, though also scattered among blue-foots, apparently shifting nesting locations (that is, changing islands) to some extent from year to year. Blue-foots occur mainly in the mid and southern areas, but white boobies were not identified.

Within the Gulf, brown boobies occur as far north as GEORGES ISLAND, a barren rock 11km from the eastern shore, which supported brown boobies (and perhaps other seabirds) in numbers enough to coat the island with guano and which Tafall noted on his visit in 1944. In June 1954 there were nesting birds all over the island and in February 1970 'many' nesting here (Anderson, pers. comm.). Brown boobies used to breed in large numbers, together with blue-foots, on SAN PEDRO MARTIR, a rocky island about 2·4km long and 319m high, in the middle of the Gulf. Late last century the brown booby population was estimated to be some 700 (birds rather than pairs presumably) nesting mostly on ledges or in niches in the rock. Mailliard (1923) said they were not nesting, but Lindsay (1962) saw some birds and one nest, whilst Anderson has many records of young, fledged and unfledged, in 1971 and 1973. In May 1973 there were around 4000–5000 pairs of brown and blue-footed boobies (though mostly the latter)—a considerable increase over 1971 and 1972 (3000–4000 and around 2000 pairs respectively, in June).

The rock, FARALLON DE SAN IGNACIO near the entrance to Topolobampo Bay (about 490m long and 137m high) may have supported the brown booby as its main breeding species and since it was reputedly the home of 'thousands' of seabirds the brown booby colony may be large. ILDEFONSO has long been the site of a large colony (e.g. Thayer 1911). Lindsay (1962) mentions large numbers with eggs (January 1962) though by April there were apparently few nests with contents (29 quoted). Anderson's (1973) records refer only to seven pairs breeding, together with 800–1000 pairs of blue-foots.

Other islands off the coast of lower California or within the Gulf, which have supported and may support brown boobies are: CAYO ISLAND, off the south west end of San José; CONSAG ROCK, which had a well-established colony in 1926 and was the species' most northerly breeding station; SAN LUIS ISLAND, also inhabited in 1926, though it had not been in 1925 (Bancroft 1927); SAN PEDRO NOLASCO; ISLA RAZA and ISLA PARTIDA (Mailliard 1923); TIBURON, common in 1932 (Van Rossem 1932). Roosting birds, often in large numbers, may be seen where they do not breed (as on SAIL ROCK).

The grand total of boobies within the Gulf used to be enormous. Vogt (1946) quotes a report stating that there were 1 525 000 boobies throughout the region, though he himself put the population very much lower, at 500 000 seabirds of which less than half would be boobies (brown, blue-footed and red-footed). Still, even this is a huge population and, if accurate, would establish the Gulf very near the top of the world list of major concentrations of boobies.

In the tropical Pacific Bight, we could by rights have included Cocos and Malpelo, but preferred to regard them as more oceanic. It remains, however, to describe some brown booby breeding haunts in the Gulf of Panama and further south to the Gulf of Guayaquil.

The volcanic **Pearl Islands,** an archipelago of 16 larger islands and more than 50 rocks and islets covering about 1165 sq. km, lie on the eastern side of the Gulf of Panama. The main seabird stations are listed by Murphy as PACHECA, SEÑORA, SEÑORITA, SANTELMO and CANGREJO. They are only some 35km from the mainland and are not patronised by the more oceanic red-footed and white boobies, but the brown booby nests on SAN MIGUEL, SABOGA, GALERA and abundantly in the northern part of PACHECA, sharing the two last named with the blue-foot. In 1915 brown boobies nested also on TABOQUILLA, near the Pacific entrance of the Panama canal (Hallinan 1924).

GORGONA ISLAND, some 40km off the Colombian coast, is the type locality of *Sula leucogaster etesiaca*, a wet-tolerating, if not wet-loving race, as well it may be for rain falls throughout the year and heavy thunderstorms occur daily. According to Murphy, who visited the area in 1925, all the seabirds (frigates, brown and blue-footed boobies) are to be found on GORGONILLA, a peninsula at the south-east corner of Gorgona, but no estimate of numbers is available. The birds nest among and beneath sodden vegetation.

Further south, off the Ecuadorian coast, lying between Manta and Salinas Point, ISLA LA PLATA is the haunt of white and blue-footed boobies but probably not of brown. Although, reputedly, the latter nests on some small islands in the Gulf of Guayaquil, Marchant (1958) believes that no boobies breed between La Plata Island and Santa Clara. PELADO ISLAND is now, he says, probably nothing more than an occasional settling ground for seabirds. It is (and presumably for a long time has been) too small to provide a breeding station and earlier claims that it did so may have been in error.

The white and blue-footed boobies go much further south, the former to San Ambrosio and San Felix off Chile and the latter to the Lobos Islands of Peru, but the brown booby stops at or before the Gulf of Guayaquil.

SUMMARY OF BREEDING DISTRIBUTION

1. The brown booby is one of three which occur throughout the tropics. Its present numbers, though very considerable, are undoubtedly but a fraction of former days.
2. It is the commonest sulid in the Caribbean, which sustains several large colonies (one of which, Desecheo, used to be one of the world's largest) and many smaller ones.
3. It occurs on coastal and offshore islands south to Rio de Janeiro, and out in the tropical Atlantic on St. Paul's Rocks and Ascension.
4. The Cape Verdes used to be a major area but are now a shadow, having been exploited for centuries.
5. There are colonies in the Gulf of Guinea.
6. The brown booby breeds in the Red and Arabian Seas, but not in large numbers.
7. Brown boobies are now rare in the atolls of the western Indian Ocean (Seychelles, Amirantes, etc.) and are absent from the central Indian Ocean (Chagos and Mascarenes) and from the Maldives, Laccadives, Andamans and Nicobars. Thus, most of the Indian Ocean is an almost empty belt for the brown booby.
8. In the eastern Indian Ocean there is a large colony on Christmas Island.
9. The only colony in Malayan waters, Pulau Perak, used to be large (5000–6000 birds) but, being savagely exploited, is now declining.
10. The status of the brown booby in the South China and neighbouring seas is little known. There are some, could be many and may be few.
11. In the Coral Sea this species is common and widely distributed, breeding on many islets off north-west and western Australia. There is a large colony on Raine Island.
12. In the western Pacific the brown booby occurs from Marcus in the north-west through the Marshalls and Gilberts.

13. The central Pacific islands are populated with (usually) small colonies. There are no large colonies in the Hawaiian Leewards, the Line Islands or the Phoenix Islands.

14. It occurs, but rarely, south-east to the Pitcairns.

15. The eastern Pacific stronghold is undoubtedly Clipperton (though Cocos also holds fair numbers). Clipperton has increased rapidly since pigs were destroyed in 1958 and in 1968 numbered over 15 000 birds and may be the world's largest colony.

16. Brown boobies do not breed in the Galapagos and very rarely visit Galapagos waters.

17. The Revillagigedos, Tres Marias, Tres Marietas and islands in the Gulf of California form a substantial brown booby breeding area.

18. South of Central America on the Pacific side, the brown booby breeds in the Gulfs of Panama and Guayaquil and on islands between. It does not penetrate as far south as the white booby (which breeds in Chile).

3. BREEDING ECOLOGY

INTRODUCTION

The ecology of the brown booby is in several ways akin both to that of the white booby and the blue-footed. The brown booby is undoubtedly a member of the 'tropical trio'—white, brown and red-footed—and as such has evolved the familiar adaptive syndrome which enables it to cope with the impoverished blue-water environment. But it is distinctly less prone than the others to forage far from its breeding place and in its relatively inshore feeding habits it resembles the blue-foot which, incidentally, it resembles also in many aspects of its behaviour (see Comparative Section) and in possessing a less-than-annual breeding cycle.

It is sympatric with the white and red-footed boobies over much of its wide pan-tropical range and is possibly, together with the latter, the most numerous and widespread sulid. Like its two congeners, it *tends* to nest in comparatively small colonies over vast expanses of the tropical oceans, although sometimes it congregates in colonies numbering many thousands of pairs.

Dorward (1962a and b), on Boatswain Bird Island (part of the Atlantic Ascension Island), was the first to study this booby and Simmons (1967b) contributed a valuable analysis of this species' set of adaptations to that particular breeding environment (see p. 476). The Pacific Ocean Biological Survey Programme has made great contributions to knowledge of its longer

(a)

(b)

Fig. 190 (a and b). Nesting habitats of the brown booby, (a) Christmas Island, Indian Ocean; the boobies nest between pinnacles of coralline limestone; (b) Los Testigos (Caribbean) nesting on boulder slope. *Photo* (b): Van Halewijn.

term breeding biology (Amerson 1971; Woodward 1972). I observed brown boobies on the Indian Ocean Christmas Island and so gained material from the third major ocean.

BREEDING HABITAT

Undoubtedly the brown booby prefers much steeper and more broken terrain than either the white or blue-footed boobies. In some places it is virtually a true cliff nester. On the Indian Ocean Christmas Island it nests on broad ledges a few metres below the cliff top and commonly on the very edge of the cliff and among broken terrain on extremely steep slopes. Simmons (1967a) says that on Ascension this booby characteristically chooses steep sites for nesting and perching—slopes, rocks, cliff tops and even cliff faces overlooking the sea (61 per cent of nest sites were on ledges, 11 per cent on eminences and 9 per cent on slopes). On Boatswain Bird Island (Dorward 1962b) it nests on the steep, high slopes and broad ledges lower down. An unusual record illustrating its abilities is that of Stager (1964) who remarks that on Clipperton (Pacific) they were nesting all over a rusting shipwreck on small pinnacles surrounded by water, thus avoiding the wild pigs which, on land, ate all their eggs. Other records illustrating its ability to use ledges and steep slopes are: cliffs and rocky stacks (Tres Marietas, Mexico), open shelves on the 91·4m high, terraced lava island of Necker (Hawaiian group), rocky escarpments on Bird Island (Hawaiian group), rocky ledges on the precipitous side of Ghardaqa (Hurghada) (Red Sea), precipitous cliffs in the Cape Verde Islands, ledges on The Brothers (Jabel Jeir) (Gulf of Aden), ledges of the precipitous La Perouse Pinnacle (French Frigate Shoals; Indian Ocean), ledges of the inland cliff of Christmas Island, Indian Ocean. Many more instances of the same kind could be adduced.

Brown boobies utilise a wide variety of nesting habitats (Fig. 190). Flat ground is perfectly congenial for them, whether it be small patches among boulders or even among high pinnacles of rock (as on much of the shore terrace of Christmas Island, Indian Ocean, where the boobies must often alight on a pinnacle and scramble down to the nest site) or flat patches well beneath a canopy of vegetation. Again on Christmas Island, some birds nested among the trees many metres into the jungle or beneath leafy evergreen shrubs on the shore terraces or among low, dense perennials many hundreds of metres inland, on raised terraces. On rain-soaked Gorgona they nest among or beneath sodden vegetation. On the Marianas they nest among the outer fringes of heavy vegetation along the beaches, usually next to fallen logs, large beach debris and under dense bushes. On many Pacific atolls, as on Kure, brown boobies nest in open spaces among vegetation, above the beach crest or in the interior, and on the bare sandy cays of the Coral Sea, they nest on bare ground without any nest material.

Clearly, greater variety of nesting habitat is open to this species than to any other booby for the white and blue-footed cannot cope with precipitous sites to any degree, whereas the brown can equal these other species in its utilisation of flat open spaces. Indeed, it comes nearest to the arboreal sulids in its ability and tendency to perch on branches, though it has never been known to nest among them.

COLONY DENSITY

Brown boobies nest in lines; large, scattered groups; small isolated ones or isolated pairs. They show as much flexibility in the size and density of their groups as do any other boobies, but are typically more widely spaced than the other ground nesters. Whilst there are some considerable colonies (see Distribution and Numbers p. 427) the species typically colonises small stacks, islets and islands or forms small, discrete nesting groups along the fringes of larger islands; isolated nests, groups of two or three and tenuous lines of nests are common. On Christmas Island, Indian Ocean, groups varied from two or three pairs to between 100–200 patchily distributed around most of the perimeter. The distance between neighbouring nests was highly variable but typically considerable. Some examples of density were: 36 nests and sites in 465 sq. m or one nest in 13·4 sq. m. In linear terms, the number of nests at a given distance from the nearest neighbour were: 0·6m (1); 0·9m (6); 1·2m (3); 1·5m (2); 1·8m (5); 2·1m (4); 2·4m (7); 2·7m (4); 3·1m (3); 3·7m (3); 4·0m (2); 4·9m (2); 5·5m (1); 5·8m (2); 6·7m (1); 7·0m (1); 7·6m (1); 8·5m (1); 9·4m (1); 10·1m (1); 27m (1).

On Boatswain Bird Island (Ascension) there were 400–450 brown boobies and another 200–250 on the nearby stacks. This was a considerably smaller population than that of the white booby and Dorward remarks that the brown booby nests were further apart than those of the white, even where the topography was favourable for the former. However, Chapman (1908) for the Bahamas refers to a colony of 1500 pairs in which nests were consistently 2–3m apart, and North (1912) remarked that the brown boobies on Bramble Cay (Torres Straits) nested so densely that it was difficult to walk between them. There are records indicating extremely dense nesting on some Cape Verde Islands. On the Malayan island of Pulau Perak, nests were 5–7m apart, all over the island. On Isratu and Wusta, of the Dahlacs (Red Sea), brown boobies were nesting in scattered groups, with never less than a few metres between nests and sometimes as much as seven metres.

It would thus be of little use to attempt to produce a figure purporting to represent this species' 'average' or 'typical' density; it is widely variable and perhaps typically rather less than that of the white and blue-footed boobies, though this generalisation may be untrue and is not important in the interpretation of this species' behaviour.

NEST SITES AND NESTS

Brown boobies are highly adaptable. 'Nests' may be placed between, among or even beneath vegetation; on ledges, bare rock or earth; alongside or beneath branches; in fairly deep and narrow gaps between pinnacles; in hollows; completely out on bare open ground (sand or rock) and even on man-made structures (ship's hulk). The only nesting places commonly used by some seabirds in brown booby areas, but not by the boobies, are true holes in rocks or trees, sites among branches, extremely narrow ledges or any sort of cliff site requiring the nest to be cemented onto it by excreta. Reports of brown boobies nesting on the tops of bushes (as Audubon said they did on Booby Island of the Dry Tortugas and as Bent (1922) attempts to support) may all be ascribed to mistaken identity. Simmons detected considerable variation in the quality of nest sites on Georgetown Stacks. Most territories held at least one suitable nest hollow but some did not, and on such 'sub-optimal' sites no young were reared.

The nest itself is a variable but often substantial structure of branches and other vegetation, (such as *Solanum*, *Tubulus*, *Verbesina*, *Eragsostis* and *Boerhavia*, stones and detritus (feathers, bones, flotsam, etc.), seaweed and grasses.

On Kure, Pacific, 10 nests measured had an average outer diameter of 33cm, inner diameter 18cm and were 4cm deep. On Ascension (Atlantic) Dorward mentions a nest 45cm in diameter, as does Hindwood *et al.* (1963) for nests in the Coral Sea. On Willis Island (Coral Sea) Serventy also gives the diameter as 45cm. On Christmas Island (Indian Ocean) they were often very substantial structures of twigs. The brown booby nest is in fact the only structurally functional one built by any ground-nesting booby excluding the excreta-using Peruvian booby. This may probably be linked with the species' liking for sites in somewhat precipitous places which could be dangerous for unprotected eggs. Nevertheless, it sometimes lays its eggs on the bare substrate, whether rock or earth. The movements of adults and young often scatter the loose structure and older young are often found on bare substrate.

THE EGG AND CLUTCH

1. *Characteristics of the egg*

Brown booby eggs are variable in size, elliptical, ovate or elongate ovate, chalky white over a bluish or often distinctly greenish shell, quickly becoming scratched and stained. Dimensions and weights from several localities are given in Table 63. The shell comprises about 12·5 per

Fig. 191. The nest is much more substantial than that of the other ground nesting boobies; on many of its steep sites, it must be necessary for safety of egg and small chick.

TABLE 63

DIMENSIONS AND WEIGHTS OF BROWN BOOBY EGGS

Area	First egg			Second egg			Position in clutch unspecified			Source
	Length	Breadth	Weight	Length	Breadth	Weight	Length	Breadth	Weight	
Christmas Island Indian Ocean	63·4 58–69 44	42·7 36–45·3 43	57·3 40–60 27	60·2 56·2–65 18	41·1 38–43 18	53·2 45–67 20				Nelson (Unpubl.)
Christmas Island Indian Ocean							56–65 10	37–45 10		Gibson-Hill 1947
Coral Sea							60·8 55·5–66·1	41·5 36·8–44·2		Hindwood et al 1963
Willis Island	60 59·5–60·5 2	41·9 41·4–42·5 2	62·5 57·5–65 3	58 56·4–59·5 2	42·7 40·6–44·7 2	59·1 52·5–65 3	63·6 59–65·9 3	41·5 40·8–41·9 3	63 60–66 2	Serventy 1959
Hawaiian Is. (Necker)							58	40		
Mariana Is. (Medinilla)							61·3 12	42·8 12		
Pacific							59·4 52·5–65·5 40	40·2 34·5–42·5 40		Bent 1922
Pacific							61 53·6–66 45	41·1 37·5–45 45		
Cape Verdes							53–64 30	37–43·5 30		Murphy 1924

cent of the egg's weight, the yolk 16·0 per cent and the albumen 71·5 per cent; actual weights were: shell 8g; yolk 9·6g (8–11); albumen 45·5g (33–51).

The first egg represents some 4·1 per cent of the female's weight, the second egg 4 per cent and the clutch of two 8·1 per cent. Thus, the full clutch requires slightly more energy than the single egg of the red-foot and almost exactly the same as that of Abbott's booby.

2. *Clutch size*

The brown booby is of particular interest as one of the two sulids (the other is the white booby) which customarily produces clutches of two eggs, but virtually never rears more than one chick.

On Boatswain Bird Island Dorward recorded that the brown booby normally laid two eggs; in three cases an egg marked in one nest was discovered in another, so this could account for some of the occasional clutches of three that are found, but a few genuine three-egg clutches probably do occur. On Christmas Island (Indian Ocean) the proportions of one, two and three egg clutches excluding replacement clutches in 72 nests were 41 (57 per cent), 30 (42 per cent) and 1 (1 per cent) and including them 46, 34 and 1. Ridley & Percy (1958) report that on Desnoeufs there were about 20 pairs in 1955, mostly with clutches of three and a few with four. They do not discuss this remarkable record. In the Gulf of California old oölogical records show 34 clutches of two, 7 of one and 1 of three.

The best information comes from the P.O.B.S.P. on Kure (Woodward 1972) where figures for four successive years, involving 93 clutches, show that 83·9 per cent were of two eggs, 8·6 per cent of three and 7·5 per cent of one. The yearly average size ranged between 1·9 and 2·1 with an overall average of 2·01.

Other counts of clutch size are: Pulau Perak (Malaya) 65 nests; average clutch size 1·6. Cocos (Pacific) 24 nests; one egg (8), two eggs (16). Bahamas (Atlantic) 35 nests; one egg (14), two eggs (21). Christmas Island (Indian Ocean) 50 nests; one egg (34), two eggs (16). Bedout Island 30 nests; one egg (16), two eggs (14). The average clutch size from the 139 clutches just listed (excluding Kure and Pulau Perak) is 1·5, so the Kure clutches appear to be significantly larger than those from other areas, but there is too little information to warrant any speculation about regional differences.

There are a few cases of broods of two; out of 740 nests examined in the Bahamas, Chapman found two with two well grown chicks of equal size and 738 with one chick and two healthy chicks about a fortnight old were found in a nest on Bird Islet (Coral Sea) (Hindwood *et al.* 1963), whilst Simmons recorded two chicks fledging successfully from one nest on Ascension. The normal fate of the second chick and the adaptive value of the two-egg clutch is discussed on p. 466.

On Kure, 3–9 days elapsed between the first and second egg (average 5·2) and hatching was asynchronous by almost as much (4·6 days, range 1–9).

Chapman suggested that the brown booby suffers a high infertility rate and this gives the two-egg clutch its value. Earlier, McCormick had mentioned that in all the clutches of two or three which he found on St. Paul's Rocks, all but one egg per clutch had been infertile. On Christmas Island (Indian Ocean) a higher proportion of clutches laid in April and May (the peak period) contained two eggs than did those laid at other times. The proportions of two-egg to one-egg clutches were: February (2nd half) 2:1; March (1st half) no clutches; March (2nd half) 1:6; April (1st half) 0:4; April (2nd half) 5:1; May (1st half) 13:3; May (2nd half) 0:13; June (1st half) 1:3; June (2nd half) 1:2; July (1st half) 1:0; July (2nd half) 1:2. Thus, 82 per cent of clutches laid in the second half of April and the first half of May contained two eggs, whilst of all clutches laid outside this period only 18 per cent contained two eggs. That two-egg clutches produce more young may thus be partly due to being laid in what is presumably the most favourable period in a seasonal environment. Also, late layers are likely to be young birds and thus prone to lay smaller clutches.

3. *Replacement laying*

On Kure, brown boobies replaced lost clutches in something less than half the cases (Woodward 1972). Thus, lumping figures for the years 1964, 1966 and 1968 and ignoring clutch size, 28 pairs lost their eggs and 13 re-laid. Although Woodward does not give the period elapsing between egg loss and replacement laying, it was obviously weeks rather than months. However, elsewhere, it may not always be easy to draw the line between a re-nesting attempt and a successive one. Thus where, as on Ascension, breeding occurs at less than annual intervals failed nesting may be followed by a new nesting attempt at a variable period less than the norm, the initiation of the new attempt probably depending on the economic situation (p. 475). However, one may take as a reasonable criterion for replacement laying that it should occur within less than six weeks of egg or chick loss. It will probably be found that almost all records fall either within that period or well outside it. On Christmas Island we recorded eight replacement laying periods as follows: 20, 21, 23, 26 (2), 27, 29 and 30–34 days.

On Ascension Dorward reported that only a small proportion of failed nesters re-laid, but Simmons found that eggs and chicks were replaced at all stages of development after an average period of five weeks, there being no consistent correlation between the stage at which the item was lost and the interval before re-laying. 87 per cent of all lost clutches were replaced within five months. Some pairs laid repeatedly (up to four times) after loss. Probably economic circumstances were different during the two study periods.

4. *Incubation period*

The five accurately measured incubation periods on Christmas Island were 43, 42, 43, 43 and 43 (average 42·8 days). Dorward gives 43–47 and Simmons (1967b) c. 42.

On Kure, the incubation period for 62 first eggs was 42·4 (range 39–48) and for 44 second eggs 42·2 (range 40–44). Since these do not significantly differ, the second egg hatches almost as far behind the first as it was laid (average interval between laying 5·2 days and between hatching 4·6 days).

5. *Incubation regime*

Dorward's figures for the length of 135 incubation spells on Boatswain Bird Island showed the following distribution: 1–6 hours (38 spells); 7–12 (35); 13–18 (33); 19–24 (24); 25–30 (4) and 37 (1). This gives a mean spell of 12 hours, excluding spells immediately prior to desertion of clutches, which tend to be much longer than normal. Simmons recorded 195 spells ranging from 6 minutes to 12 hours 30 minutes or more. Most change-overs were at dawn and any that occurred between 22.00 and 06.00 were very likely to have occurred at dawn. Of 143 observed nest reliefs 48 were at dawn; 39 between 07.00 and 11.30; 34 between 12.00 and 17.00; 20 at dusk and only 2 during darkness. The incubation spells are only just over a third as long as those of the white booby, a difference reflecting the brown booby's inshore fishing habits. Oddly enough, the incubation stints of brown boobies on Christmas Island (Indian Ocean) seemed, though on fairly inadequate data, to be considerably longer than on Ascension. Thus males averaged 40 hours (5 cases) and females 42 (6 cases). These figures probably err on the high side, but even at half their face value, which would be a considerable underestimate, they are still longer than Ascension. This may possibly reflect a tendency for Christmas Island birds to feed at certain localities some distance from Christmas Island.

THE CHICK

1. *Morphology and plumage development*

The **newly hatched** chick is naked, with a slaty-grey or pinkish-mauve skin and closed eyes, though these may open on the first day. The bill is pinkish on the upper mandible and black on the distal part, with a white tip which later may darken. The egg tooth is yellow. Already the white natal down is appearing on all dorsal pterylae, two tracts on the inner radio-ulna and on the posterior margin of the wings including the alula. There may be bluish blotches on the body.

By the age of **one week** the chick is sparsely covered with fine, white down. The bill is livid blue-grey and the forehead and orbital ring green or blue and the throat skin yellowish green. The skin, visible through the down is bluish green and the feet very pale green, a combination diagnostic of the brown booby chick. The head skin may be purplish.

Between **two** and **four weeks** the down thickens and the chick becomes completely white and fluffy, but the down is still increasing in length. By **three weeks** the primaries, though not visible, are about to erupt and the tips of the rectrices can just be felt. The primaries push through the down about a week later, although in some areas they remain hidden until the chick is between **five** and **six weeks** old. The axillary region is pale blue. At about one month the chick is roughly half the size of the adult female. There is much green on the face and gular skin and the feet are pale green. The bill is livid blue-grey.

(a) c. one week old

(b) c. one month old

(c) c. 5–6 weeks old

Photo (c): J. Warham

By **five weeks** the chick is covered with full-length down. The primaries may be (at the most) 20mm long and the juvenile contour feathers may be beginning to sprout. The plumage of breast and abdomen is the first to grow on the body tracts, appearing before that on the back (though well grown on the humeral tracts).

By **week seven**, though still covered in down, the chick can have become almost as big as its parents; primaries, scapulars and tail feathers may be conspicuous (34, 32 and 42mm long respectively on Christmas Island) though in birds of some regions they may not even be visible.

Between **weeks eight** and **nine** the longest primary may reach 89mm and the tail 97mm.

Fig. 192(a–f)

Stages in the development of the young.

(d) c. 7 weeks old

(e) left to right, c. 9 weeks; c. 9 weeks; c. 7 weeks

(f)

c. 11 weeks old

The forehead feathers are sprouting and a week later the forehead may be clear of down, as also the wings, except for the radio-ulna line.

By **nine weeks** the secondary wing feathers may be well grown and the scapulars united in the mid-line. The tail feathers have formed a good strong fan. The back and forehead are clearing of down, but it remains thick on the back of the neck and underparts, particularly the flanks and belly. By **ten weeks** down may be thinning, though thick still on head, neck, thighs, flanks and rump. The pectoral band may be apparent, the bill is still blue and the feet greenish.

At **11 weeks** wings, crown and upper breast may be clear, but thick down remains on flanks and thighs. At **12 weeks**, birds may still have down on head, neck, thighs and flanks and perhaps among the secondaries but it clears extremely quickly from now onwards. Wisps remain until, in most cases, the end of the **thirteenth** week but some birds are completely clear by then. The bill remains light blue, orbital ring grey-blue, iris light grey and feet greenish.

By the end of **week 14** the great majority are completely clear and in their new juvenile plumage. Many chicks can fly at 99 days, most can do so by day 105 and all save exceptionally retarded ones by 119 days.

Simmons' useful categorisation of the four principal stages are: 0–3 weeks, naked, becoming sparsely creamy, black-faced; 4–6 weeks, white and fluffy, becoming large; 7–11 weeks, the 'black-and-white' stage, tail and wing pins appearing from the 7th week; 12 weeks onwards, 'shedding' stage, variously dishevelled.

2. *Feeding*

The brown booby chick is fed in the normal sulid manner (regurgitation). We lack data on the frequency with which feeds are delivered, but it is clear that they are more frequent than in the red-foot and the white booby. Probably both parents forage and return at least once each day and the chick is thus fed about twice if conditions allow.

Dorward records that on Ascension the mean length of the brown booby's brooding spell was 9·3 hours (27 cases) and the longest was 20 hours. This was not uniform throughout

TABLE 64

WEIGHTS OF BROWN BOOBY CHICKS AGAINST AGE I

(From

Chick 1		Chick 2		Chick 3		Chick 4		Chick 5	
Age	Wt.	Age	Wt.	Age	Wt.	Age	Wt.	Age	Wt
6	82	8	102	8	99	6	72	8	78
11	138	10	125	10	109	9	113		
14	205	14	194	14	192	13	205		
18	300	25	609	25	389	25	564		
29	595	29	639	29	474	28	704	27	485
33	674					37	975	31	**515**
43	1025	40	925	40	700	49	1175	38	**580**
54	1175					55	1225	48	850
60	1350	57	1375	57	1050	65	1250	56	900
70	1400	67	1300	67	1200	89	**1175**	73	**850**
94	1290	90	1240	90	1100	95	**1025**	88	**675**
100	1225	103	**940**	103	**1000**	102	**900**	106	**800**
107	1140	113	1000	113	1000	112	**800**	119	**750**
				121	900	120	950		

Notes:

1. Chick 1 was normal; chicks 2 and 3, after a setback due to a twinning experiment, which ended b their separation when 25 days old, were normal up to 90 days; the remaining chicks were abnormal. Weigh showing abnormalities are printed in bold type.

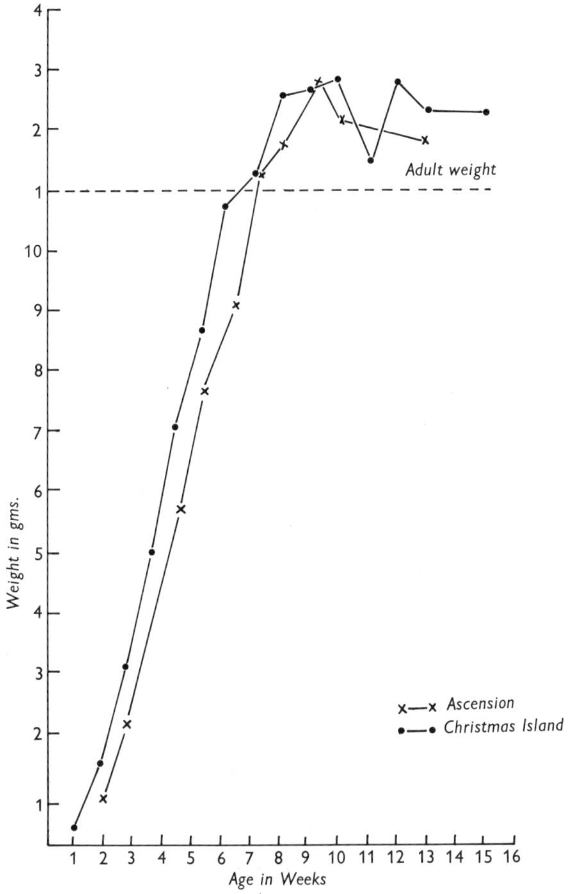

Fig. 193

Growth by weight of the young brown booby on Christmas Island (Indian Ocean) and Ascension (Atlantic).

DAYS, SHOWING NORMAL AND ABNORMAL GROWTH

Dorward 1962b)

Chick 6		Chick 7		Chick 8		Chick 9		Chick 10	
Age	Wt.	Age	Wt.	Age	Wt.	Age	Wt.	Age	Wt.
		7	72	6	53	6	65	4	54
9	115	9	107					11	118
		13	165						
16	210	24	409	16	240	16	270		
33	660	28	500	20	360	20	373	21	**200**
39	825	38	600	33	560	33	575	26	dead
46	**770**	49	975						
56	950	55	**925**	58	**840**	58	1000		
64	1050	65	**950**						
81	1150	89	1100	69	**660**	69	**890**		
85	**1000**	95	**900**	72	dead	79	dead		
14	**850**	102	**640**						
33	1000	103	dead						

2. Chick 1, normal at 107 days, may have lost weight like the others thereafter, but could not be caught. Two months later it was apparently normal. Chick 6, late in fledging, also appeared normal $2\frac{1}{2}$ months later.

development of the young, being 12·4 hours when the chicks were tiny (6–10 days) and only 6·8 hours when they were more than 25 days old. This change must be related to the greater demand of the young for food. Thus the brooding stints on tiny young and incubation stints are about the same, but stints become shorter as the young grow. Simmons' guard spells varied from 10 minutes to more than 10 hours 19 minutes.

There is disagreement about the extent to which (if at all) the brown booby is a nocturnal hunter (see p. 501), but it sometimes does return to the colony during darkness. For a description of food species, see p. 477.

3. *Growth*

(*a*) *By weight*

There are reasonably detailed growth records from two areas; Ascension (Atlantic) and Christmas Island (Indian Ocean) (Fig. 193). From the figures given in Dorward (Table 64) one may obtain points which, although only approximate, are probably valid for comparative purposes. When the Ascension growth curve is compared with that from Christmas Island, it is clear that for almost the entire time, the Ascension birds lag behind. The same is true of culmen growth. This is to be expected from what we know of the severe impoverishment which periodically affects the waters around Ascension. Similarly, the growth of the white booby on Ascension lagged behind that recorded in a more normal area (Kure).

Dorward's figures, like the Galapagos ones for the red-footed booby, reveal how extraordinarily able are young blue-water boobies to survive extreme starvation and to recover most of the lost ground (Fig. 194). Thus, one of his chicks grew normally until about 65 days and then lost weight until at 112 days it weighed hardly more than it had when a month old. As is normal, even his well-fed chicks began to lose weight after about 9–10 weeks, due to the growth of feathers and increased exertion (wing-exercising, etc.).

The Christmas Island weights fluctuated much less violently and in addition to the mean weights for most ages being significantly higher than on Ascension, the absolute maxima were much higher (nine instances of weights about 1400g, 4 of them 1500 or more and the

Fig. 194

The effect of food-shortage on the development of the brown booby. Photograph shows a fully feathered young bird from Ascension which ought to be about as big as the adult alongside.

maximum recorded weight 1590g for a 73-day-old bird, compared with only one such weight, of 1400g for a 70-day-old bird on Ascension). Although the nominate race, found on Ascension, is smaller than *S.l.plotus* found on Christmas Island, this is not nearly enough to cause the difference.

(b) By other measurements

For general comments on the adaptive value of allometric growth see p. 357.

The situation in the brown booby seems very similar to that in the white; that is, the feet reach approximately adult dimensions first, then the wings and tail, and finally the beak. Thus the juveniles can fly before their beaks are full size, which is presumably more adaptive than the other way round.

As in the white booby there are significant regional differences in the rate of growth. To be valid, a comparison should take into account sub-specific differences in adult size. The available information concerns Ascension birds (the nominate race) and Christmas Island (Indian Ocean) ones (*S.l.plotus*). The former is considerably smaller; for example, the average culmen length is about 93mm as against about 99mm in *plotus*. As a proportion of average adult culmen measurements, however, the Ascension birds lag considerably and consistently behind the Christmas Island ones (Fig. 195).

The wing and culmen growth of Ascension birds is given in Fig. 196.

4. *Fledging period*

On Kure, brown booby chicks fledged at about 95 days (range 85–103, 32 cases). On Christmas Island (Indian Ocean) they flew at 96 days (range 87–100, 11 cases, pers. obs.). Gibson-Hill gives the 15th week (i.e. 98–105 days) as the period during which the first reasonably sustained flight was made on Christmas Island. These figures compare with Dorward's estimated fledging age (no details given) of 120 days on Ascension, based on five individuals, affected in the later stages of growth by the 1958 food shortage. Simmons gives 94 days (86–103) for first flight, or completion of down shedding, whichever comes first, compared with c. 105 to completion of down shedding from Dorward.

Taken together with the differences in growth as measured by weights and culmen length this clearly shows the substantial difference between an exceptionally impoverished and a normal blue-water area.

5. *Post-fledging feeding*

The most astonishing thing about post-fledging feeding in the brown booby is its extraordinary length under some circumstances. On Christmas Island it appeared to be between

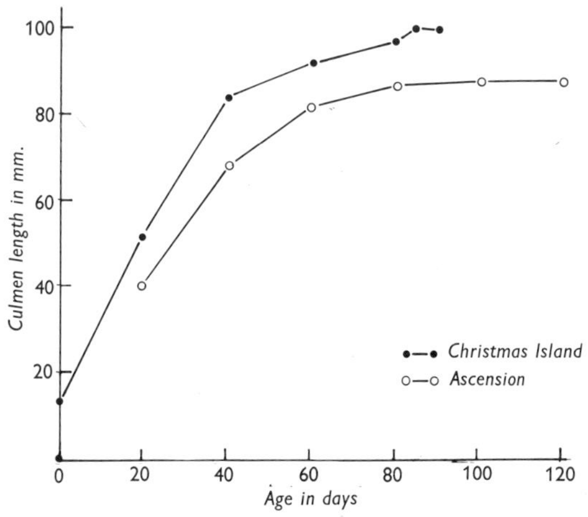

Fig. 195

Growth of culmen of young brown booby on Ascension and Christmas Island.

one and two months. On Kure it is given as about the same, but without any supporting details. For Ascension, Simmons (1967b) provides the most complete information. Here, between 1962 and 1964, the overall period during which juveniles came back to the breeding group ranged from 7 to 59 weeks (average 25). They were actually seen to be fed on average 17 weeks after fledging (range 6–37) and the last sustained food-begging behaviour was recorded 7–51 weeks (average 23) after fledging. Thus, in the extreme cases, a juvenile was seen to be fed 37 weeks after fledging, to beg sustainedly 51 weeks after and to return to the colony for 59 weeks. This is by far the longest period reliably recorded for any booby, likely to be exceeded only by Abbott's.

BREEDING SUCCESS

1. *Hatching success*

It is difficult to obtain a meaningful figure for hatching success as a specific trait; so much depends on regional circumstances. On Kure, which is perhaps fairly representative, the hatching success in five successive years was 70·4 per cent (71 eggs), 58·9 per cent (50); 55 per cent (60); 64·9 per cent (37) and 56·4 per cent (55) an overall average of 61·2 per cent, disregarding the position of the egg in the clutch (that is, whether laid first or second). My own hatching figure for Christmas Island was 51 per cent of 84 eggs. This somewhat low figure is in a sense misleading since, because obligative brood reduction occurs anyway, the meaningful figure is the proportion of *clutches* from which at least one egg hatches, the second egg being superfluous. That figure is 68 per cent.

As to the causes, considerable egg loss in the brown booby may occur as a result of desertion. Probably this is significant only in parts of its range, such as Ascension, subject to periods of impoverishment. Dorward gives details of two cases of desertion and says these were 'not exceptional'. Thus, of 89 pairs of brown boobies incubating in the first half of September 1958 (a period of food shortage) 51 lost their eggs and by far the likeliest cause was desertion due to food shortage. Overall, only 71 out of 185 clutches (38 per cent) produced a hatched chick. No comparable desertion has been recorded in other parts of this species' range. The cause of egg loss on Kure, or Christmas Island, was not obvious. However, in the case of the loss of the second-laid egg it is likely that the brooding activities of the parents following the hatching of the first-laid egg, often results in either the ejection of the second egg or its destruction, by crushing, as it hatches. Thus many of our records (9 out of 13 second eggs lost)

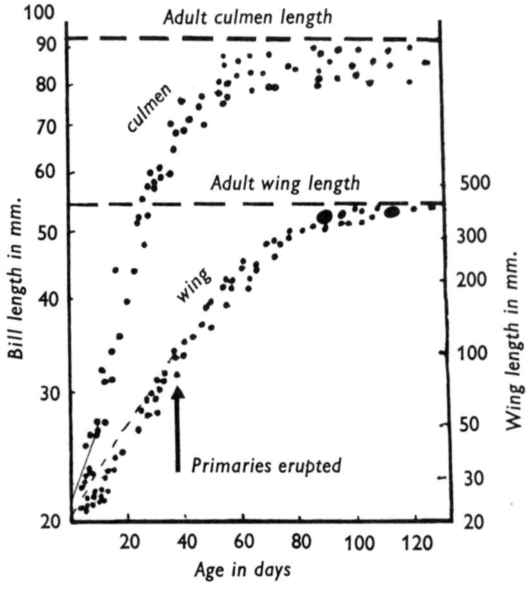

Fig. 196

Growth of wing and culmen of young brown booby, Ascension Island (after Dorward 1962b).

comment that loss of the second egg occurred just as it was due to hatch. Simmons ascribed almost 50 per cent of his egg loss to desertion. Sea swell accounted for a further 17 per cent.

The Ascension situation is of particular interest because it supplements the similar Galapagos one. Both areas are subject to periods of impoverishment, which have similar consequences. Just as the degree of these can be judged for the Galapagos by comparing the breeding ecology of the red-footed booby with that of the same species from a 'better' part of its range, so the brown booby's ecology is different on Ascension in the Atlantic, than on Kure in the Central Pacific or Christmas Island in the Indian Ocean.

2. *Fledging success*

The proportion of chicks which survive to fledging in the brown booby is also highly dependent on locality. Fortunately there are figures from three regions, the impoverished one of Ascension providing a useful contrast with the two in favourable feeding areas.

In these comparisons fledging success is not taken strictly as the proportion of all hatched chicks which survive to fledging, but as the proportion which survive taking *one* hatched chick per nest as the starting point. Where two hatch one is automatically ejected, so it would be pointless to include these in the percentage of failures.

On Ascension fledging success probably differs from year to year. In the first season studied by Dorward, 71 clutches hatched one egg or more and of these only 18 (25 per cent) fledged. The second season was not followed to completion, but fledging success was probably somewhat higher (39 chicks out of 150 hatched *clutches* survived for a month or more. The main cause of death, presumably, was starvation. Simmons, on the other hand, noted only one case of starvation in large young; chick loss was due to ocean swell (mainly in January 1964) and to falling due to displacement by adults, often intruders.

The figures given for Kure (see Table 65) do not enable one to calculate the percentage of chicks which fledged starting from one hatched chick per nest, for they are given as percent of young fledged from eggs laid, or from eggs hatched (which thus include 'automatic rejects') or from nests which held one or more eggs. The last figure, however, at least indicates the minimum fledging success and was 76, 80, 78, 96 and 65 per cent in the years 1964–68 respectively (about 79 per cent on average). This is very similar to the figure for Christmas Island (81 per cent fledging success).

Thus fledging success was extremely high on Kure and Christmas Island and very low on Ascension. Chick loss, apart from starvation as on Ascension, occurs mainly in the early stages of growth and is probably compounded mostly of inadequate parental care and a little adventitious predation. Special factors such as the heavy predation by wild pigs on Clipperton can be of only highly localised significance. The principal conclusion must be that, except in highly impoverished areas, brown boobies are extremely successful in rearing their young, thus measuring up to other sulids in this respect (see Comparative Section).

TABLE 65

PRODUCTIVITY OF BROWN BOOBIES IN THE NORTH ANTENNA FIELD BASED ON FIRST NESTING ATTEMPTS, 1964–68 (from Woodward 1972)

Year	No. of nests	No. of eggs laid	No. of eggs hatched	No. of young fledged	% of eggs hatched	% of young hatched from: Eggs	Hatching	Nests
1964	37[1]	71	50	27[2]	70·4	38·0	54·0	73·0
1965	33[1]	56[3]	33[3]	24[2]	58·9	42·9	72·7	72·7
1966	31[1]	60	33	24	55·0	40·0	72·7	77·4
1967	18[4]	37[3]	24[3]	18[5]	64·9	48·6	75·0	100·0
1968	32	55[3]	31[3]	19	56·4	34·5	61·3	59·4

Notes: [1] One not included. [2] Two young fledged from same nest. [3] Minimum figure.
[4] Eleven not included. [5] Number remaining in early July.

3. *Overall breeding success*

(*a*) *Regional differences*

The Kure figures show that over 75 per cent of nests produced a fledged juvenile. This is the really significant figure, for it shows that over three-quarters of the chicks which the parents attempt to rear, succeed. The much poorer success in terms of young reared from eggs laid, or from eggs hatched, simply reflects the fate of the second egg or small chick, which is almost always lost by 'deliberate' neglect or persecution by the sibling.

On Christmas Island the figure was equally high (fledged young were produced from 81 per cent of eggs hatched) but the success in terms of clutches which produced a fledged chick was lower (58 per cent). This reflects a higher egg loss on Christmas Island, but shows that food was readily available.

On Ascension the situation was very different. There, in 1958 only 10 per cent of nests (clutches) produced a fledged young, and in 1959, probably about 20 per cent (26 per cent produced a chick surviving to the age of a month or more but some would be expected to die before fledging). The difference between the two seasons was due to the sudden food shortage of 1958 (until that point, success was very similar to that of 1959) but even at 26 per cent the failure rate is extremely high, approaching that of the red-footed boobies in the Galapagos (see p. 700). Simmons' figures were similarly low. Of 202 cycles started between 1961 and 1964, 31 were successful, 164 unsuccessful and 7 still in progress when he left. Over half of all pairs that attempted to breed during this period were unsuccessful. The pairs that did succeed could be considered in terms of whether their sites were 'favourable' or not (criteria devised by Simmons). Of the 27 per cent of 'favourable' site birds that bred successfully, one pair reared three broods, five reared two and 18 reared one. Thus they did exceptionally well, but, overall, the considerable information now available for Ascension proves that extremely low breeding success is normal there.

(*b*) *Breeding success in relation to the two-egg clutch*

The remarks about the two-egg clutch of the white booby (p. 365) are relevant here, too. As in that species, there can now be no doubt that two-egg clutches give rise to more fledged young than do one-egg clutches, but NOT by occasionally producing two chicks. In only one certain and one probable case on Kure, one possible case of chicks surviving for 34 days on Ascension and one in which two chicks definitely fledged (in a cave which prevented eviction) were two chicks reared or part-reared. In the Kure case the eggs hatched one day apart so the chicks were almost equally matched from the beginning. Earlier records are equally decisive, most notably that of Chapman (1908) who found two chicks in only two nests out of 740 and even these were not fully grown.

There are two further points which need to be clearly distinguished here. First, the success of parents with two-egg clutches, in raising one chick, is much higher than that of parents with one-egg clutches. Second, the contribution of the second egg is NOT enough to account for the difference. In other words, although, due to the disappearance of the first egg or small chick, the second egg does produce a proportion of the fledged young, this proportion is substantially less than that by which two-egg clutches out-produce one-egg clutches. The figures from Kure and Christmas Island well illustrate this point.

On Kure, the second-laid egg was responsible for producing the fledged chick in 5 pairs out of 26 (19·2 per cent) in 1964 and 3 out of 23 (13·1 per cent) in 1966 (Woodward 1972). There is no comment on the manner in which the first egg was lost, nor whether it was lost as an egg or after hatching but before the second egg had hatched. On Christmas Island, the second egg contributed the fledged chick in two cases, in one because the first egg was lost before hatching and in the other because the first chick died before the second egg hatched. However, the extent by which two-egg clutches were more successful far exceeded this modest contribution. Thus, expressed as the relative success of clutches of one, two and three (in terms of the production of one fledged chick) the Kure figures for 1964 and 1966 together were: one-egg clutches 2 out of 7 (28·6 per cent); two-egg clutches 43 out of 51 (84·3 per cent); and three-egg clutches 3 out of 7 (42·9 per cent). Similarly, on Christmas Island, in 1967,

15 chicks fledged from 20 clutches of two (75 per cent) whereas only 14 fledged from 31 clutches of one (45 per cent).

Thus, whilst the insurance value of the second egg cannot be doubted, one must look further for the total significance of the two-egg clutch. There are two possibilities, which are probably linked. The two-egg parents may be more experienced (older) birds and they may be laying at a more favourable time for the subsequent survival of their young. The former is likely, though there is no firm evidence for it. For the latter, the figures for Christmas Island (Table 66) indicate that the majority of two-egg clutches are laid in the middle part of the main laying period whilst the one-egg clutches tend to occur either early or late. This suggestion, however, raises many questions which at present cannot be answered. If the relatively low success of one-egg clutches is correlated with their earliness or lateness, these in turn could be linked (as suggested above) with age, or the timing could itself be important. In a fairly seasonal environment, survival could depend on favourable timing with regard to food.

(*c*) *Breeding success in relation to replacement laying*

The Kure information has been analysed to show the contribution made by replacement eggs. Out of 32 lost clutches, 15 or 46·9 per cent were replaced. There were three cases in 1964 and 1966 together, in which a replacement clutch yielded a fledgling and 49 in which a first clutch did so. Thus 5·8 per cent of fledged young came from replacement clutches—a significant contribution. Replacement laying occurred on Christmas Island also and contributed 6 out of 35 fledged chicks (17 per cent). The success of replacement clutches was 67 per cent.

BREEDING REGIMES

1. *General features of attendance at colony*

Dorward reported that on Boatswain Bird Island the brown boobies were usually absent outside the breeding season and began to spend more time at their nest site, mainly at night, as the breeding season approached. He remarks that they usually left after sunrise. Nor could he locate Clubs or roosting areas, though there may have been some suitable resting places on the cliffs. Simmons (1967b) however, laid special emphasis on his observation that the birds on two of the Georgetown stacks, off Ascension, maintained daily contact with their nesting territories throughout the year, showing all the typical territorial and some sexual behaviour. He suggests that this is an adaptation which enables them to respond by initiating breeding as soon as the unpredictable food situation becomes reasonably good (see p. 475 for a full discussion of this topic). Dorward's apparently contrary observations may have arisen because many brown boobies do leave the breeding area for a time; only the adult, established breeders maintain continuous contact with their site, and perhaps not even all of these. However, there may be an anomaly here.

On Kure, brown boobies are present all the year round, though most numerous during the breeding season (April to October). Thus, between 1963 and 1969 there are records for 75 or more birds for every month of the year which represents about three-quarters of the total population. On French Frigate Shoals (Pacific), too, birds are in attendance all the year, with peaks in spring and summer.

The situation on Kure and French Frigate Shoals may well be the more typical, since the brown booby tends to forage relatively near to its breeding areas and might be expected to roost there; conceivably the Ascension birds had to forage more widely and spent more time at sea.

2. *Seasonal aspects of breeding*

The brown booby is nowhere a strictly seasonal breeder but, as with the other tropical boobies, its breeding strategy shows regional differences which are highly adaptive. On Christmas Island (I. O.), which has a fairly well marked monsoon period (November–March), egg laying was clearly seasonal. The following Figures 197 (a–f) cover the same regions as in the other two pan-tropical boobies.

Fig. 197(a–f). The timing of laying in different parts of its range.

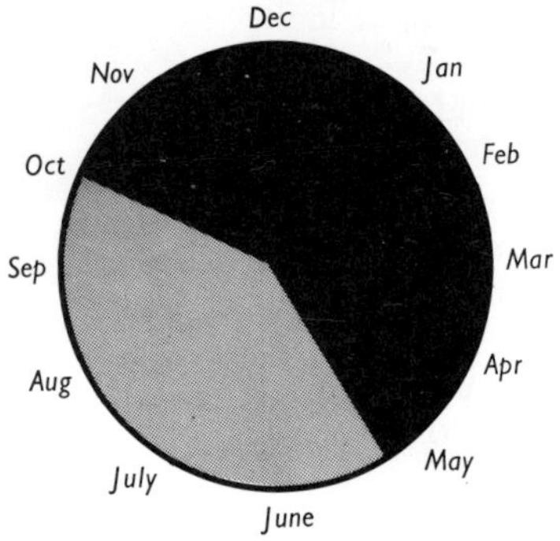

Fig. 197(a)

Caribbean and Atlantic

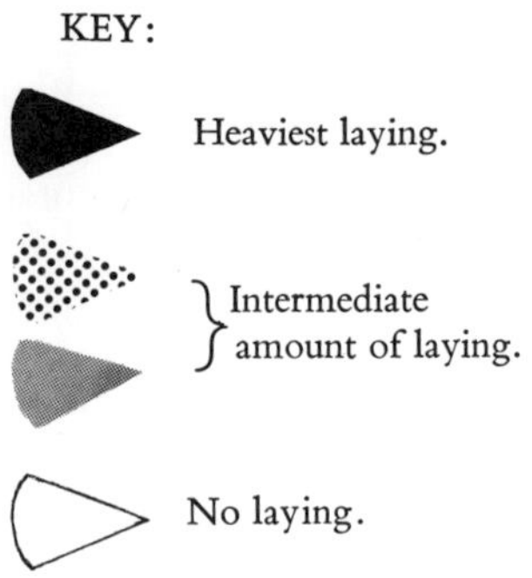

1. Bahamas	Bryant (1859) Chapman (1908)	98% of birds with young in Apr., indicates Dec.–Mar. laying.
2. Swan Island		Laying probably Sept.–Dec.
3. Isla de Barlovento; Orchila	Cory (1909)	Breeding end of Jan.
4. Desecheo	Wetmore (1918)	Laying Jan.–Mar.
5. Monito (near Mona)	Kepler (in prep).	Main peaks apparently subject to annual shifts of 3–4 months, but perhaps main laying peaks most often in 1st and 4th quarters of the year, though there is (often?) a laying peak around June to September. In general, long laying periods interspersed with periods of 2–4 months when many adults leave the island and little or no egg laying occurs.
6. St. Giles	Belcher & Smooker (1934)	Laying Oct.–Dec.
7. Little Tobago	Dinsmore (1972)	Peaks around July and Dec.
8. British Virgin Islands		Laying occurs chiefly in Feb., Mar. and Apr.
9. Isla lo Frances	Sick (1965)	Laying Mar.–June.
10. St. Paul's Rocks		Infrequent visits suggest laying in all months.
11. Ascension	Dorward (1962b)	Laying mainly in Apr. and Dec.
12. Cape Verdes	Various sources	Laying in any month, mainly Jan.–Mar.

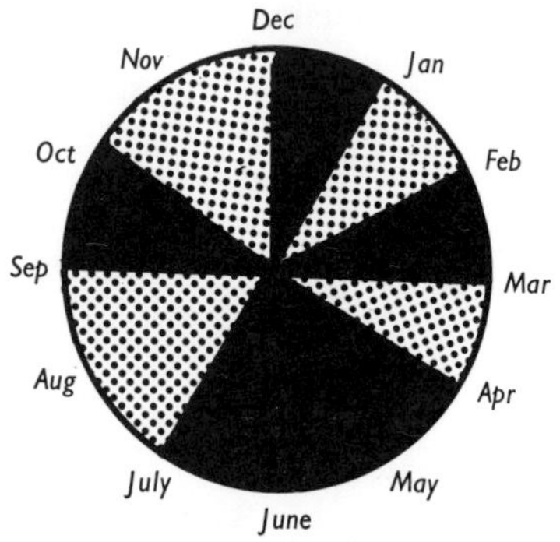

Fig. 197(b)

Indian Ocean

KEY: as in Fig. 197(a)

1. Dahlac Archipelago	Clapham (1964)	Aug. 1902, birds in every stage of breeding—laying probably occurs Mar.–Aug., peak period June.
2. Om Qamra's Islet	Al Hussaini (1939)	Aug. 23rd 1938—newly hatched young and eggs.
3. Fassan Island	Brown (1929)	Oct. 1926. Eggs and young chicks present in early Nov. No birds nesting in Apr.
4. Brothers Islands	Jones (1946)	Mid Aug. 1944. No breeding.

5. Seychelles	Vesey-Fitzgerald (1941)	Nov. One record of eggs.
6. Desnoefs	Ridley & Percy (1958)	Sept. 1955 majority of birds with eggs.
7. Farquhar Atoll	(1897)	Laying mainly Apr.–June.
8. Chagos Island	Loustau-Lalanne (1962)	Laying mainly Dec.–Mar.
9. North Keeling	Gibson-Hill (1950a)	No well-defined laying season.
10. Christmas Island	Nelson (unpubl.) Gibson-Hill (1947)	Laying in any month, Apr. and May peak, sparse laying in Jan. and July.
11. Pulau Perak		Laying Oct.–Feb.

Fig. 197(c)

Seas north of Australia

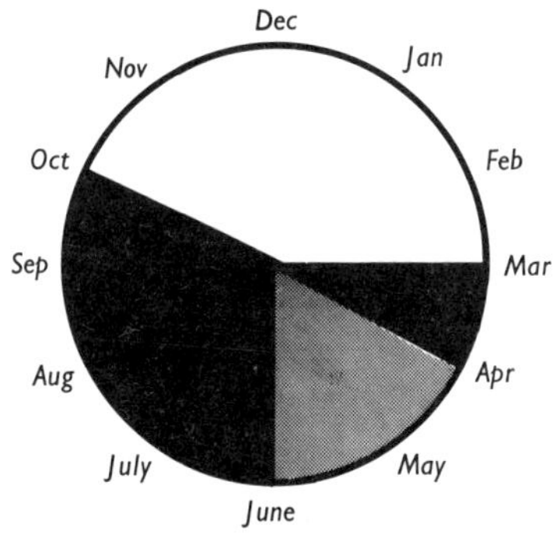

KEY: as in Fig. 197(a)

1. Bankoran, Maender and Tub Bataha Reefs	Worcester (1911)	June–Sept. egg laying.
2. Coral Sea	Serventy *et al.* (1971)	Breeding season almost continuous. Autumn and spring laying peaks.
3. Willis Island	Reithmuller (1931)	Laying 'begins' around April but eggs and young present all year.

Fig. 197(d)

Western Pacific

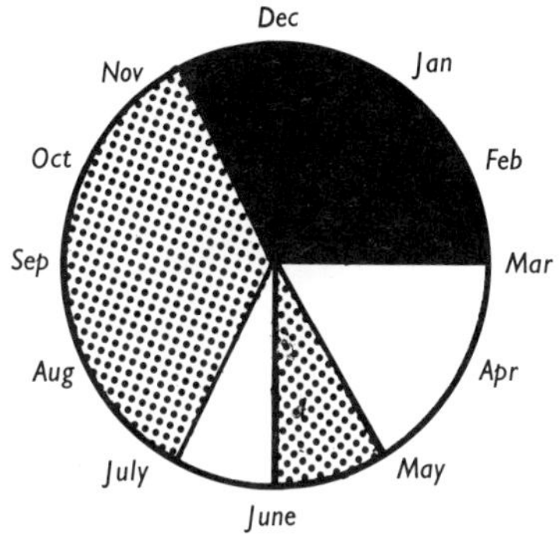

KEY: as in Fig. 197(a)

1. Bonin and Volcano Islands	King (1967)	Eggs present in May.
2. Marianas		Eggs present in Feb. 1931 but no sign of nesting in late June 1959.
3. Carolines		Jan., Feb. 1958—laying.
4. Marshall and Gilbert Islands	Amerson (1969)	Laying Dec.–mid Feb. 1966/67.
(a) Bikar Atoll	,, ,,	Laying Dec.–mid-Feb. 1966/67.
(b) Aradojurik	,, ,,	Laying July–Nov.
5. Taongi Atoll	,, ,,	Laying around Nov.

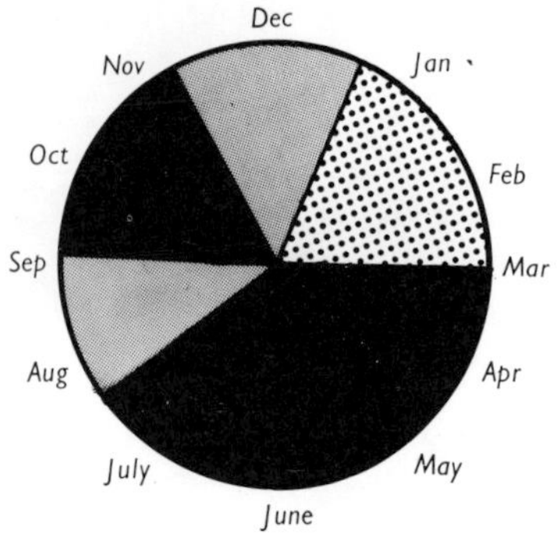

Fig. 197(e)

Central Pacific

KEY: as in Fig.197(a)

1. Hawaiian Leewards		
(a) Kure	Kepler (1969); Woodward (1972)	Laying in all months (1964–69) except Dec. and mainly from Apr.–July. Onset of laying varied between Feb. 8th and April 14th and cessation between July 1st and Aug. 28th.
(b) French Frigate Shoals	Woodward (1972)	Laying mainly Apr.–May.
(c) Necker	Various sources	Laying Mar.–May.
(d) Bird Island Moku Manu	Various sources	Laying Dec.–July.
2. Line Islands		
(a) Fanning Island	Kirby (1925)	Laying Mar.–May.
(b) Christmas Island	Schreiber & Ashmole (1970)	Laying in any month. Peaks Apr.–May and Sept.–Oct. 1967.
(c) Vostok	Clapp & Sibley (1971)	Laying Mar.–May 1965.
3. Phoenix Islands	Various sources	Laying in all months.

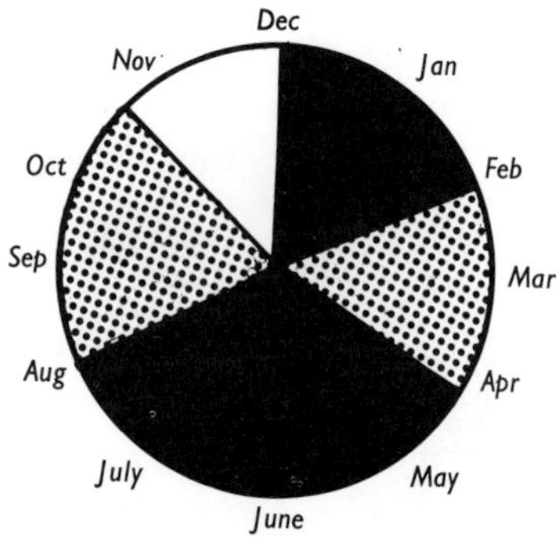

Fig. 197(f)

Eastern Pacific

KEY: as in Fig. 197(a)

1. Clipperton	Various sources	Laying at least between Apr. and Aug.
2. Cocos Islands	Various sources	Mid-Sept.—eggs, newly hatched and downy young. Dec.—eggs and young at all stages of development. No nesting Feb.–Apr. 1963. Therefore eggs laid mainly between May and Oct.
3. Tres Marietas	Grant (1964)	Laying probably occurs in all months, mainly Dec.–May.
4. Revillagigedos (San Benedicto)	Lamb (1910)	Eggs in Apr. 1940. Apr. 1909 free flying young from eggs laid the previous Sept.
5. Isla Isabela (Nayarit)	Howell (in press)	Laying mainly Apr. 1975.

6. Ildefonso	Thayer (1911)	Nov.–March eggs laid.
7. George Island		Laying at least in Jan.
8. Gulf California (general)	From zoological records, supplied by D. Anderson	Mainly Jan.–Feb. in North (earlier than blue-foot), but also Dec. and March–Apr.
9. Baja California del Norte	Bancroft (1927)	Laying starts first week of March.
10. Pearl Islands	Thayer & Bangs (1905)	No nests Mar.–Apr.
11. Taboquilla Island	Hallinan (1924)	Dec. 1915. All birds had eggs.
12. Gorgona	Thayer & Bangs (1905)	Breeding season over in June–Jyly 1904.

3. *Synchronisation*

As shown by Fig. 198 laying on Ascension occurred in concentrated bursts, with a considerable proportion of the total population laying fairly close together in time. Simmons suggests that this was the result of a number of birds responding simultaneously to the trigger of an adequate food situation and was not important as such. He noted that laying persisted for an unusually long time in 1961–62 and coincided with a major influx of fish inshore. Between April 1962 and February 1964 95 per cent of all clutches appeared in months when there were some fish inshore. Nevertheless, it is by no means certain that social factors were not involved. Sub-group synchrony was not investigated, but it would be unusual if it were absent and, if present, would probably be mediated partly through social stimulation. Simmons points out that in the a-seasonal Ascension regime, synchrony would probably not be an advantage and might even lead to competition for food, especially in view of the brown booby's tendency to fish close to the colony. The first proposition is almost certainly correct, but competition of this sort is a dubious proposition and of course sub-group synchrony could have functions in no way associated with optimum utilisation of food (see p. 911).

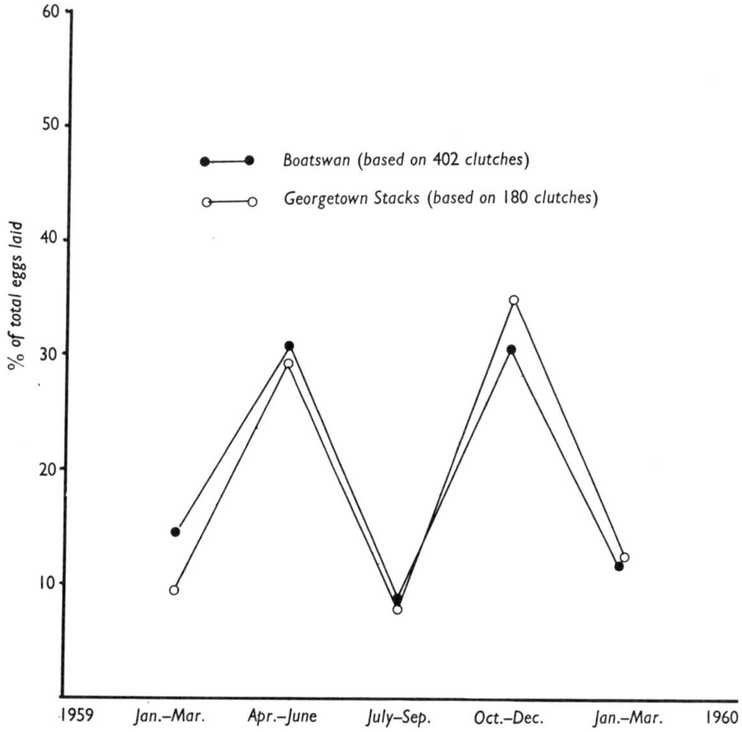

Fig. 198. The timing of laying on Ascension Island (from data in Dorward 1962b).

On Christmas Island it was evident that each of the groups around the perimeter of this sizeable island was significantly synchronised (Fig. 199). Whilst this overall effect certainly could have been produced by simultaneous response to environmental timers, the differences between groups suggests that other factors may have been involved. Again, sub-group synchrony was noted empirically, but I made no adequate investigation.

Gibson-Hill (1950c) noted that on Pulau Perak, a very large colony, the great majority of young were about the same age (10–15 weeks), thus achieving a considerably greater degree of synchronisation than, for example, in the total, scattered population of Christmas Island.

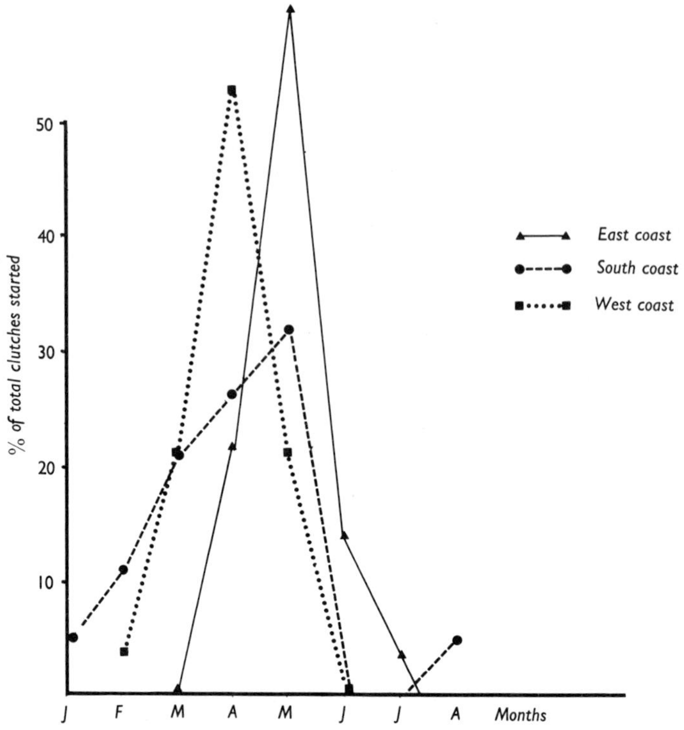

Fig. 199. The pattern of laying in different parts of Christmas Island, Indian Ocean, 1967.

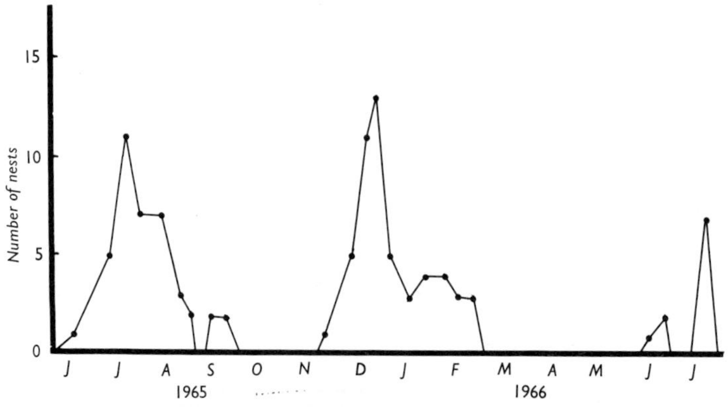

Fig. 200. The (estimated) timing of laying on Little Tobago (from Dinsmore 1972).

Laying had obviously been concentrated between November and January. A visit in March 1973 revealed that nearly all the nests had eggs (Langham & Wells 1974). Thus in both instances, considerable overall synchrony had occurred, but seasonally consistent laying had not. Dinsmore calculated (Fig. 200) that on Little Tobago there had been two clear peaks in 1965.

4. *Length and composition of breeding cycle*

Whilst the length of a complete breeding cycle shows some regional variation which is undoubtedly adaptive, the cycle is nowhere so long that the brown booby would not have time to lay at less than annual intervals. Nevertheless, only in certain parts of its range does it do so. The maximum frequency with which it could breed is determined by the length of the cycle in that particular area and the required rest period if any. The composition of the breeding cycle is thus important both because of its adaptive significance and of its role in partly dictating the frequency of breeding.

The breeding cycle involves the time spent preparing to lay, incubation, chick rearing and any necessary post-breeding activities. The only reasonably fixed periods are incubation (43 days) and rearing the chick to the free-flying stage (about 100 days) and the latter varies with locality, between about 85 and more than 120 days. Post-fledging feeding is highly variable, ranging from little more than a month to as much as 37 weeks on Ascension. Presumably its length is proportional to the prevailing food circumstances at the time when the young are gaining independence. Simmons noted that it was shortest when food was most plentiful (April–September 1962).

(*a*) *Pre-laying period*

The pre-laying (and also the post-breeding) periods are both difficult to assess and of different significance in different regions. On Ascension, apparently, some territories are defended continuously whilst on Kure many are vacated for several months each year. It is thus impossible to compute a figure typical of the species. However, to obtain a minimal length of breeding cycle in a given area, one may assume that at least three to four weeks are normally required for the pair to establish or re-establish themselves on a site and for courtship and copulations. To extend this dramatically is a regional adaptation, but not an essential prerequisite to breeding in the species as a whole, or even, probably, in any region.

TABLE 66

THE SEASONAL DISTRIBUTION OF EGG LAYING IN THE BROWN BOOBY ON CHRISTMAS ISLAND

Group	Area (sq. m)	No. of pairs	Minimum number of clutches started in: Jan	Feb	Mar	Apr	May	Jun	Jul	Aug	Total clutches recorded
South shore terrace	6000	55	2	3	4	7	4	0	0	1	21
					(Mar–May: 15)						
Lip of inland cliff	500	36			0	6	17	4	1	0	28
						(Apr–May: 23)					
Shore terrace and inland cliff		70		3	2				0	0	33
						(Apr–Jun: 28)					
West shore terrace		66	0	2	10	25	10	0	0		47
					(Mar–May: 45)						

It is possible that before our arrival, at the end of March, some clutches had been laid and lost; we could only work back from existing young. Consequently figures for Jan–Mar may be too low if many chicks died and left no trace.

(*b*) *Incubation and care of young*

The incubation period is virtually standard (43 days). There are slight regional differences in egg weight which suggest that the incubation period will vary marginally, but insignificantly in the present context.

Although the growth of the young to fledging is undoubtedly a longer process in impoverished areas such as Ascension, the difference again does not much affect the total length of the breeding cycle. Thus, on Kure and Christmas Island, it is about 95 days and on Ascension perhaps nearer 100. The fact that even underweight birds nevertheless grow their wings almost as quickly as normal ones, however, mitigates the effect of food shortage in lengthening fledging period. The Ascension juveniles may be underweight and slightly smaller when they fledge, but they do so at much the same age as birds from other areas.

(*c*) *Post-fledging period*

The period spent feeding the free-flying juvenile is the major variable in the brown booby's breeding cycle, capable of absorbing more than twice as much time as the rest of the breeding cycle combined. On Kure, post-fledging parental care lasted about six weeks, whilst on Ascension it lasted on average about 17 weeks. This average period, however, was lengthened by some pairs which fed their young for excessively long periods; others were much nearer the probable species' norm of around six weeks.

To this feeding period must be added, finally, the post-breeding attendance period. Here, one runs into the same difficulties as when estimating the pre-laying period, for apparently it lasts in some cases until the onset of the next cycle. Arbitrarily, one may assign two to three weeks as the minimum (or perhaps typical) post-breeding attendance period.

These components of the breeding cycle amount to about 34 weeks on Kure and Christmas Island and 44½ weeks on Ascension (mean 43, median 40, range 25–70 weeks according to Simmons). It thus appears that about eight months is the absolute minimum required for a successful breeding cycle in the brown booby, even where there are no severe food shortages. If brown boobies breed at predominantly eight-monthly intervals on Ascension, successful birds can do so only if they forfeit any recuperation period and shorten the period of post-fledging feeding considerably below the average that, according to Simmons, is required in that area (see below).

5. *Frequency of breeding*

Dorward's survey of the course of laying on Ascension in 1958 and 1959 and information from a few subsequent visits by others, indicated peaks of laying approximately every eight months. Thus, he calculated that there had been a peak of laying in August 1957 and that there were further peaks in April and December 1958, August–September 1959 and March–April 1960, laying thus tending to occur around April and August, rather than non-seasonally. On this time scale subsequent peaks were due in August 1961, April 1962, December 1962 and August 1963. Simmons in fact found peaks in April to September 1962 (unusually protracted); November/December 1962 and late July 1963, and deduced an August 1961 peak. This is reasonable confirmation of the eight-month periodicity.

(*a*) *Frequency in relation to successful breeding*

Simmons took up this interesting eight-month periodicity and suggested that it could be regarded as part of an adaptive complex (p. 476) fitting the brown booby for breeding in an area where food is sometimes, and unpredictably, scarce. He points out that successful breeders cannot *normally* breed once every eight months because the cycle takes longer than this. But he argues that, since most breeding attempts on Ascension fail anyway, an eight-month periodicity can still be regarded as the norm. Dorward (1962b), however, states quite explicitly (p. 182) that, of 13 pairs which laid at the peak of one season, 7 reared a chick and laid again at the peak of the next, i.e. eight months later. No doubt they were able to do this by curtailing the period of post-fledging feeding. Thus, not only failed breeders can lay again eight months after the previous clutch but, given favourable economic circumstances, successful breeders can do the same, though only by forfeiting a rest period. In 26 actual cases, an average of five weeks (range 0–14) elapsed between the end of juvenile begging and the next laying (Simmons 1967b).

(b) Frequency in relation to unsuccessful breeding

The fact remains that most breeding attempts do fail and in these circumstances the eight-month cycle is adaptive because food fluctuates irregularly and by coming into breeding condition at eight-monthly intervals instead of merely annually, brown boobies have a greater chance of coinciding with a favourable period. This advantage would, of course, be greatly increased if the boobies could maintain readiness to breed for a long time, but actually initiate breeding only if food was, or became, adequate. Simmons points out that this in fact happens and he calls this ability to hold breeding condition for a prolonged period ready to respond to the onset of favourable conditions, an 'anticipatory' adaptation and the eight-month periodicity merely 'conventional' because (unlike the mandatory periodicity of the sooty tern, for example, which brings it to successive breeding attempts precisely every 9·6 months, regardless of food conditions) it can be extended or even reduced if necessary.

In terms of the individual, a pair of brown boobies come into breeding condition, lay and either lose egg or chick or rear it. If they lose it (as most do) they are *ready* (but not forced) to lay again eight months (or earlier) after the previous laying. If they are successful, they *may* (depending on food circumstances) take more than eight months between successive layings, but alternatively may lay again eight months later. In such a case, even assuming a very short period of post-fledging feeding, the only respite of any kind between the two cycles would be the early (pre-laying) part of the second cycle, and that is not really a respite. It should be noted, however, that *in the long run*, birds on Ascension do not breed successfully any more frequently than those on Kure or Christmas Island or elsewhere; most Ascension birds fail whereas most Christmas Island and Kure ones succeed. Ascension birds get their 'rests' as a result of failure, but have had the advantage of trying more often and thus increasing their chances of hitting a favourable period.

In any case, laying dates are, it seems, determined by prevailing economic conditions. If these are bad, laying is withheld; if good, it goes ahead, even though there can be no possible guarantee that they will remain so long enough to enable successful breeding. The advantage of laying when food is plentiful is that egg laying, incubation and care of the young chick, all of which require one parent to be constantly on guard and hence unavailable for food gathering, are best done at such a time. If food then becomes scarce, at least the large chick can be left unattended and survive long periods of food shortage.

(c) Effect of success or failure on the timing of the next breeding attempt

A failed breeder need not necessarily wait eight months between successive layings, for the loss of eggs or even chicks can be followed by replacement laying within a month, but presumably only if food is plentiful at the time. Nor, as we have seen, need a successful breeder always take its normal time between successive layings. If food conditions are good, a successful pair *may* go straight on to another brood without a rest period.

If the interval between successive layings can vary so widely, it may be wondered how the clearly observable peaks arise (as in Fig. 198). This could depend on the tendencies (a) for certain periods to be avoided, (b) for large sections of the population to fail in breeding in response to the same inadequate food circumstances and (c) to respond simultaneously to the ameliorating conditions once they are ready to breed. This, however, would lead to eight-monthly cycles (and thus, if April is one of the favoured laying months, to April, December and August layings) only if these months *on average* gave the best chance of success. Thus, despite the unpredictability of food around Ascension, there must be enough predictability to lead to a degree of seasonal laying, for that is what an eight-month cycle necessarily implies. The eight-month cycle is in fact a statistical probability—and that of a relatively low order—rather than anything equivalent to the annual cycle of, say, the gannet. With regard to point (a) above, however, there is evidence (Simmons 1967b) that February can bring exceptionally big waves that destroy chicks from low nests and might reflect, also, unfavourable fishing conditions, but the latter is merely speculation.

Such a variable and potentially quick breeding system implies a number of related adaptations, which Simmons (1967b) summarises as: continuous occupation of the site; sustained relationship of the pair; a long sexual cycle (birds remain in breeding condition for much of the year) and a quick response to favourable conditions. Some other adaptations, such as brood reduction, slow growth and suspension of moult, are general adaptations to a poor food situation and not specifically traits of the brown booby (see Comparative Section). The implications of the behavioural adaptations are discussed on p. 503.

All this is based on the pattern of breeding in populations, but Dorward obtained some information about the breeding frequency of *individuals*, assumed to be the same because they nested in the same place. This gave him 111 pairs for analysis over three seasons:

(i) Six pairs laid late in season A and raised a chick. All missed the peak of season B, four of them altogether and two laying late. All six laid again at the peak of season C. So two thirds of these pairs bred twice in two years, but their two layings were *not* in the same month each time; when laying number one was in May or June, laying two was in August of the following year. The other third laid out of phase with the eight-month cycle for their second attempt but this must have failed, since they laid a third time, in phase again, at the peak of season C. All six were therefore in phase in season A and C and (even assuming season C to be successful for all) none reared more than two broods (i.e. two chicks) in the three seasons.

(ii) Thirteen pairs laid about the peak of season B and raised a chick. Seven laid again at the peak of season C whilst the other six missed the peak but laid later (possibly they, too, hit the peak but lost their eggs and replaced them). Thus, over half of this sample did breed successfully and yet managed to do so again after eight months.

(iii) Thirteen pairs laid about the peak of season B and hatched chicks which all died at varying ages. Eleven of the pairs laid again at the peak of season C (a little earlier than group (ii)).

(iv) Seventy-nine pairs laid at varying times throughout season B but lost their eggs. Seventy of them laid again close to the peak of season C. Nine were not known to lay at the peak but did so later.

This valuable set of records establishes a number of points:

Brown boobies can breed successfully, about once every eight months, but probably rather few do so.

Some birds miss entire eight-month cycles if forced to miss part, and so remain 'in phase'.

Birds which fail at various stages in a cycle can breed again at the next suitable time (peak period) because they do not have to take eight months between successive layings.

Since the system just described has, it seems, evolved to enable the brown booby to glean the most chances of successfully completing the first phases of the breeding cycle in the hostile environment around Ascension, it is not to be expected that elsewhere the same strategy will be followed. Nor is it, for in the Central Pacific, where food seems considerably more predictable and breeding success is higher, the breeding cycle is annual. As might be expected, the behaviour which has to occur to make the Ascension eight-month cycle feasible (constant site attendance and year-long maintenance of the pair bond) is not found in areas where the cycle is annual.

On Christmas Island, Indian Ocean, the breeding cycle is probably annual. Although there is no conclusive evidence, the very considerable tendency to limit laying to April–May (p. 467) would seem to preclude any possibility of an eight-month periodicity. Also, Gibson-Hill (1947) specifically records that he noted individual nesting sites to be used annually, between the same dates, and in two cases they were occupied for three successive seasons by the same pair.

(d) Non-breeding years

Dorward reports that although 109 pairs which bred in 1958 did so again the following year, 77 other pairs probably did not breed. Thirteen of the 77 pairs were ringed and of these, four were seen back at their old nest sites, but the other nine were not seen. Since no ringed pairs (32 cases) changed sites, it is unlikely that many of the missing pairs had done so. Ten of the 77 pairs may have nested but been recorded as new nests because the nest marker had disappeared, but even allowing for this and the possibility that a handful changed sites, there remains a substantial number that did not breed in the second season.

Of these non-breeding pairs, some had been successful the previous time whilst others had failed, early and late. The exact interpretation of these interesting results is impossible because of complications caused by the 'conventional' nature of the eight-month cycle (see p. 475). Thus, without precise dates it cannot be judged how much of an eight-month period was in fact missed by the non-breeding pairs.

Clearly, however, a significant proportion of the breeding population failed, (1) to breed successfully and then begin a new cycle reasonably early in the next eight-month period, (2) to begin a new cycle about eight months after the beginning of a failed attempt. Whatever the details, there was obviously much unused breeding potential, even of experienced breeders that had enjoyed a long recuperative period and even when some of the colony were initiating new breeding attempts. Why these pairs failed to initiate a new breeding attempt is not known.

OTHER ASPECTS OF BREEDING ECOLOGY

There remain a number of aspects of brown booby breeding ecology about which something (usually little) is known. These are discussed below.

1. *Food*

The brown booby's principal food items are flying fish and squid, but many other species have been recorded. Dorward examined 56 regurgitations from brown boobies, mainly (77 per cent) from adults and the remainder from chicks. By far the largest number of items measured between 5–7cm; the actual composition being:

4cm or less (13); 5–7cm (425); 8–10cm (10); c.12cm (1); 15–20cm (42); 21–25cm (11); 26–30cm (1); 35cm (1); 37cm (1). The species composition is given in Table 67.

Two-thirds of the Ascension samples contained small fish and one-half, large, which was a higher proportion of samples containing small fish than for the white booby (one-half). When only small fish were taken, the average number per sample was 20 and when only large fish were present, one or two were the rule (mean 1·6). Few of the small fish were young of

TABLE 67

THE SPECIES COMPOSITION OF REGURGITATIONS FROM THE BROWN BOOBY ON ASCENSION ISLAND (from Dorward 1962b)

	Species	No. of fish	No. of samples in which it figured
Large	*Exocoetus volitans*	46	26
	Scomberesox saurus	1	1
	Selar crumenophthalmus	6	6
	Benthodesmus simonyi	2	1
Small	*Oxyporhamphus micropterus*	9	6
	Ophioblennius webbii	260	17
	Engraulis spp.	75	4
	Benthodesmus simonyi	34*	3
	Holocentrus ascensionis	38	10
	Centrolophus niger	20	4
	Decapterus sp.	10	1
	Cephalopods (*Hyaloteuthis* spp?)	2	2

* 30 were from one sample

the larger species, even though these were obviously present in the surrounding waters (as evidenced by their occurrence in samples from fairy terns, noddies and wideawakes). Despite the brown booby's tendency to fish inshore, where one might imagine it could pick up many species not available elsewhere, it took only two more species of small fish than did the white booby.

Although 21 of the 56 samples were obtained in May 1958, when there were most chicks, the others being more or less evenly distributed over the other months, it is likely that the Dorward samples represented the brown booby's diet for much, if not all, of the year. There was some evidence that different species figure more prominently at certain times of year. *Ophioblennius*, in particular, seemed prone to be taken between January and May (11 out of 34 samples) and November to January (8 out of 11 samples), whilst between May and September it did not occur once in 9 samples. When taken, it was favoured, particularly by brown boobies and at these times formed a larger proportion of the diet than did flying fish. In July and September 4 out of 6 samples consisted entirely of *Engraulis* and there were no flying fish in this period. *Holocentrus* appeared in half the 20 samples in May, once in June and not at all at other times.

The samples thus indicated that the boobies specialised quite heavily in different species at different times, no doubt adjusting their efforts to make the most of the temporarily commonest, or most available, species.

Simmons notes that Ascension brown boobies took advantage of the lengthy (several months) invasions of inshore waters by *Selar crumenophthalmus*, taking, at other times, the inshore needlefish *Scomberesox saurus*. Inshore fishing for *Selar* is a major trait in Ascension brown boobies).

Other species recorded in the brown booby's diet are *Hemiramphus* spp. parrot fish, flat-fish and prawns (Bahamas). Gibson-Hill records that on Christmas Island its chief food is the flying fish *Cypsilurus bahiensis*, the majority of birds which he dissected containing one to three fish, ranging from 9–18cm. The largest was 27·2cm.

On Christmas Island, we recorded a regurgitated fish weighing c. 300g. On Bedout Island, Serventy (1952) saw a young brown booby disgorge a *Rastrelliger kanagurta* some 250–280mm long and about 450g; another bird disgorged two smaller specimens. In one small area of the colony other food species noted were *Trachurus*-like spp., *Chorinemus lysan*, large flying fish and squid. Serventy comments that there were no remains of *Harengula*, although these small herrings are abundant in the adjoining seas.

2. *Annual mortality*

Most of the small breeding population on Kure were ringed and from the rate of disappearance of birds (ringed as adults) it was clear that they were being replaced by young; it is unlikely that any were temporarily nomadic. From the data given in Woodward (1972) one may calculate the annual mortality rate for adults and the mortality-plus-emigration for young birds. (Table 68).

TABLE 68

SURVIVAL OF BROWN BOOBIES ON KURE ATOLL (from Woodward 1972)

Year	Number ringed as chicks	Number back on Kure, aged 2	Number alive at age: 3	4	5	6	7*
1962	18	6 (33·3%)	5	4	4	3	3
1963	30	8 (26·6%)	8	7	7	4	–
1964	29	8 (27·6%)	8	8	4	–	–
1965	23	1 (4·4%)	1	1	–	–	–

* Records run up to 1969 only.

From Table 68 it can be seen that from a total of 23 birds alive and back on Kure at the age of two, 22 or 95·6 per cent survive another year, and similarly of those 22, 20 or 90·9 per cent survive another year. Thus, the average annual mortality for these two years, based on a reasonably large sample, is 6·8 per cent. This is very close to the figure for the white booby and the gannet. A figure may be obtained, also, from birds ringed as adults. Thus, out of 66 birds ringed as adults a variable number of years prior to 1966, and breeding in 1966, 41 were still present in 1969. Thus 25/66 or 38 per cent had disappeared in three years, which is roughly 12·6 per cent per annum. One bird, banded as an adult in 1959 and still breeding in 1969, was at least 13 years old. Since some others would have been alive but unrecorded, this figure is reasonably close to the 7 per cent obtained from birds ringed as chicks. Proof that a proportion of ringed adults are either missed or absent comes from Woodward's figures, which sometimes show an increase in the percentage of ringed birds known to be alive in successive years. Simmons gives a figure of 4·5–7·7 per cent for annual adult mortality on Ascension and considers that the lower figure is the most realistic (this would give a life expectancy of about 25 years). Thus 93·3 per cent of 45 males and 86·8 per cent of 53 females survived from 1962 to 1964.

The average figure of 26·75 per cent annual adult mortality suggested by Table 70 will be much too high because some birds may miss breeding for a year or may escape detection.

TABLE 69

SURVIVAL FROM YEAR TO YEAR OF ADULT BROWN BOOBIES ON KURE (from Woodward 1972)

1959	1960	1961	1962	1963	1964	1965	1966	1967	1968	1969
9	2	2	2	2	2	2	2	2	1	1
	0									
		0								
			22	16	16	14	11	9	7	6
				28	18	18	18	16	15	13
					42	31	26	23	18	16
						17	13	11	10	8
							12	8	7	5
								7	4	3
									9	2

The bold figures are the number of adults ringed in that year.

TABLE 70

PERCENTAGE ANNUAL ADULT MORTALITY OF BROWN BOOBIES ON KURE (from Woodward 1972)

Year A	No. of adults alive in year A	No. of these adults alive in year A+1	Percent mortality
1959	9	2	77·8
1962	24	18	25
1963	46	36	21·7
1964	78	65	16·7
1965	82	70	14·6
1966	82	69	15·9
1967	76	62	18·4
1968	71	54	23·9

Nevertheless, the lowest figure (14·6 per cent mortality in 1965), even as it stands, is reasonably low. The factors mentioned above, together with the distinct possibility that some boobies are killed by man, make it highly probable that the 'natural' adult mortality figure is in fact less than 7 per cent; in other words very comparable to that of other sulids (see Comparative Section).

The mortality (or emigration) in the first year of life is of course vastly higher than the above figures. Thus of the cohorts ringed in 1959 and 1962–66 inclusive, only 4·6, 33·3, 30, 27·6, 13 and 8·8 per cent were seen back on Kure the following year, an average 'loss' of some 80 per cent. Since some of this must have been due to emigration, the actual mortality in the first year was perhaps around 70 per cent, of which probably a significant amount was caused by man. This is explicitly suggested by Woodward on the ground that the juvenile brown booby's dispersal takes it to inhabited areas, where it may be killed, presumably for bait or food.

3. *Age of first breeding*

There are no concrete records, but indications that breeding occurs, at the earliest, in the third year. An immature male, still with the mottled belly of the third (possibly second) year, and still honking like a female, was paired with an adult female and had a small chick, on Johnston Atoll in the Pacific (Amerson 1971). This is a highly unusual, if not unique, record (for a discussion of plumage and breeding in sulids, see the Comparative Section). There were indications that most brown boobies born on Kure were then absent for the first two years of life, returning during their third or even fourth year. Some three-year-old birds bred.

4. *Movements*

Young brown boobies wander extensively. An immature ringed on Kure on October 4th 1963 was captured at Wake Atoll on June 19th 1966 and later back at Kure on January 2nd 1967. Woodward (1972) suggests that there is a southerly dispersal after fledging. As in the case of the white booby, some birds which bred on Kure had been ringed as nestlings elsewhere (Eastern Island of Midway Atoll and Howland Island). The latter is a rare instance of a bird moving from a central equatorial Pacific island to the northwest Hawaiian group. But even more interesting, an adult male ringed whilst breeding on Pearl and Hermes Reef in 1967, bred at Kure in 1969. This is the first booby definitely recorded breeding on two different islands.

Extensive dispersal was shown by four birds ringed as nestlings on Kure and recovered:

Marshall Islands 1,388 nautical miles (aged 7 months);
Central Moluccas, Indonesia 3564 nautical miles (aged 21 months);
Two at Funafuti Atoll, Ellice Is. 2187 nautical miles (aged 8 months), (aged 2 years).

A Kure-ringed bird has also been recovered on Majuro and a Midway bird on Taka. There is also movement between islands in a group, as in Bikar Atoll (ringed Bikar, recovered Likiep (2)). The situation in the Central Pacific, littered with islands, is likely to differ from that on Ascension (Atlantic), Christmas Island (Indian Ocean) and other isolated islands, where the local population has little or no chance of alternative accommodation. Occasionally brown boobies turn up on inland waters. An immature lived on Parker Dam, Colorado River, for some time.

5. *Fidelity to site*

As mentioned previously, Gibson-Hill recorded brown boobies using the same site in successive years and believed them to be the same pairs. Dorward reports that 32 ringed birds nested successively in exactly the same spot and none in different spots. Simmons found that 90 per cent of birds with 'favourable' sites, 55 per cent with 'sub-optimal' and 75 per cent with 'unsuitable' sites remained faithful to them throughout 1962–64. Males showed greater site fidelity than did females.

6. *Fidelity to mate*

There are no figures on this comparable to those for the white booby, but Gibson-Hill believed that pairs often remain together. Dorward implies the same and Simmons explicitly states that, in the system of continuous site-occupation which operates in conjunction with the eight-month breeding periodicity, pairs remain together. 35/42 (83·3 per cent) stayed together from 1962–64; three partners disappeared and there were two divorces. Simmons uncovered complex extra-marital and other relationships within his community. 'Association' ranged from full acceptance, including copulation, to uneasy tolerance. Of 84 birds already paired in 1962, 29 (20 males and 9 females) were later involved in associations. The paired males were usually from 'favourable' sites and tended to associate mainly with unpaired females, 'sex' being, apparently, the attraction. Paired females associated mostly with paired males owning 'favourable' sites (successful breeding was largely confined to such sites). Of 25 unpaired birds, more than half associated with paired ones, females again being attracted to paired males (11 cases) more than vice versa (2 cases). *All* unpaired 'associating' females came from 'poor' sites, whilst seven out of eight such males came from 'favourable' sites. Most birds had only one associate, a few had two and two females each had three. Simmons distinguished association from bigamy, the latter giving rise to eggs, and noted eight bigamous males and two females, the males mainly with unpaired females.

7. *Clubs and roosting*

It seems that brown boobies are less prone to congregate in Clubs than are most other sulids. Whilst Dorward was able to recognise substantial congregations of white boobies on Boatswain Bird Island, he could not find any brown booby Clubs. Immature birds were rarely seen and never more than one or two at a time. This is to be noted, in an area where there are few alternative islands upon which immature birds could congregate. Simmons found several day roosts (inshore rocks) much used by immature brown boobies, often more than a hundred at a time.

Similarly on Kure, sub-adult brown boobies formed an insignificant proportion of the population, although a very few were present every month. Thus, in May and June, one to three were found each census night and between May and early August only six different individuals were captured. However, it must be remembered that the Kure population is very small in the first place. Roosts, sometimes of several thousands of birds, have been noted in the Gulf of California (Anderson, pers. comm.). On Kure, non-breeding birds roosted at various points outside the breeding area (Central Plain) whilst off-duty breeders usually roosted on their territories, though some roosted on the beach. It was thought that young birds began roosting on the Central Plain in the year before breeding for the first time.

The information on movements (p. 480) shows that young brown boobies travel considerable distances from their birth place and many are probably mainly nomadic until they take up breeding territories. Then, too, their habit of breeding in very small groups or even linearly may subtend a habit of returning to these to breed. Thus, immatures would be widely scattered rather than congregated in central Clubs. There are indications that one does find a few immatures scattered among breeding pairs.

8. *Relationships with other species*

Brown boobies are very often sympatric with white and red-footed boobies, and with other tropical blue-water species, perhaps most importantly with sooty terns and with some albatrosses. In the Gulf of California and off Mexico they are sympatric with blue-foots.

They are never in direct contact with the arboreal red-foot, but can be with the white booby, which is a more powerful species and probably dominant in any interspecific conflict. In fact, the brown booby's preference for extremely steep ground often sets it apart and even where, as often happens, they share common ground, the two species do not intermingle. Dorward rarely saw interspecific fighting but suspected that, at least on the plateau edges, the brown boobies were there by courtesy of the larger birds. Kepler records that on Kure, on two occasions, brown boobies were chased vigorously or received aggressive display from white boobies.

There are scattered records of brown boobies pecking or even killing nesting sooty terns, but this is an infrequent event, resulting from the few instances in which the fringe of the ternery encroaches upon the odd brown booby territory. In such circumstances the white booby, also, has been known to kill the tern.

Probably the most ecologically significant interspecific relationship is that with frigates, principally *Fregata minor* and *F. ariel*, which steal fish from the boobies and are probably often responsible for the chipped beaks which one frequently sees. The general aspects of this are explored more fully under the red-foot, which is probably the frigate's main victim.

9. *Predators*

On St. Paul's Rocks land crabs *Birgus* spp. have been known to kill and attempt to eat young boobies, after the parent has been disturbed by man. We suspected that this occasionally happened on Christmas Island, where *Birgus latro* can reach a formidable size.

The rat is the commonest man-introduced pest that might be expected to destroy at least the chicks of the brown booby. However, on the Dahlacs (Red Sea) it is said that they are not much affecting the boobies. Rats are present on most of the central Pacific islands and on some create havoc among nesting albatrosses, actually eating the adults alive, but I do not have any specific records of their effects on boobies.

Cats have been responsible for the destruction of seabirds on many islands and probably destroyed boobies on Ascension. Simmons recorded eight adults and ten juveniles killed by cats on Georgetown Stacks. The extraordinary case of the wild pigs destroying thousands of white and brown boobies on Clipperton has already been described (p. 446). For the effects of man as predator see the Comparative Section.

At sea, especially around the nesting islands, many boobies must be taken by sharks and perhaps other large predatory fish. Newly-fledged juveniles must be especially vulnerable. The high incidence of birds with damaged feet may be due mainly to attacks by fish. The white underparts could be adaptive as camouflage against attacks from beneath.

SUMMARY

1. The importance of the brown booby's blue-water environment as a principal factor in its ecology is stressed.

2. The breeding habitat is, by preference, steep or even cliff-type, but the brown booby is capable of using a very wide range. Density is highly variable but usually low and group size is small. Where large colonies occur, it is as a result of the shortage of suitable islands.

3. The nest is often a very substantial structure; not found in any other ground nesting booby except the Peruvian.

4. The clutch is usually two, often one and very occasionally three. The egg weighs about 55g.

5. Five days elapse between first and second egg and hatching is similarly asynchronous. The incubation period is 43 days.

6. Hatching success is between 60 and 70 per cent except where massive desertion occurs (as occasionally on Ascension).

7. The development of the chick is described.

8. The limited information available on food indicates preference for a smaller size of prey than that taken by the white booby.

9. The growth of the brown booby chick is fairly slow and differs with locality.

10. The chick takes about 96 days to grow to fledging age but may take as long as 120 when retarded by food shortage.

11. Post-fledging feeding is astonishingly variable in length, from little more than a month to (on Ascension) up to 37 weeks. The species' average is probably around six weeks.

12. Breeding success in a 'normal' area is probably in the region of 75 per cent of pairs producing a fledged youngster. In an area of very poor food it may be perhaps as low as 10 per cent.

13. The two-egg clutch is definitely adaptive and on Kure, in 10–20 per cent of cases of two-egg clutches, the second egg was responsible for producing the fledged chick, although

in only one certain and one probable case on Kure and one on Ascension were two chicks reared. Nevertheless, the considerably higher breeding success of pairs which produce two eggs rather than one, cannot be due solely or even mainly to the contribution of the second egg and may be attributable to some other factor(s) associated with the larger clutch—perhaps experience (age) of the female.

14. Replacement laying occurs and 5·8 per cent of fledged young on Kure and 17 per cent on Christmas Island came from replacement clutches.

15. The breeding regime of the brown booby varies with locality. Often, probably usually, it is a more or less annual breeder, but on Ascension the breeding periodicity is about eight months. This does not mean that any pair raises one chick every eight months, for the complete cycle usually takes longer than this. It means, however, that a failed pair will come into peak breeding condition eight months after the start of the previous cycle. Thus, since most pairs do fail on Ascension, there are waves of laying at roughly eight-monthly intervals. Even where breeding is annual, there is no well defined season, but a wide spread of laying.

16. The breeding cycle typically takes about 30–34 weeks, but may take over a year on Ascension (and presumably at other equally impoverished stations).

17. Synchronisation of local groups occurs, even though an entire island will not be synchronised.

18. The annual adult mortality rate is about 5 to 7 per cent or less. Where it is higher one may suspect mortality due to man's activities. Mortality in the first year is probably around 70 per cent. Expectation of life after the second year may be at least 25 years.

19. Breeding may well occur, at the earliest, in the third year.

20. Non-breeding years (or on Ascension, 8-month periods) occur.

21. Young brown boobies disperse widely (recoveries up to 3564km). They may breed on islands other than the one where they were born.

22. Brown boobies usually retain site and mate in successive years. There is a record of a brown booby breeding on two different islands.

23. Brown boobies apparently do not form conspicuous Clubs, but do form large roosts.

24. Brown boobies often breed alongside white, but typically do not intermingle, perhaps due to habitat preferences reinforced by exclusion by the more powerful white booby.

4. BREEDING BEHAVIOUR

INTRODUCTION

The brown booby's habit of nesting in well spaced-out small groups and on steep sites is an important determinant of much of its behaviour. Simmons (1967b) made a special point of this in his own studies on Ascension, which enlarged Dorward's (1962a) original account, and it provides some interesting points of comparison with the blue-footed booby which, also, is a well-dispersed breeder but on flat ground. Moreover, the blue-foot is probably phylogenetically more closely related to the brown than to any other except the Peruvian booby. It is also worth noting points of contrast between the similarly ground-nesting white booby, with which the brown is sympatric throughout much of its range. Equally important, however, is the considerable adaptability of the brown booby, for it sometimes nests densely in huge colonies. It certainly is not limited to small groups or a linear type of distribution along island fringes, though these are common.

My own observations on this species were made on the Indian Ocean Christmas Island, where brown boobies are one of the two most numerous seabirds, nesting in small groups right round the island.

ESTABLISHMENT AND MAINTENANCE OF TERRITORY

1. *Aerial and ground reconnaissance*

The brown booby, particularly the light and agile male, is extremely aerial and reconnoitres the breeding area and sometimes attacks rivals from the air. Aerial pursuits are also common.

Simmons records that unpaired females may establish sites, which males visit, as well as the other way round (the usual way), a most interesting facet, for which there is no parallel in

PLATE I

A group of Atlantic gannets on a semi-isolated stack, Bass Rock.

Photo: J. B. Nelson

PLATE 2. A dense colony of Cape gannets, Bird Island, Lamberts Bay. This species often nests far more densely than its Atlantic counterpart, preferably on flat, uncluttered ground. The dirt on the backs of some birds has been transferred from the males' webs during copulation. Note the proximity of the guano-processing factory.

Photo: G. M. Dunnet

PLATE 3. A Cape gannet brooding a three-week-old chick, on the guano-nest. After the Peruvian booby, this species is the most commercially valuable sulid. Notice the thicker black 'spectacles' and longer gular strip, compared with the Atlantic or Australasian; this may be a heat-regulating device. Notice that most birds in this picture are holding wings away from body, to lose heat. *Photo*: M. P. Harris

PLATE 4. The colony of Australasian gannets at Cape Kidnappers, New Zealand. They never nest as densely as the Cape gannet. The tail is usually partly white, compared with the all-black one of the Cape bird.

Photo: G. M. Dunnet

PLATE 5. Blue-footed boobies on nest site, Hood Island, Galapagos; male in nest hollow. There is no functional nest. The female is much larger than the male and has an apparently larger pupil.

Photo: J. B. Nelson

PLATE 6. Nesting mass of Peruvian boobies on Guañape Island, Peru. The larger chick in the foreground is about three weeks old. This species can use cliffs or flat ground and forms the largest colonies of any sulid.

Photo: J. B. Nelson

PLATE 7. The Peruvian booby on guano nest, Guañape Island. These boobies lay the biggest clutch (4) of any sulid, a fact which is related to their superabundant food (anchovies) nearby.

Photo: J. B. Nelson

PLATE 8. The colony of white boobies on Bosun Island, Ascension, illustrating unusually high density. This species, as here, often utilises nesting sites exposed to extreme sun and heat, a fact to which their conspicuous facial skin (hence 'masked' booby) and exceptionally white plumage may relate as heat regulating devices. *Photo*: D. F. Dorward

PLATE 9. Female white booby shading three-week chick, Tower Island, Galapagos. Gaping, gular fluttering and wing-loosening all help to dissipate heat. A chick of this age is unable to thermo-regulate and would quickly die of heat-stress. *Photo*: J. B. Nelson

PLATE 10

Pair of brown boobies (male on left) nesting on coralline detritus amongst pinnacles, shore terrace, Christmas Island (Indian Ocean). The nest is typically substantial, possibly because this species prefers steep sites, where such a nest could be advantageous.

Photo: J. B. Nelson

PLATE 11.
Female red-footed booby, normal white morph, with six-week chick in mangroves, Aldabra. Notice the yellowish head, as in gannets.

Photo: J. B. Nelson

PLATE 12
Red-foot (white-tailed brown morph) on unusual site (cliff ledge), Ascension.

Photo: D. F. Dorward

PLATE 13
Red-foot (all brown morph) on Tower Island, Galapagos, with three-month chick begging for food. It is nesting in a low shrub, *Cryptocarpus pyriformis.*

Photo: J. B. Nelson

PLATE 14

Female Abbott's booby, high in jungle tree, Christmas Island, with two-month-old chick, which soon will closely resemble an adult male. The colour of the bill is the diagnostic difference between the sexes. This substantial nest will disintegrate during the winter rains and wind, leaving the feathered juvenile to sit on the branch for up to eight months more before becoming independent. Most die.

Photo: J. B. Nelson

other sulids, with the possible exception of the blue-foot. Dorward indicates that it is the male who actually chooses the site, the female joining him there, probably in response to his advertising display (q.v.). But in many places the exact location of the site is not critical and beginnings are made more than once before the definitive nest hollow is acquired.

2. *Flight circuiting and outposting*

In the early stages of breeding, site owners frequently patrol from the air. Sometimes, in this territorial and sexual display context, they fly in a distinctive 'butterfly' manner, exaggerating the height of the upstroke and using a slower wing beat. Several other birds (for example, swallow-tailed gull, tropic bird, rook, razor-bill) use comparable display flights. They may land with wings held conspicuously V-shaped. Often, males on vantage points react to overflying birds by vigorous 'chuff chuff' calling accompanied by an aggressive display (see below) or by some displacement activity such as touching nest material. The male may pick up nest material and hold it high, whilst calling explosively. Although he may point towards the rival, the action is not ritualised but is merely aggressive calling directed at the other bird.

(*a*)

(*b*)

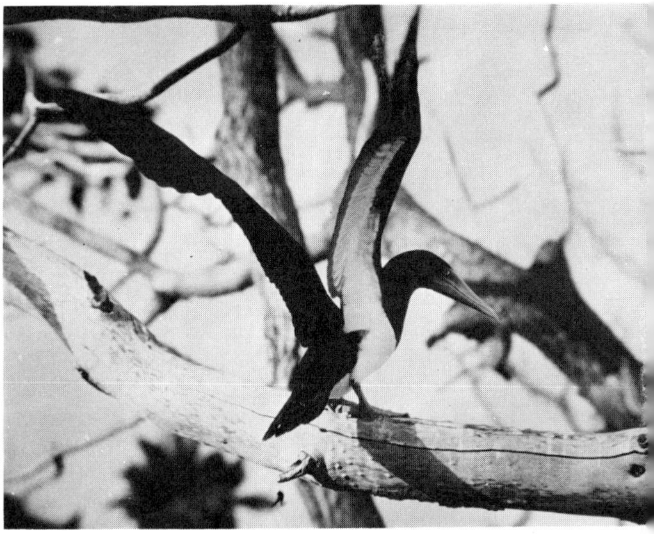

(*c*)

Fig. 201(a–c)

Flight circuiting and outposting: the male is particularly agile in the air. (a) Leaving a perch on a dead bough; (b) returning to this vantage point; (c) leaving a coral pinnacle.

3. *Fighting*

Brown boobies are aggressive birds. They fight strenuously to acquire and maintain a breeding site and sometimes damage or even kill opponents (at least, Bailey (1906) describing a dense colony on White Rock, Gulf of California, says ,'sometimes one would catch the other by the wing while he retaliated by getting his adversary by the neck, these cases often proving fatal to one or other'). A fight between two males which I watched on Christmas Island was fierce and lasted over five minutes, with the usual bill-gripping, pushing with extended neck and wing-flailing. Intruders are supplanted by the owner, who flies in with calling (a normal sulid characteristic) and plunges down on to the intruder in a shallow trajectory (Fig. 202), as if plunge diving for food, crashing on to it and seizing it by the bill. In fighting initiated from the ground, the bill is usually grasped, but sometimes the head or neck. Site owners may chase intruders for some distance and Simmons alludes to a ritualised 'fight in the air' but without giving details.

4. *Wing-flailing*

Aggressive interactions (lunging or jabbing) between rivals are sometimes interspersed with violent downward movements of the partly opened wings—behaviour which may also be directed against human intruders, accompanied by rapid forward darting of the beak and intense calling.

5. *Jabbing*

Brown boobies use jabbing movements against rivals (Fig. 208). Simmons describes them as an unritualised lunging of the bill towards the opponent, with concomitant ruffing of the head feathers, developing on occasions into a Mutual Jabbing match. In fact, however, the Jabbing or Sparring which occurs between mates (q.v.) is undoubtedly ritualised and is extremely difficult, if not impossible, to differentiate from that which occurs between rivals. In this respect, the brown booby is similar, in particular, to the blue-foot, the Peruvian and the white, all of which perform apparently identical Jabbing against rivals and 'against' mates. Brown boobies, probably as a result of their spaced nesting, tend to use Jabbing (a close-range agonistic behaviour) less than do white and Peruvian boobies, in this resembling the blue-foot (also a spaced nester). The female (which is larger) also defends the territory with extreme vigour.

Fig. 202

Dispelling rival by slanting dive (much used in fishing).

6. *Forward Head Waving or Bowing*

In the early phases of breeding, the brown booby often follows the inflying and aggressive calling by a display which I have termed Forward Head Waving (Fig. 203) because it most resembles the analogous display in the red-foot. It lands, and with stretched neck, sways its head forwards and down, from side to side, keeping its wings closed and calling. Sometimes the downward swings are more or less central and the nest material may be bitten or grasped and lifted, although the behaviour is certainly ritualised rather than an intended nest-biting movement. The downward swings often include small, jerky movements, which sometimes make the display rather like the Yes/No Headshaking of the white booby. When a Forward Head Waving bird at the same time picks up and holds a piece of nest material the behaviour seems exactly comparable to that in which the red-foot picks up and holds a twig whilst Forward Head Waving. A bird which picks up material may then roll it up and down its bill and turn it as though it were a fish to be swallowed head first, the act of handling passing over into food handling. From time to time in circumstances eliciting aggression the display may be performed on the site. A typical situation of this kind is during a 'threesome'—a territorial and sexual dispute involving much flying in to displace the rival, followed by excited whistling and Forward Head Waving. When oriented at a rival, the swinging movement may be performed with the head and bill actually inclined upwards.

Simmons suggests that the brown booby lacks a post-landing display, but goes on to describe Bowing as the site ownership display. He says it consists of bowing exaggeratedly towards the ground whilst calling and mentions that the bird may act aggressively towards nest material or even lift it. This and Forward Head Waving seem to be the same and as mentioned it does occur after landing on the site. Probably the movement is derived from biting nest material rather than arranging it, but the two types of nest handling behaviour are often difficult to separate and one grades into the other. However, the marked forward leaning swing looks quite different from the normal bending-down-to-touch-nest-material.

The display is less stereotyped than, for example, the Yes/No Headshaking of the white booby or the Yes Headshake of the blue-foot and is performed less frequently, but is nevertheless functionally an antagonistic site ownership display which may also be performed in the post-landing situation.

A bird may Forward Head Wave when its partner flies in to the territory. When partners are at separate points in the territory either or both may Bow 'at' the other, typically at rather low intensity, the bird lowering its head close to the body with bill pointing vertically downwards, towards the front or to one side of the breast or near the ventral flanks. The context in which it occurs would be consistent with an interpretation of this as low intensity Forward Head Waving. Thus, a partner flying in, or at some distance, has 'intruder valence'. Simmons, I believe correctly, regards this sexual Bowing as clearly homologous with antagonistic Bowing and, as mentioned, I believe that antagonistic Bowing and Forward Head Waving are the same thing. He mentions that in the sexual situation birds may call less as they Bow, and that low intensity versions may pass over into functional arrangement of nest material. It is typically prefaced by an intent look at the partner (see Staring, p. 490).

Fig. 203. A territorial display (Forward Head Waving).

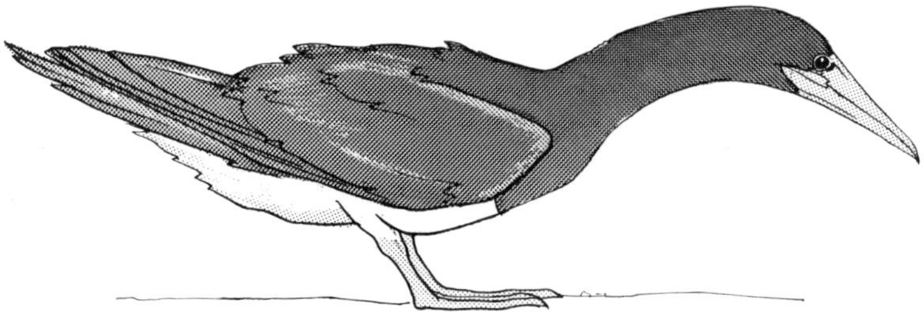

Thus Forward Head Waving (Bowing) in the brown booby is clearly fully comparable to the display of the same name in the red-foot, or to Yes/No Headshaking in the white booby and Yes Headshaking in blue-footed and Peruvian boobies, which also may be directed at the partner as well as to territorial rivals.

FORMATION AND MAINTENANCE OF PAIR

1. *Sky-pointing*

When an unmated male has acquired a breeding site he must then gain a partner. Chiefly in this context he performs a highly ritualised Sky-pointing display which he directs towards a female nearby or flying over. Typically the displaying male is on his territory but, unlike other boobies, he commonly Sky-points in flight, following the female when she flies from the site and Sky-pointing whilst gliding behind her (Fig. 204).

A Sky-pointing bird stretches his neck, points his bill about vertically upwards and raises his tail to some extent, but keeps his wings closed though slightly loosened (Fig. 204). During the display he utters a wheezy, disyllabic whistle which has individually recognisable characteristics. Several Sky-pointings may be performed in succession. Simmons gives the process of actually raising the head—a notably rapid movement—a special name (the Throw-back) although it is not an autonomous movement. In that case, the vertical, stationary position is 'the' Sky-point and the whole thing becomes the Salute (not to be confused with the quite different action in the blue-foot and Peruvian). Simmons also distinguishes the behaviour which immediately precedes the actual Sky-pointing movement as the Stretch-up-and-stare. The

(*b*)

(*a*)

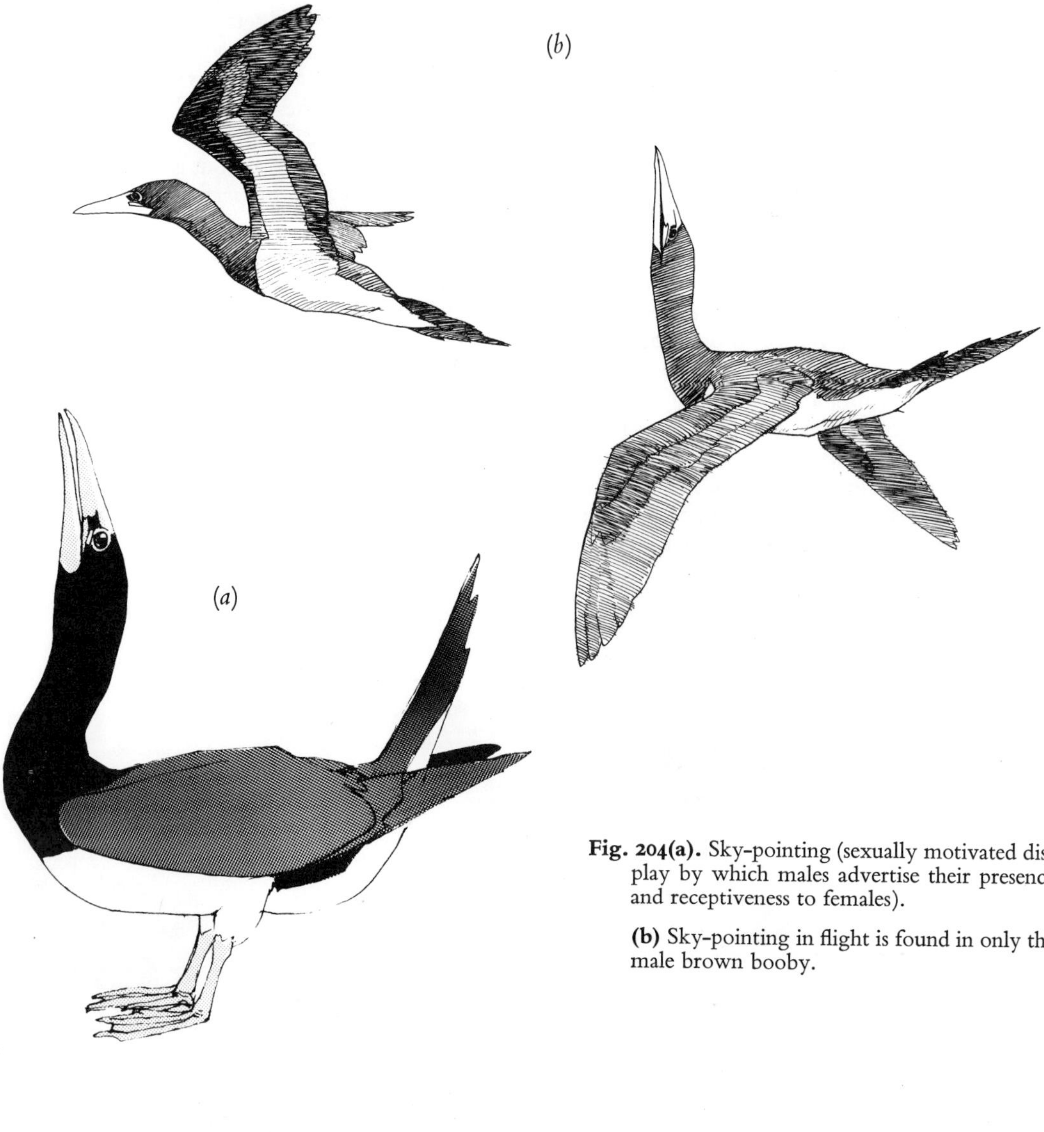

Fig. 204(a). Sky-pointing (sexually motivated display by which males advertise their presence and receptiveness to females).

(b) Sky-pointing in flight is found in only the male brown booby.

differentiation into components is useful only if some correlations are then made between, for example, the tendency to perform Sky-pointing with more or less of a particular component in particular circumstances, but I include them here to avoid confusion of terms.

Sky-pointing is performed at much the same intensity in a wide range of circumstances (this 'typical intensity'[1] is characteristic of ritualised displays) and, as in other boobies, renders the facial skin and the binocular eyes very conspicuous. In the brown booby the yellow gular area is well displayed.

The mere presence of the female is often sufficient to elicit Sky-pointing. If standing nearby she must, however fleetingly, catch the eye of the male, though if flying over she may draw

[1] Displays have 'typical' intensity when their composition and the amplitude and speed of the movements is much the same under a variety of eliciting circumstances rather than a 'bigger' stimulus producing a more intense display.

(c) (d)

(c–e) Sky-pointing followed by bill touching.

(e)

forth Sky-pointing. Simmons notes that the frequency and timing of Sky-pointing varies according to the position of the female (near or further away).

Sky-pointing is largely sexually motivated. Thus, whether the male is displaying to a female who is outside his territory or flying over; or one inside his territory but at some distance; a female who is moving away from him; or a female who is flying below and in front (the four situations by which Simmons typifies the context) he is reacting to a female—a sexual stimulus. On Ascension, the female never responds by Sky-pointing; it is solely a male display. However, on Christmas Island females did occasionally Sky-point. The two populations may differ in this respect. This would be especially interesting in view of the ecological differences between these two areas; the breeding cycles are also different.

From the contexts listed above Sky-pointing is an advertising display whose main function is to attract a female to the male's site, back to it, or to 'prevent' her from leaving it. It frequently occurs when male and female are together on the site and may help to strengthen the pair bond. This extended function is much more evident in species in which it is a mutual display. A male sometimes Sky-points, apparently spontaneously, to his nearby mate, or in response to an apparently hostile bill movement. In the latter instance, it seems similar to a greeting ceremony, but since it is unilateral this is a contradiction in terms. Nevertheless, when a hostile act on the part of a male gannet elicits attempts at Mutual Fencing (which is partly sexually motivated behaviour) it is analogous to the above situation. I have elsewhere (p. 188) discussed Mutual Fencing in terms of its possible role as appeasing behaviour, and Simmons explicitly states that the Sky-pointing display is important to the male brown booby 'undoubtedly as appeasing behaviour to the larger, more aggressive female'. There is no suggestion that Sky-pointing functions as site ownership display, repelling potential intruders.

2. *Gazing* (*Staring*)

In sexual interactions involving Sky-pointing gazing is apparently functional in ensuring the efficacy of the ensuing display (Forward Head Waving) by increasing the likelihood of it reaching its target. Presumably it is not tied to any specific motivational state. It occurs in some other boobies, too.

3. *Pair Flighting*

Pair Flighting, in which the two birds circuit the area, commonly occurs in the brown booby which has even incorporated sexual display (Sky-pointing) into the flight. This behaviour probably helps to cement the pair bond and strengthen attachment to the site. Even in those sulids which lack Pair Flighting, similar behaviour by the male alone always occurs.

4. *Mutual Jabbing* (*Sparring*), *Bill Touching, etc.*

When close together on the site, partners may jab each other in a highly ritualised way. The bill, a strong weapon, has attack-evoking properties when pointed directly at another individual, but when this situation arises between mates the ensuing behaviour is far from straightforward attack. Dorward described Mutual Jabbing or Sparring as being generally preceded or followed by Bill Pushing, the two birds with bills apposed, pushing backwards and forwards by neck movements in a see-saw motion. Then they may fling their bills at each other but without actually gripping. Simmons described this sort of close contact agonistic action as the 'mutual engagement of bills' and at its lowest intensity it may be no more than a stylised touching of bill tips, often followed by a brisk headshake. There is thus a family of movements involving bill contact, each doubtless representing a particular motivational balance and carrying its own functional overtones. We can distinguish the following types, always remembering that they may occur in an 'action mosaic' rather than in any stereotyped sequence.

A pair in close contact may engage in 'billing activities'—various movements in which 'usually without obvious signs of overt aggression, they touch, nuzzle and nibble each other's bill and facial skin, often simultaneously or reciprocally but sometimes unilaterally—in the

(a)

Fig. 205(a and b). (a) Bill alignment before landing, to be followed by (b) bill touching.

latter case more often by the male' (Simmons). As he remarks, this seems to be the equivalent of the allo-preening which is common in some sulids but not in the brown booby.

In Mutual Jabbing or Sparring the hostile element is apparent, so, equally, is the lack of intent to grip. Bill-pushing and Sparring change into each other, often in a sudden step-like manner but sometimes more gradually, following a hostile act from one member, usually the female.

Billing and Sparring usually begin by Bill Touching which has acquired special significance in the context of the pair rejoining each other on the site. The returning bird flies in calling, and whilst still in the air points its bill at the partner who similarly turns its head to face the incomer. Thus, actually as the incomer lands, the two bill tips are in apposition and are held so, momentarily in a 'frozen' bill contact (Fig. 205a, b). Should the incomer land at a distance it walks or jumps towards its partner, pointing in this distinctive manner and eliciting a similar response. Whilst it might be thought that normal landing preparations would necessarily involve pointing the bill at the site, whilst the occupier might be expected to orientate towards the incomer, the fact remains that nothing like this static Bill Touching operation is seen in other sulids in similar circumstances, except for the blue-foot (q.v.). Simmons interprets it as, functionally, a means of immobilising bills at a point when intra-pair aggression is likely to break out and indeed in some sulids an equivalent response *is* the greeting ceremony. Thus his reference to Bill Pointing as a greeting ceremony is fitting.

Occasionally, after Bill Touching, the ensuing bill movements may result in one bird putting its bill right inside the other's mouth (Fig. 206), in which case active 'pumping' movements may occur. These are obviously the behaviour patterns used in transferring food from

(b)

parent to offspring, as in all sulids, but in the case of these actions between adults no food is ever passed. Although the male may either insert his bill or accept the female's, he is the active partner in the interaction. This behaviour was recorded mainly in newly formed pairs.

Especially during bouts of Mutual Jabbing, various evasive movements of the bill may be observed. The ritualised forms are described below, but a common reaction is an undifferentiated headshaking, which is probably a response to tactile stimulation of the bill.

After Mutual Jabbing brown boobies may Stand Parallel, in the same way as white boobies, but this behaviour seems less well developed.

5. *Mutual (Allo-) Preening*

Allo-preening, in which one bird preens the other (Fig. 207), or each preens the other simultaneously, is rare in the brown booby. Dorward never recorded it and it may be that Billing largely takes its place. My own notes are equivocal.

6. *Parading*

The brown booby has a relatively large territory, though often on very steep or rugged terrain. Nevertheless, within the territory (usually but not necessarily when the partner is there) it does use an exaggerated form of ordinary walking (Fig. 208) (Parading) which Simmons describes as a 'mincing, pussy-footed gait'. It commonly occurs after a close range interaction like Sparring, when one partner, usually the male, leaves the other. Typically, the male will Parade away for a piece of nest material, preceding this movement with a special head posture (Bill-up-face-away). As in the other ground nesting boobies, Parading flaunts the webs, but (despite their gaudy colour in the brown booby) the movement is but a shadow of that seen in the blue-foot. As in other species, Parading may occur in conjunction with a variety of bill positions (q.v.). During Parading the tail is variably cocked and the neck somewhat lengthened.

No doubt its function is simply to enhance the visual impact of movements involved in intimate pair interactions and to help ensure clear communication of intent.

7. *Pelican Posture (Bill Tuck)*

During interactions and movement in the territory a common bill position, assumed by either sex but probably more by the male, is that in which the neck is arched and the bill tip is pressed to the throat (Fig. 208). Males typically Pelican Posture when moving away, for example in search of nest material (or when returning with it), after hopping to a vantage point and during Sparring (when it may be difficult to know whether it is the ritualised Bill Tucking or just an averting movement of the bill). As also in the white booby and the blue-foot, the Pelican Posture is not performed in a fully stereotyped manner, as an isolated act; often the bill is raised straight from the tucked position into the Bill-up-face-away or the other way round, whilst sometimes Bill Tucking is fleeting and repeated rather than a deeply formal, static position. Nevertheless, Dorward makes a point of mentioning that Bill Tucking in the brown

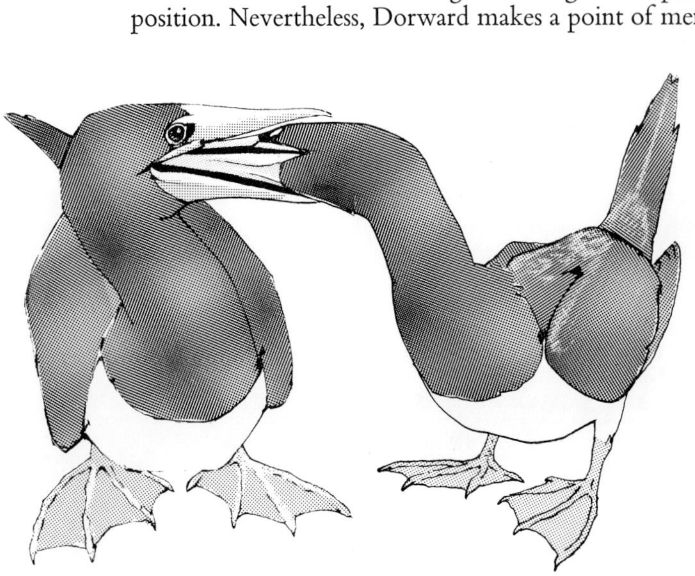

Fig. 206

Bill insertion (not courtship feeding).

booby differs from that in the white in that, in the brown, it does not occur whilst the bird is walking and running. Simmons, similarly, describes it as 'an entrenched and static position'. This is not accurate, for it often occurs during and after movement. In these contexts the bird Pelican Postures with a conspicuously arched neck, bill tip clear of the breast. Indeed, it may do so even before it actually lands (and so the Pelican Posture cannot be a recovery movement). In some such cases the posture can hardly be called a Pelican Posture, being simply a beautiful arching of the neck before or during movement.

Dorward noted Bill Tucking in birds that, from context, were largely motivated by fear or avoidance; for example, males that had been attacked and were running to the edge of the colony to take flight. In these instances the posture was maintained until the bird was in the clear. Again, birds that had been caught and handled, Bill Tucked after release. So he suggests that it is largely an appeasement posture. Thus, in the brown booby, as in the white, blue-footed and Peruvian, it does appear to be largely concerned with keeping the bill out of an attack-evoking position in an ambivalent fear-aggression motivational context, probably with fear predominating, but typically continuing beyond the distance at which physical contact (attack) could occur, and thus often seeming to have nothing to do with appeasement.

8. *Bill-up-face-away*

As, or just before, the brown booby moves away from its partner on the nest site, it characteristically tilts its bill upwards to about the horizontal, at the same time turning its head to one side, often slightly backwards as well (Fig. 208). It is movement *away from* rather than towards the partner that is accompanied by Bill-up-face-away. Simmons splits Bill-up-face-away into its two components (bill-up and the face-away) which serves to emphasise that the head can be held with the bill in any position without necessarily involving the sideways facing-away, but in fact the full Bill-up-face-away is highly typical of the situation described above, whereas it is rare for the bird to simply put its bill straight up, though relatively common for it to face-away with the bill horizontal. As in the blue-foot, Bill-up-face-away tends to precede movement which involves taking flight, though usually flight which is simply part of the social (pair) interaction and not departure for foraging. Thus the male may take off, circle, land again and resume the interaction, or the pair may take-off and flight around. The Pelican Posture is not usually performed in such a context.

Bill-up-face-away is probably a ritualised pre-flight movement, the turning away of the bill perhaps avoiding releasing attack (which often comes just as a bird moves off the site). It

Fig. 207. Unilateral allo-preening.

Fig. 208(a and b). (a) Bill-up-face-away (medium position prior to 'Parading' (a ritualised walk).
(b) Male about to 'Parade' in Bill-up-face-away Posture, whilst female bill-tucks (Pelican Posture).

is noticeable that it allows the displaying bird to keep its eye on the partner! The Bill-up-face-away of the brown booby, like the Parading, is typically less extreme than that of the blue-foot, in which the bill assumes a more vertical as well as sideways tilted, position, but nevertheless can occur in full and perfect form in the brown booby.

Whilst both the Pelican Posture and the Bill-up-face-away are extremely distinctive displays, there is an intermediate form which can be difficult to assign. Thus the facing-away movement of the Bill-up-face-away is often performed with the bill downwards, and since the arched Pelican Posture may take the bill to one side of centre, these two can be very difficult to distinguish. Bill-up-face-away and Pelican Posture are closely related anyway, both being averting movements common to the moving-away situation.

9. *Wing Rattle*

The Wing Rattle, a brisk shake of the wings, partly loosened and slightly raised at the tips, sometimes is so vigorous that the movement becomes a blur, and is commonly associated with behaviour preceding flight. It is frequently performed from the Bill-up-face-away position, itself associated with movement away, often leading to flight circuiting or a trip for nest material. Wing Rattle has signal value in this context and is not primarily concerned with care of the plumage.

10. *Upward Headshake*

When interacting with its partner, the brown booby makes considerable use of a brisk exaggerated headshake with the head tilted upwards. In long and intense bouts of varied activity this headshake acts almost as a punctuation mark. Thus, it is not tied closely to a particular situation or to another act, but occurs time after time in between, often several times in quick succession. It is common during courtship sequences and also as part of the

mosaic of activities during nest relief. Presumably it has no message as unequivocal as, say, Sky-pointing, but is just one of the many subtle mood-indicators, reflecting lightning shifts in motivational balance as events (stimuli) crowd in on the bird's awareness. When individuals interact at high intensity there is such a swift behavioural dialogue that one tends to lose the 'feel' of it if one concentrates too much on the frozen events. It is necessary to isolate the action patterns in order to recognise and define them, but in full and rapid sequence one senses the speed, complexity and variability of the interaction. It is like trying to follow a rapid conversation in an imperfectly understood language.

Probably the upward headshake in the brown booby occurs most often in connection with movement, commonly after the Bill-up-face-away or the Wing Rattle, after a hop up onto a vantage point and often after touching nest material.

11. *Nest Building*

The brown booby is the only ground nesting booby which constructs a functional nest out of conventional nest material (twigs, other vegetation and flotsam). The type of nest site used would often present great dangers to an egg or chick on the bare substrate (though even on flat ground a good nest is often built). In terms of the importance of nest building activity as pair bonding behaviour it makes little difference whether the nest is functional or not; symbolic or functional, both types involve the fetching and depositing of nest material and attendant behaviour. On Ascension the male often flew down to the sea to collect feathers. Both birds place pieces of nest material, mandibulating them and quivering the bill or raising a piece and lowering it again, at the same time vocalising, the female's 'monotonous, spaced grunts' being particularly characteristic of this situation (Simmons). During nest building the birds may bill and spar and whilst placing and mandibulating the material may reach over each other's necks (Fig. 209), as do other sulids. There is very little actual nest building behaviour; the quivering movement mentioned above may help to work some of the pieces into a united structure but the movements are so rudimentary that they can hardly do much good. Nest building, particularly the early stages, is in all sulids a time of great sexual activity. It is very important in cementing the pair bond, involving a whole gamut of interactions prior to the departure of the male (Bill-up-face-away, Parading, etc.) and the pair reunion on the site as well as actual copulation between gathering trips.

Dorward illustrates the dominance of symbolism in nest building. He says 'nests were very variable in size depending on the availability of heavy material and the exposure of the site, because feathers, although assiduously collected at times, were usually blown away; for instance, two nests on the flat top of the island were heaps of bones, feathers and shreds of old guano bags, 46cm across and with a depression in the middle, while in other places eggs were laid on bare rock with only a few small stones round them. I put a pile of stones and feathers

Fig. 209. Mutual nest building.

near one such nest before the eggs were laid and immediately the male ceremoniously carried each object over to the female, even accepting a feather from my hand.'

Male and female may change places, taking it in turn to occupy the nest centre. This is a universal trait in sulids and 'Symbolic relief' probably foreshadows the process of actual change-over (nest relief) which must function perfectly during incubation and the early life of the chick.

12. *Showing nest material*

Brown boobies Show nest material by raising it high, in a swaying arc (Fig. 210). This ritualised behaviour though less frequent than in the blue-foot, is nonetheless clear-cut. Whilst performed mainly during pair interactions, it is also to be seen during agonistic encounters, when a male may Show nest material 'at' a rival or an overflying bird (a potential intruder) often to the accompaniment of the noisy 'chuff chuff' whistle.

13. *Copulation and associated activities*

Copulation is closely correlated with nest building, particularly in the stages immediately before egg laying, when the male repeatedly brings more material and may copulate several times in less than an hour. So it usually occurs on the nest site, but birds will copulate also on vantage points within the territory. When soliciting, the female holds her head downwards, neck arched, and 'quiver-nibbles' (Simmons) a piece of nest material close to the nest bottom. 'Quiver-nibbling' is what I have called 'mandible tremoring' in other species, but it also involves tiny movements of the head from side to side. She may continue to hold and mandibulate the fragment of nest material during copulation. She also stops calling and remains in the nest centre without moving. The male may make incipient mounting movements before actually mounting. He positions himself for copulation, making movements of his bill towards her head, often from one side to the other, but not actually gripping (Fig. 211), though he may nibble her nape feathers or facial skin, or reach over and touch the nest material which she may be holding. He then moves backwards, applying his tarsi to the female's back and, with side to side movements, lowering his tail under that of the female, and achieving cloacal contact. After ejaculation (or merely cloacal contact if no insemination occurs) he transfers his weight from tarsi to feet and dismounts. Commonly he then Parades away, often with bill averted, or, as the female usually does, he may touch or build nest material. Seventy per cent of 506 observed copulations led to ejaculation (Simmons).

Simmons, who suggests a dominant role for the female in many brown booby pair interactions, describes her variable reactions to the male's attempts at copulation. She may behave aggressively by sparring during his attempts to mount, or drive him from her back with vigorous bill movements. She may even terminate the later stages of copulation in the same way. Finally she may 'exercise the avian equivalent of birth control. When receptive, her cloaca expands and contracts in spasms, thus, most probably, facilitating insemination when the male ejaculates. However, on some occasions, I noted that this activity was absent and, instead, the female defaecated copiously as the male thrust.'

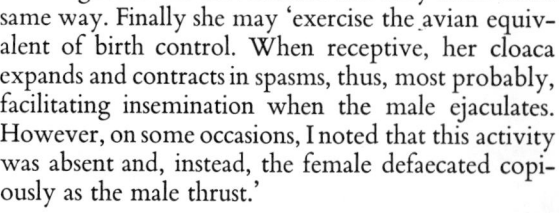

Fig. 210. Ritualised 'showing' of nest material.

OTHER BEHAVIOUR INVOLVED IN BREEDING

The preceding section has described all the ritualised behaviour used by the brown booby to control events in the breeding cycle. There remain other behaviour patterns involved in breeding, though in this species there is little with a specific flavour to report.

1. *Incubation*

Incubation behaviour is the same as in all other sulids but it is possible that this species, the white booby, and perhaps the red-foot, actually spend much of the incubation period with the egg on top of rather than beneath the webs. No precise observations have been made, but the breeding areas are often hot and keeping the egg temperature down may be important and may be better served by this alternative method. Displaced eggs are retrieved by rolling them with the bill, but only if within easy reach. Incubation stints are discussed on p. 457. They vary with locality but are in general shorter than those of the two other blue-water species. Thus, on Ascension, incubation stints were only, on average, 12 hours, but up to 37 hours and very commonly around 24 hours. On Christmas Island 24 hours was the commonest stint and the average was considerably higher than on Ascension (12 hours). Clearly, the brown booby would seem to forage less widely than the white and red-footed. In fact it is not seen as far from land and reputedly almost always seeks land upon which to roost at night, whereas white and red-footed boobies often roost on the sea.

2. *Change-over*

The incomer calls and lands at a variable distance, perhaps joining its partner in the Bill Touching position or moving towards it after first performing the Forward Head Waving. In the early stages of incubation there is much more of the behaviour chiefly associated with pair bonding—Mutual Jabbing and the various postures (Bill-up-face-away, Pelican Posture, Headshaking, etc.). Later, the relieved bird may move off the nest without having made contact and with no, or low intensity, posturing. At first, nest relief is likely to entail the fetching of a fragment of nest material and mutual interaction in dealing with it. Often, the relieved partner flies off and returns, once or several times. There are no figures for the length of time the pair spend together on the site after the egg has been laid, but it is probably little.

3. *Aspects of parent/young relationship*

Reithmüller (1931) makes the interesting observation that whereas white boobies brood tiny chicks on top of their webs because there is no nest and the ground is hot, the brown booby does not do so. He changed over small chicks of both species and noted that the young brown

Fig. 211

Copulation. Note that, as in all other boobies but in contrast to the gannets, the male does not grip the female's nape.

boobies did not climb onto the webs of their foster-parent. On Christmas Island the chick was brooded (or guarded when large) (Fig. 212) for at least the first 20 days and sometimes for as long as 61 days. On average it was 41 days old before first being left on its own. The equivalent period on Kure was 36–61 days. On Ascension it ceased to be fully covered by the adult during its fourth week. This period probably varies with locality (temperature and shade) and the pressures on adults to find enough food, but three weeks is the minimum age at which the chick is sufficiently able to regulate its body temperature (see p. 457).

The spells of brooding are as variable as those of incubation, but decrease with the age of the chick. On Ascension, the longest was 20 hours and the average of 27 records was 9·3 hours. The average length of spells on chicks 6–10 days old was 12·4 hours compared with 6·8 on chicks more than 25 days old. Simmons observed that the overall relief rate was once every 5·7 hours; males made more reliefs than females in the third and fourth periods of the day, but females more in the fifth, probaby reflecting fishing further from base.

The brown booby feeds its young in the typical sulid manner and has not been seen to regurgitate deliberately onto the ground, food always being taken by the chick directly from the adult's throat. The ratio of feeds delivered to nestlings by males and females respectively was 70 : 125 and to juveniles 59 : 127 (Simmons).

Between weeks 7–11 the chick begins to wander and a situation in which a parent might be pestered for food by a strange chick could easily arise. In a species with a feeding regime like the brown booby it would be highly disadvantageous for any individual to 'waste' food by feeding another's offspring. The ability to recognise its own chick is thus important. However, at an earlier stage it is perfectly ready to accept strange young, even when these are three or four weeks different in age from its own. The age at which the chick becomes established as 'the' offspring is not known.

BEHAVIOUR OF YOUNG

1. *Sibling interaction*

A most interesting aspect of the behaviour of young brown boobies is the method by which the brood is reduced from two to one. The eggs hatch asynchronously and it is exceedingly rare for the second chick to survive for long. It is often found trampled inside the nest or dead or dying outside it. The active rejection of the chick is not the work of the parent but of the sibling. Adults have never been seen to molest their chicks and will always accept the rejected chick if it is returned to the nest, although they will never attempt to retrieve a chick or to feed it outside the nest although Simmons once saw a neighbouring male eat a live, evicted chick. The elder chick, however, actively attacks and ejects its sibling, even though, at that age (usually a few days or a week or two old) it is itself capable only of weak and wobbly movements. We recorded a second chick, a few days old, dead and with head wounds, presumably from the sibling. In this behaviour it resembles the white booby more than the blue-foot, for

Fig. 212

Adult shading chick; loosened wings aid heat loss.

the former is an obligative brood-reducer whilst the latter is not. Nevertheless, there are slight indications that the brown booby chick is not as totally dedicated to the removal of potential opposition as the white, for there are more (though still very few) cases of two chicks growing up together. This trend, if it is real, would make sense insofar as the brown booby, like the blue-foot though to a lesser extent, is an inshore feeder and therefore ought to be better able to cope with two. The adaptive significance of the two-egg clutch is discussed on p. 466.

2. *Moving and exercising*

From the age of 4–5 weeks, the unattended brown booby chick begins to wander quite extensively, and may be found some metres from the nest site. This often allows it to seek shade when the parents have chosen an exposed nest site. All the ground nesting boobies, except the dense nesting Peruvian, wander in this way. They acquire detailed topographical memories and can find their way back from considerable distances (many metres). Often, they climb onto any available elevated perches, and exercise their wings.

3. *Begging*

The tiny chick's food begging behaviour consists simply of weak, unco-ordinated head movements and a faint 'yip' call. Later the chick crouches and turns its retracted, upward pointing head from side to side, at the same time bobbing it up and down and calling continuously. The wings may be held out and thrashed (Fig. 213), sometimes striking the ground, but the movements are not as deep and synchronous as those of the red-foot chick. It lunges wildly at the parent's beak, usually at the edge of the side plate on the upper mandible. Frenzied food begging is typical of most boobies and is absent only in Abbott's and the Peruvian; it is also absent in the gannet. In these latter three, wild begging would increase the danger of a fall.

4. *Bill Hiding*

If attacked by adults brown booby chicks do not Bill Hide. This is curious, because Bill Hiding is well developed in the chicks of white and blue-footed boobies but not in the red-foot, the reasons being obscure. Yet brown booby chicks wander, though, because of the steep terrain, less than white or blue-foot chicks. Perhaps, therefore, they are less likely to be attacked. One cannot relate Bill Hiding to a possible use in appeasing aggression between siblings, for the white booby has it, but one is always killed, the blue-foot has it, and both may survive and the brown does not have it, but one is almost always killed.

5. *Temperature regulation*

Young white boobies have been seen to adopt a posture in which the rump is raised and the

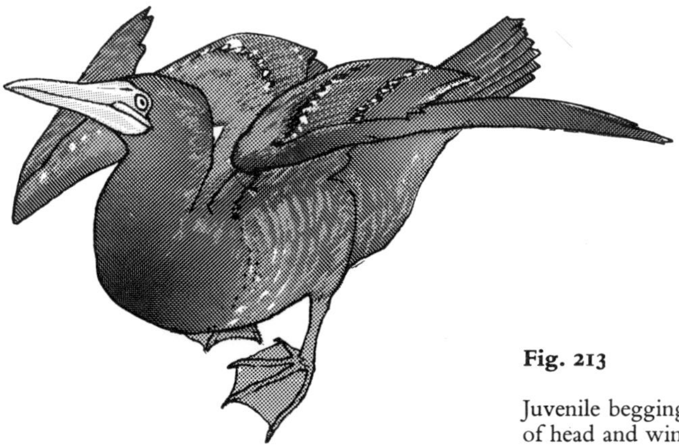

Fig. 213

Juvenile begging for food using vigorous movements of head and wings.

bare cloacal skin exposed. This is directly comparable to the 'tripod' position assumed by young red-foots. Whilst a similar posture has not been recorded for brown booby chicks, it probably does occur. Another temperature-regulating device is sideways extension of one leg, with exposure of the spread web.

6. *Ontogeny of behaviour*

Chicks perform all the usual comfort behaviour (preening, wing-limbering, leg-stretching, wing-flapping, scratching, yawning, gular-fluttering and panting). In addition, they play with nest material (biting, juggling and 'building' it). They defend their parents' site by striking out with aggressive calling and Wing Flailing. In conflict situations they may show distinct neck-tremoring and quick headshakes (the latter exactly as the adults do). From the age of about a month they interact with their parents in several ways, including jabbing and beak gripping with calling.

MAINTENANCE BEHAVIOUR

1. *Stance, movement and flight*

The brown booby, particularly the male, is a lively bird. In general stance it often resembles the white in the degree to which the body is held horizontal, but on occasions it strongly resembles the markedly upright, tail-cocked stance of the blue-foot, which the white never does. It may be no coincidence that the brown, like the blue-foot, has a very long tail and that the male has a proportionately longer tail than the female and the males of both species most often adopt the tail-cocked stance. Like the blue-foot it moves nimbly, running or hopping, though there is probably not much difference between the gait of the female brown and white boobies. It has highly conspicuous webs but does not flaunt them as ostentatiously as the blue-foot.

Brown boobies are extremely agile on the wing and are good at springing into flight, though females on flat ground often cannot take off rapidly. On Christmas Island they had to climb on to a pinnacle of limestone to gain the air. They perch well on branches, but not among fine twigs. It has been remarked that in the western Pacific, Malaysia and the Indian Ocean, brown boobies avoid ships, but in the eastern Pacific and Atlantic, perch freely on ships and roost in the rigging.

2. *Fishing behaviour*

The brown booby is of particular interest because it tends to fish closer inshore than most boobies and in this respect resembles the blue-foot. They are of course capable of the steep headlong plunges common to the entire family and differences in their fishing technique are ones of degree and of the proportion of effort spent in different types of dives and different regions of water, though none the less significant for that.

Dorward recorded anecdotal evidence that brown boobies occasionally congregate with frigates to fish close inshore on shoals of fry driven in by tunnies. They make slanting dives into shallow water just outside the breakers and will do this even in stormy weather with gales driving the breakers ashore. Bryant (1861) describes rapid dives in quick succession perhaps catching a dozen fish in the space of a minute. Brown boobies frequently feed close to their breeding islands, right inshore. Anderson (1954) says they fish alone or in pairs 16–24km offshore, often feeding on schools of garfish. Simmons (1967a) says they 'specialise in low, oblique plunge-dives and torpedo dives at a slight angle to the surface'. Inshore, both sexes capture prey in mere centimetres of water, very close to the surface and near rocks, at times under rough sea conditions. When hunting so, brown boobies look forwards and only slightly downwards, searching before rather than below. They tack noticeably and usually dive from 10 to 12m or less, often 'winnowing' down. They may dive again, almost during take-off, from a position about parallel to the surface, tail fanned, feet spread, skimming just beneath the surface and emerging quickly to repeat the process. In the Caribbean Van Halewijn (pers. comm.) saw rapid, perpendicular dives from a considerable height. They follow ships by the hour, diving in the bow wave. He saw, also, brown boobies fishing by sitting on the water and darting bill,

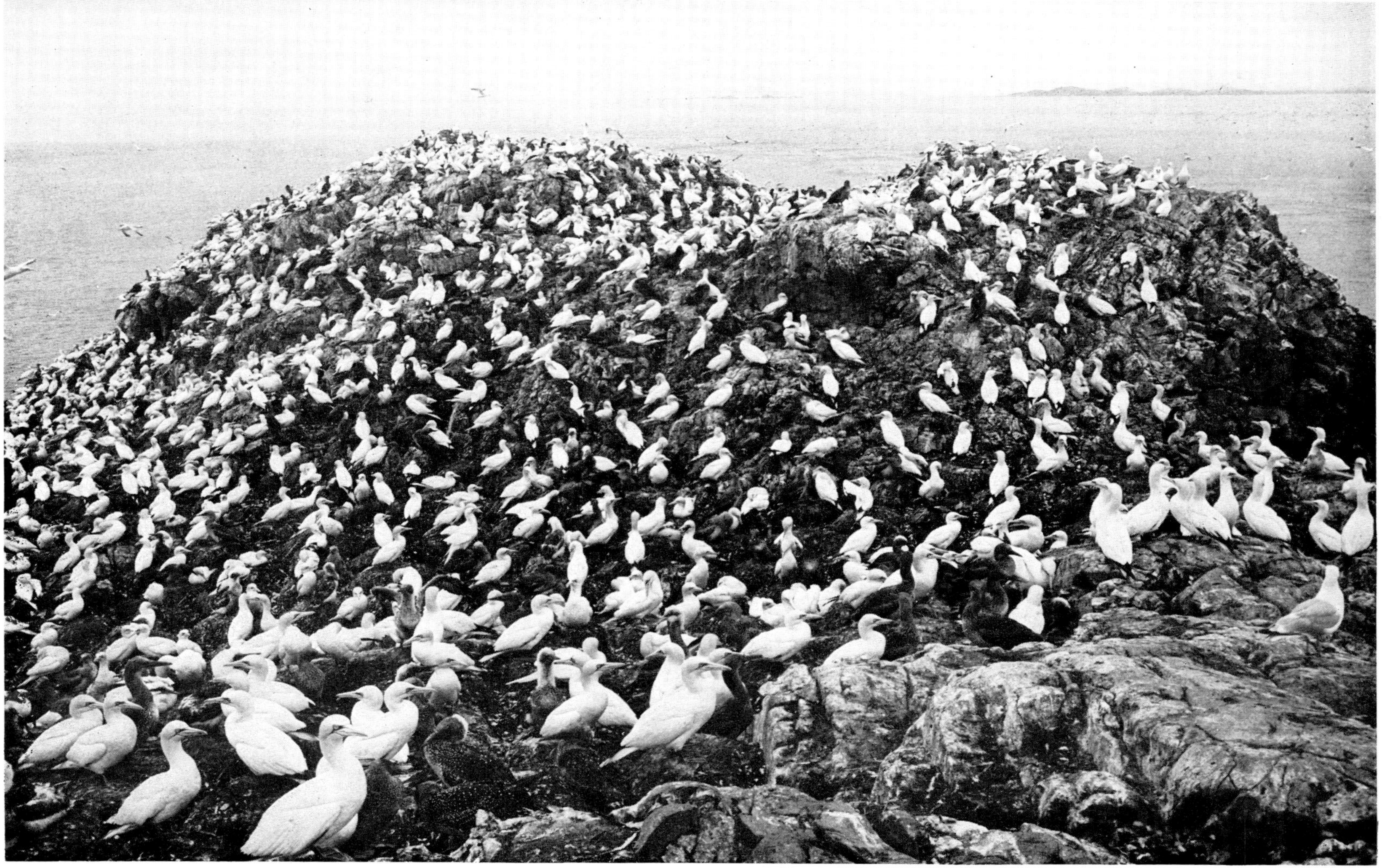

PLATE 1. Grassholm gannets in August. Most of the young birds are fully feathered and ready to fledge. The youngest chicks are in the fringe areas, but overall, there is considerable synchrony.

This and the following seventeen plates are from photographs by the Author.

PLATE 2

The gannet's greeting ceremony. The left-hand bird is just beginning to 'Sky-point', indicating that it is about to leave. Notice that all four 'fencing' birds are calling.

PLATE 3
Gannet and five-week-old chick.

PLATE 4. Neighbours.

PLATE 5. The white booby, outposted, performing its territorial display, Tower Island, Galapagos. The head is swept in an arc from side to side and nodded rapidly up and down.

PLATE 6
White booby on the alert.

Plate 7. White booby attacking a red-footed booby chick. The head of the chick has been completely stripped of down and badly lacerated. Young red-footed boobies do not 'appease' by hiding their bill, as others do, and suffer greater damage as a consequence.

Plate 8. A pair of white boobies and their two-month-old chick, Tower Island, Galapagos. The chick has its back to the camera and its down-covered wings in the 'sunning' position.

PLATE 9. Brown booby with one-month-old chick, Christmas Island, Indian Ocean. Note the large webs of the chick, which may be important in temperature-regulation.

Plate 10

Brown booby with three-week-old chick, Christmas Island, Indian Ocean. Shade is essential for the chick until it can thermo-regulate, at about four-five weeks of age.

PLATE 11

Pair of blue-footed boobies, Hood Island, Galapagos. The male is sitting. The nest material has no significance in terms of the physical structure of the nest, but the behaviour involved in collecting and depositing it has a pair-bonding function.

PLATE 12. Blue-foot with brood of two unequally-sized chicks. The eggs hatch about five days apart and survival of the younger chick depends on current availability of food. Here, it has obtained less than it needs and is retarded (it is at least two weeks old).

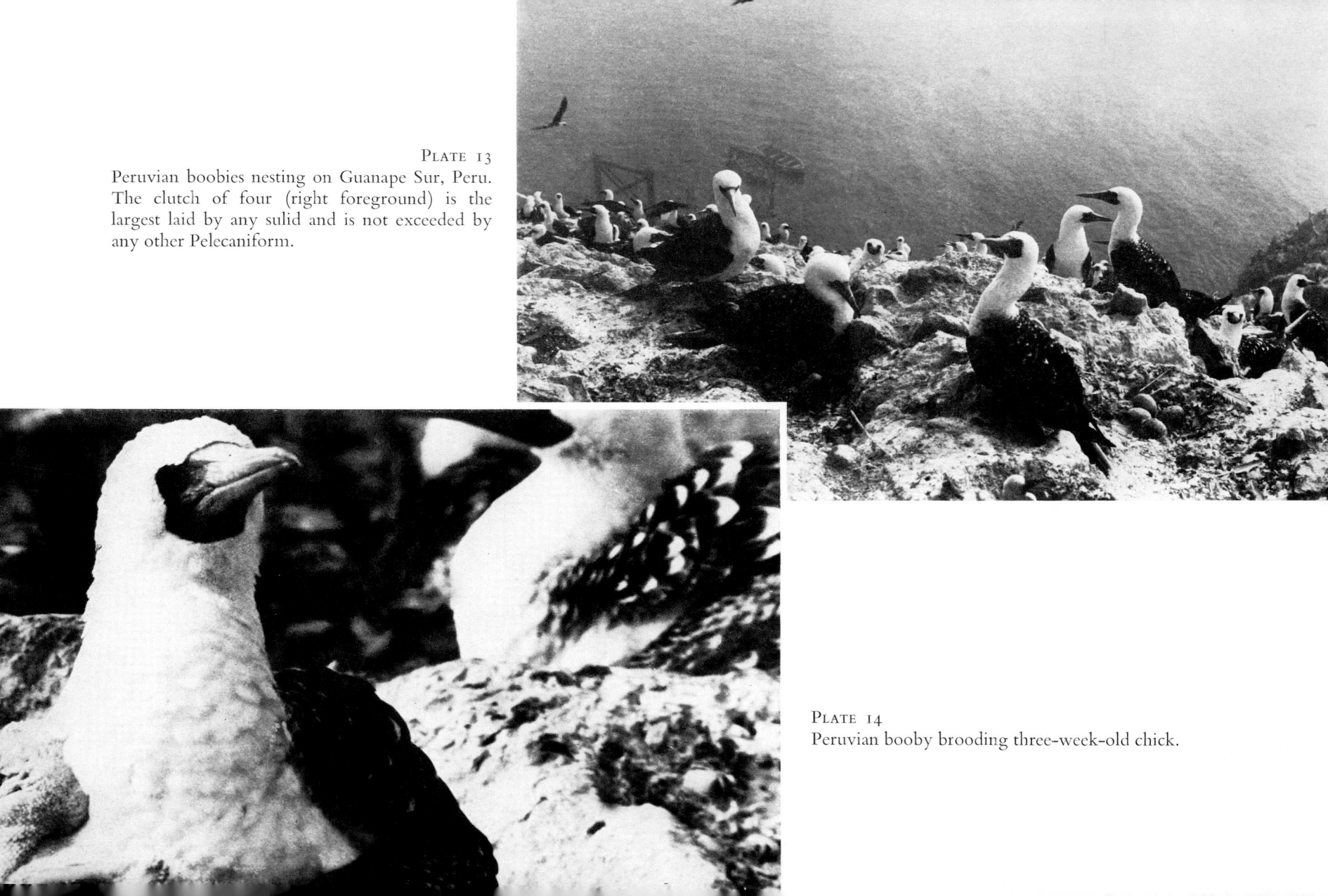

PLATE 13
Peruvian boobies nesting on Guanape Sur, Peru. The clutch of four (right foreground) is the largest laid by any sulid and is not exceeded by any other Pelecaniform.

PLATE 14
Peruvian booby brooding three-week-old chick.

Plate 15

A group of juvenile red-footed boobies on a ridge-tent, Tower Island, Galapagos. In few, if any other, places within their range are red-footed boobies as tame as in the Galapagos.

Plate 16

White morph red-footed booby, with two-month-old chick, Galapagos. The black tail of the adult is characteristic of Galapagos birds; elsewhere it is white.

Plate 17
Abbott's booby brooding month-old-chick.

PLATE 18. Abbott's booby guarding two-month-old chick. Note the loss of down on forehead (a feature of Abbott's, and not merely rubbed off during feeding) and the conspicuous black 'cape'. Frigates grow a similar cape, which may be thermo-regulatory.

(*a*)

Photos:
Van Halewijn

(*b*)

Fig. 214(a). A fishing flock of brown boobies.
(b). Compact swimming position.

head and neck below. Gibson-Hill (1947) remarks that they feed almost entirely by day, diving from a variable height but commonly from 10 to 15m and folding their wings completely as they enter the water. He gives 25–40 seconds as the period for which they remain submerged. This is a very long time, and, if correct, implies lengthy pursuit by swimming. They have, in fact, recently been filmed doing so (Howell, pers. comm.) using a flapping movement of the angled wings, and their feet, and showing considerable adroitness in twisting and turning. This again indicates that differences in hunting technique between the different sulids may be very considerable. Lamb (1910), talking about Mexican brown boobies, says that they 'fish considerably at night' and Wetmore (for Desecheo) mentions (in Brent 1922) that, though they were most active in the morning and evening, there was always much commotion among them throughout the night, which strongly suggests nocturnal coming and goings.

However, brown boobies obtain most of their food out in the ocean rather than close inshore, but usually closer to land than white or red-footed boobies. They are said to specialise in aerial pursuit of flying fish (Exocoetidae) catching it expertly on the wing, but whether they differ from the other blue water species in this respect one doesn't really know. The males especially are small and light (only the male red-foot is smaller) and could be expected to succeed better than the white boobies in opportunistic, aerial pursuit, but the male red-foot is probably quite as prone to take fish on the wing. After catching a fish, the brown booby often sits on the water juggling (killing?) it.

Brown boobies are said to specialise in individual rather than communal fishing. Simmons makes a particular point of this, suggesting that its dark plumage is an adaptation for 'hunting camouflage' and for 'social inconspicuousness' and that individuals hunt dispersed prey and are thus better off by not attracting individuals of the same or other species which interfere or compete with it (see Comparative Section for a full discussion). He ascribes this species' sexual isomorphism to selection pressures exerted in connection with fishing rather than with social factors, but the sexes are much alike in *all* sulids, except in size, in which feature the brown differs more than almost any other. On the other hand, he noted that gatherings, sometimes several hundreds strong, regularly fished inshore. The largest fishing group of white boobies was only 80–90. Brown boobies flew both to and from such gatherings in skeins of 2–27 birds. Simmons described 'hunting clubs' of up to 40 birds which settled actually during hunting and used the rocks as look-out posts. During a Pacific cruise of H.M.S. *Challenger*, MacDonald & Lawford (1954) remarked that the brown booby was by far the commonest and that, of the 300 or so which they counted, most were single or in parties of up to 10, but occasionally flocks of 40–80 were seen (between 13° and 18°s.) though these could have been one flock moving ahead of the ship. Gibson-Hill says it is usually seen singly or in small groups of 12 or less. Van Halewijn (pers. comm.) found that in the Caribbean the brown, white and red-footed boobies had different foraging and feeding techniques and remarks that though he seldom saw groups of all three species feeding together, it was commoner to see brown and red-footed fishing together and in one limited area only, brown and white together. He remarks also that the brown more often feeds inshore than do the others. Brown boobies also fish in the company of other seabirds. Clapham (1964) recorded them doing so south of Suez, in the vicinity of islands and especially in Massawa Channel.

On the other hand, there is one most intriguing record of what would appear to be co-operative communal fishing, much like that recorded in the only other inshore specialist, the blue-foot. Lowe (1909), during a cruise in the Caribbean

> . . . saw a flock of quite 1000 flying in a dense, compact mass. They were evidently following a shoal of fish, which occasionally rose to the surface, and as they watched the fish below, their movements appeared to be actuated by a single will or volition, so that they dipped or rose or inclined to right or left as if at the word of command of a single individual. Through all their movements they kept the closest order and when from time to time they dived, the whole flock fell plumb to the water as one bird, the sea being lashed and churned to white foam over a very circumscribed area in a most remarkable manner. A curious thing which we noticed was that occasionally the whole compact flock made a sort of feint at the water and then with one accord turned again to regain their former level of flight, as if the shoal of fish had been sighted but the birds realised in the middle of their dive that their prey was too deep. I have watched many thousands of gannets of different species fishing, but have never seen them hunt together in this way before. As a rule, where numbers are fishing together, each bird acts independently but this flock, which consisted entirely, so far as I could make out, of examples of (*S. sula*[1]) acted in unison as perfect as that exhibited by a flock of starlings.

Even more intriguing, it is said that brown boobies sometimes fish co-operatively at a vocal signal from one of their number. Simmons noted much calling from fishing flocks but put it down to antagonism. Gibson-Hill also says that fishing birds may call to each other. Although he was mainly concerned to say that they seldom do so, the very fact that they may do so is important. Watson (pers. comm.) observed 'co-operative feeding on flying fish in our ship's bow-wave, complete with alerting calls, in the Bay of Panama in 1965'. It is difficult to

[1] He says *Sula sula*, but was in fact referring to *leucogaster*, as the rest of the article make clear.

believe that it is mere coincidence that the two inshore specialists (brown and blue-foot) are also the only two that have evolved vocally co-ordinated communal hunting, but I have no idea why the two traits should go together. After communal fishing Ascension brown boobies often 'rafted' densely, possibly as an anti-frigate device (Simmons 1967b).

They habitually tried to rob white boobies or conspecifics, underwater by diving after them, or on the surface or in the air, mainly (or entirely) selecting birds holding fish.

DISCUSSION

Now that the breeding behaviour has been described, it is of interest to discuss in more detail the possible ways in which some of the traits may be correlated with the brown booby's ecological circumstances.

Dorward's work clearly showed the immense importance, in this species' breeding biology, of the periodic food shortages which occurred around Ascension. Simmons developed this theme and in the section on ecology several adaptations to these conditions are mentioned, of which the 'conventional' eight-month breeding periodicity is one (q.v.).

In connection with this, the Ascension brown boobies (other areas are different) show continuous (daily) defence of the site. The pair bond is maintained permanently, and there is a certain vesting of control over breeding in the female, over and above that which she necessarily possesses by virtue of the male's reliance upon her co-operation. These points may be pursued further.

For the pair to sustain their relationship between nesting periods requires either that both members are very strongly attached to the site as such, or that their pair bonding behaviour is strong and remains more or less continuously active. Possibly both phenomena are involved. In Simmons' view, selection has favoured permanent site tenacity at Ascension as an anticipatory adaptation for quick breeding in response to irregular improvements in the food supply. In other words, when conditions are good the boobies must be in a position quickly to begin breeding. This does not require aggressive behaviour at all comparable in intensity to that of the dense nesting gannets. Sites are usually not limited and there is little or no pressure in favour of concerted breeding, so competition for sites, either topographical or social, is not severe. Nevertheless, it does require sustained aggressive behaviour to repel potential usurpers and this the brown booby shows.

The female's tendency to defend the site is very strong. Simmons claims that she does so even more effectively than the male and that she sometimes establishes it. He considers that this may help her to be quicker in taking advantage of the onset of favourable conditions but of course it requires that she be able to acquire a mate. Since she does not perform the sexual advertising she presumably (under these circumstances) just waits for a male to visit her. This seems an unlikely way of doing things rapidly and I would suggest that in fact females do not establish sites. However, having acquired site and mate, the female is apparently in control of the timing of the breeding attempt, for she controls fertilisation (see Copulation p. 496).

So far as pair bonding behaviour is concerned, it is difficult to know whether brown boobies differ significantly from others. Certainly there would seem to be rather more frequent and intensive close range pair interactions than in the white and red-footed boobies, though not the blue-foot. Interestingly, some populations of the blue-foot also have an eight to nine month breeding periodicity whilst the white and red-footed are annual breeders. Again, the female blue-foot tends to dominate sexual behaviour (at least she is more aggressive in them).

Without doubt the most influential factor in deciding breeding regime is food and if the food situation is as critical, in the more impoverished blue water areas, as the evidence indicates, then it is entirely to be expected that ecology and its executive arm, behaviour, will adapt in relation to food to maximise the chances of successful breeding. The modifications of behaviour discussed here seem adaptive in this respect, and their relation to the environmental situation is further evidenced by the difference between the Ascension-type population and others. Thus, on Kure or Christmas Island, where breeding is largely annual, occupation of the site is not maintained between the end of one breeding attempt and the onset of the next. The direct effects of inshore shoals, on brown boobies, are: short feeding trips and short incubation spells; neglect of certain food items (pipefish); many birds present at the breeding colony throughout the day and more time spent guarding young; egg-laying more continuous; a higher proportion of cycles are successful; successful cycles are shorter, as are intervals between them; less desertion and faster replacement; more bigamous relationships (Simmons 1967b).

SUMMARY

1. The brown booby's habit of nesting in small groups, not densely and on steep or even cliff-type terrain is considered to have exerted a considerable influence on behaviour.

2. Brown boobies are very aerial and use aerial behaviour when establishing the site and in pair formation and bonding behaviour, the male being the only booby which performs the sexual advertising display in flight.

3. They are aggressive, but there is no serious fighting involved in site establishment or pair formation. Males usually, probably always, establish the site.

4. Ritualised behaviour used in defence of the site includes Jabbing and a display (Forward Head Waving or Bowing) probably derived from aggressive acts redirected to the nest or ground. There is no ritualised threat, probably because this is effectively close-range behaviour.

5. Pairs form when the female approaches a male in response to a special display (Sky-pointing). This display is also used, chiefly unilaterally by the male, even after pair formation and may then help pair bonding.

6. There is a lot of complicated interaction on the nest site, largely involving Bill Touching (a greeting ceremony), Sparring or Jabbing and various bill averting movements, principally Bill-up-face-away (prefacing movement away from the partner) and Pelican Posture or Bill Tucking, usually performed by stationary birds, and as the termination of movement.

7. Nest building and all the behaviour involved in fetching, transferring and building are important pair interactions. The nest often has functional value as a structure, too.

8. Copulation is usually a response to soliciting behaviour by the female and apparently she controls its success, in terms of fertilisation.

9. The smaller of the two young is almost always actively ejected by its sibling and dies.

10. Food begging behaviour by the large young is vigorous, sometimes frenzied.

11. Chicks lack the Bill Hiding behaviour.

12. Adults eventually recognise their own offspring and discriminate against strangers.

13. The role of behaviour in the brown booby's adaptive syndrome (to an impoverished blue-water environment) is discussed.

6

Sula nebouxii

BLUE-FOOTED BOOBY

1. NOMENCLATURE; EXTERNAL FEATURES; MORPHOLOGY; MOULT AND VOICE

NOMENCLATURE

1. *Common*

Blue-footed booby is the usual name. In most of Peru and Chile camanay is used but, confusingly, in northern Peru and Ecuador it is sometimes called piquero (a name usually reserved for the Peruvian booby). Captain Amasa Delano (1817) is reputed to have described the species in the Galapagos (1801). He referred to them as 'Bonaparte's army'.

2. *Scientific*

Sula nebouxii Milne-Edwards 1882, Ann. Sci. Nat. (Zoöl.), (6) 13, Art. 4; p. 37, Plate 14 (Pacific coast of America).

Coker (1920) says the original specimen described by Milne-Edwards is assumed to have come from Chile.

Sula nebouxii Ridgeway 1897, p. 596

Sula nebouxii Grant 1898, p. 435; Rothschild & Hartert 1899, p. 178; 1902 p. 407; Salvin & Godman 1901, p. 148; Snodgrass & Heller 1904, p. 248; Beck 1904, p. 6; Gifford 1913, p. 93, etc. etc.

Sula nebouxii Nelson 1899 (San Pedro Martir)

Sula gossi Ridgeway MS. Goss 1888, p. 241 (San Pedro Martir).

This species has apparently had applied to it, erroneously, the names *Sula leucogaster*, *S. brewsteri*, *S. cyanops* and *Dysporus leucogaster*.

Sub-species

Sula n. nebouxii, from California and the west coast of South America has been distinguished from *S.n. excisa* (Todd)—the Galapagos population. The differences are slight; certainly much less than in the red-footed or brown boobies, and it seems likely that the blue-foot was much more recently a single 'population', as its present distribution (p. 514) clearly indicates.

The original specimen obtained by Neboux during the voyage of the *Venus* in 1839 had no exact locality and Milne-Edwards merely surmised that it might have come from Chile. Hellmayr & Conover (1948) state that there appears to be no authentic record for the occurrence of the blue-footed booby in Chile, but the changing political boundaries between Chile and Peru may have obscured the situation.

GENERAL FEATURES

1. *Adult*

Like other boobies, the blue-foot is a large seabird, about 80–85cm in length with a longish, pointed bill, cigar-shaped body, long, angled, fairly narrow wings, about 92–106cm in complete span and a long, pointed tail. The head and bill project well forward in flight.

The adult blue-foot (sexes essentially similar, except that the female is much larger) is easily distinguishable by its densely streaked head and neck, the light tipped, often abraded and apparently split-ended feathers of which give a spiky appearance displayed by no other booby. These feathers end on the lower throat in a broadly inverted 'V' (apex anterior), the upper breast and rest of the underparts being white. The wings are a deep burnt brown, usually plain but the scapular feathers have broad pale tips which give them a barred appearance. The tail feathers are mainly darkish brown (variably bleached with age, the central ones especially pale) and all of them whitish on the basal third. The tail coverts are dark, but there is a conspicuous white rump patch, very obvious in flight, and another white patch at the base of the neck. These patches mark out the blue-foot even at a considerable distance. A brown thigh

Fig. 215. Flight outline, proportions and plumage pattern of adult blue-footed booby. Note the lean, 'flattened' appearance and long tail. The perched bird is a female (large pupil).

patch, brilliant turquoise or blue legs and feet, a dark slaty blue bill and a piercing yellow eye complete the general picture.

2. *Juvenile*

The juvenile has a plain brown instead of spiky head, brown throat and upper breast ending at the pectoral line, white underparts, plain brown wings, mantle and tail and a brown thigh patch. It is readily confusable with the juvenile white booby or juvenile or even adult brown booby. It may be distinguished from the former by its greyer underwing (whiter in the white booby), the sharp demarcation between brown upper and white lower breast (the white booby has no such pectoral band, the white running up onto the lower throat with which it merges more gradually) and above all by the white (though variable) patch at the base of the neck and in the rump area. These latter distinguish it from the brown booby (which resembles it in having a pectoral band). Also, the brown booby has a distinctive underwing pattern (q.v.). At close range, the adult brown booby is easily distinguished by its much brighter brown plumage and the colour of bill, eyes, legs and feet (q.v.).

3. *Immature stages*

These are poorly documented. In the stage following juvenile plumage, the uniformly brown head and neck feathers give way to ones with paler-tips and the scapulars, too, acquire pale or buff tips, whilst the eye becomes lighter, the bill bluish (spreading from the distal end) and the feet light (grey) blue, deepening and changing hue gradually. Even after the head has become streaked as in the adult, birds may retain traces of dark on the upper breast, down to the pectoral band and may breed in this condition.

The moult sequences required to produce adult plumage remain unknown, but it may be suggested that there is one complete replacement of flight feathers, in two cycles, the second cycle thus producing the third generation of the flight feathers concerned—i.e. juvenile, first replacement, and second replacement. The second cycle may stop short of replacing *all* flight feathers, the older feathers, in which breeding may occur, being first replacement (post-juvenile) feathers. Perhaps two body feather moults are required to transform a juvenile into the first basic (definitive) plumage. This may require some 18 months after acquisition of juvenile plumage in which case the bird would be about two years old or perhaps into its third year. This would be about the same as in the 'core' boobies (*S. dactylatra*, *S. leucogaster* and also in *S. variegata*).

4. *Flight*

It is difficult to convey in words the slight characteristics that mark out a species. Like all boobies, the blue-foot has a steady, powerful flight, alternating oaring wing beats with glides and a group or line may flap and glide almost in unison. Although the neck is somewhat extended, it never gives any impression of weakness, being 'in one piece' with the tapering body.

Robbins (1958), on a voyage in the Gulf of Panama, found that the blue-foot was rarely to be seen singly, but usually in flocks of 10-25. This may well be characteristic of the species and associated with its co-operative fishing habits (q.v.).

At the breeding colony the bird, especially the male, is an active and agile flier. It can take off from entirely flat and windless sites (though the female often has to flap-run or hop

Fig. 216 (a and b). Under and upper surfaces of juvenile about to make its first flight.

extensively) and can land in extremely restricted situations. The male is wonderfully acrobatic and performs an amazing Salute in flight (p. 550).

DETAILED DESCRIPTION

1. *Adult male and female*

The forehead is often whitish appearing as a pale band at the base of the bill. The crown feathers are deep brown or cinnamon brown narrowly tipped white, becoming large and conspicuously lanceolate on the crown, nape and sides of the neck. The streaked effect is not quite uniform, being coarser on crown and nape and finer, blending into greyish brown, on the sides of the neck and upper neck. The amount of streaking on the head and neck varies between individuals. Split tips to these feathers and a tendency to 'bristle' give the blue-foot its typical spiky appearance. The white patch at the base of the neck is variable in size and shape. A sex difference (males darker) has been claimed (Coker 1920) but is not proven.

The wings (primaries and secondaries) are blackish brown with a slight greyish brown bloom when new but subject to very considerable bleaching. The upper wing coverts and back are fuscous, but the scapulars and feathers of the upper back have broad whitish tips giving a strongly barred appearance. An irregular white rump patch, sometimes very conspicuous, passes into darker upper tail coverts. The tail feathers are brown, pale on the basal third, bleaching with age and in the case of the central ones often becoming almost white. The lateral tail feathers are fuscous and may have pale tips.

The breast, belly and under tail coverts are white; the under wing coverts greyish brown, the inner lesser coverts paler and axillaries white. There is a small brown thigh patch.

The bill is dark slaty blue with paler streaks. Palmer (1962) describes it as 'dull greenish blue' but I never saw one that seemed greenish. The gular skin merges into the slaty blue on the bill and the orbital ring is slightly darker. The legs and feet are a brilliant turquoise or shade of blue, ranging from bright ultramarine to a lighter blue. There is no consistent sex difference in the colour of feet, either male or female being darker than the partner (in a sample of 31 the female was darker in 20, the male in 3 and both were equal in 8). The possibility that leg colour varies with area has not been investigated.

There is a marked difference between the sexes in the apparent extent of the yellow in the eye. In the female the black pupil is followed by a brown iris, encircled by an irregular (sometimes star-shaped) band of brownish pigment and then a clear yellow outer zone. Thus the dark central area is large and irregular. In the male, the pupil is immediately encircled by a broad zone of yellow and thus the central area is small and round. Workers in California have noted a blue-grey eye colour following the typical brown eye colour of juveniles and have suggested that this may be a transitional stage in the acquisition of the normal yellow, adult eye.

2. *Juvenile*

The head, neck, throat and upper breast are deep brown, almost blackish, becoming browner and glossier after fledging and end sharply at the boundary of the white lower breast.

The wings (primaries, secondaries and coverts) and back are deepish brown. A variably-sized, whitish patch occurs at the junction of neck and back and another (also variable) on the rump. The tail is brownish black.

The white lower breast is sharply demarcated from the brown upper (at which junction, incidentally, down tends to persist longest). Belly and flanks are also white, the brown of the posterior part of the abdomen beginning (fairly sharply demarcated) approximately in line with the trailing edge of the wings when these are extended. The under tail coverts are also brown. The underwing is silver grey on the primaries and paler in the axillary and underwing covert areas.

The bill is almost black becoming horn or yellowish at the tip after fledging. The feet become lavender and then faint blue or purple after fledging. The eyes are brown, sometimes paler and more greyish.

3. *Measurements and weight*

The most striking feature of the blue-foot's morphology is the difference between the sexes, the male being much smaller than the female. The ratio of male to female size, however, differs according to the structure concerned. These points emerge from Table 71.

TABLE 71

SEXUAL DIMORPHISM IN THE BLUE-FOOTED BOOBY IN THE GALAPAGOS

	Male			Female			Male as per cent of female
	Mean	Range	Sample size	Mean	Range	Sample size	
Weight (g)	1283	1100–1580	23	1801	1450–2230	28	71
Culmen length (mm)	106	100–111·5	21	114	111–120	27	93
Culmen depth (mm)	33·5	32·5–35	7	35·3	33–37	6	95
Wing length (mm)	431·8	406·4–438·2	9	457·2	431·8–469·9	8	94
Tail length (mm)	236	223–251	18	237	223–250	19	99
Tail length as per cent of wing length	55			52			

TABLE 72

MEASUREMENTS OF THE BLUE-FOOTED BOOBY FROM DIFFERENT PARTS OF ITS RANGE

Area		Weight (g)	Culmen (mm)	Wing (mm)	Tail (mm)	Tarsus (mm)
MALES						
Hood Island	Mean	1283	106	431·8	236	—
Galapagos *	Range	1100–1580	100–111·5	406·4–438·2	223–251	—
	Sample	23	21	9	18	
	Mean	—	108·7	420·1	211·1	
Mexico†	Range		106–111	410–426	198–221	—
	Sample		3	3	3	
Panama	Mean	1332†	100·4	406·7	190·6	51·4
to	Range	1361†	95–107	394–421	165–226	49–56
Peru‡	Sample		10	10	10	10
FEMALES						
	Mean	1801	114	457·2	237	68
Hood*	Range	1450–2230	111–120	431·8–469·9	223–250	—
	Sample	28	27	8	19	1
	Mean	—	109·4	428·4	207·1	—
Mexico†	Range		106–114	404–449	201–214	—
	Sample		8	8	3	
Panama	Mean	1644(1)	106·1	423·3	184·1	54·1
to	Range	1758(1)	95–110	403–438	163–220	53–55
Peru‡	Sample		7	7	7	7

NOTES: * From Nelson, (pers. obs.) ‡From Murphy (1936)
† From Palmer (1962)

It may be seen that whilst the male weighs only 71 per cent of the female, his tail is almost as long (99 per cent). His tail is much longer in proportion to his body and wing length (55 per cent) than is the female's (52 per cent). Naturally his beak is smaller than hers in absolute terms, but expressed in proportion to body weight, is longer than hers. Hers is therefore disproportionately more powerful than his since his is longer in relation to body weight.

These differences clearly related to differences in hunting technique and type of prey, the male being anatomically much better adapted than the female for diving into shallow water and taking smaller, fast-moving prey, whilst she is well equipped for catching deeper swimming, larger and more powerful prey. This feeding difference in turn correlates well with the actual foraging regimes of the sexes, the male making shorter trips, and also with the male's tendency to feed the small chicks as often as, or more often than the female, but the larger chicks less frequently than she does.

Table 72 reveals some differences between blue-foots from the Galapagos and those from Peru and the Gulf of Mexico. It appears that the Galapagos birds are appreciably larger, but the figures should be treated with caution because of possible bias due to different measuring techniques. The weights are too few to show any difference.

MOULT

The chick is born naked except for short down on the dorsal pterylae and on the posterior margins of the wings and on the alula. The down that subsequently sprouts on the humeral, caudal and tertial tracts is prepennae, the remainder preplumulae through which contour feathers grow (Palmer 1962).

The first post-juvenile moult of body feathers probably produces some pale-tipped head and neck feathers and white upper breast feathers, the process continuing in the second post-juvenile moult, which probably produces the first adult body plumage. The flight feathers moult in interrupted sequence; first the inner section (half), then a pause, then the outer. The first part of a second cycle could well be completed before first breeding, thus leaving the adult with two generations of feathers in the same wing.

The moult pattern of breeding adults, as revealed by examination of Galapagos birds caught on the nest between September 9th and October 8th, 1974 is given in Table 73. A new wave of laying was just beginning and a period of acute food shortage had just ended. None of the 13 females and 8 males caught with chicks over six weeks old were in wing-moult. In the red-foot, by contrast, 88 per cent of an equivalent sample of eight birds were in wing-moult. The blue-foot's apparently anomalous case may have been due to the inhibition of moult as a result of the severe food shortage that had just occurred.

Tail feathers usually numbered 16 (26 cases) though 15 (6 cases), 14 (4 cases) and 13 (1 case) were also noted. Moult seemed irregular. There seemed a tendency for males with large chicks, in particular, to have one or more tail feathers missing.

It may be concluded that, normally, moulting of wing and tail feathers occurs during the

TABLE 73

CORRELATION BETWEEN MOULT AND THE STAGE OF THE BREEDING CYCLE IN THE BLUE-FOOTED BOOBY IN THE GALAPAGOS

	Number of primaries growing					Per cent of sample in moult
Stage	None	1	2	3	4	
Incubating	7	1	1	—	—	22
Relatively small chick	—	—	1	—	—	(100)
Relatively large chick	21	—	—	—	—	0
Unknown status but no egg or chick	4	—	1	—	—	20
Totals ..	32	1	3	—	—	11

'rest' period between breeding cycles but that a new cycle may begin well before moult ceases, thus leaving a bird with some missing or growing feathers (though few in number) during incubation and the first few weeks of the chick's growth, but rarely during the later stages.

Whilst it would be premature to build too much in the way of ecological correlates onto this, it is tempting to point out that the commencement of a new cycle whilst moult may be still incomplete is consistent with the somewhat opportunistic initiation of breeding which this species appears to practice, at least in the Galapagos.

VOICE

The male blue-foot has a light, throaty whistle varying in quality (sibilant, husky, piercing, subdued, etc.) according to context. It commonly calls in groups of three to five 'phew, phew, *phew*, phew, phew'. The advertising call (q.v.), which is such a feature of a blue-foot colony in the early stages of breeding, is a single drawn-out whistle, gradually falling away. The female shouts or grunts with a deep and pleasantly rough-edged voice 'ark, ark, ark' with a groan equivalent to the male's whistle, when advertising. The speed at which the syllables are uttered, as well as their quality, constantly varies, giving, during complicated pair-interactions, an amusing conversational effect with an odd grunt or soft whistle followed by a rapid bout of 'ah, ah, ah' calls and a piercing whistle. When several pairs 'talk' simultaneously one senses the considerable social stimulus present in an active blue-foot colony.

The chick's aggressive call is usually three or four syllables 'aa-*aa*-*aah*-ah', sometimes querulous and with a break in it. Intense alarm elicits a protracted '*aaah*-aa-aah', shouting on the first syllable. The food-begging juveniles emit about nine 'cacks' per cackle-bout, whilst pestering the adult.

Chicks gradually acquire the deep, female-type voice (though it is lighter) from the high-pitched 'yip' common to all tiny sulids. It is not known when young males begin to whistle like adults. The sex difference in voice is due to structural differences in the syrinx (Murphy 1936).

This species calls whilst fishing (q.v.) and probably uses its voice to co-ordinate the actions of the group. So far as is known, no other sulid except the brown booby does this, although all species often call excitedly when harrying a shoal or, for example, competing for fish thrown overboard.

2. BREEDING DISTRIBUTION, NUMBERS AND OTHER ASPECTS OF POPULATIONS

INTRODUCTION

The blue-foot is an interesting intermediate between booby species with a wide distribution (red-footed, brown and white boobies) and those entirely restricted to one locality (Peruvian and Abbott's boobies). In fact, the blue-foot is rarer than one might suppose; only Abbott's booby has a smaller world population. The blue-foot breeds in three areas (Fig. 217)—**islands and headlands** off the **west coast of South America**, mainly between northern Peru and Ecuador; the **Galapagos Islands,** which are some 960km west of Ecuador and therefore (even for a seabird) fairly discrete; and islands in the **Gulf of California**. The first two of these areas are probably not completely separate from each other, but there is a long stretch of central American coast, between the Gulf of Panama and the latitude of the Revillagigedos, in which it is scarce or absent. Its distribution along this enormous length of coastline is thus markedly discontinuous and, taking in the **Galapagos,** its main foci are those described above. It is thus confined to the tropical zone between the southern waters of the California Current and the northern extremity of the Peru Current.

In the following account, emphasis will be laid upon the factors which seem most likely to determine the blue-foot's distribution, chief among them being proximity to cold water. In the case of the Peruvian Islands, this is the Peru Current described on p. 596. The California Current, however, has not previously been much mentioned and will be discussed in the context of the Californian population of the blue-footed booby (below).

An up-to-date survey of the blue-foot's status off Peru and Mexico–California is badly needed; we have never known the size of either 'population' with reasonable accuracy and such figures as exist are, in addition, too old to represent the present situation. Rather more, however, is known about the Galapagos population.

BREEDING AREAS

1. *The Galapagos*

The **Galapagos Islands** extend over many thousands of square kilometres, straddling the equator and lying in the midst of strong and complex ocean currents. In particular, the cold water Humboldt, swinging northwestwards from coastal Peru, strongly affects the southernmost islands, but not the northern ones; the extent of the difference may be judged from the water temperature, which off Punta Suarez, Hood Island, is about 60°F (17°C) and in

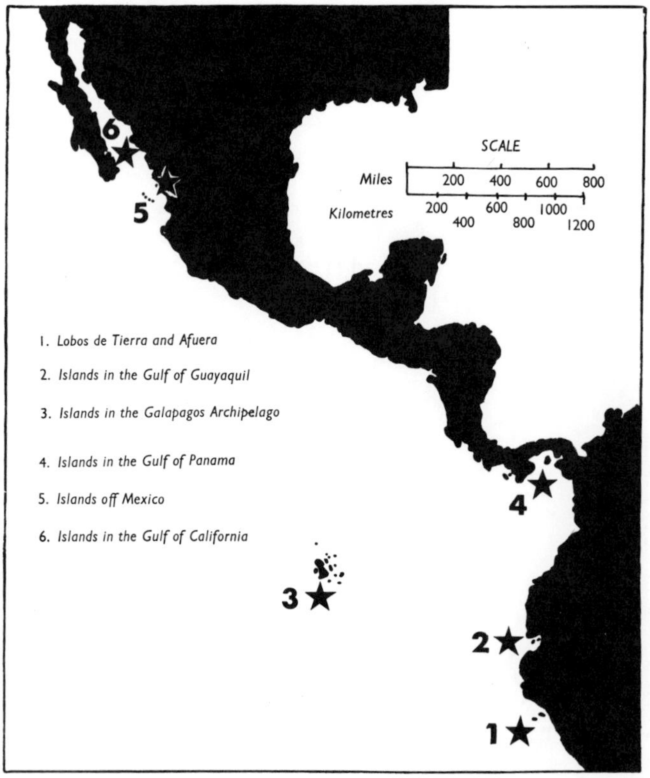

Fig. 217

Broad features of the breeding distribution of the blue-footed booby.

Darwin Bay, TOWER ISLAND 84°F (29°C). So it is hardly to be expected that the blue-foot will find both conditions equally favourable, even if other attributes such as nesting habitat are adequate throughout the archipelago. This latter point has not been critically assessed, but most, if not all the islands, offer at least some acceptable terrain. Nevertheless, distribution in the Galapagos is extremely patchy, as shown in Fig. 218 (see also Appendix 11).

There are at least 34 regular breeding stations known in the Galapagos, all on islands south of the equator, although it has bred on Tower. The main colonies are on DAPHNE MAJOR and HOOD ISLAND (Punta Cevallos and Punta Suarez).

The only actual population figures available are for DAPHNE MAJOR (some 1000 pairs) and PUNTA SUAREZ (around 500–800 pairs). However, the total **Galapagos** population must exceed 10 000 pairs and could be substantially more, even though the archipelago does not hold a single large colony. Thus it is a very major breeding area, with a population that may well exceed that of Peru.

The adaptive value of breeding in a large number of fairly small colonies rather than a few large ones, may be connected with this species' habit of fishing relatively close inshore. Tremendous numbers would obviously be incompatible with a limited foraging area unless that area happened to possess an almost inexhaustible food supply. Presumably for the same reason, one gets small colonies of cormorants or shags, which hunt near the colony, but large ones of kittiwakes, auks, tubenoses and gannets, all of which forage far from the colony.

2. *Islands off the west coast of South America between the Gulf of Panama and Peru*

Although the vast stretch of coastline between the Gulf of Panama and the **Lobos Islands** of Peru, over 3000km, holds blue-footed boobies at various points, their distribution is markedly

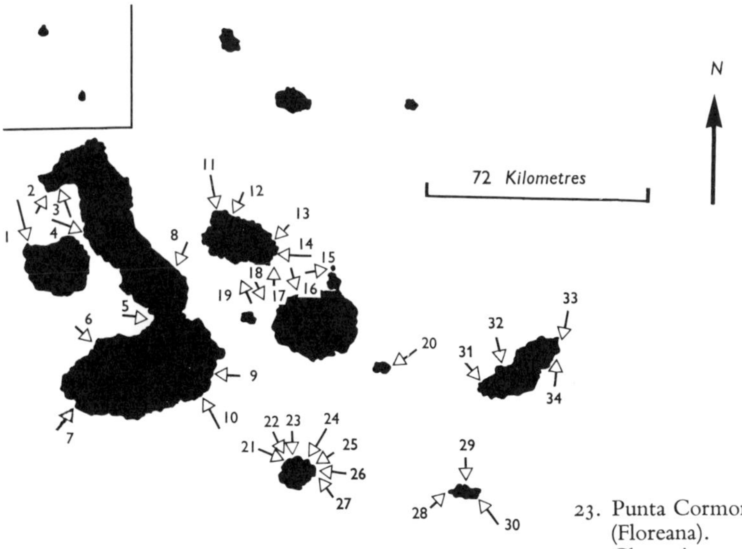

1. North Coast (Fernandina).
2. Punta Vicente Roca.
3. Banks Bay (Isabella).
4. Tagus Cove (Isabella).
5. Marielas Island.
6. Punta Moreno (Isabella).
7. Iguana Cove.
8. Cowley Island.
9. Crossman Islands.
10. Tortuga Island.
11. Albany (James).
12. North Coast (James).
13. Small Is. (near Sullivan Bay).
14. Bainbridge Rocks.
15. North Seymour.
16. Daphne.
17. ? Beagle Islands.
18. Guy Fawkes.
19. Jarvis Island.
20. Barrington.
21. Punta Daylight (Floreana).
22. Punta Cormorant.
23. Punta Cormorant (Floreana).
24. Champion.
25. Enderbury.
26. Caldwell.
27. Gardner-near-Floreana.
28. Punta Suarez (Hood).
29. Gardner-near-Hood.
30. Punta Cevallos (Hood).
31. Near Wreck Bay (San Cristobal).
32. Kicker Rock.
33, 34. Punta and Isla Pitt (San Cristobal).

Fig. 218. Breeding distribution in the Galapagos Islands (after Harris 1975).

discontinuous. The only substantial concentration is on the **Lobos Islands** (see p. 580 for a general description).

LOBOS DE AFUERA and LOBOS DE TIERRA have long been the main, if not the only Peruvian islands to hold large colonies of blue-foots, though the species ranges as far south as Pisco and, during unfavourable hydro-climatic conditions, frequently moves as far south as the **Chinchas**. It is rare or unknown off Chile. LOBOS DE AFUERA marks the southern limit of this species' breeding range. In 1919, the time of Murphy's visit, it obviously held a good number, though actual figures are not given.

LOBOS DE TIERRA was undoubtedly at one time the main stronghold of this species. In 1919 it was so abundant that, in Murphy's words, one could scarcely look from any point without seeing thousands 'here in rather dense aggregations, there scattered thinly'. Because the blue-foot is of relatively little economic importance its numbers are never recorded along with the 'big three' (guanay, piquero and pelican) in the surveys and estimates carried out by the Guano Administration. The most recent estimate (1963) puts this island's population of blue-foots at about 10 000 pairs and Tovar (1968) records that in December 1963, camanays were nesting 'over the whole extension of the island'. Nevertheless there may have been a very substantial decline since the decades between 1920 and 1940 or 50; for in the first of these Murphy states that, owing to years of undisturbed breeding at LOBOS DE TIERRA (when war-induced freightage costs rendered this island economically less viable) the blue-foot 'increased enormously'. The nests were so numerous and dense that they gave rise to a considerable increment of guano. Since this species produces a relatively miserable spattering, such a deposit could accrue only from a vast population the like of which does not exist today. It also throws further emphasis on the effects of local circumstances on colony size for whereas most blue-foot colonies are small, the Lobos colony at its peak demonstrates that relatively huge and dense concentrations can occur, given the right economic circumstances. Nevertheless, it is interesting that by the time one has reached the Lobos Islands, the anchovy, though still abundant, is notably less so than at points further south, in which areas the piquero takes over completely (the blue-foot is reputed to have bred on one of the **Guañapes,** but the record is not certain). This fact may well explain, at one and the same time, why the blue-foot is common on the Lobos Islands and why it takes over from the piquero, since the latter is very probably much more dependent on the anchovy. Elsewhere off Peru, the blue-foot is often recorded in the **Chincha** area, October to March, usually in small numbers (30–100) but occasionally in great influxes. During the 1963 exodus, hundreds went to VIEJA and SANTA ROSA from the north.

The coasts of Ecuador and Colombia are much hotter and wetter than that of Peru. Whether for this or other reasons, the coastal reaches of northern Ecuador and Pacific Colombia are without blue-footed boobies. Nevertheless, the **Gulf of Guayaquil** holds breeding blue-foots; EL MUERTO held blue-foots in abundance in 1925 and Murphy recorded 'great numbers' killed in a landslide and prevented from nesting by exceptional rains.

Further north again, the Ecuadorian island LA PLATA is still south of the belt of almost constant rain. It is covered with cacti, thorny scrub and ephemeral green vegetation and in 1925 Murphy recorded traces of occupation by this species, though the birds themselves were absent. There seems no recent information and the present day population is probably not large, if it exists at all.

There are several islands in the vicinity of La Plata, among which PELADO, much more barren than La Plata or the adjacent coast, is probably the chief blue-foot colony. Again, we lack recent information, but it is said (Hutchinson 1950) to support colonies of pelicans, frigates and blue-footed boobies. In 1925 'many' birds were actually present (Murphy 1936). However Mills (1967), who saw 150+, including immature birds, on May 5th 1966 thought that nesting probably did not occur there. He saw, also, some blue-foots on the nearby Mancora Banks. The La Plata area probably represents the point at which, moving northwards, a considerable gap begins in the blue-foot's distribution.

An exception to this statement would be provided by the colony reported to occur on the wet and humid GORGONA ISLAND (Colombia) but this record is somewhat mysterious. Bangs, in 1904, managed to collect only one (immature) bird there, which could easily have been a wanderer, and although Murphy mentions the colony (and remarks that the habitat is highly unsuitable) he does not cite the source. There are no recent records and its seems safer to assume that GORGONA is not in fact inhabited by blue-foots.

From this point there are no recorded colonies until the Gulf of Panama, over 1000 coastline kilometres to the north.

3. *Gulf of Panama*

In the **Gulf of Panama**, Robbins (1958) found the blue-foot the most numerous oceanic bird (July 15th–26th 1957). Together with the brown booby it was almost constantly in sight from **Balboa** to the **Pearl Islands**. In the waters around the Pearl archipelago there were 'many thousands' of birds (presumably not all blue-foots). There are suitable breeding islands here (PACHECA, GALERA, CAMOTE, etc.) and no doubt considerable numbers of blue-foots use them. Robbins said it was especially abundant on the rocky isle of CAMOTE and on GALERA and continued to be the most numerous species along the coast from Carachine Point to Piñas Bay. It may well nest in small numbers on many an islet off this coast and even on headlands, but there are no records.

It is very possible that between **Peru** and **Panama,** there are many offshore islets or even headlands with small colonies of blue-foots.

4. *Islands off Mexico and in the Gulf of Calfornia*

Just as, off Peru and in the Galapagos, the blue-foot is associated with a combination of arid islands and the relative proximity of cold water, so off the coast of California it is associated with arid islands and the cool California Current. This current flows southwards between latitudes 48°N and 23°N[1] along the coast of western North America, representing a slow movement of sub-arctic water towards lower latitudes; it may be the deflected continuation of the Aleutian Current of the northern Pacific. During the spring and early summer, the California Current is the northern hemisphere counterpart of the Humboldt. The wind and current both proceed along the coast causing areas of upwelling which project tongues of cold water moving southward away from the coast and interdigitated by tongues moving northwards towards it. The resultant swirls are analogous to those produced by the Humboldt off Peru. These upwellings support a large production of diatoms and thus items higher in the food chain. The enhanced productivity supports rich fisheries, particularly of the sardine *Sardinops caerulea* but also other small fish (*Engraulis mordax*, *Anchovia macrolepidota* and *Pneumatophorus japonicus*). During late summer the regular swirls disintegrate and by January a counter current flowing north to latitude 48°N has developed. It appears that phytoplankton is extremely rich within the Gulf of California, as against the Pacific coast of lower California (which in turn is richer than the open Pacific). Three areas in the Gulf are especially rich in fish—MAGDALENA BAY (24°30′N) the region off PUNTA ABREDJOS (26°40′N) and SEBASTIAN VIZCAINO BAY (28°N). There are also conspicuous upwellings at about latitudes 35°N and 41°N. Within the Gulf, fisheries are very productive and the chief food of the guano birds is said to be *Anchovietta compressa*, *A. delicatissima*, *A. helleri*, *Harengula thrissina*, *Opisthonema libertate* and *Sardinella stolifera*. Thus, both outside the Gulf proper and within it, there are rich areas of primary production (Fig. 219).

The blue-foot breeds both on islands well out in the Pacific, off Mexico and also within the **Gulf of California** itself. Among the former are the REVILLAGIGEDOS, the TRES MARIAS, and the TRES MARIETAS.

In the **Revillagigedos** (see p. 447) although Hanna (1926) makes no mention of the blue-foot on his May visit, this species nests (or nested) on SAN BENEDICTO ('hundreds of pairs nesting on the slopes July 1939'), together with white and brown boobies, but, following the 1952 eruption, Brattstrom & Howell (1956) recorded only 'several seen' on San Benedicto in November 1953 and none in March (when they should have been nesting). Their present status is not on record.

[1] This account is essentially Hutchinson's (1950) Summary of Sverdrup (1944) and Tafall (1944).

Las Tres Marias (JUANITO, MADRE, MAGDALENA and CLEOFAS) have obviously been occupied for many years; records go back into last century (Juanito, Nelson 1899). Lamb (1910) mentions blue-foots fishing all around the boat near these islands (April 1909). Hanna (1926) says that blue-foots (presumably breeding) were 'common along the shore line' of MARIA MADRE and also occurred on MAGDALENA. The islet WHITE ROCK, between Magdalena and Cleofas, about 61 metres high and nearly flat on top, was said (Bailey 1906) to possess a fine and ancient colony of brown boobies, but it seems possible that they were in fact mostly blue-foots. The thick crust of guano which covered the rock is more likely to have stemmed from blue-foots for the flat, bare top is just the sort of habitat they like, whereas the brown booby prefers steeper and more irregular ground. Furthermore, the brown booby is not common in this area which is much more the preserve of the blue-foot. Oddly enough, since writing this, I have checked the actual record cards for some of the clutches collected on White Rock and find that the correspondent (D. Anderson) who enabled me to do so, had scrawled 'sounds like blue-foot'. On the other hand, Bailey had also collected blue-foot clutches and taken specimens and photographs of the birds, so it seems unlikely that he could have been mistaken about the brown when both species were present for comparison. Stager (1957) found breeding colonies on San Juanito (some 200 pairs on the south side of the island) in April 1955 and Cleofas (just above the beach). Later, Grant & Cowan (1964) also list Juanito and Cleofas (but not Madre or Magdalena) as current breeding islands for the blue-foot.

On ISLA ISABEL or ISABELLA, 35km due west of the coast of Nayarit—'a paradise for seabirds' Hanna (1926)—the outlying rocks were covered with pelicans, brown and blue-footed boobies, the latter nesting under small trees near the shore. Presumably there must have been at least several hundred pairs and even that many would not match up to the euphoric description just quoted. Bailey collected many blue-foot clutches there in 1905 and another oologist did so in 1938. Howell (1975) visited the island from March 5th to 22nd 1975, and reported that there were 'many hundreds, possibly as much as a few thousand', courting, incubating and with well-grown young.

The **Tres Marietas** off Nayarit (Mexico), two large and one small island and a number of isolated rocks, lie merely some six km offshore. The westernmost and largest, some 1000 by 600m and 25m high, held about 550 pairs of blue-footed boobies in 1962 (Grant 1964) nesting in small groups on plateaux, among sedge and grass. These islands have long been inhabited by good numbers of blue-foots; Lamb (1910) records hundreds of nests in April 1909. However, the population may be declining slightly if Grant's records (c. 1500 individuals May 1961; 1100 May 1962 and 750 April 1963) reflect more than artefactual differences. Islands named REDONDO ISLAND and CUEVAS ISLAND, presumably the two smaller ones of the group, also held nesting blue-foots (numbers not recorded) in 1909. Human disturbance is one of the main causes of nesting failure and adult mortality in the Gulf, and presumably, also, affects the Marietas.

Within the **Gulf of California** (Fig. 219), guano birds in general have been euphorically estimated at almost 5 000 000 of which 1 525 000 were reputed to be boobies (blue-footed and brown). Even scaled down to Vogt's more realistic figure of 500 000 seabirds, this still means a lot of boobies. Indeed, arbitrarily assigning half to each of the two species suggests a figure in the region of 85 000 blue-foots which would place the **Gulf of California** as far and away the most important area in the world for this species.

The following account includes information provided by D. W. Anderson of the United States Fish and Wildlife Service, and shows that the Gulf is still an area of major importance for sulids (see also p. 448). The islands known or suspected to hold breeding blue-foots (Fig. 219) are CONSAGE ROCK (the most northerly known breeding station); ISLA SAN JORGE (George); CHOLLUDA ISLAND; SAN LUIS ISLAND; SAIL ROCK (PUERTO REFUGIO); SAN PEDRO MARTIR; SAN PEDRO NOLASCO; TORTUGA ISLAND; ILDEFONSO; FARALLON DE SAN IGNACIO and possibly some of the islands in the south-west corner of the Gulf. Most of these stations remain little known. In general, both blue-footed and brown boobies occupy the whole of the Gulf, though the former are probably more restricted to the mid and southern areas whereas the brown is most abundant in the northern part. They often share the same island; though they tend to remain apart, Anderson comments that in some cases brown boobies are 'scattered among the blue-foots', no doubt forming little enclaves rather than mixing randomly. Non-breeding birds are to be found resting on very many islands, sometimes (as on ISLA CARDINOSA) over 1000 birds. There is also a big roost, mostly brown, on SAIL ROCK.

The only specific comments for any of the above nesting stations are as follows:

SAN PEDRO MARTIR used to hold a large population along with brown boobies. This rock, 2·4km long and 319m high, has long been exploited for guano and indeed occupied over 100 Yaqui Indians continuously for about 10 years. Yet Goss (1888) estimated merely 1000 pairs though he believed that when undisturbed the island would contain

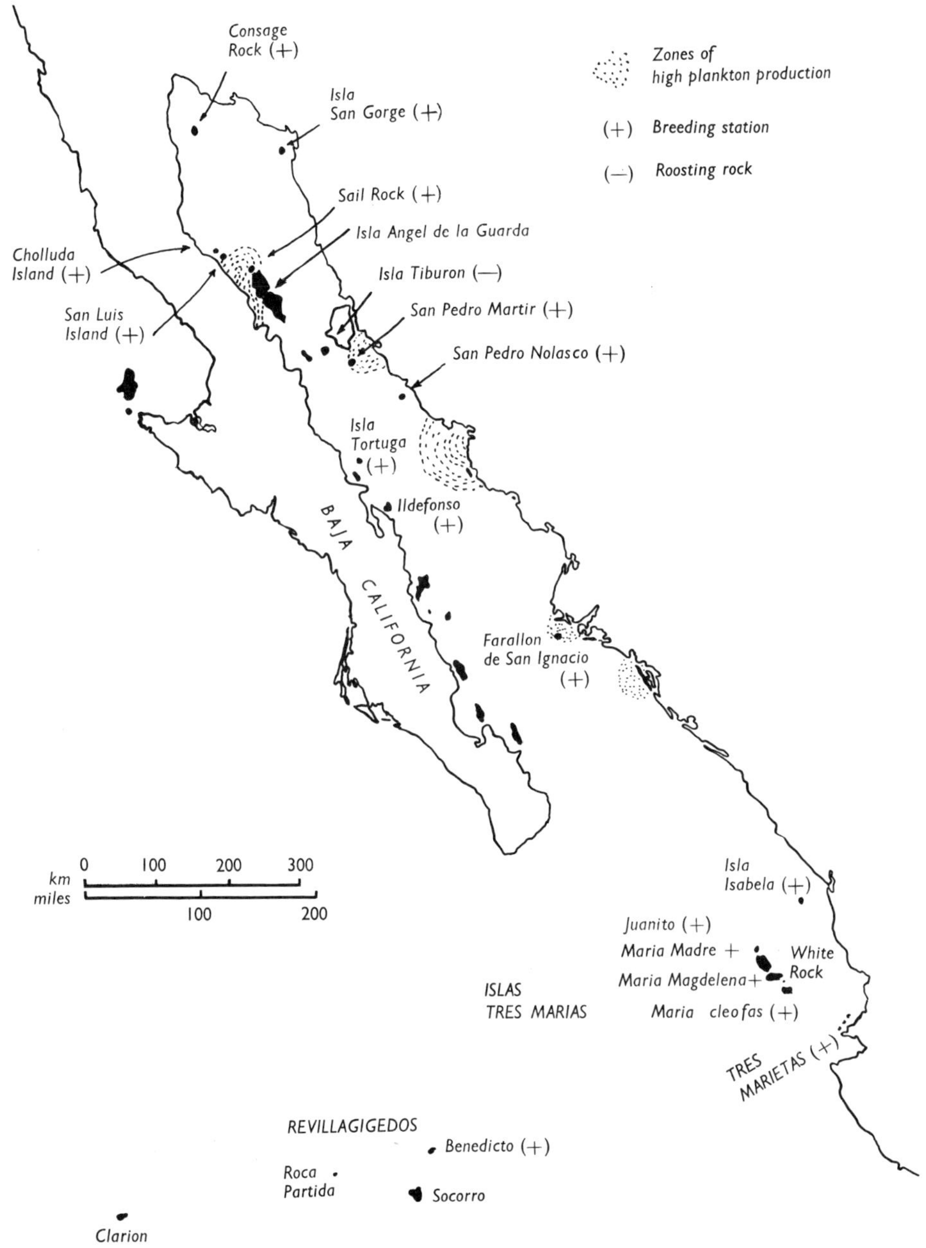

Fig. 219. Islands in the Gulf of California and off Mexico showing breeding stations (16 shown) and major plankton-producing areas. (Partly from information supplied by D. Anderson and in Hutchinson 1950).

'thousands and thousands'. Banks (pers. comm. 1962) said that it bred there 'in abundance'. In June 1971 Anderson estimated 3000–4000 pairs of blue-footed and brown boobies, the former greatly predominating. In 1972 the estimate was 2000 pairs and in May 1973, 4000–5000 pairs, again many blue-foots. He mentions 'huge numbers' flying to and from this island in May 1973. It thus emerges as one of the world's main stations for this species, possibly exceeded only by Lobos de Tierra (Peru).

SAN ILDEFONSO, according to Banks, has many fewer breeding blue-foots than San Pedro Martir and Anderson's estimate of 800–1000 pairs in March 1973 confirms this. They were nesting mainly in the lower canyon, but breeding was just beginning and numbers may have increased later.

TORTUGA ISLAND, the top of an old volcano, is fairly inaccessible. In March 1928 and 1930 it held several small colonies in shallow canyons on top. Presumably it is still a significant breeding place.

FARALLON DE SAN IGNACIO is still a good booby rock, though few details are available. It has long had the blue-foot as its chief guano bird. An accurate account of its present status is required.

Van Rossem (1932) records a few blue-foots at ISLA TIBURÓN and quotes Anthony's comment that they were common there in December 1930. He also includes GUAYMAS, SAN PEDRO NOLASCO and SAN PEDRO MARTIR, but does not make it clear that they were actually breeding on all these. They are unlikely still to do so on TIBURÓN—human persecution would ensure that. ISLA RASA, too, probably once held them (it was a major guano island) but no longer does so. Earlier this century, SAN JORGE was obviously well favoured by brown boobies (hundreds of pairs in 1926) but the status of the blue-foot there is not recorded.

At one time the islands in the **Gulf of California** undoubtedly held vast populations of seabirds, almost comparable with those of **Peru**. Nowadays only a proportion remains. There is no way of telling how the blue-foot has fared in the general decline, caused partly by guano exploitation, but the number of islands potentially suitable for nesting is large and the present population is probably a fraction of that existing a century ago. Human interference is at present a major problem there.

In conclusion, it may be noted that the world population and distribution of the blue-foot could be established much more readily and accurately than that of any other booby except Abbott's and the Peruvian. Since its distribution is much more complex than these other two it would be intrinsically more interesting to know about its colonies and to correlate these with ecological factors. At present one can merely guess at the world population and the following figure is proposed simply to give a rough basis for comparison with other sulids. There are perhaps 10 000–15 000 pairs in the **Galapagos**, the same in **Peru** and maybe 10 000 in the **California–Mexico** area. If there are several thousand scattered on various islets outside these main groupings, the total figure could be around 25–40 000 pairs.

SUMMARY

1. The blue-footed booby has a limited distribution and is the second rarest booby in the world.
2. It occurs in the Pacific ocean only, from the Gulf of California to northern Peru and out to the Galapagos.
3. The Galapagos, with at least 25 breeding stations, is a major locale for the blue-foot; there are probably more than 10 000 pairs in the archipelago.
4. Between the Gulf of Panama and Peru the only substantial concentration is on the Lobos Islands.
5. The blue-foot breeds, nevertheless, on islands in the Gulf of Guayaquil.
6. They breed also, in the Gulf of Panama (Pearl Islands).
7. The Tres Marias Islands, the Tres Marietas and the Revillagigedos all support colonies.
8. Within the Gulf of California there used to be a vast population and blue-foots are still common on several islands.

3. BREEDING ECOLOGY

INTRODUCTION

The blue-footed booby, whilst less restricted in breeding distribution than Abbott's or the Peruvian booby, is nonetheless unusual in that it breeds in only three areas in the world. It is unusual, too, in many aspects of its ecology and behaviour—apparently an 'inventive' species, which nevertheless has failed to achieve anything like the success of the rest of the family (excepting Abbott's booby). It has hitherto escaped serious attention and its behaviour and ecology have not previously been described in any detail, although there are short accounts in Nelson (1968 and 1970).

Perhaps the most useful aspect as background to this section is that, due to a combination of distribution on the fringes of upwellings in areas that are climatically fairly aseasonal, and special hunting techniques (p. 568) the blue-foot probably finds food relatively easily—at least when compared with the warm-water, pan-tropical trio (red-footed, white and brown boobies). This has a considerable effect on its breeding regime and reproductive rate.

BREEDING HABITAT

The blue-foot prefers to nest on flat ground or moderate slopes, with little or no vegetation. The largest colony in the Galapagos occupies the crater bottom on Daphne Major which is as bare and flat as a billiard table; on Lobos de Tierra, which may hold the world's largest colony, the birds nest on the pampas or on slopes and in flat valley bottoms with a variable amount of detritus. On the Tres Marietas, one small and two large islands off Mexico, they nest in the main in small groups on the plateau among grass and sedge (Grant 1964).

They tolerate a variety of substrates (Fig. 220)—completely bare, littered with irregularly sized boulders (as on Punta Suarez, Hood Island, Galapagos) or covered with a variable amount of scrub and/or zerophytic vegetation. Nests may be placed actually beneath scrub, although this must be rare in the species as a whole, but blue-foots never nest off the ground, nor can they perch in branches with any facility although they will perch on spars, rails etc. Murphy saw several which had become entangled in branches on El Muerto and (on account of this and a roosting group which were unfortunate enough to be engulfed in a landslide caused by rain) considered it to be peculiarly ill-adapted to rainy, vegetated islands! Comparably, Harris found five dead adults entangled in thorny *Parkinsonia* scrub on Champion (Galapagos).

The blue-foot avoids cliff-ledges as breeding sites but it will roost on cliffs, nest on flat areas near their edges and on Isabela (Galapagos) nests on steep slopes east of Punta Essex and

Fig. 220(a)

Blue-footed boobies nesting in t
tom of the crater on Daphne Maj
is probably the densest colony k

Fig. 220(b)

Boulder-strewn nesting habitat on Punta Suarez, Hood Island.

on the lower ledges (size unspecified) of a small island in Elizabeth Bay. This is probably the only record of the blue-foot nesting on anything which could accurately be called a ledge. In this respect the blue-foot differs markedly from its close relative the piquero and indeed is probably more closely tied to flattish ground than is any other sulid, though the white booby approaches it in this respect. It shows some tendency to choose a softish substrate rather than bare rocky ground, often selecting pockets of earth between boulders or coves where soft material has gathered. This may be correlated with the lack of nest material; the white booby is similar in this respect. Nevertheless, on Lobos de Tierra (the nests being distributed over the whole island) although most were in semi-rocky terrain, some were placed on solid rock (Galarza 1968), and an early record from San Pedro Martir notes that it preferred smooth, bare rock and made no attempt at a nest. On Isabella (off Mexico) it has been recorded nesting on bare sand a mere 3–4m from the water's edge.

Whether as a corollary or because of other factors (such as the proximity of cold water or the avoidance of dense vegetation) or as an independent factor, the blue-foot favours warm but dry areas. The wet Gorgona (Colombia), which apparently holds some blue-foots, has been cited (Murphy 1936) as an exception but details are lacking. La Plata (Ecuador) holds blue-foots, but its cover consists largely of thorn scrub and cactus and only periodically and ephemerally of lush green vegetation.

COLONY DENSITY

The blue-footed booby is undoubtedly gregarious, nesting in true colonies, although (as in all colonial seabirds) colony size is highly variable. Breeding groups vary greatly in density. On Punta Suarez, Galapagos, on July 24th 1964 there were about 230 nests with eggs or chicks plus probably at least half as many empty sites. At this estimate, some 350–500 pairs were scattered over an irregular area very roughly 2500–3000 sq metres. This means little, since they tend to nest in loose groups, perhaps separated by thinly occupied or entirely empty areas. Furthermore, due to their aseasonal and non-annual breeding, only part of the population is breeding during any one period and this fraction is not constant. Thus the density even of sub-groups can be expected to vary considerably at different times. This should be true, also, even for the much more homogeneous colony in Daphne crater (see below) though it may not hold for the Lobos colonies of Peru (see p. 516). In the top and bottom craters on Daphne Major there were 260 and 750 pairs respectively, about 0·5 pairs per sq metre, and some nests are a mere metre apart from centre to centre. This is probably near the maximum density reached by this species, which often nests in smaller, much more widely dispersed groups or sometimes even solitarily, as on Tower Island in the north of the Galapagos (an area ecologically unsuitable for the blue-foot) where a pair or two nest occasionally.

This species' ritualised breeding behaviour, which is largely based on locomotion, with its precursors and adjuncts, correlates well with the tendency to nest fairly widely dispersed.

One may speculate that its widely dispersed nesting correlates with the absence of strong competition for available space in the regions occupied (borne out by simple observations) and the lack of any other advantage (such as behavioural facilitation and thus timing of breeding) possibly associated with large and dense colonies in other species (see Comparative Section).

NEST SITES AND NESTS

The nest site is merely a scrape on the ground (Fig. 221), perhaps between two spaced boulders, beneath a shrub, in a depression or clearing within dwarf zerophytic vegetation or out in the open on bare substrate. It lies within a larger area which is vigorously defended by display, though hardly ever by fighting. Observations on colour-ringed birds demonstrated that on Punta Suarez, Galapagos, some pairs hold two or three territories, spending some time in each and gradually attaching themselves more exclusively to one of them as egg laying approaches. Later on, when the chick is partly grown, the male at least may revert to one of the other territories from which he may even advertise to overflying females. Multiple territories, as also the dispersed breeding, suggests that there is no shortage of topographically suitable nesting areas for this species. It is just possible that (as may be the case in the magnificent frigate-bird of Barbuda (Diamond 1973) the blue-foot male occasionally breeds more often than the female, leaving her to complete a cycle unaided.

There is no real nest, but merely an area from which the fragments of substrate and detritus have been picked up and deposited, during symbolic nest building, around the actual site on which the eggs are laid. A thin ring of guano surrounds the site and although it has some value as fertiliser, and indeed was considered to be a commercial proposition off Mexico, a blue-foot's deposit never remotely resembles the substantial structure of the piquero. The absence of any structurally significant nest is presumably of no disadvantage when eggs are laid on bare, flat ground, usually well away from other pairs (which are thus unable to roll them into their own nest—a slight risk in more densely nesting species) and in areas unlikely to suffer from heavy rains and thus from standing mud or water which could chill a small chick.

THE EGG AND CLUTCH

1. *Egg characteristics*

The eggs are chalky white over a distinctly blue shell and nearly elliptical in shape. Palmer (1962) describes them as departing slightly from the true ellipsoid where this is caused other than by asymmetry (one end bigger than the other), which is itself slight. He gives the average length of 19 eggs (order of laying not specified) as 62·21±2·66mm and the breadth 41·86±1·70mm. Bent (1922) gives 62·7mm by 42·5mm (range 57·8–69 length and 38·8–48·0 breadth; 62 measured). Anderson (pers. comm.) gives 59·6 (range 57·3–62·6) length and 41·8 (range 40·5–4·30) breadth, from the Gulf of California. The average weight of 39 eggs on Hood was 65g. First eggs of clutches of two weighed 65·4g (range 54–82, 25 weighed) and second eggs 64g (range 53–76, 14 weighed). In the Gulf of California, 10 eggs (position within clutch unspecified) weighed on average 53·8g (range 47·9–59·0). This is significantly less than in the Galapagos. The normal clutch of two represents some 7·2 per cent of the female's weight.

2. *Clutch size*

The blue-foot lays between one and three (usually two) eggs per clutch; four-egg clutches rarely occur. Clutch size varies with locality (see below) for it is undoubtedly an adaptation to economic circumstances. On Hood in the Galapagos, of 182 clutches 85 per cent had two eggs, 12 per cent one and 3 per cent three. Lumping five different counts in 1964 but without following individual clutches to completion, 80 per cent of 280 clutches were of two eggs,

Fig. 221. 'Symbolic' nest (merely a scrape).

18 per cent of one and 2 per cent of three. Similarly, seven spot checks on Daphne in six different months of 1963 showed 502 (71·8 per cent) clutches of two, 158 (22·6 per cent) of one and 39 (5·6 per cent) of three. A small proportion of these may have been incomplete, thus overestimating the one-egg clutches at the expense of the twos and threes, but the general picture is clear enough. On Lobos de Tierra in January 1920, Murphy records that clutches of one, two and three were about equally common. Coker (1920), writing about the same island, records that of 54 nests, 25 contained two eggs or young, 18 three eggs or young and 11 one egg or young. Of 39 nests with young only, 19 had two, 12 three and 8 one. Taking both counts together the percentages of two, three and one work out at 47·3, 32·3 and 20·4 per cent. Thus there are proportionately considerably more clutches of three on the Peruvian islands than in the Galapagos. The mean clutch size in the Galapagos is about 1·8[1] and on Lobos de Tierra 2·1. Information is scarce for clutch sizes elsewhere, but Lamb (1910) says that on the Tres Marietas, Mexico, out of hundreds of nests examined, about equal numbers had two or three and 3 had clutches of four. A series of old egg record cards which I examined included 13 two-egg clutches and 4 threes from the Marietas; 2 twos, 1 three and 1 one from islands within the Gulf of California and 6 twos and 1 one from Isabella. However, an unknown proportion of these clutches may have been incomplete, for many were taken fairly early in the season. On face value, the average clutch for this general area is 2·1.

Apart from the piquero, the blue-foot is the only sulid which regularly rears more than one chick per brood. To understand why it can do so, even on islands where white and brown boobies occur and are restricted to one chick, one must take account of its feeding strategy (pp. 530 and 564).

3. *Laying interval and incubation period*

The eggs are laid five days apart (mean interval 5·02 days; range 4–6; 13 cases). The birds attend, and at least partly incubate, the first egg. Thus the laying interval produces an equivalent hatching interval, so that the young are of dissimilar size throughout their growth. One is always dominant and can commandeer all available food if this becomes scarce. The egg takes 41 days to hatch (range 40–43; six accurately timed cases).

4. *Replacement laying*

On October 8th 1964 I removed fairly fresh eggs (none more than 12 days old) from six nests. Only one pair laid a replacement egg (24 days after loss) and they moved six metres away from the original site. Most of the remainder had not been seen again when we left on November 5th. Nevertheless, this one positive record shows that replacement laying does occur in a proportion of cases as it does in all sulids with the possible exception of Abbott's booby, for which there are no records. One suspects that the mechanism will be affected by prevailing economic circumstances, as desertion of existing eggs certainly is, and that eggs will be replaced if lost when prevailing feeding conditions are good, but not otherwise.

5. *Hatching success*

In the Galapagos, egg or chick loss was mainly dictated by economic circumstances and is best discussed together (see p. 533). Most egg loss was by desertion. The eggs for which we had precise records were deserted mainly in the first half of incubation, some almost immediately after laying, but some when almost due to hatch.

In the Galapagos predation almost certainly causes negligible loss of egg, although it is a more significant source of mortality in chicks (see below). Elsewhere, the story may well be different. Murphy records that on the Peruvian Islands, the blue-foot's principal foe is the Dominican gull, which takes eggs and small young even without the aid of human disturbance. Whilst the booby, perhaps barely uncovering the contents, defends the nest from frontal

[1] This is calculated from the figures given above, but it is bound to be an underestimate and the true figure will be 1·9 or more.

attack, another gull snatches an egg from behind. There are no estimates of the losses sustained in this way, but since there are many gulls, it could be substantial.

6. *Incubation regime*

Frequent checks showed that incubation was fairly evenly divided between the sexes. Out of a total of 186 checks, males were either incubating or attending on 50 per cent of occasions and females on 53 per cent.

Incubation stints averaged about 18 hours for males and 25 for females. Stints became shorter as incubation progressed, but there was considerable individual variation. Stint length reflects the length of the partner's foraging trips and so is an interesting guide to the species' feeding regime (see p. 530 and Table 74).

THE CHICK

1. *Morphology and plumage development*

The blue-foot chick, when **newly-hatched** and still wet, has a somewhat purple skin with sparsely distributed tracts of white down on dorsal pterylae and on posterior margin of wing and on alula. The down thickens during the first three weeks until the chick is covered with long white filoplumes. The down on humeral, caudal and tertial tracts is prepennae; the remainder preplumulae, through which contour feathers grow (Palmer 1962). The eyes remain closed during the first day or so. The following time-scale applied to Hood (Galapagos).

For the first **six weeks** the chick is entirely white and fluffy and its age can be estimated only by weight and measurements. During the **sixth week** the primaries may erupt (although six-week-old chicks may show no trace of them) and also the first 1 or 2mm of tail (usually before the primaries appear). At **seven weeks** even backward chicks show the beginnings of all primaries, the coverts are emerging, the tail may be up to 60mm long and the forehead just clearing. At **ten weeks** remiges, rectrices and scapulars are well through but down remains thick on head, neck and underparts and a thick band follows the line of the radio-ulna. The forehead may be clear and the ear-coverts thinning. Between **ten and eleven weeks**, the forehead, a thin rim round the eyes, cheeks and gular areas may be clear, but down remains thick on head, neck, throat and mid-back extending round to thighs and flanks. In some chicks of **eleven and twelve weeks** the down remains thick on the lower back and on the flanks and undersurface and some down (varying from thick to traces) remains on the radio-ulna line and on the top of the head, throat and upper breast. The forehead, mid-back, scapulars and wings are, however, free from down and the ear coverts thinning or free. The skin of the forehead may be clear of down but still bluish and unfeathered. In more advanced birds there are merely tufts of down on thighs and traces on head and neck. Between **twelve and thirteen weeks** 'late' young may still retain considerable down on thighs and under tail coverts, some on the neck and even a trace on the crown. At **thirteen weeks** the chick is usually almost or completely clear and may be almost capable of flight.

The gular skin is pale blue and the bill slightly darker than that of the adult. The legs and

TABLE 74

ATTENDANCE (INCUBATION AND CHICK CARE) IN THE BLUE-FOOT

	Length of incubation spells		Length of chick-guard spells (chick < 4 weeks)		Length of chick-guard spells (chick > 4 weeks)	
	Mean	Range	Mean	Range	Mean	Range
Male (a)	18 (33)	4–75	15 (28)	5–65	15 (31)	4–35
(b)	Eggs lost or abandoned		17 (25)	4–103	19 (20)	2–72
Female (a)	25 (35)	9–70	20 (37)	5–75	14 (32)	3–68
(b)	Eggs lost or abandoned		32 (25)	4–89	18 (27)	5–90

(a) = Before food shortage. (b) = During food shortage.

Fig. 222(a–c). Stages in the development of the young blue-footed booby. **(a)** 2–3 weeks (larger) and about 5 days less (smaller). The younger chick has been short of food; in good times the difference would be much less marked.

(b) c. 8 weeks.

(c) c. 10 weeks.

feet are variable blue/grey (sometimes lilac) turning lighter blue from the top downwards. Dark thigh feathers extend backwards to the under tail coverts.

The fully feathered youngster and free-flying juvenile is much deeper brown than the adult. The head is uniformly dark brown, without the adult's conspicuous pale flecks, and the upper breast brown, sharply demarcated from the pale lower breast and belly. The anterior edge of the pale lower breast continues the line of the leading edge of the wing so that the white underparts run continuously into the white axillaries, which are paler than the rest of the silvery-grey underwing.

2. *Feeding*

The details of begging and feeding behaviour are given on pp. 563 and 565. Here, we are concerned with feeding rates and allied topics.

The brood of two or even three chicks introduces the complicating factor of competition for food between siblings. Among the sulids, only the Peruvian booby, in its unusually rich food situation, has broods of more than one chick, so the blue-foot is clearly unusual in this respect. Even so, a clear cut dominance is exerted by the older chick with corresponding appeasement by the younger, and is used whenever there is insufficient food to satisfy both. In times of food shortage in the Galapagos the younger chicks in **all** broods of two die of starvation and even single chicks may starve. Nevertheless, for much of the time, adult blue-foots are feeding two chicks, and often rear them, a fact which is relevant to any consideration of the frequency with which they return with food.

(*a*) *Feeding frequency*

A continuous watch of pairs with broods of different ages, during the daylight part of

TABLE 75

NUMBER OF FEEDS PER CHICK, IN THE BLUE-FOOTED BOOBY, DURING THE DAYLIGHT HOURS OF A 48-HOUR SPELL

Chick	(Age) weeks	Successful bouts*	Successful entries	Unsuccessful bouts*	Unsuccessful entries
1	6	6 (2)	7	2	12
2	6	3 (2)	3	—	1
3	6	3 (2)	5	—	2
4	6	(2)	Unfed during daylight		
5	7	3 (1)	6	—	4
6	7	3	3	—	6
7	7	(2)	Unfed during daylight		
8	12	(1)	Unfed during daylight		
9	12	3 (1)	6	—	1
10	14	3 (1)	3	—	—
11	14	(2)	Unfed during daylight		

* A bout = one of a series of feeds separated from the last feed(s) by 10 minutes or more. Figures in brackets represent additional feeds deduced to have occurred during the night from changes in weight and/or a change of parent on the nest.

TABLE 76

DIVISION OF LABOUR BETWEEN MALE AND FEMALE BLUE-FOOTED BOOBIES IN FEEDING THEIR CHICK(S)

	No. of feeds per chick							
	1 (6)	2 (6)	3 (6)	5 (7)	6 (7)	9 (12+)	10 (14)	Total
Male	1	3	2	0	2	0	1	9
Female	5	0	1	3	1	3	2	15

Age of chick is given in brackets: chick number corresponds with previous table.

48 hours, gave the picture shown in Table 75. It must be mentioned that these observations were carried out on September 16–17th 1964, just after a severe spell of food shortage. Nevertheless, many pairs were beginning to court and build and a few were laying, so food was probably not exceptionally scarce just then.

The above figures are certainly too low. Evidence from weighing the chicks proved that some feeds were given during the night and direct observations at 22.00 hours, when it was very dark, showed that there had been many arrivals since 18.30. Several juveniles were begging vigorously and I recorded at the time that night feeding of young might be an important feature of this species' breeding behaviour. This makes it impossible to give an accurate figure but the following alternatives exist:

1. Taking merely the feeds seen during daylight hours and counting only the chicks fed at least once, the average number of feeds per chick was 1·8 per day.
2. Taking all chicks this figure was 1·1.
3. Taking into account deduced feeds, the overall average is 1·8.

On alternative three no chick remained unfed for 48 hours and the maximum number of feeds delivered, to chick 1, was 8, whereas on alternative 1 four chicks remained unfed. In fact, it is probably fair to take a figure of around two feeds per chick per day. Two-chick broods will require the parents to return with food more frequently than this, but unfortunately there were none which could practicably be included in the sample.

(b) Pattern of return, absence and attendance

A simple picture of the attendance regime in the different phases of the breeding cycle is provided by an analysis of the proportion of occasions on which the birds are present at the nest.

Before the egg is laid, the male attends much more frequently than the female (40 per cent of 128 checks as against 18 per cent for the female). During incubation, the sexes were recorded an equal number of times (186 checks); during the first four weeks of the chick's life the male was present on 44 per cent of 112 checks and the female on 69 per cent. Thus the male was away far more often, presumably foraging, than the female, which is consistent with his suggested tendency to make frequent, short trips, well suited to the needs of the small young. The male's attendance at chicks 4–8 weeks old dropped to 30 per cent of 161 checks, which was the same as the female's (32 per cent). Unfortunately there are too few figures for attendance at chicks older than 8 weeks to be analysed similarly, but one would expect the female's attendance to drop further; she would be away foraging, since she is the main provider for the older chicks.

The effect of the August food shortage is also well illustrated by attendance checks. Thus, attendance at chicks less than four weeks old during 'normal' conditions was 44 per cent (male) and 69 per cent (female), but during food shortage the comparative figures were 30 per cent and 23 per cent. Similarly, attendance at chicks over four weeks was 30 per cent (male) and 32 per cent (female) during 'normal' conditions but 4 per cent and 17 per cent during food shortage. It appears that during times of food shortage the female drastically shortens her attendance spells in favour of foraging and the male reduces his still further.

Analysis of the frequency with which adults returned to their site during 48 hours (Table 77) revealed that birds with large chicks had a complicated pattern of attendance. They spent a considerable amount of time on the site, departing and returning many times during a day. Most absences were short, but a few were longer than half an hour. Of 10 pairs (one of which had perhaps lost the male since he was not seen throughout the check) watched for the daylight hours of a 48 hour period, the males averaged 1·9 absences of half an hour or more and the females 1·3. If **all** absences regardless of length are counted, the figures are males 6·6 absences and females 3·7, individual males varying from 23 (a pair with six-week-old chick) to 1 (3 males all with large chicks) and individual females from 8 to 1. If one assumes, I think reasonably, that absences of less than 30 minutes are unlikely to be fishing trips, these figures agree well with the number of feeds delivered (about two per day bearing in mind the night feeds resulting from absences which we could not record). This is not a high feeding frequency, particularly bearing in mind the blue-foot's inshore fishing habit (p. 568).

The information from the 48 hour check indicates that both sexes make fishing trips of very short duration (considering the family as a whole). In view of the evidence suggesting that females tend to feed large young more than do males it is perhaps consistent that they return more frequently. On the other hand, in view of the sexual dimorphism, the smaller male could well be expected to make shorter trips and the fact that he apparently does not, may be due to some of his absences being attendance spells at one of his alternative sites rather than foraging trips. However, this factor cannot be assessed on present evidence. Also, it happens that none of the chicks were small, and it may be that it is to young chicks that the male makes the most frequent returns. It must be left to future work to show whether there really is (as I have suggested) a meaningful division of labour, with the male feeding smaller young and making on average shorter and more frequent trips than the female.

It is always relevant to record the time spent by parents actually on the site, since this represents 'dead' time so far as fishing is concerned. My figures for this represent only daylight attendance at the site; several birds were present when we began the checks at dawn and may have been present all night, so that their attendance as a proportion of 24 hours would be much higher than their daylight attendance. Furthermore, one or two birds, especially males, were suspected of resting elsewhere than on the site. The figures are thus minimal. Even so, they show that roughly a half of the daylight hours were spent by each sex on the site. Males were particularly prone to break up their attendance by short flights around the area, but these usually lasted less than a minute. There was some variation in the 10 pairs studied, but clear indications that individuals had their own pattern which they maintained for both days.

3. *Growth*

(*a*) *By weight*

The only growth figures available for the blue-foot are from Hood Island, Galapagos, July–November 1964. Since we know that for part of this time food was drastically short, the growth curves given here cannot be regarded as necessarily typical. Despite the bad period, however, a striking feature is the speed with which the chick can reach adult weight. Thus, at 65 days some chicks weigh well over 2000g (mean adult weight 1540g). The range of weight at any age is great—enhanced by the extreme differences in weight between the sexes in this species. Thus two 60-day-old birds may differ by 1000g and at 77 days the difference between heaviest and lightest chick was 1260g, the latter weighing a mere 47 per cent of the former. Figs. 223–28 show several aspects of growth.

TABLE 77

SUMMARY OF TIME SPENT AWAY FROM THE NEST BY BREEDING BLUE-FOOTED BOOBIES

Criteria of absence	Mean length and range of absences in hours and minutes Male (no. of cases)	Female (no. of cases)
Timed absence of 30 minutes or more (excluding those beginning or ending before or after observation started)	2–06 (12) Range 0–50 to 5–59	1–26 (15) Range 0–30 to 4–04
Absence of 30 minutes or more (including those excluded above)	3–39 (19) Range 0–34 to 11–46	2–24 (29) Range 0–30 to 11–30
Timed absences of any length over one minute	2–39 (27) Range 0–1 to 0–28	1–46 (39) Range 0–02 to 0–29

(*b*) *By other measurements*

As in other species the culmen is a much less sensitive index of economic circumstances than is weight and continues to grow at much the standard rate even when weight is fluctuating. Fig. 227 illustrates this by showing the growth in weight and culmen for three individual chicks.

4. *Fledging period*

On Hood, blue-footed boobies were capable of reasonably sustained flight by, on average, 102 days (8 cases, range 98–107). In one case a chick of 98 days, thrown into the air, was unable to fly, but five days later was fully fledged. Males (5 cases) fledged at 95 (1880g), 98 (1490g), 103 (1400g), 105 (1550g) and 107 (1570g) days and females at 101 (1930g), 101 (1980g) and 105 (2180g) days. These figures are too few to decide whether males fledge at an earlier age than females but, from relative sizes, one might reasonably expect them to do so. The blue-foot thus requires substantially less growing time than the blue-water boobies but not than the Peruvian, which probably just beats it despite rearing two or three chicks to the blue-foot's one or two. In fact the figures given above refer solely to single chicks (no twins were available for reasonably long series of weighings); twins may take a little longer. On the other hand, the period of food shortage may have retarded the growth even of singletons. Comparative figures for blue-footed boobies from different areas would be of interest.

Besides the absolute difference in growing time between different species, it may be noted that the blue-foot's fledging periods spread over a comparatively small range. For the slowest chick to take only just over a week longer than the fastest—and that after a period when food shortage would be expected to exaggerate any inherent variability—is notably little when compared with the Galapagos red-foot, which fledges at ages varying between 130 and 150 days. This is consistent with other indications of the blue-foot's relatively greater ability to catch more food per day.

5. *Post-fledging feeding*

There is no detailed information on this important aspect of breeding biology. Our own

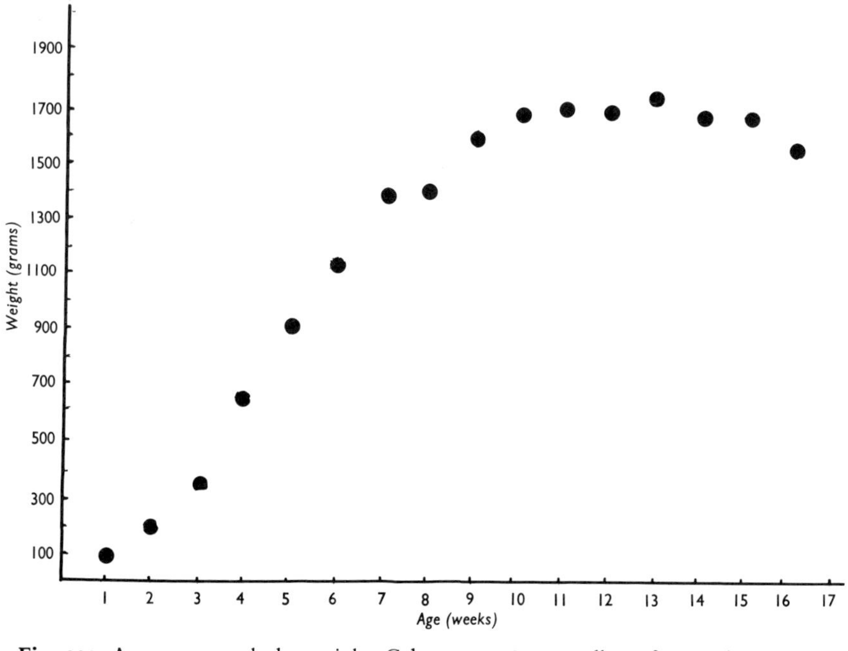

Fig. 223. Average growth, by weight, Galapagos 1964, regardless of sex or brood size.

records, though incomplete, indicate a post-fledging feeding period of at least one month. One juvenile flew about the end of July and finally left the island some time after mid-September—some six weeks after fledging. Three other juveniles were seen to receive feeds when at least 32 days beyond fledging age. Once on the wing, juvenile blue-foots go to sea each day, presumably merely for short distances, and we recorded one following its parent (female) in flight, attempting to beg as it did so and landing with her, near the site, thereupon immediately receiving food. There is no evidence that juveniles are ever fed on the sea but this seems less inconceivable than in most other sulids, since adults often fish so close to the colony and individual recognition does exist. Palmer (1962), probably from remarks made by collectors in the Gulf of California, says that where the species breeds in 'close aggregations' older chicks, though still unable to fly, assemble in groups, frequently shorewards of their nest site, and are fed there, away from their breeding territory. Presumably, if this occurs with pre-flight young it will occur also with fledged young, making any estimate of the period

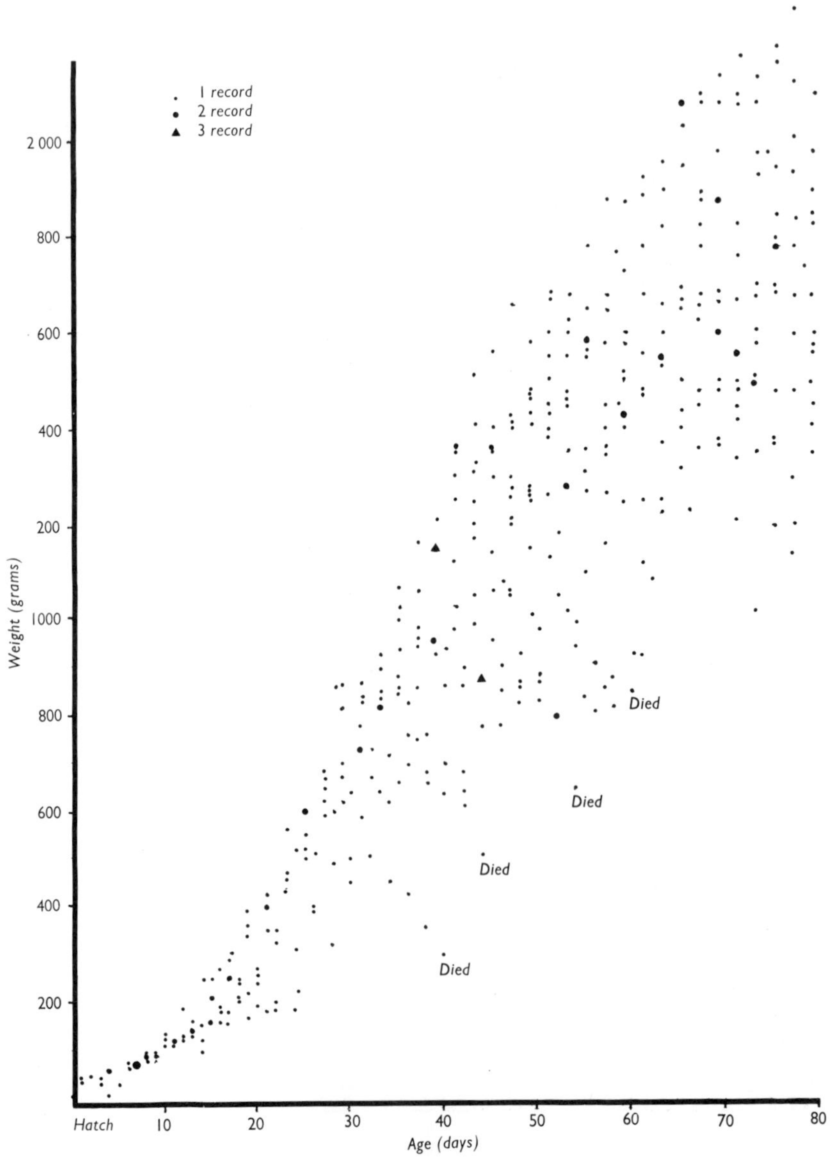

Fig. 224. Growth, by weight, showing amount of variability.

of post-fledging feeding somewhat less reliable. It is clear that there are locations, such as the Daphne craters, where this could not happen. Nevertheless, it is an interesting characteristic, apparently not found in other sulids and perhaps tied in with this species' unusual fishing tactics.

Judging from the existing incomplete information I would guess that juvenile blue-foots are rarely fed for more than six weeks after fledging and more often for four to six weeks. This is consistent with their somewhat compressed breeding cycle as a whole and forms an interesting and similarly consistent contrast with the extended cycle of (in particular) the red-foot (see Comparative Section).

BREEDING SUCCESS

In the Galapagos, even in the south of the archipelago, the blue-foot has to contend with an irregular food supply. It may well be that, owing to several adaptations, it suffers less extremely than the red-foot (q.v.) but nevertheless the importance of this economic factor in determining breeding success, both by causing desertion and loss of eggs and starvation of young, was dramatically brought home to us during our observations on the Punta Suarez colony, Hood Island. Of course, the Galapagos—indeed, for all one knows, even the Hood—situation may well be unrepresentative of the species as a whole, and comparative data are much needed.

This account of breeding success stems from two sources; a detailed study of a relatively small group of nests and a few checks on a much larger sample. Both yield figures for breeding success, but the former permits a finer picture of egg and chick loss. Out of 71 nests holding a total of 138 eggs (9 clutches of one, 57 of two and 5 of three) the pattern of loss was as follows (Table 78).

Whilst the sample is too small for the differences in the number of young produced from different clutch sizes to be significant, there is a strong suggestion that clutches of two were more successful than single-egg clutches. This is clearly because a number of nests lost merely

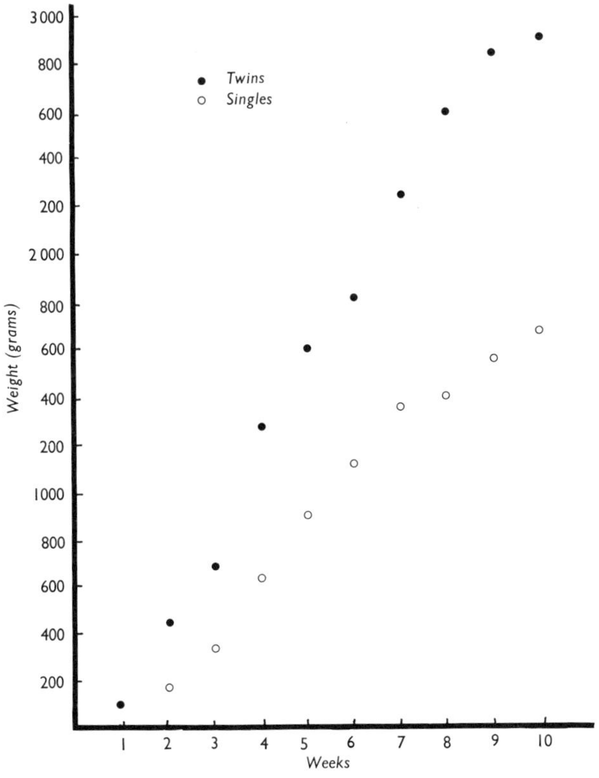

Fig. 225

Total biomass produced by pairs rearing twins and singles respectively.

one out of the two eggs (a result which need not necessarily have been expected since predators could well have eaten both of a clutch of two as readily as a clutch of one) or one out of the two chicks (mainly from starvation). From the whole sample, a substantial number (39) were lost as eggs—a loss over half as great as the total chick mortality (67). Thus egg loss can obviously be very significant. In this particular case, desertion was by far the greatest single cause and was in turn due to abnormal shortage of food. There is no reason to suspect that under normal circumstances predation is a hazard, but we were unable to discover how clutches of two lost one egg. Possibly the incubating bird left on a foraging trip and lost one egg by chance to a 'casual' predator such as a mocking bird, or the first-laid egg was unattended and

TABLE 78

PATTERN OF EGG AND CHICK LOSS FROM 71 BLUE-FOOTED BOOBY CLUTCHES

		1 egg	2 eggs	3 eggs	Total 'items'
Total nests		9	57	5	138
Lost as egg	one	4	5	2	
	two		9		29
Lost at	one	—	6	—	
hatching	two		2		10
Chick lost					
@ under	one	1	18	4	
2 weeks	two		2	1	29
Chick lost					
@ over	one	3	22	3	
2 weeks	two		4	1	38
Chick	one	1	27	2	
fledged	two		1		32
Total 'items'		9	114	15	138

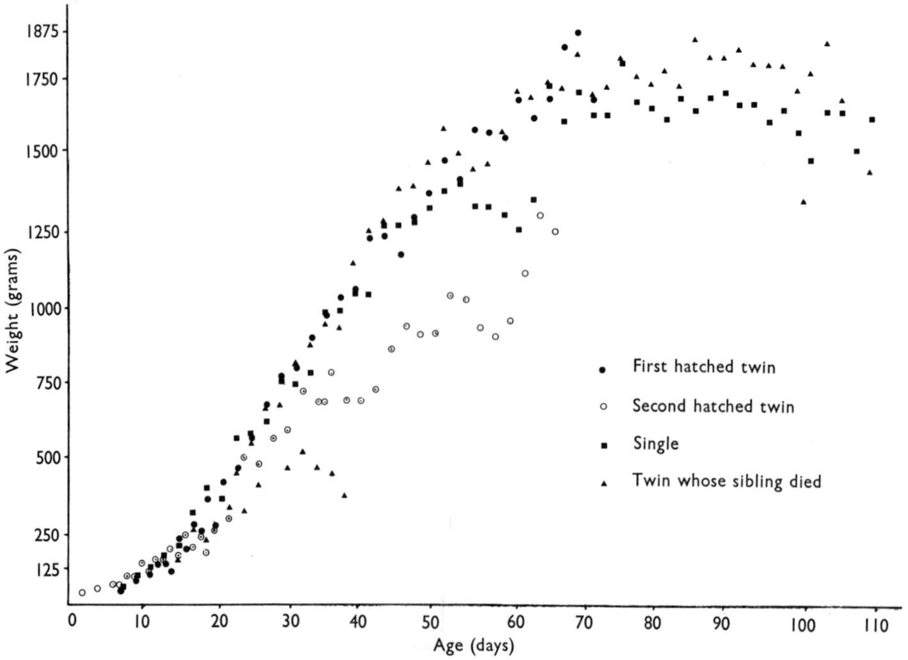

Fig. 226. Growth, by weight, of single chicks and two-chick broods respectively.

therefore vulnerable, or perhaps one egg was lost around hatching time due to difficulties in coping simultaneously with an intact egg and a hatching or newly hatched chick.

Table 79 shows that hatching success was 72 per cent of eggs laid (in terms of nests 79 per

TABLE 79

FATE OF 71 BLUE-FOOTED BOOBY NESTS

	Number of nests		
	1 egg	2 eggs	3 eggs
Laid 1 egg, lost 1 egg	4		
Laid 1 egg, lost 1 chick @ under 2 weeks	1		
Laid 1 egg, lost 1 chick @ over 2 weeks	3		
Laid 1 egg, fledge 1 chick	1		
Laid 2 eggs, lost 2 eggs		9	
Laid 2 eggs, lost 2 @ hatching		2	
Laid 2 eggs, lost 1 @ hatching & 1 chick @ under 2 weeks		2	
Laid 2 eggs, lost 1 @ hatching & 1 chick @ over 2 weeks		1	
Laid 2 eggs, lost 1 egg & 1 chick @ under 2 weeks		1	
Laid 2 eggs, lost 1 egg & 1 chick @ over 2 weeks		2	
Laid 2 eggs, lost 2 chicks @ under 2 weeks		2	
Laid 2 eggs, lost 2 chicks @ over 2 weeks		4	
Laid 2 eggs, lost 1 chick @ under 2 weeks & 1 chick @ over 2 weeks		6	
Laid 2 eggs, lost 1 egg & fledge 1 chick		2	
Laid 2 eggs, lost 1 @ hatching & fledge 1 chick		3	
Laid 2 eggs, lost 1 chick @ under 2 weeks & fledge 1 chick		9	
Laid 2 eggs, lost 1 chick @ over 2 weeks & fledge 1 chick		13	
Laid 2 eggs, fledge 2 chicks		1	
Laid 3 eggs, lost 1 egg, 1 chick @ under 2 weeks & 1 chick @ over 2 weeks			1
Laid 3 eggs, lost 2 chicks @ under 2 weeks & 1 chick @ over 2 weeks			1
Laid 3 eggs, lost 1 chick @ under 2 weeks & 2 chicks @ over 2 weeks			1
Laid 3 eggs, lost 1 egg, lost 1 chick @ under 2 weeks & fledge 1 chick			1
Laid 3 eggs, lost 1 chick @ under 2 weeks, 1 chick @ over 2 weeks & fledge 1 chick			1

Total nests		71
Total eggs		138
Total eggs lost	29	
Total lost @ hatching	10	39
Total chicks lost @ under 2 weeks		29
Total chicks lost @ over 2 weeks		38
Total chicks fledged		32
Eggs hatched from laid	99/138	= 72%
Chicks fledged from eggs hatched	32/99	= 32·3%
Chicks fledged from eggs laid	32/138	= 23·2%
Chicks fledged from total number of nests	32/71	= 45·1%

cent hatched at least one egg)—a figure which is probably lower than normal, but even at that, quite respectable.

Still considering this same sample of 71 nests it may be seen that they produced 32 fledglings (45·1 per cent). Expressed as the proportion of youngsters fledging from those hatched, this figure is 32/99 or 32·3 per cent and as the proportion of youngsters fledging from the total number of eggs laid 32/138 or 23·2 per cent. Of the 67 chicks lost, 29 died in the first 15 days of life. The remaining 38 were probably lost as a result of the unusual food shortage which drastically reduced the population of chicks on Hood and killed off at least one from nearly all nests with twins. The fledging success was thus unusually low and perhaps should not be taken as representative of the Hood blue-footed boobies, much less those of the Galapagos in general or the species as a whole. One the other hand, Harris also recorded a similar disaster on Hood in July and August, 1970. From the proportion of nests with twins (Table 80) it eesms fair to conclude that, taking average clutch size as 1·9, roughly 36 per cent of pairs that lay two or three rear two (100 pairs lay 190 eggs but rear only 126 chicks), and on this basis, the fledging success from 71 nests on Hood would have been 90 young rather than 32, had not a catastrophic spell intervened. Certainly the comparative seabird biologist would be wiser to take the higher figure as more representative of the species.

This introduces the second source of information on breeding success, the wider survey of the Punta Suarez peninsula between July and November 1964.

In late July-early August 1964, the blue-foot colony contained pairs in all stages of breeding (134 nests with eggs only, totalling 249 eggs; 20 nests with both egg(s) and chick(s), totalling

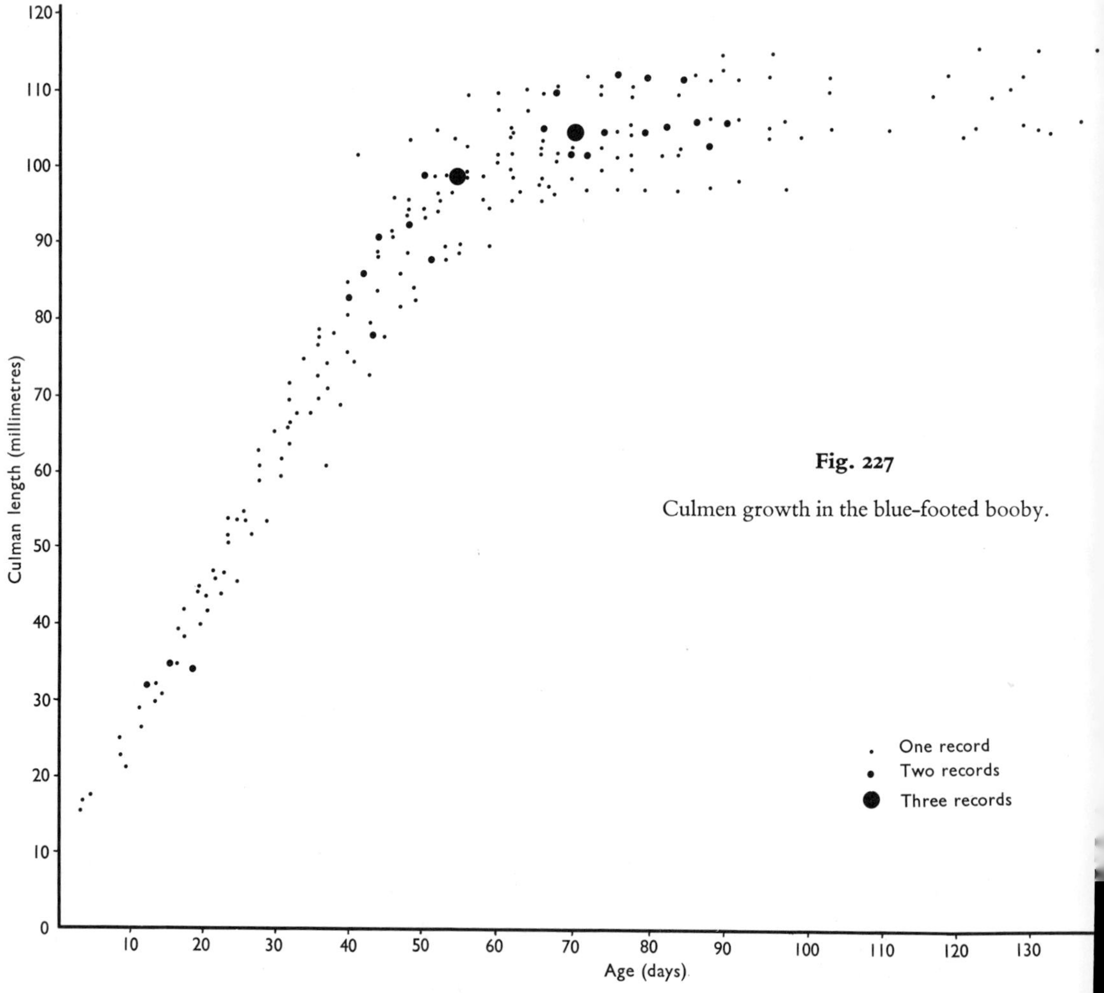

Fig. 227

Culmen growth in the blue-footed booby.

21 eggs and 20 chicks; 74 nests with chicks up to 12 weeks old, totalling 124 chicks; and 2 free-flying juveniles). Thus, at this time the colony held 230 pairs actively engaged in incubating or caring for young and also 52 pairs or singles attending sites. Altogether 416 items (eggs or chicks) were extant. Some seven weeks later, on September 22nd–28th, there were 15 nests with eggs (22 eggs), 56 nests with chicks up to 12 weeks (59 chicks) and 34 juveniles; altogether 115 items.

If all eggs and chicks up to five weeks old[1] on the August count had survived until the September count (and excluding all chicks that could have come from eggs laid between the two counts—i.e. one week old or less by the September count) there would have been 364 chicks up to 12 weeks old in September. In fact there were 58. Similarly, the 44 chicks older than six weeks in August should have been juveniles by September; in fact there were 34 although there may have been a few at sea.

As the young grow, deaths reduce the average brood-size (Fig. 229). Thus, of the eggs and chicks up to five weeks old in August, 84·1 per cent had died by September. It is not possible to separate those lost as eggs from those lost as chicks, but one can get a minimum figure. Thus, of 144 chicks up to 12 weeks old in August, 92 (including the juveniles) or 64 per cent were alive in September. Undoubtedly many of the eggs present in August would have hatched and died as chicks, but the proportion cannot be ascertained from the figures available.

Two important aspects of chick mortality are first, that it usually operates on the second of the two chicks and second, that it falls most heavily on small chicks, which are less capable of withstanding prolonged starvation. The first aspects means that, in terms of *nests* which rear at least one chick, the figure is higher than simply the percentage of chicks surviving (theoretically 100 two-egg nests could rear 100 young, which would be 100 per cent nest success, but 50 per cent chick mortality). In the situation described above, 228 nests held eggs or chicks up to 12 weeks old in August and 92 held chicks (including juveniles) in September—a 'mortality'

[1] By September they would have been 12 weeks, which is about the latest they can be aged; after that they are more or less fully feathered.

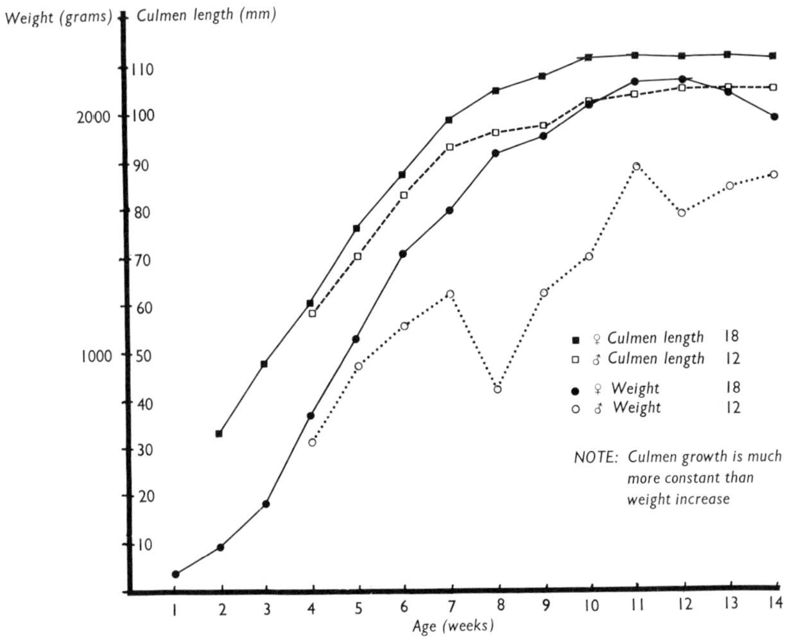

Fig. 228. Growth by weight and culmen length, of the male and female. Note that bill growth is more constant than weight.

of 61 per cent as against 84·1 per cent mortality reckoned simply as the percentage of eggs and chicks lost from those originally present. In terms of nests with one or more chicks in August and one chick in September the score is at least 83 out of 96, showing that despite, in the interval, massive egg-loss and the death of at least one chick from every two-chick brood, at least 86 per cent of nests with one or more chicks in August still held one chick in September. This figure is obtained by excluding from the September count all chicks under six weeks, since these would have been eggs in August and therefore ineligible for calculating chick survival between the two dates.

It should also be pointed out that this figure of 86 per cent includes chicks that were still newly hatched in August, when the food shortage began. The survival of chicks that were quite large in August was much better; well over 90 per cent of nests with one or more such young in August still held one in September.

Nevertheless, the dramatic effect of a sudden period of food shortage should not be underplayed. It turned the Punta Suarez colony from a thriving place to one in which dead chicks were littered everywhere, deserted clutches on all sides and surviving chicks badly underweight. There was also evidence of comparable happenings on Daphne, where there were many dead chicks in November 1964 and again on Hood in July and August 1970.

In an ecological situation of this nature and in the absence of a long run of figures it is somewhat meaningless to cite any figure for hatching success, since everything depends on whether a period of food shortage happens to intervene during the incubation period. If it does, massive desertion may occur; otherwise hatching success will be high. In the group of nests which we studied in detail, hatching success happened to be 72 per cent but this figure cannot legitimately be compared with species (like the gannet) in which there is no such capricious, environmentally-caused egg-loss. A more valid comparison would come from the Peruvian or Californian populations of blue-footed boobies, but we lack information.

Fledging success (young reared to independence from eggs hatched) is similarly at the mercy of fluctuating economic circumstances, and only an average figure taken over many years would provide a fair basis for generalisation and comparative purposes.

One of the most interesting aspects of clutch size and fledging success in the blue-foot as compared with its sympatric congeners in the Galapagos (white and red-footed boobies) is that because of its two-egg clutch it is much better able to take advantage of favourable circumstances without, it seems, suffering any disadvantage in straitened circumstances. In the Galapagos, the output per pair of blue-foots, per breeding effort, is higher than in the other two species because (a) some pairs rear two chicks and in good times this may be the norm

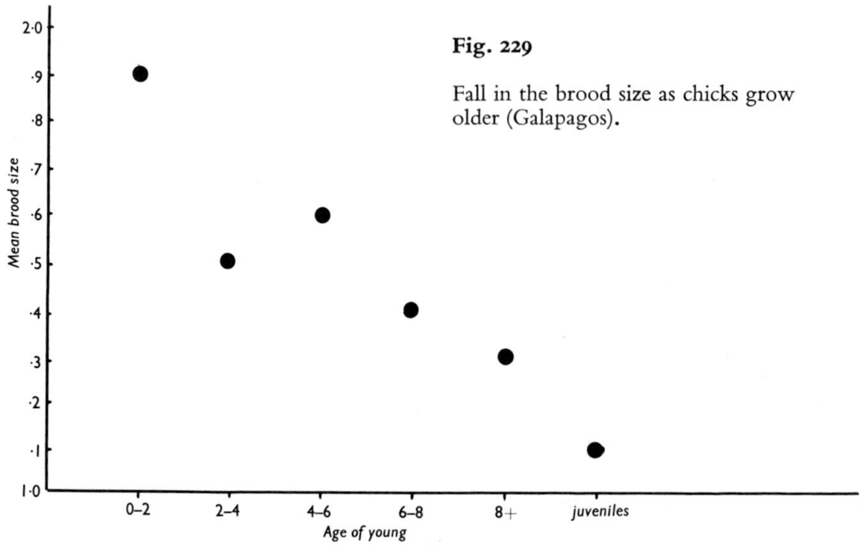

Fig. 229

Fall in the brood size as chicks grow older (Galapagos).

and (b) a higher proportion rear one chick, even though they do lose the other in lean times.

The great value of the second chick in terms of recruitment is well shown by a series of spot checks on Hood and Daphne, recording the proportions of two-chick broods of different ages (Table 80). It is clear that there are many two-chick broods even of well grown young. Whether these survive as well as singletons is not known, but (given the overriding effect of unpredictable famines which probably kill indiscriminately) they probably do.

BREEDING REGIMES

1. *Seasonal aspects*

In the Galapagos, as Appendix 11 shows, the blue-foot may be found with fresh eggs in every month of the year, although this does not necessarily mean that all months are equally favoured. Large colonies such as Daphne can easily give the impression of non-stop breeding activity, for there is rarely if ever a time when there are no birds there. On the other hand, small colonies are abandoned by the blue-foot for some weeks between breeding cycles. But even the large colonies do not sustain a steady level of breeding activity; synchronisation (see below) produces distinct peaks and troughs.

There is more information for Daphne and Hood than for any other Galapagos island, though even here there is not a sufficiently long run of records properly to establish preferred laying months. On Daphne, there seem to be very few eggs laid in July, August and September. However, in view of the blue-foot's 9–10-month breeding periodicity (p. 544) no month could be consistently avoided unless those pairs 'due' to lay in that month postponed laying

TABLE 80

THE PROPORTION OF BLUE-FOOTED BOOBY NESTS HOLDING ONE OR TWO CHICKS, AT DIFFERENT STAGES IN THEIR GROWTH

		Number of nests containing chicks aged:									
Area	Date	0—2 weeks 1	0—2 weeks 2	2—4 weeks 1	2—4 weeks 2	4—6 weeks 1	4—6 weeks 2	6—8 weeks 1	6—8 weeks 2	8+ weeks 1	8+ weeks 2
Daphne (top crater)	19.12.63	2	49	17	10	2	1	0	0	3	1
Daphne (bottom crater)	19.12.63	0	12	20	15	4	7	1	0	0	0
Daphne (top crater)	11.7.64	adults sitting		1	14	5	26	5	12	0	5
Daphne (bottom crater)	11.7.64	0	2	5	14	0	7	7	4	2	5
Hood (Punta Suarez)	26.8.64	1	27	6	4	4	2	6	9	10	5
Hood (Punta Suarez)	28.9.64	1	0	2	0	2	2	20	1	28	0
Hood (Punta Suarez)	11.11.65	3 broods of two; 14 broods of one. (M. P. Harris)									
Hood (Punta Suarez)	4.12.66	5 broods of two; 11 broods of one. (M. P. Harris)									
Hood Punta Suarez)	14.3.67	Mainly single young. (M. P. Harris)									
Daphne	8.7.70	Average brood 1·5. (M. P. Harris)									

Proportion 1:2 (a) overall = 179:242; average brood size = 1·57
(b) after 6 weeks = 82:42; average brood size = 1·26

for a few weeks longer than normal. This could happen if laying depended on an external trigger, say food, and this consistently tended to be scarce in any month(s), but this is probably not so and if it were, the breeding cycle would be expected to be much more clearly geared to avoid it than is the case. A simpler system would be to stick to a fixed breeding periodicity of optimal frequency, whilst retaining the capacity to prolong the between-cycle interval until the economic conditions were adequate for beginning a new breeding attempt. In the Galapagos, where food is notoriously liable to seasonally unpredictable periods of severe shortage, such a system would seem the most adaptive and indeed appears to have been adopted.

On Hood there is similar evidence for widespread laying (see Appendix 12). On this island, we happen to have good evidence of food-poor periods (August 1964 and July-August 1970) during which mass starvation of young and desertion of eggs occurred. By August 18th 1964 all but one of the nests which formerly had two eggs or young held one or none and corpses were everywhere. Yet, by the beginning of September there was a noticeable increase in the number of birds attending the colony and in territorial and sexual display and by the middle of the month birds began to lay. Much the same thing happened in 1970.

As already mentioned the mortality of chicks and desertion of eggs on Hood in August 1964 and a drastic failure around July-August 1963, on Isabela, show clearly that adults can neither lay so that their young do not encounter a bad patch nor even time their laying so that they themselves can continue to incubate.

Probably, in the archipelago as a whole, laying occurs mainly between October and May, perhaps particularly in April-May and October-November, but the nine to ten-month cycle brings a constant succession of pairs into approximate breeding condition throughout the year, and these await appropriate external conditions, perhaps including a suitable company of physiologically compatible neighbours, before initiating the next breeding attempt (see Synchronisation p. 541). This would account for the observed laying throughout the year with, nevertheless, the considerable degree of local synchrony which occurs and at the same time could accommodate the possibility that July-August tend to be relatively quiet months with October-November favoured for laying. It must be emphasised that this system is an adaptation to the particular conditions of the Galapagos, which permit, or even favour, a non-seasonal breeding regime and thus allow pairs to breed at intervals of a fraction of a year (as in the blue-foot), a year (white booby) or a year-plus-a-fraction (red-footed booby). The blue-foot has adopted the first of these because it fits in with other aspects of its breeding biology, which differ from those of the other two species (see Comparative Section).

Another of its main breeding areas is in the Gulf of California and off Mexico. The Tres Marietas Islands—particularly the westernmost one—hold fairly large colonies (one at least of 500–700 pairs) and were visited in May 1961, May and August 1962 and April 1963 (Grant 1964). The westernmost island held young of all stages in May 1961 and 1962 and was obviously well attended by adults. On April 17th 1963 90 per cent of at least 250 pairs had young (age unspecified, but by omission of qualifying phrases such as 'partly feathered', etc., likely to be less than two months and probably less than a month). In August 1962 there were small groups of recently fledged juveniles and only five occupied nests with young (no eggs). From this, it appears that in all three years January-February-March was the main laying period (perhaps particularly February) but with a large spread. This agrees well with observations made on an earlier visit (April 9th 1909) when eggs and young of all stages were recorded (Lamb 1910). The Tres Marias and Isla Isabella seem similar to this. Thus visits in March 1905 and February 1938, seem to have encountered mainly eggs on the Tres Marias, and Isabella's population seemed to have mainly eggs in April 1905 and February 1938. Howell (1975) found that in March 1975 there were birds courting, incubating and caring for half-feathered young. The latter must have been laid in November/December 1974. A record of a collecting visit by H. H. Bailey, on August 4th 1905, said all the birds were on eggs. On San Benedicto of the Revillagigedos, a visit in early 1939 disclosed many eggs.

This breeding regime appears to fit in well with climatic factors. During spring and early summer the California Current produces upwellings which support much food, but in late summer the pattern of currents changes and by January a counter-current has developed. Thus the most demanding period for the adult boobies coincides with the time when the higher items in the diatom-based food chain are probably most abundant. Yet it must be remarked that this climatic system is not totally fixed, which is presumably why the very considerable spread has evolved. Also, it is difficult to assess the length of the period over which food items high in the chain continue to flourish due to the earlier abundance of diatoms.

Within the Gulf, February–March again seems to be the favoured egg-laying period with a considerable spread. Early collecting records support this, and Anderson noted that in mid-March 1973 laying had just begun on Ildefonso whilst in mid May 1973 most nests on San Pedro Martir held young. Similarly in late June 1971, there were many large young (but also some eggs) on San Pedro Martir. It is not clear whether the breeding cycle is annual, or (as in the Galapagos) less than annual, but if (as seems probable), the Gulf environment is more seasonal, breeding may well be annual.

There is little recent information for the breeding seasons of the blue-foot on the Lobos Islands (de Tierra and Afuera) of Peru. In January 1920 on Lobos de Tierra Murphy found many fully grown young (thus from a September–October laying) along with downy chicks of various ages and many courting pairs, which presumably would have laid in February. Coker (1920) says breeding seems uninterrupted. At Lobos de Tierra (March 29th–April 6th 1907) he found equal proportions of eggs, new young and fully feathered birds. Again, this is consistent with laying in September–October of the previous year and continuing until March or possibly even April. In early December, the same situation apparently prevailed. If so, many eggs must have been laid in July–August and later. This certainly leaves no month of the year which could have been free from breeding activity for the species as a whole, but does not, of course, show that laying is equally distributed throughout the year, nor even that there are no marked peaks. However, on present information, it is safer to say merely that laying occurs in most or all months of the year, perhaps particularly between October and February.

There is little information specifically about the effects on the blue-foot of El Niño years (see p. 596). In the 1939 crash, the blue-foot did leave Lobos de Tierra and arrived at the Chinchas. Similarly in December 1965, another crash year, an estimated 3000 arrived at the Chinchas from the north, the high point of an influx lasting from October 1965 to March 1966. Indeed, the appearance of blue-foots outside their normal range is taken by Peruvian biologists as an early warning of atypical hydroclimatic conditions. So it is clear that the blue-foot is affected, though the smaller numbers renders this less conspicuous than in the case of the guanay and the piquero. Whether proportionately it is smitten as badly as the piquero is not known.

If one can generalise for the species, it seems that over its entire range it produces eggs in any month and is nowhere confined even loosely to any two or three month period. Nevertheless, it tends to favour November to March or April. The absence of any closely defined laying season in the Galapagos reflects the species' less-than-annual cycle and perhaps, both there and elsewhere, a degree of opportunism in choosing an economically favourable spell for the metabolically demanding process of site establishment, courtship and egg production. Presumably the period November to March is more often favourable than are other periods. In the Gulf of California and off Mexico, this may also throw the young on their own resources at a favourable season.

2. *Synchronisation*

If one takes a whole colony—for example the entire population of Punta Suarez or of the craters on Daphne Major—there is considerable overall synchronisation, though coupled with a wide spread. Records show that commonly the majority of all the breeding pairs which possess eggs or young (and the surveys quoted rarely indicate how many pairs are behaving territorially and sexually, though without eggs or young) have laid within the space of a month or so. There are several exceptions to this generalisation. For example Gifford records for Champion that on October 5th 1905 there were eggs and all stages of young, through to fully feathered, whilst the same held for Hood in late September of the same year. Similarly Harris records all stages of young on Daphne, in February 1971, and on Hood in December 1966. Some caution may be appropriate here, since despite the extremes, it is possible that the majority of nest contents fell within a much narrower range and that the observers did not distinguish between free-flying immature birds from a previous nesting cycle and juveniles from the current one. Also, a detailed examination of the records shows that there are many cases where there seems to have been two or perhaps three waves of laying, rather than a single diffuse one.

The general conclusion must be that in the Galapagos blue-footed boobies show a strong tendency towards loose but nonetheless clear-cut overall synchronisation within major groups (colonies). This may be obvious at first glance—as when a group such as the one in Daphne crater holds mainly white fluffy young (a stage which, ignoring size, lasts for several weeks) or somewhat obscured, as when a few young have just attained full feathers, whilst others remain obtrusively downy and a few pairs still have eggs. A superficial (and mistaken) reading of the latter situation could indicate complete a-synchrony. The records also show that there are considerable differences between different colonies in the timing of breeding within any calendar year, but that is another matter (see Breeding Regime p. 539).

However, the tendency towards overall synchronisation must not be allowed to obscure the spread that does occur and which one must attempt to explain. First, the overall spread itself has the important characteristic that in the main it is produced, not by odd pairs breeding early or late within an otherwise fairly homogeneous colony, but by sub-groups, each fairly well synchronised but, it may be, considerably out of step with each other. When one comes to interpret synchrony, or lack of it, overall as against sub-group synchrony must be sharply distinguished—for they cannot possibly share all the same advantages. If it were advantageous for the *species*, within a given locale, to be closely synchronised, it could not be advantageous for the sub-groups in that locale to be well out of step with each other. So far as sub-group synchrony is concerned, the situation is somewhat anomalous in that though the phenomenon is undoubtedly real—indeed obvious when one sees it in the field—no quantitative assessments have been made. On Punta Suarez, where the terrain was somewhat variable and divided by natural barriers such as lines of scrub, 'dead' areas subject to salt-spray, etc., the boobies tended to occur in irregularly demarcated and variably sized groups, within which there was considerably closer synchrony than within the colony as a whole, but between which there was considerable variation. To prove this point beyond doubt, however, would have required a proper mapping of the spatial distribution and an analysis of spread within each acceptably defined sub-area and this was not done. The nearest approach to this comes from a comparison of the upper and lower craters on Daphne, two areas which are topographically alike and separated only by some difference in height and both of substantial overall size (though the lower crater colony is much the bigger) yet which are often considerably out of step with each other, as the following records show (Table 81). Indeed, even within one crater there may be small groups (in one case tucked away in a corner) the members of which are closely synchronised but out of step with the crater colony as a whole. However there are insufficient records to pursue the matter further at this level.

Accepting the reality of some degree of overall and a higher degree of sub-group synchronisation, what 'causes' it and what survival value has it? Obviously overall synchrony would result from a reasonably standard response by the population to seasonal external changes or from an endogenously timed rhythm, whether this be circannual or based on part of a year. In a strongly seasonal environment, external timing, working through the endocrine system, accounts for the annual, fairly well synchronised breeding of most seabirds. In the Galapagos, seasonal changes are considerably less distinct, but once the members of a colony are reasonably in step, each pair taking much the same time as any other to incubate, rear young, moult and recuperate, they will tend to stay in step. On the other hand, in a relatively a-seasonal environment which, as may be observed in the Galapagos, allows breeding to occur at any time, failed breeders need not wait for a specific laying season to come round (as they must in a seasonal environment) and so can easily get out of step with the group as a whole. Together, these factors account for the overall synchrony such as it is, and also for the considerable degree of spread. The essential difference between the overall synchrony of a colony of blue-foots on Daphne and that (say) of gannets on the Bass Rock (apart from its degree) is that in the former laying may be synchronised in August one year, October the next and so on whilst in the latter it will always be around April.

TABLE 81

UPPER AND LOWER CRATERS ON DAPHNE MAJOR (GALAPAGOS) COMPARED FOR THE STATE OF BREEDING OF THE BLUE-FOOTED BOOBY

Date	Area	State of breeding
20.3.63	Upper crater	41 per cent of 70 pairs had eggs; most of remainder had variable young
	Lower crater	17–20 per cent of 250–300 pairs had eggs; most of remainder had variable young.
	CONCLUSION:	Lower crater further advanced than upper.
17.4.63	Upper crater	47 nests with eggs; 'many' with young.
	Lower crater	59 nests with eggs; 'many' with young
	CONCLUSION:	Lower crater smaller proportion with eggs, therefore probably further advanced.
21.8.63	Upper crater	Free flying young.
	Lower crater	20 nests with eggs.
	CONCLUSION:	Lower crater already starting on new breeding cycle, whilst upper crater concluding previous one.
22.10.63	Upper crater	7 per cent of some 175 pairs with eggs; most courting.
	Lower crater	Around 33 per cent of several hundred pairs with eggs.
	CONCLUSION:	Lower crater in advance of upper.
19.12.63	Upper crater	Sample: 61 with eggs; 87 with chicks. Mean development coefficient 2·3*
	Lower crater	Sample: no nest with eggs; 59 with chicks. Mean development coefficient 4·0
	CONCLUSION:	Lower crater much further advanced.
11.7.64	Upper crater	Sample: 77 eggs or small chicks. *Chicks* 0–2 weeks (1); 2–4 (17); 4–6 (31); 6–8 (17); 8 (5). Mean development coefficient 5·1.
	Lower crater	Eggs not counted, but one corner held large number of incubating adults. *Chick Sample* 0–2 (2); 2–4 (20); 4–6 (7); 6–8 (11); 8 (7). Mean development coefficient 5·0.
	CONCLUSION:	No significant different in the age of chicks in the two craters.
27.11.64	Upper crater	142 juveniles. No intermediate young. No eggs.
	Lower crater	Virtually all juveniles. 3 chicks around 10 weeks old. No eggs.
	CONCLUSION:	No significant difference between the two craters

* A crude coefficient obtained by assigning 1 'unit' for egg, 2 for two-week old chick, 6 for six-week old chick, etc. Total number of 'units' divided by sample number = coefficient of development.

Since the blue-foot can lay in any month, failed pairs can, as it were, 'choose' (no doubt depending on physiological state and prevailing economic conditions) whether to re-lay in a month (or less), two months, three months, etc. This is where sub-group synchrony enters the picture, for birds tend to join conspecifics which are at about the same stage in the reproductive cycle (the general phenomenon is discussed further in the Comparative Section p. 911).

This tendency will produce sub-group synchrony, whether operating within the framework of the colony as a whole (pairs, successful last time, returning at roughly the same time as other such pairs) or by 'persuading' a failed pair to join a group containing at least some pairs at a similar stage.

It obviously usually does not matter in which month Galapagos blue-foots lay their eggs (otherwise one would not have a 9–10 month periodicity, p. 545) so whatever synchrony there is must confer advantages other than helping in seasonal timing. The only significant advantages are social ones; by joining a physiologically compatible group one has a better chance of locating a partner and a reduced risk of interference from conspecifics.

3. *Length and composition of breeding cycle*

In any sulid the time taken for breeding includes that spent in establishing the site, gaining a mate and, at the other end, 'winding down' the season by going through a phase of renewed territorial and sexual behaviour. Its total length is a very important factor in the species' breeding strategy and it may be taken for granted that natural selection has acted on each component in the total, orchestrated pattern. The pattern adopted by a species adapts it to its particular ecological circumstances and even within a group as tightly knit as the Sulidae, varies enormously.

Perhaps the most instructive aspect of the blue-foot's cycle is its relative shortness which, in its particular environment, enables it to breed at less than annual intervals. The pre-laying phase is almost certainly variable; taking at least three weeks and possibly, under unfavourable circumstances, much longer. Incubation takes about six weeks, producing a free-flying juvenile takes another 15 and feeding it before it becomes independent about 6–8 weeks more. We do not know how long the pair continue to attend their site after the juvenile is independent; by analogy with other sulids it could be two or three weeks, but in unfavourable circumstances may be much less. This adds up to a breeding season at least 28 weeks long and probably usually 32–34.

The shortness of this breeding cycle depends largely upon the speed with which the chicks are reared to independence, which in turn probably results from the blue-foot's particular feeding techniques (p. 570) and (in most of the areas in which it breeds) its proximity to relatively productive waters. The fact that, as in the Galapagos, it is found on the same islands as the white booby, which takes longer to complete a breeding cycle (and breeds at longer intervals) reflects the white booby's adaptations, as a species, to a blue-water regime, i.e. the white booby forages much further from its breeding area than does the blue-foot. Just because the blue-foot on Daphne can rear two chicks to independence in 20 weeks or less, there are no grounds for deducing that the white booby ought to be able to do likewise.

4. *Frequency of breeding attempts*

One of the interesting aspects of the relatively non-seasonal regime in the Galapagos is that birds are less likely to be restricted to laying at certain fixed times of year and thus can breed at intervals of a year plus a bit, or a year minus a bit, as suits the species best, taking into account its other adaptive features.

On Hood we recaught 11 blue-footed boobies previously ringed as breeding birds by David Snow. In addition, we gathered records from another five nests that gave some hints about breeding frequency. The details of these records are summarised below.

1. A female was caught on January 16th 1962 with one egg; caught again on November 22nd 1963 with two half grown chicks and yet again on August 25th 1964 with one chick aged 4–5 weeks. This case gives a well-nigh perfect series of layings at precisely 40-week intervals, as detailed below:

(a) Laid January 16th 1962
.... 40 weeks
(b) Laid November 23rd 1962
.... 40 weeks
(c) Laid August 31st 1963
.... 40 weeks
(d) Laid 8th June 1964

(d) is accurately known from the chick's age; (c) is calculated assuming a six-week old chick—hardly likely to be wrong by more than one or two weeks; the difference between them is 40 weeks. Assuming the same period elapsed between (c) and the previous laying, we arrive at (b) (the laying date missing from the observed series) and another 40 week period takes us precisely back to (a) the observed date on which an egg was present. Thus, the three actual observations fit perfectly if the periodicity they indicate is intercalated to give the fourth and missing date.

2. A female was caught with one egg on January 16th 1962, again with one egg on November 22nd 1963 and with a chick around four weeks old on August 25th 1964:

(a) Laid December 25th 1961 (assuming egg half incubated)
(b) Laid November 1st 1963 (assuming egg half incubated)
....33 weeks
(c) Laid June 16th 1964

This is apparently a shorter cycle (between b and c) assuming the June 16th chick's age to be accurately gauged. Assuming that cycles of similar length occurred previously, a good fit is obtained, with three such cycles fitting into the period between November 1963 and late December 1961 (again assuming the January 1962 egg to have been half incubated when found). The potential error in these calculations lies in a false estimate of the age of the egg on two occasions, but the (b)–(c) cycle cannot be made longer than nine months. Thus this case, too, demonstrates a less than annual cycle around 8–9 months.

3. A male was caught with two chicks (age unknown) on January 16th 1962; with two eggs on November 22nd 1963; with two chicks about 2 weeks old on August 25th 1964, which later died and with three eggs, the first of which was laid on September 24th 1964:

(a) Laid perhaps October–November 1961
(b) Laid November 1st 1963
(assuming half incubated)
.... 35 weeks
(c) Laid July 1st 1964
(d) Laid September 24th 1964.
Replacement one month after loss of chicks.

The only reasonably reliable interval between successive layings obtainable from this record (b)–(c) works out at 35 weeks assuming the eggs to be half incubated when found, 38 weeks if they were fresh and 32 if about to hatch. Again a nine month cycle is indicated. It is interesting to note the short time taken for a replacement laying after the loss of chicks.

4. A male had two chicks January 16th 1962; two eggs November 23rd 1963 and one chick around ten weeks old on September 22nd 1964:

(a) Laid around October–November 1961
(b) Laid November 2nd 1963 (assuming egg half incubated) or October 10th if about to hatch.
(c) Laid early June 1964.

Thus, again, the cycle could well have been 34–36 weeks or less.

These reliable cases seem quite enough to establish the reality of the 8–10 (probably about 9) month cycle of the blue-foot on Hood Island. Thus, in nine months it courts, lays, incubates, rears its young and recuperates. None of the records quoted show that breeding occurs *every* nine months (if successful) though this seems likely. The alternative is that they occasionally miss a complete cycle and thus remain 'in step'. Since some other sulids appear to do this, the blue-foot could do so too.

In addition to the four cases quoted, there are several that give more limited information relevant to the breeding cycle. Two pairs which lost chicks under a month old *could* have re-laid about one month after the death of the chick but (since the exact date on which the chicks died and, in one case, the date on which the new clutch was started, were unknown) the longest possible interval could have been three months in one case and 11 weeks in the second.

The following cases supported the less-than-annual cycle insofar as the individuals concerned had eggs or young in widely different months in different years.

A male had a chick in January 1962 and an eight-week old chick in September 1964. Whatever age the January 1962 chick may have been, it could never have been born anywhere near July, as was the September 1964 chick. Similarly a female had a chick in January 1962 and then one around six weeks old in August 1964. In a third case a female laid in the third week of January 1962 and in the third week of June 1964 (again fitting well with a nine-monthly cycle). A female had two downy young on November 26th 1961 and a five-week old (therefore downy) chick on August 25th 1964. Finally a female had two young on January 16th 1962 and a 10-week old chick on October 5th 1964, again proving laying in widely-distanced months.

A few cases provided some circumstantial evidence that the timing of replacement layings is partly dependent on the prevailing economic circumstances. Thus, some sites whose owners had lost chicks (around a month old) contained displaying birds but were then vacated instead of receiving new eggs. Since in all cases this desertion of site occurred during a period of severe food shortage it seems likely that the two events were connected.

A final and most intriguing possibility relevant to breeding frequency in the Galapagos (and it is no more than conjecture) is that in a given time span the male blue-foot sometimes breeds more often than does the female. This was suggested by the finding that in some cases colour-ringed males known to have chicks were discovered elsewhere in the colony, occasionally advertising to females. In one case, the female had a 97-day old chick (in other words likely to be dependent on her for another 4–6 weeks) whilst the male was in the centre of the colony some 60 metres distant. Were males to leave the completion of a breeding attempt to the female, whilst themselves initiating a new one, it would be consistent with the observation that females tend to take the major share of feeding the large young. On the other hand, males sometimes do feed large young. Obviously a corollary of such a system would be to make permanent pair bonds impossible. On the whole, it is an unlikely possibility and the explanation of the observations may well be found in the males' tendency to acquire multiple territories and repair to one at intervals during the later stages of breeding. The function of multiple territories would remain to be explained, but would not involve such a radical departure from the usual type of pair relationship.

Breeding once every nine or ten months fits well with the nature of the blue-foot's cycle (rapid growth of young and reduced post-fledging feeding) but whether this is a species-specific trait, or a Galapagos one, remains unknown. It would be of great interest to know whether a similar pattern is followed off Peru and in the Gulf of California or whether it is yet another example of a population evolving its own adaptations to the Galapagos environment. The Galapagos blue-foot is probably distinct morphologically and could well have evolved a breeding regime different from those of other populations. On the other hand the relative lack of seasonal breeding throughout its range could argue in favour of a similarly non-annual regime.

We lack any information on non-breeding years but if the features of the breeding regime just described are any guide, it is likely that there will merely be extended rest periods in unfavourable circumstances, but no non-breeding calendar years.

OTHER ASPECTS OF BREEDING ECOLOGY

1. *Food*

There are extremely few records of the fishes taken by the blue-foot. Its propensity for inshore and even rock-pool fishing suggests that it takes a variety of species some of which will not figure significantly in the diet of the more oceanic boobies, but details are lacking. It is known to take flying fish (*Exocoetus* spp.), sardines, several species of anchovies, and Pacific mackerel, but this list is undoubtedly very incomplete, and all species taken by the Peruvian (p. 628) will probably figure, also, in the blue-foot's diet. Squids may well be important, as they are in the three tropical boobies.

2. *Mortality*

There are no figures for adult mortality rate. Some young blue-footed boobies on Hood fall victim to the Galapagos short-eared owl. We recorded the deaths of six large young (around 1700g) between October 7th and November 11th. Four absolutely fresh carcases had been severely bitten and clawed on the nape and then eaten from the dorsal side inwards; the fifth had not been bitten around the head and the sixth had been dead for some time and may conceivably have died from other causes. Four were killed during the night or very early morning. There are apparently no feral cats on the island and the Galapagos hawk is most unlikely to have attacked at night. Indeed, one suspects that during the day the young booby would have been quite capable of defending itself, but less so at night. Young white boobies and especially frigate birds were similarly dealt with on Tower Island, where again cats were not present, but owls numerous.

An interesting case—though more of ectoparasitism than of predation—was that of blood drinking by mocking birds. They occasionally pecked the cloacas of adult boobies until they bled, and then they drank the drops of blood. Similarly, finches on Tower drink from the bases of quills on the wings of white boobies and on Wenman, they puncture the bases of tail feathers of the red-footed boobies and drink the blood (see p. 721). These unusual methods of obtaining liquid are responses to an extremely arid environment of birds which, presumably, cannot drink sea water. Adults fall prey to sharks, etc., but it is not known to what extent. Entanglement in vegetation causes some deaths; Murphy (1936) notes their tendency to 'hang' themselves and Harris (pers. comm.) found five adults dead in thorny *Parkinsonia* on Champion (Galapagos).

3. *Age of first breeding*

By analogy with the Peruvian and brown boobies, the blue-foot would be predicted to breed first when in its third year or possibly its fourth, but there are no actual records.

4. *Movements*

Ringing has been carried out only in the Galapagos and has yielded three recoveries of birds ringed as chicks, all recovered off Ecuador. It has also indicated that adults are faithful to the 'colony' rather than a particular sub-group. All birds recovered in a breeding cycle after the one in which they were ringed, were in the original area. However, young birds may well breed in groups other than their natal one.

5. *Fidelity to site*

The blue-foot's tendency, in the Galapagos, to acquire two or more sites hints that it may have relatively loose site ties. Fidelity to mate may thus be less practicable than in a species with strong site fidelity. There may conceivably be aberrant pair relationships, in a few cases, males breaking off a cycle part way through and beginning a new one on a different site, with a new mate, but this is almost pure speculation based on a colour-ringed male which was seen to advertise to females from a site some distance from that on which his mate was still engaged with a large chick. On the other hand, some males certainly attended free-flying young.

6. *Clubs and roosts*

All sulids except Abbott's booby form 'Clubs', or gatherings of non-breeding birds, some or many of which may be adults. The only information for the blue-foot comes from the Gulf of California (Anderson, pers. comm.) where gatherings of blue-foots and brown boobies, the only two species found there, occur on rocks and islands throughout most of the area. Often they comprise under 100 birds, frequently of both species, but sometimes over 1000 occur. They are, in the main, congregations of nesting birds. There are no notes of Clubs at breeding colonies, but this probably reflects lack of observations. On Hood, there were no Clubs at Punta Suarez, though very small groups occasionally nested on the cliff edge. As in some other sulids, non-breeding adults or slightly immature birds may occur within breeding groups.

7. *Relationships with other species*

There are extremely few stations which hold only one species of booby (St. Paul's Rocks is an example); most hold two or three species. The blue-foot may breed on the same islands as the brown (as in the Gulf of California) and the white (as in the Galapagos and the Revillagigedos). In one part of its range (the Revillagigedos) it occurs with the red-footed booby and is the only booby which (on the Lobos Islands) shares part of the Peruvian's breeding range. So far as interspecific competition in the breeding area is concerned, the most likely contestants are the blue-foot and white, and the blue-foot and Peruvian. The white is almost certainly dominant and establishes the boundaries, but the blue-foot will engage in direct contest on occasions, perhaps when firmly established, and on Daphne Major the two species sometimes nest so closely that boundary disputes do occur. There are no observations on its relationships with the Peruvian booby, but one would perhaps expect the larger blue-foot female to be dominant. There are no known areas in which the number of nesting blue-foots could conceivably be limited by other seabirds acting in direct competition for nesting space. It is only rarely subjected to persecution from frigates, the Galapagos being perhaps the main area in which this happens.

SUMMARY

1. The blue-foot prefers to nest on flat ground, with little or no vegetation, but is not restricted to such a habitat.

2. It nests in colonies varying greatly in size and density. Many colonies are divided into groups (sub-colonies).

3. The nest is largely of symbolic importance.

4. Clutch size is one to three, usually two, but varies with locality. Each egg weighs about 65g and a clutch of two represents 7 per cent of the female's weight.

5. Eggs are laid 5 days apart; incubation takes 41 days and eggs hatch asynchronously. Incubation is fairly evenly divided between the sexes.

6. Replacement laying may occur.

7. Chicks are fed about twice per day.

8. The foraging trips of the parents are of short duration.

9. Growth (by weight) of the young is relatively rapid. The fledging period is about 102 days (Galapagos). Post-fledging feeding probably takes about 4–6 weeks.

10. Hatching success in a 'normal' period is probably about 72–75 per cent of eggs laid (over 80 per cent of pairs produce at least one chick).

11. Fledging success varies tremendously with year and locality. In a 'normal' year probably over 75 per cent of chicks hatched, fledge in the Galapagos; in a bad year less than 30 per cent. Breeding success figures for a less fluctuating environment are not available.

12. The blue-foot lays in all months in the Galapagos, but laying occurs mainly between October and April, with July–August probably the least favoured months.

Similarly on Lobos de Tierra, laying may occur in any month, but probably mainly October–March.

13. There is loose, but clear-cut synchronisation within major groups (colonies) in the Galapagos, and tighter synchronisation within smaller ones (sub-colonies).

14. The complete breeding-cycle takes about 32–34 weeks.

15. The blue-foot's breeding periodicity in the Galapagos is about 8–9 months. A given pair may breed successfully in successive 9-month periods, but it is likely that it occasionally misses a complete cycle.

4. BREEDING BEHAVIOUR

INTRODUCTION

The lively blue-footed booby is one of the most attractive and amusing seabirds. The only population which has been observed in any detail is that on Punta Suarez, Hood Island (Galapagos) which my wife and I watched for four months in 1964, and the following account is based almost entirely on that small colony (some 500 pairs). This species tends to form small or medium colonies at very variable but never high densities. They are extremely mobile birds and a lot of their display includes ritualised locomotion or flight. They do not perch well on branches, however, and rarely attempt to do so. They are highly vocal, and a blue-foot colony can be an amusing congregation of comically displaying birds, all grunting and whistling. The background picture so far as breeding behaviour is concerned is thus one of small colonies containing fairly well-dispersed pairs, on flat but variably littered terrain.

ESTABLISHMENT AND MAINTENANCE OF TERRITORY

On Punta Suarez several of our colour-ringed pairs divided their time between two, three or four territories separated by as much as 50 metres—an apparently unique habit of occupying more than one territory in the period before egg-laying. One pair were together on four different sites within the space of an hour. In one case, as soon as the chick could be left unguarded, the male reverted to one of his 'spare' territories, which he defended in the normal way. It remains to be discovered whether this is a habit typical of the species or peculiar to one or two localities and one can only speculate on its function (see p. 523).

Site establishment behaviour consists, in functional terms, of prospecting, contesting and maintaining the site by fighting and more or less ritualised display. But no two sulids go about it in exactly the same way. Only a proportion of the ritualised behaviour that occurs on site is actually territorial and the basis for deciding this must be its nature and effect.

1. *Aerial reconnaissance and territorial flighting*

All male boobies 'prospect' for a site by aerial reconnaissance and use territorial flighting as one means of establishing their ownership. These two forms of behaviour are, however, quite different. Reconnaissance is merely 'ordinary' flight in which the bird visually assesses the situation, but 'flighting' is highly repetitive and 'extraordinary' flight. Aerial reconnaissance is extremely well developed in the blue-foot. Where breeding birds are widely spread and the terrain is varied and concealing, preliminary inspection could obviously be useful in determining the stage of breeding of the various groups within the colony. In fact it is quite possible that birds reconnoitre as a group, for several times I saw groups of 12–15 birds flying around the colony. Nor would this be too surprising, since sub-groups are highly synchronised and one way in which this could come about would be through birds which were all at the site-establishing stage prospecting for a suitable area together. It may be relevant that in the blue-foot co-ordinated group fishing is known to occur.

Territorial flighting or aerial circuiting, takes the form of rapid flights over or around the breeding area, each flight typically lasting some 15–30 seconds, though often longer. Because it is repetitive behaviour, and is usually part of a complex which ends with a highly ritualised gesture (see Saluting) one may regard flighting as ritualised behaviour.

2. *Saluting*

After flying around the territory or when landing alone on his empty site in the early stages of breeding, the male whistles loudly as he flies in and then lands with a dramatic Salute. He Salutes, also, when flying in with the female after Pair-flighting (q.v.). Females Salute less often and neither Salute much, if at all, after the egg has been laid. Thus of 59 instances in which male Saluting was noted, 34 were to the site alone, 24 to the mate on site and 1 to the mate with chick; the corresponding figures for the female were 4, 6 and 1.

In Saluting (Fig. 230 a–c) the tautly spread feet are flung up into the air, their soles at right angles or more to the ground, and held there until it looks as though the bird couldn't possibly recover in time to pitch down, but he does so with a flourish. Usually the feet are held in front of the underparts, but sometimes stuck right out to the sides. Usually, after a Salute-landing, the blue-foot male (especially) goes straight into his aggressive site ownership display (see Yes Headshaking) and then touches or handles a scrap of nest material. This, and the calling which accompanies the flight in, indicate that Saluting is probably basically aggressive behaviour.

The Salute places the largest possible area of ultramarine web against white underparts and by jerking the feet makes them flash conspicuously. This must be effective in showing off the landing to territorial neighbours, which is probably its main function.

Since this elaborate landing has nothing to do with the aerodynamic requirements of the situation (later in the season birds land in the ordinary way) it is undoubtedly ritualised behaviour derived from ordinary landing. Its extreme development in the male is related to his unusual lightness and agility.

Important though flight behaviour undoubtedly is, during the initial stages of seeking out and laying claim to a site, the subsequent defence and maintenance of territorial integrity

Fig. 230. Landing with the foot Salute. This displays the bright blue feet and is used, particularly by the male, when landing on the site early in the breeding cycle. It is not merely braking.

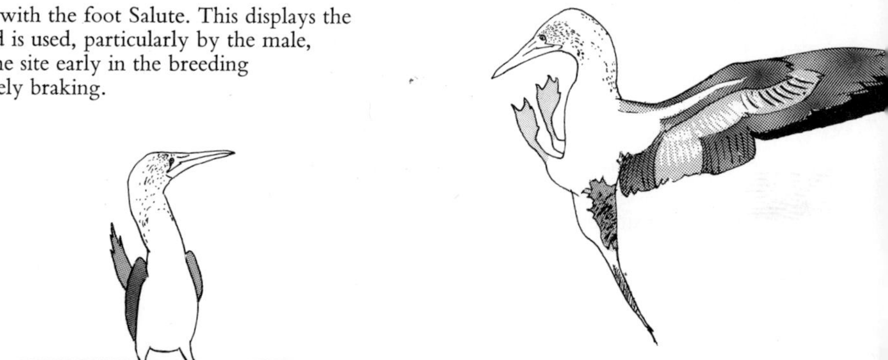

depends on a number of activities, most of them ritualised, carried out on foot within the territory.

3. *Fighting*

That most obvious and basic territorial behaviour, fighting, is almost absent in the blue-foot, which so rarely fights that, during many hundreds of bird/hour observations, we did not record one. This seems to be consistent with the holding of multiple territories in suggesting that there is little competition for nest-sites.

Aggressive (territorial) behaviour, in descending order of intensity, includes Wing-flailing, Jabbing, threatening with open bill (Menacing) and ritualised aggressive display.

4. *Wing-flailing*

Blue-footed boobies perform more or less violent and spasmodic forward beating movements of both wings, synchronously, during high intensity close-range disputes at the boundary of the territory (Fig. 231). Birds may even Wing-flail whilst running! Wing-flailing is never used on its own, but occurs as part of a mosaic of aggressive and associated withdrawal behaviour.

In the blue-foot the wings are opened and with a sharp whistle or grunt, depending on the sex, the bird darts its beak forward on the upstroke. The initial upstroke may be followed by two or three shallow downward strokes with a slight forward movement on the carpal joint. The bird may actually move towards the intruder, the whistle becoming prolonged and piercing, and in fact Flailing probably expresses a tendency to fly at the opponent. However, the tendency to withdraw is also detectable and it is often possible to interpret the balance of attack and withdrawal (aggression and fear). Thus, boundary disputes between lone males and neighbouring pairs may lead to intensive Flailing and Jabbing by all concerned but only the lone male consistently performs a beak-hiding withdrawal (see Pelican Posture p. 559) after each Flail.

5. *Jabbing*

The blue-foot, especially the small male, jabs extremely rapidly and often very vigorously, with the head flung somewhat sideways (Fig. 244). The bird calls and ruffs its head and neck feathers. However in this species Jabbing as territorial behaviour is much less frequent than in the denser-nesting Peruvian. It is also rarer in females. Neighbours are usually out of Jabbing distance and although a male will run towards a rival and engage in Jabbing at the (presumed)

Fig. 231. Wing-flailing; the left-hand bird is a female.

boundary, with or without Wing-flailing, it rarely does so after the early stages of site-establishment and pair formation, whereas the Peruvian is constantly in close contact with neighbours.

6. *Yes Headshaking*

This complex display seems to be the homologue of the Yes/No Headshaking already described for the white booby. Like that display, it signifies site ownership and thus defends the territory.

Yes Headshaking is an extremely vigorous up-and-down nodding of the head (Fig. 232), often so rapid that the head and neck vibrate and the movement becomes almost a blur. The side-to-side No component is usually inconspicuous or absent. The display is performed with a pronounced forward lean and somewhat lengthened neck. Like all aggressive displays in the Sulidae, it is accompanied by calling—usually three or four syllables with the accent on the second 'aa-*aa*-aa-a' and with a 'grunty' quality in the female. At the highest intensity it becomes disjointed and may be accompanied by Wing-flailing and Jabbing or by touching or picking up nest material. In the latter case the material may then be held during the display, just as the red-foot sometimes holds a twig during its analogous Forward Headwaving but this in no way merits the status of a separate display.

Yes Headshaking is extremely common in the male, less so in the female and occurs most typically (a) as a post-landing display, particularly after a Salute landing, early in the breeding season (like site ownership in general) and (b) as a response to territorial tension (intrusion, bird flying over, etc.) though it is by no means uncommon (c) in pair interactions (q.v.) and even (d) as, apparently, a response to general excitement and clamour in the immediate neighbourhood. Since it is associated with sexual and agonistic behaviour it frequently occurs in the behaviour mosaics which go on for hours during courtship and territorial behaviour, as the pair parade around, take-off, land and court.

Yes Headshaking is often followed by 'ordinary' headshaking, with the head upwardly inclined and when performed with nest material, often terminates by 'showing' this. Advertising (q.v.) to birds flying over, may be followed by Yes Headshaking.

The context of Yes Headshaking (its association with hostile behaviour such as Wing-flailing and particularly Jabbing and its use in repelling intruders) indicates that it is aggressively motivated and exactly comparable to similar behaviour in other sulids. It is shown mainly by individuals that are more aggressive than afraid—a survey of particular interactions and their end results showed this beyond doubt—but nevertheless, it occurs over a wide range of fear and aggression and largely in the middle of the spectrum. Thus, in high intensity aggressive interactions Yes Headshaking is not usually incorporated until the Jabbing and Wing-flailing has died down. On the other hand, it is performed less by the 'inferior' of the two parties. Its frequent occurrence during interactions between mates is fully consistent with the tendency for aggressive and sexual behaviour to occur together.

As to its origin, I have produced some evidence that all sulids have evolved ritualised, aggressive site ownership displays from re-directed aggression. Gannet Bowing has demonstrably evolved from biting re-directed to the ground and red-foot Forward Head-waving from post-landing biting of twigs. Similarly, the Yes Headshaking of the blue-foot is interspersed with touching or biting nest material and, as mentioned, may be performed with these held in the bill. Probably, therefore, Yes Headshaking conforms to a general pattern and has

Fig. 232

'Yes headshaking', a complex, aggressively motivated site-ownership display with calling. The forward leaning birds are headshaking across the boundary, female (left) to male. Shared defence of territory.

evolved from ground or nest touching or biting. The following details, which shed a little light on the sort of processes which may be involved, come from a comparison of the Yes/No Headshaking of the white booby and the Yes Headshaking of the blue-foot. When the blue-foot performs Yes Headshaking whilst holding nest material it often superimposes it on the 'arcing' movement which, on its own, is typically used to 'show' or 'present' nest material to the female (Fig. 242). This 'arcing', which is a swinging movement or arc of the head, more or less horizontally, closely resembles the 'No' movement of the white booby in its 'Yes/No' Headshaking. Whereas the white booby has now incorporated the No (arc) as a normal part of its site ownership display, the blue-foot shows it only under the additional stimulus of holding a piece of nest material (and remember the whole pattern stems from touching nest material). A clue to understanding this difference may be found in the fact that the white booby does not 'show' nest material, so there is no possibility of confusion between the No movement of Yes/No Headshaking and the arcing of showing nest material. The blue-foot, for whatever reason, *has* evolved 'showing' of nest material and may therefore have lost the somewhat similar No movement and been left with its simpler Yes Headshake. There are reasons for expecting this, since one of the requirements of a display is that it should have clear signal value, which is probably enhanced by clear differences from any other behaviour.

This completes the account of behaviour patterns which are principally concerned with site establishment and maintenance and leads on to the next main category, to do with pair formation and maintenance.

FORMATION AND MAINTENANCE OF PAIR

1. *Prospecting and Pair Flighting*

Just as reconnaissance and territorial flighting were conspicuous elements in the blue-foot's site establishment, so the prospecting by females for receptive males and subsequent pair flighting are important in pair formation. Both sexes are not only extremely active in scanning, but also highly responsive to overflying birds. This behaviour is more easily detectable in the blue-foot than in species which form vast colonies.

Female blue-foots commonly investigate from the air by flying over and around the

Fig. 233. Pair landing after courtship flight.

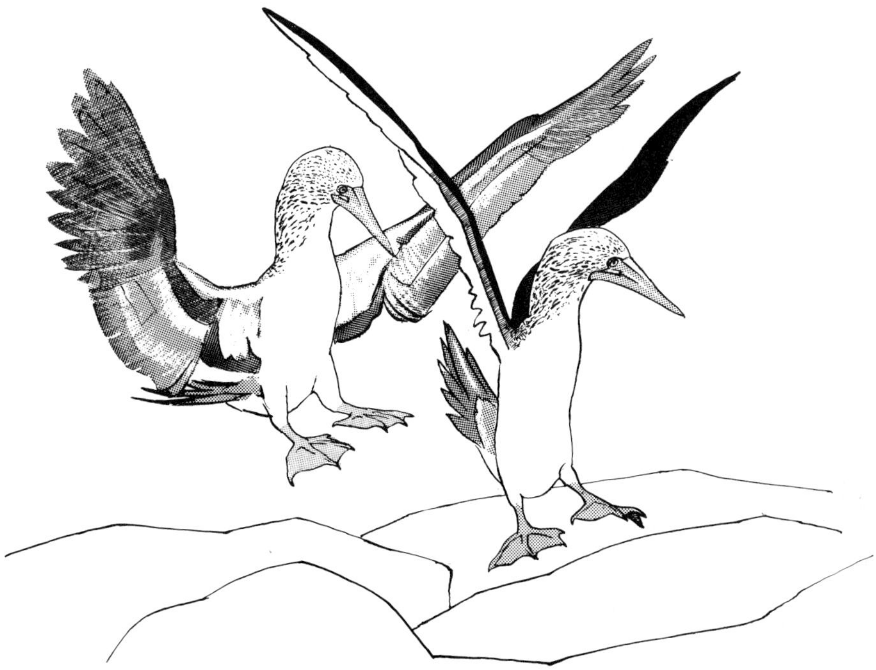

territory. Potential mates are undoubtedly located in this way and for their part show a lively response to overflying females (see Advertising p. 555).

First contacts are impossible to recognise, but one can readily see that in the early stages, the two incipient partners repeatedly take-off, fly around in tandem and land (Fig. 233) with calling and the Salute, after which they go through a variety of interactions to be described in this section. The actual flight is unremarkable, except for the obvious leading by the male, and does not appear to employ special rhythms or amplitudes of wing beat, as many comparable sexual flights do (for example, terns, the swallow-tailed gull and some corvids).

I have already mentioned the varied gamut of postures and movements that booby pairs go through in the early stages of the breeding cycle. The validity of chopping them up into their discrete parts rests on the observation that, typically linked though several of them are, they are nonetheless independent items which can occur alone and whose position within a group of two or three or more is not fixed. The following behaviour patterns are found in pair interactions in the territory.

Fig. 234

'Sky-pointing', the sexual (advertising) display of the blue-footed booby.

(a) Low intensity.

(b) Medium intensity.

(c) High intensity.

2. *Sky-pointing (Advertising)*

In two respects—form and co-operation between the sexes—Sky-pointing in the blue-foot represents the most extreme development of this display within the family. Whereas in red-footed and white boobies the neck lengthening and skyward pointing of the bill are accompanied by some elevation of the tail and busking of the wings, in the blue-foot (Fig. 234) the wings are not only rotated at the shoulder and so brought forwards—sometimes beyond the tip of the bill—but also spread laterally so that, when twisted, their upper surfaces are actually facing the partner. The tail is cocked until it leans towards the head. When that very experienced and critical ethologist, J. M. Cullen, first saw a painting of this improbable contortion he seriously thought it was a figment of an artist's imagination! As usual in the family, Sky-pointing is accompanied by vocalisation (grunt or whistle) and is much commoner in the male than in the female.

Although in the blue-foot an important context of Sky-pointing is that of a male advertising his sexual receptivity to a female—overflying females commonly elicit it from males—it has become equally or perhaps more important as a mutual display between partners that have already formed a bond. The term mutual is used to indicate that partners may actually display simultaneously—one like the mirror image of the other—rather than merely one after the other, which I have called reciprocal. In the blue-foot both mutual and reciprocal Sky-pointing are strongly developed, the pair facing each other and repeatedly performing this bizarre display.

A further aspect of Sky-pointing in a sexual context is its use in short-term co-ordination of sexual activity. Thus, it frequently precedes copulation and may be assumed to play a role in making the female receptive (or conversely, if initiated by the female, in stimulating the male). The longest bouts of persistent Sky-pointing came from females who, presumably partly as a result, then elicited copulation.

A third possible function of male Sky-pointing in the blue-foot is to entice the female to a particular site in the territory and one often sees a male parade to a chosen spot and Sky-point repeatedly and in many cases the female eventually joins him there. However, it is impossible without much more rigorous analysis to demonstrate that it is the Sky-pointing as such which attracts the female.

In all the contexts mentioned above, sexual motivation is clearly involved and the function of the display is to bring the partners together, to strengthen their bond and to co-ordinate activity. There remains a fourth context, relatively infrequent but more difficult to understand, namely that of Sky-pointing to overflying birds of the same sex, observed in both males

Fig. 235. Mutual Sky-pointing.

and females, or Sky-pointing apparently without any external stimulus, from males only. In such cases, an observed association between Sky-pointing and Yes Headshaking performed immediately afterwards, suggests that it was being used as a territorial display. Since the converse is common, Yes Headshaking used in a sexual context, it is perhaps not surprising that Sky-pointing should sometimes occur in the aggressive one. In fact, where Yes Headshaking occurred as the first behaviour pattern after Sky-pointing it did so towards what were probably prospecting females rather than ones that had been already accepted.

Finally, wherever one can detect outward signs of aggression, there are usually signs of the opposite—evinced as withdrawal or appeasement and Sky-pointing is no exception, being frequently followed by a slight Pelican Posture (bill-hiding q.v.).

Behaviour correlated with Sky-pointing

On the assumption that behavioural events closely associated in time may partly share causal factors one may analyse the events immediately following and preceding Sky-pointing (Table 82). Three behaviour patterns—*Parading*, *Pelican Posturing* and *Oblique Headshaking*—are by far the commonest displays immediately after Sky-pointing. In fact, in both male and female all three are highly correlated and in particular the tendency to Parade in a Pelican Posture makes sequential separation rather pointless. Another point is that Jabbing is commoner than Yes Headshaking as an expression of hostility during advertising—perhaps because the partners tend to be close together.

The figures for pre-Sky-pointing behaviour are smaller, because it is much more difficult to predict Sky-pointing than to follow it up. However, the trend is much as for the behaviour following it, which is hardly surprising since Sky-pointing tends to occur in bouts, so that what

TABLE 82

BEHAVIOUR ASSOCIATED WITH SKY-POINTING IN THE BLUE-FOOTED BOOBY

	Position in behavioural sequence following Sky-pointing							
	1st		2nd		3rd		Total %	
Behaviour	M.	F.	M.	F.	M.	F.	M.	F.
Pelican Posture	46	17					28	27·4
Parading	43	14			4		28·7	22·6
Oblique Headshake	24	14	10	15	5		23·8	46·8
Nothing	13						7·9	
Jabbing, etc.	6	1			3		5·5	1·6
Touching nest material	2						1·2	
Yes Headshaking	2	1	2				2·4	1·6
Bill-up-face-away	1						·6	
Show nest material	1		2				1·8	
Totals	138	47	14	15	12	0		

Fig. 236 (a–e). A series showing reciprocal and n

(*b*)

(*a*) (*c*)

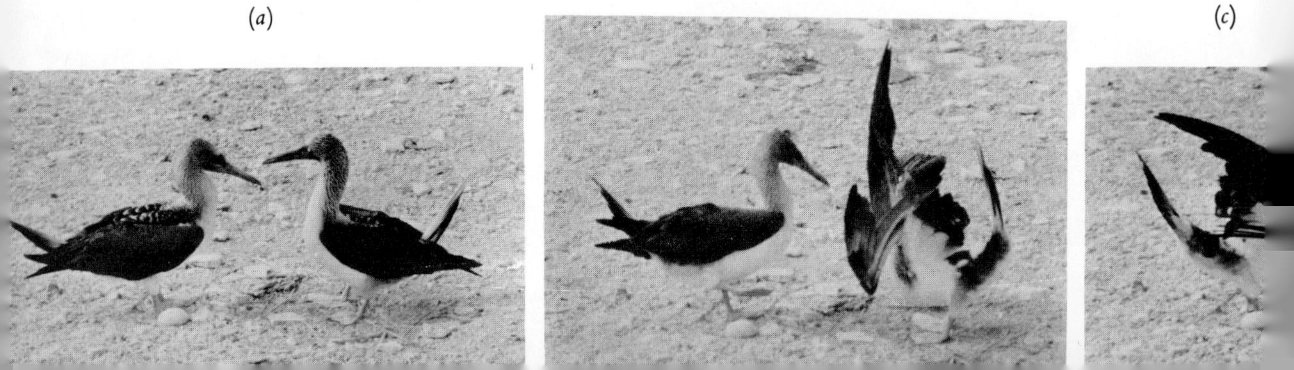

follows one precedes another. Thus Pelican Posture, Parade and Oblique Headshake were the commonest displays immediately before Sky-pointing.

3. *Parading*

In the blue-foot Parading is a highly exaggerated foot-raising, flaunting the brilliant webs upwards and outwards (Fig. 237). It often occurs on the spot but also during walking, to which it gives a ludicrous appearance. Although it is commonly linked with Sky-pointing even solitary males will parade around their territory with a ridiculously solemn air. In fact, early in breeding male blue-foots seem hardly able to walk 'normally' so prevalent is Parading in this active species. The act of collecting even a tiny scrap of nest material produces intense Parading which often continues on the spot as the bird 'shows' this material. Parading is also strongly correlated with Wing Rattling (the signal of impending flight) and the two are often performed simultaneously.

The two head positions most commonly associated with Parading are with the bill upwards and sideways (see Bill-up-face-away below) and with it tucked (see Pelican Posture p. 559). The former is highly correlated with the tendency to move and hence is quite understandably linked with Parading. The latter may be appeasing and occurs particularly as a bird Parades towards its mate.

In all these situations the bird's tendency to move is conspicuously advertised and therefore whatever behaviour accompanies the movement also gains in conspicuousness. Having become 'the' mode of walking early in the breeding cycle, all activities using locomotion (gathering nest material, approaching or leaving the mate or rival, or merely patrolling the territory,) gain visual impact, and this presumably is the function of Parading. It certainly makes maximum use of the brightly coloured feet.

It may be noted that whilst it has clearly been derived by simple exaggeration from ordinary walking, it must now be under different motivational control and has different signal value, just as the Salute landing differs from ordinary landing in the same two ways.

4. *Bill-up-face-away*

In the blue-foot, Parading is usually performed with the head held in a peculiar position—bill pointing upwards and cocked to one side (Fig. 238)—which adds even further to its visual effect. Whilst in this position the head is frequently shaken briskly with about three flicks, highly stereotyped. Although I here describe them together, they can occur independently—that is, the position alone or the headshake in a 'normal' position.

The tendency to hold the head in this Bill-up-face-away position is strong, not only when Parading but also in the following three contexts; presenting nest material (q.v.) when the head is held in the oblique position at the top of the arc (Fig. 238); after Sky-pointing; and during aggressive behaviour. For example, Yes Headshaking is typically followed by a headshake in the Bill-up-face-away position. These contexts suggest sexual and aggressive components, but the very fact that it occurs in close combination with so many other ritualised behaviours makes its own specific motivation and function difficult to evaluate more precisely. A clue may be sought in the apparent common denominator of the situations in which it occurs, which, in turn, is most evident when one looks at the same posture in the white booby. Here Bill-up-face-away is strongly linked with *the act of moving away from* the mate, an inter-

-pointing between members of a pair.

(*d*) (*e*)

pretation being that, since this situation releases attack from the partner (an observation verified in all sulids) Bill-up-face-away enables the departing bird to keep its partner in view and take appropriate action. In this way it has come to be linked with the *tendency* to move away and consequently occurs even without actual turning of the body. As further indications that Bill-up-face-away is linked with the tendency to depart, it is highly correlated with a movement (the Wing Rattle) which itself precedes flight, and with Parading, which is a ritualised form of walking.

To make some sense of its widespread occurrence in sexual and agonistic encounters in the blue-foot, it is necessary to assume that the participants are frequently 'wanting' to move away from each other. This is not unlikely, since during interactions between mates, males in particular are constantly moving away for nest material or to initiate territorial or pair flighting, whilst during agonistic encounters there is often a tendency to regain the behavioural centre of the territory (the nest site). The tendency for birds moving away from another to perform the Bill-up-face-away more than do birds moving towards another, is in accord with the interpretation just offered.

In view of the above, it is tempting to interpret Bill-up-face-away as an appeasement posture, but I consider this role to be unimportant in the blue-foot. It seemed more likely to be concerned with communicating shifting 'mood' or 'tendency' within the major motivational context (sexual or agonistic) of the encounter in question. Thus, in combination with the many other ritualised behaviour patterns which it accompanies, an impressively subtle range of visual communication signals becomes possible. The specific function of displays such as Sky-pointing or Yes Headshaking are easily understood—the former can be *seen* to attract a mate and the latter to repel another bird—but the nuances expressed by the exact composition, order and intensity of a linked series of behaviour patterns may be equally significant.

5. *Oblique Headshake*

In the blue-foot this is really a brisk headshake in what amounts to a Bill-up-face-away position, but it is a common movement in its own right—that is, usually occurring as a quick, complete action rather than the assumption of a Bill-up-face-away position followed by a headshake; the headshake is the first thing seen and only then is it apparent that the bill is pointing obliquely upwards. It is extremely frequent during pair interactions, particularly in the female after Mutual Jabbing and also occurred after Yes Headshaking and whilst Parading. It does not occur in relaxed birds. I had the subjective impression gained from watching the nature of the total interactions of which it was a part, that it signified neither aggressive tendencies strongly uppermost (as Yes Headshaking does) nor a delicate balance between aggression and withdrawal (as Pelican Posture typically seemed to do). Rather it seemed to be associated with a particular inbetween state of motivation, a shifting balance, probably involving waning or mounting aggression. Its position immediately after Yes Headshaking

Fig. 237 (a and b). Parading; this flaunting of the blue webs occurs in conjunction with two head postures, (a) Pelican Posture;
(b) Bill-up-face-away posture.

(*a*)

supports this interpretation. So, too, do the observations that Oblique Headshaking often occurs: in young birds released after handling, when fluctuations between fear and aggression are very evident; after copulation, again a time of rapidly changing motivation which probably involves aggression; and in many incidental, stimulating situations such as dispelling intruders of another species or finding an unusual stimulus (it occurred in a bird which returned to discover a donated egg in its nest). Similarly, in many animals conflict is manifested by some minor act, usually a very common one for the species and with no major signal function; for example, stretching or yawning in dogs and man; plumage shaking and scratching in birds. Since Bill-up-face-away is itself typical of such situations, the link may have arisen in this way.

Minor actions such as the Oblique Headshake occur among, and seem to qualify, the main behavioural 'phrases'. Probably they, too, convey something to the interacting individuals. In the particular case under discussion, Oblique Headshake, one could go further and suggest that even the angle at which the head is held is significant, for I noticed that in mate interactions known from their total nature to be unusually aggressive, the female held her head at an extreme angle when Headshaking, whereas this was not so in low-key interactions. The Oblique Headshake in the blue-foot thus seemed to be a punctuation mark, probably with some aggressive connotation. It occurred at frequent intervals in every mosaic of interactions between partners. Just as practically all locomotion movement in such situations employed Foot Raising and the Pelican Posture (q.v.), so behaviour involving head movement was interspersed with the Oblique or ordinary Headshake. To uncover the precise contextual and functional significance of such movements requires more sophisticated analyses of sequences than are usually possible in the field. Portable, multi-channel event recorders could be useful here.

Obviously this somewhat unusual form of Headshake has developed from an ordinary comfort movement. It was, therefore, interesting to note that on occasions a tactile stimulus (such as a fly crawling on the head) elicited several Oblique Headshakes. Here, the ritualised Headshake occurred in response to a stimulus that originally elicited the ordinary form, even though this stimulus is normally no longer the one eliciting the ritualised Headshake. In other words, the ritualised Headshake now occurs in response to the original *and* the derived stimulus. Its ritualisation is evinced by the head position and the emphatic and consistently structured 'shake'. Thus it rarely appears hesitant, containing just one shake, or several, fast or slow (as does ordinary headshaking) but is typically about three brisk movements (starting from centre, these would be left, right, back to centre or left of centre) without hesitation or prolongation.

6. *Pelican Posture*

This bill-hiding posture, tip pressed to breast (Fig. 239), has already been mentioned in connection with Parading. The blue-foot uses it a great deal when moving around its territory, exactly as do the white and brown boobies. Also, this posture commonly accompanies hostile interactions between territorial

(*b*)

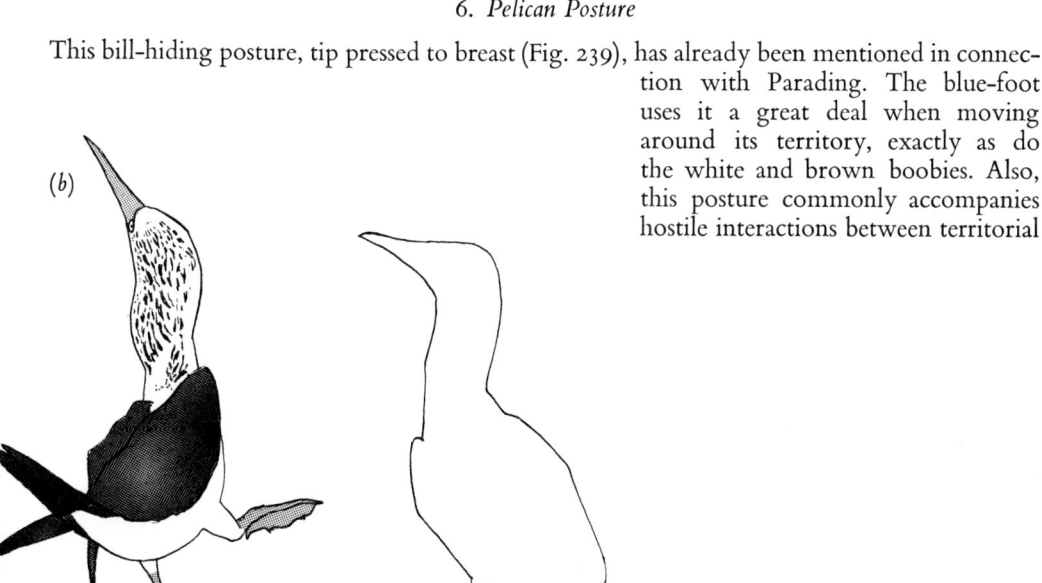

rivals or between mates. Thus during and after border disputes with Flailing, Jabbing or Yes Headshaking, participants Pelican Posture deeply and so do mates, often Bill-touching or Jabbing. In understanding its motivation and function, therefore, one is faced with a problem similar to that of Bill-up-face-away; it is a matter of disentangling its role in a behaviour complex.

It seems to occur usually when aggressive and withdrawal tendencies are in tension; the sexual element seems not to be essential. For example, a threat to the young, say from man, may elicit the Pelican Posture from the parent, in which aggression is strongly evident in its attack and fear in its withdrawal and eventual panic. A similar but milder ambivalence is evident in some boundary disputes, where the Pelican Posture seems most characteristic of the more aggressive individual. Whilst one may conclude that the Pelican Posture occurs over a fairly wide range of relative intensities of fear and aggression, it is also the case that it commonly marks interactions between strongly bonded mates. Does this indicate merely that an extremely low level of these motivational components can elicit the Pelican Posture or, more likely, that ambivalent motivation involving components other than merely fear and aggression can also elicit it?

Functionally, the Pelican Posture would seem to be appeasement behaviour, but this interpretation is based purely on the form of the movement. There seem to be two similar but distinct forms of the Pelican Posture in sulids, one, found in the red-foot, resembles a post-hop recovery movement, with the neck strongly arched and the other resembles a bill-hiding posture, with bill tip pressed to breast as chicks of some sulids do when attacked. It is the latter that the blue-foot's Pelican Posture resembles and in fact, its young, unlike those of the red-foot, do show beak-hiding.

7. *Wing Rattle*

Parading, Bill-up-face-away and Pelican Posture are all concerned with locomotion and the next behaviour pattern with communication value in the pair context, namely the Wing Rattle, is a logical extension, since it precedes take-off. In the blue-foot, the vigorous shake of slightly raised wings (Fig. 240), often with head held slightly upwards and forwards, is not simply concerned with arranging the plumage, but has become exaggerated and stylised. It is strongly correlated with impending flight and therefore with other behaviour typically preceding departure—particularly Parading. Flight by no means certainly follows, but conversely, it rarely if ever occurs after Parading and Bill-up-face-away without prior Wing Rattling. Presumably through its connection with flight, Wing Rattling is correlated with alarm.

8. *Symbolic nest building, 'Showing' nest material and Bowing to touch it*

These behaviour patterns are probably best described together because they are typically performed as a group.

The blue-footed booby does not build a nest which has any importance as a structure for holding eggs. In this sense it is merely symbolic—a faint scrape with fragments of nest material

Fig. 238 (a–c). Bill-up-face-away: (a) male about to tur

(*a*)

(

round the edge. However, as in the case of the white booby, the behaviour involved in building it must surely be extremely important, if time, effort and ritualisation be any guide. Each expedition of a few feet for a scrap of dried excreta, with the corresponding return, presentation and mutual interest in its placement (Fig. 242), involves intimate interaction which probably forms and strengthens the pair bond.

The blue-foot's habit of moving in the showy Parading manner, often with the Bill-up-face-away posture, is the preliminary to a highly ritualised 'showing' or presentation of the nest material, followed by a smooth Bow down to touch it and then, for a longer period, by handling it or 'building' it. These are now discussed in turn.

When presenting nest material a male blue-foot picks up a fragment and then, calling loudly, continues the upward movement of the head in a smooth, high arc (Fig. 242) before depositing the material. He may repeat this several times in quick succession. Sometimes he takes off with the nest material, flies round, lands and presents it. The mere act of picking up or holding a fragment sometimes stimulates the 'showing' movement as a superimposition on another display—for example, Yes Headshaking—which then occurs in a nodding arc instead of the usual straight up and down manner. Again, the act of raising the head in the beginning of the arc sometimes leads to the Bill-up-face-away position, which is held briefly and relaxed.

Despite its normal context, there is clearly an element of aggression in this behaviour, as indicated by its occurrence in territorial disputes, when a male may pick up and present nest material 'at' rather than 'to' the rival. Here, though, the actual touching of the nest material may be the aggressive element, the remainder following on through postural facilitation.

Touching nest material in a smooth Bow is usually performed after landing at the site. It is a rather slow, forward sweep, neck strongly arched, different from the way in which the bird normally bends down to touch nest material in conflict situations. It tends to be obscured because it usually occurs with the other post-landing behaviour and is itself often followed by 'ordinary' nest touching movements. The blue-foot sequence landing with calling and Salute, Yes Headshake and Bow is comparable to landing with calling, Yes/No Headshaking and touching nest material in the white booby and landing with calling, Forward Head Waving and touching twigs in the red-foot. The blue-foot Bow is perhaps a first stage in the elaboration of a nest touching movement, which has reached an advanced stage in, for example, the gannet, where the Bow is very complex.

Finally, in this group of movements to do with nest material in the blue-foot, the apparently unritualised touching of nest material is exceedingly common and very often performed by the pair together. It is presumably the relic of actual nest building and follows every acquisition of new nest material. As in many birds, nest material has become a convenient external directing stimulus and so figures prominently in conflict situations, where it often releases and directs touching or biting movements, for example in members of very new pairs, in territorial disputes and when danger, man for example, threatens.

Bill Touching, Mutual Jabbing, and allo-preening

Jabbing in the blue-foot has already been described in the context of territorial behaviour.

vay from, and leave, a female; (b) female about to leave a Sky-pointing male.

(c) Female parading in Bill-up-face-away.

Mutual Jabbing is simply thrusting open beaks at each other, usually without gripping. Though the actual motion is somewhat variable—for example sometimes with a twist—it is not easily distinguishable from ordinary aggressive Jabbing. Bill Touching (Fig. 243) is probably a somewhat stylised precursor to Jabbing. Both are fairly common in the pair context, where they illustrate what is clear in every sulid—that there is considerable aggression between mates. They have not, however, become ritualised, probably because withdrawal is easy.

Yes Headshaking and Pelican Posturing are the activities which in the male most commonly follow immediately after Jabbing (and before the female has reacted by performing any obvious act). In the female Oblique Headshaking and Pelican Posturing are commonest. The Yes Headshaking tends to confirm that Mutual Jabbing is aggressively motivated even in the pair context and the Pelican Posture reflects the fear aspect of aggression and is perhaps functionally appeasing here. The blue-foot sometimes adopts a 'parallel' position but it is not prolonged or obvious. Reciprocal allo-preening does occur in the blue-foot, but is comparatively rare.

10. *Copulation and associated activities*

The preliminaries to copulation in the blue-foot entail more movement than in most boobies, particularly Parading. Females stand and males generally mount from a more or less parallel position. Copulations take between five and ten seconds and are followed by Parading with Pelican Posture or Bill-up-face-away and Headshake, Jabbing, further Sky-pointing (unilateral or reciprocal) and touching or Showing nest material. No reverse copulations were noted, but a male was seen to attempt copulation with a ten week-old chick.

OTHER BEHAVIOUR INVOLVED IN BREEDING

The next major category of behaviour in the breeding cycle could embrace all that occurs after the egg has been laid, at which time the early stages may be considered complete—the site assured, the pair functioning as a unit—and incubation and care of young become the main activities. This is a much less active time so far as ritualised courtship and territorial behaviour is concerned.

1. *Incubation and incubation stints*

The blue-footed and Peruvian boobies are the only sulids which commonly lay more than two eggs; four is the maximum clutch for both species. Three donation experiments gave conflicting results. In the first, two eggs were given to a pair that had already prepared a scrape. The male reacted very strongly, shying away and circling the nest warily before the female arrived, whereupon both participated in an intensive bout of Showing and building nest material. Then there followed a highly telescoped series of nest reliefs, performing in a few minutes what would have taken two or three days. This pair, therefore, by a bit of 'quick stepping' got into the normal rhythm. The other two pairs, although judged to be near laying, rejected the eggs. The correct

Fig. 239. Pelican Posture.

conclusion is probably that the first pair were actually nearer to laying and, as in gannets, can then slip into the appropriate behaviour without having actually laid.

The blue-foot commonly stands off its eggs or even leaves them completely unattended in the early stages before the clutch is complete. Presumably this habit does not exist where there are many egg-predators (as on the Peruvian islands with 'kleos', Dominican gulls and Belcher's gulls). It also shades them and incubates them on top of, as well as beneath, its webs, presumably relying on heat receptors in its feet to determine which treatment is appropriate.

The length of the spells of incubation duty are important ecological indicators in sulids, varying with the type of foraging typical for the species and with the particular circumstances (food availability) at the time (see Comparative Section). Blue-foot incubation stints are medium length, the average of 33 spells for males being 18·0 hours and of 35 for females 25·0 hours (see Table 74).

2. *Change-over*

The blue-foot has no elaborate change-over ritual, either on egg or chick. The time taken to effect nest-relief on chicks varied, in the ten cases timed, from less than five seconds to 55 (less than 5 (two cases), 7, 10, 15, 40 (two), 45 (two), 55). After change-over actual departure of the relieved bird from the vicinity of the nest often occurred within seconds and usually in less than ten minutes.

In most cases there was no actual contact; one bird moved off, perhaps after the incomer had displayed a little (Yes Headshaking, Sky-pointing, Oblique Headshaking, Parading were all noted) and the other moved on. Usually the outgoing bird moved off with Parading, etc. and occasionally a male flew off after the appropriate Wing Rattle and returned with Saluting, before finally departing.

3. *Brooding of young*

Blue-foot chicks broke out of the egg at the broad end and the parent removed or tossed the shell to about one metre from the nest.

The young were brooded continuously in the usual way for about the first two weeks and thereafter guarded until between three and five weeks of age. Even then, the adults spent much time at the nest, as shown in Table 74, and the average spells of attendance were remarkably lengthy. Thus, throughout August, which was undoubtedly a time of considerable shortage of food, males were in attendance, mainly on young, on about 20 per cent of checks, females on over 25 per cent and the pair together on about 10 per cent of checks. The average length of the attendance spells was about 17 hours for males and 23 hours for females. It may be that lengthy periods of rest are essential for adults, regardless of the food situation.

4. *Feeding of young*

The average duration of the blue-foot's absences from its chicks, and hence the presumed duration of the foraging trips, was between two and four hours (max. 12 hours).

Fig. 240 (a and b). (a) Male Wing Rattling (a pre-movement display) in the context of leaving the nest at change-over time.

(b) Female Wing Rattling before moving away from site.

(*b*)

Feeding frequency is determined by the length of foraging absences; short trips mean frequent feeds. Foraging behaviour is in turn related to the nature of the feeding environment; in general, scarce food or that which is difficult to locate, means long hunting trips. All species have evolved species-specific adaptive responses to the demands of their feeding environment, but they have done so in two different ways; either both sexes are about equally adapted to the same food situation or the sexes show more or less differentiation enabling them to exploit different feeding niches.

Within the Sulidae, the blue-foot (and to a lesser extent the brown booby also) has taken morphological sexual differentiation (see p. 511) and with it different feeding roles, to the extreme. The small males tend to hunt in inshore waters, sometimes mere tidal creeks or rock pools, and the large females tend to hunt offshore (though even they are relatively inshore feeders in the family spectrum). This difference could be highly significant in enabling the species to rear two, or even three, young, whilst the white booby on the same island lays two eggs but never rears more than one chick. The blue-foot can achieve this by reducing the chances of long starvation periods early in the chick's growth, when the male can make short, quick trips for food. The habit may even partly account for the chicks' relatively short period of dependence and hence the species' short breeding cycle (8–10 months) whilst most other sulids breed at yearly or less than yearly intervals. The role of sexual differentiation and division of labour here may be to exploit alternative and more dependable food resources.

Whilst it is not possible to discover the nature of the selection which originally favoured the evolution of the small males, it seems likely that it was a response to radiation into food-poor areas. Having started on this path, display behaviour utilising the associated aerial skills co-evolved and resulted in the spectacular Salute. Probably, also, the emphasis on displays derived from locomotion (Parading, Bill-up-face-away, etc.) was partly encouraged by smallness and agility. If this is correct, we have here a good example of the interlocking nature of the evolution of behaviour and of course the ramifications are still more extensive, for they begin to affect the nature of social relationships.

5. *Other aspects of parent/young relationship*

The few experiments which we carried out on parent/young recognition showed that adults and strange young would accept each other so long as the latter were not more than about three weeks old. However, parents eventually respond selectively to the chicks they have reared, rejecting strangers, and chicks eventually respond selectively to their 'own' site and 'own' parents by returning home from strange areas (we never made exchanges which precluded this). This state of affairs is not quite clear-cut, for adults may accept chicks older than three weeks or one partner may accept it and the other reject it. However, in general the findings supported the idea that by the time chicks became liable to wander, discrimination had 'matured'.

BEHAVIOUR OF YOUNG

1. *Relationships between siblings*

The behaviour of sibling blue-footed and Peruvian boobies to each other is of great interest because these two species are the only members of the family which rear more than a single youngster, though white and brown boobies often hatch two eggs. In the latter two species

(*a*)

(*b*)

and especially in the white booby, the older chick actively evicts the younger at a very early age. The tendency of two young white boobies to fight remains extremely strong for at least three to four weeks and always leads to the death of one, even when their period together is artificially prolonged. In the blue-foot this obligative sibling murder has become facultative; frequently, the older 'allows' the younger to co-exist but asserts its dominance when necessary, driving the sibling from the nest site. In this way, as in many birds, brood size is adjusted to the current food situation. Because the eggs hatch at intervals of about five days, the older chick retains dominance throughout development and so one strong chick is produced in hard times, rather than two weak ones. The extent to which the blue-foot's mechanism still resembles that of the white booby is indicated by the observation that when food becomes scarce the stimulus, even of a tiny chick, becomes sufficient to release hostile behaviour from the older, though neither yet require much food. On Hood, severe food shortages did occur and one could then see the advantage of brood reduction, whilst, on the other hand, two or three chicks were sometimes reared, so that the system seemed a better one than obligative reduction. A factor which may be critical in allowing the blue-foot system is the sexual division of labour.

2. *Food begging*

The begging behaviour of the young blue-foot (Fig. 246) is vigorous and somewhat uncoordinated and in form resembles that of the white booby. The chick lifts its wings at the elbow joint and moves them spasmodically, sometimes violently, but not as synchronous flapping movements like those of red-foot chicks. It may rotate them forwards, as in Sky-pointing. Simultaneously it jabs at the base of the parent's bill, uttering a fast 'chuck-chuck' note. Even small chicks, less than a month old, use wing beats. Full-winged juveniles may beg with small-amplitude trembling of outspread wings and a head movement indistinguishable from Yes Headshaking or with violent flailing and jabbing. In such high intensity begging the juvenile's bill may rattle against that of the adult. In lower intensity begging there is often a more horizontal or even downward inclination of the bill; the head is much retracted and the wings half open.

3. *Interactive behaviour*

There is much to be learned about the differences in the rates at which the adult behaviour patterns develop in the young and about differences between species in the development of analogous behaviour patterns. Young gannets almost never show adult patterns of territorial and sexual behaviour before they fledge. Yet young blue-footed boobies, even when still completely downy, may Sky-point to over-flying adults, complete with call and rotation of stumpy wings. By Jabbing and Yes Headshaking in the adult manner, chicks from about six weeks of age defend the site against intruders. A fluffy chick performed the Oblique Headshake after displacing a mocking bird. Similarly, young brown and white boobies defend their parents' territory against intruding young or adults, even though subsequent attack by the latter may enforce appropriate beak-hiding. In those species in which the young do not defend the site (gannet, red-foot and Abbott's booby) there would be great danger in doing so. The adult gannet is highly aggressive and could easily dislodge the young with fatal results. The

(*c*)

Fig. 241 (a–c)

Wing Rattling and extreme Bill-up posture followed by flight preparations (neck lengthening and crouch, preceding the leap).

other two are arboreal and thus undergo strong selection pressure favouring behaviour which lessens the risk of falling. Attacks on adults would certainly increase this risk.

When the blue-foot's down thins conspicuously, the young begin to wander from the site and chicks from adjacent nests occupy many different positions with respect to each other, yet their parents must obviously recognise them, since when necessary they always go to them immediately. Indeed, parents may accompany them up to 20 metres from the original site, which accords with other evidence indicating that in the blue-foot actual site attachment is relatively weak (see p. 547).

4. *Fledging behaviour*

Young blue-footed boobies wander quite extensively in the late stages of growth. Before they can fly, they perform long bouts of vigorous wing-flapping, often rising from the ground. Wandering, with wing-exercising, eventually culminates in more or less protracted flight. It is probably common for several fully feathered young to gather on the fringes of the breeding group. Their first flights take them but a little way from land, for they return and spend most of their time near their parents' territory, where they are fed.

MAINTENANCE BEHAVIOUR

As before, this is merely a heading of convenience, to include aspects not covered by other major groupings.

1. *Stance and movement*

The human eye accurately registers tiny features of posture and movement which, though difficult to describe, nevertheless convey the essence of a species. The blue-foot is particularly idiosyncratic, indeed comical, in this way. It stands rather upright, a spare bird with a lean look and a long dagger-like bill that goes well with its piercing yellow eyes. Its gaudy blue tarsi are a shade spindly. The tail is cocked appreciably more than in other species and the blue-foot moves rather like a shag, with somewhat sinuous neck movements and a tendency to point the bill downwards as a result of curving the neck rather than angling the head. It is agile on the ground, walking and running with less of a waddle than, for example, the white booby.

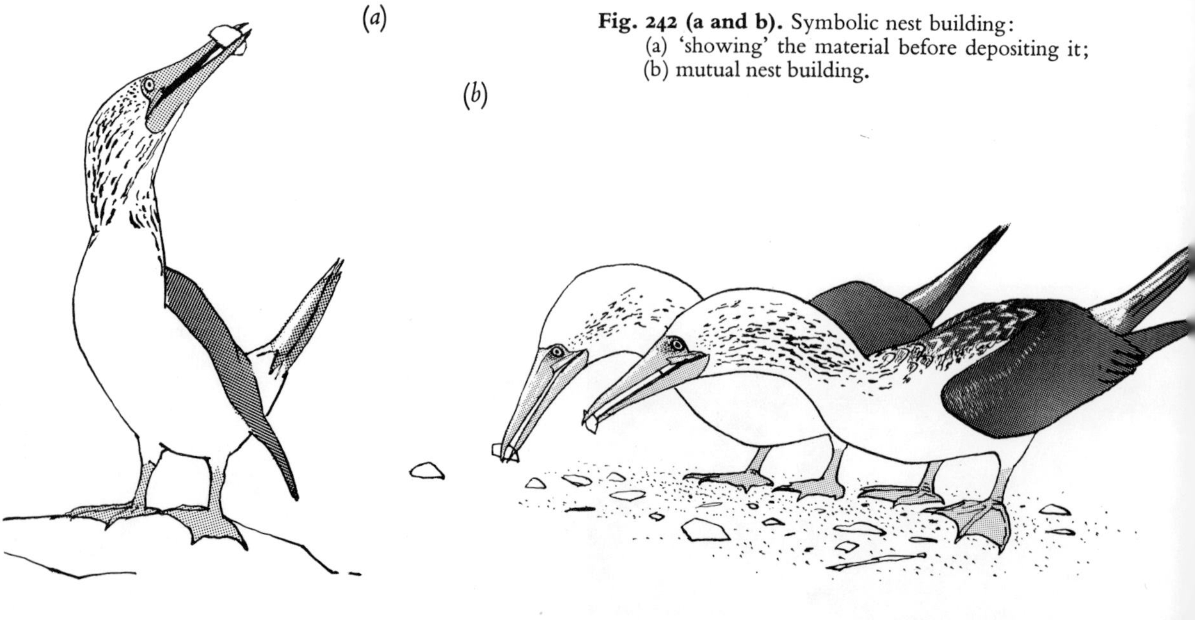

Fig. 242 (a and b). Symbolic nest building:
(a) 'showing' the material before depositing it;
(b) mutual nest building.

2. *Wing Flapping and Headshaking*

Ordinary wing flapping is a common comfort movement in sulids, often associated with a vigorous rotating shake of the head and a fluffing of body plumage. It is associated with moult and preening. Nevertheless, in some sulids, wing flapping is also unquestionably elicited by a rising tendency to fly and hence by alarm. It is often impossible to know which motivation is involved and indeed both may share the final common path (tactile stimulation, in the case of alarm caused by nervous 'tightening' of the feather follicles).

In the blue-foot, the Rotary Headshake, if it occurs at all, follows rather than accompanies the Wing Flapping. Occasionally, the Oblique Headshake may follow it—another apparent case of an 'ordinary' tactile stimulus eliciting this special headshake, now usually associated with aggressive situations (see p. 559). The Rotary Headshake is much less frequent than in the gannet and even when it occurs the actual turning movements of the head are relatively slight. Nor is it associated with alarm, as Wing Flap and Rotary Headshake so noticeably are in the gannet. The side-to-side wag of the tail commonly terminates the wing flap.

Whilst it is difficult to deduce much from these fragments, it is clear that the status of Wing Flapping, Rotary Headshaking and indeed ordinary sideways headshaking in the blue-foot is quite different from that in the gannet. In the latter, even allowing for the fact that one is usually observing hundreds of individuals instead of tens, the frequency of Wing Flapping, with or without Rotary Headshaking, and of ordinary sideways headshaking is one of the striking features. Since these three are all simple behaviour patterns one wonders why this difference exists, and there seem two possibilities. First, in the dry, clean habitat of the blue-foot 'cleansing' headshakes are rarely needed, whereas the reverse is true for the gannet. Second, the blue-foot has ritualised a form of headshaking (the Oblique) which has therefore acquired signal value. Dilution with similar headshakes would presumably weaken this function.

4. *Heat regulation*

Adults 'sun' themselves, loosening their wings, ruffling their dorsal plumage and turning their backs to the sun. Incubating birds sometimes do this.

The blue-foot may pant, with open and slightly lifted beak, in quite moderate heat and overcast. Both adults and young vibrate or flutter the skin between the rami of the lower mandible, presumably to increase air flow over it and so lose more body heat. A critical study of thermo-regulation in boobies would be of great interest; it might turn out to be an important factor in the energy budget (see p. 692).

Fig. 243. Bill Touching.

5. *Fishing behaviour*

One can scarcely better the earliest description, that of Delano (1817) quoted in Murphy as follows:

> 'These birds collect together in small flocks for the purpose of diving. They fly round in a circle and continue to rise till they get to the height of from 60–100 yards in the air, when one of them makes a pitch to dive, at which motion everyone follows, they fly down with remarkable swiftness, till within 4 or 5 yards of the surface, and then suddenly clasp their wings together and go into the water with the greatest velocity that can be conceived of, exceeding anything of the kind that I ever witnessed. They go into the water with such force as to form a curve of 30 or 40 yards in length before coming to the top again, going to a great depth under water. They glide under water at almost as great a degree of swiftness as when flying in the air.'

Although plunge diving (Fig. 248) is so spectacular, we know remarkably little about all aspects of fishing behaviour in sulids. How deep do they dive; how do they catch fish; what are the respective merits of solitary as against flock feeding; how far do they go; how nocturnal are they? There are certainly important differences between species and the blue-foot is probably the most specialised of all. The two aspects of its fishing behaviour which seem to me the most unusual are its inshore fishing and its group co-operation.

The physical characteristics of the male, small, light and extremely long-tailed, have already been described (p. 511) and help one to understand how it is possible for him to perform almost incredible feats. Long before I saw one hurtle down into two feet of water in a rock pool on Tower Island, Murphy had recounted its abilities and, even earlier, Coker noted its tendency to fish in shallow water, in sharp contrast to the Peruvian booby. In fact he saw one dive vertically into 15cm of water, whilst another dropped onto its feet there and secured its prey. Verrill saw one dive from a height of 15 metres into water about 0·5 metres deep and Murphy quotes a colleague's opinion that, in the smoothness and lack of splash with which this species enters the water, it excels all other diving birds. A valuable feeding niche has thus been opened up, for one can observe that small fish are often abundant in the extremely shallow water close to the shore. Even the female blue-foot which, as mentioned, is not lighter than other boobies, tends to feed relatively close inshore, though her specialisation is of a quite different order, for the tendency to feed within a few km of land and rarely to go as much as 160km away (both of which are characteristic of the female blue-foot) can hardly be correlated with the physical ability to dive at speed into shallow water. Rather they seem to reflect this booby's restriction to relatively cool waters, where it may rarely be profitable to forage hundreds of km in search of fish, whereas this may often be necessary for those blue-water species (such as the red-footed and white boobies) which feed chiefly on flying fish and are in fact known to feed at least 500km from land.

The tendency to co-operate in fishing is perhaps a separate phenomenon. It is to be distinguished from the phenomenon of group fishing, in which many individuals congregate, but do not collaborate, except perhaps inadvertently (however, even this distinction is not so clear as it may seem). The best account of blue-foot co-operation (Parkin *et al.* 1970) describes how small groups (2–13 birds) of both sexes work a small area, flying at 5–30m above the sea,

Fig. 244 (a and b). (a) Bill Touching and (b) jabbing between members of a pair.

and, as one bird whistles and dives, some or all of the others dive almost simultaneously, without calling. There can be no doubt that the call acts as a signal, presumably enhancing the chances of more birds diving simultaneously. This must, on average, make it more likely that each individual will catch something. This is likely to be true if they are diving into a shoal, which would scatter when disturbed by the first bird. The first bird could itself benefit by the total confusion caused by a simultaneous mass descent of boobies. Basically the same argument should apply to sulids feeding in deeper water, in the open sea, and in fact there is reason to believe that concerted diving is advantageous there, too, and is only 'inadvertent' collaboration in the sense that it does not employ a timing signal. In the sense that the birds (and gannets are a good example) have become highly responsive to the signal of conspecifics diving and may have evolved brilliant marker plumage to facilitate this response, it is in evolutionary terms 'deliberate'. Nobody has suggested a likely reason why a 'timer' like the blue-foot's whistle has not evolved in other species, but it probably has to do with the type of prey upon which each feeds most. Closely 'staggered' rather than simultaneous diving may be more effective for gannets perhaps by thus exhausting the fish's 'quick-swim' mechanism which fatigues rapidly if triggered in quick succession, thus giving an active underwater pursuit by the gannet more chance of success if the fish is using the slow-swim mechanism. In this situation, great penetration would obviously help and this is allowed by the gannet's weight. In other species, again, quite different circumstances obtain. The capture of flying fish is probably not helped by collaboration and red-footed and white boobies may usually fish singly. The mass presence of anchovies in the feeding area of the Peruvian booby, plus the almost inevitable presence of thousands of other fish eaters, such as cormorants and sea lions, creates, there, a very different situation, in which mass diving may have little practical advantage, but occurs just because there are so many birds and fish in such a small area. A particularly interesting comparison would be the case of the brown booby, which also tends to fish inshore and might benefit from a mechanism similar to that of the blue-foot. Timed, co-operative fishing, however, has not been observed in this species (but see p. 502).

Coker describes blue-foots descending in a spiral to the appropriate height for the final plunge. He considered it far inferior to the piquero in pace and elegance, but this is a subjective judgement, perhaps heavily dependent on circumstances. Murphy records 'cautious, slanting dives' but, out at sea, 'long straight plunges with very nearly as much verve as the Piquero'.

My observations on the blue-foot's fishing behaviour, apart from inshore and group fishing, showed that diving from the surface is common. A male interspersed some 100 plunges from 3 to 6m with 15 surface dives, at least two of which were successful. Altogether it caught at least five fish, three of which it brought to the surface before swallowing. It submerged more or less on the spot with sharply inclined head and neck and a high, vigorous flip of the wings. Sometimes it lifted its wings and moved over the surface before diving or jumped almost clear, rather like a shag though less gracefully, before submerging. This diving seemed

Fig. 245

Mutual preening (reciprocal allopreening).

awkward but effective. Often it came up from a plunge and cleared the surface in a more or less continuous movement before plunging again. From these low slanting dives, the booby always emerged in line with the direction of the plunge, whereas steep ones allowed it to reverse its direction under water and emerge going the other way. There are no observations on surface diving in other boobies, so it would be unjustifiable to suggest that the blue-foot shows more tendency to do so, but its facility in this direction hints that, in the shallows which it often frequents, underwater pursuit from a surface dive could be a useful method of feeding, perhaps especially in the male. In the Galapagos, Harris (1974) recorded three blue-foots fishing by power diving at about 10° to the horizontal, apparently to achieve speed rather than penetration. One bird 'hardly broke flight at all . . . but bounced off the wave top or passed through the wave'. It was successful in capturing fish.

I saw surface diving in juveniles, also, which swam quickly over the surface with head submerged before flipping completely under. Here it could be a significant step towards acquiring the full fishing technique, by starting with surface dives and small dives. This is probably the way in which all sulids acquire this difficult art.

The ecological aspects of inshore fishing and possible sexual division of labour in the blue-foot have already been mentioned; besides helping the blue-foot to raise two or three young, these fishing abilities may be partly responsible for reducing the length of its breeding cycle, increasing breeding frequency, allowing the male to hold an extra territory whilst the female is still completing the previous breeding cycle and perhaps may thus affect the system of mate fidelity by facilitating overlapping cycles in which the male starts with one female and acquires a different one for a new attempt before the old has been finished. If these conjectures are correct, this is an intriguing example of interrelationships between behavioural and ecological systems.

SUMMARY

1. The breeding behaviour of the blue-footed booby is much influenced by the species' agility, both in the air and on the ground, and by its flat-ground habitat.

2. The male 'prospects' for a site from the air and aerial patrolling is one form of site defence.

3. More than one territory may be held simultaneously.

4. In addition to actual fighting (rare) or Wing-flailing, the following ritualised behaviour patterns are used in connection with site ownership:

Fig. 246 (a and b)

Food begging in the young blue-footed booby.
(a) medium intensity.
(b) high intensity.

Aerial Saluting
Yes Headshaking—an aggressive head nodding
Ritualised Jabbing
Various postures associated with ritualised walking (see Pair Maintenance)
Ritualised forms of handling nest material.

These are often expressed as a rapid succession in no fixed order and may involve both members of a pair.

5. Pair formation is preceded by Prospecting by the female and then by Pair Flighting.

6. The male 'advertises' for a female by means of the Sky-pointing display, which is extremely well developed. Sky-pointing is used also as a mutual display between mates and probably helps to strengthen the pair bond. It is homologous with Sky-pointing in other sulids and is derived from a pre-movement posture.

7. Several ritualised behaviour patterns are closely associated with Sky-pointing—particularly Parading, Pelican Posture and Oblique Headshake.

8. Bill-up-face-away is associated with Parading and particularly with movement away from the partner. It may be an appeasement posture.

9. Another common bill position is 'tucked'—the Pelican Posture, used extensively as an accompaniment to locomotion.

10. Departure from the site is often signalled by a ritualised wing-shaking movement, Wing Rattle.

Fig. 247. Panting, gular fluttering and ruffling of dorsal feathers as heat-regulating mechanisms.

Fig. 248 (a and b). (a) Plunge diving. (b) Group, or co-ordinated diving.

11. A trio of activities centred on the nest and used a great deal during interactions between mates are Showing Nest Material; building it (mutually and symbolically) and touching it in a smooth Bowing motion.

12. Pair members engage in Bill Touching and Jabbing, the latter in a form very similar to that used by rivals.

13. Reciprocal allo-preening is rare in the blue-foot.

14. Incubation stints are about 18 hours in the male and 25 in the female. Behaviour during nest relief is discussed.

15. Foraging trips are short (about 4–7 hours).

16. Parents will accept strange young chicks but eventually come to recognise their own and will not then accept strangers.

17. The older of the two siblings does not automatically kill or eject the younger as happens in the white and brown boobies; the second blue-foot chick dies only if food becomes scarce and is monopolised by the first-born.

18. Some examples of the performance of 'adult' behaviour patterns by chicks are given.

19. Body maintenance behaviour is described.

20. Blue-foots have specialised fishing techniques particularly plunge-diving into shallows and communal fishing. These and other aspects of fishing behaviour are discussed.

7

Sula variegata

PERUVIAN BOOBY

1. NOMENCLATURE; EXTERNAL FEATURES; MORPHOLOGY; MOULT AND VOICE

NOMENCLATURE

1. *Common*

Peruvian booby or piquero or piquero comun are perhaps the most frequently used names; others being variegated booby, lancer and camanay (camanay is usually given to the blue-footed booby, but in northern Peru camanay and piquero are interchanged, the former applying to *S. variegata* and the latter to *S. nebouxii*).

2. *Scientific*

Sula variegata (Von Tschudi 1844), Fauna Per. Orn. p. 313.

Binomial synonyms have included:

Dysporus variegatus and, erroneously, *Sula cyanops* and *S. fusca.* Skulls from northern Chile have been called *Sula antiqua.*

GENERAL FEATURES

1. *Adult*

The adult piquero's (sexes alike) distinctive *combination* of characters is the pure white head, neck and underparts together with the variegated white and brown wings and back giving a scaly appearance. The primaries are warm darkish brown, merging into fuscous black on the outer webs and distally, but paler on the inner web and basally. There is comparatively little sexual dimorphism in size; overall length is about 74cm and wing span some $1\frac{1}{2}$m from tip to tip.

The booby with which it is most likely to be confused (the blue-foot) has a streaked head and neck, whilst the only other booby (Abbott's) with white head, neck and underparts and black back is confined to the Indian Ocean around Christmas Island, whilst the piquero is restricted to the belt of the Pacific off Peru, Chile and, more rarely, Ecuador. It would be a miracle if the two came into contact!

The lower back and flanks of the Peruvian booby are variegated brown and white. The tail is variably brown and white. Some birds have the central tail feathers white whilst others have brown tips (or more) to some or all tail feathers (it is not known whether birds with some brown on the tail are younger than ones with white tails).

The bill is variously described as lead grey, horn, slaty or purplish blue, becoming redder in the breeding season. The eyes are ruby red and the legs and feet bluish grey, sometimes rather dark. The female may have brighter feet than the male.

2. *Juvenile*

The juvenile is conspicuously dingy-greyish, buff or light fuscous below, with feathers of breast and belly widely bordered white, after a large, sub-terminal brownish patch. A somewhat darker band extends from the sides of the lower neck, onto the breast in a pectoral band (a similar demarcation band is found in most juvenile sulids). The head and neck are finely ash-streaked. The wings and back are duller and darker than in the adult due to the narrower white borders of the feathers of the dorsal plumage. White down persists on the rump longer than anywhere else but is usually clear by the time the bird first flies properly.

The iris is yellowish grey, becoming brown and then red; the bill and face bluish and the legs and feet a lighter blue-grey than those of the adult.

The juvenile acquires adult plumage probably in two incomplete moults, the intervening stages being little different from the adult once the dull feathers of the head and underparts have been replaced by pure white. One slightly immature bird had a white head but somewhat ashy flanks and slightly off-white ventral surface. The iris remains light brown until into the second year and the facial skin, legs and feet are lighter than those of the adult.

3. *Flight*

With the exception of Abbott's, boobies are all so similar in flight that it is difficult to say much that is diagnostic about one species. Piqueros are probably slightly stiffer-winged than the blue-foot. They have a steady fairly shallow, oaring wing beat (approx. 2·7–2·8 complete flaps per second, Coker (1919), Blake (1948) interspersed with glides. They use the wind expertly and can hang, poised and motionless except for a sinuous twisting of the head and neck, above and alongside their nesting places. Often they travel low over the water, but may fly in skeins at a greater height, often among files of guanays.

DETAILED DESCRIPTION

1. *Adult male and female*

(*a*) *Upperparts*

The head and neck are pure white, with the rest of the upperparts variegated brown and

Fig. 249(a). The Peruvian booby. **(b)** showing underwing pattern.

Fig. 251. Flight silhouettes.

white. The mantle feathers are fuscous, with broad, white distal margins which tend to disappear with abrasion, giving an overall browner appearance.

(*b*) *Underparts*

Breast and entire ventral surface white, except for mottled brown patch on flanks.

Primaries and primary coverts mainly brown, but blackish on outer webs and lighter basally. Secondaries and scapulars brownish black, with whitish bases and slight white borders on outer webs.

The tail feathers are mainly whitish, the central feathers completely so, the lateral ones becoming progressively darker, at least the outer webs of the outermost pair being fuscous black.

(*c*) *Bill, feet, etc.*

Because there is only the one race of Peruvian booby, there is no geographical variation in the colour of bill, facial skin and feet. Nor is there much sexual or seasonal variation so far as I can make out. The bill is lead-blue more or less tinged with brownish red, sometimes quite markedly. Murphy describes it as 'purplish blue, sometimes almost pinkish'.

The facial skin is dark grey or bluish, slightly darker than the orbital ring. It does not look as conspicuous as on the white booby, mainly because it is hardly darker than the bill and so does not contrast with it. Nevertheless, the extent of the facial skin is not much, if any, less. The eye is red brown, sometimes with a deep orange tint.

The legs and feet are lead grey, or bluish grey, looking much darker in dried skins than in life.

MEASUREMENTS AND WEIGHT

The piquero is a medium-sized booby (overall length c. 740mm). The male's weight is approximately 85 per cent of the female's, a ratio which, although somewhat sexually dimorphic, is far less so than that of the blue-foot. Whilst the female Peruvian is smaller than the female blue-foot, the male is larger

Fig. 250

Juvenile plumage.

than the male blue-foot; the gap between the sexes, thus narrowed from both sides, giving a medium-sized, less dimorphic booby.

The tail measures approximately 24 per cent of the total body length in the male and 25 per cent in the female. Thus in both sexes the tail is much shorter than in the blue-foot and in particular, there is markedly less difference between the sexes in this important characteristic than there is in the blue-foot. This may be correlated with the fact that male and female fish in much the same way, whereas in the blue-foot there is substantial difference between the sexes in hunting technique (p. 568).

Table 83 gives some of the available measurements for the Peruvian booby.

MOULT

There are no detailed published observations on the progress of moult in this species. Murphy says that the wing and tail feathers are moulted during incubation, the new feathers being conspicuously darker than the old worn ones. Doubtless, as in all sulids, moult proceeds in overlapping cycles, each involving only part of the flight complement, rather than as a complete annual replacement of flight feathers (see White booby p. 324). Of four breeding birds, two males and two females, I examined, all had either two or three primaries and up to six tail feathers growing. All had chicks, ranging from newly hatched to a month.

VOICE

At the breeding colony the piquero is a noisy bird with an expressive range involving distinctive differences in pitch and timbre difficult to describe. The impact of a stupendous colony of whistling, grunting and loud-calling piqueros is unforgettable. My notes describe, from females, soft bickering and grunting, rising and falling in pitch and amplitude and continuing for 30–40 separate articulations though usually 6–12, and a loud, cow-like call. Fighting females may maintain a moaning call. Males bicker and chitter in a high pitched voice but have no piercing whistle, so that in voice as well as morphology there is less difference between the sexes than in the blue-foot. Vogt describes the female's voice as a goose-like honk (probably my 'cow-call') and the male's as a trumpet-like note and a whistle. Murphy describes them as the noisiest of the guano birds, producing a medley of whistles, gabblings and trumpet-like calls.

As in all sulids, the piquero calls when flying in to its site, often starting with one or two isolated calls followed by a full, fast run. Females seem noisier than males and constitute the main source of sound in the colony.

The piquero may call when fishing (which it often does in dense flocks).

TABLE 83

PHYSICAL CHARACTERISTICS OF THE PERUVIAN BOOBY

	Male			Female			Male as % of female	
	Mean	Range	Sample Size	Mean	Range	Sample size		
Weight (g)	1300	1250–1350	2	1520	1500–1540	2	86	Nelson
Culmen length (mm)	92·6	88–99·6	14	98·2	96–101	9	94	Murphy (1936)
	94	93–95	2	99	98–100·5	2		
Culmen depth (mm)	30			32				Nelson
Wing length (mm)	379·5	361–394	14	395·4	378–415	9	95	Murphy
	394		2	413		2		Nelson
Tail length (mm)	163·5	146–181	14	172·5	161·5–190	9	94	Murphy
	175		2	185		2		Nelson
Tarsus (mm)	48	45–50	14	50·4	48–53	9	94	Murphy
	40		2	48		2		Nelson

2. BREEDING DISTRIBUTION, NUMBERS AND OTHER ASPECTS OF POPULATIONS

INTRODUCTION

It is interesting that, of the seven sulid species in existence, the entire world population of three (*Sula variegata*, *S. abbotti* and the *S. bassana* superspecies) is fairly accurately known and that of a fourth (*S. nebouxii*) could in principle easily be ascertained.

The Peruvian booby is of particular interest because of the phenomenal fluctuations in its numbers imposed by the periodical disappearance of its principal food fish. Also, because it is of restricted distribution and long-standing commercial importance, something is known about its population changes over many years.

At the present day, it breeds mainly on islands off the coast of Peru, between LOBOS DE TIERRA and the islets known as JESÚS and IÑANA. Many general texts claim that it breeds along the coast of Chile. Thus Johnson (1965) says 'fairly large nesting colonies are to be found at certain points along the Chilean Coast' but he gives no supporting details. However, Millie (pers. comm.) has recently photographed a colony in Coquimbo (Fig. 252). It occurs

Fig. 252

Colony of Peruvian boobies on Isla Pajaros, Coquimbo Province, Chile, Sept. 1974. *Photo:* G. Millie.

only in small numbers south of the Ballestas group and north of the Lobos Islands, its main colonies lying between lats. 6° and 10°s. and around 13°s. The main concentrations are on the **Lobos Islands**, MAZORCA, the **Guañapes,** the **Ballestas** and CENTRAL CHINCHA (R. Jordán 1963 and pers. comm.). But it breeds or has bred on a large number, probably hundreds, of other islands and islets and mainland puntas (see Table 84). As an indication of the number of breeding stations occupied by guano-producing birds, at least 147 islands and 21 mainland localities were still yielding guano in 1950 (Hutchinson 1950). To this figure must be added the many islets which are not now, or perhaps have never been, commercially viable. Not all of these breeding stations are used by piqueros, but probably most of them are or have been (there is reason to think the booby population was once much larger than it is now). It must be remembered that Peruvian islands can lose or gain huge populations over the years or even in successive years. DON MARTIN acquired a colony sometime between 1821 and 1847 and is now a very important source of guano. ASIA and SANTA ISLANDS, too, are now important, but were not significant sources of old guano. The description of the main piquero colonies which follows provides several examples of huge changes in the population of an island in two successive years. The oceanographic conditions around the Peruvian islands are not uniform, and therefore neither is the concentration of fish. Hutchinson shows that, around some islands such as the **Chinchas** and **Guañapes**, there are many more fish shoals to be seen than there are around others, such as LOBOS DE TIERRA. One would expect the distribution of guano birds to coincide fairly well with that of fish, and on the whole the largest concentration of birds does so, though in such a rich area and with birds as mobile as piqueros, one cannot expect a very precise correlation.

THE GUANO ISLANDS (GENERAL)

The Peruvian guano islands are utterly fascinating. They are near to the coast (Fig. 253) mostly lying a mere 16 or 19km offshore. ISLA LOBERIA, near Cerro Azul, is actually connected to the mainland by cable car, though the **Lobos de Afuera** group (two irregular islands and several islets) lie some 54km from the nearest mainland point. Most of them are small—merely a few tens of acres in area. Almost all are utterly barren, often jagged, excreta-encrusted rocks and slopes thrusting from an oily swell into a hazy blue sky, their inhospitable, cavernous bases ringed with surf. The exceptions are islands like SAN GALLÁN, SAN LORENZO and LA ISLA VIEJA, which reach an altitude of more than 300m and support, from cloud moisture, luxuriant pockets of vegetation.

The two **Lobos** groups, separated by some 70km, are quite different in character and in their bird life, marking as they do the area in which the piquero becomes scarcer and the blue-foot becomes dominant (on LOBOS DE AFUERA they are roughly equal but on LOBOS DE TIERRA the piquero is greatly outnumbered).

Lobos de Tierra

This is the northernmost Lobos, a mere 6°s; a moon-like island 'its scarred surface a chiaroscuro of white convexities and purple shadows'. It is 9km long and 3·2km across at the widest point—the largest of the Peruvian bird islands and as large as the combined Lobos de Afuera group. Its hills are mainly less than 60m, but one at the southern end reaches 91m. LOBOS DE TIERRA is a metamorphosed rock much folded by pressure, with high peaks coated with a hard glass-like substance—'guano glass'—probably formed by the action of moisture on guano. The western side is steep and irregular; the eastern slopes more gently and possesses sandy beaches. The island is unusual among low-liers in that it supports thorny, acacia-like trees. It used to be popular with pelicans and blue-footed boobies, less so with piqueros and possessed few Peruvian cormorants but this picture has now changed (see p. 589). Presumably because it is relatively near the humid tropics, it gets a little more rain than the other islands, though the amount remains almost negligible.

Lobos de Afuera

This is in one of the most eroded groups of all the Peruvian islands. Its surface has been drastically gashed and pulverised by man's activities, so that heaps of rubble lie everywhere.

Murphy describes it as a constantly folded island of metamorphic rock, much shattered and crumpled. The summits, like those of Lobos de Tierra, are coated with guano-glass. LOBOS DE AFUERA was famous for its huge colonies of pelicans, but these are now much reduced.

North, South and Central Chincha

NORTH and CENTRAL CHINCHA are 1·2 and 1·3km long respectively; SOUTH CHINCHA is much smaller. All are cliffy islands of granite with deposits of water-worn pebbles, betraying their origin as parts of erstwhile coastal Peru, later upraised. They form, with the Ballestas (8km distant) a twin group of islands off Pisco. The legendary Chinchas are the most famous of all the Peruvian islands. No fewer than 346 sailing vessels are said to have loaded up with guano there in 1858. Between 1850 and 1872 nearly 11 million tons of guano are said to have been exported from the Chinchas alone (Coker 1920). Murphy's vivid words capture the essence of this dramatic area:

> '... small though the Chinchas are, their name is known in the farthest seaports of the world and their share in making fortunes and abetting calamities, in debauching men and demoralising administrations, and in serving as the inanimate cause of greed, cruelty, extravagance, economic ruin and war has given them a historic place quite out of proportion to their size.
>
> Central Island is the highest of the group, its peak having today an altitude of 78·3m to which another 30m may have been added by the former blanket of guano. As a lookout, the summit presents a panorama so beautiful that an observer must be stolid indeed if he can resist a feeling of exultation when he beholds it.

Fig. 253. The distribution of the colonies off the coast of Peru.

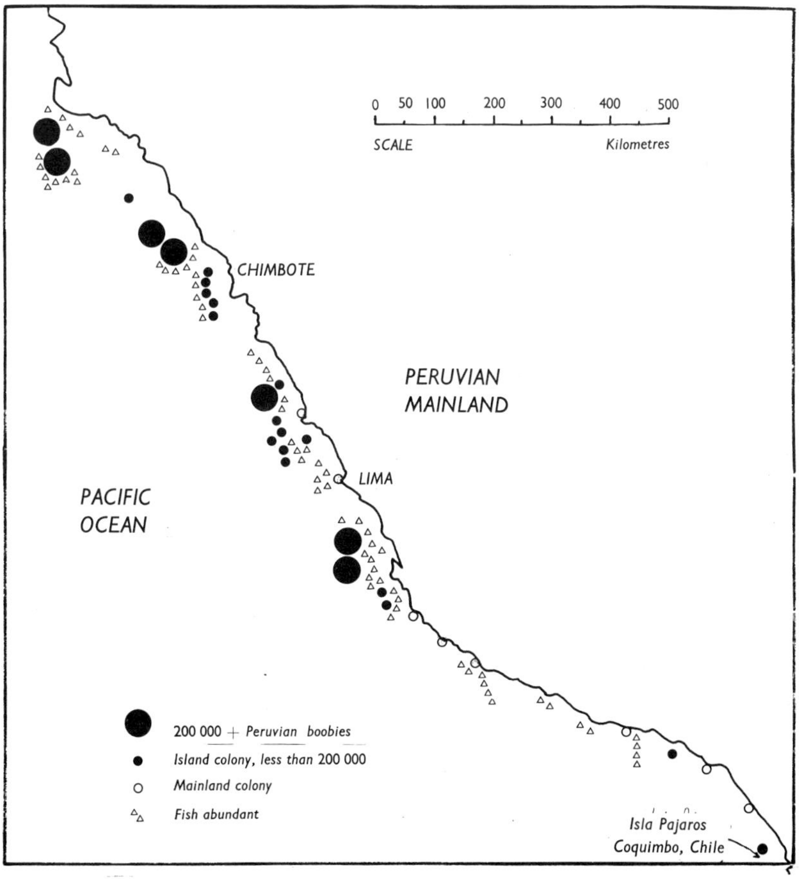

> The two sister isles, especially the lower and more distant North Island, round which a hundred square-riggers used to rock their spars, seem to lie at one's feet like white stars in the blue field of the sea. The western half of the circle of vision is taken up with the ever-varying Pacific, often covered with netted foam-streaks, and by the prevailingly cloud-filled sky in which feather-wisps and mare's-tails form all summer above the Humboldt Current. The offshore layers of cloud usually hang low in the west to hide the sun just before it nears the horizon and blazes forth again at the end of day. On this side, too, beyond South Island, stand the picturesque twin cones known as La Goleta (The Schooner). To the northeastward one looks towards Tambo de Mora, the Pampas de Noco, and the crests of the cordillera, beyond which still higher crests, of a thinner and colder blue, reveal themselves on the clearest days. In the southeastern quarter lies the bay of Pisco; the mountain-in-the-sea of San Gallán, with its westerly peak always hidden under a mantle of fog; the Ballestas and Isla Blanca; the red hills of Paracas Peninsula, which all but conceal the deep cove behind them; and the desert south of Pisco, blocked at the southern end by coal-bearing ridges, but stretching inland towards the vine-growing country of the Ica Valley. When the weather is calmest and brightest, the great Indian symbol of the Tres Cruces, which is carved on the seaward mountain slope, can be seen with the naked eye from Central Island, although its distance is 11 sea miles. The bay of Pisco is dotted with ruffled or shimmering areas where schools of anchovies or herrings are moving near the surface, the myriads of individual fishes straining out with their gill-rakers the invisible plant life which thickens the water; birds and seals in turn pursue the massing fishes, and oftentimes one can watch from the hilltop small groups of humpback whales which breach and blow, and then point up their flukes for the 'long dive'. Finally, the white hillsides about one are likely to be darkened by vast, huddled crowds of guanayes, while waving lashes of the same birds are silhouetted against the sky in all directions.'

North and South Guañape

The two GUAÑAPES are among the most famous of the islands and indeed hold the Peruvian record for the amount of guano yielded up to 1944: (408 334 metric tons). The south island, steeper and smaller than the north, is 690 by 570m and 165m high and almost entirely covered with piqueros whose nesting ranks, rising into the sunlit mist, form the finest bird spectacle I have ever seen. The north island, which holds fine old guano-administration buildings, is 1050 by 700m and rises from the sea to a terrace and from there by a steep slope, almost a cliff in places, to a flat interior pampa. It, too, holds an enormous population of piqueros, but also many cormorants.

The islands so sketchily described in the preceding paragraphs are perhaps the most famous of this astonishing string, almost any one of which, were it alone, would deserve special comment as a seabird breeding station. It is beyond the present scope to describe the other seabirds which share the islands with the piqueros, but the Peruvian cormorants (guanays), red-footed cormorants, burrowing petrels, penguins, pelicans, terns, gulls and skuas are all numerous, some of them abundant, and together create the incredible Peruvian seabird metropolis. At present, it is probably partly recovering from an all-time low.

THE GUANO ISLANDS (BOOBY POPULATIONS)

The most important and recently published source of information on the numbers and distribution of the piquero and the other chief guano birds is the report by Jordán (1963) of the aerial censuses of 1960 and 1962, covering the breeding seasons 1960–61 and 1961–62. These produced estimates based on the areas covered by the species concerned using a standard density which, for the piquero, was $1\frac{1}{2}$ pairs per square metre. Altogether, figures for 45 islands and puntas (headlands) are given (Table 84).

Seven colonies (LOBOS DE TIERRA, LOBOS DE AFUERA, GUAÑAPE NORTE, GUAÑAPE SUR, MAZORCA, CHINCHA NORTE and BALLESTAS) held more than 100 000 individuals each, the largest being Mazorca (total 732 700).

It is of considerable biological as well as practical import, to realise the extraordinary extent to which the populations on some of the islands fluctuate. Obviously, mass movements onto and away from islands lead to vast increments or decrements, often in successive years. This has implications for several aspects of breeding—such as fidelity to site and mate. However, not all populations fluctuate in this way and some islands continue a steady upwards climb for several years. Also, most islands always retain a substantial population even in falling years and it is comparatively rare for an island to gain a species or lose one entirely.

The main piquero colonies (some of which are no longer important) are described below, followed by a general history of the species and the impact on numbers of periodic catastrophes.

Guañape Norte

The GUAÑAPE islands are today one of the species' major strongholds. In November 1960 the population of the north island was an estimated 249 000 adults, rising to 424 000 by January 1962. When we were on the Guañapes in December 1964 the population of north island was estimated by the chief guardiane to be over 356 000. At each of these times the population was probably near its height, most pairs having laid or taken up territories.

Guañape Sur

On our visit in December 1964 this island seemed to be exclusively occupied by piqueros, as it was also in 1920 when (Murphy 1936) 'not one guanay lived on the high island of South Guañape and except for the narrow domain of Inca terns and chuitas around the shore line, it was occupied by but a single species, the piquero. The breeding grounds of this bird spread from the magnificent western precipice, more than 120m high, over to the pampa of the eastern slope, where the nests filled extensive spaces and presented one of the most beautiful scenes that could be imagined.' This is a good example of the piquero dominating an entire island for an appreciable span of years, even though the general area is suitable for other guano birds and GUAÑAPE SUR is topographically adequate for guanays. So it is of great interest to find (Jordán 1963) that in November 1960 this island held 425 700 guanays and in January 1962, 238 200. A vast population had suddenly arrived and (if my impression in 1964 was correct) had just as suddenly left again.

Estimated figures for the piquero population of SOUTH GUAÑAPE are 278 800 in 1960–61 and 370 800 in 1961–62. Thus, in the latter year the north island held even more than the south, but by February 1972 GUAÑAPE SUR again held most (Jordán pers. comm.). So far as earlier records are concerned, a mid-nineteenth century one definitely records piqueros on Guañape but does not specify which island. Probably both have been occupied from time immemorial for there are general statements to the effect that the Guañapes have been a stronghold for as long as there are records.

The Chinchas

CENTRAL CHINCHA holds more piqueros than NORTH or SOUTH CHINCHA; Jordán (pers. comm.) includes it in his list of the four major stations of today. Yet in 1960 it was NORTH CHINCHA that held most (340 300) whilst CENTRAL CHINCHA's population was a mere 600. In 1962 the respective totals were 305 600 (North) and 240 000 (Central).

Coker (1919), describing his visits in 1908–9, was presumably referring to Chincha Centro when he wrote 'thousands of nests overflowed the cliffs' and that here was the only place where he saw piqueros' nests on real table-land. Earlier (1869) piqueros were nesting here.

North Chincha has been the site of the most intensive ecological work yet carried out; both Vogt and Galarza conducted their studies here, where the birds' habit of nesting on man-made constructions makes them suitable for marking and handling. Neither Vogt (1942) nor Galarza (1968) estimated the population, the latter commenting that it breeds in ravines

TABLE 84

THE NUMBERS AND DISTRIBUTION OF CORMORANTS, PERUVIAN BOOBIES, AND PELICANS ON PERUVIAN ISLANDS AND HEADLANDS FROM AERIAL CENSUS 1960 AND 1962

	Cormorants		Peruvian boobies		Pelicans		Total	
	Nov. 1960	Jan. 1962	Nov. 1960	Jan. 1962	Nov. 1960	Jan. 1962	Nov. 1960	Jan. 1962
Lobos de Tierra	0	X	500 000	470 100	15 000	800	515 000	470 900
Lobos de Afuera	0	0	400 900	220 800	1 500	0	402 400	220 800
Punta la Farola	0	10 500	0	4 000	0	2 200	0	16 700
Punta Malabrigo	—	0	—	1 000	—	600	—	1 600
Macabí	439 300	385 600	54 500	45 500	0	0	493 800	431 100
Punta Cerro Negro	100 800	0	0	4 000	0	1 000	100 800	5 000
Guañape Norte	770 600	531 000	249 000	424 000	0	0	1 019 600	955 000
Guañape Sur	425 700	238 200	278 800	370 800	0	0	704 500	609 000
Chao	9 600	27 400	500	10 700	0	0	10 100	38 100
Corcovado	4 500	15 700	21 200	24 500	0	0	25 700	40 200
Santa	55 200	268 000	800	14 900	100	2 700	56 100	285 600
La Blanca	700	1 300	500	1 000	1 600	1 000	2 800	3 300
Ferrol	13 600	75 200	4 200	8 000	0	300	17 800	83 500
Tortugas	0	400	0	7 000	0	0	0	7 400
Punta la Grama	0	0	0	0	0	0	0	0
Punta Culebras	798 400	1 877 300	0	200	46 600	49 000	845 000	1 926 500
Punta Colorado	11 200	1 700	0	700	300	0	11 500	2 400
Punta Litera	88 600	800	0	0	19 500	1 000	108 100	1 800
Don Martín	389 100	471 200	5 600	42 800	59 400	64 800	454 100	578 800
Mazorca	261 600	225 800	732 700	112 200	0	0	994 300	338 000
Huampanú	—	57 500	—	7 300	—	2 800	—	67 600
Punta Salinas	424 000	441 000	5 000	10 000	9 000	15 000	438 000	466 000

Punta Chancay	0	0	0	0	0	0	0	0
Pescadores	594 600	314 200	23 100	4 200	6 200	300	623 900	318 700
La Cruz	0	200	400	2 500	200	0	600	2 700
Cabinzas	0	0	0	300	100	0	100	800
Palominos	9 000	2 100	3 000	3 000	500	200	12 500	5 300
Pachacamac	7 200	40 400	5 400	0	3 900	6 000	16 500	46 400
Asia	23 200	378 600	600	2 800	10 800	28 600	34 600	410 000
Punta Centinela	0	0	0	0	0	0	0	0
Chincha Norte	1 414 800	752 300	340 300	305 600	48 900	63 600	1 804 000	1 121 500
Chincha Centro	1 300	660 800	600	240 000	0	23 300	1 900	924 100
Chincha Sur	0	1 818 000	600	232 800	0	0	600	2 050 800
Ballestas	10 300	553 400	221 400	424 600	0	0	231 700	978 000
Santa Rosa	516 800	531 800	0	0	7 600	7 400	524 400	539 200
La Vieja	1 975 000	2 271 700	0	0	0	17 500	1 975 000	2 289 200
Punta Lomitas	100	191 800	0	0	200	4 400	300	196 200
Punta Lomas	56 000	899 000	0	500	25 200	14 200	81 200	913 700
Punta San Juan	818 500	365 000	0	0	12 300	6 000	830 800	371 000
Punta Autico	—	10 400	—	0	—	600	—	11 000
Punta La Chira	71 500	45 900	0	0	0	0	71 500	45 900
Punta Islay y Hornillos	97 000	209 500	0	100	0	3 200	97 000	212 800
Punta Jesús y Cocotea	50 000	0	0	0	2 000	200	52 000	200
Punta Coles	2 200	25 000	0	0	0	800	2 200	25 800
Punta Morro Sama	0	300	0	0	0	100	0	400
Totals	9 440 400	13 699 000	2 849 100	2 995 900	270 900	317 600	12 560 400	17 012 500
	75·16	80·52	22·68	17·51	2·16	1·87	100·00	100·00

X = colony disappeared — = no record

and on cliffs and on islets off North Chincha. Earlier, Murphy referring to his 1919–20 visit said it was moderately common on North Chincha, entirely on cliffs and the edges of plateaux. As already mentioned, the 1960 and 1962 figures were 340 300 and 305 600 respectively. Obviously, there has been a vast increase since the 1920's.

On SOUTH CHINCHA piqueros bred on the southern extremity (Vogt) but no idea of numbers is given. In 1960–61 there were only some 600 but in the following breeding season, 232 800. Again, vast transference had obviously taken place. Even taking the three Chinchas as a unit, the 1961–62 total was 436 900 up on the previous year.

Huara Islands

MAZORCA is another of today's 'big four' piquero stations with 732 700 in 1960; 112 200 in 1962 and a place among the four largest colonies in 1972. It is a fine example of a massive change in proportions of guanays and piqueros. In 1960 there were 261 600 guanays—about a third as many as the piquero—whilst in 1962 there were 225 800, which was twice as many as the piquero. There is little about this island in the literature. Murphy recorded 'many thousands' in 1919–20. Forbes (1913) noted piqueros breeding on the cliffs and there is an old (1852) reference in Hutchinson to an island Mazorque, where large numbers of piqueros were taken for food. Obviously, Mazorca has been well favoured by piqueros for a long time.

EL PELADO, another of the **Huara** group, is implicated in the 1852 record mentioned above, to the effect that vast numbers of birds (piqueros and guanays) and eggs were taken by Indians. 24 000 birds and 12 000 eggs were said to be taken annually.

The Lobos Islands

LOBOS DE TIERRA is the northernmost guano island and is of particular interest as the point at which the blue-footed booby, with its main distribution to the north, takes over from the piquero, whose main colonies lie to the south. It has been inhabited by piqueros for as long as there are records. Coker cites it as an example of an island which has been favoured by the piquero for centuries. Murphy found that the blue-foot far outnumbered the piquero, but this is not now the case. In 1960 there were 500 000 piqueros on de Tierra. This was in fact the second largest concentration in the entire Peruvian string. It was (within the limits of the observations) exactly the same size as the population on LOBOS DE AFUERA. In 1962 Lobos de Tierra (470 100) outnumbered Afuera (220 800). This again is noteworthy, since Murphy found that the piquero was much commoner on Afuera, though even here it was equalled by the blue-foot. Obviously a very substantial northward shift of piqueros has occurred within relatively recent years and the islands once regarded as the northern limits of its range (though still the most northerly colonies of any size) are now among the main centres of population. Oddly enough, no guanays had moved north with them. On Lobos de Afuera it breeds (or bred) on steep slopes.

Macabí

These islands are among those of pre-eminent importance in the production of guano (half as much as the Guañapes and the Chinchas). Though mainly given over to guanays, they held 54 500 and 45 500 piqueros in 1960 and 1962 respectively. Earlier Forbes (1913) recorded them on the pampas and scarps.

Corcovado Group

This is one of five islands (LA VICIDA, CORCOVADO, SANTITA, SANTA and MESIA) lying between Chao and the Bay of Ferrol and collectively referred to (for purposes of guano production) as the Santa Group (Hutchinson 1950). Corcovado is small and low and has a long history of guano production. The 1960 census revealed 21 200 piqueros there (five times as many as the guanays) and in 1962, 24 500 (less than twice as many). Here again is an island suited to both species and undergoing huge changes in absolute numbers and proportions of each in very short periods of time.

Ferrol Islands

NORTH and SOUTH FERROL held 4200 piqueros in the 1960 census and 8000 in the 1962 one. On both occasions they were heavily outnumbered by guanays.

Don Martín

Guano was first collected from this small island (20m high) in 1922 and by 1944, 237 115 metric tons had been yielded. This very considerable amount must have been largely newly deposited, for it is known that in 1821 it had neither birds nor guano though by 1847 there were birds and the beginnings of a deposition of guano. By 1945 it was said to contain a dense breeding population of guanays and a smaller number of piqueros (389 100 guanays and 5600 piqueros; and 471 200 guanays and 42 800 piqueros in 1944 and 1945 respectively). Even so, a population of 43 000 piqueros is far from negligible.

Pachacamac

This is a group of four islands. PACHACAMAC held 5400 piqueros in 1960 but none in 1962, the guanay population having risen from 7200 to 40 400. Earlier it was said to hold mainly guanays with a few piqueros.

Asia Island

ASIA was not an important guano station last century, but when Murphy visited the island in 1919, the bird population was considerable (mainly guanays) and in 1960 and 1962 there were large numbers of guanays but fewer piqueros (600 and 2800).

Pescadores

THE PESCADORES, like the Pachacamacs, have always been mainly guanay stations, with a few piqueros. Murphy recorded it as moderately common. In fact the 1960 census showed 23 100 birds but this dropped to 4200 in 1962 and in any case was merely a fraction of the guanay numbers.

Ballestas

Finally, in this treatment of the main piquero island colonies, there are the three BALLESTAS in Pisco Bay, south of the Chinchas. They have yielded much guano and are obviously well favoured and ancient sites. The piquero population (221 400 in 1960 and 424 600 in 1962) has probably increased in recent years, and together with half a million guanays, gave a population of almost a million in the latter year.

San Gallán

Murphy found it breeding here and Vogt (1942) recorded it as breeding on the south-facing cliff.

Mainland colonies

Some mainland guanay colonies are as big as any of the island ones, thus PUNTA CULEBRAS held 1 877 300 guanays in 1962 and was exceeded only by the island of LA VIEJA. Of the Puntas, however (La Farola, Malabrigo, Cerro Negro, La Grama, Culebras, Colorado, Litera, Salinas, Chancay, Centinela, Lomitas, Lomas, San Juan, Atico, La Chira, Islay y Hornillos, Jesús y Cocotea, Coles and Morro Sama) only Salinas held any piqueros at all in 1960 (5000). In 1962, however, six headlands were occupied by piqueros, the largest colony (10 000) being again on Salinas, though two others (La Farola and Cerro Negro) held 4000.

These very substantial mainland colonies owe their success to the conservation and management measures taken by the Guano Administration and are recent (post 1945) phenomena.

ASPECTS OF TOTAL POPULATION

1. *Historical, with reference to the piquero's relationship with other guano birds*

Within a restricted locale, the piquero is a numerous species, forming vast colonies and addicted to particular islands, which it may dominate for many years. It does, of course, share most of these islands with hordes of other seabirds, its potential competitors being, in particular, the guanay and the pelican and the history of the piquero's population changes possibly involves directly related changes in these other species. This would be so only if an increase in guanays or pelicans either displaced and prevented piqueros from breeding, or caused significant mortality amongst breeding piqueros. There is no clear evidence for the former and it is far from certain that disruption by pelicans (though it did sometimes occur) had a significant effect. Nevertheless, for what it is worth, the evidence bearing on this topic should be examined.

As a starting point it may be recalled that the guano birds have shared these islands as comparable groups of seabirds have shared similar zoogeographical areas, for millions of years They are actually recorded in pre-Incan times, on ceramics (one shows piquero nests on cliffs) but there are no written records until the eighteenth century, and few useful details until the nineteenth century naturalists discovered the Peruvian Islands

Their records are useful indications of the relative abundance of the main guano species although the interpretation of them is fraught with difficulties Here, the sources of information, which influenced many later works of reference, are the reports of the famous Von Humboldt (1806), Von Tschudi (1846) and Raimondi (1856). Von Tschudi incorporated information from a study by Rivero (or Ribero) originally published in 1827 (details in Hutchinson's bibliography). Von Tschudi, who visited the islands in 1842, was impressed by the abundance of the piquero and rated it as the most important of the guano birds. This may have been a false impression, due perhaps to greater mortality among guanays in the previous year (which happens to be one of the hypothetical 'catastrophe' years calculated by Vogt on the basis of a seven-year cycle, now known to be an unreliable prognostic). However, a little later, and probably before he had seen Von Tschudi's report, Raimondi (1852) also testified to the abundance of the piquero, but some confusion attaches to his account, since it seems he did not know what a guanay was. This appears from Raimondi's (1876) annotated reprint of the earliest literary reference specifically to guano birds (that of Juan and de Ulloa 1806, writing of conditions not later than 1748) where he says that 'guanays' are marine birds belonging to the genus *Sula*. Another early author (Markham 1880) also speaks of 'the guano bird' as *Sula variegata*. A further confusing possibility is that the word was used as an inclusive term for *all* guano birds.

Perhaps we may take Von Tschudi at face value and conclude that the piquero's status relative to the guanay has changed markedly in the last 100 years, for until very recently the guanay outnumbered it 4 to 1, and had done so for over 50 years at least. Coker (1920) noted with surprise that the piquero was often stated, in works of reference, to be the chief guano bird, whereas in his own experience the guanay far surpassed it in numbers and the pelican came second as a guano bird.

Hutchinson, after a scholarly review of the circumstantial evidence for the fluctuations of guanay populations on the Chinchas, does indeed conclude that the piquero and pelican held sway on islands with undisturbed guano caps, such as the Ballestas and South Chincha, until about the middle of last century. Then, the human onslaught on the guano, with the colossal disturbances involved, drove away the dominant species and, for reasons not explained, the guanays, rather than the piqueros and pelicans, subsequently returned and thrived best, building up to their present superior position. Probably guanays are less susceptible to human disturbance than are piqueros and, particularly, pelicans, and have responded best to protection, which, on account of their better guano production, may even have been preferential. This explanation, however, does not show how the guanays ever lost their position of chief guano bird (if in fact they did), for Hutchinson believes that prior to about 1825, they were the most abundant guano birds and responsible for the bulk of the vast old guano deposits laid down over the years.

Hutchinson makes a point of basic importance with respect to their distribution in the past. He points out that the extensive guano deposits which occurred along the coast of what is now northern Chile but was, prior to the war of 1879–82, southern Peru, mean that a substantial shift in the location of guano birds has occurred within relatively recent times (that is, in the last very few thousand years). For now there are no concentrations of guano birds in this area, but once, before the deposits in central and northern Peru were laid down (the Chilean material is considerably older than, say, the old Chincha deposits) there must have been considerable numbers of guano birds there. Only so can one explain the huge fossil deposits of Pabillon de Pica, Punta de Lobos and Hornillos. The difference in age between these deposits and those from central and northern Peru (that is, roughly, a difference between areas south and north of Independencia Bay) mean that deposition was not proceeding contemporaneously. Evidently the southern area eventually became uninhabitable whilst the northern one became attractive to guano birds. Hutchinson (on evidence from the probable age of deposits) places the colonisation of central and northern Peru at about 2000–3000 years ago and suggests that, until then, it may have been ecologically unsuitable. He suggests that 'the only reasonable explanation of such a change is that the phenomena of the abnormal years, with warm water and violent rain, formerly occurred so much more frequently that permanent colonisation and deposition could not take place. It is in fact necessary to suppose that the conditions now met with north of the Lobos Islands formerly extended as far south as the Chinchas'. The factors which led to the decline of guano birds on the (now) Chilean coast may have been oceanographic in two ways—a change in currents with an associated change in the centres of distribution of food fish and a change in sea level, leading to the submergence of many islands off Chile. Even today, (although there is no direct evidence) the astonishingly rapid desertion of some islands and the formation of new colonies on others may be a response to changes in the distribution patterns of anchovies.

It is possible that, for a period, the total population of guano birds was very considerably larger than it is now; there may have been contemporaneous colonies in all the places where guano has been found. Speculatively, in such a case, the massive decline could have resulted from climatic changes or from disease (Vogt 1942) or both. It is just possible that the introduction of avian disease via domestic poultry could have combined with the weakening effects of periods of warmer, wetter weather to produce kills much more massive than those which would have resulted from the bad periods alone. In any case, the possibility that past populations were much larger is interesting in view of the present day habit of nesting so densely.

The probability that the guano birds as a whole have fluctuated in the past does not mean that the proportions of the various species have remained constant. As mentioned earlier, there is good evidence that piqueros and pelicans were once more plentiful than guanays. It is relevant here, therefore, to discuss the matter of interspecific competition, though as usual there is little enough concrete information.

When piqueros, guanays and pelicans share an island they never intermingle. Each species forms its own dense congregations clearly demarcated from those of other species (Fig. 262c). Consequently relatively few individuals would even be in a position to engage in direct, interspecific aggressive encounters. It would be astonishing if, in fact, there were no 'incidents' where species adjoin and in such cases one would expect the piquero, aggressive and with a formidable beak, to be capable of displacing the guanay and of course the pelican should dominate the other two. However, it is far more likely that meaningful competition, if it occurs, takes the form of 'swamping out'—one species, once established and undisturbed by man, more or less continuously occupying traditional areas and merely by its presence excluding others. Guañape Sur was for a period given over entirely to piqueros, although it used to hold many guanays and has recently acquired some again.

Thus, probably, whilst there are some areas which one or another species finds uncongenial, there are others which have certainly, at different times, been occupied by at least two species and it would be of great interest to have the details over several years for one or two such areas. Nevertheless, though there is here the basis for 'passive' competition in the sense that ground suitable for two or three species is occupied merely by one, there is no hint of evidence that individuals of one species are actually debarred from breeding by exclusion from an area. In other words, whilst it may be true that, for example, the piquero, by occupying much of South Chincha, kept out the guanay for a period, and in that sense competed with it, it may not be true that the *total* population of guanays ever suffered, as a result of exclusion by piqueros from breeding habitats. Certainly within the last 50–100 years, there have been unoccupied areas on many, if not most, islands and also some unoccupied islands. Yet, as noted previously, pelicans and piqueros *have* declined relative to guanays in the last 70 years or so and Vogt attributes the piquero's decline mainly to competition from the guanay. But this is probably due more to man's interference, affecting the piquero and pelican more than the guanay.

One may probably conclude that neither the total numbers of any single species, nor their status relative to each other, have been determined by shortage of breeding habitat and associated, active competition for space. Probably the present day Peruvian seabirds owe their species composition more to basic traits specific to each, such as reproductive success (compounded of clutch size, breeding frequency, age of first breeding, etc.) feeding habits (such as degree of dependence on anchovies) upon which are superimposed the effects of man's interference and possibly predation, than to interspecific competition for breeding areas. At

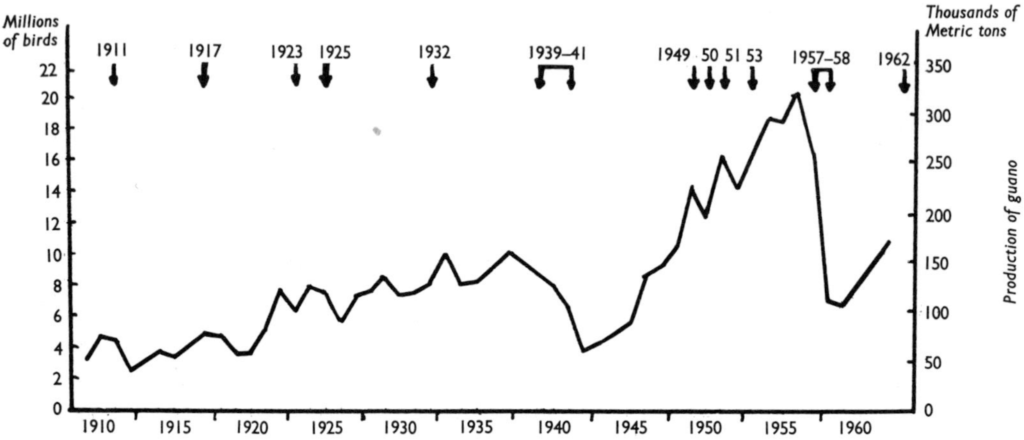

Fig. 254

Fluctuations in the population of guano birds, 1909–62, based on the amount of guano deposited, assuming one bird deposits 15·9 kg per annum. Years of serious population crashes marked with arrows (from Jordán & Fuentes 1966).

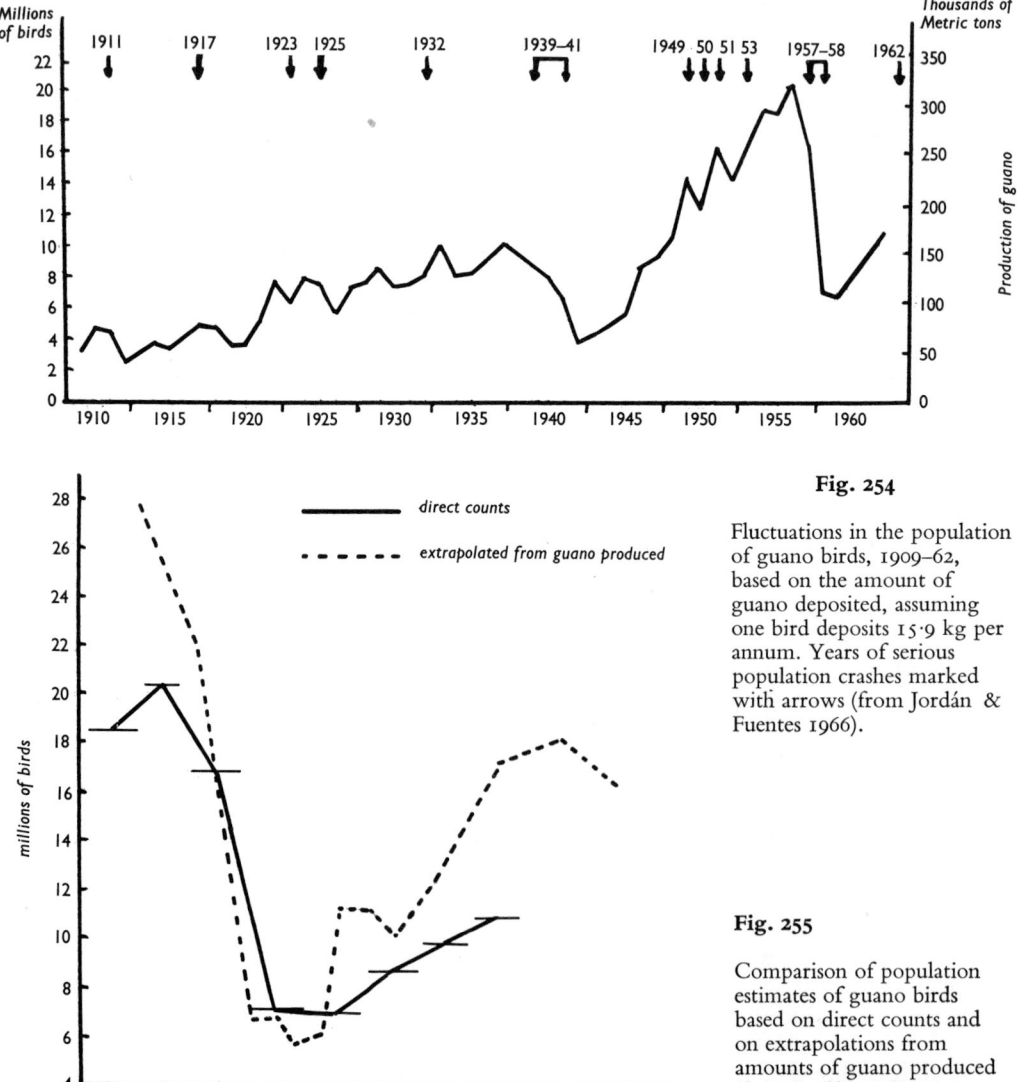

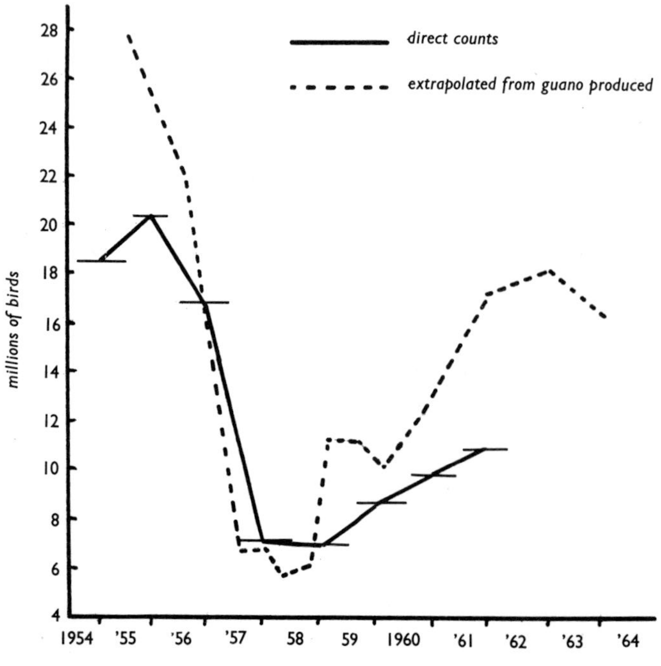

Fig. 255

Comparison of population estimates of guano birds based on direct counts and on extrapolations from amounts of guano produced (from Jordán & Fuentes 1966).

the present time, an unprecedented effect on the population of guano birds is being exerted by the Peruvian anchovy fisheries. Birds are suffering directly (caught in nets and killed by fishermen) and (pp. 602, 606) indirectly as a result of the depleted anchovy stocks (Jordán & Fuentes 1966). Guanays are suffering proportionately far more than piqueros. Thus the composition of the seabirds is being influenced by a new set of man-made circumstances.

2. *Total population in the Twentieth Century*

Although direct figures for the total population of adult piqueros in Peru over many years do not exist in the literature, it is possible to gain a fairly accurate picture from two sources. The first (Fig. 254), covering the period 1909–62, is a graph in Jordán & Fuentes (1966) which gives the total population of guano birds (not just piqueros) estimated from the yield of guano for each year, a method which (as Fig. 255 shows) is surprisingly accurate. The second (Fig. 256) is a graph in the same publication which gives guano bird populations for the years 1955–66, based on actual censuses taken by the guardianes at the main breeding stations. These are obtained by estimating the area occupied by the birds and multiplying by the average density, In addition to these sources there are, more recently, aerial censuses, those for 1960–61 and 1961–62 being given in detail in Jordán (1963). Finally, Jordán (pers. comm.) provided me with straight figures for the total population of piqueros for the years 1963–72.

From source one, the piquero population over the years may be calculated on the basis of the 1963 figure (an indirectly estimated 12 million guano birds) of which an actual 2·8 million (Jordán's figure) or 23·3 per cent were piqueros. Whilst it is almost certainly inaccurate to assume that, just because piqueros constituted 23·3 per cent of the guano bird population in 1963, they would do so, also, in the years back to 1909, it is impossible to apply adequate

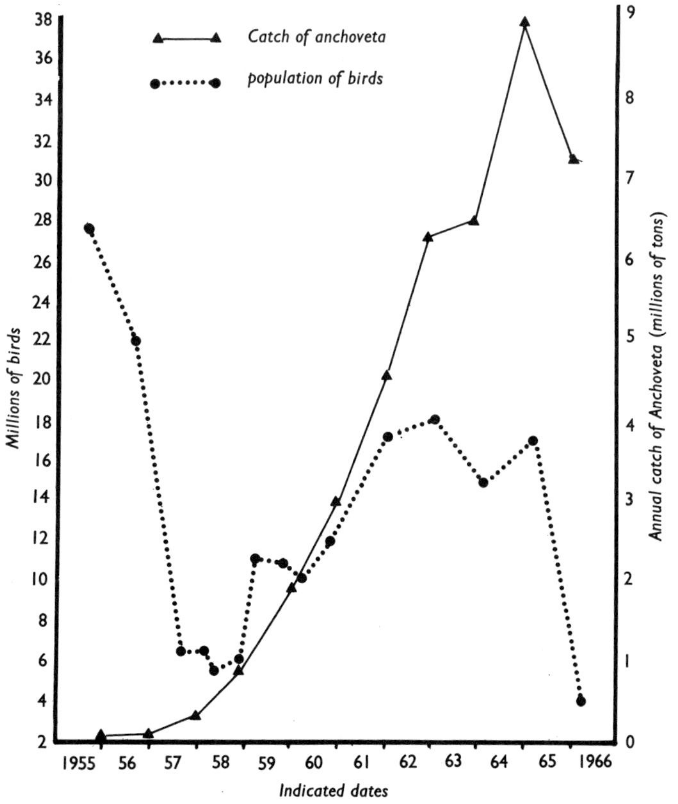

Fig. 256. Population of guano birds, 1955–66, based on censuses and graphed against the anchoveta catch (after Jordán & Fuentes 1966).

correction factors and in any case the accuracy of the figures based on guano production is too low to warrant such sophistry. In most years, piqueros are more likely to comprise around 15·5 per cent of the total guano birds, but since 23·3 per cent was the actual figure in 1963 and furthermore the estimates of guano birds based on guano deposition will err markedly on the low side (for which a high percentage estimate will thus compensate) 23·3 per cent is used in the calculation. Applying this figure as a constant, therefore, the piquero population thus gained is presented in Table 85.

Source two, the censused guano bird population, should give more accurate figures, though over a much shorter span of time. Here, the proportion of piqueros in the guano bird population is known for the years 1963–6 (Jordán pers. comm.) and works out at 15·5, 14·2, 16·6 and 25 per cent respectively. When calculating a constant proportion to apply to the census figures back to 1955 it is wise to omit the 1966 figure of 25 per cent because 1965 was a catastrophe year and the 1966 proportion of piqueros was abnormally high due to relatively higher mortality among guanays. The average of the remainder is 15·4 per cent. Assuming that in each year for which census figures are available, 15·4 per cent of the total guano bird population consisted of piqueros, we get a piquero population as set out in Table 86.

In addition, Table 86 includes the straightforward piquero population given by Jordán (1963) and Jordán (pers. comm.) from actual censuses.

Since the 1960 census (for the breeding cycle 1960–61) and the 1962 census (breeding cycle 1961–62) were the first attempts at an aerial census, and moreover give additional information, on proportions of adults and chicks and adult breeders and non-breeders the, figures will be given in some detail (Table 87). It is not worth attempting to assess the absolute validity of the methods used (based on an estimate of the area occupied by breeding adults,

TABLE 85

POPULATION STATISTICS FOR THE PERUVIAN BOOBY 1909–54
BASED ON AMOUNT OF GUANO DEPOSITED

	Peruvian booby population calculated from total guano bird population in turn calculated from guano deposited			Peruvian booby population calculated from total guano bird population in turn calculated from guano deposited	
Year	Guano birds	Peruvian boobies	Year	Guano birds	Peruvian boobies
1909	3 100 000	0 722 300	1932	8 000 000	1 864 000
1910	4 300 000	1 001 900	1933	9 700 000	2 260 100
1911	4 150 000	0 946 950	1934	8 000 000	1 864 000
1912	2 300 000	0 535 900	1935	8 300 000	1 933 900
1913	3 200 000	0 745 600	1936	9 000 000	2 097 000
1914	3 500 000	0 815 500	1937	10 000 000	2 330 000
1915	3 300 000	0 768 900	1938	9 400 000	2 190 200
1916	3 900 000	0 908 700	1939	8 600 000	2 003 800
1917	4 800 000	1 118 400	1940	8 000 000	1 864 000
1918	4 300 000	1 001 900	1941	6 750 000	1 572 700
1919	3 300 000	0 768 900	1942	3 750 000	0 873 700
1920	3 500 000	0 815 500	1943	4 400 000	1 025 200
1921	5 000 000	1 165 000	1944	5 000 000	1 165 000
1922	7 500 000	1 747 500	1945	5 800 000	1 351 400
1923	6 300 000	1 467 900	1946	8 700 000	2 027 100
1924	7 700 000	1 794 100	1947	9 250 000	2 158 200
1925	7 500 000	1 747 500	1948	10 500 000	2 446 500
1926	5 600 000	1 304 800	1949	14 400 000	3 355 200
1927	7 100 000	1 654 300	1950	12 600 000	2 935 800
1928	7 500 000	1 747 500	1951	16 200 000	3 774 600
1929	8 500 000	1 980 500	1952	14 400 000	3 355 200
1930	7 300 000	1 700 900	1953	16 500 000	3 844 500
1931	7 500 000	1 747 500	1954	18 600 000	4 333 800

PIQUERO POPULATION FIGURES, OBTAINED DIRECTLY AND INDIRECTLY FOR THE YEARS 1955–1972

	Calculated from guano deposits assuming 23·3% piqueros		Calculated from direct estimate of guano birds, assuming 15·4% piqueros		Direct estimate of piqueros	Comment
Year	Guano birds	Piqueros	Guano birds	Piqueros		
1955	18 400 000	4 287 200	27 700 000†	4 293 500		*Direct* counts of piquero not available until 1961; using a figure of 15·4% piqueros based on direct counts, the piquero's population for the year back to 1955 can then be calculated from the direct estimate of total guano birds.
1956	20 350 000	4 741 600	22 000 000†	3 410 000		
1957	16 600 000	3 867 800	6 600 000†	1 023 000		
1958a	7 000 000	1 631 000	6 700 000†	1 038 500		
b			5 600 000†	0 868 000		
c			6 300 000†	0 976 500		
1959	6 800 000	1 584 400	11 100 000†	1 720 500		
			11 000 000†	1 705 000		
1960	8 400 000	1 957 200	10 100 000†	1 565 500		
			12 000 000†	1 860 000		
1961	9 900 000	2 306 700	12 560 400†	1 934 200	2 849 100§	Census taken Dec. 1960. But covers 1960–61 breeding.
1962	10 700 000	2 493 100	17 012 500	2 635 000	2 995 900§	Census Jan. 1962 covers 1961–62
1963	12 000 000	2 796 000	18 100 000†	2 805 500	2 800 000‡	Piqueros 15·4% of total
1964	9 000 000	2 097 000	14 800 000†	2 294 000	2 100 000‡	Piqueros 14·2% of total
1965	—	—	17 000 000†	2 635 000	2 800 000‡	Piqueros 17·0% of total
1966	—	—	4 000 000†	0 620 000	1 000 000 Jan.	
			4 700 000*	0 728 500	1 400 000 Nov.	
1967	—	—	—	—	1 200 000 Jan.	
			4 100 000*	0 635 500	1 000 000 Nov.	
1968	—	—	—	—	1 400 000 Feb.	
			4 100 000*	0 635 500	1 500 000 Nov.	
1969			5 400 000		2 000 000 Feb.	
					1 000 000 Nov.	
1970					1 600 000 Feb.	
					1 700 000 April	
					1 300 000 Nov.	
1971					1 800 000 Feb.	
					1 500 000 Mar.	
					1 400 000 Nov.	
1972					2 200 000 Feb.	

Key: * Figures from Schaeffer's reproduction of a graph from Jordán
† Direct guano bird census figures from Jordán & Fuentes (1966)
‡ Direct census figures supplied by R. Jordán
§ Direct census figures for piqueros from Jordán (1963)

non-breeding adults and chicks and multiplying up to reach a total occupying the area observed to be covered by the species concerned). The criteria adopted were that seven individual breeding guanays, or five piqueros, or three pelicans, occupied one square metre. Similarly, 15 non-breeding guanays, or five piqueros or three pelicans and 10 guanay chicks, or five piquero chicks or four pelican chicks, occupied a square metre. The survey obtained figures for each of the islands and headlands occupied by significant numbers of guano birds (see Table 84).

A curious shift in distribution seems apparent from the figures obtained in the two successive censuses, but this is explained by Jordán on the grounds that the big population on SOUTH CHINCHA in 1962 was merely transitory, having arrived there only a week before the census. The piquero showed the greatest variation in distribution in the two years—a finding which, incidentally, could reinforce my deduction, made in another context—that piqueros shift breeding locations and therefore, presumably, often change mates during their breeding lifetime.

The phenomenal increase, from 12·5 to 17 million adults between 1960–61 and 1961–62 must be emphasised and must be partly due to the return of dispersed individuals.

Returning to the general theme of populations considered over the long term, it will be seen that in the years 1963–66, for some of which the piquero population has been arrived at by three different methods, there is not a gross inconsistency. The 1963 figures are bound to agree because the figure of 2·8 million provided by Jordán (pers. comm.) is the one used to calculate the proportion of piqueros both from guano deposition and from censused birds. But the subsequent divergence in the one year for which the comparison can be made (1964) using this same proportion, is not completely unacceptable, though it is fairly substantial.

Bearing in mind the very large approximations involved in acquiring the census data in the first place, the errors involved in calculating the piquero population from the census and even from the guano deposition are not likely grossly to falsify the general picture.

So, if Tables 84 and 85 are broadly acceptable, it appears that, this century, the population of piqueros in Peru (and therefore the world) has fluctuated between less than a million and possibly over four million adult birds. It started the century at a perilously low ebb, doubtless due to the ferocious exploitation of guano and the concomitant scaring and killing of guano birds in the uncontrolled days of the latter half of the nineteenth century, but the protection later afforded by the Guano Administration (from 1909) began to take effect and the population rose (as also did that of the guanay). It did particularly well in the 1950's as a result of the extension (in the 1940's) of breeding habitat, provided by the administration's policy of walling-off certain headlands and creating suitable nesting sites there. It dropped again in the 60's and

TABLE 87

AERIAL CENSUSES OF PERUVIAN GUANO BIRDS

	Totals and % of totals			
	1960–61		1961–62	
	Adults	Young	Adults	Young
Cormorant:				
Phalacrocorax bougainvillei	9 440 400 (75·2%)	3 756 500	13 699 000 (80·5%)	9 084 900
Peruvian booby:				
Sula variegata	2 849 100 (22·6%)	1 058 200	2 995 900 (17·6%)	2 135 400
Pelican:				
Pelecanus occidentalis	270 900 (2·2%)	91 100	317 600 (1·9%)	381 600
Total	12 560 400	4 905 800	17 012 500	11 601 900

the 1965 catastrophe hit it particularly hard (though less than it hit the guanays) but by 1972 it had apparently recovered fairly successfully and reached a population (2·2 million) comparing favourably with that obtaining for most years during the present century. At the time of writing, the piquero thus seems to be holding its own, despite the adverse effect, on guano birds in general, of the anchovy fishery industry, which by consistently exceeding the maximum sustainable catch, appears, at last, to have entered into direct competition with the birds (p. 606). Since writing this, another crash in 1972–73 has reduced numbers again.

Finally, special mention must be made of the astonishing recent shift in the relative

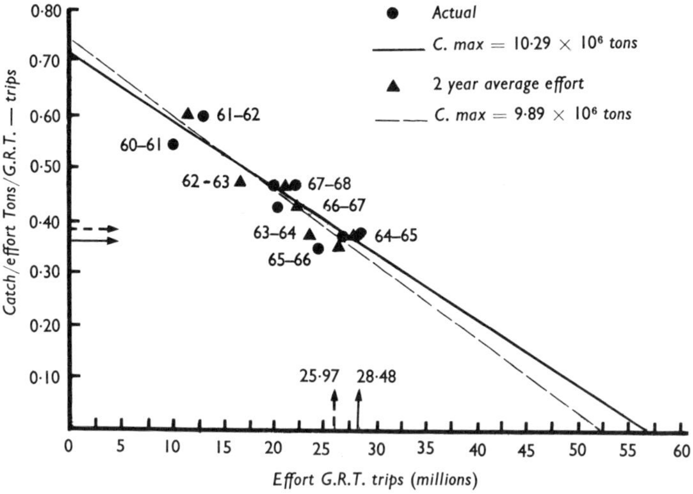

Fig. 257

Relationship between effort by commercial fisherman and birds combined, and anchoveta abundance, 1960–61 through 1967–68, with estimates of maximum sustainable yield to both predators (C max). Arrows indicate levels of effort and abundance corresponding to estimates of C max (from M. B. Schaeffer 1970).

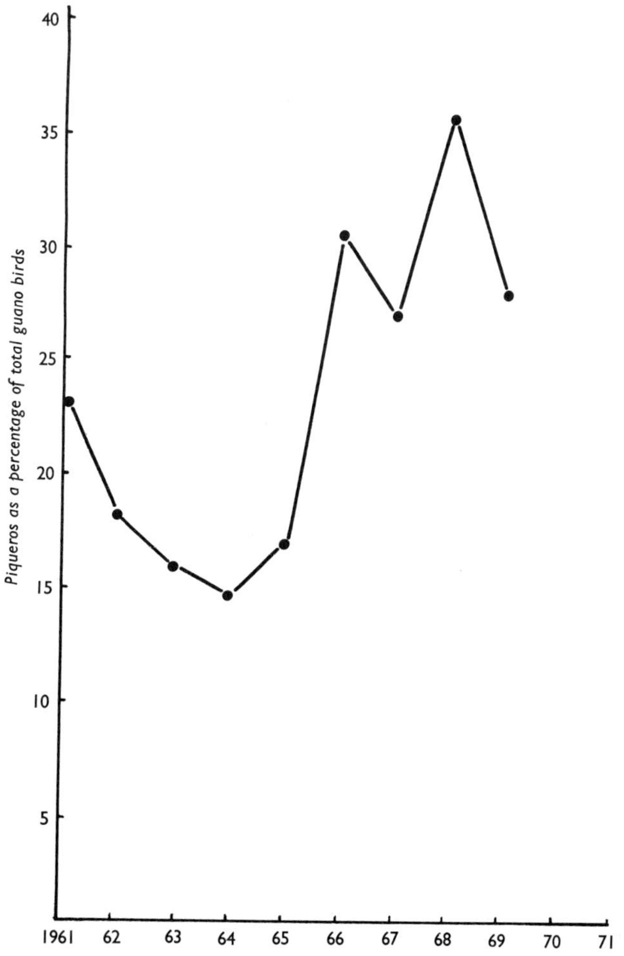

Fig. 258

Piqueros as percentage of total population of guano birds (1961–70).

proportions of piqueros and guanays. Due to the failure of the guanay to recover after recent heavy losses, the piquero is coming to achieve a much greater prominence in the guano bird population. This is shown in Figs. 303 and 305.

3. *Population 'Crashes'*

(*a*) *Introduction*

Second in fame only to the abundance of the Peruvian anchovies is their habit of disappearing every so often, causing catastrophic mortality among the guano birds which depend so heavily on them. Recurrent disasters of this magnitude are unknown anywhere else in the world for nowhere else occurs an equivalent combination of superlative abundance capable of disappearing virtually overnight as the result of climatic and oceanographic changes.

These catastrophes, dependent as they are on phenomena which may have existed from time measurable in geological rather than historical terms, must have exerted tremendous selection pressure on the guano birds, favouring traits, such as large clutches and rapid breeding which lead to rapid recuperation of the population. These traits must have been particularly strongly selected because food is superabundant in the periods between crashes and therefore in itself leads to the evolution of large clutches, etc. Were it otherwise, large clutches etc. would be impossible; no amount of decimation of a population could lead to the evolution of such rapid breeding if the 'normal' level of food did not permit rapid growth of large broods. Population crashes, therefore, are phenomena to which the guano birds have become adjusted by a web of adaptive devices including behavioural mechanisms (see Section on Behaviour p. 649).

The general phenomenon of catastrophes has been graphically described by Murphy (1926) who happened to observe the effects of a particularly dramatic one (1925) and Hutchinson reviews the information up to 1950. The effects of catastrophes upon piquero populations is described later. Here, the nature of the phenomenon, the event itself, its effects on fish and guano birds and finally the crashes which have occurred this century, in particular that of 1965, will be discussed.

(*b*) *The nature of the phenomenon*

Coastal Peru is bathed by cold waters, sometimes (but misleadingly) called the Antarctic, Peru or Humboldt Current. Periodically, abnormal conditions arise and warmer water approaches the coast. This so called aguaje may occur at any time of year and very locally or it may become serious and widespread, as in the major catastrophe years. The causes of local as against widespread aguaje may, however, be different (see below). Coinciding with a rise in the temperature of coastal waters there may be rain in areas that are normally completely rainless. These conditions tend to recur with a periodicity of seven years, though their variability is such that some episodes are barely noticeable, thus obscuring any strong pattern. It is important to realise that the incursion of warmer water into Peruvian coastal areas normally free from it is not a rare, all-or-none phenomenon, but occurs to a variable extent, as a frequent, indeed normal event. The point is that, in most years, it has few, if any, untoward effects. When it does adversely affect the birds, it usually comes in two 'waves', the first around April/May and the second rather precisely at Christmas time. The term El Niño (derived from this fact) is usually reserved for the second phenomenon (but see below). The duration of the disturbance, as well as its severity, is highly variable. Sometimes three successive years are abnormal to some extent, whilst at others a relatively brief but catastrophic disturbance is followed by a return to normality. The 1965 phenomenon, described below, illustrates the nature of the oceanographic changes that occur.

The underlying causes of the oceanographic and climatic changes which result in the warming up of Peruvian coastal waters are complex (Fig. 259). First, the coastal waters of Peru are extremely deep. There is no shallow continental shelf, but an abrupt plunge into the Peru–Chile Trench. The Milne-Edwards Deep (6216m below sea level) just off the coast, is virtually a continuation of the 6768m Mount Huascaran. This feature—an undersea 'wall'—helps bring about upwelling in the area. Basically the cold Peruvian water (17°–20°C.)—much colder than would be expected from its position well within the tropics—results not from a cold current running northwards from Antarctica (as Von Humboldt's theory held) but from cold water upwelling off the Peruvian and north Chilean coasts and then flowing northwards from Valparaiso almost to the Gulf of Guayaquil in Ecuador, before swinging west and joining the westward flowing South-Equatorial Current. There is a similar upwelling and southward flowing current in the northern hemisphere, the California Current.

The Peruvian upwelling is caused by global current systems acting on the west coast of South America. The general direction of the fundamental current system of the area (the southern anticyclonic circulation of the southern Pacific) in the form of the South-Equatorial Current, is north-west, varying to west. The normal wind direction is south-east (the South East Trades) deflected by the Andes to blow parallel to the Peruvian coast. Out to sea, the westward setting current tends to draw water away from the land and this is replaced by cold water from beneath. The northwards moving current generated by the South East Trades also turns westwards, deflected by coriolis force, thus adding to the compensating upwelling. This northwards moving Peruvian Current moves at different speeds in different places and in fact local reversals may occur, the current flowing southwards. This is because the upwelling which replaces the deflected water moving offshore and the water drawn westward by the South Equatorial Current, forms huge eddies and spirals. Also, tongues of warmer water move southwards and coastwards to compensate for the general north and west movement of the Peruvian Current and produce various 'swirls'. As a result of these local variations in the distribution of warm and cold water, the distribution of fish, though tolerably uniform, is also to

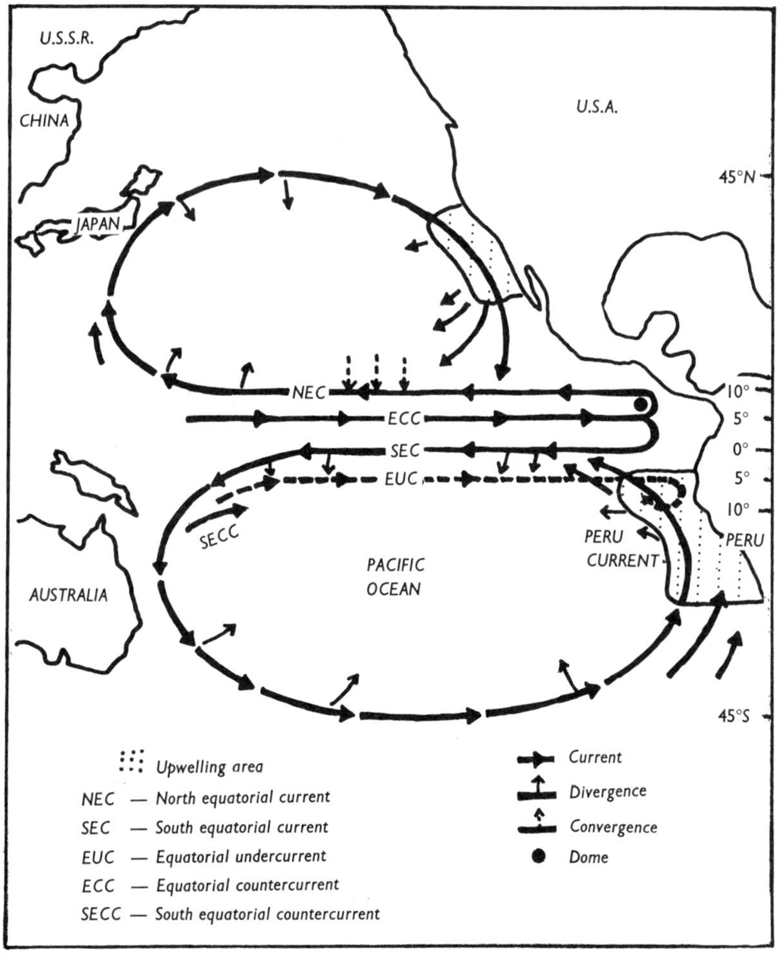

Fig. 259. The Peruvian current in the context of Pacific Ocean circulation (from Paulik 1970).

some extent patchy and hence so is the distribution of seabirds. A small secondary upwelling, mainly caused by wind, is often generated at about 100km from the shore, where some of the original upwelling sinks (Paulik 1970). These areas, however, are not constant or closely defined, which may explain periodic shifts in fish and bird distribution, though man's effects, superimposed, are likely to obscure the bird changes.

Finally, the intensity of the upwelling varies seasonally with location. Over most of the Peruvian littoral a strong upwelling in winter (May to August) seems to disperse the anchovies, which, at this time, are harder (for man) to catch. It may be noted in passing that this, insofar as the piquero can be said to have one, is the non-breeding season.

This basic situation is altered, from time to time, as we have seen, by the abnormal impingement of warm water from the north and north-west. In Schweigger's view, a warm and strictly coastal counter current, El Niño, flows southwards from the Gulf of Guayaquil and washes the Peruvian shore. This is a relatively local phenomenon and not in itself of major importance. Far more important is a massive movement to Peru from the north and west, of warm, oceanic water. This warm water is 'allowed in' whenever the upwelling weakens and the colder, denser coastal water can no longer keep out the warm oceanic water. This, as does also the incursion of the coastal El Niño, tends to happen annually, at the height of the southern summer, (hence its association with Christmas and 'The Child') but is usually not well marked. In catastrophe years, however, it is strongly pronounced

The direct result of the rise in water temperature is that the fish become unavailable both to man and to birds. Authorities disagree about whether they move right away from their normal centres of distribution, perhaps mainly southwards, or merely seek cooler, deeper waters, perhaps rising to the surface at night, in concert with the nocturnal ascent of plankton. Vogt (1942) favours the first of these hypotheses, whilst Schweigger (1943) and Fiedler, Jarvis & Lobell (1943) favour the second. The latter describe how, during February and March 1941 (a year of high mortality among birds) they encountered at night several small shoals and one huge one at a time when guano birds were abandoning their nests. Jordán & Fuentes (1966) also give concrete evidence showing that, during the 1965 Niño, anchovies were present, but in deep, fragmented groups. Obviously there is some nocturnal vertical migration of fish during such times, but whether only a small proportion of the anchovies are involved, the remainder having moved right away, remains unknown. Whatever they do, very probably most of the anchovies do not die during a bad El Niño, although the stock does become reduced, mainly by an inhibition of spawning.

In any event, during bad years, the guano birds obviously find it impossible to cope with the changed situation and they abandon their breeding activities and die or emigrate in millions, the survivors returning after a variable period of absence. The birds mainly emigrate southwards, to cooler waters, but this is by no means always the case and many go northwards as far as the Gulf of Guayaquil and even up the Rio Guayas itself. Their movements are on a colossal scale. Thus, in 1939, an estimated 11 million guanays built up in the vicinity of the Chinchas, and five days later this locality was almost entirely deserted. The time elapsing between the onset of bad conditions and the death of seabirds may be very short. In 1925, for example, conditions did not begin to deteriorate until January 18th, and yet, by the end of the month, sick and dead birds were numerous in northern Peru, and desertion of the Lobos and Guañape Islands occurred in March. Also, even before the rains began in northern Peru (late January) hordes of guanays went ashore at Coquimbo. On the other hand, as in 1938–39, there may be some months between the onset of abnormal conditions and the detection of observable effects on the birds.

Essentially, therefore, the phenomenon of warm water incursion into the coastal waters of Peru is normal, probably two-pronged and relatively harmless. Periodically, however, a weakening of the Peruvian upwelling allows an abnormal incursion which disturbs the whole biotic community, with inevitable and severe dislocation at the top.

(*c*) *Resumé of crashes in the nineteenth and twentieth centuries*

The climatic changes—rise in sea temperature and onset of rain—which precede and accompany the reduction in the availability of anchovies show some regularity. Hutchinson sets out all the information on rainfall from 1790 to 1940 and shows that, at least between

1864 and 1939, there is a good fit between 'expected' high rainfall years (assuming a seven-year cycle) and observed wet years (though much of the information here is qualitative and has to be assessed somewhat arbitrarily).

According to Hutchinson the periodic declines in guano birds do not occur strictly every seven years. This is a pity, since Vogt (1942) on this basis explained so neatly why Darwin evidently did not see enough birds to elicit any comment, Tschudi obviously was not impressed by the guanay's numbers, nor was Raimondi; and Lucas saw few guano birds. All these observers visited the islands in the nineteenth century soon after a theoretically calculated 'crash' year and it would have been economical to explain their observations or lack of them, in this way.

There were crashes of varying magnitude in or around 1618, and in 1824, 1848, 1869–71, 1891, 1899, 1911–12, 1917, 1923, 1925, 1926, 1932, 1939–41, 1949–51, 1953, 1957–8, 1963–5 and 1972. The guano bird populations from 1909 to the present time are given in Tables 85 and 86 which may be used in conjunction with the present account to gain some idea of the magnitude of the disasters. The earlier crashes (prior to 1917, which was the one described and interpreted by Lavalle (1924), whose contribution forms the basis of our understanding of the phenomenon) are not adequately documented, but Hutchinson garners information to make a reasonably coherent account, which may be summarised as follows.

1618. About this year Vazques de Espinosa visited Arica and comments that enormous numbers of seabirds, fish and seals die there and rot.

1824. There are not even descriptive remarks to go on here but merely a statement (Rivero 1827) that certain islands which used to produce a lot of guano have, in recent years, produced very little. However, there is evidence of extraordinary rains in northern Peru in 1814 and good rain in 1817, 1819 and 1824.

1848. This crash essentially rests on the verbal communication (to Cookson) of a man who lived 40 years on Pabellon de Pica and describes how about 1848 a 'plague' attacked the birds, which died by the million so that their bodies covered the beach for miles. The birds were pelicans, gannets and terns. Here, too, there is a possible correlation with the wet years 1844–6.

1869–71. Again Cookson records information given to him by somebody else—this time an English engineer (Hindle) who visited Guañape (or perhaps one of the Lobos islands) probably in 1871, and found the surface of the island covered with dead gannets and guanays. Again, 1871 was a wet year, but apparently the reduction had begun in 1869 or sooner.

1891. There is here only the indirect evidence of widespread anomalies (Murphy 1925, 26, 36) affecting many marine organisms and presumably, therefore, affecting the seabirds too.

1899. Murphy (1923) records that on August 10th and 11th 1899 a ship passed for 300 miles through areas of dead pelicans and other seabirds off northern Peru.

1911. Here, for the first time, there is concrete comment on the scale of the disaster, as it affected one island (Chincha) for Forbes (1914) records that in November 1911 almost the entire avian population of the Chincha Islands began '. . . to take their departure, leaving both eggs and young to their fate. . . . By December 1911, hardly a score of birds remained'. Almost all other islands were similarly affected, but not synchronously, for as late as May and June 1912 Forbes saw many dead birds near Lobos de Tierra. It was the end of that year before birds began to breed again. It seems likely that all the broods from eggs laid later than August 1911 died, together with an unknown but presumably colossal number of adults. Forbes himself attributed the disaster to earthquakes, but he was almost certainly wrong.

1917–18. March signalled the onset of the 1917 catastrophe, which hit the Guañapes, Pescadores, Cabinzas Island and the Ballestas. Dead birds were found, though others were apparently merely weakened. Lavalle noted the extension southwards of warm water and concluded that it destroyed plankton and caused the fish to withdraw. A third of the dead birds were infected with the fungus *Aspergillus fumigatus* which could have been the immediate cause of death consequent upon malnutrition. The effects of this particular episode seemed to be protracted, for the population apparently continued to decline during 1918.

1923. There was apparently some mortality in May and June of 1923 (Lavalle 1924) but it was probably relatively slight and restricted to a limited area, and Peruvians do not count 1923 as an abnormal year.

1925–6. The catastrophe from January to March 1925 has been made famous by Murphy

(1926) who was in Peru at the time. By the end of January many guano birds were already dead or dying, although conditions had, apparently, been normal until about January 18th. By March mass desertions of breeding stations had occurred and huge numbers of guano birds moved up and down the coast and inland, appearing in numerous bizarre situations. The influx to Chile was thought to number millions. However, deaths were actually recorded by the thousand rather than the million (20 000 or more dead or dying at San Antonio) though those counted represented a tiny fraction of the real mortality.

Evidently 1926 was also abnormally wet and there were again exceptional movements of birds north to Ecuador. There are no records of the mortality in this year, but presumably there was some and in addition it seems unlikely that much breeding would occur.

1932. May and June of this year saw another massive emigration and high mortality, particularly of guanays, but also, substantially, of piqueros and other guano birds.

1939–41. Water temperatures began to rise in October 1938 but the birds were not much affected until March or April. In the latter month virtually the entire population of Lobos de Tierra left the islands and blue-footed boobies turned up on the Chinchas (this, incidentally, is the first time that the blue-foot is specifically implicated in mass movements or mortality and it could well be that, in fact, it suffers less than the piquero, for reasons discussed elsewhere (p. 541).

The numbers involved in these movements are graphically illustrated by the observation that the abandonment of the more northerly islands led to a congregation of some 11 million guanays on the Chinchas by June 5th 1939 and five days later the islands were virtually deserted.

1940 was also highly abnormal with massive desertion recorded for the Chinchas (three-quarters of the guanay population left the islands on February 11th).

Although, in 1941, there was no real dearth of anchovies, they nevertheless tended to remain deep by day, and this year saw further heavy mortality, so that this particular episode exerted heavy pressure on the guano birds for three years, during which time they were highly unlikely to have produced many young, whilst nevertheless suffering massive losses of adults. The guano bird population was very low by 1942 (see Table 85) numbering some 3·75 millions, the lowest total since 1920, at which time it was still recovering from the ravages of exploitation terminated by the formation of the Guano Administration in 1909. Of this total probably less than a million were piqueros.

There followed a number of normal years, though 1949, 1950, 1951 and 1953 are indicated by Jordán & Fuentes (1966) to have been mildly abnormal.

1957 was a bad year and 1958 was also abnormal, the result being that the 1959 population of guano birds was down to 6·8 millions from the 20·3 millions of 1956. The 1957–58 crash ranks as one of the worst ever and Jordán (1964) states that the population was reduced by some 70 per cent from the previous 27–30 millions. He adds that by February 1963 the population had climbed back to some 18 million adults and 8–10 million juveniles. Thus, after the crash, a population of 6–7 millions had in four years increased by somewhat more than 60 per cent—well over 20 per cent compound increase per annum. The discrepancy in the figures for the population before the crash stems from the fact that the 20·3 millions was extracted from a graph in Jordán & Fuentes (1966) whilst the 27–30 millions was an unamplified statement in Jordán (1964). It is not clear why they should differ.

1963, and to a limited extent 1964, were also abnormal.

1965 was another catastrophic year and the population plummeted to 4 million in 1966.

Desperate though these mass mortalities may appear to be, the subsequent recoveries have typically been almost equally spectacular, but this situation has now changed drastically.

At the time of writing, the 1972 crash is still too recent to be fully assessed, but there seem to be three important points. First, the catastrophe was very serious, in particular further reducing the already low population of guanays, which had failed to recover from the effects of the 1965 crash (the reasons for this failure are discussed on p. 608). Second, the anchovies disappeared for longer than usual and at the time of writing had not returned to their usual abundance, though in 1974 they appeared to be doing so. Third, the piquero fared notably better than the guanay, possibly because it is less dependent on anchovies (p. 648). At the present time, therefore, the piquero proportion of the total guano bird population is higher than it has ever been since records began.

(d) The 1963 and 1965 crashes

The 1963 and 1965 crashes have been far more fully analysed than previous ones. These reports make several points of basic interest and the following account of the crashes with which they deal probably has a general validity for the phenomenon as a whole. Although I prefer to make these points in the context of the specific years and events concerned, the reader could keep an eye open for their wider significance.

The first months of 1963 seemed normal and the main colonies were breeding as usual. However, signs of instability developed in June, with local emigrations. Autumn and winter saw a considerable exodus of guano birds from their breeding islands. It is clear, as might well be expected, that there are significant differences in the times at which various colonies are deserted. Emigration is not a synchronous event, but is much influenced by the conditions around each breeding station, which in turn are highly variable throughout the vast, complex coast alwaters. Thus, on a reconnaissance flight in August, only Guañape Norte and Santa in the north and Chincha Norte and Alacrán in the south, held large colonies.

The subsequent arrival of birds beyond their normal limits, with the associated mortality, was analysed in some detail (Jordán 1964), though mainly for guanays and pelicans. The emigrés apparently did not disperse uniformly along the coast. More go south than north and there are apparently favoured localities which attract the displaced birds, though it is not known why. There are also considerable differences in the mortality occurring in different areas. South of Lima and especially in the Chincha area, it is, as a general rule, considerably (and presumably disproportionately) greater than in the north (Jordán 1964). Why, under such circumstances, south should be the favoured direction for emigration, seems somewhat anomalous. It is also interesting that mortality on and around the islands is usually considerably less than on the mainland beaches, but this is probably to be explained in terms of birds dying at sea and being carried to the beaches by currents.

The analysis, by month, of recoveries of corpses from previous crashes, had shown that far more were recovered in March, April and May than in other months.

Some species suffer heavier mortality than others. Thus, of 410 corpses of five species found on June 24th 1963 (before the main effects had been felt) only 10·4 per cent were piqueros, whilst by the end of the abnormal period the proportion was even lower at 4·5 per cent (Table 88). The pelican suffers most, the guanay almost as badly, but the piquero much less.

TABLE 88

DIFFERENCES BETWEEN THE THREE MAIN GUANO BIRDS IN THE EXTENT OF THEIR MORTALITY IN THE 1963 'CRASH' (from Jordán 1964)

	Total no. of corpses found	Percentage of deaths falling to each species	Percentage which each species contributed to total population before the 'crash'
Cormorant: *Phalacrocorax bougainvillei*	6566	73·4	82·4
Pelican: *Pelecanus occidentalis*	1973	22·1	2·3
Peruvian booby: *Sula variegata*	375	4·5	15·3

NOTES: 1. In addition to the three species compared in this table, 313 corpses of other species were found.

2. The population census before the crash was taken in February 1963 and the counts of dead birds were made between June and August 1963.

One would expect juvenile birds to be affected more than adults. Even in normal years it is believed (Jordán & Cabrera 1960) that some 50–60 per cent of young guanays die in their first year of life (a surprisingly high figure in such a favourable area). In abnormal years, juvenile guanays and pelicans die before adults and proportionately in greater numbers (about 70:30). One would expect the same to hold for the piquero, but Jordán's (1964) account indicates otherwise (65·5 per cent of recoveries were adult and only 34·5 per cent juveniles). This, however, is almost certainly a misleading result due to the great difficulty of establishing the age of young piqueros after the middle of their first year.

Differential mortality must be a complicated phenomenon. Jordán (1964) comments on the fact that even at the same breeding colony, some guanays are obviously emaciated whilst others are fat and healthy and the same is true for pelicans (piqueros are again not mentioned in this connection). It is of interest that, after the 1963 famine, some guanays were apparently going to breed, even though they were not in first class condition. Thus, on Don Martín on October 23rd, 20 guanays caught near the main colony (the report doesn't say whether they were actually breeding) were on average 142g lighter than birds in good condition. This amounts to about 7 per cent of the normal adult weight.

A most interesting finding was that several birds had died by drowning. No interpretation is offered and it seems almost silly to suggest that these starving birds had gone too deep in their efforts to locate prey!

Just as the unfavourable conditions may increase gradually so, too, their withdrawal may be anything but clear cut, with local variability adding further complications. In this situation, some colonies may resume breeding before others and may even be forced to abandon it or make slow progress. In 1963, piqueros began to display on Macabí and Chincha, but several weeks later than usual.

The 1965 catastrophe is of particular interest for two reasons. First, there is detailed documentation in Jordán & Fuentes (1966) of the extent of the mortality including an assessment of its effect specifically upon guanays and piqueros and second, it occurred at a time when the meteoric rise in the Peruvian anchovy fishery was beginning to pose fundamental questions about the maximum sustainable yield of this resource and about the possibility that birds and fishermen might at last be coming into direct competition.

Jordán & Fuentes found that, basically, the 1965 crash, like previous ones, was mainly the result of usual patterns of abnormal hydrobiological conditions, though exacerbated by man's activities. As early as the end of 1964, it was clear from conditions in the northern coastal waters, that 1965 was likely to be a very abnormal year. By March 1965 tropical water of temperature 24°–26°C. and salinity 34·1–36·4 per cent was advancing southwards and coastwards, confining the Peruvian current to a variable fringe some 10–40 miles wide, with a temperature of 19°–22°C. and a salinity of 34·9 per cent (Schweigger (1940) regards 22°C. as the upper limit for 'green' water and 23°–25° as the lower limit for full oceanic 'blue' or warm water). As a result the anchovies gathered close to the coast, particularly opposite Pacasmayo, Huarmey and Ancon, at a depth of 20–25m. Conditions continued abnormal in April, with a tongue of warm water between Huarmey and Callao. The thermocline, though very marked, was variably deep (between 0–60 metres). Littoral plankton was confined to small areas in the waters off Supe, Pisco and Atico. In general, the water was more than 3°C. higher than the average for April (1939–56). The anchovies remained very close to the coast, fragmented rather than in huge shoals and at depths of 8–70m. Throughout May the bad conditions continued and the anchovies remained 15–43m deep, rising nearer to the surface at night. The fishermen were able to catch them only at dusk and dawn. By the southern winter, although a marked improvement was underway, the temperature was still 1·5°C. higher than the average for the previous 17 years and anchovies were scarce and 5–75m deep. Catches in July, September and October were low (August is a closed month). From October to December the region continued to be affected by sub-tropical water, the influence of the equatorial current in the north being particularly evident, with sea temperatures 3·5°C. higher than they should have been, though central and southern waters were only 1°C. higher. Anchovies were more abundant and more widely and uniformly distributed, with some significant concentrations in the south.

The 1965 conditions were notably similar to those of 1957, also a particularly abnormal year, with high mortality among the guano birds. The poor catches reflected the great scarcity of fish; they were particularly low (the lowest since 1959) from July to September and for 1965 as a whole, down by two million tons on the previous year despite increased fishing effort and at greater depths than usual.

The effect on the guano birds was calamitous. In the first fortnight of February, towards the end of the breeding season (such as it is) there were an estimated 17 million adult individuals (79 per cent guanays, 20 per cent piqueros and 1 per cent pelicans) and 9–10 million chicks. Thus breeding in the 1964–5 season was moving towards a fairly successful conclusion, though down on 1962 and 1963 (if 9–10 million chicks be taken as about 50 per cent of the adult population, the corresponding percentage in 1962 and 63 was about 70 per cent). By January 1965, birds in the north began to abandon nests. Later, in February and succeeding months, birds from further south followed suit, with considerable mortality of chicks and juveniles, particularly on the Lobos and Guañape islands, Isla la Vieja and Punta Culebras. At the beginning of May massive emigration commenced. Birds ringed prior to 1965 were recovered south to Lat. 42° from the beginning of June onwards. Other birds fled northwards, ending up on the beaches of Ecuador and Colombia, especially in August. Recoveries of dead birds on beaches, though not carried out systematically, was enough to show that there were two 'waves' of mortality, the first between February and April, mainly of juveniles and the second in June and July, including more adults. This fits with the known tendency of juveniles to succumb first. At the same time, many birds were found dead on the sea.

Whilst it may be safely assumed that all the preceding remarks apply to piqueros as well as to guanays, the records show that, as in 1963, the guanay suffered much heavier mortality than the booby. This is probably because the piquero can dive deeper, forage further and catch a wider variety of fish than the cormorant. The net result of the 1965 crash was that from the original 17 millions only 3–4 millions of guano birds survived; a mortality of 76–82 per cent.

Jordán and Fuentes noted that the numbers of dead birds on Peruvian beaches in 1965 were similar to those during the much more modest disturbances of 1963 and conclude that the bulk of the 1965 birds died in Chile and Ecuador. When they reported, there seemed little likelihood that the birds had merely migrated and would return and the subsequent failure of islands and headlands to be re-populated confirms this. This contrasts with the situation after the 1957 crash for then the population was only 5–6 millions in May 1958 but had increased to 11·1 millions by March 1959. This was due to the return of birds which had left the area and the mortality was thus considerably less than at first appeared.

In the longer perspective, the 1965 crash ranks as one of the worst ever. The following Table gives figures for the crashes of 1917, 1925, 1939–41, 1957–8 and 1965 showing how far the population crashed on each of these occasions and how long it took to build up to the peak reached before the next crash. The reader is reminded that the figures apply to the main three guano birds and not merely to piqueros.

Table 89 shows two important points. First, the mortality among adult piqueros as a result of the 1965 conditions was about 73 per cent compared with only about 50 per cent as a result of the 1957–8 conditions, notwithstanding the fact that the 1956 population had been very high at 3·410 millions. This suggests additional factors operating in 1965, probably the effects of man's fishing activities.

Second, the failure of the population to increase significantly up to the end of 1968 is in clear contrast to the situation following the 1957–8 conditions, for then the birds climbed up to 18·1 millions (2·8055 million piqueros) in 1963 from 11·1 millions (1·7205 million piqueros) in 1959. Again, this implies that unusually stringent conditions obtained after the 1965 episode and these are likely to have resulted from the diminution of anchovies due to over-fishing by man. The fortunes of the piquero and guanay both in absolute terms and relative to each other, are shown in Fig. 260.

It is clear that the guanays suffered heavier losses and showed far poorer recoveries than the piqueros, although formerly (as shown elsewhere) they had recovered magnificently.

Finally, in this consideration of the 1965 phenomenon, it is important to make it quite clear that, as in 1963 (Jordán 1964), actual starvation rather than epizootic disease or rampant parasitism consequent upon debilitating malnutrition, was the cause of death (Jordán & Fuentes 1966). This was because, in response to the hydrobiological disturbances (rise in temperature, etc.) anchovies went to depths at which the birds couldn't catch them. Thus, the

TABLE 89

MAGNITUDE OF 'CRASHES' OF GUANO BIRDS AND RECOVERIES BETWEEN 1917 AND 1965

Year of crash	Population in year before crash	Population in year after crash	Lowest population reached after crash and before next one	Highest population reached after crash and before next one
1917	3 900 000 (1916)	4 300 000 (1918)	3 300 000 (1919)	7 700 000 (1924)
	908 700	1 001 900	768 900	1 794 100
1925	7 700 000 (1924)	5 600 000 (1926)	5 600 000 (1926)	10 000 000 (1937)
	1 747 500	1 304 800	1 304 800	2 330 000
1939–41	9 400 000 (1938)	3 800 000 (1942)	3 800 000 (1942)	27 700 000 (1955)
	2 190 200	873 700	873 700	4 293 500
1957–58	22 000 000 (1956)	11 100 000 (1959)	10 100 000 (1960)	18 100 000 (1963)
	3 410 000	1 720 500	1 565 500	2 805 500
1965	14 800 000 (1964)	4 000 000 (1966)	4 000 000 (1966)	4 100 000 (up to
	2 294 000	620 000	620 000	635 500 end 1968)
1972	—	—	—	—

NOTES: 1. The figures up to and including 1954 are based on guano deposition. The figures after 1954 are based on actual censuses. There are large discrepancies between these two methods, the former greatly under-estimating actual numbers.

2. Piquero figures are given below the total guano bird figures. — = figure not available for 1972.

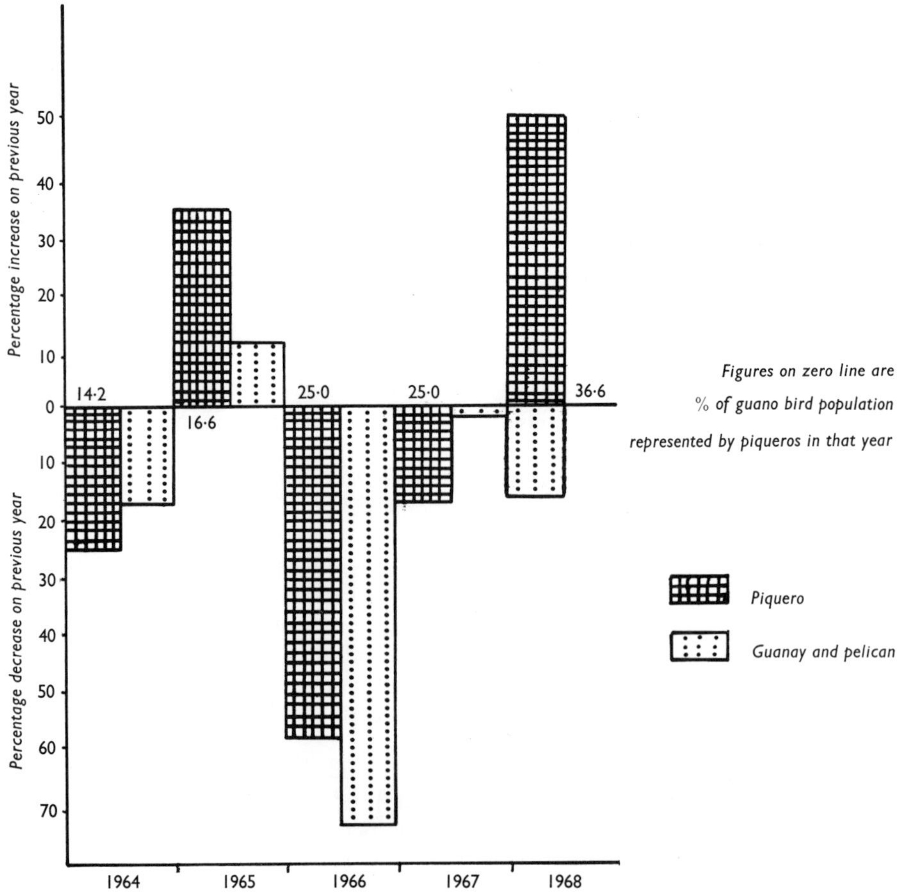

Fig. 260. The magnitude of population fluctuations in the Peruvian booby and guanay cormorant, 1964–68.

cause of the mortality among the birds was essentially the same as on previous occasions, but may have been exacerbated by unusually low stocks. Almost certainly the delay in the recovery of the bird population was due to depleted anchovy stocks which had been overfished by man. On the other hand, in the abnormal year of 1917–18 a third of the dead birds were said to be infected with *Aspergillus fumigatus*. In an autopsy of 29 corpses from the 1963 deaths no gross infections were found. Most birds had a very few nematodes (one pelican had 24) and a few ectoparasites (*Mallophaga*) but nothing exceptional and only one bird showed pathological symptoms (general septicaemia).

4. *The relationship between man and the piquero*

There are three ways in which man is affecting the population of guano birds in general and thus of the piquero, at the present time. First, he is conserving them in several ways. Second he is destroying them directly. Third, he is affecting them indirectly, through their food supply.

(*a*) *Conservation*

Since the Guano Administration instituted protection for guano birds in 1909, probably the single most effective measure has been the stationing of official guardianes at the main breeding stations, to prevent people from landing and disturbing or taking eggs or birds, and to control predators such as foxes, gulls, condors and turkey buzzards. Some of the other regulations, though law, are difficult to enforce; thus all boats are supposed to remain at least two miles away from the breeding islands; fishing boats are supposed to refrain from operations within a three-mile belt around all stations, and five miles around Guañape, Chincha and La Vieja, and over the islands planes are supposed to fly no lower than 500 metres.

The next most effective measure has been the provision of extra nesting areas on headlands of the Peruvian coast. Not only have peninsulas been isolated by walls of concrete 3m high, from trespass and interference, but actual nesting areas have been enlarged and nesting sites created. Since the introduction of the measure in 1945, up to 1956, there has been a dramatic expansion of the mainland population (see Table 84). Before this guano birds had been virtually confined to islands, but then began to form mainland nesting colonies which grew progressively larger. At the present time headlands accommodate a total population of some 15–20 000 piqueros. Punta Salinas held 10 000 piqueros, 441 000 guanays and 15 000 pelicans in January 1962. There are few, if any, comparable examples of the creation by man of new colonies of seabirds.

(*b*) *Destruction*

It may seem anomalous that, at the same time as he protects them, man also destroys them, but the anomaly rests on the conflicting interests of the Guano Administration and the newer fish-meal industry. The anchovy fishing industry is discussed below. Here, it need merely be said that fishermen kill many guano birds by accidentally catching them in nets, either drowning or strangling them; actual figures are not available. This could be much reduced if the belt of fishing-free water around the breeding stations was respected, but in fact it is largely ignored. Secondly, there is some deliberate killing of guano birds at breeding stations. In 1966 there was considerable dismay among conservationists because (and I quote from a letter written to the Duke of Edinburgh, June 8th 1966 by a leading Peruvian conservationist) 'thousands of birds are being massacred daily by the fishermen, to prevent these hungry birds from spoiling their nets or interfering with their catch. I have evidence of more than 43 000 birds being clubbed to death in 8 days'. The same facts were reported to Dillon Ripley of the I.C.B.P. Most such episodes have probably been spontaneous rather than systematic attempts to exterminate the birds, but deliberate extermination or elimination as it has been euphemistically called, has been seriously suggested. The grounds for rejecting this terrible proposal are three-fold—it would be a moral outrage; it would destroy a valuable and continuing asset; and it would probably not achieve the desired objective, which could be realised in other ways (see below). Up to now, the damage wrought in these direct ways has not been nearly so great as the benefits extended by the Guano Administrations' measures.

(c) *Guano birds and the anchovy fisheries*

Where many millions of seabirds are annually extracting enormous numbers of fish from a limited area whilst at the same time a fishing industry booms at a rate without precedent in the world, the possibility that birds and man are competing, inevitably arises. Before attempting to answer this question some background information is necessary. I take the facts about anchovies from Paulik (1970) and about primary productivity from Ryther (1969). First, the immensity of the anchovy shoals is unimaginable. In about seven months in 1969–70 Peruvian fishermen officially caught 11 million metric tons comprising more than ten trillion (10 000 000 000 000 000 000) anchovies. In fact, more than 13–14 million metric tons were actually caught, the difference being due to operational losses and under-reporting of catches, and even this ignores the fact that, due to loss of juices, the weight of fish is some 25 per cent less than the fresh weight caught. Peru has built up this phenomenal annual catch, virtually from nothing, since 1951 and takes it from a strip of sea a mere 1280 by 48km. Yet, and this is perhaps the most astounding fact of all, a further ten million metric tons are thought to be taken annually by other predators such as birds, sea lions, bonito and squid. Although calculations of this kind are liable to gross error, it is nonetheless of great interest to know that the estimated productivity of such an area of upwelling is about 20 million metric tons. Thus, if natural predators are removing ten million tons each year, the absolute maximum sustainable yield for man cannot be greater than ten million. This is the same as the maximum sustainable yield of about 9·5 million recently agreed upon by the international fishery experts, but less than the amount that has been taken annually for the past few years (see Table 90 and below).

Anchovies depend only partly on zooplankton; they also browse directly on phytoplankton. Five–15g of phytoplankton are needed to produce one g of zooplankton, so herbivorous anchovies eliminate a wasteful step in the energy conversion ladder and gain access to a great amount of additional energy. This, and the vast amount of nutrients and hence phytoplankton in the upwelling off Peru, helps to account for the anchovies' numbers. Other, related factors are their rapid growth to maturity (12–18 months) and the method of reproduction (large numbers of eggs can be laid because they do not need yolk stores, food being virtually guaranteed for the newly-hatched anchovies).

An understanding of the food and population dynamics of the anchovy is necessary if one is to estimate what the Peruvian waters can produce and what man and other predators (fish,

TABLE 90

DATA CONCERNING CATCH AND EFFORT BY THE COMBINED FISHERY OF MEN AND BIRDS ON THE ANCHOVETA OFF PERU

(M. Schaeffer 1970. Trans. Amer. Fisheries Soc.)

Fishing year	Catch by fishermen 10^6 tons	Catch/effort tons/G.R.T. trip*	Fishermen's effort 1000 G.R.T. trips**	Adult bird population 10^6 birds†	Catch by birds 10^6 tons‡	Combined catch 10^6 tons	Combined effort 1000 G.R.T. trips§
1960–61	3·934	0·551	7,134	12·0	1·88	5·81	10,544
1961–62	5·502	0·603	9,129	17·0	2·67	8·17	13,549
1962–63	6·907	0·478	14,447	18·0	2·83	9·74	20,377
1963–64	8·006	0·376	21,285	15·0	2·36	10·37	27,580
1964–65	8·037	0·376	21,374	17·3	2·72	10·76	28,617
1965–66	8·096	0·356	22,741	4·3	0·68	8·77	24,635
1966–67	8·242	0·435	18,948	4·8	0·75	8·99	20,667
1967–68	9·818	0·472	20,800	4·5	0·71	10·53	22,309

* Effort units are in terms of 1960–61 efficiency. This column is essentially a measure of apparent abundance. From I. Tsukiyama, corrected for effects of closed season, strikes etc. related to variable seasonal availability; corrected for changes in gear efficiency.

† From R. Jordan and H. Fuentes I.M.A.R.P.E. Informe No. 10 and unpublished information for recent years.

‡ Calculated at 430 grams of anchoveta per bird per day (157 kg/yr).

** Total catch divided by catch-per-unit-of-effort.

§ Combined catch, by man and birds etc., divided by catch-per-unit-per-of-fishing-effort of the fishermen, giving combined effort of both predators.

mammals and birds) can take without exhausting the stock. Such an understanding also provides clues about the ways in which the breeding biology of the piqueros and other guano birds is related to anchovy biology.

Anchovies spawn mainly around September (but also throughout the year) with a smaller peak in April–May. A female may spawn over 20 000 eggs and the young anchovies grow rapidly, joining the adult schools when about five months old. Thus the progeny of the first spawning peak enter the fishery in January or February, which is just about the time when most guano birds have rapidly growing young in the nest. However, because of its short life span, the anchovy cannot afford to confine its spawning to restricted periods. If it did, and it happened to hit a disastrous spell, the whole of a breeding effort would fail and the population, with short-lived adults relatively few of which would survive either, would be seriously endangered. Therefore, it spawns all year. Correspondingly with food assured, guano birds can breed all year.

Peruvian anchovies suffer high mortality. Probably only 8–15 per cent of adults survive from one year to the next, at the level of fishing as it was prior to 1969–70. During the mid-1960's, the fishery industry probably accounted for half the mortality, the rest falling to natural predators and disease. However, the 1969–70 season, which took 13–14 million metric tons (including wastage), probably increased man's share to 60 per cent at the expense of new recruits which otherwise would have survived. Stocks were being exploited at a size and age considerably before first maturity and the danger of reducing the number of spawners below some unknown but critical threshold already existed at that level of exploitation. Presumably for this reason, among others, a 1970 meeting of experts sponsored by F.A.O., U.N.D.P. and I.M.A.R.P.E. determined the best estimate of maximum sustainable yield to be about 9·5 million metric tons.

Against that background, the role of the guano birds must be examined. From the fairly reliable estimate that a guanay weighing 2kg eats on average 430g each day, it can be calculated that a population of 5·4 millions (the 1969 figure which is hardly a fifth of the 'normal' bird population) eats about 0·84 million metric tons, on top of which the young consume perhaps as much again. Thus, in 1969–70 birds and man between them, extracting at least 16 million metric tons per year (to say nothing of other predators) were taking a dangerously high proportion of the total anchovy population, and man himself was taking far more than the maximum sustainable yield.

Jordán & Fuentes (1966) emphasise that an analysis of the graph of guano bird population with fishery catches (see Fig. 256) during the period of rapid expansion of the fisheries show that about 16 million birds co-existed with fishery catches of about 6–9 million tons. Moreover, the birds were able to recover rapidly from the 1957–8 crashes even though the fisheries were expanding rapidly. Thus, birds increased from 11 million in March 1959 to 18 million by the beginning of 1963, an average annual increment of about 20 per cent, even though the fishery reached the (then) notable peak of 6·3 million tons in 1962. At that level, man was obviously not reducing the stocks to any appreciable extent, otherwise the birds would have been affected.

On the other hand, the dramatic failure of the guano birds to recover from the 1965 slump strongly suggests that, by then, anchovies were being adversely affected; the fisheries did not *cause* the 1965 crash, but they almost certainly retarded recovery from it. The indications are that from 1963 onwards, the anchovy stocks began to suffer significant depletion, though this was masked, so far as absolute fishery yields were concerned, by vastly increased fishing effort and more advanced fishing gear. Thus, Jordán and Fuentes purport to show that the reproductive success of guano birds in 1963–4 and 1964–5 was less than in previous years. They use, as a rough measure of reproductive success, the number of young produced by adults, censused as described previously. By this measure, the reproductive success from 1962–65 was as follows:

Year	No. of adults (millions)	No. of chicks (millions)	Reproductive success %
1962 (Jan.)	17·0	11·6	68
1963 (Feb.)	18·1	12·8	70
1964	15·0	6·0	40
1965 (Feb.)	17·3	8·6	49

Most of these birds were guanays, 96 per cent of whose food is anchovies, so their decreasing breeding success presumably reflected reduction in anchovies. Then the 1965 crash intervened and it was not until it became evident that the guano birds were failing to recover that there was further indirect evidence for a decline in anchovies. This reduction in bird breeding success and particularly the failure to recover at a time when the anchovy catch was still rising has two important aspects. As already mentioned, it suggests that competition was at last entering into the equation—first, the stocks were no longer absorbing the total drain from man and other predators, as they had in the past, without diminishing. Second, it probably meant that the reduced bird population, artificially kept low by a reduction in the abundance of fish, 'freed' anchovies for the fishing industry. This, together with increased fishing effort, enabled the total catch to continue rising, thus further obscuring the real and progressive diminution in anchovy stocks.

By 1969 some fishery experts were, however, extremely worried, even though the total catch continued to rise. Paulik wrote as follows:

> 'Destruction of the world's greatest single species fishery is unthinkable. Could it really occur? Consider the following scenario: heavy fishing pressure has so reduced the abundance of one and two year old anchoveta that the bulk of the catch is taken from recruits before their first birthday. Most of the catch is made from January through May. A moratorium on vessel construction has held the size of the fleet to 300 000 tons of hold capacity. In the year 197(?)

(since this was written, there has been a spectacular failure of anchovies in 1972)

> adverse oceanographic conditions cause a near failure of the entering year class and low catches in the southern spring and early summer (September through December) cause fish meal prices to climb to $300 per ton.[1] Weak upwelling currents in January, February and March concentrate the residual population in a narrow band extending about 10km from the coast.

(see the account of the 1965 phenomenon, where this happened)

> The total catch during the first four months of the season is one million metric tons and the total biomass of the entire residual population plus the entering recruits is about five million metric tons. Although many danger signals are flashing and scientists warn the industry that fishing effort must be curtailed immediately, the industry's creditors are clamouring for payment of short term loans and many factories and fleets are unable to meet payrolls and pay operating expenses (even) while fish meal prices are at an all time high. The January catches total 0·5 million metric tons instead of the 2 million expected. The industry rationalises that recruitment is later than usual and will occur during the February closure. When the season re-opens in March the entire fleet is poised and the residual population is vulnerable. Within two months the entire 4·5 million metric tons is caught and sold at record prices. The government imposes an emergency closure when the catch-per-unit drops to zero at the end of April. The fishery is closed during May but it is too late. The Peruvian anchoveta stocks have been fished into oblivion. Only small, scattered schools of anchoveta remain; dead birds, rusting bolicheros and idle fish meal factories will soon litter the beaches from Chicama to Aricá.'

It is as yet too early to say how far reality now matches this awful scenario, but there are some ominous signs. 1972 was one of the worst El Niño years on record, affecting the climate until August. There were no anchovies to the Chilean border and the fishing plants were idle at least until November (the time of writing). This situation had a tremendous impact on the guano birds already low after the 1965 crash and its aftermath. The population of birds at the end of the year was almost an all time low.

It seems beyond doubt that the combination of the naturally-occurring catastrophes and the vast over-exploitation of the anchovy stocks by the fishing industry has led to a serious

[1] At the time of writing it already far exceeds that price.

reduction in the population of guano birds and can be expected to do so even more in the future. The piquero, however, has survived much better than the guanay and in 1972 its population remained around the level occupied for much of this century It thus happens that, precisely as I write this, a major shift in the balance of guano birds, in favour of the piquero, is occurring.

Since the above was written it seems that the anchovy stocks have partially recovered and in May 1974 were estimated at 8–10 million tons. Yet the birds have not recovered with them. Nobody has explained this apparent anomaly.

SUMMARY

1. At present the main concentrations of Peruvian boobies are on the Lobos Islands, Mazorca, the Guañapes and Central Chincha. However, in 1950, or thereabouts, at least 147 islands and 21 mainland sites were still yielding guano. A full list of present day stations is given.

2. A brief account of some of the main islands is given.

3. Aerial censuses carried out in the breeding seasons 1960–61 and 1961–62 produced estimates of 12·5 and 17 million Peruvian boobies. Seven colonies each held more than 100 000 individuals, the largest being Mazorca (732 700).

4. Massive changes in the absolute numbers and relative proportions of piqueros and guanays on any one island take place from year to year.

5. Some aspects of past changes in numbers and proportions of the guano birds are discussed.

6. Figures for the population of piqueros for the years 1909–72 are given, based on calculations from guano deposited and, latterly, direct censuses.

7. This century, the population of piqueros has fluctuated between less than one million and possibly over four million adult birds. In 1972 it stood at about 2·2 millions.

8. The phenomenon of population 'crashes' is discussed. Until the present time, these have always been due solely to the operation of 'natural' factors (hydroclimatic).

9. The crashes of the twentieth century are reviewed and discussed and in particular those of 1963 and 1965, which have been the most fully analysed.

10. However, a new factor (man's over-fishing) has now entered into the equation, depressed anchovy stocks to an all-time low and prevented seabird population recoveries after the last two crashes.

3. BREEDING ECOLOGY

INTRODUCTION

It is perhaps surprising that this enormously interesting and economically important species has never been investigated in detail and Vogt's (1942) study carried out nearly 40 years ago is still the main source of information on breeding biology, though there is also much of interest in Coker (1919) and in Murphy's (1936) classic. Vogt's series of reports also contain some information on breeding biology, and Hutchinson's (1950) work is an invaluable compilation of all those aspects of Peruvian booby biology which relate to guano. Recently, Galarza has studied the breeding biology of the Peruvian booby on Chincha and promises a detailed treatment. Two features of this species' breeding biology are of such basic importance that they should be introduced straightaway. One is the catastrophes that periodically befall it, wiping out 90 per cent of the population. These have already been discussed at length but it is important to have them in mind. The other is the prodigal nature of its food supply (anchovies) except during the catastrophe periods, when it becomes unavailable to all the Peruvian seabirds.

BREEDING HABITAT

All the breeding areas of this booby are bare and arid, the substrate consisting of guano and debris-littered rocky surfaces, but within that general condition there are two major habitat types—cliffs and flat ground, with of course the intermediate stages. The Peruvian booby is able to breed on completely flat surfaces devoid of any eminence other than the ring of guano that constitutes its nest, and also on small ledges or protruberances on almost sheer rocky faces. Bearing in mind that a fall even of a few feet into a mass of other birds would invariably prove fatal to any youngster unable to fly properly, it is clear that cliff nesting adaptations are as important to it as they would be if it nested above a precipice.

The types of habitat occupied are shown in Fig. 307 a–d but it is more difficult to ascertain the proportions of individuals using cliff, slopes and flat sites. Nevertheless, on the two

Fig. 261. Small rocks off Guañape Norte, with colonies of Peruvian boobies.

Guañape Islands, the strongholds of the piquero, probably two-thirds nest on variably steep slopes particularly on the higher, windward side of Guañape Norte, and most of the remainder on cliffs. On the Lobos islands there is a higher proportion of flatter ground and consequently of boobies using it. On Mazorca there were many thousands, mainly on cliffs at either end but spilling onto the pampa and even on boulders in the midst of guanay territory (Murphy 1936). The Pescadores were occupied mainly on cliffs and plateau-edges; on Asia the piqueros were entirely on cliffs and plateau edges. The Chinchas were occupied near the tops of cliffs and on scarps; San Gallán's south-facing cliff held birds (Vogt 1942) and Lobos de Afuera was occupied on its steep and rugged slopes (Coker 1919). A modern survey of habitat preference is wanting, and on all the islands named, things may well have changed. However, overall, it is probable that this species breeds mainly on cliffs or steep slopes, and is indeed far more addicted to this habitat than any other sulid except the North Atlantic gannet.

Several authors since Coker (1919) have pointed out that the species has undergone significant changes in habitat over the years. Von Tschudi (1852) in his account of travels in Peru between 1838 and 1842, clearly implies that the piquero nested in rookeries on flat ground (the pampas) in the interiors of islands. Similarly, Raimondi (1856) records that in 1853, the piquero confined itself to the interiors of islands, but later (1874) said merely that some, at least, nested on the tableland of the Chinchas, beyond the cliff top. These naturalists made their observations just before and after (respectively) commercial exploitation of guano began in earnest—in other words whilst there was relatively little human disturbance.

By the time Coker carried out his work in 1907 and 1908, the species was almost exclusively a cliff-nester and none were to be found on the pampas. Some ten years later, however, Murphy visited some of the islands that Coker had described, and photographed piqueros nesting in great rookeries on flat or gently sloping ground. Today, they still nest in large numbers on flattish ground on Guañape, Lobos and Chincha. There seems no reason to doubt that some of the boobies forsook flat ground for the cliffs and then later reclaimed the flat ground.

There are two possible reasons why the piquero abandoned the pampas and concentrated on the cliffs. One is that the direct pressure of human interference drove them onto the inaccessible ledges. The other is that a large increase in competitors, particularly guanays and pelicans, achieved the same result, the increase being itself the result of a greater tolerance of human disturbance, at least by the guanay, and possibly even to preferential protection afforded to it as the better guano bird (Vogt mentions and disapproves of the suggestion made by some Peruvian officials, that the piquero be exterminated to provide more room for guanays). The piquero has indeed been well overtaken in numbers, by the guanay at least,[1] for whereas Coker (1919) described it as 'almost omnipresent on the Peruvian coast and undoubtedly the most abundant sea fowl' and Murphy, visiting Peru in 1920, agrees that it is the most numerous of the guano birds, Vogt (1942) ranks it far behind the guanay, and not far ahead of the pelican. Modern censuses have shown that the guanay comprises some 70 per cent of guano birds, the piquero usually around 15–20 per cent and the pelican less than 5 per cent (see Numbers and Distribution p. 594). The assumption that these two species *could* successfully compete with piqueros for the flatter sites is also supported by Vogt's statement that the piquero nests only in places that the guanay cannot use, and that the guanay has expanded at the boobies' expense, whilst Murphy comments that piqueros on the pampa are liable to be jostled, and their eggs and young trampled on by the pelicans. Thus, whatever may have been the cause of a rise in guanay and pelican numbers (and man's activities seem by far the likeliest candidate), the result so far as the piquero is concerned would probably be displacement from many of the

[1] In 1973 the guanay had dropped to a very low level and may have been less numerous than the piquero.

Fig. 262(a)

Peruvian boobies nesting on absolutely flat area at about max. density.

Fig. 262(b)

Nesting on slopes.

Fig. 262(c)

Nesting on slopes, with guanay cormorants; note clean boundary between the two species.

Fig. 262(d)

Nesting on cliff face ledges.

flatter areas. Of the two competitors, the guanay has probably been the most effective in interspecific competition of this kind, and Vogt specifically names it as the most important cause of the piquero's decline.

The subsequent reinvasion of flatter ground by the piquero, seems likely to be a result of the conservation measures that were introduced in 1945.

The intriguing question of whether the piquero basically prefers flatter ground or cliffs is not easily answered. Hutchinson thinks it probable that, when the population of piqueros was relatively small and nesting sites were determined by density independent factors, they first chose ledges on cliffs but then spread onto pampas. Later still, pressure from an increasingly large population of guanays forced them off some of the pampas. The section on Behaviour (p. 649) adduces some evidence suggesting that the species possesses adaptations for nesting on ledges and cliffs; birds certainly seem much more at home (less wary of a close approach by humans for example) than those on flat ground, which often flee when approached. On the other hand, there is nothing to suggest that it takes to flat ground only as a last resort when all cliffs are full. Indeed, and despite its adaptations, cliffs still represent a dangerous habitat; thousands of young piqueros die by falling out of their nests. Also, the piquero is undoubtedly most closely related to the blue-footed booby which is par excellence a flat-ground nester. It is perhaps impossible to distinguish between the possibilities (a) that the ancestral piquero was largely a flat-ground nester whose numbers eventually forced it onto cliffs and that it then continued, and continues subject to transitory changes due to man's activities, to utilise both kinds of habitat, and (b) that the reverse process occurred.

At present, the piquero is mainly a cliff nester, though vast numbers do nest on slopes and flat ground, as on Guañape, Chincha and the Lobos islands, (where there were seven groups on flat ground in 1920) and under protection on some mainland puntas.

It probably prefers, above all, the cliffs and scarps on the higher reaches of islands, as on Guañape Sur, whose magnificent upland slopes and small inland peaks are crammed with these snowy birds and are reputedly the first areas to be re-colonised each year. In these areas, as on sea cliffs, it utilises extremely narrow ledges, which is the reason why many young fall off.

The slope of the ground is probably not the only factor affecting the distribution of the piquero, for one may frequently observe unoccupied areas which seem physiographically adequate. The suggested reasons for avoiding an area are that it is too hot, too windless, too infested with ectoparasites or too recently disturbed by guano operations. The last named is likely to be much the most important of those, and indeed the first two can often be ruled out altogether in view of the fact that the area concerned has been occupied in the recent past.

Vogt records that piqueros nest variously in cool, hot, wind-swept or relatively windless areas, which indicates that they are able to use a wider range of habitats than the guanay. Guanays are more susceptible to heat, and on Chincha South, for example, there was an area between the south-facing cliff and a point inland, which (due to the cliff's deflection of the prevailing southerly winds) lay in a calm pocket with a high ground temperature. Here, the piqueros nested, being abruptly replaced by guanays at the point where the wind reached the ground (Vogt 1942). Murphy suggested that piqueros actually like sunlight and avoid shade, remarking that on Asia Island they avoided the shady parts of a great chasm, their nests forming 'a sort of sundial line along a stretch of the wall reached daily by late afternoon rays'.

COLONY DENSITY

If one accepts the behavioural evidence that the ancestral form was probably a flat-ground nester, no doubt the pressures which encouraged the Peruvian booby to take to cliffs—namely competition for nesting space—also encouraged dense nesting (though space shortage was probably not the only factor).

Vogt gives a figure of 1·6 pairs per sq. m for Chincha but mentions that the birds were recovering from a decline and were steadily increasing in density. My measurements of a flat area on Guañape Norte gave 300 pairs in 198 sq. m or 1·5 pairs per sq. m.

Reference to the Comparative Section shows that this figure far exceeds that of any other sulid except the gannet super species. Piquero colonies become vast, exceeding half a million birds on one island (see Table 83 for distribution and size of colonies).

It is interesting to note that, notwithstanding its extreme gregariousness, this species will nest in solitary pairs out of sight of others, and (as on the south cliffs of San Gallán) in small groups, the nearest average-sized colony being miles away on another island (in this case, the Chinchas). The guanay does not show a comparable range of gregariousness, nor does it in its fishing activities, being on both counts more compulsively sociable than the piquero.

NEST SITES AND NESTS

The minimum width of ledge which the piquero can utilise is about 25–30cm. In many cases there is space around the nest upon which one member of the pair can perch, and this applies also to those nesting on flat ground. In this respect piqueros differ from North Atlantic gannets, which are rarely able to perch anywhere except on the nest itself.

The nest is constructed entirely of fragments of guano, small pebbles and miscellaneous debris such as feathers. Guano constitutes most of the bulk and forms a mound about 15cm high, hollow in the centre. The guano itself is a hard grey substance. The large amount required to produce a reasonable nest can be produced only if the bird excretes mainly on the nest site and relatively little whilst at sea. This withholding of excretion is an adaptive behavioural mechanism resulting from the need to produce a nest of some kind, even in an area devoid of traditional material. A nest is undoubtedly necessary to contain the eggs and small young on cliff ledges and is therefore functional in the structural sense in contrast to that of the closely related blue-foot, which has a merely symbolic significance.

THE EGG AND CLUTCH

1. *Egg characteristics*

The slightly pointed egg is chalky white over a bluish background but as in all other boobies it becomes chipped and discoloured.

The dimensions (Coker 1920) are: length (mm) 53, 59, 60, 61 (2), 62 (3); breadth (mm) 39·5, 40, 41, 42, 43 (3), 44. Johnson (1965) gives the average dimensions as 61·4 × 42·2mm. There is no published information on their weight, but from the approximate weight of the newly hatched chick the egg weighs about 50g.

2. *Clutch size and incubation period*

Peruvian boobies lay between one and four eggs per clutch, most commonly two or three. On North Chincha Galarza records that 41 per cent of 97 nests contained two eggs, 41 per cent held three and 18 per cent only a single egg. A total of 263 eggs were laid in 105 nests, giving an average completed clutch size of 2·5. My own figures from Guañape were 36 per cent two eggs, 53 per cent three eggs, 9 per cent one and 2 per cent four eggs. In addition several authors make general statements indicating that two or three eggs are by far the commonest clutch sizes. It is very possible that the proportion of nests with higher clutches rises after the population has suffered heavy mortality, though firm information is lacking.

No other sulid lays clutches as large as those of the piquero and it is clear from the comparative account that in many if not all species, the clutch size is adjusted to the prevailing economic circumstances. In other words, it usually represents the largest number of young that parents can feed. The piquero's uniquely abundant food supply is undoubtedly the reason why it can rear two, three or sometimes four young, whilst some species cannot do so and may have great difficulty rearing even a single chick. Moreover, the piquero rears its brood more quickly than others rear their smaller ones. Corroboratary evidence for the effect of anchovies on the clutch size of the guano birds is to be found in the fact that in other species, too, clutch sizes tend to be larger than average for the taxonomic group in question. Thus, the penguin lays two to four eggs; the Dominican gull usually three, the guanays three or four and the pelican one to six (usually two or three).

In the piquero, the eggs are laid four or more days apart (Vogt 1942) and incubation begins with the first egg. Under normal circumstances incomplete clutches are never even momentarily left unattended. The incubation period is about 42 days (Vogt 1942; Galarza 1968). The latter gives 11 incubation periods (40 (5); 42; 43 (2); 44; 47; 48; mean 42·4) eight of which refer to egg number two of the clutch, one to a first egg (40 days) and one to a third egg (48 days). The laying intervals between successive eggs result in corresponding differences in hatching, so that piqueros' nests often contain young of vastly different sizes. There is a slight indication that the later eggs may also take longer to hatch than the earlier ones, thus increasing the age gap between brood members.

3. *Rate of laying*

Galarza followed the progress of 97 nests, all of which held eggs by December 29th 1965. The rate at which the number of nests holding an egg (or eggs) increased is given in Fig. 263. This is probably not representative and large groups, perhaps under more favourable food conditions (1965–66 was not an outstandingly good year), may well lay at a much faster rate than indicated here.

4. *Hatching success*

Galarza observed a group of 155 nests on top of a water storage tank on North Chincha between November 25th 1965 and May 19th 1966. Of these, 124 were nests remaining from the previous breeding season and 31 were newly built during his period of observation. 263 eggs were laid in 105 nests (2·5 eggs per nest). Due to intermittent observations, he was unable to follow their fate precisely, but noted the loss of 54 eggs and 35 eggs or chicks. Of the 54 eggs lost 39 simply disappeared (perhaps accidentally displaced, although Galarza thought that the Dominican gull may have been the culprit), 13 were broken, it is not known how, and two definitely fell victim to the gull. Thus, if we assume that the 35 entities lost as eggs or chicks were in fact chicks, then hatching success works out at 79 per cent.[1] If we assume half the 35 were lost as eggs, it is 73 per cent and if all were lost as eggs, 66 per cent. Probably 70–75 per cent may be taken as the hatching success in this particular group. It would not be surprising

[1] Galarza's figures for total eggs laid are wrong; he inadvertently omits 27 lost eggs from the total (lost before December 30th; Cuadro 4).

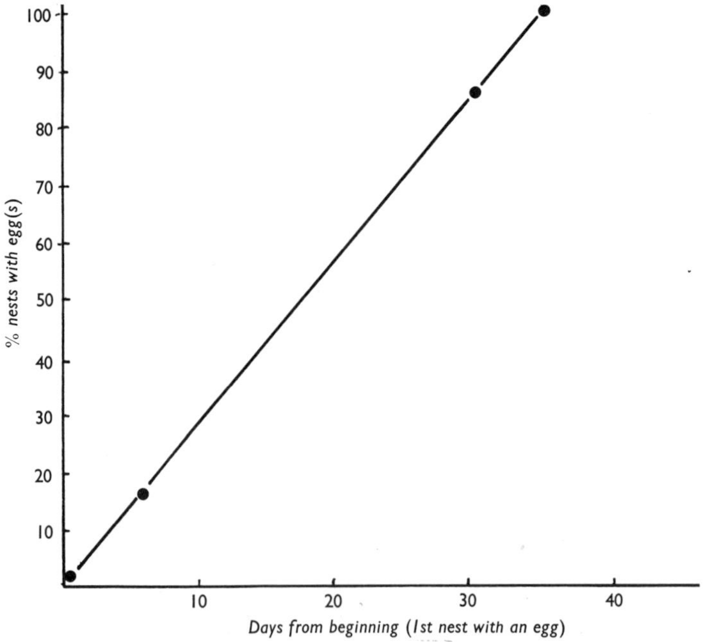

Fig. 263. The rate of laying in a group of Peruvian boobies.

if in fact the hatching success were often considerably higher than this, for there seems to have been a fair amount of unexplained disturbance at the colony from which these figures came. It is not known whether the position of the egg within the clutch (1st laid, 2nd laid, etc.) influences its chances of hatching.

Egg loss in the piquero is caused in three main ways; by human disturbance, by natural predators (gulls, turkey buzzards and condors) unaided by man and by intraspecific activities (interactions between mates and neighbours).

Nobody describes the methods used by the predators to get at eggs or small chicks, which are defended by adults with formidable bills. Coker mentions that the red-headed gallinazo or turkey buzzard manages to rob piqueros by apparently co-operative hunting in which, whilst one bird distracts the piquero, the other sidles in from behind and snatches the uncovered eggs or young. Vogt mentions that cliff nesting piqueros are less prone to predation from turkey buzzards but that this is not a serious factor anyway. Murphy describes how he shot a condor from whose gullet slid about a dozen unbroken yolks of guanay eggs and it is unlikely that piquero eggs will escape their attention completely even though the booby is undoubtedly more pugnacious. Here, too, the cliff-nesters should fare better than the pampa birds. If it is true that piqueros are relatively immune from predation, they differ in this respect from guanays for Murphy (1925 p. 204) records truly enormous havoc wreaked by gulls, vultures and condors among the guanays of Asia Island.

5. *Incubation regime*

Both sexes incubate, but the male takes the greater share. This tendency for the male to spend more time on site than does the female probably runs through the whole season and his greater share of incubation simply reflects this rather than having any special significance. Thus, Coker states (and Galarza confirms) that the male established the site, and the former implies that he attends it more assiduously than does the female in the period before the egg is laid. Furthermore, the male is even more persistent than the female in attempting to take over incubation duties after returning to the nest; both sexes may have to wait for up to three hours before change-over occurs, but the male persists so strongly in his efforts to displace his partner that she may be stimulated to threaten him. In this connection, it may be suggested that nests with three or four eggs may sometimes lose one or more in the process of vigorous and perhaps resisted change-over. The length of incubation stints on Guañape Norte was about 4–10 hours. Whilst these may vary from island to island, they are much shorter than those of most other boobies (see Comparative Section) probably because their food is close at hand and easily procured. As mentioned above, the eggs hatch at intervals, roughly corresponding to the laying intervals, and the chicks are therefore unevenly sized.

THE CHICK

1. *Morphology and plumage development*

So far as I am aware, the various stages of development of the chick have not been described.

Fig. 264(a). 3-day-old chick.

(b). 2-week-old chick (left).

However, they are extremely similar to those of the blue-footed booby and the reader wishing to compare sulids from this point of view is referred to the section on blue-foot development (p. 526).

2. *Feeding*

The young are fed in the normal sulid manner, by incomplete regurgitation. There is little information on feeding frequency and none on the relative shares taken by the sexes. My own observations indicated a return frequency of approximately 2·5 per day per adult and assuming that one chick receives all the food (by no means necessarily a valid assumption), all the individuals of a brood of three would be fed approximately 1·7 times per day. Assuming that 2 young share the food on each parental return, they could receive food twice as often and whilst for comparative purposes it would be interesting to have more detailed information on the frequency with which young are fed, the central fact is that they usually grow quickly, and few die (see below) except in the years of mass mortality due to almost total disappearance of fish (p. 596). Details of the fish species known to be taken by the Peruvian booby are given elsewhere (p. 628). Here, it may merely be noted that the chief prey is anchovy *Engraulis ringens*, pejerrey *Odontesthies regia*, caballa or mackerel *Pneumatophorus peruanus*, machete *Brevoortia maculata* and lisa (*Mugil* spp.) (Galarza 1968).

3. *Growth*

(*a*) *By weight*

The rate of growth of chicks in different species is of great comparative interest. The piquero has larger broods than any other sulid, but its food is both abundant and near at hand, and as a result the species produces a lot of chick weight, and quickly. The accompanying figures are based on Galarza's records, and since growth is such an important aspect of breeding biology and has hitherto never been published in any detail, it is necessary to go into some detail about the basic data.

Galarza weighed young from 25 nests, almost all of them containing two chicks for most of the time concerned, though 7 of them held three for a short period before losing one. Weighings were carried out on five occasions between February 6th and April 6th, but each time, a proportion (apparently arbitrary) of the nests were ignored, so that no single youngster was followed right through. For 10 of the nests, the precise date of hatching of one egg (usually the second laid) was recorded, thus giving 10 accurately aged chicks and datum points from which I have worked out the ages of the other chick(s) in those broods. All these chicks of known age and weight provide a fairly sound base for estimating the age of the remainder at their first weighing. For any given age, a comparison between the mean weight obtained from chicks whose ages have been *calculated* from the known hatching date of one of the brood, with the equivalent weight obtained from *all* chicks, including those merely '*estimated*' reveals very little difference. The lumped curve (Fig. 265) may therefore be accepted as a reasonably accurate representation of the Peruvian booby's growth.

Several important points emerge from these figures. First, growth is extremely rapid, and the maximum weight is reached between 50–60 days, the curve falling thereafter in the usual manner, as feather growth and wing exercise proceeds. Second (Fig. 266) there is no significant difference between the weight achieved by a first-hatched chick at x days and that reached (also at x days) by a second (or probably third) hatched. In other words, the younger members of a brood do not fall behind the older ones, although they are of course lighter on any given date because they hatched later.

This strongly suggests that the parents easily find enough food for all, otherwise one would expect the smaller and weaker ones to fall behind, as they often do, with fatal results, in the blue-footed booby. The related point, namely that in this species there is no brood reduction by sibling murder, as there is in the white and brown boobies, hardly needs making (see Comparative Section).

However, this should not be allowed to obscure the fact that the growth of chicks from broods of three is sometimes slightly poorer than that of chicks from broods of two. This difference is presumably due to the limited food-gathering abilities of the adults, notwithstanding the superabundance of food. Presumably they simply cannot capture prey quite fast enough to feed three as adequately as two, whatever the abundance of fish. Nevertheless, the difference is rather slight and in a normal year should not result in differential survival of young from broods of two and three respectively. Perhaps the high proportion of two-egg clutches, however, does reflect a slightly better survival overall—that is including somewhat abnormal years. Certainly in very abnormal years a weight difference in newly independent young from broods of two or three respectively would be expected to be important. It is known that the juveniles and young birds suffer a much higher mortality than adults in an abnormal year and a difference in fledging weight could prove critical. The piquero would be particularly well suited to a long-term study of this and related aspects of breeding biology.

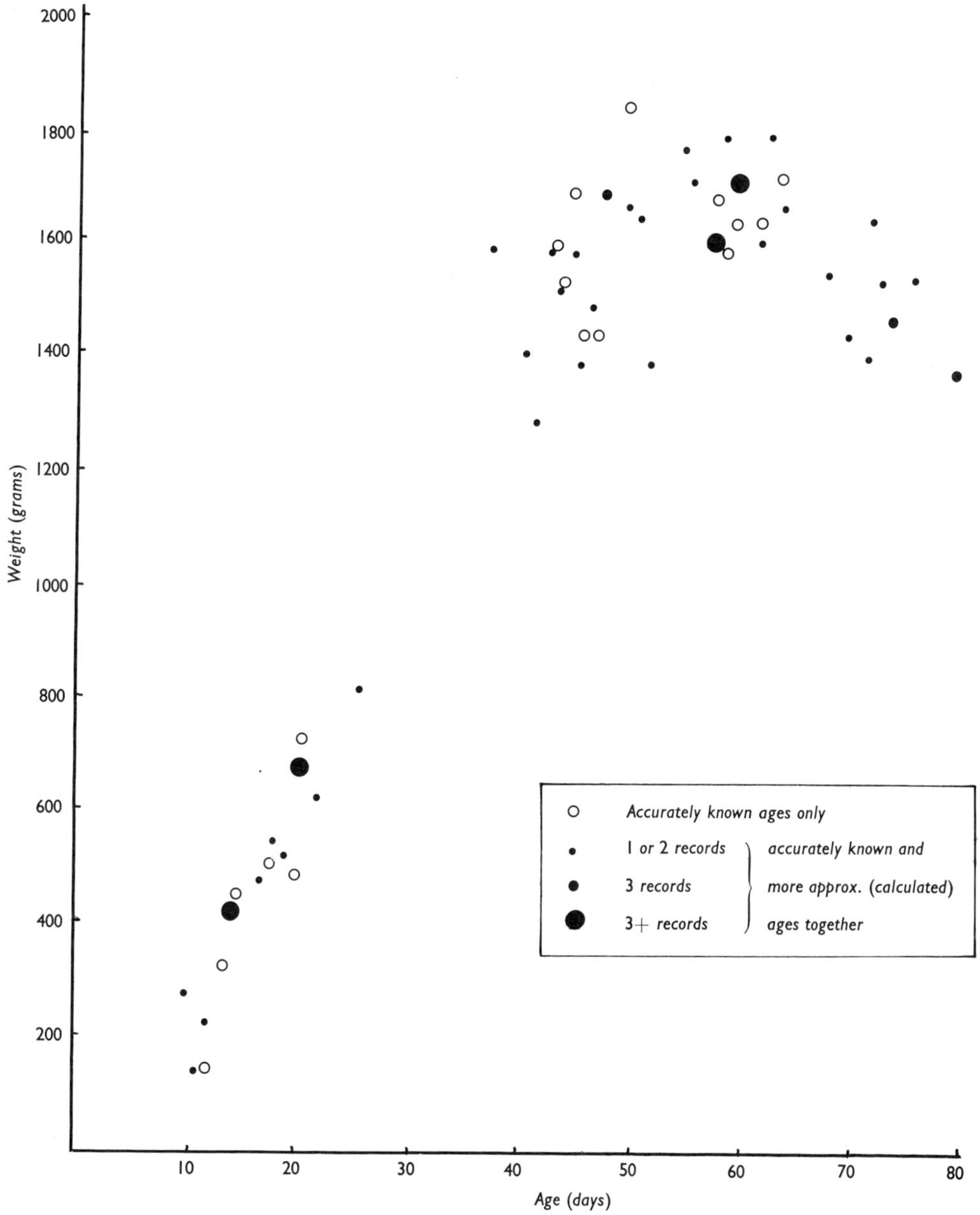

Fig. 265. Growth, by weight, of young Peruvian booby.

If one calculates the total chick biomass (Fig. 267) reared by a pair of piqueros, the richness of the food source becomes even more apparent, though to appreciate the full extent of the achievement one must compare the performance with those of the other members of the family (see Fig. 390).

Finally and notwithstanding the extraordinary growth which does occur, the scatter of individual weights with age (Fig. 266) shows that there is considerable variation at all ages. This implies that, despite the prodigal nature of the food supply, individual variation in parental behaviour (not necessarily hunting skill) is still sufficient to affect breeding success.

(*b*) *By other measurements*

There are no figures for the growth of wing, culmen or tarsus.

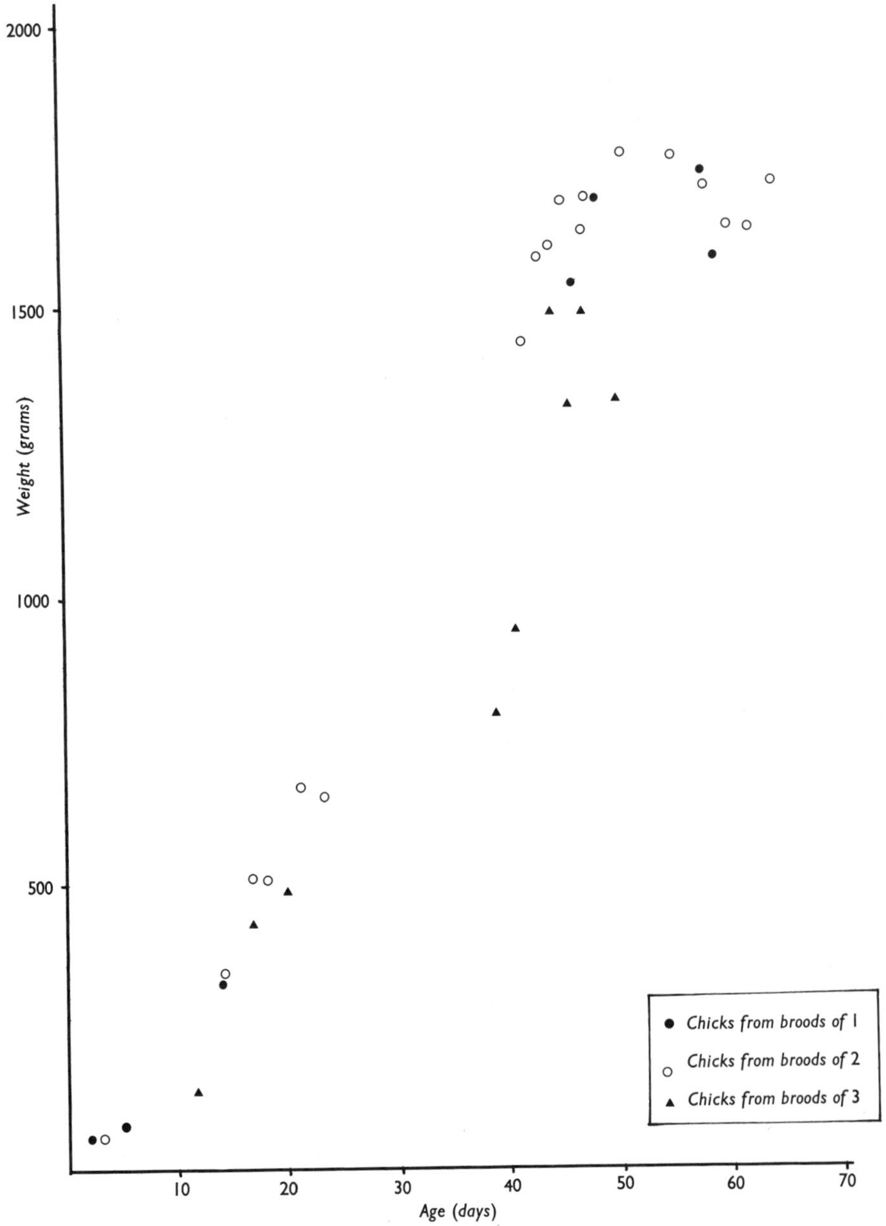

Fig. 266. Growth, by weight, of chicks from different brood sizes.

4. *Fledging period*

Piquero chicks begin to fly when about 14 weeks old (Galarza). Vogt suggested a figure of 2–3 months but this was not based on actual observations and is certainly too short. Even 14 weeks represents rapid growth compared with other boobies, particularly in view of the brood size. They acquire flight gradually by exercising and letting the wind lift them. Those nesting on flatter ground begin to wander and fly for up to 100m (Vogt) before essaying a

Fig. 267. Growth (total biomass) of broods of 2 and 3 chicks of the Peruvian booby.

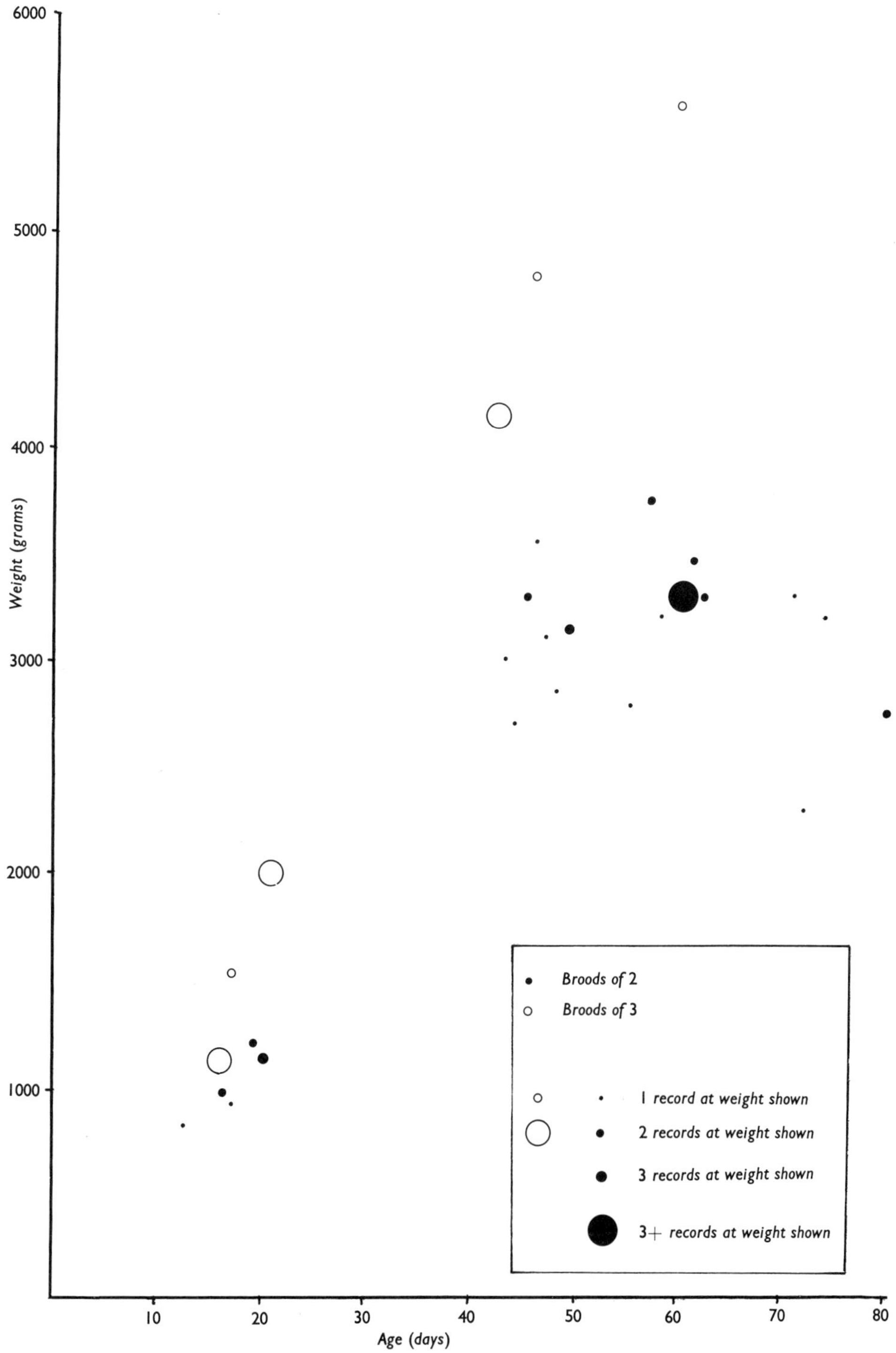

TABLE 91

CENSUS OF JUVENILES ON PERUVIAN ISLANDS AND HEADLANDS 1960 AND 1962
(from Jordán 1963)

	Peruvian cormorants		Peruvian boobies		Pelicans		Total	
	Nov. 1960	Jan. 1962	Nov. 1960	Jan. 1962	Nov. 1960	Jan. 1962	Nov. 1960	Jan. 1962
Lobos de Tierra	0	X	400 000	470 100	20 000	0	420 000	470 100
Lobos de Afuera	0	0	259 500	220 800	0	0	259 500	220 800
Punta la Farola	0	0	0	0	0	3 000	0	3 000
Punta Malabrigo	—	0	—	0	—	0	—	0
Macabí	400 000	550 900	54 500	45 500	0	0	454 500	596 400
Punta Cerro Negro	—	0	0	0	0	0	0	0
Guañape Norte	484 600	720 100	218 700	356 700	0	0	703 300	1 076 800
Guañape Sur	(H) 0	328 300	(H) 0	342 400	0	0	0	670 700
Chao	(H) 0	1 300	0	1 100	0	0	0	2 400
Corcovado	7 200	16 000	19 800	21 500	0	0	27 000	37 500
Santa	20 000	299 400	300	14 000	0	0	20 300	313 400
La Blanca	0	0	0	0	0	0	0	0
Ferrol	17 800	107 200	6 200	8 000	0	300	24 000	115 500
Tortugas	0	0	0	0	0	0	0	0
Punta la Grama	0	0	0	0	0	0	0	0
Punta Culebras	1 126 000	1 229 000	0	0	29 100	17 000	1 155 100	1 246 000
Punta Colorado	0	0	0	0	0	0	0	0
Punta Litera	0	0	0	0	0	0	0	0
Don Martín	500 000	476 000	3 000	0	10 000	79 900	513 000	555 900
Mazorca	263 200	283 000	39 100	77 000	0	0	302 300	360 000
Hiampanú	—	25 000	—	300	—	0	—	25 300
Punta Salinas	150 000	560 000	0	10 000	(H) 0	20 000	150 000	590 000

Punta Chancay	0	0	0	0	0	0	0	0
Pescadores	400 000	165 800	—	400	—	300	400 000	166 500
La Cruz	0	0	0	0	0	0	0	0
Cabinzas	0	0	0	0	0	0	0	0
Palominos	200	3 200	0	0	0	0	200	3 200
Pachacamac	0	2 000	0	0	0	800	0	2 800
Asia	0	540 800	0	0	2 000	37 100	2 000	577 900
Punta Centinela	0	0	0	0	0	0	0	0
Chincha Norte	89 600	114 100	(H) 44 800	158 900	(H) 0	140 200	134 400	413 200
Chincha Centro	0	233 000	0	45 900	0	31 100	0	310 000
Chincha Sur	0	0	(H) 0	0	0	0	0	0
Ballestas	7 400	295 200	12 300	362 800	0	0	19 700	658 000
Santa Rose	(H) 0	647 000	0	0	0	9 500	0	656 500
La Vieja	(H) 0	1 539 000	0	0	0	23 300	0	1 562 300
Punta Lomitas	0	0	0	0	0	0	0	0
Punta Lomas	0	200 000	0	0	30 000	8 000	30 000	208 000
Punta San Juan	(H) 290 500	733 600	0	0	0	10 400	290 500	744 000
Punta Atico	0	15 000	0	0	0	300	0	15 300
Punta La Chira	—	0	—	0	—	0	—	0
Punta Islay y Hornillos	0	0	0	0	0	400	0	400
Punta Jesús y Cocotea	0	0	0	0	0	0	0	0
Punta Coles	0	0	0	0	0	0	0	0
Punta Morro Sama	0	0	0	0	0	0	0	0
Totals	3 756 500	9 084 900	1 058 200	2 135 400	91 100	381 600	4 905 800	11 601 900
%	76·58	78·3	21·57	18·4	1·81	2·3	100·00	100·00

X = colony disappeared — = no record (H) signifies the presence of eggs.

proper flight out to sea. The precise details of this part of the life history have never been recorded. Murphy, for example, says that on Guañape Sur he encountered fully feathered young, which had left the vicinity of their nests, scrambling around all over the island exercising and trying to fly. It would be most interesting to know how far and for how long a young piquero *will* wander before actually flying and whether it returns to its nest from various distances before its first flight over the sea. Since the species is extremely territorial, it would seem a dangerous procedure for a young bird to have to run the gauntlet of nesting adults, in order to regain its nest after exercising, and indeed Vogt specifically records that young which leave their nest are attacked by neighbours and may be killed. On the other hand, if it doesn't stray far from the nest until it is about ready to fly properly, and then returns on the wing, the process requires rather precise timing if the juvenile is not to endure a debilitating period of starvation at a critical point in its development.

5. *Fledging success*

In normal years the piquero undoubtedly enjoys an extremely high fledging success (chicks which reach the free-flying stage from eggs hatched). Vogt records a phenomenally high percentage of chicks surviving from about three weeks through to fledging; on North Chincha he ringed 1005 young birds of which only six (less than 1 per cent) died in the colony. This was on flat ground, and he emphasises that there is continuous mortality among cliff nesters, due to chicks falling out of the nest. This, in fact, is his main reason for suggesting that the species is not really adapted to cliff nesting. Murphy notes the same thing and suggested that some nests break away, a phenomenon not uncommon in the kittiwake, which similarly cements its nest by excreta. He remarks 'the drift lines to leeward of the Peruvian Islands are likely to be well punctuated with the corpses of nestling piqueros of all ages'.

Galarza records 163 chicks fledged from between 174 and 209 eggs hatched (the precise number was not known because 35 entities from a total of 263 eggs laid could have been lost either as eggs or chicks, in addition to 11 chicks known to have been lost). This gives a fledging success of 78–94 per cent, the latter figure approximating to the true one. It thus seems that, on flat ground, and in a normal year, something over 90 per cent of all eggs hatched give rise to fledged young. On cliffs the figure may be significantly lower, though there are merely empirical statements to this effect. This figure is far higher than in any other booby and of the same order as that of the North Atlantic gannet which, like the piquero, is a densely colonial breeder in a food-rich habitat.

The only existing figures for total breeding success are those of Galarza, who recorded 163 fledged from 263 laid—a breeding success of 63 per cent. However even this represents 163 young from 105 nests, which is 1·5 young per pair of adults, compared with a maximum of 0·9 in the gannet. An interesting and new method of discovering the productivity of nesting piqueros was the aerial census by Jordán, who calculated that on November 22nd 1960 there were 1 058 200 juveniles on the Peruvian islands and headlands (Table 91) and 2 849 100 adults (Table 84). This implies that by November 1960 less than one juvenile per pair of adults (1959–60 breeding attempt) had survived (see below). The actual figures of the census are so useful that the counts are included in full.

6. *Post-fledging mortality*

The censuses referred to above provide a rough method of estimating post-fledging mortality occurring in the first few months of free-flying life. This is an extraordinarily difficult statistic to obtain and any indication is better than none. Thus, on the basis that 1 424 550 pairs of piqueros (derived from the November 1960 census) would have produced 2 136 825 fledged young (on the basis of 1·5 per pair—see above) but that in fact there were only 1 058 200 in November 1960 (the direct census figure) 50·5 per cent were 'missing'. Since they do not emigrate in normal years and the census covered the entire Peruvian littoral, one may perhaps assume that about half the chicks produced from the 1959–60 breeding effort had died by November 1960. However, there are very serious objections to this figure. Thus:

1. The figure of 1·5 young per pair may be considerably in error.

2. It is not clear from the accounts of the census how the 'polluelos' (juveniles) were defined and identified from the air.
3. There would have been an unknown proportion of juveniles at sea at the time of the census.
4. The validity of the mortality figure depends on the assumption that the November 1960 figure for adult pairs (the one used in the calculation of juvenile mortality) is about the same as the 1959–60 figure (which produced the juveniles).

Caveat 1. probably would make the estimate of mortality too low rather than too high; *2.* could conceivably have either effect and *3.* would make it too high.

Despite these uncertainties, it is interesting to note that the figure of 50 per cent mortality accords closely with the unamplified statement in Jordán (1964) that about 50–60 per cent of young guanays die in their first year of life, so it may not be too far out.

7. *Post-fledging feeding*

There is little information on this aspect, but Vogt makes it quite clear that the young piqueros return to the nest to be fed for some time after they can fly competently. He describes how in certain situations, they may intercept their parents some 50m from the nest, but are not fed except on the nest. This is an interesting behavioural point. Unfortunately, neither Vogt nor Galarza put any figure on the length of the period of post-fledging feeding, but it is possibly safe to assume that this lasts for some 4–8 weeks. The length of the post-fledging feeding is, in the different booby species, undoubtedly related to the food situation (see Comparative Section), and it is conceivable that the unusual abundance of the anchovies and the ease with which even an inexperienced bird can locate them (thanks to the vast commotions caused by fishing guanays and boobies) render a long period of parental subsidy unnecessary. But the actual hunting skills have nevertheless to be acquired, and for this, six weeks would seem a reasonable period (see Comparative Section).

BREEDING REGIMES

1. *Seasonal aspects*

In the Peruvian booby one is not faced with the wide variation in environmental regimes that attend the more widely distributed sulids and which, in them, lead to very different breeding regimes within the species. But conditions in coastal Peru and northern Chile though far from seasonally uniform, are not in themselves of critical importance in determining breeding seasons. In the hottest months, October to February, air temperatures average about 22°C. and sea temperatures remain between 19° and 20°C. except in abnormal years. The south-east trades blow for most of the year and there is normally no rainfall on the islands.

Nevertheless, despite these climatic conditions and although the piquero has been recorded as laying in every month, it is a markedly seasonal breeder. Coker simply remarks tersely, that breeding is continuous throughout the year and in 1919–20 Murphy found eggs and every stage of young on all the islands he visited and on many mainland cliffs. But undoubtedly the laying season is mainly between September and February and within that period, November and December are the principal months. Thus the young are dependent mainly between January and April, and perhaps most demanding in February–March. Murphy simply states that a large proportion of eggs are laid between September and February and at Mazorca, on December 28th 1919, notes that the great majority of many thousands of nests contained eggs or callow chicks. Six years earlier, on the same island, Beck had found plenty of young but few eggs in June, which (if the young were mainly large) could be consistent with a January–February or even earlier peak of laying. Vogt states that eggs are laid mainly in November.

On Guañape Norte, in late December 1964, most nests held eggs, small young (less than two weeks) or nothing, and there was a big increase in birds establishing sites. These pairs could presumably lay three or four weeks later (it takes that time for site establishment and pair formation). In Galarza's study group on North Chincha, laying began on November 25th and at least 97 out of 155 (62·5 per cent) nests that eventually held eggs did so by December

29th. By February 12th all eggs had hatched or been lost, so, ignoring the latter, and taking a 42 day incubation period, the latest eggs must have been laid very early in January which means that almost all the eggs in the group were laid within about five weeks. On January 20th 1962 most colonies held chicks between four and thirteen weeks old, the most developed being active fliers. Thus, these eggs had been laid about late September 1961.

An interesting point thrown up by the aerial censuses reported in Jordán (1963) was the extent to which, mainly within the seasonal framework outlined above, different localities within the whole Peruvian breeding area varied in the stage of breeding reached. Although there are no details given, it seems clear that in November 1960 certain areas contained a higher proportion of unhatched eggs than others. Similarly, in January 1962 most colonies contained chicks between three and 13 weeks old but the group of islands Don Martín, the Pescadores, the Ballestas and Punta San Juan contained displaying birds and birds just beginning to incubate. This phenomenon is hardly surprising in Peruvian waters, where there are no compelling pressures restricting breeding within narrowly defined seasonal limits, but it does imply the importance of local factors in timing breeding, though within a broadly defined seasonal framework valid for the whole Peruvian littoral.

The facts to be interpreted are thus that piqueros may breed at any time of year, but normally lay within a reasonably defined season. There must be advantages in both traits. Before discussing the probable explanation however, it may be noted that the other Peruvian seabirds are fairly comparable in this respect. The guanay resembles the piquero; the penguin lays during much of the year but probably mainly in September and October, and the pelican lays mainly in November.

The explanation is to be sought in the pattern of abundance of the principal food fish, the anchovy. Anchovies are unimaginably prolific fish, which spawn all year round, but with a major spawning peak around September and a secondary peak in April–May. A fully mature female may lay 20 000 eggs and the young fish are recruited to the fishery when about five months old, which means that around February the shoals of anchovies, already vast, are further augmented by the influx of young. The laying regime of the guano birds would seem to be broadly adapted to this fish pattern, by producing young which make their main demands on the adults during and soon after the rise in anchovy numbers. On the other hand, the protracted abundance of anchovies is adequate reason why the guano birds need not confine their breeding within strict seasonal limits (a more detailed analysis of anchovy numbers and related topics is to be found on p. 606). It should be remembered that generally, in birds, breeding must be timed so as to minimise mortality among the young once they become independent. This is particularly important in species, like seabirds, whose prey is difficult to catch. Here, too, the year-long availability of anchovies permits newly independent juveniles to acquire their skills at any time of year. Had there been a marked 'scarce period' the laying would presumably have had to be timed so as to produce newly independent young outside this period, even at the cost of compromising the adult's chances of taking full advantage of a marked peak in anchovies by suitably timing their feeding of dependent young. As it is, the guano birds get the best of both worlds. Alas, however, they have to contend with man!

2. *Synchronisation of breeding*

The spread of laying over the Peruvian littoral as a whole is very considerable but a survey of a major piquero colony in the middle of breeding is enough to show that, wide though the spread of laying may be in the colony as a whole, local groups are closely synchronised. Unfortunately, there are no quantitative figures to support this statement, but on both Guañape Norte and Sur in December 1964 it was so obvious, simply by looking, that nobody could possibly have doubted the phenomenon. The functional value of sub-group synchrony in colonial species is a subject of intrinsic interest, and will be discussed in the Comparative Section (p. 911). Here, I am concerned merely to emphasise its occurrence in the piquero.

3. *Length and composition of the breeding cycle*

Piqueros are to be seen on most of the breeding stations at any time of year. Between breeding seasons they do disperse throughout some 2250km of coastal sea but roost and rest on the islands. Thus there is probably no period during which a breeding station is always deserted (as may happen with some of the more oceanic boobies). Nevertheless for any individual, the breeding cycle is probably as distinctly demarcated as for any other species. In other words, I suspect that no piquero returns regularly (if at all) to its nest between the termination of post-breeding behaviour (that is, the period immediately after the offspring have severed all links with their parents), during which the latter show a temporary recrudescence of territorial and sexual behaviour and the onset of the next breeding cycle. It may continue to frequent the same island—though this has never been proved—perhaps favouring it but also using others. Certainly it congregates in non-breeding aggregations on the island on which it will later breed, for Vogt records that in the very early stages of the breeding cycle, the male will spend some time in such a congregation, from which it will fly to its site. However, once it has really begun to show territorial behaviour and to perform the sexual 'advertising' display (p. 637), it attends the site most assiduously, and after pair-formation has occurred, customarily never leaves it unattended. This period lasts for about a month—perhaps longer if one begins to count from the very first spells of attendance.

The incubation period (42 days) and the period during which the chicks are in the nest (14 weeks) occupies a further 20 weeks. If the period during which the adults continue to feed the free-flying young is accepted as about a month, and the post-breeding territorial behaviour two to four weeks (it could even be absent altogether), the length of the period during which *some* breeding activities are being performed by any given pair totals 26–30 weeks or less. This is still a very short period when compared with some boobies. In fact, it is so short that it raises the distinct possibility of less than annual breeding (see below).

4. *Frequency of breeding attempts*

It is usually stated that the piquero breeds annually but the wide spread of laying, proving that food is not strictly seasonal, together with the relatively short breeding cycle, makes more frequent breeding quite possible, under certain circumstances. The spectacular population crashes (p. 596) provide special circumstances—that is a relaxation of any possible density dependent competition, or of any social inhibition (could this occur) and it has been stated though without any details, that after a crash the guano producing birds do breed with increased frequency and with larger than average clutches. If these two phenomena could occur they would help to explain the wonderful ability for recovery of the population (Table 89; p. 603) shown by this species and the guanay. Unfortunately, there is no information involving known pairs. However, the phenomenon should be obvious enough if large numbers of pairs rear successive broods without, or with less than, the usual rest period, and the statements that they do so may well be correct. The implications—viz. that under normal conditions the breeding frequency is maintained at a merely annual level by counter selection pressure(s) or by social inhibition as an intrinsic population regulation mechanism—raise many interesting points about which, however, nothing is known.

5. *Non-breeding years*

Galarza records that in his study group on North Chincha, 1965–66, only 105 pairs laid eggs, out of 155 pairs that built nests. It is virtually impossible that the remainder all lost their eggs and whilst it is possible that a few represented pairs that had finished or failed breeding prior to the commencement of his observations one must conclude that nearly a third of the pairs did not breed. The further assumption that they were experienced adults is not necessarily justifiable, for they could have been young pairs with no previous breeding experience. Nevertheless, the possibility of 'rest' years among experienced adults remains and it would be of great interest to know more about this.

6. *Age of first breeding*

Vogt ringed a large number of young piqueros but I have been unable to trace any published reference to their reappearance as breeding birds. They are said to acquire adult plumage by the beginning of their second year and may well begin to breed, or at least to attend the colony, whilst in their second year. Almost certainly they will actually breed in their third year. Thus, in concrete terms, a chick born in, say, January 1960 might look like an adult in January 1961, when it may well be attending a breeding colony, perhaps even laying in February, March or April or alternatively merely acquiring a site. By October–November–December–January of 1961–62, however, it might be expected to breed. By February 1962 it would be just over two years old, but actually in its third year. The variability inherent in such a system would of course provide a further potential mechanism for regulating recruitment to the population and, as such, for coping with the effects of population crashes.

7. *Fidelity to group*

Here again, marked individuals would clarify the issue, but the evidence from guano operations indicate that birds certainly change islands and if they remain on an island, they may change the areas they occupy. Thus, when digging operations make it impossible for them to use certain favoured slopes, they settle elsewhere, perhaps in recently cleared zones. The phenomenon of changing islands occurs on a colossal scale (see for example Table 87) and has obviously been going on for a long time. Vogt records that in August 1939 there were no piqueros on the Lobos islands, though there were birds on the Chinchas to the south, and both Lobos de Tierra and Lobos de Afuera normally hold boobies. From the detailed censuses of 1960 and 1962 it is clear that huge populations of piqueros may simply desert a particular island completely and appear en masse on another, without any period of build-up. It would be fascinating to know whether a population tends to move as a unit or simply to split up, other populations doing the same and combinations of the fragments thus giving new colonies. One suspects that, even before commercial guano operations, changes in the distribution of anchovies may have provided grounds for adaptive shifts by the bird populations, but there can be little doubt that, at present, guano operations are largely responsible for the yearly movements from island to island.

Most of the productive islands are cleared every second or third year, but the work is, so far as possible, carried on outside the breeding season. Thus any given pair could conceivably be disrupted relatively infrequently, or even not at all and it is therefore difficult to decide just what effects human interference have on the piqueros breeding biology. Is it practicable to remain faithful to site and mate more often than not? The probable answer is that neither site nor mate fidelity are very important in this species, although a proportion of pairs doubtless reunite on the same site in two or more successive years. The tendency to change both site and mate fairly often is present in the closely related blue-foot and it is likely that, encouraged by circumstances, the Peruvian booby takes the tendency a step or two further.

We do not know whether pairs that remain together enjoy higher breeding success or whether failure predisposes divorce, but since breeding success is so high anyway, these peripheral factors are unlikely to be important.

8. *Food fish*

Murphy (1925) quoting Everman & Radcliffe (1917) and adding 11 species to their list, records that around 163 species of marine fish had been collected from the coastal waters of Peru and he comments that several more certainly occur. But of this wealth by far the most abundant species, of paramount importance to the guano birds and perhaps particularly to the guanay, pelican and piquero, is the anchovy or anchoveta *Engraulis ringens*. Upon the unimaginably immense shoals of this fish the millions of the 'big three' guano birds depend and usually with success, to feed themselves and their large broods.

Anchovies are 15cm or less in length. Their huge schools, containing adults and immatures, travel usually near the surface, where they feed on marine phyto- and zoo-plankton. When conditions are favourable these fish are liable to occur at any point along the entire 2090km length of the Peruvian coast, but they do favour certain areas (see Fig. 298) and it seems that the distribution of seabirds bears some relationship to the centres of distribution of their food fish.

I cannot resist quoting another of Murphy's vivid descriptions; this time of anchovetas on the move. 'Their appearance, from above, is amazing, for the quivering silvery creatures seem to be packed together like sardines in a tin, except their heads point all in one direction as their legion, which somehow seems more like an individual organism than a conglomeration of millions, streams through the gauntlet of its diverse and ubiquitous enemies.' If, as Murphy describes, whole herds of sea-lions can loll amongst the anchovies gorging themselves, the schools must be so dense that seabirds simply pack their stomachs and crops in no time. Over 70 anchovies have been recovered from one guanay.

The anchovies are by no means the only abundant fish available to seabirds in these essentially temperate waters. The sardine *Sardinella sagax* and machete *Potamalosa notacanthoides*—both herring types—occur in enormous shoals, as do the delicious silver-sides, of which the pejerrey *Basilichthys affinis* is perhaps the commonest and is widely taken by guano birds. Then there are the mullets, of which *Mugil cephalus* is abundant, the mackerels, of which the caballa *Scomber japonicus* and the bonito *Sarda chilensis* are the most important, the carangids, basses, flounders, blennies, croakers and drums.

The piquero certainly takes many of these and may well rely on some as a secondary source when anchovies become unavailable. Coker and Murphy simply state, in effect, that anchovies are its staple diet and that it doubtless takes other species, as available. Jordán (1967) says that anchovies constitute 96 per cent of the food of guanays, but only 'at least 80 per cent' of the food of the piquero and the pelican. Jordán (1964) records that a concentration of some 300 000 guano birds were fishing near Callao in September 1963 and taking mainly 'Eljorobado' (*Vomer* spp.), machetes, pejerries and anchovies. Recently, Galarza (1968) has provided a more detailed account. In a sample of 105 regurgitations he found *Engraulis ringens* a pejerrey *Odontesthes regia*, a mackerel *Pneumatophorus peruanus*, a herring *Brevoortia maculata* and a mullet *Mugil* spp. The detailed breakdown of the sample showed (Table 92) that anchovies figure most commonly in the regurgitations (in 83 per cent) followed by pejerries (18 per cent).

The ability to catch species other than the anchovy and thus move onto secondary food sources, may well be a vital factor in the piquero's ecology, enabling it better to survive the temporary disappearance of its principal prey. Its population figures (see Table 88) seem to bear this out and its fluctuations are much less dramatic than those of the guanay.

There is no information on the relative frequency of different sizes of anchovy in the piquero's diet, but guanays are known to take all size groups between 2 and 14·5cm; mainly 10–12cm (Jordán 1967). Since piqueros often, if not usually, feed on the same shoals, it is likely that they also will capture a similar range.

SUMMARY

1. Peruvian boobies nest on either cliffs or flat ground; the proportion of the population using flat ground has varied within recent times and this is discussed.

TABLE 92

COMPOSITION OF 105 REGURGITATIONS OF THE PIQUERO

Fish species	% of regurgitations in which present
Anchovies only	70
Anchovies and pejerries	10
Pejerries only	6
Caballa	4
Caballa and anchovies	2
Machete	2
Unidentified species and combinations of above species	7

2. The minimum width of usable ledge is about 30cm.

3. The nest is highly functional compared with the symbolic ones of the blue-footed and white boobies.

4. The clutch size is one to four, usually two or three, average clutch size 2·5. This represents some 10 per cent of the female's weight.

5. Eggs are laid four or more days apart and hatch asynchronously.

6. The incubation period lasts about 42 days.

7. Hatching success in a normal year averages 70–80 per cent.

8. Both sexes incubate, but males slightly more than females.

9. The appearance of the chick from hatching to fledging is similar to that of the blue-footed booby.

10. Growth curves for the young are given. Second-hatched chicks do not fall behind first-hatched and both grow relatively quickly compared with other sulids.

11. Peruvian boobies take about 14 weeks from hatching to fledging.

12. Fledging success is normally extremely high; probably around 90 per cent of all eggs that hatch give rise to fledged young.

13. Mortality in the first year of life is probably about 50–60 per cent.

14. The main laying season is September to February, but eggs may be found in any month.

15. The breeding regime is timed so that the heaviest demands of the young coincide with the period of great abundance of anchovies.

16. Local synchronisation occurs within a colony, members of a small group laying more or less at the same time.

17. The total breeding cycle lasts 26–30 weeks.

18. It seems likely that, as in other boobies, adults sometimes 'miss' a breeding cycle although they may nevertheless attend the colony. The frequency with which, on average, they do this is unknown.

19. Probably piqueros breed for the first time in their third year.

20. Birds may breed on different islands in successive breeding cycles and therefore almost certainly change mates.

21. Some characteristics of the principal food fish *Engraulis ringens* are described and food fish listed.

4. BREEDING BEHAVIOUR

INTRODUCTION

The behaviour of the piquero is of outstanding interest because, alone among the boobies, it breeds in huge dense colonies and moreover on cliffs, a habit which all the others, with the partial exception of the brown booby, carefully avoid. This immediately provides two behavioural 'themes' with comparative import. A third is to be found in the unusually close behavioural (and morphological) resemblance between it and the blue-foot, the only sulid with which the piquero overlaps in breeding distribution (on the Lobos Islands of Peru). But the blue-foot is pre-eminently a flat-ground nester and the two species reflect their different habitat preferences in their behaviour, particularly the form of their displays.

The seabird colonies of Peru are among the most spectacular sights in the bird world The islands, incomparably set against the green sea and the backcloth of the Andes, are thronged with snowy piqueros, covering the pampas, climbing the scarps and festooning the pinnacles. This point is worth making repeatedly, for the complete and deliberate destruction of the guano birds has been seriously suggested in the past and may be again.

Yet piqueros have been valued almost solely for their economic worth and, whilst protected in many ways since 1909, their behaviour, as indeed much of their breeding biology, has been much neglected. Murphy (1925, 1936) and Vogt (1942) wrote before ethology had become established and their writings contain very little about behaviour. My own visit to the Guañapes in December 1964 therefore forms the basis of the present account.

ESTABLISHMENT AND MAINTENANCE OF TERRITORY

Piquero colonies are undoubtedly highly traditional and ancient references to them on several of the guano islands show that the same islands have been inhabited probably for many hundreds of years. Nevertheless, since guano exploitation began (and probably before) piqueros and the other guano birds have been forced to change their nesting location, either on or between islands, at relatively frequent intervals. This, together with the young birds entering the breeding population for the first time, means that at any colony, almost at any time (since these birds lay in most months of the year) there may be some birds establishing territories. A second general point is that an 'attraction of equals' operates, 'equals' here being birds in roughly comparable reproductive states. Thus, normally, males on the look-out for a nesting site are attracted to areas where other males are doing likewise or have just established sites, rather than to areas where most birds are incubating and-or feeding young. So it is that a huge colony of piqueros with, overall, birds in every stage of breeding, nevertheless consists of locally synchronised groups. As in other sulids, the male acquires the site.

1. *Aerial reconnaissance and territorial flighting*

A bird looking for a ledge in a densely occupied area must either simply land wherever it can and await possible reactions from returning owners or spend much time in aerial reconnaissance. Gannets spend many hours or days reconnoitring and so, probably, do piqueros, though this has not been established by observation.

Having settled on a place the male repeatedly flies out and returns, each time calling as he comes in and performing the post-landing display (p. 634). This may be considered territorial flighting, for even though it is not flight above the actual territory, it is flight functionally concerned with the establishment of territory. Similar behaviour is important in all sulids, though it is not until one counts the number of times that a male performs the act, and realises how conspicuous is each occasion in terms of the demonstration to immediate neighbours, that its significance becomes apparent.

2. *Saluting*

The flight into the site terminates with a throwing up of the feet, soles spread, in a 'Salute' (Fig. 268). This might, at first sight, be interpreted as braking behaviour, but in fact it is a display emphasising landing. It occurs much more dramatically in the blue-foot but is recognisably the same behaviour in the piquero. The reduced form may be correlated with duller feet. The

Fig. 268

Male landing with foot Salute. This is a signal and not merely a braking action.

muted Salute, in which the feet are not thrown up so high nor held there till the last split second, may be made necessary by the difficulties of such an athletic manoeuvre whilst coming in to land on a crowded cliff. Incidentally, it provides a minor clue to the evolutionary relationship of Peruvian and blue-foot, hinting that the former evolved from a blue-foot-type ancestor; one would not expect a Salute to evolve *de nouveau* in a cliff environment, but might expect a pre-existing version to be toned down.

The female piquero Salutes less often than the male. However, the fact that she shares territorial defence, as do all sulids, is noteworthy.

3. *Fighting*

Piqueros are pugnacious birds. A dense group on fairly flat ground is in a constant ferment of aggressive activity. They defend their territory by overt fighting in which birds, with head feathers bristling, stab, lock bills and with frequent changes of grip force the opponent away from the site. The fights are noisy and vigorous but relatively short-lived (usually less than two minutes) and probably harmless, at least compared with those of the gannet. Nevertheless, they represent the extreme within boobies, being far more frequent, long-lasting and intense than in any other and particularly than in the blue-foot. This is doubtless correlated with the keen competition for sites, which imposes strong selection pressure favouring aggressive individuals. Comparably (though for different ultimate reasons) the gannet has evolved fierce competition and fighting. Both male and female piqueros fight, though only against members of their own sex. In fact, most of the 20 or so fights which I recorded were between females. Again, in sharing fighting, the piquero resembles the gannet rather than the other boobies.

4. *Wing-flailing*

This behaviour, essentially similar to that described for other boobies, is not frequent in the piquero, probably because cliff ledges are unsuitable for it and because in their crowded colonies, expansive movements trespass on neighbouring territories and draw reprisals (Fig. 269).

5. *Jabbing*

In the Peruvian booby Jabbing in defence of territory is performed by both sexes. It is repetitive, at fairly high speed (about one jab per 1·4 seconds) and there may be 12 or more jabs in quick succession, performed with an open beak (Fig. 270), accompanied by rapid calling and often with head feathers ruffed. Jabbing contains an inbuilt withdrawal and is sometimes followed by a rapid shake of the head, although this is not a regular part of the total behaviour. It is quite clearly ritualised, since in most cases it is not a preliminary to actual contact, though

Fig. 269 (a and b)

(a) Wing-flailing; here, birds have newly taken up territories on a cleared area.

(b) Wing-flailing and low intensity threat, evoking bill tucking.

it may lead to gripping. In other words the Jabbing as such has signal value rather than being merely an abortive attempt to get hold of a rival. Often it includes a shake so that open bills rattle and clash and this, with the associated withdrawal, oft repeated, gives it a stylised appearance. Nevertheless, it is quite different from the ritualised Jabbing of the gannet, which has a slow withdrawal often followed by a Pelican Posture. But it functions as a close-range spacing-out mechanism, as much in the gannet.

Jabbing between mates has become a ritualised pair interaction and is described in that context (p. 642).

6. *Threat-gape or Menace*

As mentioned, Jabbing occurs with a throwing motion of the open beak and in the piquero a version of this, with less of the jab and more of the gape, occurs as lower intensity territorial aggression. Interestingly, the only other sulid which habitually uses this simple threat-gape—so common in birds—is the gannet, whose Menace is however more ritualised (it includes a twist and withdrawal) than the equivalent in the Peruvian booby. Like Jabbing it is essentially close-range behaviour, which is presumably why it is so common in the piquero but does not occur as a typical part of the behaviour of the closely related blue-foot.

7. *Yes-Headshaking*

All sulids have one main display which is performed by both sexes, signifies their ownership of a territory and is in large part aggressively motivated. Whether they are homologous is a question for the Comparative Section (p. 929), but even a person completely unfamiliar with display in this group would immediately recognise the similarity between the behaviour which a piquero performs after landing on its site or after a fracas, and that which a blue-foot or even a white booby performs in similar circumstances. This display was called Yes-Head-

Fig. 270(a). Distance between nests is maintained partly by Jabbing.

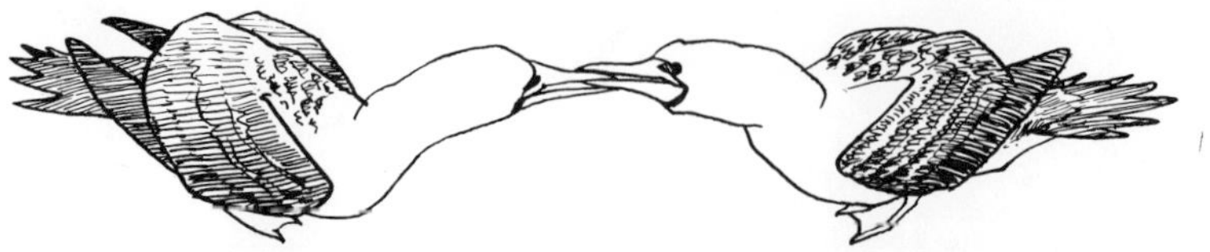

(b)

Jabbing grades into bill gripping or sometimes into fighting.

shaking in the blue-foot because it is a rapid up and down nodding. In the Peruvian the same movement is used (Fig. 271), but it is much slower, of greater amplitude and more emphatic (when the bird is standing the Headshake may take the bill down to the nest). This is enough to give it its own unmistakable character. Piqueros headshake about two to three times per second whereas the blue-foot headshakes at least three times as quickly. Timed bouts in the Peruvian lasted between one and six seconds (mean—3 secs.). As in all sulids it is accompanied by calling—a fluctuating high-pitched call in the male (Vogt described it as a neighing call) and a deeper call in the female (Vogt's 'goose-like honk').

The Peruvian booby Headshakes whilst standing, sitting, walking, running, with head held back (see Head-back position, below) or forwards. Thus, like its counterpart in the blue-foot, this display has numerous secondary aspects which, no doubt, are all related to the precise state of motivation at any instant. The origin of the display is discussed in detail for the blue-foot and the reader is referred to this (p. 552).

8. *Attendance*

Between establishing their site and laying eggs, a pair of piqueros attend it for at least three weeks and perhaps more. At first the male, who establishes the site, may not spend very long there, merely flying to it from some non-breeding aggregation on the island, probably in the early morning (Vogt 1942) but leaving it unattended for much of the day. After pair formation, however, the site is attended continuously. The attendance spells of the male are longer than those of the female (Vogt 1942 and pers. obs.). Both sexes are able to catch enough food relatively quickly and so foraging trips are short.

The constant attendance at the site after pair formation and before laying is interesting, for gannets behave similarly, although most boobies do not. Again, it may be associated with the keen site competition and so the need to guard it constantly, particularly since a group at the site-establishing stage attracts birds bent on doing likewise.

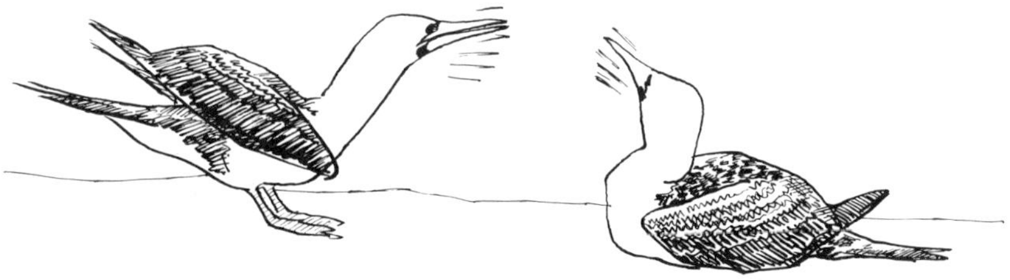

(a) 'Yes-headshake', a stylised, site-ownership display consisting of an up-and-down movement of the head.

Fig. 271 (a and b)

(b)

The calling bird is 'Yes-headshaking' at the long-necked bird moving towards it.

FORMATION AND MAINTENANCE OF PAIR

In many ways it is not helpful to try to separate behaviour which brings about the formation of the pair from that which strengthens their relationship; the one grades into the other. I do so here only to make the point that there is special behaviour whose function is to bring male and female together for the initial meeting and that this can be distinguished from a group of other activities which occur later during interactions between the partners. A single and receptive male certainly would not respond to a 'prospecting' female by performing the behaviour that normally preceeds take-off for instance, but he would probably perform a sexually-motivated display called Sky-pointing. After that, if the female joined him, the pair would go through a whole gamut of interactions. It is these kinds of behaviour with which the present section is concerned. Many of the behaviour patterns occur in almost identical form in the blue-foot and the reader will sometimes be referred there.

Courtship, taken as the period between initial pair formation and egg laying, probably lasts about a month, during which the nest is constantly attended but this period is sometimes significantly shorter. The actual process of acquiring a mate in all boobies involves a special 'advertising' display by the male, to which the female, who obviously must be on the look-out, responds. Thus the pair engineer the initial meeting, after which the association either breaks

Fig. 272 (a–e)

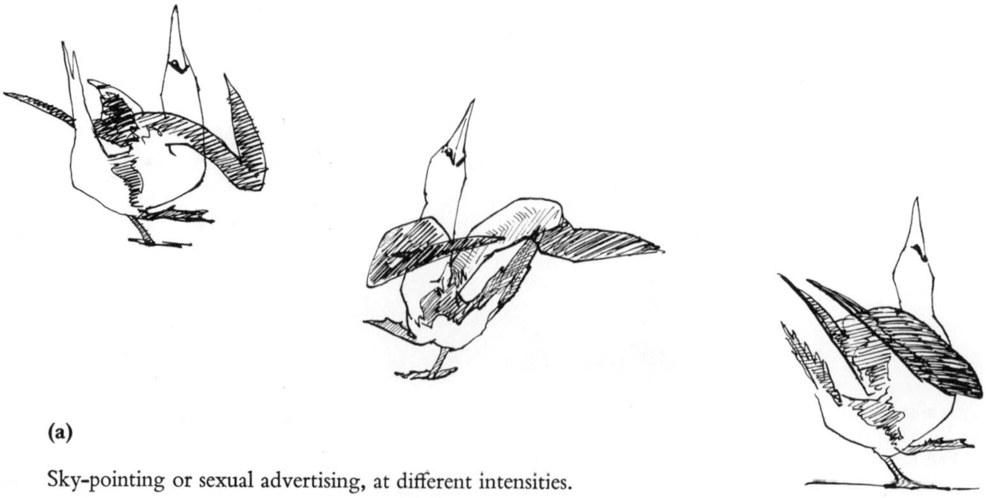

(a)

Sky-pointing or sexual advertising, at different intensities.

up or develops into a stable relationship. In the latter case a bond is formed between the mates. The advertising display is Sky-pointing.

1. *Sky-pointing*

In the piquero it consists of stretching the neck and pointing the bill skywards, simultaneously spreading and swivelling the wings so that their upper surface faces forwards, calling and (often) lifting one foot, web spread, clear of the ground (Fig. 272). The wing lifting proceeds in one smooth movement as the beak is pointed upwards and is accompanied by a whistle. In the male foot lifting was incorporated in 119 out of a sample of 129 cases of Sky-pointing, and oddly enough the male raised his right foot significantly more than his left. The female's Sky-pointing is used mainly after the pair has been formed, as part of the pair-cementing behaviour.

The Sky-pointing of the piquero resembles that of the blue-foot far more closely than that of any other booby, but differs from it in two ways. Its typical intensity form is slightly less extreme, the wings are not spread quite so widely, rotated so extremely or brought quite so far forwards. The whistle accompanies the wing raising and is shorter in the Peruvian than

Fig. 272(b)

Highest intensity Sky-pointing.

(c) Male Sky-pointing to female (out of picture), who then joins him. Simultaneously another male (second left) is interested in the female (left foreground) who is prospecting.

(d) Low-intensity Sky-pointing by the male on left is directed towards the female (second left) whose tendency to move towards the male elicits an intention movement of threat from the female of the other pair (third from left).

(e)

Her male then Sky-points again.

in the blue-foot (about a third to a half as long). If the Sky-pointing proceeds in two or three jerks, there are corresponding breaks in the whistle (or grunt if from a female). Also, and unlike the blue-foot, Sky-pointing incorporates foot-raising. Probably because of the dense nesting, it is often performed with the partners actually touching, though where space permits a male will follow his female, Sky-pointing all the time.

Sky-pointing is clearly associated with sexual motivation and one of its functions, probably the main one, is to bring the pair together. However, I observed that in the Peruvian booby Sky-pointing by the male was not infrequently followed by attempted reverse copulation (female mounting male) which I did not see in the blue-foot. Also, the female Peruvian occasionally oriented her Sky-pointing to neighbouring males, even when her partner was present, giving the impression that she was using it to attract him to the site, again reversing what is usually the male role (see the brown booby, p. 490). It is, therefore, possible that there is some difference between the species in the precise balance of the roles of Sky-pointing.

That Sky-pointing birds were also aggressive was evident both from the nature of accompanying acts (see below) and the sometimes aggressive response (Jabbing) from the Sky-pointing bird once it had been joined by the other, particularly when a female Sky-pointed to a male. The tendency for a Pelican Posture (bill-hiding) to follow Sky-pointing perhaps indicates that, in this sexual context, whatever aggressive and withdrawal tendencies occur, do so in variable states of balance. Parading (q.v.) probably indicates a tendency to approach the partner, either for sexual or aggressive acts. An idea of the importance of Sky-pointing in the pair relationship may be gained from the following figures: in one continuous bout, lasting about three minutes, a male Sky-pointed 35 times, whilst the female did so nine times. These activities were intermixed with many others in one complex mosaic.

Vogt records that Sky-pointing may continue for up to two months and still be unsuccessful in attracting a female. However, his observations were carried out on North Chincha when the population was recovering from a decline.

Sky-pointing is never long performed alone; it is usually part, even though central, of a group of activities, the precise composition of which is doubtless significant, though a much more detailed analysis would be required to elucidate the difference in motivation associated with complexes of different natures. In the piquero the ritualised postures or movements which comprise the mosaic of activities characteristic of early (pre-laying) pair interactions on the site, and of which Sky-pointing is an important constituent, are: Parading; facing away with the bill held upwards (Bill-up-face-away) or backwards; a headshake in this position (Oblique Headshake); Pelican Posturing; Mutual Jabbing; Bill-touching; ritualised nest building; and a brisk shake of partly raised wings (Wing Rattle). It is important to mention again that none of these activities are totally restricted to the context of pair formation and maintenance, though all, except Jabbing, are far more typical of it than of any other.

2. *Parading*

Parading is the exaggerated walking which piqueros (and most boobies) use when walking around in a territorial or sexual context. It is not 'normal' walking, but employs a flaunting upwards and sideways movement of the feet, with webs spread (Fig. 273). Although it looks comically exaggerated, it is nevertheless much less extreme than that of the blue-foot. This is understandable in the cliff habitat. As in the case of aerial Saluting, the lesser use of the webs in a ritualised display is correlated with their duller coloration. The incorporation of foot-raising (which is on-the-spot Parading) into the Sky-pointing of the Peruvian booby seems readily understandable along the lines suggested above. Thus, Parading in the blue-foot is very commonly associated with sexual interactions, but in the piquero is restricted by the habitat. Foot-raising (the reduced form of Parading) however, can be used and so is incorporated into mosaics of which Sky-pointing is the main constituent. In this line of interpretation I assume that piqueros stemmed from a blue-foot type (flat-ground) ancestor (see p. 649).

As already indicated Parading is often one of a mosaic of behaviour patterns in the territorial and/or sexual context. It often occurs with the head held so that the bill points upwards and/or sideways, or is tucked (Pelican Posture). The former is often assumed by birds which are about to move and so is understandably linked with Parading. The latter is particularly common when Parading towards a mate and may be appeasing (q.v.). Parading is strongly correlated with Wing Rattle (a signal of impending flight) again understandably since often the first act in the sequence leading to flight is walking, which in a territorial context means Parading. Then comes the Wing Rattle, sometimes whilst the bird is still Parading.

One must advance much the same functional interpretation as for the blue-foot—namely that Parading emphasises both the bird's tendency to move and its actual locomotion, which presumably is of advantage in co-ordinating pair activities and in minimising conflict between neighbouring birds.

Although derived from ordinary locomotion, it must now have acquired a different set of motivating factors, for it is shown only in special (i.e. breeding) circumstances.

3. *Bill-up-face-away*

I have already discussed this conspicuous, ritualised posture in some detail under the white booby and particularly under the blue-foot, and most of the remarks made there apply here, too. The posture itself (Fig. 274) is very similar and it is performed in the same contexts—that is, when moving around the territory or moving about during an interaction with the partner. In one respect, however, the piquero is distinctive; it often adopts a posture in which the head, rather than being pointed upwards and tilted sideways, is held in an extreme backwards position, though still with the neck elongated. This Head Back was adopted whenever a bird had to run the gauntlet of hostile neighbours on its way to a take-off point. It may be that in this situation, an oblique posture which helps the bird to keep an eye on one individual in the rear, but at the expense of a vast blind spot to the opposite side, is less useful than one in which forward vision is maintained, whilst the bill is lifted somewhat out of harms way. In fact it is by no means clear that Head Back is merely a form of the Bill-up-face-away. It may be an unritualised posture with different motivation (primarily avoidance or fear). A detailed analysis of contexts and associated behaviour would shed light on this point. Certainly it has no exact counterpart in any other booby, nor does a gannet ever adopt such a posture when it runs the gauntlet; instead it strains upwards and forwards. It is intriguing that in such similar circumstances two closely related birds should differ in this way.

4. *Pelican Posture*

Piqueros often tuck their bills when moving around their territories or when interacting with

Fig. 273 (a and b)

(a) Parading: an exaggerated web-flaunting movement, here performed on the spot and with the beginnings of a Bill-up-face-away posture, which usually accompanies movement away from the partner.

(b)

Parading in low-intensity bill-tucked posture.

their mates. On 10 occasions out of 30, the male bill-tucked after Sky-pointing. Much more observation would be needed to elucidate the motivation and function of this posture, but I have the impression that it is associated with motivational flux, in which aggression-fear are certainly involved. It may well serve to reduce the likelihood of aggression between mates, which is commonly, though not solely, where it occurs (see the other species for fuller comment).

5. *Wing Rattle*

Before a piquero launches into flight, it may simply perform small preparatory movements such as slightly lengthening the neck and crouching a little. On the other hand, it may lift its wings slightly, still mainly closed, and rattle them briskly (Fig. 275). This is unquestionably a ritualised behaviour pattern rather than a necessary precursor of flight. It is typically a signal of impending take-off when the pair are together on the nest and one of them is about to leave.

The correlation with flight tendency was well shown by two sets of comparisons of the frequency of Wing Rattling. In the first, birds on nests with eggs or chicks were compared with those on empty nests (0·27 Wing Rattles per bird with egg or chick; 1·4 on empty nests) and second, birds with eggs or small chicks against Club birds (0·05 as against 0·5). Thus in one comparison the two categories differed by a factor of 6 and in the other by 10 and in both it was the birds whose circumstances would allow flight that showed the highest incidence of Wing Rattling. Sitting on eggs or chicks inhibits the tendency to fly and hence the tendency to Wing Rattle. The comparison was made the more meaningful by comparing, in the same periods, the incidence of Wing Flapping, which is plumage maintenance rather than flight signal behaviour. Here, there was virtually no difference between the three categories of birds.

The context of Wing Rattling suggests that it must be of some advantage for a bird to know when its partner is about to leave and it may be that Wing Rattling thus serves to

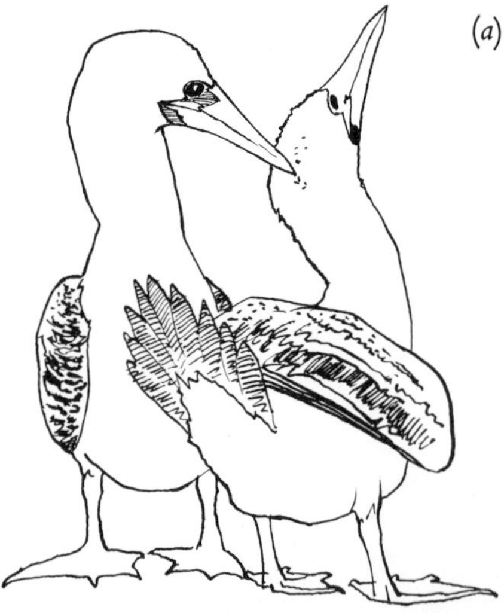

(*a*)

Fig. 274 (a–c)

(a) Bill-up-face-away: a posture assumed by a bird about to move away from its partner.

(b) Low-intensity Bill-up-face-away.

(c) Bill position (face away) which grades into Bill-up-face-away. Note the spread web (Parading).

(*b*)

(*c*)

co-ordinate pair interactions during courtship and perhaps when relieving each other from incubation and spells of guarding the chick. If both birds left it would expose the eggs or young to the risk of predation by gulls (kleos) and it is also possible that unattended nests would be visited and their contents harmed by other piqueros.

6. *Nest-building, Showing Nest Material and Bowing to Touch it*

The piquero builds a nest which, in many situations, is undoubtedly essential for the safety of eggs and chicks. Because ordinary nest material is non-existent on most Peruvian islands, which lack vegetation, and there is little seaweed available, the nest has to be made of the bird's own excreta, together with small stones, fragments of earth and detritus, etc. and in this way a sizeable structure is formed. The bird often bends its tail and directs the excreta on to the side of the nest. Thus, one certainly cannot speak of Symbolic Nest Building comparable to that of the blue-foot, where the actual structure is not in the least significant, but the activities involved are extremely important as pair bonding behaviour. Nevertheless, the two species are very alike in their nest building activities and very probably the nest building (and associated) activities have a pair bonding function in the piquero, as they do in the blue-foot. Vogt makes a particular point of emphasising the 'psychological' significance, as he terms it, of nest material and describes in detail the intense excitement which a male evinced when his female brought nest material to him (usually it is the other way round).

In boobies with relatively large territories on flat ground, the males, in particular, spend much time fetching material (using a ritualised walk) and interacting with the female in placing it, etc. The small territory of the piquero, however, precludes this. Hence the preliminary steps in the normal sequence have more or less disappeared. Perhaps correlated with this, the piquero has a far weaker tendency than the blue-foot, to perform the other ritualised behaviour associated with nest building. Thus, for example, the Presenting or Showing of a scrap of nest material (Fig. 276), in which the bird, whilst holding a piece of nest material, swings its head, bill more or less vertical, through a wide arc before placing the fragment on the nest site, is rarer in the piquero. Also, it is less likely to occur as pure 'Showing' and more likely to incorporate the aggressive Yes Headshaking (p. 634). In these instances, it can still be recognised as Showing because of the 'arcing' movement, but the aggressive display is superimposed. Another indication that ritualised nest building is less strongly developed, is the less stereotyped form of the Bow by which the bird touches the nest material which has been placed. In the piquero it is a variable movement and can hardly be considered ritualised behaviour at all. The third pattern associated with nest building, that in which the pair, with heads together, handle or build in the fragments, seems fully comparable in piquero and blue-foot and is an intimate interaction which doubtless helps to strengthen the relationship of the partners. In sum, therefore, the piquero nest building complex is obviously a weak version of the cluster of symbolic acts that one sees in the blue-foot. The piquero, of course, could, even where ritualised walking to collect material is impossible, pick up and Present a scrap from the already-formed nest; but it rarely does so. Even where proper excursions on foot are possible,

Fig. 275

Wing-rattle: a brisk shake of the partly raised wings, signalling impending flight.

the male, though he will return with nest material in the Parading Walk, is much less prone to Present it. Probably symbolic nest building, like Saluting and Parading have been reduced in the piquero due to the exigencies of cliff nesting. Piqueros collect material mainly around the nest but will occasionally fly in holding a fragment.

7. *Mutual Jabbing*

Mutual Jabbing between mates in the Peruvian booby is characterised first, by its high frequency and greater degree of stylisation. Bills are pointed at each other, opened and with rapid calling the birds perform jabbing motions (Fig. 277), usually without touching though bills may overlap. Often, heads are kept motionless, but the birds open their bills and call 'past' each other. Secondly, it occurs in bouts, rather than merely as one or two jabs. Thus, it is a primitive meeting ceremony, though it lasts only a few seconds (22 timings were 10 seconds, 8(2), 5(5), $4\frac{1}{2}$(4), $3\frac{1}{2}$(3), 3(3), $2\frac{1}{2}$(2), 2(3)). Thirdly, and unlike the blue-foot's Mutual Jabbing (but like most 'true' greeting ceremonies, the gannet's being a good example) it persists throughout the breeding cycle. On all counts, therefore, it may be considered more highly developed, as ritualised behaviour, than in the blue-foot.

In the Peruvian booby there is a marked tendency for Yes Headshaking to be interspersed with Mutual Jabbing—which is hardly surprising since both are basically aggressive. The greater tendency for Peruvian partners to jab each other may be linked with the species' greater tendency to fight, etc. and the enforced close proximity of mates. This, in turn, may have encouraged some ritualisation of the behaviour. A similar situation exists in the dense and highly aggressive gannet, though here the female has become highly inhibited from attacking the male, whereas this is certainly not the case in the Peruvian. Nevertheless, there are many

(*c*)

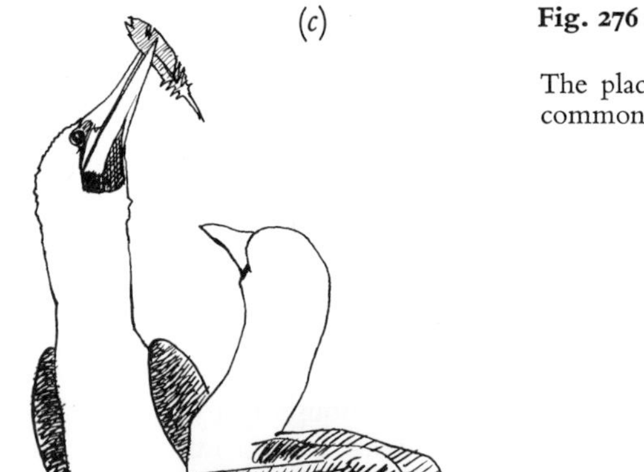

Fig. 276 (a to c)

The placement of fragments of guano (nest-building) is a common interaction between members of a pair.

In (a *lower left*) the male (with calling) bends to pick up a fragment. In (b *lower right*) the pair call as they bend to touch the ground (nest site).

In (c *upper left*) 'Showing' nest material is a part of ritualised nest building.

similarities between gannet Mutual Fencing and Peruvian booby Mutual Jabbing. Both occur on meeting, are seasonally protracted, involve aggression, are interspersed with touching nest material over the partner's neck, are elicited by intrusion, etc. Furthermore, both often terminate in Mutual Preening, which may be interpreted as derived from aggressive behaviour rather than functional body care. The blue-foot lacks this, though the male sometimes preens the female.

In sum, therefore, the Peruvian booby has certainly gone further than the blue-foot in elaborating a meeting ceremony (though it is crude compared with highly developed ones, such as those of the gannet or Abbott's booby) and there may be a connection between this and its aggressiveness and dense nesting. However, the pair relationship involves the sum of the behaviour patterns enacted in each other's company and these are partly dictated, indirectly, by many other factors, such as the nature of the habitat, agility and the behaviour primarily evolved in non-pair contexts.

8. *Bill Touching*

This behaviour, in which partners appose bill tips, is probably just a low intensity form of Jabbing and may indeed develop into it. Its main interest is comparative (see p. 929).

9. *Mutual Preening*

Piquero partners often preen each other simultaneously (Fig. 278). There is no quantitative investigation of this behaviour, but the fact that it occurs is interesting enough (see Comparative Section p. 938). In a dense nesting species in which withdrawal is difficult this behaviour (like ritualised greeting behaviour) is adaptive insofar as it forms a pair bonding mode of expression of aggressive motivation in the pair context.

10. *Copulation and associated activities*

As in all other boobies, but not the gannet, the male piquero copulates without gripping the female with his beak (Fig. 279) although he places his bill alongside her head and makes nibbling movements. Females usually stand, which is interesting because species highly adapted to cliffs often squat, as does the gannet, the kittiwake and the black noddy for example, so here is another scrap of evidence indicating a flat-ground ancestry for the blue-foot/Peruvian stock. When females are incubating their first egg(s) males often attempt copulation with the female in a sitting position, but a high proportion are unsuccessful, the male sliding off. Some soliciting females assumed a horizontal position, quivering the tail. Preliminaries by the male included preening the female's nape and Foot Raising (a prelude to mounting).

During copulation males may keep their wings closed or hold them partly or fully out and wave them. The tarsi are usually laid along the female's back and 'pattered'. Timed copulations, from mounting to dismounting, took 14, 12, 11, 9½, 9(2), 8 and 7 seconds.

Fig. 277 (a and b). Pair calling together before Mutual Jabbing (a). Mutual Jabbing between mates (as here) is indistinguishable from that between rivals (b).

(*a*) (*b*)

The commonest behaviour after copulation was touching nest material (both sexes), Yes Headshaking (both sexes) and Mutual Jabbing, all of which probably indicated disinhibited aggression. Males tend to fetch nest material after copulation and so one finds, also, the usual precursors of movement (Parading, Bill-up-face-away, etc.). Two reverse copulations were seen.

This concludes the account of behaviour which brings the pair together and establishes their full and co-operative relationship. From this point, they become involved in incubation and the rearing of the chick, and though ritualised behaviour by no means disappears, it plays a reduced role in the activities of the pair and other behaviour becomes important.

OTHER BEHAVIOUR INVOLVED IN BREEDING

1. *Incubation*

The piquero, with its clutch of up to four, must have reached about the limit with respect to the number of eggs which can be incubated underfoot, in the normal sulid manner.

Incubation (about 42 days) is shared unequally, the male taking somewhat more than the female. Vogt (1942) states this empirically and our observations on known pairs, though few, confirmed it.

2. *Change-over*

When the incomer lands on the site (almost always directly from its flight in from the sea), usually it cannot simply push its way on to the nest. First the pair must greet each other and then wait, or interact, until the shifting motivations of each bird activate one to vacate the nest and the other to assume the centre. This may take some time, for the occupier may still be broody. Often, particularly if the incomer is a male, it flies off again and returns, sometimes with a fragment of nest material. Sometimes, the occupier has to be forced off the nest by the incomer. The few change-overs that I was able to time took between ten seconds and ten minutes, but Vogt records that 2–3 hours may elapse. The interactions following the arrival with calling, commonly involve a vocal exchange, Mutual Jabbing of variable intensity, touching of nest material, the partners often bending over the other's neck, and (if the incomer is about to leave again) the ritualised postures which precede and accompany movement (Bill-up-face-away, Parading and Wing Rattling). Also, the return of a partner is often followed

Fig. 278. Mutual (allo-) Preening between mates.

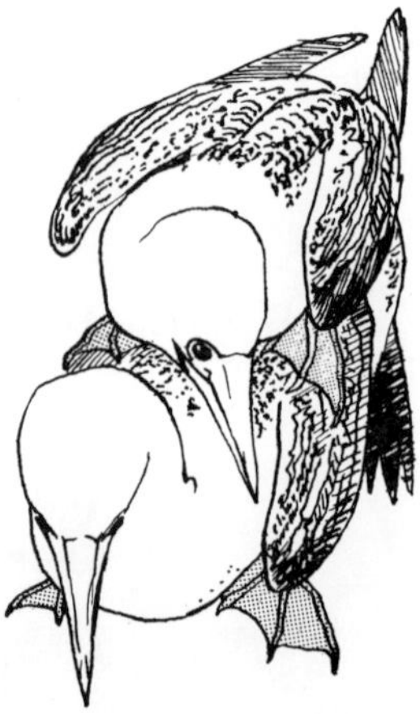

Fig. 279. Copulation: note that the male does not grip the female's head, though often he lays his bill alongside and makes nibbling movements.

by lengthy and intensive preening and oiling, which may precede or follow change-over and by reciprocal allo-preening. Vogt says that the latter is usually initiated by the incomer and may last for a few moments. There is usually no overt aggression, although males particularly insistent on taking over the nest may elicit threat from their mates. After change-over the relieved bird may bring nest material.

3. *Aspects of parent-young relationship*

There is very little precise information on the care of young in the Peruvian booby, but equally no reason to suppose that the species differs in any important way from the other members of the family insofar as egg-shell removal, transference of newly-hatched young to the dorsal surface of the webs, etc. are concerned.

The frequency with which the young are fed is an important ecological indicator, and the piquero's foraging trips, if the length of absence be an accurate guide, are between 3 and 24 hours. The brood, as an entity, is fed about 2–4 times per day. How the feeds are divided up amongst the two, three or even four unequally sized young has never been studied, but their growth indicates (see Figs. 265, 266, 267) that even the smaller members manage to get about as much food as did their siblings at a comparable age. This must mean that the parents bring back enough food to satiate the bigger chicks, which then allows the youngest to feed. This could happen only if the adults were able to collect food very quickly and in large amounts; otherwise the bigger chicks would almost always be hungry and the youngest would get much less than did its siblings. We know that the unique position of the piquero normally does in fact allow them rapid and successful foraging trips and the situation is thus in the greatest possible contrast to that of the blue-water boobies with their extremely long foraging trips and their single, often ill-fed, chick.

BEHAVIOUR OF YOUNG

1. *Relationship between siblings*

In the piquero the two to four chicks live amicably together. We did not observe obvious aggression between them or, in the smaller siblings, any bill-hiding, such as one often finds in the blue-foot, which is the only other sulid frequently raising broods of more than a single chick. Undoubtedly the rich food supply is the ecological factor which has made it unnecessary for the piquero to evolve brood reduction mechanisms or marked sibling dominance. It would

Fig. 280. Young Peruvian booby begging for food (centre nest).

be interesting to have observations on the brood's behaviour during times of food shortage. No doubt under conditions of starvation, the older chick would claim all the food.

2. *Food begging*

The young piquero solicits food by rubbing its bill tip up and down the underside of the long axis of the adult's bill (Fig. 280). The begging which I saw was restrained, in marked contrast to that of the blue-foot. This was probably because the young were less hungry and also, possibly, because restrained begging has evolved as an adaptation to nesting on cliffs. A similar situation exists in the gannet (q.v.). Feeding is by incomplete regurgitation, the chick inserting its head into the mouth and crop of the adult and transferring boluses of food direct.

3. *Fledging behaviour*

Piqueros fledge after about 14 weeks in the nest. From Vogt's (1942) comments it appears that young piqueros, after wing exercising in the normal manner, essay small, trial flights by allowing the wind to lift them, hanging in it for a while and then dropping back onto the nest. When they have become proficient, after flights of about 100 metres, they make proper flights some distance from the nest. Evidently some do this before they are competent, for Murphy gives an amusing description of the way in which fledgling piqueros tumble from the sky, landing with a disconcerting thump.

> Still older chicks which had left the vicinity of their nest were encountered all over the island, resting and sleeping, striving to scramble up hill, or launching out into space. One could never tell when such a youngster might come hurtling down from aloft, to alight with a thud close by. These fledglings were all extraordinarily tame; almost any of them could be touched or picked up.

There is, in fact, an element of mystery in these accounts, since it is clear that the fledgling of a pair nesting on cliffs must do one of two things: either (like the gannet) it makes a once and for all departure, with no return, or it does not risk flying from the ledge until it is fully competent, otherwise it would run a substantial risk of death. Obviously, the piquero should belong in the second category—as all other boobies do—since it has a period of post-fledging dependence on its parents. Even if one assumes that the incompetent fledglings of Murphy's account were from slopes or flatter ground rather than cliffs, it still leaves a question mark over the method by which they regain their nest, if they are too incompetent to fly back. Certainly they would not be allowed an unmolested passage through the nesting ranks. Vogt describes how young piqueros are attacked by neighbours if they leave the nest and may be killed. This, of course, is a problem that does not beset the ground-nesting boobies, like the blue-foot, which can hop and part-fly back from wherever their bungled flight lands them. Yet regain their nests the piqueros do, for Vogt describes how they attempt to intercept their parent on its return with food, some distance (say 50m) from the nest (obviously, in this case, on flatter ground) but are fed only on the nest.

4. *Ontogeny of behaviour*

Unfortunately there is no information on this aspect of behaviour. Other boobies, even before they are fully feathered, begin to show most of the ritualised behaviour patterns of the adult—such as the sexual advertising and the aggressive site ownership display. This is certainly the case in the blue-foot and since the piquero is equally if not more intensely territorial, it is likely that the same applies. A gap in the piquero's ethogram, which could be easily filled, concerns the ages at which the various behaviour patterns first emerge.

MAINTENANCE BEHAVIOUR

Returning now to the behaviour of the adult piquero, there remain those activities which do not fall into the main functional categories already described and which are themselves somewhat difficult to group under any unifying theme.

1. *Stance and movement*

The piquero is distinctly less shag-like than the blue-foot, but also less heavy and deliberate than the white booby. Usually the tail is carried slightly above horizontal, but not cocked as much as the blue-foot's. The piquero walks and runs with facility, waddling less than the white booby. In general stance and movement, there is undoubtedly most resemblance between the piquero, blue-foot and brown booby.

2. *Preening*

There is nothing to add to the accounts of preening and oiling already given for other sulids. Piqueros bathe communally, great rafts of birds, congregating densely and usually in groups entirely separate from similar bathing groups of guanays and pelicans. They 'roll-bathe', turning onto their sides, duck-like, and exposing the ventral surface. They also duck, thresh the water with partly loosened wings, roll the back of the head on the back and flap their fully opened wings, rising partly from the water.

The tendency to bathe in dense groups is interesting. There may be little or no direct advantage in so doing but it is noticeable that colonial seabirds, when on the water in non-feeding groups, almost always congregate in dense groups. It may simply be a generalised response to conspecifics, functional in the breeding colony and of no disadvantage outside—particularly if the species is a group feeder.

3. *Wing Flapping and Headshaking*

These behaviour patterns were fully discussed for some of the other sulids. Ordinary wing flapping is a comfort movement associated with preening and particularly common during moult. It was shown, for the gannet, that it is associated with alarm and has a very clear seasonal pattern, being much commoner early and late in the season, when the birds' fear of land is less inhibited by the attraction of the site than it is when egg or chick are present. It was also pointed out that birds may simply wing flap (with or without a subsequent tail wag) or they may incorporate a rapid headshake which I termed Rotary because the head rotates from side to side rather than simply being wagged from side to side (the latter is a sideways headshake). The piquero's repertoire includes the ordinary wing flapping, the Rotary Headshake, sideways headshake and a quick headshake with the head tilted to one side—the Oblique Headshake.

The wing flap is performed with body fully upright, wings fully out and flapped at increasing speed. It was clearly commoner without the Rotary Headshake—indeed it was extremely frequent—and in this form associated with alarm. In this respect, it corresponded with the gannet, but not with the blue-foot, whose wing flapping was usually associated with the Rotary Headshake and a fluffing of body plumage and was apparently largely concerned with plumage-care. The association with alarm in the piquero was clear from a comparison of the incidence of wing flapping in groups of breeding birds as against birds in non-breeding congregations. The latter were much warier and showed a far higher incidence of wing flapping.

The ordinary sideways headshake is not a usual behaviour pattern in the piquero, as it is in the gannet, and it may be suggested that this is because the former inhabits a clean, dry habitat and therefore has not used headshaking so frequently in its primary context (dirt-dispelling) and so has not incorporated it into signal situations to the same extent as the gannet. It has, however, evolved the Oblique Headshake, which the gannet has not.

4. *Heat regulation*

Piqueros use panting and gular fluttering to regulate their body temperature. Adults 'sun' themselves with loosened, crossed wings.

5. *Fishing behaviour*

Apparently, piqueros fish during daylight hours, beginning at dawn (Jordán 1967). Like all sulids, they locate their prey by scanning from the air, though if others or other species have already done so, the piqueros simply join them, falling like hailstones into massed regiments of other seabirds. Sometimes (unlike guanays) they fish solitarily, on non-shoaling fish. The actual dive is like that of all other sulids; a headlong plunge with wings partly open and constantly adjusted during the dive, extending right back as the bird enters the water. From all accounts the height of dive varies from immediately above the surface to an estimated 40 metres.

They may penetrate very deeply or pursue extensively by swimming since Murphy states that they may remain underwater at least as long as a minute, which is some six or seven times as long as gannets.[1] Obviously the anchovies at times of El Niño are out of reach at 40m or more though the boobies survive better than the guanays and pelicans.

On occasions a number of birds all dive together, but there is no reason to suppose that this is due to anything other than simply seeing a shoal and diving into it simultaneously. A mechanism such as the signalled group diving of the blue-foot would seem unnecessary in the presence of vast shoals of uniformly sized fish, nor would marked sexual dimorphism, with its implied differentiation in feeding technique, seem useful. Agility in pursuit of small, lively fish would obviously help and might be one of the selection pressures which have kept both sexes medium sized.

The piquero hunts in close company with many other species of birds and with the sea-lions and large predatory fish thronging the green sea lanes. Whether it hunts in competition or collaboration with any of these is not known. Indirect evidence clearly shows that there is not density-dependent competition for food—there is more than enough for everybody (or has been until recently)—but it is possible that hunting piqueros benefit from the confusion and disorientation caused amongst the massed fish by the assaults of other species. This is really the same as saying that hunting in flocks is, under certain circumstances, advantageous to the individual, whether the flocks be mixed or of one species only. Certainly, they do respond to the fishing activities of other species besides their own; in this way, they benefit from shoals located by them, and doubtless the process works the other way round.

Normally the piquero's food supply is close at hand and it does not usually remain at sea for more than a very few hours at a time. Jordán (1967) says that piqueros may be encountered more than 80km offshore, but that they prefer to fish nearer the coast. Detailed figures for all stages of the breeding cycle are unfortunately not available, but from Vogt (1942), my own observations and Galarza (1968), it seems that absences from nests attended by the partner vary between 2 and 12 hours and males tend to spend less time at sea and longer at the nest than do females.

The main conclusion is that normally piqueros are able to find and gather food abundantly and quickly, and this is of basic importance to their breeding biology.

For a vivid account of the massed dives of the piquero one cannot do better than to quote Frank Chapman:

> The Boobies fished from the air, plunging headlong and with great force from an average height of fifty ft into the water almost directly. Like a great flying spear-head they strike the water and disappear in the jet of foam which spurts upward as they hit the surface. It is a more thrilling, reckless performance than even the plunge of the Fish Hawk. The dive of a single Booby, like that of the Hawk, is always a notable exhibition of skill, strength and perfection of the winged fisherman's art. Only a person rarely gifted in the use of words could adequately describe it. How, then, can one hope to paint a pen picture of a thousand Boobies diving, of a skyful of Boobies which, in endless stream, poured downward into the sea? It was a curtain of darts, a barrage of birds. The water below became a mass of foam from which, if one watched closely, hundreds of dark forms took wing at a low angle to return

[1] Duffy (pers. comm.), however, timed 34 dives at a mean 2·6 secs (1·7–4·4 secs) which is very short.

to the animated throng above, and dive again; or, their hunger satisfied, they filed away with thousands of others, to some distant resting place. It is difficult to understand why the birds emerging from the water are not at times impaled by their plunging comrades and how the Cormorants, always fishing on or near the surface, escape. But the most amazing phenomenon in all this amazing scene was the action of flocks of Boobies of five hundred to a thousand birds, which, in more or less compact formation, were hurrying to join one of the Booby squalls which darkened the air over the fishing grounds. If, unexpectedly, they chanced to fly over a school of fish, instantly and as one individual every Booby in the flock plunged downward and in a twinkling the air, which had been filled with rapidly flying birds, was left without a feather! This spectacle, the most surprising evolution I have ever seen in bird life, was witnessed repeatedly during the day.

BEHAVIOURAL CONVERGENCE IN PERUVIAN BOOBIES AND GANNETS

This account has described many similarities between blue-footed and Peruvian boobies, but these, it has been argued, stem from a close phylogenetic relationship between the two species, the differences being due to the differences in habitat. Conversely, however, one can detect a few behavioural similarities between the Peruvian and a much more distant sulid, the gannet, which may have resulted from the similar nesting habits (dense and preferably on cliffs) of the two species. Traits which the Peruvian shares with the gannet, and not with the blue-foot, are thus of special significance in establishing convergence:

1. Overt fighting is common in the gannet and Peruvian booby, but not in the blue-foot. This is because the gannet must compete for a limited number of socially adequate sites and the Peruvian for a limited number of physical sites. This is a fundamental difference, but, nevertheless, the competition which is involved necessarily leads to more, and more extreme, aggression in these two species than in all other sulids, in which neither restriction applies.
2. As a corollary of (1) and also a direct result of crowding and the associated need for close-range spacing-out behaviour, both gannets and Peruvian boobies, but not the blue-foot, have evolved ritualised threat-gaping (Menacing).
3. In gannets and Peruvian boobies, the behaviour of the pair upon meeting is necessarily close-range. Both species have ritualised contact greeting ceremonies, though that of the gannet has become more complicated and polished than that of the Peruvian booby. Blue-foot mates tend to interact at a distance rather than by actual contact.
4. Both gannets and Peruvian boobies have evolved nest-cementing, probably as a result of somewhat different selection pressures though the basic need to anchor material to an unsafe site is often common to both.
5. Gannets and Peruvian boobies, but not the blue-foot, have evolved reciprocal allo-preening. Like (3) this may be a response to enforced, close proximity of aggressive partners, allo-preening being a modified expression of hostility rather than functional grooming.
6. Gannet and Peruvian booby young beg passively, those of the blue-foot frenziedly. This may be (in the case of the gannet it certainly is) to reduce the risk of falling, but other factors may be involved. Blue-foot young are far more likely to be starving than are those of the other two.
7. Copulation seems less cliff adapted in Peruvian boobies than in gannets; the latter squat, whereas the former may stand, as do blue-foots. Copulations take over twice as long in gannets and males are heavier than females, which may mitigate against standing. But male gannets bite their mates during copulation whereas boobies do not and (though this is speculation) I believe that it has been critically important in gannets to link male biting with sexual behaviour so that females can 'accept' it (males that are 'allowed' by natural selection to bite females are probably more adequate (aggressive) territorially than if their biting in the sexual context had been inhibited). If this is so,

lengthy copulations with biting could be thus indirectly favoured, which in turn could mean squatting rather than standing. The same line of argument does not apply to the Peruvian for the simple reason that males are not nearly so aggressive to females (and one may add, not so aggressive territorially).

One may conclude that some convergent evolution has occurred and that both Peruvian boobies and gannets show behaviour, effective in close-range spacing and adaptive on cliff ledges, which is absent in the blue-foot.

SUMMARY

1. The piquero nests in huge, dense colonies, primarily on cliffs. These factors are important determinants of its behaviour.

2. Territory is established, by the male, after aerial reconnaissance, by repeated flights from and returns to the chosen site, landing each time with loud calling and a ritualised throwing up of feet (the Salute) which display continues to be shown in the early stages of breeding.

3. The site may be contested by actual fighting. Other agonistic behaviour patterns are Wing Flailing, Jabbing, Menacing and Yes-Headshaking—a ritualised site ownership display. All are performed by both sexes.

4. The site is attended punctiliously for three or more weeks prior to egg laying. Absences are relatively brief (a few hours).

5. Pair formation occurs after the male has advertised by a special display (Sky-pointing) which attracts a female (the display, however, continues to occur after pair formation has taken place, when it may be mutual as well as merely from male to female).

6. A whole range of ritualised activities occur in the period before egg laying and are doubtless effective in cementing the pair relationship. They include ritualised walking (Parading), often in a special posture (Bill-up-face-away and Pelican Posture), Mutual Jabbing (a low intensity form of which is called Bill-touching), mutual preening, joint nest building activities, including ritualised presentation of nest material. Another ritualised behaviour pattern associated with pair interactions is Wing Rattle (signalling impending flight and also used in nest relief).

7. Copulation is performed with the female sitting or standing. Behaviour patterns associated with it are described.

8. Incubation stints average about 6 hours. Change-over takes a variable length of time and commonly involves various interactions between the pair rather than a rapid interactionless encounter.

9. Some aspects of the relationship between parent and young are described.

10. The young behave amicably towards each other, presumably because food is usually plentiful.

11. There is slight mystery about the exact fledging procedure, for it seems that many young leave the nest before they are competent fliers. How, then, do they regain their nest to be fed?

12. The stance, movement, flight and body maintenance behaviour of the piquero is described.

13. Fishing behaviour is discussed.

14. Behavioural convergence between the piquero and the gannet is detailed.

8

Sula sula

RED-FOOTED BOOBY

1. NOMENCLATURE; EXTERNAL FEATURES; MORPHOLOGY; MOULT AND VOICE

NOMENCLATURE

1. *Common*

Red-footed booby; red-faced booby; red-legged gannet; white booby; white-tailed booby; tree booby; Webster's booby; Webster's red-footed booby; lesser gannet; brown booby; Australian red-footed gannet; bush gannet.

Pajaro bobo blanco (Brazil); Bubi blanco; Fou bête (Seychelles); Fou blanc; le petit fou brun; Burong puteh (adults), Burong main-main, Burong bureh, Burong belorek (juveniles), the words signifying patterns of mottling in immature stages (Malaya); Nana (Marshall Islands); Kota (Gilbert Islands); Tra-tra (Mauritius); Taitai or Austin bird (Pitcairns); Kena or Karinga hopetea (Tuamotus).

2. *Scientific*

The several colour morphs, often co-existing and usually imperfectly described, have always sabotaged attempts to place red-footed boobies from various regions in clearly defined subspecies.

The type locality has been assigned to the West Indies (Barbados) by Grant & Mackworth-Praed, a decision which Murphy (1936) supported. Besides the Caribbean, *Sula sula sula* includes birds from the south Atlantic.

Sula sula rubripes is the race found in the Indian Ocean, eastwards into the extreme western Pacific, and *Sula sula websteri* is the eastern Pacific race northwards to the Revillagigedos.

As Murphy long ago remarked, it is absurd to treat the many colour morphs as distinct sub-species. It is equally absurd to describe one of the commonest brown morphs as a distinct species (the white-tailed red-footed booby, alias *Sula nicolli* Grant & Mackworth-Praed 1933) since this form sometimes occurs on the same island as and interbreeds with other forms. Also, the form to which they assign specific status has intermediates which would make it necessary to treat merely the white tail as the diagnostic feature, thus excluding the all-brown morphs (which exist solely in the Galapagos and on Cocos Island). In this case, either the brown morph would then be assigned to the other red-foot species, along with the all-white morphs, etc. or it would constitute a third species. In either case, the lack of white on the tail would be the only justification for specific status, regardless of other (huge) plumage differences and of interbreeding. Murphy was undoubtedly right to reject *Sula nicolli*!

The basic problem is that selectively unpenalised polymorphism has, for some obscure reason, spread throughout a single, perfectly good species, largely (but by no means entirely) divorced from regional influences. Even recognition of the three sub-species listed above means that a white morph from the Galapagos (*websteri*) and one from the Indian Ocean Christmas Island (*rubripes*) are supposedly distinct, though there is certainly less difference between them than between the form which predominates on say Canton (all white but for a dark back) and the white morph of the same island, both of which on the above scheme would be placed in the same sub-species. Perhaps the phenomenon is theoretically most meaningfully described in purely genetical, rather than taxonomic terms, but since it is necessary to name forms this should be done, as for the white booby, by assigning sub-specific rank to putatively 'isolated' regional populations of considerable size—essentially Indian Ocean, west and central Pacific (*rubripes*), eastern Pacific (*websteri*) and Atlantic (*sula*).

The following scientific names have been used for the red-footed booby.

BINOMIAL

Pelecanus sula,[1] Linnaeus 1776, Syst. Nat. Edit. 12, 1, p. 218 (Barbados).
Sula sula (Linn.).
Pelecanus piscator, Kitlitz, Obser. Zool., in Lutké, Voy. 'Le Se'niavine', 3, 1836, pp. 296, 299, (Lukunor).
Sula piscator, Ogilvie-Grant, Cat. Birds Brit. Mus., 26, 1898, p. 432 (Pelew).
Sula piscatrix, Wiglesworth, Abhandl. und Ber. Zool. Mus. Dresden, no. 6, 1890–91, p. 72 (Pelew, Luganor).
Dysporus piscator, Hartlaub, Proc. Zool. Soc. London, 1867, p. 831 (Pelew); *D. hernandezi*; *D. fiber*.
Sula rubripeda (= rubripes); *S. erythrorhyncha*; *S. brasiliensis*; *S. candida*; *S. hernandezi*; *S. coryi*; *S. websteri*; *S. nicolli*; *S. autumnalis*; *S. cyanops*; *S. fiber*.
Morus piscator.

TRINOMIAL

Sula sula sula, Linnaeus (see above).
Sula sula rubripes, Gould, Synops. Birds Austr. pt. iv, 1838, app. p. 7 (Raine Island, North Queensland).
Sula sula websteri }
Sula piscator websteri } Rothschild 1898a, p. lii (orig. descr.).
Piscatrix sula rubripes, Kuroda, in Momiyama, Birds Micronesia, 1922, p. 34 (Pelew).

GENERAL FEATURES

1. *Introduction*

Recognition of the red-foot is more complicated than for any other booby because there are three major adult plumage types and several intermediates. The term 'morph' is preferable to 'phase' since the latter implies transitoriness and these plumage types are permanent. Much confusion stems from a mistaken belief that the intermediate plumages are immature stages

[1] All Linnaeus's references under his *P. sula* refer to the brown booby *Sula leucogaster* (Grant & Mackworth-Praed 1933).

(a) (b)

(c) (d)

Fig. 281 (a–d). The distinctive flight profile of the red-foot: (a) long wings; (b) long tail; (c) the conspicuous white-tailed brown morph (Caribbean); and (d) the white morph (Aldabra).
Photos: (a) J. Warham; (c) R. Van Halewijn.

and will develop into the white morph. Since, obviously, there are stages in the progressive development from brown juvenile to white adult, it is easy to confuse permanent (adult) intermediates and immature white morphs. Undoubtedly, however, there is a complex genetical basis for the types and ratios of the major morphs and the many intermediates and it is certainly not a question of immaturity. Of course, as in brown skuas, for example, the brown and part-brown morphs are wearing plumage which is phylogenetically more primitive and also occurs first ontogenetically, but has acquired adult phenotypical expression.

So far as we know the colours of the soft parts cover the same range in all morphs, but there are seasonal and sexual differences and maybe regional ones also. These are best expressed in table form (Table 93).

2. *Adult*

The red-foot is the smallest booby (overall length of male roughly 70cm; female 71cm), long-winged (male 374mm; female 380mm) and long-tailed (see Fig. 281c), with a light build and a graceful, more flexible and faster flight than other boobies, tending to skim and shear the waves and often gliding for long distances. Red-footed and white boobies are met with further from land than any other booby.

The white morph, the commonest form throughout the species' range and sole representative in the Indian Ocean, is all white except for the yellow head and neck (sometimes a yellow tinge colours all the white plumage) and blackish primaries, secondaries and some coverts. The Galapagos white morph has a blackish tail. The presence or absence of black secondaries has been suggested (Serventy *et al.* 1971) to vary with locality but in fact all white morphs, everywhere, have dark primaries and secondaries, though the tertials are white. This leaves a white gap between the innermost black secondary and the body, whereas in the white booby black wing feathers extend to the body, in addition to which, the humerals are black. The bill is blue, the facial skin often reddish, the irises dark brown and the legs and feet bright red; all these features provide diagnostic differences from the white booby in a good view. To confuse matters, however, the irises of white morphs are sometimes light coloured or yellowish.

The brown morph is entirely, though often not uniformly, brown; the wings may be darker and the tail and head lighter than the body. Sometimes the head has a warmer tinge, tending to ginger. A lot depends on the degree of bleaching. A completely brown morph predominates in the Galapagos and occurs on Cocos and possibly elsewhere in the eastern Pacific but overall is apparently much rarer than the white-tailed brown morph (see below).

The white and brown morphs are the two extremes, but another well-marked one is brown with the tail, rump and lower back pure white. This form occurs widely (Caribbean and much of the Pacific and probably on Glorioso, Indian Ocean) but not ubiquitously. It is entirely absent from the Galapagos, even though white and brown morphs interbreed there.

In addition, there are three intermediates:

(a) brown, including the tail, but with noticeably paler scapulars, common in the Galapagos.
(b) dark brown back but white head, neck and upper breast and white tail, typical of Canton in the Phoenix Islands but also of much wider occurrence in the central Pacific.
(c) as (b) but with mottled back. It is not absolutely clear that these could not be immature white morphs.

Between them, the three main morphs provide the basis for all the regional variations. Basically these involve the permutations and combinations of more or less pale (even white) scapulars and more or less pale head, neck and underparts, with brown back and wings and white tail. Thus, in the Coral Sea, a form has brown wings and back and white tail but variable amounts of white on scapulars and a variably pale head and underparts, shading to buff with a strong golden tinge. Those individuals with brown head, merely pale or brown scapulars and brownish underparts, are thus very similar to Galapagos birds except for their white tails, whilst those with almost white head and fairly brown scapulars along with the rest of the brown back, are much like Canton birds.

3. *Juveniles and immatures*

Newly-fledged juveniles of all morphs are similar; all are brown with darker primaries, black bills, blackish facial skin, light grey irises (sometimes yellowish or dark brown) and variably dark grey, khaki, orangy or puce feet.

Birds part way towards adult plumage have mottled grey-brown heads, variably grey-brown and white backs and wings and increasingly white underparts. Brown feathers remain longest on the back. The tail is brownish grey. The bill, face and feet move from the dirty shades of the immature through blotched and dull colours to adult hues.

DETAILED DESCRIPTION

This section should be used in conjunction with the previous one, which it supplements.

1. *Adult plumage*

(*a*) *White morph*

The head and neck are variably washed with yellow, which in some parts of its range (e.g. Christmas Island, Indian Ocean) extends also on to the wings, body and tail, the entire bird being creamy, several shades deeper than the dazzling white of the white booby. Almost certainly, different populations of white morphs show different shades of white. The primaries, primary coverts, alula, greater upper wing coverts and outer webs and distal portions of secondaries are blackish brown with variable hoary 'frosting' on outer webs, the bases of the secondaries becoming white.

The under wing coverts are white except for median and greater, which are mostly greyish brown (fuscous) showing as a conspicuous patch. An albino was seen on Cato Island, Coral Sea; its beak and legs were pale pink and irises pale grey (Serventy *et al.* 1971).

(b) Brown morph

This can be uniformly warm brown except for slightly darker primaries and secondaries, but a wide range of subtle shades results from differential fading of different plumage regions. These, allied with genetical variation, give a range of individuals from extremely pale (the 'grey' of some accounts) to a deepish brown. The heads of brown morph breeding females go streaky, as does that of the female gannet.

(c) Other morphs

See General Features, above. More detailed notes are superfluous because of gradations between the types cited.

2. *Bill, feet etc.*

Details are given in Table 93.

3. *Juveniles and immatures*

(a) White morph

The depth of juvenile brown colour probably varies with morph or even area. Christmas Island (Indian Ocean) and Coral Sea juveniles of white morphs are grey-brown, paler on belly and lower breast with, in some, under tail coverts and ventral area white. Tromelin juveniles are chocolate brown. The early, 'dusty' appearance of the plumage later gives way to a shiny brown some weeks after fledging, the head and neck often becoming golden (Diamond 1974). Often, there is a noticeably dark thigh patch.

The bill is black, facial and gular skin and eyelids dark grey blue or purplish, iris grey or grey-green or, on Tromelin, clear yellow, and legs and feet grey, dark khaki or greyish pink, deeper on the webs. Some juveniles apparently have pinkish gular sacs at first and these darken from the edges inwards. At about eight months the plumage is still brown, the bill mid-grey, feet redder and iris browner.

Next, the head becomes mottled grey-brown, stronger on the nape; mantle and rump and some wing coverts grey-brown, in some golden-brown; wing and tail feathers greyish with some white feathers among the secondaries; axillaries grey-brown with pale tips; breast and belly pure white and throat greyish.

This gives way increasingly to adult white morph plumage with brown feathers remaining longest on the back. The mantle and back are streaked or mottled white and pale brown; wing coverts largely white and body feathers white; tail feathers white or pale brownish grey except perhaps the central pair. The thigh feathers may be dark brown.

The bill becomes pale blue, pinkish at the base of the lower mandible and across the forehead, but retains a dark horn tip longest; the facial skin becomes bluer, the inter-ramal skin and eyelids pale blue, the iris putty coloured, yellowish-brown and then brown, perhaps varying with locality, and the feet deep pink to coral red.

The white morph may attain adult plumage before it is fully three. From Woodward's (1972) data, birds ringed as nestlings in June 1966 were still all brown in June 1967 and one banded as 'immature' in May 1966 was still brown a full year later, when probably at least 18 months from hatching. This means that, well into their second year, immature birds can still be very similar to juveniles. On the other hand, a bird ringed as a nestling in June 1966 was partly white a year later, being thus more advanced than the bird just mentioned even though younger.

Most birds around two years old are brown and white; 21 nestlings ringed in 1966 were brown and white when recaught around June 1968. However, variability obviously persists, for two birds ringed as immatures in July 1966 were still brown and white in July 1967 (age unknown but probably between two and three) whilst nine sub-adults in June 1966 were still brown and white in June 1967 when they must have been at least three years old. Birds ringed as immature in June 1964 were white in June 1967 when either three or four and five birds, sub-adults in 1966, were white in 1967 when three. However, two birds ringed when 'immature' in 1963 were still 'sub-adult' in July 1966 (Woodward 1972).

TABLE 93

COLOUR OF BILL, FACE, IRIS AND FEET IN DIFFERENT MORPHS OF THE RED-FOOTED BOOBY

Area	Morph	Feature	Breeding Season		Non-Breeding Season	
			Male	Female	Male	Female
West Indies	White-tailed brown	Bill	Blue grey			
		Face	Greenish blue; orange at base of bill	Pinkish around eyes		
		Gular	Black			
		Iris	Grey			
		Feet	Pale red			
Cocos-Keeling Eastern Indian Ocean	White	Bill	Light blue-green; base greener than in non-breeders		Bluer rather than greener	
		Face	Green with pink flush		Green at base of mandibles; orange-pink line across fore-head	
		Gular	Black		Black, but paler than breeding	Paler than male
		Iris	Dark brown	As male	Dark brown, orbital ring light green and prussian blue	
		Feet	Rich crimson		Rich crimson	
Christmas Island Eastern Indian Ocean	White	Bill	Pale blue, pink basal $\frac{1}{6}$ lower mandible and thin line along longitudinal edge of each ramus of lower mandible			
		Face	Pink on forehead and round gape; blue round eye			
		Gular	Blue-grey with hint of mauve, becoming dull purple, then black. Fades after egg hatches	As male	Blue-grey; skin in angle of gape pinkish	As male

		Iris	Dark brown, orbital ring blue, lower eyelid pink	As male	
		Feet	Red, slightly orange on legs claws grey-blue to pink	As male	
Coral Sea (season and sex not specified)	White and White-tailed brown	Bill	Blue or greenish blue	As male	
		Face	Pink at base of both mandibles, more extensive on lower, where either black or deep blue line at the junction of the feathers extends to gular skin. Around eyes rich blue or purple blue, occasionally paler, with greenish tinge and with dark blue spot in front of eye		
		Gular	Velvet black to grey	As male	
		Iris	Dark brown to blackish	As male	
		Feet	Coral red	As male	
Mainly Pacific but amalgamating Caribbean	White	Bill	Light blue, pinkish at base	As male	
		Face	Pinkish across forehead and round eyes, tending to orange. Green lores	Lores bluer	Less vivid
		Gular	Variable but dark or wholly black	Greyer, centre pinkish	
		Iris	Chestnut, reported yellowish in some central Pacific birds		
		Feet	Red	Red	
Galapagos Eastern Pacific	Brown morph and White morph	Bill	Light blue	As male	Similar to breeding season
		Face	Great variance in depth of colour		
		Gular	Black		
		Iris	Brown		
		Feet	Maroon or purple red or brighter red (age?)		

[a, b, c, d in this column]

[e, f, g, h in this column]

In sum, immature birds moving towards white plumage can be brown or brown and white at one year; brown and white at two years; brown and white or like adults at three years. There is no evidence that they can still retain immature plumage at the age of four or more.

(b) Brown morph

Juveniles of the brown morph are an almost uniform dark brown, the head slightly darker than the throat and upper breast. The feathers of wing coverts and scapulars often have pale edges and the primaries and secondaries are dark, often with a silvery bloom. There is too a conspicuous darkish pectoral line even though the abdomen may or may not be considerably lighter in colour, and there may be a dark patch on the thighs. Later the plumage becomes lighter. The bill and facial skin are black, iris pale or deeper brown, greyish or yellowish, and feet blackish tinged red or, even before fledging, puce coloured. Later, the feet pass through pale orange and purple-red, the skin between the digits most purple. The bill lightens and becomes suffused with purple (as if stained with blackberry juice). The bill tip remains dark longest. The facial skin and orbital ring turns blue and the forehead ridge pink, these changes becoming noticeable as little as two months after fledging.

4. *Distribution of different morphs*

Whilst the proportions of the morphs in areas holding more than one type, are rarely known, a broad picture of morph distribution can be drawn.

Area	Morphs present
Caribbean	White morphs and white-tailed brown morphs; latter apparently greatly predominates (Orquilla, Little Cayman, Giles Islets—Tobago). Van Halewijn gives a ratio of 20:1 (pers. comm.).
Atlantic	
Ascension	White and white-tailed brown morphs.
Fernando Noronha	White and white-tailed brown morphs—latter with belly white also.
West Indian Ocean	
Aldabra & Cosmoledo	White morphs only.
Tromelin	66 per cent white morph; rest white-tailed brown morph with variably pale scapulars, head, neck and underparts.
East Indian Ocean	
North Keeling & Christmas Island	White morphs only.

Fig. 282 (a–h) *on facing page. Photos:* (c), (d), (e), (g) K. Hindwood; (f), F. Staub.

(a) White morph, Indian Ocean (Aldabra). This is the commonest form in the species' range as a whole.
(b) White morph with blackish tail, eastern Pacific (Galapagos).
(c) White-tailed brown morph with darkish head, a widespread morph in the Pacific (except Galapagos), Caribbean and Atlantic, but absent from the Indian Ocean. This specimen was photographed on Lord Howe Island.
(d) and (e) Ventral and dorsal surfaces of white-tailed brown morph with *pale* head and underparts (Lord Howe).
(f) Similar form, western Indian Ocean (Tromelin).
(g) As (e), but with pale scapulars possibly as a result of bleaching (found, too, in some all-brown morphs, Galapagos).
(h) A similarly pale-headed brown morph, but with brown tail (Galapagos). Note thigh patch and short tarsi.

Coral Sea	White and white-tailed brown morphs; latter varying between birds more or less white on head, neck and underparts and ones more golden brown in these areas. Also, some individuals have variably white scapulars and others brown ones. There are no complete brown morphs here.
Western Pacific	Mainly white morphs. In the vast Tuamotu group, most are said to be 'grey' (probably the paler brown of other areas), a few with white tails.
Central Pacific	On Kure, all are white morphs. In the Hawaiian group, almost all are white morphs. In the Line and Phoenix Islands all birds are white morphs. On Canton, perhaps 1 per cent are white; most are white but for variably dark brown backs; none are all brown. Other south-central areas have variably dark birds (Gifford 1913).
Eastern Pacific	
Clipperton	0·3 per cent white, 33 per cent white-tailed brown morphs; rest brown but not certain whether morphs or simply immature.
Cocos	Only brown morphs; white or white-tailed brown very rare.
Galapagos	Brown morphs; some 5 per cent white morphs; many intermediates—largely brown but with variably pale scapulars and variably pale brown head, neck and underparts. *No* white-tailed birds. The proportions of white and brown morphs (see Nelson 1969a) followed, exactly, a Hardy-Weinburg distribution. This theoretically means that both forms were maintaining their proportionate representation within the population, without either of them being at a selective advantage, and that the Galapagos population is not subject to immigrants. How the former could possibly be true is a mystery.
Revillagigedos	White morphs; various combinations of brown and white (unspecified). White morph commonest.

5. *Measurements and weights*

Table 94 gives measurements of red-footed boobies from different areas of their range.

Three important aspects of morphology are absolute measurements, regional variation and sexual dimorphism. From the first, a species' position within the family can be gauged, whilst the second and third shed light on adaptations. The Comparative Section discusses all these (p. 823). Here, it may be remarked that the red-foot is the smallest and lightest sulid. Although a very small male blue-foot or brown booby may be as small as a female red-foot, the latter is smaller, sex for sex. Its proportions differ from those of other sulids (Fig. 364).

Fig. 282 (i)

All brown morph, Galapagos.

It is relatively long-winged and long-tailed (wing-length as a percentage of total length is about 53 per cent and tail-length 30 per cent). This, and its lightness, can be interpreted as an adaptation to a particular feeding niche (p. 826). Regional variation is not extreme (Fig. 373) but the eastern Pacific form (*websteri*) is relatively large. This, too, may be partly an adaptation to an impoverished environment, enabling the female to produce large eggs (p. 685). The Canton (central Pacific) birds seem particularly tiny. Detailed weights and measurements on a global scale would doubtless reveal many adaptive differences in morphology. Sexual dimorphism is not extreme (Fig. 365), largely because the female red-foot is particularly small for a female sulid. Female brown and blue-footed boobies, by contrast, are large whilst the males are small. This, too, is probably a feeding adaptation; both sexes of the red-foot are oceanic foragers whereas brown, and particularly blue-footed, males tend more to a specialised inshore fishing habit.

(*a*)

(*b*)

(*c*)

(*d*)

Fig. 283 (a–d)

(a) Juvenile, western Indian Ocean (Tromelin). Eastern Indian Ocean juveniles are identical to this.
Photo: F. Staub.

(b) Juvenile, eastern Pacific (Galapagos).

(c) Presumed immature (first- or second-year bird) white form, Galapagos.
The areas which are turning white are those which first do so in the gannet.

(d) Sub-adult, white morph, Christmas Island (Indian Ocean).

TABLE 94

MEASUREMENTS OF THE RED-FOOTED BOOBY FROM DIFFERENT AREAS

Area	Overall length		Wing length		Culmen length		Culmen depth		Tarsus		Tail		Weight	
	Male	Female	Male	Female	Male	Female	Male	Female	Male	Female	Male	Female	Male	Female
Caribbean	690–760 9	720–790 7	372·1 362–385 9	389 278–405 7	81·2 76·3–85 9	83·7 80·5–86 7	—	—	33·7 32·7–36·9 9	37·3 35–40·3 7	217 206–231 9	207·4 198–215 7	—	—
Tromelin				370 386		86 87				46 47		200 200		900 900
Cocos-Keeling	705 681–730 15	706 681–754 6	377 356–395 15	379 370–396 6	85 83–90 15	87·3 84·5–94 6	—	—	38 37–41 15	39·5 38·5–40 6	215 183–233 15	205 177–219 6	—	—
Christmas Island	694 685–719 6	707 701–726 3	386 376–390 5	380 373–392 3	85 83–89 6	89 86–91 3	—	—	34 32–35 6	34 34–35 3	201 192–208 5	200 193–207 3	860 810–900 3	950 930–970 2
Indian Ocean	682·5 1	686 1	379 375–383 6	403 387–419 2	83·3 79–86 7	86·2 83, 89·5 2	27·9 27–29 7	28·3 28, 28·5 2	—	—	228 212–243 5	229 213, 245 2	874 810–920 4	950 930–970 2
			376 S.D. 16·4 5		86·9 S.D. 3·0 5								982 S.D. 26·4 5	
Aldabra — Adults														
			380 S.D. 11·8 50		84·7 S.D. 3·0 50								918 S.D. 99·5 50	
— Intermediates														
			382 S.D. 17·2 3		86·6 S.D. 1·7 3								895 S.D. 77·8 2	
— Juvenile														
			376 S.D. 10·1 4		86·1 S.D. 2·4 4								888 S.D. 71·9 2	

Area	Overall length		Wing length		Culmen length		Culmen depth		Tarsus		Tail		Weight	
	Male	Female	Male	Female	Male	Female	Male	Female	Male	Female	Male	Female	Male	Female
Coral Sea													928	1068 1040 928
Line Islands Vostok			378 369–387 4	378 371–388 5	84·3 82·8–86 3	83·9 79·8–88·8 5							803	873 766
Canton			355 344–371 5	—	75·3 72–78·6 5	—								
Galapagos and Revillagigedos	—	—	382 404	384 402	85·6 78–92 18 86 87	90·3 85–95 22 88 92			36 37	38 40	189 221	197 211	938 850–1160 20	1068 850–1210 20
Amalgam—includes some of above	—	—	371·2 355–382	383 370–391	78·8 74–84	83·6 80–86	—	—	35 33–38	36·6 35–38	223·5 205–235	219·4 199–231	—	—

Note: Hyphen shows range, followed (below) by sample size. Adults unless specified otherwise.

MOULT

The following information concerns Galapagos and Aldabra birds caught at the breeding colony, but the moult sequences which occur between the juvenile and the first adult (basic) plumage are likely to be similar to those of the white booby, about which more is known (p. 324).

Primary moult begins with the innermost (number one) probably about five (not later than seven months after fledging (Diamond 1974). Probably the second wave begins when the first reaches primary seven. Immatures on Aldabra had two (not three, as in adults) waves of moult apparent in the wing and so Diamond suggests that immatures may moult at longer intervals than adults (in which the same stage of primary moult recurs every 13–14 months).

The correlation between moult and the stage of the breeding cycle is shown in Table 95.

Although the tendency to pause in moult in the early stages of breeding may seem indistinct, five out of the 15 Galapagos birds with eggs or small chicks were in suspended moult, compared with only three out of 24 in other stages. Similarly the four out of nine Aldabra birds without egg or chick that had paused in moult, and the 12 out of 47 incubating birds that had done likewise, indicate a considerable pause in moult in the early stages of breeding—probably in particular, before laying. In early July, on Tower, there was extremely heavy moulting of flight and body feathers at most of the old (empty) nests and well used perches. Breeding activities were at a low ebb and it seems likely that the moulting birds were either (or both) failed breeders from the highly unsuccessful February/March layings (see p. 708) or successful birds from still earlier, moulting between cycles.

On Christmas Island (Indian Ocean) the indications, from a very small sample examined, were that the pattern was similar, incubating birds being in suspended moult and those with fairly well grown young in moult again. Most wings in moult had either one or two primaries missing or partly grown, but several had three and one four, a situation similar to that in the white booby, the pattern of moult doubtless being much the same in all boobies. An incubating bird captured twice, a month apart, had *begun* moult at three foci (primaries 1 and 2, 4 and 5, and 10) between captures (Diamond 1971). This type of moult, at spaced intervals along the wing, is typical of sulids, and also of some other tropical seabirds such as white terns and tropic birds.

TABLE 95

CORRELATION BETWEEN MOULT AND THE STAGE OF THE BREEDING CYCLE IN THE RED-FOOTED BOOBY IN THE GALAPAGOS (G) AND ON ALDABRA (A)

Stage		Number of primaries growing: None	1	2	3	4	% of sample in moult
Incubating	G.	3	3	3	—	—	66
	A.	12	18	13	4	—	74
Relatively small chick	G.	2	2	2	—	—	66
	A.	NR	NR	NR	—	—	NR
Relatively large chick	G.	1	5	2	—	—	88
	A.*	4	16	14	4	—	89
Failed breeders	G.	1	—	2	4	1	88
	A.	NR	NR	NR	NR	—	
Unknown status but no egg or chick	G.	1	1	4	2	—	88
	A.	4	3	1	1	—	55
Immatures	G.	NR	NR	NR	NR	—	NR
	A.	0	18	5	0	—	100
Totals (birds)		28	66	46	15	—	

* Aldabra data is from Diamond (1971), who does not divide his chick category

VOICE

The red-foot is a noisy booby in the early stages of breeding and on many a hot tropical island the harsh, brassy notes create a quarrelsome atmosphere. The commonest is a sharp, indignant and variably protracted 'karrk', often from a booby molested by frigates. The tone and intensity varies and may be distinctive enough, in birds with full crops, to be used as a cue by frigates. The red-foot often calls at night.

A grating 'karr-uk, karr-uk' is run together in a series of rapid, harsh, metallic notes uttered by birds flying in to land and during territorial display. Commonly, birds (particularly males) call when hopping from place to place within their territories, the sound rising to crescendos and trailing off with each new hop or bout of display. The notes are higher pitched and more metallic in the male, like a cheap wooden rattle revolving slowly. The difference in voice between the sexes is very much less marked than in other boobies (except Abbott's) and the male red-foot has no whistle. There are softer, conversational notes in some pair interactions and sometimes a clattering of the mandibles, primarily used in 'settling' fish.

During copulation the male utters a harsh, drawn-out call and is the only booby to do so. Since it often copulates at night, this call provides a source of auditory stimulation which may contribute to local synchronisation of breeding.

The young beg with a passionate, rapid and repetitive 'chuck' call, rising and falling and sometimes maintained for an hour or more.

2. BREEDING DISTRIBUTION, NUMBERS AND OTHER ASPECTS OF POPULATIONS

INTRODUCTION

The large distributional overlap between white, brown and red-footed boobies has already been emphasised. However, one important factor affecting the red-foot's distribution, and perhaps even its numbers, is its habit of nesting in trees or shrubs. This has enabled it to share islands with its two tropicopolitan congeners when it is conceivable that it would otherwise (as the smallest of the three) have been excluded. Like these others, it has suffered much persecution by man, with the extra dimension of destruction of habitat by him and the goats he introduces. On the other hand, its arboreal habit has often saved it. If, as is probably the case, the red-foot is today the world's most abundant booby, it may be in no small part due to the protection afforded by this habit, particularly against man, but also against alien mammals. The wild swine that wiped out the teeming thousands of white and brown boobies on Clipperton could not have affected a tree nesting population, except by destroying the trees, nor would rats and cats be as effective against a tree nester.

This survey follows the same lines as the sections on the distribution of the white and brown boobies. Although the ranges of the various colour morphs are discussed in another section (p. 661) a mention of the morph(s) typical of each population is included here.

Perhaps surprisingly, the largest of the red-foot's colonies is bigger than any formed by the brown or white and its mean colony size (if such a figure is meaningful) is probably larger too. This may be partly related to its far-foraging habit, which opens up a vast feeding area for a colony, but such an 'explanation' is not wholly convincing (p. 861).

A notable feature of the red-foot's distribution is its close correspondence with a frigate bird, usually the great frigate. Since the latter is in no way beneficial to the booby, but the reverse, the association is to be explained by the frigate following the booby.

BREEDING AREAS

1. *Caribbean and Atlantic*

The red-foot of the Caribbean and Atlantic is *Sula sula sula* and breeding birds occur in two colour forms, the white and the brown-with-white-tail. There are no all-brown adults.

There are no red-footed boobies nesting in the Gulf of Mexico. The most northerly Atlantic (Caribbean) station is Half Moon Cay the site of Verner's 1958 study. At that time he estimated some 3500 birds and counted 1389 nests. There used to be thousands on Little Cayman and it still breeds there (C. Bernard Lewis in litt. to Hutchinson 1950) though no estimate of numbers is available. The Swan Islands used to hold a colony on Eastern Island (Lowe 1911) and Murphy (1967) includes it in his map of breeding distribution.

To the south-east lie two famous bird stations, Serrana Bank with (in 1956) an estimated 100 000 seabirds of eight species and to the south of it Roncador Bank. Serrana holds large numbers of red-footed boobies and Roncador Cay was 'covered with boobies' in May–June

1966 (Milliman 1969) and, though not identified, these were presumably brown and red-footed. It may breed, also, on Serranilla Cay. The red-foot breeds, also, on ALBUQUERQUE CAY, to the south-west of Roncador. NAVASSA ISLAND reputedly holds a colony.

On the Puerto Rican island of DESECHEO Wetmore (1918) recorded some 2000 (birds or pairs not stated) and even so it was outnumbered by the brown booby. On the nearby island of MONA the red foot was 'abundant' (Bowdish 1902) but is so no longer and may not breed there at all.

In the **Virgin Islands** it breeds on COCKROACH and SULA CAYS. Following the sweep of the Lesser Antilles, the red-foot breeds in the **Grenadines** on BATTOWIA and DIAMOND ISLANDS, and CARRIACOU 32km north of Grenada used to hold some (Wells 1902) but may not do so now. GILES ISLET off Tobago holds red-footed boobies and formerly they nested on the coasts of Trinidad and Tobago themselves (Belcher & Smooker 1934).

Off Venezuela, the red-foot occurs all along the coast from La Guaira to Trinidad, probably on scores of unrecorded small islands. Van Halewijn provides estimates of at least 1000 pairs on ISLAS LAS AVES and well over 1000 pairs on the ARCHIPEL LOS ROQUES. He recorded several dozens 40km north of ORCHILA, which supports extensive mangrove areas and certainly used to support a red-foot colony. There may be over 1000 pairs on the small islands east of Blanquilla (the most numerous of the three booby species nesting there). On LOS HERMANOS it was the commonest booby in 1908 (Lowe 1911) even though the brown bred there in 'great abundance'. There are small colonies on the smaller of the seven islets comprising LOS TESTIGOS. Van Halewijn never observed it south of an imaginary line connecting Chichiriviche–La Tortuga–Los Testigos–North Trinidad and found it most numerous north of Curaçāo and Los Hermanos to Los Testigos, also north and east of Tobago, around Grenada, Grenadines and east of Trinidad

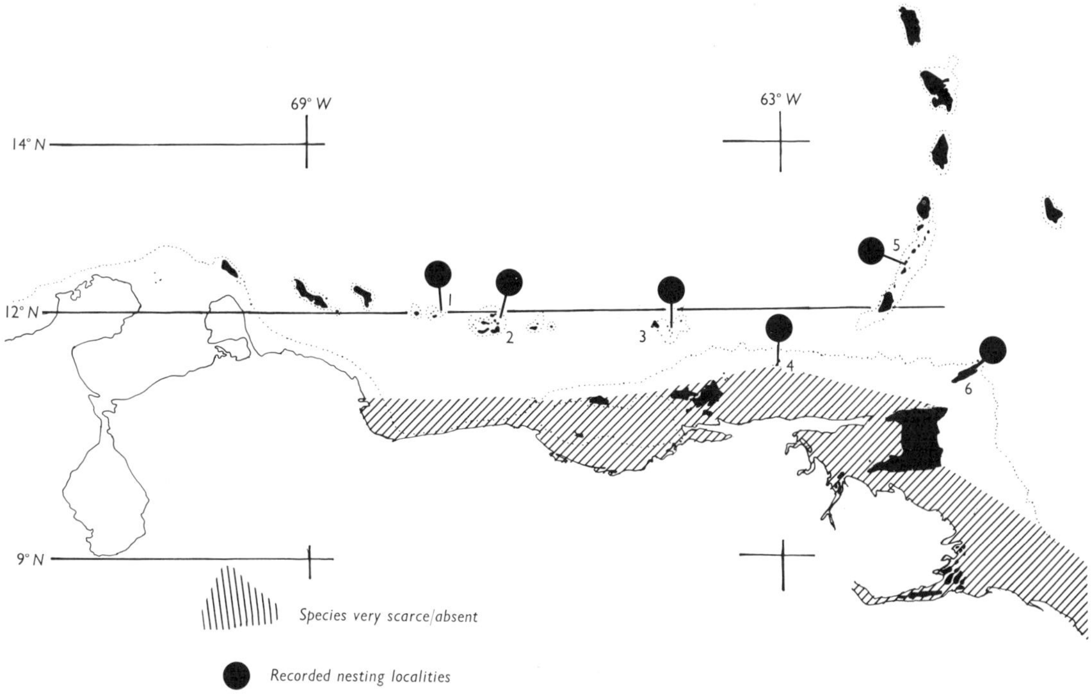

Fig. 284. The breeding distribution of the red-footed booby in the south-east Caribbean (from R. Van Halewijn, pers. comm.).

1. Islas Las Aves.
2. Archipel Los Roques.
3. Between Blanquilla and Los Hermanos.
4. Los Testigos.
5. Grenadines.
6. Tobago.

Fig. 285. The breeding distribution in the Atlantic, the Caribbean, and eastern Pacific.

1. British Honduras (Half Moon Cay).
2. Little Swan.
3. Little Cayman Island.
4. Albuquerque Cay.
5. Roncador Bank, Serrana Bank, Serranilla Bank.
6. Navassa Island.
7. Monito.
8. Islas Las Aves.
9. Archipel Los Roques.
10. Hermanos and Los Testigos.
11. Mona and Desecheo (Puerto Rico).
12. Virgin Islands (Cockroach Cay, Sula Cay).
13. Grenadines.
14. Tobago.
15. La Guaria, Trinidad.
16. Fernando do Noronha.
17. Ascension.
18. South Trinidad (Brazil).
19. Revillagigedos.
20. Cocos Island.
21. Galapagos.

Given the vast size of some of these Caribbean colonies in the past, the large number of islands holding them and the presence of all three cosmopolitan boobies, it is clear that the area is, or was, one of the world's strongholds. It is, of course, a rich fishing area and supports a vast number of other seabirds.

The red-foot breeds on RATA ISLAND of the **Fernando de Noronha** group, along with white and brown boobies. It appears from old accounts that it used to nest, also, on GRAND CONNETABLE.

ASCENSION ISLAND is another tropical Atlantic station where the red-footed booby has declined, in this case perhaps due to the disappearance of trees or shrubs which compelled them to nest on the ground or cliffs, followed by the introduction of rats and cats, the latter being probably responsible for their elimination (and also that of the white boobies). Now the red-foot barely survives. There were some 30 birds resident on BOATSWAIN BIRD ISLAND, nesting and roosting on inaccessible cliffs (Stonehouse 1962) and none on Ascension itself, though it almost certainly bred there in numbers in the past (Ashmole 1963).

Fig. 286. The breeding distribution in the Indian Ocean.

1. Amirantes (North and South Islands).
2. Aldabra Atoll.
3. Assumption Island (?).
4. Astove Island (?).
5. Cosmoledo Atoll (Wizard Island, Menai Island, East North, South, Polyte, Chauve-Souris).
6. Gloriosa.
7. Farquhar Atoll (South Island, Desnoeufs).
8. Agalega Islands.
9. Tromelin Island.
10. Chagos Archipelago (Eagle Island, Ile aux Vache Marine, Tres Frères, Danger Island, Nelson Island).
11. Peros Banhos.
12. Cocos Keeling (North Keeling).
13. Christmas Island.
14. Manoek.
15. Pulau Kakabia.

Another south Atlantic island which has suffered almost total loss of its vegetation within historic times, is South Trinidad, steep-sided and once beautifully vegetated with brazil-wood trees *Caesalpinia* but destroyed, probably by goats liberated last century. Red-foots used to nest here in great numbers, especially on top of the island, around 700m above sea level, and continued to do so on the dead boughs for years after the forest had decayed.

2. *Indian Ocean*

Throughout the entire Indian Ocean (and probably the Pacific) the sub-species is *Sula s. rubripes*. On Aldabra all adults are of the white morph. However, on Tromelin there are white morphs and brown forms with white scapulars and tails. There are no completely brown adults. The situation on the other west Indian Ocean islands is not documented. On Christmas Island all the breeding birds are white morphs.

Early this century large flocks of red-footed boobies were reported from the seas around Socotra and Abd-el-Kuri, but there are no breeding records.

The western Indian Ocean is a considerable stronghold for the red-foot. In the general area of the **Seychelles** it nests or nested in large colonies on the southern, limestone islands. The following list moves from north to south and broadly west to east. On North and South

ISLANDS of the **Amirantes** there were breeding colonies but these, in common with those of other seabirds, have seriously declined in recent years due to egg collecting from Mahé in the Seychelles. The BIRD ISLAND colony must also now be considered defunct (Ridley & Percy 1958).

On **Aldabra Atoll,** Diamond (1974), after a careful survey, estimated about 5000 nests scattered over many sub-colonies and calculated that 6–7000 pairs breed there.

Red-foots used to nest on ASSUMPTION. There are now very few trees left, but four birds were seen in 1967. This used to be a beautiful, wooded island, but the largest guano reserves in the western Indian Ocean proved its undoing and there are now only a few stunted bushes in holes and pits. Nevertheless, the red-foot may still nest (the white booby has also been recorded, but not breeding). As a seabird station Assumption has been ruined.

ASTOVE now has more trees than Assumption and the red-foot may be the only breeding seabird there. There are still areas covered with deciduous scrub, with frequent *Pisonia* trees and dunes covered with *Suriana* on the windward side and *Scaevola* and *Tournefortia* on the leeward. Despite this, Bayne *et al.* (1970) consider that there is no suitable habitat for tree nesters and no red-foots were seen on either of two visits in 1968 (March and September).

On **Cosmoledo** the red-foot nests on WIZARD ISLAND (well over 150 pairs at the south end, in dense low bushes 2–3m high and at least 20 pairs in *Avicennia* on the lagoon shore). In early March the nests were either empty or with eggs, a new season just beginning (Stoddart 1970). On MENAI ISLAND many had half-grown chicks in March, in tall *Rhizophora* on the landward fringe. The red-foot breeds also on EAST NORTH ISLAND, SOUTH ISLAND, POLYTE and CHAUVE-SOURIS. On the latter there was a large colony with many young in October 1965. 200 (chicks?) per year are taken for food (Stoddart 1967). ST. PIERRE formerly had an immense colony, now largely destroyed. There are none on Providence.

In this general area Parker (1970) found the red-foot the commonest booby. It used to breed on GLORIOSA, one of two sandy islands (the other is Ile du Lise) with a grass-covered rock between. However, visits in 1970/71 failed to disclose any and the colony may be extinct. Gloriosa is 3km long with high dunes and used to be covered with forest. It is possible that Abbott's booby once bred there (see p. 757).

On **Farquhar Atoll** the red-foot nests on SOUTH ISLAND (Vesey-Fitzgerald 1941) and many roost, with frigates, in the coconut trees on DESNOEUFS. Further east, the AGALEGA ISLANDS reputedly hold them.

Clearly, before large scale destruction by man, the red-foot must have numbered well over a million birds in this section of the Indian Ocean.

On ST. BRANDON'S (**Cargados Carajos**) around 300 birds nested on ILE ALBATROS in 1956, but these succumbed to cats. Visits in 1964–65 confirmed that there were indeed no longer any red-foots, though the cats had been eliminated (Staub & Gueho 1968). However, birds roost there, probably from Tromelin and may re-colonise.

On RODRIGUEZ there are probably no sulids today (Gill 1967) though these islands were once a notable centre (see p. 759). In the eighteenth century Ile Frégate, in particular, held vast numbers of the white and the white-tailed (and pale-bellied) brown morph (Staub 1973). On TROMELIN ISLAND around 200 pairs nested on *Tournefortia* in 1954. The situation seems somewhat better now, with 300 pairs in August 1968 in a strip 100×5m and 200 pairs along the southern half of the island (Staub 1970). About two-thirds are white morphs and one-third white-tailed brown (Brygoo 1955).

The birds of the **Chagos Archipelago** have recently been reviewed by Bourne (1971). The archipelago is inhabited and consists of five island groups scattered over some 3000 sq. km 'nearly as far from land as it is possible to be in this area'. Red-foots are now much reduced on the inhabited islands and no longer occur on DIEGO GARCIA, the largest. EAGLE ISLAND, ILE AUX VACHE MARINE and TRES FRÈRES, which are now uninhabited, may hold significant colonies again. Since this was written Hirons (pers. comm.) gives estimates, for Sea Cow, North, Middle and South Brothers, of 850, 460, 450 and 50 pairs respectively. DANGER ISLAND, forested on the crown, is also now uninhabited and apparently many seabirds are in evidence around the island, including adult and immature red-foots, so it seems certain that they breed there, perhaps in good numbers. NELSON ISLAND (uninhabited), visited in 1970 and apparently still largely untouched, holds colonies of red-footed and brown boobies, together with noddies, white terns and great frigate birds. Hirons's estimates for these islands are 4200 (Danger) and 300 (Nelson) pairs.

The atoll of **Peros Banhos** (some 30 islands and islets) apparently still contains considerable seabird colonies on the many smaller eastern islands and whilst red-foots are not specifically mentioned they may well occur.

Thus the Chagos group do not follow the geologically similar Maldives and Laccadives in the latter's apparently complete lack of sulids. It is possible, incidentally, that the Chagos Islands may once have been a breeding station of Abbott's booby, for some islands used to support fine timber. It is interesting that Bourne mentions a sighting of two possible Abbott's, at sea (3° 55′S.; 70° 25′ E.) on January 13th 1961, and Hirons *et al.* (1976) claim definite sightings.

In the eastern Indian Ocean the red-foot used to breed in considerable numbers on COCOS at the southern end of the main atoll but its flesh proved too much to the liking of the Malays and once the atoll was settled, the boobies were driven to the island of NORTH KEELING, where in 1941 there were some 3500–4000 pairs breeding in the *Tournefortia*. They occur all round the atoll except along the west side and there are some in *Pisonia* trees on the points called Pulo Latim and Pulo Bill and also among frigates in two big clumps of *Pemphis* (Gibson-Hill 1950a).

To the east, on CHRISTMAS ISLAND, there are a very large number of red-footed boobies. They nest in trees on the shore terrace around much of the island's perimeter (several hundred km) but particularly on the mid-north coast, around North West Point and at South Point. The most conservative estimate put the total population at not less than 5000 pairs and it may possibly be ten times as many. This, however, is doubtful because there are many stretches where red-foots do not occur and the depth of the occupied zone is usually not great. In some areas, for example Lily Beach before persecution by Malays, they used to nest in low scrub.

3. *Seas north of Australia*

The birds of this region are white and white-tailed brown morphs, probably belonging to the race *Sula sula rubripes*.

The distribution of the red-foot in most of these seas is little known and the recent discovery of an enormous colony, estimated at around 10 000 pairs, on MANOEK, a small island in the Banda Sea (Simpson 1970), shows how little is on record. There is a colony on PULAU KAKABIA (Baar's Island) in the Banda Sea, along with brown boobies and frigates, but no details of numbers are available. Palmer lists BANG KORAN, CAVILLA ISLAND and THE PARACELS as breeding islands in the Sulu Sea. I am indebted to Iaian C. Orr for translating a Chinese account (Jing-Xian and Zi-Yu 1975) of the red-footed booby in the Xisha (Paracel) islands. It is one of the commonest seabirds ('thousands') on EAST ISLAND (Hewu or Dong Island) which is covered with *Pisonia grandis* and (on the shores) the usual *Scaevola frutescens* and *Tournefortia argentea*. The birds nest mainly in the *Pisonia*.

On RAINE ISLAND, an ancient colony, Warham (1961) estimated about 300 birds, nesting at a height of less than one metre in *Tribulus* bushes. The red-foot is the least common booby on the island, almost equalling the white, but far behind the brown, which numbers 7000–9000 birds. In the Coral Sea, excluded from the unvegetated cays, it has a more limited distribution than the white or brown boobies.

WILLIS ISLAND often has a few roosting and they have been mentioned as nesting on shrubs about one third of a metre off the ground, but Serventy (1959) found only one bird on the island, in June 1954. Prior to 1960 these were the only two breeding stations of the red-footed booby known in the south west Coral Sea. However, the expedition already mentioned (Hindwood *et. al.* 1963) provided information on ten more colonies in the area. Some of these were substantial. There were well over 1000 pairs on North East Cay of the HERALD GROUP and other 'considerable' breeding colonies were situated on South West Cay (Herald group), SOUTH WEST CORINGA CAY, CHILCOTT ISLAND and MAGDELAINE CAY. The four islets of the DIAMOND CAYS are also breeding stations. It breeds also on WRECK REEF (Bird Islet) and CATO ISLAND (20 pairs) and further south may nest on the West Island of ASHMORE REEF (Serventy *et. al.* 1971). On those islets where *Messerschmidia* trees were growing, the red-foots nested in them, but seldom more than about one metre off the ground. However, on Bird Islet of Wreck Reef and on Cato Island, a total of nine pairs nested on the ground, among vegetation.

4. *Western Pacific*

The red-foot is reputed to breed in the northern **Marianas** (King 1967) and the **Carolines.** Brandt (1962) recorded it breeding on **Truk Atoll.** It is abundant on EAST FAYN and the young are killed in large numbers for food. The breeding colonies are fairly dense—several nests in the same tree, often together with frigates and mostly 5–10m from the ground. In former years, and perhaps now, Brandt suggests, it bred on ALIA ISLET, **Satawan Atoll,** 113km south west of Truk and has been recorded also, at **Lukuna Atoll,** 16km from Satawan and breeding on **Oroluk Atoll** 320km north-east of Truk. Very probably it breeds, too, on many other remote Micronesian islands.

The red-foot breeds in the **Gilbert and Marshall Islands,** but apparently only visits the Ellice Islands (unsubstantiated suggestions of breeding on TAPUKU, KETA and MAKITABA and possibly at BAKATOROTORO in the Gilberts). Excellent information on numbers and distribution in the Marshall and Gilbert Islands has recently been obtained by Amerson (1969).

Taongi Atoll, 3·45 sq. km of dry land, comprising 13 islands, is a red-foot stronghold. In October 1964 SIBYLLA held an estimated 3000 birds, BREJE 1000 and KAMOME 500, whilst in April 1967 the estimated population of SIBYLLA was 2000. These birds nest in *Scaevola* and *Messerschmidia* on all the islands.

Three islands of **Bikar Atoll,** 0·5 sq. km of dry land comprising six low islands, support red-foot colonies. In October 1964 JABWELO and ALMANI each held over 1000 birds and BIKAR some 200, whilst in May 1967 the totals were Jabwelo 500, Almani 300, Bikar 200 and some 20 by the lagoon.

Taka Atoll, is obviously a nesting area but it was evident that many birds had been killed by natives and the red-foot may have been driven from the atoll.

On JEMO ISLAND there were an estimated 1000 red-foots in October 1964 and 2000 in May 1967. On the first of these visits some 200 nests were counted in *Pisonia grandis*, of which there are many fine specimens up to 35m high on the west side of the island.

The red-foot also breeds or may breed on a number of other atolls. In the first category falls **Jaluit** (c. 1500 roosting on LIJERON in November 1964 and five nests with eggs), **Onotoa, Kwajalein, Bikini** and **Mili Atolls,** whilst in the second fall **Tabitevea, Abaiang, Makin, Namu, Ujae, Ailinginae, Rongelap, Eniwetok, Majuro, Erikub** and **Likiep Atolls.**

It breeds on WAKE ISLAND.

It is not known from the **Bismarcks, Solomons, New Hebrides** or **Kermadecs.** From the SANTA CRUZ Islands, east of the Solomons and north of the New Hebrides, Hadley & Parker (1965) saw only brown boobies at sea.

In the **Fiji Archipelago** it breeds, as do the other two tropicopolitan boobies. Fortunately, J. B. Smart and R. K. Templeton have recently made valuable observations in this area, which significantly extend our knowledge. Smart (pers. comm.) summarises its status (up to 1971) as 'one of the commonest, most widely dispersed seabirds throughout the Fiji group with nesting colonies dotted over the whole area on suitable islets'. Nesting islands named by Smart were: VATU IRA, MUMBUALAU off Viti Levu, islet off north-eastern end of VATULELE, YABU ISLAND (Kadavu group) around 100 nests in 1973, islet north of ONO ISLAND off Kadavu, NAMENA ISLAND between Vanua Levu and Koro (large numbers visible from the air), islet off the southern end of NGAU, VANUA MASI to the north-east of Lakemba (by repute only), YANYUA ISLAND at Oni-i-lau (where Templeton found a colony estimated to be between 3000 and 13000, beginning to nest in June 1971). Finally, Templeton records a hearsay colony at VATOA. Brown boobies are, by contrast, rare and Smart has no breeding records, whilst white boobies were not even recorded. Shorthouse (1967) records red-footed, brown and white boobies breeding on Vatu Ira.

It breeds also in the **Samoan Islands** ('several hundreds' on ROSE ATOLL, 1924 and 'enormous numbers of white boobies with young' in 1938), and the **Austral and Society Islands,** but beyond these general statements it is difficult to go.

5. *Central Pacific*

In the central Pacific the red-foot is probably now the commonest booby. Its numbers in the past have obviously been substantially greater but even today many small islands whose populations of other sulids number tens or hundreds support, by contrast, thousands of red-foots. Earlier records usually employ the term 'abundant'.

The adult birds of this region are typically white on head, neck and underparts, with dark wings and back. A few are white morphs. They probably belong to a separate sub-species as yet undefined, or alternatively to *rubripes*.

On Kure, the red-foot nests in moderate numbers, mainly in the higher clumps of *Scaevola*. Kenyon & Rice (1958) estimated 240 nesting pairs, all of the white morph. Nest counts by the Pacific Ocean Biological Survey Programme between 1965 and 1969 were fairly consistent at around 200 pairs, but in 1967 a maximum count of 429 nests gave a 147 per cent increase from 1966 and 74 per cent increase from 1965—the previous maximum count. The causes of the increase were unknown. The maximum number of individuals in the P.O.B.S.P. estimate was 1075 between May and July 1967 (Woodward 1972). On Midway in May 1945, one colony on Eastern Island contained all the birds left after military activities had taken their toll. There were some 200 nests and some 450 birds, including immatures (Fisher & Baldwin 1946) and at this, the red-foot was more successful than the other two boobies, both of which had been eliminated (the brown is reviving slightly now). In March 1957 there were 76 red-foots on nests in the largest discrete group on Eastern Island (Kenyon & Rice 1958).

Laysan had a small colony of old standing. Fisher (1903) reported scattered groups nesting in shrubs on the inner slopes near the lagoon and Dill (1912) mentioned 125 birds (or pairs) in the north-west of the island. Wetmore (1925) said 'one tree supported some'. Now, however, there is a breeding population of some 1200 birds (maximum estimate 1963–68). Considerable numbers of birds from other islands frequently roost here, as they do on most other islands of the chain (Clapp, pers. comm.). Up to 3000 individuals have been recorded.

Lisianski's highest breeding estimate (1963–68), based on a partial nest count during a peak breeding period, was around 1000 birds and the highest population estimate around 3000.

A few red-footed boobies nest on French Frigate Shoals, on East Island (4 or 5 pairs) and on Trig (4 nests in a single heliotrope bush less than a metre high). Earlier, Fisher (1903) called it 'not uncommon'. Pearl and Hermes Reef hold at most just over 100 breeding individuals, mainly on Southeast Island. The islets of this reef present relatively little adequate nesting habitat. Disturbance and associated interference by frigates appear to be having some adverse effect (Clapp, pers. comm.).

On Oahu, there is a fairly large colony on Ulupau Head, Mokapu Peninsula; there were some 500 birds in April and December of 1947 (Richardson & Fisher 1950) and in March 1964 there were at least 500 nests (Ashmole & Ashmole 1967).

There is also a colony on Moku Manu, an island about one kilometre from Ulupau Head, which had about 200 nests in February 1947 (Richardson & Fisher 1950). The nests were chiefly on the high east end of the island and the upper parts of the south slopes. In 1947 some 40 nests were concentrated in a small area at about 0·04 nests/sq. m. It was suggested that the spread to nearby Mokapu Peninsula might have been caused by shortage of nesting bushes but this seems unlikely. Apparently the frigates molest the Moku birds but rarely harry those on the peninsula. There are no red-foots on the nearby island of Manana, which lacks good bushes and is disturbed by man.

Fisher (1951) found them to be abundant in the channel between Kanai and Nihua Island and suspected that they bred on the steep cliffs on the east side of Nihua. He recorded around 3000 individuals on Lehua, a small island off the northern extremity of Nihua; they had by then (August 12th–16th 1947) finished breeding. They were found, 'not uncommon' near the East Horn of Kaula (40km west-south-west of Nihua) by Caum in 1931 and 1932. Earlier, Fisher (1903) found them to be abundant in *Chenopodium* and *Sesbania* on Necker and plentiful on Bird Island (Moku Manu). The P.O.B.S.P. checks (1963–68) recorded a conservative estimate of 1000–1400 individuals (breeding population) on Necker. On Nihoa, the maximum estimates of the breeding population were 3000–3400.

The **Line** and **Phoenix Islands**, with which may be included **Johnston** and **Caroline Atolls,** provide some major red-foot breeding stations. On Western Islet of Sand Island (Johnston Atoll) there is a small colony (about 100 birds) nesting on the girders of collapsed

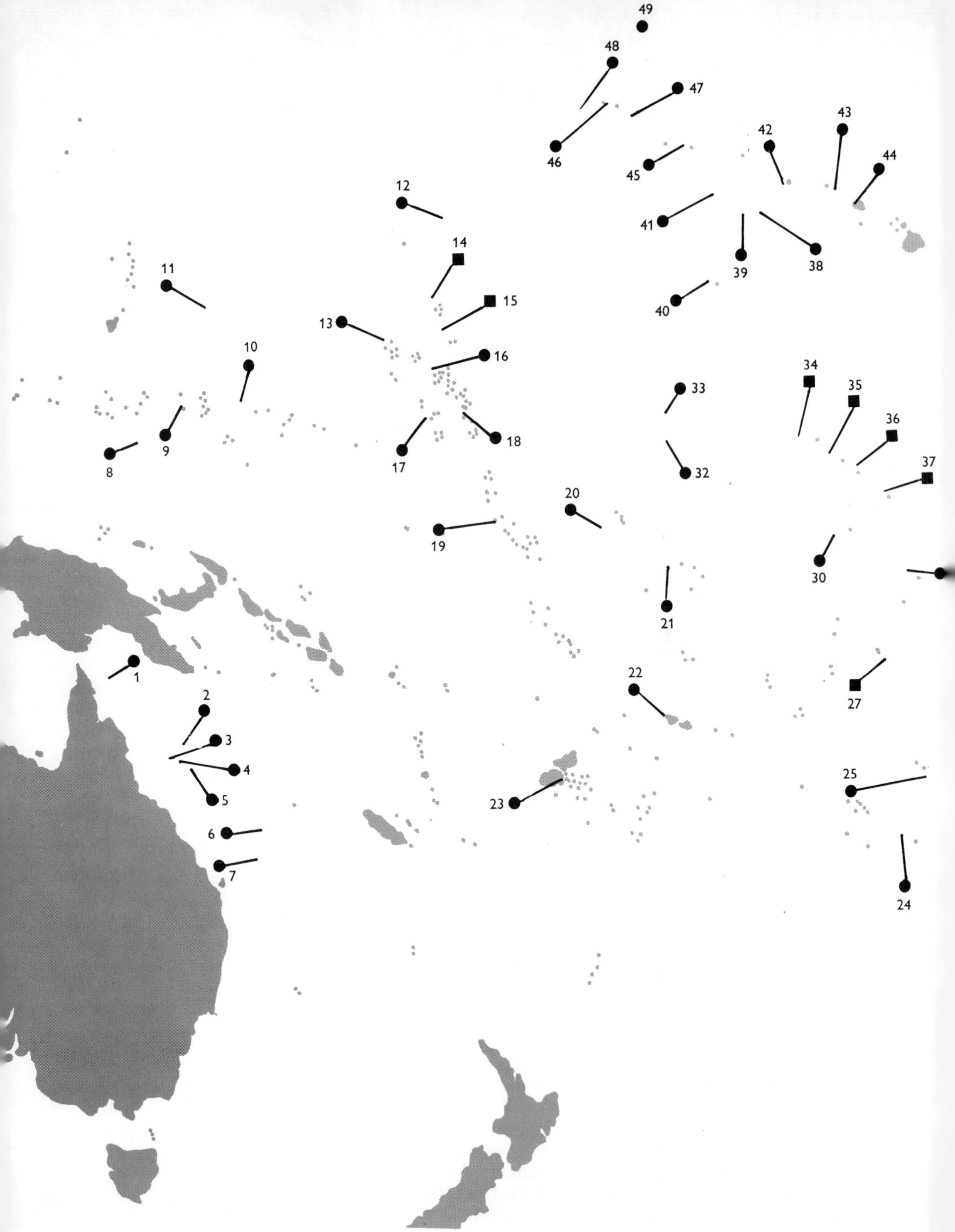

Fig. 287. The breeding distribution in the Pacific.

NOTE: Key to the colonies located on this Fig. is on next page.

radio towers (personnel left the island in October 1956). However, counts of more than 3500 birds, adult and immature, have been made on Sand in February (Harrington, in press) and preliminary information from the P.O.B.S.P. cites a nesting area limited to the highest ridge on the eastern part of Sand Island, with numbers around 300, July–November (most immature) and a sudden increase in December to c. 1600 (adults). But there are few nests.

The islands of Caroline Atoll are an ancient site for red-footed boobies. Clapp & Sibley (1971b) found them nesting on almost all the islands except the South, in a wide variety of plants, and estimated 3000–5000 breeding individuals.

The Line Islands proper are a major central Pacific stronghold of red-footed boobies. FANNING has been a considerable rookery for a long time. Kirby (1925) found it the most abundant bird and Bakus (1967) described it as abundant. There is a colony with a diameter of 400m at GREEN TREES, an island with mature *Pisonia* in which the birds nest as much as 25m above the ground. At Lake Napanaiaroa it nests in *Tournefortia* as low as 5m above the ground. Visits between 1963–68 produced a maximum estimate of 5000 birds and a maximum breeding population of 1200 birds (in March).

On CHRISTMAS ISLAND, where the red-foot has been on record since 1777, it nests in widely scattered colonies primarily in the central lagoon area, where it is interspersed with frigates. Schreiber found that in May–June 1967 there were 2000–3000 red-foot nests, 8000–9000 adults and a few flying juveniles on the island (Schreiber & Ashmole 1970). This means that between 2000 and 5000 adults were not nesting at that time. In November–December there were less than 500 nests and not more than 5000 adults, but 1800–2200 juveniles (and very few sub-adults). Thus the non-nesting adults of May–June had not begun to nest by November. This fact alone strongly suggests that breeding on Christmas Island averages out at less than once per year for many adults, for a proportion of those 2000–5000 adults must have taken at least six months 'rest' (from May or earlier to November or later) and the breeding cycle takes more than six months (p. 712).

Kirby (1925) reported it to be 'abundant' on WASHINGTON and the maximum P.O.B.S.P. estimate (1963–68) was 2000 birds, the breeding population in one December being 500 birds. The population is subject to severe 'hunting' pressure (Clapp, pers. comm.).

The heavily vegetated island of PALMYRA, from which the red-foot was first recorded in 1802, supports the largest population in the south central Pacific. Some 25 000 birds have been estimated as the maximum population and the minimum between 1963 and 1968 was around 8000. JARVIS has a much smaller population, probably because there is little cover and Kirby recorded it nesting on the ground. Between 1963–68 the breeding population has typically been of the order of 300–500 birds, though in some years it may have been much

Key to colonies located on Fig. 287.

1. Raine Island.
2. Willis Island.
3. Herald Group (N.E. Cay, S.W. Cay).
4. Coringa Group (S.W. Islet, Chilcott Island).
5. Diamond Group.
6. Wreck Reef (Bird Islet).
7. Cato Island.
8. Satawan Atoll (S.W. of Truk) and Lukuna Atoll.
9. Truk Atoll.
10. Oroluk Atoll.
11. Marianas.
12. Wake Island.
13. Bikini Atoll (Ralik Chain).
14. Taonga Atoll (Sibylla, Breje, Kamone), Ratak Chain.
15. Bikar Atoll (Jabwelo, Almani, Bikar), Ratak Chain.
16. Kwajalein Atoll (Ratak Chain).
17. Jaluit Atoll (Ralik Chain).
18. Mili Atoll (Ratak Chain).
19. Onotoa Atoll (Ralik Chain).
20. Howland Island.
21. Phoenix (Enderbury, Phoenix, McKean).
22. Samoan Islands.
23. Fiji Archipelago (Vatuira, Mumbualan, Yabu Island, Vatulele, Ono Island, Namema I., Ngau, Vanna Masi, Yanyua I.).
24. Austral Islands.
25. Society Islands.
26. Tuamotu Archipelago (Makarea, Henderson Islands).
27. Vostok.
28. Caroline Atoll.
29. Marquesas.
30. Jarvis.
31. Malden.
32. Taka Atoll.
33. Jemo Island.
34. Palmyra.
35. Washington.
36. Fanning Island.
37. Christmas Island.
38. Nihoa.
39. Necker.
40. Johnston Atoll (Sand Island).
41. French Frigate Shoals.
42. Lehua and Nihua.
43. Moku Manu.
44. Oahu.
45. Laysan.
46. Midway Island.
47. Lisianski.
48. Kure Atoll.
49. Pearl and Hermes Reef.
50. Revillagigedos (Clarion, San Benedicto, Socorro).
51. Clipperton.
52. Cocos Islands.
53. Galapagos (Tower Island, Culpepper, Wenman).
54. Pitcairns (Oeno, Dulcie).

higher (R. Clapp, pers. comm.). The maximum number ever recorded there (not all breeding) was about 2500 birds. MALDEN typically has a breeding population of some 1500–2000 birds and the maximum number recorded was around 5000. Red-foots are apparently mere visitors to STARBUCK.

The well-wooded VOSTOK, in the Southern Line Islands, held an estimated 1000 nests in *Pisonia*, 4–5m high in small trees on the east to some 27m in taller trees on the west (Clapp & Sibley 1971a). The total flying population (age structure unspecified) was estimated at 2000–4000 birds.

In the **Phoenix Islands** the principal population is now on ENDERBURY, with a maximum breeding population of about 1000–1200 birds (1963–68). The red-foot used to be extremely abundant on CANTON. No numbers are given in Murphy *et al.* (1954) but in mid-April they found birds perching and nesting over all large shrubby areas in several parts of the island, particularly at the south-east tip. At a guess there were thousands rather than hundreds, but they have now been exterminated by man. Low level aerial surveys over the island in 1971 and 1973 failed to reveal any nesting groups (Clapp, pers. comm.) and the last known nesting occurred about 1963. In ten years a major and probably ancient colony has been needlessly destroyed. PHOENIX ISLAND itself has a small but variable population (maximum number of breeding birds 102 in 1967) possibly influenced by yearly variations in the amount of the shrub *Sida fallax*. The same applies to MCKEAN (maximum breeding population around 180 birds) but variations are less marked because of alternative nest sites (stone walls). No other islands in this group are now well populated. The highest numbers breeding on GARDNER were around 500 and on HULL a few birds occupy a mere fraction of the available habitat. It now no longer breeds on BAKER or (probably) SYDNEY and possibly never did so on BIRNIE. HOWLAND holds a few pairs (highest number of individuals, about 80 but usually many fewer) among a large colony of lesser frigates; they tend to be markedly unsuccessful (Clapp, pers. comm.).

To the south-east the red-foot—mainly white-tailed brown morphs—breeds in the **Tuamotu Archipelago,** on MAKATEA and HENDERSON ISLANDS and probably elsewhere. The latter is quite a large coral island (9km by 5km) 15–25m high, covered with dense scrub and *Pandanus* (Ogilvie-Grant 1913) and could hold large numbers of red-foots, but no details are known. There was a small colony on KAHONGI ISLAND (Raroia Atoll) in 1952 (Morrison 1954) and probably it breeds, also, on KENA and KORINGA HOPETEA but the birds of the Tuamotus are much persecuted for food.

Red-foots are common in the **Marquesas** (King & Pyle 1957) but details are lacking.

In the **Pitcairns** they breed on OENO and probably also on DUCIE; they are white-tailed brown morphs, the white extending onto the rump, vent and thighs (Williams 1960).

6. *Eastern Pacific*

The great seabird stations of CLIPPERTON and MALPELO are largely unsuitable for red-footed boobies, which thus face an even greater expanse of island-less, tropical Pacific than their two invariable congeners. Nevertheless, there is a colony on Clipperton. In 1958 there were a few to be seen, but not breeding, (Stager 1964) and in 1968 293 individuals were counted (Ehrhardt 1971) mainly brown, with lighter coloured tails and underparts. They were nesting in coconut palms.

The red-foot nests, and for long has nested, abundantly over much of forested COCOS, occupying the steep slopes and ridges around Wafer Bay (and elsewhere) in such numbers that the trees seem dotted with white blossoms (the downy young) (Slud 1967). There is no estimate of numbers, but there are certainly likely to be tens of thousands. All are completely brown morphs.

The other great eastern Pacific red-foot area is the **Galapagos Archipelago** (Fig. 288). There are fewer stations than in the cases of the white and blue-footed boobies, but nevertheless five islands are occupied (CULPEPPER, WENMAN and TOWER in the north and GARDNER-BY-FLOREANA, PUNTA and ISLA PITT in the south). Roca Redonda and Punta Moreno (Albemarle) have recently been cited too, but I cannot find details. This distribution is certainly not accountable for in terms of available islands with trees or bushes, for HOOD is well vegetated and yet unoccupied. It is far more likely that the controlling factor is the temperature of the surrounding seas, which are suitably blue and warm in the north, but 20°F. cooler in the south, where the Humboldt Current exerts a strong effect. Why this does not affect the white booby as much is not clear.

The population on Tower was estimated in 1964 to be around 140 000 pairs. This figure was arrived at by means of five sample counts and appropriate multiplication. The areas counted were chosen at random, but away from the extreme fringes which, as at the head of Darwin Bay, were sometimes unrepresentatively heavily populated. Only nests or evidence of past nests, were counted. Nevertheless, the figure is only a rough approximation and a more thorough survey would be of interest, particularly since, as it now stands, the Tower population is the largest in the world, which I find difficult to believe.

Unfortunately there are no comparable figures for the other occupied islands but the Wenman and Culpepper ones are likely to be very substantial. Altogether, it is likely that the three together hold over a quarter of a million pairs, thus making this species by far the most abundant sulid in the archipelago. Culpepper holds 'great numbers, in places almost every (croton) tree having one or two nests' (Fosberg 1965) whilst on Wenman they were also abundant, nesting in fallen as well as living trees.

It nests in small numbers on LA PLATA ISLAND (Ecuador) along with the masked booby. The morph recorded (Owre, pers. comm.) is all brown, rather pale on head and beneath, exactly like many of the Galapagos birds.

In the **Revillagigedos** red-footed boobies used to nest abundantly in *Euphorbia* thickets on CLARION and on SAN BENEDICTO Hanna (1926) described them as nesting on grass mounds in the absence of trees or shrubs. On SOCORRO they roosted but did not nest. In March 1953 Brattstrom & Howell (1956) found three nesting areas on Clarion, all of them small. There were about 30 birds on the north side of the island and two groups on the lower slopes of the south-east part. The total population was only 150–200 birds. The breeding birds were variably white and brown but white birds greatly predominated. None were recorded from the other islands but in the check list the authors include SAN BENEDICTO as a breeding island, thus making it the only known island upon which four species of sulid nest (red-foot, blue-foot, white and brown).

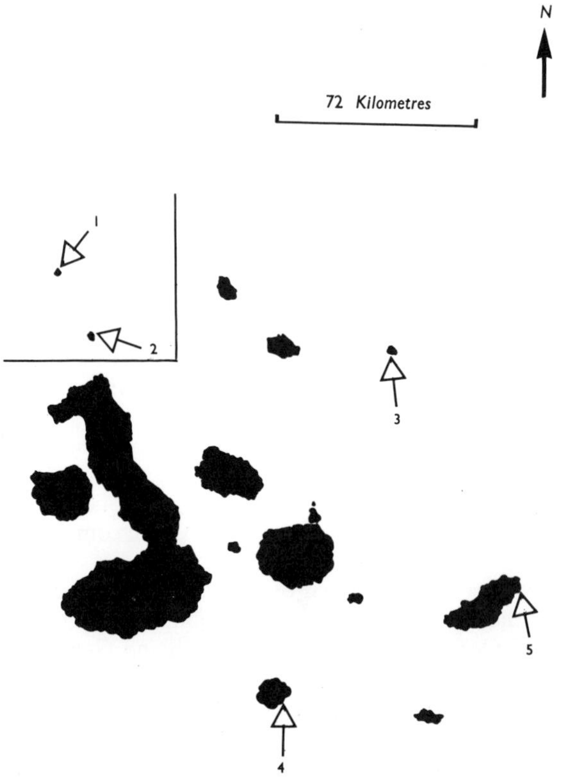

Fig. 288

The breeding distribution of the red-footed booby in the Galapagos. (After Harris 1974.)

1. Culpepper
2. Wenman
3. Tower
4. Gardner-by-Floreana
5. Punta and Isla Pitt (San Cristobal).

3. BREEDING ECOLOGY

INTRODUCTION

Red-footed and white boobies are the most oceanic members of the family. The red-foot breeds in tropical, often impoverished oceans, within which it forages far from the colony, a habit undoubtedly correlated with many features of its breeding biology. Perhaps the most striking of these features is the syndrome of associated adaptations in areas such as the Galapagos, where food is often extremely scarce. As the Peru Current and its anchovies are prime determinants of piquero breeding ecology, so, albeit in stark contrast, relatively poor and widely dispersed food determines much of the red-foot's. Slow growth, low clutch size and relatively infrequent breeding are straightforward adaptations, but vary greatly between populations, for in such a wide-ranging species conditions in different areas vary tremendously.

Observations in the Galapagos and the Indian Ocean Christmas Island (Nelson 1969a), in the Caribbean (Verner 1961), and on Aldabra (Diamond 1971) allow a reasonably widely-based assessment of the species' breeding ecology.

BREEDING HABITAT

Most red-footed booby colonies are on small or very small oceanic islands or on peninsulas of somewhat larger islands (as on Mokapu Peninsula, Oahu, Hawaii). None are on the shores of large land masses.

The red-foot nests almost only in trees or shrubs. These may be low growth at sea level, with their roots in the water, trees on mountain slopes (as on Mount Gallegos, Clarion Island), on the upper parts of islands (as on the south slopes of Moku Manu), on the tops of islands as high as 700m above sea level and two or three km inland as on South Trinidad Island. It may well be that red-foots prefer to nest in trees on shore terraces, as on Christmas Island, but their readiness to use sites quite far from the sea opens up considerably more habitat. They can nest on cliffs; Fisher (1951) records them frequenting steep cliffs on the east side of Nihoa (Hawaii), though they were not actually breeding there, and a very few nest on cliffs on Ascension.

There is an interesting record of red-foots nesting on deserted buildings 'and other rubble' on East Island, French Frigate Shoals (Amerson 1971) and on McKean (Phoenix Islands) it nests on stone walls (Clapp, pers. comm.).

Since even small, low lying islands generally support some vegetation, red-foots are rarely forced to use the ground, though often, as in the Galapagos, they may be much less than half a metre off it. However, on Jarvis, in the Line Islands, several colonies breed on the ground, building nests of twigs up to almost half a metre high and on Willis Island in the south west Coral Sea they build near or on the ground. On San Benedicto of the Revillagigedos they are also ground nesters.

So long as they can find branches they are willing to accept almost any locale—swamp, lagoon, shore, lava-spread, beach or tree lodged in a cliff face. They are similarly catholic in their choice of vegetation (Appendix 40). Mangroves, *Pisonia* and *Tournefortia* may well be the most frequently used trees in the red-foot's range as a whole. The only detailed correlation of nest numbers with tree types is that of Verner (1961) for Half Moon Cay (Table 96).

TABLE 96

TREES UTILISED AS NESTING COVER BY RED-FOOTED BOOBIES, ON HALF MOON CAY, BRITISH HONDURAS (from Verner 1961)

Species	Total nests	Total trees	Average number of nests per tree
Cordia sebestena	783	363	2·16
Bursera simaruba	232	77	3·01
Bumelia retusa	210	130	1·62
Pouteria campechiana	86	45	1·91
Ficus sp.	50	25	2·00
Ximenia americana	22	7	3·14
Pithecellobium keyense	4	2	2·00
Neea choriophylla	2	2	1·00
Total	1389	651	2·12

Fig. 289 (a–c). Red-footed boobies in canopy:

(a) South Point, Christmas Island. Height of nests about 10m.

(b) Nesting with great frigate birds, Tower Island, Galapagos, in scrub c. 1m. high.

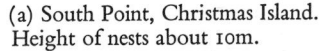

Red-foots usually nest somewhat within the tree or bush, beneath the canopy rather than in the crown and they often choose the centre of vegetated areas rather than the edges. Perhaps 5–10m is the commonest height, but they have been recorded up to 27m in *Pisonia* on Fanning and above 16m in unidentified jungle trees on the Indian Ocean Christmas Island. Low scrub is frequently used, as on Cosmoledo (dense bushes) and Tower Island (dense *Cryptocarpus*) mainly less than 1m high.

The red-foot is often exposed to extremely high temperatures and insolation. Whilst it often breeds beneath the canopy, it is capable of withstanding extreme exposure. On Tower, some of the red-footed boobies in the Darwin Bay colony nested almost fully exposed to the sun in bare, dry trees which remained leafless for 50 weeks each year. The temperature often rose to 100°F. or well above on occasions—a stifling, oven-like heat amongst the tortured basalt.

COLONY DENSITY

An important aspect of any colonial nester is the nature of its spacing in relation to colony size and density. If we take a colony to be the island occupied by breeding red-foots, since they almost always choose islands small enough for any bird on it still to be near the locality of its birth, then a red-foot 'colony' can be very large indeed or merely a few pairs. Large colonies are composed of sub-colonies separated by relatively large distances and each with a density considerably greater than that obtained simply by dividing the total island area by the number of breeding pairs. Even on small islands such as Green Island, Kure Atoll, they breed in groups, leaving large areas unused, rather than scattering widely over the available space. On the other hand on Tower, in the interior, nests were very widely scattered. In any case there is never any shortage of nesting sites, where they occur at all.

Large colonies are rarer than small ones and in many cases may be caused by shortage of habitable islands. Vast areas of tropical blue-water oceans are suitable for the highly pelagic red-foot, but thinly supplied with islands. This is obviously true for the Galapagos and it is probably no coincidence that Tower Island, with an estimated 140 000 pairs (Nelson 1969a) is the largest recorded colony though a thorough check on this estimate is highly desirable. Similarly, the Indian Ocean Christmas Island (5000–10 000 pairs or more) is quite remote and moreover, single. Other large colonies are the Indian Ocean Aldabra (more than 10 000 birds) the Pacific Ocean Christmas Island (2500 ± 15 per cent nests, but 8000–9000 adults) and Palmyra, the largest colony in the central Pacific, with probably more than 20 000 birds. But these large colonies are no denser than small ones, and in fact (as mentioned) are usually composed of many sub-colonies.

Thus a great red-foot colony is not nearly so impressive as one of gannets or piqueros;

(c) Nesting in mangroves, Aldabra, 1–7m above water.

the birds are largely hidden in foliage and there are no great concentrations. My own recollections are of hot sunshine punctuated with the vibrant, brassy calling of an incoming or displaying bird and perhaps a short raucous interchange, but nothing comparable to the sustained roar of a great gannetry. The small groups number tens, scores or perhaps several hundreds; there were some 300 pairs in a strip 100 × 5m on Tromelin Island (Staub 1970). On the other hand, on Half Moon Cay, the entire colony (1400 nests) was concentrated in one small area some 4·38 hectares in extent, though they were not evenly spaced throughout. As Verner remarks, even at this density territories are non-contiguous and most of the breeding area is in fact 'unowned' and undefended, each pair having only a relatively small territory. There are areas within a colony where non-breeders can gather.

Most commonly there are several pairs in one tree, but a pair or two may nest in isolation. In such a situation, average densities merely indicate the order-of-magnitude densities at fairly large and well established red-foot colonies. Expressed as pairs per 1000 sq. m there were 53 in the *Cryptocarpus* bushes on Tower, 40 on the most populated part of the south-east slope of Moku Manu, Hawaii (Richardson & Fisher 1950), 27 in the trees of Half Moon Cay, British Honduras (Verner 1961), and a quite exceptional 600 in a strip of *Tournefortia* on Tromelin Island (Staub 1970). Within such groups, spacing between nests is highly variable. In the *Cryptocarpus* colony just mentioned, of 146 measured inter-nest distances, 21 were less than 1m, 25 between 1–2m, 27 between 2–3m, 69 between 3–4m and 4 between 4–5m. On Little Cayman (Caribbean) nests were mainly 1–2m apart, but some distances were up to 7m. On Tromelin they were around 1m apart, a density comparable to that found in a gannetry but which was probably an average figure comprised of rather irregular inter-nest distances. The record for proximity was a mere 17·5cm, rim to rim, noted by Verner on Half Moon Cay.

Thus the red-foot is not compelled by shortage of nest sites to breed densely, albeit, as a member of a basically highly colonial family, and doubtless because of other advantages, it nevertheless does breed in true colonies, in which the optimal distance between nests is between one and two metres.

It is clearly a great advantage for a pan-tropical species to be free from obligatory ties with a cliff-type nesting habitat, for many islands well situated for an oceanic forager are without cliffs. Whereas white and brown boobies have taken to the ground, the red-foot has exploited trees and bushes. Having done so, adequate specialisation has opened up a wide range of nest sites, free from any possible competition with congenerics. Perhaps this has contributed to the red-foot's notable success as a species.

NEST SITES AND NESTS

Little attention has been paid to the detailed features of nest sites, such as access, aspect, twig topography, etc. Diamond (1971) notes that on Aldabra nests were usually built fairly deeply into the mangrove foliage and in most cases sheltered from the South East Trade Winds. Whilst it is rare for them to use dead trees or branches, it is not unknown if this is all they can get (as used to be the case in South Trinidad). Verner noticed that most nests were placed near the tops of trees (a nearly continuous overhead canopy about 6–15m above ground level) or on their outer edges where the birds could utilise winds or drop from their perches when

Fig. 290. (a) Typical red-foot nest. Here the female is adding a sprig of green material even though the egg has been laid.

(b) An abnormally large nest, Tower Island, Galapagos.

taking flight. Nests were placed on top of criss-crossing networks of small branches or in the angles of wide, flat crotches or on top of nearly level limbs. Nests on Moku Manu had fresh branches a foot or two long on top of a low bush, packed down to form a flat platform.

On Tower, 38 were measured for height above ground level; 5 were 0–15cm; 20, 18–30 cm; 8, 33–48 cm; 2, 48–61 cm; 2, 64–76 cm and only one above 90cm. Verner found the highest nest on Half Moon Cay to be 12m above ground, the lowest 1·8m and the average height of 100 nests 6m. He remarks 'I found no records of higher nests in any part of the world'. Some parts of the Indian Ocean Christmas Island exceed that and Amerson records nests on Jemo Island (central Pacific) in *Pisonia* 25–33m high. Clapp & Sibley (1971b) record nests up to 27m high on the west side of Vostok. But Verner is undoubtedly right when he remarks 'apparently the nest height depends primarily upon the height of available vegetation'. The San Benedicto birds (Revillagigedos) are said to nest on piles of vegetation (mainly grasses) on the ground, 0·3–0·6m high and Jarvis Island birds (as mentioned earlier) construct twig nests 30cm or more high, on the ground, this island lacking trees (though how it acquires twigs is not clear).

The nest is a variable structure of twigs; at its flimsiest, it is a small, frail platform through which an egg could be lost and at its most massive a structure nearly two metres deep with several barrow-loads of twigs incorporated in the base (Fig. 290); doubtless the accretion of years. Usually it is a reasonably solid base, with a shallow or very shallow cup, lined with finer twigs and often incorporating sprays of leafy twigs, or the stems of coarse herbaceous plants. Among species which the red-foot has been known to use are *Cryptocarpus*, *Solarium*, *Ipomoea*, *Scaevola*, *Boerhavia*, Mangroves, *Cordia*, *Tournefortia*, but it uses any vegetation in the area. Whole areas may be stripped of green vegetation, but there seems to be a tendency to restrict gathering to one or two localities.

Verner measured 27 nests; 24 were circular and 3 oval. The former measured between 26 and 42cm (average 30·6) in diameter. The outside depths—top of rim to bottom of compacted portion—measured between 7·5–18cm (average 11·3). These measurements are similar to 10 on Kure Atoll (outer diameter 33·5cm, inner diameter 14·7cm, depth 7·9cm). On Christmas Island, nests measured 30–40cm and on Bird Islet, Coral Sea, 38–45cm and 10–13cm high.

In some locations the nest may persist for several years, but perhaps more normally it disappears. Thus, on Half Moon Cay, three-quarters of 81 nests 'occupied' by juveniles (they usually stood nearby) had been pulled to pieces before the young became independent and any nests remaining would probably disintegrate in the stormy season.

THE EGG AND CLUTCH

1. *Characteristics of the egg*

The egg is variable in shape; elliptical ovate, long or short, but typically elongate and slightly broader at one end (measurements in Table 97). The outer, limy layer is chalky white. The shell beneath the chalky layer is light blue, bluish green or bluish-white, but we saw distinctly pinkish shells; it is about 0·4mm thick, and soon becomes deeply scratched and stained with juices from leaves in the nest.

In relation to the size of the female red-footed booby (which is the lightest of the family) the egg is fairly heavy, particularly in the Galapagos (5·1 per cent of female's weight as against 4·9 per cent on Christmas Island and probably the same on Half Moon Cay; a significant difference). The Line Island eggs, judged by measurements, are also large when compared with Caribbean and Indian Ocean samples. Staub (1970) produces measurements of five eggs from white-morph birds on Tromelin Island which average significantly larger than six eggs from brown-and-white-morphs.[1]

2. *Clutch size*

Together with Abbott's, the red-foot is the only booby which has never been known to produce more than a one-egg clutch. There are several old references to two-egg clutches,

[1] Measurements in mm: Brown-and-white—54 × 37; 52 × 37; 59 × 38; 54 × 37. White—63 × 42; 59 × 38; 63 × 37; 60 × 40; 63 × 39.

TABLE 97

CHARACTERISTICS OF THE EGG OF THE RED-FOOTED BOOBY
FROM DIFFERENT AREAS

Area		Sample size	Length (mm)			Breadth (mm)			Weight (g)		
			Max.	Min.	Mean	Max.	Min.	Mean	Max.	Min.	Mean
Half Moon Cay		100	72·2	53·3	59·4	48·7	36·7	39·8	58·3	35	47·1
Christmas Is., Indian	(i)	6	63	54	59	41·5	36	39	54·0	40	47·3
Ocean	(ii)	10	59	56	—	40	36	—	—	—	—
Tromelin		11	63	52	57·9	42	37	38·2	NR	NR	NR
Laysan		NR	71	60	65★	43	35	42★	NR	NR	NR
Truk Is.		1	NR	NR	64	NR	NR	43·2	NR	NR	NR
Tobago		NR	NR	NR	58	NR	NR	39	NR	NR	NR
Tower		48	NR	NR	NR	NR	NR	NR	66	41	54
Various sources mainly Pacific from Bent (1922)		38	72·2	59	62·7	48·5	40·5	41·4	NR	NR	NR

★ Not actually a mean value but 'the most prevalent size' (Fisher 1903).

but none of these writers gives the slightest supporting evidence and may be safely disregarded. Verner recorded two instances of two-egg clutches on Half Moon Cay, but in each case one egg was obviously very old and the other appeared fresh. All the remainder in his group (515 nests) contained one egg or chick.

3. *Replacement laying*

Red-footed boobies will replace lost eggs. In the Galapagos, about 9 per cent of lost eggs were replaced within 10–40 days (Table 98).

Verner noted replacement laying in the Caribbean 25, 27 and 28 days after egg loss. It is clear from a record by Richardson & Fisher (1950) concerning widespread destruction of nests and eggs by storm on Moku Manu (Hawaii) that replacement on a large scale may fail to take place. Probably, in any locality, only a small proportion will be replaced.

4. *Incubation period*

Incubation begins within minutes or a few hours after laying. On Tower Island, 21 incubation periods measured with variable accuracy were, 43–47 days (1); 44–45 (1); 44–49 (1); 45 (4);

TABLE 98

REPLACEMENT LAYING IN THE RED-FOOTED BOOBY IN THE GALAPAGOS

Month	No. of eggs laid	% lost of total remaining	No. re-laid	No. of days between loss and re-lay	Month in which re-laid
January	53	23	5	10+, 13+, 15+, 16+	January and February
February	58	18	6	14+, 16+, 24★, 25★, 40★	February
March	11	43	0		
April	0	4	0		

★ Known accurately

45–46 (4); 45–47 (2); 46 (1); 46–47 (6); 48–49 (1); the mean value of the periods measured to within 24 hours being 46 days. It is not necessarily to be expected that incubation periods will be the same from all parts of the red-foot's range; in the Caribbean it is 44·5 (42·5–46, 12 cases, Verner 1961) and on the Indian Ocean Christmas Island, 45 days. This fits with the observation that Galapagos eggs are larger and heavier.

5. *Incubation regime*

The egg is incubated in long stints. On Tower, these averaged about 60 hours, with no significant difference between the sexes (Table 99). The female tends to spend up to several days at the nest immediately before the egg is laid and her first spell on the egg is usually shorter than average.

If one assumes that off duty adults are foraging, long absences must be spent looking for and catching food. It then appears that extremely long hunting trips are often forced on the species even when they endanger (and sometimes cause the death of) the chick, especially when the chick is very young and has few reserves. Table 99 shows that seven of the eight longest incubation spells were in the last three weeks of March, which in fact included, in most cases, the final incubation stint. Chick 91 hatched when the female had been incubating for about 24 hours, but the male did not return for a further 120 hours and the chick died around this time. Chick 48 hatched after a very long incubation stint and another long period without nest relief followed; the chick died when about 12 days old. The maladaptiveness of this regime is obvious but it is forced on the red-foot by difficulty in gathering food. In British Honduras incubation shift lengths averaged only 24 hours (Verner 1961), on Aldabra 37 hours (Diamond 1971) and on Christmas Island, Indian Ocean 53 hours (actual figures were males: 48; 24; 54; 72 and 66; average 53 hrs; females: 72; 24; 48; 96; 30; 48; average 53). Again, this is consistent with the supposition that the Galapagos is a more 'difficult' feeding area. In the Caribbean, even the longest shifts were only 36, or occasionally 48 hours. On the

TABLE 99

INCUBATION STATISTICS OF RED-FOOTED BOOBIES ON TOWER ISLAND, GALAPAGOS, IN 1964

Nest no.	Date egg laid	Sex	No. of stints	Maximum stint (hours)	Min. stint (hours)	Total no. of hours incubated	Av.	Dates of longest stints	Length of stint immediately prior to hatching
48	25 Jan.	M.	10	96	24	508	51	5– 9 Mar.	96
		F.	11	96	24	644	59	9–13 Mar.	96
56	22 Jan.	M.	6	80	12	256	43		
		F.	6	80	10	215	36		
89	10 Feb.	M.	9 (7)	128 (96)	19 (24)	555 (332)	62 (47)	14–19 Mar.	48
		F.	9 (7)	109 (100)	27 (24)	568 (299)	63 (50)	9–14 Mar.	65
91	3 Feb.	M.	8	138	24	564	71	11–17 Mar.	138
		F.	9	144	25	609	68	17–23 Mar.	144
97	14 Feb.	M.	10 (5)	96 (96)	24 (54)	533 (366)	53 (73)	26–30 Mar.	96
		F.	10 (5)	199 (96)	24 (24)	547 (336)	55 (67)	21–26 Mar.	119

NOTES: Figures in brackets refer to incubation stints on infertile eggs beyond the expected hatching date i.e. extra to the normal quota. In these cases, the length of stint 'immediately prior to hatching' is that prior to the date on which the egg should have hatched, taking the mean incubation period for the species.

Nest 56 lost its egg before the end of the incubation period.

Overall averages: male 56·2 hours per incubation stint (58·4 excluding next 56). female 57·4 hours (60·7 excluding nest 56).

other hand, on only seven occasions were two exchanges noted at the same nest in one day and five of these were 12 hours apart. Thus, even there, virtually all red-foot foraging trips require at least 12 hours and nearly all require 24.

(a) Month-old chick; Galapagos (development slower than typical for species).

(b) 6-7 weeks; Galapagos.

(c) c. 6 weeks; Raine Island. *Photo:* J. Warham.

(d) c. 12 weeks; Galapagos.

(e) c. 16 weeks; Galapagos.

Fig. 291 (a–e). Stages in the development of the young red-footed booby.

THE CHICK

1. *Morphology and plumage development*

The **newly hatched chick** (about 120mm long) is pinkish, mauve or purplish but may be grey, with darker face and bill which may be almost black. The egg tooth may persist for at least five weeks. Feet and legs are dark grey. The eyes are closed but they can just open during the first day and fully during the second. The irises are light grey or a darker, purplish brown; in some areas they later turn yellowish. The down (pre-plumule) grows fairly quickly and by the 7–10th day the chick is covered with short white down on the dorsal pterylae and the posterior margin of the wing. The down which eventually appears on humeral, caudal and tertial tracts is pre-pennae, the remainder pre-plumulae (Palmer 1962). There are strips of naked skin above and behind the eyes, on the throat, the upper and under surfaces of the wing and around the uropygium. During the third and fourth weeks, the down thickens and lengthens and the chick becomes a fluffy ball. From this stage on, development depends on the availability of food and shows marked regional differences.

The following descriptions apply to birds from Christmas Island (Indian Ocean). Development in the Galapagos is considerably slower. By the end of **week five** the contour feathers have emerged but remain hidden beneath the down, becoming visible about a week later, and the forehead may be beginning to clear. The facial and gular skin has lightened to a pale bluish and the feet are pale grey/green with a hint of orange. By the end of **week six**, primaries, rectrices and scapulars are clearly visible. The secondaries appear during the **seventh week** and by the **eighth** the scapulars have united in the mid-line, and most of the upper back is covered with adult feathers. By **week nine** the tail feathers are over 10cm long, the longest primary about 2cm and the down is thinning over the breast and on parts of the head. Between weeks **nine and eleven**, down is replaced by feathers over breast, upper belly and lower back. By the end of **week 11** in good feeding areas, the wings are virtually clear of down (some may linger among the secondaries) but there may be a thin remnant on the radio-ulna line, but in impoverished areas, birds entering their **13th week** may still retain much down on wing coverts. By the **11th week** the 'pectoral band' may be clearly marked. By the **12th and 13th week**, in good areas, down is left in appreciable amounts only on the back of the head, neck, rump, belly and thighs, though wisps on the head may persist until the **15th week** (100 days). By then, the general plumage is fairly dark brown, primaries and secondaries blackish brown with a hoary bloom and tail dark brown with paler tips and shafts. In the Galapagos, however, at **12 weeks**, the throat was clearing but the forehead was downy and thick down remained on underparts and thighs and even at **16 weeks** birds were not quite clear on back and wings, whilst down remained thick on belly, near axillaries and on thighs. At **20 weeks**, there were variable amounts of down on head and neck, wisps on coverts and sides and (in some) thick on thighs, though advanced individuals may be free-flying and almost clear of down. As before, a combination of plumage characters and culmen length is recommended as the safest method for estimating age.

During development the feet change colour from the greyish or blackish of the first four or five weeks to a khaki, pale orange, tomato or puce colour by 11 weeks (probably depending on morph and region). These darken into red usually during the first year. In some populations the iris remains light greyish or blue for some months but eventually becomes brown (see also Table 93 and, for juvenile and adult plumages, p. 56).

2. *Feeding*

A continuous 48-hour feeding check (Table 100) showed that in the Galapagos each chick was fed on average 0·92 times per day. A series of weighings, four times each day for a fortnight, showed that each chick received 0·9 feeds per day. This implies that adults with young return more frequently than adults with eggs and raises the question of how they can do this if the length of foraging trip is dictated by circumstances outside their control (see Comparative Section p. 950).

Adults return and feed their chicks mainly in the early morning or, particularly, the evening.

During the 48-hour watch, feeds took place at 06.00; 06.20; 15.39; 15.50; 16.04; 16.22; 18.06; 18.31 and 18.50. Other timed feeds fell mainly in the period after 18.30 (27 feeds); 15.30–18.30 (22); 12.30–15.30 (10) and 9.30–12.30 (1). A substantial number of feeds take place during the night, perhaps more than in other boobies, though the red-foot is by no means unique in this.

The weight of food delivered was calculated from the weight increases of the young, based on the three-hourly weighings. Whilst even these figures will inevitably under-estimate the mean weight of feeds, the fact that many were in the late evening, but the young were not weighed until 06.00 hours the next morning, means that the overall mean weight will be substantially below the true figure and that large feeds are disproportionately absent from the figures, having been partly or even largely assimilated. With these provisos, the weights of feeds (in gm) were: 0–50 (2); 51–100 (6); 101–150 (9); 151–200 (10); 201–250 (9); 251–300 (3); 301–350 (1); 451–500 (1). This averages 126g per feed. Probably the true figure is at least 200g, which is about one fifth of the adult's weight—a proportion comparable to that regurgitated by the much heavier gannet.

Verner's observations in British Honduras indicated one feed (i.e. bout of feeding) per day, almost always in the evening (the rate of feeding in his observation group, size not mentioned, was 0·26 per hour between 05.00–07.00, none between 07·00–15.00; 0·78 between 15.00–17.00 and 3·04 per hour between 17.00–1900.

Diamond conducted similar investigations on Aldabra and concluded that chicks were fed at intervals of just less than a day (0·9). He also deduced from weighings that the weight of feeds delivered on Aldabra was significantly less than on Tower. However, two-thirds of Aldabra feeds occurred between 17.00 and 07.30 which, since he weighed his chicks between 17.00 and 17.30, meant that he may well have been weighing, in the main, chicks that had been fed many hours before, (my weighings were more frequent and later). Diamond accommodates this factor by assuming 10 hours' difference between feeding time and weighing time in one-third and allowing a weight loss of eight g an hour (a figure obtained from captive chicks). Even so, his figure for the average weight of a meal is only 144g, which is not significantly more than the absolute minimum for Galapagos birds and is less than the probable true Galapagos figure.

This is an interesting point because on all counts Aldabra birds are less prone to suffer food shortage. A much longer series of figures and more direct estimates would be needed to show whether Aldabra adults do deliver more food per day than Galapagos birds, but it seems that, for much of the time, the latter manage to return as often as their Aldabran counterparts and with as much food, but are more likely to encounter one or more really drastic food shortage during the chick's dependency. This would explain the overall slower growth (see Fig. 292) of Galapagos chicks. The apparent lack of any difference in feeding frequency and meal size is partly because my checks fell during a period when food was not really short around the Galapagos. Close examination of the red-foot's growth characteristics in the two places indicates that, throughout, there is far more variability in the Galapagos birds (slower growth throughout is a different matter because that could have evolved in the long term as an adaptation to periodic shortages).

TABLE 100

THE RATE AND TIME OF FEEDS GIVEN TO RED-FOOTED BOOBY CHICKS IN THE GALAPAGOS

						Av./chick/day
No. of feeds in 14 days	15 [59]	13 [57]	12 [74]	12 [59]	8 [61]	0·9
No. of feeds in 48 hours	2 (3)	2 (3)	2 (3)	2 (2) 2 (2)	1 (1)	0·92
Time of feeds in 48 hours		Before 07.00 hours		07.00–15.00 hours		15.00–19.00 hours
		2		0		9

Figures in parentheses are [ ] age of chicks concerned;
( ) total number of regurgitations in feeds concerned.

3. *Growth*

(*a*) *By weight*

The information on growth in different localities allows interesting comparisons. In the Galapagos, growth between hatching and flying was obtained by weighing and measuring 22 chicks every second day and a representative sample four times a day for two weeks. The generalised growth curve is shown in Fig. 296, detailed scatter of weight in Fig. 293 and four individual growth curves in Fig. 294. The two latter and Fig. 295 show how considerably an individual may fluctuate during growth and also indicate a relationship between the time of year and the peaks or troughs; chicks of various ages tend to do well or poorly together, presumably in accord with relative availability of food. This is an important possibility which can be explored further. One could not even expect a comparison of the growth (by weight) of chicks which differ greatly in age to show clear and concurrent variations related to differences in food (assuming there were such), the intake of small young being only a fraction of that of larger young. However, if it were possible to compare the growth actually achieved, at various ages, with that which *could* have been achieved under optimal conditions, information on any differences in availability of food could be obtained. This can be done simply by comparing the average weight of a number of, say, four-week-old chicks with the optimal weight for that age and doing the same with 6, 8, 10, etc. week-old chicks. This process, carried out over the year, results in a generalised curve of growth related to 'season' for the year in question, there being, of course, no guarantee that it would be similar in other years unless conditions were similar which, in an unpredictably fluctuating environment, would not be the case. Thus, let us say that on a date in March 10 chicks of various ages together weighed 5000g when they could, under good conditions, have weighed 10 000g (as shown by actual weights recorded for such chicks) the growth 'index' for that date would be 50 per cent—or in other words, the gap between 'achieved' and 'possible' weights would be 50 per cent. Fig. 296 shows the results of such a comparison for February to June 1964 and clearly reveals that March, and particularly April, were very much poorer than February or May. Such a demonstration gives useful insight into feeding conditions at sea and provides a sound basis for correlating breeding regime (p. 701) with availability of food in the year in question. Thus, in 1964, the least favourable period of growth, and thus of food availability, coincided with egg-desertion,

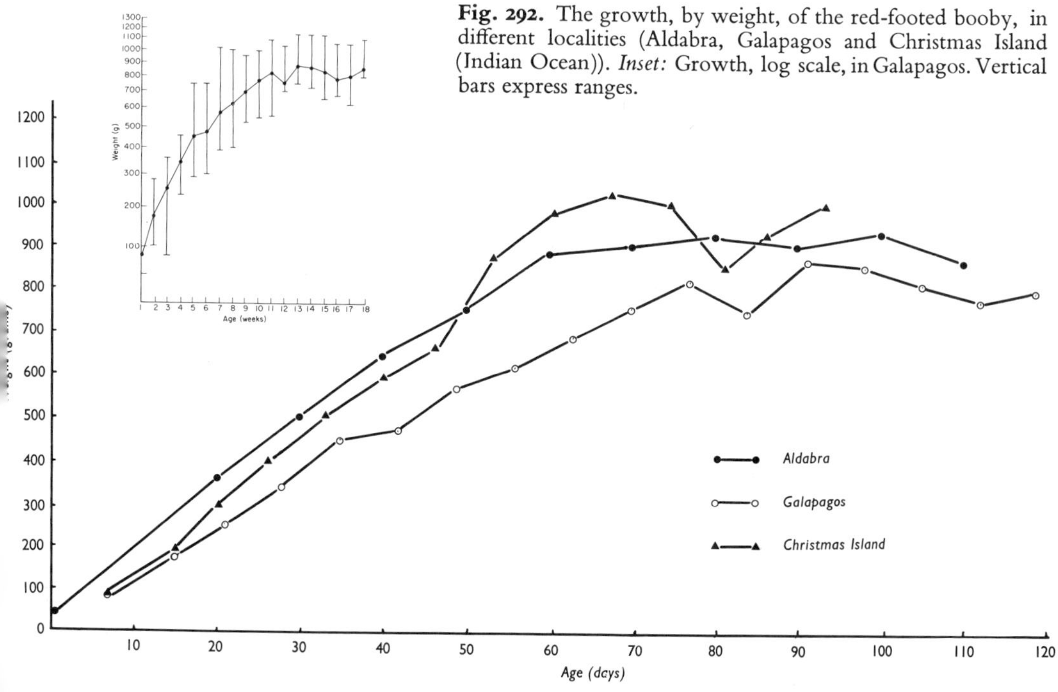

Fig. 292. The growth, by weight, of the red-footed booby, in different localities (Aldabra, Galapagos and Christmas Island (Indian Ocean)). *Inset:* Growth, log scale, in Galapagos. Vertical bars express ranges.

abandoned nesting attempts and death, by starvation, of chicks of various ages. The most favourable periods coincided with the initiation of a new 'wave' of breeding.

In general, therefore, the growth of Galapagos chicks convincingly showed that food shortages could hit breeding pairs at any time; wild fluctuations and slow growth were the hallmarks of Galapagos red-foots. Over the shorter term, growth showed some interesting features which will be discussed in a moment, but first it is instructive to look at the situation elsewhere than in the Galapagos.

Diamond's figures for the growth of Aldabra chicks are the most detailed and Figs. 292 and 295 compare these and Galapagos birds, from which it is clear that the former grow faster and show less variation at comparable ages.

I have interpreted the slow growth and starvations which we found in the Galapagos to mean that food was often scarce, and I believe this conclusion is correct (it is buttressed by a series of observations on other Galapagos seabirds). Diamond has pointed out, however, that there may be factors in addition to shortage of food at sea, which will retard chick growth and (he suggests) may even interrupt nest building and egg laying. Heat stress could be such a factor. Tower gets extremely hot and February–March is the hottest time. Galapagos chicks probably

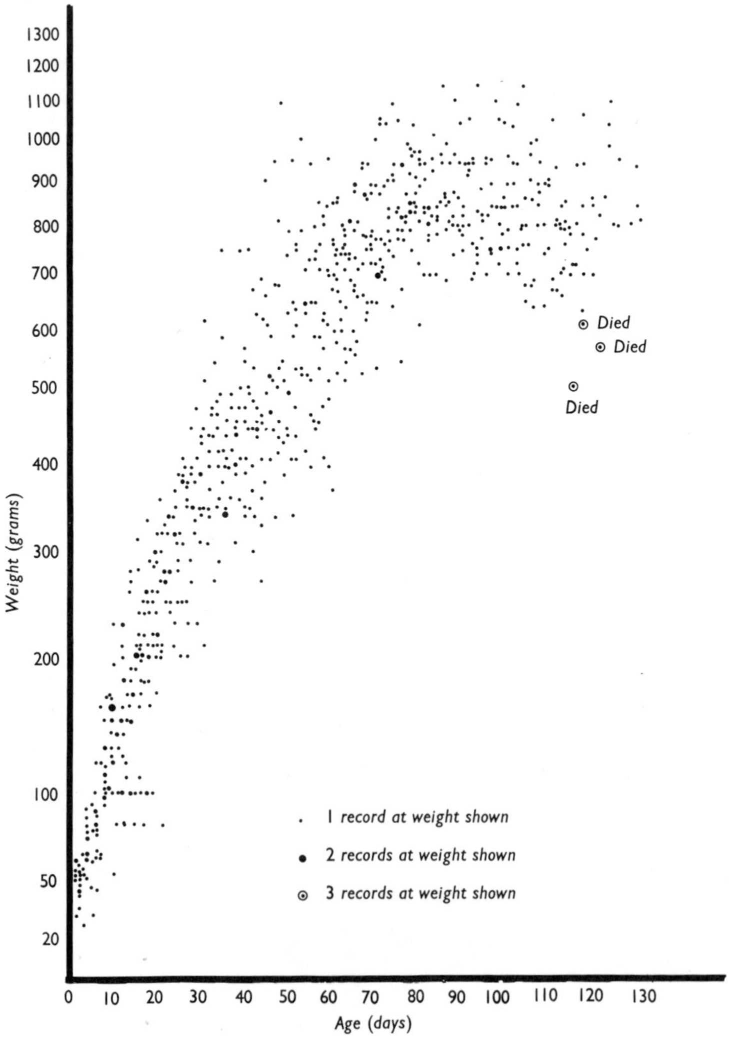

Fig. 293. Detailed weight records for the growth of the red-footed booby on Tower, Galapagos, Jan.–July 1964.

do need to use more energy in maintaining an acceptable body temperature than do those from Aldabra. As Diamond says, the increase of metabolic rate and of evaporative water-loss becomes marked above an ambient temperature of about 32°C. Above 42°C. there is, in some birds, a marked increase in the rate of panting, which may well cost a significant amount of energy. It is thus of interest to note that whereas the temperature of the mangrove breeding areas of Aldabra exceed about 32°C., that of the hotter parts of Tower reached over 42°C. Galapagos chicks adopt special postures to facilitate heat loss by radiation and these have not been recorded from Aldabra chicks. However, it is self evident that the slow growth and starvation recorded above cannot be attributed solely to heat stress. More to the point though, heat stress could be no more than a relatively minor contributory factor in determining the adaptive responses of Galapagos red-foots to their environment, principally to food. The magnitude of the starvation and retarded growth, the sudden resumption of vigorous growth with no concomitant change in ambient temperature, the lack of any consistent correlation of starvation with hottest time of year—all this speaks far more of severe and erratic food shortage than of heat stress.

Returning to the matter of the short-term fluctuations in weight (Fig. 297) it can be seen that each increment in weight is followed by a rapid weight loss. The differences in the pattern of weight loss with period of day are set out in Table 101.

There is some indication that the greatest loss occurred in the morning (which is the hottest three-hour period) but this may be partly due to the slower rate of weight loss with increasing time since the last feed.

Table 102 shows how rapid the assimilation of food can be, with a loss of 200g overnight. The large increases (e.g. 460g) probably result from a feed just prior to the weighing.

Finally, this concentrated series of weighings illustrated in a way which more spaced weighings could not, just how drastically the individual chicks, even within such a small group, changed in weight relative to each other. One chick may do well for a period and then suffer a drastic decline which may take a long time to repair, and can even effect its chances of survival. One, for example, weighed no more at the end of the fortnight that at the beginning (less than 700g) despite having soared to more than 1200g at one stage. This, incidentally, shows how extremely misleading a spot weight check can be if used on its own to estimate age.

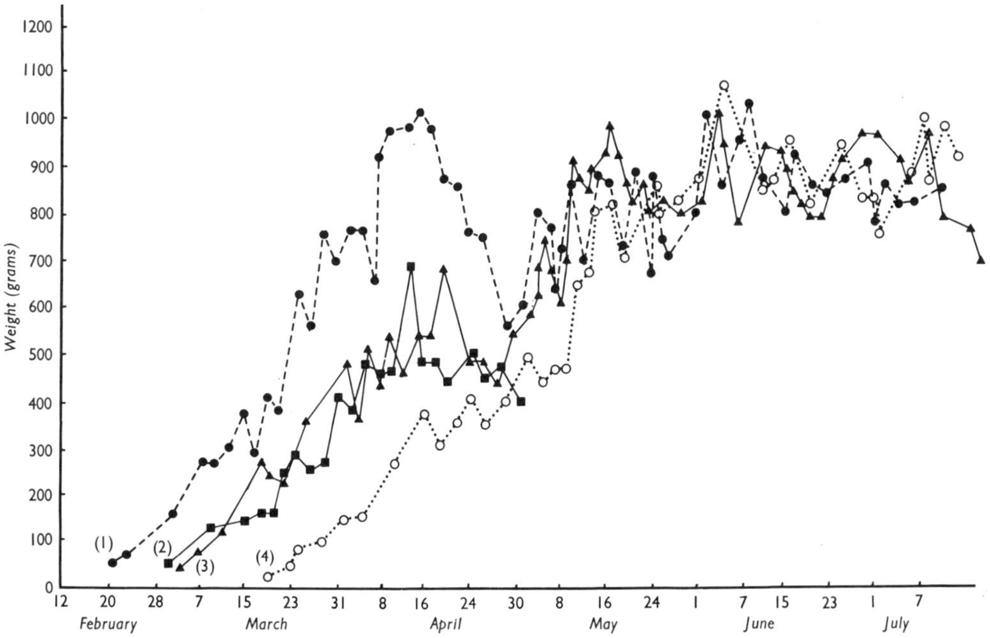

Fig. 294. Four individual growth curves of different ages, arranged according to time of year. Note great fluctuations in all curves. Despite age differences, the four individuals rise and fall approximately in concert.

No. 2 died after 1, 3 and 4 had suffered large weight losses.

TABLE 101

PATTERN OF WEIGHT LOSS IN RED-FOOTED BOOBY CHICKS IN THE GALAPAGOS

Period	Av. weight loss (g.)	Percent of weighings where loss occurred	No. of feeds
09.30–12.30	31	94	1
12.30–15.30	23·2	73	10
15.30–18.30	19·8	41	22

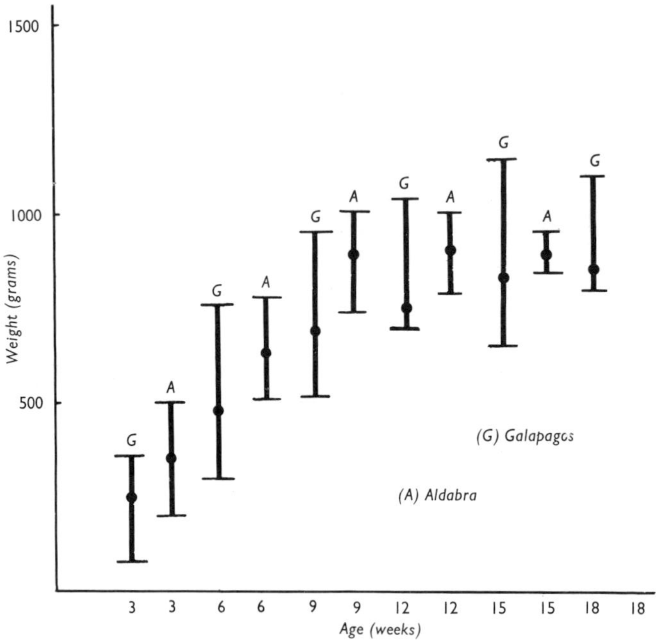

Fig. 295

A comparison of the mean, maximum and minimum weights of red-footed booby chicks from Aldabra and the Galapagos.

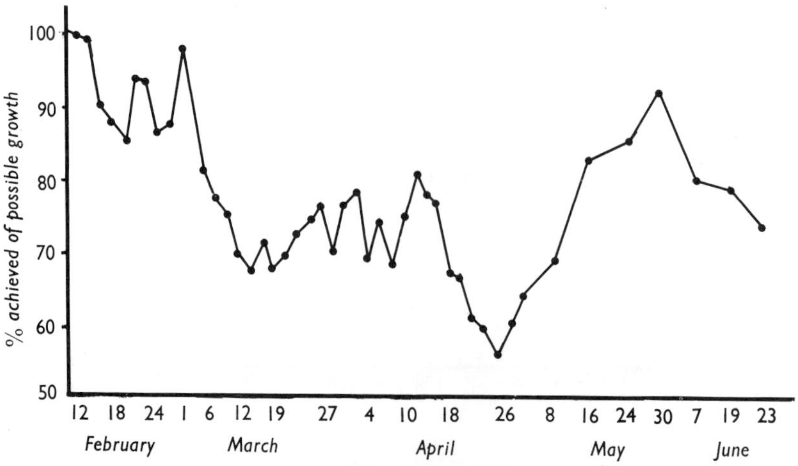

Fig. 296. Generalised growth curve, expressed as growth achieved out of that which was 'possible', thereby indicating the degree of food shortage.

(*b*) *Growth by other measurements*

The main points of interest when comparing the rate at which culmens and wings grow (Figs. 298, 299) are first that they do not follow exactly the same curve as each other, nor as weight, and second that regional differences are less marked than with weight. Culmen growth follows a relatively unimpeded course compared with weight (growth proceeds by utilising stored energy and thus despite weight loss). For the same reason, regional differences are minimised. However, culmens do not reach adult size as soon as do wings. This is probably because adult wing size is necessary for efficient flight whereas adult culmen size is not required immediately upon fledging, since it is probably not critical and in any case fledglings are still fed by parents. Figs. 300, 301 show the correlation between weight and culmen, and weight and wing length. Expressed as a percentage of the adult figure (Fig. 302), the point at which the culmen growth levels out (to be completed later) and weight drops (to be regained later), but wing growth continues, is about 12 to 14 weeks, or just before fledging occurs.

4. *Fledging period and associated aspects*

Young red-foots take an exceptionally long time to grow, even in 'good' areas. This is a specific adaptation to the far-foraging habit. On Aldabra they fledged at about 110 days; on

TABLE 102

THE GREATEST WEIGHT INCREASES (g) AND DECREASES, IN RED-FOOTED BOOBY CHICKS, BETWEEN 18.30 AND 09.30 THE FOLLOWING DAY, DURING TWO WEEKS

Chick age (days)	Greatest increase	Greatest decrease	No. of increases of 150g or more	Average increase
57	190	130	4	90
59	220	90	4	121
59	240	140	6	137
61	280	120	5	140
74	460	200	4	142

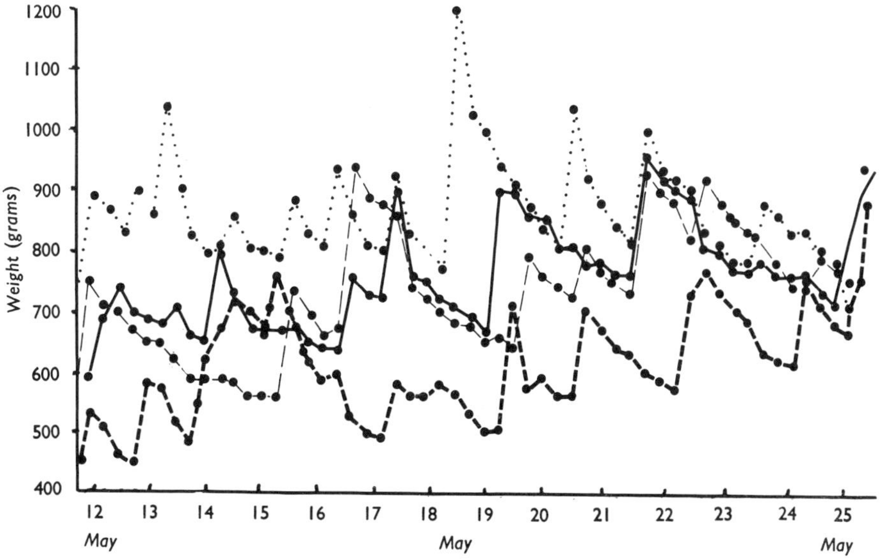

Fig. 297. Weight fluctuations in four young red-footed boobies weighed four times daily for 14 days.

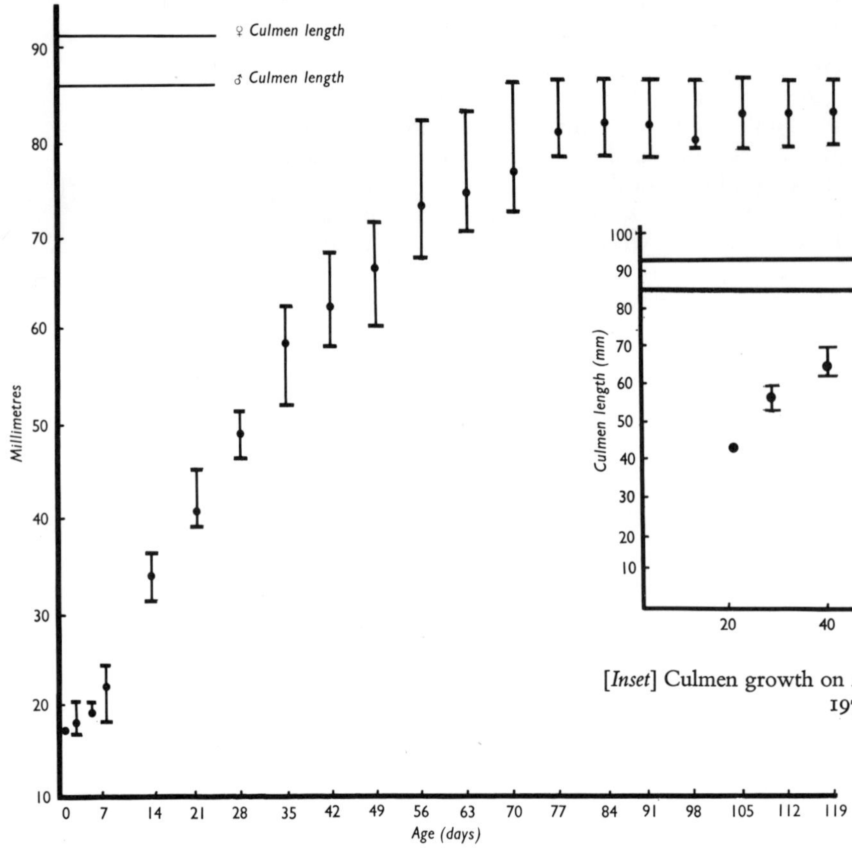

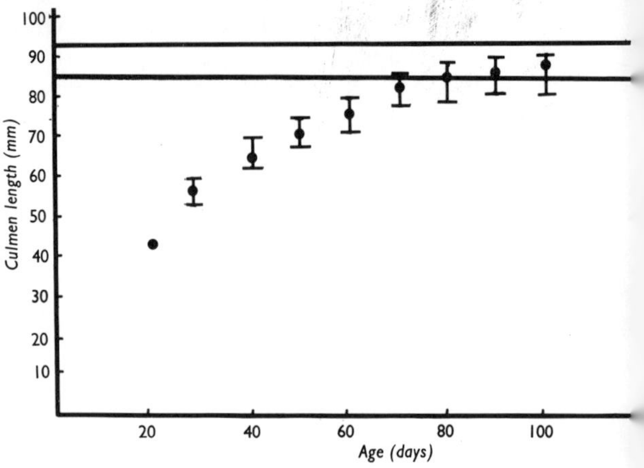

[*Inset*] Culmen growth on Aldabra (data from Diamond 1971).

Fig. 298. The growth of the culmen in the red-footed booby, Galapagos.

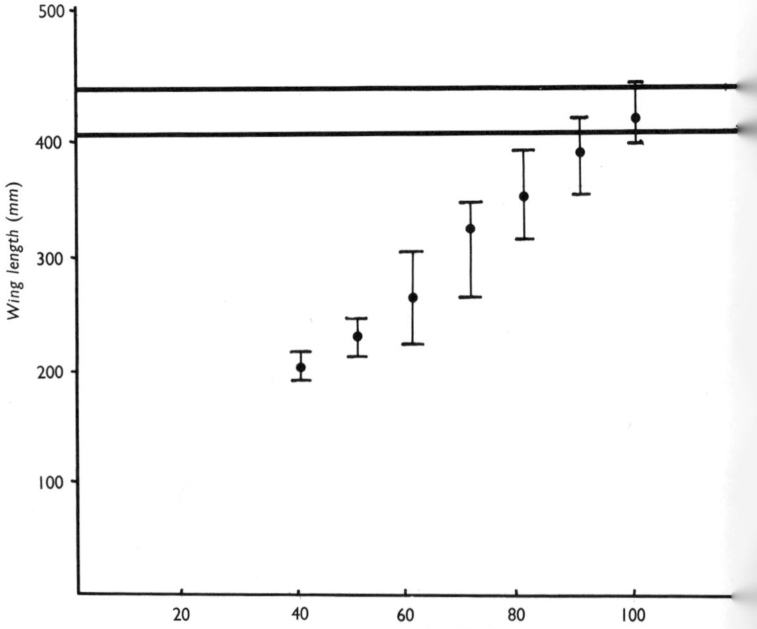

Fig. 299. The growth of the wing, Aldabra (data from Diamond 1971).

Half Moon Cay 91–112 days; on Christmas Island, Indian Ocean 100–110 days and in the Galapagos 139 days or more. Our two most accurately known fledging ages were 135 and 136 days, which is over six weeks longer than the most advanced Caribbean birds. This tremendous difference underlines the contrast between these two areas and the adaptive response of the species. When one compares the Galapagos red-foot's fledging period with that of the blue-foot rearing twins, the difference is convincing evidence of the differentiation that has occurred (see Comparative Section p. 898).

The weight of the red-foot chick when it fledges is considerably less than its maximum weight during growth (Table 103).

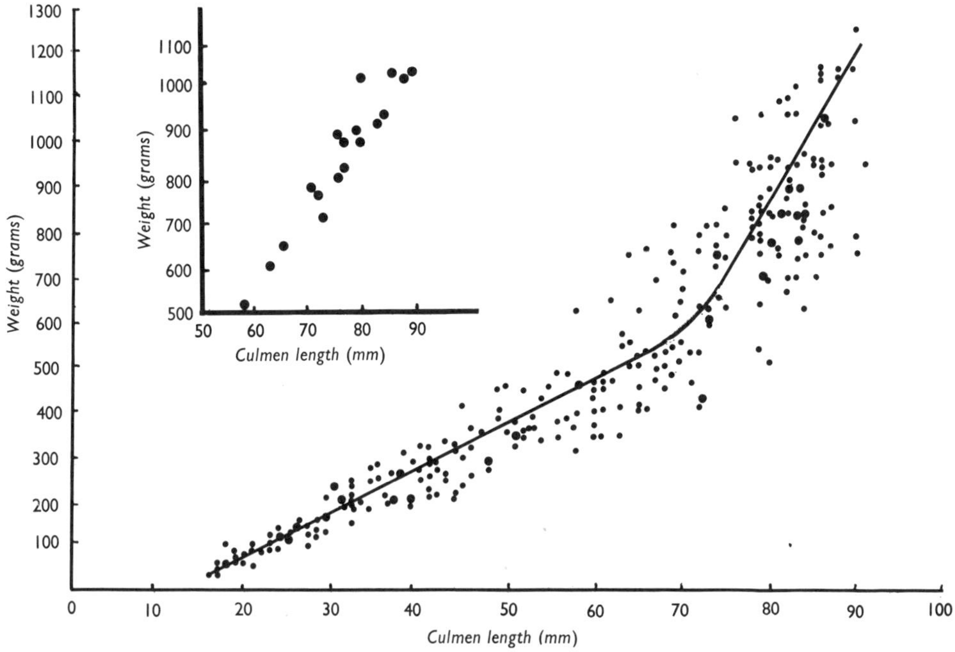

Fig. 300. The correlation between culmen and body weight during growth on Aldabra (data from Diamond 1971).

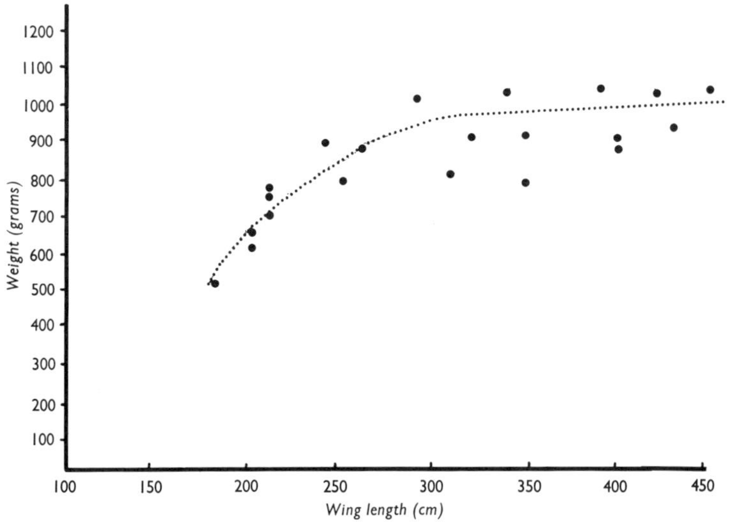

Fig. 301. The correlation between wing length and body weight during growth on Aldabra (data from Diamond 1971).

TABLE 103

FLEDGING PERIODS AND WEIGHTS OF RED-FOOTED BOOBY CHICKS ON TOWER ISLAND

Age at fledging (days)	Fledging weight	Age of maximum weight	Maximum weight
120–139	900		
120–	840		
126–	1000		
135–140	950		
136–146	930		
139–	1100		
140–149	1000		
140–160	900		
143–153	1050		
147–157	750		
133–	900	123	1060
135	780	90	1100
136	920	98	1240
Chicks still not fledged when we left			
112		73	1040
116		89	960
118		75	1090
118		84	1010
118		87	990
120		81	950

Average fledging period 139 days; fledging period taken as time between hatching and making the first sustained flight; not the period between hatching and independence.

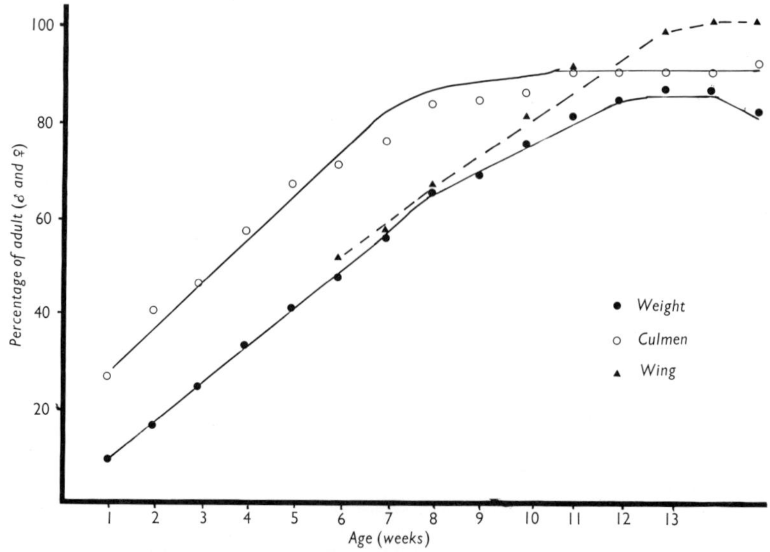

Fig. 302. The growth in weight, culmen and wing, as per cent of adult.

5. *Post-fledging feeding*

Just as a long incubation period often correlates with a long fledging period, so in most of the sulids, the latter goes with long post-fledging feeding. It is difficult to gather accurate information on this, because the frequency of feeds falls off progressively and the figure one gets is always the minimum. However, we obtained records for 11 juveniles, which were fed, as fully flying individuals, for between 78 and 103 days (average 90). Figures from elsewhere are scarce, but Diamond provides the interesting information that no Aldabra juveniles were seen to be fed for more than a month after fledging. This is in full accord with all other observations indicating a situation harsher in the Galapagos than on Aldabra. Vastly extended post-fledging feeding is a very significant indicator.

In British Honduras, Verner found that post-fledging feeding lasted for at least one month. He believed that, on one site a juvenile 'certainly nearly a year old' was being fed, but it seems possible that it was merely an unusually advanced bird from the current breeding.

BREEDING SUCCESS

Breeding success has two important aspects; the specific traits, some species having characteristic patterns of egg or chick loss, and the local pattern, which may vary considerably within a species. The red-foot as a species tends to lose more eggs and small chicks than the gannet, yet the Galapagos red-foot undoubtedly has its own local pattern of egg and chick loss, which probably tends to run true to form most years and differs from that found on Christmas Island, Aldabra or Half Moon Cay. When discussing breeding success, both these aspects are important, the former illuminates adaptive radiation within the family but must not be based so much on one locality that it becomes less than fully representative.

1. *Hatching success*

In British Honduras, Verner found that 90·7 per cent of 86 eggs were fertile, though whether this figure represented the actual hatching success is not clear. On Kure, the hatching success in a sample of 32 nests was 67·9 per cent (Woodward 1972) which is much the same as in other boobies. Diamond says merely that whilst he was on Aldabra loss of eggs (or chicks) was low, which could presumably mean anything from 10–30 per cent but not much more. In the Galapagos, egg loss was high due to the special nature of the environment which encouraged desertion. In the two *Cryptocarpus* colonies on Tower, 109 eggs were laid between January and March 1964 and 13 were already present when we arrived. Of these 122 eggs no less than 70 per cent were lost before hatching. Of these, nine were infertile and almost all the remainder were deserted during periods of food shortage. Thus 15 eggs were simply abandoned and a further 57 were lost, some almost certainly from temporary inattention.

Accidental displacement accounts for a very small amount of egg loss from unusually frail nests, as it does in other species, such as frigates, which build flimsy nests.

Interference from conspecifics was noted on Tower, but it is probably negligible. Some egg loss was caused by frigates looking for nest material. We could not gauge the importance of this, but it could have been of some significance locally—that is where 'nuclei' of frigates' nests occurred close to a group of boobies. Over the island as a whole it was certainly totally insignificant. Diamond makes the interesting suggestion that on Aldabra the red-foots may have been influenced in the timing of breeding by the need to avoid interference by frigates (see p. 711).

2. *Fledging success*

Again, there are considerable differences between localities. Verner was unable to see how many young died on Half Moon Cay, but from the lack of comment it is safe to conclude that, at least for the first three quarters of their period of growth, there was no obtrusive mortality; probably no more than 20 per cent died. Fledging success on Kure averaged around 90 per cent (see Table 104) which is extraordinarily high and is not significantly surpassed by any sulid in any locality. In the Galapagos, by contrast, following the substantial loss of eggs, came heavy mortality of chicks. Of all young that hatched 72 per cent died before fledging; a mortality at least five times as great as that on Half Moon Cay and Aldabra. Twenty three Galapagos chicks were lost at a variety of ages (Table 104). Most deaths were due to straight starvation and some others to inadequate parental care due to excessively long absences, presumably foraging. This did not happen on Kure, Aldabra, Half Moon Cay, and Christmas Island, Indian Ocean.

When these losses were plotted against the generalised curve (see Fig. 296) which is the barometer of the food situation, it is clear that most of them occurred when food was scarce. A detailed analysis of events within the colony at the time of food shortage showed that not only were chicks starving and eggs being abandoned, but also that a large number of pairs that had started displaying and building suddenly abandoned these activities. One must conclude that the poor economic situation directly and indirectly caused egg and chick loss and at the same time led to the termination of newly-initiated breeding attempts.

The predation suffered by young red-foots was mainly from Galapagos short-eared owls. We saw five cases, in all of which the booby had been attacked around the head, as were the blue-footed booby chicks on Hood. There do not appear to be records from elsewhere, of direct predation of young birds, though when a red-foot colony is disurbed by man in at frigate-bird area, eggs and small young may be picked up and dropped by the latter, particularly if they are building at the time. A few deaths were caused by attacks from unemployed white boobies—but these cannot be significant in the wide context.

It has been recorded that bad weather in the form of heavy rain with wind may so waterlog and disturb the nests that they tip sideways, losing eggs or young and that young may die from chilling. This must be a relatively rare phenomenon. Whilst there is no evidence for loss of embryos and chicks through overheating, this must be an ever-present danger in any area where the ambient temperature reaches much over 40°C. No doubt this is one reason why red-foots place their nests within rather than on the canopy, however low this may be.

3. *Overall breeding success*

On Half Moon Cay overall breeding success was probably at least 70 per cent. On Kure it was even higher (Table 105). The Kure information provides an excellent base line, because it spans several years, several groups and, unlike the Galapagos, the area is probably not environmentally too severe. The figures for Kure as a whole are supplemented by figures for 1969 only, of breeding success in three different groups (Table 106).

Apart from their interest in the interspecific comparison, these figures emphasise the intraspecific differences. In the Galapagos in 1964, only 8·4 per cent of eggs laid gave rise to fledged young, whilst on Kure the figure was over 70 per cent. This means that the red-foot's population dynamics in these two types of area, the highly impoverished and the normal, are quite different. Presumably the Galapagos adults live longer or the population is declining or is stable

TABLE 104

AGE AND MANNER OF RED-FOOTED BOOBY CHICK DEATHS IN THE GALAPAGOS

No. of deaths due to	Age in weeks 0–1	1–2	2–4	4–8	8–12	12–20	20+	Total
Starvation	6		3		1	2	1	13
Attacks due to inadequate parental attendance			4	1				5
Unknown		2	1	1				4
Disease			1					1
Totals	6	2	9	2	1	2	1	23

even at that low potential recruitment rate, which implies that the Kure-type population produces excess recruits which presumably emigrate, or that the population is expanding. At the Galapagos success rate, each pair of adults would need to produce over 20 chicks simply to replace themselves, which would take them at least 25 years. Whilst this may be achieved by highly exceptional birds, it is probably not a normal life span. Thus 1964 must have been a particularly bad year; the population could not maintain its numbers with this level of reproduction. Nevertheless, in the Galapagos, reproductive success probably usually is low compared with other populations.

Summarising breeding success, it seems that over much of its range it is similar to that of other boobies—perhaps particularly the white and brown and of the order of three quarters of eggs laid hatch and about the same proportion of chicks survive from hatching to fledging. In certain areas, however (the Galapagos is obviously one) massive loss of eggs and chicks may occur and is probably not uncommon—reducing breeding success to less than 10 per cent. Food shortage is by far the most likely cause of this high failure rate.

BREEDING REGIMES

Among the ways in which a seabird can cope with or take most advantage of its local environment, breeding strategy (timing and duration of breeding) ranks with clutch size as perhaps the

TABLE 105

BREEDING SUCCESS OF THE RED-FOOTED BOOBY ON KURE ATOLL (GREEN ISLAND) 1964–69 (based on Woodward 1972)

Year	Max. nest count or est.	Max. egg count or est.	Max. chick count or est.	Est. of young fledged	% laid that hatched	% hatched that fledged	% laid that fledged
1964	200†	NR	200†	200	NC	NC	NC
1965	241*	189*	200*	200	NC	100	NC
1966	174†	170†	150†	135	89	90	80
1967	429*	395*	324*	300	82	92	76
1968	297*	121†	256*	225	NC	88	NC
1969	390†	350†	250†	NR	71	NR	NR

NOTES: * Count † Estimate NR Nor recorded NC Not calculable

TABLE 106

BREEDING SUCCESS OF THREE DIFFERENT GROUPS OF RED-FOOTED BOOBIES ON KURE ATOLL IN 1969 (from Woodward 1972)

	No. of nests	% hatched of eggs laid	% fledged of eggs hatched
Group 1	27	70·4	NR
Group 2	43	NR	93*
Group 3	26	65·4	NR

* Actually 58·1 per cent were still on the nest but well grown.

major ones. However, it is now clear that not only are there large differences between species, but also within them. One cannot assume that because a species is an annual, seasonal breeder in one area, it is so in all areas. The red-foot is typically an annual breeder, but it is not a highly seasonal one and, of course, its breeding 'seasons', such as they are, vary enormously with locality.

1. *General features of attendance at the colony*

On Aldabra, where there are several peaks of laying in a year, there was no period during which all birds were absent from the island. Some were in roosts and resting areas but others were in the breeding areas even when there was little actual breeding. Thus, during July and August, when very few birds were breeding, the trees in the breeding colony held about half the number of adults present at the height of the breeding season (November to April). Similarly, Verner records that there was some breeding for most of the year on Half Moon Cay and he even suggested that some pairs may maintain their territory throughout the year. Diamond suspects that the birds absent from the Aldabra breeding colony were at sea, rather than in roosts or Clubs elsewhere on the atoll, but they could have been both (see below). In any case, it seems likely that most adult boobies belonging to Aldabra roosted there, at least fairly regularly, throughout the year. Another important point about roosting or resting birds on an island where red-foots breed, is that one cannot use counts of the numbers in roosts as any indication of the numbers engaging in breeding activities or of the population of the island. Thus, on Kure Atoll, Woodward (1972) records that the numbers in the roosts did not ever equal the number of incubating or brooding adults. He states that in fact the roost *did* contain some of the breeding adults—an important point based, presumably, on positive information, though this is not given.

In the Galapagos one could never visit Tower without finding some red-footed boobies, but there were certainly periods during which the island was dead so far as adults were concerned, with nothing but the infrequent visits of parents with chicks to feed. Then, suddenly, there would be a sharp increase in the number of birds attending the colony; territorial and sexual display would become obtrusive and nest-building commence. Such upswings in attendance and activity were undoubtedly part of the response to fluctuating economic circumstances. As such, they were a-seasonal fluctuations with, perhaps, a mild seasonal bias (see below).

So it appears that, as in the white booby, there may well be area differences in the pattern of use of, or attendance at, the breeding colony, some birds returning more often, out of the breeding cycle, than others. This would seem reasonable if the fishing habits vary with locality, some birds foraging much further away (as in the Galapagos) and being 'caught' at sea at nightfall, more often than others (say, Aldabra birds). When established birds that have bred do return, even when not engaged in breeding, they may well go straight to their old territory rather than elsewhere, thus following the pattern suggested by Verner and Diamond. We lack evidence about the status of adult birds which frequent Clubs; these could all be non-breeders, or a proportion could be erstwhile breeders which, perhaps from time to time, go to Clubs rather than always to their old sites. Probably the latter is the case.

2. *Seasonal aspects of breeding*

This section attempts to bring together in diagrammatic form scattered records concerning the months in which red-foots lay in different parts of their range. As a general orienting statement, it may be said that, typically, the red-foot is a very loosely seasonal, annual breeder, but often with an enormous spread of laying, and sometimes with two or more widely separated peaks, and that there are significant regional differences in the timing of breeding. Where records refer merely to 'breeding' I have assumed that laying was meant; without this, interpretation is impossible. In the Paracels it is said (Jing-Xian and Zi-Yu 1975) to have 'three breeding seasons' which together account for the entire year, but the account is totally ambiguous. Apparently, typhoons cause much damage between July and October, smashing nests with eggs and downy young to the ground.

Fig. 303. The timing of breeding in different parts of its range.

KEY:

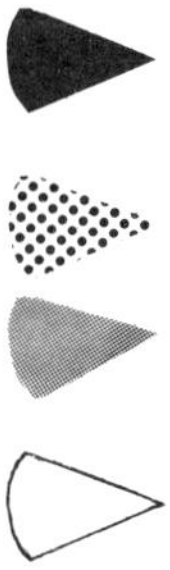

Heaviest laying.

Intermediate amount of laying.

No laying.

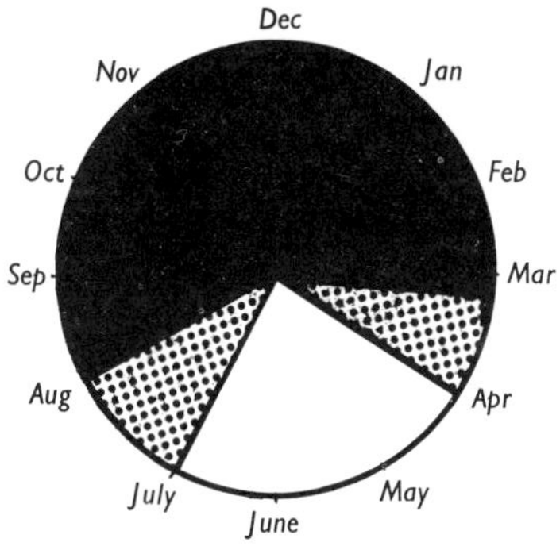

Fig. 303(a)

Caribbean and Atlantic

1. Half Moon Cay	Verner (1961)	Colony active all year. Laying mid-Nov.–mid-Apr. 1957/58.
2. Little Cayman	Nicoll (1904)	Laying in Nov.
3. Los Hermanos	Lowe (1911)	Birds started laying in Sept.
4. St. Giles	Dinsmore & Ffrench (1968)	Laying July to Sept. In Aug. 1968 all nests examined had eggs; laying continued until following March.
5. South Trinidad		All stages of young but no eggs Jan. (1906).

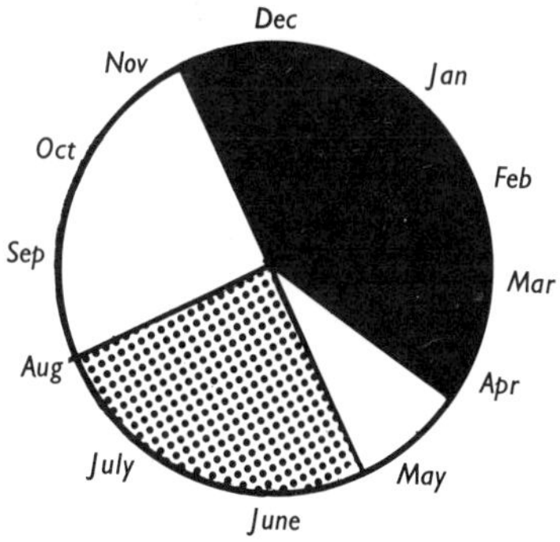

Fig. 303(b)

Western Indian Ocean

KEY: as in Fig. 303(a)

1. Aldabra	Diamond (1971) and pers. obs.	Laying concentrated between Nov. and Apr.
2. Wizard Island	Various sources	Laying Nov.–Apr.
3. Menai Island	Various sources	Laying mid-late Nov.
4. Chauve-Souris	Various sources	Possible June laying.
5. Farquhar Atoll	Various sources	Laying Apr.
6. Tromelin Island	Staub (1970)	Laying at least from May to Aug.
7. Chagos Archipelago	Bourne (1971)	Some evidence for July laying.

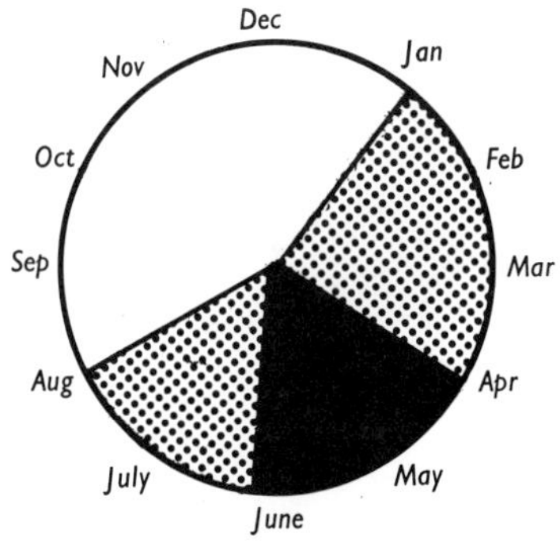

Fig. 303(c)

Eastern Indian Ocean

KEY: as in Fig. 303(a)

1. Cocos Island	Gibson-Hill (1950a)	Laying Jan.–July, mainly between Apr. and June.
2. Christmas Island	Gibson-Hill (1947) Nelson (1972)	Laying mainly between Apr. and June, peak late Apr.–May.

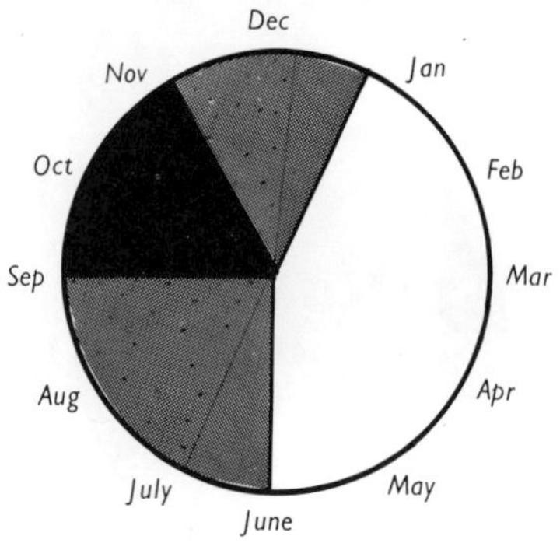

Fig. 303(d)

Seas north of Australia

KEY: as in Fig. 303(a)

1. Coral Sea	Hindwood *et al.* (1963) Serventy *et al.* (1971)	Laying probably June–Jan., main period Sept.–Oct.

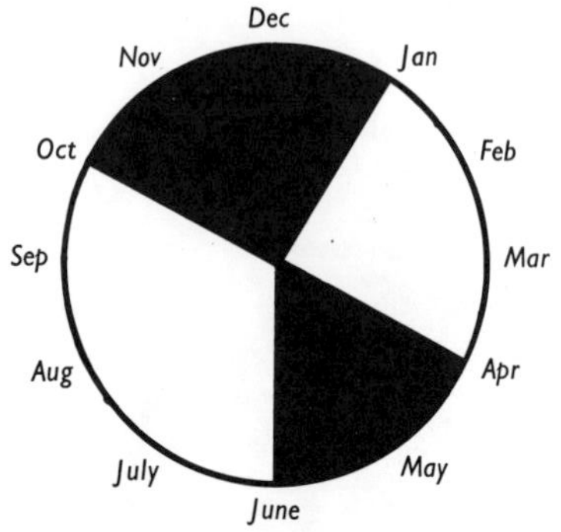

Fig. 303(e)

Western Pacific

KEY: as in Fig. 303(a)

1. Marshall Islands	Data mainly from Amerson (1969)	Laying Oct.–Jan.
(a) Taongi Atoll	,,	Laying Oct.–Nov.
(b) Bikar Atoll	,,	Laying Oct.–Jan.
(c) Jemo Island	,,	Laying Nov.–Dec.
2. Majuro Atoll	,,	Birds not nesting in June 1966.
3. Milli Atoll	,,	Breeding in southern winter and spring.
4. Bikini Atoll	,,	Laying May.
5. Truk Island	Brandt (1962)	Laying starts at the end of April.

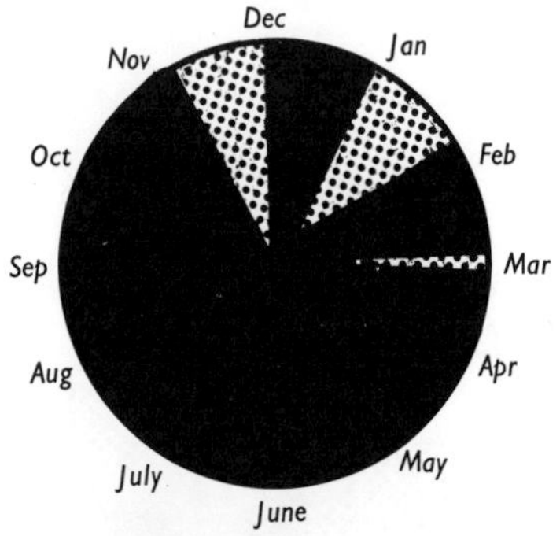

Fig. 303(f)

Central Pacific

KEY: as in Fig. 303(a)

1. Hawaiian Leewards		
(a) Kure Atoll	Woodward (1972)	Laying Mar.–Nov. Peak laying May–June although much seasonal variability.
(b) Laysan	Fisher (1951)	Laying probably Jan.–May.
(c) Moku Manu	Richardson & Fisher (1950)	Laying throughout the year, peaks in Feb. and possibly Oct.

(d) Oahu	Ashmole and Ashmole (1967)	Laying late Feb.–early June, mainly Mar.–May, occasional eggs Aug., Sept.
(e) French Frigate Shoals	Amerson (1971)	Laying Jan.–June, mainly late Feb.–Apr.
(f) Necker Island	Clapp *in* Harrington (in press)	Laying March and Apr.
2. Line Islands		
(a) Christmas Island	Schreiber & Ashmole (1970)	Laying mainly Apr.–Nov. Peaks in June–July 1959, Dec. 1966, Mar.–Apr. 1967, Dec. 1876.
(b) Fanning	Bakus (1967)	Laying early Apr.–early May.
(c) Vostok	Clapp & Sibley (1971a)	Eggs laid around April.
(d) Caroline Atoll	Clapp & Sibley (1971b)	Laying around Jan.
(e) Palmyra	Streets (1877)	Main laying Sept.–Oct.
3. Phoenix	Buddle (1938)	Laying protracted and non-seasonal.
4. Samoan Islands	King and Pyle (1957)	Laying mainly in Nov.
5. Tuamotus Archipelago	King and Pyle (1957)	Laying mainly in Aug.
6. Pitcairns	King and Pyle (1957)	Laying in Oct.

Fig. 303(g)

Eastern Pacific

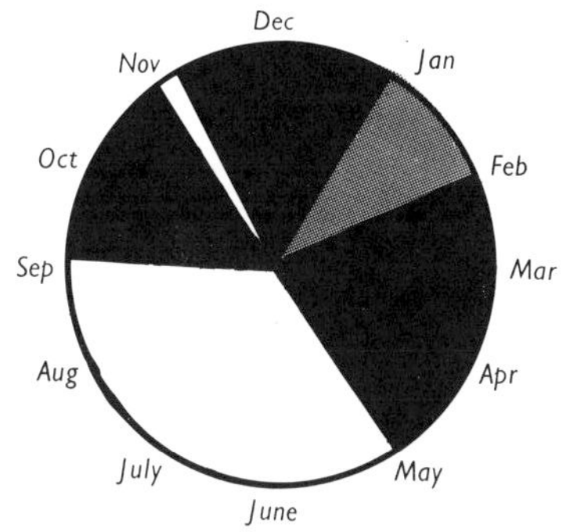

KEY: as in Fig. 303(a)

1. Cocos Island	Slud (1967)	Laying Nov.–Dec., probably no regular annual laying period.
2. Galapagos Archipelago	Nelson	Wave of laying Sept.–Oct., less marked Feb.–Apr. peak, although great annual variation. See Appendix 12
3. Revillagigedos	Brattstrom & Howell (1956)	Laying probably Mar.–Apr.

3. *Synchronisation of breeding*

The section on seasonal breeding, by revealing how widely laying is spread, has shown that nowhere can the red-foot be considered to lay in a highly synchronised manner even though in some places it is to some extent seasonal.

(*a*) *Sub-group synchronisation and rate of laying*

Much of the preceding material has involved some mention of local synchronisation. In theory this could be synchronisation in time alone, or in time and space. In the former, one would have, in say a colony of 1000 pairs, a number laying closely synchronised in time but scattered throughout the colony, then a few days, or weeks, with very few birds laying followed by another scattered laying, again synchronised in time. If the overall spread was considerable such synchrony would be extremely difficult to detect, for one could have eggs, small, medium and large young scattered throughout the colony. In the time and space synchrony (which probably always occurs) a group of neighbours is more or less synchronised and clearly separated in time from other groups. In fact, 'time alone' synchronisation probably does not occur in pure form; it would imply timing by external factors excluding social ones (since there would be no correlation with the neighbour's condition) and social factors almost always are involved.

The distribution of laying within large colonies has not been recorded in enough detail and enough colonies to make possible any comparison between areas. All one can say is that sub-groups are significantly more closely synchronised than the colony as a whole. Observations, such as Schreiber's for the Pacific Christmas Island, that even sub-colonies can contain as wide a laying range as the entire colony do not disprove sub-group synchrony; they probably show that the sub-group as a unit was too large to reveal it, whereas smaller groupings within it may have done so.

Even on Tower, Galapagos, where, as will later emerge, it is advantageous for the red-foot to stagger its breeding so that all do not fail due to one unfavourable spell, it was obvious that laying was significantly synchronised in the two small groups studied (Fig. 305). We obtained some evidence (Table 107) that birds starting to build when many neighbours were

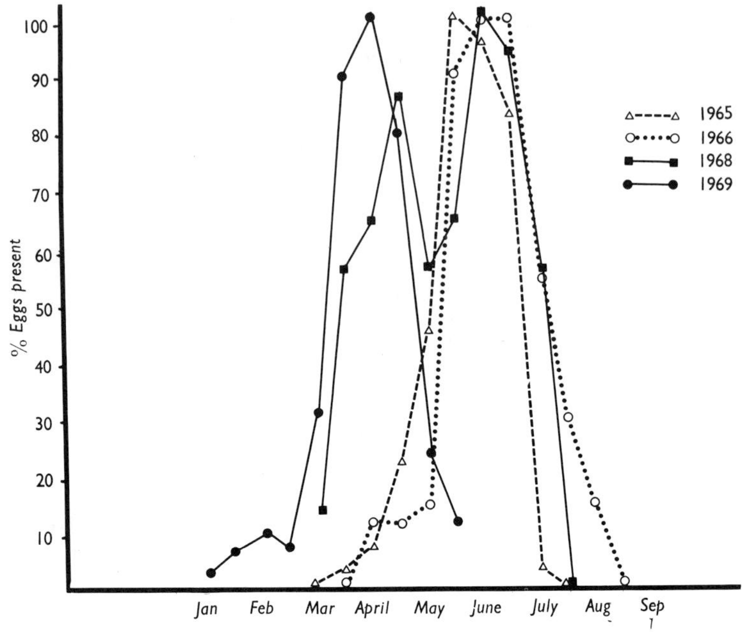

Fig. 304

The pattern of egg laying on Christmas Island (Pacific). From data in Schreiber & Ashmole (1970).

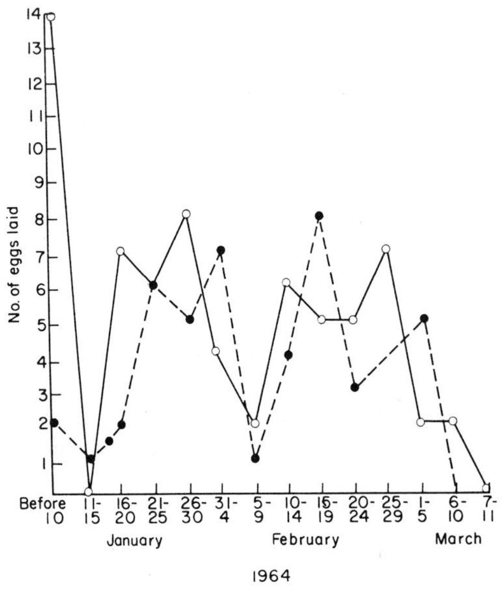

Fig. 305

The progress of egg laying in two separate groups, Tower Island, Galapagos, 1964.

also building took less time between beginning to build and laying than those doing so at a quieter time.

On Aldabra, Diamond found that on Middle Island laying was concentrated mainly between November and January, though with some in August, September and through to April. He summarised the situation as 'a wide spread of laying but most in the wet season with another peak in some colonies in the late dry season'. From his histogram of the number of eggs laid in two areas (Bras Takamaka and Main Colony) it is possible to get some idea of the rate of laying. Unfortunately the figures were worked back from the ages of chicks and therefore (quite apart from the difficulty of estimating laying dates by such means) do not take account of egg loss. On face value, they indicate a much slower incremental rate of laying than in the *Cryptocarpus* colony on Tower, but this could well be an artefact. Certainly, however, the degree of synchronisation cannot have been high. In the main colony, 23 eggs were spread over almost five months; even if as many again were lost and thus unrecorded by Diamond, the rate would still have been about 0·6 per cent eggs laid per day compared with 2 per cent per day on Tower.

It appears from Woodward's data from Kure Atoll that in 1969 (a year of exceptionally high population) something over 60 per cent of the eggs laid (about 400) were laid between mid-March and mid-April, which is about 2 per cent per day as on Tower at the height of laying. We do not yet know that sub-group synchrony is a universal phenomenon. Maybe there are colonies within which eggs are randomly distributed over the period of laying but this is very unlikely. And of course whatever the degree of synchrony, even if all females of a colony or sub-colony laid on the same day, we would not know whether this had been caused by external, non-social factors, or external factors including social ones. One could painstakingly gather inadequate snippets of evidence for synchrony within sub-colonies, but it is hardly worthwhile. The phenomenon is obvious enough at the superficial level and beyond that nobody has yet scratched the surface.

This, however, may be the best point at which to introduce some information on the related topic of the role of external factors in controlling (initiating and terminating) laying in the red-foot and the features of one such laying wave which was analysed in some detail.

(*b*) *External factors controlling breeding*

The case to be described seems to demonstrate the role of food as a proximate rather than an ultimate factor in the timing of breeding. The events occurred on Tower, Galapagos, and whilst something comparable may happen in other areas poor in food, it should, perhaps, be treated as a special case (see p. 474 for the parallel situation in the brown boobies of Ascension). Some other Galapagos seabirds, for example Audubon's shearwater and the swallow-tailed gull have evolved similar, presumably adaptive, responses to food as a proximate factor (see Harris 1969).

It should be recalled that in the Galapagos the red-foot may lay in any month of the year. In August 1963 there were young of all ages and a few eggs; many young were dying. By late December the colony held 121 pairs attending sites, 21 attending nests, 9 pairs with eggs and 99 nests with chicks of various ages, but mainly up to six weeks old. Thus there must have

TABLE 107

TIME, IN DAYS, BETWEEN BEGINNING TO BUILD AND EGG LAYING (ACCURATE TO WITHIN 24 HOURS) IN THE RED-FOOTED BOOBY IN THE GALAPAGOS

Pairs building in	No. of cases	Average	Range
First half of January	7	27	20–35
Second half of January	11	20+	13–28
First half of February	24	17	11–27
Second half of February	6	16	14–21

been a wave of laying around September and by late December, another wave was being initiated. This one was studied in detail.

Early in January 1964 there was an upsurge of building and laying, which then, in mid-February, sharply declined. Yet, at the time of the decline, many birds had already formed pairs, built nests and were almost ready to lay. Others had begun pair formation or nest-building and yet others had started to 'attend' their territory seriously. Thus, suddenly, the ongoing process was halted, though as would be expected, those pairs which had progressed farthest

TABLE 108

EGG LAYING IN THE DARWIN BAY (GALAPAGOS) COLONY OF RED-FOOTED BOOBIES IN RELATION TO THE NUMBER OF PAIRS WITH NESTS

	Quarter-monthly periods										
	January			February				March			
	1–2	3	4	1	2	3	4	1	2	3	4
No. of nests being built	38	49	52	54	75	70	56	19	5	0	0
% that never had an egg	13	20	20	26	41	60	71	84	100		
% that had an egg in the next $\frac{1}{4}$ month	45	33	17	26	20	26	13	16			
% that eventually had an egg	42	47	63	48	39	14	16				
No. of sites or nests being attended but not built	9	11	17	27	28	27	16	5	2	1	0
% that never had an egg	11	45	53	70	82	93	88	100	100	100	
% that eventually had an egg	89	55	47	30	18	7	12				
Total number of attended nests or sites	47	60	69	81	103	97	72	24	7	1	0

TABLE 109

CHANGES IN THE STRUCTURE OF THE DARWIN BAY (GALAPAGOS) COLONY OF RED-FOOTED BOOBIES BETWEEN JANUARY AND MARCH 1964

		Quarter-monthly periods										
		January			February				March			
	Nest category	1–2	3	4	1	2	3	4	1	2	3	4
+	Newcomers beginning to attend	10	4	8	17	13	4	2	0	0	0	0
+	Newcomers beginning to attend and build	38	15	12	14	19	7	11	1	0	0	0
+	Attended beginning to build	0	3	3	11	15	12	4	3	0	0	0
–	Built becoming merely attended	0	0	0	4	4	8	3	2	1	1	0
–	Attended becoming unattended	0	0	1	0	2	1	13	10	4	2	2
–	Built becoming unattended	0	0	1	3	2	8	18	32	10	4	0

+ means progression towards laying; – means regression from point of laying after having begun the initial stages of a breeding cycle.

The stages distinguished in this analysis are 'attending'—returning frequently and spending time as a pair in the territory, and 'building'—adding new nest material to the nest.

A nest counted in one category for one quarter-month period can move + or – in succeeding periods until it is laid in or abandoned. It is not countered thereafter. The quarter-month period in which the egg was laid is excluded.

tended to be halted less readily than those newly started when the inhibiting circumstances arose. The extent of the breeding wave thus stopped in its tracks can be gauged from the following figures. Out of 197 nests built between January and mid-March only just over half (101) actually received eggs, whilst a further 50 partly built nests were never completed. This is important because it shows that whatever factor(s) halted breeding, they must have been external, since they acted on birds that were obviously in the right internal (physiological) condition, having already initiated breeding (and in some cases actually laid eggs) when they were stopped. In other words, the decline was not that of a late group well past the peak breeding season, but of an up-and-coming one. This analysis of the situation is supported by Table 108 and Figs. 306, 308. Here it can be seen that the point at which negative responses begin to gain ascendancy is about the second half of February.

The question is, what external factor(s) were responsible for this dramatic switch in breeding activity and (by implication) for the preceding 'stop-go' events? In a mainly constant climate such as the equatorial one around Tower successive waves of breeding activity demonstrate that when favourable external factors come into operation, some birds are ready and

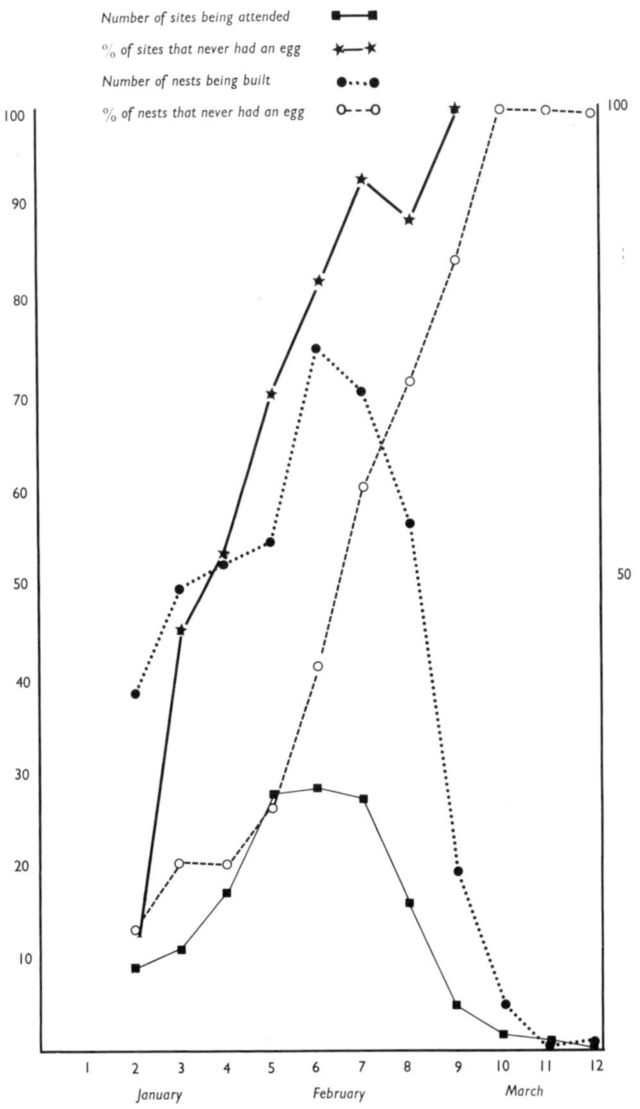

Fig. 306. Pattern of attendance, nest building and nest abandonment, Tower Island, 1964.

able to respond. How can there be, at all times of year, a supply of birds poised for release into a new breeding cycle and what releases them?

At any time, the population (or any group) consists of birds in several categories of physiological condition, for instance birds that ended a successful breeding attempt a variable time ago and those that terminated an unsuccessful one. In a place like Tower, there are many in the latter category having lost eggs or chicks of various ages through abandonment, starvation or predation. In the Galapagos a failed breeder may begin a new cycle after a variable interval and even successful ones show great variability in the length of the interval before the next attempt. This state of affairs is in striking contrast to that in a temperate species with a strong circannual rhythm. Thus, a failed gannet lays again the next year at its 'normal' time and in step with other failed and with successful breeders. Galapagos red-foots reach a state of 'potentiation' for breeding rather than trying to breed *whatever* the circumstances, after an internally-fixed period of time as the sooty tern does. The supply of 'potentiated' birds is mediated as described and in this state they are susceptible to an external trigger.

An obvious possibility is that breeding commences in physiologically prepared birds when food is relatively plentiful but is checked or inhibited when food becomes or remains scarce. This seems to be the case, for we found that the period of initiation and progression of a laying wave corresponded to that in which food was plentiful, whilst the regression of breeding activities was marked by dire food shortage as measured by the growth of chicks of various ages. Fig. 308 shows the generalised growth curve matched against the progressive and regressive breeding activities. It appears that at the time when most chicks were starving, reflecting scarcity of food in the foraging areas of the adults, the number of abandoned breeding

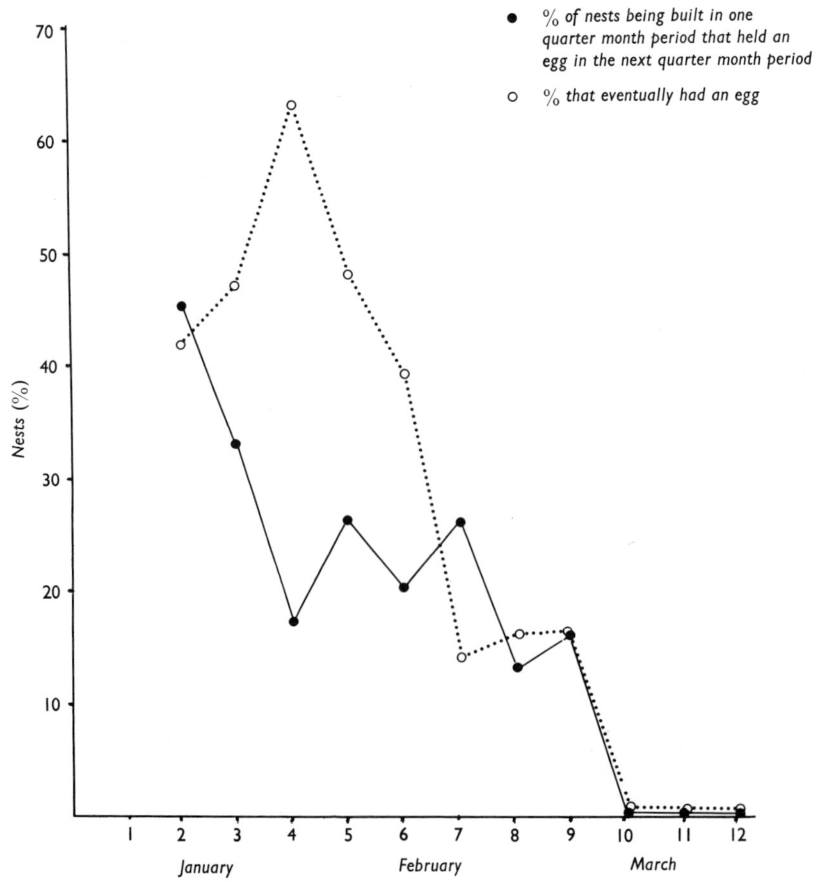

Fig. 307. Pattern of laying, Tower Island, 1964.

attempts was highest. Conversely, when new nests were being built and eggs laid, chick growth was good.

It seems that this pattern is repeated over and over again in the Galapagos, for numerous scattered visits tell of starving young at various times of year. Yet the adaptiveness of using the current food situation as a trigger for breeding is by no means obvious, for plentiful food at the time of building and laying is no guarantee of the same when the chick is making heavy demands. This is all too clear in the record of chick starvation. Yet, if food is truly unpredictable (and were it not, one would expect the evolution of better ability to avoid famine times) nothing can be done to safeguard the young. But it is possible to ensure that energy-consuming territory establishment, pair formation, nest building and nest attendance and (for the female) egg production, are all performed when food is relatively plentiful. Thus, these tasks are commenced at such times.

It may seem maladaptive, though, to get as far as laying and then abandon the attempt. But the task of incubation, especially in heat, is highly demanding of energy and six or seven days without food may be as long as a red-foot can endure without jeopardising its survival. Also it may be more economical to abandon the egg and try again later, than to persevere, probably lose the chick (since most do) and thus waste a greater proportion of one's reproductive life span.

Finally, there may be a positive correlation of slight but sufficient survival value, between food availability at the time of laying and later. There seems to be a tendency to lay between January to March and September to November, rather than the intervening months.

There is no evidence that food acts as an external timer in other red-foot populations, but the very wide spread of laying and the multiple peaks which obviously occur in some places indicate either that inherent variability is alone enough and works independently of external factors to produce waves of laying (no doubt socially synchronised to some extent) or that some external factor(s) are involved. Diamond (1974) suggested that, on Aldabra, food acts only as a broad timer and that frigate birds are an important external factor, the boobies laying mainly when the frigates have ceased to rob nests for building material. Food operates as an external timer in the brown booby on Ascension, too (see p. 474).

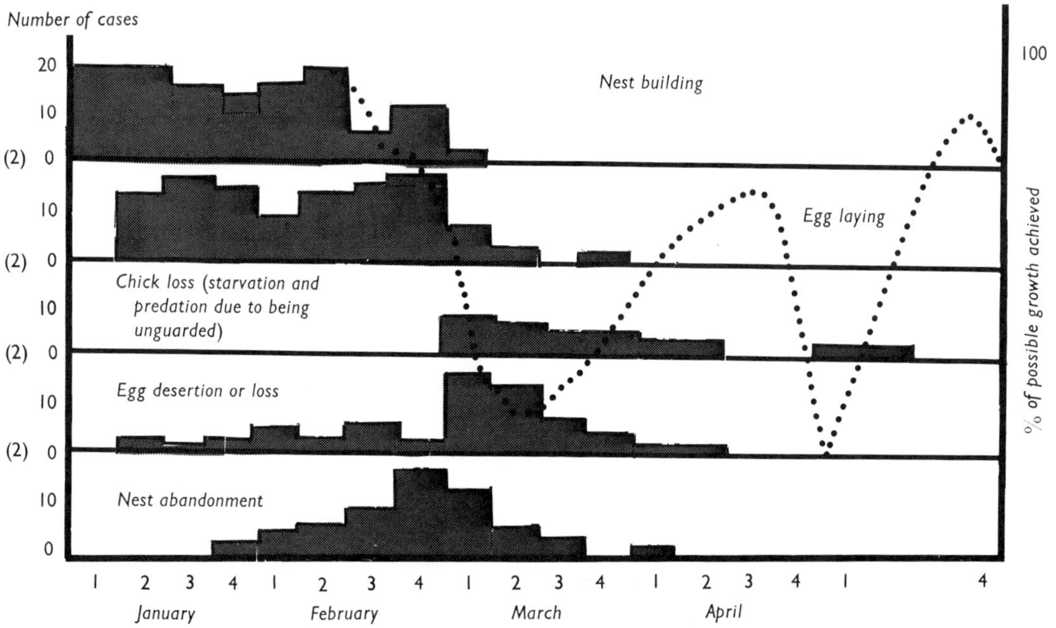

Fig. 308. Seasonal relationship between progressive and regressive breeding activities related to generalised representation of food situation as revealed by growth of young.

4. *Length and composition of breeding cycle*

(*a*) *Pre-laying period*

Three weeks is about the minimum time between beginning serious attendance at the colony and laying. Since desultory attendance can precede this for a very variable period and there are no records other than for the Galapagos, it is impossible to be precise about the duration of this phase, but it is an essential one and its length no doubt depends largely on local conditions. Very little is known about regional variation in the attendance pattern outside the breeding cycle and large adaptive differences are to be expected.

(*b*) *Incubation and care of young*

Table 110 shows that the length of the incubation period is standard but that there is very considerable regional variation in the length of time devoted to care of young. This is because growth is much slower in impoverished areas and the period of post-fledging feeding can be extremely long. As a result, the total length of the cycle shows considerable regional variation, in fact to a greater degree than in any other sulid except the brown booby. There is no information on the length of the post-breeding period of attendance at the site and Table 110 therefore excludes this when comparing total cycle lengths.

The significance of variable cycle length, apart from its adaptive role in allowing boobies to cope with impoverished habitats, lies in its effect on the frequency of breeding.

TABLE 110

THE LENGTH AND COMPOSITION OF THE BREEDING CYCLE OF THE RED-FOOTED BOOBY IN DIFFERENT AREAS

Area	Pre-laying breeding activities	Length in days of: Incubation period	Fledging period	Post-fledging feeding	Total breeding cycle	Source
Half Moon Cay	N.R. allow 14–35	45	91–112	c. 30	180–222+	Verner (1961)
Aldabra	N.R. allow 14–35	45	110	c. 30	199–220+	Diamond (1971)
Christmas Island	21–35	45	100–110	N.R. allow 30–50	196–240+	Nelson
Kure Atoll	N.R. allow 14–35	c. 42*	90–100+	N.R. allow 30–60	176–240+	Woodward (1972)
Tower Galapagos	18–56+	46	139+	78–103	281–344+	Nelson (1969a)

N.R. = No record * Probably an underestimate

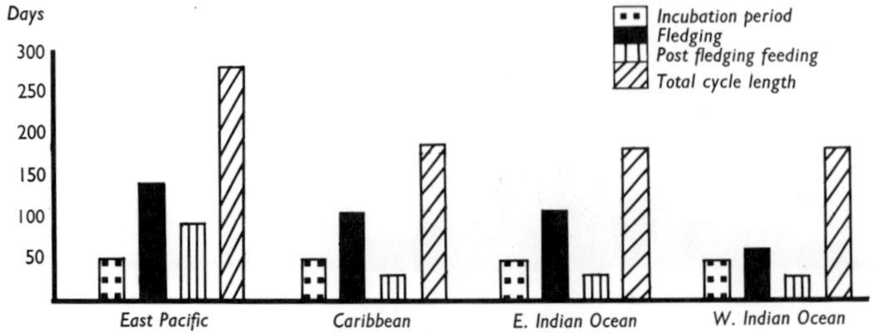

Fig. 309. Regional variation in the lengths of components of the breeding cycle.

5. *Frequency of breeding*

In most places the red-foot does not require more than twelve months in which to complete a successful breeding cycle and recuperate ready for the next one, but in others it needs more than this between successive layings. Whether even the former do breed every year is discussed below, but they certainly could, in so far as they could fit their cycle into a twelve month period. If, excluding the Galapagos, we take 33 weeks as a reasonable length for the red-foot's entire cycle, there is ample time left for recuperation within the twelve-month period and annual breeding is easily possible. In the Galapagos this is not the case and the red-foot must breed at intervals of more than a year. Diamond attempted to obtain this figure directly by following the fortunes of marked birds over a 21-month period. He emerges with a figure of 11 to 15 months (mean 12·7) between successive layings, in assumed successful pairs. This may be too short. Thus, if (on a checking visit, of which there were only three) a bird was occupying an empty nest, he assumed it would lay in about three weeks. Whilst this is a fair assumption for such a bird in an actively laying group in the Galapagos, it is also true that under other circumstances, birds occupied nests for much longer without laying. Secondly, some of his birds may have been failed breeders from the previous cycle and such pairs would have a shorter laying interval than successful ones.

In the Galapagos I obtained some figures for intervals elapsing between successive layings, both for successful birds and those that did not fully complete the first cycle (Table 111).

There was some evidence that one pair took 80 weeks or more between successive layings, the first cycle having taken almost a year from occupying the territory to stopping feeding the juvenile. It thus seems that Galapagos red-foots lay at intervals of slightly more than a year—probably, on occasions considerably more.

A fair general conclusion for the species as a whole would be that if successful the red-foot breeds at intervals of between 12 and 15 months (probably usually near 12), more than annual intervals being allowable in its relatively aseasonal breeding regime. Failed breeders try again at somewhat shorter intervals. The laying of a whole population is thus considerably spread, again as the aseasonal environment allows.

(*a*) *Non-breeding years*

The only evidence of this comes from nests which I marked on Tower and which M. P. Harris subsequently visited at infrequent intervals over several years. The results are too inconclusive to warrant details, but indicated that a high proportion either bred substantially less than once per year, or at best, laid and lost eggs or young. I strongly suspect that the

TABLE 111

CYCLE LENGTHS IN RED-FOOTED BOOBIES OF DIFFERENT CATEGORIES (SUCCESSFUL AND FAILED AT VARIOUS STAGES IN PREVIOUS CYCLE) IN THE GALAPAGOS

	Time (weeks) between successive layings (or a laying and the prior abandoned cycle)		
Result of previous egg laying	Mean	Range	No. of cases
Young reached independence or died when fully feathered	56	49–65+	6
Egg lost, or chick lost before four weeks old	37	31–44	26
Nest built but abandoned before laying	35	30–41	10

I had no records for nests which lost chicks between one month and fully feathered.

Subsequent visits by M. Castro (pers. comm.) produced a possible instance of 80+ weeks elapsing between successive layings in the case of a pair whose chick took 46 weeks from hatching to full independence.

period between successive nesting attempts is highly variable regardless of success and may be many months. Non-breeding 'periods' if not actually a year, are almost certainly common in such areas. Whether they occur, also, in more seasonal and productive areas is unknown.

OTHER ASPECTS OF BREEDING ECOLOGY

1. *Food*

The red-foot tends to feed far from the colony, over deep, blue water. Flying fish and squid figure largely in its diet and most general references to its food cite these. Diamond provides a most valuable analysis of food of Aldabra birds (Table 112). The staple is flying fish, supplemented in the wet season by a considerable proportion of squid. Squid figure less prominently in the dry season when the proportion of *Cypselurus furcatus* rises. Diamond shows (Fig. 310) that most of the red-foot's prey are between 50–100g with very few over 100g and mostly measure between 10–22cm.

TABLE 112

COMPOSITION OF FOOD SAMPLES REGURGITATED BY RED-FOOTED BOOBY CHICKS ON ALDABRA (Diamond 1971)

	Wet season			Dry season		
	%F	%N	%W	%F	%N	%W
No. samples	27	96	901	47	129	2278
Fish	93	57	79	100	95	99
Exocoetidae (unidentified)	44	22	—	62	52	—
Exocoetus volitans	25	10	29	17	11	25
Cypselurus furcatus	25	11	41	50	17	73
Oxyperhamphus micropterus	4	1	6	4	3	—
All Exocoetidae	70	44	76	94	83	98
Hemirhamphidae	4	4	—	2	1	2
Others	7	2	4	6	1	—
Squid	50	43	21	10	5	1

NOTES: 1. F = frequency, N = number, W = weight.

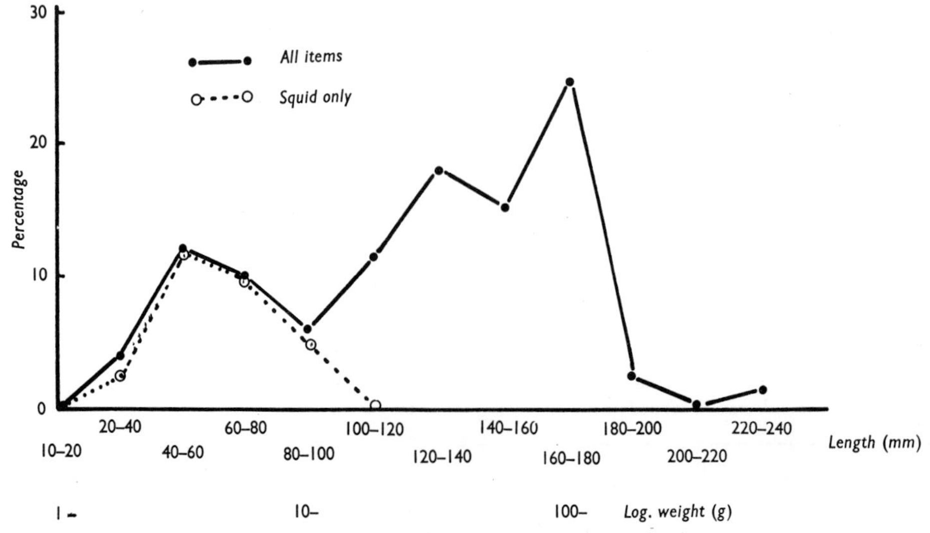

Fig. 310. Length and weight of fish taken (after Diamond 1971).

Elsewhere, the food of the red-foot has been recorded as mainly squid (Christmas Island, Indian Ocean) and squid and flying fish (Christmas Island, Pacific) in 58 samples (Schreiber & Ashmole 1970). In the Galapagos, squid and flying fish were the main items seen in accidental regurgitations, but no details were recorded. Ashmole & Ashmole (1967) report that a small series of samples from Oahu, Hawaii, averaged nine items each, of which 64 per cent were fish and 36 per cent squid. The fish were mainly Exocoetidae and Gempylidae while all the identified squid were Ommastrephidae, probably all of the genus *Symplectoteuthis*. Half the fish were 8–12cm long and appreciable numbers were 12–16cm. Only a few squid had mantle lengths of more than 8cm. In another paper (Ashmole & Ashmole 1967) it is pointed out that the investigation of the food of seabirds around the Pacific Ocean Christmas Island reveals the astonishingly large contribution made by squid (34–97 per cent of the diet of those species taking least and most squid respectively). It is suggested that squid may rival, in available biomass, the whole of the fish fauna, even in a relatively rich fishing area. In the Paracels the main food is said to be 'bajiao' (*Cybium commerson*?) but this comes from a Chinese account and may be wrongly interpreted.

2. *Annual mortality*

The only information on mortality comes from Kure Atoll (Woodward 1972). The P.O.B.S.P. personnel ringed large numbers of adults, sub-adults and chicks and saw or recaptured many of these in subsequent years. The considerable movement between islands and the differences

TABLE 113

PERCENTAGE ANNUAL MORTALITY OF BREEDING ADULT RED-FOOTED BOOBIES ON KURE (from Woodward 1972)

Year A	No. of adults alive in year A	No. of these adults seen in year A+1	Percent apparent mortality
1964	32	14	56·3
1965	14	13	7·2
1966	22	14	36·4
1967	72	36	50·0
1968	39	23	41·1

TABLE 114

PERCENTAGE ANNUAL MORTALITY OF NON-BREEDING ADULT RED-FOOTED BOOBIES ON KURE (from Woodward 1972)

Year A	No. alive in year A	No. seen in year A+1	% apparent mortality
1962	28	13	53·6
1963	139	80	42·4
1964	329	216	34·3
1965	301	255	15·3
1966	545	306	43·9
1967	350	262	25·1
1968	339	210	38·1

in effort put into recapture and observation of marked birds in different years (which meant that unknown proportions remained alive but were not seen) makes it impossible to deduce accurate mortality rates. Nevertheless, they give valuable indications of the maximum possible mortality. Table 113 gives the results from breeding adults ringed and subsequently observed on the same island between 1964 and 1969.

A maximum possible 81·2 per cent of the original 32 ringed in 1964 had disappeared by 1969. This averages 16 per cent mortality per annum. For the reasons given above, this figure may be regarded as higher than the true one and 10 per cent or less is probably more realistic. The lowest figure for adult mortality in any year (7·2 per cent) indicates how low mortality can be, and is itself a maximum.

Details of re-sightings of birds ringed as non-breeding adults and subsequently seen on the same island are given in Table 114. The fact that they were caught as non-breeders means that at least some probably belonged elsewhere and the imponderables mentioned above also apply.

TABLE 115

PERCENTAGE ANNUAL MORTALITY OF RED-FOOTED BOOBIES RINGED AS SUB-ADULTS ON KURE
(from Woodward 1972)

Year A	No. alive in year A	No. seen in year A+1	Percent apparent mortality
1963	74	32	56·8
1964	119	68	42·9
1965	79	70	11·3
1966	220	87	60·5
1967	122	57	53·3
1968	118	35	70·3

TABLE 116

RECAPTURE RATES OF RED-FOOTED BOOBIES BANDED AS NESTLINGS AT KURE ATOLL AND RECAPTURED THERE (EXPRESSED AS PERCENTAGES), 1959–69
(from Woodward 1972)

Year banded	n.	Year recaptured 1959	1960	1961	1962	1963	1964	1965	1966	1967	1968	1969
1959	28	100·0	3·6 (0·0)	3·6 (0·0)	3·6 (0·0)	3·6 (0·0)	3·6 (0·0)	3·6 (0·0)	3·6 (0·0)	0·0 (0·0)	0·0 (0·0)	0·0 (0·0)
1962	71	—	—	—	100·0	19·7 (0·0)	19·7 (0·0)	19·7 (1·4)	19·7 (11·3)	14·1 (7·0)	9·9 (4·2)	7·0 (7·0)
1964	9	—	—	—	—	—	100·0	55·6 (11·1)	44·4 (22·2)	22·2 (22·2)	11·1 (11·1)	0·0 (0·0)
1966	127	—	—	—	—	—	—	—	100·0	24·4 (3·9)	22·1 (18·1)	6·3 (6·3)
1967	141	—	—	—	—	—	—	—	—	100·0	14·9 (11·4)	5·0 (5·0)
1968	198	—	—	—	—	—	—	—	—	—	100·0	1·5 (1·5)
1969	33	—	—	—	—	—	—	—	—	—	—	100·0
	607											

First figure represents the percentage of birds known to have been alive and the second figure is the percentage of birds captured.

The figure of 15·3 per cent apparent mortality from a sample of 301 birds (1965–66) indicates the possible survival and in adjusted terms probably means about 8 per cent annual mortality. The figures for birds ringed as sub-adults (Table 115) provide a similar range.

An additional unknown variable in this set of figures is the age at which the birds were ringed. If some were juveniles, whose mortality rate is higher than one- or two-year-olds, the overall survival will be lower than for adults, whereas if all were at least a year old when ringed, this difference would be much slighter.

Mortality during the first year of life (Table 116) is particularly difficult to estimate because of the very considerable movement between islands. Table 116 indicates that of 607 chicks ringed, an average of only 20 per cent were seen in the following year, the figures ranging from 55·6 per cent (but from a sample of only 9) to 1·5 per cent (of 198). Many of the missing birds were undoubtedly elsewhere, but on the not entirely safe assumption that almost all survivors would eventually return to their native island to breed and would do so in their third year, 12·9 per cent of 235 nestlings were actually seen alive three years later. Since this is a minimum figure for survival, probably no more than 75 per cent of nestlings had died in those three years of which (assuming a mortality rate independent of age after the first year) 16–20 per cent had died in their second or third years, leaving about 55–60 per cent as the figure for mortality in the first year of life. This is very comparable with the equally approximate figures derived for other boobies (pp. 379, 478) and suggests that it is fairly safe to assume a first year mortality rate in the order of 50 per cent.

3. *Age of first breeding*

There is no direct evidence on this point. However, red-foots usually do not acquire adult plumage until their third or fourth year and usually do not breed in immature plumage (the brown morphs are not immature) although an immature-plumaged bird collected in the West Indies, was marked 'breeding'. Very probably many birds are in their third year and others in their fourth; the laying season is usually protracted and moult is variable in all sulids so that, for example, of ten chicks born in June 1960, some may have acquired adult plumage by May 1963 (in their third year) whilst others do so in July 1963 (their fourth year) though all may breed as adults in 1963.

4. *Movements*

Woodward (Table 117) records a substantial amount of movement between islands in the north-central Pacific. In 1966, 1967 and 1968, 60 per cent, 40 per cent and 23·8 per cent respectively of banded birds controlled by personnel of the Pacific Ocean project had been banded, as young or adults, elsewhere, though probably very few were breeding when recaptured. 141 ringed birds were recaptured on French Frigate Shoals, from Johnston (61), Laysan (24), Kure (14), Lisianski (14), Oahu (10), Kanai (6), Midway (6), Wake (4), Pearl and Hermes (2). Similarly, 100 birds ringed on French Frigate Shoals were recovered elsewhere, Johnston (60), Kure (19), Laysan (2), Lisianski (10), Pearl and Hermes (3), Midway (2), Wake (1), Oahu (1) and at sea (2). It seems that, genetically, there are vast areas within which the population is essentially one great gene pool. This is perhaps to be expected in climatically homogeneous areas in which there is relatively little selection pressure for local populations to become specially adapted, a point which has implications for any theory of group selection (p. 905) and is germane, also, to any interpretation of morph distribution. The situation may be analogous to that in the Peruvian booby and the Atlantic gannet, where it is known for certain that there is considerable interchange, at least of young birds, between colonies (see pp. 64 and 583).

Movement of adults probably mainly concerns non-breeding birds. From the 1011 adults ringed on Kure mainly as non-breeders, 36 were recaptured on other islands and 10 of these recaptured a second time, back on Kure. Probably some of the birds ringed on Kure stemmed from other islands, for three were captured breeding on Midway. Without an analysis of the effort put into recapturing birds on the different islands it is impossible to detect any trends towards particular types of movement, but it seems likely that birds from islands spread over thousands of square kilometres wander in this huge area, roosting or perhaps basing themselves for some time, on any one of several islands, but usually returning to their native one to breed. Thus, an island may be used by many more boobies than are to be seen there at any one time. In 1963–69, 2070 red-foots were banded on French Frigate Shoals, but the maximum number ever recorded there was 757, of which only a proportion bore rings. Probably the tendency to wander far from the native island is greatest in juveniles, some of which may remain away for their first year or two (recapture figures, Table 116, suggest that this is so). Since there are usually large numbers of sub-adults at Kure (and presumably other stations) a proportion of these will be from other islands. Twenty-nine of the 607 red-foots ringed on Kure as chicks and 20 of the 425 ringed as sub-adults, were recaptured elsewhere. Twelve birds were ringed on Kure when less than a year old, in 1964, and handled there again in 1966, when still immature.

Nevertheless, many birds either do not leave the vicinity of their native island or return from their juvenile wanderings in their first year, for Woodward (1972) records that the 1966 cohort were present in May–July 1967 and the 1967 one similarly in 1968. Thus, year-old birds were in the colony. By contrast, it is rare to see immature birds on the Indian Ocean Christmas Island and there may well be important differences between populations in this, as in other respects.

The large number of red-foots ringed on other islands and recovered on Kure enabled Woodward to draw the following conclusions:

1. Only red-foots from the Hawaiian islands Wake and Johnston travelled to Kure.
2. Proportionately more young travelled than adults and whereas adults moved both north and south, immatures mainly moved south.
3. Movement dropped off with distance but considerably more birds moved to Kure from Wake and Johnston than would be expected if movement between islands were only a function of distance. This suggests there might be a migratory movement between these areas.

Large congregations of birds may build up on islands where few or none breed. On Johnston Atoll numbers build up from October (maximum 500 birds) to late February (up to

TABLE 117

MOVEMENT TO KURE ATOLL OF RED-FOOTED BOOBIES BANDED ON OTHER ISLANDS (BY P.O.B.S.P.), 1965–69 (after Woodward 1972)

From:	Midway Atoll	Pearl and Hermes Reef	Lisianski	Laysan	French Frigate Shoals	Johnston Atoll	Wake Atoll	Main Hawaiian Islands
Distance to Kure (naut. miles)	49	135	266	379	695	838	978	1072
Number of adults banded	174	150	664	604	617	153	144	2441
Number of young banded	159	18	199	256	1168	646	320	1703
Total number banded	333	168	863	860	1785	799	464	4144
Number banded as adults recaptured at Kure	4 (2·3)	3 (2·0)	0 (0)	1 (0·2)	3 (0·5)	3 (2·0)	1 (0·7)	0 (0)
Number banded as young recaptured at Kure	18 (11·3)	2 (11·3)	6 (3·0)	5 (2·0)	10 (0·9)	12 (1·9)	15 (4·7)	3 (0·2)
Total number recaptured at Kure	22 (6·6)	5 (3·0)	6 (0·7)	6 (0·7)	13 (0·7)	15 (1·9)	16 (3·4)	3 (0·1)

Figure in brackets is percentage.

6000 birds (Harrington in press from whom comes the information in the remainder of this section). During this time, the proportion of birds in their first and second years increases until by late March they comprise 92 per cent of the roosting birds. Virtually all these birds come from the Hawaiian Islands, with a few from Wake. None, apparently, come from the Line and Phoenix Island groups to the south. Adults and immatures were noted east of 169°w. in about equal numbers. Both categories were commoner there than in the area west of 170°w., where adults outnumbered immatures. In other words adults, particularly, tended to disperse eastwards from the Hawaiian Islands.

5. *Fidelity to site*

There is one record of a red-foot breeding on two different islands in the Hawaiian group, but this is probably highly exceptional. However, it is probably quite common for them to change sites within the same general area. There is too little firm data to warrant detailed discussion, but certainly a high proportion of my marked nests on Tower were not replaced in subsequent years. This is not surprising, since adequate sites are common and nests often completely disintegrate after use.

6. *Fidelity to mate*

Here, too, data is lacking. On Tower a few pairs certainly remained together for two successive broods. At least in an aseasonal environment, however, it is probable that many partners get out of step and therefore do not rejoin their previous mate. This, too, might well differ between populations. It seems that the other tropical boobies also show less mate fidelity than does the North Atlantic gannet and this may be connected with the former's reduced site fidelity and the non-seasonal environment.

7. *Population structure*

The breeding population on Kure, in 1967, had the following age structure extrapolated from a sample catch of 79 ringed birds:

	Age								
	3	4	4+	5	5+	6	6+	7+	8+
Number	21	28	179	34	28	–	150	69	6

Whilst it is difficult to explain the low proportion of five and six year olds, it is interesting to note the high number of birds more than six and seven years old. In 1966 an estimated 20 per cent of the Kure population consisted of sub-adults, up to 200 of which were present between May and July but some, also, between April and October.

Within the Kure population there are many immature birds. These are distributed throughout the population rather than concentrated into discrete Clubs. The composition of this immature population on Green Island in 1967 and 1968 was as follows:

	Percentage of each age present in:	
Age	May–July 1967	May–July 1968
1	19·7	50·9
2	55·3	37·0
3	25·0	12·1
	76 cases	108 cases

The high proportion of one year olds in 1968 was probably due to a higher breeding success of the population in 1967 than in 1966. Nevertheless the very fact that there were 51 per cent of one year olds in May–July 1968 means (given the mortality in the first year) that most of the previous year's surviving juveniles were in the colony.

It appears that significant fluctuations in the Kure population occur from year to year. The increases tended to occur after a year in which unusually few bred, and after a late breeding season. 1969 saw a 31·3 per cent increase in the breeding population, over 1968. This may be connected with the possibility that, in some years, unfavourable conditions inhibit a proportion of the population from breeding. Thus, in 1966, there were as many adults present in the central area of Green Island, but markedly fewer were breeding. This intriguing phenomenon suggests important questions—such as whether the inhibitory factors were physical or social, but without more detailed information little worthwhile interpretation is possible.

The considerable movement between islands discussed above leads one to expect that populations will be subject to increase or decrease (or change in relative proportions of age groups) independently of their particular productivity and that new islands may suddenly acquire a population. Trig Island (French Frigate Shoals) for example, increased eightfold between 1963 and 1969, in this case due to colonisation following an increase in vegetation. Whale-Skate Island increased from one nest in 1963 to 33 in 1968 and dropped to 18 in 1969.

8. *Clubs and roosts*

Non-breeding, immature and perhaps some off-duty breeders are to be found in red-foot colonies, either scattered throughout the breeding birds or in more discrete gatherings. It is useful to distinguish between the non-breeding congregations, however composed, that occur in breeding colonies and the non-breeding congregations or roosts that occur on islands where there are no breeders, or none at that time.

Fairly dense gatherings of non-breeding, mainly immature, red-footed boobies were observed by Diamond on Aldabra, mainly at the lagoonward end of a belt of mangroves, or trees on the sheltered side of an offshore islet. These groups were small and numerous rather than one or two large gatherings. Diamond remarks that many were on isolated *Pisonia grandis*—a tree much favoured in the Pacific for roosting and nesting but rare on Aldabra. In the Galapagos, Tower Island Clubs frequented the fringe of the *Cryptocarpus* area or the trees on the edges of the cliffs beyond the colony and in some cases were comprised mainly of juveniles. Diamond noted both completely juvenile and also fully adult-plumaged individuals in his Clubs. As described in the Behaviour Section (p. 741) there are many interactions in Clubs, but mainly playful (juggling and toying with nest material) or low intensity agonistic interactions. There is little evidence that off-duty breeders join Clubs (but see p. 702 for the statement that they may join roosts; the distinction between Clubs and roosts is not always easy). Almost certainly they are merely temporary gatherings of birds with time on their hands. Having congregated, the presence of others, particularly at close quarters, and when mature individuals are involved, elicits many of the behaviour patterns concerned with breeding.

It emerges from the findings of the Pacific Ocean project that, on several islands, there are large numbers of non-breeders, sometimes totalling about as many as the breeding population. Unfortunately, the criteria for deciding that they are not off-duty breeders is not given. However, it seems certain that in some years a large part of the total population does not breed. Probably the composition of these gatherings changes throughout the season, birds from other islands, perhaps, entering and leaving. It is not known whether they are anything more than resting and roosting congregations that happen to be near, or among, breeding birds. Certainly, however, red-foots do rest and roost on islands which do not support any nesting birds—for example, the bare, rocky island of La Perousse (French Frigate Shoals). Red-foots are notably oceanic and may be seen on or around islands far outside their breeding range, for example, in the many south-west Pacific island archipelagos, which they visit but do not colonise.

9. *Relationships with other species*

The red-foot's arboreal habit removes it from any possible competition for space except, in some local areas, with frigate-birds. Between great frigate-birds and red-foots, however, there is a very close relationship; the two co-exist over much of their range and very often they intermingle intimately when breeding. An intriguing case of a ringed male red-footed booby caught in two successive years on Enderbury Island (Pacific) whilst brooding a nestling great frigate-bird (Woodward 1975) may have resulted from the booby having been reared by frigates. Possibly a booby egg fell into a frigate's nest. Undoubtedly the frigate is the sole beneficiary from the sympatry which must be assumed to stem at least partly from deliberate 'policy' on its part. Not only do incoming red-foots provide some food for the piratical frigates, but their nest-building activities often give the frigate a chance of acquiring material by flight rather than by twig pulling. The red-foot is parasitised more than any other booby, but little is known about the frigate's methods of selecting victims or the significance in the frigate's economy, of the booty thus gained, or the effect on its victim's economy, or sexual and interspecific differences in piracy. I have suggested that victims are selected on the basis of their vocalisations, the pressure of a full crop producing a recognisably distinct call. Rarely do the numbers of frigates in a colony approach the number of boobies, but on Aldabra they even outnumber them. Diamond has suggested that there may have been selection pressure on the boobies to lay at different times than frigates to minimise loss of nests. There are indications that in some areas, male great frigates are more piratical than females, but in magnificent frigates this may not be so. Verner (1965) recorded 86 attacks by magnificent frigates on red-foots; all were by females. On Aldabra I noted that most attacks by great and lesser frigates were by females. Males of both species, however, use precisely the same 'flying down' method to secure nest material from boobies, and in the Galapagos male great frigates chased boobies for food more than did females. The significance of the sex differences in frigate klepto-parasitism is completely obscure. The success rate of chases also seems to vary with region. Twelve per cent of attempted piracies by *minor* on red-foots were successful in the Galapagos, 18 per cent on Aldabra and 63 per cent on the Pacific Christmas Island. Most attacks occur when boobies are returning in the afternoon and evening with full crops, and they seem selective in that some pursuits are quickly abandoned whilst others persist with the utmost determination.

An odd relationship, in which, again, the booby is the loser, concerns the habit of the small-billed Darwin's finch of drinking blood from the roots of the booby's main tail feathers (Fosberg 1965).

SUMMARY

1. The red-footed booby prefers trees (often mangroves) or bushes near the shore, but can nest on cliffs or the ground or two or three kilometres inland.

2. Colony size and density vary enormously, but the red-foot never nests in vast, dense congregations. Usually small groups or single pairs are scattered over a fairly large area.

3. The nest ranges from a flimsy platform to a large, shallow-cupped structure, usually about 30cm in diameter.

Fig. 311

Female lesser frigate 'tipping' red-footed booby to encourage it to disgorge.

4. Clutch size is invariably one; no larger clutches have ever been reliably recorded. The fresh egg weighs about 50g.

5. Lost eggs may be replaced after 10 or more days.

6. The mean incubation period is 45–46 days depending on locality.

7. Incubation stints vary greatly with locality, but are probably typically between 24 and 36 hours.

8. The stages in the development of the chick are described.

9. The chick is fed about once per day, mainly on flying fish and squid.

10. Growth by weight is slow compared with most sulids and is subject to considerable variation between regions. In impoverished areas, growth may be grossly retarded for long periods.

11. The fledging period varies with area, from less than 100 days in a 'good' area to 135 or more in an impoverished one. Probably the most typical period is around 100–110 days.

12. Post-fledging feeding is similarly variable; in good areas it is probably about a month and in impoverished ones anything up to three months.

13. Breeding success (young fledged from eggs laid) varies with area, from less than 10 per cent to at least 70 per cent. In the Galapagos, severe mortality can occur due to shortage of food.

14. Laying is nowhere confined to a short period of the year; seasonal aspects are summarised diagrammatically.

15. Evidence showing food to be the proximate factor controlling the timing of breeding in the Galapagos is discussed in detail.

16. The total length of the breeding cycle varies considerably, according to region; it can be more than 12 months, but is usually substantially less.

17. Probably the red-foot typically breeds annually, but some pairs in the Galapagos must take longer than 12 months between successive layings. In some environments, the interval between successive layings is probably highly variable in the population as a whole. Non-breeding 'periods' (extended rest periods), even if not full years, probably occur.

18. Flying fish and squid are the main food items.

19. Annual adult mortality is probably not more than 8 per cent and may be less.

20. Probably, the red-foot first breeds when in its third or fourth year. Breeding in immature plumage has been recorded.

21. There is substantial movement between islands in general areas (such as the north-central Pacific).

22. The degree of fidelity to site and mate is not known, but at least in the Galapagos, indirect evidence suggests that it may not be very high.

23. Groups of immatures and (some presumed) non-breeders are to be found within breeding colonies.

24. Frigate-birds are often found breeding alongside or among red-footed boobies, which they klepto-parasitise.

4. BREEDING BEHAVIOUR

INTRODUCTION

This species shares with Abbott's booby the distinction of being the only arboreal sulid. The habit of perching in trees has naturally affected the behaviour which the red-foot has evolved, as it has to some extent, its morphology. This point is worth remembering in relation to the details of its behaviour.

ESTABLISHMENT AND MAINTENANCE OF TERRITORY

1. *Aerial Reconnaissance, Flight Circuiting, 'V'-flighting, and Outposting*

We lack information on the first steps of site establishment and have no evidence that this species uses flight reconnaissance, with intense scrutiny of the colony, so important in the gannet. But there is rarely any lack of spare perching places in the vicinity of nesting red-foots, so that no particular problems face the site-establishing bird, who probably in any case returns to the general area of his birthplace, which he has often visited as a free-flying juvenile and as an immature bird.

Once he has settled on an area which will hold his nest, however, (and the exact place is almost certainly decided only late in the proceedings) he begins territorial Flight-circuiting, repeatedly flying from the site and back again or circuiting the immediate area. If there is no female present, the solitary male just jumps into the air, flies off and returns. In other circumstances he may interrupt pair interactions to take-off, fly around and return again.

This behaviour advertises his association with that particular area, for the return always involves landing with loud calling (rah-rah-rah) followed by a post-landing display (see below). Often, the inflying bird holds the wings in a V position, tremoring rather than beating vigorously. So the circuiting behaviour has conspicuous signal value in the context of establishing the ownership of a territory.

Flight-circuiting and V-flighting are rarely if ever seen after egg laying, until the brief recrudescence of territorial and sexual behaviour late in the season. In fact, even the post-landing display largely disappears once the egg has hatched.

The strong relationship between the site and Flight-circuiting, V-flighting and post-landing display is shown by the fact that, even before egg laying, birds do not Flight-circuit from starting points other than their territory, nor land in such places with V-flighting followed by display.

2. *Fighting*

Territorial fighting in the red-foot was relatively rare and brief on Tower, on Christmas Island (Indian Ocean) and also in the Caribbean. This is not to imply that aggressive behaviour is unimportant in this species—far from it—but that (in common with the situation in most other sulids) site competition is insufficiently severe to have placed a premium on the most extreme form of aggression.

When it does occur it involves the stabbing, beak-gripping with pushing, aided by Wing-flailing, common to the group. They do not strike each other with wings or feet. I saw a violent fight between members of a pair that had just reared a chick, but this was unusual. It is worth noting that even though the red-foot nests in trees, it is not much endangered by fighting since, if it slips and falls, it is usually able to recover or climb back up, using the beak as a lever and gripping with the very flexible webs. The red-foot is remarkably agile among branches; much more so than Abbott's booby. Frequently vegetation intervenes between aggressive birds and aggression may then be redirected to the twigs, as a biting or shaking movement. In fact, aggression directed towards twigs is probably the source of the red-foot's main agonistic display, Forward Head Waving (see below), which usually occurs immediately after the bird lands in its territory.

Once established, or re-established, the territory is maintained largely by mere presence (attendance) but also by agonistic behaviour which grades from the rare fighting, through Wing-flailing, Jabbing (or sparring) to a highly ritualised display (Forward Head Waving).

3. *Wing-flailing*

This behaviour usually accompanies either fighting or the lower intensity aggressive behaviour. Against a territorial rival, Jabbing or Forward Head Waving may be accompanied by a violent synchronous movement of the partly spread wings which are raised on the jab and then brought downwards as though the bird were urging itself against the intruder (Fig. 312). At the same time, the bird screeches raucously and may show a variable amount of feather-erection (Ruffing) especially around the head, neck and back.

The same behaviour occurs in defence of small young, when the adult may become extremely frenzied. In this situation it is obvious that the bird is highly afraid as well as aggressive and it is probable that the Ruffing (which here is extreme) always betrays some avoidance (fleeing or fear). This point is of interest because Ruffing may accompany other behaviour and it is interesting to know what it denotes.

The form of the movement is very like that used by large young in vigorous food-begging (q.v.). There, too, the movement is smart and synchronous. Since in other boobies, where the begging wing movements are somewhat different, the Wing-flailing differs correspondingly, it may proably be taken that begging Wing-flailing is in all species the origin of the movement used in the agonistic situation.

4. *Jabbing*

Territorial rivals may Jab at each other (Fig. 313) rapidly and repeatedly, though often without gripping. When boobies do grip, they may get hold of the rival's bill or other parts of the body, perhaps particularly the neck. At its lowest intensity (and very commonly in the pair context) it is merely a slight reaching movement towards the other bird. The typical movement does not appear to be ritualised and is probably just hostile behaviour of medium intensity. At higher intensity it incorporates Wing-flailing and harsh calling and may alternate with bouts of the territorial display Forward Head Waving (see below). In this context it is obviously concerned with defence of territory. Jabbing of a virtually indistinguishable kind quite frequently occurs between members of a pair (see later).

Jabbing is used by the red-foot against other species. It is part of the aggressive behaviour by which the species defends its young and in the Galapagos was frequently used against encroaching great frigate-birds, since these two species nested in very close association. Lawrence (1972)[1] has recorded it, also, against iguanas.

5. *Sparring*

Although earlier (1969b) I recorded that Jabbing 'may also involve violent sideways flicks as though each were flinging its head at the other with bill open, thus resembling the Mutual Jabbing of the white booby' I did not give this form a special name. However, in British Honduras Lawrence called it Sparring (a term which Dorward (1962a) used for the white booby) and noted that it occurred in border conflicts and between mates. The distinguishing features were that, in Sparring, the somewhat opened bills were flung at each other with a sideways shake of the head, rather than as a direct jab. Sparring frequently occurred apparently as a result of mates bringing their bills near to each others', as in Bill-touching or allopreening. This fits with comparable behaviour in

[1] This and subsequent references are to material in preparation for publication. At the time of going to press I have no reference.

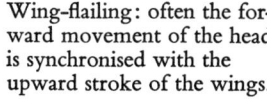

Fig. 312

Wing-flailing: often the forward movement of the head is synchronised with the upward stroke of the wings.

other boobies, where such proximity appears to trigger a hostile reaction, but this takes a variably ritualised form. Bouts lasted about 5–10 seconds and the female usually reacted by Facing-away (see below).

I recorded Sparring associated with Menacing from juveniles in Clubs. It grades into Jabbing, from which it is not always separable. It is clearly a weakly ritualised version of basically hostile Jabbing, particularly common between mates.

6. *Forward Head Waving*

Immediately after landing in the territory and almost as a continuation of the post-landing movement, both sexes perform a violent display which consists of rapid movements of the head down to the twigs, alternately on either side. The neck is stretched, the body sleeked with wings wrapped tightly to it and the whole posture inclined forwards and downwards (Fig. 314). Sometimes the movement is mainly sideways, with a downward direction at the end; at others the swaying is more sinuous. There is often an impression of wildness about the display, accentuated by rapid and vibrant calling, rising and falling throughout, in the harsh, metallic high pitched timbre of the male and the lower one of the female. Usually there are about five swings of the head and body, often extending down to the twigs, which may be gripped fiercely and shaken. Although the movement usually looks somewhat disjointed and uncoordinated it is undoubtedly a highly ritualised display. The so-called twig-waving display (Verner 1961) is simply Forward Head Waving performed whilst holding a twig—a likely contingency because these are often gripped and may be detached. The act of holding a twig and/or taking the bill down to the branches sometimes releases nest-building movements, probably through postural facilitation or as transition movements.

Although utterly predictable as a post-landing display in the period preceding egg-laying, Forward Head Waving is also performed, particularly by the male, at intervals whilst the bird is in its territory. Indeed it may occur in lengthy bouts after territorial disputes or, spasmodically, by tense-looking (stretched and sleeked) birds even where no discernible external stimulus has triggered it. Lawrence recorded a bout of Forward Head Waving that lasted for 28 minutes during a border dispute, the bills of the contestants often being within centimetres of each other. In the early stages of breeding when males are hopping from place to place in their territories they may intersperse bouts of Forward Head Waving. In this situation they are effectively landing again in their territory. If, by contrast, the bird lands away from its territory—say in search of nest material—it does not call or perform the Forward Head Waving. Lawrence observed that on 16 out of 74 occasions on which a bird returned to its nest after a

Fig. 313. Aggressive jabbing.

fairly long absence, the Forward Head Waving of the incomer was matched by Head Waving from the occupier. Though he does not say so, it is likely that in these instances the occupier was the male, reacting to the intruder qualities of the female. This is probably the way in which the gannet's Mutual Fencing display arose from simultaneous Bowing (q.v.).

Although largely concerned with the early stages of breeding, Forward Head Waving may occur even when the birds have chicks and becomes more frequent again very late in the breeding cycle.

Forward Head Waving is an aggressive display. The very act of biting the twigs indicates this and is clearly equivalent to the similar biting of ground (and mate) shown by the male gannet after he lands. The context, too, supports this interpretation, for the display is given as a response to territorial intrusion and in concert with obviously aggressive behaviour like fighting, Wing-flailing, and Jabbing. By contrast, it is not performed by vanquished individuals. Nevertheless, one cannot assume that Forward Head Waving birds are solely aggressive, for (apart from the fact that such 'pure' motivation is inherently very improbable) one can observe that Forward Head Waving may occur in response to disturbance by man or intrusion by a rival—both situations which involve some fear.

It seems likely that Forward Head Waving has been derived from re-directed attack. In fact, this particular display is rather obviously re-directed aggression and has not been elaborated into a highly polished display; its origin thus remains clear. As mentioned earlier, nest building movements may be incorporated, but Forward Head Waving is unlikely to have been derived from them. The fact that the red-foot has not transformed this redirected biting into a highly ritualised and frequently performed display comparable to gannet Bowing may reflect the weaker territoriality of the red-foot, which lacks comparable site competition.

The function of Forward Head Waving is to signify the bird's ownership of a territory and thus to repel potential trespassers.

In sum, the red-foot defends its territory in several ways, from overt fighting through Jabbing to Forward Head Waving. The site ownership display, however, is relatively weakly ritualised re-directed attack and somewhat seasonally restricted in occurrence.

FORMATION AND MAINTENANCE OF PAIR

This is merely a convenient head under which to group a number of behaviour patterns which are related in that their primary context is to do with pair relations. We have already seen that several behaviour patterns occur both between mates and rivals and the same applies to some behaviour to be described in this section.

In the red-foot's large arboreal territory, birds are unable to move about freely on foot, but are nevertheless able to perch well apart (in the Galapagos, even well established mates usually perched more than one metre apart) and to retreat from each other when necessary. Thus they are not constantly on the move in their territories, with the attendant mosaic of communication behaviour patterns, but tend to have fewer interactions. Although they have to meet and to co-ordinate sexual and nest building activity, for example, and mates show considerable hostility towards each other, they have not evolved much appeasement or meeting behaviour.

Pair formation is brought about by territorial males attracting females by Sky-pointing. Presumably females which are ready to breed either return to their previous site or, if they are unable to do so or are breeding for the first time, they Prospect in the colony and react to the appropriate male display.

1. *Sky-pointing (advertising)*

The Sky-pointing bird lengthens its neck, points its bill upwards or even slightly backwards, raises its tail and, by rotating its wings at the shoulder, raises their tips without spreading them (Fig. 315). Thus, the two wing tips, the beak and the tail all point upwards and the display has been called four-pointing. Birds repeat this movement many times, relaxing into a normal position in between. Each time they stretch their necks they utter a long drawn grating call, deeper in the female and more metallic in the smaller male. The extreme position is held for about two seconds, during which the black inter-ramal and gular skin and to a lesser extent the coloured facial skin is prominently displayed. Before and after the display the bird fixes its eyes on the partner ('Gazing' or 'staring') and seems particularly stimulated to Sky-point when it 'catches the eye' of its partner. Between performances the male, in particular, often reaches towards the female (Fig. 315b) and frequently Jabs her—sometimes so fiercely that she retreats, whereupon he Sky-points repeatedly only, perhaps, to launch a further attack when she returns. The display may continue for an hour or more, during which the male, in particular, may Sky-point many scores of times. During Sky-pointing the feathers are sleek. Between times, in the female at least, they may be ruffed—an important indication of her ambivalent motivation (see below).

Whilst Sky-pointing by the male is elicited by females perched nearby or even flying past, it is by no means confined to that situation. Partners often Sky-point to each other, sometimes for very long periods and sometimes females Sky-point to nearby or overflying males. Males often Sky-point between their trips for nest material, at which times they also copulate. Sky-pointing as a mutual display becomes very common after pair formation; females do not usually Sky-point much until the pair bond has been formed.

Sky-pointing is largely sexually motivated behaviour; the context and the nature of the eliciting stimuli make that clear. In the male, aggression is also involved, as the interspersed reaching movements and Jabbing and occasionally Wing-flailing or even overt attack reveal. The female to whom it is directed is often ruffed and may be so between (but not during) her own Sky-pointing, which indicates some fear. She may Face-away or even retreat, but this is usually when the male is Sky-pointing unilaterally rather than when both are displaying together.

Sky-pointing has at least two functions. First, it attracts unmated females and so helps to bring about the initial contact. This is probably its primary function to which, being conspicuous and noisy, it is well adapted.

Second, it establishes rapport between partners, which is particularly important in the copulating and nest building phase. A pair of red-foots is by no means totally inhibited from attacking each other when they are close together and moreover have nothing like the gannet's Mutual Fencing to cope with aggression aroused between mates. Thus, after pair formation but before egg-laying, they often Sky-point to each other at fairly close range, sometimes for over half an hour continuously and it is in this situation that, it seems to me, Sky-pointing fulfills its second function. It will be recalled from the description of Jabbing and Sparring that red-foots are ill equipped with close range 'reassuring' interactions and their habitat precludes the mosaic of behaviour patterns derived from locomotion and its precursors, which are so conspicuous in the ground nesting group of boobies (see p. 557). It therefore seems that in the

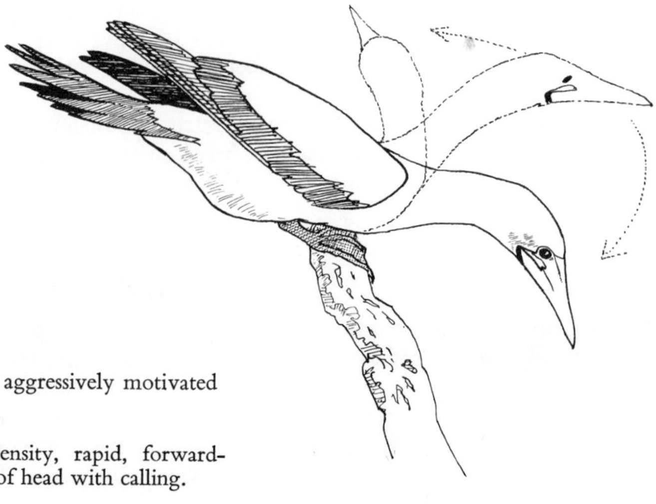

Fig. 314 (a, b, c)

Forward Head Waving display, an aggressively motivated site-ownership display.

(a) Typical intensity, rapid, forward-leaning swings of head with calling.

red-foot Sky-pointing of this kind may compensate. The parallel between its use in these circumstances and that of Mutual Fencing in the gannet is quite close; the male red-foot has a conspicuous habit of interrupting his Sky-pointing to fly out from the site, circle and return to resume Sky-pointing and eventually to copulate. This corresponds to the gannet's habit in early pair formation of performing the meeting ceremony, flying out and returning to resume Mutual Fencing followed by copulation. In both cases the pair members are repeatedly parting, meeting and interacting, which presumably strengthens the pair bond. The fact that reciprocal Sky-pointing is virtually confined to these early stages of the breeding cycle seems to fit this interpretation since later, when it is absent, pair co-operation is minimal, each partner simply taking its share of incubation and chick care with little additional interaction. This stress on the reciprocal nature of Sky-pointing should nevertheless be treated sceptically because neither Verner (1961) nor Lawrence saw reciprocal Sky-pointing at all frequently in the red-foots of Half Moon Cay. It seems improbable that the behaviour could be important in one population but hardly exist in another. This in no way invalidates the suggestion that Sky-pointing as such could function as I suggest, but merely implies that the reciprocal form of the behaviour is unimportant.

If Sky-pointing helps to synchronise the pair's breeding condition—and evidence on the effect of display in general, in birds, suggests that it will (it is known, for example, that in some species, females return to the breeding colony with gonads considerably less well developed than those of males), this would be a function closely related to the above. Thus, ardent display from a sexually advanced male may hasten maturation in the female and reduce any inequality in their physical condition. However, such an effect would not be restricted to Sky-pointing—all pair interactions probably achieve it.

It has been suggested that male Sky-pointing may be directed towards other males and serve as a site ownership display. This is perhaps somewhat unlikely, both on account of its rarity in such a context and because the species *has* a conspicuous display—Forward Head Waving, which clearly fulfils this very function. In fact, whilst, in birds, aggressive behaviour almost invariably enters into courtship, sexual behaviour more rarely functions secondarily as aggressive behaviour.

(b) Forward Head Waving with low-intensity wing action.

(c) Forward Head Waving with high-intensity wing action.

Finally, with regard to derivation, the Sky-pointing movement is almost certainly homologous throughout the sulids (see p. 932). In the gannet the display is indisputably a pre-movement signal (probably its ancestral function) and not a sexual display. One may convincingly derive Sky-pointing from pre-flight neck lengthening and chin lifting, exaggerated by pointing the bill upwards. Thus the red-foot's Sky-pointing may also stem from an ancestral pre-flight movement, though it has since become functionally and motivationally emancipated.

Apart from Sky-pointing and of course copulation itself, there probably is no other behaviour that is primarily sexual, although the pair do interact in many more ways, which are described below.

2. *Jabbing*

Jabbing, whether mutual or otherwise, has already been described as territorial behaviour, but it is also common between mates. When pair members meet at the site after a prolonged absence (though not when one returns after a brief flight) they often Jab each other hard and rapidly. This hostile behaviour seems fully overt (that is, not hesitant or restrained) and early and late in the season, when presumably aggressive motivation is high and for some reason insufficiently inhibited, even old pair members may actually fight. One such struggle lasted for several minutes and forcibly illustrates the part played by aggression in pair relations. It also,

Fig. 315 (a and b)

(a) Sky-pointing (sexual advertising display). Each partner Sky-points to the other, but not simultaneously.

(b) Between 'Sky-points' the male often reaches (aggressively) towards the female, who ruffles her head feathers, tremors her neck and Faces-away.

incidentally, illustrates one of the contrasts between the red-foot and the gannet, for it could not have happened in the latter species, despite the aggressiveness of the male; the female gannet simply will not fight her mate.

(a) A male flies (calling) from a perch in his territory to one nearer the female, who is showing some fear (long necked, head withdrawn, slightly ruffled).

(b) Male moves (calling) towards a female (both long necked and sleeked).

(c) As he gets close both become ruffed and the female threatens male.

(d) A male Sky-points to a female who shows some fear (ruffed).

(e) The male reaches (aggressively) towards female, who Faces-away.

Fig. 316 (a–e)

Aggressive and sexual interactions between mates.

Jabbed birds, usually females, squawk, Ruff their feathers and take evasive action, sometimes violent, at others merely Facing-away (q.v.). There seems no obvious difference between the Mutual Jabbing of rivals and that of mates, though the latter tends more towards Sparring (q.v.). It usually elicits corresponding withdrawal rather than an attempt to grip and is itself followed by withdrawal.

There is nothing to suggest that Jabbing between mates, either unilateral or mutual, has any obvious function though it may possibly have a more subtle one as a 'cathartic' expression of aggression. It seems better to interpret it merely as an expression of their tendency to attack each other, usually sufficiently inhibited by antagonistic ones to be expressed merely as Sparring, Bill-touching, Reaching or even just Staring. Certainly there is nothing in this species to suggest that the male's aggression has become sexually stimulating to the female, a situation quite contrary to that in the gannet.

Intimate pair relations requiring more co-operation than simple territorial tolerance are, as already mentioned, characterised by bouts of mutual Sky-pointing which may thus subserve one of the functions filled by ritualised greeting behaviour in some other species.

3. *Sparring*

The more frequent occurrence of Sparring (see p. 725) between mates than between rivals, is consistent with its role as relatively low intensity agonistic behaviour in the territorial context. It has not progressed significantly towards becoming a ritualised pair interaction, comparable even to the white booby's Mutual Jabbing.

4. *Bill-touching*

Bill-touching occurs during close contact between mates and is also probably low intensity agonistic behaviour. It is relatively infrequent and unpredictable. Bill-touching birds usually evince either aggression (more forward posture and sleeked feathers) or fear (withdrawal and ruffed feathers) the male typically showing the former. Bill-touching is probably low intensity Jabbing in which the actual jab appears as an intention movement; it is often interspersed with or precedes Jabbing.

5. *Facing-away (including Tremoring)*

This behaviour occurs during interactions between neighbouring territory owners but mainly between mates. In the former it accompanies Jabbing or Sparring.

Unlike the gannet, where the male shows violent unilateral attack and the female marked appeasement behaviour, the aggression of red-foot pairs is mutual though more frequent and intense in the male. A common response to attack is a turning of the head Facing-away (Fig. 316). In both sexes the gesture is often so unobtrusive and fleeting that it could be overlooked as simply a random head movement or flinch, though it is in fact a clear response to the movement, or intention movement of Jabbing from the other bird. Thus it is particularly common when the male is constantly Reaching towards the female (incipient aggression) and she just as frequently Faces-away. It is also performed by, for example, trespassing birds when engaged in agonistic interaction with territory owners.

Birds Facing-away tend to show ruffled plumage and Tremoring. The latter is a shivering or sometimes strong trembling of the head, neck and lower breast. Aggression by the partner is only one of the stimulus situations eliciting Tremoring; any in which fear and aggression are in conflict are likely to cause it. Thus, birds guarding new born young Tremor when man approaches and juveniles Tremor strongly when others 'crash' their individual distance barriers or launch an attack with Menacing (q.v.). At such times, every member of a group of juveniles, perhaps 20 or more, might Tremor simultaneously.

The contexts in which birds Face-away make it plain that the behaviour is induced mainly by fear and tends to occur in the less aggressive of two interacting birds. The fact that it is often accompanied by Tremoring and Ruffing is consistent with this interpretation since these, too, occur in situations which offer danger and thus arouse fear.

In a strongly territorial bird in which the sexes are very much alike, appeasement behaviour would be one way of controlling aggression between mates. In fact, it has been observed that birds which Face-away are very rarely attacked and although this simple correlation does not prove that Facing-away inhibits attack, it suggests so.

If it is indeed appeasement behaviour, it seems somewhat anomalous that it is so very inconspicuous. In the absence of plumage markers to confine aggression to individuals with the appropriate releasers (conspecifics of the same sex) and of a greeting ceremony equivalent to the gannet's (q.v.), one might have expected something more dramatic. Perhaps the fact that red-foots can easily withdraw tends to reduce the need for conspicuous appeasement.

If one concludes that the red-foot lacks really effective appeasement behaviour it makes some sense of the fact that this species lacks mutual allo-preening. One sex may roughly preen the other on the head but usually the partners do not preen each other simultaneously. The male's preening of the female is usually directed to one spot on the head or nape and is rough and aggressive, with twig biting often interposed. The female often reacts by Tremoring and Facing-away. The lack of mutual preening may reflect the danger, inherent in an aggressive species with weak appeasement, of two individuals pointing bills at each other at close range, as would be necessary in mutual preening (see Comparative Section p. 945).

6. *Copulation*

Red-foots copulate only in the territory and in my experience on or very close to the nest site, usually early or late in the day and frequently, also, during darkness—their activity betrayed by the male's peculiar grating call. The female shows no obvious soliciting behaviour, although when the male mounts she is in fact often bending forward to touch or handle nest material (Fig. 317). This is partly because the male usually precedes copulation with trips for nest material. The male shows no essential preliminaries to copulation, though the normal intention movements of locomotion—neck lengthening and Wing-flicking—often precede the hop onto her back and similarly, Wing-flicking, the usual post-hop Pelican Posture or even full post-landing territorial display (Forward Head Waving with calling) may occur after he alights on the female's back or hops down from it. In both the above cases, the behaviour

Fig. 317. During copulation (no head gripping) the male utters a grating call. No other sulid calls during copulation.

patterns are probably causally linked with the locomotory movement involved in copulation rather than with the sexual aspect.

As he mounts, and also during copulation, the male utters a grating call which is higher and less drawn-out than the Sky-pointing call; he may repeat it more slowly during copulation. The red-foot male does not grip the female's head, nor does he open his wings or patter with his feet. During copulation the female frequently grips, and builds or quivers nest material, and ruffles her feathers. Cloacal application is achieved by the female raising her tail sideways. The entire process takes only ten seconds or less; copulation in the gannet takes almost three times as long and involves much more stimulation for both sexes—an interesting point for the Comparative Section. The male may fly straight from the female's back or dismount. Sometimes the pair briefly touch bills afterwards, but normally the female makes nest building movements and the male flies off for nest material.

7. *Movements signalling impending flight*

(*a*) *Wing Flick*

More than any other booby, the red-foot often performs a quick flick of the wings, rapidly jerking them half open and shut, before taking flight. Wing Flicking also occurs prior to hopping, though it is rarely performed unless flight is imminent, and also before mounting or dismounting in copulation. The liberal use of this behaviour pattern, particularly in situations in which actual flight does not immediately follow, strongly suggests that in this species it has signal value. In fact it could serve a useful function in co-ordinating nest relief, as Sky-pointing undoubtedly does in the gannet (q.v.). A female red-foot may react to male Wing Flicking by responding similarly and moving; thus when both are off the nest and the male Wing Flicks, the female may move onto the nest as though anticipating the male's departure, which usually follows.

The extreme use of Wing Flicking in this species is particularly interesting since it has 'lost' pre-flight neck lengthening, or Sky-pointing, as a signal of movement (Sky-pointing is now a sexual display, p. 728) and because its habitat precludes walking about, has not had the same chance to develop another pre-walking posture, such as Bill-up-face-away in the white booby (q.v.). It seems to have compensated by using the next link in the sequence leading to flight as a pre-movement signal.

(*b*) *Wing Rattle*

This is a brisk, jerky, mainly horizontal shaking of the loosened and slightly raised wings, with bill inclined upwards. It probably originated as a plumage settling movement after preening or bathing and in preparation for flight, but now undoubtedly has signal value and is incorporated into display. Like Wing Flicking, it occurs during bouts of Sky-pointing, when the male frequently takes off and returns, and during the interactions preceding nest relief. It seems to possess a signal value similar to that of Wing Flicking.

8. *Pelican Posture*

The Pelican Posture belongs here because it is clearly associated with movement, which it follows. When moving about in their territory, red-foots assume this distinctive posture, neck arched and bill pointing downwards (Fig. 318), after each hop. They usually hold the bill tip well clear of the throat and the movement is almost a continuation of or recovery from the hop. The posture is fleetingly held and then the neck slowly and gracefully straightened. However, the Pelican Posture is more than simply a necessary part of the mechanics of recovering from a hop, for birds which are about to hop (as shown by precursors such as Wing Flicking) may also Pelican Posture. Also a red-foot may assume the Pelican Posture in ambivalent situations, as when its chick is unduly aggressive during food begging. Nevertheless, its signal value is obscure. The Comparative Account (q.v.) helps only a little. So far as the red-foot is concerned, it would be mere guesswork to define the function, but of course its form immediately suggests appeasement.

It seems odd that the adult red-foot should possess the Pelican Posture and Facing-away, but the chick lacks bill-hiding, which would seem the likeliest source of both.

This completes the account of behaviour mainly to do with forming and maintaining the pair. It is not yet known how often the red-foot keeps the same mate in successive breeding attempts (though it sometimes does so), but behavioural evidence hints that often pairs may not re-form. Thus the pair-bond is relatively ill-formed, (deduced from the relative lack of pair interactions). If this is so, the trait may (at least in the Galapagos) be correlated with an environment in which long term stability of pairs is often impracticable (see Ecology Section pp. 710 and 713).

OTHER BEHAVIOUR INVOLVED IN BREEDING

The previous section concentrated on communication behaviour, but of course successful breeding depends on a large number of behaviour patterns that have a perfectly obvious and straightforward function.

1. *Nest building and associated behaviour*

The nest in the red-foot is a variably substantial structure. The largest may consist of a vast pile of twigs, the smallest are flimsy platforms which occasionally allow the egg to slip through. Most are more or less robust but temporary structures with shallow cups and often a lining of smaller green sprays. Green sprays on nests in the interior of the island showed that birds must have journeyed more than a mile to the nearest *Cryptocarpus* shrub. Material may be gathered within 5 or 6 metres of the nest, but not plucked from the immediate vicinity. Abbott's booby shares this trait. Thus some cover remains to shade the young. Other members of the family frequently gather nest material from the territory and immediately around the site. That there is not a total inhibition against gathering nest material from the vicinity of the site is shown by the red-foot's habit in British Honduras of pilfering from nearby nests. Oddly, the Galapagos birds ignored unattended nests, which remained intact even though other pairs were building nearby.

The nest is built mainly by the female from twigs brought by the male, particularly during the pre-laying phase of frequent copulation and prolonged attendance. The main, perhaps the only, contributions of the female are at change-over when the relieved bird often gathers nest material. This, incidentally, means that the presence of green material cannot reliably be used to date the nest and eggs.

Females usually begin the actual building, though once I saw the male place the first twig (or at least a twig where there were no others). Perhaps either sex chooses the site, though the male chooses the territory. At first, successive pieces of nest material may be placed in three or four different spots before enough accumulate to guide subsequent placings. Solitary males may

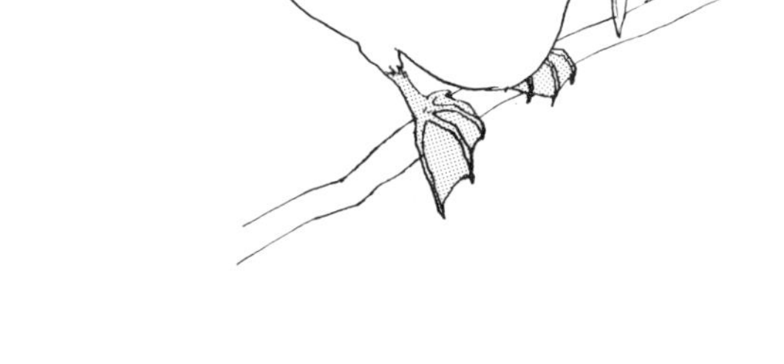

Fig. 318

Pelican Posture, following a hop.

collect nest material but in my experience a female always appeared before a proper nest had been built.

Records of about 200 nests which were subsequently laid in showed that in the Galapagos one to three weeks normally elapsed between starting the nest and laying the egg, if the building occured in a period of concerted activity in the group concerned, leading to a clear peak in egg laying. Sometimes desultory building continued for weeks or even months without culminating in laying though usually the nest was abandoned after a relatively short period of building, if there was to be no laying.

Twigs are placed in front or to one side and vibrated or quivered into position with stereotyped side to side movements of the head, sometimes of very small amplitude. As a result the material is pushed in between existing pieces in a crude and haphazard way rather than skilfully interwoven. The mandibles are not vibrated rapidly up and down, as they are in the gannet, when letting go of a sticky piece of nest material. The act of nest building is not invariably followed by a side to side headshake as it is in the gannet, again probably because the red-foot does not need to shake off dirt or water as the gannet does.

So far, I have described nest building in terms of its primary function—the construction of an adequate nest. There are two other aspects—nest building as a pair bonding activity and as a displacement activity. Mates may simultaneously grip a twig and make building movements with it. Other sulids do the same with their respective nest materials and in some species, for example the white booby, the shared nest building is purely symbolic. In all cases, one may suspect that the pair bond is slightly strengthened by this habit.

Nest building movements are often performed during courtship, even when there is no nest. They may be interspersed with Sky-pointing, Jabbing and Facing-away and are common, from the female, during copulation and from an occupying bird upon the arrival of its mate. The female may perform quivering during allo-preening, or either bird as a response to the approach of an intruder—whether another booby, another species of bird, or man. In all such cases they are probably facilitated displacement acts, elicited and oriented by the external stimulus provided by twigs and the nest. This kind of phenomenon is well known in conflict situations and the role of the external environment in influencing which particular 'irrelevant' act shall occur is well documented. It is understandable that in the red-foot conflict behaviour should take the form of nest or twig touching, biting or nest building movements. In such situations the handling of nest material frequently seems to elicit conspicuous swallowing movements.

In addition to cases such as those cited above, which clearly involve conflict in varying degrees, nest building movements (quivering) occur simply because the nest or a twig, is there to release it, though at that particular instant it is neither functional in building nor is there conflict. Quivering is a very common activity among Club birds, where it may be associated with breaking off, juggling or tossing twigs and also occurs in chicks. The red-foot reaction to twigs is thus extremely strong. Even when away from their territory, resting or preening, birds will usually attempt to catch twigs that are thrown to them whereas a ground nesting booby will not.

Several boobies have evolved the habit of exhibiting to the partner the fragment of nest material which they are about to deposit. They do so by swinging the twig or whatever it is high into the air in an arc. The red-foot, however, has not evolved this behaviour.

2. *Nest digging*

Red-foots dig and probe vigorously into the bottom of the nest with slightly parted mandibles, afterwards shaking their heads with a violent flinging motion in the manner employed when shaking strongly adhering matter from the bill. Presumably the function of this behaviour is to remove lumps which might puncture the eggshell when this is supporting the weight of the incubating bird, or damage the new chick.

3. *Incubation and incubation stints*

By the time the egg is laid both sexes, and particularly the female, are spending long periods at the site, attendance having risen steadily since the beginning of the nesting attempt. Thereafter the pair spend little time together. Because neither bird stays long away from the nest just before laying, it is usually possible for the female to relinquish the egg soon after and go to sea, leaving the male to take the first long stint. As a species, the red-foot takes long incubation stints. In the Galapagos they averaged about 60 hours (Table 99) though in the Caribbean they were only about 24 hours. This trait is related to the length of the foraging trips, which in turn is an adaptation to their feeding habitat (see Ecology Section p. 681). Thus, in the Galapagos, each sex took about ten stints. Probably the red-foot chick begins to vocalise after piercing the air space and so the parents know when their egg is about to hatch. Thus, it should be possible for them to react by shortening their foraging trips so that the possibility of a newly hatched chick left without food for several days would be minimised. This, in fact, happens in some species. In the Galapagos, however, adults sometimes remained at sea for over twice as long as the average off-duty spell, itself long, even when the egg was due to hatch or the chick was very small. Thus the unpredictable scarcity of food made it impossible to avoid long absences, as a direct result of which some newly born young died.

Each partner tends to take time off about equal to the time it had to incubate before relief, which suggests that it has to make good considerable weight loss (in the great frigate-bird this amounts to some 20 per cent of its body weight per stint) or else that it takes a long time to locate and catch enough food.

The egg is incubated beneath the webs and its position adjusted by tucking movements using the closed bill. The webs are shifted on top of the egg and clasp it more or less completely (heat transference is discussed in the Comparative Behaviour Section p. 946). During the heat of the day the egg may be shaded rather than incubated. If it is deserted at any stage of the normal incubation period or fails to hatch after more than the maximum, incubation behaviour stops gradually. The adult may stand in the territory, leaving the egg uncovered and then return to it for a short spell before flying right away.

Earlier, I described the results of some experiments designed to show whether a gannet would incubate before she had laid her own egg (p. 201). In similar substitution experiments with the red-foot, a female at the nest building stage accepted a partly incubated egg and hatched it. Furthermore, she then fed and cared for the chick at the same time as she incubated her own egg which she had by then laid.

4. *Brooding of young*

Like other sulids, red-foots do not systematically dispose of egg shells; they often drop them over the edge of the nest or leave them near the rim. Chicks are brooded on top of the parent's webs for the first few days and parents boldly defend the nest, striking at human intruders, simultaneously bristling their feathers, screeching and Wing-flailing. Apart from brooding the chick and tucking it gently into position from time to time by placing their closed beak beneath it and with small, controlled jabs shifting it on their webs and occasionally preening it, the main interaction between chick and parent is during feeding.

The young are at first unable to regulate their body temperature and so are shielded from the sun and kept warm at night. This protection, which of course is also against predators, lasts until the chick is about four to five weeks old, by which time it is well clothed in down, though by no means able to defend itself against all predators (see p. 700). After that, it is left unguarded whilst both parents forage. This contrasts totally with the state of affairs in the gannet, where normally the chick is never left unattended from hatching until it flies from the nest.

5. *Change-over*

It has already been mentioned that red-foots do not perform complex meeting ceremonies, but simply brief and apparently hostile Jabbing, with some Facing-away by the female. Often the sitting bird simply rises and departs after its partner flies in and performs the Forward Head Waving display. Relieved males in particular, may make several trips for nest material and then often fly round in a wide semi-circle, before heading out to sea. Alternatively they may move slightly off the nest and preen before departing. Again, the strong tendency for pair members to move away from each other is evident, whereas gannet pair members spend about a sixth of the day together on the nest during chick growth. Almost all change-overs, of which we recorded hundreds accurate to within three hours, were in the hour or two before or after dark.

6. *Feeding of young*

Probably from the first day, the chick periodically protrudes and raises its head in the uncoordinated manner of nidicolous young, ruffling the parent's breast feathers. This stimulates the adult to lower its head and triggers off the chain of food-giving behaviour in which the parent, with widely opened beak, engulfs the chick's head and regurgitates food fragments in a semi-controlled fashion. Often, however, the adult first repeatedly touches the chick's head as though to stimulate begging, or feeds it apparently without any external stimulus other than the chick's presence. When the chick is newly hatched, it seems that gannets provide a more or less *internally fixed* number of feeds and if there are two young each gets less (p. 101). Later in their growth this is not the case. Unfortunately we could not obtain similar evidence for the red-foot because of the enormous variation in normal growth due to prolonged starvation even in the early stages and the inadequate supply of synchronously hatched young.

Adults returning with full crops are usually eager to feed their young and begin to stretch their necks and show intention movements of regurgitation even before the chick has touched them. The chick thrusts its head violently into the adult's mouth (Fig. 319) and makes strenuous pumping movements which probably help to transfer fish from throat to throat. A bout of feeding comprises one to six successive entries into the parent's mouth. Red-foot chicks are fed on average slightly less than once per day after they are about a month old. However, growth is very irregular and may be suspended for many days; according to locality, well over 30 weeks may elapse between hatching and fledging.

7. *Other aspects of parent/young relationship*

Whilst some species of brids discriminate against strange young, others do not, though this does not prove that they cannot recognise their own. The red-foot will accept foster chicks up to at least a month old and probably more, irrespective of the age of its own youngster. Thus it fails to discriminate between objects which are physically poles apart. Chicks will, for their part, accept foster parents and a donated sibling (cf. white booby). Things change, however, at about the time when the young become capable of flight. Then, adults will attack strange young and drive them away. This is probably what people see when they claim that parents force their fully feathered young to fly by knocking them off their perch. Verner (1961) specifically noted that whereas adults did not discriminate against strange, fluffy young, they did so against fully feathered ones. Thus, discrimination, if not recognition matures late in the latter's dependent phase, when it becomes advantageous by ensuring that strange young are not fed. Earlier discrimination would be of no advantage since the young always remain in or near their own nest—a situation which does not apply to ground nesting boobies. The adult red-foot does not, however, restrict its food-giving to young which are actually on the nest (as the gannet does). I found that red-foot chicks were tolerant of other chicks when artificially twinned, but Verner (1961) noted that 'nestlings fiercely resisted intrusion by other young' and young on their own nests usually subdued even larger, introduced chicks.

BEHAVIOUR OF YOUNG

From hatching until independence, the young red-foot's behaviour is concentrated exclusively on survival—in terms of combating hunger, the environment and attack from other birds. In a treatment of behaviour ordered in relation to function, these categories are as good as any for a framework.

1. *Feeding*

The greatest hazard facing the young red-foot, at least in some parts of its range, is starvation.

Some newly-hatched chicks shrivelled up because the parent, absent when they were born, remained away four or five days and the other had no food, or large chicks lost so much weight that they ended up six or eight weeks 'behind' the weight they should have been—hardly more than skin, bone and feathers. Yet at other times all thrived and the ones who had survived the

Fig. 319

(a) When begging for food, juveniles use a synchronous wing beating and head bobbing.

(b) About to insert its bill in parent's mouth (the chick is calling repeatedly).

(c)

Probing for a bolus.

testing time rapidly recovered. Obviously there must have been severe selection pressure in favour of any adaptation, physiological or behavioural, that helped to cope with this situation. The only behaviour which could have a direct effect on the adult's willingness to give food would seem to be begging (Fig. 319). At first, the small, naked and wobbly-headed youngster can do little except lift and move its head in a weak and unco-ordinated manner. However, as the chick gets older it begs progressively more vigorously. From about a month onwards, it bobs and feints (Fig. 319) with rapid ducking and side to side head movements, simultaneously giving violent down strokes of its wings. This may pass into a frenzied onslaught on the adult, with vigorous lunges and jabs at the basal half of its beak. From about six weeks onwards the young bird incorporates a 'chucking' call and in starving young hunger is so powerful that this is ceaselessly maintained even during sleep, with head in scapulars. Unsatisfied chicks may continue high intensity begging long after the parent has flown right away from the territory. Since the extreme form of this frenzied begging surpasses anything found in the other sulids, it may well have evolved as adaptive behaviour, maximally stimulating to the parent and therefore more likely to elicit regurgitation, which could be critically important for the chick.

2. *Resting and sleeping*

If it is impossible to get enough food it is helpful to reduce energy expenditure. A considerable amount of energy is used in maintaining the right body temperature. In parts of the interior of Tower the temperature of the air may be over 38°C and it then becomes difficult for a bird to lose body heat. Since bare areas radiate heat most effectively, the best position would be one in which these are most exposed to air currents. The red-foot chick achieves this by sticking its rump—the bare skin around the cloaca—high into the air, with the bill forming a forward prop. It sleeps or rests like this only during the hot part of the day. In another resting or sleeping posture the head and neck dangle vertically downwards. Often, too, the head is inclined slightly upwards and the gular skin fluttered. This provides a flow of air over the bare skin and probably helps to regulate heat loss. Judged by the rate of weight loss, the time of greatest energy expenditure is during the hot period of the day, which is when the behaviour patterns just described come into play. The same tripod position was adopted by young birds on Half Moon Cay and is thus not a special adaptation to an unusually hot environment.

3. *Moving, exercising, etc.*

Boobies are not anatomically suited to tree nesting, but the young red-foot is fairly nimble among branches. It seeks shade and moves freely, balancing adeptly where others would fall. Even when the nest is virtually on the ground the chick is rarely found there, preferring to remain higher. Nor is the nest itself necessary, once the chick has reached about four weeks of age. We followed the fortunes of more than 100 young on Tower, many of which had little or no nest and only two fell to the ground. At the age of four to six weeks chicks often climb onto exposed perches and exercise their wings. Fully feathered young spend long periods 'feeling' the wind with outspread wings, balancing in it and allowing it to lift them slightly off their perch. Because they are so light they can easily make short practice flights and on Tower it was not uncommon to see young with considerable down on the head and neck actually fly from the nest and return. I doubt whether this would be possible in all red-foot habitats. On Christmas Island it might be difficult, when so unpractised, to return to a nest high in a jungle tree. There could be no greater contrast than with the comparable situation in the gannet p. 214.

4. *Interactive behaviour*

(*a*) *Bill-hiding*

The red-foot chick has little need of social behaviour other than seeking shelter and food from its parents. Once it has become fluffy it is left alone for much of the time and its arboreal habitat precludes much wandering. Even downy young will, however, defend their parent's territory against intruding adults either of their own or another species. This behaviour revealed a surprising weakness. It sometimes happened that an adult white booby wandered on to a red-foot territory and attacked the chick, as it would also attack a white booby chick, but whereas the latter would hide its bill—a stereotyped appeasement posture—the red-foot chick lacked this behaviour and retaliated. It may seem astonishing that such simple avoidance behaviour, which one might have thought to be a reflex withdrawal, can in fact be absent in one species though present in other members of the genus. This raises three points; the efficacy of beak-hiding as appeasement behaviour, the reasons for its absence in the red-foot and the implications for adult behaviour thought to be derived from it.

The natural experiment already mentioned strongly indicated that beak-hiding is effective in saving young from injury or even death. Whereas the white booby chicks were pecked until the nape, which the chick presented, bled profusely, they were not severely damaged, but the red-foot chick, pitting its soft bill and fluffy body against the steel and feathers of the adult white booby, was mauled and even killed.

One can only surmise that beak-hiding has dropped out of the red-foot chick's repertoire because in the large arboreal territories there is normally no likelihood of severe attack by adults of the same species who have, concurrently, evolved an avoidance response to youngsters who attack them. The Tower red-foots were just unlucky to nest in low shrubs where white boobies could get at them—normally the two species do not nest cheek by jowl, and the red-foots are in much higher trees, such as the jungle of Christmas Island (Indian Ocean) or the mangroves of Aldabra.

Infantile beak-hiding may be the source of two adult behaviour patterns—the Pelican Posture and Facing-away. The lack of it in the red-foot could imply that the Pelican Posture and Facing-away are derived from a different source from their apparent homologues in the gannet (q.v.) which seem so clearly related to chick beak-hiding.

(*b*) *Juvenile behaviour, including Clubs*

The red-foot is fully feathered when about 14–17 weeks old. Strictly it becomes a juvenile when it is free-flying and theoretically capable of fishing for itself, but this demarcation has little practical meaning here. The young red-foot becomes free-flying some time before it has any hope of catching anything and long before it could possibly sustain itself.

On Tower, for months after its first extended flight, the juvenile returned to its territory where it showed normal adult territorial behaviour, displacing intruders and giving the Forward Head Waving display after landing. Then, as shown by colour-ringed individuals, in some cases whilst still being fed by its parents, it joined dense Clubs on the fringes of the breeding areas. The Clubs, about 50–60 strong and often composed entirely of juveniles, appeared suddenly in early June. Club juveniles settled almost in bodily contact with neighbours, there was considerable coming and going and the Club's strong social attraction was shown by the way in which foci shifted; where a few gathered others joined. Even on the sea, dense rafts formed, the birds apparently being attracted mainly by the presence of others rather than by food; there was much traffic and no fishing dives, though birds arrived in shallow landing dives.

Juveniles showed marked agonistic conflict behaviour in these gregarious Clubs. Tense Neck Tremoring was shown by almost every bird, particularly soon after it first arrived. Neighbours often Jabbed each other, much as adult pair members do on meeting in the territory and showed the same Sparring followed by quick sideways headshaking. Sometimes one preened or nibbled its neighbour's feathers, eliciting a startled 'aark', but there was no reciprocal allo-preening. Birds constantly provoked each other by tweaking the feet, wings or tail of even a peaceable neighbour. Then they threatened each other with open bill and neck tremoring. Thus, when densely grouped they used threat behaviour as gannets do, even though this is not used by adults in territorial encounters. Occasionally they Faced-away from each other, much as a female Faces-away from an aggressive male. They also adopted the Pelican Posture when moving from place to place. Frequently they plucked sprays, tossed and juggled twigs and made nest building movements. At this stage all adult behaviour patterns, except copulation and Sky-pointing were already being performed, but not yet organised into the adult pattern.

From the beginning of June until we left in July, there was a growing tendency for groups of adults and slightly immature birds to congregate on the fringe of the areas which held breeding birds. These groups were not composed of birds on fixed sites and seemed comparable to gannet Clubs. The Club birds were unusually wary and took flight long before site attending birds. They tended to keep apart from the juveniles. On Aldabra, groups of variably immature birds either gathered in favoured resting trees or in small groups among breeding birds.

In a territorial but colonial species like the red-foot the development of the necessary spacing-out behaviour must occur simultaneously with the development, or maintenance, of 'clustering' behaviour—a complex process to which interactions in non-breeding groups may contribute significantly.

MAINTENANCE BEHAVIOUR

So far in this account the emphasis has been on those groups of behaviour patterns, often ritualised, which bear a direct relationship to major events in the breeding cycle. Whilst this may have imparted some form to what might otherwise have been a mere list, it has meant that a number of 'ordinary' activities have not yet received due mention, simply because they do not fit anywhere in particular in such a functional scheme. The following section describes these under the convenient heading of maintenance activities, though they are not all strictly concerned with body maintenance.

Fig. 320

Sunning posture.

1. *Stance and movement*

In the relaxed position the red-footed booby perches with retracted head and smooth plumage but when alert becomes more upright and long-necked. The alert position is easily recognised and useful as an indication that the booby is paying attention to some external stimulus, in which the observer, also, might be interested! The tarsi are, both in absolute terms and relative to the bird's size, shorter than in any other sulid, which may be an adaptation to tree-nesting. Red-footed boobies perch extremely well; by contrast, most other boobies are hopeless in trees. Among branches they usually hop with both legs together, probably because their short tarsi prevent them taking long steps, or they may sidle along uncluttered branches. If they crash-land among twigs—as they not infrequently do in their haste to escape the attention of marauding frigates—they may use their closed beak to level themselves up, but they never pull themselves up by gripping. One would suspect that it would be more efficient to do so but birds, at least those as primitive as this group, are not great innovators. On the ground they shuffle hesitantly and awkwardly with their tarsi inclined at a shallow angle. On Tower they rarely alighted on the ground, and they are certainly by far the least efficient boobies at walking.

Curio (1964) recorded a curious phenomenon in which birds trying to take flight under conditions of stress, as when quickly approached by man, became totally disorganised and fell to the ground. His interpretation, that flight paralysis was induced by powerful conflict, may seem less likely than that failure resulted from over hasty movements. Some birds fell when attempting to escape from me under difficult conditions, but not usually from favourable perches.

2. *Preening and associated behaviour*

All boobies often spend many consecutive hours, days or perhaps even weeks at sea and therefore have fully waterproof plumage which they spend much time preening and oiling. The actual preening movements, nibbling, stropping against the lie of breast and belly feathers, running the vanes of wing and tail feathers through the serrated bill and so on, are alike in all and need not be repeated in detail. The red-foot, however, has one curious trait. The bird suddenly stabs savagely at the root of the tail or the flank area with a violent swinging motion, often alternating from side to side. Simultaneously it may squawk as though unpleasantly stimulated. This 'stab' preening hardly seems likely to be a normal habit and may perhaps be restricted to the Galapagos birds, which may have been infested with a particularly troublesome ectoparasite. Red-foots very often, if not invariably, preen their tails, primaries and back

Fig. 321

Resting posture in the chick. Exposed cloaca, loosened wings, and exposed webs (which may also be excreted onto) may all be heat-losing devices.

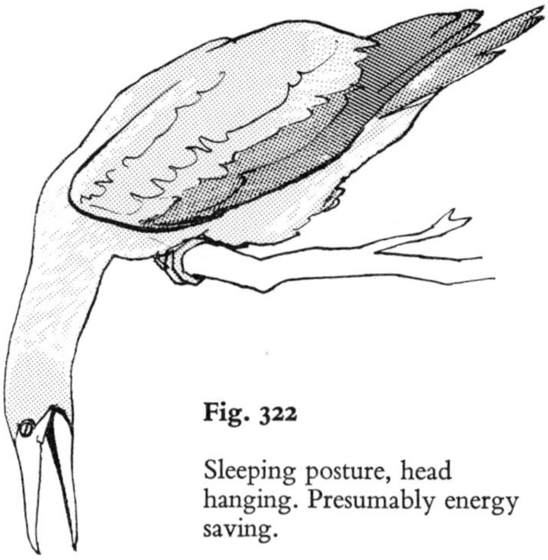

Fig. 322

Sleeping posture, head hanging. Presumably energy saving.

with eyes closed, but keep them open when preening breast feathers and wing bow.

The waterproofing of feathers is achieved by applying the oily secretion of the preen gland, at the base of the tail. Birds roll the back of the head on the gland and then roll or rub it on wings, back or other parts. They occasionally take up the gland secretion on their bills and apply it directly to the feathers.

All boobies frequently scratch the head and neck region as part of their toilet behaviour. The movement is direct, the foot being brought forwards beneath the wing, not over the top of it as in indirect scratching.

3. *Headshaking and Wing-flapping*

(*a*) *Headshaking*

The quick headshake from side to side in its ordinary context is largely concerned with dispelling matter adhering to the head or bill—fish fragments, water or fragments of nest material being the commonest—or settling fish in the crop. It also occurs, quickly and forcefully, after Mutual Jabbing and sometimes after Sky-pointing. In both it may still be a response to tactile stimulation, in the former due to contact and in the latter to feather tightening (neck lengthening). It could conceivably play a minor role as a social signal, communicating

Fig. 323. A group of roosting red-footed boobies, Raine Island. Note the different plumages (morphs). *Photo:* J. Warham.

ambivalence in the same way that the several components of a behaviour mosaic probably indicate subtle motivational shifts, but there is of course no direct evidence of this. Certainly it has not become prominent in pair and other social interactions as it has in the gannet, which may reflect the fact that it is very much rarer in the first place. Much the same is true for other boobies (see Comparative Section p. 952).

(*b*) *Rotary Headshaking*

The Rotary Headshake is simply a special way of headshaking—a rapid and vigorous rotation of the head and neck preceded and accompanied by a fluffing of the head and neck feathers. It accompanies all prolonged preening and is particularly frequent during moult of body feathers, which it helps to displace. It is worth distinguishing by a special name because it is in fact morphologically distinct and because in the family as a whole it has become somewhat variable and involved with other behaviour.

(*c*) *Feather Ruffing*

This action—a variable raising or fluffing of feathers—has been mentioned in connection with apparently fearful behaviour (Facing-away, Tremoring, etc.). Usually the head and neck and breast feathers are partially erected in this way and in the conflict situations associated with threat and courtship this is an autonomic response. Doubtless it communicates the ambivalence which the bird feels. Fully feathered, non-flying young show it when frightened by man and may also show violently disordered body plumage.

Feather position also regulates heat loss to the surrounding atmosphere and when Sunning (q.v.) red-foots usually ruff their plumage. They also ruff during preening, when the action separates the individual feather for attention.

(*d*) *Wing-flapping*

Wing-flapping consists of ordinary, vigorous and prolonged forward flapping of the fully spread wings with the body at about 45° and the tail partly fanned. It is primarily a feather maintenance activity performed after bathing and preening and there is no indication that it has acquired any signal function. It is not, for instance, a prelude to flight.

4. *Heat regulation*

The Sunning position (Fig. 320) is adopted under warm, sunny conditions. The wings, with

Fig. 324. A flock of red-footed boobies fishing off Christmas Island, Indian Ocean.

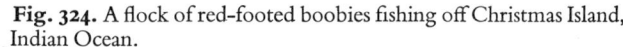

tips crossed, are slightly relaxed and their dorsal surfaces presented to the sun. The feathers of the back and wings are slightly raised and the tail feathers widely separated. The habit is somewhat puzzling. Exposing the skin to insolation should heat it and this might be understandable if the habit were practised during the early morning, but it often occurs during the heat of the day. Nor, conversely, can it be an effective cooling device since the ambient mean radiant temperature is probably higher than the skin temperature and therefore will impart heat to it. Red-footed booby chicks sometimes rest in a tripod position with tail raised, cloaca exposed and wings loosened (Fig. 321). This presumably helps to dissipate heat. Although the habit has never received specific comment in this species it is possible that deliberate excretion onto the webs is used as a thermo-regulatory device (see p. 263).

5. *Sleeping*

Adult red-foots usually sleep with head in scapulars, but sometimes they dangle it vertically downwards, neck fully stretched (Fig. 322). Such a position is possible only in a tree nester, but seems otherwise comparable to the supine posture adopted by the young of all sulids. It may require less energy. They may roost on the ground (Fig. 323).

6. *Fishing behaviour*

The red-foot may be encountered up to 100–150km from the nearest breeding colony and more than 70km from the nearest land of any sort. Often, it fishes singly or in small groups, but larger flocks are common and I have seen gatherings of many hundreds fishing close to Aldabra and over 200 off Christmas Island. Van Halewijn (pers. comm.) in the Caribbean, noted that red-foots usually fished in flocks up to several hundreds strong, almost invariably mixed with other seabirds, such as sooty terns, common noddies, shearwaters and the other two tropical boobies, particularly the brown. Similarly, mixed feeding is found in other areas too. Two or more are said to accompany every flock of white-capped noddies in the Fiji Islands. Anderson (1954) describes it as fishing 'frantically' from a school. He notes that (at least in white morphs) birds converge from afar over a shoal, and makes the interesting but unsubstantiated suggestion that they can 'sense' a school 30km or more away. Perhaps this is a chain-effect, birds too distant to see the school nevertheless recognising the purposeful flight of those who can, and so on down the chain. The size of fishing flocks may be expected to vary with region and may be greater in the Caribbean than, say, the eastern Pacific. Although it never fishes in muddy inshore waters, it will fish in lagoons as well as the open sea.

The red-foot plunges like other boobies, sometimes from a height of at least 7m. Van Halewijn noted that it dived from a greater height than brown boobies, when exploiting the

Fig. 325. Swallowing a fish in flight.

same shoal. Undoubtedly, though, it tends to take fish in the air more than other species. It often makes shallow, slanting dives in quick succession. It may bring large fish to the surface and swallow them there or as it flies up (Fig. 325). Where flying fish are breaking the surface in scores, it often changes direction rapidly and hounds them down, taking them just after they re-enter (Fig. 326). Boats disturb fish, and red-foots often accompany ships, sometimes for several hundred kilometres. Occasionally (but less than the brown booby) it snatches at surface fish whilst sitting on the water, using its wings for momentum. On the basis of this superficial account and having seen the dives of all the other species except Abbott's, I would guess that the red-foot's small size and long wings and tail correlate with a tendency to take fish at, and particularly above, the surface. In this it may most closely resemble the brown booby, among the pan-tropical trio; the latter, too, has a very small, long-tailed male, but tends to specialise more in inshore fishing (see p. 500) and is notably less oceanic.

Red-foots leave the colony to go fishing mainly in the early morning, often in very large numbers two or three hours after sunrise, but also throughout the day and even shortly before sundown. In the Caribbean, birds departing from Half Moon Cay often used updraughts, in which soaring groups formed. The mean size of groups flying out to fish decreased steadily during the morning; in the early morning and late evening it was 2·4 (n = 2143). The most ever seen in one group was 36, leaving before sunrise (Verner 1965). On Aldabra groups up to 150 strong left the colony, mainly at low altitude, though singles and small groups were also common. Most groups invariably contained at least one adult, juveniles rarely leaving the atoll solely in the company of other juveniles. Perhaps they discover particular foraging areas by accompanying adults. They fly out from and return to land in such direct flight that a course may be set by their direction 200km from land.

Red-foots, probably more so than any other sulid, are markedly nocturnal, flying back to the colony long after dark even on moonless nights. Chris Huxley was astonished when, in February 1974, at Middle Camp, Aldabra, at 20.30 hours on a dark, rainy night, four adult boobies in succession crash landed in the forefront of the open hut, presumably attracted by the light. All had full crops and had been flying in filthy weather and almost total darkness. How they could have located a particular mangrove or even landed among twigs at all, it is more than difficult to imagine.

7. *Flight and soaring*

Verner (1965) noticed that many birds spent a long time soaring in updraughts in the evening at Half Moon Cay. Birds that had just been relieved from the nest may have formed the bulk of such groups. It did not seem to be used to gain height for departure and its function, if any (other than to satisfy an urge to fly, in birds that had been sitting all day), remains obscure.

They fly at 50–70km per hour, usually close to the surface and soaring in a gentle rise and fall motion.

Fig. 326

Aerial pursuit of flying fish.

SUMMARY

1. Territories are established mainly by display (fighting is rare), involving Flight-circuiting and ritualised landing followed by a site ownership display (Forward Headwaving) and Jabbing.

2. The male attracts a female by 'advertising' (Sky-pointing), a display which is later used, also, to strengthen the pair bond and synchronise mating behaviour.

3. There is virtually no meeting ceremony. Males are aggressive to females (jabbing) and females either Face-away or actually move away. They show 'fear' by tremoring and feather ruffing.

4. Copulation is accompanied by a grating call from the male, the only booby to do so.

5. Other communication behaviour in the territory includes a bill-tucking (Pelican Posture), probably appeasing, a wing-rattle and wing-flick signalling impending departure.

6. Nest-building and associated behaviour is well developed.

7. Incubation stints are long when compared with other sulids. Change-over is often during darkness.

8. Chicks are brooded or attended until 4 or 5 weeks old.

9. They are fed slightly less than once per day on average, which is less frequently than other boobies, though much depends on locality.

10. Young red-foots will accept donated siblings, and adults also accept them until their own young are feathered, at which time they begin to discriminate against strange young.

11. Red-foot chicks lack bill-hiding (on appeasement posture).

12. Their food begging behaviour is exceptionally vigorous, which probably is adaptive.

13. Temperature regulation is aided, in young, by special postures.

14. Maintenance behaviour (preening etc.), is described.

15. Red-foots forage further from land than any other booby except possibly the white. They probably specialise in taking fish in the air, and in nocturnal fishing.

9

Sula abbotti

ABBOTT'S BOOBY

1. NOMENCLATURE; EXTERNAL FEATURES; MORPHOLOGY; MOULT AND VOICE

NOMENCLATURE

1. *Common*

The only common name is Abbott's booby, named after the American naturalist W. L. Abbott, who visited Assumption in September 1892 and collected a specimen (Ridgway 1893, 1895). The Malays call it burra burong.

2. *Scientific*

Sula abbotti Ridgway, 1893, Proc. U.S. Nat. Mus. XVI, p. 599 (Assumption Is.)

GENERAL FEATURES

Abbott's is a large booby about 79cm long with snow-white head, neck and underparts, black and white back, and black wings and tail, a distinctive combination found in no other sulid except one of the immature stages of the gannet. The adult white booby also has black wings, but the large expanse of white on wing coverts and on the back are quite different from Abbott's, with its black upper surface to the whole wing. The striped appearance imparted by the white on the inner webs of the flight feathers impressed Gibson-Hill as an obvious flight character and the dark flank patch is also conspicuous.

Abbott's booby has a distinctive shape. The wings appear noticeably long and narrow (in fact the humerus is unusually long (see Comparative Section p. 810)) and the forward projection of the head and neck is unusually prominent, giving a long, rakish line; perhaps it simply flies with its neck rather more elongated than other boobies. The head is massive. The tail does not seem long and at rest is noticeably square cut, rather than with the conspicuously

Fig. 327. Flight positions. Note the unusually long humeral part of the wing.

longer central feathers characteristic of some sulids. At rest, the wing tips extend to or slightly beyond the tail.

The sexes are alike except for bill colour, which is pink in the female and greyish in the male. The juvenile cannot be distinguished from the adult male except, possibly, in the hand. The steady flight is rather casual and employs a 'wristy' wing action, the distal part beating with a shallow motion whilst the wing as a whole appears to move less than in other sulids. In steady, oaring flight the wings beat about three times per second, though Abbott's booby glides long and frequently between flapping bouts (Fig. 327).

DETAILED DESCRIPTION

1. *Adult male and female*

(*a*) *Upperparts*

The head and neck are pure white, the feathers appearing somewhat long and loosely placed rather than lying in a dense, smooth mass. In display they are expressively raised and lowered, giving the head a range of sizes and shapes further enhanced by the unusual trick of keeping the feathers of the forehead flat whilst raising those of the crown. The scapulars and wings are deep blackish when new, becoming bleached to a deep, burnt brown, with variably buff-edged coverts. Thus some birds appear paler than others on the dorsal surface. There may be a few tiny, part-white covert feathers on the wings, variably apparent depending on the way the plumage happens to be lying. The carpal joint is spotted with white, which extends on to the leading edge of the wings and is conspicuous in flight. The inner webs of the black primaries each have a broad white stripe except on the distal fifth, the white spreading first over the entire inner web and then over both webs towards the base. These white areas are conspicuous during display with spread wings (Fig. 344). The shafts of the primaries may be a dark yellowish horn, probably darker when new. The secondaries also have white inner webs and bases. The basal part of the inner webs and the extreme base of the outer webs of the coverts are white.

The back between the wings is white, boldly patterned with black blotches of variable size and shape, visible mainly in flight. The upper tail coverts are white, or white with black centres.

Fig. 328. Pattern of markings on thigh and rump.

The tail feathers are black with irregular white tips of variable size, often only one or two millimetres.

(*b*) *Underparts*

The throat, neck, breast and abdomen are white. The axillaries and the undersides of the wings are white except for the undersurfaces of those (distal) parts of the primaries not covered by the under wing coverts, and the extreme tips of a few inner secondaries. There is a very large and conspicuous irregular black patch on the flanks, just posterior to the line of the leg and reaching right up to the under tail coverts. This is composed of feathers with triangular dark patches, confined to one web, not placed medially.

(*c*) *Bill, feet, etc.*

The large, deep bill has coarser teeth (Fig. 329), continuing further back than in other sulids, the distal end of the lower mandible is flattened or 'keeled'. Towards the tip, which is noticeably hooked, there is a slight gap between the opposed cutting edges.

In the male the bill is a livid blue-grey faintly but distinctively tinged pink, whilst in the female it has a deep, rosy pink hue. In both it is broadly tipped with black.

The skin of the face, including around and particularly behind the eye, is bluish black and the gular skin lead grey with a delicate greenish line separating it from the throat. The orbital ring is blackish and this, together with the black skin behind the eye and the dark brown iris, make the orbital region look like a huge, dark eye. The eyelid is white, bordered black. The face is thus unusually sober for a booby but the eye is very conspicuous and it seems no coincidence that Abbott's booby alone has used the eye and white eyelid in communication behaviour between mates.

The tarsi and feet are deep grey, with the distal third of the web black. The tarsal scutes are particularly robust.

2. *Juvenile*

The remarks made above apply almost equally to the juvenile, except that the latter has slightly more buff edges to scapulars and wing coverts, though this characteristic is too slight to be of much use in the field, especially when adult wings have become bleached. As mentioned, the juvenile's bill is blue grey, like that of the adult male, but slightly greyer, without the pinkish tinge.

The descriptions given above are my own from living birds in the field and differ slightly from some to be found elsewhere. Thus, Gibson-Hill (1947) describes the 'soft parts', including bill, as the same in both sexes but the bill as fleshy white to fleshy grey or green. The grey/green must refer to the male and perhaps the fleshy white to females seen in intense sunlight or judged from dead and somewhat faded specimens.

Chasen (1933) notes that Ridgway's original description of the Assumption birds fits

Fig. 329

Abbott's bill is unusually large and coarsely toothed.

those from Christmas Island exactly and quotes 'Iris dark brown; bill pale waxy pink to greyish pink, blackish at tip; skin at base of lower mandible and gular pouch light bluish green; skin at base of upper mandible and orbital skin, blackish, a light patch on the lower eyelid. Tarsus and first two joints of digits, greenish grey; part of webs bounded by first two joints greyish blue; distal joints of digits and remainder of webs blackish; claws whitish.' Here, too, the sex difference in bill colour was seen but not specified.

3. *Discussion*

The most remarkable aspect of the plumage of Abbott's booby is the extraordinarily close resemblance between the juvenile and the adult male. Any interpretation of this most unusual situation must necessarily be speculative.

First, we may assume that the adult's plumage is adaptive and therefore the sooner it is reached by the juvenile the better. The reason why other young sulids differ from their parents presumably is at least partly concerned with appeasement and the more necessary this is, the more the two differ. Thus, in the gannet, the juvenile is about as unlike the adult as it can be (see p. 209). In Abbott's booby, however, as this account shows, the internal threshold for aggression is clearly extremely high; even the external stimulus of an intruder male fails to elicit overt aggression from a territory owner. If a male is unlikely to attack an intruder male, he is unlikely to attack his own chick, which can therefore be 'permitted' to acquire the (presumably adaptive) adult plumage whilst still in the nest, for the vestiges of brown plumage can apparently be produced and discarded very quickly (see p. 775). This suggestion fits well with the point made in connection with the long breeding cycle—namely that everything possible must be done to make the breeding attempt successful, for with such a low reproductive rate (one chick in two years) there are relatively so few chances for adults to replace themselves. A Peruvian booby could produce six or more in that period. Hence the very long post-fledging subsidy, taking the chick through into a favourable part of the year following its birth, and the adoption, whilst still subsidised, of what is presumably the best plumage in which to hunt fish. This is tantamount to saying that if the young Abbott's booby cannot become proficient under those circumstances, it cannot do so at all. Everything is in its favour, in stark contrast to the situation in the young gannet (p. 133).

The long narrow wings may be an adaptation for far foraging. This and other morphological features which have a bearing on the species' ecology are discussed later (pp. 825, 832).

4. *Measurements and weight*

The measurements of ten live adult Abbott's boobies are given in Table 118.

When Gibson-Hill (1950b) wrote, there were 15 Abbott's booby skins in museums—5 in the British Museum (Andrew's 1897 and 1908 skins), 2 in Cambridge (Fryer's 1911 Assumption skins), 3 in New York (the original Assumption skin and 2 donated by the Raffles) and 5 in the Raffles (the 7 Raffles skins taken from Christmas Island between 1932–40). Gibson-Hill gathers together measurements for all 15, given in Table 119.

There is some sexual dimorphism, the males scaling only about 94 per cent of the females' weight. This, however, is less difference than in any other booby (see Comparative Section p. 826). The bill of Abbott's booby is notably large and female number 2 in Table 119 with a bill of 120×39mm is unmatched by any other sulid for which I have a record. The tarsus is long when compared with that of the only other arboreal sulid—the red-footed booby—but proportionately about the same as in other sulids.

The only[1] free-flying specimen of a juvenile had the measurements shown in Table 118.

MOULT

Chasen remarks that the moulting specimens in the Raffles Collection have some faded brown feathers, whilst the birds in fresher plumage are black and white.

I examined nine adults for moult. Three breeding pairs with young showed no moult in

[1] There are now others (Nelson and Powell, in prep.).

TABLE 118

WEIGHTS (g) AND MEASUREMENTS (mm) OF ABBOTT'S BOOBY

Specimen number	Age, sex, status	Weight	Culmen-length	Culmen-depth	Wing	Tail	Tarsus
1}	Adult ♂	1620	108·5	40	—	—	—
2}	Adult ♀	1470	120	39	439	213	—
3}	Adult ♂	1520	108	38	—	—	—
4}	Adult♀	1630	111	40	493	—	—
5}	Adult ♂	1370	101·5	35	—	—	—
6}	Adult ♀	1700	114	43·5	—	—	40
7	Adult ♂ grounded	1300	108	38	464	220	41
8	Adult ♂ grounded	1320	107	37·5	442	215	39
9	Adult ♂ grounded	1300	103·5	36·5	440	205	—
10	Adult ♀ grounded	1330	108	36	450	—	41·5
11	Juvenile grounded	1214	108·6	36·8	495	—	—
12	Shot off Java	—	109·5	39·6	454	242	48
	Mean of ♂♂	1405	106·1	37·5	449	219	40
	Mean of ♀♀	1532	113·3	39·8	461	—	41
	Mean of ♂♂ (excluding grounded)	1503	—	—	—	—	—
	Mean of ♀♀ (excluding grounded)	1600	—	—	—	—	—

Note. Brackets indicate a pair.

TABLE 119

MEASUREMENTS (mm) OF ALL EXISTING ABBOTT'S BOOBY SKINS

Collection details	Year	Sex	Live length	Tail*	Wing	Tarsus	Culmen
Abbott's type specimen Assumption Island	1892	Male	—	213	447	51	112
Fryer's 2 specimens Assumption Island	1911	NR	—	247	447	—	112
		NR	—	227	462	—	115
Andrew's 5 specimens Christmas Island	1898	Male	—	223	432	—	108
	1908	Male	—	220	436	—	109
	1908	Female	—	224	437	—	110
	1908	Female	—	231+	462	—	116
	1908	Female	—	230+	458	—	115
Raffles Mus. 7 specimens (6 collected by Tweedie; 1 by Gibson-Hill) Christmas Island	1932	Male	772	247 (200)	436	43	109
	1932	Female	787	265 (206)	460	45	113
	1932	Female	761	249 (203)	435	47	111
	1932	Female	787	248 (213)	458	48	110
	1940	Female	785	203	447	43	112
		Male	761	200	441	42	110
		Female	770	203	450	45	112

* The figures in brackets for some entries are Chasen's measurements of the bird.

August and September, though they had some primaries more bleached and abraded than others, as one would expect in a sulid, since the flight feathers moult in cycles spreading over more than one year and suspended at intervals. These six birds each had 16 tail feathers, also of different ages. The other three adults were grounded during tree felling. One female was almost certainly still feeding a juvenile (grounded nearby) and showed no moult. Of the other two, both males, one showed no moult (August 2nd) and the other (August 28th) had primaries 1, 2 and 7 growing (counting from inner to outer) with primaries 8–10 oldest on the left wing and 8–9 on the right wing. In addition we found moulted flight feathers beneath many occupied trees in late July and August, when many pairs had just stopped feeding their juveniles. The same was true in 1974.

It seems from this that moult is suspended during the main part of the breeding season and resumed during the last stages of feeding the juvenile, though the sample is too small to allow a firm judgement.

VOICE

Abbott's booby possesses the deepest and loudest voice of any sulid, resonant and commanding. Its vocabulary is varied for a booby. One or two deep and abrupt shouts and grunts are given just before and after landing. During the meeting ceremony it shouts lustily with great carrying power and with changes in amplitude and pitch, 'aaw-ah-err' or 'oya oya' or 'aaah-ooaah', pleasantly sonorous. Intimate pair reactions may be accompanied by deep, prolonged croaks which occasionally become glottal stops and during copulation change into a repetitive 'click-grunt'. In association with a special posture (neck held at 45°) Abbott's has a soft, sonorous and drawn out groan.

Large young and juveniles beg with an unmistakable drawn out and harshly grating call, (duration 1–2 seconds) each interspersed with several short, rapid, half-formed throaty sounds—'ah, ah, ah, ah, aa-arr-rr-rr' pause 'ah, ah, ah, aa-rrr-rr' etc. They maintain this for hours and it is one of the most distinctive sounds of the jungle.

Gibson-Hill gives the voice as 'ko-ark, ko-ark' repeated several times in a descending key and he was probably referring to the calls given when the pair greet each other at the nest site. He records a single, loud, deep croak as a response to aerial attack by a frigate-bird. The deep, prolonged croak given during pair interactions he describes as a deep-bellied rumbling sound. All these efforts to phoneticise bring out the unusually deep and resonant quality of Abbott's voice.

2. BREEDING DISTRIBUTION, NUMBERS AND OTHER ASPECTS OF POPULATIONS

INTRODUCTION

Abbott's booby is the world's rarest sulid and since it has only one known breeding station the problem is not so much understanding its present distribution as the factors which have led to it, for it is hardly possible that it has never had a wider one. But, because of its breeding habitat (dense forest) it is a secretive species, until recently one of the world's least-known seabirds. There is room, however, for a new assessment of the evidence that exists regarding its earlier distribution.

DISTRIBUTION IN THE PAST

Abbott's booby now nests only on the Indian Ocean Christmas Island. It is always *said* to have nested on Assumption Island until 1926 and, as mentioned, it was there that Abbott collected the specimen that is now in the American Museum of Natural History. There are, however, some reasons for doubting that it ever bred on Assumption. To begin with, the statement 'a few nest', though positive enough, is unfortunately bare for such an important matter, particularly in view of the fact that Abbott was not aware of the extreme rarity and restricted distribution of the species. Furthermore, as Gibson-Hill (1950b) pointed out, Abbott himself makes a peculiar error in relation to it. 'He labelled the type specimen "Assumption Island" but in the rough description of the island which he sent to Washington he makes no mention of the presence of the new booby.' On the other hand, in his description of Glorioso (about 160km south east of Assumption and 144km from Cape Amber, Madagascar) which he visited on the same expedition, he says 'among the seabirds there is a booby, which seems to be peculiar to the island. They breed in large numbers upon the "fouche" trees, in company with frigates and common boobies.' Ridgway added a footnote to this which pointed out that the two booby species collected by Abbott were in fact *Sula cyanops* (=*S. dactylatra*) and *Sula piscator* (=*S. sula*) Only the second of these nests in trees or bushes; *S. dactylatra* never does. As Gibson-Hill says, it would seem that Abbott put the wrong locality on the skin which he sent back to Washington and that the booby was actually taken on Glorioso. The assignation to Assumption is, however, repeated in a note by Abbott, published later by Ridgeway, which says 'a few breed on Assumption. Said not to be found on any other island in these seas.' The repetition is perhaps not too surprising if Abbott had got the two localities crossed in his own mind in the first place.

This little mystery in Abbott's account will probably never be cleared up, but there can be no doubt about Fryer's (1911) record. Fryer stayed in the Aldabra group from August 1908 to February 1909. In his account of Assumption he mentions 'a gannet (*Sula abbotti*) which is peculiar to Assumption and Christmas Island (Indian Ocean)' and he shot two adults (unsexed). Fryer, however, makes absolutely no mention of whether these boobies were breeding; he says merely that 'it inhabits the large dune, never descending to low parts of the island and only going a few kilometres to sea to fish'. As Gibson-Hill perspicaciously remarks, 'seemingly he was not particularly interested in them, since, two years after his return to England he admits that he had still not compared his specimens of Abbott's booby with examples from Christmas Island'. Since Fryer's is the only other first hand record of Abbott's booby on Assumption, it means that the sole reason for accepting that it ever nested there is Abbott's simple statement, quoted earlier, with the accompanying peculiar comment concerning Glorioso. Thus, J. M. Nicoll, who visited Assumption in March 1906, does not mention the rare booby, though he even photographed the red-foot on its nest, and at that time only two specimens of Abbott's booby were extant. Both Betts and Vesey-Fitzgerald, both of whom visited the island in the late 1930s found no Abbott's booby and their comments are based merely on hearsay. The former says 'I was told that no nesting had been attempted since 1930 . . . and none had been seen since 1936', whilst the latter says 'a single individual, which disappeared about 1926, had been mateless for many years'.

Altogether, one feels uneasy about accepting that Abbott's booby nested on Assumption. Gibson-Hill notices the remarkable discrepancy between the habitat in which it supposedly nested on Assumption and its Christmas Island habitat—the one, low, scrubby bushes on dunes which were mostly a mere 6m above sea level, rising to 27m at the south-east corner, the other, fine jungle trees, topping 30 or 45m, on the elevated inland plateau above the 150m contour. Whilst it is true that the other arboreal sulid, the red-footed booby, breeds in a wide range of habitats, and Abbott's booby may have done likewise, it is also true that the latter is a much more specialised bird, with a much more restricted range of habitat-types on Christmas Island, where both species occur. Indeed, if Abbott's booby really did nest on Assumption, this would have important implications for the present, when much of its jungle

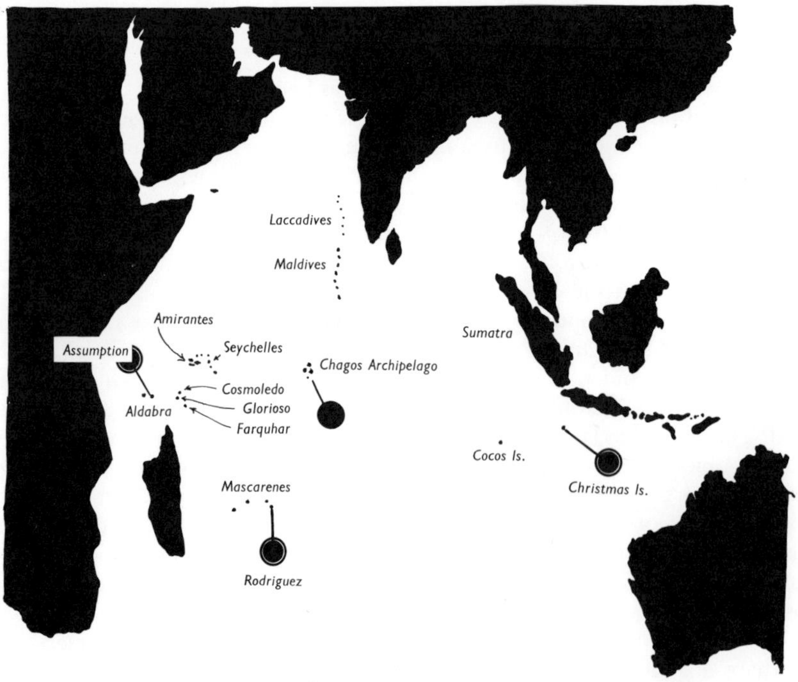

Fig. 330. Probable past, and present distribution.

habitat is being destroyed and its ability to utilise the sparser growth at lower altitudes may spell the difference between survival and extinction for the species.

Nesting or not, however, Abbott's booby was to be seen on Assumption and must therefore have nested somewhere in the western Indian Ocean, for they could scarcely have been Christmas Island birds. Glorioso would seem to have been a more suitable island for it. There were fine trees there and if the objection be raised that it was never reported after Abbott's visit the answer could be that, even in 1892, many of the large trees had been cut down and a few years later (in Gibson-Hill's view) Abbott's booby could have been expected to be scarce or absent. It could be that they were driven from Glorioso and visited and roosted on Assumption, without breeding, finally dwindling and dying (no doubt vigorously helped out by guano workers on Assumption). Such a long lived bird could easily persist the 20 or 30 years necessary to account for the 1926 (or 1936) record. That, in my view, is more likely than that Assumption ever (within historical times) had a breeding colony of Abbott's boobies.

There is, however, a much more positive clue revealing a hitherto unsuspected nesting locality of Abbott's booby. It seems that it formerly nested, probably in good numbers, on Rodriguez, the smallest of the Mascarene Islands, in the middle of the southern Indian Ocean. Bourne (1968) points out that in the eighteenth century Rodriguez was covered in dense forest. He attempts to identify, from the descriptions in French, the species of seabirds which nested there. One of these he identifies as *Sula dactylatra* but probably it refers in fact to Abbott's booby. In Bourne's words, 'The Boeuf, said c. 1730 to bellow like a bull and in 1761 to be a sort of Fou (French for gannet), in both accounts to be white with black flight feathers and in 1761 to be rather larger than a duck but like it in front, with a longer, conical, slightly hooked grey bill with traces of red and a black tip and grey-black webbed feet . . . agrees well with *Sula dactylatra*.' In fact, it presents three characters which fit extremely well with Abbott's. Thus, no other adult sulid has a black tip to a grey bill, but both the adult male and the juvenile Abbott's do, whilst adult females have black-tipped pinkish bills (the 'traces of red' in the above account). Immature red-foots often have a black-tipped bill but the other characters (below) seem to rule it out.

No sulid except Abbott's could be said to make a noise even remotely like a bellowing bull; a female white booby honks or quacks, but 'bellow' has never been a term chosen to describe its vocalisation. A bull-like bellow, however, is a very fitting description for a full-blown Abbott's booby call when the pair meet at the nest. Thus I have described it as possessing 'the deepest, loudest voice of any sulid, resonant and commanding'.

Only Abbott's has grey-black webbed feet. Its feet are in fact mainly grey, but black on the distal third or so. Since the description says 'grey-black' and not grey tipped with black one may accept this as slightly less than diagnostic but taken with the other two it seems to clinch the matter. Since I wrote this, Bourne has looked at some booby bones found on Rodriguez and concluded that they belonged to Abbott's.

There may, of course, have been other breeding localities of Abbott's booby at that time, but Rodriguez alone provides an important link between Christmas Island and a possible breeding locality or localities in the western Indian Ocean. It also provides a slight hope that it may yet be found elsewhere than Christmas Island. One other possible or even probable past breeding station is the Chagos Group, in mid Indian Ocean, which, like Rodriguez, was formerly heavily forested with magnificent trees. The French felled them in the eighteenth and early nineteenth century, just when Rodriguez was also being despoiled and its Abbott's boobies destroyed. Since writing this, Hirons (1976 and pers. comm.) has reported three sightings of Abbott's booby in the Chagos group, between islands. He noted the black wings, dark thigh patch and the black-tipped bill but did not mention the shape or long wings and compared its size to a red-foot, than which it is in fact considerably larger.

It has uncritically been reported from other islands, such as Cocos Keeling (Chasen 1933) and suggested as possibly breeding in Java. Such records can almost certainly be discounted. Chasen's inclusion of Abbott's booby as a Cocos species was based on acceptance of a misidentification by Wood-Jones (1909). The latter described Abbott's booby as breeding on bare ground on North Keeling, but did not mention the white booby, which in fact breeds there. There can be no doubt that he confused the two species. Unfortunately the Wood-Jones record has been quoted in later lists, including Chasen's.

There has never been any suggestion that Abbott's booby has nested outside the Indian Ocean, but a recent paper by Slud (1967) on the birds of the Pacific Ocean Cocos Island contains a mysterious and intriguing reference to an 'unknown' booby. His description is given in full below.

> This booby appeared to be entirely a dusky dull, brownish, including the underwing, toned a bit grayish at close range. Thus it differed from the young of the brown booby, which have the under parts paler than and abruptly demarked from, the solid breast. This patterned appearance of the young brown, foreshadowing that of the adult, is apparent both in the field and in a collection of skins. Also, one of the nameless boobies showed a white spot or two on the upper side of one wing when in flight. Viewed in the telescope, the perched bird had a heavy conical black beak, a hazel iris, bluish skin behind the eye and the legs drab like the under parts. The webs joining the toes appeared a translucent yellowish or ocher against the sky.
>
> This booby impressed me as being larger and longer tailed than the brown booby. Its more frequently flapping, heavier-bodied flight caused it to appear considerably slower on the wing, yet it could outfly the brown at will. Sporadically, it worried the brown, not only overtaking the latter but also engaging at times in 'half-hearted' pursuit; once I saw it rob a red-footed booby (*Sula sula*). In contrast to the plunging brown it had the shearwater-like habit of flapping and coursing very close to the surface and entering the water for fish with its body barely downslanted from the horizontal. A bird or two could be noted almost daily either heading inland up Wafer Valley or flying out of the interior to the bay, which I never saw the brown booby do, though the red-footed did so all the time.
>
> When occasionally I saw this booby come to rest it was, as is often the case with the brown, on the limbs of trees. One day, however, a bird attempted to perch in a manner foreign to the brown booby at Wafer. Manoeuvering and lighting awkwardly on a thin low branch, which immediately snapped, bird and branch tumbled several yards to the ground. The booby struggled to gain its feet and stood looking 'stupidly' about. Its attitude could have been that of a person attempting to feign a face-saving indifference. Early that same morning, incidentally, I had noticed an individual, perhaps the same one, standing alone and exposed on an open sand flat in what struck me at the time as an idiotic manner. The brown booby in my experience at Cocos never behaved in such a way.
>
> This booby was generally separable, too, by its heavy, bullfrog-like croak, deeper than the quacks of the brown booby and different in quality. It also made a croaking growl, when bothered by noddies, that brought to mind the cry of a red-footed booby being pursued by *Fregata*.

Slud could have seen a hybrid sulid (see p. 814) presumably a cross between the white and brown, which would account for the larger size and be consistent with the ochre feet. The reference to the voice, however, intrigues me, for it is a perfect description of a juvenile Abbott's booby. The plumage, except for the white spots in the wing, is wrong, however, and could fit only on the wild assumption that the brown juvenile feathers which are virtually absent in Christmas Island Abbott's boobies, were retained in this 'Cocos *abbotti*'.

The reference to the bird flying *inland* (i.e. to the forested interior) is also tantalising, for one would expect this only of Abbott's or red-footed boobies and the latter, apparently, can be ruled out.

Abbott's booby owes its present status as a species isolated on one forested oceanic island, largely to destruction of habitat and Rodriguez is a case in point. It may never have been common, as the arboreal red-foot is common, but the reasons for this can never be known (but see Comparative Section p. 858).

NUMBERS AND DISTRIBUTION ON CHRISTMAS ISLAND

In 1897, Dr. C. W. Andrews found Abbott's booby nesting on Christmas Island, Indian Ocean and shot an adult male. In 1908 he collected another male and three females and these skins are in the British Museum. The Raffles Museum collected seven more (2 males, 5 females) between 1932 and 1940, of which two were sent to the American Musuem of Natural History, New York.

Until 1967 Abbott's booby was thought to be in grave danger of extinction. Christmas Island was largely untracked forest, some of it very difficult to penetrate, and there were certainly areas that had never been trodden by man. Any estimates of the size of the population of Abbott's boobies was mere guesswork but, following Gibson-Hill's (1947) estimate of 500–700 pairs, Pearson's (1966) opinion that there might be less than 100 pairs seemed to indicate a severe decline and it was included in the list of endangered species by the International Union for the Conservation of Nature. One can easily see that in this awkward and extensive terrain (over 4000 sq. km) it was impossible to carry out any count of nests, which were widely scattered and located in the sub-canopy at a height of about 21m.

By good fortune, however, our 1967 visit (March to September) coincided with the clearing of an island-wide grid of survey lines, 123m apart, which proved ideal for census work and transformed the situation. Areas which one had been able to reach only by many hours, or even some days, of difficult travel on foot, suddenly became accessible by jeep. We could see into all the trees on each side of a cleared line and comb the areas between lines. Line numbers and intersections, referred to maps provided by the surveying office of the island, gave locations and contour heights accurate to within a few metres. Since we are here considering the world population of a species whose future is in some danger, it is worth giving full details of the way in which the figure is reached. The population was estimated by direct search and as a check birds were counted on their evening return to the island.

The direct search used four sources of information—nests actually seen; nest sites indicated by the presence of a free-flying juvenile which has a distinctive call; nest sites revealed by the loud and unmistakable calling of greeting pairs and finally, sites revealed by piles of droppings beneath the tree (these could have belonged to a pair, a single adult or a juvenile). All records and all negative searches were marked on a large scale map.

The results—786 pairs actually pinpointed—represent only a proportion of the true figure.

TABLE 120

DETAILS OF THE POPULATION OF ABBOTT'S BOOBY ON CHRISTMAS ISLAND

Map segment	% of area searched	Located in areas searched			Presumed missed in areas searched			Presumed missed in areas not searched			Total pairs
		Calling pairs	Juveniles	Nests	Pairs	Juveniles	Nests	Pairs	Juveniles	Nests	
1	38	129 (70)	40 (70)	91 (90)	55	17	9	210	93	165	809
2	69	225 (70)	57 (70)	148 (90)	96	24	16	144	36	73	819
3		15	3	3			50				71
4		19	4	4			20				47
5		22	8	18			50				98
		410	112	264							1844

Notes. (1) The island was divided into five segments (Fig. 1). The boundaries of the populous segments 1 and 2 were drawn where the boobies became noticeably rarer, so although no thinly populated areas were taken as dense, the total population may thereby have been under-estimated.

(2) The proportion of segments 1 and 2 actually searched was taken as the percentage of the total length of the survey lines that we searched. A more complex method was considered superfluous.

(3) The figures in brackets (percentages) represent our estimate of the proportion actually located in the areas searched. They assume an improbably high success on our part and the final total will therefore err on the low side. From 2 (above) and calculating the total pairs in that proportion, the total for the whole segment can be obtained.

(4) Segments 3–5 contain too few located birds to form the basis for an acceptable calculation for such large areas. A small overall figure has therefore been allowed for the number of birds presumed to occur in each.

Apart from the pairs we missed in the areas we searched, there were tracts of the island that we did not search. By assuming that we located 90 per cent of actual nests in areas searched (an improbably high figure) and 70 per cent of calling pairs and calling juveniles (even more improbably high, since the chances of them being absent at the time of our visit must have been considerable, despite the fact that we searched between 16.00 and 18.00 hours when most breeding birds were at the nest) and allowing a figure for the areas unsearched, the total population can be estimated. Obviously this figure will err on the low side. The results are given in Table 120.

The validity of Table 120 depends on the accuracy of the estimate of undiscovered pairs and, in the absence of a uniform distribution, the fairest way to treat this is to divide the island into areas, each of which is known by spot checks to be roughly homogeneous, and estimate the population in each, on the basis of the densities established for the searched parts of those areas. The validity of this procedure, in turn, depends on drawing the boundaries in the right places and here, too, we erred on the side of caution, by ensuring that the boundary of, say, a high density area, was drawn through points at which the densities were known to be still high. In other words, these high density areas may have projected a little further into assumed low density ones, but not the other way round. So, again, our figure should tend to err on the low side. The results are given in Figs. 331 and 332.

From all this we emerge with a figure of 1844 pairs, but since we almost certainly over-

Fig. 331. Actual distribution of located pairs, Christmas Island 1967, in relation to topography. Subsequent part check (1974) revealed substantial agreement, though small parts of the densest areas (segment 2) had by then been destroyed by mining operations.

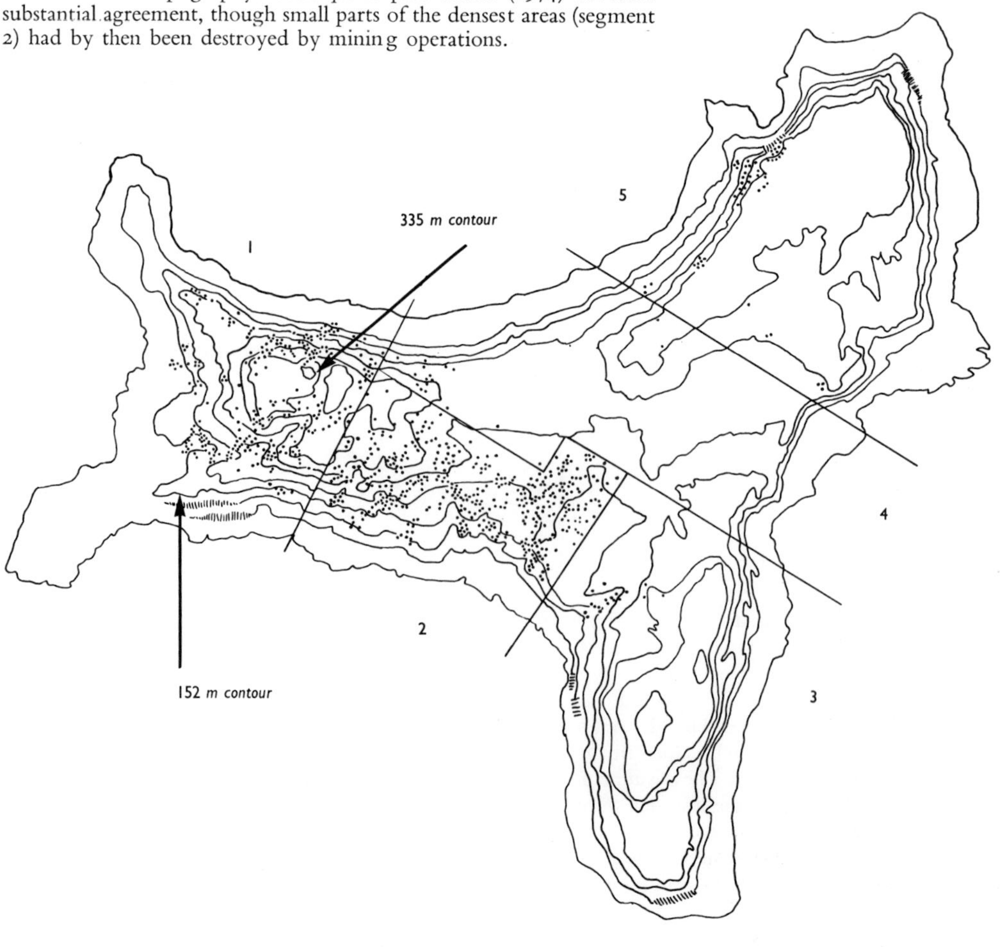

estimated the success of our search, the total population was probably at least 2300 pairs and perhaps even 3000 or more. In addition to these, the young birds (other than free-flying juveniles) and any immature birds or non-breeding adults, perhaps dispersed at sea, must be added to arrive at the world's total. On the basis of 1850 pairs, 282 chicks and a very roughly estimated 200 immatures, a figure of around 4200 individuals is obtained. Based on 2300 pairs, the total becomes around 5100 individuals.

It was possible to cross-check these figures, at least roughly, by counting the number of birds flying in to the island during daylight. We noticed that Abbott's booby seemed to drift in, often high, from the north-west and not from any other direction. We discovered a good vantage point on a high ridge in the north-west of the island, over which most of the incomers passed on a narrow front. From a series of counts (Table 121), one of them continuous from dawn to dusk, we obtained figures from which, making certain assumptions, we could calculate the size of the population. The result, given in Table 122, was a figure of 3030 individuals, which made no allowance for incomers which we missed, nor for non-breeders and immatures dispersed at sea. A conservative estimate of the total number of free-flying Abbott's boobies at the time of our count would be about 3500 to 4500 individuals and more probably 5000 to 5500. Since then, a much fuller series of counts has been carried out by D. Powell (Table 121) and these have shown that the population is probably significantly larger than was thought. His counts present some puzzles, chiefly the enormous difference in the number of incoming boobies at different times of year and the large variations within a matter of days. The former show two main features—first, the marked decline in October/November as much of the population leaves the island for the 'winter' followed by the April return, and second, a notable

Fig. 332

Simplified representation of the distribution of Abbott's booby on Christmas Island.

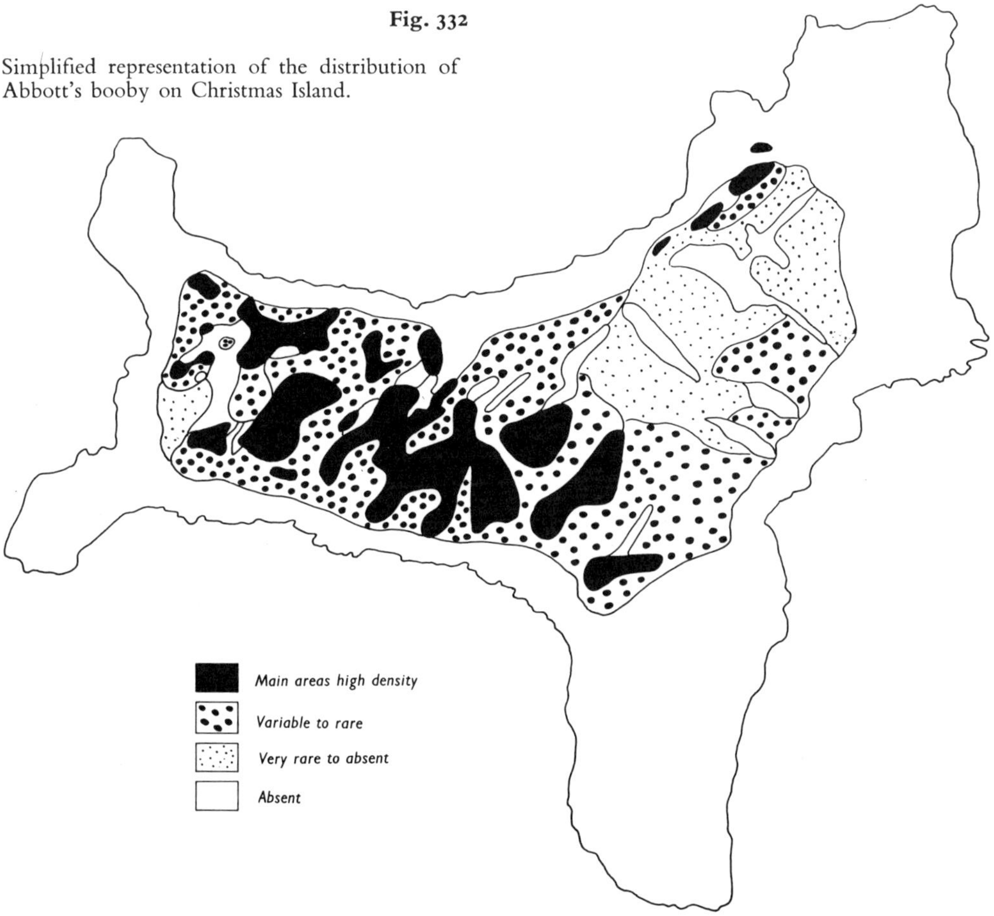

TABLE 121

THE NUMBERS OF INFLYING ABBOTT'S BOOBIES COUNTED FROM TOM'S RIDGE BETWEEN APPROXIMATELY 16·00–18·00 HOURS.
(Counts by D. Powell)

		1975 Greatest	1975 Least	1975 Mean	No. of counts	1976 Greatest	1976 Least	1976 Mean	No. of counts	Comments on 1976
		No. of inflying Abbott's				No. of inflying Abbott's				
January	1	8	8	8	2	9	1	6	3	(all 16·00–17·00)
	2	72	1	33	3	38	3	17	3	,, ,, ,,
February	1	14	1	5	4	—	—	—	—	
	2	—	—	—	1	55	4	21	3	(all 16·00–17·00)
March	1	29	3	11	4	1	0	1	2	
	2	10	1	4	4	44 in 1½ hrs.	4 in 1 hr.	24	2	
April	1	358	2	125	5	1528	23	665	3	
	2	452	14	144	7	1527	1010	1268	2	
May	1	1745	253	962	3	1705	139	875	6	
	2	999	105	492	3	1303	484	893	—	
June	1	1038	325	681	2	744	387	608	3	
	2	867	239	553	2	891	740	815	2	
July	1	1826	503	1034	3	1710	853	1364	3	
	2	1451	741	1096	2	2073	297	1477	6	
August	1	936	515	705 (592 (2))	3	1653	205	995	7	
		1188	865	1026	2 (1967)					
	2	—	—	—	—	2415	1155	1777	5	
September	1	1989 (473 (1))	—	—	1	1556	548	841	5	
		700	—	—	1 (1967)					
	2	—	—	—	—	2327	1279	1702	4	
October	1	747 (669 (1))	—	—	1	2162	787	1391	5	
	2	15 (609 (1))	—	—	1	834	100	470	5	
November	1	604	128	332	3	189	93	150	3	
	2	233 (174 (1))	111	173	3	40	30	35	2	
December	1	104	7	32 (67 (6))	5	157	14	85	2	
	2	86	14	50 (7 (4))	2	14	—	—	1	

Notes:

The *total* number flying in during the last 4 or 5 hours of daylight is often larger, but variability in the duration of the count precludes direct quotes. Figures in brackets refer to 1974 counts (sample number in sub-brackets) except in those cases bracketed '1967'.

July/August peak in numbers. The decline very probably marks the departure of all the non-breeding and failed-breeding birds. The reasons for going are probably to do with a change in foraging and feeding regime during the monsoons and with unpleasant or dangerous conditions for landing and being in trees during this period. The July/August peak is probably due to a temporary influx of immature birds (and perhaps also some non-breeding adults). This would be entirely analogous to the situation in other sulids, and since it is extremely probable that Abbott's maturity is long-deferred, there should be the recruits from several breeding seasons somewhere around. The short-term fluctuations in numbers of incomers, sometimes very large, may be correlated with weather. D. Powell believes this to be so, but a full analysis would be premature. The possibility that the standard watching point is sometimes by-passed by a highly variable proportion of the incomers cannot be entirely ruled out, though there is no evidence for this.

The largest influxes yet recorded (3259 in $4\frac{1}{4}$ hours, July 26th 1976; 2095 in 4 hours, August 10th 1976; 2215 in 4 hours, August 11th; 2411 in $4\frac{1}{2}$ hours, August 14th; 2547 in $4\frac{1}{2}$ hours, August 18th; 3131 in $5\frac{1}{2}$ hours, August 20th; 3190 in $5\frac{1}{4}$ hours, August 21st; 2939 in $4\frac{1}{2}$ hours, August 25th and 3221 in 5 hours, September 18th) are considerably bigger than my 1967 counts and although an unknown proportion were immature or non-breeding birds,

TABLE 122

ESTIMATION OF THE POPULATION OF ABBOTT'S BOOBY ON CHRISTMAS ISLAND IN AUGUST 1967, FROM COUNTS OF INCOMING BIRDS

Basis: approximately 2000 incoming individuals each day.

Assumptions:
(1) Adult population roughly in two halves, breeding in alternate years. This is more than an assumption since observations proved that the same pair could not breed successfully in two successive years.
(2) Of the pairs which laid in 1966, 80% assumed successful and still visiting the nest, the remaining 20% permanently at sea at the time of the count.
(3) For every ten breeders there is one current non-breeder visiting the island, and non-breeder pair members return on alternate days (at the time of the counts non-breeders were usually seen singly at the nest-site).
(4) 1967 breeders will, each day, have one bird on the nest and one bird returning (supported by observations).
(5) In pairs with juveniles, both members will return daily (supported by observations).
(6) 75% of juveniles, at time of count, assumed to be free-flying and returning daily.

Calculation: On the assumptions and observations given above, the incoming birds will consist of the following categories:

	Proportions	*Comments*
Non-breeders	1	Only half the non-breeders return each day
1967 breeders	5	10 1967 breeders for every 10 1966 breeders, but 50% of 1967 breeders on nest
1966 breeders	8	20% of 1966 breeders failed and absent
Juveniles	3	75% of juveniles from 80% of 1966 breeders arrive daily

Applying these proportions to the 2000 incomers:

Non-breeders	118
1967 breeders	588
1966 breeders	941
Juveniles	353
Total	2000

Population composition at time of count, as individuals:

Non-breeders (2×118)	236
1967 breeders (2×588)	1176
1966 breeders with juveniles	941
1966 breeders away at sea	236
1966 juveniles (353+25%)	441
Total	3030

the same applied in 1967. Whilst it would be misplaced effort to recalculate Table 122, it seems probable that, as I remarked then, the calculated figure was too low, and the total population of free-flying Abbott's probably at least 8000 individuals.

Despite the very different approaches and the incompleteness of the information, these two estimates agree remarkably closely. One could be highly satisfied with the state of this magnificent species were it not for the destruction of habitat which it now faces. Since the above was written, however, a great deal has happened. Following upon the clearing of densely occupied areas and the destruction of many birds in 1970, a much greater concern has been shown by the mining company. In 1974, after recommendations by a Standing Committee of the Australian Parliament, to which I made a submission, and the Canberra Conference of the International Council for Bird Preservation, which showed great concern for Abbott's booby, a full-time conservator in the employ of the Phosphate Commissioners was appointed. Since that time few, if any, Abbott's boobies have been destroyed. All areas to be cleared are carefully searched and every Abbott's tree left standing until the nesting attempt is definitely over. This year (1977) a full-time Government Conservator goes to the island to implement a comprehensive conservation policy submitted by a team of three Australian and New Zealand government biologists after a visit in 1975. This provides for a limited area to be completely safe and most of the remainder of the plateau area, including virtually all the Abbott's booby habitat, to be 'controlled'. Mining and development are thus vetted. After a visit early in 1977 I have added slightly to these proposals. The net outcome is that destruction of birds is a thing of the past; destruction of their habitat goes on, but if suggestions for an appropriately large reserve area are heeded, all should be well (see, also, next page).

There are a number of puzzling features about the actual distribution of Abbott's booby on the island. As the map shows, it is far from uniform and this poses two main questions: why does Abbott's booby favour some areas over others and (a quite different point) within favoured areas, what determines distribution? On the first point, as recorded by Gibson-Hill, they nest mainly above the 150–180m contours and are much more concentrated on the western half of the island, which is hillier and more dissected than much of the middle and east, huge areas of which seem virtually empty of Abbott's boobies.

Abbott's booby generally occupies dense forest, with large trees. Areas sparsely covered with poor trees, as in the extreme south-west and many parts of the east, are unoccupied as, also, are poor trees on drier, stony slopes even within generally favoured areas such as Segment 1 on the map (see Fig. 331). Yet there are large areas of magnificent trees that are extremely thinly populated or empty. Segment 4 and much of the eastern half of the island are covered with fine trees, but virtually ignored by Abbott's booby. The entire eastern seaboard lacks them even above the 150m contour, though they begin to occur further towards the centre, the first pairs just inland of the inland cliff (as in Segment 5). Suitable trees are obviously not the only requirement and it occurred to us that the eastern slopes, exposed to stronger and more persistent winds (the north-easterly gales of January to May and the persistent south-easterly trades for most of the year) produced a noticeably closer-knit canopy, which also had a less rugged underlying terrain than in the west. Since, in calm conditions, we observed Abbott's boobies fall 9m or more, after taking off; before getting under way, we surmised that its choice of habitat partly depended on the need for safe entry to and departure from nesting trees. Typically, it nests at heights of 18m or more in trees which are either fully emergent or contain large gaps which the birds can enter or leave (nests are placed on a broad limb beneath a section of canopy or among thinner lateral branches not in the crown). Extremely broken terrain—spurs, hillsides and valley sides—provide far more of these 'emergent' facilities, lacking in dense and even jungle canopy, even of fine trees of the right species and this may partly explain the preference of Abbott's booby for the dissected western half of the island. In fact, as we mapped the distribution of more and more pairs, it seemed to us that the booby did indeed tend to concentrate on spurs and the sides of small valleys, even when these were not obvious to us on the ground. On the other hand, whilst in some areas the correlation between distribution and map contours was clear, in others it was poorer. But this could have been due to the fact that map contours are often insufficiently detailed to reveal topographical irregularities, even though these might be significant to the birds. Map readings of larger features and ground exploration of less obvious ones eventually satisfied us that the distribution of Abbott's booby was much affected by topography. Besides emergence, Abbott's boobies choose trees with gaps on the western side, since they can enter these upwind.

This still leaves the problem of the patchy distribution within the favoured areas. Abbott's booby, in common with all other sulids, is basically gregarious, although it has lost this tendency to a far greater extent than any other and in fact often nests solitarily. Nevertheless, we found many cases of two nests in one tree and a few of three nests in one tree. In scores of cases nests were in adjacent trees. In terms of actual densities, in two widely separated but densely populated areas of 876 000 and 854 000 sq. m we located 90 and 65 pairs, which gives approximately 9700 and 13 000 sq. m per pair respectively and even here distribution was uneven, so that small patches showed considerably higher densities. One patch, for example, held 18 pairs in 20 000 sq. m. This gregarious tendency, in a small population (the factors limiting which are completely unknown) could explain its patchy distribution even within suitable areas of the island. There simply are not enough boobies to fill them to the optimum density, if this is anywhere near the level of the more favoured patches.

Alternatively, or in addition, it is possible that even broadly favourable areas are not uniformly attractive. Landing, for example, may be easier in some places than others.

Finally, I suggest that it must be of very considerable survival value for the juvenile, after its first proper flight (and whilst it is still wholly dependent on its parents for food), to have a visual fix—an easily recognisable locality to home on to, rather than be faced, with the task of re-locating its own tree in a vast, uniform sea of jungle canopy. Maybe 'recognisability', too, plays some part in determining what is a suitable breeding spot.

In brief, the non-uniform distribution of Abbott's booby on Christmas Island may be explicable on the hypothesis that the favoured western part, by virtue of its dissected nature and irregular canopy, provides more scope for landing and departure. The patchiness within favoured areas may depend on the basically gregarious tendency of boobies, together with small differences in suitability.

At the time of writing (October 1976) the conservation prospects can be more realistically assessed than in 1967. In the intervening years an area in the heart of Abbott's booby country has been cleared and mined and a considerable number (probably in sum between 100 and 200) of adults, juveniles and nests destroyed. In July–August 1974 I revisited the island and found that the distribution of Abbott's booby (so far as could be judged in the short time available) was the same as in 1967 (see Nelson 1975); there had been no movement into new areas. Birds were nesting around the perimeter of mined areas and almost certainly were those displaced by the clearing operations. Thus, despite the noise, disturbance and altered landscape they were remaining as close as possible to their original location. Furthermore, they were nesting in two small 'islands' of trees which had been left standing near Fields 20 and 21. These facts alone indicate that for conservation planning purposes one can confidently assume that Abbott's booby remains faithful to its preferred localities from year to year and secondly that it is well worthwhile leaving patches of trees in the most favoured spots. Longer term reclamation of devastated areas by reafforestation is now being put in hand by the Phosphate Commissioners' Conservation Officer. At the moment then, and thanks mainly to the dedicated safeguarding of nesting pairs by D. Powell, for which, in turn the Phosphate Commissioners themselves deserve credit, the population remains healthy and viable and reasonably generous conservation measures (Nelson, 1977) can ensure that it remains so.

In the reasonably long term, even a slightly increased adult mortality rate and/or a reduced breeding success, both of which could quite conceivably be brought about by an enforced transference to a sub-optimal breeding habitat, could run down the population to a level at which it could become non-viable. There are indications from David Powell's work that the breeding success of Abbott's booby is very much lower than I predicted from my limited period on the island. In such a case, an appreciation of the dangers could come too late, since a very small population with extremely low recruitment rate, largely dependent on weather, has poor powers of recovery.

SUMMARY

1. Although usually said to have nested on Assumption, this probably ought to be treated with serious reservation. However, it can now be accepted as having nested (probably commonly) on Rodriguez (Mascarene Islands) in the eighteenth century and perhaps later.

2. Today, Abbott's booby is, so far as we know, entirely confined to the Indian Ocean Christmas Island.

3. It inhabits the forest canopy, mainly on the western half of the island, above the 150m contour.

4. Its distribution within this area is patchy, and seems to be determined partly by underlying topography, the birds favouring that which provides broken canopy and emergent trees, since it can enter and leave these more easily and safely.

5. The population on Christmas Island was estimated to be 4000–5000 individuals but new figures indicate that it may be as high as 8000 individuals (Nelson, 1977).

6. There is a potentially serious conservation problem since much of its Christmas Island habitat is being and will be destroyed, but efforts to minimise damage are being made.

3. BREEDING ECOLOGY

BREEDING HABITAT

Christmas Island, the only nesting place of this booby, lies 312 km south of Java Head and 852km east of Cocos Keeling; a single island of volcanic origin, perhaps the shattered cone of an old volcano, with a superstructure of coralline limestone. Much of its 166 square km is over 152m high and at two points in the western part (Ross Hill and Murray Hill) it reaches a height of 323m and 356m. Almost the entire island is covered with rain forest. The peaks descend by gentle slope and precipitous coralline limestone cliffs, particularly prominent on the south side, to shore terraces of sea-fretted, pinnacled limestone which terminate in low, undercut sea cliffs with fantastic caves and shelves.

The sea cliff, some 9 to 15m high, is interrupted, particularly on the north and east sides, by small shingle or coral-sand beaches, many of which are inaccessible except by boat. The eroded limestone pinnacles of the shore terrace are a rusty blackish colour, brittle and razor sharp. There are pockets of vegetation (succulent evergreens) and, often, a dense fringe of spiny shrubs and *Pandanus*. Noddies nest on the sea cliffs and brown boobies on the shore terrace between the pinnacles and on gentler rocky ground a few metres further inland. At a variable distance inland there is an irregular 60 to 90m inner cliff leading to the first of the forested inland terraces and boulder strewn slopes. The inner, forested parts of the shore terrace are used by frigate birds (*Fregata andrewsi* and in a few places *F. minor*) and red-footed boobies and the inland cliffs by noddies, brown boobies and red-tailed tropic birds.

The present structure has obviously arisen as a result of the growth of coral on the highest parts of the old volcano, now the island's three hills, and a succession of uplifts which raised these peaks over 300m above the sea. The periods of time between upraisings have allowed new sea cliffs and fringing reefs to form, the latter, when in turn raised, to become the new shore terrace. The brittle coral pinnacles are now mainly covered with humus but, even far in the interior, exposed tracts remain, festooned with thorny scrub and a nightmare to negotiate. Cracks, too wide to span and up to 6m deep have to be painfully traversed and at its worst, this terrain can demand several hours to yield a few hundred metres.

The soil that covers much of the island is thin and easily dried out and the porous limestone fails to retain much moisture. Thus, in the dry season (July to November or December) plants face considerable drought. The present climax jungle is obviously a finely balanced ecosystem and once the soil cover and vegetation have been destroyed, there is no possibility of rapid regeneration.

Between the limestone pinnacles there are deposits of calcium phosphate. The usual theory is that it represents transformed guano, laid down under an ancient, dry climatic regime by an astronomically huge seabird population rather than the paltry few thousand of today. I find this hard to believe. Quite apart from the climatic changes that must be hypothesised and the vastness of the bird population required, there are no skeletal remains in the phosphate, whereas, by comparison, the Peruvian guano deposits contain many. It seems far more likely that the phosphate stems from marine sediments deposited in the crevices of the coralline limestone with which it combined to form calcium phosphate.[1] Now it lies beneath a layer of earth, which has to be scraped off before the phosphate can be dug out by mechanical grabs. It takes but a few weeks via bulldozing, burning and phosphate extraction to reduce virgin jungle to naked limestone pinnacles.

In addition to Abbott's booby, Christmas Island is the sole nesting place of the lovely golden bosun bird and probably the only nesting place of Andrew's frigate bird. It also supports an endemic owl, goshawk, imperial pigeon, emerald dove, white-eyed warbler, swiftlet and ground thrush. To biologists Christmas Island approaches the same level of importance as the famous Galapagos Islands. The prospect of significant destruction by phosphate mining is appalling to contemplate and plans for conservation are a matter of urgency.

Returning now, to the theme of the habitat of Abbott's booby on Christmas Island, this booby has without doubt the narrowest breeding niche of any sulid, for it has been recorded only in trees, whereas even the arboreal red-footed booby uses low bushes and, very exceptionally, the ground. The significance of the remarkably sharp contour boundary, around 150m, above which all Abbott's boobies nest, remains obscure, if it is not merely an aspect of its tendency to choose strongly contoured ground. Within its favoured habitat, of fine trees on irregular ground on the central plateau of Christmas Island, however, there are significant preferences.

The plateau forest is dominated by three emergent species whose crowns project above the main-storey canopy. These are *Planchonella nitida*, *Eugenia gigantea* and *Hernandia peltata* (Mitchell, undated but around 1970) which achieve a maximum height of around 45m in sheltered areas, though only 20–35 in the least favourable ones. The under-storey consists of saplings of all the plateau species together with *Pisonia excelsa*. Only *Planchonella* and *Eugenia* are of prime importance for Abbott's booby (D. Powell, pers. comm.). *Planchonella* is probably the most widespread tree on the island, occurring on all terraces and comprising perhaps 15 per cent of the tree cover on the plateau. It has a long, uncluttered bole, buttressed to about 3–5m. The branches are regular, horizontal and spreading. *Eugenia*, almost as common as *Planchonella* on the plateau, is commonly excessively buttressed, sometimes to more than 7m up the bole. Branches, usually borne high on the bole, are irregular and spreading and the canopy is normally light and open.

COLONY CHARACTERISTICS

Abbott's booby is by far the least colonial of all sulids and many pairs are almost solitary. Yet it is undoubtedly gregarious; uneven though its nesting density is, the densest groups

[1] Lately, the B.P.C. Geologist, Peter Barrat (in prep.), has developed a complex hypothesis based on localised, volcanic heat combination of guano with coral limestone proceeding simultaneously with bird-occupation. I find this, too, hard to believe.

Fig. 333 (a). Shore terrace, Christmas Island, used by red-foot and brown booby but not by Abbott's booby.

(b). Typical jungle in the mid-western part of the island – a good area for Abbott's booby. The cleared area in the foreground has been recently mined.

(for example, 18 pairs in 20 000 sq. m) clearly represent considerable aggregates and the very common habit of nesting two or three to a tree or in adjacent trees is even more indicative. In fact, it is extremely rare for any pair to be out of earshot of another pair or more. Having stressed this point, however, it remains true that it is the contrast between the highly social sulids, as a family, and this single, aberrant, relatively solitary nesting member that stands out. This comparative aspect and the functions of colonial nesting are discussed later.

NEST SITES AND NESTS

There are many ways in which one can attempt to characterise the nesting sites of Abbott's booby. I have already mentioned its predilection for the higher and more irregular parts of the island and for fine and emergent trees. The following account is a more detailed description of the precise types of nesting sites which it uses, delineated in terms of tree-species, height, type of branches used and the aspect of the nest—whether placed on the north, south, east or west side of the tree or in the centre. Of 76 nests found in August 1974, 55 (72·4 per cent) were in *Planchonella nitida*, 15 (19·7 per cent) in *Eugenia gigantea* and 6 (7·9 per cent) in *Tristeriopsis nativitatis* (D. Powell, pers. comm.). I give these figures in preference to my larger 1967 sample because the former did not distinguish adequately between *Planchonella* and *Eugenia*. Undoubtedly, however, almost all nests were in these two species though a few were in banyan (*Ficus* spp.).

Of 67 nests whose height was estimated (entirely by eye and therefore possibly far from accurate but most likely to err on the low side) 24 were placed between 18–21m high, 16 at 21–24m, 15 at 15–18m, 9 at 12–15m, 2 at 9–12m and 1 above 24m.

It was most interesting to note that Abbott's booby used a wide variety of types of sites but preferred to place its nest out among thin lateral branches. Thirty-nine of a sample of 68 nests were described as among thin laterals. Mostly these were thin branches, in some cases twigs, far out from the main trunk, usually beneath the canopy, but in two cases right up among the canopy twigs. They were usually more nearly horizontal than vertical. The next most favoured site (12 cases) was a fairly vertical crotch or fork, often substantial but sometimes thin, and either fairly central or more lateral. Thick or fairly thick branches upon which the nest was placed, perhaps at a junction or against an upright lateral, accounted for seven cases. In five more, nests were placed among thin uprights, mainly peripheral, in four among medium thick laterals and in one among thick uprights.

Over 80 per cent of these nests were in large trees, but one was 10–12m up in the middle of a small tree and another among extremely thin laterals in what, at the time, I described as a 'tiny' tree though even here the nest was perhaps 15m high. These are important cases because they reveal the ability of Abbott's booby to use this kind of habitat. The fact that very few now do so may not mean that they would be unable to change to this sparser growth if their preferred habitat was largely destroyed, as it may well be unless the conservation case is heeded.

Fig. 333 (c). Typical example of impoverished growth on the low stony ground in the south-west of Christmas Island. Abbott's booby does not use this habitat.

(d)

Mined-out area.

Abbott's booby prefers west facing nests (35 out of 55 cases) followed by south facing (12). Two north facing nests were recorded and six more were north-west or south-west. This preference probably reflects the general west facing tendency of the slopes, the trees being on the whole more open and easily entered from that side, and also the prevailing south-easterly wind. D. Powell recorded, in terms of compass bearings, which segment of the tree the nest was in and thus the direction 'faced' by the nest; a nest located at (say) 285° would face about north-west and the bird would normally approach it from the north-west. Of 72 nests, 48 (66 per cent) were in the north-west segment (between 270° and 360°); 16 (22 per cent) in the south-west segment (180°–270°); 5 (7 per cent) in the north-east segment (0–90°) and 3 (5 per cent) in the south-east (90°–180°) and almost all the east facing nests were in trees which lacked open canopy on the west side.

By far the greatest number of Abbott's booby nests were found among thin lateral branches on the west side of the tree, beneath the canopy, in fairly emergent situations and with good access to the site itself. An exceptionally interesting case (Fig. 334) found in 1974 was that of a nest in a completely dead tree. Almost certainly, the pair had been displaced by clearing operations.

Abbott's booby builds a substantial nest of twigs, always living when plucked (in contrast to Andrew's frigate-bird). The nest measures about 0·75–0·90m across the base and is of considerable though variable depth. The cup, which is moderately deep, is lined with the

Fig. 334 (a)

Nest placed on fairly thick lateral, usually at a fork.

(b)

In 1974, the only pair yet known to have built in a dead tree. They did so following the clearing of jungle in a favoured booby area, obviously preferring the locality even in the absence of a normal nesting site.

leaves and terminal leafy parts of larger twigs. The nest structure incorporates some of the branches on which it rests and is therefore much more secure than if it merely sat on top of them. Even so, the strong winds which not infrequently catch the tree, particularly emergent ones, displace the branches to such an extent that the nest must often be severely strained. The heavy rain which characterises Christmas Island's climate, usually does not fall until about November, by which time the chick is almost or quite fully grown. The combination of wind and torrential rain must lead to the disintegration of many nests, since it is common to find juveniles begging from branches or in crotches where no nest remains but where, from behavioural evidence, the nest had been situated. The importance of the nest in supporting the chick for several months is no doubt the reason for its substantial nature. Frigate nests are pathetic platforms of dead twigs, but these birds are better perchers than Abbott's booby and build in situations where perching is easier. Furthermore, they build lower down, in more sheltered positions.

THE EGG AND CLUTCH

Abbott's booby lays a single, whitish egg, covered with the chalky deposit common to the order and eventually staining a brownish yellow with the juice from crushed leaves in the nest.

I obtained the measurements and weights of three eggs (78×51mm; 84×54; 82×53; 100·5g; 124; and 112). As a percentage of the weight of the female that laid them, these eggs were 6·9, 7·6 and 6·7 respectively. Thus, both in absolute terms and relative to the female's weight, the egg of Abbott's booby is larger and heavier than that of any other sulid.

The incubation period (57·5; 56 and c.56; mean 57 days) is 11 days longer than any other sulid, the next longest being that of the red-foot, which also lays the next heaviest egg relative to its own weight. The adaptive significance of the red-foot's large egg almost certainly lies in the production of a well-developed chick better capable of withstanding the starvation to which it may be, and in the Galapagos often is, subjected. Whilst there is no evidence that the same holds for Abbott's booby, there are indications that it, too, is habitually an offshore (far-foraging) feeder, in which context the large egg would be adaptive.

There is no information on replacement laying.

The egg loses about 11 per cent of its weight during incubation, which is in line with the other members of the family.

Incubation regime

Both sexes incubate. On the two nests sufficiently accessible for regular observation, the respective males averaged 48 and 61 hour shifts (range 7–95 hours and 7–96) and the females 48 and 51 hours (range 16–119 and 30–74). On one nest we obtained complete coverage for the first 39 days of incubation during which the male took seven spells (71, 24, 72, 25, 95 and 7 hours) whilst the female took eight, starting with one prior to the male's first spell (31, 48,

Fig. 335

Abbott's booby settling on egg.

50, 96, 119, 24, 16 and 24 hours). Over this period the averages worked out almost exactly equal (male 52 hours, female 51). For the remainder of the incubation period the pair reduced the length of their incubation stints and averaged 36 and 37 hours respectively, the overall average for incubation stints working out at 48 hours for each. For the second nest, the male's stints were 80, 96, 20, 7, 72 and 94 and the female's 74, 30, 46, 49, 73 and 73, but there was insufficient coverage to demonstrate the reduction in length of stint as incubation progressed.

These stints are extremely long for a sulid; four days away, at the most, gives time enough for a vast range, as does even 52 hours (the mean for all four birds). Since there is every reason to believe that Abbott's booby lives in a region where food is not scarce—probably quite the contrary—this may mean that instead of spending the time looking for food, much of it is used in getting to and from some distant and reliable feeding area (see p. 883). This, of course, assumes that when Abbott's booby is not to be seen at the nest, it is in fact away at sea.

THE CHICK

1. *Morphology and plumage development*

From the first starring of the egg to the complete emergence of the chick takes 36 to 48 hours. The eyes can be opened during the first day, but are kept closed most of the time. The skin is purplish. The down is thicker than in other sulids and this, together with the open eyes, indicate the chick's relatively advanced development on hatching. The lead-grey bill has a black tip and white egg tooth. The iris is brown and the orbital ring deep grey. At first, the

Fig. 336 (a). Abbott's booby with month-old chick. Note the white eye-lid of the adult (displacement sleeping).

(c). Abbott's booby with two-month old chick.

(b)

Abbott's booby with chick about five weeks old, showing characteristic feather tracts on forehead and well developed black scapulars.

webs lack black on their distal part, but after 30 days the orbital ring blackens and the webs begin to gain the dark edges characteristic of the adult.

The chick differs from those of all other boobies. By **six to seven weeks** the body down has become extremely thick and short, like cotton wool. From about 31 days (in one case 37 days) the forehead is clear of down and a wide band of barish skin extends backwards beyond the eyes, ending sharply where the down of the crown begins. The bare area develops short, buff-tipped feathers in two fan-shaped tracts, apices forwards, but the tips must eventually abrade or the feathers be quickly replaced, since fully grown juveniles have pure white heads like adults. Except for the forehead, the down of the head and neck is extremely long, with deeply dissected tips giving a distinctive loose appearance. By the time feathers develop, the bill has turned pale greyish blue, less vinous than the adult male's.

The primaries erupted between days 40 and 42 in one chick, but not until the 50th day in another. The feathers of the greater wing-coverts, which together with the scapulars later form the distinctive black 'cape', began to show at about 15–20 days. The down on humerus and radio-ulna is pushed out by brown-tipped feathers which, as on the forehead, seem mainly transitory, though some juveniles have a few small brown scapulars. Perhaps these brown and brown-tipped feathers are all that remain of the brown juvenile plumage common to all other sulids. The primaries show no such brown tips. The tail erupts at about 46–50 days. As the black feathers on the wing and scapular region extend, the young Abbott's booby becomes astonishingly like a miniature adult. Growth transforms it into a juvenile virtually indistinguishable from the adult male. Table 123 gives some measurements at different ages.

2. *Attendance by parents*

After the chick hatched the duration of attendance spells dropped further (it had already declined during the last third of incubation). In nest 1 the egg hatched on July 26th and the female took the first guard spell. It lasted 24 hours, as did her two subsequent ones and the alternating ones of the male. After that our records were slightly less complete, but the following figures are probably not far out: Female spells 20; 42; 24; 8; 12; 15; 18; 24; 24; 24 and 24 and the alternating spells of the male 60; 24; 16; 26; 21; 30; 10; 22; 20; 26 and 24. Overall, the male's guard spells averaged 27 hours (range 10–60) the first three averaged 32 and the subsequent 11 spells 25 hours (not a significant difference). The female's spells averaged 21 hours (range 8–42) the first three 24 hours and the subsequent 11 spells 21 hours. Thus male and female took equal guard stints and kept up a fairly consistent return rate for the first month or so of the chick's life.

In nest 2 the figures were less comprehensive but worked out at an average 17 hours for the male (24; 24; 24; 24; 18; 7; 24; 9 and 7) and 22 for the female (24; 24; 24; 18; 27; 24; 17; 17 and 19). Again the sexes took equal shares and a 24-hour return rate or near it, seemed the norm.

TABLE 123

MORPHOLOGICAL DEVELOPMENT IN ABBOTT'S BOOBY BASED ON THREE CHICKS

Age (days)	Culmen	Length (mm) Longest primary	Longest greater wing covert	Tail
10	26			
20	37·5		0·5	
30	50		11	
40	65	Erupting	15	
50	74·5	14–21	23–44	Erupting
60	82	28–44	46	34
70	91	53	50	53

3. *Feeding*

The frequency with which the young are fed could be accurately determined only by a continuous watch. We were able to do this for one 30-day old chick during the daylight part of a 48-hour period and recorded one feed delivered by each parent (the feed consisting of several separate insertions of the chick's head into the parent's mouth). Probably the female, who returned before dark on the second day, fed the chick again during the early night. If so, he chick received 1·5 feeds per day.

The visits by parents to our three observation chicks, assuming that each return following a reasonable time lapse resulted in a feed, indicated that young are fed about 1·2 times per day between about three and eight weeks of age and less frequently thereafter. Between hatching and about three weeks, although parental attendance spells averaged about 22 hours feeds were not similarly spaced, since we found that parents can produce small amounts even mid-way through such spells. Later, the young take food more immediately, though even then three to four hours may elapse between the adult returning and feeding the chick. Food may be brought at any time but there is a very strong tendency to return between 15.30 and 18.00 hours and particularly between 16.00 and 17.00 hours.

Recalling the sexual division of labour in the blue-footed booby, we looked for a similar trait in Abbott's booby. Of 13 pre-fledging feeds the male: female ratio was 4:9 and of 11 feeds given to juveniles 7:4, the difference is not significant.

4. *Food*

There is little information. One specimen seen on its way between parent and chick was large

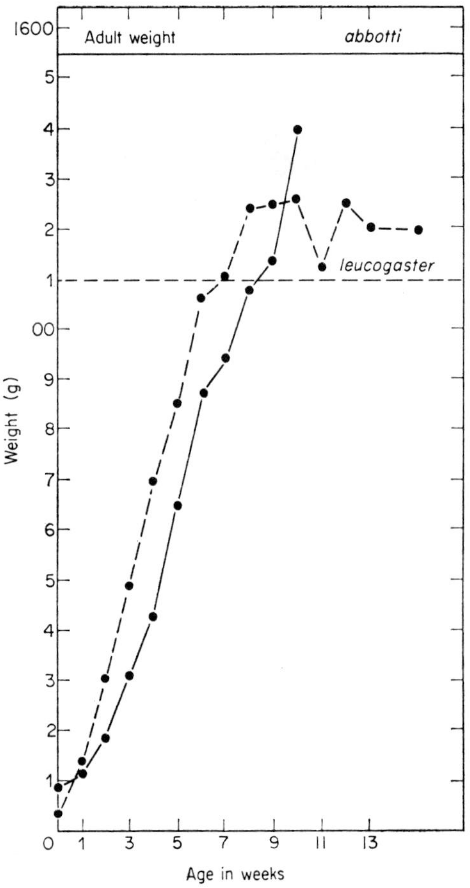

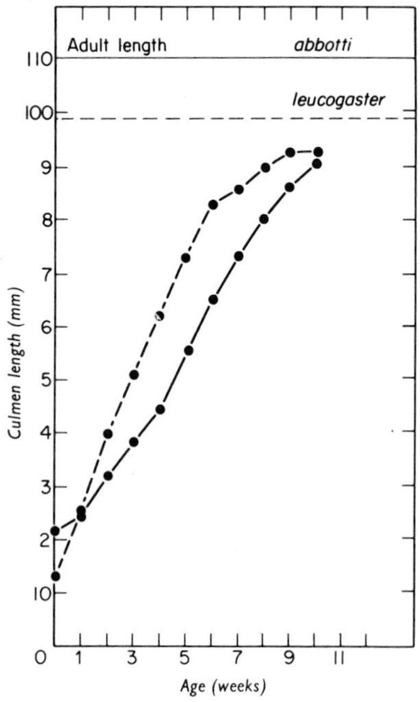

Fig. 338. Culmen growth in Abbott's booby, compared with the brown booby on Christmas Island.

Fig. 337. Rate of growth by weight of Abbott's booby and the brown booby, on Christmas Island.

(perhaps 15–20cm) and orange/red in colour—possibly a grouper of some kind. Flying fish and squid are commonly taken.

5. *Growth*

The chick's growth is remarkably slow. This point can best be brought out by contrasting the growth of another species, the brown booby, on the same island and for the same period. Figs. 337 and 338 compare weight increases and culmen growth in Abbott's and brown boobies. Although Abbott's weighs twice as much at hatching, the situation is reversed within three weeks, even though the adult brown booby is a much smaller bird. It takes ten weeks before the growth curves cross again. Similarly, a brown booby chick weighs half as much as an adult by 3½ weeks, where Abbott's takes 5½ weeks; and the brown booby reaches adult weight when just over seven weeks old, whilst Abbott's booby is only 90 per cent of the adult's weight at 10 weeks (when our weight records ended). The brown booby grows faster on Christmas Island than on Ascension, at least in some years (Dorward 1962b). Abbott's booby nevertheless grows even more slowly than the Ascension Island brown booby. Similarly, the red-footed booby chick on Christmas Island grew much more rapidly than Abbott's booby in the year of this study. The significance of this is discussed later. By extrapolation, it is probable that Abbott's booby requires at least 24 weeks to become free-flying.

Individual growth curves (Fig. 339) showed a meagre increase in weight during the first three weeks and then a relatively rapid one. This may reflect the full adoption of the normal sulid feeding mechanism (taking large boluses of food directly from the adult's throat) after the earlier tendency to pick it inexpertly from the nest bottom (see p. 804).

The culmen growth rates of brown and Abbott's boobies endorse the points revealed by weight increases. By the age of one week the brown booby has a longer culmen than Abbott's booby despite hatching with one only 13mm long, 9mm shorter than in Abbott's booby. By the age of 10 weeks the culmen of the latter measures 83 per cent of the adult's length against 94 per cent for the brown booby and is still 2mm shorter in absolute length although the adult culmen of Abbott's booby is 11mm longer than that of the adult brown booby.

6. *Fledging period*

Extrapolation from the growth rates shown in Figs. 337, 338 and Table 123 suggests that Abbott's booby nestlings do not reach adult weight until they are at least 12 weeks old. If 60 per cent is taken as a reasonable figure for the proportion of the fledging period required by the chick to reach adult weight (derived from the growth curves of four other booby species)

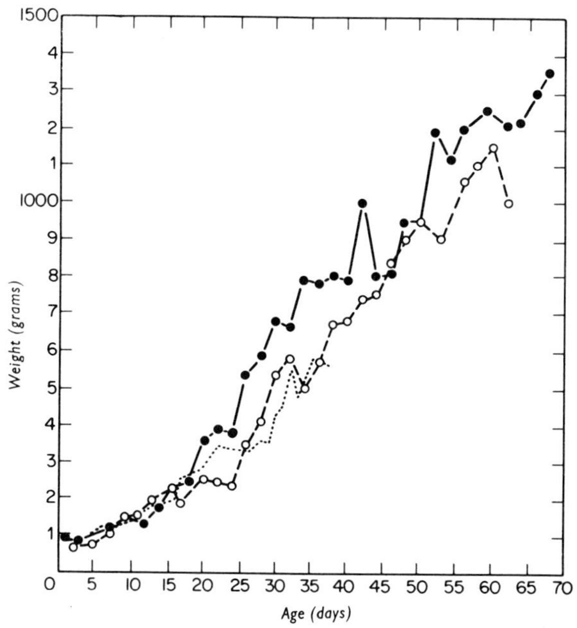

Fig. 339

Growth, by weight, of three Abbott's booby chicks.

the fledging period of Abbott's booby would be at least 20 weeks. Probably it is much longer than this, because in addition to the chick's very slow growth the dangers of the jungle top prevent practice flights. The young bird will be under strong selection pressure to delay its first flight until it is fully competent whereas, by contrast, the red-footed booby may make small and wobbly practice flights whilst still retaining some down. It therefore seems highly improbable that Abbott's booby will fledge before it is at least 24 weeks old.

This is the longest fledging period of any sulid and is particularly interesting because the causes are probably not the same as those which force extremely long fledging periods on half starved Galapagos red-footed boobies or Ascension brown boobies. The growth of Abbott's booby is steady and slow rather than the interrupted and frequently retarded one of the other two species. Its adaptive significance is perhaps to be understood in the context of its long breeding cycle and biennial breeding frequency (p. 781).

Since this was written, D. Powell has followed the progress of 10 young Abbott's boobies right through the winter (October/March) of 1974/75. This is the period when Abbott's boobies largely disappear from Christmas Island, being seldom seen or heard. It seems that Powell's adults visited their young relatively infrequently and he found that these suffered heavy mortality, directly or indirectly through starvation. Apparently few if any of these young birds were free-flying, at least up until February, so perhaps they were from late eggs.

7. *Post-fledging feeding*

After fledging, young Abbott's boobies still require to be fed. Of four juveniles that were fully grown when first found in March 1967 but whose age was otherwise unknown.

1. One was last seen to be fed on May 30th, but continued food-begging until the end of July and was sporadically present throughout August. Post-fledging feeding lasted at least 90 days.
2. One was definitely absent in early May but probably flew earlier. The last feed actually seen was on June 26th, but it was almost certainly fed until mid-July. From July 19th the parents began to show interest in nest building and ignored the juvenile, which continued to beg until August 8th, when it disappeared. Post-fledging feeding lasted 80–100 days or more.
3. One was located by its calling early in April but was often impossible to see. It was present daily until mid-July and feeds were seen June 14–18th. Begging frequently during latter half of July and August and probably being fed. Begging waned in September and the juvenile probably left some time in the third week. Post-fledging feeding probably lasted 90 days or more.
4. One was located early in April and was definitely free-flying by the third week. It continued begging and was almost certainly fed until early July. The parents began collecting nest material in the third week of July and probably stopped feeding the juvenile shortly before that. Post-fledging feeding lasted 80–100 days or more.

Elsewhere on the island, we recorded isolated instances of juveniles being fed as late as July 11th. In 1974 juveniles were being fed in August and September. Although their ages were unknown it is highly likely that they hatched the previous July or August.

David Powell continued our own observations on one of our known-age birds and thus provided a valuable record, then the only one, of the postfledging history of Abbott's booby. After fledging some time in December 1967, the juvenile was regularly, if not almost constantly present at the nest, often actually in it, until June 22nd 1968. After that, birds kept appearing at the nest in July, August and September, but the parents had been sporadically in evidence since mid-April (for some time prior to that, exact period unspecified, they had not been seen) and there is a possibility that adult male and juvenile were not distinguished. However, Powell considered that he did not lose track of the juvenile until about mid-July; after that he said 'the juvenile often disappeared but never for long periods', though by September 7th he thinks that the juvenile was 'gone'. Thus, although this case does not add to our knowledge of the post-fledging feeding periods, it shows that a chick which hatched on July 4th 1967 was still around the nest one year later and that the adults which laid on May 10th 1967 had not laid again by September 7th 1968.

From these examples it seems that Abbott's booby young are dependent on their parents for at least 30–40 weeks and almost certainly for up to a year.

The fact that three of our juveniles disappeared from their nesting tree and were not seen again, though formerly they had been attending fairly regularly, suggests that they had gone off to sea.

Fig. 340

Abbott's booby feeding fully grown juvenile, aged about one year (August 1974). The juvenile is begging on the exact spot where the nest used to be. Note that the juvenile closely resembles the adult.

8. *Breeding success*

We recorded the death, by falling, of one month-old chick, out of four that we followed. One cannot base anything on that, but falling may be one of the principal dangers, especially in high winds and may be one reason why the east side of the island, which receives most of the wind, is less favoured, though this suggestion hardly fits with the species' tendency to inhabit the upper reaches of the island—even to the near summit of Murray Hill. There are no very significant predators although the Christmas Island goshawk occasionally takes small young (D. Powell). Breeding success is therefore probably high, in terms of *fledged* young produced, but mortality between fledging and competent independence may be very high. D. Powell's (pers. comm.) observations on nests containing young Abbott's boobies throughout the winters (October/March) of 1974/75 and 1975/76, provided startling evidence of high mortality; by March, 90 per cent had fallen and those which he recorded were seriously underweight. During the unusually dry and calm winter of 1976/77, fully grown (mainly fledged) young in January did well up until early March but then several died. Low success thus seems usual and with Abbott's booby's other restraints on recruitment, indicates extreme longevity.

BREEDING REGIMES

1. *General features of attendance at the island*

There is some irregularity about the yearly pattern of the presence of Abbott's booby on Christmas Island. Early statements to the effect that it leaves the island around October, returning perhaps around March, are not entirely correct. Whilst such a pattern would roughly fit with those of other seabirds, it is impossible for Abbott's booby, for the simple reason that it is still feeding its chick or juvenile throughout the period November to March. Yet it is certainly true that Abbott's booby is much less in evidence at this time and this is probably because all those not tied with chicks are away from the island and those with chicks are quiet and undemonstrative at this time. Since Abbott's booby is hard enough to see at any time, it is little wonder that to a casual observer it seems to be altogether absent. David Powell (pers. comm.) illustrated this point most powerfully when in a letter dated February 24th 1968 he commented that, at that time, Abbott's boobies were 'as rare as the proverbial dodo'. He had just spent two weeks working in the Tom's Ridge area where there are quite a lot of breeding Abbott's, without seeing or hearing a single adult or even a juvenile. Yet, at that time, there must have been juveniles in the canopy; the juvenile in one of our observation nests, hatched the previous July, was still to be seen sitting in its nest. This shows how inconspicuous they must have been.

Since I wrote this, D. Powell (pers. comm.) has shown that birds with dependent young continue to visit the island throughout winter but usually very few are to be seen flying in, and they come much less frequently than when the young are growing in the nest.

About March or early April, however, they suddenly become more apparent and can be seen circling (often just one or two at a time, extremely high) above parts of the island, landing in the high canopy and calling (see Behaviour Section, p. 784). These are probably, in the main, adults about to begin a new breeding cycle. This was the time of year at which we arrived on Christmas Island in 1967 and David Powell reports that in 1968 Abbott's boobies re-appeared on the island on April 3rd. The next day adults were calling in various places and on the 15th adults were seen back at our observation nest, which still held the juvenile and which continued to do so until late July, at least. Powell comments 'what this does not convey is the sudden and complete return of the Abbott's. I would be out in the bush and would never see one. Then, on that particular afternoon I . . . sensed something different and, looking up, saw two or three birds circling a banyan tree. It seemed at the time so utterly complete.' As I remarked earlier, these are likely to be birds about to initiate a new breeding attempt. The winter elusiveness of adults feeding juveniles probably depends partly on weather; in 1976/77 they were commonly seen.

In the case of experienced breeders, almost certainly the same territory is used year after year and partners remain faithful. The old site is re-occupied and attendance becomes progressively more intensive. The time spent at the site is very considerable for at least six weeks before the egg is laid. Thus, in one of our observation pairs, which laid on May 10th, both male and female were recorded in attendance on 70 per cent of days in April and this must under-represent the true figure. These pre-laying attendance spells were not just brief visits; 13 male spells whose length could be calculated averaged 21 hours (range 6–41) and nine female spells 30 hours (range 6–42). Absences during this time averaged, for the male, 25 hours (range 9–120; 11 cases) and for the female 42 (8–127; 10 cases). This pattern, with the male attending the territory more than the female, is typical of sulids. The female's longer absences might be slightly adaptive in helping her to meet the cost of egg production, but at 7 per cent of the female's weight this can hardly be very important.

In the only other pair for which we gained some information on attendance before laying, both male and female averaged attendance spells of 19·5 hours (range 6–30) the period over which the figures were gained was too short to make meaningful comparison.

The pattern of attendance during incubation and the chick guarding stage is dealt with under those headings. Here, it may be said that the young are guarded continuously for 4–6 weeks and then visited intermittently for feeding. Our own detailed observations ended long before the chicks were fully grown, so the period of post-fledging care was worked out indirectly (see p. 777). However, it was probably at least three to four months. It remains completely unknown whether Abbott's boobies attend the site for a period after completely severing its connections with the juvenile. In view of the length of the cycle (p. 782) it is very possible that it does not, instead merely progressively reducing the frequency of its return with food.

Thus, whilst the pattern of attendance for the six weeks or so prior to egg laying, during incubation, and throughout the first two months' of the chick's life are satisfactorily known (if two pairs can be taken as reasonably representative) there are still hardly any observations on events at the tail end of the breeding cycle.

2. *The breeding cycle and frequency of breeding*

Some of the preceding sections have given details of each stage of the breeding cycle, the whole of which is summarised in Table 124.

With such a protracted breeding cycle, it is clearly impossible for Abbott's booby to breed annually. The crucial question in determining the frequency of breeding then becomes: when does Abbott's booby lay? If it can lay in any month, then breeding can occur at intervals of a year and a half or a year and three-quarters or whatever would be necessary to accommodate the breeding events plus a recuperative period. If, on the other hand, it lays only within a fairly circumscribed part of the year, then obviously it can breed, at the most, only every second year, because a bird laying in June or July of one year will not be finished in time for the next June or July and must (if restricted to a June or July laying) go on to the one after that.

On this crucial issue we gained good evidence that Abbott's booby lays only between April and August. This seasonal egg laying we could, of course, establish only for the year of our study (1967) when laying was recorded between April and July with a clear peak in May. The actual laying dates recorded in 1967 were: 10, 13, 14–20, 15–20, 20 and 29 May, and 29 June; and the estimated 1967 dates were: May (three cases), May–June (two cases), early June (one case) and late June (one case). The evidence strongly suggests that the 1966 breeding season was similar. Thus in March and April 1967 extensive search disclosed, apart from some pairs in early courtship, solely fully grown juveniles. The eggs must have been laid earlier than the preceding August but probably later than March–April; in other words, probably April to July 1966. No eggs had been laid between approximately August 1966 and April 1967. The estimated laying dates for 1966 were late April (one case), late July or August (three cases), but it must be emphasised that these are approximate.

The length of the breeding cycle had to be established by combining observations on the post-fledging dependence of juveniles hatched in 1966 and on additional data from D. Powell, with those on pre-laying activities, incubating and fledging periods from pairs laying in 1967. These activities total more than 16 months (see Table 124).

Seasonal breeding is a feature of Christmas Island's seabirds, presumably because the main rainy period, between about November and April, associated with gales from the north east, is not a suitable time either for fluffy young to be exposed to the weather or for adults to provide for them. Abbott's booby is therefore as much in line as it can be, consistent with its long cycle, for it lays and produces a fully grown youngster in much the same months favoured by the other seabirds. For some reason(s), as yet unknown, but probably to do with its habit of feeding far from the island, it has evolved such a slowly developing chick (and its antecedent large egg) that, by the time December comes, the juvenile would, with but the normal sulid post-fledging feeding period of a month or six weeks, find itself newly independent at the worst time of year. This would hardly be the time at which to launch the single, expensive product of a long and arduous reproductive attempt on its independent course. Having got thus far, so it seems to me, Abbott's booby does the 'logical' thing and maintains its youngster until the new season. In the usual way, having gone in for slow development as a response to some set of environmental factors, evolution has pushed this adaptation as far as possible. Annual breeding has become impossible and yet seasonal breeding remains advantageous, so Abbott's booby has lengthened its cycle right out and gone for biennial breeding. To make this practicable it must have resulted in a greatly increased chance of survival for the one youngster that it does produce, and again, the longest possible post-fledging support would certainly help here. Then, too, there is the contingent factor, already mentioned, of the unusually demanding nesting environment, which means that the juvenile must be very competent (and therefore relatively old) before it attempts to fly. Also, it is quite possible that Abbott's booby is adapted to a special feeding area, which may require prolonged dependence of the juvenile so that it can acquire the information and perhaps the skills necessary for efficient feeding.

TABLE 124

THE BREEDING CYCLE OF ABBOTT'S BOOBY

Phase	Length (days)	Comments
Pre-laying (pair-bonding and nest building)	56–70+	This figure is based on firm observations of pairs building and mating
Incubation	56	
Chick growth to fledging	150–170+	Acceptable extrapolations from growth data plus definite record of nest 1
Post-fledging feeding	200+	Variably firm observations on 4 juveniles plus information on several nests from D. Powell
Post-breeding recuperation	180+	Judged on the concrete case of nest 1 which (given 3 months post-fledging feeding of young) went from mid-March till at least the beginning of September without beginning a new breeding cycle. Unless this pair laid in September or later and hence had small young in the NE and NW monsoon period (for which all our evidence was contrary) it must go 2 years at least between successive layings
Total	642–676+	

Note. In 1964 some chicks of *S. sula* in the Galapagos took 133 days to fledge and were dependent on their parents a further 119 days (Nelson 1969a) whilst for *S. leucogaster* on Ascension the figures were 112 days to fledge (Dorward 1962b) and 160 of post-fledging dependence (Simmons 1967b). Both of these were examples of growth under conditions of severe food shortage and yet probably required less time than *abbotti* to gain independence. Compared with the same two species on Christmas Island, *abbotti* required *much* longer.

Thus, the unusually protracted breeding cycle and the need to lay its egg within a relatively circumscribed period, restricts Abbott's booby to breeding once every two years, and this specialised system has many advantages.

SUMMARY

1. Christmas Island, the habitat of Abbott's booby, is coral limestone on basalt, 165 square km rising to 356m and covered with jungle.

2. Abbott's booby often nests solitarily, but it is not randomly dispersed; it shows slight but definite tendency to 'clump', some areas being much more thickly populated than others.

3. Nests are usually placed 18 to 21m high, in thin laterals, on the west side of the tree, by far the most favoured species being the two commonest emergent canopy species, *Planchonella nitida* and *Eugenia gigantea.*

4. A single large egg is laid (c.112g and 7 per cent of the female's weight) and takes 57 days to hatch.

5. Incubation is by both sexes equally, averaging about 50 hours per stint.

6. The chick is guarded equally by both parents; usually for 24-hour spells at a time. It is fed about 1·5 times a day.

7. It grows extremely slowly—far slower than any other booby—even though Christmas Island is not in a food poor area. This slow growth is an adaptation and not due to enforced starvation. The fledging period is probably at least 24 weeks.

8. Post-fledging feeding lasts at least 6 months and often (or usually) much longer.

9. Thus the complete reproductive cycle takes much longer than a year.

10. All the available evidence indicates that Abbott's booby lays only between April and July, therefore, in view of the long reproductive cycle, it must breed once every two years.

4. BREEDING BEHAVIOUR

INTRODUCTION

In its behaviour, as in its ecology, Abbott's booby is in many ways aberrant. Its family connections are always evident, but its behaviour is not strikingly similar to that of any other sulid, as the blue-footed and Peruvian's are to each other or even to that of the brown and white boobies. Nor does Abbott's resemble the only other arboreal sulid, the red-footed booby. Whilst we can know little about the evolutionary history of Abbott's booby—it may well have diverged from the ancestral sulid stock before the others (see p. 813)—it is helpful to look at its behaviour as being strongly moulded by its tree-top environment. The most important thing for Abbott's is to avoid falling to the ground, for this means certain death. It tends to reduce or altogether avoid 'contact' behaviour, in particular violent or vigorous contact because, one reasonably supposes, this is too dangerous. Much of the behaviour of Abbott's booby is more easily understood if one constantly recalls this factor. For example, there is no fighting; much of the behaviour between mates is long range and the food-begging of the young is remarkably restrained.

ESTABLISHMENT AND MAINTENANCE OF TERRITORY

1. *Site acquisition*

In March and April we frequently saw Abbott's boobies circling round and round high above their breeding areas, though of course we did not know their status. At closer range, non-established (presumed young) males intensively investigated areas already containing other Abbott's boobies. Established birds, conspicuously outposted in their nesting trees clearly attract these 'prospectors', which patrolled repeatedly along favoured lines, 'looking in' at them. Often they landed nearby forming 'threesomes' and then awaited the reaction of the occupants. To an observer sitting in the branches at the same height as the established bird, it is clear that it watches over-flying individuals with keen attention and may even react to them by low intensity display (Head Jerking). Areas already colonised will obviously be suitable localities for breeding and so, as in other sulids, young birds will doubtless tend to return to their area of birth. It may be that the threesomes are often parents and their prospecting offspring, now two, three or more years old. Aerial prospecting is common to all sulids and Abbott's booby shows no special features. By reacting, with appropriate avoidance, to the agonistic displays of territory owners (see later) the prospecting bird eventually demarcates its own tree or part of one, but it does not choose a precise nest site until after pair formation. In this it differs from most other sulids, in which the male usually demarcates a site.

Territorial defence is markedly inhibited. Established males usually do not go within touching distance of intruders; in no case did we see rivals fight,[1] grip beaks or even jab. Nor do they use the violent wing flailing shown in high-intensity situations in all other sulids except the gannet. I interpret this unusual state of affairs as an adaptation to minimise the risk of falling but it should be realised that it involves a failure to respond to external stimuli which in other sulids almost invariably elicit aggression and thus implies an internal inhibitory mechanism in Abbott's booby. In high-intensity territorial behaviour a male displaces the rival simply by determined approach or, more often, vigorous display. The main agonistic display is Head Jerking. Wing Waving, though used mainly as a meeting ceremony between mates (where it will be described) also frequently occurs in indistinguishable form as a hostile display. Both displays are highly ritualised.

2. *Head Jerking*

Head Jerking commonly occurs as a display between rivals and mutually or unilaterally between mates. It is oriented towards the rival or mate even if this means turning the head over the shoulder. It is an extraordinarily violent, spasmodic up and down movement of the head involving lengthening and shortening of the neck as well as jerking of the head (Fig. 341). The unusual twists and retractions reminded me of wryneck movements. At low intensity it is an abrupt upward nod. With increasing intensity the neck is more fully stretched, the upward snap takes the bill into the vertical position and as it descends and the neck shortens, side to side twists and jerks occur in a frenzied mosaic which may become so vigorous that the bird lifts from the branch with the energy of its movements. Forward lunges occur with the sideways jerks. At low intensity the wings are closed; at high intensity they open and close or are held out for the duration of a bout. The tail is widely fanned. The head and neck feathers are conspicuously ruffed and the displaying bird swallows repeatedly. At high intensity the head is jerked about once every one and a half to two seconds. Bouts may last for more than five minutes. Usually Head Jerking is accompanied by vigorous biting of the branch or twig.

When performed between mates, the male, or sometimes both, may pull off and hold a single leaf or small spray, which they replace if dropped. Either sex may perform the more vigorously, but usually the male does. Stretching movements made during the display resemble incipient jabs, though without opening the bill or making contact.

In pair relations, intense Head Jerking occurs between potential or new mates (see Pair Formation p. 789) but long established pairs, even with well grown young, also often perform vigorous Head Jerking, particularly after nest relief when the bird moving away from the nest Head Jerks violently at its partner and often bites branches, or a male moving away from the nest prior to departing for nest material, Head Jerks (perhaps just once) before taking off. This display, however, is not a part of pair meeting interactions as consistently as is Wing Waving.

In the period before egg laying, the male Head Jerked in all the instances where I noted his behaviour during the five minutes before parting from the female. In six instances of arrival at the nest to join the partner, neither Head Jerked during the following five minutes, but in one instance where they arrived more or less simultaneously both did so. The most extreme

[1] In one instance, in a high nest much obscured, there was a terrific commotion and violent action of some sort with crescendos of calling. Here, I thought there was protracted bill gripping (I could not be sure because of intervening foliage). This was the only instance, but worth recording even in its incomplete state because it may undermine the generalisation that Abbott's booby *never* fights.

examples of its involvement in sexual interactions occurred in bouts of pair behaviour which included copulation—the male, off the nest, suddenly Head Jerking briefly with intention movements of jabs towards the female. During incubation I twice recorded Head Jerking from a male following reunion at the nest; once the male was the incomer, once the female.

During territorial encounters, when it occurs most predictably, violent Head Jerking may occur in response to the rival landing nearby. I never noted it in the absence of an external stimulus provided by another bird.

The examples cited suggest that Head Jerking is mainly aggressively motivated behaviour. When it occurred in pair (sexual) encounters one partner had usually moved away, so weakening its strength as a sexual stimulus. On the 'disinhibition' hypothesis, the expression of an aggressive tendency had previously been blocked by the simultaneous arousal of an incompat-

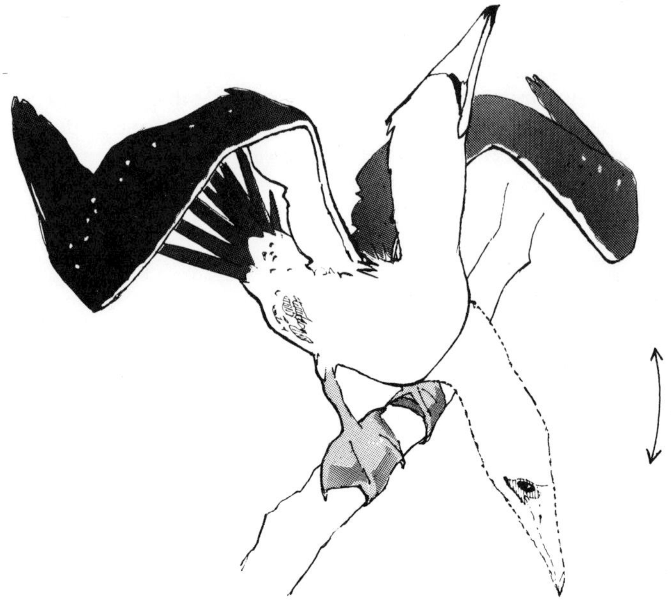

Fig. 341 (a–c)

(a) Head-jerking: here, an upward position of the head.

(b)

Head jerked to the left and downwards.

ible sexual tendency. In all sulids aggression between members of a pair is most likely to occur when one partner moves off the nest. Head Jerking in the new pair situation parallels the occurrence in other sulids of their respective aggressive pair interactions. Further, the incorporation of intention movements of jabs and the biting directed to nearby twigs indicates aggression.

In territorial rivalry there is, of course, no reason to suppose that Head Jerking is other than mainly aggressive behaviour directed at an opponent. However, it contains a genuine element of sexual motivation (see p. 789). The occurrence of Head Jerking at such length and with nest material held in the bill in the new pair situation is an interesting aspect, particularly since Abbott's booby in fact lacks sexual advertising. One is reminded of the comparable instances in which other sulids occasionally perform one of their 'normal' displays but with the additional element of holding nest material. No doubt, since all displays are motivated by more than one tendency, the 'holding nest material' version reflects a particular balance. In time it could conceivably differentiate into a discrete display performed under more clear cut circumstances.

It is also worth recalling that, besides using Head Jerking in territorial and pair situations, Abbott's booby also uses Wing Waving in these two contexts, but whereas Head Jerking is largely agonistic, Wing Waving is largely sexual behaviour. It appears that Abbott's booby has not achieved fully discrete nervous (and release) mechanisms for its two main ritualised displays and a possible reason for this will be discussed later.

The discussion of context and motivation indicate that Head Jerking is mainly an agonistic, distance-evoking display directed against rivals. However, Head Jerking with nest material (absent in later Head Jerking displays) may be functionally an 'invitation' display, but a much more complete analysis of Head Jerking in its various contexts would be necessary to decide (a) whether there are slight differences in its form and (b) if there are not, whether it could subserve two such distinct functions.

Fig. 341 (c)

High intensity Head-jerking, an aggressively motivated display.

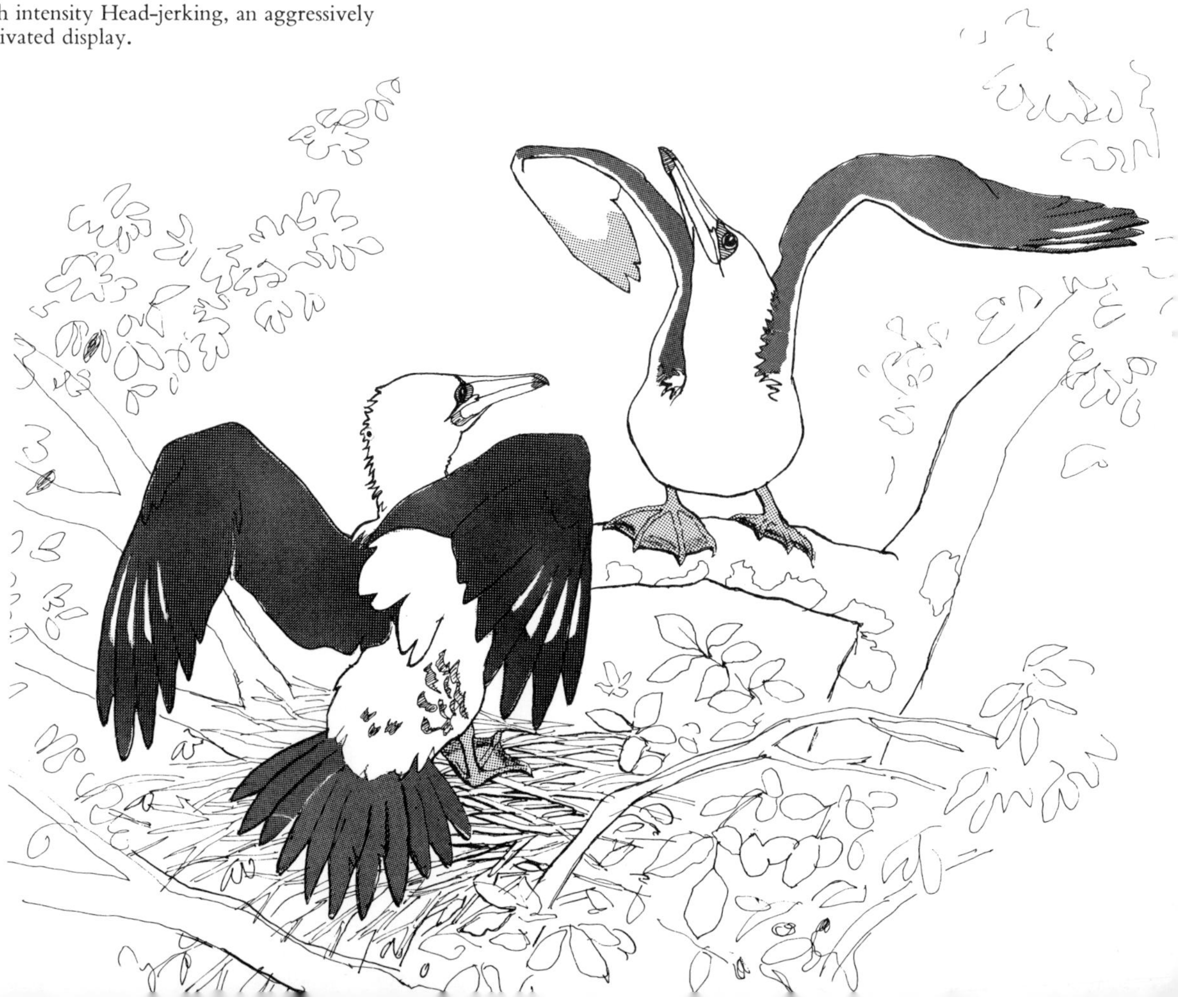

(*a*)

(*b*)

(*c*)

(*d*)

(*e*)

(*f*)

(*g*)

(*h*)

(*i*)

Fig. 342. The movements in the Head Jerking display are unusually abrupt; sequence shows representative positions of head and wings, into each of which the displaying bird quickly 'snaps'.

FORMATION AND MAINTENANCE OF PAIR

1. *Pair formation*

Early pair formation is difficult to observe because of the obscuring canopy and the relatively solitary nesting. The most notable feature is negative; the surprising absence of an advertising display equivalent to the conspicuous Sky-pointing of other boobies. We scrutinised scores of encounters which would certainly have elicited advertising in other boobies but which did not evoke any special action from Abbott's. Yet, potential partners must locate each other and this is achieved by conspicuous outposting (both sexes) and prolonged flight reconnaissance. There seemed no special behaviour by which unmated individuals signified their sexual status; birds investigate, perhaps particularly the more densely colonised areas, and by landing near and interacting with outposted individuals they gain information about the status of these. Thus, one frequently sees three birds together in a tree, presumably usually at least one 'visitor' or 'intruder' and the resident pair which is being investigated. Why Abbott's booby should retain this presumably more primitive, since less specific and sophisticated, method is a matter for speculation, but unlike all other sulids the prospecting Abbott's booby does not have to contend with a large or dense colony and the attendant dangers of repeated errors and wasted interactions. A less immediate and precise mechanism may therefore be adequate.

The cases involving three or more birds at one site (not necessarily all at once) were of six kinds:

1. Intruder male visited resident male and was displaced.
2. Intruder male visited pair and was displaced by the male.
3. Intruder male visited incubating female and remained till rightful male arrived and displaced him.
4. Two intruder males simultaneously visited a mated female who was within 24 hours of laying.
5. Intruder female visited mated pair and was displaced by pair Mutual Wing Waving.
6. Intruder female visited incubating male and departed when male called and performed conflict behaviour.

In all cases there was a notable lack of overt aggression (all the more remarkable by contrast with other sulids), the owner never approaching and attacking the intruder. It seemed that the intruder remained until the status of the visited bird(s) had been revealed. These observations provide circumstantial support for the mechanism of pair formation suggested earlier. It should, however, be noted that assumed intruder males could possibly have been immature birds, the offspring of the pair in question, from a previous year.

We observed in detail one instance of a probable first meeting and initial pair formation. The case is instructive and worth describing in full. The two birds were probably young, since they had no established site and the season was so far advanced that they would be unlikely to breed until the following year. When first seen, they were flying around a particular area and continued to do so for some time before the male, and then the female, landed. The female moved nearer and for half a minute both performed high-intensity, silent Wing Waving, followed by an extremely long bout of high-intensity Head Jerking, dominated by the male, during which each held a small piece of nest material, in the male's case a single leaf. Twice he dropped his leaf and plucked another. Frequently he stretched towards the female in a low horizontal posture. Eventually the female flew off and after peering intently, the male followed. Both landed in a tree about 50 metres away, near to an incubating female, and this time both performed Wing Waving with calling. The male then resumed high intensity Head Jerking. After a few minutes he took off, flew round and returned and both again performed the noisy greeting ceremony, this time briefly, though with Bill Touching and Jabbing (rather rarely seen in established pairs). Once more Wing Waving graded into Head Jerking, the male orienting strongly towards the female, even turning his head over his shoulder to do so and holding nest material. Eventually the pair became inactive and the female flew off.

This interaction demonstrated that:

1. Initial contact can be made without either bird having a definite site.

2. Head Jerking can occur in a sexual situation with no established territory. We also know that it is frequently an aggressive display.
3. In a sexual context, Head Jerking may include the showing of nest material, a ritual element which we did not see in aggressive Head Jerking.
4. Wing Waving may occur as the initial meeting behaviour, at first without vocalisation, which may require a higher level of sexual motivation and/or a lower fear/aggression element. Thus, the second and third meetings involved calling.
5. Wing Waving and Head Jerking may grade delicately into each other as the stimulus changes, apparently at least largely internally.
6. In a situation providing all the conditions for sexual advertising, none occurred—at least not as a special display equivalent to that of other sulids.
7. On establishment of close contact, Bill Touching and Jabbing occurred as in other boobies, even though both are markedly infrequent in most Abbott's booby pair interactions.
8. The pattern of flying out and returning followed by meeting behaviour occurs in Abbott's booby as in all other sulids.

2. *Sky-pointing*

Abbott's booby is very unusual in that it lacks any conspicuous display whose main function is to reduce distance between partners or potential partners. It will be recalled that all the other boobies, without exception, have a homologous (advertising) display--Sky-pointing, which fulfills this function and is extremely common and conspicuous in the early stages of breeding, when the pair is formed and the pair bond forged.

Yet, on fairly rare occasions, Abbott's booby performs what can be described as a 'forward-point' (Fig. 343). It stretches the head forward and upward at a variable angle, sometimes croaking or groaning deeply. In what appears to be an extreme version, head and neck are stretched forwards almost as low as the branch and held there for several seconds. I saw it only from birds either approaching or just after leaving the nest, usually the latter, and particularly, by the departing bird, after the behaviour accompanying nest relief (Wing Waving and Head Jerking). The resemblance between it and low intensity Sky-pointing in other sulids, both in posture and in the accompanying call, was certainly noteworthy and also the fact that it was performed by the partner off the nest. However, as in the gannet, it was connected with movement rather than directly with sexual behaviour as it is in all other boobies. It was not an invariable or even usual part of the behaviour accompanying nest relief and this seemed rather odd, since it undoubtedly has great potential signal value. There may, however, be little survival value in such a signal in Abbott's booby, whereas it has obvious and considerable value in the gannet by co-ordinating nest relief and avoiding exposure of egg or chick to predation or pilfering.

If the Sky-pointing of Abbott's booby is homologous with that of other sulids (and since

Fig. 343

Forward point – a visually conspicuous but rarely-used posture whose significance remains obscure.

every other sulid possesses it this seems likely) it is derived from pre-flight behaviour. Abbott's, however, is rather different in that the wing movements seem lacking and the forward or even horizontal orientation is unusual. It is also relatively uncommon compared with its presumed homologues.

3. *Wing Waving with Forward Bowing*

This is the commonest and most conspicuous display of Abbott's booby and a very impressive one. Seen at close quarters against the sunlit tracery of the green canopy, it is one of those especially evocative displays, in the same category as albatross dancing. the geese triumph ceremony and the frigate's sexual display. Among sulids, only the ecstatic Mutual Fencing of long separated gannets equals this greeting ceremony of Abbott's booby. Long may the jungle of Christmas Island resound to it. It is always performed mutually by mated birds meeting at the nest or site and is first and foremost a meeting ceremony. It commonly occurs, also, as a reaction to intruders, and even to birds that are merely flying past. Clearly, its role as a reaction (presumably hostile) to potential intruders is important. A bird flying past may electrify a resident pair into intense mutual Wing Waving, just as a gannet blundering through a gannetry electrifies the pairs it affects into vigorous Mutual Fencing. This comparison may be taken further, for Wing Waving in Abbott's booby may occur solo, just as Bowing (a form of Mutual Fencing) is solo in the gannet. Wing Waving was also seen from birds that landed in trees other than their nesting tree, but only if there was another adult there.

Wing Waving is a slow, powerful flapping, not mainly up and down, but backwards and forwards with cambered wings (as though braking) often in a figure of eight movement (Fig. 345). There is distinctly loose articulation in the shoulder region. The body is held at about 30° to the horizontal and the head and neck outstretched and kept in line with it, but moving vigorously up and down, now absolutely prone, then swinging far upwards. Head movements often lose the beat of wing movements and continue slowly in a trance-like way. The fanned tail moves up and down and head feathers stand on end.

The displaying birds shout loudly, periodically quietening down and building up to a new frenzy. Sometimes a pair will perform a long bout of mutual Wing Waving completely silently. At low intensity, they simply half raise their wings and turn their heads sideways without calling. Sometimes between bouts of Wing Waving or Head Jerking, Abbott's boobies stare fixedly at each other—possibly the orienting phase of these displays.

Wing Waving is strongly oriented to the eliciting object and may be interspersed with reaching movements, though, significantly, it rarely occurs within touching range and is typically conducted at a distance of some metres, particularly early in the bout. Immediately after Wing Waving, the distinctively marked flank or rump is touched in a ritualised preening movement.

The duration of this meeting ceremony depends on the length of the preceding separation, the status—old or new—of the pair and the stage of the breeding cycle (see below). New bouts, usually initiated by the newcomer, often break out after quiet periods. But Wing Waving may be omitted when the pair are repeatedly meeting after brief separations, as when the male is gathering nest material.

Wing Waving is largely a pair interaction with the sexual and agonistic elements usually present in such situations. It seems directly comparable to Mutual Fencing in the gannet which occurs in equivalent circumstances. There, it was shown that the main components of the motivation could be detected from certain quantitative differences between male and female versions of the display. Thus, the aggressive component (dipping towards the ground, a movement derived from nest biting) was more marked in the male, who was, on other counts, the more aggressive. In addition, there were revealing temporal relationships between Mutual Fencing and aggressive behaviour (fighting, threat, etc.) and Mutual Fencing and sexual behaviour (copulation frequency). Observations indicated a comparable situation for Wing Waving in Abbott's booby. However, whereas Mutual Fencing in the gannet seems to be a modified form of the quite distinct agonistic site ownership display Bowing, Abbott's booby Wing Waving seems indistinguishable in both agonistic and sexual contexts, as indeed does Head Jerking. However, the comparison is not easily made, since gannet Mutual Fencing is always contact behaviour and it is difficult to see just how similar each bird's actions are to those it would perform if Bowing.

The habit of Wing Waving from a distance could suggest a fear element, whilst the marked forward reaching suggests incipient distance-reducing behaviour, sexually and/or aggressively induced. When (rarely) Wing Waving occurs at close quarters, the forward lunges may become Bill Touching, Jabbing or even gripping, which suggests aggressive motivation. Displays conducted with the participants at a distance have obvious advantages in the tree top environment.

Wing Waving may occur between three birds at a time, during these not-infrequent three-somes. In such cases it must be partly aggressive, for at least two of the participants must be of the same sex.

Bouts of Wing Waving are longer when sex motivation is high. Thus on average less than one minute elapsed between the cessation of lengthy bouts of Wing Waving (more than 60 seconds) and copulation, whereas up to seven minutes elapsed after short bouts (less than 15 seconds). Also, the number of copulations was higher in the ten minutes following the cessation of lengthy Wing Waving than after short. As in the gannet's Mutual Fencing, Wing Waving in Abbott's booby is longest (up to five minutes) and most intense following long separation early in the breeding cycle.

By these measures, the intensity of the display is positively correlated with sex motivation, and probably also with agonistic motivation. The same combination of external conditions, later in the year, elicits no comparable response, which clearly shows the importance of the bird's internal state to this display.

Fig. 344 (a). High-intensity Wing-waving, the non-contact greeting ceremony between mates, here occurring before egg is present.

A stable pair bond is beneficial in birds whose breeding success depends on co-operation over a long period and many such species have evolved displays which maintain it. Abbott's booby, with its unusually protracted care of young, may have special need of a strong pair bond, though this interpretation is not entirely satisfactory because some other birds, with equally protracted parental care do not have a strong pair bond (e.g. frigate-birds). Probably more likely, a suitable site is a valuable possession, fidelity to which automatically renders fidelity to mate easily practicable—a situation which certainly does not hold for frigates.

It seems clear that mutual Wing Waving is either basically an agonistic display which has acquired pair bonding function or a sexual display which has secondarily acquired the function of dispelling intruders. The first interpretation follows a pattern now widely recognised in bird courtship. Females are intruders, but the aggression thus elicited must be inhibited, or better, be expressed as 'reassuring' behaviour the performance of which actually rewards the performers as well as fulfilling the important function of permitting two hostile individuals to remain together on the nest. Thus the hostile, unilateral Bowing of the gannet has given

Fig. 344(b). Pair with half-grown chick greet each other.

rise to Mutual Fencing in the pair (even the male's direct attack, in the form of nape-biting, seems to stimulate rather than repel the female). Similarly, it seems, the agonistic Wing Waving of Abbott's booby has become the pair-bonding display mutual Wing Waving, with little or no change in form but with suppression of the hostile 'approach' which displaces intruders. Thus Wing Waving, at least initially, occurs at a distance until both are 'reassured' and the aggressive motivation has achieved outlet without displacing the partner.

Wing Waving possesses a marked braking action and may be a ritualised recovery movement, though it is now certainly no longer tied to the mechanics of landing. On the other hand, the forward reaching movements are somewhat comparable to aggressive touching or biting of the substrate. It may be significant that the main agonistic display, Head Jerking, and even Wing Waving itself, may be performed with nest material held in the bill, though whether this results from genuine nest material plucking or re-directed aggression, it is impossible to say. Nevertheless, one suspects the latter, since there are clear cases of an exactly comparable phenomenon in, for example, Forward Head Waving with aggressively plucked nest material in the red-footed booby and Bowing with nest biting in the gannet.

(*a*)

(*d*)

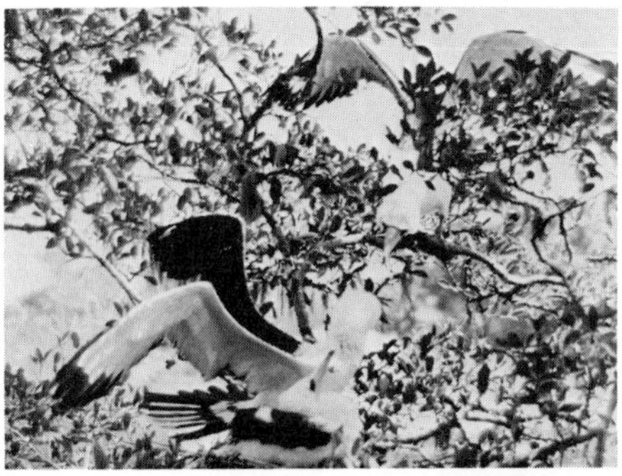

(*b*)

(*e*)

(*c*)

Fig. 345 (a–e)

Arrival (upper bird) followed by mutual Wing-waving and a closer approach by incomer, then more high intensity Wing-waving and finally change-over at the nest. Note the bold jump in (c) and the deepening of the gular pouch in (d) as the bird (on right) croaks.

4. *Bill Touching and Mutual Jabbing*

Bill Touching (Fig. 346) and Jabbing are relatively rare in Abbott's booby and probably commonest in new pairs, when, as in other boobies, the aggressive component of sexual behaviour tends to be most manifest. Jabbing may occur in among Head Jerking; sometimes it is accompanied by a loud, deep groan. During nest relief, partners often make intention movements of jabs or briefly and vigorously jab or touch bills, although they do not engage in bouts of jabbing. A brief example of an actual nest relief encounter illustrates the sort of interaction involved. The male was on the nest when the female arrived. After a bout of mutual Wing Waving the female sidled nearer; the male, with head feathers ruffed, frequently Head Jerked. As the female drew near, the male initiated several short jabs to which she responded similarly; there was no gripping but the jabs were very vigorous. After Jabbing two or three times, the female, with ruffed head feathers, pointed her bill at 45° and shouted. In another encounter, both members of the pair were together on the nest, and touched beaks. They then kept their bills opposed for some seconds by deliberate, fine adjusting movements. When one partner moves off the nest, the other sometimes resumes Jabbing, the male, in particular, occasionally jabs at the female after he has vacated the nest. No retaliation was seen in this situation.

Mutual Jabbing between mates shows no obvious signs of ritualisation, but it proved impossible to compare its form in the pair context with that between rivals since none of the reactions between owner and intruder ever led to contact. Between mates, however, it was never accompanied by indications of fear (flinching, tremoring, facing-away) and it was obviously not important for Abbott's booby to avoid situations bringing them close together; indeed they spent much time together on the nest in the period before egg laying.

It is interesting that Abbott's booby shows Mutual Jabbing (of which Bill Touching is probably a low intensity form) since it occurs in sulids as a family trait. The extent to which this relatively simple aggressive behaviour has become differentiated varies but none has lost it.

When an adult female and a juvenile were introduced in captivity, the female, who was quite aggressive towards the juvenile, opened and closed her wings when Jabbing. This, no doubt partly balancing (compensating) movement, was the nearest thing to Wing Flailing that we ever saw.

5. *Pelican Posture*

Bill-tucking or the Pelican Posture (Fig. 347), occurs throughout the Sulidae. It occurs in two forms which may be derived from different sources. In one form (A) the bill tip is pressed against the upper breast and in another (B) the neck is arched and the bill tip pointed downwards clear of the breast. Abbott's booby shows mainly the first form. In the gannet form A is an ambivalent fear/aggression posture occurring during territorial hostilities but not as an accompaniment to locomotion. In ground nesting boobies, on the other hand, form A invariably

Fig. 346

Bill Touching.

accompanies locomotion around the territory even in quiet, single individuals. In Abbott's booby the full Pelican Posture (A) occurs not as the bird moves around its territory, nor immediately after a hop (as B does in the red-footed booby) but mainly in fear/aggression situations. Thus during intimate pair interactions, when male and female repeatedly come into close contact, vacating or taking over the centre of the nest, both tend to Pelican Posture deeply. Again, during an experimental introduction of a juvenile to an adult female, the latter Pelican Postured deeply and repeatedly, re-assuming the position each time the juvenile moved and jabbing at and sometimes even gripping it. It is possible that in Abbott's booby the Pelican Posture has acquired an appeasing function in response to selection pressure exerted by the dangerous environment; strict control of potentially aggressive interactions is necessary.

Because the Pelican Posture is not tied to movement in Abbott's booby, as it is in some other boobies, it is understandably less frequent. Also, Abbott's relatively restrained behaviour (due to internal inhibition) in situations which would elicit aggressive interaction in other sulids, reduces the extent to which it must rely on formal appeasement postures (external inhibiting mechanisms) to avert conflict.

6. *Ruffing of head feathers*

Abbott's booby greatly enhances the signal potential of its behaviour by expressive raising and lowering of the head and neck feathers. The head may be enormously enlarged and altered in shape by raising all the feathers, or the forehead feathers may remain flattened (Fig. 348) whilst behind a sharply demarcated line on the crown the feathers stand on end. No other sulid does this. The flattened part of the head is that area in which, in the chick, the two tracts of brown feathers appear (p. 775) and there is doubtless some ancient significance to this fact. Perhaps Abbott's booby is nearer to the pelicans than are other boobies and retains more of their differentiation of head feathers.

Raising the head feathers is particularly prominent during Head Jerking, Wing Waving and copulation, but other intimate pair interactions elicit it. Thus nest building, when performed by the pair together, and change-over on the nest are accompanied by some degree of Feather Ruffing. A close watch reveals the extraordinary sensitivity of Feather Ruffing. Once, at the exact moment at which the male moved off the egg, he flattened his forehead and raised his crown, the shift in motivation being thus reflected in the position of the head feathers. Other activities during which head feathers are often raised include ritualised preening and ritualised sleeping.

So Feather Ruffing is elicited by ambivalent motivation involving sex and

Fig. 347

Pelican Posture (bill tucking).

fear/aggression. During a complicated bout of behaviour the head feathers may be sleeked with every act lacking such motivation (e.g. stretching the wings or defaecating) but immediately re-erected for the next bout of Head Jerking, Twig Biting, etc. Head feathers are typically smooth during genuine sleeping and preening, during low intensity and solitary nest building activity and also high intensity nest building after high intensity and consummated sexual behaviour. However, head feathers may be raised by solitary birds on the nest and when tending the chick.

7. *Wing Rattle*

In the Sulidae a group of somewhat similar behaviour patterns involve shaking movements of the wings and/or plumage. It is not always obvious which should be considered signal and which simply plumage care behaviour (cleaning and settling the feathers) though comparative study shows that the Wing Rattle is, in all boobies, a ritualised signal of impending flight.

Abbott's booby performs the Wing Rattle (a brisk shaking of the slightly lifted wings) usually as it is moving around, though probably less frequently than other boobies. I had insufficient evidence to show whether it had signal value. Certainly it occurs in non-signal situations, as when a single bird awoke and Wing Rattled.

Wing Flicking—a rapid, fractional opening and closing of the wings immediately before flight was not seen in Abbott's booby, though it is common in the red-foot.

8. *Ritualised preening*

Most common acts are potential material for ritualisation. The Sulidae have ritualised head-

Fig. 348 (a–c)

(a) The pair are interacting at the nest in the period before egg laying. Excitement is high and head feathers are used expressively; the flattened forehead can be seen in profile.

(b) The completely smooth head of the lower bird contrasts markedly with (a).

(c) In this interaction at the nest the incomer is showing the Pelican Posture and the occupier (left) a withdrawn position with ruffled head feathers.

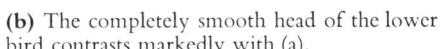

shaking, walking, wing-limbering, biting, neck-lengthening and others. Yet a striking omission is ritualised preening. Displacement preening occurs in all species but generally without obvious stylisation or direction of the act to particular morphological 'pointers', though detailed analysis might reveal significant tendencies to direct displacement preening to particular areas. Abbott's booby is the marked exception, since (Fig. 349) it directs ritualised preening to its two boldly patterned areas—the flanks and rump, and also the wing-bow, where there is a conspicuous black and white margin.

Ritualised preening occurs during pair and rival interactions, particularly after Wing Waving. It may involve actual preening, or bill movements which do not groom the feathers, or simply touching the areas. Often the bill is held in the preening position for several seconds. It seems mainly conflict behaviour performed in somewhat ambivalent motivational situations. It may be interpreted as partly aggressive, possibly redirected onto a substitute object (here the bird itself). The conspicuously marked areas direct the preening but may possibly have no other significance. Re-directed aggression is now well known, but this case would be of interest if it were in fact aggression re-directed onto the bird's own self.

9. *Allo-preening*

Many hours of watching in appropriate situations convincingly showed that Abbott's booby entirely lacks allo-preening, both unilateral and mutual. Even when pair members stand so close that a head movement brings the bill of one into contact with the head feathers of the other, there was never any suggestion of allo-preening. Yet they spend much time together on the nest. Again, one may suggest that in Abbott's booby internal inhibition of aggression is so strong that 'outlets', like mutual preening, are not required. This implies, of course, that allo-preening is modified aggressive behaviour, for which interpretation see Harrison (1965).

10. *Ritualised sleeping*

Abbott's booby possesses an eyelid, white over its middle two-thirds, which it draws across its eye during ritualised sleeping. The bird is alert, but seems to have its eye closed, though the contrast of white lid with black facial skin in fact makes them unusually conspicuous and no other sulid has any comparable feature. When genuinely sleeping, Abbott's booby closes its eyes by apposing top and bottom edges of the orbital ring, thus hiding the white membrane,

Fig. 349

Ritualised preening directed to flank patch and to Wing bow. No actual preening of feathers occurs.

and puts its head in its scapulars. In conflict situations, however, it uses its 'false eye' even to the extent of presenting it on the 'danger' side whilst keeping the other eye open (Fig. 350). The apparent complacence of an Abbott's booby that 'slept' whilst I cleared tree ferns and hammered wooden rungs on the trunk immediately below, was really displacement sleeping. By 'cutting off' (Chance 1962) disturbing stimuli, Abbott's booby may be less likely to flee in panic. It may even function to cut off the visual stimulus of the partner and so reduce contact interactions when the pair are near to each other. In both these ways, the habit could thus be adaptive in the jungle-top environment. It seems highly unlikely that the false eye is a warning device, as it is in so many invertebrates.

11. *Choice of nest site*

In only one case could we actually observe Abbott's booby searching for a site; usually the first pieces of nest material were present or the pair were resorting so regularly to a particular fork that the choice had obviously already been made. One pair, however, had the limb bearing their nest blown down. The loss of the nest elicited repeated aerial reconnaissance from male and female, who made the usual approach again and again but failed to complete it because the topography of the shorn tree was 'wrong'. When they eventually landed they omitted the inflying calls. Soon afterwards the female was actively looking for a site, peering around with concentration and eventually clearing away obtruding growth from a particular area.

Despite the obvious searching of this female, who was in fact within a few days of laying, the male probably chooses the nest site. He often occupies a definitive location long before a nest is built and attends the site more assiduously than the female. He also gathers the nest material and does most of the building—at least until the female begins to take over the nest before egg laying and builds from the material brought by the male. After the choice of nest site, but in the complete absence of nest material both male and female may perform extensive nest building movements on the precise spot where the nest is to be built.

12. *Nest building*

Before egg laying, nest material is gathered almost entirely by the male, usually from a distance and often from a particular tree. However, females will on occasions pluck nest material even before the egg is laid and more often later as part of nest relief interactions. The male may bring several lots of nest material in succession, often flying in without the calling usually associated with approach and landing on the site, but sometimes calling whilst holding the nest material. On one occasion, the only time the male brought nest material with calling, he also

Fig. 350

A pair of Abbott's boobies here 'cut-off' the sight of each other by displaying their 'false' eye, whilst keeping the other one open in the normal way.

followed it by Head Jerking. This is consistent with the interpretation of Head Jerking as aggressively motivated behaviour, for we know from other evidence that the inflying calling is also aggressive. In other words, the one time the male was sufficiently aggressive to call as he flew in was the only time he followed this by Head Jerking. Later, a male that is incubating, or guarding young, will accept even a purely symbolic offering (e.g. a single leaf) from the female. Such offerings may follow Head Jerking which has been performed by the incomer

Fig. 351. Nest building behaviour in Abbott's booby. Note the considerable length of the twig.

whilst still holding a leaf and the bird accepting it may then 'present' it (see later) before building it into the nest. When starting a nest on a more or less horizontal branch Abbott's booby was seen to lay long leafy twigs so that they hung over each side. In a crotch the formation of a base presents fewer problems.

Nest building behaviour is primitive. Material is deposited, the stem inserted and the twig then shaken and vibrated into position with side to side head movements. These movements eventually work one end into the structure and the other is then bent and similarly inserted. Projecting pieces are persistently worked and a strong, crudely interwoven structure results. Both partners may simultaneously build in material brought (usually) by the male. This mutual nest building is a frequent and intimate pair interaction, probably important in strengthening the pair relationship, but either partner will nest build on its own. During nest building activities the crown feathers may be raised and the forehead kept flat, a sign of the excitement, probably sexual, involved in this activity. The state of the head feathers is probably a sensitive indicator of mood; we noticed that even if they have previously been ruffed, they smooth down, partly or completely, when nest building activities begin. Also, when building, Abbott's booby often utters the 'click-grunt' heard during copulation. This is not surprising since, as mentioned, sexual motivation and the bringing of nest material go together; copulations often occur between trips for nest material. In one case, two copulations were interspersed among six trips for nest material. Mandible tremoring or vibrating, common in the gannet, seems absent in Abbott's booby. Constant application of the large webs, as the bird turns in the nest, rounds out and flattens the cup. Unattended nests remain intact even when other pairs are building nearby—there is no pilfering as in gannets and frigates.

13. *Presenting nest material*

Often the female takes nest material from the male's bill and lifts it high into the air in a conspicuous swinging arc (Fig. 352), 'showing' it before building it into the nest. 'Showing' might appear to be simply a non-ritualised evaluation of weight, length, etc., but as well as being stylised, it is performed with items that require no evaluation such as a single leaf. The movement is in fact like that shown in similar circumstances by the blue-footed booby, where it is certainly symbolic since the nest is composed of structurally useless fragments. The inference is that functional nest building was ancestrally important in the Sulidae, and even those members that no longer need a functional nest have nevertheless retained nest building movements derived from ancestors that handled functional nest material, as Abbott's booby still

Fig. 352

Abbott's booby 'showing' nest material. This behaviour is clearly ritualised in some sulids, and probably in Abbott's too.

does. On the other hand, functional nest building movements may remain unritualised as in the red-footed booby and it is not at all clear why Abbott's booby should have developed this display whilst the red-foot has not.

Despite the obvious importance of the nest to Abbott's booby and its conspicuousness as a 'directing' object, nest touching or building movements were rarely shown as displacement activities.

14. *Copulation*

Like all other boobies, the male Abbott's mounts and copulates without gripping the female's head. The female solicits by raising her fanned tail, lowering her head and crouching low in the nest. The female's Wing Waving, in a bout immediately preceding copulation, grades into soliciting movements; the wing movements become looser and less vigorous and are combined with fanning and raising the tail. Cloacal dilation may also precede copulation. The male makes intention movements of mounting, from the side, after facing her. After mounting he lays his bill alongside her head and spreads and waves his wings. His feet may shift position slightly, but do not patter or tread as they do in the gannet. During copulation both sexes raise their head feathers and may utter low guttural, almost glottal clicks. There is no immobile phase such as characterises the final stages in the gannet. Copulation takes about 10 seconds compared with about 25 seconds in the gannet. Shortly before egg laying it may occur at less than five-minute intervals, and between copulations the male may fly off for nest material. The behaviour immediately after copulation is variable. The female may build, move off the nest, displacement preen flank and rump or simply remain motionless with head feathers raised. The male often leaves the nest, Head Jerks (sometimes violently), and stands for a variable period before leaving for nest material. I never recorded mutual Wing Waving following copulation, as the equivalent Mutual Fencing often does in the gannet. We recorded copulation five weeks before egg laying but it probably begins earlier than that.

OTHER BEHAVIOUR INVOLVED IN BREEDING

1. *Incubation behaviour*

Like other sulids, Abbot's booby incubates its egg beneath or on top of its webs and shades it during heat. Shortly before the egg hatches it is transferred to the top of the webs. Incubating

Fig. 353. Change-over on the nest, here accompanied by low intensity mutual Wing Waving. Note the ruffled crown feathers but smooth forehead.

adults tend to sit with their backs to the sun and often click-grunt as they change position, which they tend to do in 90°–180° shifts. Head feathers are mainly smooth, but are often ruffed for the first minutes of an incubation stint.

In our single observation of a male's first reaction to his female's egg, he showed concentrated attention, staring fixedly at it with his head feathers conspicuously ruffed. He then moved on to the nest, made many exaggerated foot movements, tucked the egg, preened in the ritualised way and performed low intensity Head Jerking. Thus the first sight of the egg obviously stimulated him and aroused somewhat conflicting tendencies.

2. *Change-over*

The relief of the partner at the nest is always preceded by display, which begins as the incoming bird lands in the outer branches and continues at intervals as it approaches (in the red-foot, by contrast, it is often rapid and undemonstrative). The soft click-grunt used in copulation may be given by the incoming bird when it gets near the nest and as it settles on the egg. The incubating partner may move off the egg within two minutes or remain for up to half an hour, but is not closely approached by its mate until it does show signs of leaving. Close proximity, always accompanied by intense feather ruffing, may then lead to brief Bill Touching or Jabbing intermixed with brief Wing Waving (Fig. 353) and usually followed by displacement preening of the dark thigh patch or the inside (humeral) part of the wing. Slow withdrawal of the outgoing bird is accompanied by signs of aggression such as Head Jerking, Twig Biting or brief Wing Waving. Departure from the nest or branch is occasionally preceded by a curious forward crouching posture (see Sky-pointing p. 790) sometimes horizontal and held absolutely motionless for up

Fig. 354

Adult brooding and feeding 3-4 week old chick.

to a minute. The departing bird often gives the Wing Rattle or Rotary Headshake before it flies. However, it usually takes some time to reach the flight threshold and may move extensively among the branches before departing. Even then, it may circle two or three times and return again, then fetch nest material and finally depart to sea. The bird taking over always performs nest building movements and once on the nest ignores the partner. Frequently it preens and oils intensively.

Once, a female returned after a very short absence. The mate refused to leave the nest, whereupon the female maintained violent Head Jerking and Twig Biting with ruffed head feathers for one and a half hours. On the other hand, a male returned to a recently laid egg and literally pushed the female off it and began to incubate.

3. *Aspects of parent/young relationship*

Abbott's booby guards its young continuously during the first four to six weeks and thereafter attends it for a few hours or less with each feeding visit. The nest cup is cleaned and probed and fragments of food are flung aside. The young are preened desultorily. Large young, five weeks or more old, are brooded as much as their size allows.

Abbott's booby is unique among the Sulidae in combining complete regurgitation with the family method of incomplete regurgitation. For the first fortnight the adult often deposits food on the floor of the nest and the chick makes feeble and only partly successful attempts to pick it up. The parent often re-swallows and regurgitates several times, which further softens and fragments the firmer boluses. Later we saw only the normal method of feeding, with a maximum of seven entries into the adult's mouth.

Even after the nest had completely disintegrated, the one juvenile whose feeding position was visible from the ground always moved to the exact nest site whenever a parent arrived. Later the adults began to rebuild there. D. Powell noted that pairs that fed young during the winters of 1974/75 and 1975/76, but failed, rebuilt in exactly the same places.

BEHAVIOUR OF YOUNG

A small chick begs for food by gently jabbing and attempting to insert its beak near the base of the parent's beak, occasionally nibbling at the parent's breast feathers and calling repetitively. At about four weeks a specific, stylised form of begging develops and is retained to the end of post-fledging dependence. The young bird stands on the nest or the site of it and sways the head from side to side, holding it retracted and backwards with beak pointing downwards (Fig. 355), whilst uttering a quickly repeated 'qua qua qua'. Every few seconds the note changes to the drawn out grating call and with this the head is brought forwards and down with slight

Fig. 355. Restrained begging of young.

Fig. 356

Prone sleeping position.

or pronounced swaying motion. The gape is distended with each long call. The movement is not fully stylised; sometimes the head movements become disorganised and the bill oriented upwards. The wings are raised from the back or variably spread and re-settled, but not waved or flailed violently as they are in other boobies, so that Abbott's begging is restrained and inhibited compared with the frenzied activity of all other sulids except the gannet. Even during highest intensity begging, the juvenile never touches the adult and this is probably another

Fig. 357

Wing exercising and the beginning of scratching.

behavioural precaution against falling. On cliffs, the gannet faces an equivalent danger and is the only other sulid to show markedly restrained begging. Young Abbott's boobies, from an early age, avoid fouling their nest, although the habit of backing to the rim before defaecating is not without danger; one chick fell to its death. Young Abbott's boobies tuck their bills beneath their bodies in fear/aggression situations, as for example when approached for weighing. They were not seen to show it in reaction to any adult behaviour. Sleeping and resting positions may be prone (Fig. 356). Wing exercising is performed from an early age (Fig. 357). The Pelican Posture appeared at about five weeks. Incipient Head Jerking was observed in young about seven weeks old, in the absence of an adult. Wing Waving was not seen at all, even in juveniles. Unlike some boobies, free-flying juvenile Abbott's boobies apparently do not show adult patterns of territorial behaviour, perhaps because their territory is not threatened.

MAINTENANCE BEHAVIOUR

1. *Movement in trees*

Abbott's booby, despite its size and weight, can move skilfully among branches, aided by notably prehensile feet, although its movements are usually cautiously competent rather than lively. After landing, perhaps among terminal twigs, it often sidles along thicker limbs or hops boldly across large gaps, sometimes launching itself up to 2½m from a higher to a lower branch. It can turn completely round, through 180°, in a single twisting hop, on a branch. If it has to move far, it employs an alternate-foot, sideways sidle, suitable for a thick branch. Occasionally it uses its beak to lever itself out of an awkward position—a behaviour pattern common to all sulids and possibly inherited from an ancestral cliff-nesting form.

2. *Take-off*

Landing and departure are the danger points for Abbott's booby. As mentioned it sometimes falls 9 to 12m before getting under way. It launches into flight without any posturing and

Fig. 358

Abbott's booby just before landing.

usually without prior Wing Rattling or Wing Flicking. It merely lengthens its neck, peers around, makes slight, forwardly inclined intention movements and then launches abruptly into flight. Sometimes it hesitates, partly opening its wings once or twice before launching off. Other sulids employ signal movements before they depart, the movements being exaggerated versions of flight preparation. One may speculate that Abbott's booby has, as it were, to be quite sure of its take-off before attempting it, so the threshold for flight is very high and the rising flight motivation, instead of eliciting actual motor movements as in other boobies (part flight as it were) builds up until the actual departure can occur.

When coming in to land, it lowers its feet whilst far out, to aid braking, which is mainly accomplished by extreme braking movements of the wings. The whole performance looks considerably less agile than that of the red-footed booby.

3. *Defaecation*

Abbott's booby half squats and partly raises its wings before defaecating from a branch. If on the nest, it moves to the rim, although much excreta fouls the broad base.

4. *Oiling and preening*

Abbott's booby oils the back of its head on the oil gland and then transfers the oil to the wings and tail, or from the beak to the underparts. In ordinary preening, plumage is drawn through the coarse teeth of the lower mandible, nibbled, stropped, etc. in the normal way. Preening may be followed by the usual type of wing limbering, scratching, yawning with gular distention, etc.

5. *Plumage shaking and Headshaking*

In Abbott's booby the Rotary Headshake (a movement in which the head is rapidly rotated whilst the body plumage is fluffed and shaken) is not very distinct from the simple all-over shaking of plumage (Dogshaking) and it seems that Abbott's booby has not ritualised this body maintenance activity. It sometimes performs it in mid-air after take-off as the gannet almost invariably does. It seems likely, therefore, that the Rotary Headshake-Dogshake complex are body maintenance activities, unritualised and less frequent than in the gannet (this may be linked with the dirtier nesting environment of the latter).

The common, simple sideways headshaking by which sulids dispel water, dirt, etc. occurs in Abbott's booby, though infrequently and unpredictably. Thus, the secretion from the salt gland is often allowed to drip unheeded, though it is sometimes shaken off. However, the headshake obviously does not depend on external tactile stimuli, since I observed it in birds that had spent many hours at the nest and were not settling fish in their crop or secreting from the salt gland.

6. *Heat regulation*

Abbott's booby uses the normal methods common to all sulids—gular fluttering, with bill inclined upwards; panting and raising the tail. Nesting below the crown canopy presumably helps to avoid overheating.

7. *Fishing behaviour*

So far as I know, nobody has ever recorded an Abbott's booby plunge-diving, though there is not the slightest chance that it will differ radically from other boobies in this respect. Gibson-Hill records that one can get them within shot range (a miserable thought) by throwing fish, on a line, into the sea. I find this somewhat surprising, since, unlike brown boobies, Abbott's did not seem to frequent the waters near the island. It's possible habit of fishing in an upwelling area off Java is discussed on p. 883.

DISCUSSION

Two aspects of the behaviour of Abbott's booby which seem open to useful, if speculative, discussion, concern its relatively solitary habits and its high internal threshold for aggression. Associated with the latter is the lack of appeasement behaviour in the juvenile and its adoption of adult male plumage whilst still in the nest; this has been discussed under Morphology (p. 754).

We do not know whether Abbott's booby nests so thinly because there are few really suitable sites or just too few birds, though the latter seems overwhelmingly the more likely. In any case, severe competition, in so far as it is judged by overt aggression, has clearly been ruled out as too dangerous. Perhaps there really is little or no need for competition, in which case there is doubtless selective advantage in avoiding aggression. However, the very clear indications that Abbott's booby is by no means unaggressive—only extremely restrained in expressing it by contact actions—goes against this. Why Abbott's booby has come to rely so heavily on internal restraint rather than a system of response to external signals, is difficult to recognise. In other sulids, behaviour signals play a larger part in controlling the expression of aggression.

Associated with the solitary habit and restrained behaviour is a conspicuous lack of many other communication behaviour patterns found in other sulids. Apart from its highly developed Wing Waving and Head Jerking, Abbott's booby shows few ritualised interactions between mates and rivals; there is much less need for them. Other sulids may fight, threaten, appease, parade, jab, proclaim site ownership, advertise, proclaim departure, signal arrival, attack their mate and so on, but Abbott's booby sits placidly in its territory, usually ignores trespassers, never fights, threatens, proclaims its site ownership by a special display or advertises. The meeting ceremony, however, is, with the exception of that of the gannet, by far the most highly developed in the family and its very vigour and complexity may reflect the behavioural burden which it has assumed, in providing some motor-outlet for aggression in such a way as to reinforce the pair bond, in the absence of so many intra-pair activities.

SUMMARY

1. Unusually for a sulid, Abbott's booby does not show overt aggression (attack) when establishing or defending its territory.

2. Its main agonistic display is Head Jerking, performed at a distance.

3. It lacks a specific advertising display.

4. It has a long and impressive meeting ceremony (mutual Wing Waving) performed with the partners at a distance. Partner interactions do not usually involve much contact.

5. There are several other ritualised behaviour patterns employed in the pair context (Pelican Posture, ritualised preening, ritualised sleeping, etc.).

6. Nest building involves ritualised handling of nest material.

7. Attendance prior to egg laying is slightly more intensive in the male than in the female.

8. Chick care is unusual in that feeding is sometimes by regurgitating food into the nest bottom to be picked up. No other sulid does this.

9. Chicks beg in a very restrained manner. This and numbers 1, 3 and 4 above are interpreted as adaptations minimising the risk of falling in the highly dangerous jungle top environment.

10

The Sulids Compared

1. NOMENCLATURE; EXTERNAL FEATURES; MORPHOLOGY; MOULT AND VOICE

INTRODUCTION

The aims of this section are to examine the case for including all sulids in the genus *Sula* as against putting the gannets in *Morus* and/or relegating the aberrant Abbott's booby to a separate genus; to discuss the gannets as races, allo-species or species; to comment on certain familial and specific external and morphological characters; to construct a key for identification and to discuss moult and voice in the Sulidae.

NOMENCLATURE

1. *Generic discussion*

'To regard nomenclature as more than a means to an end is pedantry, and to take a minority course in a matter of convention is merely a nuisance' (Thomson 1964). It does not really matter whether the gannets are split off from the boobies and future authors will make their own choice anyway, for there clearly are differences sufficiently large to persuade many that both groups deserve generic status. But a genus is merely a device for indicating a degree of relationship within the context of the larger taxon and those who emphasise broad relationships consider that the similarities are great enough to justify calling both gannets and boobies '*Sula*'. Neither course is perfect and I have myself dithered between the two. If we try to decide merely on the basis of extant sulids, ignoring the fact that they are but the living representatives of a much larger group (see Appendix 16), we may arrive at a different answer than if extinct sulids are also considered.

Extant sulids

There are nine sulids if all three gannets are counted separately. Four of them, possibly five, may be called 'core' sulids (white, brown, blue-footed, Peruvian and possibly red-footed boobies), one is distinctly aberrant (Abbott's booby) and the three gannets are closely related and differ from the core boobies about as much as (probably no more than) does Abbott's booby. The strong inclination shown by many authors, perhaps especially those familiar with both gannets and boobies in the flesh, to use two genera is probably mainly subjective, a partly intuitive assessment of what is useful and biologically 'right'. This is by no means to be despised and indeed it is commonly (and naturally) found that intensive study of a group inclines one to split it in order to emphasise differences which the generalist might overlook. But it is worth pointing out that on morphological, ecological, behavioural and biochemical (protein analysis) criteria, there is no clear separation.

Bourne (1976) has brought together some measurements (Table 125) of wing bones and tarsi lengths in the Sulidae. One of the basic differences which has been used to separate gannets from boobies has been the relative lengths of the distal and proximal part of the wing. The boobies supposedly possess relatively short humeri and long 'forearms' (radio-ulna-hands) whilst the gannets show the reverse. The two conditions may have arisen by the elimination of intermediates, such as existed in some ancestral sulids, and by the selection of the two types of wing as part of adaptive syndromes correlated with two different modes of flying and diving (see below). Alternatively, booby and gannet types may have been distinct even as miocene forms, in which case today's two groups of descendants would each merit generic status. On the other hand, the differences in wing proportion existing in today's gannets and boobies may have arisen anew, both groups having descended from the same ancestral sulid. In this case, even though the distinction appears to be fairly basic, the conclusion to be drawn is not so clear, since the difference is transgressed by Abbott's booby, which has a long humerus. Thus on the criterion of wing proportion, one would place the gannets in *Morus*, the boobies (except Abbott's) in *Sula* and Abbott's booby in a separate genus. I would be loath to do this, preferring to emphasise its similarities to the other boobies.

The condition of the aortic arches is not a dependable taxonomic indicator at this level; it may be intra-generically inconsistent and the implications of Glenny's (1955) work for the Sulidae are not clear.

So far as ecological separation is concerned, there are no qualitative differences which would serve as criteria to separate the two groups, even if such differences could be handled in this way. All plunge-dive similarly, all lay small eggs, clutch size does not differ consistently; the fundamental aspects of breeding regime and breeding success are similar, etc. Distributional separation does, however, occur. None of the three gannets overlaps in breeding distribution with any other sulid, whereas every booby is sympatric with another.

Behaviourally, the two groups superficially do appear to differ, but I have striven unsuccessfully to define these. Such differences as there are—for example, nape biting by the male gannet during copulation—grade through intention movements of so doing in boobies and there are very few behaviour patterns in either group which do not have what appears to be a close homologue in the other. Even though Sky-pointing has a different function in gannets and boobies, it is homologous in them.

Sibley & Ahlquist (1972) report that egg-white protein patterns are uniform in the Sulidae; though they have not sampled all species, they have included gannets.

I conclude from all this that, to be consistent, one should keep the gannets and Abbott's booby within the genus *Sula*. But the matter certainly is not clear-cut, and perhaps most of those who are familiar with the group may, as does Simmons (pers. comm.) still prefer to put the gannets into *Morus*, whilst others, as Voous (pers. comm.) prefer to stress similarities and use only the genus *Sula*. The two genera have in any case been so widely used in the past that it will make little practical difference whether or not they continue to be so.

Extinct sulids

The fossil sulids, more of which have recently been discovered (Norfolk and Lord Howe Islands, Van Tets, in prep.), are reviewed for this book by J. C. Harrison (Appendix 16). It would appear that two distinct 'types' did exist, which could suggest that the modern boobies and gannets have sufficiently different origins to qualify as distinct taxa at a relatively high level. However, much depends on an interpretation of the evolutionary paths followed and it is

TABLE 125

MEAN, STANDARD DEVIATION AND RANGE (IN mm), AND PROPORTIONS OF BONES OF THE SULIDAE (BOURNE 1976)

	Reference/origin	Number	Skull	Humerus	Ulna	Tarso-metatarsus	Ulna/humerus	Tarsus/humerus
Californian Miocene fossils								
Palaeosula stocktoni	Miller (1935)	1	—	264	175	—	0·63	—
Miosula media	Miller (1925, 1935)	1	—	181	140	64	0·77	0·35
Morus lompocana	Miller (1935)	1	—	230	201	—	0·87	—
(*Sula*?) *willetti*	Miller (1925)	1	129	156	147	41	0·94	0·26
Sula pohli	Howard (1958)	1	—	150/145	170/148	—	1·13/1·02	—
Extant species								
Morus bassanus	North Atlantic	3	179±2·2	226±4·6	196±4·0	59±0·5	0·87	0·26
Gannet			(176–181)	(220–231)	(190–199)	(59–60)		
Morus (*b*?) *serrator*	New Zealand	16	158±4·1	213±6·0	185±4·0	54±1·0	0·87	0·25
Australian gannet	(one Australia)		(150–167)	(202–228)	(177–193)	(53–56)		
Sula abbotti	Christmas Island	1	185	—	228	49	—	—
Abbott's booby	Mascarene Islands	?	—	224	225	51	1·00	0·23
Sula d. dactylatra	Ascension	3	147±4·0	178±3·6	186±1·7	54±1·2	1·04	0·30
Masked booby			(144–153)	(175–183)	(184–188)	(52–55)		
Sula d. personata	Phoenix and	2	149±0·5	184±3·0	195±1·5	56±0·5	1·06	0·30
	Lord Howe Island		(150, 149)	(181, 167)	(194, 197)	(56, 57)		
Sula variegata	W. South America	2	142	171±3·0	181±2·0	51±1·0	1·06	0·30
Piquero			(142, —)	(167, 173)	(176, 180)	(50, 52)		
Sula nebouxi	Miller (1935);	2	160	179±10·0	194±9·0	57	1·08	0·32
Blue-footed booby	Gulf of California		(—, 160)	(169, 189)	(185, 203)	(—, 57)		
Sula l. brewsteri	W. North America	4	136±5·2	156±5·9	169±5·7	46±2·4	1·08	0·29
Brown booby			(132–143)	(148–162)	(163–177)	(43–49)		
Sula l. plotus	Indo-Pacific area	4	143±6·0	159±8·4	173±7·3	47±1·7	1·09	0·30
			(138–153)	(152–173)	(166–185)	(46–50)		
Sula l. leucogaster	St. Paul's Rocks	3	164±1·6	169±2·5	188	50±0·5	1·11	0·30
			(162–166)	(166–172)	(—, —, 188)	(50–51)		
Sula sula rubripes	Indian Ocean	5	132±3·3	166±3·5	184±3·3	37±1·5	1·11	0·22
Red-footed booby			(129–138)	(161–171)	(178–188)	(36–40)		
Sula sula subsp.?	(Central Pacific?)	1	112	146	167	33	1·14	0·23

Note: The nomenclature is taken from Miller (1935) and Howard (1958). The longest measurements were taken; all measurements were not available for every specimen, and the two figures for *S. pohli* refer to the right and (shortened?) left wings. Dr G. F. van Tets provided the measurements for *Sula serrator*, *Sula dactylatra personata*, and some specimens of the other species. The last measurements are from a skeleton without data from the Rothschild Collection.

conceivable that either the large or small fossil sulids, whatever their wing proportions, could have given rise to both the present-day gannets and the boobies. Form and function are intimately related and much depends on an interpretation of the nature of the adaptive radiation shown by the sulids. It is not worth a long and speculative discussion, particularly since Olson may shortly review the North American fossil sulids, and incorporate new material.

2. *The status of the gannets*

Regardless of generic name, should each of the three gannets be accorded specific status, sub-specific or something between? One should reject sub-specific status; as the species accounts have shown, the differences between the Atlantic and the other two are fairly considerable, both in size, plumage, ecology and behaviour. Jarvis (1972) concludes from his intensive study of the Cape gannet that it would be unlikely to interbreed with the Atlantic even if the two came together, and I agree. The Cape and Australasian gannets differ from each other considerably less than either does from the Atlantic, but it would be hair splitting to give these two different status from the Atlantic. Nevertheless, the close similarities, between these two in particular, do indicate that full specific status would probably not be justified, though for practical reasons one might nevertheless decide to confer it (Voous, in press). One may encompass the biological realities by indicating the special relationship between the three gannets, neither minimising the differences, as sub-specific rank would do, nor yet over-emphasising them, as specific status would tend to do. The gannet super-species, containing three allo-species, *sensu* Amadon (1966b), seems a fair compromise. The trinomial nomenclature indicates the close affinities and the use of the square bracket around the specific name indicates special rank (allo-species). Thus, if the generic name *Sula* were chosen, one would define *Sula* [*bassana*] *bassana*, *S.* [*b.*] *capensis* and *S.* [*b.*] *serrator*. This method indicates that the three gannets form a closely knit trio, closer to each other than to any other member of the genus (which is self-

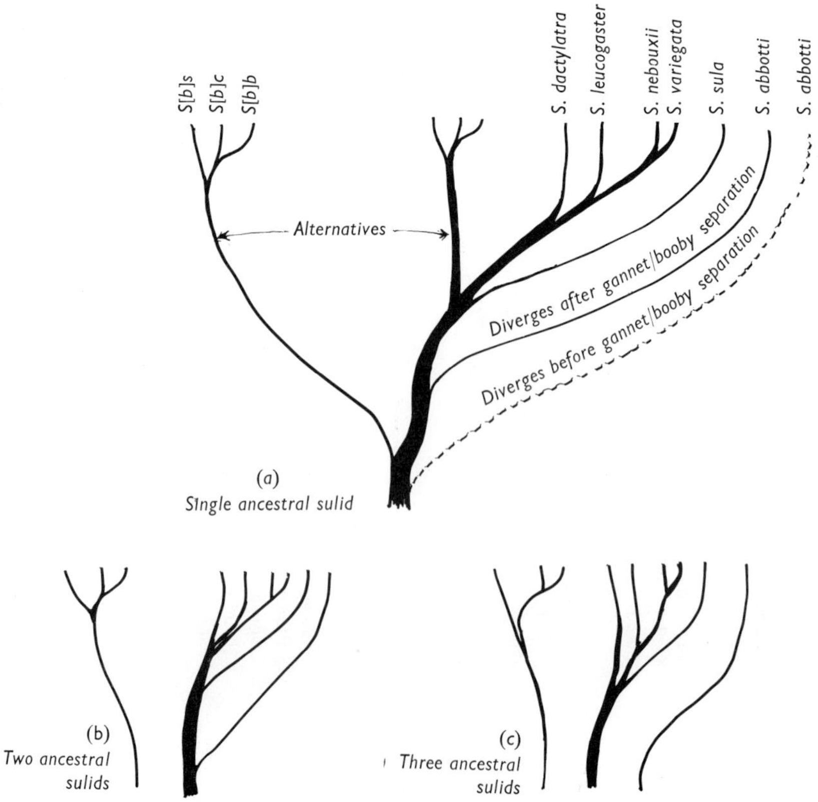

Fig. 359. Speculative evolutionary trees, Sulidae.

evident) yet without being clear-cut species or mere sub-species (which also is true). My inclination is thus to place the gannets as a super-species, within the genus *Sula*.

3. *Evolutionary relationships within the Sulidae*

The modern sulids between them cover the seas from almost the sub-Antarctic, through the tropics, to the Arctic oceans. They could not be expected to have achieved this dispersion without evolving considerable divergence in feeding and breeding habits (see Comparative Morphology p. 833). These differences are served by corresponding morphological ones and to some extent by plumage and behaviour, and it is to all three that one turns for an evaluation of affinities within the group.

Probably the Sulidae originated in the southern hemisphere at least 50 million years ago. The living representatives are clearly not equally closely related to each other. The periods during which the several divergences occurred cannot be estimated with any accuracy because we have no idea, for example, whether it has taken longer for the gannets to evolve their differences from an ancestral sulid stock than it has taken Abbott's booby to do so. Three presumably possible evolutionary trees are suggested in Fig. 359.

First, we do not know whether present-day sulids stem from one or more ancestral form(s), but on fossil evidence it is possible that as far back as the Miocene, distinct booby and gannet types were separable. In this case, and assuming that the present-day gannet group stems from the gannet ancestral form and the booby group(s) from the booby form(s), one would have to give generic status to each. On an alternative hypothesis that both present-day groups diverged from the same ancestral form during the period when this was but one of several sulid-types, we then ask when this occurred and when the divergences giving rise to the present-day booby species occurred.

The ancestral sulid may have been common in what is now the vast region of the western and south-western Pacific. The ancestral Australasian gannet may have split off as a result of the climatic changes which occurred in the lower regions of the southern ocean. Later, as a relatively cold-adapted form, it may have crossed the Indian Ocean as a result of an over-shoot in migration in a westerly direction (which still occurs) and become established in the equivalent cold water area of the Benguela. Later still, this form may have given rise to the Atlantic gannet, as a result of an over-shoot in northerly migration (which still occurs). This northern form became markedly cold-adapted, as detailed on p. 915, but retains the need to migrate south as a juvenile (as the other two gannets still do), to waters sub-tending a different feeding regime.

Meanwhile, the warm-adapted sulid stock differentiated into the ancestors of the present-day boobies. There appear to have been three major divergences—into ground nesting (white, brown, blue-footed and Peruvian boobies), tree nesting (red-footed booby) and tree nesting (Abbott's booby). The ground nesters, possibly coming into competition with each other or co-existing forms now extinct, or, perhaps more likely, radiating into different feeding niches and evolving anatomies which then pre-adapted them to exploit different types of ground nesting habitat, split into the white/brown and blue-footed/Peruvian. The two first named still interbreed on occasions (p. 814) whilst the two latter are in all respects closely related, the Peruvian being merely a specialised form of blue-foot which has become adapted to the particular conditions of the Humboldt area.

The nature of the spread shown by each ancestral form of today's boobies can be only dimly conjectured, for each set of speculations raises problems. Perhaps inter-specific competition played an important part during periods when the sulid population was probably many times greater than it is today. The adaptive radiation in morphology related to feeding indicates that, despite the retention of the serviceable sulid form and techniques, specific specialisation was adaptive.

So far as the wider relationships of the Sulidae within the Pelecaniformes are concerned, I have nothing useful to add to existing schemes (see Salvin & Godman 1879–1904, Blanford 1898, Reichenow 1901, McGregor 1909, Hartert 1912–21, Reichenow 1913, Paris 1921, Wetmore 1927, Baker 1929, Forbush 1929, Bannerman 1930, Peters 1931, Chapin 1932, Kuroda 1936, Murphy 1936, Tugarinov 1947, Hellmayr & Conover 1948, Baker 1951,

Dementiev & Gladkov 1951, Bouet 1955, Wetmore 1965, Dementiev & Gladkov 1966, Ali & Ripley 1968) (from Blackwelder 1972).

Behaviourally, the nearest relatives to the sulids seem to me to be the Pelecanidae rather than the Phalacrocoracidae and Anhingidae, but perhaps both pelicans and sulids should be classified as separate sub-orders Pelecani and Sulae (Verhayen 1961). The intra-ordinal relationships given by Wetmore (1960) however indicate a closer relationship between sulids and cormorants than between sulids and pelicans.

Order Pelecaniformes (or Steganopodes)
- Sub-order Phaethontes
  - Family Phaethontidae, tropic birds (3 species)
- Sub-order Pelecani
  - Super-family Pelecanoidea
    - Family Pelecanidae, pelicans (7 species)
  - Super-family Suloidea
    - Family Sulidae, boobies, gannets (7 species)
    - Family Phalacrocoracidae, cormorants (29 species)
    - Family Anhingidae, snakebirds or darters (2 species)
- Sub-order Fregatae
  - Family Fregatidae, frigate-birds (5 species)

The following synonyms and types have been used for the Sulidae:

	Type
Sula Brisson 1760	*S. sula* (= *leucogaster*)
Pelecanus Gmelin 1789	*S. leucogaster*
Dysporus Illiger 1811	*S. bassana*
Plancus Rafinesque 1815	*S. bassana*
Sularius Rafinesque 1815	*S. sula* (= *leucogaster*)
Moris Leach 1816	*S. bassana*
Morus Vieillot 1817	*S. sula* (= *leucogaster*)
Disporus Agassiz 1846	*S. bassana*
Piscatrix Reichenbach 1850	*S. piscator* (= *sula*)
Abeltera Heine 1890	*S. sula* (= *leucogaster*)
Parasula Matthews 1913	*S. dactylatra*
Sulita Mathews 1915	*S. bassana*
Hemisula Mathews 1913	*S. leucogaster*

Hybridisation

The only sulids which are suspected to have interbred are the white and brown boobies, which are not only highly sympatric but often breed cheek by jowl. R. W. Schreiber (pers. comm. and Fig. 360) has recorded a presumed hybrid breeding on Moku Manu, Oahu (September 1967) and R. L. Pyle photographed one there with a two-month-old chick, in the following

Fig. 360(a) Hybrid, from brown and white boobies, Moku Manu, Oahu 1967. Photo R. W. Schreiber.
(b) Ditto, Boatswain Bird Island, Ascension, 1961. Photo D. F. Dorward.

(*a*)

(*b*)

June. Dorward photographed one on Boatswain Bird Island (1962b). It seems almost impossible that the intermediates were merely unusual immature plumages of the white booby, with prolonged retention of the dark feathers of head and neck. The report that these two species interbreed on Latham Island was probably due to a misinterpretation of observations (see p. 332).

CHARACTERISTICS OF ORDER AND FAMILY

Before comparing in detail the external features of the various sulids, a brief synopsis of the principal morphological characteristics of the order and family is given, basically from Witherby (1940) and Thomson (1964).

The Pelecaniformes or Steganopodes, some 53 species altogether, are globally distributed fish-eaters distinguished mainly by having webs between all four toes (three complete webs), the hallux (lower and turned forwards) being connected to the inner toe. In all except the frigate-birds, the webs are efficient structures for swimming. The external nostrils are slit-like (tropic birds), nearly closed (cormorants and darters) or obsolete (pelicans, frigates, gannets and boobies). The palate is customarily defined as largely desmognathous (vomers small or absent, maxilla palatines bróad and meeting each other or the vomers in the mid-line) but this condition is not a clearly demarcated type of neognathous palate, which in turn is now known not to be a valid major category, being imperfectly distinguishable from the major alternative condition (palaeognathous) (McDowell 1948). The basipterygoid process is missing. The sternum usually has a single sternal notch (rarely, two or none) and the furcula is largely fixed (ankylosed) to the keel. The posterior margin of the *bony* aperture of the nares (as against the aperture in the external covering of the bill) is rounded (holorhinal). There are 14–20 cervical vertebrae. The tongue is small. The carotids may be paired or single. The leg muscle formulae (though, apparently, Garrod's notation is now inadequate) are AXY (tropic birds), AX (cormorants, darters, pelicans and sulids) and A (frigates). (A = caudi-femoralis, part of caud-ilio-femoralis; B = accessory = pars-ilio-femoralis; X = semitendinosus = caud-ilio-flexorius; Y = accessory part of semitendinosus = flexor cruris lateralis). ABXY, all four muscles present, represents a primitive condition; ABX, AXY and BXY are derived conditions, whilst AX, BX and XY represent further reductions. A (as in frigates) is highly specialised.

There are 11 primaries, the outermost minute; the aftershaft is vestigial or absent; the fifth secondary remex is apparently absent (diastataxis). The oil gland is tufted and there is down on the apteria and pterylae (pterylae are tracts of skin from which feathers grow and apteria are the areas between). The naked skin between the rami of the lower mandibles and on the throat is variably developed, most markedly in pelicans and frigates. Subcutaneous air-sacs are best developed in the heavy plunge-divers (pelicans and particularly gannets and boobies). Chicks are born blind and naked, except those of tropic birds, which are downy.

The Pelecaniformes are variably colonial, near water. The largest colonies, of millions, are formed by guanay cormorants. Nesting sites are highly variable (cliffs (ledges or holes); the ground; trees (branches or holes); bushes). Nests may be substantial (only two sulids and some cormorants construct ones entirely of excreta) or virtually absent (sóme sulids and tropic birds). Clutch size is usually 2–4 in pelicans; 3–6 in cormorants and daters; always 1 in frigates and tropic birds; 1–4 (usually 1 or 2) in sulids. The reproductive period is-protracted or (in some sulids and all frigates) very protracted (more than a year).

Fish-catching is by diving from the surface (cormorants); splash-plunging (pelicans); plunging with complete immersion (tropic birds); deep plunging (gannets and boobies) and picking from the surface (frigates), and only frigates are habitual kleptoparasites. Tropic birds are probably the best adapted, among Pelecaniformes, for hovering, probably mainly in connection with feeding. Reproductive display is well developed in most groups (see Van Tets 1965 for a comprehensive survey).

Skeletally, the sulids are particularly characterised by their strong, fairly long and pointed bill, tapered but only slightly curved at the tip and never hooked and with even the apertures of the nostril chambers blocked in the bone of the bill; a linear groove on each side of the culmen; tomia (cutting edges) of the beak serrated; mouth rictus large, extending beyond the eye; upper mandible movable via naso-frontal hinge; bones of the lower jaw incompletely fused in the region of the os spleniale and with special articulation with the quadrate, permitting wide opening of the mouth (the three last-named features are adaptations for swallowing large prey); palatines fused in mid-line, with slight median keel; post-orbital process emarginate; greater part of the carina sterni and the region of the sternum bearing the coracoid grooves extending far beyond the anterior lateral process of the sternum; the keel of the sternum extending slightly more than half the sternum's length; outer and middle toes longer than inner; claws broad, flat and somewhat curved with serrations on the inner edge of the middle toe; 18 cervical vertebrae. The skulls of sulids are compared in Fig. 361. Notable external features are the opening of the preen (oil) gland via five apertures; bare skin of the face and

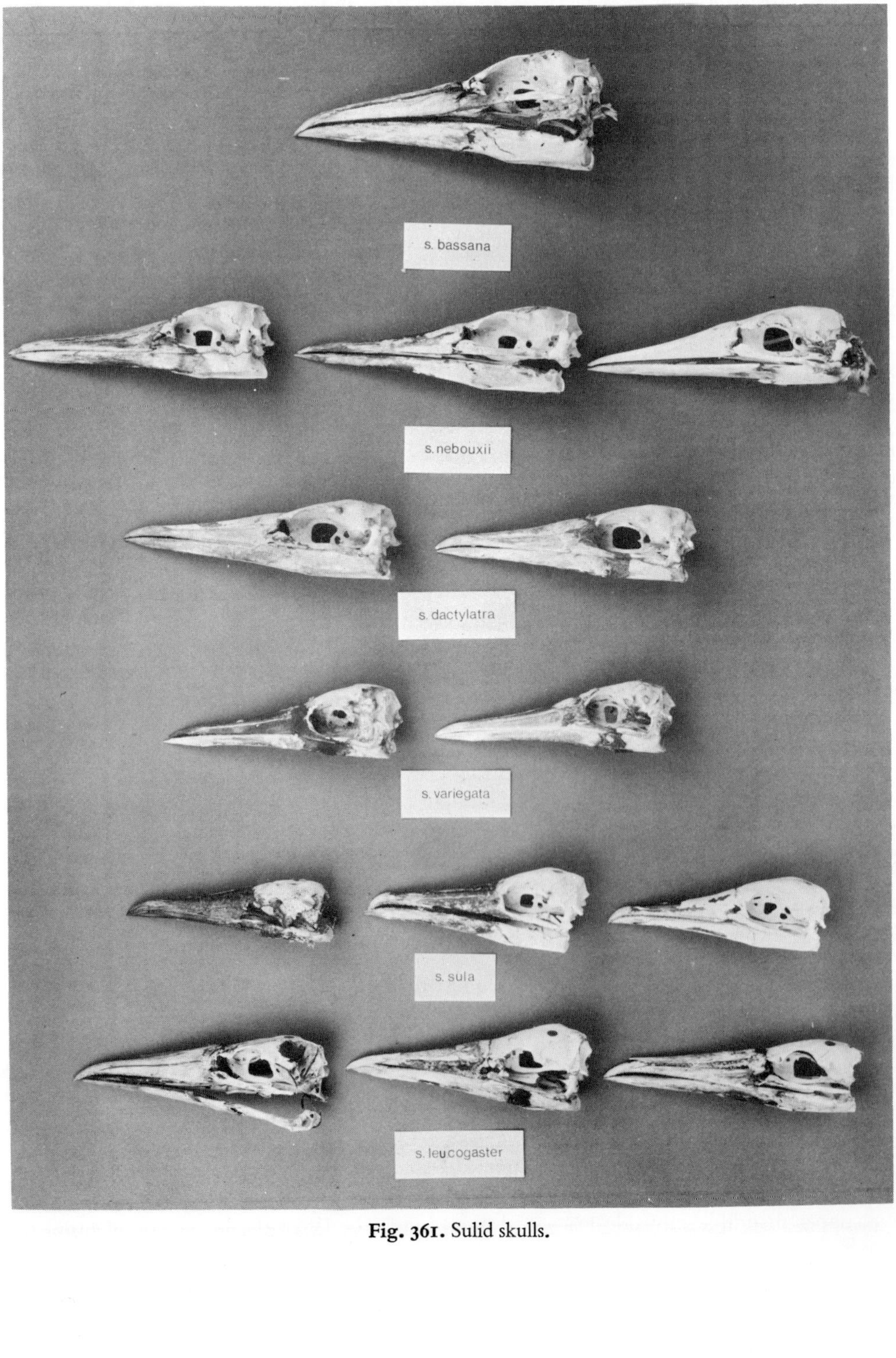

Fig. 361. Sulid skulls.

gular region; long pointed wings with emarginated outer primary (Appendix 15); long, variably cuneate tail (12–18 feathers) with middle rectrices longest; tarsus medium-short (shorter than the foot) with reticulated surface, that of the upper toes continuing up the tarsus as rows of small scale-like plates (scutes). The facial skin, bill, eyes and feet are usually brightly coloured. See Fig. 367 for the size and shape of the bill and the patterns of head and face.

COLOURED PARTS

1. *Faces, bills, feet and 'cosmetic' colour*

Although there are considerable differences within the Sulidae in size, proportions and colouration and indeed these even vary with region, there is little evidence on their adaptive significance. This section discusses, albeit speculatively, the function of morphological and allied variation and also problems of identification.

The feet, and particularly the faces of sulids, with their ornamental skin, are among their most striking features. The colours are caused by pigments, of which melanin, eumelanin, phaeomelanin, carotenoids and xanthophils are probably among the main ones. Between them, these could produce the blacks, yellows, oranges, reds and presumably the greens and blues. It is well known that red pigment can come from astaxanthin in crustacea, and other pigments such as the carotenoids, which cannot be manufactured, must also come from the birds' food. This could account for the regional variation in the colour of soft parts, which is so marked in sulids and is unlikely to have any adaptive significance.

Ornamentally coloured parts may help to emphasise signal behaviour patterns. The black inter-ramal skin, extending onto the throat, is conspicuous in Skypointing (Fig. 124); the brightly coloured bills and faces of white, brown and red-footed boobies are prominent in close range ritualised behaviour and are brightest in the early part of the breeding cycle. The feet are flaunted; the gannet droops its webs, displaying the dorsal lines, and the blue-foot spreads them. The red-foot, however, does not use its feet in any conspicuous way (the tree habitat may preclude it) and the brown booby, though it has extremely colourful webs, flaunts them much less than the blue-foot. This may be partly connected with the latter's longer tarsi and associated tendency to walk about more.

By facilitating heat loss, facial and gular skin also help to regulate body temperature, which explains the hypertrophy of the inter-ramal skin in the Cape gannet when compared with the Atlantic. This function may be particularly important in the white booby and partly explains its conspicuous black mask, since it breeds in intensely hot and sunny habitats whereas, of the two boobies sympatric with it, the arboreal red-foot nests in shade and the brown is often on draught-cooled slopes, cliff-edges and among vegetation. Perhaps comparably, the Cape gannet's 'face' is blacker and more extensive than that of the Atlantic.

The yellow head colour in gannets and red-foots (white morphs) is difficult to understand. It could be 'cosmetic' colour transferred from the preen-gland, in which all sulids roll their heads, but this explanation fails to accommodate the sexual and seasonal differences, which are particularly noticeable in gannets (p. 8). Since the buff head colour is so similar in these two species it seems odd that in the gannet there is never any trace of yellow on the body plumage, whereas there often is in the red-foot. It is also odd that the white booby never shows the slightest trace of yellow.

2. *Sexual isomorphism*

In all sulids the sexes are remarkably alike in plumage, but only in the gannet and to a lesser extent the Peruvian and white booby are size and coloured parts also so similar that the sexes are hard to tell apart. It may be more than coincidence that it is in two of these species, and above all in the gannet, that shared defence of a highly competed for site is most important. Also, similarity in size is 'permissible', if not even advantageous, in their particular feeding environments (p. 915).

PLUMAGE

1. *Genus-characteristic plumage features*

Certain plumage characteristics recur throughout the sulids, at least in the juvenile and immature stages, having been phylogenetically much more persistent than others. They are found also in the immature pelecanid plumages. All juvenile and/or immature sulids have a dark thigh patch though only the Peruvian, blue-foot and Abbott's booby show it as adults. All except possibly Abbott's have at least an indication of a pectoral band though only the brown booby retains it as an adult. It is particularly well-marked in the juvenile blue-foot and in some juvenile and immature red-foots. In the white and Peruvian boobies and the gannet it is merely a boundary between the upper breast, which moults its down relatively quickly, and the lower breast and belly, which retains it longer and subsequently tends to be slightly paler. In all sulids except Abbott's, the head and neck are first to lose down and, eventually, to gain adult plumage (this is particularly marked in the gannet, which may have an adult head in its second year). However, the back of the neck and mid-upper neck tend to retain immature feathers longest. These may be a carry-over from a primitive condition in which the head and neck had a special external embellishment, perhaps even a stabiliser! The blue-foot's spiky head feathers are unique in the family and so is the ability of Abbott's booby to raise the crest feathers whilst keeping those of the forehead flat. Incidentally, the gannet's extremely strong tendency to keep its head feathers sleek reflects its unusually high fear threshold, so far as conspecifics are concerned, rather than any structural difference. The scapulars are the first true feathers to develop in the chick and, with the secondaries, the last to attain adult colour. Their precocious development may be connected with heat regulation for they are used to cover the head when sleeping. The nape and collar and the rump are white in most immature sulids but only the blue-foot has retained these two features as adult marks.

2. *Regional variation in plumage*

Regional variation in plumage is conspicuous only in brown and (particularly) red-footed boobies. The chief variants of the former (*etesiaca* of humid regions and *brewsteri* of arid areas) conform to the 'rule' that dark forms go with high temperature and humidity and light ones with high temperature and dryness. The advantages are not clear. Crypsis, often an advantage of light colouration in deserts, could not apply to the booby; the effects of dryness and temperature may be physiologically determined and selectively neutral, or the characteristics may perhaps play a role in temperature regulation. The striking morphs of the red-foot are still an enigma so far as their functions are concerned, but the following theoretical possibilities may be mentioned. First could be the evolution of plumage variability as a device to confuse prey by complicating its task of recognising its predators. This, however, might be expected to produce populations with a great deal of polymorphism whereas instead the trend is for a particular region to possess only or almost entirely one morph. Second, the principal function of the two main morphs (white, and brown or part-brown) could be the enhanced camouflage value (see also p. 820) of each under different weather and sea conditions. Broken, sun-lit water has different refractive properties than smooth water under a dull sky and the plumage morphs cannot be equally visible to fish under all conditions. This principle is obviously capable of much more sophisticated speculative analysis but the main point seems plausible. A special case along these lines is the suggestion that brown morphs tend to be more nocturnal but this is certainly not a clear-cut difference and seems unlikely (p. 747). Third, the general principle of variability in an organism as an adaptive response to a variable environment could be invoked but fails to explain why the red-foot alone among the three sympatric boobies should have developed so much plumage variability. However, it does inhabit impoverished waters and probably overlaps with more seabird species, in terms of food spectrum, than does the white (which is the only other blue-water far-foraging sulid). Thus its plumage differentiation may be an intra-specific form of adaptive radiation, helping it to exploit food more efficiently. Finally it is probable that in some polymorphic species one form enjoys better breeding success than another under certain conditions. However, there is no evidence on this for any polymorphic population of the red-foot.

The white booby shows no regional variation in plumage. The whiteness is noticeably more intense than that of the white-morph red-foot and it seems likely that its dazzling quality has an important function. This seems unlikely to be signal (but see p. 821) and (like the mask) could be thermoregulatory in the open, intensely insolated habitats typical of this species.

3. *Moult*

All sulids are born with a few tracts of neosoptiles (Fig. 40) and go on to develop a massive plumage of white down (Fig. 362), followed by several immature (pennaceous, teleoptile) plumages and finally the adult plumage. The length of the down filaments varies with species but the characteristics and function of downy plumage in sulids have not been investigated. Some birds, for example hawks, have two downy plumages, the first of which grows from the same follicles as the pennaceous feathers and is pushed out by them, and the second of which grows from other follicles and is retained, in part, beneath the contour feathers. In gannet chicks there are two generations of down. The first is short and finely divided at the tip and the main coat is long and woolly, varying greatly in length according to the part of the body. It is shed as the feathers grow but although, during development, it lies thickly on the surface of the true feathers, these do not grow from the same follicles nor, apparently, does the down lying beneath the feathers. Witherby *et al.* (1940) says this under-down may replace the chick down but is not continuous with it.

Immature sulids gradually move from the juvenile plumage to the adult, requiring two to five years according to species. By contrast some birds (for example the bald eagle) moult from a fully immature plumage, of which they have more than one, straight into adult plumage. The adaptive significance of the sulid-type transition has never been interpreted.

Amadon (1966a) considers that even minor plumage changes between breeding and non-breeding 'seasons' qualify a bird for inclusion in the category of those which possess two

Fig. 362. Down from (a) Abbott's booby and (b) gannet. The latter is typical sulid down, which varies in number and length (but not structure) of filaments, according to position.

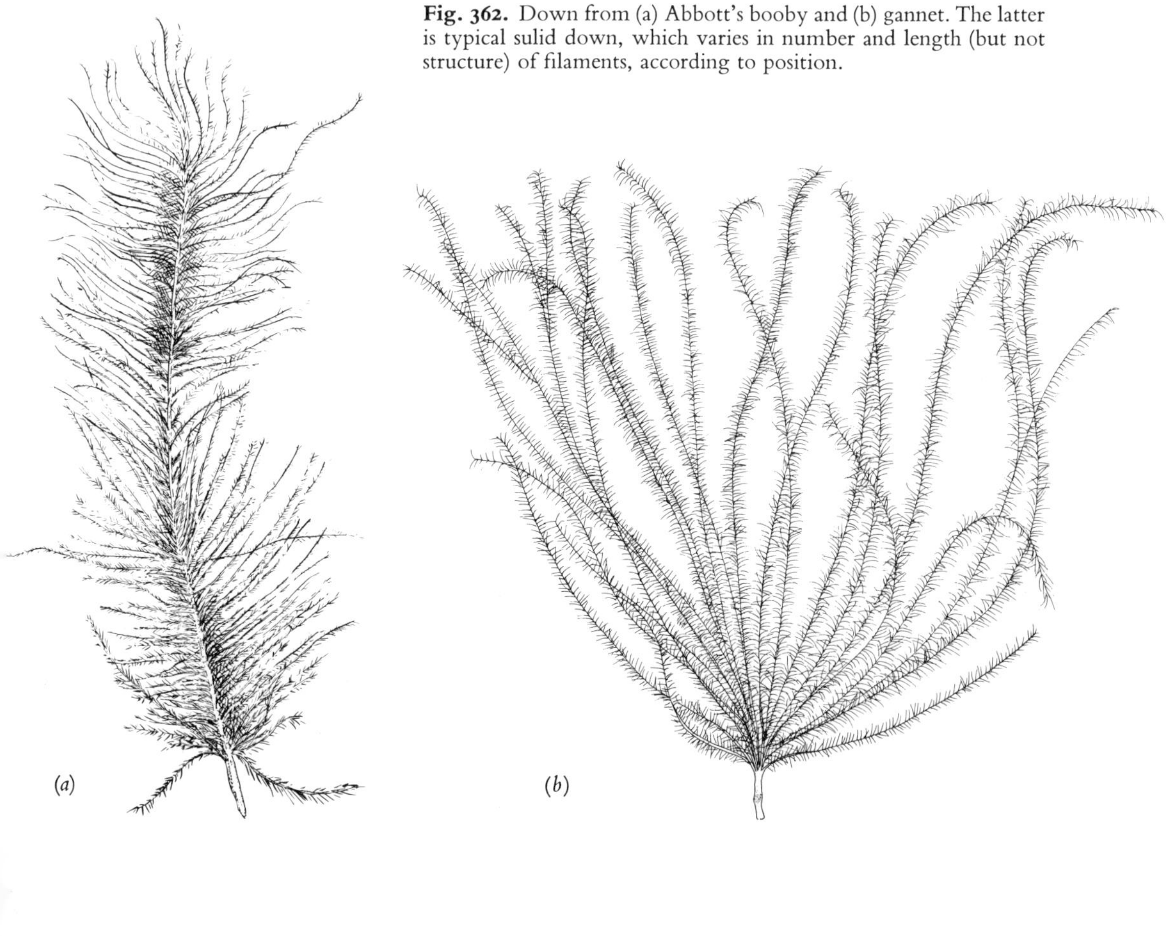

distinct adult plumages. The gannet, which acquires a deeper yellow head in the breeding season, and probably, also, the white-morph red-foot, thus qualify. Other sulids, however, do not acquire any distinctive plumage colouration, though abrasion may, in individual cases, produce a paler and less uniform appearance on dark parts of the plumage in some species, notably the Peruvian and the blue-foot. Skin colours, nevertheless, show distinctive changes in the breeding season (see under 'species'). In all sulids the sexes are alike in plumage but often dissimilar in size, colour of face and bill and in voice. This marked sexual isomorphism, an almost universal trait in seabirds, may be correlated with shared defence of territory frequently found in colonial species. Plumage polymorphism, as distinct from regional variation, is found only in the red-foot and even there not within all populations (see p. 661).

On account of the energy involved in feather replacement the pattern of moult is bound to be highly sensitive to natural selection. In all adult sulids the major 'fixed point' in the moult cycle is soon after the egg hatches. At this time the moult of flight feathers, usually interrupted for the duration of the pre-laying and incubation stages of the breeding cycle (which almost certainly demand most energy) is resumed. Thus two or three generations of feathers often co-exist in the same wing (p. 324). However, whereas (at least in the gannet) body feathers are moulted massively, starting around hatching time, primary moult may not resume until the chick is well grown. The precise pattern of events is undoubtedly influenced by local conditions, particularly food. In all sulids, flight feathers are shed evenly throughout the interval between resumption of moult and the onset of the next breeding attempt, when moult ceases.

Using Amadon's (1966a) criteria, sulid moult can be described as follows:

Name of plumage		*Name of subsequent moult*
	1. *YOUNG BIRDS*	
	A. Downy plumages	
Downy plumage (apparently only one)	....	Post-natal moult.
	B. Pennaceous plumages	
Juvenile plumage;	....	Post-juvenile moult.
immature plumages (1st, 2nd, 3rd and 4th)	....	Immature moults.
	2. *ADULT BIRDS*	
Breeding plumage	....	Post-breeding moult.
non-breeding plumage	....	Possible pre-breeding abrasion.

4. *Plumage adaptations for hunting*

Simmons (1972) divides seabird plumage into three main 'types' according to the relative amount of dark (black, brown and grey) and light (white or pale grey). In Type 1 birds are mainly or wholly dark with restricted light areas and dark frontal aspects. Examples are frigates, some albatrosses, petrels and shearwaters, cormorants, skuas and some auks. Type 2 birds are dark above and white below, with dark and light areas about equal but the frontal aspect mainly dark. Most shearwaters, penguins, some cormorants and most auks are of this type. Type 3 are wholly or mainly light with restricted dark areas and a light frontal aspect. Almost all gulls and most terns belong here, also some shearwaters. Most sulids fit broadly into Type 3, none in Type 2 and a very few in Type 1. White predominates, especially on the ventral surface.

Sulid plumages fall into four categories:

1. All white except for a little black on wings and in some cases tail (adults of all three gannets, adult white booby and adult red-foot, white morph).

2. White beneath and on head, but dark above (adult Peruvian booby, adult and juvenile Abbott's booby, second year gannets and white booby).
3. Mostly white beneath but head and in some cases part of throat and upper breast brown (adult and juvenile blue-footed booby, adult and juvenile brown booby, juvenile white booby, some immature stages and some intermediate morphs of the red-footed booby, some cases of juvenile and first year Australasian and Cape gannets).
4. Dark above and below, including the head (juvenile gannets, adult and juvenile of the brown-morph red-footed booby).

The adaptive significance of these plumage types is probably mainly connected with hunting, an activity upon which constant and severe selection pressure operates, particularly in periods when food is difficult to obtain, a condition which applies, even if only transiently, to all sulids. The great range of plumages listed above, the many different modes of hunting practised by sulids and the variable climatic conditions under which all of them must operate, however, preclude any chance of a neat and convincing set of 'explanations'.

There are three ways in which plumage could affect hunting success and they are not mutually exclusive. It could act as a signal, to which others respond by joining the 'first-finder' (social enhancement by social conspicuousness) or it could act as camouflage making it difficult for the prey to spot the hunter (hunting camouflage) or it could help to make the 'first-finder' inconspicuous to other birds when viewed against the sea (social camouflage by social inconspicuousness). These possibilities have been discussed by Simmons (1972) following pioneer suggestions by Armstrong (1944) and Craik (1944) and stimulated particularly by Phillip's unpublished work (1962).

Seabirds may be divided into many types according to feeding method (Simmons uses 10). In six the bird remains airborne throughout (aerial pursuit, aerial dipping, contact dipping, pattering, hovering, and stepping) whilst in the others flying is interrupted by plunging to the surface, plunge-diving, surface-diving and surface-feeding. Broadly, the types that feed in the air or by picking from the surface, tend to be dark (petrels, frigates, skuas, some terns) whilst those that plunge-dive usually have pale frontal aspects and, often, ventral surfaces.

Before getting down to details, it remains to make three further general points. First, in my opinión (and it seems most others) white birds are more easily seen by other birds than are dark ones. This is particularly true when viewed against the sea, but holds, also, against several conditions of sky. Second, Cowan (1972) has demonstrated that pale undersides have in fact a smaller 'undersides contrast' against the sky than black ones (but not than partly white ones) and are thus less conspicuous to fish. Third, there are reasons for believing that a first-finder which attracts conspecifics to a shoal is itself likely to gain thereby.

Returning to the four categories of plumage listed above, of the three all white sulids, the gannets are birds of cold water, food-rich areas and the white and red-footed boobies are two extremely far-foraging species in tropical blue waters. Gannets plunge more steeply and deeply than other sulids (p. 915) and both their ventral and dorsal aspects may be presented during the plunge. Their all-white plumage (apart from the pigment-strengthened wing tips) may thus be interpreted as hunting camouflage rendering the diving bird less easily spotted by fish. However, white hunting camouflage is probably not very important when birds dive from a great height into a dense shoal, but may be more so when plunge diving from just above the surface, with less speed. The conspicuousness of a diving gannet—quite remarkable in sunlight—attracts others. Social enhancement obviously helps the birds thus summoned. It may also help the first-finder to catch more than it could have done on its own by confusing the fish (their escape actions use the rapid-swim mechanism which quickly tires when repeatedly activated) and preventing them forming into dense packs. These, as Simmons points out, can be an effective barrier to penetration;

> '. . . pelagic fish driven inshore (to Ascension) by predatory fish, or coming in to spawn, often grouped into dense, conspicuous, circular shoals or "packs"; at times, these extended for several metres in diameter on or near the surface and were of unknown depth. A dark, seething throng of fish was formed with the individuals so close to one another that they were pressed tight in a solid mass, splashing and bubbling on the surface. These shoals were primarily defensive against the underwater attacks of large predatory fish, to which

they presented an impenetrable barrier; additionally, they served as a defence against the aerial attacks of seabirds. On all but one occasion, these fish packs had not a single seabird—not a booby or even an Ascension Frigate-bird *Fregata aquila*—in attendance.'

This interpretation seems much more convincing than the only alternatives, namely that white plumage evolved for some non-feeding function and that first-finders are simply compelled to tolerate having to give away the location of food, mitigated by the fact that often there is so much that nobody's intake is thereby reduced or, secondly, that it is an altruistic mechanism.

When applied to the white and red-footed boobies, however, this interpretation seems less cogent. These two species usually feed solitarily or in very small groups, on widely dispersed prey which, particularly in the red-foot's case, is often taken from the air or followed down as it re-enters the water. Furthermore, the wide variation in red-foot plumage types, even though all take largely flying fish and squid, suggest that neither the hunting camouflage effect of white plumage, nor its social conspicuousness, is as important as it is in the gannet. In the red-foot, therefore, there seems a more complicated balance of advantages. The 'confusion-effect' on prey may be one (above); the social inconspicuousness of brown plumage, perhaps reducing the likelihood of being seen and persecuted at sea by frigates, may be another. Thus, whilst white remains, on balance, the commonest presumably because of its hunting camouflage, the plumage polymorphism also persists.

The white booby is undoubtedly the most dazzling of all sulids and is moreover monomorphic in plumage. Yet social enhancement of feeding can hardly be an important function since this is relatively so rare and so often inappropriate. Here, the very quality of the white (high light reflectance) may suggest that an important function is at the breeding colony, as a thermo-regulatory device, for it is certainly true that this species inhabits the most open and highly insolated breeding places of any sulid. Perhaps equally important may be its value as hunting camouflage. Simmons, on the other hand, stresses its value in social enhancement of feeding, but as mentioned, what little we know about it suggests that the white booby does not usually feed in large groups.

The second category, white beneath and on the head but dark above, confers much the same hunting camouflage as the first group but may be less socially conspicuous. This, however, is by no means certain. Abbott's booby, especially, with its boldly patterned black and white dorsal surface (see Fig. 328) may be almost as conspicuous as a pure white bird. The Peruvian booby, though, probably is less socially conspicuous. Here it may be recalled that it is probably a modified blue-foot (see p. 813) than which it has already achieved a much whiter frontal aspect. Furthermore, the extreme abundance of anchovies may reduce the value of social enhancement of feeding. Thus, its basic adaptation could well be that of hunting camouflage; the rest could be unimportant.

The third category has forfeited or, more likely, never gained a fully white frontal aspect. The fact that this group contains so many members, if one includes temporary ones, is perhaps surprising if one considers hunting camouflage to be very important, and particularly surprising in young birds, for whom even slight handicaps should be important during their months of inexperience. When attempting to interpret this situation one may look for general trends and then take each case on its merits for specific characters. First, the white ventral surface is present in all, except the juvenile Atlantic gannet, for which a convincing 'explanation' is available (p. 209). So there is in fact a great deal of 'hunting camouflage'. In the case of the juvenile white booby, social inconspicuousness could well be an advantage. As already mentioned, its type of foraging and prey dispersion do not lend themselves to social facilitation of feeding, in fact quite the reverse, in addition to which, inconspicuousness to frigates is probably a significant advantage. Furthermore, one advantage suggested for the adult white booby's plumage (thermo-regulation) is temporarily in abeyance for the juvenile is not forced to spend long periods at the breeding colony in fierce sun. The brown booby, both in adult and juvenile plumage, is exceptional among sulids in possessing a completely dark upper breast and head, sharply demarcated from the white belly. Two of its feeding habits could be relevant to this; it often feeds by air-to-air and air-to-surface encounters with prey and it has a marked tendency to fish inshore, often in very rough water. In both these situations its plumage pattern would seem to offer more effective camouflage than an unbroken white frontal aspect. Simmons cites, also, its tendency to dive obliquely from low heights and suggests that the need for a white frontal aspect here and when attacking dense shoals inshore, is minimal. Its completely brown dorsal surface makes it inconspicuous from above and so perhaps aids against frigates, though conversely this species reputedly robs frigates in Australia!

The blue-foot is distinguished, on the other hand, by conspicuous rump and nape patches. Perhaps significantly it often hunts in groups (p. 568) suggesting that this pattern could aid social conspicuousness. Its inshore feeding presumably benefits from the white ventral surface.

The final category contains the all-dark birds, rare among sulids. Since the dark juvenile gannet has already been discussed it leaves only the adult brown morph and the juvenile of all morphs of the red-footed booby. Social inconspicuousness is probably an advantage to these. Their dispersed food in impoverished seas (and this applies particularly to the Galapagos which is in the only area in the world possessing all-brown adults) does not induce social feeding, whilst of all boobies the red-foot is most parasitised by frigates and so stands to gain most from social camouflage. Yet the commonest form is all or mainly white, which goes to show how impossible it is to pigeon-hole a complex situation. Obviously several selection pressures operate (see p. 822) and each locality has its own combination of these. To add to the difficulties of interpretation, the proportions of white to brown morphs in the Galapagos exactly fit a Hardy-Weinberg ratio, which implies that these plumage characters are selectively neutral! Furthermore, each species employs several hunting methods for each of which there is presumably an optimal type of plumage. Thus brown boobies hunt shoaling fish gregariously but also hunt solitarily, both inshore and at sea, both by diving and by pursuit of fish in the air. On Ascension they even robbed white boobies (Simmons 1972).

In sum, therefore, probably the most important functions of the plumages of sulids are in hunting, either as hunting camouflage in plunge diving, primarily involving white ventral and frontal aspects or as social signals to facilitate communal feeding (the best case being that of the gannet) or as social camouflage to prevent conspecifics from joining in or to evade the attentions of klepto-parasites. However, there is such variety in plumage and in selection pressures that no simple 'rules' are valid and each case must be considered in the light of the species' distribution, prey types, hunting methods and breeding habitat.

MORPHOLOGY

Weight, both absolute and in relation to wing area, beak characteristics and length of tail and tarsus (Table 126), determine many of a bird's capabilities, particularly in connection with feeding. Obviously, even within a group of closely related species one cannot expect these features to vary in concert; the proportional difference between the weights of heaviest and lightest may be vastly greater than the comparable differences in say length of wing or bill. Each set of characters, such as the combination of light weight, medium wings, long tail and slender bill (which roughly describes the male blue-foot) implies a corresponding set of abilities and restrictions which in principle must be relatable to the bird's feeding and breeding biology. This general theme is the concern of the present section.

Fig. 363 shows the extent to which different morphological features vary within the Sulidae and reveals the enormous difference in weights compared with relatively slight ones in the lengths of bill, wing and tail. Fig. 364 emphasises these differences by expressing the absolute extent of the range in measurements of weight, wing, culmen and tarsus in each species. This brings out the extent of the differences between species in these features; for example there is clearly a greater range of weight and wing length in the blue-foot than in any other sulid (which in fact reflects its marked sexual dimorphism). Weight and wing length clearly show the greatest *absolute* range but, whilst this is useful when comparing the same features from sulid to sulid, it means little when comparing different features, since obviously a large object such as a wing will show a greater absolute range than a small one such as a bill. Fig. 364 (inset) however compares these ranges as percentages and reveals that both between species and within all species, weight is again the most variable character. Culmen and wing length are not so consistent; in some species bill length is more variable than wing length,

TABLE 126

COMPARATIVE MEAN MEASUREMENTS IN THE SULIDAE

Position within family* for each measure	Weight (g)	Wing (carpal joint to tip)	Tail (mm)	Tarsus (mm)	Beak length (mm)	Beak depth (mm)
1	♂ Atlantic gannet ♀ Atlantic gannet (3100)	♂ Atlantic gannet (513)	♂ Blue-foot ♀ Blue-foot (237)	♂ Atlantic gannet ♀ Atlantic gannet (59)	♀ Blue-foot (114)	♀ Abbott's (39·8)
2	—	♀ Atlantic gannet (510)	—	—	♀ Abbott's (113·3)	♀ White (38·1)
3	♀ Cape gannet (2670)	♂ Cape gannet (480)	♀ Abbott's (231)	♀ White (57)	♀ White (109·3)	♂ Abbott's (37·5)
4	♂ Cape gannet (2620)	♀ Cape gannet (477)	♂ Abbott's (219)	♂ Cape gannet ♀ Cape gannet (est. 56)	♂ White (106·8)	♂ White (37·3)
5	♂ Australian gannet (2350)‡ ♀ Australian gannet (2350)‡	♂ Australian gannet (463)‡	♂ Red-foot (215)	—	♂ Abbott's (106·1)	♀ Blue-foot (35·3)
6	—	♀ Australian gannet (463)‡	♂ Atlantic gannet ♀ Atlantic gannet (215)	♂ White (55)	♂ Blue-foot (106)	♂ Atlantic gannet (35)
7	♀ White (1880)	♀ Abbott's† (461)	—	♂ Australian gannet ♀ Australian gannet (54)‡	♀ Brown (102)	♀ Atlantic gannet (34·3)
8	♀ Blue-foot (1800)	♀ Blue-foot (457)	♂ Australian gannet ♀ Australian gannet (215)‡	—	♂ Atlantic gannet (100)	♀ Brown (34·2)
9	♂ White (1630)	♂ White (456)	—	♂ Blue-foot ♀ Blue-foot (54)	♀ Atlantic gannet (99·8)	♂ Blue-foot (33·5)
10	♀ Abbott's (1600)	♀ Abbott's† (449)	♀ Red-foot (205)	—	♀ Peruvian (98·2)	♀ Peruvian ♂ Brown (32)
11	♀ Peruvian (1520)	♂ Blue-foot (432)	♀ White (192)	♀ Peruvian (50)	♂ Brown (96·2)	♂ Cape gannet (est. 32)

* For example, '4' means it is fourth largest in the measurement concerned.
† The overall wing length of Abbott's booby is longer than in other sulids due to a longer humerus.
‡ Data not separated into sexes, though there must be a difference.

Position within family* for each measure	Weight (g)	Wing (carpal joint to tip)	Tail (mm)	Tarsus (mm)	Beak length (mm)	Beak depth (mm)
12	♂ Abbott's (1500)	♂ White (432)	Cape ♀ gannet (191)	♂ Peruvian (48)	Cape ♂ gannet (94) ♂ Peruvian (92.6)	—
13	♂ Peruvian (1300)	♀ Brown (396)	Cape ♂ gannet (189)	♀ Brown (47)	—	Cape ♀ gannet (est. 31)
14	♂ Blue-foot (1280)	♀ Peruvian (429)	♂ White (188)	♂ Abbott's ♀ Abbott's (45)	Cape ♀ gannet (91)	Australian ♂ gannet (est. 30·5)
15	♀ Brown (1260)	♂ Brown (380)	♂ Brown (186)	—	♀ Red-floot (90)	Australian ♀ gannet ♂ Peruvian (30)
16	♀ Red-foot (1070)	♀ Red-foot (385)	♀ Brown (181)	♂ Brown (44)	Australian ♂ gannet (89)‡ Australian ♀ gannet (89)‡	—
17	♂ Brown (960)	♂ Peruvian (386)	♀ Peruvian (171)	♀ Red-foot (40)	—	♀ Red-foot (28)
18	♂ Red-foot (940)	♂ Red-foot (379)	♂ Peruvian (164)	♂ Red-foot (38)	♂ Red-foot (86)	♂ Red-foot (27·5)

whilst in others the reverse occurs. Weight thus seems the most appropriate characteristic to which to relate other measurements.

1. *Weight and wing length*

The weight of male sulids (Fig. 365 line 1) falls progressively from the gannet (about 3150g) to the red foot (about 900gm). Female weights (line 2) follow a slightly different pattern. Whilst in all boobies females are heavier than males, the male gannet is as heavy or heavier than the female (this may be correlated with site defence, p. 17). Also, the degree to which the sexes differ in weight varies between species and is greatest in the blue foot, which may be correlated with hunting techniques (p. 950). The very considerable range in the family as a whole has evolved as adaptive radiation in feeding (p. 914).

Wing lengths (lines 3 and 4) do not follow exactly those for weights. Thus Abbott's booby, though lighter than the white booby, has longer wings (in fact, the difference is much greater than here indicated, because Abbott's unusually long humerus is not represented in these measurements). The female blue-foot, though no heavier than the white, has longer wings. The Peruvian booby is heavier than the brown but its wings are not much longer. Expressing the weight/wing-length relationship as a single index, Fig. 366 reveals a striking degree of separation, due in large part to sexual dimorphism. The gannet's wing loading is almost three times as great as that of the red-foot, at the bottom end of the scale. As with bill shape, there is far more sexual dimorphism in the brown and blue-footed boobies than in any other, and virtually none in the gannet and the Peruvian booby (see p. 914).

Weight and wing-length are correlated with foraging behaviour and fishing techniques, (see p. 915 for a discussion of weight). It is more efficient for sulids with large foraging ranges in impoverished areas to have a higher ratio of wing span to weight than those in rich zones. This is because in impoverished areas and given the booby's method of feeding and transporting fish direct rather than converting it to oil, it is both difficult to find enough fish to support a high body weight, and to transport great weight over large distances is an inefficient way of exploiting widely dispersed food. In addition (and of equal importance), wing shape and loading directly affects the manner of flying and diving. Here too, we lack any precise information, but the gross differences revealed by Fig. 366 are obviously significant. Thus, the red-foot's extremely low wing-loading (its wings are very long in relation to its weight) is probably associated with its tendency to take flying fish on the wing. Conversely, the gannet's high one is due to its great weight, used in deep diving (p. 915). Sexual dimorphism in the blue-foot and brown is associated with different fishing techniques in male and female (p. 568), and lack of it in the Peruvian with its standard-sized and superabundant food. As mentioned, the relative length of the proximal and distal parts of the wing varies in sulids. The gannets have longer proximal parts relative to the 'hand' than have the boobies (except for Abbott's, which is highly aberrant in this respect). The red-foot, in particular, has a relatively long 'hand'. This difference may be connected with diving technique. In the gannet's heavy, powerful plunge, a long 'hand' may be subjected to severe stress, whilst in the red-foot's more aerial and shallow diving, it may confer greater manoeuvrability. On this argument, Abbott's booby might be expected to dive powerfully and deeply, which may well be the case. The mechanics associated with the wing shape and loading of sulids, related to their feeding techniques, might repay thorough investigation.

Though the main shaping factor, food is not the only one. Breeding habitat makes its demands and the red-foot's lightness is undoubtedly an advantage in trees, just as (conversely) the gannet's weight demands cliffs or windy slopes (p. 79). In the main, though, the ground

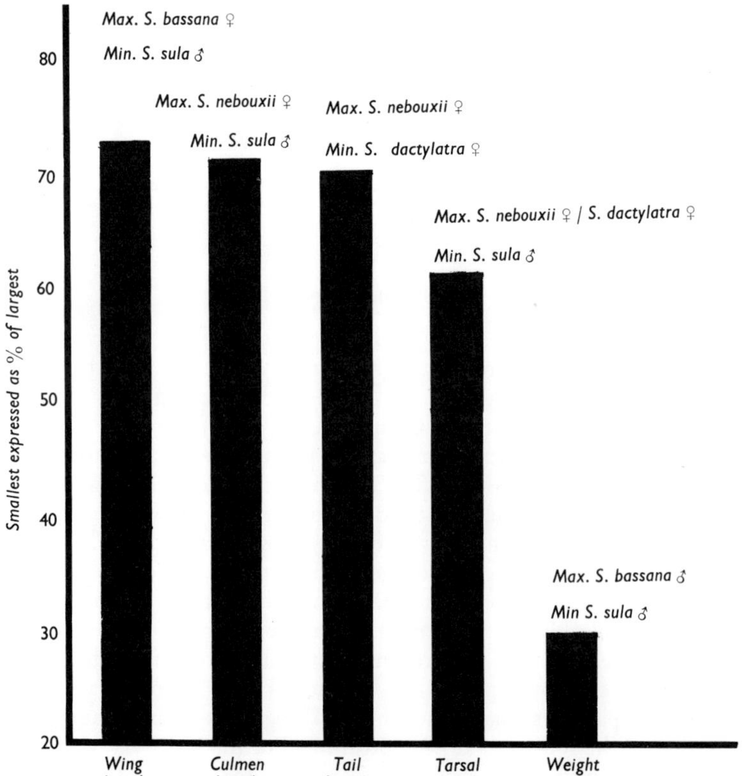

Fig. 363. The degree of variation in different morphological features in the Sulidae. Max. and min. refers to the species with the greatest and least mean measurements in the parameter concerned.

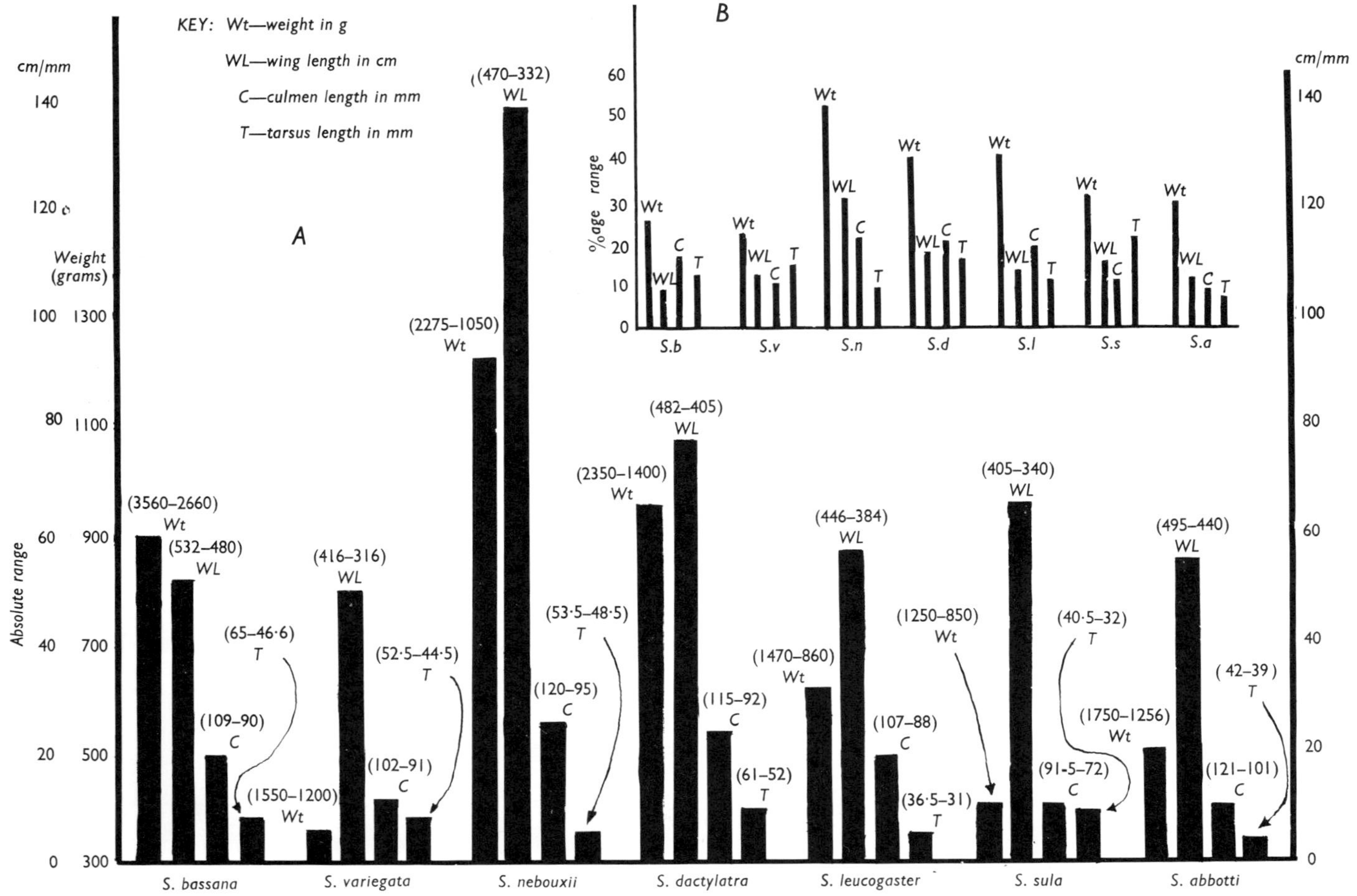

Fig. 364. The variation in morphological characteristics expressed for each sulid (*A*) in absolute and (*B*) in percentage terms. In (*B*) the difference between greatest and least is expressed as a percentage of the greatest.

Note.

Figures in brackets are the absolute measurements and weights, the difference between which gives the range. It is the *range* which is plotted here.

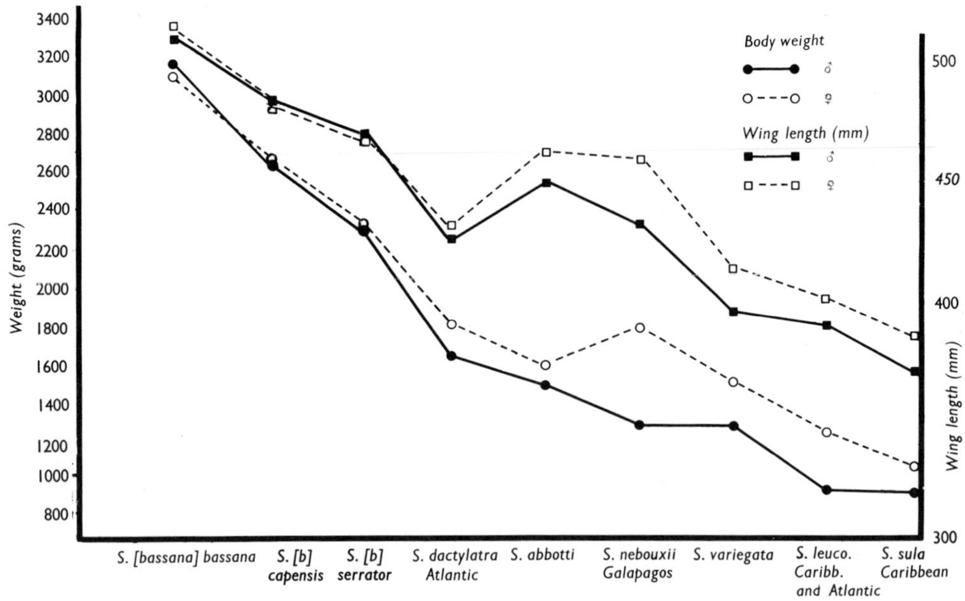

Fig. 365. Adult weight and wing-length in the Sulidae.

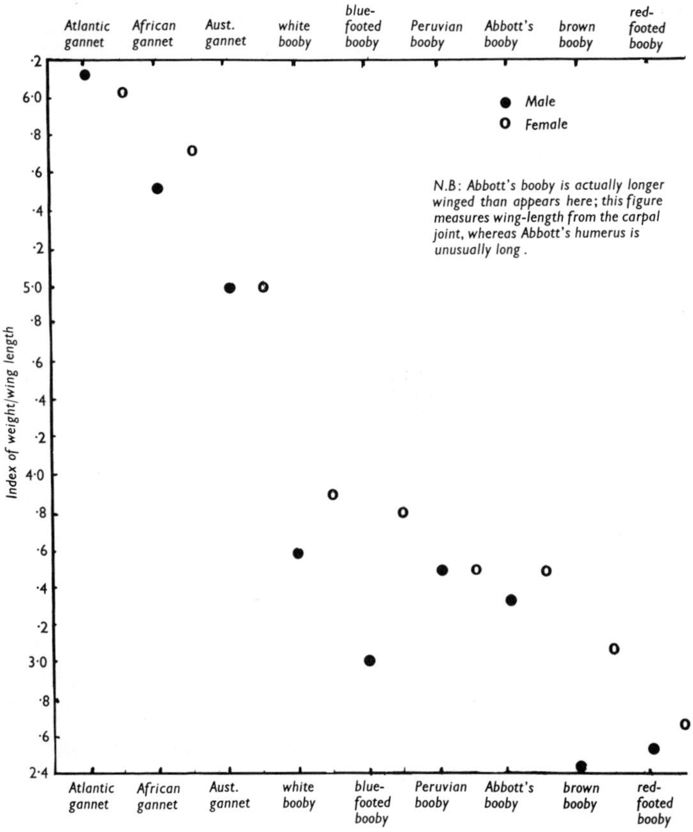

Fig. 366. Variation within the Sulidae in the ratio of weight to wing-length.

nesting boobies are not critically dependent on their particular wing-loadings for choice of habitat; most can nest where any of the others can do so.

2. *Weight and bill characteristics*

Bills have evolved to deal with food, therefore the differences in length, depth and shape reflect prey preferences. On the assumption that deep diving enables the bird to catch larger and stronger prey one would expect heavy birds to evolve beaks which are deep in relation to their length,[1] since this gives greater gripping power. The following series of figures shows the relationships between: bill length and depth merely in relation to each other (Fig. 369); weight and bill length (Fig. 370); weight and bill depth (Fig. 371) and weight and bill depth/length ratio (Fig. 372). Of course, the same principles operate in conferring adaptive value upon differences between *sexes* of the same species, as operate between *species*. In both cases we know so little about foraging and feeding that it becomes mere guesswork to interpret morphological characters, but without doubt significant feeding-niche diversification does result.

Perhaps the most helpful way of working through the information is to take one species at a time right through the series of figures.

(i) *Gannet*

Fig. 369 shows that both male and female gannets fall near the middle of the family, exceeded in bill length by the white booby, blue-foot and Abbott's booby and in bill depth by the white and Abbott's booby. The gannet is not sympatric with any other sulid and for this reason, and its abundant food, experiences little pressure for developing separate feeding niches. Fig. 368 reveals its great superiority in weight whilst its bill remains relatively short. Fig. 370 clarifies the degree of divergence both in the family, and between the sexes of each species, in terms of a *combined* bill-size and body-weight difference. Thus, the graph-gap between the weight of the gannet and its bill length is only half that between these measures in the blue-foot. This is because the female blue-foot is exceptionally long-billed and the male blue-foot exceptionally light. In neither character, however, is there much sex difference in the gannet, for reasons mentioned above. Fig. 371 expands on Fig. 370 by showing bill depth relative to weight. The gannet, though so heavy, has only a medium deep bill. Finally, in Fig. 372 it may be seen that the gannet equals any other sulid in the depth of its bill in proportion to length whilst far exceeding them in weight and therefore gripping power. It is thus the most powerful-billed sulid.

(ii) *White booby*

This species is sympatric particularly with the brown and red-footed booby and also with the blue-foot. It is notably large-billed, equalled or exceeded only by Abbott's and well clear of all its sympatric congeners (Fig. 368). The degree of sexual dimorphism is not great (Fig. 369). It is about the heaviest booby of all; the female is in fact the heaviest sulid after the gannet superspecies and falls on exactly the same line (Fig. 372) as Abbott's and the female brown in terms of its ratio of weight to bill depth and length. Thus only the female brown emerges as a comparably large-billed (though considerably lighter) sympatric booby and it is interesting that this species has evolved marked sexual dimorphism. The red-foot, its principal congener, falls right at the other end of the scale. No other tropical plunge-diver of any kind equals the white booby in weight and bill size, which presumably implies that this species has sole access to a particular feeding niche.

(iii) *Abbott's booby*

This is very much an aberrant species, sympatric with the brown and red-footed. The female has the largest bill of any sulid, whilst that of the male is exceeded by no other species. Its serrations are unusually coarse. There is only moderate sexual dimorphism (Fig. 369).

[1] I am here comparing birds of the same family rather than intending a general statement covering birds with different feeding methods.

Fig. 367. Comparative morphology of beak and head in the Sulidae.

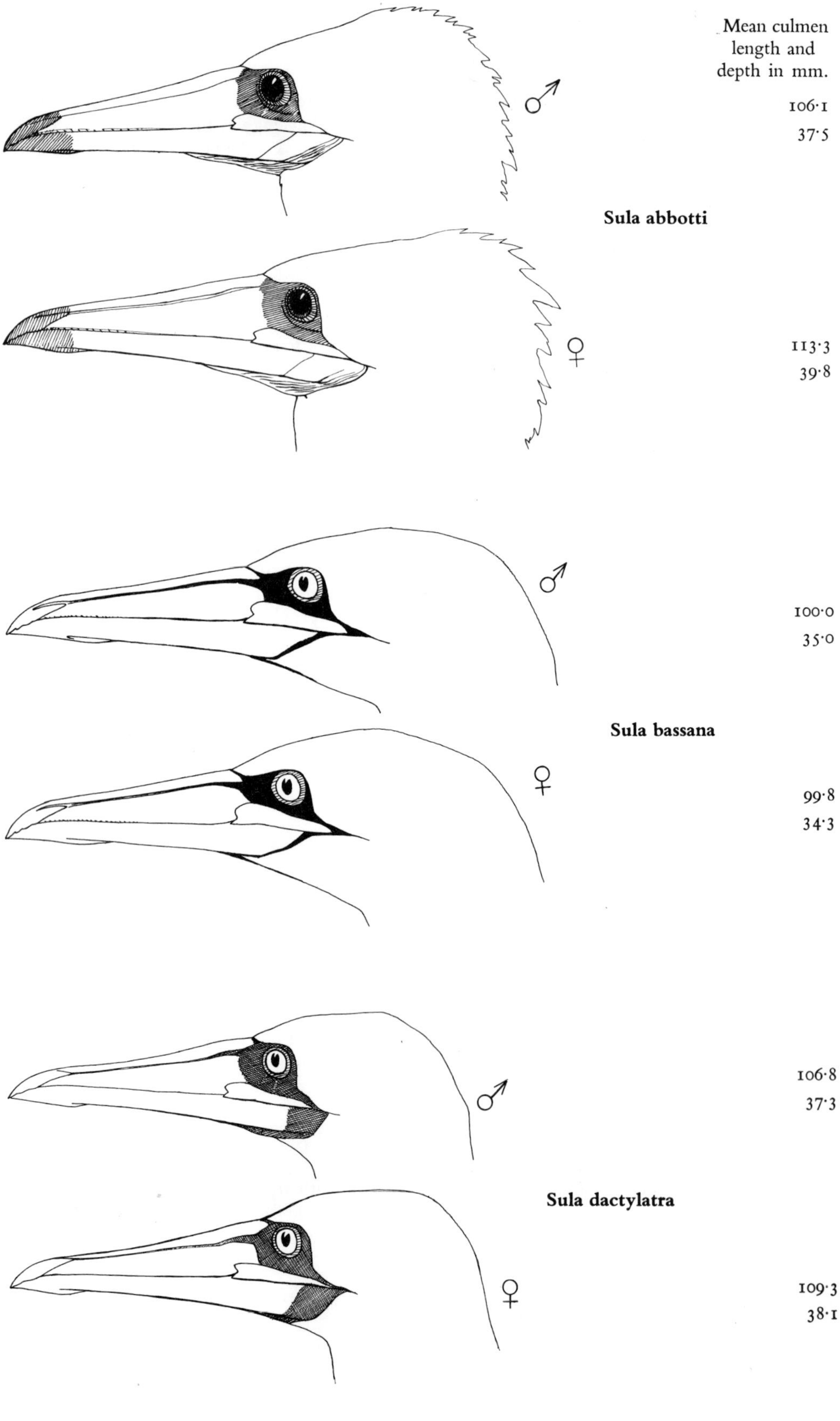

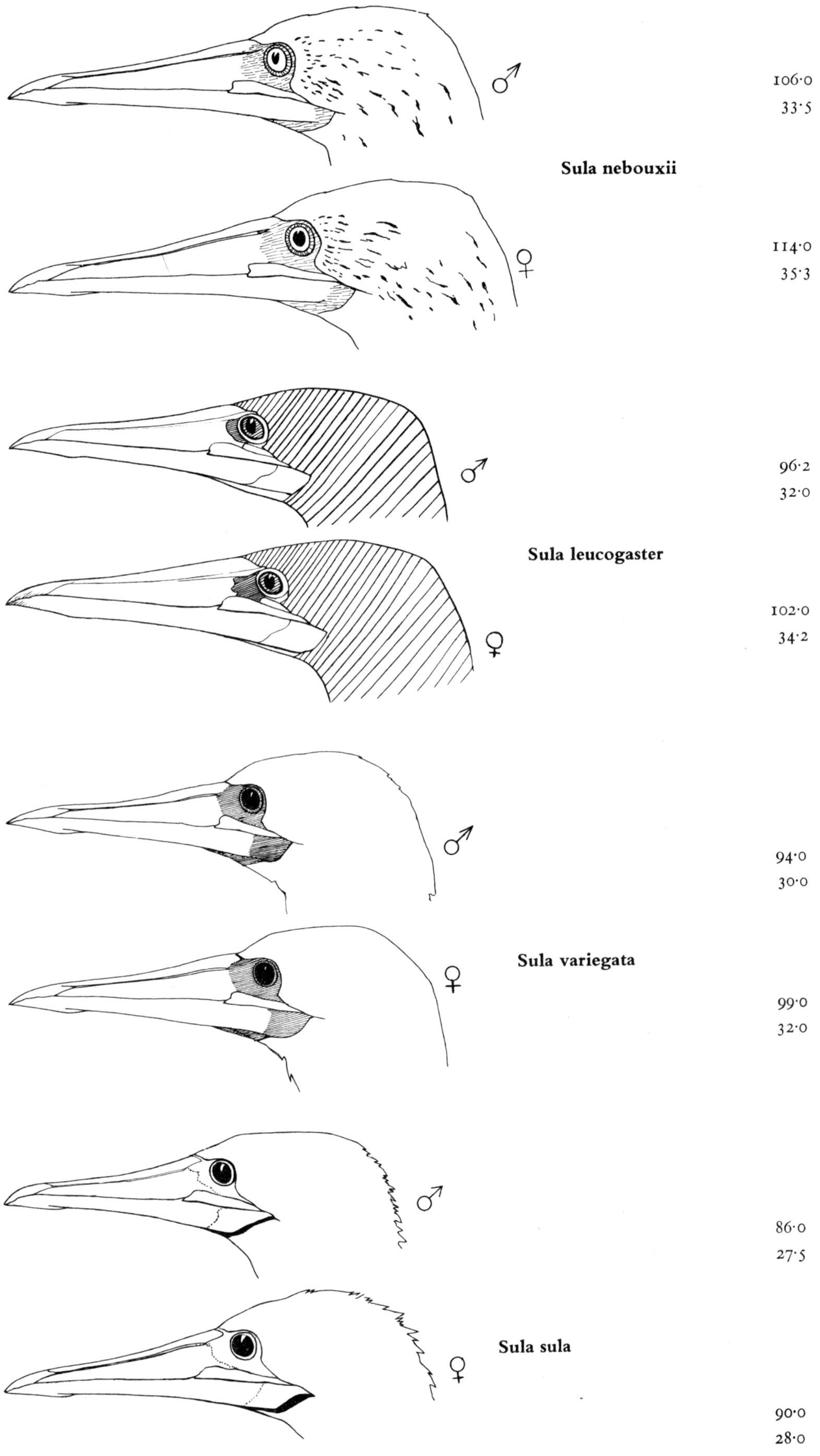

♂
106·0
33·5
Sula nebouxii
♀
114·0
35·3
♂
96·2
32·0
Sula leucogaster
♀
102·0
34·2
♂
94·0
30·0
Sula variegata
♀
99·0
32·0
♂
86·0
27·5
Sula sula
♀
90·0
28·0

Abbott's is not particularly heavy, which in conjunction with its large bill produces an considerable differential between bill-size and body weight (Fig. 370) compared with most other sulids. Fig. 372 places Abbott's equal to the other large-billed sulids in ratio of depth to length, but lighter than all except the brown. Its exceptional bill and peculiarly long and narrow wings distinctly suggest a specialised feeding method and perhaps a different balance of prey sizes, if not species, but nothing concrete is known. The wing proportions might imply particularly powerful plunging. It once enjoyed a wider distribution (p. 757) when it may have been sympatric with the white booby as well as the brown. In this case, three large-billed species overlapped in bill characters to some extent but diverged in absolute size (Abbott's largest), body weight (white booby heaviest) and degree of sexual dimorphism (greatest in the brown).

(iv) *Blue-footed booby*

The blue-foot is nowhere the only sulid; it overlaps with white, brown, red-footed and Peruvian. Its bill is exceptionally long, both in absolute terms (so far as the female is concerned) and particularly in relation to depth. The degree of sexual dimorphism in bill-size is the greatest in the family (Fig. 369) and is associated with marked sexual dimorphism in weight, though this is equalled by the brown and red-footed boobies (Fig. 370). In terms of body weight and bill depth alone (Fig. 371) the male falls close to the brown (also a highly sexually dimorphic species) whilst the female is nearest to the male white. In terms of the ratio of bill depth/length to weight, however, the relative positions fall out somewhat differently (Fig. 372). Here, the female has the thinnest bill in relation to weight of any sulid whilst the male falls equal with the male Peruvian (the female Peruvian has the same bill depth/length ratio but is heavier). The browns become widely separated from both sexes of blue-foot. This difference is due to the great length of the blue-foot's bill which thus reduces its depth/length coefficient. It carries both sexes clear of all congeners except the Peruvian which (assuming feeding diversification is the advantage) does not matter where food is superabundant. The great sexual dimorphism is associated with the inshore fishing technique of the male and the sexual division of labour (p. 530).

(v) *Peruvian booby*

The Peruvian, 90 per cent of which are the sole sulids in their area, clearly falls among the

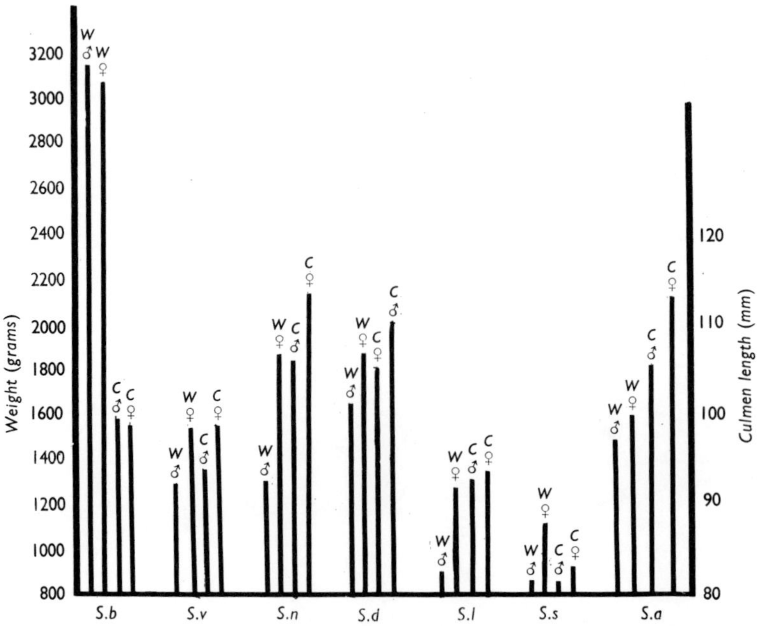

Fig. 368. Absolute weights and culmen lengths for all sulids.

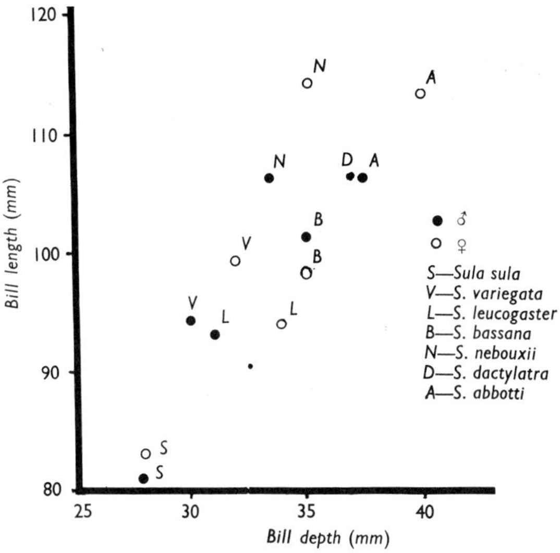

Fig. 369

Bill-length and depth in the Sulidae.

small-billed sulids (Fig. 369) with medium sexual dimorphism in bill-size (Fig. 370). Its weight mirrors these characteristics and thus the combined bill-length and weight sex difference (Fig. 370) is almost the slightest in the family, along with the gannet. In terms of bill depth in relation to weight (Fig. 371) both male and female have a relatively thinner bill than those sulids of the same weight, whilst in Fig. 372 the Peruvians fall out near to the male blue-foot. This type of bill certainly should be adapted to dealing with small or medium fish since anchovies are the Peruvian's staple diet, which accords well with the male blue-foot's inshore fishing. As mentioned, interspecific competition is not important to the Peruvian and there is no reason to expect marked divergence between it and the blue-foot.

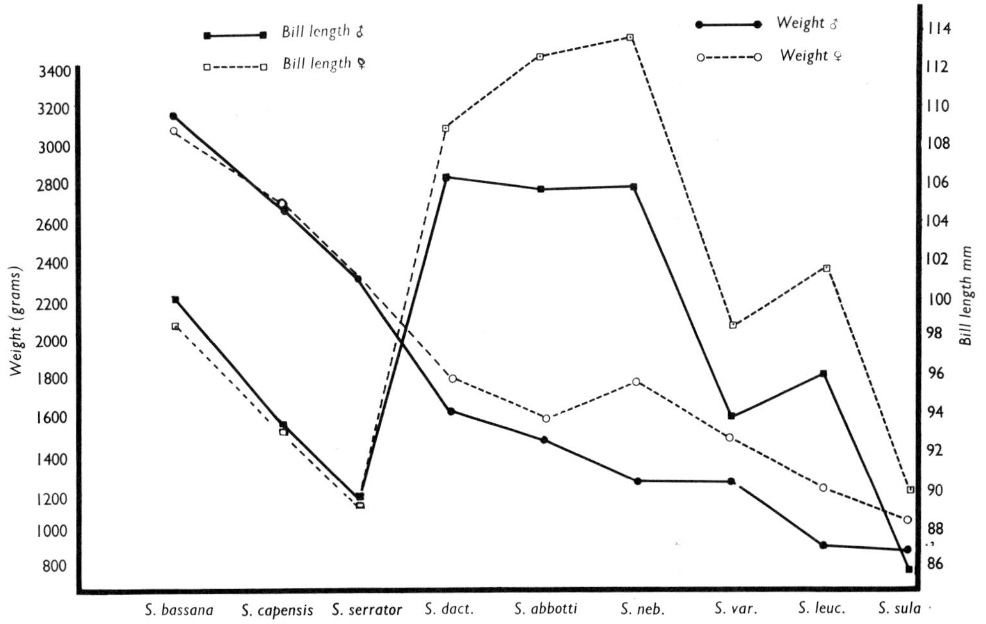

Fig. 370. Body-weight and bill-length in the Sulidae.

(vi) *Brown booby*

The white and red-footed boobies are the main species sympatric with the brown, whilst the blue-foot overlaps with it in the Gulf of California, in one large area. Brown boobies are relatively small-billed (Fig. 369) with considerable sexual dimorphism (Fig. 370) with which is associated corresponding dimorphism in weight. The combined bill-length and body-weight

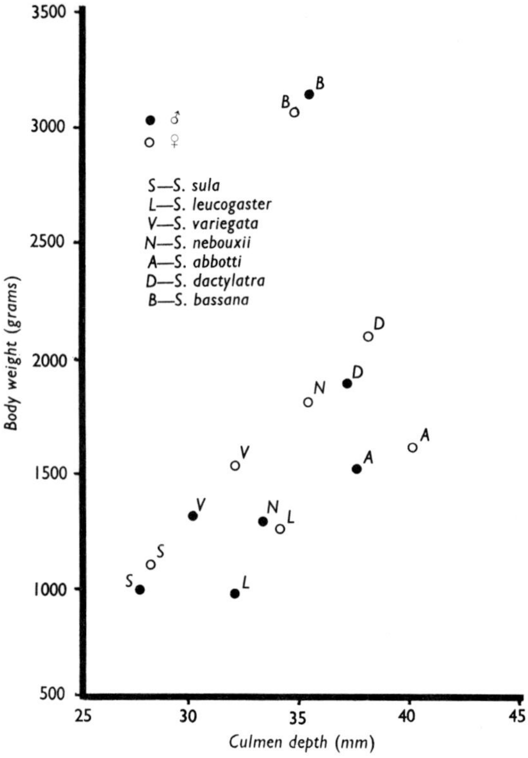

Fig. 371

Body-weight and bill-depth in the Sulidae.

Fig. 372

Relationship between the ratio of bill-depth/bill-length and body-weight in the Sulidae.

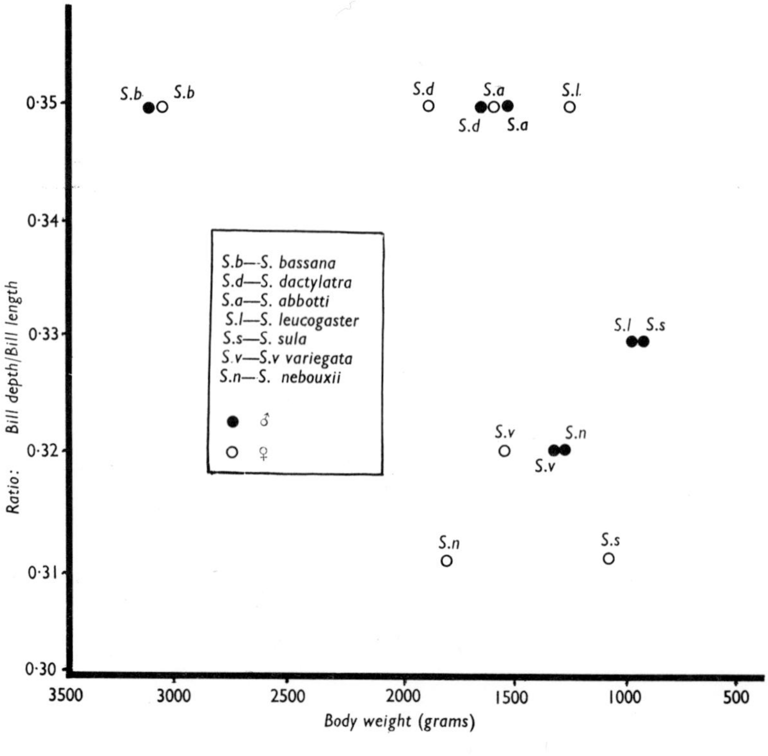

differential between sexes (Fig. 370) is not, however, as great as in several other sulids because the female's bill is not very large in absolute terms. The male's bill approximates most closely to the red-foot's, but is thicker. Similarly the female's bill is thicker than the equivalent-weight Peruvian's or blue-foot's. Their bills are thus slightly more powerful than these. In the ratio of depth/length to weight this emerges more clearly and the female brown ranks as the equal of the large-billed sulids, though considerably lighter and so less powerful. The male falls out alongside the male red-foot. This is interesting because these two are sympatric. Nevertheless, ecological separation is very evident since the male brown booby is much more of an inshore feeder than the far-foraging red-foot.

(vii) *Red-footed booby*

The red-foot is the smallest-billed sulid (Fig. 369) with relatively little sexual dimorphism in bill-size (Fig. 370). Overall, it is also the lightest species, though with more dimorphism in body-weight than bill-size. Its combined bill-length and weight difference (Fig. 370) is slight. In terms of bill depth in relation to weight the male is much thinner billed than the male brown, of equal (and very low) weight, and even the female, which is heavier than the male brown, is thinner billed than him. In the ratio of bill depth/length to weight the female red-foot becomes the smallest-billed sulid whilst the male falls alongside the male brown. The red-foot's small bill, light weight and long wings are all adaptations to its mode of feeding (p. 747) and to its extreme blue-water, offshore feeding habitat, which it shares to any large extent only with the white. It may thus be significant that the latter falls right at the other end of the weight and bill-size spectrum.

Clearly, there has been much adaptive radiation in weight and bill-size within the family, both between and within species, and this presumably has resulted in a more efficient exploitation of the prey spectrum. In no case does either sex of one species closely resemble either sex of another sympatric species both in these characters and in foraging and fishing techniques. The Peruvian and male blue-foot come close to doing so, but are a special case in an area of superabundant food. The Sulidae thus appear to be another example of the widely accepted phenomenon of adaptive radiation in feeding perhaps comparable to sympatric tropical terns (Ashmole 1968). Judging from the subtle differences in the relationship between bill structure and body weight, each species, and in some cases, each sex, may have its own fishing technique and particular preferences in prey size and/or species, perhaps if only at certain times of the year.

3. *Regional variation in measurements*

Differences between species have arisen as a result of geographical isolation and subsequent divergence in response to local conditions. So it is to be expected that between races or even distinct populations of the same race there will be adaptive differences in morphology, as there are in ecology, these two being in any case interrelated.

Fig. 373 shows the degree of regional morphological variation in both sexes of the four species which have a wide distribution and therefore experience a range of environmental conditions. It is not practicable to interpret these morphological differences in detail and Fig. 373 must be taken simply as a guide to the degree of variability that exists, and as implying significant adaptations. Each column represents the extent of known variability (though the figures are not always adequate) in the feature (and sex) concerned; the smaller the column the more the geographical variation between the populations (named in relation to the number above each column). Note that the localities furnishing the largest and smallest measurements respectively need not be the same for each feature or sex. In fact they probably should be (unless, say, bills are smallest in one area but wings in another, or the smallest-billed females come from a different area than the smallest-billed males). Thus, from the Figure it may be seen that in the white booby, the male from Kuria Muria is only 83 per cent as heavy as the male from Kure Atoll and the female from the Southern Line Islands only 81 per cent as heavy as the Kure female. In wing-length however, the smallest male is 93 per cent as large as the largest, and the female 89 per cent.

Many comparisons may be drawn from the Figure but I will simply indicate three.

1. The white booby seems geographically more variable than the other three species. This may be because, as the largest booby, with the least sexual dimorphism, it has most room for morphological manoeuvre. The others, especially the blue-foot and brown have, as a result of marked sexual dimorphism, already pushed intra-specific variation fairly far, irrespective of geographical variation.
2. The relatively great variation in culmen length in the male red-foot (between Galapagos and Phoenix Island males) reflects the fairly large Galapagos form adapted to an impoverished environment (p. 692) and the extremely tiny Central Pacific form represented on Phoenix. Why the female should vary proportionately less is not clear.
3. The extremely little variation between different populations of male blue-foots may reflect the well-marked sexual dimorphism which has already produced a small, specialised male.

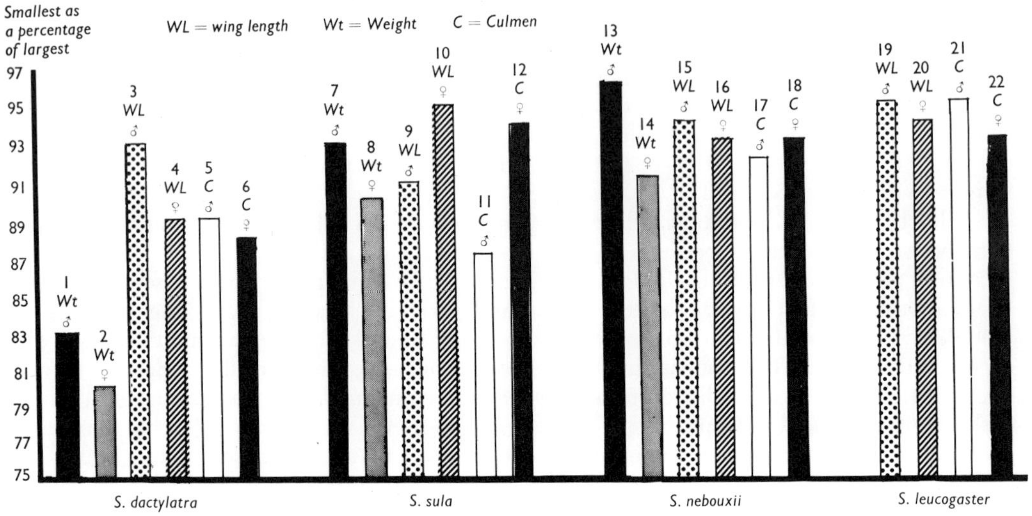

Fig. 373. Comparative measurements in the Sulidae showing geographical variations in species with a wide distribution. Christmas Island refers to the one in the Indian Ocean.

1. max. Kure. *S.d. personata.*
   min. Kuria Murias. *S.d. personata.*
2. max. Kure.
   min. S. Line Is. *S.d. personata.*
3. max. Ecuador and Peru. *S.d. granti.*
   min. Kuria Murias.
4. max. Galapagos. *S.d. granti.*
   min. Atlantic. *S.d. dactylatra.*
5. max. Galapagos.
   min. Atlantic.
6. max. Ecuador and Peru.
   min. Atlantic.
7. max. Galapagos. *S.s. websteri.*
   min. Christmas Is. *S.s. rubripes.*
8. max. Galapagos.
   min. Christmas Is.
9. max. Christmas Is.
   min. Phoenix. *S.s.* (? race)
10. max. Caribbean. *S.s. sula.*
    min. Tromelin. *S.s. rubripes.*
11. max. Galapagos.
    min. Phoenix.
12. max. Christmas Is.
    min. Caribbean. *S.s. sula.*
13. max. Panama and Peru. *S.n. nebouxii.*
    min. Galapagos. *S.n. excisa.*
14. max. Galapagos.
    min. Panama and Peru.
15. max. Galapagos.
    min. Panama and Peru.
16. max. Galapagos.
    min. Panama and Peru.
17. max. Mexico. *S.n. nebouxii.*
    min. Panama and Peru.
18. max. Galapagos.
    min. Panama and Peru.
19. max. Christmas Is. *S.l. plotus*
    min. Central. Amer. *S.l. etesiaca.*
20. max. Christmas Is.
    min. Central Amer.
21. max. Christmas Is.
    min. Central Amer. *S.l. etesiaca* and *brewsteri.*
22. max. Christmas Is.
    min. Ascension. *S.l. leucogaster.*

COMPARATIVE IDENTIFICATION FEATURES

Adult sulids pose few problems but immature birds can be difficult. The key (Table 127 below) should permit a sulid to be tracked down without checking laboriously through species' accounts. This Table is an attempt to define the areas of possible confusion and to provide enough diagnostic features to eliminate these. The main unsatisfactory group is that containing the variable immature, but post-juvenile, forms of white and red-footed boobies. It becomes impracticably complex to try to define all the possible permutations and combinations, further confused by several adult morphs of the red-foot. But size is usually diagnostic and at close quarters, the colours of beak and face and feet. The identification Figures 374 and 375 should also help.

To help identify dead birds, or wings which may be in poor condition, Appendix 15 gives outline characteristics of three outermost primaries for all species.

TABLE 127

IDENTIFICATION

Species	Normal distribution	Overlaps at sea with	Adult may be confused with	Size
North Atlantic gannet	North Sea N.E. Atlantic offshore south to Senegal	None Cape gannet Brown booby	Cape gannet White booby Red-footed booby	Large
	N.W. Atlantic offshore south to Gulf of Mexico	Brown booby White booby Red-footed booby		
Cape gannet	S.E. Atlantic	Atlantic gannet Brown booby White booby	Atlantic gannet White booby Red-footed booby	Large
	Indian Ocean	Brown booby White booby Red-footed booby		
Australasian gannet	Pacific around New Zealand and off S. and E. Australia	Brown booby White booby Red-footed booby	White booby Red-footed booby	Large
White booby	Tropical Atlantic	Atlantic gannet Cape gannet Brown booby Red-footed booby		Large
	Tropical Pacific	Australasian gannet Brown booby Blue-footed booby Peruvian booby Red-footed booby	All gannets Red-footed booby	
	Indian Ocean	Cape gannet Brown booby Red-footed booby Abbott's booby		
Brown booby	Tropical Atlantic	Atlantic gannet Cape gannet White booby Red-footed booby		
	Tropical Pacific	Australasian gannet White booby Blue-footed booby Red-footed booby	None	Male medium Female large
	Indian Ocean	Cape gannet White booby Red-footed booby Abbott's booby		

OF THE SULIDAE

Principal and diagnostic features of adult	Juvenile or immature may be confused with:	Principal features of juvenile or immature
All white except black primaries; yellowish head; blue bill. Distinguished by: size, white tail and secondaries combined with blue bill, white humerals.	Immatures of: Cape gannet White booby Brown booby Red-footed booby	Not certainly distinguishable from Cape. Black rather than brown non-white areas, bluish bill and iris distinguish it from white booby. Ventral pattern and underwing distinctive in brown booby. Red-foot much smaller.
As Atlantic, except for having black secondaries and tail.	As Atlantic	As Atlantic
As Cape, but only central tail feathers black and feet blackish	Immatures of: Brown booby White booby Red-footed booby	As Atlantic
Dazzling white, black primaries, secondaries, tail and humerals. Orange bill and eyes and black face. Distinguished by: Black humerals, orangy beak and eye.	Immatures of: All gannets Brown booby Blue-footed booby Peruvian booby Red-footed booby	Large; white extends on to throat, lacks pectoral band or white rump patch, otherwise brown. Post-juvenile is so variable that no diagnostic pattern distinguishes it from all possible plumages of other species, but size easily distinguishes it from red-foot.
Brown above; brown head, neck and upper breast. Greenish yellow bill. Distinguished by: Sharp demarcation between brown upper breast and white belly. Yellowish feet and bill.	Immatures of: All gannets White booby Blue-footed booby Red-footed booby	Diagnostic underwing pattern also usually distinct though dull version of the adult pectoral demarcation line.

TABLE 127—*contd.*

Species	Normal distribution	Overlaps at sea with	Adult may be confused with	Size
Blue-footed booby	Eastern Pacific from Gulf of California to Peru	Brown booby White booby Peruvian booby Red-footed booby	Brown booby Peruvian booby	Male small Female large
Peruvian booby	Off Peru and northern Chile	Brown booby White booby Blue-footed booby	Adult blue-foot, late immature white booby	Medium
Red-footed booby	Tropical Atlantic	White booby Brown booby	White morph with: White booby Cape and Australasian gannets	
	Tropical Pacific	Australasian gannet Brown booby White booby Blue-footed booby	Brown morph with: juveniles of: White booby Brown booby Blue-footed booby	Small
	Indian Ocean	Cape gannet White booby Brown booby Abbott's booby		
Abbott's booby	E. Indian Ocean within 500km of Christmas Island rarely mid-Indian Ocean	Brown booby White booby Red-footed booby	White booby Red-footed booby	Large

Principal and diagnostic features of adult	Juvenile or immature may be confused with:	Principal features of juvenile or immature
Streaked head and neck, white underparts, white nape and rump patch. Distinguished by: Streaked head, white nape and rump, bright blue feet.	Immatures of: Brown booby, White booby, Peruvian booby, Red-footed booby	Head not streaked. White rump and nape patch. Most likely to be confused with brown, but this has distinctive underwing and lacks rump and nape patches, as does paler, drabber Peruvian.
White head, neck and underparts. Brown back, wings, tail and flanks, drab feet.	Immatures of: Brown booby, White booby, Blue-footed booby	Generally drab, fawnish underparts, grey-brown head and neck; darker back and wings. No abrupt demarcation line or white patches. Smaller than white.
1. White morph a. Black primaries and secondaries, black extending to flanks. Tail white. b. As above but black not extending to flanks (inner secondaries white). Tail white. c. As (a) but mainly black tail (Galapagos) 2. All brown morph (Galapagos, Cocos). 3. White-tailed brown morph (tail and rump white). All have blue bill and red feet. Distinguished from white by: Blue bill, red feet, no black humerals, smaller size. Distinguished from gannets by: White tail, red feet, smaller. Distinguished from juveniles by: Blue bill, red feet and lack of white nape or rump patches.	Immatures of: Cape gannet, Austral. gannet, White booby, Brown booby, Blue-footed booby	Juvenile has black bill; lacks any white patches or sharp demarcation lines; lacks brown's diagnostic underwing. Immatures not distinguishable from all possible plumages of other species, but smaller than gannets or white booby and lacks specific features of juvenile brown and blue-foot. Also bill blue or turning blue and feet reddish.
White head, neck and underparts, black wings and tail. White back with black blotches and bold black blotches on flanks. Distinguished from white by black wings and thigh patches. Red-foot much smaller and mainly white-winged.	As adult	Resembles adult

TABLE 128

COLOURED PARTS IN SULIDS (LIVING BIRDS; SKINS ARE COMPLETELY UNRELIABLE)

	Gannets (all three)			White booby		
	Adult	Immature	Chick	Adult	Immature	Chick
Beak	Light grey-blue	Turning non-descript to clouded and mottled bluish	Black	Yellow to orange or greenish	Turning to dull yellowish	Greyish horn
Facial skin	Black	Black	Black	Black	Darkening until black	Creamy or pinkish turning to pale grey or bluish
Feet	Grey to black with yellow/green-blue lines	Grey to black. Lines distinct by 2nd year	Dark grey	Dark grey to olive/khaki to orange	Nondescript. Brightening to adult shades	Greyish
Iris	Pale grey with more dark pigment in Cape & Australasian	Turning pale (nondescript, suffused grey-blue by end 2nd year)	Deep (blue or brown)	Yellow to orange	Brightening from grey to yellowish	Lead grey

	Brown booby			Blue-foot			Peruvian		
	Adult	Immature	Chick	Adult	Immature	Chick	Adult	Immature	Chick
Beak	Yellowish to lime green, bluish at tip	Pale and drab (bluish) to yellowish	Livid blue-grey to greenish	Dark, slaty blue	Becoming bluish	Black	Lead grey to reddish or purplish	Bluish	Bluish
Facial skin	Yellow to green, with blue areas or tinge	Pale greyish-green	Yellow-green or bluish	Dark greyish	Dull greyish-blue	Grey	Dark grey or bluish	Grey-blue	Pale greyish
Feet	Green to chrome yellow	Dull greenish	Pale greenish	Bright blue or turquoise	Becoming brighter blue	Dull grey-blue	Lead grey or bluish	Greyish, lighter than adult	Grey
Iris	Pale greyish or yellowish to whitish, to dark	Pale grey	Pale grey	Pale yellow	Becoming lighter and yellowish	Dark hazel to brown	Red-brown	Yellowish becoming brown and red	Dark

TABLE 128—*contd.*

	Red-foot			Abbott's booby		
	Adult	Immature	Chick	Adult	Immature	Chick
Beak	Blue	Becoming grey and bluish, tip sometimes dark, sometimes horn-coloured	Blackish	Pale grey-blue (male) pink (female) blackish tip	Presumed grey-blue	Pale grey-blue
Facial skin	Red, blue and greenish	Becoming pale and bluish	Blackish	Blackish	Blackish	Grey
Feet	Red	Khaki/orange/reddish	Greyish becoming puce/khaki	Dark grey; ends of webs black	Dark grey	Grey, becoming darker
Iris	Variable. Grey, yellowish or brown	As chick	Variable. Light grey, or blue through yellowish to brown	Dark brown	Brown	Brown

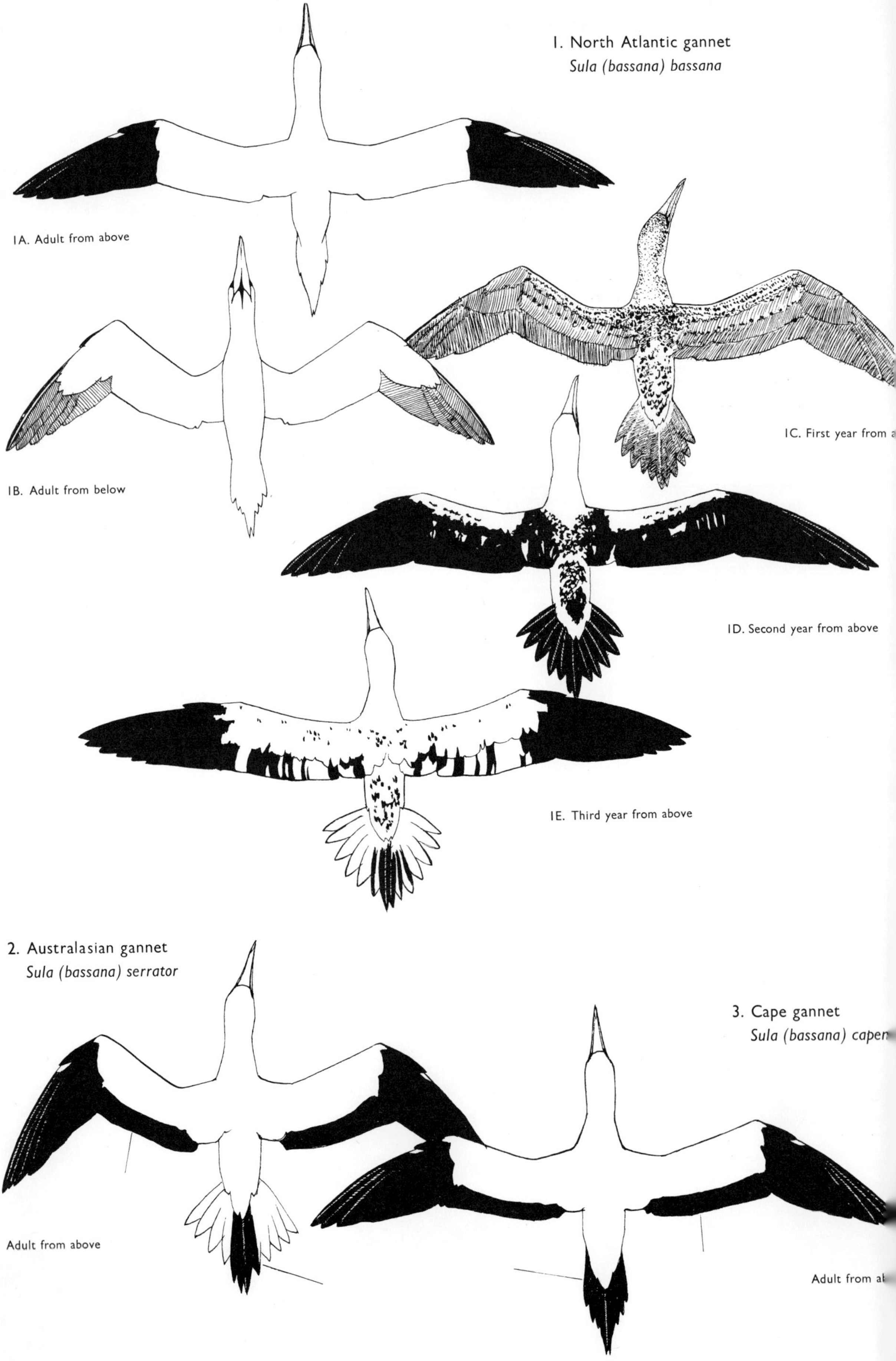

1. North Atlantic gannet
Sula (bassana) bassana

1A. Adult from above

1B. Adult from below

1C. First year from a

1D. Second year from above

1E. Third year from above

2. Australasian gannet
Sula (bassana) serrator

Adult from above

3. Cape gannet
Sula (bassana) capen

Adult from ab

(Leaders indicate diagnostic features)

Fig. 374. Comparative identification drawings of sulids in flight.

1. *North Atlantic gannet.* C–E. Plumages common late in the first year, second year and third year respectively.

2. *Australasian gannet.* Distribution makes confusion with the Atlantic gannet impossible. Immatures more finely marked than Atlantic birds. Tail of adult variable in amount of black.

3. *Cape gannet.* The tail of the adult is variable (see Fig. 104). Confusion with advanced third year Atlantic gannets is obviated by the unbroken black secondaries of the Cape bird and (usually) much more black in the tail. Immatures are probably much as in the Atlantic bird and probably often indistinguishable. The main area of overlap is probably in the Gulf of Guinea.

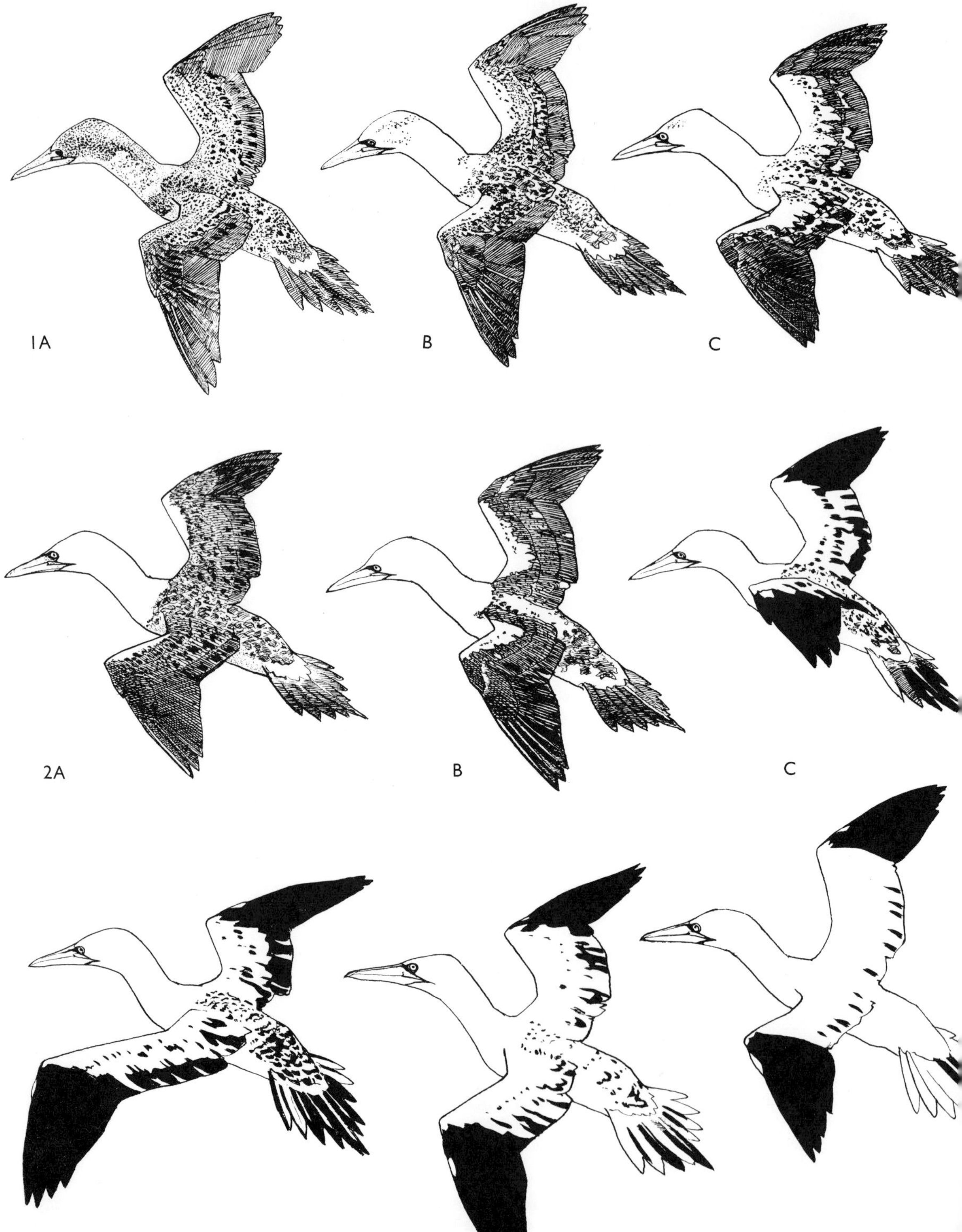

North Atlantic gannet: variation in plumage
in first, second and third years

Fig. 374—contd.

1A. Typical of a bird during the latter part of the first half of its first year. The juvenile plumage in which it fledged has already abraded or been replaced on parts of the neck, producing a hint of the 'collared' appearance common in late first-year birds. Often, the wings and back are browner than at fledging. Occasionally seen in home waters in this plumage.

B. Common late in the first year and often into the second. The head may remain completely dark into the second year.

C. Unusually advanced plumage, occasionally found at the end of year one, probably in birds which have assumed year two plumage early. Such birds may be late year one or any stage of year two.

2A. Common early in second year; head and underparts are usually the first areas to become white. May be found late in first year.

B. The 'epaulette' stage. Very common in mid- or late-second year. Often, the white on rump encircles the darker patch, giving a 'rosette' rump. The bill may now be pale blue.

C. An advanced two-year old which may retain this plumage in part of year three. Bill blue and head may be yellow.

3A. Common early in third year, except rarely so much black on back and rump, though scapulars often retain black feathers.

B. Perhaps the plumage most typical of mid- to fairly late-third year.

C. A very common plumage in late-third and part- or all-of-the-fourth year, with black secondaries gradually disappearing to give a four-year old with only one or two and/or one or two black tail feathers (central). A few birds acquire perfect adult plumage in their fourth year.

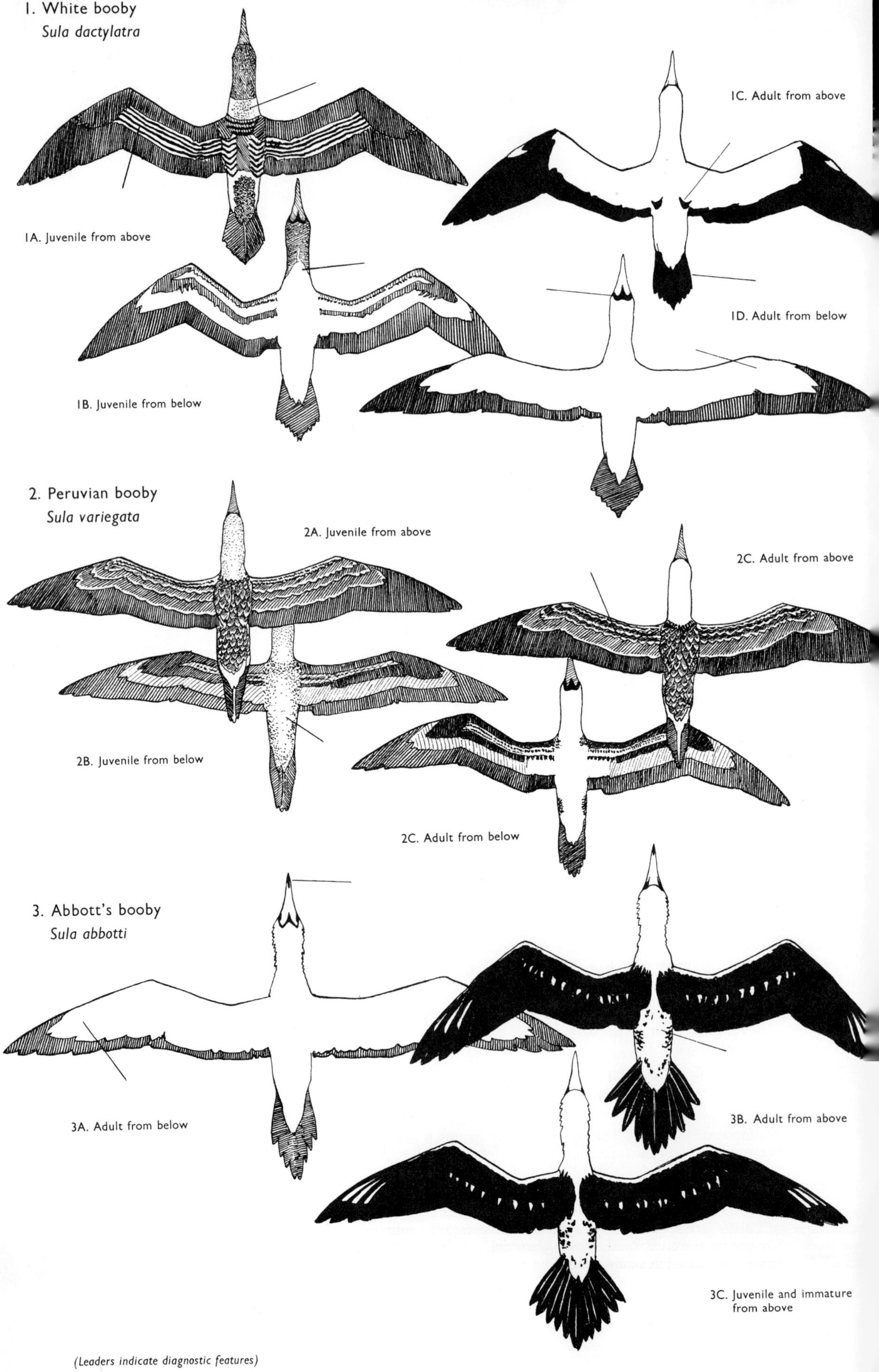

(Leaders indicate diagnostic features)

Fig. 374—contd.

1. *White booby*. A. Juvenile and first year. Collar may be more or less pronounced; pattern on back and wings shown semi-diagrammatically.

   B. Demarcation of inverted 'V' on throat sometimes vague.

   C. Black humerals distinguish it from white morph red-footed boobies, most of which also have a white tail.

   D. Lack of black patches in carpal region distinguishes it from the red-foot (Fig. 374).

2. *Peruvian booby* A. Juvenile and first year; the head is dingy, pale brown indicated by speckling on drawing.

   B. Underparts variably suffused fawn or pale brown, sometimes looking vaguely barred.

   C. Upper wing often 'ripple-patterned' due to buff-edged coverts. Sometimes uniform deep brown. Tail variably bleached.

3. *Abbott's booby*. B. Diagnostic combination of pure white head, neck and underparts; black wings and tail and patches of black on lower back and flanks. White feathers in wing coverts not always visible.

   C. Juvenile resembles adult.

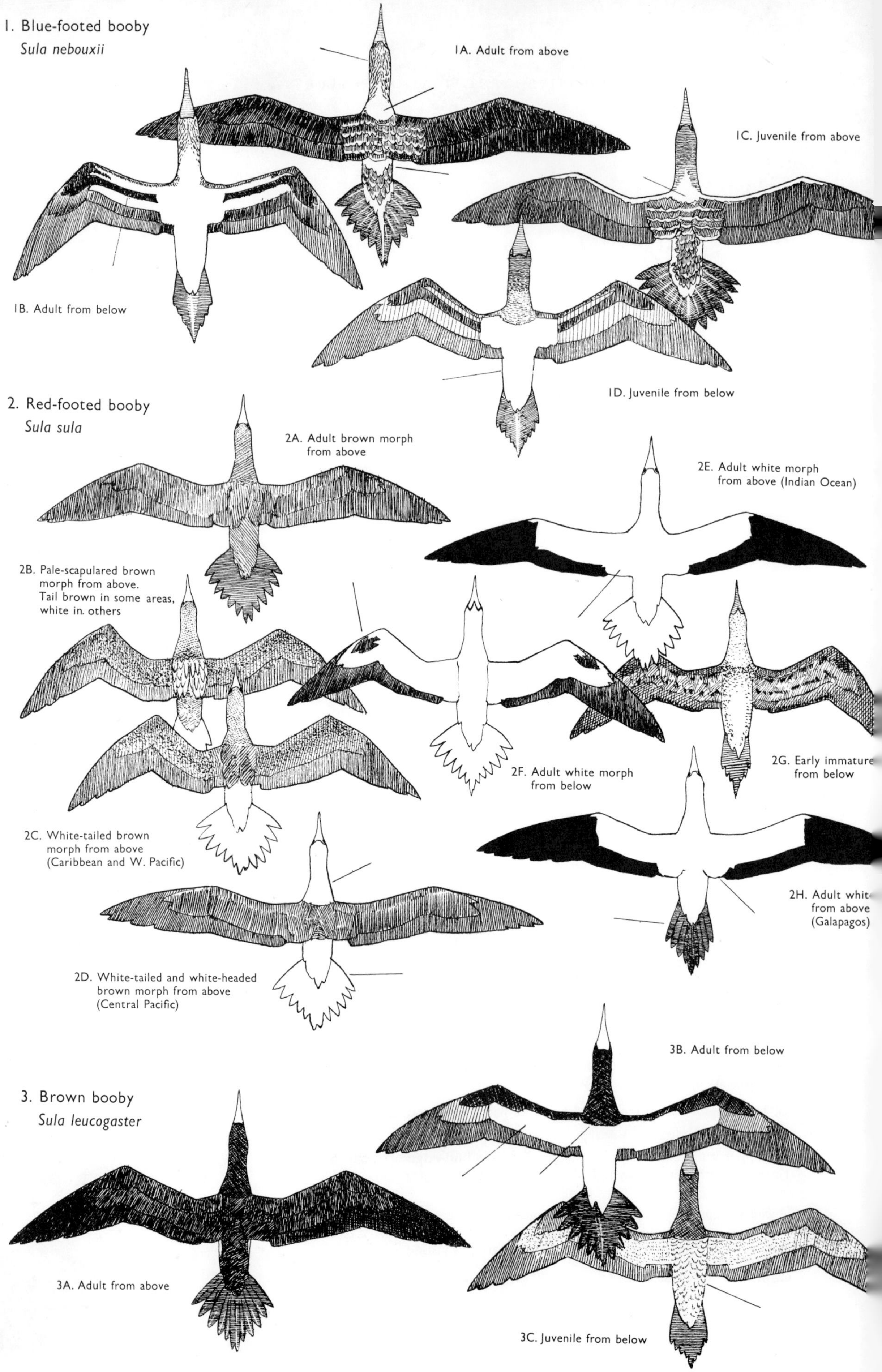
1. Blue-footed booby
Sula nebouxii
1A. Adult from above
1B. Adult from below
1C. Juvenile from above
1D. Juvenile from below
2. Red-footed booby
Sula sula
2A. Adult brown morph from above
2B. Pale-scapulared brown morph from above. Tail brown in some areas, white in others
2C. White-tailed brown morph from above (Caribbean and W. Pacific)
2D. White-tailed and white-headed brown morph from above (Central Pacific)
2E. Adult white morph from above (Indian Ocean)
2F. Adult white morph from below
2G. Early immature from below
2H. Adult whit from above (Galapagos)
3. Brown booby
Sula leucogaster
3A. Adult from above
3B. Adult from below
3C. Juvenile from below

(Leaders indicate diagnostic features)

Fig. 374—contd.

1. *Blue-footed booby*. A. Streaked head, white nape and rump patches are diagnostic.

   C. White rump patch sometimes more obvious than here.

   D. Upper breast region variable but often with clear demarcation line and never with inverted V of juvenile white booby.

2. *Red-footed booby*. A. The adult all-brown morph (Galapagos and Pacific Cocos Island). The exact shade and degree of uniformity is variable.

   B. An adult brown morph with pale buff to whitish scapulars. In some regions the tail is brown (Galapagos) and in others white (west Indian Ocean and parts of west and central Pacific).

   C. White-tailed brown morph (e.g. Caribbean).

   D. A central Pacific (e.g. Canton Island) form, particularly small and with white (or very pale) head and neck and white rump and tail; back and wings dark brown, fairly uniform.

   E. Adult white morph.

   G. Juveniles are uniformly brown above and paler below. The back later becomes patchy brown and white and the underparts variably patterned brown and white.

   H. Adult white morph with tail blackish e.g. Galapagos.

3. *Brown booby*. A. The uniformly dark 'cowl' is usually diagnostic, but one form (*Sula leucogaster nesiotes*) has a lighter coloured head. The uniformly deep brown back and wings are also diagnostic.

   B. This distinctive underwing pattern is diagnostic.

   C. The brown crescentic markings are not found in all juveniles, tending to appear in immatures as the more uniformly drab belly becomes patterned with more white.

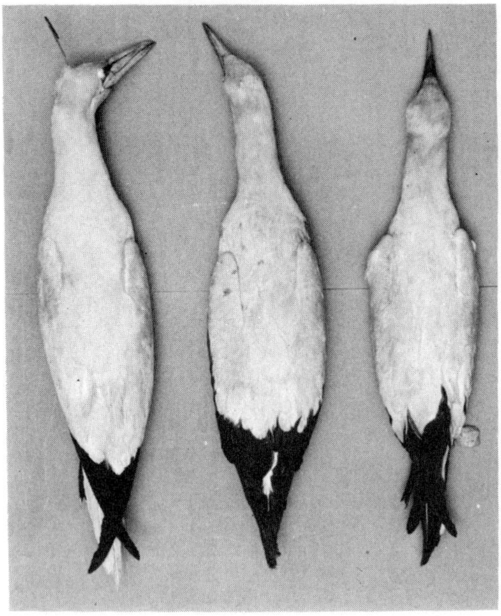

(1) *S.* [*b.*] *bassana, S.* [*b.*] *capensis* (Cape Gannet). *S.* [*b.*] *serrator* (Australasian gannet), adults, dorsal.

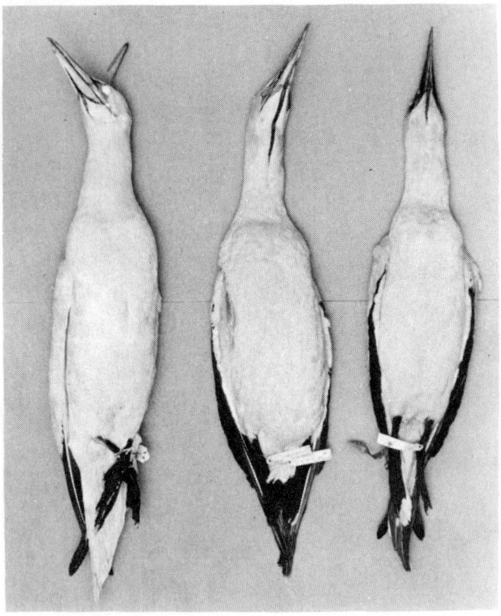

(2) *S.* [*b.*] *bassana, S.* [*b.*] *capensis, S.* [*b.*] *serrator*, adults, ventral.

[The skins on these plates are mounted *left–right*].

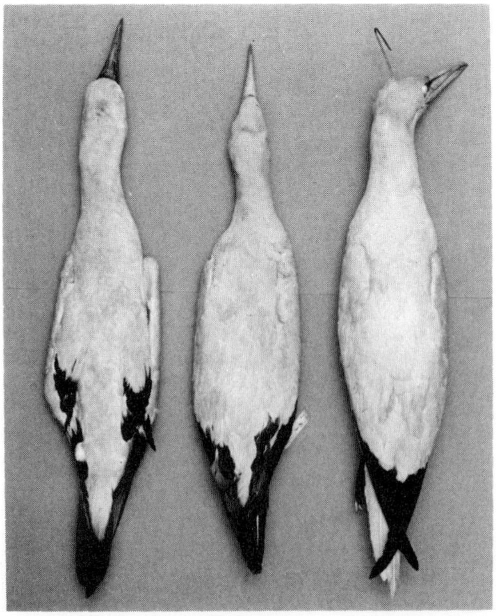

(3) *S. dactylatra, S.* [*b.*] *capensis, S.* [*b.*] *bassana*, adults, dorsal. Note black humerals on *dactylatra*.

Fig. 375. Comparative identification photographs (museum skins).

(4) [*S. b.*] *capensis*, *S.* [*b.*] *bassana*, *S.* [*b.*] *serrator*, juveniles, ventral.

(5) *S.* [*b.*] *capensis*, *S.* [*b.*] *bassana*, *S.* [*b.*] *serrator*, juveniles, dorsal. Despite variability, the paler underparts on *serrator* is typical.

(6) *S.* [*b.*] *capensis*, *S.* [*b.*] *serrator*, *S.* [*b.*] *bassana*, immatures, dorsal. The degree of immatúrity may not be exactly the same in all; *S.* [*b.*] *bassana* is late second year. *S.* [*b.*] *capensis* may be younger.

Fig. 375—contd.

Fig. 375—contd.

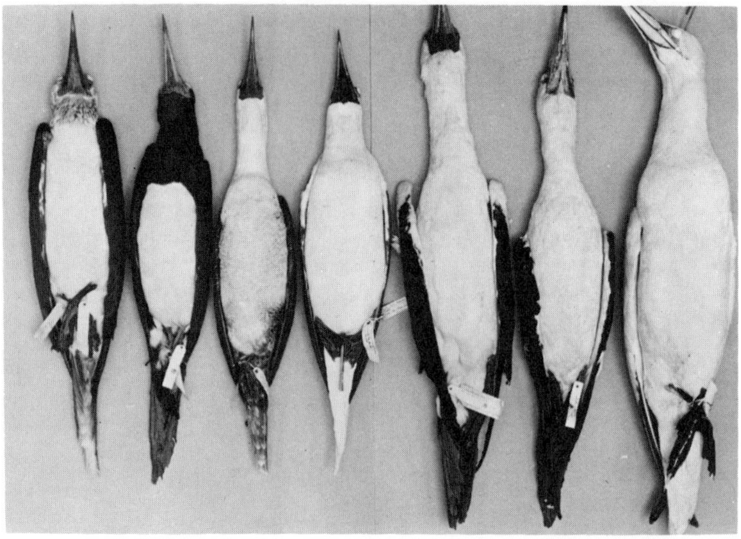

(7) *Sula nebouxii*, *S. leucogaster*, *S. variegata*, *S. sula*, *S. dactylatra*, *S. abbotti* and *S.* [*b.*] *bassana* (Atlantic gannet); ventral. All adult except *S. variegata* which is slightly immature.

[Skins mounted *left–right*].

(8) *S. nebouxii*, *S. leucogaster*, *S. variegata*, *S. sula*, *S. dactylatra*, *S. abbotti* and *S.* [*b.*] *bassana*; dorsal.

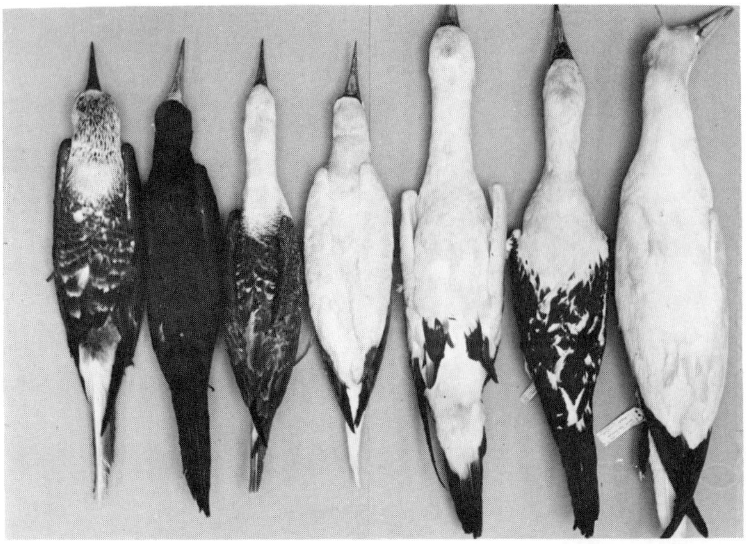

(9) *Sula dactylatra,* stages of immaturity.

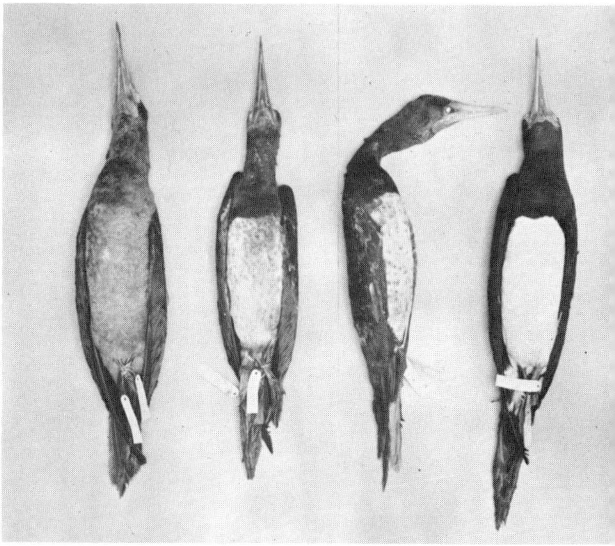

(10) *Sula leucogaster* (brown booby). Juvenile, two immatures and adult.

(11)
Two *Sula leucogaster* and two immature *S. dactylatra* to compare pattern of ventral surface.

Fig. 375—contd.

Fig. 375—contd. [Skins mounted *left–right*]

(12) *Sula variegata* (Peruvian booby), immature, ventral.

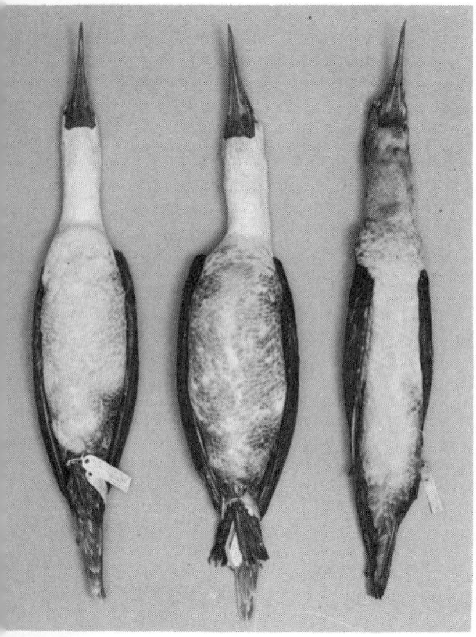

(13) *S. variegata*, immature, dorsal.

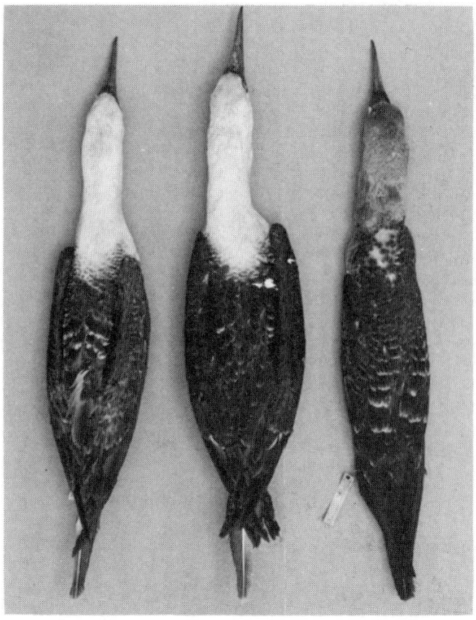

(14) *S. variegata* (almost fully adult), *S. nebouxii* (blue-footed booby; adult), *S. nebouxii* (immature).

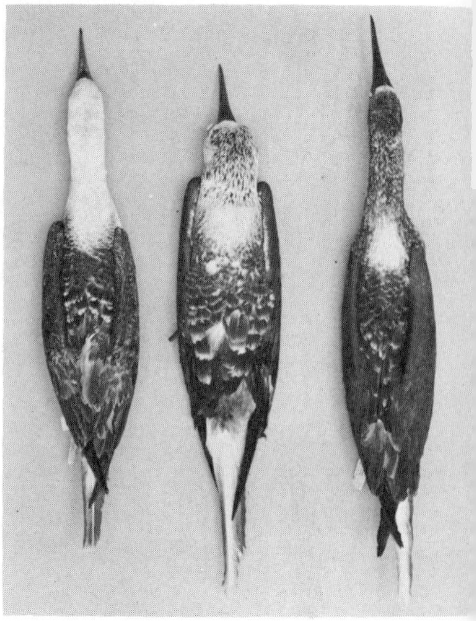

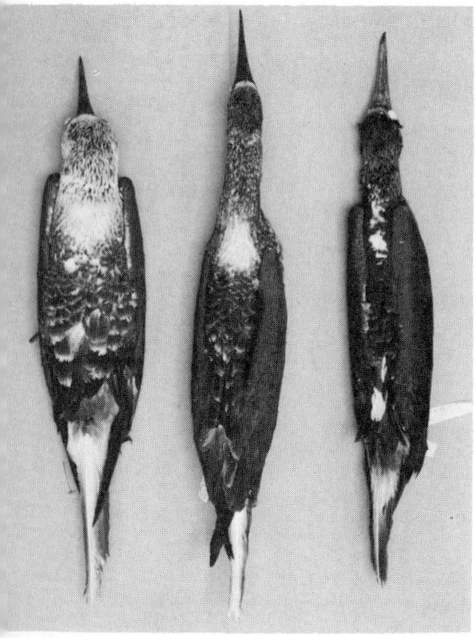

(15) *S. nebouxii*, adult and two stages of immature, dorsal.

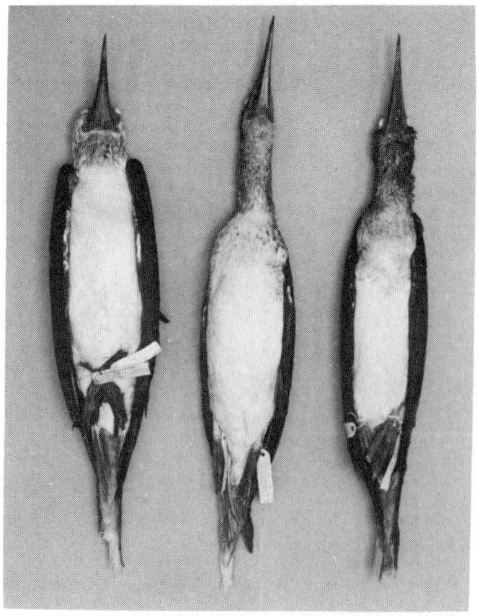

(16) *S. nebouxii*, ditto, ventral.

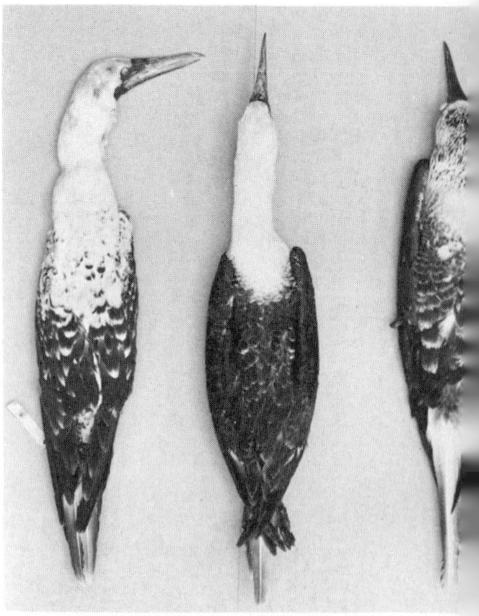

(17) *S. dactylatra* (white booby, immature); *S. variegata* (adult); *S. nebouxii* (adult).

(18)

Sula sula (red-footed booby).

Brown morph (dorsal)

Brown morph (ventral)

White-tailed brown morph (ventral)

White-tailed brown morph (dorsal)

White morph.

[Skins mounted *left–right*]

(19)

Immature stages of white morph *Sula sula* (ventral).

Note pectoral band.

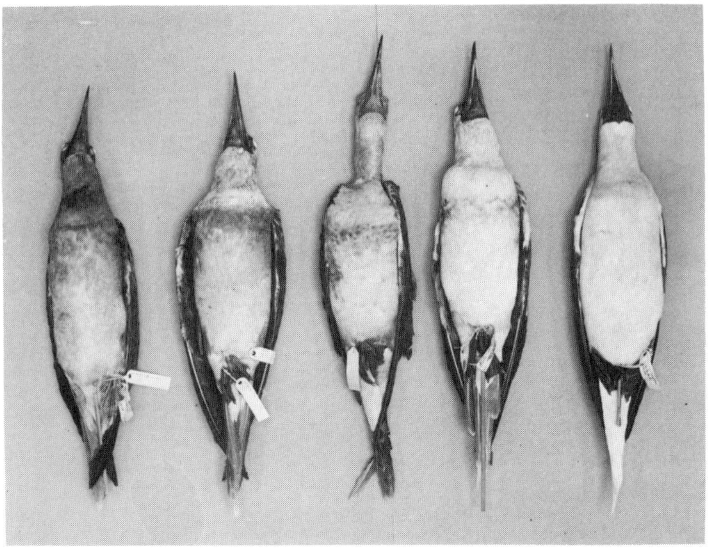

(20)

Immature stages of white morph *Sula sula* (dorsal).

Fig. 375 completed.

2. NUMBERS AND DISTRIBUTION

INTRODUCTION

The Sulidae is an ancient and successful group, widespread and numerous. Adaptive radiation into areas differing greatly in climate and oceanography has imposed different feeding methods and therefore different reproductive regimes and patterns of breeding success and of mortality of young. Similarly, radiation into different breeding habitats has imposed different sets of selection pressures. These factors have largely determined present-day numbers and distribution. It will rarely be possible to say *why* one of two common species is the more numerous and widespread, but in some cases there are pointers. This section seems the most appropriate place to discuss colony size, also.

COMPARATIVE NUMBERS IN THE SULIDAE

Compared with petrels, terns or auks no sulid is really numerous, but few large seabirds greatly outnumber the three tropical boobies and, but for the great man-wrought reduction that has undoubtedly occurred, they might have been the world's most numerous large seabirds.

Sulids fall into two distinct groups (Fig. 376). The pan-tropical trio and the Peruvian are about 10 to 40 times as common as the others. This is largely because the white, brown and red-footed occur over vast (though sometimes impoverished) areas whereas the others are highly restricted. The Peruvian, too, is highly restricted but the small area which it inhabits is uniquely rich and can support an enormous local population.

Since there is usually no shortage of nesting sites for any of the three tropical species, and little difference in their natural (man-independent) recruitment and mortality rates, the red-foot's dominant position may depend largely on the protection afforded by its tree-nesting habit. In many areas, man may have exerted extremely heavy pressure on the large, highly palatable ground-nesting boobies, the adults of which would be particularly vulnerable to sporadic raiding parties. The population of an entire island could easily be exterminated over a relatively short period, and indeed the Mascarenes, Marquesas, Mauritius, Assumption, Glorioso and many islands in Micronesia, to name but a few, have entirely lost certain species through man's agency. Some present-day anomalies in distribution may be due to this.

The remaining sulids are more specialised. Abbott's booby once had a much wider distribution in the Indian Ocean and the main factor in its decline appears to have been destruction of habitat. However (disregarding the threat of further destruction on Christmas Island) it is impossible to say what controls its numbers today. Man certainly has not been responsible for keeping the Christmas Island population down to its present level, nor is there any lack of nesting sites. Though still common, the blue-foot almost certainly has decreased in the Gulf of California. Indeed touristic and other development of this area is now giving conservationists good cause for concern. It has decreased, too, in the once populous Lobos de Tierra island, off northern Peru, but its Galapagos population thrives. Its restriction to the fringes of productive, cold-water areas is partly responsible for its relatively small world population. Its penetration into the Humboldt area was followed by specialisation and subsequent, relatively recent, divergence to give the present-day blue-footed and Peruvian boobies. The three gannets, also, are fairly clear cases of specialisation and restriction to well-defined and relatively small areas. The Atlantic population is presumably climbing back to a previous ceiling, though it is impossible to say how high this once was. Again man was responsible for the huge drop in numbers. Much the same applies to the Australasian gannet. The Cape gannet may well now be declining, but its erstwhile optimal numbers are unknown.

COLONY SIZE—A GENERAL DISCUSSION WITH PARTICULAR REFERENCE TO SULIDS

The nature of any species' breeding dispersal is one of its most fundamental attributes. The hows and whys of colony structure, size and density inevitably lead to blind alleys because speculation requires much more data on age structure, breeding success and the reasons for it than are usually available. The mounting number of studies on social aspects of breeding (see for example Crook 1965 and Nelson 1970 for references) are revealing the great complexity of social adaptations and long-term studies on a variety of species with varying recruitment rates, life spans and social structures are still badly needed. Coulson's (1966, 1968) classical work on kittiwakes has shown what can be achieved.

Are species colonial because of shortage of sites, relative safety from predators, or some more subtle advantages to do with social stimulation? Within relatively homogeneous habitats such as those occupied by many penguins, gulls, terns and boobies, what, if any, advantages accrue from *position* within a group (central or peripheral) or from membership of a *particular kind* of group (large, small, dense, sparser)? If, for example, central nests seem to succeed best, what factors mediate this? Are they mainly intra- or inter-specific? If the former, are the central

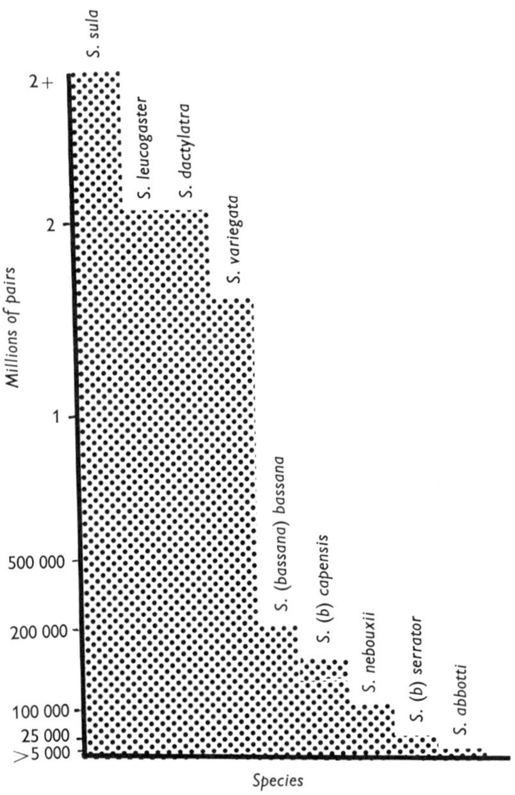

Fig. 376

A rough estimate of the world population of the sulids.

birds older (more experienced) or fitter in some way (bigger and heavier)? Do they lay earlier and if so how does this affect success? Are central nests sought after by peripheral birds and if so what does this imply about site and mate fidelity? We can rarely answer more than a few of these questions.

What is 'a' colony? Colonial implies visual and/or auditory contact with a number of conspecifics. The degree of contact and the numbers involved are highly arbitrary; populations, demes, colonies and sub-colonies or groups grade into each other and it is often quite impossible to demarcate them. In practice it rarely matters and one is usually concerned with a physiographically or arbitrarily defined group. But for comparative ecological and behavioural purposes it may be useful to define a species as colonial if its *typical* breeding dispersion is such that each individual sees, hears or frequently interacts with 'many' conspecifics, usually throughout breeding, but always at least in the pre-laying stages. 'Many' means tens, scores or hundreds. This definition accommodates the observation that many colonial species, even of the most extreme kind, *can* breed in very small groups or even solitarily; gannets typically congregate in thousands, but one or two pairs can breed, cut off by over 160km from the nearest colony. Most colonial species breed in crowded conditions and if terrain separates them (as in burrowing species) they interact densely in flight, or in congregations outside, as do petrels and shearwaters. An important property usually implied by colonial, is that members of a colony have, theoretically, a fair chance of interbreeding. This could be important in the evolution of groups with their own characteristics, behavioural and ecological as well as morphological. Usually birds remain faithful to their natal colony and indeed to their own group within it.

Sulids are not in the first rank when it comes to colony size. By far the biggest sulid colonies are those of the Peruvian booby (up to one million pairs) but the colonies of all other sulids rarely exceed 50 000 pairs, most are well below 10 000 and many, perhaps most, below 1000. This may be compared with the auks (several million guillemots on Bear Island; some five million little auks at two east-Greenland localities; until recently more than a million pairs of puffins on St. Kilda), shearwaters and petrels (some two million pairs of great shearwaters on Nightingale of the Tristan Islands; several colonies of Wilson's storm petrels holding more than a million pairs), terns (several estimates of colonies of many millions of wideawakes in various localities), albatrosses (more than 100 000 pairs of Laysan albatrosses on Laysan) and penguins (about 300 000 Adelie penguins at Cape Crozier, Ross Island).

Most colonial seabirds show variation in colony size by factors of many thousands. I know of none that actually *require* to breed in the company of at least 1000 neighbours and none always adjusts the size of its colonies to within reasonably constant limits. Even the size of a particular colony can vary enormously over sufficiently long periods. This implies (a) that absolute numbers are not important with respect to their social qualities, an obvious conclusion since even in the largest colonies each pair can be influenced socially by only a fraction of the total number, and (b) that colony size is imposed by external factors such as the location of the colony within the distributional range of the species, the availability of suitable breeding habitats and the nature of the surrounding food supply.

Although seabirds vary markedly in the upper limits of colony size, some seeming practically unlimited whilst others, including the sulids, have a loosely typical, though highly variable, colony size, there is no reason to think that size as distinct from density (discussed on p. 892) is ever regulated by behavioural mechanisms such as the exclusion of new breeders by old. Small colonies may be new ones growing bigger, old ones decimated by predators, disease or starvation, or distributional outposts with low breeding success and low recruitment. In the orthodox view, it is hardly surprising that intrinsic factors rarely if ever limit the size of seabird colonies, since the large colonies are in fact populations (or at least demes) and one would thus be postulating intrinsic population control (see p. 905).

If, however, demes are so controlled, then one would indeed expect to find social (behavioural) mechanisms limiting the component sections of the population, which are the breeding colonies or sub-colonies. Such mechanisms still have not been unequivocally demonstrated in seabirds and the circumstances outlined above, perhaps in combination, seem enough to explain the vast range in colony size.

Given the variation between and within sulids in colony size, one must ask what are the ultimate controlling factors. Food and nesting requirements are two vital ones which conceivably could regulate the total numbers of seabirds in any area and so influence colony size.

1. *Food and colony size*

Table 129 gives the upper and lower limits and a broadly estimated typical size for breeding colonies of sulids. The species with the largest typical colony size are those which breed near to a rich food supply. Within a species, the largest colonies are those situated near to a productive area or within a vast area of relatively impoverished sea but containing very few islands (this latter does not concern us at the moment).

Concerning the first point, the piquero's numerical relationship with the anchovies of the Humboldt has been fully discussed (p. 606) and is an indisputable example of superabundant food supporting vast booby and other seabird colonies; the largest recorded blue-foot colony was also on the fringe of this area (Lobos Islands). The proximity of the Benguela Current to the large colonies of Cape gannets and other seabirds is another case and the great colonies of Atlantic gannets in the vicinity of the prolific fisheries of the Grand Banks on the west and the rich herring, sprat, saithe, codling, whiting and mackerel fishing grounds (Icelandic Banks, Solan Banks, Ballantrae Banks, Minch, North Sea, Farne Deeps, etc.) in the east Atlantic, again associated with vast numbers of other seabirds, further illustrate this positive relationship between abundant local food and the tendency of whichever sulid species is present, to have a large 'typical' colony size.

Obvious though this may seem, its implied corollary is by no means proven. To suggest that a species could not form such large 'typical' colonies if food were scarcer is to imply that this is because competition would exist within the foraging area if numbers were large. This, however, is a theoretical postulate. There is no reason to suppose either that density-dependent competition occurs among piqueros, with their abundant anchovies, or among gannets in the North Sea or among the many thousands of red-foots ranging the often-impoverished Pacific around the Galapagos. Nor has one good reason to believe that the effects of a population of any sulid twice or ten times as great as the present one, in any area, would have the slightest effect on either the absolute numbers or the availability of their prey. In other words, plentiful food attracts large numbers of birds to an area, but this does not mean that it necessarily sets

TABLE 129

COLONY-SIZE IN THE SULIDAE (IN PAIRS)

Species	Maximum	Minimum	Very approx. 'typical' size at present day
Peruvian booby	360 000 (Mazorca 1960)	< 400 (Coquimbo 1972)	50 000?
Cape gannet	100 000 (Ichaboe 1956)	1 or 2 pairs (Bird Island, Lamberts Bay 1912)	20–30 000?
Atlantic gannet	55–60 000 (St. Kilda 1973) 125 000 (Bird Rocks, before 1850)	2 (Bempton 1930's)	5–10 000?
Australasian gannet	6000 (White Island 1971)	< 6 (Wedge Light, early 1970's)	1–2000
Blue-footed booby	10 000 + ? (Lobos de Tierra, 1930's)	2 or 3 (Tower, 1960's)	< 1000
Red-footed booby	140 000 (Tower Island 1964)	< 10 (Ascension 1960's, La Plata, 1976)	2000 or less?
White booby	5000 + (Malpelo, 1940's)	< 10 (some Line Islands)	1000 or less?
Brown booby	8–10 000 (Desecheo 1927)	< 50 (some Line Islands)	1000 or less?
Abbott's booby	one existing 'colony' of 2–3000 pairs, Christmas Island, Indian Ocean		

Note: The 'typical colony size' has strictly limited meaning, since (a) a 'colony' is impossible to define satisfactorily; (b) artefactual influences could be extremely important, but nevertheless it serves to illustrate certain points (see text).

the upper limits to population via direct competition. Thus it does not determine the precise size of the local population. Contrast, again, the piquero and the red-foot. When anchovies are abundant the number of piqueros almost certainly has no effect on the catch of any individual bird; the limits to the catch are simply those imposed by flying out, locating a shoal and then by the mechanics of diving repeatedly into the incalculable squadrons until replete. Alternatively, when anchovies fail, they disappear almost entirely, and there can be no real question of actual competition affecting an individual's catch; it is surely more a matter of luck in finding the rare shoal near enough the surface, or of greater ability to withstand starvation or willingness to fly further afield. In the case of the red-foot, it is probably facile and erroneous to assume that when chicks are starving by hundreds, things would be even worse if the population were twice as big. Whatever the factors which render food temporarily unavailable (probably oceanographic) feeding is not likely to be either better or worse as the result of less or more red-footed boobies quartering the vast areas of unproductive seas. If red-foots forage some 300km from Tower (and their range is probably much greater) their potential feeding area is some 300 000 sq km. Even if they do not forage evenly or singly over the vast expanse, is it conceivable that a population half or twice the size of the present one would result in meaningful differences in the catch of individual birds? The likelihood of a competing booby being at hand to catch a flying fish is, to say the least, remote. Far more important are the factors which control the movements and numbers of the flying fish and these factors are certainly not birds.

This does not dispute the widely accepted view that food is the main ultimate factor limiting seabird numbers and regulating their distribution; it simply suggests that, in practice as against theoretical possibility, the numbers of any sulid species do not rise to the level at which the logically inevitable competition would take effect.

What, then, prevents the attainment of this local population level?

1. So far as sulids are concerned, it seems possible that one mechanism is simply the fluctuations in food, operating independently of bird populations. Thus, piqueros increase until a catastrophic year vastly reduces their numbers. This increase would need to be truly exponential if one is to exclude the operation of some regulating factor, and we do not know whether in fact it is so between crashes. By contrast, red-foot breeding success in impoverished areas is so low that recruitment barely keeps pace with mortality; again the low success is certainly food-*mediated* but not competitively induced. This perhaps naive theory which excludes the importance of feed-back (regulation) from the existing numbers, encounters most difficulty in accommodating species such as the gannet, or populations of boobies in relatively productive areas such as the Indian Ocean Christmas Island, where there are no periodic catastrophes as in the piquero and no massive nestling mortality as in the Galapagos red-foots. The fluctuations in such species may be longer-term, perhaps much longer, but still correlated with food changes that are not mediated by direct competition between individual birds. The populations *depend* on the food, but do not themselves materially affect it. An important proviso here could be the possibility that the pressure of seabirds on their food supply is additive and that inter-specific competitions may be important. If density-dependent competition within a species is contentious and impossible to demonstrate, however, the mind boggles at the implications of interspecific density-dependent competition.

2. It has been suggested (Wynne-Edwards 1962) that the attainment of a population level sufficiently high to engender actual competition is prevented by various social (behavioural) mechanisms, themselves, no doubt, hormonally regulated, which reduce the rate of recruitment appropriately. This theory has great appeal but encounters some difficulties, which are best discussed under Recruitment Rates (p. 901). In the present context, the implication is that in any species the population 'carried' by the local food supply is adjusted to and maintained at a level which can be supported without depleting stocks and that if it rose much higher, depletion and competition would occur. As mentioned, it often seems that the population of any one species is relatively unimportant as a regulator of fish stocks (as for example, in the piquero) and therefore that a rise in the population of that particular fish eater would not lead to competition. If, on the other hand, the species-additive effect is considered to be paramount, then the problems of *inter*-specific mechanisms regulating populations of all food-sharing species, yet below the level of over-exploitation and competition, are formidable.

Thus the alternative theoretical explanations for the control of the size of a local sulid population through food are:

(a) food becomes limiting due to population growth, over-exploitation and competition (and this mechanism could work even if food were the object of competition for only a *small* part of the year, or less frequently still). Populations thus oscillate but cannot remain permanently below the exploitation level because when they are there, reproductive rates rise until populations come up against the ceiling. This process may involve interspecific competition via an additive effect on food. This view maintains that populations *are* in fact regulated, and hinges on actual competition for food.

(b) Food is limiting, but the population keeps itself below the ceiling by social means (reduced recruitment). The mechanism envisaged would seem to preclude ones which could work interspecifically, yet these would seem necessary for the model to operate efficiently. Furthermore, the theory depends on the 'voluntary' reduction of breeding effort, and/or the social control of recruitment, which even within any *one* species encounters theoretical difficulties and in some cases (such as the gannet, p. 126) apparently makes demands which actual observations do not support.

(c) Food limits population but *neither* through over exploitation and subsequent competition nor through socially mediated controls. It does so simply by periodically (and the periods may be frequent or very infrequent) becoming variably scarce so that mortality exceeds recruitment. The scarcity results not from overfishing by any one species but from other basically important factors such as changes in water temperature, alterations in primary productivity and in food items low in the food chain upon which fish are dependent. There are at least two objections to this. When food becomes scarce, competition would necessarily ensue. This may or may not be so, but in any case, firstly the birds need not have *caused* the scarcity by overexploitation and their populations at the time of the shortage would *not* have been up against a ceiling and secondly the shortage would not have been avoided by a lower bird population brought about by social control. The second objection is more basic. It seems that in higher vertebrates a model which supposes that there need be no actual regulation of population, and that numbers could be indefinitely buffered by chance, without a countering mechanism, could not work. I cannot comment usefully on this except to suggest that, for the reasons given above, the sulids—or at least some of them—are exceptions to this.

If (c) is a plausible model, it seems possible that, when food does become scarce, exploitation by the sum of all species which overlap in the food items taken, may for a period lead to interspecific competition.

2. *Nesting requirements and colony size*

Theoretically, shortage of suitable nest sites could limit the size of a colony or even a population, but, among sulids, the only possible candidate for such a situation is the Peruvian booby. The distribution of others, particularly the red-foot, depends on suitable habitats but the numbers on any island usually do not.

It would be taking a sledgehammer to crack a nut if one were to slog through a representative series of colonies for each species to prove that, in the great majority of cases, there was some—usually much—unoccupied habitat. It is usually obvious, and in any case, the point is dealt with in more detail under Density (p. 892), since dense nesting has often been held to result from shortage of nest sites.

DISTRIBUTION IN THE SULIDAE

INTRODUCTION

Understandably, most studies of seabirds are of breeding biology. It is extraordinarily difficutl, though crucially important, to study their activities at sea. There are many sources of confusion, and information is so patchy and incomplete that interpretation is dangerous. Most of this introduction concerns the bird at sea, but the section includes a brief analysis of sulid breeding distribution, before going on to their distribution at sea.

Except near their breeding places, most seabirds, and certainly sulids, are seen too infrequently to allow detailed analysis and the figures that *have* been obtained are apparently not highly replicable (contrast for example, the voyages of Gill (1967) and Bailey (1968)). Also, various factors inevitably associated with observations from a ship (its presence and movement, conditions at sea, seasonal effects etc.) can greatly affect the figures. Finally, information on the nature and amount of food at the places where the seabirds are actually counted is rarely available. Indeed, it is comparatively rare to see seabirds actually feeding; most of their time is spent searching for food. Moreover, though many species (including boobies) depend heavily on flying fish, Bailey (1968) was unable to correlate the presence of any species with the abundance of flying fish, even though this was one of his aims. Recently, however, a big programme of studies of birds at sea has been carried out by the P.O.B.S.P. (1963–68) and the first computer-based report, on pelagic studies of seabirds in the central and eastern Pacific Ocean, has appeared (King 1974). However, the sulids are not included in this volume. Recent authors (Ashmole 1971, Brown 1975) have stressed the need for a co-ordinated attack by oceanographers, marine biologists and ornithologists, on the problems of seabird distribution. In the past, observations from ships have usually been casual, sometimes more methodical and occasionally have involved long transects for the specific purpose of exploring rarely visited stretches of deep ocean. Particularly in Britain, sea watches from the coast have yielded much information about seabird movements, and this will be reviewed for the gannet. Recoveries of ringed birds have revealed routes and patterns of movement, and shooting at sea has provided data on stomach contents and thus on the food resources of the area concerned. Records gathered by the Royal Naval Bird Watching Society are valuable and have been incorporated into Figs. 378 to 386.

In this section I have separated observations on occurrence at sea from those on breeding distribution. Generally, sulids are seen within about 200km of their breeding place, so that a map of breeding distribution extended by this amount would largely cover their occurrence at sea. The scattered information from watches at sea, though considerable, is not worth detailed analysis for the simple reason that it would still not advance our knowledge of the *quantitative* relationships between sulids and specific sea areas. Nevertheless it is useful to show the limits of their distribution and (where possible) areas in which they are common. However, the underlying oceanographic factors, with which this section opens, are relevant to both.

OCEANOGRAPHIC INFLUENCES

1. *General*

General accounts of oceans are to be found in Sverdrup, Johnson & Fleming (1942), Hill (1963) and Fairbridge (1966). A few marine ornithologists have attempted to define the important determinants of seabird distribution (Murphy 1914; 1936; Jespersen 1929; Wynne Edwards 1935 and latterly Bourne 1963; Ashmole 1971) having recognised its patchy and essentially zonal nature.

The patchy constitution of the oceans in temperature, salinity, nutrients, plankton and thus in higher life (predatory fish, mammals and seabirds) is caused, and maintained in consistent patterns, by the movement of water masses (currents) impelled by winds and Coriolis force, secondarily affected by the shape of the land masses which bound them and by underwater topography. Minerals from deeper layers reach the surface by a process of vertical mixing, generated by turbulence created by winds or by heating and cooling of the surface layers. Upwellings bring cold, richer water from deeper layers. Convergences, where water masses of different temperatures meet, also cause mixing. These processes are affected by the depth of the sea, which has been classified as neritic (over continental shelves) or oceanic. A similar classification divides the marine habitat into inshore (out to about eight km) and pelagic (the deep ocean). Upwelling is a particularly important phenomenon for seabirds. Usually the water comes up from not more than a few hundred metres. It occurs mainly off the western coasts of continents, especially North and South America and southern Africa, where prevailing winds carry surface water away from the coast and cold water upwells to replace it. It can, however, occur in the open ocean (references in Smith 1968). Convergences occur at the boundaries of latitudinally defined water zones. Especially at high latitudes, these support particular groups of species. Ashmole (1971) has summarised zones mainly from an ornithological viewpoint. The antarctic zone extends from the edge of the antarctic continent to the antarctic convergence, which varies in latitude in the three major oceans. No sulids occur within it.

The sub-antarctic zone lies between the antarctic convergence and the sub-tropical convergence. This belt of rich water, well mixed due to the sinking of colder antarctic water at the antarctic convergence and the action of strong westerly winds, has a temperature boundary of 19°C (surface layer, February). The Australasian gannet ranges into this zone. The sub-tropical, and tropical or equatorial zones, are separable mainly on the basis of the seasonal changes in stratification shown by the former. In the tropical zone a permanent thermocline means that production varies little throughout the year. On this criterion the tropical zone comprises the areas in which the sea temperature remains above 23°C all year, since seasonal changes in stratification and productivity seem minimal at or above 23°C. This definition extends the sub-tropical ocean areas to include all the major upwellings associated with eastern boundary currents, but away from these, the boundaries between sub-tropical and tropical are near to the Tropics of Cancer and Capricorn. The tropical and sub-tropical communities include all the boobies and (as breeders or visitors) all three gannets.

The boreal (sub-arctic) zone extends between the northern limit of the sub-tropic and the southern limit of the low arctic. It is a complex area of enriched water. The arctic zone includes the Arctic Ocean and areas of mixing of arctic and non-arctic water, as in the belt from Newfoundland to the Barents Sea. The Atlantic gannet breeds mainly in the boreal, but also in the arctic, zone.

The major ocean currents and upwelling areas (see Fig. 377) are briefly described below for the major oceans or ocean segments. Currents arise from global wind systems. At the equator, where the earth's diameter and thus the speed of rotational movement is greatest, rotation from west to east generates currents from east to west. By blowing from the east, the tradewinds between Cancer and Capricorn move water which has been warmed in the tropics, against the east coasts of Australasia, the Americas and Africa. These water movements, or equatorial currents, are about 1000 to 1500km broad and are separated by a 500km countercurrent flowing the opposite way. They are eventually deflected eastwards after first flowing south-west and south in the southern hemisphere and north-west and north in the northern and converge with cold water from the polar areas, where they form the boundaries at the sub-tropical convergencies.

In the 'forties the winds are strong westerlies, producing in both hemispheres an eastward flowing, west-wind drift. In the southern hemisphere icy water is taken east along the west facing coasts of South America (the Humboldt) and South Africa (the Benguela), supporting vast populations of piqueros and Cape gannets respectively. In the northern hemisphere the circulation of water is impeded by land masses. As part of the west wind drift, cold water from the arctic enters the North Pacific through the Bering straits and eventually flows south-east to cool the western coast of North America, in part as the Californian Current supporting large concentrations of four booby species off Mexico.

Warm water intrusions into colder areas are also important, as in the boreal and arctic seas warmed by the Gulf Stream and kept ice-free the year round as far as 70°N. In the west Atlantic at comparable latitudes, a rich zone is produced by the meeting of the southward flowing Labrador current with a weak branch of the Gulf Stream in which area (the Grand Banks) the Canadian population of the Atlantic gannet flourishes.

2. *Characteristics of major oceans*

The Indian Ocean

The information on this section comes from the general references cited on p. 864. With an area of some 73 000 million sq km, the Indian Ocean is the smallest of the 'big three'. Its thermal equator lies at 10°N. and the western sector is warmer than the eastern at the same latitudes, by 1–3°C. Over the tropical zone, the surface temperature is between 23°–30°C.

It is strongly affected by the monsoons which cause much greater seasonal changes than analogous shifts in the wind systems (south-east and north-east Trades) of the Pacific and

Atlantic. Its surface currents change due to wind changes. North of the equator, between about October and March, the dry, light north-east monsoons blow, giving a westward drift over the whole of the northern Indian Ocean. Also, the westward flowing north equatorial current is well developed north of 4°s. (below this the eastward flowing counter-current takes over). From about May the north-east monsoon is replaced by the much stronger south-west monsoon and the surface currents reversed over the entire Arabian Sea. Until September the current generated by the south-west monsoon flows east and causes upwelling off the coasts of Arabia and off Somalia from Ras Mabber to Ras Hafun. At this time the counter current does not exist as a distinct flow but an easterly flow of surface water extends south to about 6°s. The seasonal upwelling attracts many seabirds, though not sulids, to feed (Bailey 1968), and presumably is influential in determining breeding season in these parts. In the southern hemisphere the south equatorial current flows strongly west throughout the year, most strongly in the northern summer when the south-east winds are flowing. In the northern winter, the winds are mainly south-west monsoonal. In the Indian Ocean, because the equatorial counter currents do not exist comparably to those in the Pacific, there is no source of upwelling equivalent to that at the northern boundary of the Pacific Ocean counter current. The tropical convergence is less well defined than the others and is not such a complete barrier to organisms and thus to seabirds. Bailey (1968) suggests that there may be an area in the central Indian Ocean, at the centre of the great gyral of surface currents, equivalent to the Sargasso Sea of the North Atlantic and similarly devoid of seabirds.

Important upwellings besides those off Somalia and Arabia, occur south of Java (Wyrkti 1962) and off the west coast of Australia. In both these areas, the density of seabirds is higher than in surrounding waters. The Timor Sea and seas north of Australia are consistently rich upwelling areas and support very many more seabirds than the open Indian Ocean at the same latitudes west of Australia. The low concentration of birds in the Arafura Sea is apparently difficult to explain, since there is upwelling, high mineral concentration and large numbers of flying fish. Yet birds are almost completely absent.

The Pacific Ocean

The Pacific occupies some 165–178 000 million sq. km. To the west, its limit is the coast of Asia as far as the Malay Peninsula, then the length of the northern part of the Malacca Strait and the west and south coasts of the East Indian Archipelago. South of New Guinea it crosses the Torres Straits to the east coast of Australia then west of Bass Strait to Tasmania. It follows the meridian 147°E. to the antarctic. To the east, it is bounded by the coasts of North and South America. To the north the limit cuts across the Bering Strait. Surface temperatures in the tropical Pacific are between 25° and 28°. The Pacific is extremely complex. Huge currents, far below the surface, are still being discovered, like the Cromwell which flows eastwards beneath the westward flowing equatorial drift. It is about 200m deep and 400km wide. Even well used theories such as upwelling at the northern boundary of the counter current are not unchallenged. However, since I am unable to say much about pan-tropical sulid distribution in relation to food in the Pacific, such uncertainties are not immediately relevant, though they serve to underline the difficulties of interpretation. In the equatorial Pacific, the boundaries between the equatorial currents and the counter current are important sources of mixing and hence of primary production. The equatorial currents, some 1000–1500km broad, flowing clockwise in the northern hemisphere and anti-clockwise in the southern, are separated by an eastwards-flowing counter current some 500km wide. The north and south equatorial currents are analogous to the north-east and south-east trades and the counter current to a region of low winds. Since the intertropical covergence, which separates the north-east from the south-east trades, is mostly 300–700km north of the equator, the counter current also lies north of it.

The south Pacific equatorial drift to the south-west extends to 20°–25°s. and goes further south in the eastern half than in the western. In the north, its equivalent extends to about 20°N. near the Asiatic Islands. The south equatorial current is present on both sides of the equator and extends to about 5°N., but the north equatorial current remains entirely in the northern hemisphere.

There appears to be an equatorial front separating dense upwelled water near the equator from the less dense surface waters of the south equatorial current. Horizontal convergence and sinking are associated with this front which does not, however, coincide with the boundary of the equatorial counter current.

The north Pacific counter current changes position with season; moreover it widens with depth and parts of it underlie the equatorial current. Its northern boundary is near 10°N. but at times it recedes almost to the equator. The south equatorial current, about 450km wide, flows east. The north equatorial counter current branches off well before reaching the western boundary of the ocean, north to the Japan current and south to feed the north Pacific counter current. The south equatorial drift is weaker than in the north. Since more than half the equatorial drift is in the northern hemisphere there is less eastward-moving water in the south.

Although the Pacific is less affected by seasonal winds than is the Indian Ocean, there are important changes in the position and extent of some of the upwellings, particularly in the east. The major upwellings are the California Current, which is cold water from high latitudes that has flowed south-eastwards across the Pacific, and the Peru Current system. The former is arbitrarily assigned to a position 1000km offshore and produces upwelling varying seasonally with the wind. It is most marked north of 35°N. in mid-summer, though occurring earlier (March/May) off Baja California where it presumably influences the breeding seasons of the sulids in this region. It has an annual range in temperature of more than twice the central Pacific at the same latitude. Within the Gulf of California a low pressure system to the east produces strong northerly winds in the winter which blow surface water out of the southern Gulf and cause a sub-surface inflow of warmer Pacific waters. As a result, cool water upwells in the lee of capes and islands (see Fig. 219) mainly along the eastern side. In summer, southerly winds drive Pacific water into the Gulf and upwelling occurs primarily along the peninsular coast. Thus, plankton is abundant at all seasons, particularly in the central Gulf.

The Peru (Humboldt) Current has been described in connection with the Peruvian booby (p. 596).

Atlantic Ocean

The Atlantic covers about 106 500 000 sq m. To the west it is limited by the east coasts of North and South America from Hudson Bay in the north to Cape Horn in the south. The limit then follows this meridian as far as the north coast of the antarctic continent, which forms the southern boundary of the ocean. To the east, the meridian of the Cape of Good Hope (20°E.) forms the boundary, which then follows the coasts of Africa and Europe. To the north it is separated from the Arctic Ocean by a line drawn through the most northerly point of Norway, the most southerly of West Spitzbergen, the Denmark Strait and Greenland. The north Atlantic is connected with the Arctic Ocean and exchanges vast amounts of water with it. The same applies to the Mediterranean and Atlantic.

The counter current, flowing east between the west-flowing equatorial currents of both hemispheres, is relatively weak compared with that of the Pacific, since its strength depends on the volume of water which the equatorial current piles up on the continental coast which receives it. The bulge of the north-east coast of South America deflects the Atlantic equatorial current northwards and therefore less flows back to the east. Because of complex circulation patterns, the northern boundary of the counter currents and the equator represent lines of divergence which cause upwelling and which augment the effect of the Benguela. This enhances plankton levels towards the west, from the coast of Africa.

The Atlantic equatorial currents are deflected by the coast of Brazil. The warm south-flowing Brazil current is part of the south equatorial current, which has crossed the equator, but the greater part of its water flows north-west as the Guiana Current, through the Lesser Antilles and into the Caribbean and Gulf of Mexico, where its identity terminates. The main surface outflow of this warm water from the Gulf (the Florida Current) goes into the north Atlantic as the Gulf Stream, which at first flows in a north-easterly direction but Coriolis force deflects it towards the right until between latitudes 40–50 it flows eastwards across the Atlantic (as the North Atlantic Current). Further deflection turns it south to join again with the North Atlantic Equatorial Current. This vast circulation of water surrounds the relatively motionless mass of the Sargasso Sea.

As the North Atlantic Current moves eastwards, north-westerly winds (the westerlies) deflect some of this warm water to the north-east to form the North Atlantic drift which flows along the west and north of Britain and eventually enters the northern part of the North Sea. It also flows far up into the arctic, along the west and north coasts of Norway, and some flows round Iceland. So far as the Atlantic gannet, and the vast population of other seabirds in this area is concerned, it is vitally important in keeping this rich, cold water open, and enables the gannet to remain in these northern seas throughout the year to make an early start to the breeding season.

3. *Some minor seas*

The *North Sea* (575 000 sq km) is a shallow sea with enormous fish stocks (now much depleted), and important to gannets. It occupies the shelf area between the British Isles and the Continent. In the north-west its border is from Dunnet Head to the Orkneys and Shetlands and then up meridian 0·53′W. to 61° 00′N., and east to the coast of Norway. The February surface temperature increases from 2°C off Denmark to 7·5°C in the north and the August one from 13°C to 18°C. The western parts rarely freeze but in eastern and southern areas sea-ice becomes general even in mild winters. By April, however, the entire North Sea is ice-free.

Comparably, the Continental shelf off Nova Scotia, some 190km wide and only 40–300m deep, is the stronghold of the Canadian population. The Grand Banks are fed by the Labrador current (surface temperature 3°C).

The *Caribbean* (2 640 000 sq km) is an important area for boobies. It enjoys steady winds (from the east and north-east) and the water is warm (late summer sea surface temperature 28·3°C in the south and 28·9°C in the north; winter temperatures 3° lower). Fish are abundant because the Caribbean receives water from both the north and south Atlantic with much mixing and strong currents, *The Mediterranean* and *Baltic* are not attractive to sulids, or to seabirds in general. The former is the most impoverished large body of water in the world and the latter is brackish, with precipitation greatly in excess of evaporation.

COMPARATIVE ASPECTS OF BREEDING DISTRIBUTION

Here, I have done more guessing than is wise, but perhaps somebody who blends an understanding of oceanography, palaeogeography and speciation with specialist seabird knowledge, will now analyse sulid distribution.

Sulids need a lot of fish. They are large, and compared with an albatross or frigate, their flight is fairly costly in terms of energy. Two species have extended their foraging range beyond that which is typical of the family as a whole, but the remainder are wedded to life in productive areas, typically feeding within less than 200m of their breeding station and committed to the annual production of a fairly considerable biomass.

Their present-day distribution is equalled by no other family of comparable size. Sulids fall into three clearly defined groups: the specialists in exceptionally rich areas (piquero and the three gannets); the widely-distributed oceanic species (white, brown and red-footed) and the relict with highly restricted distribution dependent on a partly unknown combination of present-day requirements and past evolutionary mis-adventures (Abbott's booby). The blue-foot falls between groups one and two.

It is hardly surprising that sulids generally occur in productive areas. In the cases of the two extreme examples (the Peruvian booby and the Atlantic gannet) the factors limiting their breeding distribution seem fairly clear. The Atlantic gannet breeds as far north as it can, given open water for a sufficiently long season and (less clearly) as far south as the distribution of its principal prey-species in the breeding season. To the east, it lacks adequate breeding islands. It is the only sulid in this area because the ecological circumstances require a particular combination of characteristics which no other fills (see p. 915). A small, light sulid probably could not succeed and any northward excursions of the brown booby would be rebuffed. Interchange between colonies has presumably effectively prevented differentiation in the eastern Atlantic gannet population. The Peruvian booby could perhaps penetrate a little further south but has become so dependent on the superabundance of its special prey that even slight inadequacies in the availability of anchovies may limit it.

In its nesting behaviour the blue-foot gave Murphy the impression of 'falling between stools' and its distribution, too, is somewhat puzzling. Why is it so restricted and discontinuous? Part of the answer may lie in its relations with the brown booby which, apart from the Peruvian, is probably its nearest relative. The blue-foot has largely escaped from competition with the 'big three'. It is true that it overlaps with all of them, but mostly they are clear of the blue-foot. It is adapted neither for a thorough-going blue-water regime (as they are) nor can it compete with the Peruvian. It is an essentially tropical species locked into the narrow belt of seas west of the Americas, with an outpost in the Galapagos but barred from expansion westwards by vast blue-water belts, to the south by the Peruvian, to the north by temperature and perhaps other factors and to the east by the Isthmus and (beyond it) the equatorial Atlantic. Only if it crossed the Isthmus, which apparently it does not, and penetrated as far as the Benguela, would it reach the cool, rich waters which apparently suit it best. And there, nesting islands are scarce until, further south the hordes of Benguela seabirds, including the flat-ground nesting Cape gannet, take over.

Perhaps an ancestral brown booby/blue-foot sulid differentiated, the brown continuing (or beginning) to compete with the ancestral white and red-footed boobies, and probably with others too, and the ancestral blue-foot beginning to evolve adaptations to a specific set of conditions which appear to include fringe proximity to cool and relatively productive water. This divergence may have originated in the present north-eastern part of the blue-foot's range, an area which it still shares mainly with the brown. In such a case, the latter may have re-invaded the area after exclusion of the ancestral form by the evolving blue-foot. The blue-foot does indeed predominate in the Gulf and on the Tres Marias and Revillagigedos.

In the widespread and highly sympatric pan-tropical boobies niche differentiation (both nesting and feeding) as a correlate of morphological divergence, including unequal degrees of sexual dimorphism, implies advantage in sharing these commodities. However, there is much overlap in the food taken by all three and in nest sites between brown and white. Although there are many locally enriched areas supporting large populations of all or some of these three species, for example—the Arabian Sea, Red Sea, Coral Sea, Caribbean, Gulf of California, Revillagigedos and Tres Marias, this enrichment is generally of a low or medium order rather than the extreme of the Humboldt, Benguela, Grand Banks, North Sea etc. And, although it is true that the distribution of these boobies broadly conforms to areas of convergence etc., it is also true that they are nonetheless often relatively impoverished areas. In achieving the adaptive syndromes which enables them to exploit these wide, blue-water areas these three species have presumably forfeited the ability to penetrate the 'specialist-rich' areas. They are in fact those species which have adapted to the average features of the ocean-type which comprises the world's greatest area of bird-habitable sea. This means that their feeding habits preclude them from feeding in some richer cold water areas. For example, the upwelling off Arabia does not attract the warm-water boobies, probably because flying fish are mainly absent (Bailey 1968). Again, the only times when white boobies penetrate further south than usual, off Peru, is when warm water extends further south than it normally does and when, therefore, fish are scarcer than usual!

An evaluation of the distributional relationships between them is beset with artefacts, particularly the effect of man. I have already mentioned the relative safety of the arboreal habitat, favouring the red-foot. The brown is helped by its ability to use a wider range of nesting habitats than the white and by (probably) a wider spectrum of feeding behaviour, but it is hardly worth attempting a detailed analysis.

The final category of boobies, that of relict species, contains only Abbott's. Even when it had a wider distribution it was, as far as we know, restricted to a few localities in the Indian Ocean. In the east, it probably at one time co-existed with several large sulids now extinct and perhaps took to trees to gain an empty niche, but its other specialisations decreed a very different arboreal niche than that which sufficed for the red-foot. It needed high emergent trees for safe landing and take-off. Its feeding requirements obviously played a crucial role in determining its distribution but apart from its present association with upwellings we know nothing about these.

The flexibility of most sulids in nesting habitat makes it unlikely that, except in the vast ocean tracts containing few or no islands, nest sites limit its distribution or, in the great majority

Fig. 377. World distribution of gannets and boobies, major ocean currents and zones marked in. Oceanographic data from sources cited in text.

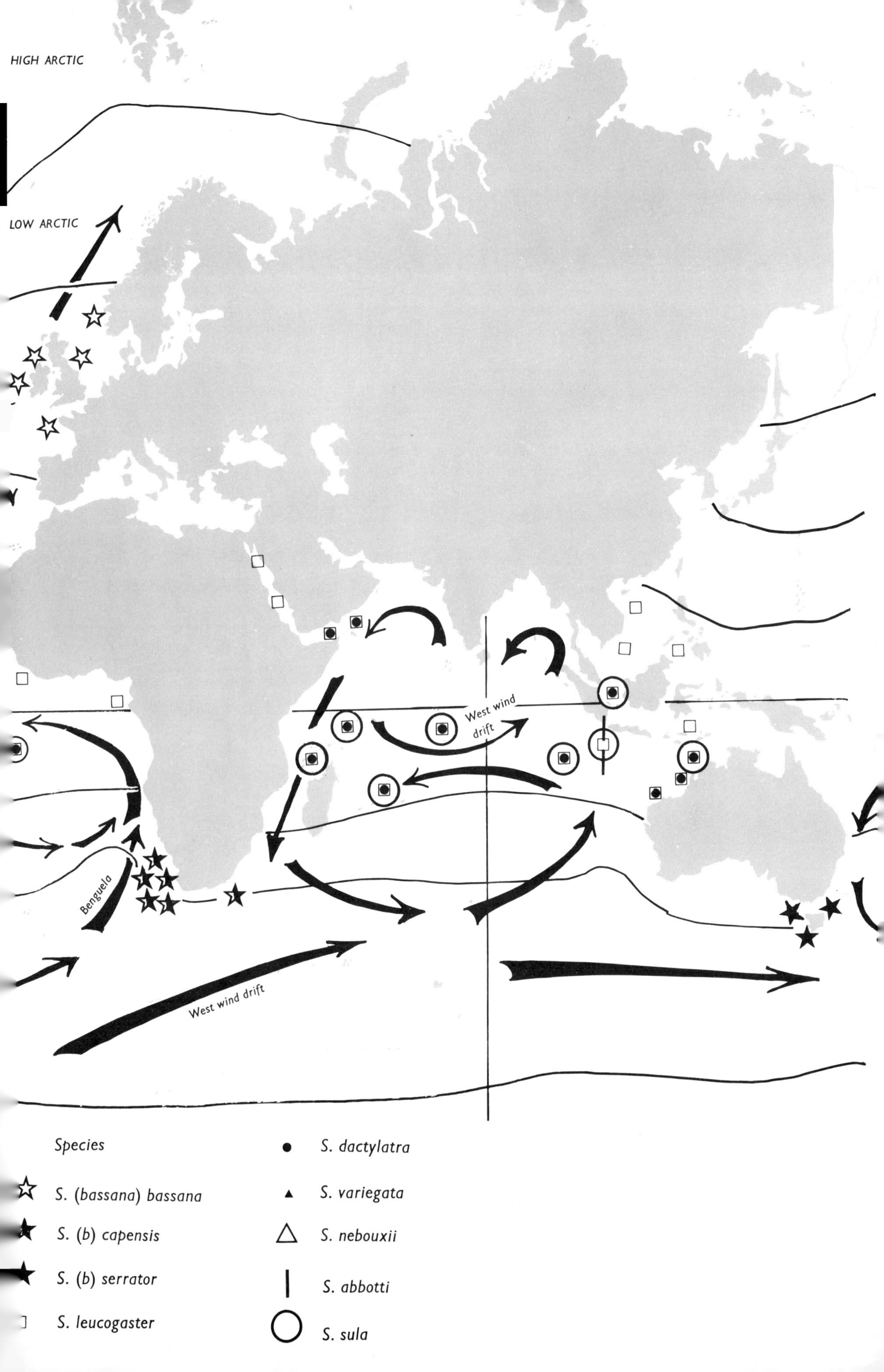

HIGH ARCTIC

LOW ARCTIC

West wind drift

West wind drift

Benguela

Species

☆ S. (bassana) bassana

★ S. (b) capensis

◅★ S. (b) serrator

▯ S. leucogaster

● S. dactylatra

▲ S. variegata

△ S. nebouxii

| S. abbotti

◯ S. sula

of cases, its numbers. It is not necessary to buttress this statement with examples further to those given in the species accounts. Other determining factors (apart from food) can only be highly marginal. They include possibilities such as insect pests (mosquitoes have been known to cause seabirds to desert an island or fail to breed), extreme weather conditions and possibly predators, though I cannot think which.

There are odd gaps in sulid distribution. For example, a large area in the south-west Pacific (Micronesia and Melanesia) is very poorly populated. It contains thousands of islands within the distribution limits of flying fish, but very few boobies. Pre-historic human pressure may have been a potent factor here, but one cannot rule out a possibly marginal food supply. The Maldives and Laccadives in the Indian Ocean lack sulids, yet offer suitable habitat. But in most cases where an archipelago or an island within a generally favourable area, lacks sulids, the explanation is likely to be either human destruction or some subtle combination of socio-ecological factors precluding colonisation. Even when an island supports one or two species, it is often impossible to see why it lacks a third or fourth. For example, Christmas Island in the eastern Indian Ocean, and Aldabra Atoll in the west, lack white and brown boobies respectively and yet both support red-footed and have suitable nesting habitat. But little useful purpose would be served by analysing such cases in detail. The apparent puzzle posed by the absence of gannets from the vast central and northern Pacific area may be explicable in terms of this species' many adaptations to cold water (see p. 915) which would certainly bar it from breeding in warm water, with all the latter's concomitant effects on food.

COMPARATIVE ASPECTS OF OCCURRENCE AT SEA

Watching at sea presents its own problems, amongst which may be mentioned the difficulty of concentrating when nothing is seen for hours or days on end; the effect of varying weather conditions and times of day; the difficulties of identification at distance; the effects of observation position (high or low) and the enormous difficulties of interpreting one's observations. Nevertheless, observations of empirical importance certainly can be made, such as that of an Atlantic gannet in mid-Atlantic, or a red-footed booby over 1000km from the nearest land, or a brown booby in Galapagos waters where it never breeds. For reasons mentioned earlier, this section makes no pretence to completeness. It should, however, enable the observer to place his observation within its order of importance and relevance to the known facts. The maps of breeding distribution are helpful in conjunction with this section.

1. *Brown booby*

Atlantic adults are more tied to the vicinity of their nesting islands than are the white and red-footed boobies and more likely to occur in muddy coastal waters. Post-breeding dispersal, particularly (but not solely) of juveniles and immatures provides sightings hundreds of kilometres from the nearest island. In general, however, all three tropical species (as others) are extremely thinly and patchily spread over the open ocean and many travellers record voyages of several thousands of kilometres without seeing a booby. The following comments supplement the general features shown in Figs. 378–386.

In the south Atlantic it is fairly casual south of southern Brazil. Harris & Hansen (1974), travelling between Europe and Rio Plata, picked it up, first, near Fernando Noronha (where it breeds), and then up to 120km from the Brazilian coast, most commonly between Cabo São Tomé and Cabo Frio. They remark that it was the only seabird present in the muddy outpouring of the Rio Docé. In the south-west, it has been recorded from Argentina and (doubtfully) in the Falklands (possible confusion with the juvenile white booby). In the east and south-east it is common in the Gulf of Guinea where it overlaps with the Atlantic and Cape gannets and reputedly straggles all the way to the southern tip of Africa, but in fact is rarely seen at Lagos (6° 30′N.) and is merely an extreme vagrant to south-west Nigeria, despite thousands in the Gulf of Guinea.

Further north, on the western side of the Atlantic, it occurs throughout the Caribbean, where it is locally abundant and penetrates right into the bays. In contrast to the red-foot, the entire Venezuelan coast is a great haunt, from the Golfo de Venezuela to the Peninsula de

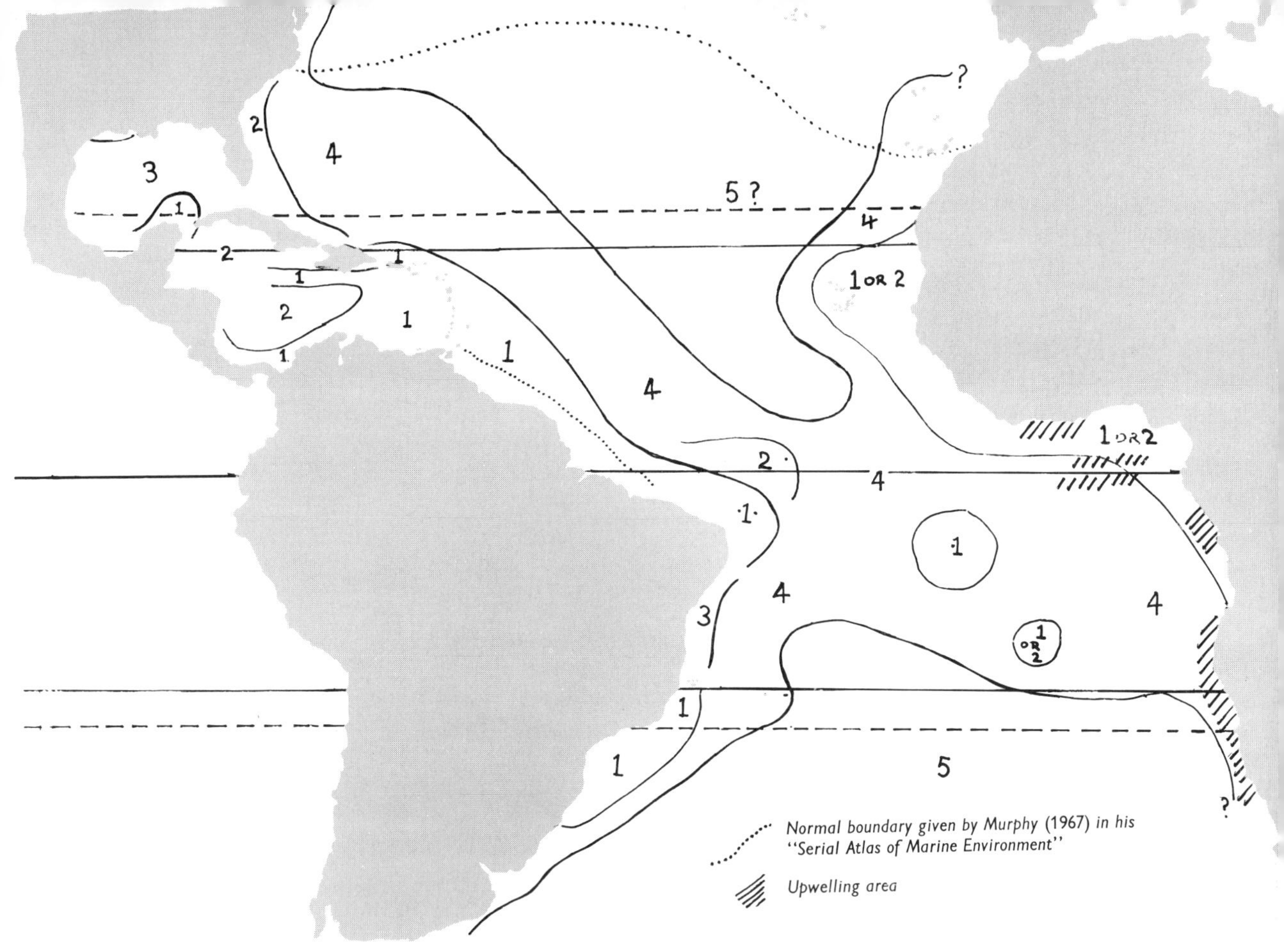

Fig. 378. The distribution of the brown booby in the Atlantic Ocean.

Key: 1. Common or abundant.
2. Fairly common or possibly common.
3. Possibly fairly common but could be uncommon.
4. Uncommon to rare.
5. Extremely rare or unrecorded.

N.B. This applies also to Figs. 379–386.

Paria, with thousands between Margarita Island and the mainland (Van Halewijn 1975). Numbers vary with locality, from almost none between La Vela and San Juan de los Cayos to 'quite numerous' near Chichiriviche and between Puerto La Cruz and Carúpano. Large sections of the Venezuelan coast are frequented only by juveniles. The coast of Trinidad is well frequented especially in winter.

There are numerous records in the Gulf of Mexico for every month except November and it visits the Dry Tortugas and Bermuda (Palmer 1962). It straggles as far north as Cape Cod. On the eastern side of the Atlantic it has been recorded as far north as the Canaries but apparently rarely gets much further, though there is a possible record from the east coast of Britain (never accepted by the Rarities Committee). In fact it is rare in the Atlantic adjacent to the Caribbean and there are even few records from waters east of the southern Windward Islands or of Trinidad.

Indian Ocean

It occurs very commonly around the southern Red Sea islands and, mainly when not breeding, off the south coast of Arabia but rarely to the east of Ras Fartak (Bailey 1966). However, Bailey (1971) did not see it at all during his survey off Somalia, July to September 1964, though white boobies occurred. The area around 4°–5°N., 48°–52°E. is rich in flying fish but maybe too far offshore to attract many brown boobies. Off Cape Gardafui it can be abundant ('great flocks', Elkington 1930) along with white boobies. It is said to occur off the

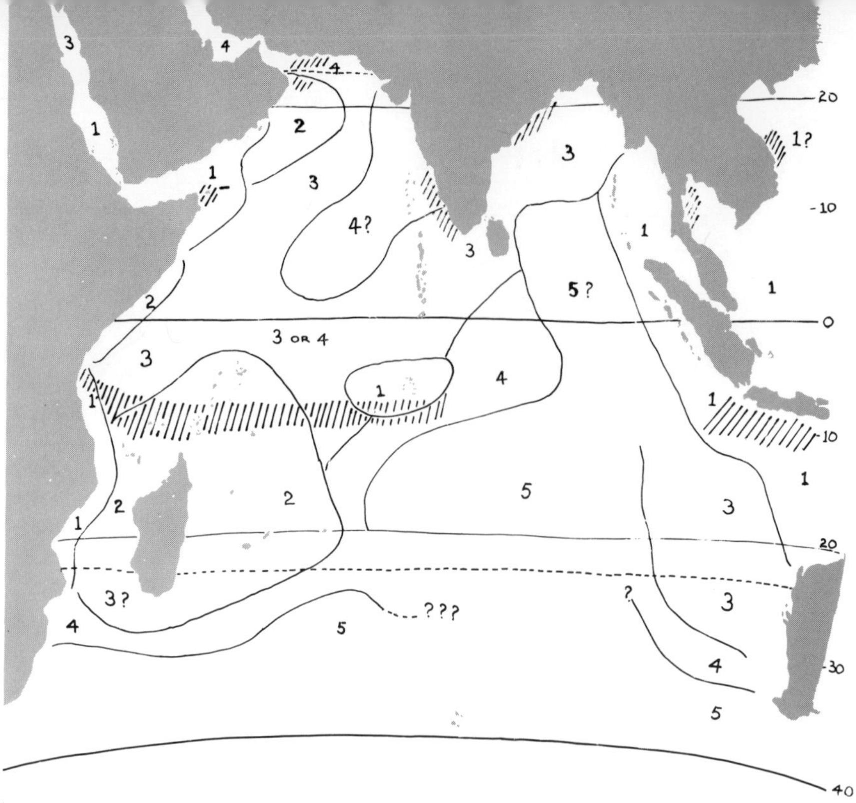

Fig. 379. The distribution of the brown booby in the Indian Ocean.

entire eastern coast of Africa and across the width of the Indian Ocean from approximately south of Madagascar, but in this tract, probably there are enormous areas in which the brown booby is rarely or never seen.

The two major papers on the distribution of seabirds in the western Indian Ocean are those of Gill (1967) and Bailey (1968). The latter does not even mention brown booby, despite the vast area covered though he records one in Kuria Muria Bay in his 1966 paper, and Gill merely records four near Socotra in February. This illustrates how restricted in biological value are maps which merely outline distributional limits and cannot quantify. Gill further remarks on the paucity of seabirds over most of the Indian Ocean, noting that they are relatively numerous only in the western Arabian Sea, below the sub-tropical convergence and around the Seychelles and Mascarenes.

In the eastern Indian Ocean it is the commonest booby (mainly when immature) off the east coast of Ceylon and straggles to the west coast during the north-east monsoons. The only formal record for India appears to be from the Malabar coast. It occurs off the coast of Malaysia and Sumatra/Java, doubtless birds from Pulau Perak, Cocos Keeling and Christmas Island. Birds commonly pass through the Sunda Straits into the extreme east of the Indian Ocean.

Further south and east again, it occurs commonly off western Australia as far south as the Dampier Archipelago (it breeds on Bedout Island) and off northern Australia through to the western Pacific (it breeds in the Gulf of Carpentaria). It has straggled as far south as Melbourne (May 1965) and off New South Wales and the Hauraki Gulf of New Zealand.

In the Arafura, Timor and seas off north-west Australia it was commoner than the red-foot or white, comprising in these localities respectively, three per cent of 264 seabirds noted, seven per count of 3112 and ten per cent of 1495 (all north of 20°s.), in May–July 1967 (Shuntov 1968, 375 counts).

Pacific Ocean

It thus ranges without a break through into the Pacific, its south-westernmost breeding area being the south-west Coral Sea. The Challenger Expedition recorded it as by far the commonest booby in the south-west Pacific in the longitude belt of roughly 137°–165°E. as far south as 23° 15′s., from whence it straggles south to New Zealand. In a single month,

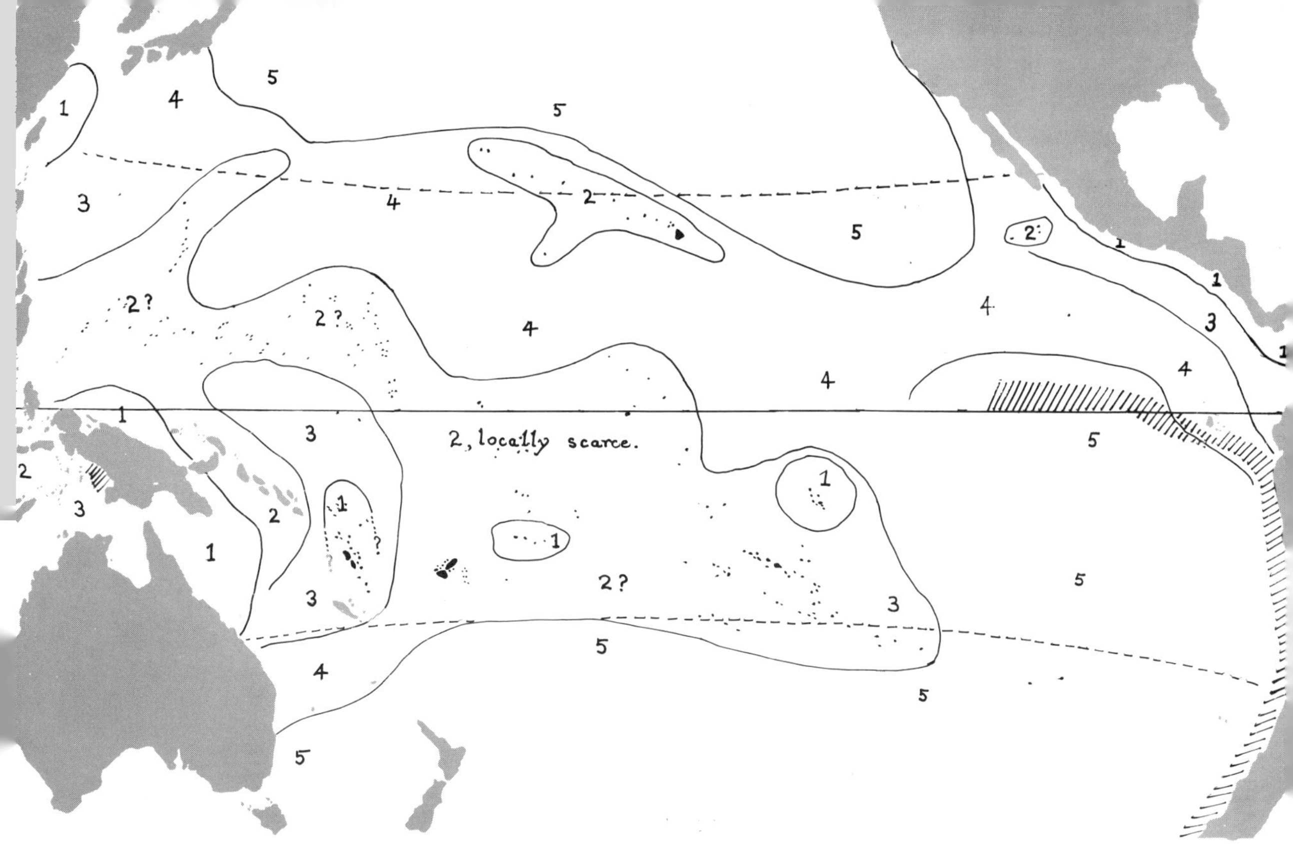

Fig. 380. The distribution of the brown booby in the Pacific Ocean.

incidentally, Challenger recorded it north to 20° 31′, thus spanning practically the full range of tropical latitudes. Further north, in the extreme western Pacific, it is a year-round regular visitor to the coast of Sabah (North Borneo) both east and west, though commonest on the west, from December to May (Gore 1968). Island groups in which it has been specifically recorded include Santa Cruz Islands (good numbers) and the Gilbert Islands from Butaritari in the north to Tabitenea in the south, though not abundant. In his report of the *Dana*'s research voyage, Jesperson (1932) calls it undoubtedly the commonest booby in the Pacific, though he did not see it between the Marquesas and New Caledonia. It was abundant off northern New Guinea and in the Celebes Sea and through into the Indo-Malayan Archipelago. Moving northwards in the western Pacific, it occurs (rarely) in the Palau Islands and abundantly in the South China Sea and north to beyond the Bonins and Volcanos. However, in 6000 nautical miles, Kuroda (1960) saw no sulids in the north-west Pacific (northernmost point 57° 28′N.).

Eastwards across the Pacific between the tropics, it is theoretically possible to encounter brown boobies anywhere until the Marquesas, where they are abundant (though King & Pyle (1957) report none more than 140km from land) beyond which begins an equally vast tract virtually lacking islands. In King (1970) the transects for the central Pacific showed brown boobies mainly near to their breeding islands. Of 81 seen, all but seven were within 80km of Oahu, but those seven were between 300–1500km from the nearest breeding place. Several casual transects across the empty tract from the Marquesas, over 4000km, have failed to record any booby, let alone brown. Fleming (1950) records them as 'plentiful' at 5° 46′N., 83° 21′W. and 1° 12′N., 94° 15′W., in the region of the Galapagos, but these are likely to have been blue-foots, for the brown does not breed in the Galapagos and is very rarely seen there at all. As the breeding areas off California, Mexico and Central America are approached, brown boobies become abundant. They are extremely common in the Gulf of Panama, along with the blue-foot, especially around the Pearl Islands. They cocur commonly off the Mexican coast and, away from the immediate vicinity of Cabo San Lucas, only rarely off Baja California (3 records, McCaskie 1970). An immature bird at 31° 30′N., 117° 00′W. probably represents about the northerly limit for this species in the eastern Pacific. It straggles to south-west U.S.A., mostly

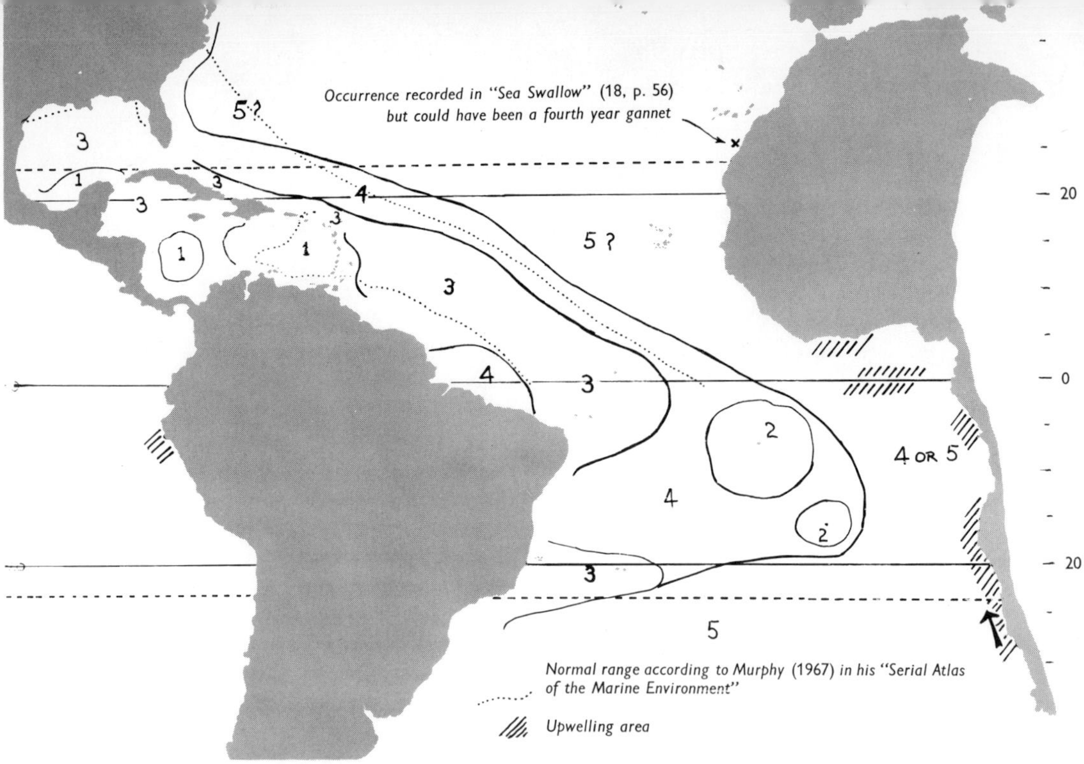

Fig. 381. The distribution of the white booby in the Atlantic Ocean.

along the Colorado Valley and Salton Sea. Southwards it becomes rare off northern Ecuador though it may be seen as far south as Isla Pelado.

2. *White booby*

Atlantic Ocean

In the south Atlantic it has apparently not been recorded more than about 300km away from known breeding places, but juveniles and immatures are often hard to identify. Murphy (1914) travelled from 3°s., 31°w. to 53°s., 35°w. and back without seeing any sulids. A record of scores of immature white boobies off West Africa at 15°N., 17° 55′w. (Bierman & Voous 1950) were probably immature Atlantic gannets and Oreel & Voous (1974) have since corrected the earlier record. Further north, on the eastern side of the Atlantic, it is common in the Caribbean, though more local than the brown and red-footed. In the area covered by van Halewijn's voyages (see Fig. 150) it occurred in the area enclosed by Cumana—Tortuga—Margarita—Los Testigos—Carupano, and particularly off Margarita, where it foraged in flocks of many dozens, possibly throughout the year. It was common, also, around La Blanquilla and Los Hermanos. Elsewhere it was recorded only five times, all 'doubtfuls', in addition to definite singles off Cabo Codera, La Tortuga, La Orchila, west of St. Lucia and Grenada and, more or less commonly east of Tobago and Grenada. Halewijn specifically remarks that he failed to see a white booby anywhere in the entire western half of the area covered by the transects. However, there is a record of c. 200 in the central area of the Caribbean at 16°N., 68°w. (Sea Swallow, 1965).

It breeds in the south of the Gulf of Mexico and is common in the Dry Tortugas, casual to the northern Gulf coast of Texas, Louisiana and Florida, and has been reported at Cape Hatteras (Palmer 1962). On the eastern side of the Atlantic it does not cross into the northern hemisphere. An oceanographic survey carried out right across the north Atlantic in parallel courses between 10° and 34°N., showed very few boobies. Apart from an area of upwelling off north-west Africa and off the Lesser Antilles, the sub-tropical waters covered by these transects are impoverished. However, even in areas where squid and flying fish were seen daily, practically the only birds seen were a few roving tropic birds and some petrels (Tuck 1966).

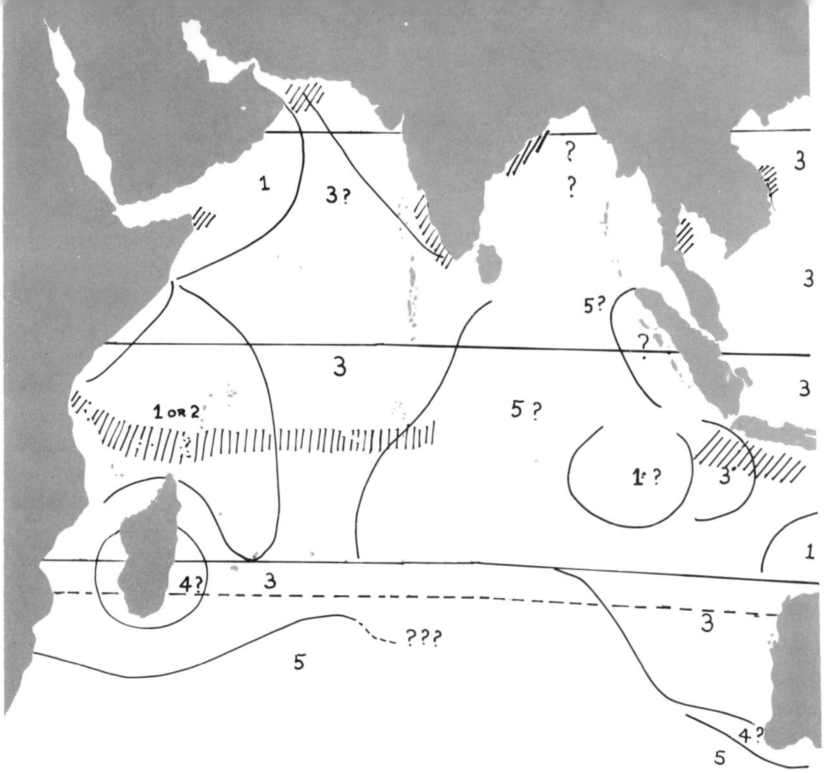

Fig. 382. The distribution of the white booby in the Indian Ocean.

Indian Ocean

White boobies occur throughout the Red Sea but mainly in the southern part and are common all year off Arabia and into the southern Persian Gulf. Probably adults range further from the offshore breeding islands between November and March, but Bailey (1968) saw only one in the central Arabian Sea. Fishing flocks may be seen commonly in the Gulf of Aden and between Socotra and Cape Guardafui (white boobies breed near Socotra). Off the Kuria Murias it has been seen in large numbers ('an uncountable carpet' Sea Swallow 1962) and 30 per cent were immatures. It appears to be rare off the coast of eastern Somaliland, south of Cape Guardafui (Bailey 1971) though immature birds may be seen on occasions and it occurs off East Africa, south to southern Madagascar (it breeds on Latham). Bailey notes the apparent gap between the Arabian Sea population and the birds to the south and east. In the western Indian Ocean it occurs over a wide span south of the equator and around the extended Seychelles area. Parker (1970) saw several adults and immatures at 4°S., 40–31°E. and so did Bailey (1968). The former suggests a strong correlation between abundant seabirds and the east-flowing equatorial counter-current.

From its stations off Somaliland in the Arabian sea it strays east to Sind and the Karachi coast, continuing, by repute, as far south-east as the Laccadives, though it does not breed there. Possibly it straggles to Ceylon (from Cocos?), for there are two old specimens said to have been taken on the west coast of Ceylon (Gibson-Hill 1953). It is distinctly uncommon in the Malay Archipelago and, altogether, it is rare within the eastern Indian Ocean, where it breeds only on Cocos and on islands off northern Australia. It occurs off the north-west coast of Australia (Dampier Archipelago) but straggles either from here or, perhaps more likely, from Lord Howe Island in the south-west Pacific, to the south coast of Australia (an adult, Victoria Harbour, December 1966) where it could easily be confused with the Australasian gannet.

Shuntov (1968) in his transects in the Arafura, and Timor Seas and waters off north-west Australia, did not separate this species from the red-foot. However, the two together comprised only 3, 15 and 7 birds in these three areas respectively.

Pacific Ocean

The white booby may be encountered from the Tasman Sea (at least 32°S.) through the Coral Sea and to at least 31°N., but nothing quantitative can be said about its occurrence

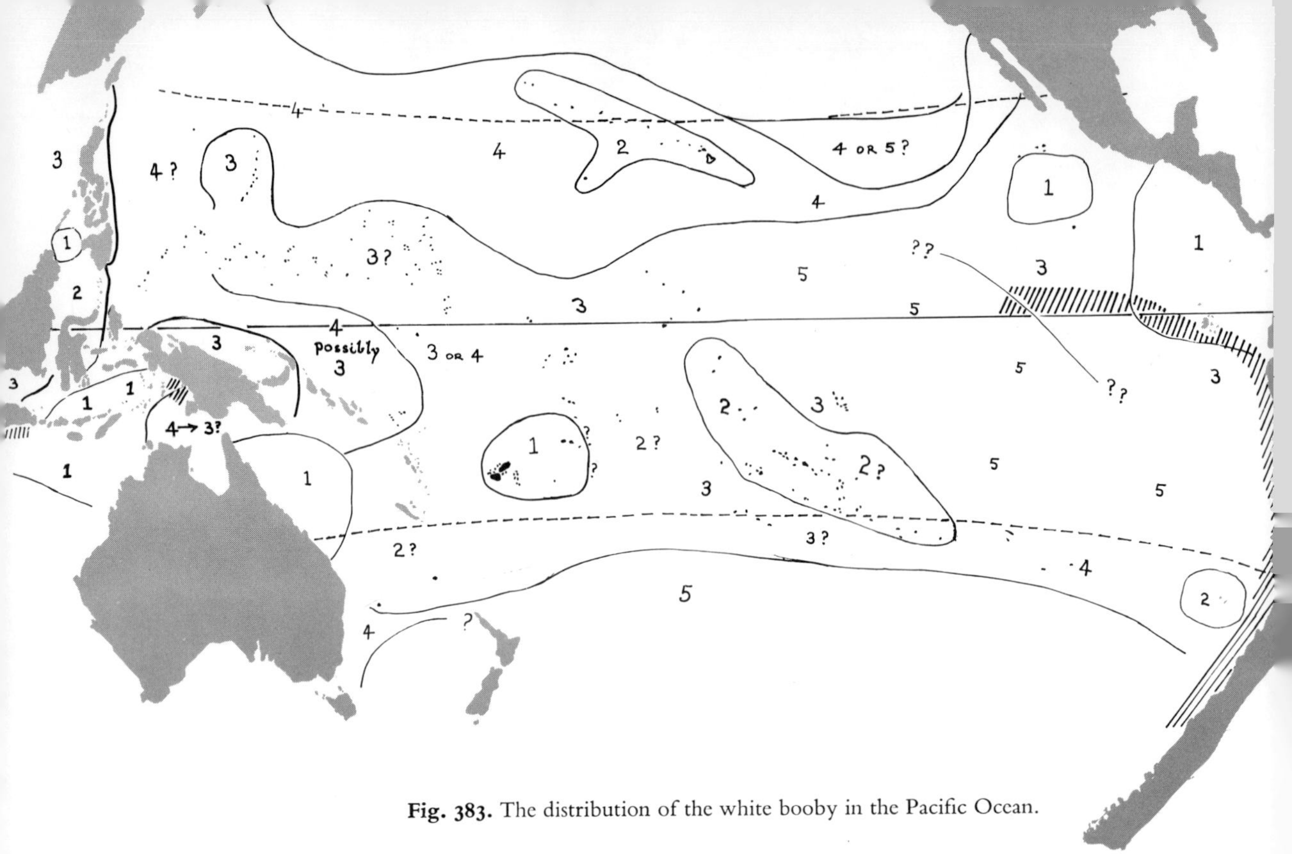

Fig. 383. The distribution of the white booby in the Pacific Ocean.

within the south-west and west Pacific, where it is relatively uncommon. It visits several areas, such as New Caledonia, where it does not now breed. Thus it occurs in small numbers throughout the Gilberts but is not known to breed there. King (1967) lists it as a vagrant in, or entirely absent from, the extreme south-west and north-west Pacific (New Caledonia, New Hebrides, Solomons, Bismarcks, Carolines, Palaus, Bonins and Volcanos) but there are scattered records from the extreme south-west (for example 23°s., 178°E.) and it breeds on Lord Howe and islets off Norfolk Island.

Theoretically it occurs throughout the central tropical Pacific but so thinly and unevenly that it may not be encountered for thousands of kilometres. Wilhoft (1961) saw it on only seven occasion on two crossings of the Pacific, whilst on 17 replicate cruises totalling 122 070km, east, north and south of the Hawaiian Islands between March 1964 and June 1965, only 45 were seen and all except one were immature (King 1970). King & Pyle (1957) in an earlier report of a 22 218km cruise between September and December in the equatorial region of the central and eastern Pacific, an area not frequently visited by ornithologists, recorded only four white boobies except in the vicinity of known breeding places (Christmas Island and Palmyra). Murphy & Ikehara (1955) report on their sightings of oceanic bird flocks (290km or more from land) for 205 days between 20°N. and 10°s. and 110°w. and 170°w. Unfortunately they lump boobies, frigates, terns and tropic birds and so it is impossible to disentangle the position of boobies and quite probable that in fact most of their birds were sooty terns and tropic birds. The average number of birds per day was 37 and the maximum (at 10°N., 120°w.) was 234. In the north equatorial current, north of 20°N. birds were few; between 10° and 20°N. they were still rather few but in the counter-current area they were common. In the south equatorial current birds and fish were relatively scarce between the equator and 5°N. Further south they were commoner. It seems that near islands zooplankton is most abundant around the Line Islands, then the Phoenix and the Hawaiian Islands and this correlates with fish abundance as revealed by experimental trolling. However, in oceanic areas there are considerable discrepancies between the abundance of zooplankton and that of fish and birds. Similarly, Morzer-Bruyns (1965) reported that all boobies were few and far between on a trans-Pacific transect along 7°N. in the region of the equatorial counter-current.

In the eastern Pacific it disperses widely in all directions from its breeding islands in the north (Galapagos, Clipperton, Malpelo and Revillagigedos) and ranges off Baja California. In the south it disperses more than 200km south-east of its breeding island, San Ambrosia, though rare and widely scattered. On the island itself it was roosting in hundreds or thousands

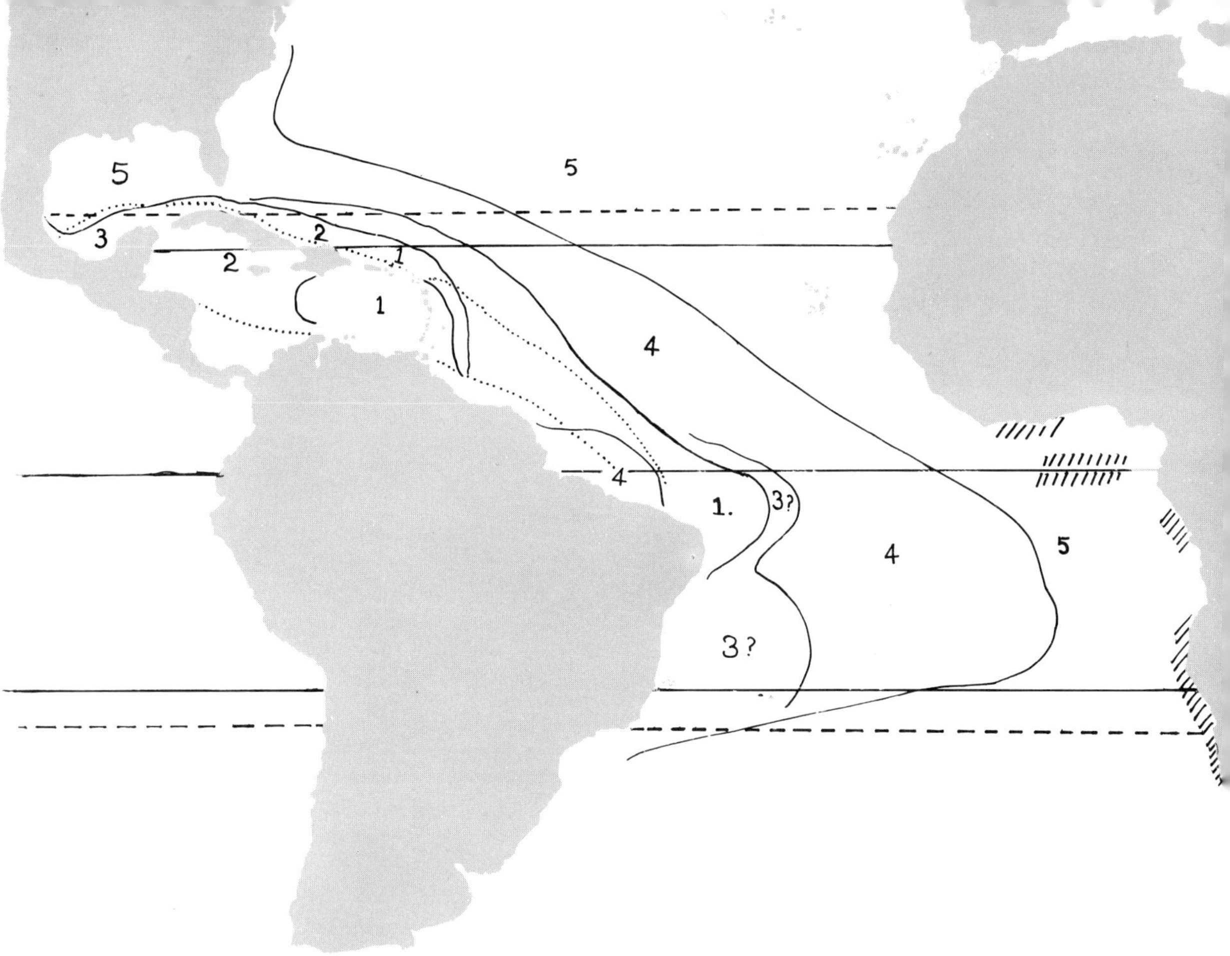

Fig. 384. The distribution of the red-footed booby in the Atlantic Ocean.

in June 1972. Between these extremes, covering more than 50° of latitude, it is especially common in the Bay of Panama, off the Gulf of Quayaquil and in Santa Elena Bay, but is replaced by the blue-foot and Peruvian boobies on the inshore islands of the Humboldt. When warm water extends unusually far south, however, the white booby moves with it.

3. *Red-footed booby*

Probably the most oceanic of sulids and, with the brown, the most numerous, this species should be the most commonly encountered at sea. In fact, it is probably recorded less than the white or brown, perhaps partly because it is harder to identify.

Atlantic Ocean

North of the equator, the only Atlantic area in which one encounters the red-foot is the Caribbean, the area off the north coast of South America and, rarely, both coasts of Florida and the Gulf of Mexico. The latter must be the only place in the world where the red-foot could overlap with the Atlantic gannet. Van Halewijn (1975) found it commonly but patchily in the south-east Caribbean. It avoided the continental shelf areas (though others have recorded it there) and he never saw it south of an imaginary line joining Chichiriviche–La Tortuga Los Testagos–North Trinidad. He found it most numerous north of Curaçao, Los Hermanos and Los Testigos and north and east of Tobago, around Grenada, the Grenadines and east of Trinidad. There were almost no records from the area enclosed by the islands of Barbados–St. Vincent–Dominica, nor from the Guayana shelf. It was common at sea between the line connecting Margarita and the chain of islands containing Curaçao and Los Hermanos. It was not very numerous west of Curaçao. Further west, it is common throughout the year in the Netherlands Antilles (probably from the Islas de Aves) particularly off Bonaire. It visits the Gulf of Mexico and the east coast of Florida.

Red-foots did not forage within a few kilometres of the breeding place but rather within ten to more than 100km of it, but this is not always the habit everywhere. Usually they were

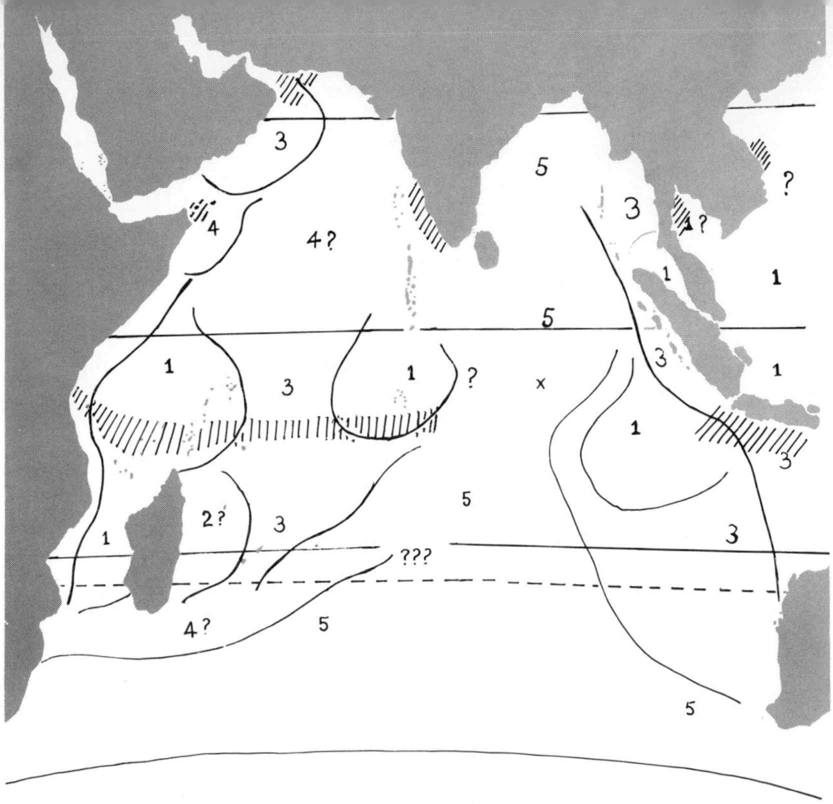

Fig. 385. The distribution of the red-footed booby in the Indian Ocean.

in flocks up to several hundred strong, typically mixed with terns, shearwaters and brown boobies. Immatures wander much further than adults and a few were seen in the adjacent Atlantic. Occasionally they stray very far from land, as in the case of the bird seen in the west Sargasso Sea at 25° 11′N., 62° 46′W., 940 km from the nearest land.

Further south it occurs commonly around Fernando Norhona and for at least 320km to the north-east (and probably equally in other directions except where this takes it too close to shore). However, its breeding places in the south Atlantic (Ascension and South Trinidad) have been to all practical purposes lost, and it must be extremely rare in this ocean. Murphy travelled from 3°S. to 53°S. and back again (around 31°–35°W.) without seeing a single sulid.

Indian Ocean

The red-foot is uncommon in the Red Sea (it has been recorded 20km from Port Sudan) and relatively so in the Arabian Sea and off Somaliland. Most of Bailey's (1968) records in the western Indian Ocean were near to known breeding places but he recorded 'fair numbers' both of adults and immatures between the Seychelles and East Africa in September and October and several immatures in the southern Arabian Sea in September, probably representing the northward dispersal into the Arabian Sea which occurs in several oceanic seabirds around that time.

It is common at sea in the greater Seychelles area (Seychelles, Amirantes, Farquhar, Cosmoledo, Astove, Assumption and Aldabra) and north and north-west of Madagascar but, oddly, Gill (1967) does not mention it. It may be seen fishing in flocks of several hundreds off Aldabra, along with terns and frigates and even far from land, is sometimes in the company of sooty terns (Parker 1970). A juvenile ringed on Aldabra was recovered some 500km to the south-west, as a five-year-old (by which time it could well have been breeding). Almost all are white morphs but white-tailed brown morphs breed, for example, on Tromelin and may be seen in the western Indian Ocean off northern Madagascar.

The red-foot reputedly wanders more extensively than does the white booby, but immature birds have reached Ceylon and perhaps the Laccadives and the Bay of Bengal (Gibson-Hill 1953). Further east it breeds on Cocos Keeling and in large numbers on Christmas Island. At 11° 42′S., 96° 38′E., 18km from North Keeling, an enormous concentration, estimated at 6000 birds, nearly all immatures except for one group of 500–1000 adults, has been noted

Fig. 386. The distribution of the red-footed booby in the Pacific Ocean.

(*Sea Swallow* 17). It is seen, locally common, in Malaysian waters. Shuntov (1968) made 618 counts (375 on the shelf of northern Australia and 243 along transects between south-west Australia and the Sunda and Lombok Straits) all between May and July except for one in January Red-footed and brown boobies, which he did not separate, occurred only between 5° and 15°S. on the transect between south-west Australia and the Sunda Straits, but with these ten degrees of latitude, their abundance varied astonishingly. Thus in May 1965 they comprised only one of the 80 seabirds seen between 5°–10°S. whereas in June 1966 they comprised 409 of the 594 birds seen. Both months are in the middle of the breeding season on Christmas Island, so why should the proportion differ so? In January 1966 the comparable figure was 22 of 61 birds seen. Their presence between 10° and 15°S. fluctuated less widely.

Off northern Australia, north of 20°S., in the Arafura and Timor Seas (May–July 1967) red-footed and white boobies (not distinguished) together comprised less than one per cent of the 264 birds counted.

Pacific Ocean

The red-foot occurs off the entire north coast of Australia through to the waters of north-east Queensland and the Coral Sea, where it breeds. It occurs widely throughout the western Pacific, visiting (though apparently uncommonly) the New Hebrides, New Caledonia and the Gilbert Islands, breeding abundantly in the Fijis (though this has only recently been put on record) and ranging north to the Sulu Sea (where it is 'very abundant' Sea Swallow 17) and China Sea (it breeds abundantly in the Paracel group) and north-eastwards to the Society Islands and the Marquesas, in both of which it is common. It has even been recorded in the U.S.S.R. (Tatar Strait). However, the Challenger Expedition (Macdonald & Lawford 1954) identified it only rarely and in widely scattered localities in the western Pacific. It occurs throughout the central Pacific between or beyond the tropics (it nests on Kure at 28° 25′N.) and wanders many hundreds of kilometres from its nesting islands, in addition to the much more extensive dispersals of mainly immature birds. In the 17 central Pacific cruises (122 070km) reported by King (1970) 22 out of the 1082 red-foots seen were more than 80km from Oahu and of these 11 were immature and only four recorded as adult. Further east it breeds in large numbers in the Galapagos and on Cocos and a few on the Revillagigedos. It rarely strays as far east as the west coast of Mexico. It is virtually absent from enormous stretches of the south-east Pacific and in four trips between Panama and New Zealand (some 41 860km in all)

Fleming (1947) failed to see one. King & Pyle's (1957) 'Eastropic' cruise failed to locate any in 22 218km, except around the Marquesas and off Christmas Island and Palmyra.

4. *Blue-footed booby*

The blue-foot is essentially an inshore species. Adults are unlikely to be encountered more than 80 to, at most, 160km from their breeding areas, but there is no reason why immature birds should not wander and odd ones have been recorded more than 1000km from breeding stations. The Isthmus of Panama apparently constitutes an impassable barrier (as it does, also, to the brown booby) thus confining the blue-foot to the Pacific side where its limits appear to be Chile (Pisco) and north as an extreme straggler to Vancouver Island. Even as far as southern California and western Arizona, however, it is casual. A few may fly north-west from the Gulf of California but there is no evidence of any northward movement up the coast of Baja California. One in Puget Sound (23 September 1935) is the most northerly record (Jewett *et al.* 1953). In southern California and western Arizona a total of 61 have been recorded in 12 years, 32 of them in 1969. Most records are from the Salton Sea (42) and Colorado River Valley (6) but 10 birds have occurred north-west of the Salton Sea (Cochella Valley, San Bernardino area and the north-west portion of Los Angeles, Phoenix Arizona and west of Salton Sea. Lamb (1927) reported a flock of five off the wharf at La Paz. McCaskie (1970) says they arrive in California, mainly immatures but including a few adults, from late July to early September, probably due to 'faulty' breeding dispersal from the Gulf of California. Blue-foots can survive for months on inland waters. Of seven birds found away from water, five were on highways which, possibly, they had mistaken for ribbons of water.

Within the Gulf of California it is common, but it is not found off the west coast of Baja California, away from the immediate vicinity of Cabo San Lucas. It then occurs southwards off the west coast of the Americas but, from northern Mexico to northern Peru, apparently not commonly until the Panama region, where it is abundant. Many thousands of blue-footed and brown boobies are to be seen in the Gulf of Panama where they may be the commonest seabird, especially abundant around the Pearl Islands, in the vicinity of the rocky islet of Camote and at Galera. It is easily the most numerous species along the coast from Carachine Point to Pinas Bay. Apparently, numbers fall sharply from the Pearl Islands north to Balboa, though it does not become scarce. It is common off the coast of Ecuador to which, as ringing records show (Harris 1975) some Galapagos blue-foots migrate. There, it occurs with immature white boobies (for example more than 150 immature and adult blue-foots with about 300 immature white boobies at Isla Pelado (Mills 1967), and continues south to the Lobos Islands off northern Peru (Robbins 1958)). At sea it is usually found in flocks of 10–25 and rarely either as single or mixed with brown boobies. Travellers passing the Galapagos often see blue-footed boobies, and records of the Peruvian and the brown booby in this area are almost certainly mistaken and refer to this species or, possibly immature white boobies. The Peruvian has *never* been reliably seen in the Galapagos.

The blue-foot thus conforms to the invariable sulid pattern of post-breeding dispersal of juveniles and to a lesser extent, adults. Its restricted breeding distribution and relatively inshore habits, however, combine to confine it to a narrow belt of sea off the Americas.

5. *Peruvian booby*

In normal years, Peruvian boobies are not seen more than 200km away from a breeding area, except during the post-breeding dispersal which may take it further south. In the south of its range it is fairly common inshore in large bays between Golfo de Aranco and Valparaiso and widely distributed but uncommon north to 29°S. (Jehl 1973). It has, however, been recovered much further south, at 42°S. (Jordan 1958). Its distribution in Peru may be seen from Fig. 253 and Table 84. It penetrates north to about 2°N., but not far out to sea. It does not reach the Galapagos. In El Niño it wanders more extensively and some are recovered inland.

6. *Abbott's booby*

Abbott's booby has been recorded in the vicinity of Christmas Island and on at least three occasions away from it. I saw two birds at 7° 26′S., 105° 16′E. on 4 August 1974 and a female was shot on 12 September 1938 from the beach of Muara Cipuduj 6° 49′S., 102° 13′E. on the southern coast of west Java (Becking 1976). There is a record, in a review of material collected by the Royal Naval Bird Watching Society (Bourne 1957b) of an Abbott's booby seen on passage from Mombasa to Mauritius in late September at 10° 04′S., 50° 32′E., one day after passing Assumption Island! However, in such an important case, the possibility that it was an immature white booby cannot be discounted. Hirons (1976) reported several sightings off the Chagos group. It is highly desirable to have more records of this species at sea. Its apparent adaptations, both morphological and ecological, for far-foraging, and its known flight path into the island (p. 763) led me to predict that it would feed in the upwelling off Java and the flimsy evidence up to now confirms this. Unless it travels high, it should be fairly readily encountered in the belt connecting feeding and nesting areas.

7. *Atlantic gannet*

(a) British inshore waters

There is much information about gannet movements around our coasts, but interpretation is hazardous because we do not know how many move unseen further out or at night, how many are non-breeding birds whose pattern of movement may be quite different from that of foraging breeders, how much the direction of movement at a particular observation point depends on local topography (Cape Clear, for example, is said to lend itself to westerly movement) and how many colonies contribute to particular passage movements. Apparently confusing pictures may result from the inevitable complexity of movements which involve four major components; seasonal movements of (i) adults and (ii) immature birds, and foraging movements of (iii) breeding adults and (iv) non-breeding adults and immature birds. Thus, simultaneous movements north and south, or east and west, are not surprising. Nevertheless, several generalisations can be made. The following section owes much to the efforts of sea-watchers, mainly members of the Seabird Group.

Seasonal movements. In September and October, British, Irish and no doubt Faeroese, Norwegian and Icelandic adult gannets move in large numbers to waters south of the British Isles and back again in the early months of the year, though it is by no means clear what proportion of the adult population does so and it is clear that, despite statements to the contrary, gannets are common in the North Sea and around the west coast of Britain, all year round, though scarcest between December and February. Immatures do likewise, though they are later to move north and earlier to move south. Birds of the year move south in August and September in large numbers, but without a corresponding northward passage in spring. In these mass movements up to 4000 birds may pass close inshore in an hour at favoured spots, though heavy passage more usually amounts to 200 or 300 per hour and a good rate is 100 or more.

Passage has been logged at many points mainly in Britain but also from the French, Spanish and North African coasts. Whilst many gannets remain all winter around Britain (including the Shetlands) and Ireland and their feeding movements confuse the picture, it is clear, as mentioned above, that major movements do occur. The details are perhaps best relegated to Appendix 6 and merely the main trends and speculations given here.

The northward movement of adults from southern waters (possibly not usually south of Biscay) is not well documented. Of 1477 birds moving north off Morocco in April to June, a negligible proportion were adult (Hopkins 1969), but this would in any case have been too late to detect breeders returning north, supposing there had been any. Similarly, in April 1968, almost all the birds moving north off Cape Verde, the most westerly point of the bulge of Africa, were immature (Gaston 1970). Off Brittany, between 3–9 April 1966, 65 per cent of passing gannets were adult but again were too late to have been experienced breeders. However, Cape Clear is more or less directly north of the sea areas off Biscay, Portugal and North Africa, to which we know large numbers of gannets migrate. At Cape Clear, considerable numbers of adults (well over 100 per hour) are moving in January (the trend throughout the year is westerly) representing a distinct increase over the November and December figures, and are probably birds moving northwards to their breeding colonies. Passage peaks from March to mid-May and immatures are virtually absent until mid-April (Sharrock 1973 and Seabird Bulletin No. 3). Immatures then flood through in May and June which fits well with the timing of their appearance and increase at breeding colonies. The picture is thus of a part of the adult breeding population and a considerably higher proportion of immature birds, wintering south of Britain and moving north between January and April. The many adults which take up their territories before that are presumably birds which have remained nearer to home since their dispersal the previous autumn. The alternating north and south movements of gannets off Aberdeenshire between January and May (Elkins & Williams 1969) could have been foraging movements of Bass birds, but there were some predominantly northerly movements in April which could have been birds returning to colonies to the north and west.

Once gannets are back in residence at the breeding colony, which may be as early as January, local feeding movements can greatly confuse any other type of movement. As an example of the scale involved, Kersley (1975) recorded an hourly passage of 2646 birds, two-thirds going north to one-third south, during one period in June 1975, off Lamba Ness, Unst, Shetland. The average hourly rate over nine days was 625 north and 299 south.

The autumn records are fuller and show clearly the early southward movement of near-adult and adult (presumably non-breeding) birds in August, followed by birds of the year in September and October and more adults, presumably breeders. Off Aberdeenshire the autumn movement is mainly north, peaking between 13–21 October (Henderson 1974) and presumably representing Bass birds moving out of the North Sea via the Pentland Firth. Of the birds moving north between 27 August and 21 October, 56·5 per cent (of 3540 birds) were adults, 23·8 per cent sub-adults and 15·2 per cent first year birds. There was, however, also a southerly movement, of which 41·9 per cent (of 227 birds) were first year. This presumably means that relatively few Bass juveniles go north and then through the Pentland and south, but quite a lot of west coast juveniles move east and then south, unless they were all Shetland or Icelandic young. Probably large numbers of gannets (and other seabirds) from Atlantic areas north of Scotland move into the North Sea and thence south in spells of favourable weather.

Off the west coast of Britain and Ireland, heavy autumnal passage has been recorded at several points and there is some passage along the east coast of Ireland, sometimes with a large proportion of immature birds, for example 50 per cent in August at Clogher Head (Moore 1974). The Irish passage is complex but shows some consistent trends. The complexity results from the concentration of large gannetries with potentially (and doubtless actually) overlapping foraging ranges in the west. The overlapping, in time, of breeding adults on foraging trips and non-breeders moving out of (and into) home waters must also complicate matters. Nevertheless, at any one point the trends in direction of movement are consistent. The movement of adults at St. John's Point is mainly north (March, April, August and September) but at Malin Head mainly west, at Tory Island and Erris Head mainly south or south-west, at Armagh Head mainly south and at Cape Clear westerly all year (see Hounsome 1967). The westerly movement off Cape Clear apparently spoils an otherwise anti-clockwise movement around Ireland, which could speculatively have been related to good fishing areas in the Irish Sea (the Liverpool area is rich in fish) and a fast, wind-aided return. However, topography may produce artefacts here. In sum, the trend is south down the west coast, west along the south coast, mixed in the north-west and south-west corners and north along the north-east coast. The heaviest movements occur from August through October.

Heavy south-west passage in autumn has been noted off Wales (for example, Strumble Head) and Cornwall and accords with expectation, but on the east coast of England, at Spurn Head, a strong northerly component in October is puzzling, since at that time Bass birds are leaving or have left, so that return (northerly) movements of foraging breeding birds seem unlikely to be the explanation. Passage off the south-east coast of England (for example, Suffolk) is notably poor, probably because birds pass out of observational range. Had it occurred, a very heavy passage off the east coast of Britain would have seemed easy to interpret, since we know that birds from the north and west pass into the North Sea and could well have been expected to move from there into the Atlantic via the English Channel.

KEY

⊞ Area broadly within foraging distance of colonies. Gannets common throughout the year in East Atlantic (April to October in West) but most abundant March-October. Immatures flood into area May, June. Non-breeders and immatures wander widely

▨ Common (locally and seasonally may be abundant)

⊡ Fairly common

▽ᵥ▽ Occurs, but may be only rarely or very rarely

○ Adult
● Immature } bigger symbol denotes preponderance

2 11 etc. Month (February and November here) in which actual records of many birds have been made

⊙ Ocean weather station from which observations made

✕ Location of some actual observations

⇨ Spring } passage; when it occurs in both directions in the one season.
➡ Autumn } Double head denotes preponderance in that direction

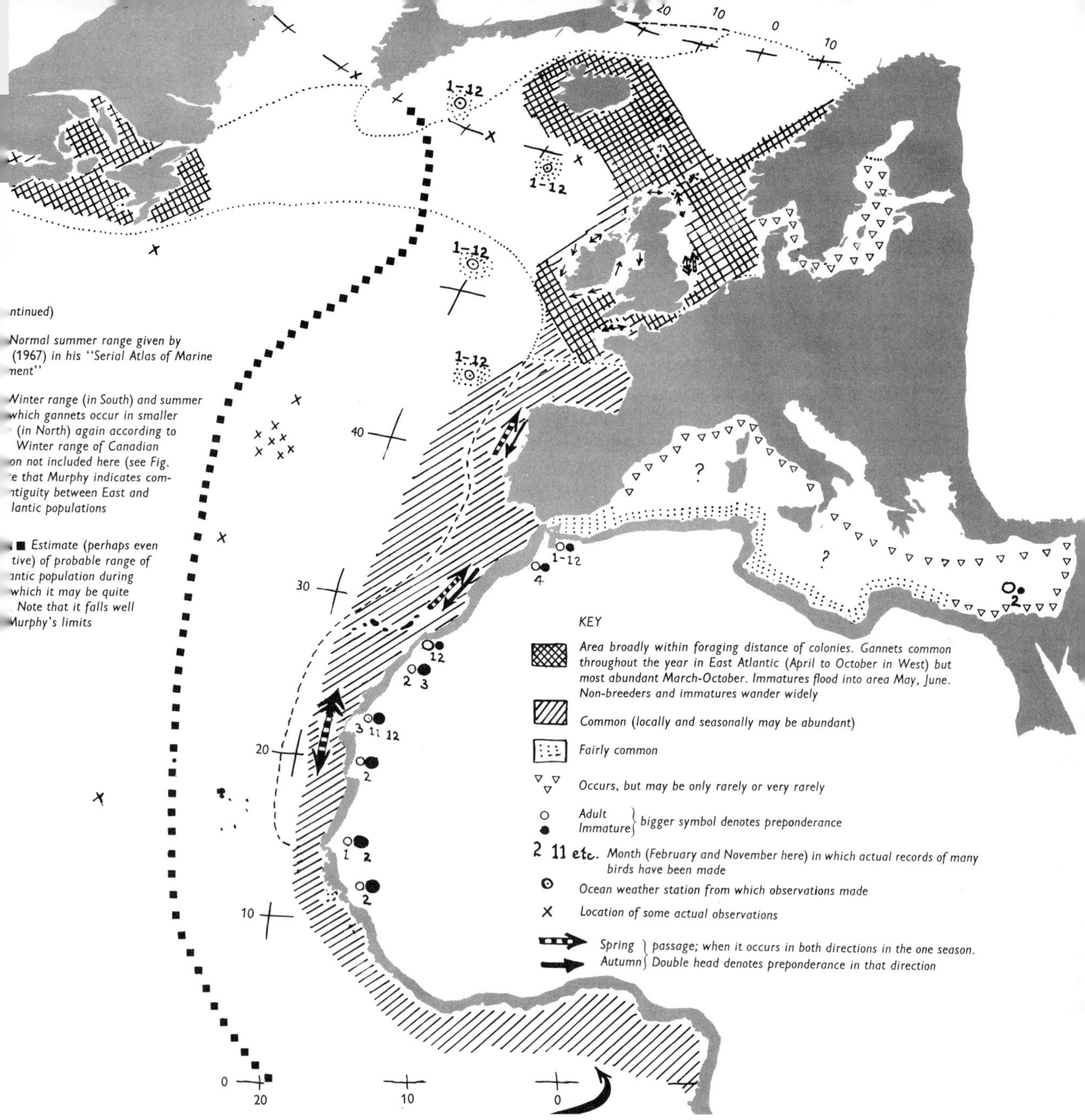

Fig. 387. Main features of the distribution of the gannet in the North Atlantic Ocean.

South of Britain, autumn watches from the Cherbourg Peninsula (18 August to 10 November) gave an average daily number of 200–300; the maximum was 783 on 9 November. As elsewhere, the proportion of immatures rose markedly in September and October and the passage was overwhelmingly westwards (Wooldridge 1974). At Cap Gris Nez in 1966 there were few gannets until early September and the main passage was probably in October (or later) though again movement both east and west confuses interpretation. In October 1969 1100 gannets passed in nine hours.

on not included here (see Fig.

■ Estimate (perhaps even

Off north-west Spain (Estaca de Bares, Galicia) the rate of autumn passage climbed steadily from early September to early October, from about 20 to 180 per hour. The bulk of early September birds were birds of the year, which illustrates the rapid passage made once they achieve flight. The number of immatures climbed from early to late September. Adults or near-adults appeared a little later and became about as numerous as juveniles (Pettitt 1969). On 5 October 1967 3279 gannets were counted in 11 hours of which 954 were apparent adults. This represents a massive movement. Pettitt calculates that in 1968 some 29 000 juveniles passed south, off north-west Spain. Out in the Bay of Biscay on 17 October, 820 adults, 115 sub-adults and 42 juveniles were seen (Clugston 1969) and there are many records of very large numbers in Biscay. It may not be too wild to suggest that more than half of the breeding population and a much higher proportion of younger birds move right out of home waters in autumn. There are some old records of great concentrations of gannets off Iberia and North Africa, for example between Lisbon and Corunna (Alexander 1898), about 15km off Morocco (Bannerman 1927) and off Cape Blanco (Blyth 1930). In this respect, there may be two consistently different components of the population, one of which regularly winters in northern areas, around Ireland, Scotland, Shetlands and Iceland. We know that many Bass, Ailsa and Icelandic birds are back at their sites by February, or in the case of the Bass, much earlier and that gannets remain right round British coasts all year. Or perhaps there is a massive post-breeding movement to southern waters followed by a slow and highly variable and age-dependent return or even more than one southward and return movement.

The Straits of Gibraltar are reached by adults mainly in the latter half of October and in November, though some are present all year. The wintering population in the Mediterranean is probably hundreds rather than thousands (Garcia 1971), though Gibraltar gatherings may number 100 or more, of which up to 70 per cent may be adults. They move out mainly in March and April. Whitaker (1903) says juveniles are often seen there.

Other aspects of movement. On passage, gannets generally move singly or in small, loose groups. However, groups of up to 100 are not uncommon and up to 1000 have been seen off Cape Clear. Henderson (1974) showed that birds moving north off Aberdeen did so in significantly larger groups than those moving south. They fly low or fairly low and have never been recorded flying in the high, direct manner of some migrants. In other words, they use their normal foraging behaviour. Often they are moving over a featureless seascape and in a fairly loosely oriented fashion, but coasts act as strong guiding lines, since gannets virtually never voluntarily cross land and if drifted towards a shore will fly parallel to or away from it. In this connection there is slight evidence that juveniles are more strongly affected by wind than are adults. Pettitt (1969) remarks that, off north-west Spain, north-westerly winds drifted juveniles inshore more than they did adults. Thus juveniles occurred in substantially greater numbers than adults on days following north-westerly winds.

Gannets seem little affected by weather conditions and it is clear from a number of reports that they move in winds up to force 6–8, or in calm anticyclonic conditions. However, several authors correlate southerly movements with brisk north-westerly winds and Hopkins (1969) observed peak northerly migration off Morocco after strong north-easterly winds, whilst further north, off Brittany, maximum passage occurred with strong south-easterly winds. Henderson (1974) found that most movement occurred in calms between depressions or in clearing, frontal conditions. Almost everywhere, gannets tend to move mainly in the early morning, although some passage occurs throughout the day and off the Manx coast passage is heaviest in the evening. Night migration has not yet been recorded. The proportion of adult to immature birds varies greatly according to time of year. First, the northerly movement of second, third and fourth year birds results in a big increase of immatures around May, June and July and second, the southerly movement of juveniles in September and October is always heavily reflected in sea-watch records. From Cape Clear (1959–64) 320 286 gannets were counted of which 82·2 per cent were separated into adult or immature. Of these, immatures represented less than 10 per cent in January, February, March, April, November and December; 20–30 per cent in August, September and October and between 40 and 50 per cent in May, June and July (Sharrock 1965), (see also Appendix 6 for further records from specific areas).

(*b*) *Records made at sea*

Although gannets are normally birds of shallow, continental shelf areas, and Wynne-Edwards (1935) stresses the sharpness of the boundary which they observe between pelagic and offshore waters, they are sometimes encountered far offshore (Fig. 387), particularly outside the breeding season. Even between April and August, non-breeding adults and immature birds wander very extensively, remaining away from their colony probably for many days at a time and, in the case of immature birds at least, visiting other colonies in their wanderings. In the fisheries off the east coast of Scotland, gannets are numerous in October and least numerous in February and March. But in *any* month large numbers of adults and immatures, including some early second year birds which look very dark and even a few first year birds, may be seen in areas offering good fishing (for example, off north-east Scotland for sprats). It is possible, however, that the North Sea is more favoured than the Atlantic from November to February. The only work attempting to correlate meteorological conditions at sea with the presence or absence of gannets, is that of Manikowski (1971) (Fig. 388). He found that numbers decreased with wind speeds above force 6 but, below this speed, gannet numbers rose with increasing wind speed and associated wave size. They also rose 24 hours after an increase in visibility (presumably correlated with clearing frontal conditions). Gannets became common in the fishing areas at the time of the passage of an occlusion and behind it, in the vicinity of other fronts and in advance of a low. In general, the number of gannets increased when low pressure systems were active and decreased during a high; the mean number per observation period in a depression was 57 and in a high 15.

South of Britain and Ireland, adults and all stages of immatures may be encountered commonly throughout the year in the Channel, Biscay and off Iberia, but adults are relatively scarce south of Biscay between April and October. Further south, to the equator, adults and immatures are again found throughout the year, but with increasing proportions of first year birds as one moves south. Adults are distinctly uncommon south of 5°N., especially between February and October.

(c) *Canadian records*

Although there are several records of gannets in mid-Atlantic, and Murphy (1967) shows complete continuity between the normal range of east and west Atlantic birds, it is probably safe to assume that the two populations remain largely separate. On the other hand, records from Greenland and northern Labrador provide possible stepping stones. The fact that the two populations have not evolved any detectable morphological differences and are extremely similar in all other respects, could indicate some gene flow. Canadian gannets have not been much watched from the coast, but their southward migration is known from ringing recoveries (Fig. 65). Recently, Brown (pers. comm.) has investigated their distribution and abundance at sea in the area of Nova Scotia, St. Lawrence, Newfoundland and Labrador. From distribution maps covering March to December it is clear that, except within foraging distance of the

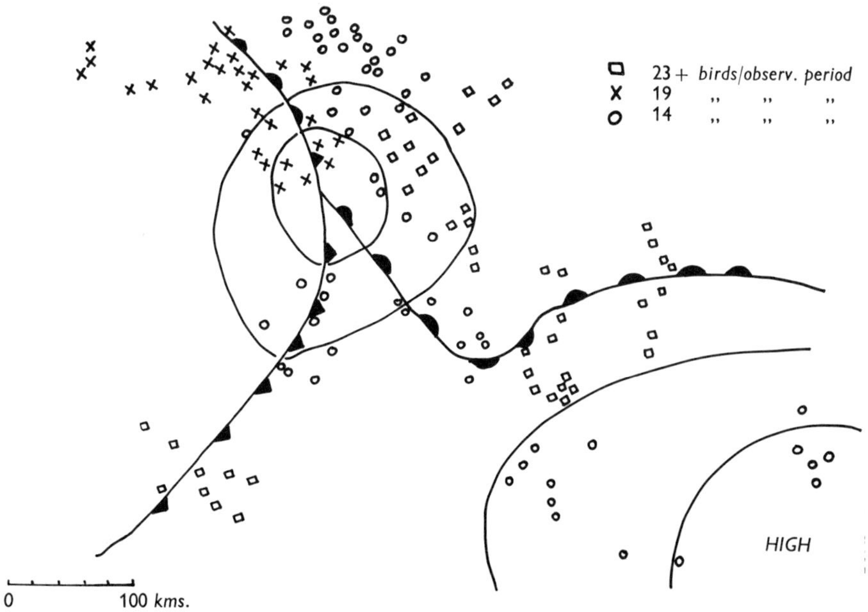

Fig. 388. Correlation between the mean number of gannets in an observation period, and the meteorological features of the locality (from Manikowski 1971).

colonies, there are extremely few gannets to be seen in the north-west Atlantic. His transects extend to 40°W. but the extremes at which *any* gannets were seen (and then usually only one bird per hour or less) were: March 53°W.; April 48°W.; May 48°W.; June 48°W.; July 46°W. (probably nomadic non-breeders as in the eastern Atlantic); August 48°W.; September none east of Newfoundland; October 47°W.; November and December none east of Newfoundland. Northwards, the transects ranged from 40° to 58°N. and gave the following results: March 43–47°; April 42–47°; May 42½–52°; June 43–53°; July 43–52½°; August 44–54°; September 44–49°; October 42½–49°; November/December 44–47½°N. Apparently they are sometimes common off Cape Breton Island in November. Of 686 10-minute transects, only 52 yielded one or more birds and only one gave as many as 100 and that was near to a colony. Birds were seen mainly in the Gulf, off the east coast of Newfoundland, off Cape Breton and in and around the Bay of Fundy. Other people's casual observations indicate the area around the confluence of the Gulf and Labrador streams (around 41°N., 66°W.) as a good area for gannets. Gannet migration reaches south to the Gulf of Mexico, but apparently merely in a strip of inshore water, out to about 300km offshore (Baker 1947). This author suggests they range as far east as the western edge of the Gulf Stream.

In the cases of the Cape and Australasian gannets, little useful can be added to the information given by ringing recoveries (pp. 251 and 293). Pakenham (1943) took two adult Cape gannets off north-west Zanzibar in July–August 1932, which shows that this species reaches far up the east coast of Africa, as well as the west. Gross (1960) records an adult on 11 May, when he must have been well into the northern hemisphere (he was at 1°S., 19°W. on 8 May and travelling steadily north-west), but this is an unusual record and could easily have been a slightly immature Atlantic gannet. Rand (1963c) saw none whatever in transects from Cape Town to 47°S. 50'W., June to July.

The Australasian gannet is seen throughout the year, but is not common, on the west and south-west coasts of Australia. Storr (1964) recorded 96 (47 adults, 22 immatures and 27 undetermined) in 85 crossings of the strait betweeen Fremantle and Rottnest, mainly between June and October (none in January or February, one in March, two immatures in April, four in November and two in December). The biggest number was 15 on 1 October. On the east and south-east it is much commoner but there are no quantitative details available.

3. BREEDING ECOLOGY

INTRODUCTION

The aim of this section is to focus on the trends within the family and on those major elements of ecology which reveal the nature of a species' relationship with its environment. Much of the discussion centres around food and its correlates—clutch size, growth-rates, breeding regimes and recruitment rates. The three gannets are compared in a separate account. A summary of the major ecological differences between sulids is given in Table 130.

BREEDING HABITAT

Sulids occupy seas right around the world and between Arctic and sub-Antarctic latitudes. Within this enormous range there is much geographical overlap between species. Only the gannets never share a breeding island with another sulid. Within the boobies it is therefore to be expected that adaptive radiation into several habitat types will have occurred. Although initially one might suppose otherwise, the process has in fact gone quite far and different boobies now habitually nest on trees, shrubs, cliff ledges, slopes and entirely flat ground, on islands of vastly differing types and sizes. This is a greater degree of catholicity than that shown by almost any other family of seabirds. Albatrosses and petrels, for example, fall far short though terns perhaps equal it. On the other hand, the sulid's primary commitment is to the sea and to its mode of hunting, so that like almost all true seabirds they are closely tied to its shores.

Where, as in the three tropicopolitan species (white, brown and red-footed) there is almost total sympatry and very considerable overlap in food and feeding areas, one might expect to find fairly extreme division of breeding habitat. Yet, acting against extreme specialisation there may be limited availability of nesting area, so that a species' success in colonising a region might depend on its ability to use a variety of habitats. So we see good examples of both processes—enough specialisation to enable division of the available habitat in many cases, with its concomitant avoidance of direct competition coupled with (in some sulids) considerable versatility. These are perhaps the factors with the most explanatory value in any consideration of sulid breeding habitats.

A third general point is that the well marked tendency for sulids to eschew the edges of land masses is probably both anti-predator (particularly man) and also because such areas are often either some distance from good feeding grounds or are logistically unsuitable by reducing the foraging area available to the bird. There is no natural law which restricts sulids to small islands; there are, for instance mainland colonies of piqueros in Peru, gannets in Britain and Canada and white boobies in Australia and no doubt there were many more prior to man's emergence. However, the supreme advantage of small islands, for most species, is probably that they are better positioned for feeding.

Cliffs, flat ground, and trees or shrubs provide discrete niches on the many islands inhabited by the three mainly sympatric species. The red-foot has reaped substantial advantage from its arboreal habit. Few islands are devoid of vegetation and since the red-foot can nest on almost anything that raises it slightly off the ground or in tall trees, it avoids confrontation

TABLE 130

COMPARATIVE ECOLOG

Species	Habitat type	Density pairs/m²	Clutch size	Brood size	Egg wt. as % ♀	Incub. period (days)	Approx. typical length of incubatio stints (hrs
Atlantic gannet	Cliffs (preferred), slopes, flat ground	2·3	1	1	3·4	43·6	33
Cape gannet	Flat ground, preferably uncluttered	2·0–6·8 (mean 2·5?)	1	1	3·9	44·0	41
Australasian gannet	Flat ground, slopes, cliffs	2·6	1	1	3·9	43·6	27
White booby	Flat ground, slopes, rarely cliffs. Usually needs some slope, or good wind. Sometimes on or among vegetation	Highly variable 0·005–0·3	1–2 (2)	1	3·6	43·7	12–14 accordin to area
Brown booby	Cliffs and cliff-edges, slopes, flat ground. Often among or under vegetation	Highly variable 0·001–1·0	1–2 (2)	1	4·0	42·8	12–24, probably usually < 24
Blue-footed booby	Flat ground, slopes, occasionally broad ledges. Sometimes among vegetation	Highly variable 0·01 (or less)–0·5	1–3 (2)	1–3 (2)	3·6	41·0	21 Galapago
Peruvian booby	Cliffs (preferred?), slopes, flat ground	1–2·0	1–4 (3)	1–4 (3)	3·0	c. 42·0	12
Red-footed booby	Trees, bushes, occasionally low herbaceous growth, very rarely, cliffs	Variable 0·003–0·6	1	1	5·0	45·0	24–60 accordin to area
Abbott's booby	Tall trees below top canopy	< ·00001	1	1	7·0	57·0	52

Note: Clutch size given as 1–3 means 1–3, usually 2.
(2)

with the larger and stronger species and evades ground predators (though only alien species introduced by man are important).

The arboreal habit may be correlated with the evolution of special body proportions which in turn correlate with specialised fishing techniques. There is reason to suspect that red-foots depend less on plunge diving than other species and snatch more food from the surface (squid) or catch it in flight (flying fish). The short legs (a trend carried to extremes in the frigate which specialises in the techniques just mentioned) may be primarily a help in getting around among twigs and the species' smallness and lightness must also help.

Between the ground nesting white and brown boobies competition is much more likely. Both use a wide variety of nest sites, the main difference being the brown booby's greater preference for steep sites and its greater facility among and beneath vegetation. There is rarely an absolute shortage of sites for either booby and only in areas where islands are extremely scarce (as, for example, in the tropical Atlantic) will the relative preferences and abilities of the two species become important. Thus, on Boatswain Bird Island (p. 431) there is a marked division of habitat along the lines indicated above. However, the ability of both to nest in a wide variety of habitats and to be equally flexible in colony size and density seems more important than the differences in habitat preference, real though these are. In this respect the brown perhaps goes further than the white, to which factor one could partly attribute its greater range and numbers.

OF SULIDAE

Fledging period (days)	Approx. frequency with which young fed per day	Max. wt. of chick as % of adult	Length of post-fledging feeding period (weeks)	Type of post-breeding movement Adult	Young	Approx. annual adult mortality
91	2·7	137	0	Mainly dispersal	Southward migration up to 5000km+	6
97·2	NR but prob. c. 2·0	109	0 (but see text)	Mainly dispersal	Northward migration up to 4000km+	5–8
102	2	138	0 (but see text)	Mainly dispersal	Westward migration up to 5000km	4–5
c. 120	1·4	114	c. 8	Dispersal	Wide ranging dispersal (up to 1000's of km)	5–7
85–105	Variable 1·5–2·0 ?	100–110 ?	Typically 4–8 but up to 36	Typically dispersal but may remain at breeding col.	Wide-ranging dispersal (up to 1000's of km)	3–10 prob. c. 5
102	2·0	112	4–6	Dispersal	Less wide-ranging dispersal	?
c. 78	3·0	120	4 +?	Minor dispersal	Minor dispersal	?
100–139	1·0	85–90	4–13 or more	Wide dispersal	Wide-ranging dispersal (up to 1000's of km)	< 10
168 or more	1·2	< 100 ?	30–40 or more	?	?	?

The blue-foot likes flat ground. Although it has a highly restricted distribution, it is nowhere the only booby in the area. In Peru it overlaps with the piquero; in Panama, off Mexico and in the Gulf of California with the brown and/or the white or even the red-footed and in the Galapagos with the white booby. With a few local exceptions, such as the crater on Daphne Major, there are no habitats suitable for the blue-foot, but not for the brown or white boobies. Thus, where the former is sympatric with either or both the latter, there is either no important competition or (if blue-foot overlaps with white) the white is dominant and (if with brown) the brown's steep-ground preference divides the habitat. An example of the white taking first choice occurs on Punta Suarez (Galapagos) where the white takes the strip facing the open sea and inland of this the blue-foot takes over. On Daphne crater rim the two have adjacent territories actually within threatening distance, but there is no information on which is dominant.

It is a curious and unexplained fact that, whilst there are innumerable cases of three species nesting on one island (red-footed with brown and white, with brown and Abbott's, brown and blue-footed and white and blue-footed; and brown also with white and blue-footed) there is only one case (in the Revillagigedos) of four nesting on the same island. It seems largely a matter of distribution rather than habitat, for with the exception of Christmas Island (Indian Ocean) with its Abbott's booby, there are few islands within the distributional limits of four species.

COLONY DENSITY

The size and density of colonies is, in some sulids, enormously variable whilst in others only colony size is variable, the spacing within large and small colonies alike falling within narrow limits. Colony size and the factors which may control it are discussed (p. 859) under Numbers and Distribution (see also Recruitment Rates p. 905). Here I am concerned with density.

This raises several questions:

(a) Is each species densest where sites are scarcest? (b) Where sites are abundant is there still a tendency to clump? (c) Does this clumping tendency vary between species? (d) If so, what are its functions?

(a) Several cases have been cited which show that isolated islands tend to hold large and dense seabird populations. The limited supply of suitable islands enforces a high degree of coloniality on sulids, as upon all other seabirds. This situation has provided the basis for the evolution of differing degrees of density which have co-evolved with the species' other traits, but usually it has *not* dictated that degree. Indisputably, gannets on the Bass, piqueros on Guañape or red-foots on Tower have to be colonial, but it would be completely wrong to assume that their respective densities are enforced by the extent of the site shortage (see below).

(b) Even where there are almost unlimited suitable sites, the tendency to clump, and the nature of the clumping is comparatively little altered. This independent tendency to retain a typical density is by no means equally marked in all sulids (see below) but it shows conclusively that factors other than the supply of physically suitable sites operate on each species.

(c) When breeding, the spatial characteristics of each species are different and important (this is true of gatherings outside the breeding area and season, but these are not our present concern). The details have been given in the species accounts, but a brief summary in comparative terms follows. The gannets and the Peruvian booby nest very densely and with extremely little regard to available space. In the Atlantic gannet this characteristic is developed to an extraordinary degree (see p. 82), so that perfectly good sites are ignored if they are more than a certain distance from existing nests and (in an expanding colony) one therefore gets the apparently anomalous situation in which there is fierce competition for a limited area whilst, a few metres distant, physically perfect sites go begging. This in turn means that a gannet colony expands in a characteristic way. Males are inhibited from acquiring sites far from existing nests and so the colony creeps outwards, though usually not symmetrically. Because tenuous lines of advance and far-out 'pioneers' are, on flatter ground, avoided, there are rarely gaps in the colony, which tends to blanket the ground. For the same reasons the outer edges are clear cut. On cliffs, this pattern is much more at the mercy of topography. Peruvian boobies are similar, but with a significantly greater tendency to set up groups apart from the main body. Thus one gets more gaps, unless the pressure on space (which, unlike the gannet's, is shared with several other abundant species over which the boobies are not dominant) closes them all. This, in fact, often happens when the seabird population is at a high level between 'crashes'. However, even when there is free space the piqueros still clump at much the standard density, leaving gaps between clumps rather than dispersing more widely within them.

White, brown, and blue-footed boobies show much more variable spacing, responding to 'free space' by spreading out. Also, they are far more likely to nest in small enclaves or even solitarily. Christmas Island (Indian Ocean) is a particularly good example for the brown booby. Groups, some containing as few as two or three pairs, others several hundreds, are scattered right round the island and their density varies considerably.

Similarly in the red-foot, the density on Tower varied enormously. Yet even the three ground nesters and the red-foot have their own typical colony structure. In particular, they never crowd together as densely as gannets or Peruvians and secondly, in the vast majority of cases, the group, even if it contains as few as ten pairs, has a fairly typical spacing. Of a thousand trees of equal size on Christmas Island, many will contain the same number of red-footed booby nests at much the same spacing. Similarly, groups of brown boobies are more alike in spacing than topography dictates.

The main points thus are that these four species nest less densely, are tremendously more variable in density than the gannet and piquero, but nonetheless have a species-typical spacing pattern and that they strongly tend to nest in small groups rather than *en masse*.

Abbott's booby is more solitary, but unquestionably retains a colonial habit, the colony being divided into groups within which spacing is on average wider than in comparable groups of red-foots.

(d) These facts need interpreting and this can lead far afield. Broadly, the choice so far as sulids are concerned, lies between social grouping as a device to use scarce sites most efficiently, or to group as an anti-predator device, or for some other social advantage. We have already discussed the first. The second seems superficially attractive, particularly in the light of the effective mass anti-predator behaviour shown by some gulls, but no sulid shows any concerted attack behaviour, nor is subject to predation except by the very animals (introduced pests and man) against which dense nesting is a hindrance rather than a help. The anti-predator argument is thus completely inadequate here. Clearly, colonial nesting is an integral part of the exploitation of a marine habitat, but to explain the pressures controlling density we must look elsewhere than to site scarcity or predation.

The other social advantages of dense nesting inevitably involve joint consideration of numbers and density. These advantages are *information transfer* and *effects on the timing of breeding*. The idea that social groupings may perform a valuable function in facilitating the most efficient use of food within the species' foraging area has been developed by some authors with particular reference to roosts. It is suggested that where food tends to be clumped, and particularly where no individual suffers much from the, albeit inadvertent, disclosure of its source of food to another, temporarily less informed member, it is possible that a system of signalling the whereabouts of food could develop. This could work very simply if a bird learned the cues (perhaps different flight mannerisms) associated with another's departure to a known food supply as against departure on a searching errand. One can see great potential advantages here, but since this could not be important in any sulid, it is unnecessary to go further into details. The reasons are that in the tropical seas most food is thinly dispersed and fast moving and in food-rich areas no such 'leading' behaviour is necessary. Thus, either the feeding areas are relatively limited, are discoverable in the pre-breeding life of the individual and are signalled by the conspicuous plunge diving techniques which all sulids use, or they are fast moving clumps to which a bird cannot return (and thus to which it cannot lead others) after a period away from the area. So, although off-duty sulids often roost at the colony, the dense congregations represented there could not conceivably have the main function of dispensing information.

There remains the extremely important effect of density and spatial distribution on the timing of breeding. This is discussed under Synchronisation of Breeding (p. 911).

THE EGG AND CLUTCH

1. *The egg*

Tyler (1969) gives thicknesses for the Atlantic gannet (shell 420μ, with cover 90μ thick), brown booby (375μ and 106μ) and red-footed (252μ and 80μ), but on extremely small samples. In general in bird orders there is a very close relationship between shell thickness and weight per unit area, and the apparent density thus differs also. However, in the Pelecaniformes (and the Gaviiformes) there is practically no effect of thickness on density. The apparent density of Pelecaniform egg shells is lower than that of Gaviforms, which suggests a different shell structure. However, the four orders described in the above paper (Gaviiformes, Procellariiformes, Podicipitiformes and Pelecaniformes) all had simple shell pores, round in cross section with a slight funnel opening, and a typical true shell structure with no noteworthy differences. Tyler could not distinguish between the pelicans, gannets and boobies, cormorants, darters or frigates by any of the characters studied.

Whilst all sulid eggs look very much alike, they differ substantially in weight and as a proportion of the female's weight (Fig. 389). The smallness of each individual egg, regardless of species or clutch size, and the concommitant altricial nature of the young, reflect the whole feeding and social system of the adults which are quite different from those of seabirds with precocial young.

The weight of the egg depends on the volume of yolk, two important aspects of which are the cost of production and the adaptiveness of egg size. Individually, sulid eggs are small compared with those of almost all other seabirds. Even allowing for the inversely proportionate ratio between body size and egg weight, sulid eggs are small compared with those of terns, auks, shearwaters and petrels (up to 25 per cent of female's body weight) whilst birds heavier than sulids nevertheless, in some cases (notably albatrosses) lay proportionately larger eggs (up to 12 per cent of female's body weight). This partly reflects the sulids' altricial rather than precocial nature. It might seem odd that the red-foot, an inhabitant of impoverished oceanic zones, produces a bigger egg than the Atlantic gannet, which lives in rich waters. However, it produces a chick better able to survive initial starvation, an interpretation which is supported

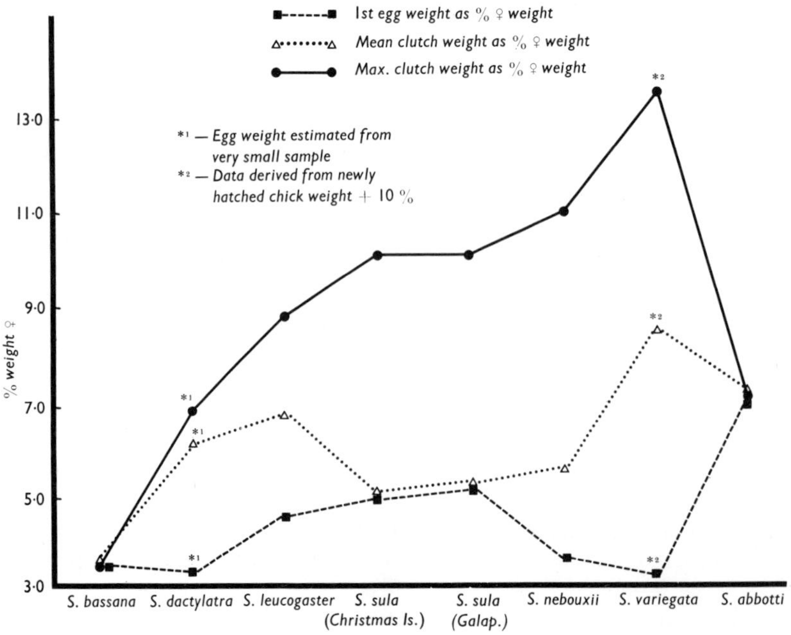

Fig. 389. The variation in egg and clutch weight, as a percentage of the female's weight, in the Sulidae.

by the fact that birds from food-poor areas lay proportionately bigger eggs than those from better areas (p. 685). The largeness of Abbott's booby's egg, however, is difficult to explain in these terms. The one-egg clutch is a derived condition and in Abbott's case, it may be that, since two or more young would be incompatible with prolonged safety, the reserves have been put into one, there being no counter-pressure favouring a reduction in the total amount of energy put into the eggs. Also, the adults feed far from the breeding island and the small young are perhaps often fed less frequently than those of other species. Individual eggs of the multiparous sulids are proportionately slightly smaller than those of the single egg species and the relevant question, here, concerns the adaptive value of clutch size (see below).

The smallness of the gannet's egg is difficult to understand. It is possible that it slightly relieves stress on the male, since he already spends vast amounts of time guarding the site before egg-laying occurs and loses weight. If the female stayed away longer, this would be exacerbated, but seems hardly enough to explain the phenomenon. Presumably it is simply unnecessary to invest more in the egg.

The unusually long interval (up to 5 days whereas in the great majority of birds it is 24 or 48 hours) between the first and second egg, in sulids which lay two or more, is probably *not* to be regarded as evidence suggesting difficulty in forming the egg as Lack (1967) suggests, but as an adaptation to potentially intermittent feeding of young. If both hatched together and encountered a period of food shortage, the insurance value of the second egg would be largely lost, since both would die.

2. *Clutch size*

The red-foot, Abbott's booby and the gannet are the only uniparous members of the family. The red-foot is restricted to one because it can feed only one chick. In impoverished areas such as the Galapagos, this is completely beyond doubt and, in general, the red-foot is a creature of blue-water belts. Abbott's booby is uniquely slow-growing and has a long post-fledging period of dependence. It is highly unlikely that it could feed two. The gannet's position is more anomalous for there is good evidence that it can rear twins. However, this is discussed in detail elsewhere (p. 99) and here it may simply be noted that it remains possible either that twins would survive badly enough to be selected against or (more likely) that two-egg clutches were abandoned in the past and have not yet re-evolved.

The remainder of the family have retained the habit, common to most Pelecaniforms, of laying clutches of two or more. Again, as with the one-egg members, there are two entirely different sets of circumstances to which the larger clutches are adapted—food-poor, and food-rich. The two-egg clutches of the white and brown boobies represent about as much, in terms of the female's weight, as the single egg of Abbott's booby and considerably more than that of the red-foot. Both brown and white boobies (1) live in areas of poor food (2) do not (and in most areas *could* not) rear more than a single young even though they lay two eggs and (3) on indirect evidence do not find the energy-requirements of producing eggs negligible (some populations time egg production to fit in with optimal food availability and others, with a fairly constant laying season, are affected by locally bad conditions during the pre-laying period). The two-egg clutches must therefore have considerable advantage even though they do not lead to the production of two young. This has been fully discussed (p. 365) and shown in these circumstances to be the significant contribution to the production of fledged young made by the second egg. This outweighs the potential advantage of a single but larger egg, though why it evidently does not do so in the case of the red-foot is a matter for conjecture; it may be connected with the fact that the female of this species is considerably lighter and also with the red-foot's more extreme specialisation for far foraging for which a large egg is a valuable adaptation. The survival value of two spaced but weaker young as against a single stronger one must, in species occupying the same environment and with much the same feeding techniques (particularly true of the white and red-footed boobies) be very finely balanced and we know too little to judge. That the two-egg clutch is not wholly advantageous is indicated by the fact that a proportion of brown and white boobies lay single egg clutches, and this is not simply an effect of age. As with the red-foot, however, there can be no doubt that one young represents the most these two species can feed.

On the other hand, the correlation of larger clutches with more plentiful food is not surprising and is itself of two kinds—connected with special feeding adaptations and with locally superabundant food. The blue-foot, which lays 2 or 3 eggs, is a somewhat special case because of its inshore fishing technique (p. 568) and its tendency as a species, to live relatively near to productive areas. Here, it is clear that the larger clutch size *does* reflect the increased chances of rearing two or more young, which puts it into a quite different category from the two-egg clutches of the white and brown boobies. Coincidentally, the cost to the female is comparatively less (Fig. 389), a fact which may also relate to the relatively great frequency with which she breeds. A similar but more extreme position holds for the Peruvian which lays 2–4 eggs, the largest clutch of all, and rears on average the most young per brood. This is indisputably due to the superabundance of anchovies around the Peruvian boobies' nesting islands. Throughout the family, therefore, clutch size can convincingly be related to food.

3. *Incubation*

The incubation periods for all sulids are, with the exception of Abbott's booby, remarkably consistent and fall between 42 and 46 days. Abbott's long incubation period (55 days) obviously reflects the larger egg, whose possible adaptive value has just been discussed. In relation to the absolute size of the egg, sulid incubation periods are undoubtedly long, for example, auks, gulls, penguins, and geese laying eggs of roughly the same size take up to a fortnight less to hatch though Procellariforms take as long or slightly longer, than sulids.

The length of the incubation shifts is to a large extent determined by local conditions and the differences between species can be quite obscured. Every population must adapt to conditions in its own area and where these differ as drastically as, for example, between the Galapagos and the Indian Ocean Christmas Island, feeding patterns will differ with them.

The red-foot and the white booby clearly have the longest attendance spells, which are the mirror images of foraging spells. These are the boobies most frequently encountered far from land and protracted foraging is their response to few and widely scattered food fishes. The difficulties of interpretation are shown, however, by the figures for the brown booby's incubation stints on Ascension and Christmas Island. On the former, in one of the most rigorous feeding habitats known, incubation stints are actually shorter than on Christmas Island, which has a much superior record for chick growth (p. 462). In such circumstances one must compare species from the same island. On Ascension, the brown averages substantially shorter stints than the white and what we know about the former's fishing habits supports this, the brown frequently fishing inshore, which the white rarely does. On these criteria, the blue-foot would be expected to show short incubation stints and does so.

During the different phases of the reproductive cycle, the pattern of attendance varies. Where there are reasonably complete figures, as for the Atlantic gannet, it is clear that quite sudden and substantial changes in the lengths of absences occur (they become much shorter immediately after the egg hatches) and the sketchier information from other sulids agrees. If these changes are often independent of changes in the availability of food, as clearly seems to be the case, it means that foraging behaviour is a complex phenomenon which the bird is constantly altering to subserve the needs of the moment, though we know next to nothing about this. It might, however, serve as a warning against any simple view of factors governing feeding behaviour.

4. *Hatching success*

Mean hatching success in all sulids (if undisturbed) is between 70 and 90 per cent though in certain areas and some seasons it can be much less. At its highest, it equals that known for any bird. Low hatching success could be due to inadequate behaviour (mainly desertion and dislodging eggs during change-over) or to infertility, or could be positively correlated with clutch size, or with environment (local factors) or with predation.

Desertion is probably fairly common in the three tropical boobies. It can be a direct response to unfavourable feeding circumstances which cause long foraging stints and thus unacceptably long incubation stints for the partner. It has been recorded on a substantial scale for brown and white boobies on Ascension, red-foots on Tower (Galapagos), blue-foots on Hood (Galapagos) and particularly for the Peruvian booby but seems unknown in the gannets.

A second behavioural phenomenon which could reduce overall hatching success is a correlate of clutch size—the tendency for the second egg to be chilled or lost after the first has hatched. At this time, the adult's behaviour switches to brooding of young, rather than incubation and the two cannot be carried out perfectly together. However, this should show up in a comparison of hatching success of first and second eggs, which in fact showed little difference in the brown booby on Kure. Loss of eggs at change-over may be fairly common and Dorward's many records of white boobies acquiring several eggs shows that it can happen on a significant scale.

Little is known about infertility in boobies; there are anecdotal comments which indicate that in some localities substantial numbers of eggs fail to hatch but the incidence of true infertility has not been established. Adverse weather can cause catastrophic losses in Australasian gannets, heavy swell affects some brown boobies (as on Ascension), and possibly white boobies. Toxic chemicals may be responsible for reduced hatching success in Bonaventure and some Norwegian gannets.

Finally, egg predation other than by man and, in one case by wild pigs introduced by man, seems unimportant (see species accounts for details).

THE CHICK

1. *Morphology*

Sulid chicks are much alike in their development of long white down by the age of about three weeks, the chief function of which is to regulate body temperature. Whilst the extent of the guard period is significantly dependent on economic circumstances its normal minimum length of about three to four weeks in all species is undoubtedly dictated by the chick's prior inability to thermo-regulate.

The body down of all sulids has the structure shown in Fig. 362, though the length of the filaments varies with body region. The areas with longest down are those which retain it longest. The only sulid chick to exhibit down of a basically different structure is Abbott's booby, whose head down differs both from its own body down and from all down of other species. The significance of this is not clear. The down came from a five-week chick with an apparently downy head, but the down structure is simply that of an under-plumage feather with a loose rather than cohesive vane. It seems possible that, even so early, the true head down may already have been lost. However, the sequence and nature of Abbott's head is obviously unusual (p. 775) and clearly merits proper investigation.

The rate at which, in different species, down is lost from various regions of the body bears a general relationship to the rate of development which in turn shows regional variation. It would not be useful to attempt a detailed comparison but three points may be made. 1. The pectoral band occurs in all sulids, even those with uniformly coloured underparts. Thus during development, if not actually in newly acquired juvenile plumage, there is a clear demarcation line below which the down persists longer and the plumage is paler. In the brown and blue-footed juvenile and in some brown-morph red-foots, the line persists in the juvenile (see Fig. 283(b)) and darker lower breast is clearly demarcated from paler belly whilst in all other juvenile sulids either the underparts are completely white (Abbott's) or largely white (white booby) or the belly and areas posterior to it are paler than the rest of the underparts, (piquero and all three gannets). Whilst pale underparts are adaptive in plunge divers (p. 821) it also seems possible that the pectoral line is a phylogenetically primitive characteristic. 2. Similarly the head down, particularly on crown and nape, is very persistent in all sulids, much more so than on other, equally innaccessible areas. Subsequently, acquisition of adult head plumage proceeds more rapidly. Thus the head (and the ventral surface already mentioned) is always the first to turn white or (in the blue-footed booby) paler. Even less than a year after fledging some young gannets have lost all their dark head feathers though the remainder of the upper parts remain dark (Fig. 4(a), (b)). 3. Another general feature of juvenile sulid plumage is the prevalence of thigh patches. Here, too, there is an associated persistence of down. Thigh patches, which may be marked in juvenile white boobies, gannets and red-foots, never persist in these adults but do so in the blue-footed, Peruvian, brown and Abbott's booby. They are not used in display except by Abbott's but again seem likely to be a phylogenetically primitive character. The tendency of all juvenile sulids (except Abbott's booby) to be darker than adults is probably of ancient standing and could indicate a link between the sulids and the pelicans; the adult brown pelican (probably representing the original pelicanid plumage) is basically similar to juvenile sulids.

A striking feature in sulids is the rapid growth of the scapulars. These are used to protect the facial skin during sleep, presumably as a thermo-regulatory device. Sulids have precise control over the scapulars and can raise them to form two walls of feathers, one on each side of the head. In Abbott's booby they are black, strongly reminding one of the black 'cape' of the frigate chick. This, too, may be a thermo-regulatory device. In the red-foot the scapulars, together with the tail feathers, produce polymorphism within the brown form, for they can be either white, brown or intermediate (see p. 662). The scapulars, in particular, seem highly variable in this respect. In gannets, white morph red-foots, and white boobies, the scapulars are among the last feathers to attain adult colour. It is not clear why this should be so.

The colour of skins, faces, bills, feet and irises in sulid chicks and juveniles shows no immediately meaningful pattern, except the universal tendency for melanin to produce a grey or black colouration. Irises may be darker or lighter than in the adult and bills darker or an entirely different colour. In general the tendency is for coloured parts to become lighter and brighter-coloured with age and the onset of sexual maturity.

2. *Growth rates*

Growth curves have many important implications. They reveal a species' adaptations to particular feeding regimes, indicate local availability of food and may show whether clutch size is optimal in terms of what parents can feed.

(*a*) *Inter-specific adaptations to particular feeding regimes*

One of the best examples of the way in which adaptations occur in interrelated 'complexes', is that of adaptations to feeding. Fig. 390 shows the different growth rates of sulids.

Clearly (and with caveats to be made in a moment) the sulids are divisible into fast growers and slow growers, so far as the growth of individual young and the production of total biomass is concerned. These categories are correlated with the feeding environment in a simple and direct way. The fast growers (gannet, Peruvian and blue-footed boobies) live in food rich areas, the details of which have been discussed under each species. This conclusion does not rest merely on the evidence which it is supposed to explain, but also on knowledge of productivity in the foraging areas of the birds.

The Peruvian and blue-footed boobies have the largest brood sizes in the family and the quickest growth, gannets excepted. The Atlantic gannet, in particular, shows extremely rapid growth. Its single chick may lay down far more in fat than some boobies weigh in their entirety. The demographies of these species are very different (p. 902); the large biomass of the Piquero's brood is produced as two or three young, leading to rapid growth of the population, which is periodically catastrophically depleted, whilst the gannet produces a single chick, facing very different selection pressures (p. 219) and recruiting into a population equally under different pressures from those operating on the Piquero.

The four slow-growing sulids are all single-chick species. The three pan-tropical boobies, as has been amply demonstrated, may suffer from serious food shortages, to which their slow growth is an adaptive response. Abbott's is a slow grower for reasons to do with specialised feeding and nesting habits (p. 777). Thus in all cases growth rate is readily interpretable in terms of the species' economic circumstances and clearly related to definable environmental features.

(*b*) *Intra-specific (population) differences in growth rates*

Reference to the species accounts shows that even allowing for racial differences in size there are, in some species, substantial regional differences in the rate at which chicks grow. This reflects the feeding environment, knowledge of which in turn helps in understanding many intra-specific differences in physiology, morphology, ecology and behaviour.

The species known to grow at different rates in different areas are white, brown and red-footed boobies. The remainder either grow at equal rates throughout their range, as do the gannet (p. 95) and Peruvian booby, or has only one breeding area (Abbott's booby); there are no data on this for the blue-foot.

The first three occupy vast areas and are adapted to relatively slow growth. We do not know whether there are now physiological differences between populations of the same species,

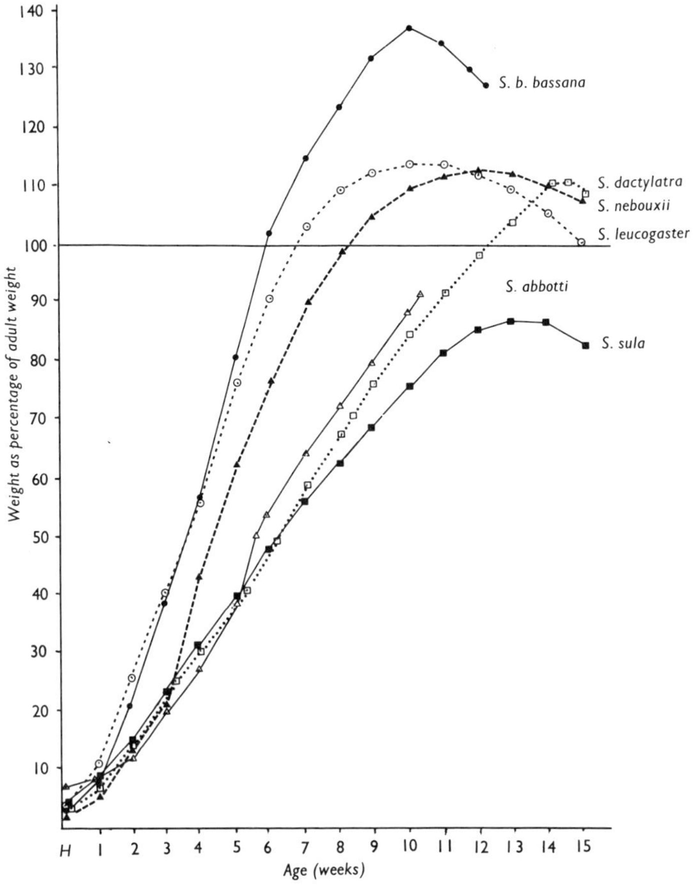

Fig. 390

(a) Growth by weight in the Sulidae.

(b) Growth of bill length in the Sulidae.

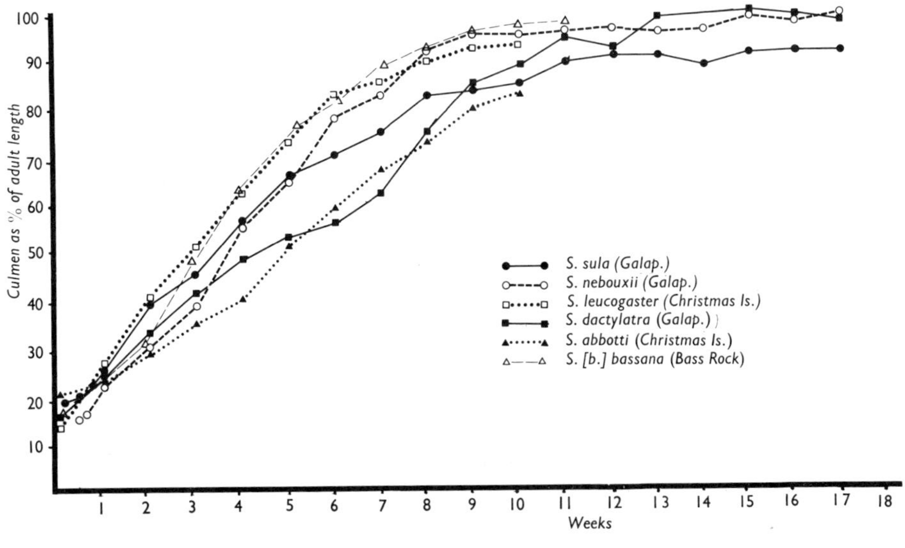

but this seems possible. The ocean belts which this trio occupy are so varied that adaptive radiation must have occurred. Morphologically, these three species have each evolved considerable, but unequal, regional differences, but as yet we cannot relate racial differences to ecological factors (but see p. 663).

The ecological effects of an impoverished and aseasonal food supply are many and have been detailed under their respective headings for the appropriate species: low clutch size, long growth periods and post-fledging feeding and non-annual breeding frequencies. *Intra*specifically most of these same differences apply. The behavioural correlates of slow growth are equally complex; thus not only are foraging stints longer, but much of the pattern of attendance at the colony and many interactions between mates may be modified (see brown booby p. 503).

The species (gannet and piquero) in which chicks show rapid growth do not show population differences in chick growth rate, since all are characterised by a rich and dependable food supply. Adult polymorphism is negligible and sexual dimorphism relatively slight. All other concomitants of abundant food are also shown (pp. 78, 624).

(c) Growth rate as an indicator of optimal clutch size

Clutch size has already been discussed. The view taken here is that in most sulids brood size is one of the species' many adaptations to the nature of its food supply. In all cases except the gannet, there seems little doubt that it corresponds to the number of young which can be fed adequately. This can be satisfactorily deduced from growth rates and related survival. Who can doubt that the white, brown and red-footed boobies would usually, if not always, be unable to feed two? Even one grows slowly or starves. Conversely, the relationship between food and the piquero's swiftly growing brood of three or four is obvious. Between the extremes

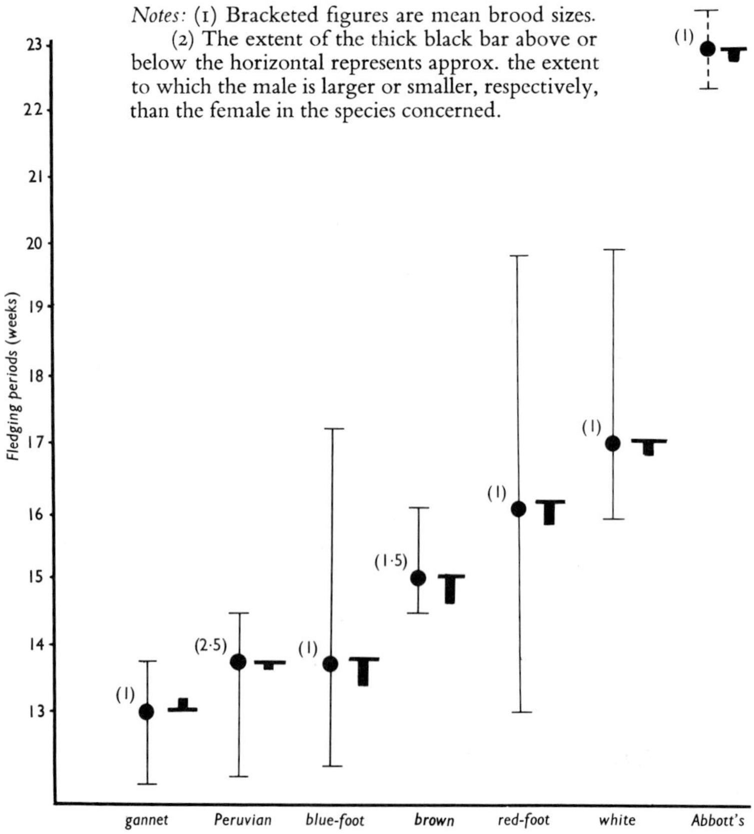
Notes: (1) Bracketed figures are mean brood sizes.
(2) The extent of the thick black bar above or below the horizontal represents approx. the extent to which the male is larger or smaller, respectively, than the female in the species concerned.
Fledging periods (weeks)
13
14
15
16
17
18
19
20
21
22
23
(1)
(2·5)
(1)
(1·5)
(1)
(1)
(1)
gannet
Peruvian
blue-foot
brown
red-foot
white
Abbott's

Fig. 391. Fledging periods in the Sulidae (max., min., mean).

lies the blue-foot, rearing one, two or three as conditions dictate, rather faster than the blue-water boobies but slower than the piquero. The gannet's special case is discussed in detai elsewhere (p. 913).

3. *Fledging period and post-fledging feeding*

Fledging periods (Fig. 391) merely reflect growth rates and like these tell much about differences between and within species. Extreme intra-specific variation, as in the three tropical boobies, makes it difficult to compare means. In Fig. 391 I have taken what is probably the most typical fledging period rather than attempting to obtain a mean using figures from different areas. The astonishing effect of impoverished areas in prolonging the fledging period in blue water boobies is clearly shown. Similarly, the short period and reduced variation in the rich water species (gannet and piquero) is revealed. The brown and blue-footed boobies are intermediate cases with extreme sexual dimorphism. In the blue-foot this enables faster growth and greater brood size. In the brown, whilst the blue water habitat precludes broods of more than one and imposes long fledging periods in extreme cases, the typical fledging period for the species is much reduced compared with white and red-footed boobies. Abbott's booby is completely idiosyncratic (p. 778).

Post-fledging feeding shows much the same thing. Both the length and the variability co-vary and are greatest in the species with longest fledging periods. The Atlantic gannet's unique position in lacking any post-fledging feeding should be specially noted.

BREEDING SUCCESS AND RECRUITMENT RATE

All adaptations, in the end, are to be seen in the light of recruitment rates. The maintenance of a healthy population (meaning, here, world numbers) is the measure of biological success and in a sense the larger that population, so long as its size is not leading to a crash, the more successful the species. Clearly, therefore, one can hardly ask more important questions than those concerning breeding success.

Throughout this book, the adaptive theme has been pursued—not in order to show that any sulid is 'better' adapted than any other, but to display the structure of the adaptive web. In comparing breeding success, therefore, we will look for the relationship between each species and its environment, asking: does productivity vary between them; what are the differences; how do these relate to the environment; what is the overall recruitment? Breeding success shows great differences between and within species.

The first part of this discussion is limited to breeding success. This is not the same as recruitment nor as productivity. Breeding success is fledged young produced from eggs laid (with the special proviso in the case of the two obligatory brood-reducers that it is fledged young from *clutches* laid). Recruitment includes mortality after the offspring reach independence (the criterion of breeding success) but before they breed (which is their main importance in terms of recruitment to the population). Productivity is young produced per pair per standard time unit (conveniently per year). The calculations made later in this section are simply order of magnitude attempts to see if, given certain assumptions, the apparent population dynamics of the species can be understood. If a 'fit' requires outrageous assumptions, these must be discarded. Otherwise, they form a basis for future verification.

1. *Comparison of breeding success within the Sulidae*

The so-called 'typical' hatching, fledging and overall breeding success figures are intended to represent those obtaining in most populations of the species concerned. They are not simple averages from known figures because there is too little information to allow proper weighting of each local figure, whose contribution properly depends on the proportions of that type of habitat in the species' distribution. The reader who wishes to compute his own figure is referred to the actual details under each species and to the sections on distribution. The figures for 'lowest' and 'highest' are actual records.

The pattern of success varies tremendously between species. All three blue water boobies (white, brown and red-footed) display the same syndrome of potentially massive egg and/or chick loss and therefore of potentially low overall success. The lowest actual figures for breeding success are almost identical at around 10 per cent. With this is linked slow growth and minimal brood size. Although breeding success can be extremely high (80 per cent) is it still valid to categorise these species as basically adapted to scarce or irregular food, since *wherever* they occur their growth is relatively slow and brood size minimal. In other words, adaptation has been to relatively impoverished ocean belts and these are so effective that breeding success is typically fairly high; in extreme adversity, it is low. Reference to the Ecology and Behaviour sections will show the red-foot's many adaptations to this kind of feeding habitat and at the same time will reveal why the species has been unable to eliminate substantial loss of eggs and chicks.

This contrasts strongly with the two rich water species (gannet and piquero). The Atlantic gannet has a high or very high breeding success and there is no evidence that it falls far short of this anywhere in its range. With this is linked extremely rapid growth. The low brood size is a special case (p. 913) and is emphatically *not* to be interpreted as an adaptation to scarce or irregular food. The piquero usually has a high or extremely high breeding success with which is correlated rapid growth and large brood size. There are no differences between populations in breeding success. However, it is subject to 'crash' years in which success can drop to zero, a situation without parallel in the Sulidae. These special years are not simply an extreme case of the kind that often affects the boobies of impoverished waters, for unlike the latter, they are not something to which the birds can adapt. The blue-water boobies are adapted to scarcity; the piquero to plenty. Possibly the latter's adaptations are influenced by the fact that scarcities *do* occur, in that adaptations which result in massive recruitment must take account of long term population dynamics which are very much affected by the crashes. But the sets of adaptations to the two situations are basically different.

Little can be said about the blue-foot's breeding success. It breeds mainly in rich waters (Peru, Gulf of California and areas affected by the California current), but also in impoverished ones (Galapagos though even here only in the south of the archipelago, touched by the Humboldt) and comparative figures are lacking upon which to base an overall assessment. Probably it more resembles the species with high breeding success than those from poorer areas, but in any case its productivity is a more important guide (see below).

Abbott's booby is a special case and because of its biennial breeding, best discussed under 'productivity'.

In sum, therefore, the main divisions within the family, with respect to breeding success, are between relatively low success, high success and 'special case' species. The first show great regional variability, the second do not and in the third category, the blue-foot probably does but mitigates it by special mechanisms.

2. *Comparison of productivity and recruitment within the Sulidae*

The number of young produced per year depends partly on brood size and breeding frequency. Whilst the Peruvian booby may fledge only 70 young from each 100 eggs laid and the red-foot, in some areas, may do likewise, the former produces 2½ times as many young. Table 131 lists productivity for all sulids.

Peruvian booby

The piquero is by far the most productive. Even at the conservative estimate of 70 per cent breeding success and assuming annual breeding, each pair produces 1·75 young per year. At an estimated 50 per cent pre-breeding mortality (p. 625) and an estimated breeding life of 10 years, each pair would, during its life, contribute 8·75 breeding birds to the population. This accounts for the species' rapid recovery after disaster. In fact, there must be checks on the breeding output during the later part of a population recovery or, ten years after a crash, numbers would far exceed those known to occur. For example, starting from a population remnant of 20 per cent of that which existed before a crash—say 2 000 000—the 400 000 survivors would, on the above premises and the additional ones (a) that birds commence breeding at 3 years of age and (b) that annual adult mortality is 10 per cent, give 3 273 570 birds in 10 years. This large excess is achieved in the calculation notwithstanding the fairly unfavourable assumptions made. Checks could take the form of exclusion of potential breeders due to lack of space, bearing in mind interspecific competition with guanays and pelicans, or limitation by social mechanisms. The former certainly appears to operate but so, also, may the latter (see p. 627). It seems certain that checks could not be imposed by density dependent competition for food, even for a relatively short period of the year.

Thus, the piquero's breeding biology is adapted to producing a large output of young in good years. The population never grows beyond a fairly consistent level because (a) periodic catastrophes intervene and (b) there may be finer control imposed by either (or both) space limitations and intrinsic mechanisms. Extension of range is effectively forbidden by the piquero's highly developed dependence on a particular type of food which has itself a limited distribution.

Blue-footed booby

The blue-foot is the piquero's closest relative and comes second to it in productivity (1·2 young per pair per year). Assuming 50 per cent pre-breeding mortality, an adult breeding life of ten years and 60 per cent breeding success (see p. 535) each pair would contribute 6 breeding birds to the population. This figure, however, is likely to be a considerable over-estimate. Thus, the breeding success is likely to be considerably less than 60 per cent where breeding frequency is every nine months (i.e. in the Galapagos). Where breeding success is higher than 60 per cent (probably Peru and Gulf of California) breeding *frequency* is probably lower. At 40 per cent breeding success and nine-month breeding frequency, output per year is 0·82 and, allowing 50 per cent pre-breeding mortality 4·1 per lifetime per pair. A further reduction may result from frequent abandonment of breeding before laying (see p. 533), thus reducing real breeding frequency, on average, far below once per nine months, even though this frequency often *is* attained. At half this figure, the population would be about stable. Whilst such a regime provides a very rough fit with known Galapagos data, nothing is known for other regions. However, since, in Peru, blue-foots are severely affected by periodic catastrophes, average productivity between times could afford to be much higher than in the Galapagos and long term population stability still maintained.

Compared with the piquero, the blue-foot is less able to take advantage of superabundant food, but, by the same token, less dependent on it. Its distribution is thus wider, but tied to at least the fringes of productive areas. Here, as in other aspects of its biology, the piquero is a specialised blue-foot; its specialisation has paid dividends in absolute numbers, but has decreased range and adaptability. It seems most likely that the piquero stems from an ancestor which resembled the present-day blue-foot, rather than the other way round.

Brown booby

The brown booby is divisible into two demographic 'types' more clearly than the blue-foot. In impoverished areas, assuming 30 per cent breeding success and 8 monthly breeding

TABLE 131

PRODUCTION OF YOUNG PER PAIR PER YEAR IN THE SULIDAE

	Production	Brood size	Per cent breeding success	Breeding frequency
Peruvian booby	1·75	2·5	70	12 months
Blue-footed booby	1·20	1·5	60	9 months
Brown booby	0·45	1·0	30	8 months (Ascension)
	0·65	1·0	65	12 months (Christmas Island)
White booby	0·40	1·0	40	12 months (Galapagos)
	0·65	1·0	65	12 months (Kure)
Red-footed booby	0·24	1·0	30	15 months (Galapagos)
	0·70	1·0	70	12 months (Caribbean)
Abbott's booby	0·1	1·0	20 (?)	24 months
Gannet	0·80	1·0	80	12 months

frequency (p. 474), its productivity is likely to be around 0·45 young per pair per year or less. In 'normal' areas, assuming 65 per cent breeding success and an annual cycle, its productivity would be 0·65, or less. We do not have figures for enough years to decide whether 30 per cent breeding success is a reasonable estimate for an impoverished area, but 65 per cent for good areas is probably valid. If birds with an eight-month cycle miss a cycle merely as often as birds with a twelve month cycle, this would cancel out and the difference in productivity between the two types could fairly easily be insignificant and due mainly to inaccurate estimates of success in the impoverished types. In this case, the impoverished birds would make up by breeding more frequently what they lost by failing more drastically, the 'normal' birds being (presumably) prevented from breeding more frequently by the relatively seasonal nature of their environment. On the other hand, birds with eight-month cycles could well rest *more* frequently and their success would thus be lower. If the figure of 30 per cent success is accurate this would exacerbate the difference even more and it would then be highly significant. At present it is impossible to choose between these alternatives, which have important demographic implications.

White booby

This species is in one respect less complicated than the brown in that its breeding frequency is always about annual. Its productivity, however, probably differs significantly between areas. In impoverished ones a productivity of 0·4 per pair per year (which is about what the available figures indicate) is about replacement level given 10 per cent annual adult mortality and 50 per cent pre-breeding mortality of immatures. Productivity in good areas should provide a surplus. Unlike the Peruvian, production over and above that required for replacement of the local population *could* be absorbed elsewhere in the species' range, for the white booby is a great wanderer and will breed on other than its natal island. Furthermore, man-induced mortality may in many areas greatly exceed the 10 per cent allowed here. In addition, non-breeding years certainly occur and could adjust recruitment to about the level required for mere replacement. The factors controlling such years remain to be shown. In these respects, the white booby closely resembles the brown, compared with which it seems to have slightly (though probably not significantly) lower productivity in impoverished areas and the same productivity in good areas.

Red-footed booby

The productivity of the red-foot closely resembles that of the white booby, but possibly fluctuates between slightly greater extremes. In the only impoverished area yielding records for both species (Galapagos) the red-foot probably breeds slightly less frequently, more pairs taking more than a year between successive attempts and with slightly less success. On this basis its productivity is 0·24 per pair per year against 0·4 for the white. Applying the same figures for adult mortality and mortality of immatures prior to breeding, this would not maintain the population. Probably the year upon which the breeding success figure of 30 per cent was based was unusually severe. At the other extreme, the high success apparently enjoyed in good areas such as the Caribbean and the Indian Ocean Christmas Island, probably yields 0·7 per pair per year, which is about the same as the white booby in good areas, and allowing 50 per cent immature mortality is well in excess of replacement requirements. How much of this is absorbed by less productive areas, or whether recruitment is intrinsically maintained well below the level suggested by these figures, is unknown. What does seem probable is that density dependent curtailment of output is unlikely to operate via direct competition (see p. 862).

The lowest productivity for the red-foot and the figure for the Peruvian differ by a factor of more than seven, which is a graphic comment on the environmental differences between them, and on their respective adaptations.

Abbott's booby

Even with a moderate breeding success, which may well be an invalid assumption, Abbott's booby appears to have extremely low productivity, resulting from its biennial breeding and minimal brood size. There seems little scope for more than replacement productivity unless post-fledging and adult mortality are significantly lower than in other sulids. However, little is known about this. On the face of it, this species appears to have paid for excessive specialisation by lowered productivity. Other species—notably frigates—appear to have biennial breeding and, moreover, a fairly low breeding success and yet have a high enough productivity to build up large populations. One major difference is that frigates are not restricted to a scarce breeding habitat, whereas Abbott's booby is. However, this does not explain why the latter has apparently been unable to build up a large population on Christmas Island, which is but thinly colonised (but see p. 780). Red-foots with a low productivity in the Galapagos have been much more successful, but they have a lower post-fledging mortality.

Gannet

The gannet (all three forms) is the most productive of all uniparous sulids. However, it alone lacks post-fledging feeding and as a result its chick suffers heavy post-fledging mortality. Seven or eight out of every ten die before breeding; thus, with a 15 year breeding life, each pair produces 2·4 breeding recruits in its life time. This is slightly more than replacement rate, even at such a heavy pre-breeding mortality and, in the case of the Atlantic gannet, a British breeding population of 100 000 pairs would produce 40 000 in excess of replacement per generation of gannets. Over 15 years this number would be available to re-stock differentially depleted gannetries and to expand others. It is difficult to judge whether the increase in British gannets now occurring, is of a different order of magnitude than can be accounted for in these terms. However, the fit seems reasonable. In particular, the rate of increase on the Bass (p. 48) which is probably the most useful indicator because it is likely to be independent of other colonies, is about right using the breeding success and mortality rates just quoted. The situation in the other two gannets is roughly comparable (p. 310) although mortality before fledging is probably higher and mortality after fledging probably lower than in the Atlantic gannet.

3. *Recruitment in general terms*

Having briefly stated the facts for each species, it remains to draw general conclusions. Since recruitment involves not only productivity and mortality, but emigration, immigration, non-breeding years and delayed maturity, these will be included here.

Basically, the questions are whether recruitment and population levels in the sulids are controlled by mechanisms which maximise productivity, thus seeming to accord with neo-Darwinian principles or whether recruitment and population levels are controlled intrinsically, that is by checks on recruitment imposed as it were by the population on itself. Related to these two alternatives is the different problem of whether the first system would inevitably lead to density-dependent external restraints on recruitment, via reduced breeding success and higher mortality. The second (intrinsic control) theory implicitly accepts that such external checks would in fact occur if other restraints did not keep the population at a non-exploiting level.

On the first, most widely held, hypothesis, one would expect clutch size to correspond to the most young that could be adequately fed; breeding to occur as frequently as possible with due regard to its stress on adults; breeding to occur as soon as possible with a similar proviso and populations to rise until something halted or reversed the process. Do these things happen?

Brood size corresponds to the most young that the parents can feed adequately; reference to the appropriate sections demonstrates this beyond much doubt except for the Atlantic gannet whose case remains somewhat anomalous. The twinning experiments leave very little room to doubt that a substantial reproductive advantage would accrue in most years, to most pairs rearing twins and with little if any adverse effects on the parents. Even at 10 per cent below normal fledging weight, mortality among twins would have to be almost impossibly higher than among singles to offset the advantage. Given the great variability in fledging weight among singles anyway, and the very large part played by chance in gannet survival at this stage, it is hard, but not impossible, to deny the conclusion that gannets could gain advantage by laying two eggs instead of one. To accept this conclusion means *either* that gannets are now in a different feeding situation than in the past, that their one-egg clutch represents as many young as they formerly could feed (i.e. maximum productivity) and that probably the clutch will in time revert to two (or the population rise till one egg again represents maximum reproduction), *or* that the one-egg clutch is a mechanism to minimise productivity *or* that there is some reason other than food (perhaps the dangers of falling) prohibiting twins.

There is no sure way of weighting these possibilities at present. They all appear to contain inherent improbabilities and yet one of them must apply. Thus, the first, which I favour, implies that the relationship between gannet numbers and food was once substantially less favourable and that one-egg clutches survived best (it does not require that competition operated). How long could one expect a long-lived bird, like the gannet, with low reproductive rate, to take to revert back to a two-egg clutch once one-egg clutches had become almost universal (nowadays certainly no more than 0·01 per cent lay two eggs and in fact there is no unequivocal case on record)? It could possibly take thousands of years. Perhaps, at that period, things were different.

The second possibility ostensibly requires the operation of altruism and group selection, as suggested by Wynne-Edwards (1962). It implies that at some time in the past the population of gannets became in balance with the food supply at a level which did not exploit the 'capital' but merely the 'interest'. Presumably, to stay there required that those females laying two or more eggs reduced their clutch size to one, as the simplest method for reducing productivity. This could happen only as a result of selection pressure against the two-egg genotype. If this selection could not operate on the breeding pair on the principle of advantage to those parents producing the greatest number of 'fit' offspring, it must operate on the principle of the greatest good to the long-term interests of the group or population sharing the resource (food). Towards this idea there has been much empirical scepticism based on inability to see how selection could favour breeding units (pairs) which *under*-produce for the long-term benefit of others who are *not* closely enough related for kinship benefits to operate. It would seem that if a population were to consist of breeding units, some of which produced more than others (which in fact happens) the under-producers would automatically contribute less to posterity and their genotype would be eliminated. It is this principle which many are unable to relinquish. And it is particularly difficult to relinquish in a species which, like the gannet, invariably lays one egg. In species which, like the great tit, lay vastly different clutch sizes, it is clear that natural selection cannot be operating by maximising average productivity. If it were, as Mountford (1971) points out, clutch size would not be variable. The function of the variability is to maximise the chances of the population surviving. In other words, natural selection insures against all possible contingencies in a variable environment by maintaining clutches which are both smaller and larger than that which on average produce most young. But this argument cannot be applied to a species with an invariable clutch size.

Nevertheless, Mountford's comments on the biological significance of clutch size seem so pertinent that I quote part of the final paragraph of his discussion: 'The usual measure of the fitness of a genotype ill-describes the evolutionary movement of a population in a varying environment. In current usage the fitness of an individual is defined as the average number of gametes contributed to the next generation. The emergence of the fittest genotype is thus in exact correspondence to the evolution of the most efficient clutch size in the sense defined by Lack (1947). Hence the criticism in this paper of Lack's criterion applies equally to the conventional measure of fitness; in a varying environment both measures are misleading and inappropriate.'

The third alternative mentioned the possibility that something other than food could have made it on balance disadvantageous for gannets to produce more than a single chick. The candidates appear to be increased probability of falling from cliffs (which may at one time have been a more dominant nesting habitat than it is now) and unacceptable stress on adults. Both these have been fairly convincingly dismissed (p. 102), but there may be other possibilities as yet unthought of.

With respect to clutch size, therefore, all the sulids except the gannet appear to lay maximum clutches which accord with the food situation; where food is plentiful clutches are larger and where food is short they are minimal.

The remainder of the devices which affect recruitment rate can be discussed more briefly because the underlying principles are the same. The frequency with which sulids breed (Fig. 392) has been shown to vary not only between species, but also within them, though basically the sulid breeding frequency is annual. There are two quite separate aspects to this: first, the normal time interval between two successive clutches and second, the frequency with which an entire cycle is 'deliberately' missed.

The first depends on the time required for a complete breeding cycle and on the nature (seasonal or aseasonal) of the environment. Thus, in an aseasonal environment a pair can theoretically breed, at most, every *x* months, where *x* equals the length of the breeding cycle. Usually, but not always, a rest period is added on. This maximal frequency, without rest, is in fact sometimes achieved by brown boobies on Ascension (p. 474) and only slightly less frequent breeding is shown by the blue-foot in the Galapagos. In a seasonal environment breeding may be restricted to part of the year and thus can occur only annually even though the rest period may not need to be so long. This is basically the situation for the brown booby in those parts of its range where it is an annual breeder but in fact takes no longer to complete a cycle than the birds that breed every eight months. The same may be true for the blue-foot, but this has not been shown.

By contrast, the *red-foot* in the aseasonal Galapagos because of its protracted care of young, may take more than 12 but less than 24 months between successive layings, whilst in most other areas it takes less time to complete a cycle and breeds annually. Whether taking less than a year, a year or more than a year, however, all these species appear to be breeding as often as they can. The same holds for the *Peruvian booby*, which requires much less than a year but occupies a somewhat seasonal environment. It is not clear whether it ever packs more than one cycle into a year, but even if it does not, the size of its brood may require it to forage for them only within the season when anchovies are most available. The *white booby* breeds only once a

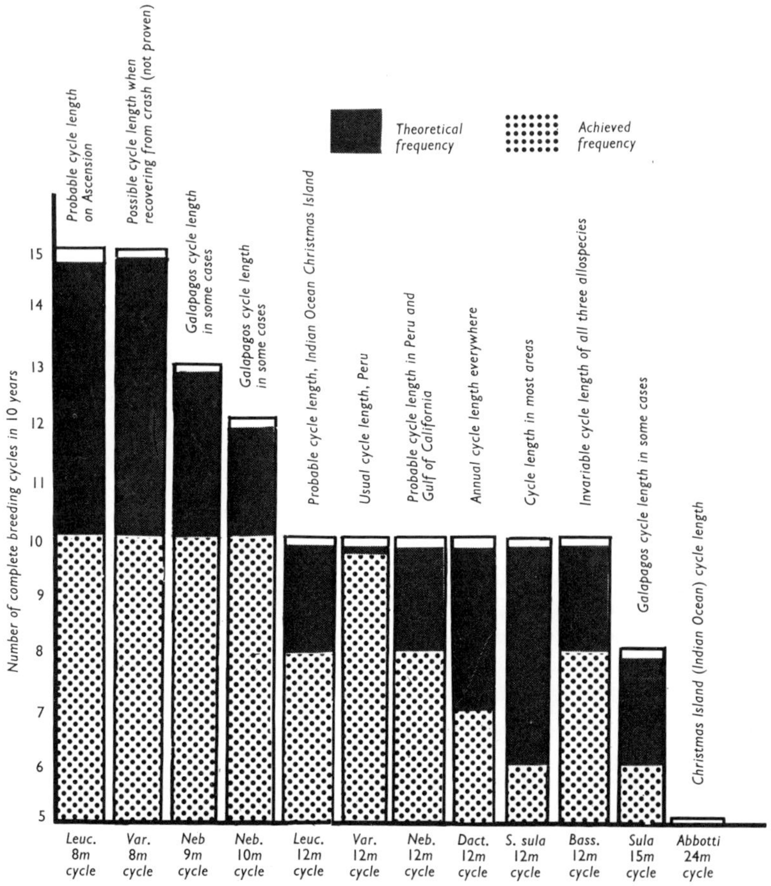

Fig. 392. The frequency of breeding in the Sulidae; theoretical and actual compared.

year whether in a seasonal environment or otherwise. The breeding cycle is somewhat longer than in the brown, but it is not clear why, in an aseasonal environment such as Ascension, it cannot breed almost as often as this other species. *Abbott's booby* with its biennial breeding, has the lowest breeding frequency of any sulid but is highly specialised and probably (p. 781) could not breed annually, nor at intervals of a year-plus-a-fraction. The *Atlantic gannet* inhabits a highly seasonal environment which certainly restricts it to breeding once each year and the same is true for the other two gannets.

Nowhere in the family, therefore, is there a hint that breeding could be more frequent. The annual cycle has been abandoned in several cases where more frequent breeding is possible (cycle length reduced) or where conditions permit cycle-length to be extended as an adaptive measure.

Concerning the second of the two aspects of breeding frequency—the deliberate omission of whole breeding cycles—it seems (see Species Accounts) that at least white and brown boobies, and possibly, also, red-foots, blue-foots and Peruvian boobies, have rest years. On the other hand, the gannet makes little if any use of them. Almost all, or all, 'missed' seasons are due to loss of egg or of mate. Thus, even if a bereaved male replaces his mate, she may not lay the first year and the pair thus appear to be missing a season. Even if rest years are genuine in the blue water boobies, it is difficult to interpret them, because one does not know how they relate to the fluctuations in population or whether they are physiologically necessary and therefore devices to maximise rather than reduce productivity. Proponents of intrinsic regulation regard them as control mechanisms, reducing output where necessary, but the mechanism by which the necessity is so finely gauged remains highly obscure so far as sulids are concerned.

Delayed maturity is similar. Again, the question is whether the 3, 4, 5 or more years pre-breeding life helps productivity by avoiding stress on young birds, whose attempts would largely fail anyway, or whether the period is often longer than it need be and thus represents a potential reservoir of breeding power, to be tapped when circumstances dictate. For most sulids, there is no information on the first-time breeding success of young birds as against that of older ones, so one simply cannot say whether it is more productive to breed first at 4 than at 3 and even if it were, whether the advantage gained by the younger birds would be offset by stress. There are figures to show that inexperienced gannets breed less successfully than experienced (p. 110) and this is true for many other seabirds too, but this proves nothing about age. It is likely that there *would* be a reproductive advantage to be gained by breeding at 4 instead of 5, for even if young and inexperienced birds were slightly less successful than older, inexperienced birds, they would probably produce significantly more young in their reproductive life (but see below). All this may hold for boobies too. Thus, whilst an orthodox interpretation would insist that delay in breeding confers advantages that outweigh the extra young that would have been gained, absolutely no proof of this has yet been adduced. A relevant point is that all the evidence for the gannets indicates (p. 102) that young inexperienced breeders *can* cope with the actual collecting of food equally as well as can older, experienced ones. This strongly suggests (as I have repeatedly stressed in other contexts) that populations are not high enough to induce actual competition for food between individuals. If they did, younger, less experienced birds should be at a disadvantage in obtaining food. Because they evidently are not, it is difficult to believe that breeding stresses them significantly more than it does experienced birds. Yet many gannets withhold breeding until they are 5 or even 6 years old.

It may be that such birds are simply late in reaching some undefinable but nonetheless precise level of fitness. On this view, neither 3, 4, 5 or 6 years are necessarily required before breeding, but the attainment of a level of fitness is. This is tantamount to saying that the delayed maturity is not a device to lower productivity, but rather to ensure that the individual does not impair its total productivity. It should also be remembered that in a long-lived species the younger the bird the less significant is the loss of a breeding season. Rest years would presumably be subject to the same 'explanation'.

We may now propose a general reply to the question: is productivity maximal or is it reduced by intrinsic means? Brood size is maximal in all except gannets; breeding frequency is maximal in terms of the time relationships of normally consecutive breeding efforts, but may conceivably be less than maximal in species which have rest years; delayed maturity may be necessary, not as any fixed period but as an individually variable requirement for reaching perfect fitness. Overall, there is more evidence to suggest maximum productivity than to indicate the witholding of recruitment.

In the population control mechanism suggested earlier (p. 861) there is no need to postulate either density-dependent competition or the intrinsic regulation of populations. Instead, each pair reproduces maximally and the population rises until cut back by shortage of food, that shortage, however, NOT having been caused by the increased population but by some other factor or factors, such as climatic change, oceanographical factors, or even biological factors affecting the distribution and or availability of food. These latter could be alterations in prey-predator ratios *below* the surface, or changes in the food-chain at low trophic levels. Thus, it is easy to accommodate the observation cited above and (for the gannet) several others which make it impossible to believe that there is actual *competition* for food. Also it becomes unnecessary to postulate fine, intrinsic controls aimed at keeping the population below some hypothetical level. Food remains the ultimate controlling factor, but one is spared both the strain on one's credulity of a concept in which a few thousand more or less of a seabird species introduces actual competition and the equally difficult feat of conceiving a mechanism by which both the food supply and the population levels necessary to avoid over-exploitation are monitored by each species. The latter situation becomes even more complex when, as they must be, the effects of competing species are considered. Reduction in food would, if severe and long maintained, automatically lead to reduction of clutch size and to all the other features associated with scarce food, but competition *as such* would not be important. Conversely, ample food would lead to larger clutches (or their equivalent) greater productivity and increasing population, but again, rarely, if ever to the point of competition. It is possible that, although populations of most or perhaps all invertebrates could rise and fall by non-selective and density independent mortality, as imposed, for example by climatic factors, vertebrate populations could not remain as stable as they do without density-dependent control. In this case, the suggestion made above would be untenable. There seems no logical incongruity in it, however, and it should be stressed that the mortality induced by such food shortage would be selective; superior individuals would survive best.

Food, though the main factor affecting population growth, may not be the only one. Many other factors, such as availability of nest sites, a possible increase in mortality by predation or disease or interference from conspecifics consequent upon higher numbers, would have to be taken into account in any general model.

BREEDING REGIMES

Most sulids spend part of the year away from the breeding colony. This is obviously adaptive in opening up a wider foraging range than during the breeding cycle and reducing energy costs by eliminating journeys to and from the colony. Exceptionally, as in the brown boobies of Ascension, this pattern is modified as an adaptive response enabling the birds to maintain constant readiness to breed (p. 474). Here, there is daily attendance throughout the year. The pattern of attendance at the colony is extremely flexible in all species, except perhaps Abbott's booby. The most unusual case is that of the Atlantic gannet which spends about 4 months at the breeding site in addition to the time needed for incubation and chick rearing. This extra period is used in defence of the site and consolidation of the pair bond.

In general, where there are marked seasonal (climatic) changes which affect food, birds breed annually. Where the climate is equable and food is mainly constant or unpredictably scarce, birds may breed non-seasonally, with annual or non-annual cycles (the former can occur when a population lays through much of the year but each individual lays annually). The sulids fit fairly well into this scheme. Except for Abbott's booby, those (few) that are restricted to areas with highly seasonal climates show appropriately timed annual breeding. Those with a distribution embracing different climates show an appropriate range of breeding regimes: annual and seasonal; loosely or very loosely seasonal and annual or even largely aseasonal and annual; loosely seasonal and less-than-annual.

The species accounts give details of the relationship between breeding and seasonal factors, from which it is clear that in all cases far-reaching sets of linked adaptations have evolved; the Atlantic gannet (p. 118) is perhaps the clearest example. It is difficult to generalise about the three pan-tropical boobies, spread, as they are, over such vast areas throughout which there could be so many unknown variables. From an examination, on a global scale, of the seasonal breeding characteristics of all the Sulidae, several trends may be discerned, albeit grossly obscured by inadequate and uneven records. In the three pan-tropical species, breeding seasons are often at opposite periods of the year in northern and southern hemispheres, even where the latitudinal differences are not great. The extreme eastern and western sections of the Indian Ocean subtend significantly different laying seasons. On Christmas Island the brown and red-footed boobies are annual, fairly seasonal breeders, laying mainly April–July, whereas in the western Indian Ocean, on Aldabra, the red-foot lays more continuously but with a marked peak in the southern spring and summer (November to April). Both areas are subject to strong, seasonal climatic changes. Christmas Island experiences the dry south-east trades from March–November and the monsoons between November and February–March, during which the wind is often strong, from the north-east or north-west. Aldabra also experiences the south-east trades from April–October and light and variable predominantly north-west winds between November and March. However, Aldabra is not typical of an oceanic island at 10°S.; islands further east than Farquhar are probably little affected by the north-west monsoon. The situation in the Pacific is even less clear cut. Birds in the east tend to avoid laying in the second quarter more than those in the west. However, across the whole vast belt of tropical Pacific the main influences (the North Equatorial current (north of the equator)), the South Equatorial current (south of about 5°S.) and the equatorial Counter-current flowing between them) are relatively non-seasonal. Breeding, is correspondingly aseasonal. In the tropical Atlantic laying is not seasonal but in the Caribbean it often occurs in the first and second quarters thus avoiding the heavy precipitation late in the year. Often all three species lay during the same periods of the year, but overall the brown lays in those months more than do the other two, a trait which, on Ascension, is correlated with its greater breeding frequency. In every ocean segment, however, all three species show a wide spread of laying, which emphasises the lack of clearly adaptive seasonal regimes.

The departure of some *populations* of sulids from an annual breeding regime is perhaps unusual in that, where other seabirds do so, it is more usually a specific rather than a local adaptation. It is a further example of the evolution of an adaptation which involves the modification of the bird's physiological responses to external timers.

The white booby is the only member of this tropical trio which, regardless of its extremely wide spread of laying, in some localities amounting to several months, *nowhere* departs from a strictly annual cycle. Even in the northern hemisphere, in the Arabian Gulf, it has a protracted laying seasonal though other seabirds breeding there lay much more restrictedly (Bailey 1972). The other two are slightly more flexible. The red-foot is probably an annual breeder almost everywhere, but may lengthen its cycle in the Galapagos and possibly elsewhere whilst the brown is certainly typically an annual breeder but may shorten its cycle on Ascension and possibly elsewhere. In both places, the white, also, occurs, but remains annual.

Probably, the blue-foot is typically an annual and fairly seasonal breeder, as in the Gulf of California, and the Tres Marias and Marietas, the Revillagigedos and the Lobos Islands of northern Peru. In all these areas, and especially in the area affected by the California current and its associated upwelling, which is seasonal, there seems good reason to lay seasonally. The Gulf, too, has its cyclic upwellings. So far as is known, all other sulids (brown, white and red-footed) found in some of these areas breed at the same season as the blue-foot. In the relatively aseasonal Galapagos, however, the blue-foot lays more or less continuously and here it has shortened its cycle. Again, the white booby breeds on the same islands, but annually.

The Peruvian's restricted distribution precludes geographical comparison of breeding regime and the same applies to Abbott's. In both cases laying is seasonal (though with a very wide spread in the Peruvian) and the climatic regimes are also seasonal, particularly for Abbott's.

The three gannets are all restricted to seasonal or highly seasonal areas and time their strictly annual breeding adaptively, the Atlantic laying almost entirely in April and May and the Cape and Australasian mainly in October and November. However, the two latter are markedly less seasonal than the former and this probably reflects differences in food and in the weather conditions which affects the survival of fledglings.

SYNCHRONISATION

In general in birds, synchronisation is adaptive either as an anti-predator device or (if seasonal also) because precise timing of laying enhances survival of young, or because it reduces interference from conspecifics. Close synchronisation, furthermore, almost certainly always depends partly upon social stimulation. Social stimulation itself is a function of numbers and density. There are in the Sulidae four main colony types and associated breeding regimes:

1. Large, dense 'blanket' colonies, notably as in the three gannets on the tops of islands. These show considerable overall synchrony but also substantial spread. The synchrony depends partly upon social stimulation (p. 123). Atlantic gannets nest at a highly invariable density and so it is impracticable to distinguish between the onset and synchrony of laying in equal-sized groups of dense as opposed to sparse nesters, but it is fair to infer that dense nesting, as such, enhances social stimulation. Looked at from another angle, small groups, whether semi-isolated parts of a large colony or small, separate colonies (and in both cases experienced breeders) begin laying later, have a later mean laying date and proportionately a wider spread than bigger groups (see p. 120). The difference is due to the difference in social stimulation, to which both size and density contribute. Since colonies are usually large and density is high, social stimulation is maximal. The advantages of the earlier and more synchronised laying to which these factors contribute has already been discussed (p. 104). In the comparative context the essential point is that these advantages hinge entirely on the seasonal nature of the gannet's environment, particularly in its effect upon the post-fledging survival of juveniles. Probably it is highly adaptive to fledge early in the season and this is aided by the regulatory effect of social stimulation on laying. However, these circumstances apply only to gannets and only gannets show this type of social structure.
2. The second major type of sulid colony is that found in the three tropical boobies. Here, there is great variation in colony size (though on average they are medium-small), in group (sub-colony) size and in group density, which on average is low. Colonies are composed of clumps, variably separated. With this structure is associated, overall, an extremely wide spread of laying, yet within groups there is indisputably more synchronisation than would result from chance. This is to be expected from such a colony structure, so far as the contribution of social stimulation to timing is concerned. Large distances between groups permit these to be out of phase with each other more easily than if the same groups were closely adjacent. Relatively greater synchrony *within* groups is facilitated by the converse. Functionally, these results accord perfectly well with the aseasonal environmental regime. There is probably little difference in the survival of young born at different seasons. Thus, social stimulation is not important as a seasonal timer. Indeed, there is probably advantage in having staggered output, for extreme versions of the same reasons that maintain spread in the gannet (p. 104). The advantage of synchrony within groups may be to minimise intraspecific interference

   The factors producing 'species-typical' density are unknown but at least those densities are much more variable than in the gannet. Correspondingly, so is synchrony, and the respective advantages are consistent with what we can deduce about the selection pressures imposed by each species' environment.
3. The third type, found in the Peruvian, is intermediate between the gannet and the three blue-water boobies. Thus, like gannets, the colonies are huge and dense and tend to form 'blankets' but, like boobies, they are more readily separable into sub-colonies. Correspondingly, like gannets, there is a considerable degree of seasonal timing, but like boobies much more overall spread allied with sub-group synchrony. Both sets of characteristics are simply explained and highly adaptive to what is basically an environment correspondingly intermediate between that of gannets and tropical boobies. The straightforward pressures on space enforce large size and dense nesting. Unlike the gannet, however, the Peruvian booby faces no strong selection pressure to ensure that its young fledge during a fairly limited seasonal period. Similarly, unlike the boobies, it

is not dealing with a largely non-seasonal and unpredictable food supply. It falls between the two. Food is somewhat seasonal and breeding is somewhat seasonal (p. 625). But a colony of Peruvian boobies resembles a concentrated blue-foot colony—that is a spatially compressed congregation of out-of-phase groups, rather than a gannetry which is a vast, fairly homogeneous whole in so far as this is consistent with the inevitable variation caused by age, etc. Despite superficial similarities, there is an important difference between the gannet and piquero in colony structure and its synchronising results and the adaptive significance of this timing effect.

4. In the fourth case, Abbott's booby, there is greatly reduced colony size and density. Social stimulation certainly exists and breeding is broadly seasonal, but the relict nature of the one existing population and its major specialisations, such as biennial breeding, make it difficult to deduce the role of density in this species. There probably is sub-group synchrony.

The foregoing analysis of density in relation to the timing of breeding attempts to show some of the differences between sulids in the selection pressures bearing upon their reproductive success. Colony size and density cannot be understood if social stimulation is ignored. The precise advantages conferred are composite and represent a balance different for each species. In particular, much remains to be discovered about the function of typical sub-group synchrony via sub-group density.

LENGTH AND COMPOSITION OF THE BREEDING CYCLE

The breeding cycle has already been discussed in several contexts. It has been shown to vary adaptively in length (pp. 907, 909), thus affecting breeding frequency, this variation being itself related to climatic (and associated food) factors.

No two sulids have breeding cycles similarly composed. Fig. 393 depicts the differences. By far the most variable components are the duration of chick growth and of post-fledging feeding. The latter alone (aseasonal environment permitting) can control the possibility of less than annual, or enforce more than annual, breeding. The differences between species are enormous, ranging from the three-month chick rearing period of the gannet to more than 12 months required by Abbott's booby and some brown boobies and red-foots. The latter take four times as long to rear 1000g as the gannet takes to rear 4500g!

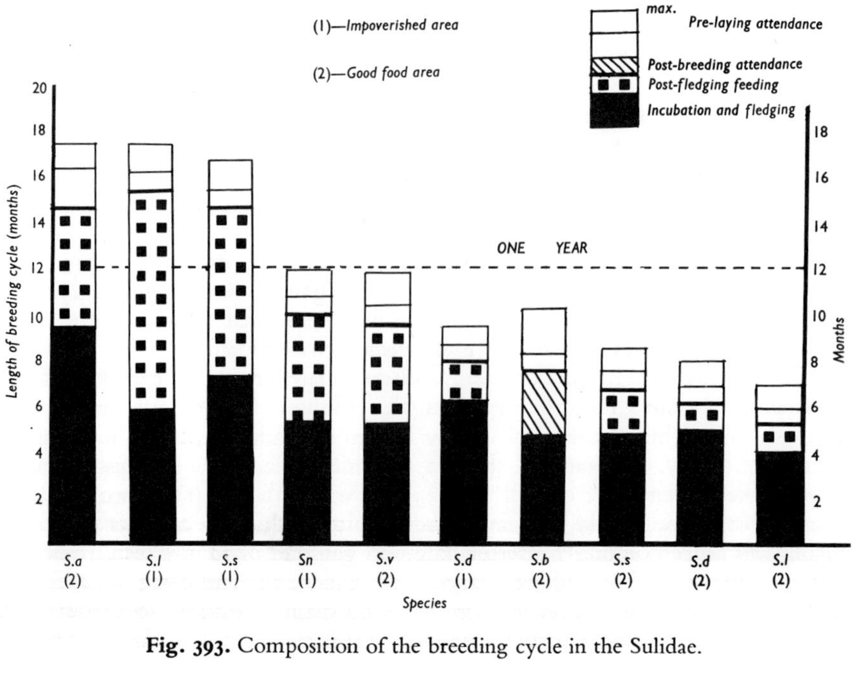

Fig. 393. Composition of the breeding cycle in the Sulidae.

The length of the breeding cycle is one of the main adaptive variables in the reproductive strategy of any bird and this is true both of the overall length and of the particular relationship of the parts. The gannet has been able to compress the growth of its young into a very short period because nutritious fish are abundant at the time its chick is growing. In this situation, however, it has been faced with the problem of optimal usage. It is practicable for chicks to be fed so much that they deposit fat, and very heavy chicks cannot fly. So, as pointed out earlier, the gannet had to 'decide' where to draw the line. Fat young, once they have jumped off the cliff ledge, cannot return and cannot be fed at sea. A mortality-laden independence is thus necessarily part of the evolutionary packet. On the other hand, early young are at an advantage and since quick growth makes them early and quick growth is highly feasible between June and September in the North Sea and North Atlantic, the gannet had either to use the available food to the maximum, so producing fat young after 13 weeks with all that implies (p. 217) or eschew maximal use and produce leaner young (perhaps at 11 weeks) with the hypothetical but reasonable corollary that such young would be able to return to the nest to be fed. It has 'chosen' the former and by so doing become the only sulid to relinquish the considerable reproductive advantages of post-fledging feeding. One can never know the precise balance of advantages over penalties that this entrained but it seems a clear example of the evolutionary ploy of using an important environmental advantage to the full, and adapting to the disadvantages involved, rather than compromising. One can visualise several disadvantages of retaining post-fledging feeding in the gannet's situation and equally important advantages of its adopted method (above). The interest lies in the balance of forces and the deployment of the evolutionary jig-saw pieces thrown up. Thus, rapid growth and no post-fledging feeding speedily accomplishes the main business of breeding, with great advantage to the young gannet. Apparently paradoxically, however, one sees that the gannet has, in fact, a long breeding season. Some are present at the colony for nine months of the year or more. Instead of abandoning the relatively dangerous colony for the safety of the seas, gannets defend an empty nest for perhaps five months of the year. This is entirely consistent with all one can observe about the importance of the site to the gannet—the astonishing competition, elaborate site-oriented displays and so on (p. 162). Half or more of the entire breeding season is devoted to site activities rather than the basic business of incubating and chick rearing. The cleverness of the use to which evolution has 'put' the environmental factors is thus evident: good, seasonal feeding is followed by rapid seasonal deterioration of weather; good feeding enables quick chick growth and consequent evasion of bad weather; the timing involved is helped by social stimulation; this in turn is facilitated by dense nesting; this involves site competition, and site maintenance and defence is strenghtened by the release of time and energy consequent upon the rapid completion of chick growth which was advantageous and environmentally feasible in the first place! All the behavioural adaptations flow from this environmental equation which is based on optimal use of food.

In complete contrast, the Galapagos red-foots, whilst equally adapted to the nature of their food (p. 681) which is non-seasonal and scarce, have evolved the opposite sort of adaptive web. Laying occurs at all seasons. Chick growth is prolonged instead of rapid and above all post-fledging feeding is exceptionally protracted. Except for incubation and care of young, the time spent at the colony is restricted to the three weeks or so required for re-establishing a site, forming or re-forming a pair and building a nest. These responses do not depend on the timing of breeding by social (behavioural) factors and since there is no lack of sites, there is thus little or no site competition. This in turn correlates with, and in a sense 'explains' much red-foot behaviour just as the corresponding site competition in the gannet 'explains' its behaviour. The link between environment and the length and competition of the breeding cycle is further confirmed by the intra-specific variation in the red-foot. In more seasonal localities, such as Christmas Island, breeding is approximately annual and loosely seasonal, the fledging period is much shorter and post-fledging feeding greatly reduced. Thus the contrast with the gannet is not so marked. Unfortunately it is not known whether there are any social and behavioural differences between the two types of red-foot population.

The remainder of the family fit between these two extreme situations. The brown booby is an unusual case, in that it is apparently hugely variable in the length of time devoted to post-fledging feeding even within the same, impoverished, environment (p. 463). This makes its cycle length either considerably less or more than a year, a phenomenon which is not recorded for any other sulid.

Abbott's booby is a different case, for although it has the longest cycle of all, it is in response to a seasonal rather than an aseasonal environment and also, probably, to a special feeding technique and to the demands of the jungle habitat (see p. 781). It is thus not comparable to the long Galapagos red-foot cycle.

In sum, within the Sulidae, breeding (egg-laying) occurs at intervals of a year, a year plus a fraction, less than a year and two years, the cycle being in each case relatable to environmental factors. At least three species vary the frequency of breeding, viz. annually in some regions but less than annually in more impoverished areas (red-foot), annually or more than annually in more impoverished areas (brown and probably blue-foot), this being correlated with different adaptive approaches to the problems of breeding in a food-scarce area.

OTHER ASPECTS OF BREEDING ECOLOGY

It remains to make comparative remarks about some other aspects of breeding ecology.

1. *Food*

The type of food taken, its distribution, abundance and seasonal aspects underly virtually all of an animal's biology. It shapes morphology; it is usually the ultimate factor controlling population size; it may be the proximate factor initiating breeding and it determines much breeding strategy culminating in the production of young at the best time for survival. All these factors have constantly obtruded in this account of the sulids, which are all highly specialised plunge-diving fishers. Unfortunately, we still lack any detailed comparative study of fishing behaviour and food species taken in the various boobies and gannets and all that I can do here is to mention some general points.

Form and feeding

The behavioural response to the nature of the available food lies primarily in hunting technique with its concomitant morphological correlates, whilst the ecological response lies in the use to which the acquired energy is put—the strategy of deployment. Morphological features are discussed in the section on comparative morphology. The main difficulty in interpreting their relation to food is the paucity of information about the food spectra of sympatric species and the complete lack of information about the preferences of males and females (morphologically often very dissimilar). Yet these morphological differences subtend different prey-catching abilities, since weight, body and bill proportions, and plumage pattern are important correlates of feeding. Even if the same prey species are taken, species or sex differences in the boobies can be expected to affect at least the proportion of each size class taken.

In general, sulids have not developed great differences in size and structure. Although the lightest sulid weighs only a quarter as much as the heaviest (see Fig. 363) there is considerably less variation in size and nothing approaching the range found for example in the petrels, terns or auks. This suggests that deep plunge diving basically requires a fairly high minimum weight which, in correlation with an adaptive shape, produces a medium-large size (all smaller plunge divers penetrate less deeply than sulids).

Nevertheless, significant adaptive radiation has occurred. Nowhere in the world is there an area in which only a small or large booby occurs. The only areas in which only a large or medium-sized *sulid* occurs are cold water and rich in food. They concern only two species, the gannet superspecies and the Peruvian booby. Elsewhere, size differentiation has been a universal response to sympatry. Morphologically the family is divisible into three well defined groups (see Figs. 364–72):

(i) Extremely heavy; large (Atlantic gannet).
(ii) Medium heavy; large (Cape and Australasian gannet; male and female white booby; male and female Abbott's booby; female blue-foot; female brown).

(iii) Small and light (male and female red foot; male blue-foot; male brown and, though less appropriately accommodated here, male and female Peruvian).

The selection pressures responsible for shaping them have concerned not only feeding but also energy budgets and the requirements of the breeding habitat. Although feeding is under discussion here, the others must also be considered. The whole system is an excellent example of interrelationships in an adaptive web.

(i) The Atlantic gannet is exceptionally heavy and has responded to the presence of large and powerful prey by evolving weight for deep diving and a large, deep bill to provide gripping strength. To these, it allies far-foraging. This is a complementary system. The large size and related food reserves mean that prolonged and fruitless searching at relatively high energy cost, often in extremely harsh conditions, is perfectly acceptable since it is associated with the ability to utilise large prey to a remarkable extent once located (and location is aided by signal-plumage). This ability depends partly on penetration (weight) and on the related capacity to ingest vast quantities in one feeding bout. The system depends on the presence of large shoaling fish which, even if hard to locate, yield large rewards. This is not to say that smaller fry or solitary fish are ignored but merely that the dominant factor is the presence of large and in many cases extremely muscular prey. The evolutionary rationale of the gannet's breeding system (quick growth and large fat deposits) rests on this base. Of important complementary value, however, are climatic and breeding-habitat factors, for this gannet inhabits climatically extremely severe northern seas with low temperatures, blizzards of sleet and snow and persistently high, cold winds, and has windy islands with large cliff-ledges readily available. The first factors encourage insulating and food-storage fat (weight) and the second provides the necessary breeding environment in which a heavy seabird can land and take flight. The other two gannets live in warmer seas and nest on flat ground, a combination which may account for their much lower weight even though they are about as large. The Atlantic gannet's sexual isomorphism is explicable on the grounds that both must cope with the same environmental factors and both must have the ability to catch large quantities of large prey if the opportunities of their particular region are to be fully exploited. The same argument does not apply to boobies (below). The role of sexual isomorphism in shared site defence is also more important in gannets than in other sulids.

(ii) Most sulids fall into the second category. Thus, a weight of about 1600–2000g and a bill length of 100–110mm with large size (almost as large as the Atlantic gannet) is the most favoured combination for a sulid. All species included in this group inhabit tropical or warm-temperate seas, where thermo-regulation is often concerned with facilitating heat loss rather than conserving it and extensive fat deposits would probably not be an advantage, even if the available food made them practicable. Concomitantly, the most numerous nesting islands are flat, and in fact all these species are flat ground nesters. This, too, favours lightness. The only heavier seabirds inhabiting this sort of feeding and breeding environment are some albatrosses, and their feeding regimes are quite different.

The bills of this group include the longest in the family, though they are slightly thinner, relative to length than that of the Atlantic gannet. Prey size is often large, but it is doubtful whether as many items are as heavy and muscular as, for example, the large mackerel which form a staple prey for gannets, especially during the most demanding period of chick growth. Almost certainly, the species in this group do not penetrate as deeply as gannets, a large part of their prey consisting of flying-fish and squid from surface layers, whereas mackerel shoals are often 10 metres or more deep.

(iii) The considerable gap in sizes between groups two and three presumably reflects a significant difference in prey-spectra. Excluding the special case of the piquero, four boobies (three of them males) weigh less than 1000g. All of them have a tropical distribution, often in impoverished areas, but with the exception of the blue-foot and to a much lesser extent the brown, with their inshore diving, it is difficult to see precisely how small size is adaptive. It may confer such rapidity that small prey is easily caught but eludes larger birds. It will also subtend a different energy budget. However, only one *species* (that is, including both sexes)—the red-foot—has gone in for such lightness. With lightness it has linked long wings and tail which suggests that its fishing methods may be significantly different from those of other sulids. It is also the only tree-nester apart from Abbott's, and its lightness is undoubtedly a help in this context. The fact that the very smallest boobies are all males (red-foot, blue-foot and brown) seems merely an exaggeration of the normal trend in sulid sexual dimorphism, the selective basis of which may have to do with egg production, among other things.

The Peruvian booby does not fit exactly into this third category. Its medium weight and size and relatively slight sexual dimorphism probably relates to the nature of its food. Anchovetas are not only super-abundant but are also relatively small and uniform and there can be little selective advantage in specialising either on different prey-species or sizes. They are also often fairly deep and good penetration must be advantageous, particularly in el niño years, when prey is deeper anyway, and selection pressure immense (p. 598).

In sum, the inter-specific variations in weight and the intra-specific ones in weight and size within the Sulidae relate to definable environmental factors—feeding, climate and nesting habitat—conferring advantages which are broadly discernible, even though quantitative evidence for these is almost always lacking. The nature of the food supply, whether relatively sparse and unpredictable, necessitating lengthy foraging trips, or richer and more dependable, obtainable by shorter trips, is perhaps the major determinant of the species' breeding biology. This theme has been elaborated in the species accounts and the main components may be drawn together in the following scheme (Table 132).

TABLE 132

THE RELATIONSHIP BETWEEN FOOD AND FORAGING HABITS AND BREEDING ECOLOGY IN THE SULIDAE

Far foraging (food scarce and/or difficult to locate; fishing trips long, up to 300 miles or more)	Red-footed booby	Clutch of one relatively large egg; slow growth; high starvation rate of young in some areas; breeding cycle may take more than a year; laying may be aseasonal.
	White booby	Clutch of two but obligatory brood reduction; slow growth in some areas; may be high starvation rate of young; laying may be only loosely seasonal.
	Abbott's booby	Clutch of one; relatively large egg; extremely slow growth; breeding cycle takes more than a year, laying fairly seasonal and thus, because of length of cycle, can breed only once in two years.
Near foraging (food relatively rich, rich, or abundant, *or* special feeding mechanisms not used by far foragers)	Atlantic gannet	Clutch of one; small egg; rapid growth with deposition of large fat reserves; no starvation of young; laying annual and highly seasonal.
	Peruvian booby	Clutch of 2–4 (average 3); young grow quickly. No starvation except in catastrophic years; laying annual but only loosely seasonal.
	Blue-footed booby	Clutch of 1–3 (average 2); facultative brood reduction; young grow fairly quickly; starvation rate variable but mainly low; special feeding mechanism; laying seasonal or aseasonal, annual or less than annual, depending on area.
	Brown booby	Clutch of 1 or 2 but obligatory brood reduction; young grow fairly quickly; starvation rate variable but mainly low; special feeding mechanism; laying seasonal or aseasonal, annual or less than annual depending on area.

2. *Age of first breeding*

The relevance of this to recruitment has been mentioned (p. 908) but some specific points remain. In general, in birds, this phenomenon cannot be related in any simple way to body size. Geese breed sooner than storm petrels and woodpigeons than kittiwakes or fulmars. The sulids are all slow to begin breeding and in this respect are similar to albatrosses, penguins and frigates, all of which may reach more than seven and sometimes more than ten, years of age before breeding for the first time.

Their common feature is a highly specialised feeding technique, to which must be added (in the case of most frigates) a breeding distribution in relatively impoverished ocean belts. It may be taken for granted that in all sulids the motor skills of plunge-diving take some time to learn, but certainly not four or five years. Within the family, however, there is considerable variation, both between and within species. Gannets apparently require a longer pre-breeding period than any other sulid. Information is sketchy, but indicates that white, brown and red-footed boobies first breed in their third year; Peruvian boobies may breed in their second year (but will probably be into their third before the breeding cycle is over). Gannets usually begin their first breeding attempt when in their fifth year and will be into their sixth before that breeding season is over.

One may speculate, first, whether it is likely to be easier for boobies to acquire the necessary feeding lore. It seems somewhat anomalous that the gannet, breeding where food is abundant, has a longer deferred maturity period than the pan tropical boobies. However, it seems probable that gannets use well defined feeding areas and it needs little imagination to realise that, in the North Sea and North Atlantic, success must depend on hunting in the right area for the weather at the time and on taking account of the habits and movements of the food fish through the season. There is no difficulty whatsoever in reconciling the fact that food is abundant with the need for expert hunting lore (a reconciliation which, by contrast need not be made for the piquero). This would seem to be enough to explain a reasonably long apprenticeship, but hardly sufficient to require five years. There is, however, the additional factor, that gannets spend their first year or two well outside the normal adult range. The selection pressures which have led to this are not relevant here, but the effect is to reduce the number of pre-breeding years spent in 'home waters' to two or three. When it is recalled that a pre-breeding year within the colony is usually necessary to establish a site and form a pair bond and that this requires considerable time and energy, the average male is being called upon to do this after less than two years in home waters or in other words almost the minimum if it is to experience seasonal phenomena. In concrete terms (Fig. 53) a male born in June 1960, which returns in May 1962, establishes a site in March or April 1964 and has an egg the following April or May, will have less than two years full freedom to explore feeding areas. Comparably, the royal albatross has a low mortality during the four (or more) years during which it wanders at will, but a quarter of them then die in the year following their return to the breeding grounds. This, it has been suggested (C. J. R. Robertson pers. comm.), may be due to the restriction of feeding area enforced by attendance at the colony.

The pan tropical boobies are a different case. The unpredictability of their food supply probably makes it impossible to acquire information comparable to that open to the gannet. For opposite reasons (the great predictability of food fish nine years out of ten) the piquero, too, probably need not acquire much local lore.

It is also possible that gannets live longer than boobies and therefore (since in vertebrates age of first breeding is inversely correlated with life expectancy) do not breed as soon. Another factor may be the greater physical demands which site establishment makes on gannets (p. 173). In these ways, the apparently unduly long deferred maturity may be part of the gannet's complex adaptive syndrome, which is linked with the crucial matter of competitive site-establishment. To say merely that the time is required for learning to fish would be grossly simplistic.

The points just advanced provide, also, possible explanations for intra-specific variation in deferred maturity, at least in the gannet. The variation within each sex is marked (p. 127) but one can merely suggest that the great demands of breeding exacerbate and thus show up the effects of normal physiological variability in 'fitness'. The difference *between* the sexes, however, may perhaps be understood in terms of the greater demands made on the males (p. 128) requiring them to be older than females before first breeding. Unfortunately, there is no information on differences between the sexes of any of the boobies, in the length of deferred maturity. In giant petrels, some penguins and gulls, however, the difference corresponds with that in gannets.

If fitness requirements are so high that first breeding is precluded by marginal inadequacies, it is to be expected, and is found, that first time breeders are as good as experienced ones in feeding their young. If they make the grade at all, they make it fully in this respect and the concept of younger breeders in direct and penalised competition with older birds for food, must be discarded. On the other hand, it would remain true, on the above suggestions, that breeding was occurring as soon as possible. This of course conflicts with the view that deferred maturity is a social mechanism for reducing recruitment rate (p. 908). Hard evidence on this matter is scarce and it is therefore worth emphasising that, on the basis of direct observation, there is no exclusion of new breeders by established birds in a gannetry—either within a stable group or at the fringes of an expanding one. Any social role of deferred maturity would therefore necessarily depend on self-imposed postponement of breeding by perfectly fit individuals. Since there are some adult-plumage birds in the Clubs and there are no means of telling how fit they are, this remains a possibility. Elucidation would depend on fine enough estimates of physiological condition in non-breeders. It could be suggested that a reserve of mature individuals which have never bred would be better able to withstand extreme conditions and could thus be an insurance policy for the population. But, quite apart from the doubtful assumption that breeding weakens adults, this still leaves the question of what decides which individuals shall so penalise themselves. Also, the suggestion is particularly inappropriate in a maritime species which very rarely encounters the extreme conditions postulated.

In sum, therefore, it seems to me that deferred maturity in sulids means that the time is necessary for the acquisition of motor skills, hunting lore and in the gannet's case, enough physical fitness to enable the male to establish a site. Direct exclusion of young, inexperienced birds by established ones emphatically does not occur, but self-imposed postponement remains a theoretical possibility.

3. *Clubs*

Clubs are curious phenomena. They occur probably in all sulids except Abbott's booby and certainly in gannets, white, brown, red-footed and Peruvian boobies (see Species Accounts).

TABLE 133

TYPES OF CLUBS WITHIN THE SULIDAE

BREEDING SEASON	1	Various stages: immature birds; non-breeding adult-plumaged birds and off-duty breeders at the breeding colony, e.g., *S. dactylatra* on Ascension.
	2	Immatures; non-breeding adult-plumaged birds but NO off-duty breeders, e.g., *S. bassana* on Bass Rock.
	3	Solely off-duty breeders; no example known.
	4	Solely adult-plumaged non-breeders; no example known.
	5	Solely immature-plumaged birds at the breeding colony, e.g., *S. sula* in the Galapagos.
NON-BREEDING SEASON	6	Clubs and/or roosting aggregations, immature and adult-plumaged, at the breeding colony, e.g., *S. dactylatra* and *S. leucogaster* on Ascension.
	7	Clubs and/or roosting aggregations, immature and adult-plumaged, on non-breeding islands, e.g., *S. dactylatra* and *S. leucogaster* in the Central Pacific and *S. variegata*, Peru, *S. nebouxii* in Gulf of California.
	8	No Clubs or roosting congregations on land, but may roost communally at sea, e.g., *S. bassana*.

The main questions concern their composition and function, consideration of which, in turn, devolves around the nature of the congregations concerned. Table 133 shows the main types of gathering.

Category 1 is probably common in the pan tropical boobies, particularly in localities where there are few islands, but it is usually not possible to distinguish between off-duty breeders and non-breeding adults. The presence in Clubs of off-duty breeders has been specifically proved by sightings of colour ringed individuals only for the white booby on Ascension but is likely to be more general. There seems nothing intrinsically improbable about their attendance in Clubs, but it would depend to some extent on the absence of selection pressure favouring constant attendance at the nest site. It would be theoretically possible for attendance at the Club to be made conditional upon the partner's attendance at the site, but almost certainly this has not happened; unattended chicks are common. A positive inducement to vacate the nest site for the Club could be escape from the chick's food pestering, which in these three species is often severe.

Category 2 is a more specialised type, regulated by the selection pressures operating on Atlantic gannets (p. 154). Thus, there is good reason to believe that breeding gannets do not spend any time in the Clubs and (unlike boobies) they never leave nests unattended. There is strong selection pressure encouraging gannets to guard their sites continuously and for the pair to spend time together there (p. 116). Attendance at the Club has no comparably strong advantages. Nevertheless, in the somewhat special circumstances of Bempton gannetry breeding birds do use what can be considered to be Club ledges (p. 135). Category 5 is rare and probably fortuitous; that is, occasionally it just so happens that only immature birds are present, but not as a result of any behaviour excluding or avoiding adults. Certainly as a species the red-foot does form mixed gatherings (as on Aldabra) containing all stages of immatures and some adults. Category 6 is similar to Category 1 and, where breeding is largely seasonal, virtually indistinguishable from it. In this case, the label 'non-breeding season' applies merely to individuals and not to the population as a whole. Category 7 is similar to Category 6, applying to areas in which there are many available nesting islands. Category 8 is again a special situation applying only to the gannet. So far as we know, outside the breeding season gannets do not congregate on land. It is not even clear that gannets are less prone to roost ashore than boobies, for much depends on the number of islands and birds and on the number of pertinent observations. However, it seems probable that gannets mainly roost at sea, except in the breeding season.

The functions of sulid Clubs are two-fold—resting and preparation for breeding. The latter is really the Club's main function, in the sense that birds can rest and preen solitarily but cannot interact, as they do in Clubs, without their fellows. Clubs are phenomena of the breeding season. Birds may and do rest and/or roost in Clubs, which thus fulfil both functions, but conversely, congregations outside the breeding season do not perform the social function (below) and are thus simply roosts.

The performance of territorial and sexual behaviour common in Clubs, presumably conditions individuals so that their capacity for appropriate responses in a whole range of situations is enhanced. This could be particularly valuable in a dense colony of aggressive individuals, as in a gannetry. Also in the gannet's case, at least, fear of land is considerable and the experience of a year or two in Clubs may facilitate eventual site establishment. This seems less applicable to boobies, which may be connected with the fact that they have experienced weeks or months of daily returns to the colony as dependent juveniles, whereas gannets experience merely a traumatic departure followed by a long period of nomadic, ocean-based life.

It has been suggested that Clubs help to regulate populations. This role would depend on their being reservoirs of potential breeders capable of being incorporated into the colony as part of a homeostatic mechanism (Wynne-Edwards 1962). The presence of non-breeding, adult plumaged birds, conveniently poised on the edge of the breeding colony may thus seem plausibly interpreted, but the points made earlier, that such individuals are of unknown physiological status and that, in gannets, there are no signs of behaviour functioning to regulate their entry into the breeding ranks, must be taken into account. Clubs undoubtedly hold hundreds of birds which are at least five years old, an age at which successful breeding can occur, but until we know that they are fit, but being prevented from breeding by a mechanism which does not involve established birds, Clubs cannot convincingly be considered recruitment regulators of a social kind. Probably the adults within them are young (or remotely conceivably, very old) and physiologically imperfect. However, consistently with my interpretation of other population phenomena, I would not consider this state to be density dependent. The role of Clubs as congregations within which individuals may rest and preen is simply explained on the basis of social attraction (in highly gregarious birds the mère proximity of conspecifics may be rewarding), limited islands and, possibly, enhanced safety. Outside the breeding season these same factors would be expected to operate.

Finally, their possible role as vehicles for the transmission of information (mainly about the location of food) must be mentioned, though it is almost certain that the feeding behaviour of sulids precludes such a mechanism (p. 893).

4. *Movements*

As in several other aspects of breeding biology, gannets and boobies show marked differences in the post-breeding movements of the young. All juvenile boobies, except Abbott's about which nothing is known, typically disperse from the breeding colony, the pan tropical species travelling large distances in several directions.

Juvenile gannets, of all three allo-species, show true migration (p. 293). Again, the difference seems related to the feeding environment. The juvenile Atlantic gannet for example, migrates south to Biscay and North African waters, regions which, climatically and with respect to available fish, are perhaps favourable for the acquisition of fishing skills (p. 252) at a time when worsening weather in home waters would impose severe trials on a newly independent and totally unskilled juvenile. Similarly, the Cape gannet migrates northwards to broadly the same areas and the Australasian migrates swiftly across the Tasman Sea to coastal waters of Australia, though it is not clear whether they thereby move into better feeding areas. As already mentioned, it may be of great survival value if, regardless of absolute plenitude, fish in the areas to which young gannets migrate are more likely to be encountered within a given time period, easier to catch or of a certain size (too big might be difficult, too small an inadequate return for effort). Also, the matter of thermoregulation (by and large they move to warmer areas) may play a part in the energy budget at this critical period in their life.

The pan tropical boobies, on the other hand, are not unskilled when post-fledging feeding ceases, nor are they faced with seasonally adverse weather, so they simply disperse, feeding over wide areas and roosting on convenient islands, upon many of which their species never breeds. The advantage of this behaviour as against remaining near the colony, is presumably that it increases the chances of locating food. Peruvian boobies tend to remain noticeably closer to their breeding locality, probably because locating food is rarely a problem except in Niño years.

The tendency to return to the natal colony is strong in all sulids, but by no means complete. Whilst, on present information, it is impossible to differentiate between species, it can be said that all (except Abbott's) are attracted to some degree to 'strange' colonies. This may be important in the growth of a particular colony (p. 69). There must be considerable but not overwhelming advantage in returning to one's own colony, and all sulids conform to this pattern. In the piquero it is probably not uncommon to breed in two or more different colonies. Whilst this may be to a large extent artificially enforced, it is probably related, too, to the easily locatable fish shoals which reduce the premium on local lore. It is consistent with this general idea that, in the Atlantic gannet, exchange between colonies on the west side of the British Isles is considerable, whereas between east and west it is probably almost nil (p. 887). Nevertheless, all sulids are typically philopatric.

5. *Parasites*

Sulids are often heavily infested with ectoparasites, notably feather lice (Mallophaga) flies (Hippoboscids) and ticks (Argasids). The Mallophagans *Eidmanniella albescens*, *Pectinopygus annulatus* and *P. sulae* have been recovered from white and red-footed boobies on many central Pacific islands (Amerson & Emerson 1971). Uchida (ref. in Baker 1951) obtained *Menopan brevipalpe* and *Lipeurus potens* from the brown booby from the 'sea off Mariana Islands'. The hippoboscid *Olfersia aenescens* has been collected from a brown booby in the Tuamotus (Morrison 1954) and the feather mite *Sulanyssus caput medusae* (Freyanidae) from red-foots on Sand Island (Johnston Atoll) (P.O.B.S.P.). The tick *Ornithodoros* (*Alectorobius*) *muesebecki* has been found on white boobies on Hasikiya, Arabian Sea (Hoogstraal 1969) and is closely related to *O. amblus* from Peruvian boobies. Reithmuller (1931) says that on Willis Island young brown boobies were greatly troubled by ticks on their legs and heads and sometimes died from the effects.

Owre (1962) suggests that pelicaniforms are continuously infested by nematodes but that they do not necessarily damage the birds and may even help in digesting prey.

The fungus *Aspergillus fumigatus*, a rare pathogen of many animals, has been recorded, as a fatal case, from a wild Cape gannet (Uys *et al.* 1966). It may have picked it up by using the same roost as gulls or cormorants, which in turn transmitted it from mainland soil or vegetation. Similarly, the virus causing Newcastle's disease in poultry has been isolated from a wild Atlantic gannet, which may have become infected in the same way. Salmonella has also been isolated from the Atlantic gannet. But epizootic disease, such as has been recorded from Manx shearwaters (puffinosis), has never been recorded in a gannetry, nor has massive mortality from any disease. Cactus lobes have been noted adhering to a brown booby and this and other plants may have been spread, in part, by sulids.

6. *Predation*

(*a*) *Natural*

Adult sulids are fairly immune from predation. Some individuals fall prey to large fish, principally sharks. An adult white booby was removed from the stomach of a shark and an Australasian gannet from a four-metre tiger shark, and there are several anecdotal records of boobies being drawn under by large fish. Possibly this source of predation is much more important than I have implied and may have been a factor in the evolution of pale underparts in boobies (see p. 821). Particularly near the breeding colony, and on young birds, predation could be substantial. One sees many boobies with slightly damaged webs and toes. No doubt the sea-eagle took some gannets in northern waters, whilst the harassment by frigates may cause one or two deaths among red-footed boobies which try to crash land in trees. These and similar incidents, however, are of no general importance, and predation can have had no effect in shaping breeding behaviour (colony size and density and breeding regime). This remains true of predation on young sulids although here there is more evidence that it does occur. Galapagos short-eared owls preyed upon young red-footed, white and blue-footed boobies (pp. 547, 700) and on young frigates, as well as upon other seabirds (swallow-tailed gull chicks and adult storm petrels in particular). The large gulls which breed alongside several sulids (herring and black-backed gulls in northern gannetries, southern black-backs in Australasian gannetries, Dominican gulls in Peruvian islands) are largely or entirely incapable of stealing young from normal, undisturbed adult gannets or boobies but wreak havoc in a disturbed colony. Turkey-vultures, however, have some success among Peruvian boobies (p. 617). No doubt, on tropical islands, a few young boobies die from scorpion or centipede bites, or are absconded by large land crabs.

(*b*) *Man as predator*

In this section it is convenient to bring together the effects, direct and indirect, which man has had upon the world's sulids, whose fortunes (or misfortunes), as those of so many other creatures, he has massively determined. Naturally other seabirds have suffered as much or more; a short general review may be found in Bourne (1972). Today there are hundreds of islands which have entirely lost their breeding populations, thousands more have had them greatly reduced. It may not be widely appreciated that in global terms the sulid population has probably diminished by over 50 per cent since the beginning of this century. This statement cannot be fully substantiated because there are no early estimates, but the qualitative impression in several areas is undoubtedly one of erstwhile huge booby populations now exterminated.

The catalogue of interference is a long one: direct killing of adults and young and the collection of eggs for food; interference in the pursuit of guano; accidental or deliberate killing during fishing or other operations; the introduction of pests; the destruction of habitats and finally and most recently, several forms of pollution.

In several areas, boobies have for hundreds or thousands of years been taken for food (even today the red-foot is greatly esteemed and the brown booby and gannet still eaten). Prehistoric middens have yielded albatross bones (Brodkorb 1963b) and no doubt sulids were equally vulnerable. Ancient shrines have been found in the Phoenix Islands which must have been visited by Polynesians for hundreds of years. Within the last hundred or so years, especially, many colonies have been exploited on an extremely large scale. The brown booby population of the Cape Verdes has been reduced to a remnant; truly vast numbers of eggs and birds have been taken from several Caribbean Islands (pp. 330, 430); almost certainly many more have greatly reduced populations; many booby populations in the Seychelles have disappeared; the Mascarenes have lost two or three species; the vast populations of the Marquesas have gone; innumerable atolls in the south-west Pacific and to a lesser extent the central and north Pacific have been exploited, in the case of the Micronesian Islands probably for thousands of years, which may partly explain the curiously thin and patchy distribution of some boobies in this segment of the Pacific; the great colony of brown boobies on Pulau Perak, in Malaya, has been brought low (p. 437). Some of the seabird colonies off north-east Australia, for example islands off Ashmore Reef, are regularly pillaged by Indonesian and no doubt other fishermen; several huge Australasian gannetries, such as Cat Island, Matapia and South West Island of the Three Kings Islands, were virtually exterminated, some having probably been exploited by Maoris prior to Europeans. Where I have found precise information, I have included it in the remarks on the colony concerned; the general point here is to indicate the scale and widespread nature of the decrease. If fishermen visit a colony several times a year, and kill large numbers of birds, even a vast colony can soon be reduced to a remnant. The excess productivity of other areas may go into replenishing such colonies.

Guano operations have affected relatively few areas. The Peruvian booby has probably benefited in the long term (p. 605) but booby populations on some islands in the Gulf of California, for example White Island, have probably suffered. The prime cause of concern, however, is undoubtedly Christmas Island, whose population of endemic seabirds, including Abbott's booby, is endangered as a result of phosphate mining (but see p. 767.)

Accidental or deliberate killing during fishing operations covers a multitude of sins. A significant cause of death in Atlantic gannets of all ages is entanglement with nets and to a lesser extent, drowning through swallowing baited hooks thrown overboard from a line fishing boat (p. 132). Peruvian boobies also suffer from net entanglement and the three tropical boobies occasionally take baited hooks. These misadventures are, however, totally insignificant in their effects upon numbers. By contrast, deliberate killing in connection with man's fishing activities is both actually and potentially of great importance. The petty killing at sea which goes on all the time, whereby for example, a French or Portuguese fisherman shoots a few gannets which are annoying him (not a few ringing returns come this way) or native fisherman spear, shoot or club imprudently hungry gannets or boobies, is again unimportant. But serious slaughter has occurred where fishermen go into breeding colonies and kill adults for bait. This reduced the famous Bird Rock gannetry of Newfoundland from probably over 50 000 pairs to a few hundred in 30 years, and the Cat Island gannetry from at least 2500 pairs to less than 20. Again, the main danger to the birds lies in the substantial depletion of breeding adults, which are many times as valuable to the species as eggs or young birds. Another facet of the bird–fisherman interaction, which could be most important of all, lies in the potential deliberate destruction of seabirds *en masse*, urged by some Government advisers with a view to eliminating what they wrongly construe as direct competition for fish. This has been suggested in the case of the Peruvian booby (p. 605) and the Cape gannet (p. 235). It would be an absurd and thoroughly reprehensible policy to pursue, but nonetheless entirely typical of man. Its absurdity would lie in the naivety of the assumption that direct competition exists (see p. 861) and its reprehensibility in the arrogance of the assumption that whole populations of birds can be eliminated on such a thin pretext. Whilst on this familiar and depressing theme one might mention the cases, notably in the north Central Pacific, in which the creation of air-strips and military bases has, either by policy or simply man's capacity for enjoyment in killing, led to the slaughter of scores or hundreds of thousands of boobies and other seabirds, principally albatrosses and terns. Nearer to home, it might not be suspected that the pleasure of sailing up to a great gannetry and taking pot-shots at sitting birds, with the usual crop of maimed individuals did not die out with the Victorians, and the passing of the Seabird Protection Act. In 1973 Ailsa Craig was thus treated (p. 35) to its annual desecration,

The introduction of pests (mainly rats, dogs, cats, goats and pigs) can have a drastic effect. Destruction of cover and/or direct predation has expelled boobies from Ascension, St. Helena, South Trinidad, Assumption, Glorioso, Rodriguez and many more. The pigs introduced to Clipperton virtually exterminated the vast population of white and brown boobies (p. 343). Rats, however, seem insignificant in the teeming colonies of piqueros and among Atlantic gannets (as on Ailsa), because they are unable to combat the adult's lethal beak.

Three forms of pollution affect sulids: oil, toxic chemicals and synthetic fibres (old netting etc.). Oil is a lesser threat to sulids (it affects mainly gannets) than to auks and ducks, presumably because the former rarely dive into an oil slick, whereas the latter often swim, drift or surface into one, and since most of their time is spent on or below the surface, they are at considerably greater risk. Nevertheless Atlantic gannets contribute a significant number of corpses to the sad toll (p. 132), particularly on the British and European coasts. Presumably the Cape gannet is equally at risk. Something like a million tons of oil per day pass round the Cape. Recently (1974) Bird Island (where most of Jarvis' work on the Cape gannet has been done) was badly polluted by another kind of oil. Something like 5000 Cape cormorants, 700 gannets and over 100 jackass penguins were killed by oil discharged from a nearby fish factory. The greatest imaginable damage would occur in the event of a large oil spill near to a major breeding colony, a scenario which is now being set up in the Shetlands and Orkneys, where giant tankers are liable to make unpleasant history in the near future. Nothing is known about oil and boobies, but probably they have suffered little damage. Toxic chemicals are building up to alarming concentrations in some sea areas (Appendix 17).

We now know that residues from organochlorine compounds are present in many seabirds throughout the world and, in certain areas, that the effects of these have been extremely harmful. The brown pelicans off Florida now lay totally useless, soft-shelled eggs. Eggs from the gannets in the Gulf of St. Lawrence are much more contaminated than those from the Bass, and there is some suggestion that this may contribute to their lower breeding success (p.108). The gannetries on Ailsa Criag and Grassholm and possibly Ireland would appear to be the most threatened from this point of view. The massive industrial discharges from the Clyde and South Wales complexes respectively may not be altogether or even mainly responsible, for the currents are complex. Water tainted by the discharge of grossly polluted European rivers may be affecting the west coastal waters of Britain.

Synthetic fibres are an unexpected hazard. A high percentage of nests in British gannetries (p. 132) embody pieces of netting, in which both young and adults may easily become entangled with fatal consequences. Grassholm seems particularly vulnerable to this tragic form of pollution, which causes a particularly slow and nasty death. Much more publicity should be devoted to an attempt to persuade fishermen not to throw their unwanted lines or bits of net into the sea.

Man has thus exerted a strong influence on sulids, almost wholly to their detriment. However, the Atlantic gannet is doing well at present, partly as a result of much reduced persecution since the beginning of this century. Its main threats are probably oil and toxic chemicals, but even these seem less dangerous to it than to the auks. The only sulid in danger as a species, and that due to the unfortunate occurrence of a commercially valuable mineral at its sole breeding place, is Abbott's booby on Christmas Island and recent highly commendable efforts by the Phosphate Commissioners and the Australian Government, subsequent to my 1974 visit, may well save not only Abbott's but also the other birds (particularly Andrew's frigate) of this lovely island.

(*c*) *Mortality*

Annual adult mortality seems remarkably similar in all sulids, at between three and ten per cent per annum and (except in the Peruvian booby) probably rarely more than five per cent if the effects of man are excluded. All sulids suffer heavy mortality (of the order of 70–80 per cent) between fledging and breeding (this is only an assumption so far as Abbott's is concerned) though its precise timing depends on whether, the species feeds the free-flying juvenile or not. There may well be slight differences between species, and gannets (perhaps all three 'species') are likely to suffer most. Life expectancy is roughly 15–20 years, probably substantially more in some species (perhaps particularly gannets and Abbott's booby). There are now several records of live Atlantic and Australasian gannets well over 20 years old and a substantial proportion must be over 30 or even 40 (see p. 292). This is merely in accord with the information now accruing for several other seabirds (particularly Procellariiforms) which encompasses individuals now known to be 30, 40 and even more than 50 years old.

We know nothing about possible fluctuations in mortality rates at different stages of maturity. Probably, after about two years, the annual mortality rate becomes constant, as we know to be the case in many birds. My figures for annual adult mortality in the gannet, over many years, show no significant fluctuations. It would appear that Atlantic gannets, at least, are not susceptible to decimation by exceptionally bad years, probably owing their immunity to the factors discussed earlier (food reserves, powerful flight etc.). Among sulids, only the Peruvian booby is known to suffer, periodically, massive mortality.

4. BREEDING BEHAVIOUR

INTRODUCTION

The comparative accounts are intended to deal mainly with ideas and generalities. A comparison of behaviour involves discussion and interpretation but illuminates the adaptive characteristics of each subject. It should usually be found possible to move readily between any species account and the appropriate comparative discussion but it is not always possible to use the descriptive name for a particular behaviour pattern as the heading of a comparative section, for each species has its own display. Instead, the functional grouping must be used. For example, discussion of Bowing and its equivalents such as Forward Head Waving, must be grouped under the appropriate functional heading, in this case 'Territorial Display'.

A stranger to sulids, presented with a series of skins representing the family, would easily recognise their close relationship. Perhaps in only one other family of seabirds (the frigates) is there so little difference in size and plumage. One might expect a corresponding similarity in behaviour. All are plunge divers; all are social yet strongly territorial; in all, there is elaborate courtship and pair bonding behaviour; they feed their young in the same way. They all show variants of particular categories of behaviour; for example, in the early stages of the breeding cycle all of them repeatedly fly from their site (after first performing some ritualised behaviour pattern) return, calling loudly as they fly in, and perform a site ownership display. Yet there are considerable differences in behaviour. For instance one would not immediately equate the acts performed by a male white booby when it returns to its site with those of the gannet. The comparative approach, by analysing both the resemblances and the differences, can sometimes help identify the source from which and the selective influences under which, a given pattern has developed. In so doing, the general behavioural phenomena themselves may become clearer.

All references simply to 'the gannet' are to the North Atlantic gannet. The behavioural differences between the three gannets are too slight and imperfectly documented to allow further differentiation (but see p. 311). In the series of stylised comparative drawings which follows, any species unrepresented under a particular heading, and not covered by an explanatory note, in fact lacks that behaviour.

ESTABLISHMENT AND MAINTENANCE OF TERRITORY

1. *Aerial and ground reconnaissance*

Aerial reconnaissance over the breeding area is a useful way of assessing the local situation and is used by many seabirds with suitable flight; fulmars, frigates and gulls do it but shags and auks, unless there is a very considerable updraught, do not. It is in no way ritualised, but simply protracted and repeated investigation. Since all sulids are colonial and highly territorial, this obviates the risk of unnecessary clashes. Although one might not suspect it, even males of well-established pairs often spend time flying over the colony 'looking in'.

The only sulid which has developed this so much that throughout the season there is constant dense traffic over the colony, is the gannet, and it seems particularly the Atlantic gannet. The Peruvian booby seems most similar. One may correlate this with the gannet's extreme competitiveness for a socially adequate site (see p. 82).

The tendency for a gannetry to grow in bulges depends to some extent on well-developed aerial reconnoitring. Certain areas, for whatever reason, begin to attract a relatively high number of new breeders and this gives that group a characteristic 'behavioural look', since the nature and frequency of some behaviour patterns are different in newly established birds. Overflying birds see this and those which are in the site-establishing phase tend to be attracted to expanding areas. The advantages are probably that site establishment is easier, since new pairs are less antagonistic to incomers than are old-established ones; pair formation is easier (receptive females tend to prospect in such areas) and there is probably an advantage in being at the same stage of breeding as one's neighbours. There is much more to be learnt about these aspects of the colony's infra-structure.

None of the boobies except possibly the Peruvian are characteristically short of sites, topographical or social. Nor do brown, blue-footed and white boobies usually nest in places inaccessible to conspecifics. This even applies to the two arboreal boobies to some extent, but a specific area among massed gannets or Peruvian boobies is usually impossible to investigate on foot. Thus, most boobies make less use of aerial investigation.

2. *Flight circuiting*

All established male sulids repeatedly leave and return to their sites and so consolidate their attachment, signal their ownership and condition newly acquired females to remain on the site. Male brown boobies (exceptionally aerial) have exaggerated the flight movement and both they and the white and red-footed boobies show a slightly specialised landing (V-flighting).

Pair flighting (Fig. 394) follows much the same family pattern, the aerial brown and blue-footed boobies are the only two which regularly take-off and fly in tandem over the breeding area. They then land together and display. Similarly, the brown manages to perform the sexual advertising display in mid-flight, though it must perforce do it quickly. Even when performed on the ground it is a noticeably quick movement compared with that of other boobies. One may note, also, the correlation between these evidences of aerial skill in the male brown and blue-footed boobies and their unusually small size and long tail, and between these features and the specialised fishing methods of these two males.

Gannets never Pair-flight and there are many reasons why it would be highly maladaptive to do so. It would mean leaving the nest unguarded and therefore open to pilfering, pose considerable physical difficulties when landing and unduly complicate the change-over ritual since this uses a signal which obviates the possibility of both partners leaving simultaneously. If at one stage of the cycle they frequently did so, whilst later it was risky to do so, things would be complex and inconsistent. In my opinion evolution does not work that way. Nor do red-foot and Abbott's booby pair flight. The former would often lose its nest to frigates, and the latter would greatly increase the number of landings to be made in the tree tops, a procedure to be minimised for safety's sake. One might expect white boobies to pair flight but this behaviour has not been recorded. Peruvian boobies probably do so.

3. *Fighting*

Blue-footed boobies rarely fight whereas Peruvian boobies frequently do so. Gannets fight ferociously and Abbott's boobies not at all. Yet all sulids are territorial; it is merely that the importance of territory differs and hence so does the intensity of the aggressive behaviour that is justified by enhanced reproductive success. Also, the balance of opposing selection pressures varies between species. A gannet can (and does) fight to exhaustion and if it falls off the ledge, the chances are that it will survive. An Abbott's booby dies if it falls to the jungle floor.

Whilst a physically suitable breeding site is obviously equally important to all species,

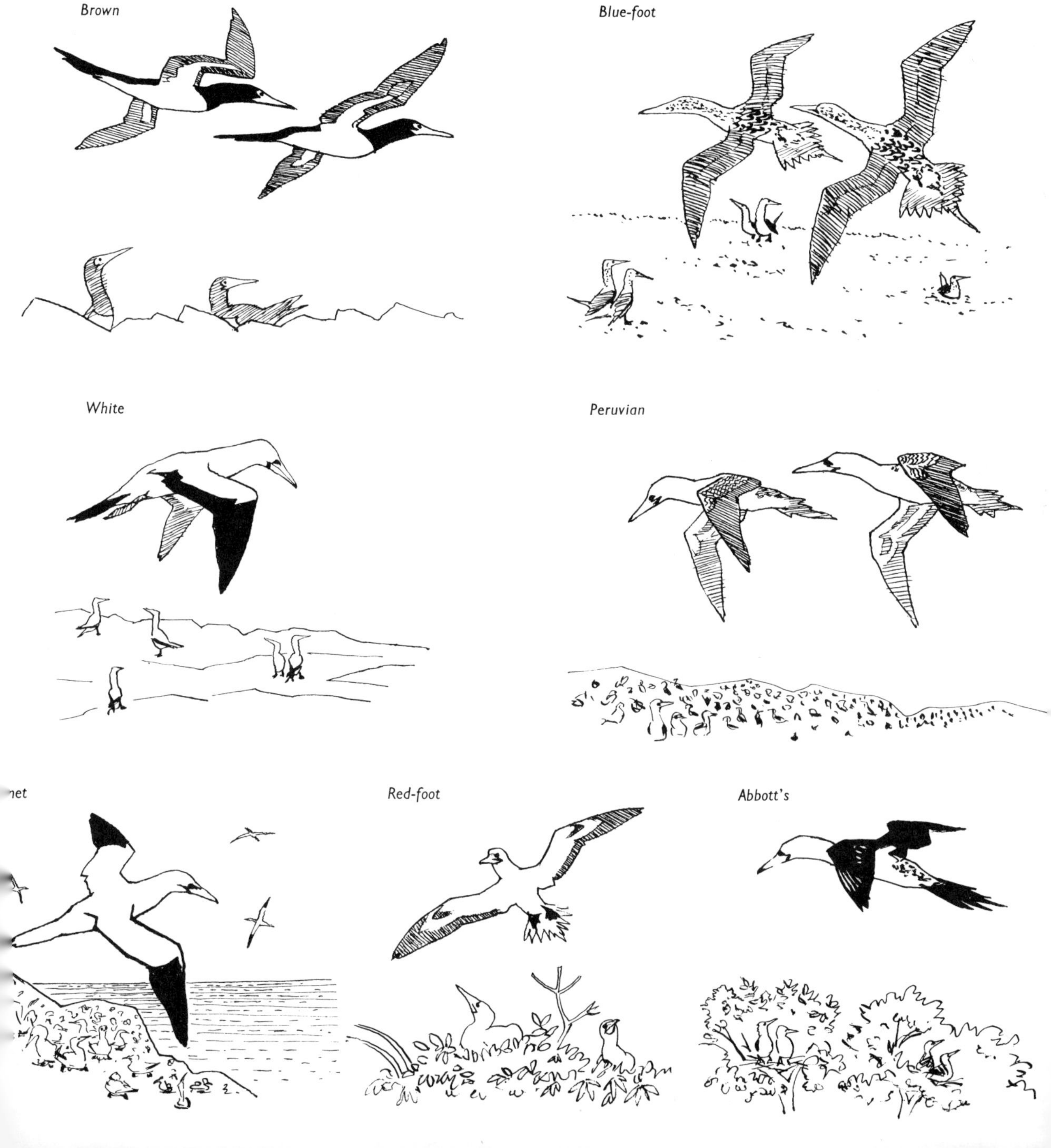

Fig. 394. Flying over the colony is part of the behaviour involved in site establishment and (together with the associated landing) has become variably ritualised in the sulids. In this drawing, the type of habitat and relative density are depicted for each species; both have an important influence on the nature of the species' display (see Table 135).

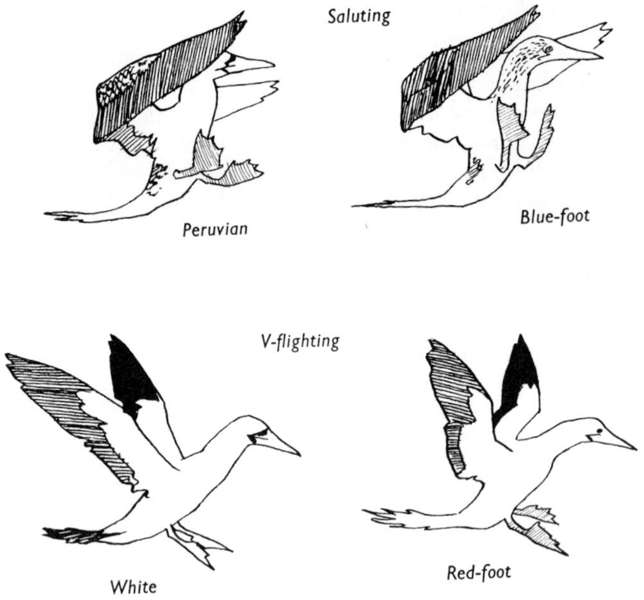

Fig. 395

Ritualised in-flying is not greatly different from ordinary landing; Saluting is most highly developed in the blue-foot, and is undoubtedly a conspicuous and highly ritualised form of landing.

there are other considerations. A site's *social* qualities may affect breeding success differently in different species. In the gannet, social factors are much more important than in Abbott's booby (see p. 82). Even competition for physical territory is bound to differ according to local conditions. Thus, Christmas Island brown boobies did not fight much; terrain was plentiful and forbade it in any case, whereas on crowded Boatswain Bird Island and the White Rock (off Mexico) fighting was apparently commoner and on the latter, if Bailey's (1906) account is accurate, often fatal. But these are usually trivial and easily interpreted differences; it is the big interspecific differences that are of interest.

The only four sulids which fight frequently and engage in fairly prolonged bouts are the three gannets and the Peruvian booby. The wider aspects of the gannets' case are deferred; the Peruvian seems often to fight for fiercely contested space. Whilst this is consistent with the known crowding on the guano islands of Peru, it is interesting that, much as does the gannet, the piquero keeps a standard density whatever the available space and this density enhances territorial conflict. Either the crowding is so typically enforced that appropriate behaviour has become the norm or perhaps the uniquely high reproductive rate (itself a response to the rich food and periodic population crashes both of which strongly favour rapid population increase) depends partly on a high level of social stimulation.

Fig. 396

Fighting is always solely by gripping, stabbing and pushing. Only in the three gannets and the Peruvian booby is it common, and only in the former is it prolonged and severe. These four are the only sulids which nest densely.

4. *Threat behaviour*

All aggressively motivated display with a repelling function implies threat. As the manifestation of a tendency to bite, threat-gaping is widespread among animals and is often unritualised. It is simply the first step towards actual attack, which is prevented by the simultaneous arousal of fear. It may, however, become highly ritualised. In sulids, both forms occur. When a hesitant female gannet, prospecting on the fringe of a group, is suddenly jabbed by a nearby bird, she may instantly menace the offender, but in an uncontrolled, spasmodic manner. This is quite different from the slow, controlled, stereotyped Menace-plus-withdrawal which often occurs between two long established neighbours. The latter is clearly ritualised. Only the gannet has evolved a ritualised Menace, and only the gannet and Peruvian booby regularly use unritualised menacing as distance-evoking behaviour. These are the only species which nest densely enough for it to be effective. For a threatened bite to be effective, there must be the ability to bite.

Other sulids come into close range contact at territorial boundaries, but jab (Fig. 398) rather than threat-gape. This is frequent in all sulids except Abbott's. It is clearly ritualised in the gannet, Peruvian, and white boobies and maybe in other species. There are two related points here. First, Jabbing occurs between mates, where the ritualised nature is obvious, and second, as in threat-gaping, there may be both a ritualised and an unritualised form in the same species. Ritualised and unritualised Jabbing between rivals simply reflects slightly different motivational states. They are distinguishable partly by effect; 'real' Jabbing is actually an attack and is accompanied by biting and gripping. Ritualised Jabbing, as in the Sparring of white and brown boobies and piqueros, and in the Jab with twisting and withdrawing motion in the gannet, does not result in gripping and is clearly a 'feint' or modified version of the real thing. Furthermore, real and ritualised Jabbing grade into each other; encounters may be made up entirely of one or the other, or a mixture. It is not surprising that all sulids use aggressive jabbing in territorial disputes. They have appropriate beaks and are adept at rapid head movements (used in hunting). A raptore, for example, is not pre-adapted in the same way and does not use similar methods even when close enough and when there is an object of competition. It is thus also to be expected that sulids will use Jabbing in the pair context.

5. *Territorial display*

These are the aggressively motivated site ownership displays (Fig. 399) by which all sulids proclaim their territorial status at a distance. They are largely equivalent in context, motivation and function. The question is whether they are homologous or merely analogous.

It will be recalled that these displays (Bowing in the gannet; Yes/No Headshaking in the white booby; Forward Head Waving in the brown booby; Yes Headshaking in the blue-footed and Peruvian boobies; Forward Head Waving in the red-footed booby and Head Jerking in Abbott's booby) occur most typically in two situations: after landing in the territory in the early stages of the breeding cycle and as a response to any set of circumstances which elicit aggression.

Gannet Bowing is derived from biting the ground or nest, the act performed in the conflict which arises after the bird has landed on its site when aggression and fear are so obviously aroused simultaneously. This is a likely primary source for behaviour suitable for ritualisation; displacement acts often occur in conflict situations and may become ritualised. But must the same argument hold good for all sulids in similar contexts? It seems that some sulid site ownership displays are derived from re-directed biting of the substrate, but it is possible that others may stem from a different source. The same function can be served by displays which arise from different sources, as we see clearly in the case of the two kinds of sexual advertising in the sulids.

In all sulids the site ownership display either incorporates or is interspersed with redirected aggression (biting and/or holding the substrate); for details, see Species Accounts. However, it is not clear that all these booby displays are *derived* from re-directed aggression as against incorporating it. In particular, the displays of the three boobies which use the Yes/No or the Yes Headshake, strongly resemble food begging of the young. If the site ownership display

Fig. 397

Ritualised, close-range threat is highly developed only in the gannets; it is common but less highly ritualised in the Peruvian and is not found in the other (more widely spaced) sulids.

Fig. 398. Meeting ceremonies: Jabbing is a common form of aggressive interaction between sulids (both between mates and between rivals), as one might expect in species which use their beaks in hunting. In most sulids, Jabbing forms the only meeting ceremony, and as such is variably ritualised. However gannets and Abbott's booby have evolved elaborate meeting ceremonies. The former retains Jabbing (ritualised) between rivals, but not between mates, whilst the latter does not show it either between rivals or mates.

derives from juvenile food begging, the ground touching and handling of nest material has been superimposed. In this case, two simple primary sources would be implicated—re-directed biting and modified food begging. White, blue-footed, Peruvian and Abbott's boobies would, on this hypothesis derive their respective site ownership displays from food begging (the detailed descriptions agree with this) and gannets and red-footed boobies from simple substrate biting.

Whatever the full relationships within the family might be, it seems clear that the site ownership displays in the white, blue-footed and Peruvian boobies are closely related, and especially in the two latter. At the same time they illustrate how effectively variation in extent and speed of constituents give specifically distinctive character to homologous displays.

The post-landing context, with its associated conflict, was suggested as the probable source of the site ownership display, especially in the gannet and red-footed booby. Van Tets (1965) suggested, I believe correctly, that a very few simple primary sources gave rise to the majority of pelicaniform displays. Examples are, infantile behaviour, especially food begging; locomotion and its precursors (for example neck lengthening) and post-landing recovery movements. The latter, Van Tets suggests, gave rise to the post-landing display (in this example, to Bowing in the gannet). The recovery movement concerned is arching the neck and pressing the bill tip to the breast (Pelican Posture). In fact, however, the gannet or booby typically does not do this immediately after landing. The gannet first bites its mate (if present) or Bows and *then* assumes the Pelican Posture. Similarly, the newly-landed red-footed booby first swings its head downwards from side to side, maybe biting the twigs as it does so. When the red-foot hops from place to place it does follow the hop with the Pelican Posture and in this situation it may be an exaggerated post-hop recovery, but as the source of the post-landing display (Bowing and its homologues or analogues) the post-landing recovery movement is certainly not a candidate. Post-hop recovery and post-landing territorial display ought to be clearly distinguished.

Fig. 399. Territorial display. All sulids possess an aggressively motivated display whose function is to repel potential intruders. Possibly all are derived from re-directed aggression (substrate biting) though this is not certain for all species. The display is most frequent and most highly stylised in the gannets, which are, by other measures, the most strongly territorial.

FORMATION AND MAINTENANCE OF PAIR

A pair bond may be defined as the special relationship between partners which facilitates co-operation during part or all of the breeding cycle. We know of no seabird in which mates remain together outside the breeding season and away from the nest site. This is obviously because, unlike many raptores, they do not hunt mainly within a large territory in which there are a number of potential meeting points. For seabirds each new breeding cycle means a re-union of mates or the formation of a new pair. It must be extremely rare, even in long-lived species with a strong tendency to form permanent partnerships, for any bird to have but one mate in its lifetime. Thus, on a few, several or many occasions, the ability to attract and retain a mate is crucial.

In species with complicated breeding cycles involving shared defence of the territory, shared incubation and chick rearing and prolonged support of the young, and this includes all the sulids, co-operation plays a key role. Some of these characteristics are difficult to reconcile. For example, shared defence of territory is probably best achieved if the sexes look alike but this means that the partner has aggression-releasing key stimuli and thus throws a heavier burden on appeasing or pair bonding behaviour. A further complication is that the sulids are highly colonial, so that the close proximity of aggressive neighbours adds to the pressures demanding clear communication between mates. A gannet or Peruvian booby cannot with-draw from the immediate proximity of its mate, however tense the situation may be. Also, the pair relationship is part of the species' overall adaptedness. The type of ritualised interactions between mates is determined partly by habitat and by the degree of territorial behaviour which the species has evolved.

The pair bond begins with the first coming together of the partners and is subsequently strengthened and maintained by behaviour which modifies the interactions by feed-back. In other words the behaviour between mates changes over time due to the pair's interactions rather than merely to the passage of time. A special relationship grows up and is not transfer-able.

1. *Pair formation*

The special displays by which a male sulid attracts a female, Headshake-and-reach in the gannet, Sky-pointing in all the boobies except Abbott's (Fig. 400) though functionally equiva-lent, are two quite different displays. The origin of the gannet's Headshake-and-reach seems plain (p. 176) and it is easy to understand how it has come to be used in the sexual context; it is simply modified threat display aroused by the potential trespass of the approaching female. The origin of Sky-pointing (p. 192) is also fairly plain—it is modified flight preparation—but it is not clear why it has become a sexual display. There are no concrete grounds for further interpretation; one can merely point out that since both gannets and boobies possess the Sky-pointing display (that is, they all show a version which clearly has a common origin) but use it for different functions, one or other function must have come first. There must once have been an ancestral sulid that Sky-pointed (it seems impossible that both gannets and boobies independently acquired it, with all its resemblances, since the stock diverged). Later, either the boobies or the gannet, or both, changed its meaning. The first of these alternatives is probably the correct one. Thus, the display is clearly derived from flight intention and, in the gannet, this is precisely what it communicates. Therefore its present message is exactly what the deriva-tion of the movement would suggest that it was originally. If so, the boobies have changed and not the gannet. But one is unable to say convincingly why the boobies chose Sky-pointing to take up the new function. Having done so, however, they then each modified the pattern as they evolved. Now, no two boobies Sky-point exactly alike (Fig. 400). Thus, evolution has produced diversity in form and concomitant changes in function. The variations in form in-volve wing movement, (in the Peruvian and blue-foot a complete swivelling which turns the back of the wings forward rather than a mere lifting of the tips). Correspondingly, the more it swivels the further it opens. Foot-lifting, which the Peruvian incorporates, is simply a form of walking and locomotion is usually a necessary precursor of flight. Parading is intimately as-sociated with Sky-pointing in the blue-foot but is precluded by space limitations in the Peruvian, whose compromise is a prolonged Foot-raising as an accompaniment to Sky-pointing. A fourth element (vocalisation) has been retained by all boobies just as gannets have retained it during movement in a Sky-pointing. This may add to the effectiveness of the behaviour over a distance.

Since behaviour is a valuable taxonomic tool one can use Sky-pointing as a behavioural measure of similarity. There are no surprises here. The two boobies most alike in Sky-pointing (the blue-foot and Peruvian) are most alike on all other criteria. Apart from this the picture is unclear.

Fig. 400. Sexual advertising displays in the Sulidae. In the boobies, the Sky-pointing displays are homologous. The gannet's sexual advertising display is merely analogous. Gannets use the homologue of Sky-pointing for another communication function.

In the brown and white boobies, the male Sky-points to the female but not the other way round. In the red-foot, the male Sky-points to the female and she responds similarly but they do not display simultaneously. In the Peruvian and most of all the blue-foot, male and female Sky-point both in response (reciprocally) and together (mutually). These are strictly observed characteristics. One never sees a pair of white boobies Sky-pointing repeatedly and mutually any more than one sees them open and swivel their wings like a blue-foot. These differences in reciprocity and some differences in the amount of time the different species devote to the display, suggest substantial differences in function, to which we now turn.

The crux of the difference is that in, notably, the white and brown boobies, Sky-pointing is confined almost entirely to the period of pair formation and to the post-breeding period of resurgence of sexual activity. During these short periods it is an opportunistic response by a male to attract a nearby female. She does not respond by the same display, and subsequent pair interactions take some other form. In the other boobies (except Abbott's) the male does not confine his Sky-pointing to the pair forming phase, but displays frequently and for long periods, after the pair have formed. In these species it has become, in addition, a pair bonding activity.

Prolonged Sky-pointing seems to be the equivalent of a meeting ceremony between partners which lack a well developed one. The red-foot is certainly poorly equipped with greeting behaviour and intimate pair interactions and uses Sky-pointing extensively in the early stages of the cycle, when co-operation is most required. Conversely the white and brown boobies have fairly well-developed greeting behaviour, and other intimate pair interactions and (see above) do not use Sky-pointing in this way. But the blue-foot, which has a plethora of intimate pair interactions, and the Peruvian, which has a simple greeting (Mutual Jabbing), are the two which not only have excessively conspicuous Sky-pointing but also use it mutually and outside the initial pair formation context. This sort of apparent anomaly can be resolved only, if at all, by a more rigorous analysis of pair bonding behaviour.

2. *Pair maintenance*

Besides the extended function of Sky-pointing in strengthening pair bonds there are two major sources of essential rapport, the greeting ceremony and the miscellaneous group of activities involving co-operation (pair flighting; gathering, presenting and 'building in' nest material, etc.).

(*a*) *Meeting ceremonies*

The mutual performance of ritualised behaviour upon meeting occurs in several groups for example (herons, geese, fulmars, storks, penguins). Meeting ceremonies are not, however, common. Much behaviour which might at first seem to belong in this category does not do so. Mutual display, such as the dancing of albatrosses or the head waggling of frigates is not performed on meeting; almost certainly its function is to increase rapport, but it is not strictly a meeting ceremony. Among the sulids (Fig. 398) only the gannet and Abbott's booby have a true meeting ceremony. Each time they reunite on the site after a reasonably long absence they go through long and ecstatic-looking mutual display.

The detailed account of Mutual Fencing (p. 184) shows that it derives from aggressive behaviour and particularly in the male is accompanied by obvious signs of aggression. However, it is also associated with sexual behaviour. Unlike some of the simple forms of 'meeting' (such as sparring in boobies) it is never performed between rivals and is performed at the fullest intensity between old and long established mates after a long separation. On one occasion, a female disappeared from a nest containing a small chick. For five weeks the male cared for the chick single handed, tailoring his fishing trips to short forays and somehow finding enough food. One evening his mate returned and on that occasion, which luckily was observed, a remarkably long and intense bout ensued. For over 17 minutes without ceasing, the pair fenced and shouted at high intensity (S. Wanless pers. comm.).

Part of its function is to facilitate pair co-operation by providing a means of expression of the aggression which exists between mates. This links directly with the paramount position of territorial-defence behaviour in the gannet. If the male is to retain his full tendency to respond to intrusion, he must attack any object with certain primary releasing stimuli, which includes his own mate. Equally important, he must not only retain that mate, but condition her so that her attachment to the site (through him) becomes almost as strong as his, and she will defend it wholeheartedly. The meeting ceremony achieves this. I doubt if anybody who had really watched a major reunion, with its attendant greeting behaviour, would feel unconvinced of its immense potential for creating a strong pair bond. Here, it seems, evolution has been extremely 'clever'; the more intense the territorial tendencies of the male, the more intense is his greeting behaviour and the stronger the pair bond which he thus creates with its guarantee of a faithful co-defender. He wins three ways at once. A similar argument probably applies to nape biting.

I suggest, therefore, that in the gannet, the unique development of the greeting ceremony is an indirect result of the selection pressures encouraging the development of the utmost territoriality in response to site competition. The links in this chain of events were outlined in the preceding paragraph (for a full discussion of factors which lead to such unusually severe competition see pp. 82 and 118).

There is a further element in the web of relationships between territory and Mutual Fencing. Gannets consistently nest densely. The more densely they nest (the more incompressible their territory) the greater the pressure to defend it and the less possible becomes even the slightest withdrawal as a response to aggression by the partner. Therefore, the stronger the pressures which make Mutual Fencing more intense and (if it works the way I have suggested) the more effective becomes Mutual Fencing as a means of coping with the aggression, 'satisfying' the participants and keeping them harmoniously squashed together in their tiny territory. It is a system in which the strengthening of one part strengthens, rather than weakens, the others. Therefore the whole process can reach a higher level of efficiency than would otherwise be possible.

This interpretation centres on the acquisition and defence of a socially adequate site. Pair bonding relates primarily to this, and the hypertrophied meeting ceremony subserves pair bonding. Thus we can understand why it is that gannets should have acquired such a conspicuous greeting ceremony whilst other sulids (with the exception of Abbott's booby, to be discussed in a moment) have not. Superficially one might well have expected the boobies, which take longer to rear their young, to need as much pair co-operation and therefore pair bonding behaviour. The crucial difference, however, is that the boobies do not suffer such strong selection pressures over sites. There is less need to develop powerful pair bonding because there is less territorial aggression to be accommodated in the pair relationship. Neither is there the same degree of co-operation in defence of site. Boobies leave their site completely unguarded once the chick can regulate its body temperature. This reduces the need for precise co-ordination of pair activities. Often a booby flies in, feeds its young and departs without even seeing its mate. A gannet must accurately co-ordinate every change-over at the nest. It must wait until its mate arrives, however hungry, soiled or heat-stressed it might be. To do this it must become firmly conditioned, and part of the 'reward' is the activity which the reunion provides. Only for a relatively short period is that activity overtly sexual (copulation) though since copulation and Mutual Fencing are closely linked, this may partly explain the rewarding property of Mutual Fencing. This argument applies particularly to the female, for she is less strongly tied to the site itself. Thus it seems perfectly explicable that gannets have a degree of co-operation and associated pair bonding that most boobies do not.

To preserve the flow of the argument I did not consider why site competition should be less severe among boobies than gannets, but the reasons are fairly obvious. First, among boobies, sites are usually not limited; second, there is usually no survival value in seasonal production of young, an objective facilitated by social stimulation (see p. 123) and very important in the gannet. Consistent with the argument that sites are less important among boobies than gannets, they are changed frequently; similarly mates are changed more than in the gannet.

The gannet's situation coheres well because, perhaps, more is known. Abbott's booby, the other sulid which shows notable greeting behaviour, is less easily understood (see p. 793). The question is why has Abbott's developed such marked pair bonding behaviour? When mates meet on the nest, though they show evident signs of excitement and aggression (Feather Ruffing and vigorous Head Jerking, which is an aggressively motivated display) they usually

(*a*) *Peruvian. Bill-up-face-away*

(*b*) *Blue-foot. Bill-up-face-away*

(*c*) *White. Bill-up-face-away*

(*d*) *Brown. Bill-up-face-away*

Fig. 401. Ritualised locomotion and associated postures. Bill-up-face-away typically precedes movement away from partner; such movement often uses web-flaunting (Parading) and may be accompanied by Bill-tucking. All the ground-nesting boobies show these behaviour patterns; the red-foot and Abbott's do not, nor are they found in the gannets, which typically use Sky-pointing when moving away from site or partner.

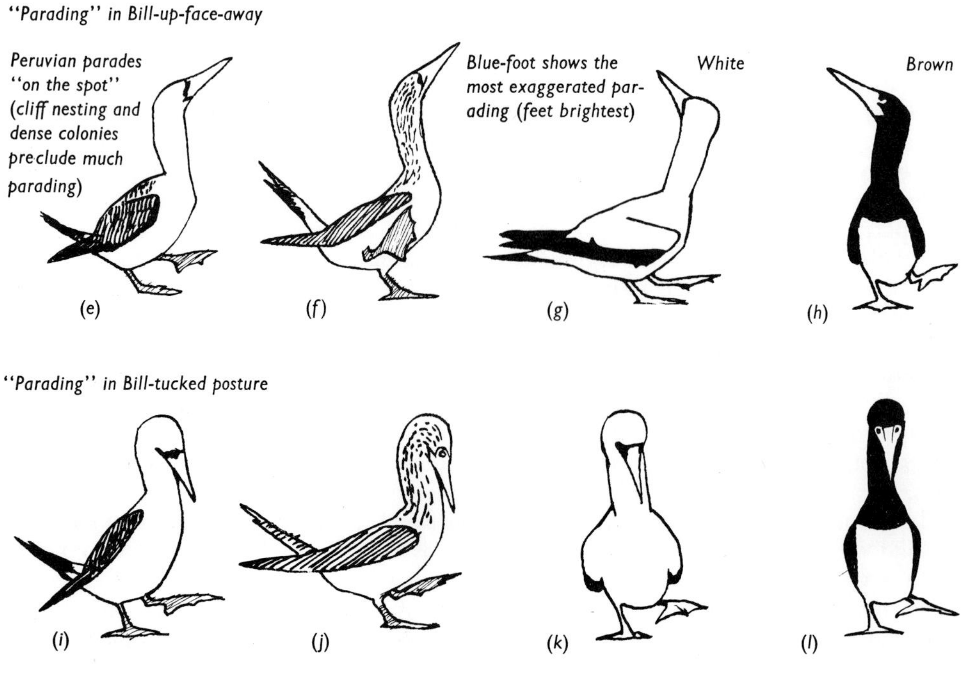

do not jab or spar as other boobies do. This may be because prior to contact, they have gone through a lengthy meeting ceremony. They have conducted their vigorous aggressively motivated behaviour at a safe distance. They have reached the motivational state which gannets reach at the end of their Mutual Fencing. On this view, the long and ecstatic meeting ceremony of Abbott's booby would have, as a primary function, the attainment of a high threshold for further aggressive acts, thus making it safe for the pair to interact at close quarters. This is not the same as simply saying that a long range meeting ceremony is adaptive because it directly reduces the likelihood of falling. That is true also, but the present point is that it affects thresholds. Again, it is a double mechanism.

One may relegate the Jabbing of the remainder of the family to the status of relatively unimportant interactions. In the white, brown and Peruvian boobies particularly, they are clearly ritualised but brief and simple. In the red-foot the Jabbing of the pair is indistinguishable from that of rivals and neither seems obviously ritualised. The blue-foot Jabs relatively little. Jabbing appears to form a vehicle for the immediate discharge of aggressive tendencies in pair contact, but has not become a fully developed meeting ceremony.

The next few paragraphs summarise the pair interactions which occur in sulids other than the gannet and Abbott's booby, with interpretative comments on the relative importance of the pair bond.

In the white booby Sky-pointing is confined to promoting initial contact and Mutual Jabbing is brief and simple. Much time is spent in locomotion within the territory, often in the service of symbolic nest building. Thus the pair members are constantly parting, as the male, with appropriate posturing (Fig. 401), leaves the female, Parades away (Fig. 401(g)), returns, often with a fragment of nest material and ceremoniously deposits it, after which both of them 'build' it (Fig. 402(c)). Flight circuiting adds further to the number of times the pair interact. Pair bonding thus appears to be delegated to a number of apparently minor, closely interwoven behaviour patterns rather than one or two major patterns comparable to Mutual Fencing. Most of these occur early in the breeding cycle and for much of the later stages the pair interact relatively briefly and infrequently until the post-breeding recrudescence of sexual activity. In this respect it sets the pattern for the other ground nesting boobies, the differences being mainly in varying use of flight and locomotion. The white booby is less aerial than the brown or blue-foot; the male is considerably heavier. It seems (p. 382) that pairs not infrequently break up after one breeding cycle.

The brown booby emphasises aerial displays, a trait which is facilitated by the agility of the male and its predilection for steep nesting sites. The blue-foot has exaggerated the role of locomotion and associated postures (by flaunting its incredibly bright feet), and of pair flighting and Sky-pointing (by making it more conspicuous, reciprocal and protracted). It has developed the interactions involved in nest building, particularly showing nest material. Much of the Peruvian's pair bonding behaviour is a muted version of the blue-foot's. It cannot Parade around and, perhaps significantly, it has reverted to vigorous Mutual Jabbing, much as in the white booby. This may be partly correlated with the reduction in other activities but mainly with the more severe competition for sites, with concomitant evolution of aggressive behaviour. The phenomenon is the more convincing because Jabbing is so markedly reduced in the blue-foot; the assertiveness of the piquero is evident by comparison. It would be interesting to have comparative figures for the strength of the pair bond, as measured by fidelity in successive, undisturbed cycles, in blue-foot and Peruvian boobies.

The red-foot might be expected to resemble Abbott's, the other arboreal species, but so far as pair behaviour is concerned they are almost opposites. The red-foot virtually lacks a meeting ceremony and its threshold for aggression is very much lower, so that in the early stages of the breeding cycle overt aggression is common between red-foot mates. Allo-preening occurs commonly in the red-foot. Later in the breeding season when mates re-unite, for instance during nest relief, they usually do not interact at all except to change-over. On the other hand, and again in keeping with the family tendency to subserve pair bonding by several means, increasing the role of one behaviour pattern if another is diminished, the red-foot makes extensive use of Sky-pointing as a pair display after it has functioned to bring them together. Thus, reciprocal Sky-pointing at close quarters and of very long duration is common in the pre-laying period when it is closely associated with copulation.

The use of Sky-pointing by the red-foot, so frequently and at close range, after pair formation, is instructive in view firstly of this species' lack of meeting behaviour, secondly, its low threshold for aggression at close quarters (males may attack females and fighting occasionally takes place, whilst females show marked fear responses, trembling, flinching, feather ruffing and facing-away) and thirdly, its inability, due to the restrictions of the habitat, to use ritualised locomotion and associated behaviour as do the ground nesting boobies. The options open to the red-foot have probably been: to elaborate the already sexually motivated pair formation display; to develop special greeting behaviour (cf. gannet and Abbott's booby); or to reduce pair interactions altogether except for essentials like nest building and copulation, and by withdrawal, to avoid pair disrupting aggressive interaction.

The last is not practicable on its own since the proximity and co-operation involved in, say, copulation require behavioural compatibility and in fact options 1 and 3 have been combined. Sexually motivated Sky-pointing apparently functions as the display ensuring temporary compatibility for mating and nest building as well as for bringing the sexes together. Reduced interaction and withdrawal characterise later pair relations. Allo-preening does occur, mainly the male preening the female in a rough and aggressive-looking manner and the female flinching, ruffing her head feathers, tremoring and facing-away. This, too, indicates the species' difficulty in coping with the aggression-arousing stimuli involved in close-range pair interactions.

(*b*) *Allo-preening*

Allo-preening is widespread in sulids (Fig. 403). Gannets, white and Peruvian boobies preen each other simultaneously (mutual allo-preening). Unilateral allo-preening occurs in

(a) Collecting symbolic fragment and returning to site, often using web-flaunting.

(b) 'Showing' (in an arc) the fragment (or in the case of the brown and Abbott's, the functional piece) of nest material.

Fig. 402. Display used in collecting, 'showing', and building in nest material.

blue-footed and brown boobies (but is relatively rare) and red-footed boobies (largely male preening female) and there is no allo-preening in Abbott's. This form of preening is undoubtedly aggressive and its distribution fits fairly well with the suppositions that aggressive species show it most, especially when they have other behaviour (Mutual Fencing or Mutual Jabbing) which can 'take care' of close range hostilities should they flare up as a result of the close proximity of bills, potentially an aggression-eliciting situation. Thus, the gannet is highly aggressive in the pair context, but with extremely well developed close contact display (Mutual Fencing). The Peruvian is also aggressive and has Mutual Jabbing. It is consistent with Abbott's booby's lack of close range pair interactions (for reasons fully discussed) that it should be the only sulid to lack Mutual Preening. Mutual Preening may thus be interpreted as another mode of behaviour by means of which aggression can be accommodated in the pair relationship.

(*c*) *Appeasement behaviour*

Appeasement is important in the pair context in birds as aggressive as gannets and boobies. The concept is deceptively simple. Behaviour appeases if it reduces the likelihood of attack or switches off an attack already launched. But many responses which would not usually be classed as 'appeasing' do this. In fact, the term is commonly applied to a category of acts in which, either by removing its weapons of offense from a potentially attacking position or by putting itself

Fig. 402 (c). Mutual nest building: in the blue-foot, white, and some brown, the nest is merely symbolic (but 'building' it is an important pair-interaction). In the other sulids, the nest is functional in the obvious sense, but still provides intimate pair interactions.

into a vulnerable position, the appeasing individual conspicuously renders itself incapable of launching an aggressive act. In this sense, the sulids are both surprisingly tardy and somewhat uneven in their deployment of appeasing behaviour (Fig. 404). In a wider sense (discussed later) they are remarkably well equipped.

The most obviously appeasing behaviour in the pair contest is Facing-away. However, in no case is this highly developed and in several boobies it is altogether absent. Female gannets Face-away from aggressive males but with very limited success (p. 179). Female red-footed boobies fleetingly Face-away from aggressive males but usually add prudent retreat. The remainder of the family do not Face-away; that is they do not typically avert their face and bill when attacked or threatened. Nor do any sulids, gannets included, use this appeasement gesture during aggressive encounters with rivals of the same sex. Even when it does occur, Face-away looks more like an ordinary response than a highly ritualised gesture.

White and brown boobies have evolved a mutual appeasement gesture, in which both sexes Stand Parallel (p. 398). This reduces potential bill contact and is clearly a stereotyped act. Four boobies (white, brown, blue-footed and Peruvian) have evolved exaggerated and stereotyped Bill-up-face-away postures principally in the context of movement (on foot) away from the partner and therefore typical of the four ground nesting boobies with large territories. Paradoxically, they are probably appeasement postures which work by *not* turning the weapon fully away. The instant at which a bird is most likely to attack its mate is just as the latter has turned away and is moving off the site. In Bill-up-face-away a bird simultaneously signals its intention to move (neck lengthening) enhanced, incidentally, by exaggerated flaunting of the feet 'on the spot' and at the same time keeps an eye on the partner. The tree nesting boobies lack Bill-up-face-away just as they lack ritualised locomotion. The gannet uses Sky-pointing where boobies use Bill-up-face-away.

Bill Tucking is a third bill averting posture. If it is the case that there are two distinct types (p. 944) the Bill Tucking type seems most likely to be homologous with infantile beak hiding. This is discussed on p. 213 but so far as adult Bill Tucking is concerned, the evidence for its

Fig. 403. Allo-preening is basically aggressive behaviour, which serves to maintain the pair bond, or at least to facilitate harmonious proximity between mates. Abbott's booby lacks it.

appeasing function is thin. One hindrance to interpretation is that the context of Bill Tucking is not the same in all sulids. White, brown, blue-footed and Peruvian boobies Bill Tuck as they move around their territories or even when they are alone. Gannets Bill Tuck in high intensity fear-aggression situations and the red-foot does not Bill Tuck in this precise way at all (it uses the neck arched Pelican Posture as a post-hop recovery movement). Because Bill Tucking accompanies movement in the ground nesting boobies, the partner is often approached with Bill Tucked, but it is a moot point whether this reduces aggression between established partners. Whatever its function, however, there is little doubt that in these four (and probably the gannet

Fig. 404

Appeasement behaviour in adult sulids.

(a) White booby, "parallel standing" in which bills are ostentatiously not pointed at the partner; not as clearly found in the other ground nesters but some instances of incipient Bill-up-face-away look similar

(b) Female gannet Faces away from male; never vice-versa

Female red-foot Faces away from male. Not as clearly shown in other boobies

(c) Pelican posture (bill tucking), found in all sulids but in two rather different forms; motivation complex and function not clear

Gannet

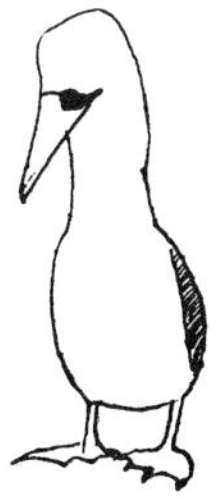

Peruvian

Blue-foot

White

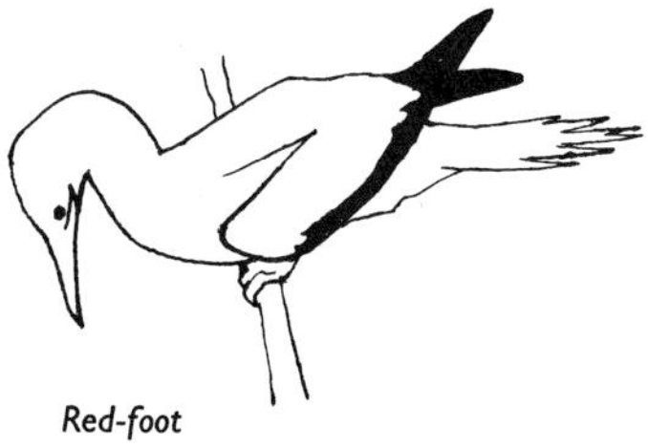

Red-foot

Abbott's

also) it is homologous and it is of interest therefore, to find that the chicks of all five show Bill Hiding—the suggested source—whilst the adult red-foot does not Bill Tuck and its chick does not Bill Hide. Abbott's booby corresponds with the rest of the family in showing adult Bill Tucking and infantile Bill Hiding.

In my opinion, the above facts do not point to a major role for appeasement behaviour. At least in the gannet I would place more emphasis on the role of Mutual Fencing as the behaviour responsible for affecting the balance of motivation. It does this by a process of negative feedback. The partner, by co-operating in Mutual Fencing, permits the aggressive individual to raise its own threshold for subsequent aggression. If both are aggressive, they do this 'to' or 'for' each other. Thus both reduce their own tendency to behave aggressively, in the usual sense of 'aggressively' (overt attack). Because this mechanism is so highly developed in gannets, ordinary appeasement is not much needed. Much the same mechanism could work in Abbott's booby, which would explain why it is the only other sulid with a magnificently developed meeting ceremony; the threshold for aggression here being controlled at a distance to obviate contact aggression in the tree top environment (p. 784).

Having now encompassed nearly all the ritualised behaviour patterns of breeding sulids, I have set out the relationships in Table 134.

TABLE 134

INTERSPECIFIC DIFFERENCES IN BEHAVIOUR WITHIN THE SULIDAE

Behaviour	Status		Differences
A. TERRITORIAL			
1. Flight reconnaissance	D	U.R.	Common to all sulids; differs in extent to which practised; most in gannets and (probably) Peruvian booby.
2. Fighting	D	U.R.	All sulids except Abbot's booby fight, using beak only. Severe fighting only in gannet. Of the boobies, Peruvian fights most and blue-foot (and possibly red-foot) least. Peruvian also forms biggest and densest colonies and suffers most competition for sites.
3. Threat gaping (menacing)	D	R	Ritualised Menacing found only in gannets correlated with need for highly repetitive and seasonally protracted close-range threat.
		U.R.	Unritualised menacing occurs in all sulids (including gannets) except Abbott's, but is infrequent in all except Peruvian.
4. Site-ownership display White — Yes/No Headshaking Blue-foot — Yes Headshaking Peruvian — Yes Headshaking, slow Abbott's — Head Jerking Brown — Forward Head Waving Red-foot — Forward Head Waving Gannet — Bowing	F	R	All sulids have one, but not all are immediately recognisable as being related in form. The site ownership display of white, blue-footed and Peruvian boobies seem clearly homologous (certainly the two latter are); all of them are head nodding displays. That of Abbott's (basically head jerking) is also reasonably similar in form. Those of brown and red-footed boobies look fairly similar to each other (they are head waving displays) and the gannet's is basically similar (forward and downward movements of the head). Alternative

Status: D = Descriptive name
F = Functional name (where descriptive inappropriate)
R = Ritualised
U.R. = Unritualised

Behaviour	Status	Differences
		derivations are: (a) all from redirected aggression, as the gannet's so clearly is, (b) some so derived but others from either juvenile food-begging *or* post-landing recovery movements. The most complex and highly ritualised (gannet Bowing) is the one performed most frequently and for longest period.
B. PAIR FORMING		
5. Prospecting by female	F U.R.	Receptive females have no special behaviour; their prospecting reveals their status.
6. Advertising by male All boobies—Sky-pointing (except Abbott's) Abbott's—None Gannet—Headshake-and-reach	F R	Best example of homologous display in sulids. Differs in form but recognisable as basically same display in all except gannet and Abbott's. Differs merely in extent of movement. Derived from pre-movement signal. Gannet has retained this in original context and evolved different display for advertising. All except Abbott's have Sky-pointing. Has achieved additional pair bonding rather than merely pair forming function in red-foot, blue-foot and Peruvian.
C. PAIR BONDING		
7. Pair flighting	D R	Found only in brown, blue-footed and possibly Peruvian. Males of these species exceptionally aerial.
Interactions on site involving ritualised locomotion and associated postures, ritualised nest building, etc.		
8. Leave and return	D U.R.	In principle, same in all sulids; male flies out from site, circles (variably) and returns. Associated pre-flight and post-landing behaviour differ in each species. Key role in conditioning female to remain on site when male leaves.
9. Pre-flight signals Sky-pointing Wing Rattle Wing flick	F R	All sulids have some pre-flight signal, used in intensive bouts of pair bonding activities and nest relief ceremonies. Gannet pre-flight signal typically Skypointing. Boobies use Sky-pointing as advertising, so it is not available for use as pre-flight signal; Wing Rattle used instead. This is a modified comfort movement (gannets have a version of it but not as a pre-flight signal). Wing Rattle does not vary significantly throughout the boobies though in some (especially blue-foot, but also white and brown) it has become more strongly linked with movement on *foot* and hence often performed in the Bill-up-face-away posture, which is associated with movement on foot. In the red-foot it has been largely replaced by a single wing-flicking movement.
10. Ritualised locomotion Parading—Web flaunting Web drooping	D R	All ground nesting sulids use ritualised locomotion, which means (a) the locomotion itself, (b) the postures preceding, accompanying or

TABLE 134—contd.

Behaviour	Status	Differences
		following it. (a) White, brown, Peruvian and blue-foot in that order, flaunt their webs with increasing ostentation (webs spread). Gannets droop webs, which display markings better.
Bill-up-face-away	D R	(b) The commonest posture preceding Parading is Bill-up-face-away, virtually identical in white, brown, blue-foot and Peruvian. The arboreal boobies lack it. The gannet uses Sky-pointing and also lacks Bill-up-face-away. Bill-up-face-away has replaced Sky-pointing as a signal of impending movement on foot in boobies (Sky-pointing having been taken over as advertising) just as Wing Rattle has replaced Sky-pointing as a signal of impending flight. Gannets still use Sky-pointing for both.
Pelican Posture	D R	Precedes, accompanies and follows movement in all sulids. Difficult posture to understand because probably two differently derived kinds—one post-hop recovery and the other derived from infantile beak hiding. The first type (neck arched) is typical of post-hop recovery in the red-foot and is probably not an appeasement posture. The second type (bill tucking) typically occurs during Parading in blue-foot, white, brown and Peruvian. The gannet, which does not have a territory large enough to walk around in, Pelican Postures in ambivalent fear-aggression situations, which may be motivationally equivalent to those in which the bill-tucking type occurs in boobies. The gannet often hops, but does not typically show the post-hop Pelican Posture. Abbott's booby Pelican Postures in ambivalent fear-aggression and also post-hop; it certainly uses the bill-tucking type but not so clearly the neck-arched type. This is probably a phylogenetically extremely primitive posture and more work is needed to get a clear picture.
11. Nest building activities	D R U.R.	The sulids divide into three groups (a) those in which a proper nest is more or less essential (North Atlantic gannet, red-foot, Abbott's booby); (b) those in which it is undoubtedly useful but not essential (brown and Peruvian boobies, Cape gannet) and (c) those in which it is always merely symbolic (white and blue-footed boobies). Yet in all sulids gathering, presentation and 'building' of nest material is an important activity. Building behaviour may, correspondingly, be divided into functional and symbolic. In the former a stereotyped sequence of simple movements are used (see species' accounts) the main elements of which are movements of the head from side to side; 'quivering' the material into place and vibrating the mandibles to disengage sticky material. Concentrated bouts of building are carried out by pairs or by birds alone

Behaviour	Status	Differences
		on the nest, i.e. with no pair bonding potential. In the latter there is no real building (the material doesn't allow it) but much mutual handling of nest material.
Presentation of nest material (Showing)	D R	Ritualised presentation of material is not confined merely to symbolic builders; it occurs in blue-foot (symbolic); Peruvian and brown (functional grade b) and Abbott's (functional grade a). In the first three species it is a highly comparable movement. The Presentation of Abbott's may be non-homologous with these (more precise observations are required). Showing does not occur in the gannets, white or red-footed boobies. Pair bonding effects, therefore, may stem from mutual, functional nest building in groups (a) and (b) above, but must surely be the main 'purpose' of Symbolic Nest Building. Each trip for nest material (functional or symbolic) involves the associated posturing before leaving on foot or by air and the posturing on return (or the post-landing behaviour). Thus nest building is a major pair bonding activity. Nest building was undoubtedly a characteristic of the ancestral sulid—indeed of the ancestral pelicaniform—and the loss of a nest has only gone as far as the loss of the structure; the behaviour patterns have not been lost but have been pressed into use in the context of pair bonding. The headshaking movements originally functional in nest building (among other things) have also been frequently incorporated into displays in the sulids.
Interactions upon meeting at the site		
12. Meeting ceremonies	F R	Only gannets and Abbott's booby have evolved a 'proper' meeting ceremony. These are not superficially alike. but conceivably both derive from re-directed aggression (the gannet's almost certainly does). The incorporation of unilateral (male to female) overt attack into a pair bonding behaviour pattern has occurred only once in the family—in the gannet, whose aggressiveness has been prominent in shaping relationships between mates. The remainder of the sulids either have no activity which is particularly characteristic of meeting (red-foot and blue-foot) or merely a simple Bill Touching and/or Jabbing. However, all sulids Jab, whether on meeting or during interactions involving a whole range of other acts and this (and the low intensity or orientation form, Bill Touching) is another basic sulid trait, probably attributable to their territorial nature and pre-adaptation (movement used in fishing). The jabs are not sufficiently dissimilar in form to allow separation, though ciné analysis might permit this. There seems to be an inverse correlation between a well developed meeting ceremony and
Nape Biting	R	
Mutual Fencing	R	
Mutual Wing Waving	R	
Mutual Jabbing	R	
Bill Touching	R	
Mutual Preening	R	

TABLE 134—contd.

Behaviour	Status	Differences
		the development of a wide range of other types of pair interaction. Mutual allo-preening occurs in gannets (frequent and intense), Peruvian, white and blue-footed boobies (less frequent). Unilateral allo-preening occurs in the brown and red-foot. It seems relatively rare in the first and largely an aggressive male to female act in the red-foot. Abbott's lacks it altogether. The form of the behaviour is the same throughout; its occurrence correlates with aggression (see Mutual Preening in Comparative Account, p. 938).
13. Copulation	F U.R. R	All sulids except the gannet copulate without the male gripping the female's head. At least in the brown and the Peruvian, the male makes clear intention movements of biting during copulation. This has not been noticed in the remaining species but could have been overlooked. The gannet's biting probably enhances the stimulation imparted to the female and linking Nape Biting with sexual stimulation has probably been the mechanism by which females have been conditioned to accept male aggression as a positive element in pair relationships. Gannets 'patter' more during copulation and take much longer than boobies, thus enhancing its bonding function.

OTHER BEHAVIOUR INVOLVED IN BREEDING

1. *Comparative aspects of incubation and the care of the young*

All sulids incubate by applying their webs to the egg(s) but little is known about any specific differences. Four eggs (as occasionally in the Peruvian) seem to be the upper limit with which this system could cope but since one two or three form the usual clutch this factor has not operated in limiting clutch size. The mechanism of heat transfer seems puzzling. Howell (pers. comm.) to whom I am grateful for permission to quote the following, recently demonstrated that the temperature inside the egg of the blue-footed booby (37·2; extremes 35·0 and 38·5°C) was greater than that of the web (33·2; extremes 31·5 and 35·0°C) and concludes that webs are not the means of transferring heat. Other considerations suggest that they are (blood flow through them increases and webs become hot during incubation; they are tightly applied to the egg; there is no brood patch and the insulation of the feathers precludes transfer of heat from the skin; incubation behaviour differs according to the ambient temperature in a perfectly understandable fashion). Until an alternative explanation is forthcoming, I conclude that heat for incubation flows from the web and that Howell's result is an artefact (such as vascular constriction of the web due to puncture, or heat temporarily passed to the egg from some extra source such as the hot ground, or loss of heat from the web between seizing the bird and inserting the thermister).

No booby systematically disposes of eggshells. In the arboreal species they usually drop over the edge of the nest or are placed among nearby twigs, and in ground nesters remain nearby. Predators such as rats, cats, crabs, gulls and turkey vultures are either there anyway or use cues other than eggshells or are incapable of dealing with an adult booby. The case is thus quite different from that of a gull or tern, whose cryptic chick would be betrayed to predators by the conspicuous white inside and edge of a broken eggshell. No sulids bring water to their young, and chick excreta is not removed. Adults of all species pick up and eat or fling away spilt food. Nevertheless dense colonies often become foul.

The age at which young are first left unattended is largely dependent on physiology and ecology and only in the case of the gannet on behavioural factors. Thus, all boobies first leave their young unguarded at 3–5 weeks, when they can regulate their body temperatures. This applies only to dry chicks, but since all boobies nest in areas that are either dry or so hot that wetness would not lead to dangerous cooling, there is no problem. In fact, the main danger is overheating. This is where the equation becomes ecological, for the balance of advantage between guarding the chick from overheating and fishing on its behalf must often be a fine one. In food-poor areas the scale must usually tip in favour of food, for in most cases a chick with energy to spare for thermo-regulation has a better chance of survival than one which is well shaded but starved; starvation is invariably critical whilst ambient temperature usually is not. This is consistent with the known tendency for chicks in impoverished areas to be left unguarded earlier than those in richer ones, even when the latter are also cooler. The behavioural aspects are however paramount in the gannet, which typically never leaves its chick (which means its nest) unguarded. From the moment it hatches until the moment it fledges, a young gannet will normally never have been left on its own for so much as a second.

Whereas gannets never identify their own young, red-foots do so only when they become free-flying and the three ground nesting boobies seem to be selective by the time their young can wander. The behaviour of the adult gannet and red-foot is adequate, since chicks of the former cannot wander and those of the red-foot are discriminated against once they can. There are no critical observations on parent-young recognition in white, brown and blue-footed boobies and it may be that the marked tendency of these young to remain within their parent's territory (or return if artificially displaced) and to attack strangers, is enough to preclude potentially harmful usurpation, without discrimination by adults. In general, therefore, parent-young recognition may be seen as environmentally-induced adaptive behaviour in the Sulidae.

A further difference between gannets and boobies is the post-fledging feeding practised by all boobies, but entirely absent in gannets. The reasons for this deep divergence are ecological and are discussed on p. 913.

All adult sulids lower body temperature by gular fluttering, panting, feather ruffing, tail raising (exposing cloacal skin), holding the wings slightly out from the body and orienting with backs to the sun so that direct radiation does not fall on naked vascular areas (principally the feet, gular and facial skin) (Fig. 320). At 41°C (Bartholomew 1966) their body temperature is higher than that of the surrounding air, to which they can therefore, by convection, lose heat from their bare skin, if this is in shade. The Atlantic gannet, at least, often points its face and throat skywards, thus perhaps radiating heat to the 'cold' sky. Water balance is no problem in sulids, which can afford as much as they need for evaporative cooling. In this connection, the gular area could (in shade) lose heat from the outer surface (by convection) and from the inner (by evaporative cooling). Cape and Australasian gannets thermo-regulate by excreting onto their own feet (p. 263). Perhaps this habit has been overlooked in other sulids.

The maintenance of *enough* heat depends on metabolic rate and insulation. In this connection it may be significant that the North Atlantic gannet, in its cold regions, has apparently a slightly higher body temperature than the white booby (mean 41·4°C (McNab 1966) against 40·7°C) and certainly has far more subcutaneous fat and thicker 'quilting' plumage. It has, also, less bare facial and gular skin and in fact has markedly less than its warm-area, superspecific relative the Cape gannet (Fig. 375) than which it is also fatter. The huge webs are obvious vehicles for heat loss and there must be a mechanism for varying their temperature, not merely to allow incubation but to aid thermo-regulation outside the breeding season.

BEHAVIOUR OF YOUNG

Most behaviour characteristics are common to all young sulids; the few that are specific are directly related to environmental pressures.

1. *Begging, feeding and sleeping*

Sulid chicks are divisible into the restrained and the active beggers. All of the former (gannet, Abbott's booby and Peruvian booby) would find it dangerous or impossible to flail around frenziedly, but in addition, none of them normally suffer from shortage of food. With the remaining boobies it is often very much otherwise (p. 740) and their begging is typically extremely vigorous. Of the undoubted differences that exist between species in the begging movements, nothing useful can be said. They require detailed analysis.

Feeding, by incomplete regurgitation is essentially similar in all sulids. Very young Abbott's, however, not infrequently take food regurgitated for them into the bottom of the nest. All will pick up food spilled by accident, but there are specific differences which are not dependent solely on the state of hunger of the individual. Gannet chicks are extremely reluctant to do so whereas white and brown boobies do so with alacrity.

Sleeping postures vary between species. Once large enough to be unattended, chicks of the ground nesters (white, brown, blue-foot), and often similarly sized Peruvian too, spend proportionately more time standing, with head in scapulars or just resting, than do gannets or the tree-nesters. This may be because a supine position usually means that the body covers the webs, which in hot environments may hinder thermo-regulation. The red-foot's tripod position seems unique to that species. Abbott's spends much time lying, rather like a gannet.

2. *Thermo-regulation*

Thermo-regulation is effected in different ways. To lose heat, all gular flutter and pant; young gannets, whilst lying down, protrude one spread web and red-foots raise their posteriors (with exposed cloaca) high into the air. Cape and Australasian gannet chicks lose heat by excreting onto their webs and evaporating the moisture. All sleep prone with head dangling over the nest rim or lying on the ground, and all start sleeping in the adult manner at about four to five weeks old. Scapulars are precociously developed in all and may prevent heat gain or loss (when the mean radiant temperature is above or below the bird's body temperature). To gain heat, all shiver.

These methods of regulation are effective only when the chick has acquired reasonably thick down. Until then, brooding by the parents is essential; whatever the equability of the tropical environment, the micro-climates endured by the ground nesting boobies are often extreme, whilst even in more temperate species the sun or the cold can quickly kill young chicks. Bartholomew (1966) established that in the white booby the temperatures of hatching eggs and small chicks, when taken from beneath adults were between 38·0 and 40·3°C; this stability being achieved entirely as a result of the parent's attention, for very small chicks show almost no capacity to maintain body temperature above the ambient. When 400g in weight (about 21 days old), however, they can maintain normal body temperature when in shade. The mechanism used to produce heat is shivering, which (in experiments) first appeared when chicks were about 200g (10 days) and became strong and sustained when about 380g. The larger the chick, the higher the body temperature at which shivering first appeared. Naked chicks never shivered visibly; sparsely covered chicks shivered when their body temperature declined to 36–37°C; well covered chicks (375–500g or 17–24 days) shivered powerfully even when their body temperatures were as high as 38·5°C, which is in the lower range of body temperatures experienced whilst being brooded.

Similarly the ability to keep body temperature down increased. Chicks weighing less than 100g, placed in direct sun, would have died within 20 minutes; sparsely downy chicks gained heat more slowly, whilst young weighing 400–500g stabilised their body temperatures at about 42°C, which is a little over the comparable mean adult temperature of 40·7°C.

Under heat stress, gular fluttering may occur immediately after hatching, even at relatively low body temperatures (40·4 $\pm$ 0·45°C in the 8 instances determined). Bartholomew interprets the lack of shivering by tiny chicks to mean that gular fluttering can be elicited by peripheral receptors and thus comes into operation almost immediately the chick is exposed to direct insolation. Since it is only minutes away from death through overheating, it would be adaptive to activate the cooling mechanism prior to any significant rise in body temperature. An early shivering mechanism would be useless, since in a mainly naked chick, the heat thus generated would simply be lost.

Slightly distressed chicks (too hot, cold or hungry) vocalise steadily at about once per second and fully downy ones may preen the synsacral region, possibly as a displacement activity.

Parents cope with the chick's thermo-regulatory needs simply by brooding the small ones on top of their webs, thereby shielding them from the hot ground, shading them from the sun and transmitting appropriate heat to them, through the webs. Larger chicks are shaded by the adult's body. On Tower, the steady seasonal decrease in the length of time for which the chick was constantly guarded was probably due to the progressively cooler days from January to March.

The arboreal species do not face the overheating problem as acutely as the ground nesters and although parents brood and guard their small chicks in much the same way, some red-foots on Tower were left unguarded when they reached the age of three weeks (mean c. 28 days), whereas white boobies on the same island typically guarded them for longer and in some cases for over 60 days (mean 42 days).

3. *Appeasement behaviour*

This aspect of chick behaviour has not been properly studied. Insofar as one can generalise, there seems a tendency for the chicks of those species in which 'conventional' appeasement plays a significant role in adults, to bill-hide more than those in which this is not so. Gannet chicks show extreme bill-hiding; red-foots apparently not at all and Abbott's only in a mild form. Adults of the three ground-nesters show marked bill-averting postures and their chicks Bill-hide quite strongly.

4. *Territorial and sexual display*

The difference between gannets and the ground-nesting boobies in this respect is extremely marked. Even fluffy boobies defend their parents' territory by display and also 'advertise'. Territorial defence by feathered young is often very effective against intruding adults. Gannet chicks, however, whilst extremely boisterous and playful with their parents (p. 212) do not display or defend the territory against strange adults. Clearly the reason is that the danger of eliciting reprisals from a gannet is too great, in addition to which intrusion is rarely possible. The situation in Abbott's is not clear but probably there is little or no display or 'contact' defence by the young, whilst red-foot chicks were never seen to display. It is clear from the Species Accounts that the chick displayers are those in which there is least danger involved but the advantage seems obscure. Probably there is none and it is more a case of maturation of these behaviour patterns having been selectively depressed in those species in which their expression would pose danger.

5. *Wandering, exercising and fledging*

The tendency to wander from the nest site, stringently discouraged in Atlantic gannets piqueros and the two arboreal species, is advantageous in the ground nesters by allowing the young to find shade, which is particularly important in the pantropical species, where saving energy is at a premium. As feathers grow, wing exercising is common to all. This behaviour is clearly important, for it has persisted despite being the most important single cause of mortality among piqueros and gannets (pp. 106 and 624).

The fledging of young sulids also bears a direct and simple relationship to environment. Those species (white, brown, blue-foot and red-foot) in which trial flights are practicable show them; Abbott's booby and Atlantic gannets do not. Cape and Australasian gannets, however, wander more and show a different pattern of growth of the flight feathers (p. 306).

MAINTENANCE BEHAVIOUR

1. *Preening, etc.*

Whilst considerable effort has gone into the analysis of breeding behaviour, particularly displays, little has been expended on a detailed study of comparative preening, oiling, bathing, sleeping, scratching, yawning and various ways of distending the gape; wing-stretching; resting and 'inactive' behaviour, if such is not a too contradictory term. All sulids perform exactly the same range of maintenance activities, which are obviously highly stable compared with communication behaviour.

2. *Fishing*

Despite similar plunge diving, sulids undoubtedly possess their own specific feeding methods. These have been discussed in relation to morphology elsewhere (pp. 825, 914) and the Species Accounts give more detailed information. Here it is sufficient to summarise the differences in broad terms.

(a) Within the sulids there is not the size range found in most other seabird families, but weight varies by a factor of 3·5 and is correlated with fishing technique, particularly penetration. The degree of morphological sexual dimorphism varies between species and is likewise correlated with foraging and fishing techniques.

(b) The nature of the feeding environment (local sources; mean time taken to locate adequate fish; prey species and size classes; range and frequency of different weather conditions; etc.) varies between species and often between different populations of the same species. It may also vary seasonally for some but not for others. Feeding and foraging must therefore be flexible, hence the great similarities and overlaps, but it must also be specifically or even locally adaptive. Hence differences in foraging techniques, degree of nocturnal fishing, proportion of time spent hunting in particular manners such as in groups or taking surface or aerial prey; fishing inshore, etc.

(c) The 'average' method of feeding is adapted to ecological circumstances and deeply inter-related with breeding ecology (Table 132).

SYNTHESIS

The behaviour account has been built in two tiers—details of species, followed by an attempt to draw out the important similarities and differences. The (rare) enquirer who has read both should now have a picture of a small seabird family with related but specifically distinct behavioural repertoires, in each case strongly correlated with certain features of the environment. The final tier should summarise the general phenomena which have been and are involved in producing sulid behaviour as it exists today.

All the sulids have evolved many complex behaviour patterns. So far as unritualised behaviour is concerned they have, like other birds, developed those non-ritualised behaviours (e.g. hunting) which serve with their way of life. They have also, however, developed considerable repertoires of highly ritualised behaviour patterns. In this, they accord with most other colonial seabirds, but have probably gone further than many, and exceed all other families within their order. Any attempt to quantify these large statements would be pointless because so much hinges on correct identification (separation) and enumeration of the behaviour patterns themselves and there has not been comparable effort expended on the families concerned. But even a superficial glance through the main seabird groups and through the families within the Pelicaniformes, broadly substantiates both points. Thus, the auks, penguins, petrels, shearwaters and fulmars have relatively few and simple behaviour patterns to gain territories and regulate intraspecific contacts and to form and co-ordinate pairs. However, some albatrosses, gulls and terns probably use as many complex, situation-specific behaviour patterns as any sulid. Within the Pelicaniformes, though, the pelicans themselves use mainly simple variants of head shaking behaviour (Schreiber, pers. comm.); frigates have extremely poorly differentiated territorial and pair behaviour; tropic birds use mainly ritualised flighting and phalacrocoracids have complex ritualised agonistic and pair forming behaviour but fewer behaviour patterns regulating contact within the pair and between neighbours. Comparing a sulid with a raptore, which is perhaps the most suitable land-bird and which has virtually no display, it seems plausible to suggest that it is the complexity and spatial restrictions of colonial life which make it necessary for the former to develop so much more 'on-the-spot' communication behaviour. But it is more difficult to account for differences between colonial seabird taxa. Why should gannets need a higher number of obviously distinct communication behaviour patterns than guillemots, or boobies than tropic birds? The question, as presented, may be misleading or unanswerable. However, the following factors may be involved:

1. All sulids are large, powerful and agile birds with bills much more capable of inflicting damage than those of most other seabirds.
2. They are highly territorial and yet gregarious.
3. There is considerable site and mate fidelity and they live a long time.
4. Their nesting habitat renders visual signals effective. I would suggest that all seabirds to which *all* these factors apply (and they do so in no other Pelecaniform) possess extremely well developed communication behaviour. Most seabirds, however, cannot be thus categorised.

It is for communication between itself and neighbours, mate and offspring that an adult sulid develops ritualised behaviour. The communication, by transmitting 'intent' or (what amounts to the same thing) the communicator's mood or balance of tendencies, influences the receiver's behaviour. Thus, it may cause the latter to approach, withdraw or remain, or trigger some specific response such as attack, mounting or appeasement. Clear and often complex signals thus arise (in general, complex signals can carry more information and so are more unambiguous). Territorial and pair behaviour is extremely (but within the family, variably) important in sulids. It is difficult, in several instances, to see why, but given that it is so and also points (1) and (2) above, the elaboration of displays which repel at a distance is advantageous, and the more important the territory, the greater the role of territorial displays. This is demonstrated by the differences between the gannets and the less territorial boobies (q.v.). Communication between mates also ranks high among sulids but, whereas all (except gannets) employ complex and arresting performances for attracting mates, their subsequent pair bonding behaviour differs much between species, being particularly strong in gannets. It is in accord with these points that site and mate fidelity are higher among gannets than boobies. Communication between adults and young need only be extremely simple and the only ritualised behaviours which young show to parents are Food Begging and Bill-hiding (appeasement). Adults show no ritualised behaviour towards or in combination with young. Sulids, perhaps particularly the blue-foot, well illustrate the potential of 'behavioural dialogue'. Not merely the acts themselves, but their setting, in terms both of the acts which precede and follow and of the detailed context (for instance, distance from centre of territory) play a part in communicating fine nuances of mood. This dimension of behaviour warns the analyst against a too-rigid separation and isolation of component acts.

Complex displays do not appear *de nouveau* any more than do complex organs; they derive from simpler, pre-existing patterns which become modified or combined. The sulids provide excellent examples of this. Two points emerge: simple patterns primarily associated with a variety of functional categories, such as comfort movements, feeding, locomotion, landing and recovery, and flight, form the modifiable behaviour 'pool'. The modification is either straight exaggeration, distortion in the form or plane of the movement, alteration in timing or combination with another movement. Examples are exaggeration of the headshake in gannet advertising and soliciting; change of plane in booby Oblique Headshake; exaggeration of flight preparation behaviour in the Wing Rattle; of locomotion (foot movements) in Parading; of chin-lifting (flight preparation) in Sky-pointing and Bill-up-face-away; pre-landing preparation in Saluting and post-hop recovery in the Pelican Posture. The best example of combination is in gannet Bowing, where the dip (biting re-directed to the nest) dirties the bill and the ensuing cleansing headshake has become ritualised and completely tied to the dip, whether or not the bill touches the ground.

Secondly, one may ask what decides which of the many possible candidates for ritualisation shall be chosen. Watching sulids, it has become clear that there are very many extremely conspicuous and unambiguous movements which *could* form the basis for display and yet have not done so. One of my tame gannets occasionally performs a stereotyped head jerking quite unlike anything I have seen in the wild. The movement associated with oiling is extremely conspicuous but has not been modified for communication in any sulid. And there are many more. I was even half tempted to sketch a series of postures which sulids 'could' have evolved, to show the possibilities. The point has wide application; the movements selected for ritualisation are but a few of those possible. Probably there is a strong tendency to 'choose' movements which are commonest and most practicable in that species' situation. A good example is the gannet's massive incorporation of headshaking into displays, whereas this is not the case in boobies, the point being that headshaking in the gannet is very common non-display behaviour correlated with the muddy, dirty environment and the constant handling of glutinous nest material. The boobies find far less use for ordinary cleansing headshaking and

TABLE 135

THE RELATIONSHIP BETWEEN NESTING DENSITY

DENSE NESTING
(mainly on cliffs)

caused by number of available sites limited by species' SOCIAL needs	Number of available sites PHYSICALLY limited
ATLANTIC GANNET	PERUVIAN BOOBY
1. Strong site competition giving rise to: (a) Severe fighting. (b) High frequency, ritualised, short range threat. (c) Highly developed territorial display. (d) Seasonally protracted site attendance. (e) Continuous guarding of site. (f) Male highly aggressive to female: (i) Nape-biting on meeting and during copulation not paralleled by any other sulid. (ii) Lengthy meeting ceremony (basically aggressive). (iii) Intense mutual preening (basically aggressive). (iv) Development, by female, of high tolerance to attack by male. (v) Female's appeasement behaviour well developed.	**1. Strong site competition giving rise to:** (a) Fighting more prolonged and frequent thar in any other booby. (b) High frequency short range threat. Other correlates of dense nesting absent or les marked than in gannet because *social* aspects o dense nesing less important (see below) and because the Peruvian is essentially a modified bluefoot and has retained much more booby-like behaviour than has the gannet.
2. Enhanced social stimulation (SOCIAL needs) **contributing to:** Seasonal and synchronised breeding allows optimal exploitation of seasonally abundant food and fledging of young at most favourable time of year.	**2. Enhanced social stimulation giving rise to:** Enhanced *local* synchrony but breeding not seasonally highly synchronised; food relatively aseasona and little selection pressure for fledging at particular time of year.
3. Cliff-nesting adaptations: (a) Reduction of aerial and locomotory displays (b) Nest cementation etc.	**3. Cliff-nesting adaptations:** (a) Reduction of aerial and locomotory displays (b) Nest cementation.

perhaps correspondingly use it less as part of communication behaviour. Locomotion, on the other hand, seems to contribute much more to booby display than to gannet's and is obviously more practicable in their spaced, flat ground groups. If begging behaviour is the source of some booby territorial display (p. 394) this could suggest a correlation with the vast amount of intense begging which they have to perform as chicks. The correlation of modified flight behaviour with aerialness as in the blue-footed and brown boobies, and the use of nest building movements in boobies lacking functional nests, are further cases.

Sulid behaviour illustrates the further general and fairly obvious point that form is related to function. The most conspicuous displays, such as Bowing in gannets and Sky-pointing in boobies, are those which must often communicate, with impact, over a distance. Conversely, as in gannet advertising, inconspicuous displays are restricted to close-range situations, in which category also belong all the slight, mood-communicating behaviour such as tremoring,

ESTING HABITAT, AND BEHAVIOUR IN THE SULIDAE

SPACED NESTING

GROUND

lentiful physical sites; social stimulation ss important as a mechanism for timing reeding.

UE-FOOT — WHITE BOOBY — BROWN BOOBY

TREES

Plentiful physical sites; social stimulation less important as a mechanism for timing breeding.

RED-FOOT — ABBOTT'S

Site competition reduced correlating with:

(a) Little or no fighting (none in Abbott's due to dangerous tree-top nesting sites).
(b) Little short range threat.
(c) Territorial display well developed, nevertheless.
(d) Reduced post-breeding site attendance compared with Atlantic gannet.
(e) Greater tendency to leave site unattended.
(f) Less aggression from male to female.
  (i) No nape-biting.
  (ii) Meeting ceremony relatively simple or absent, except in Abbott's booby where it is extremely well developed, probably for reasons to do with special habitat (see p. 792).
  (iii) Allo-preening reduced or absent.
  (iv) Female not tolerant of male attack.
  (v) Female's appeasement behaviour not well developed.

SOCIAL stimulation gives rise to:

cal synchrony only; all species, in at least some areas, show little or no overall synchrony of breeding; atively aseasonal environment.

Flat-ground nesting adaptations

(a) Elaboration of aerial and locomotory display, particularly in the blue-foot.

Tree-nesting adaptations

(a) Reduction of aerial and locomotory display.
(b) Elaboration of non-contact behaviour, particularly in Abbott's booby.

ruffing, eye movements, etc. Thus, functionally equivalent displays can, in closely related species, be very different in form, depending on circumstances.

Primarily non-ritualised behaviour such as preening, bathing, oiling, nest building, egg-shell removal, feeding and caring for the young, fishing, etc. does not vary so much within the family and cannot be so much used to trace relationships. Where the primary function of the behaviour has become unnecessary as in nest building in some sulids, some of the movements have become ritualised and are extensively used. But there can be relatively little meaningful interspecific variation in the form of incomplete regurgitation (given the sulid anatomy) or in preening, oiling, etc. Here, of course, the main interest, in terms of division of habitat and resources, lies in the familial priorities, when compared with other seabird families.

This leads to the final point, which is the close and intricate connection between ecology and behaviour. This applies to all birds, but is exemplified for the sulids in the above scheme (Table 135) which is perhaps the best way to conclude this comparative behaviour synthesis. This Table should be read in conjunction with a similar one in the Ecology section (Table 132).

APPENDIX 1

FACTORS RELEVANT TO COUNTS AT GANNETRIES

The results of counting gannets depend not only on the accuracy of the count but on the proportion of 'possible' attenders that are actually there at the time.

There are three aspects to this problem:

1. The seasonal attendance of *nesting* birds.
2. The seasonal attendance of site-owning and transitory birds.
3. The proportion of pairs attending, with regard to (a) season and (b) time of day.

Seasonal attendance of nesters is not a problem because counts are usually done in June or July. However, Fig. 1 shows attendance between the beginning of March and mid-October, at the Bass, and from the 'absent' line, it can be seen that between May and August a negligible proportion of nests are unattended. In fact even the April non-attendance records are of site-owners rather than nesters (this sample contained several such, though it was mainly composed of pairs that subsequently nested).

Site-owners and transitory attenders are a problem and may significantly affect counts. It is literally impossible to separate site-owners clearly from 'nesters' since they may have a

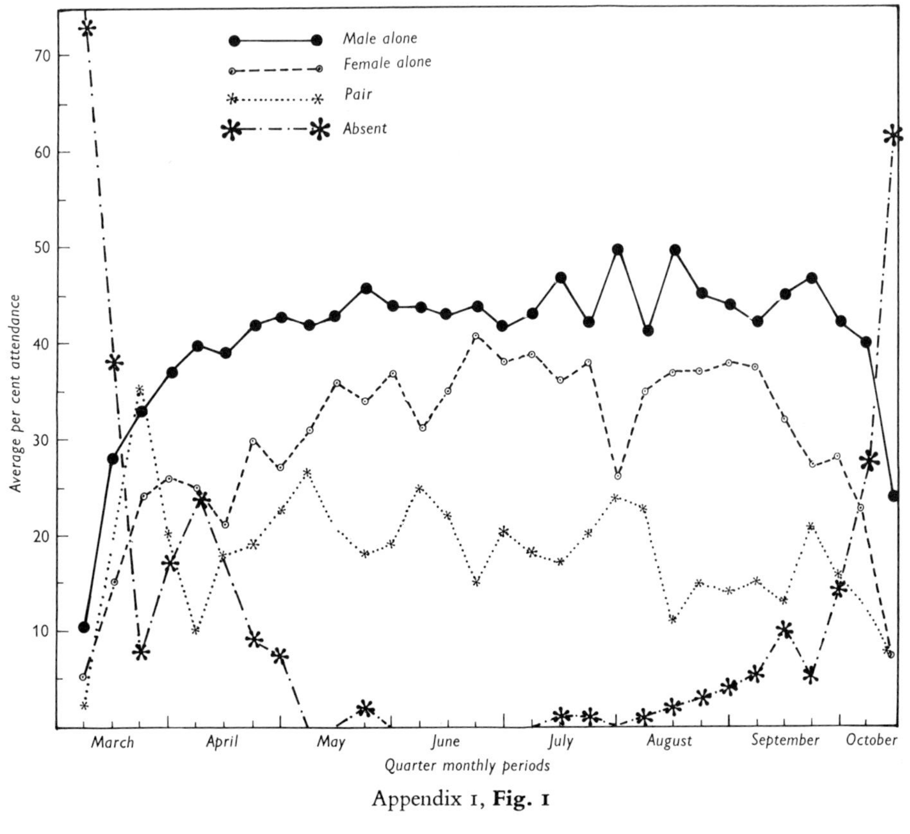

Appendix 1, **Fig. 1**

little bit of nest material and by July (when all nesters will have eggs or young) they may have lost these. Likewise it is impossible to separate transitory attenders from 'seriously' attached birds. And transitory attenders spend relatively little time at the site, or may be there only once or twice, grading to 'club' birds at some gannetries. So (taking account of season and time of day) how can one add an appropriate number for site-owners missing at the time of the count, when one doesn't know the proportion of the whole count that may be attributed to site-owners and cannot, therefore, correct that proportion for the number that one knows must be absent? The short answer is that one cannot, but can merely assume that between 10 and 30 per cent of any gannetry (locally, within a gannetry the range may be greater) will be occupied by site-owners and that the serious site-owners will attend about 80 per cent as much as do nesters. From this one can calculate a correction figure. If a gannetry holds 5,000 occupied nests or sites on a count in June, and 20 per cent (1,000) are assumed to be sites, this 1,000 will represent an 80 per cent attendance so another 250 (for the missing 20 per cent) should be added making 5,250. The rule of thumb ought to be to assume the highest percentage of site-owners at vigorously expanding gannetries.

Transitory or casual attenders are even more difficult to incorporate into a count. When they are there, one will inevitably count them as 'sites', but when they are absent, it is impossible to put a meaningful figure on the probable number that 'should' have been there. However, both absent site-owners and absent transitory birds will make the count too low, and this will be a healthy antidote to inflated estimates. It must be remembered, however, that apparent discrepancies between counts at the same gannetry, in roughly the same time-period of the same year, could well differ substantially on account of this.

The proportion of PAIRS present at the time of the count can very significantly affect counts from photographs, and also visual counts of large masses where it is impossible to distinguish between a pair and two neighbours. Therefore *such areas* should be counted as heads and a pair-factor allowed. The seasonal attendance of pairs is shown in Fig. 2. Again it is mainly for nesting pairs, but in view of the other imponderables there is no point in making slight corrections for site-owning pairs. The daily rhythm of attendance is also important. Basically, counts before 09.00 hours and *especially* after about 17.00 hours in June/July will include substantially more pairs than inbetween times. Therefore the average reading for pairs, which is all that Figure 2 gives, should be modified somewhat, by adding roughly 10 per cent if the count was made after 17.00 hours and subtracting 10 per cent if it was made around the time of day when fewest pairs are in attendance.

Having decided the proportion of nests likely to hold pairs, allowance is simply by subtraction:

100 'heads' counted, if no pairs present = 100 nests or sites.
100 'heads', if 10 per cent of nests/sites occupied by pairs = 90 sites. (10 pairs = 20 'heads' on 10 sites; 80 heads of single attenders = 80 sites; total 100 heads but 90 sites).

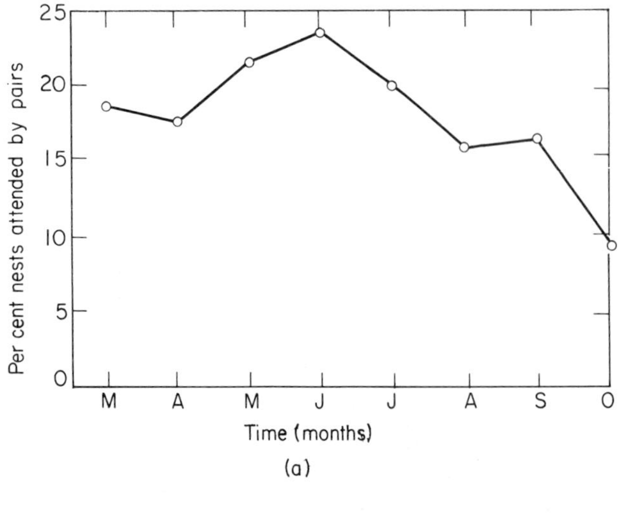

Appendix 1

Fig. 2

Finally, a word about the merits of visual versus photographic counts. The latter, providing they are crisp, are always preferable where large gannetries or sections of gannetries are being counted, for it is simply impossible to cope accurately with these by visual count from a boat and hardly less so from land unless one devotes hours to the job. A photograph can be examined at leisure, if necessary under a binocular microscope with grids. Even when taken with a standard lens from a boat, a good camera will offer results so sharp that the behaviour patterns of constituent birds can often be discerned. Furthermore, since to take it occupies but a few seconds, it need not interfere with either a rough visual estimate or a detailed visual count and can be used to check these. However, cameras are normally quite incapable of yielding details which could establish the status of the birds photographed, whereas visual observation can often do so. Thus, the ideal combination for a large gannetry would be photographs and a series of small samples, counted visually with relevant details of whether the birds were on sites, good nests or poor nests, and were pairs or singles. For small gannetries, detailed visual counts are best, but even there photographs are good, permanent supporting evidence. Counts or estimates of large colonies may be wrong by 50 per cent or more; counts from good photographs are unlikely to err by more than 5 per cent (S. Wanless, pers. comm.). Finally, it is wise to count colonies in May, since in June and July there is liable to be a variable, possibly high proportion of 'transients', and this adds significantly to the chance of confusion when comparing counts between years.

APPENDIX 2

VARIATIONS IN THE COUNTS OF GANNETS ON AILSA CRAIG FROM YEAR TO YEAR, BASED ON FIGURES FROM J. A. GIBSON

Year	Total pairs	% increase on previous year	% decrease on previous year
1936	4800		
1937	5945	24	
1938	5387		
1939	5419	1	
1940	6232	15	
1941	3518		44
1942	4829	37	
1943–1946	No figures		
1947	5383	11	
1948	5190		4
1949	4947		5
1950	6579	33	
1951	7833	29	
1952	7987	2	
1953	8249	3	
1954	8555	4	
1955	10402	22	
1956	8063		22
1957	7742		4
1958	9506	23	
1959	9390		1
1960	13532	44	
1961	8504		37
1962	9573	13	
1963	11699	22	
1964	11715	0	
1965	13273	13	
1966	12747		4
1967	10518		17
1968	10924	4	
1969	13054	20	
1970	12729		2
1971	14347	12	
1972	15219	6	
1973	15892	4	
1974	17367	9	
1975	12246		28
1976	14051	15	

Note: The very large difference in the number of occupied sites between 1974 and 1975 (J. A. G. visual counts) was not recorded by S. Wanless (photographic counts). Some of the previous differences may have been artefacts.

APPENDIX 3

CALCULATION OF PER CENT PER ANNUM INCREASE

In this section on Numbers and Distribution, many 'per cent per annum' increases have been calculated. Where this is done for a long span of years containing few known datum points the actual increase may, during that time, have been exponential or it may have been fast over a short period, but slow, none existent or the population may even have decreased over another part of the span. However, the exponential growth model is a fully acceptable one and is used here. The figures given in the accompanying Table have been derived from regression lines calculated from the equation:

$$\star \log_e N_t = \log_e N_o + rt \text{ where the per cent increase } = (100 \times e^r) - 100$$

Nevertheless, the yearly increase which one calculates depends on the slope of the regression line and hence on the section used to extrapolate backwards to the year in which the colony (theoretically) began.

(Dr. J. G. Ollason worked out the results in this Appendix)

$\star$ t = time counted in years from 1900

N_t = population size at time t

N_o = population size at time o

r = growth rate constant

SOME FIGURES FOR ANNUAL INCREASE RATES, BASED ON AN EXPONENTIAL GROWTH MODEL, OF CERTAIN GANNETRIES

Colony	Period of growth	Correlation co-efficient (R)	Growth rate constant (slope of graph)	Per cent per annum increase
GRASSHOLM	1909–1969	0·931	0·065	7·0
	1924–1933	—	—	10·1
	1939–1949	—	—	4·6
	1964–1969	—	—	0·8
SCAR ROCKS	1949–1974	0·953	0·080	8·3
	1968–1974	—	—	1·5
ST KILDA	1909–1973	0·932	0·042	4·3
	1949–1959	—	—	10·1
	1959–1973	—	—	2·1
HERMANESS	1909–1969	0·918		15·7
	1965–1969	—		10·8
FAROES AND ICELAND	1909–1939		0·002	0·2
	1939–1969		0·014	1·.4
BIRD ROCK	1900–1972	0·994	0·061	6·3
BONAVENTURE	1900–1972	0·964	0·036	3·7
	1961–1966			10·0
FUNK ISLAND	1936–1945		c·372	45·4
	1945–1956		0·163	17·7
	1956–1959		0·277	31·9
	1959–1967		0·006	0·6
	1967–1972		0·067	6·9

Note: Increases above 5 per cent per annum mean immigration.

APPENDIX 4

EXPLOITATION OF THE GANNET BY MAN

Seabirds provide a readily accessible source of fat, protein and feathers, all of which have been extremely valuable to man in the past. Gannets, and particularly young ones (gugas) offer by far the largest and easiest 'crop' of any North Atlantic Seabird. One large youngster provides over 3000 gms of fat and protein and it is perfectly feasible to gather 2000 birds in one 'raid'. One can readily imagine the pressures, from pre-historic man, which could have helped to drive gannets to nest on inaccessible islands.

Gurney (1913) devotes a chapter to the topic of gannets as food, and describes the curative properties of their fat. In 'Ein Mittelenglisches Medizin Buch', of the fifteenth and sixteenth centuries, gannet's grease is recommended (along with fat of badgers and boars) as a cure for gout—'Pro Gutta: Item unguentum; Also an oyntement for the same. R tak cattes grece, ganates grece, banfones grece, bores grece, mery of an hors, 7 grece of a dogge, 7 alle these tempre togeder'. Again, from Hector Boece, 1526, ... 'within the bowellis of thir geis, is ane fatness of singulaire medicine; for it helis mony infirmities, speciallie sik as cumis be gut [such as come by gout] and cater [catarrh] disceding [diseasing] in the hauches or lethes [groins] of men and wemen' (Gurney, 1913, p. 179, where details of derivation are given). Barrels of gannet's grease were so valuable that a dispute, concerning some, between the Prioress of North Berwick and Robert Lauder, owner of the Bass, was arbitrated by Pope Alexander VI in 1493. As late as 1766, ten gallons fetched £2.13s.5d, and in those days, in Scotland, one could get a cottage built for labour costs of under £1. Feathers sold at 10 shillings per Scottish stone (24 lbs) in 1767 and eighteen shillings in 1874. This meant almost 300 gannets to stuff one featherbed. Two hundred and forty stones comprised the rent of St. Kilda, paid by the islanders in the mid-nineteenth century, though not all were gannet feathers.

Gannets were once highly esteemed as food. We do not know what St. Baldred (upon the site of whose call we lived) thought of them, but in 1684 Sir Robert Sibbald pronounced that 'the art of cookery cannot form a dish of such delicate flavour, and combining the tastes of fish and flesh, as a roasted Solan Goose'. Charles II did not agree, apparently remarking that there were two things in Scotland which he did not like—the Solan Goose and the Solemn League and Covenant. My own verdict inclines towards Sibbald's. In the hey-day of collecting, when between 1300–1900 birds, ninety per cent of them young, were taken from the Bass each season and sold in Edinburgh, at The Poultry (market), every week day in August and September. In 1634 they fetched 2s. 1d. a piece and in 1710, 24 pence. After that they sold at 20 pence up until the early years of the nineteenth century. By mid century the price had dropped to ninepence and in another decade the trade in gannets, as food, had virtually ceased, and that in grease and feathers seriously declined. However, as late as 1876, some 800 gannets a year were being taken, and many of them cooked and sent to Sheffield, London, Birmingham, Manchester, and Newcastle. A decade later, gathering still went on, particularly in years when many Irish harvesters were in the area. Then, across at Canty Bay, occurred scenes which, sitting outside the Bass Chapel late in a summer evening, I have often imagined. The heaps of young gannets being handed ashore from the boats and cooked in brick ovens, to be eaten, by the score (200, it is said, in one 'feast'), out in the open air, by the rough Irish labourers.

Besides roasting, gannets may be pickled, dried and eaten raw, or simply boiled in water and eaten with potatoes. Many Lewis people at the present day eat them this way. Gannets' eggs (6s. per dozen around 1856) were also eaten and an advertisement claimed that they were highly appreciated at the Royal Table and 'admitted to be indistinguishable from plover's eggs' (Gurney, 1913, p. 253). The St. Kildans took thousands per year (for instance, 14000 from merely the summit of Stack Lee on May 14, 1902). Finally, in the list of usages to which gannets have been put, must be cited that of the breast bone as a lamp, the stomach and gullet (capable of enormous distension) as a skin-bottle for (among other liquids) fulmar-oil; the ulna for a pipe-stem and the web for a pouch or purse.

Exploitation (approximate dates) ceased on Ailsa in 1880; Bass 1885; St. Kilda 1910; Sule Stack 1932 and Eldey 1940 and continues at the present day only on Sula Sgeir, Myggenaes (Faroes) and the Westmann Islands. Details of culls are now given for individual gannetries, taken mainly from Gurney (1913) and Fisher & Vevers (1943).

The *maximum* yearly numbers taken from various gannetries were: Bass (1900); Ailsa (500); St. Kilda (14000); Sulisgeir (3000); Sule Stack (1000); Faroes (900); Westmann Islands, (3000) and Eldey (4000), but no doubt bad weather greatly reduced the toll in some years.

St. Kilda. The culls may have been grossly over estimated, for although Martin Martin writes that 22,600 gannets were eaten by the St. Kildans in 1696, Neil Mackenzie, minister there between 1829 and 1843, gives 2000 gugas and the same number of adults as the biggest annual total ever killed in this period and goes on to say that they probably never took more than 5000 gugas and 2–3000 adults, which totals less than half Martin's figure. In June 1847, 1100 gannets were said to be taken in one night. In June 1847, 1100 gannets were said to be taken in one night. In April 1885, 660 adults were killed in one night. By 1895, 1280 young and 1920 adults were taken but in 1902 only 300. In spring 1910, 600 adults were caught, and this appears to be the last record.

On *Myggenaes,* 600–800 young (no adults) were being taken in the 1930's (Vevers & Evans 1938).

Bass yielded a yearly max. of 2000, min. 1000 and mean probably around 1500–1600 between (known dates) 1511 and 1865 (though not necessarily every year). Less than 1000 in the 1870's until 1876. Fewer still after that and probably last taken around 1885. Eggs taken up to and including 1885.

Ailsa has been culled since (at least) 1635, though earlier references to abundance (1526) probably indicate culls. Max. 500 young taken per year (1853–1860) possibly up to 1880. Thus Ailsa was exploited much less than the Bass. Eggs, however, probably taken until 1929.

Sula Sgeir has long been exploited (1549) from Ness (Lewis). In the 1860's 'several thousand'; 1880's 2000–3000 taken; 2800 in 3 days in 1884, 2500 1898 are totals of young birds (though also some adults) culled in the nineteenth century. Then 2200 in 1912; 1100 in 1915; 2000 in 1931; 2000 in 1933; 1400 in 1934; 2060 in a fortnight in 1936; 2000 in 1937; 2000 in 1938 and some in 1939. Raids have continued in post-war years.

Sule Stack. Raided from Orkney sometime before 1795; also by Ness men, but less than Sula Sgeir. 'Never more than 1000' young were accessible. None taken for 'many years' prior to 1937.

In the *Westmann Islands* 400–500 were taken each year from Sulnasker prior to 1862; 562 or 662 killed in 1898 (depending on account), 480 (1913); 363 (1914); 427 (1915); 526 (1916); 162 (1917); 159 (1918); 228 (1919); 480 (1920); 384 (1921); 668 (1922); 376 (1924); 368 (1925); 656 (1926); 864 (1927); 824 (1928); 632 (1929); 536 (1930). These figures likely to be considerable under statements.

Eldey. Westmann Islanders took thousands; 4100 and 1908. Between 1910 and 1939 the average kill was 3257 (200–4000) 2000 were taken in 1939 but in 1940 the island became protected.

APPENDIX 5

EXAMPLES OF THE LAYING DATES OF THE SAME FEMALE IN SUCCESSIVE YEARS; GROUP 6, BASS ROCK

	Date of laying in:												
Female	1961	1962	1963	1965	1966	1968	1970	1971	1972	1973	1974	1975	1976
1	19/4	][8/5	2/5	1/5	25/4	26/4	15/4	15/4	13/4	11/4	NR	Dead	—
2	25/4	24/4*	26/4	⟨1/5	11/4	NR	20/4	20/4*	⟨20/4*	4/4	NR	3/4	Gone
3	28/4	20/4	20/4	⟨1/5	18/4	NR	][28/4	Dead	—	—	—	—	—
4	23/5*	20/5*	NR	⟨1/5	9/5	NR	][20/4	20/4	17/4	13/4	NR	3/5	19/4
5	—	—	—	—	16/5	26/4	][28/4	⟨20/4	17/4	⟨12/4	16/4	10/4	17/4
6	28/4*	11/5[I]	20/4	⟨ 1/5	11/4	NR	][12/4	⟨20/4	7/4	10/4	⟨16/4[I]	14/4	Gone
7	—	—	—	⟨1/5[1st]	⟨30/4*	NR	20/4	13/4	17/4	4/4	23/4	1/4	5/4
8	27/4	24/4	26/4	⟨ 1/5	27/4	NR	20/4	20/4	13/4	Gone	—	—	—
9	10/5*	NE	NR	][⟨1/5	⟩ 2/5[I]	NR	15/4	20/4	13/4	7/4	16/4	18/4	NR
10	28/4	22/4*	20/4	⟨1/5	2/5	NR	16/4	⟨20/4	13/4*	][⟨12/4	26/4	21/4	NR

Notes: * Egg lost; often retards laying in following year.
I Infertile.][Change of mate. NR No record.
1st First-time breeder. NE No egg.

APPENDIX 6

GANNET MOVEMENTS OFFSHORE

In the section on the distribution of the gannet at sea I omitted details of counts. However, some of them are worth including as examples of the types of passage which can be seen round our coasts.

1. *East Coast passage*

Gannets have been intensively 'sea-watched' off Yorkshire and Aberdeen (Spurn Point and Rattray Head Area respectively). Very probably the birds come mainly from the Bass Rock. The watches are not detailed enough, nor over a sufficiently long period, to resolve the nature of feeding movements, but, clearly, these complicate any interpretation of seasonal, migratory or dispersal movements. The main point seems to be that, between August and October inclusive, the main (indeed almost the only) movement off Aberdeenshire is northward whilst off Spurn, it is predominantly southwards, though with a strong northerly component. There is only one year (1973) available for Aberdeen, but 5 years for Spurn, so I will summarise the latter before drawing the comparison. Counts at Spurn between 1st August and 22nd October yielded the following results;

	North	South	
1970	593	958	
1971	959	1723	
1972	1706	1336	
1973	742	1051	
1974	1108	2293	
	5108	7361	or 1:1·44

Observer effort was not equal each year so the absolute figures are relatively meaningless; it is the overall preponderance of southerly movement that is significant. In August, the southerly movement barely predominated (2005 to 1575 or 1:1·30 over 5 years) but in September it was significantly greater (5724 to 2911 or 1:1·97). This probably implies that the southwards passage along the coast south of the Bass is largely feeding movement until late September, when it then becomes a significant passage southwards, though with substantial northward (return) movements of birds that had merely been foraging. This picture is broadly substantiated by R. Appleby's (pers. comm.) counts from Filey Brigg. Between 1960–74 inclusive his August counts totalled 812 north and 274 south, whilst in September 65 went north to 1083 south and in October 100 to 114. There are probably some artefacts involved here, since almost never were north and south passages recorded on the same day, whereas this was entirely normal at Spurn. But the overall trend seems clear.

Off Aberdeenshire the picture is different. Henderson (1974) detected a clear southerly passage on only one day (29th September). The great bulk of the movement was north. His figures cannot be directly compared with those from Spurn since they are given as birds/hour and no time limits are available for Spurn, but the main points are that the passage rate rose from mid-September to early October.

The conclusion seems to be that Bass gannets send out foraging birds, north and south, and at the same time, birds dispersing or migrating for the winter. In August the latter are hardly evident but become so in September and October. Probably more birds move out of the North Sea southwards, than northwards, but clearly both routes are followed.

Henderson's data on the differences in the proportions of adults and immature birds passing north off Aberdeenshire is given in Fig. 1.

The following notes summarise observations made at several places which as yet remain unintegrated or uninterpreted.

(1) *Sutherland.* Equal movement east and west (October 5th and 6th) but 27 per cent moving west were immature, and only 7 per cent moving east were immature.

(2) *Rattray Head.* Mainly north, September—December. After mid-January trend became south but with substantial movements both ways in February/March. Then the trend became mainly northerly in the latter half of April but, in reduced numbers and much more random by early May and further reduced in June. (Elkins & Williams, 1969). The latter observation is probably explained by the shorter foraging trips of birds with small young.

(3) *Blavand, Jutland.* Up to 900 birds per day passing, mainly north in May, June, July and south in August, September and October. Immatures increased in May, June

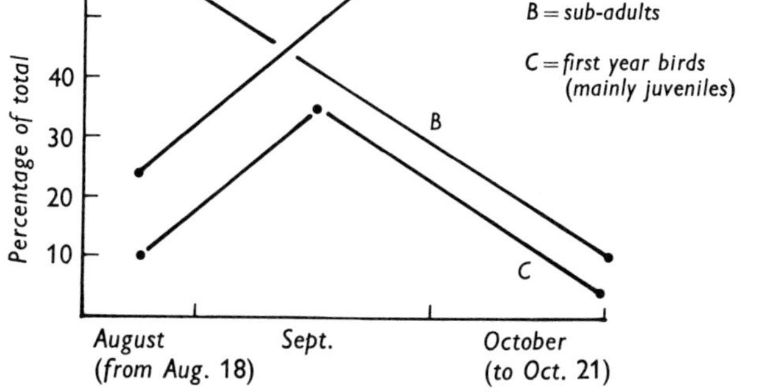

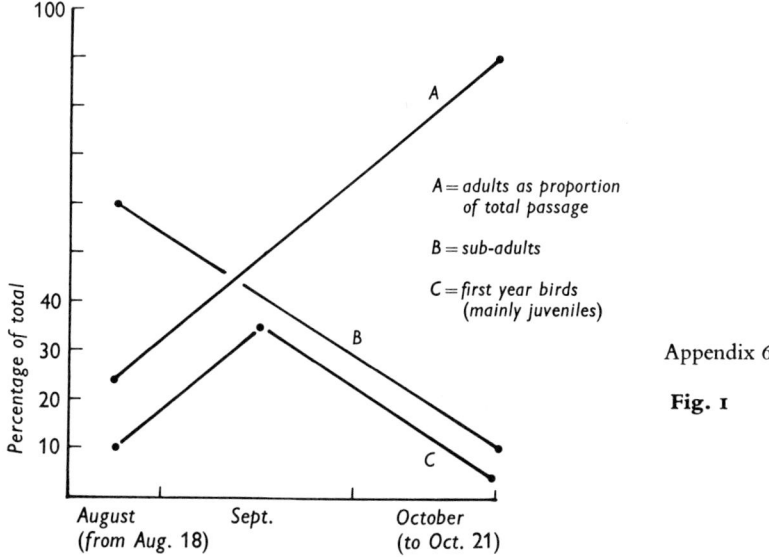

Appendix 6

Fig. 1

and July (17 per cent first-year birds: 34 per cent second year; 22 per cent third year and 27 per cent fourth year in period September 21st–October 31st). Most birds in westerly winds force 4–6. Significant morning peak (Meltofte and Overlund, 1974). In addition to these movements, up to 400 birds per day were seen foraging off the coast.

(4) *Bradda Head, Isle of Man*. Earlier considered to be common throughout summer only, but now occurs throughout the year. Southward movement not studied over long period, but late July/early August. A reasonably heavy southward flow (96 per cent adults) with a few moving north, has been noted. Movement was in groups of 1–6 birds.

(5) *Strumble Head*. 822 gannets moved south-west in three hours, September 9th. (Pettitt, 1969).

(6) *Clogher Head* (*E. Ireland*). Peak movement in August (presumably south) at 150/hours. Fifty per cent immature (Moore 1974).

(7) *Erris Head, Mullet Peninsula, County Mayo*. A steady drift to the south-west in autumn at 50/hr. adults about half the total and very few first-year birds. Observers noted a passage both ways, all year, up to 100/hr. with a maximum of 2000/hr.

(8) *Malin Head*. Very heavy October passage, mainly west, (Hounsome 1967) probably of Scottish birds.

(9) *Slyne Head* (*Galway*). 1090 gannets passed north and 31 south, September 4th. 1969 (Sheldon & Bradshaw, 1970).

(10) *Cape Clear*. Passage (mainly westerly all year) peaks from March to mid-May (160/hr.) and August–mid-October (279/hr.), the maximum being 4000/hr. Immatures virtually absent from mid-January to mid-April, but exceed adults mid-May–mid-June. Largest number of immatures are in early August and of adults, early October. (Sharrock, 1973).

(11) *Cap Gris Nez*. Very large October passage (mainly west but some east), but few until early September. Of 220 in 8 hours, October 22, 55 per cent were adult.

(12) *Morocco*. Main peaks, going north in April–June, were 400 in 1½ hrs. Only 53/1477 were adult and 5–10 per cent of remainder sub-adult, (Hopkins, 1969).

(13) *Cape Verde*. Up to 50 birds/hr. passing north; total 400. 36 passed south (Gaston, 1970).

APPENDIX 7

FORTH/CLYDE CROSSINGS BY GANNETS

Autumn observations of gannets in the upper Forth (skinflat area).
Data from Taylor, Potts and Fleming, (pers. comm.)

Year	*Summary of observations*
1960	One first-year bird*, October 2nd.
1961	3 juveniles in river, September 10th; 3 fishing mid-river, September 22nd.
1963	c. 58 first-year and 2 adults fishing in river and Grangemouth Bay, September 14th; one first-year, September 28th.
1966	1 adult left river and flew SW, August 27th; 13 first-year flew up river, September 24th; 12 first-year flew up Forth, past road bridge, 1 left river and flew SW, September 25th.
1967	One first-year over Falkirk, 3½ miles inland, flying SW, September 13th; one first-year over Carronshire, 2 miles inland, flying SW, September 17th; 3 first-year, left river and flew SW, September 27th.
1970	Three first-year, August 28th; several first-year, September 14th.
1971	Five first-year, August 22nd.
1972	13 first-year birds resting on the river between Grangemouth and Kincardine Bridge, September 2nd; in which area 7 were patrolling on September 20th and 4 on September 23rd. Adults (able to fly when released) were twice found in fields West of Kincardine Bridge.
1973	One first-year bird flying upstream, September 6th; one first-year bird flying downstream towards Grangemouth, September 8th.
	These records are inconclusive in terms of a regular passage, but it is possible that, whilst up-river a few juveniles do respond to the urge to move South, overland.

* 'first-year' almost certainly means newly fledged juveniles.

APPENDIX 8

RECOVERIES OF RINGED CAPE GANNETS

Cape Gannet pulli ringed at Malagas (W) and Bird Island (E) and recovered at various localities west and east of Cape Agulhas

	% Birds recovered		Distance (Km)	
AREA WEST OF AGULHAS	Ringed Bird Island	Ringed Malagas	From Bird Island	From Malagas
Cape Agulhas—Cape Point	8·8	6·7	370–480	170–300
Cape Point—Malagas Island	1·8	2·9	480–660	0–170
Malagas—Orange River	1·8	0·0	660–890	0–540
Orange River—Wolvis Bay	0·0	0·0	890–1330	540–1250
Wolvis Bay—Mossamedes	7·2	11·5	1330–1890	1250–2180
Mossamedes—Lobito	16·0	5·8	1900–2060	2180–2470
Lobito—Luanda	17·9	12·5	2060–2320	2470–2890
Luanda—Cabinda	7·2	3·8	2320–2570	2890–2390
Cabinda—Port Gentil	5·4	13·4	2570–2970	2390–3960
Port Gentil—Bata	7·2	7·7	2970–3130	3960–4200
Bata—Victoria	1·8	3·8	3130–3290	4200–4460
Victoria—Lagos	1·8	3·8	3290–3590	4460–4920
AREA EAST OF AGULHAS				
Cape Agulhas—Port Elizabeth	3·6	5·8	0–600	300–1050
Port Elizabeth—East London	3·6	0·0	0–250	1050–1120
East London—Port Shepstone	5·4	8·6	250–620	1120–1460
Port Shepstone—Durban	3·6	1·0	620–730	1460–1570
Durban—Laurenco Marques	3·6	5·8	730–1210	1570–2000
Laurenco Marques—Beira	1·8	4·8	1210–1960	2000–2700
Beira—Cape Delgado	—	1·9	—	2700–4000
Beira—Mocambique	1·8	—	1960–2870	—

APPENDIX 9

ABERRANT PHYSICAL FEATURES

Most of the abnormalities recorded for sulids have referred to Atlantic gannets and they include albino chick (Ailsa, 1973); deformed mandibles (crossed with upper lengthened and down-curved; also elongated lower mandible, Bass, 1962; 1963; unusual pigmentation of iris 'star-shaped pupil' of a Bass bird recorded in Gurney (1913); chipped bill covering, sometimes with 'peeled' piece projecting in odd shapes, possibly from skua attacks or from fighting; holes and tears in webs. Blind gannets are often mentioned among fishermen but there seems no real basis for the tale.

APPENDIX 10

GALAPAGOS BREEDING RECORDS FOR *SULA DACTYLATRA*

Locality	*Date*	*State of breeding*	*Authority*
Hood Island	1.2.06	Abundant; eggs and/or very small young.	Gifford (1913)
,, ,,	23.9.57 and 16.10.57	Pre-laying attendance but no eggs or young.	Bowman (C.D.R.S.)
,, ,,	Late May 1962	Large to fully-feathered young only.	M. H. Hundley (C.D.R.S.)
,, ,,	10.12.1962	Sample: 70 nests with no eggs or young, 15 nests with one egg and 5 nests with two eggs.	J. Hatch (pers. comm.)
,, ,,	23.7.63	A few feathered but ground-fast young; free-flying juvs. "Many" young recently gone from Punta Suarez and Punta Cevallos.	D. W. Snow (C.D.R.S.)
,, ,,	30.8.63	No young; some inactive adults.	M. Castro (C.D.R.S.)
,, ,,	22.11.63	Pre-laying activity; 3 nests with eggs.	D. W. Snow (C.D.R.S.)
,, ,,	12.2.64	Mostly eggs; some small young also.	G.I.S.P. (C.D.R.S.)
Culpepper	10.12.1898	Pre-laying activity; few eggs.	Snodgrass & Heller (1904)
,,	18.2.63	Many eggs and young.	E. Curio & P. Kramer (C.D.R.S.)
Daphne	23.11.05	Eggs and young.	Gifford (1913)
,,	20.3.63	Young of many sizes.	M. Castro (C.D.R.S.)
,,	30.5.63	Many flying juveniles.	M. Castro (C.D.R.S.)
,,	31.7.63	Small number downy young, primaries growing.	M. Castro (C.D.R.S.)
,,	21.8.63	No further breeding.	M. Castro (C.D.R.S.)
,,	22.10.63	Many nesting; sample: attended nest but no egg or young (38); egg(s) (30); young (1).	D. W. Snow & M. Castro (C.D.R.S.)
,,	19.12.63	Sample: young (variable, up to large downy) (21); egg(s) 4.	D. W. Snow & M. Castro (C.D.R.S.)
,,	8.2.64	Most young half to nearly full grown.	D. W. Snow (C.D.R.S.)
,,	27.5.64	Nesting almost over.	J. Fitter (C.D.R.S.)
Tower Island	22.6.1899	Some adults; not nesting.	Snodgrass & Heller (1904)
,, ,,	20.11.62	Mainly well incubated eggs or small young.	J. Hatch (pers. comm.)
,, ,,	Late May to early August 1963	No breeding.	E. Curio & P. Kramer (C.D.R.S.)
Wenman	13.12.1898	Considerable numbers of eggs and small young.	Snodgrass & Heller (1904)
,,	January 1963	Pre-laying activity.	E. Curio & P Kramer (C.D.R.S.)
Kicker Rock	7.6.63	Adults with young.	M. Castro (C.D.R.S.)
Punta Pitt area	8.6.63	Few pairs nesting; 4 nests with young.	M. Castro (C.D.R.S.)

Note: C.D.R.S. refers to records from the Charles Darwin Research Station files, Santa Cruz, extracted by J. B. Nelson in late 1964. G.I.S.P. refers to records collected by the Galapagos International Scientific Programme of 1964.

APPENDIX 11

EGG DATA, BLUE-FOOTED BOOBY (ISLA SAN PEDRO MARTIR 1971)

FROM D. ANDERSON

Degree incubated	Weight	Length/Breadth	Shell weight	Percent lipid
Fresh	53·25	6·09/4.13	5·30	3·50
,,	57·02	5·93/4·30	5·94	3·80
,,	47·88	5·73/4·05	4·82	4·40
,,	51·92	5·96/4.13	4·94	3·70
,,	51·57	5·89/4·11	4·71	3·90
,,	55·05	6·06/4·18	5·51	3·60
5 days	52·34	5·82/4·14	5·51	3·70
,,	59·13	6·26/4·20	5·39	4·00
one-third	55·04	5·98/4·29	5·57	4·40
,,	55·07	5·93/4·28	5·20	3·90

APPENDIX 12

BREEDING DISTRIBUTION OF BLUE-FOOTED BOOBY IN THE GALAPAGOS

(see also Fig. 218)

Island	Location(s) on island	Approx. no. (pairs)	Assessment of status
Daphne Major	Upper & lower craters & surrounding areas.	1000+	Abundant & regular breeder, large colonies dense for this species. Has bred there prob. for at least 100's of years (e.g. present 1905).
Hood Island	Punta Suarez Punta Cevallos	500+ 1000+?	Abundant & regular breeder. Colony less homogenous than Daphne; long-established (e.g. present 1906).
Gardner-near-Charles		Abundant breeder. January 10th 1963	

Island	Location)s) on island	Approx. no. (pairs)	Assessment of status
Wenman		Large colony	Curio & Kramer, in January 1963, found eggs & young in all stages & recorded 'burst of laying'—so obv. many pairs.
Culpepper		'Many'	Regular breeder; long-established; breeding pop. currently healthy.
Champion-near-Charles		Obviously many.	Long established e.g. present 1905. Common breeder 1963 and since.
Jervis		Breeds: numbers not on record.	
Guy Fawkes		c. 40 pairs (1967).	
Isobella	Cape Berkeley. Tagus Cove (both sides), Island in Elizabeth Bay.. ..	Many	Numerous and regular, in total; exact sizes of contributory colonies not documented.
	slopes east of Punta Essex, Cowley Island	Small colony	
San Cristobal	Punta Pitt.	30	These records refer to 1963 but from numbers, seems likely that it is well-established and regular here.
	Isla Lobos.	100	
Tower		'One seen' 1906 (Gifford) 'Locally common on cliffs' Nov. '62 (Hatch C.D.S.R.) '6 or fewer pairs, one locality' May–Aug. 1963 (Curio-Kramer, C.D.S.R.).	Difficult to judge but obviously very few and prob. in some years does not breed.
Brattle			Long established (e.g. present 1905). Current status?
North Seymour		Breeds: number not on record.	
Tortuga Island		'Many'.	

APPENDIX 13

ANNUAL VARIATION IN BREEDING OF THE RED-FOOTED BOOBY IN THE GALAPAGOS

Year	Date	State of breeding	Source	Deduction of main laying period
		TOWER ISLAND		
1899	June	Nesting; eggs; none with young	Snodgrass & Heller (1904)	April/May/June
1906	Sept.	Nests all over; 2 or 3 fresh eggs seen; 1 juvenile just able to fly	Gifford (1913)	—
1962	Nov.	Most with egg	J. Hatch (pers. comm.)	Oct./Nov.
1963	Aug.	Few eggs; young all ages, many dying.	E. Curio & P. Kramer	April/Sept./Oct.
1964		Most eggs laid Jan. & Feb.	Nelson	Jan./Feb./Oct./Nov.
1965		Most eggs laid Sept./Oct.; some in January	M. Castro (pers. comm.)	Sept /Oct.
1966	Feb.	Mainly large young; some building; no eggs	M. Harris (pers. comm.)	March/April/Sept./Oct.
	April	Starting laying	,,	
	July	Fluffy to fully feathered young. No eggs	,,	
	Aug.	More nests; still no eggs	,,	
	Dec.	Fluffy to fully feathered young; few eggs	,,	
1967	Jan.	Large chicks; few eggs	,,	April/May
	March	Mainly juveniles; no eggs	,,	
	July	Young just showing feathers; a few eggs. Little activity	,,	
1968	May	No breeding	,,	—
1970	Feb.	Little activity; some nest building; no eggs; 1 fully feathered young	,,	March/April/Oct.
	April	A few eggs	,,	
	June	Mostly display; a few eggs; a very few large young	,,	
	Sept.	Building; some eggs	,,	
1971	Feb.–May	No breeding activity	,,	Poss. Sept. peak
	July	Many more adults, display, no nests	,,	
1972	Nov.	Many breeding & have been for some time	,,	Poss. Sept. peak
		WENMAN ISLAND		
1906	Sept.	Most apparently without nests; no eggs seen; 1 juvenile	Gifford (1913)	
1971	Feb.	A few eggs and small young	M. Harris (pers. comm.)	
		PUNTA PITT (ISLAND)		
1965	Dec.	Mainly attending sites or empty nests (12 pairs); 4 with young	,,	
1966	April	No activity	,,	
1967	May	5 with eggs	,,	
		PUNTA PITT (MAINLAND)		
1966	July	Mainly eggs or small young (80 out of 97) but 11 juveniles and 6 large young	,,	April
1967	May	8 eggs; 17 small young; 6 large young; 17 half-feathered; 21 juveniles	,,	Fairly continuous Sept./April

APPENDIX 14

TYPES OF VEGETATION IN WHICH RED-FOOTED BOOBIES BUILD THEIR NESTS

Avicennia spp.—Seychelles, *A. marina*—Aldabra, Cosmoledo
Brugieria spp.—Seychelles, *B. gymnorhiza*—Aldabra
Bumelia retusa—Cayman Islands
Bursera spp.—Galapagos, *B. simaruba*—Cayman Islands
Ceriope tagal—Aldabra
Ceriope tagal—Aldabra
Chenopodium spp.—Necker, *C. sandwicheum*—Laysan
Cordia spp.—Caroline Atoll, Galapagos, Howland, *C. sebestena*—Cayman Is., *C. subcordata*—Seychelles
Cryptocarpus pyriformis—Galapagos
Euphorbia—Clarion Is.
Ficus spp.—Cayman Is.
Lycium spp.—Hawaii
Morinda spp.—Caroline Atoll
Neea choriophylla—Cayman Is.
Pandanus spp.—Henderson Is.
Pemphis acidula —Seychelles.
Pisonia spp.—Caroline Atoll, Fanning Is., Seychelles, *Pisonia grandis*—Manua Group
Pithecellobium keyense—Cayman Is.
Ponteria campechiana—Cayman Is.
Rhizophora spp.—Menai Is., Seychelles, *R. mucronata*—Aldabra
Sauriana maritima—Seychellse
Scaevola spp.—Kure Atoll, Seychelles
Sesbania tomentosa—Nihoa, Necker
Tournefortia spp.—Caroline Atoll, Christmas Is. (Pacific) Tromelin Is.
Coconut palms—Clipperton
Kiawe tree—Mokapu peninsula

APPENDIX 15

THE SHAPE OF THE OUTERMOST THREE PRIMARIES IN THE SULIDAE.

Outlines traced direct from specimens and reproduced here half size.

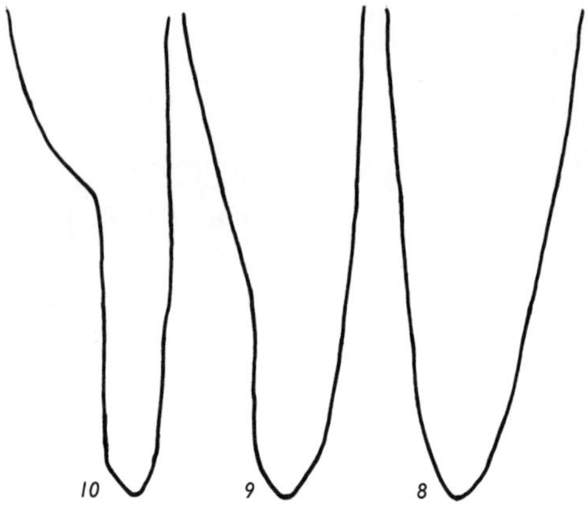

Atlantic gannet; right wing

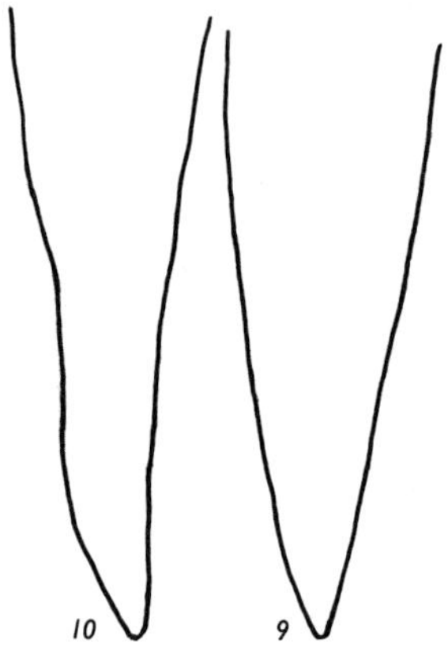

Cape gannet; adult, right wing

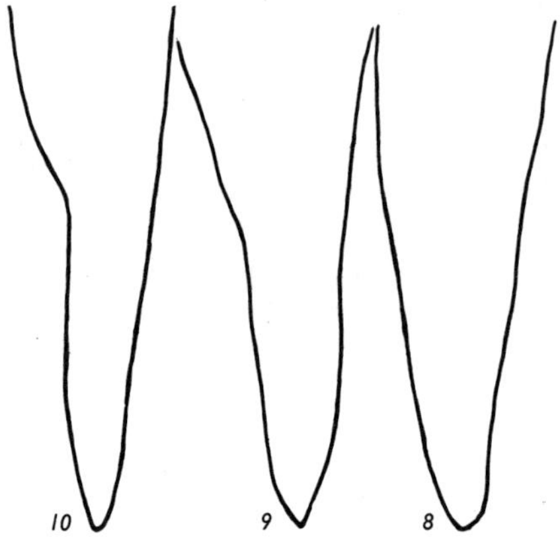

Australasian gannet; right wing

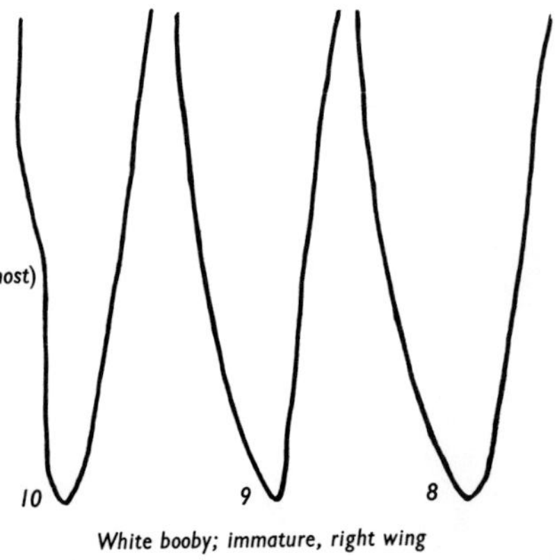

White booby; immature, right wing

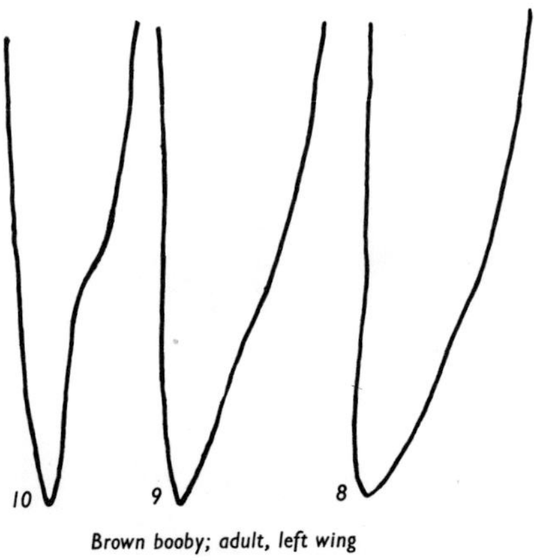

Brown booby; adult, left wing

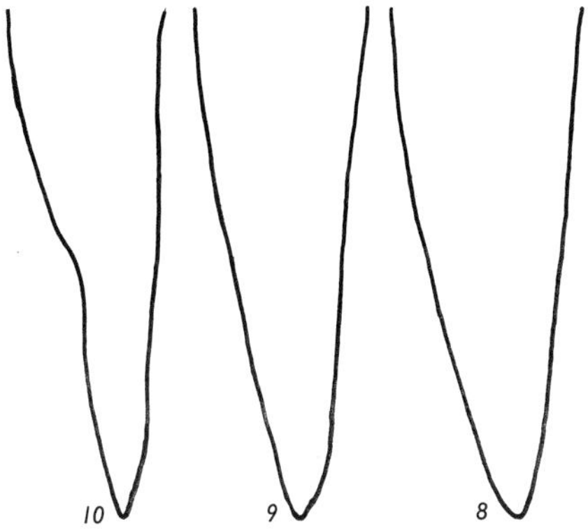

Blue-foot; adult, right wing

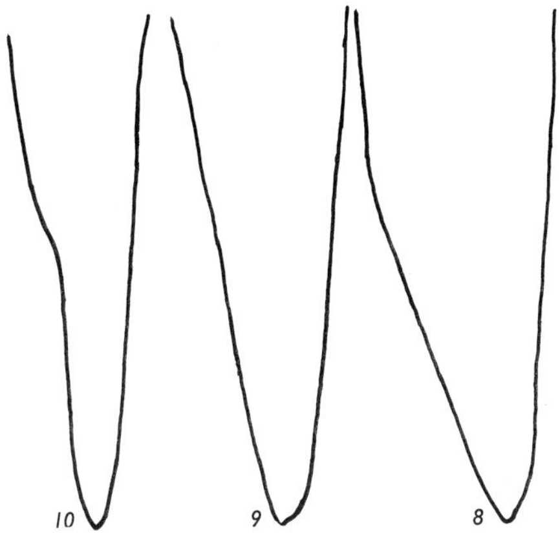

Blue-foot; adult, right wing

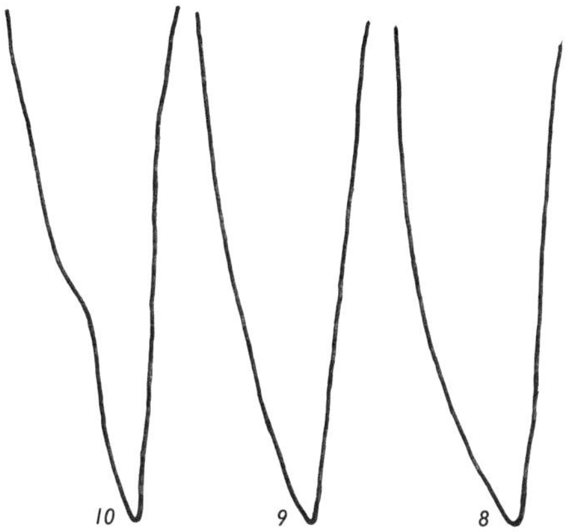

Peruvian booby; immature, right wing

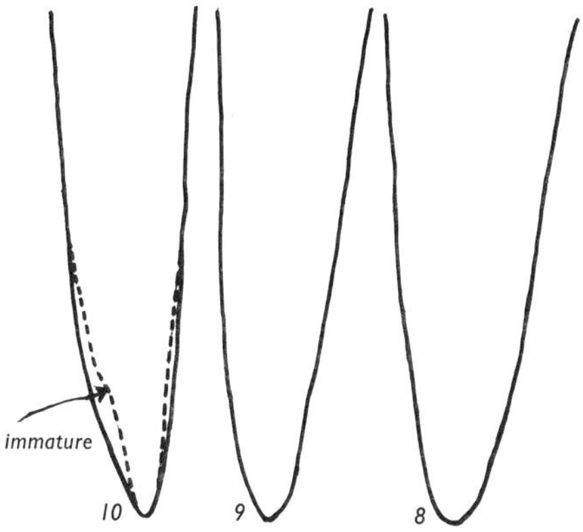

Red-foot; adult, right wing. The only sulid with hardly any, or no emargination on inner web of outermost primary.

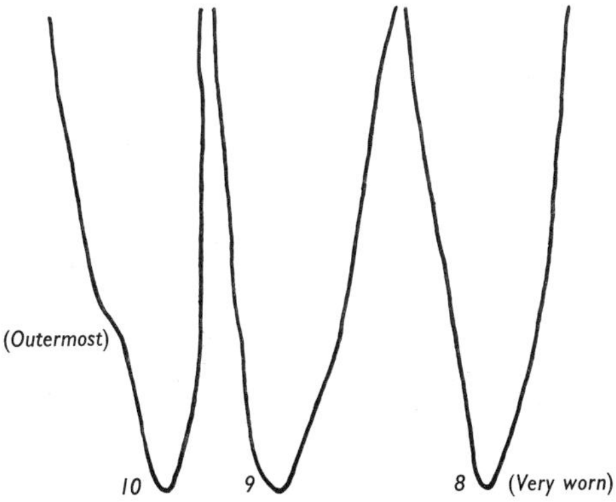

Abbott's booby; right wing

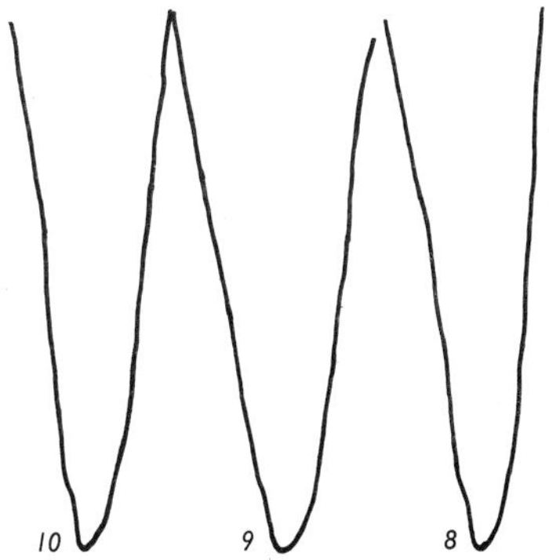

Red-foot; adult, right wing

APPENDIX 16

FOSSIL BOOBIES AND GANNETS

BY C. J. O. HARRISON

A number of species of fossil boobies and gannets have been described, but in studying them one encounters the same limitations and problems that occur with other bird fossils. Sulids appear to have a good chance of being preserved as fossils. The rock strata in which such remains occur are usually sediments laid down in seas and lakes. As a result the bones of sea and fresh water birds are more likely to be preserved than those of land birds. In addition bird bones are fragile and the bones of larger birds are more likely to be preserved, and to be found than are those of smaller species. Boobies and gannets are reasonably large sea-birds with fairly stout bones and stand a good chance both of becoming fossil and being found.

In most bird remains the bones tend to become separated during decay and the disintegration of the body, and many known fossil species are based on a single bone, or a few scattered fragments. It is fortunate that a number of sulids died in places where they appear to have sunk quickly into soft mud or sand, or have been rapidly covered, and now occur as associated groups of fossil bones within the rocks, rather than as scattered fragments.

When fossil bones of birds are studied they are compared mainly with the bones of Recent species and assigned to the family and genus with which they share most of their characters. If they are sufficiently peculiar in character a new genus or family may be created for them. However, such work is limited by the material available. If a palaeontologist bases a new fossil species of *Sula* on a single bone he infers that the bone closely resembles those of other *Sula* species and differs from those of other genera in its visible characters, but has certain individual peculiarities which may justify its separation as a species. His comments can only apply to the bone available and while a similarity in the remainder of the structure is implied he cannot be certain that the rest of the skeleton will be as similar to that of *Sula* as the bone which he is studying.

In general fossil evidence is likely to indicate how long sulid birds have been in existence, and the degree of variability that they may show in some parts of the skeleton. It may also give an indication of general trends in sulid evolution, but there will be gaps in the record and much of the detail will be missing.

The known fossil species of gannets and boobies have been listed by Brodkorb (1963b) in his *Catalogue of Fossil Birds*. A work of this kind cannot critically appraise every species and must list the forms described by a number of authors. The criteria used for taxonomic separation of the various birds has changed over a period and the early workers in this field had a very different and usually much broader concept of what constituted a genus or any other taxon than did those who came later. Because of this inconsistency in classification the final picture is a little different from the one that might be formed from merely examining the list of names.

Alphonse Milne-Edwards was the earliest worker on this group and he also described the geologically earliest species. *Sula ronzoni* Milne-Edwards 1867 is based on a pelvis which appears to be that of a cormorant rather than a gannet (Harrison, 1975) and should not be included in the present survey. Similarly *Sula pygmaea* Milne-Edwards 1874, assigned by Brodkorb to the genus *Microsula*, is based on a humerus which shows very generalised characters and cannot certainly be assigned to the Sulidae.

The earliest species which can be regarded as a member of the Sulidae is therefore the third one described by Milne-Edwards, which he assigned to *Sula* but which appears to differ from these and has been assigned to a separate genus as *Empheresula arvernensis* (Milne-Edwards) 1867 (Harrison, 1975a and b). This is based on a fossil from the Upper Oligocene of France partly embedded in matrix and showing on one side the upper surface of the pelvis and on the other the incomplete lower surface of the sternum. The pelvis is typical of sulids but rather long posteriorly. The sternum tapers anteriorly in normal sulid fashion but towards the posterior it is broader with prominent, incurving lateral processes, deep sternal notches and the central portion terminating in three prominent processes. The typical pelecaniform sternum is rather short, and that of the Sulidae is longer than in other families. The sternum of the present species is longer still posteriorly and shows some superficial similarity to those of divers and grebes. Extrapolating from this one might suggest that the species could have been more aquatic in its way of life than the present sulid species. We do not know if this longer sternum was an ancestral character of the Pelecaniformes or just a divergent peculiarity of this bird. This fossil sulid from France is the only one recorded from Europe, all the other fossils known at present having been described from North America.

The main evolutionary radiation of the Sulidae appears to have occured in the Miocene. Recent workers have described a *Sula* species from the Lower Miocene and a *Morus* species from the Middle Miocene, others of these genera appearing in subsequent periods. It is therefore evident that the differences in osteology which define these genera were already apparent about thirty-five million years ago, although the record is too incomplete for us to assert with any certainty that such divergence in structure occurred only once and that subsequently there was an independendent evolutionary line from the earliest form assigned to each of these genera to those of the present day.

It was in the Miocene also that other divergent forms occurred. *Microsula arvita* (Wetmore) 1938 of the Middle Miocene is based on a distal end and a shaft of a humerus, and a carpometacarpal. It was smaller than any other species. Well-developed pneumatic foramina are characteristic of the carpometacarpi of *Sula* and *Morus* but were almost closed in this fossil species. Apparently on the basis of this peculiarity Wetmore separated his new species in the subgenus *Microsula* of the genus *Sula*, and subsequently Brodkorb elevated *Microsula* to a full genus. This reduction in pneumaticity may indicate a modification for a more aquatic existence.

The genus *Miosula* first occurs in the Upper Miocene. *Miosula media* L. Miller 1925 is based on a partial skeleton embedded in a slab of matrix. It is the remains of a sulid with a body size slightly larger than that of a gannet and with stouter legs and feet, shorter wings and a less straight humerus. It appears to have been evolving towards a cormorant-like form. The shorter wings and stouter legs suggest a bird that relies mainly on swimming rather than flying for its food-finding activities. Together with *Morus lompocanus* and *Sula willetti* it was found in deposits believed to have originated in the quiet waters of bays used for spawning by a species of herring which attracted a number of fish, birds and mammals as predators. The genus *Miosula* persisted at least until the Middle Pliocene when *Miosula recentior* Howard 1949 occurred. The latter is described from a tibiotarsus, part of an ulna and a broken humeral shaft. The remains show similar characters to those of the earlier species. *Miosula recentior* appears to have had an even more slender wing than *M. media* and to show a further trend towards a more aquatic form, but from the absence of any later fossils it may be presumed that the line became extinct in the Pliocene, before reaching the fully cormorant-like stage.

Palaeosula stocktoni L. (Miller) 1935 of the Upper Miocene appears to have been a more extreme example of the divergent and more aquatic trend shown by *Miosula*, although existing at the same time as the earlier species of that genus. It was described from incomplete remains embedded in a matrix slab, and Howard (1958) later referred another humerus to this species. It had a larger body size than that of both the gannet and *Miosula media*, and a shorter wing, the ulna being much shorter and the humerus large with a massive proximal end. The species would appear to have shown further adaptation to a more aquatic existence than did either *Miosula* species.

Microsula of the Middle Miocene shows evidence of the possible beginnings of divergence, but *Miosula* and *Palaeosula* in the Upper Miocene and Pliocene are the only sulids which diverge markedly from the typical *Sula* and *Morus* stock. In view of the apparent increase in divergence over a period of time it seems likely that this is a true evolutionary trend rather than evidence of a modified form which has persisted from a much earlier period but has only been found in later deposits. Although these forms show an interesting attempt to utilise a more aquatic, cormorant-like niche, in terms of evolution over the fossil period as a whole their success was short-lived.

The typical boobies of the genus *Sula* have the longest record. The earliest, *Sula universitatis* Brodkorb 1963, occurred in the Lower Miocene of Florida. It is based on an incomplete carpometacarpus which shows characters of *Sula* and differs from *Morus*. The species would have been similar in size to *Sula leucogaster* and smaller than *Empheresula arvernensis*. *Sula willetti* L. Miller 1925 of the Upper Miocene is known from a fairly complete and a partial skeleton, both embedded in blocks of matrix. It was about the size of *Sula piscator*, but like *S. universitatis*, and also *Palaeosula* and *Miosula*, it has an ulna which is shorter relative to the humerus than those of Recent *Sula* species, and in this respect is more similar to *Morus*. The digital portion of the wing is proportionally longer than in Recent *Sula* species, the tibiotarsus shorter, the tarsometatarsus longer and the forehead of the skull more concave. Possibly these two earlier *Sula* species should be treated taxonomically as a separate subgenus or genus.

Sula pohli Howard 1958 of the Upper Miocene is known from an incomplete skeleton embedded in matrix. Although it co-existed with *S. willetti* it differed from it in having the ulna longer than the humerus as in Recent *Sula* species, and also having a longer coracoid of differing proportions. Two *Sula* species are known from the Lower Pliocene. *Sula guano* Brodkorb 1955 is known from incomplete coracoid, ulna and tibiotarsus, similar in size to those of *S. sula* but stouter and in many respects more similar to *S. nebouxii*. *S. phosphata* Brodkorb 1955 occurs in the same deposits and is known from several incomplete coracoids, resembling in some respects those of *S. leucogaster*.

The last known fossil *Sula* species prior to Recent birds is *S. humeralis* L. Miller and Bowman 1958 of the Middle Pliocene, known from partial humerus, femur and coracoid. It is a little larger than other fossil species, but smaller than the Recent gannets. In some osteological characters it resembles *S. leucogaster*. It occurred at a similar period to *Miosula recentior*. Following the occurrence of this species there is a gap in the records of the genus until Recent species occur.

The earliest gannets of the genus *Morus* occur later than the earliest *Sula* species, two being found in the Middle Miocene. *Morus loxostyla* (Cope) 1870 was originally described as a *Sula* species, based on a damaged coracoid. Shufeldt (1915) described *Sula atlantica* from the same period, based on a more complete coracoid, and stated that Cope's specimen was not a gannet or booby and was figured upside-down. Both statements were incorrect. Wetmore (1926) concluded that both specimens were from the same species and also referred a humerus to it. He considered that the characters present indicated a gannet and not a booby. *M. loxostyla* was a little smaller than the Recent Gannet. *Morus vagabundus* Wetmore 1930 occurred at the same period, and is known from portions of a humerus and an ulna. It was smaller than the previous species and about the size of *Sula piscator*.

Morus lompocanus L. Miller 1925 occurred in the Upper Miocene of California together with *Sula willetti* and *Miosula media*. It is known from a partial skeleton embedded in a block of matrix. It was similar in size to *Morus bassanus* but had longer wings and the pelvis is weaker, with more prominent lateral projections above the acetabula.

Morus peninsularis Brodkorb 1955 was found in the Lower Pliocene of California together with *Sula guano* and *S. phosphata*. They occur in the Bone Valley formation which contains phosphate deposits; and the presence of numerous remains of a cormorant, *Phalacrocorax wetmorei*, led Brodkorb to suggest that these seabirds were breeding colonially on guano-covered islands in this region during the early Pliocene. *M. peninsularis* is known from two coracoids and a vertebra. It appears to have been considerably smaller than *M. lompocanus* but larger and of heavier build than *M. loxostyla* and *M. vagabundus*.

Following *M. peninsularis* there is a considerable gap in the record until *Morus reyanus* Howard 1936 occurred in the Upper Pleistocene. This species is known from a coracoid. It was similar to modern gannets but with minor osteological peculiarities which justify specific separation. It was present on the Pacific coast of North America where gannets do not now occur.

The overall picture of evolution in the Sulidae as indicated by these fossil remains is of an apparent ancestral form in the Upper Oligocene, with the two extant genera *Sula* and *Morus* appearing early in the Miocene and occurring as a series of forms subsequent to this. The two earliest *Sula* species appear to have had a shorter wing of the type which is now characteristic of *Morus*. During the Miocene forms appeared showing divergent adaptation to a more aquatic and cormorant-like way of life and one at least persisted until the Middle Pliocene, but there is no later evidence of these. It is not possible to be sure why this line should have become extinct but it seems possible that as they evolved towards a more cormorant-like form they may have come into competition with the already successful true cormorants.

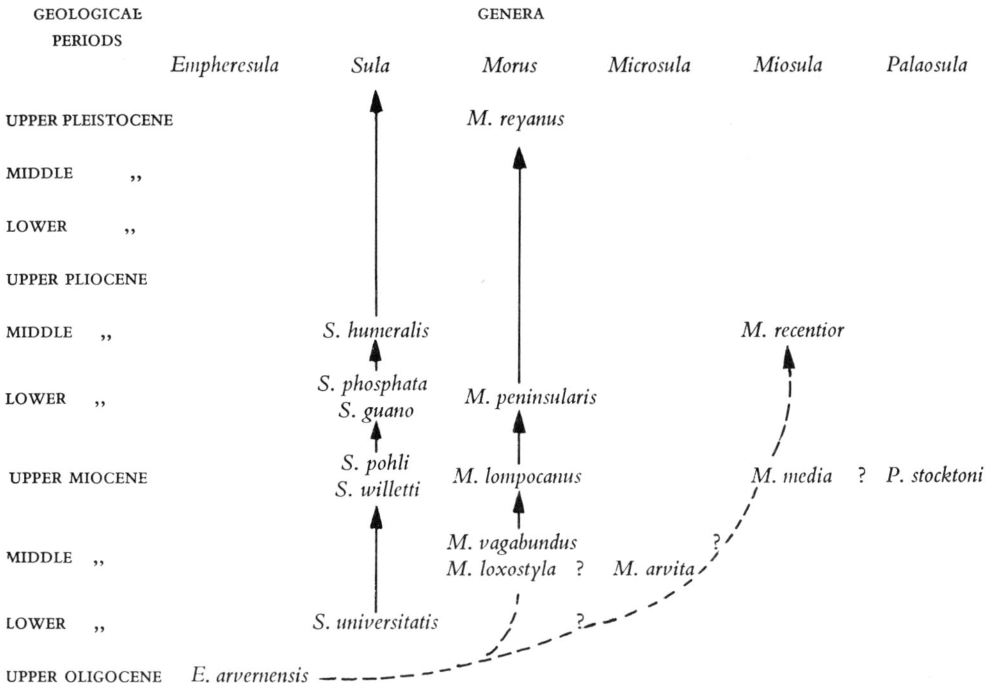

The geological periods are arranged with the earliest at the bottom. The bold, dashed, lines represent possible evolutionary pathways. The three right-hand genera show increasing divergence towards a cormorant-like form.

APPENDIX 17

POLLUTION AND THE SULIDAE

BY W. R. P. BOURNE, J. A. BOGAN AND SARAH WANLESS

Populations of long-lived predators with low reproductive rates are particularly vulnerable. Human predation has long had an important influence on their welfare, and more recently pollution has had a growing impact (Bourne 1976). Gannets form between one and two per-cent of the bird bodies washed up on north-west European beaches, which is roughly in proportion to their abundance compared to other birds at sea, and many of these gannet bodies are affected by pollution. About half are oiled, which is an average level for beached bodies in this area; more aquatic species such as the auks, sea-duck, grebes and divers tend to suffer more severely from oil pollution, and more aerial species such as the gulls and terns less so. It seems likely that many of the bodies only become polluted after death. Problems also occur where the birds collect oiled nest-material, as occurred at the French colony on the Sept Iles after the Torrey Canyon disaster (Jouanin 1967). In addition to its affect on the plumage of the birds, destroying their insulating and waterproofing capacity, oil blocks the pores of eggs and asphyxiates the embryo. Some gannets also become entangled with a variety of artefacts drifting

TABLE I

CHLORINATED HYDROCARBONS IN

Origin	Character		Date	Weight(g)
Sula bassana, Atlantic gannet				
	Ailsa Craig, juvenile			
411/J751	,, ,, ,,	juv ♂	20.8.75	3500
364	,, ,, ,,	juv, k	5.9.74	3000
	Ailsa Craig, immature			
243	,, ,, ,,	2y ♂, bw	2.8.72	2562
407/7548	,, ,, ,,	3–4y ♀	21.7.75	3100
415/7511	,, ,, ,,	3–4y ♀, i	22.4.75	3550
410/7534	,, ,, ,,	4y ♀	24.6.75	2900
412/7532	,, ,, ,,	4y ♀	22.6.75	2450
418/7530	,, ,, ,,	4y ♂	18.6.75	2600
363	,, ,, ,,	6y ad, k	10.7.74	3300
	Ailsa Craig, healthy adults			
244	,, ,, ,, ,,	ad, k	2.8.73	2872
382	,, ,, ,, ,,	ad, bw	20.4.74	heavy
409/7631	,, ,, ,, ,,	ad ♀, bw, db	28.7.76	3100
414/7515	,, ,, ,, ,,	ad ♂, bw	1.5.75	2800
416/7512	,, ,, ,, ,,	ad ♀, bw	24.4.75	3100
417/7522	,, ,, ,, ,,	ad ♀	3.6.75	2950
419/7518	,, ,, ,, ,,	ad ♂	22.5.75	2800
420/7514	,, ,, ,, ,,	ad ♂	29.4.75	2700
421/753	,, ,, ,, ,,	ad ♀, bw	12.4.75	3000
	Ailsa Craig, debilitated birds			
362	,, ,, ,, ,,	ad ♂, db	25.5.74	light
245	,, ,, ,, ,,	ad ♀, bw	3.8.73	2320
413/7526	,, ,, ,, ,,	ad ♂, bw	8.6.75	2300
408/7619	,, ,, ,, ,,	3–4y ♀, db	6.6.76	1550
	Miscellaneous			
199	Cumbrae, W. Scotland	ad, fd	24.3.73	
236	St. Kilda, Hebrides	ad, k	19.8.73	
80	Lewis, Hebrides	ad, fd	May 72	2700
181	,, ,,	ad, fd	21.5.73	
204	,, ,,	ad, fd	6.6.73	2000
205	,, ,,	ad, fd	12.6.73	1800
210	Orkney	ad, i	July 73	
62	Shetland	ad, oil	May 71	
64	Fife, E. Scotland	ad, fd	March 72	3500
355	Tenby, S. Wales	i	1973	
165	St. David's, S. Wales	ad, oil	28.1.73	
369	Massachusetts	juv, fd	26.10.71	1590
S. (b.) serrator, Australasian gannet				
383	New Zealand	ad, fd	1.9.74	
Sula leucogaster, Brown booby				
402/1307	Jalisco, West Mexico	ly, k	8.4.75	
403/1310	,, ,, ,,	ly, k	8.4.75	
404/1306	,, ,, ,,	ly, k	8.4.75	
405/A	,, ,, ,,	ly, k	8.4.75	
Sula dactylatra, Masked booby				
401/1320	West Guatemala	ad, k	12.4.75	
406/1321	,, ,,	ad, k	12.4.75	
381	Chagos group	ad, k	17.3.75	

Also three eggs of *Sula dactylatra* from Desnoeufs Id., Amirantes, in the summer of 1975 contained 5·5, 4· and 8·6 percent lipid, 0·08, 0·06 and 0·13 ppm DDE and traces of PCBs.

THE SULIDAE (PPM. WET WEIGHT)

Liver				Muscle				Fat		
% lipid	DDE	PCBs	HEOD	% lipid	DDE	PCBs	HEOD	% lipid	DDE	PCBs
3·3	0·01	0·05	0·003	9·7	0·06	0·35	0·01			
				13	0·11	0·48	0·02			
4·6	0·14	0·7	0·1	8·3	0·5	2·5				
1·9	0·40	2·2	0·09	8·4	1·8	11	0·49			
7·3	1·9	9·8	0·32	3·8	0·64	4·8	0·14			
6·7	0·9	5·6	0·23	5·1	1·0	5·9	0·24			
1·6	0·24	1·8	0·08	7·0	1·5	8·8	0·37			
5·8	1·2	9·7	0·33	2·0	0·38	3·2	0·08			
				9·6	1·6	6·2	0·42			
5·5	3·9	15	1·1	4·6	4·6	18				
3·1	1·6	7·7	0·22							
2·4	0·39	1·6	0·12	2·5	0·44	2·7	0·08			
2·2	2·4	11·6	0·19	8·3	10	20	0·62			
11	2·3	14·9	0·42	13	2·9	15·7	0·69			
7·4	5·3	14·6	0·62	5·4	4·9	23	0·54			
5·6	2·2	13·8	0·73	4·1	2·1	16	0·60			
1·7	0·12	1·49	0·08	6·3	0·75	6·6	0·18			
9·6	1·0	11·2	0·34	3·2	1·2	12	0·40			
				3·3	71	453	15·9			
3·4	17	70	4·3	13	89	355				
1·5	1·7	10·8	0·59	8·1	11	103	2·8			
2·8	3·8	36	0·75	12	15	79	2·1			
30	13	54		19	10	41				
5·3	1·3	4	0·2	12	5	15				
5·3	0·5	3		4·4	0·54	3·2		76	5	30
2·8	10·7	32	1·4	0·61	2·3	7				
3·7	7·8	39		0·57	1·0	5				
1·9	2·2	7·5	0·03	0·97	3·4	11	0·04			
				1·3	7·0	21	1·5			
1·5	8·9	44		6·6	2·6	12·9				
2·5	0·31	2·2		2·4	0·3	2·1		82	2·5	17
1·7	4·4	37		1·2	3·7	21				
3·8	5	41		1·3	5	43				
3·8	1·6	3·37								
11	0·20	0·17		8·6	0·20	0·14				
6·7	0·22	trace		8·5	0·47	trace				
7·4	0·14	trace		7·4	0·23	trace				
4·2	0·16	trace		5·2	0·24	trace				
3·5	0·17	trace		3·7	0·29	trace				
10	10·9	trace		4·6	7·5	trace				
6·3	5·5	trace		2·7	6·2	trace				
4·2	0·02	0·01		7·5	0·06	0·03		61	0·46	0·22

Ad=adult, y=years of age when known, juv.=less than one year, k=presumably healthy bird which died suddenly, bw=broken wing and possible delay in death, i=injured in other ways, oil=oiled, fd=found dead, db=disturbed behaviour possibly due to toxic effects. Healthy Atlantic gannets normally weigh at least 2800 g. when full grown.

at sea, especially nylon fishing-nets and lines, and here also some of the worst problems occur when these are collected for nest-material and ensnare the birds or their young (p. 132). Some of the bodies washed up on British beaches, especially those facing the Irish Sea, also contain considerable amounts of toxic chemicals (Parslow *et al.* 1973, Parslow & Jefferies, in press). These have also been blamed for a decline in numbers at colonies in the Gulf of the St Lawrence on the opposite side of the Atlantic (Pearce *et al.* 1973, Nettleship 1976).

Two groups of toxic chemicals currently cause concern. The heavy metals are leached naturally from mineral-bearing rocks and are also found in industrial effluents and sewage, and tend to be deposited in the tissues of birds. Organochlorines manufactured as pesticides and for industrial purposes are highly soluble in fat, and tend to accumulate in the birds' lipids. They are mobilised as the fat is consumed if the bird starves, so that they may exert their greatest effect when it is exposed to other stresses as well. The more complex organochlorines may only be metabolised very slowly by animals which lack natural detoxification and excretory mechanisms for synthetic products, so these are liable to accumulate first in individual animals and then along food-chains. In addition, predators may preferentially capture intoxicated prey. So far the heavy metals only appear to be causing severe contamination above the natural level locally, but the synthetic organochlorines have become very widely distributed. The results of analyses of 42 sulids from different parts of the world for the three most prominent compounds, DDE and HEOD derived from the pesticides DDT and dieldrin, and a mixture of isomeric polychlorinated biphenyls (PCBs) used in industry, are given in Table 1.

Estimates of organochlorines require careful interpretation, since they particularly depend on the amount of fat in the body and in individual tissues. The most constant levels are possibly found in the brain, which tends to have a constant lipid content, and the level there may have an important effect on the nervous system. It is not always easy to obtain specimens of nervous tissue, however, and we have usually tested the level in muscle as a measure of the general contamination of the bird, and the liver since organochlorine tends to accumulate there in starved individuals. Since the heavy metals do not move around the body so freely it is usually sufficient to test one tissue for them, usually the liver. It will be seen from Table 1 that the highest level of organochlorine contamination, usually with PCBs with some DDE and less of the more highly toxic HEOD, is found in the Atlantic gannet, with a considerable amount of DDE in Masked boobies feeding out at sea off the west coast of tropical America, though young Brown boobies feeding inshore in that area, Masked boobies from the Indian Ocean, and an Australasian gannet from New Zealand contained only low levels of organochlorine, with more DDE than PCBs. Similar low levels have been reported in Brown boobies from Panama in the tropical Pacific (Risebrough *et al.* 1968) and Ascension in the tropical Atlantic (Johnston 1973), except that like Atlantic gannets the latter contained more PCBs than DDE.

Organochlorine in gannet eggs from north Norway inlets on opposite coasts of Britain and the Gulf of the St Lawrence in eastern Canada on the opposite side of the Atlantic are compared in Table 2. It will be seen that the eggs from Ailsa Craig at the northern outlet to the polluted Irish Sea contain over twice as much organochlorine as those from the Bass Rock overlooking the inflow of purer water from the Atlantic into the North Sea on the other side of Scotland. The only results available so far indicate that the eggs from the Gulf of the St

TABLE 2

CHLORINATED HYDROCARBONS IN GANNET EGGS

	Nordmjele, N. Norway 10 eggs, 1972	Bass Rock E. Scotland 10 eggs, 1974	Ailsa Craig, W. Scotland 11 eggs, 1974	Bonaventure Id., Quebec, Canada 21 eggs, 1969
PCBs	166 ± 52·6	194 ± 29·4	412 ± 64·4	224 ± 37
DDE	44·8 ± 13·9	25·6 ± 3·7	54·2 ± 6·6	458 ± 64
HEOD	2·57 ± 0·55	11·4 ± 1·2	26·9 ± 4·1	17 ± 2·7

Means and standard errors in ppm fat weight from Fimreite *et al.* in press, Parslow & Jefferies, 1977, and Gilbertson & Reynolds 1974, figures recalculated by J. A. Keith.

Lawrence contain less PCB derived from industry but more DDE derived from forestry and agriculture than the European eggs. The mercury levels in eggs from five north-west European gannetries are compared in Table 3, where it will be seen that the highest level is found in the north Irish Sea, with less in the Firth of Clyde to the north, and lower levels, which may be natural, in south-west Ireland, eastern Britain, and north Norway. Reports of chlorinated hydrocarbons and mercury in adult gannets are summarised in Table 4. It will be seen that the birds from Ailsa Craig show a progressive increase in their organochlorine levels as they mature, but that the levels in healthy adults are not very high. They are much higher in wasted birds found there and on beaches elsewhere, notably around the Irish Sea. Raised mercury levels are also found in the Irish Sea, with one slightly high result from the St Lawrence.

The effect of these toxic chemicals is still uncertain. They were blamed at one time for a limited mortality of gannets around the coasts of Britain in the spring of 1972, but the situation is complicated because some birds which died early along the east coast were in good condition and contained only limited amounts of toxic chemicals, whereas others found dead later in the west contained higher levels of contaminants (Parslow *et al.* 1973). It seems possible that at

TABLE 3

MERCURY IN EGGS FROM FIVE NORTH-WEST EUROPEAN GANNETRIES

Origin	Date	No. eggs	Mean and standard error
Scar Rocks, N. Irish Sea	1972–3	18	10·47 ± 0·71
Ailsa Craig, SW Scotland	1971–4	29	4·54 ± 0·36
Bass Rock, SE Scotland	1973–4	18	2·62 ± 0·17
Little Skellig, SW Ireland	1973	7	3·21 ± 0·35
Nordmjele, N. Norway	1972	10	2·90

Measurements in ppm dry weight, taken from Parslow & Jefferies 1977 & Fimreite *et al.* 1974; wet weight levels given by the latter multiplied by five.

TABLE 4

ORGANOCHLORINES AND MERCURY IN NORTH ATLANTIC GANNETS, 1963–1976

Origin	Sample	Liver							Other tissues				
		No.	DDE	PCBs	No.	HEOD	No.	Hg	No.	DDE	PCBs	No.	HEOD
Ailsa Craig	Juveniles	1	0·01	0·05	1	0·003	–	–	2	0·08	0·41	2	0·02
	2nd year	1	0·14	0·71	1	0·1	–	–	1	0·5	2·5	–	–
	3–4 year	5	0·72	4·62	5	0·18	–	–	5	0·96	6·15	5	0·22
	healthy adult	9	1·35	7·80	9	0·30	–	–	9	2·17	11·2	8	0·37
Ailsa and Clyde	wasted adult	4	6·15	34·8	3	1·24	–	–	5	25·3	140	3	4·5
Irish Sea	mixed	9	12·0	175	3	1·24	8	23·8	–	–	–	–	–
Bristol Channel	mixed	4	8·38	57·2	–	–	3	12·1	4	4·94	25·2	–	–
East Britain	mixed	6	3·29	12·3	2	0·12	6	11·8	4	3·14	14·7	–	–
N. Scottish Is.	mixed	6	3·21	13·0	3	0·20	2	13·1	7	2·34	9·07	2	0·24
Iceland	healthy adult?	–	–	–	–	–	–	–	1	1·5	12	1	0·34
Funk Id.	healthy adult	–	–	–	–	–	–	–	10	1·14	–	–	0·06
Bonaventure Id.	healthy adult	–	–	–	–	–	–	–	10	3·20	–	–	0·10
St Lawrence	dead or dying	–	–	–	–	–	1	16·0	3	11·8	24·1	3	0·69

Taken from Table 1, Parslow & Jefferies 1977, Dale *et al.* 1973 (Britain), Sproul *et al.* 1975 (Iceland) and Pearce *et al.* 1973 (Canada). Chlorinated hydrocarbons in ppm wet weight, mercury in ppm dry weight, geometric means. The other tissues were liver in the case of mercury and muscle for organochlorines except in Canada, where they were brain; five specimens of mixed origin from Britain contained geometric mean levels of 5·42 ppm DDE and 18·81 ppm PCBs in the brain. The Canadian results have been revised by J. A. Keith, who will be publishing a fuller study elsewhere.

least some of the birds may have been affected by a virus such as Newcastle Disease, which previously caused mortality among Pelecaniformes including a gannet during a widespread epidemic which also affected poultry in the late 1940s (Wilson 1950, Blaxland 1951). It was present in the country again in 1972, but full pathological investigations of the gannets were never carried out. It seems likely that an adult male gannet found in a stupefied state, unable to balance and with a slow pupillary reflex, on Ailsa Craig in May 1974, which proved to contain 453 ppm PCBs, 71 ppm DDE and 15·9 ppm HEOD in its muscle (the first and last the highest levels yet recorded in sulids) was affected by them, but it was exceptional at that site. Birds containing similar levels are also washed up from time to time around the Irish Sea, where one also contained 98 ppm (dry weight) of mercury, which may also be in the toxic range. Some British gannets with high DDE levels also lay eggs with thin shells, another toxic effect of this compound, though this is not a general phenomenon yet in Britain (Parslow & Jefferies 1977). It has been suggested that the number of gannets breeding on Ailsa Craig is declining (Sharrock 1976), but further information indicates that this may have been a temporary fluctuation (p. 35.)

The gannets which are apparently most highly contaminated with DDE, breeding at Bonaventure Island in the Gulf of the St Lawrence, eastern Canada, are reported to be laying eggs with shells 17 per cent thinner than those of eggs laid before 1915, and to have a low fledging rate (Pearce *et al.* 1973), though in the latter case the sample investigated may not be typical. The colony on Bonaventure Island declined by 16 per cent from 20 511 pairs in 1969 to 17 281 pairs in 1973 (Nettleship 1973), at a time when colonies off less polluted coasts of Canada were participating in the general increase seen throughout the rest of the North Atlantic (Nettleship 1976). There appears to be little information available about the Masked boobies found to be contaminated with DDE off the west coast of tropical America, but it seems possible that they may have come from colonies far to the north washed by water from the California current contaminated by effluent from a Los Angeles pesticide factory, which is known to have caused havoc among the local Brown pelicans *Pelecanus occidentalis* for some years (Anderson *et al.* 1975).

We are indebted to many people for the specimens listed in Table 1, notably Dr J. Jehl for those from western tropical America, Mr. M. Hirons and Dr. C. J. Feare for those from the Indian Ocean, and Mr. David Crockett for that from New Zealand. Mr. J. L. F. Parslow provided much assistance and advice in the preparation of this note, and Drs. N. Fimreite and J. A. Keith also provided details of unpublished work.

REFERENCES

Anderson, D. W., Jehl, J. R., Risebrough, R. W., Woods, L. A., Deweese, L. R. & Edgecombe, W. G. 1975. Brown pelicans: improved reproduction off the southern California coast. *Science* **190**: 806–8.

Blaxland, J. D. 1951. Newcastle Disease in Shags and Cormorants and its significance in the spread of this disease among domestic poultry. *Vet. Rec.* **63**: 731–3.

Bourne, W. R. P. 1976. Seabirds and pollution. In Johnston, R. (ed.), *Marine Pollution*, Academic Press: 403–502.

Dale, I. M., Baxter, M. S., Bogan, J. A. & Bourne, W. R. P. 1973. Mercury in seabirds. *Mar. Pollut. Bull.* **4**: 77–9.

Fimreite, N., Bjerk, J. E., Kveseth, N. & Brun, E. in press. DDE and PCBs in eggs of Norwegian sea-birds. *Astarte*.

Fimreite, N., Brun, E., Froslie, A., Frederichsen, P. & Gundersen, N. 1974. Mercury in eggs of Norwegian seabirds. *Astarte* **1**: 71–5.

Gilbertson, M. & Reynolds, L. 1974. DDE and PCB in Canadian birds 1969–72. Canadian Wildlife Service Occasional Paper 19.

Johnston, D. W. 1973. Polychlorinated biphenyls in sea birds from Ascension Island, South Atlantic Ocean. *Bull. Envir. Contam. Toxicol.* **10**: 368–71.

Jouanin, C. 1967. La naufrage du Torrey Canyon. *Courr. Nat.* 1–2: 18–19.

Nettleship, D. N. 1975. A recent decline of Gannets *Morus bassanus* on Bonaventure Island, Quebec. *Can. Field Nat.* **89**: 125–33.

—— 1976. Gannets in North America: Present numbers and recent population changes. *Wilson Bull.* **88**: 300–13.

Parslow, J. L. F. & Jefferies, D. J. in 1977. Toxic chemical residues in British gannets. *Brit. Birds.* 70: 366–372.

——, —— & Hanson, H. M. 1973. Gannet mortality incidents in 1972. *Mar. Pollut. Bull.* **4**: 41–3.

PEARCE, P. A., GRUCHY, I. M. & KEITH, J. A. 1973. Toxic chemicals in living things in the Gulf of St Lawrence. Proceedings of the Canadian Society of Fisheries and Wildlife Biologists, Canadian Society of Zoologists Symposium: Renewable Resource Management of the Gulf of St Lawrence, 5 January 1973, Halifax, Nova Scotia.

RISEBROUGH, R. W., REICHE, P., PEAKALL, D. B., HERMAN, S. G. & KIRVEN, M. N. 1968. Polychlorinated biphenyls in the global ecosystem. *Nature* **220**: 1098–102.

SHARROCK, J. T. R. 1976. *The Atlas of Breeding Birds in Britain and Ireland.*

SPROUL, J. A., BRADLEY, R. L. & HICKEY, J. J. 1975. Polychlorinated biphenyls, DDE and dieldrin in Icelandic birds. Final report on contract 14-16-0008-672 submitted to Patuxent Wildlife Research Center, Fish and Wildlife Service, U.S. Department of the Interior.

WILSON, J. E. 1950. Newcastle disease in a Gannet. *Vet. Rec.* **62**: 33.

APPENDIX 18

AMOUNT OF TIME SPENT ON THE SITE BY BLUE-FOOTED BOOBIES WITH CHICKS DURING THE DAYLIGHT HOURS OF A 48-HOUR PERIOD

Nest No.	(Chick's) age (in weeks)		Male Longest	Male Shortest	Male Total	Female Longest	Female Shortest	Female Total
			Length of time spent on the site (in hours and minutes)					
1	6	Day 1	7—30	1—18	8—48	5—58	3—27	9—25
		Day 2	11—30	—	11—30	3—35	2—29	9—4
2	6	Day 1	11—9	—45	11—45	5—21	3—1	8—22
		Day 2	6—4	1—58	8—2	10—31	—	10—31
3	6	Day 1	6—46	—	6—46	6—45	3—15	10—
		Day 2	12	—	12	5—16	—	5—16
4	6	Day 1	4—21	2—27	9—48	—30	—	—30
		Day 2	6—9	—8	7—5	—1	—	—1
5	7	Day 1	9—34	—10	9—59	3—53	—6	4—57
		Day 2	10—27	—	10—27	2—24	—	2—24
6	7	Day 1	3—22	—15	4—58	7	2—25	9—25
		Day 2	1—57	—56	4—27	8—22	—10	10—7
7	7	Day 1	—	—	—	3—20	—	3—20
		Day 2	—4	—	—4	3—27	—	3—27
9	12+	Day 1	Not seen			5—34	5—28	11—13
		Day 2				6—57	—2	9—55
10	14	Day 1	2—20	—	2—20	6—39	—20	6—59
		Day 2	1—16	—2	1—49	10—16	—	10—16
11	14	Day 1	—	—	—	6—28	4—38	11—16
		Day 2	—12	—10	—22	11—28	—3	11—31

Day 1 Male average 5–50
Female average 7–24
Day 2 Male average 6–12 Excluding attendances under 30 min. 7–54
Female average 7–15 Excluding attendances under 30 min. 8–3
Total averages excluding attendance spells of less than 30 minutes
Male 6–52
Female 7–43

APPENDIX 19

Main laying months of the blue-foot in the Galapagos

Island	Months in which considerable laying occurred (no. of occasions, 1962–72).											
	Jan.	Feb.	March	April	May	June	July	Aug.	Sept.	Oct.	Nov.	Dec.
Daphne	4	7	7	7	7	5	2	1	4	5	6	5
Hood	1	3	3	5	5	3	3	3	4	10	8	3
Champion		1		1	1					2	2	2
Seymour	2		1		1	1	1	1				1
Jervis			1									
Wenman	1									1		1
Culpepper	1	1										
Isabella					1	1	1					
Gardner										1	1	
Tortuga				1	1						1	
	9	12	12	14	16	10	7	5	8	19	18	12

LIST OF BIRDS MENTIONED IN TEXT

Albatross, Black-browed: *Diomedea melanophris*
　　Laysan: *D. immutablis*
　　Royal: *D. epomophora*
Auk, Little: *Plautus alle*
Bosunbird, Golden; see Tropic-bird, white-tailed
Chuita: see Cormorant, Red-footed
Condor: *Vultur gryphus*
Coot: *Fulica atra*
Cormorant: *Phalacrocorax carbo*
　　Cape: *P. capensis*
　　Guanay or Peruvian: *P. bougainvillei*
　　Red-footed (legged): *P. gaimardi*
Darwin's Finch, Small-billed: see Finch, Darwin's Short-billed
Dove, Christmas Island Emerald: *Chalcophaps indica*
Eagle, Sea or White-tailed: *Haliaetus albicilla*
Finch, Darwin's Small-billed: *Geospiza difficilis*
Frigate-bird, Andrew's: *Fregata andrewsi*
　　Great: *F. minor*
　　Lesser: *F. ariel*
Fulmar: *Fulmarus glacialis*
Goose, Grey Lag: *Anser anser*
Goshawk, Christmas Island: *Accipiter fasciatus*
Guillemot: *Uria aalge*
　　Black: *U. grylle*
Ground-thrush, Christmas Island: *Turdus javanicus*
Gull, Belcher's: *Larus belcheri*
　　Black-headed: *L. ridibundus*
　　Dominican: *L. dominicanus*
　　Great Black-backed: *L. marinus*
　　Herring: *L. argentatus*
　　Kelp or Kleo: see Gull, Dominican
　　Lesser Black-backed: *L. fuscus*
　　Red-billed: see Gull, Silver
　　Silver: *L. novaehollandiae*
(Gull), Southern Black-backed: see Gull, Dominican
　　Swallow-tailed: *Creagrus furcatus*
Kittiwake: *Rissa tridactyla*
Mocking-bird, Galapagos: *Nesomimus melanotis*

Noddy: *Anous stolidus*
Black: *A. tenuirostris*
White-capped: *A. minutus*
Owl, Christmas Island: *Ninox forbesi*
Galapagos Short-eared: *Asio flammeus*
Pelican, Brown: *Pelecanus occidentalis*
Chilean: *P. thagus*
White: *P. erythrorhynchus*
Penguin, Adelie: *Pygoscelis adeliae*
King: *Aptenodytes patagonica*
Yellow-eyed: *Megadyptes antipodes*
Petrel, Galapagos Storm: *Oceanodroma tethys*
Giant: *Macronectes giganteus*
Storm: *Hydrobates pelagicus*
Wilson's: *Oceanites oceanicus*
Pigeon, Christmas Island Imperial: *Ducula rosacea*
Wood: *Columba palumbus*
Puffin: *Fratercula arctica*
Raven: *Corvus corax*
Razorbill: *Alca torda*
Shag: *Phalacrocorax aristotelis*
Shearwater, Audubon's: *Puffinus lherminieri*
Great: *P. gravis*
Manx: *P. puffinus*
Short-tailed: *P. tenuirostris*
Wedge-tailed: *P. pacificus*
Shelduck: *Tadorna tadorna*
Skua, Great: *Catharacta skua*
Starling: *Sturnus vulgaris*
Storm Petrel: see Petrel, Storm
Storm-petrel, Galapagos: see Petrel, Galapagos Storm
Wilson's: see Petrel, Wilson's
Swiftlet, Christmas Island: *Collocalia esculenta*
Tern, Arctic: *Sterna paradisaea*
Crested: *Sterna bergii*
Fairy: *Gygis alba*
Inca: *Larosterna inca*
Sooty: *Sterna fuscata*
Thrush, Christmas Island Ground; see Ground-thrush, Christmas Island
Tit, Great: *Parus major*
Tropic-bird, Red-billed: *Phaethon aethereus*
Red-tailed: *P. rubricauda*
Yellow-billed or White-tailed: *P. lepturus*
Vulture, Turkey: *Cathartes aura*
White-eye, Christmas Island: *Zosterops natalis*
Wideawake: see Tern, Sooty
Woodpigeon: see Pigeon, Wood

BIBLIOGRAPHY

ABDULALI, H. 1964. The birds of the Andaman and Nicobar Islands. *J. Bombay Nat. Hist. Soc.* **61:** 483–571.

—— 1971. Narcondam Island and notes on some birds from the Andaman Islands. *J. Bombay Nat. Hist. Soc.* **68:** 385–411.

ALEXANDER, B. 1898. An ornithological expedition to the Cape Verde Islands. *Ibis:* 74–118.

AL-HUSSAINI, A. H. 1939. Further notes on the birds of Ghardaqa (Hurghada) Red Sea. *Ibis:* 343–347.

ALI, S. & RIPLEY, S. D. 1968. *Handbook of the birds of India and Pakistan together with those of Nepal, Sikkim, Bhutan and Ceylon.* London.

ALLEY, R. & BOYD, H. 1950. Parent–young recognition in the coot *Fulica atra. Ibis* **92:** 46–51.

AMADON, D. 1964. The evolution of low reproductive rates in birds. *Evolution* **18:** 105–110.

—— 1966a. Avian plumages and molts, *Condor* **68:** 263–278.

—— 1966b. The superspecies concept. *Syst. Zool.* **15:** 245–249.

AMERSON, A. B. 1969. Ornithology of the Marshall and Gilbert Islands. *Atoll Res. Bull.* **127:** 348 pp.

—— 1971. The natural history of French Frigate shoals, northwestern Hawaiian Islands. *Atoll Res. Bull.* **150:** 383 pp.

—— & EMERSON, K. C. 1971. Records of Mallophaga from Pacific birds. *Atoll Res. Bull.* **146:** 30 pp.

ANDERSON, W. G. 1954. Notes on food habits of sea birds of the Pacific. *Elepaio* **14:** 80–84.

ANDERSSON, M. 1976. Predation and kleptoparasitism by skuas in a Shetland bird colony. *Ibis* **118:** 208–217.

ANDREWS, C. W. 1900. *A Monograph of Christmas Island.* London.

APLIN, O. V. 1915. Gannet nesting in Orkney. *Zoologist* **19:** 433.

ARMSTRONG, E. A. 1944. White plumage of sea birds. *Nature* (London) **153:** 527.

ASHMOLE, M. J. 1963. *Guide to the birds of Samoa.* Pacific Sci. Inf. Centre. Bernice P. Bishop Mus.

—— & ASHMOLE, N. P. 1967. Notes on the breeding season and food of the red-footed booby (*Sula sula*) on Oahu Hawaii. *Ardea* **55:** 265–267.

ASHMOLE, N. P. 1963. The regulation of numbers of tropical oceanic birds. *Ibis* **103b:** 458–473.

—— 1968. Body size, prey size and ecological segregation in five sympatric tropical terns (Aves: Laridae). *Syst. Zool.* **17:** 292–304.

—— 1971. *Sea bird ecology and the marine environment.* In *Avian Biology*. London.

—— & ASHMOLE, M. J. 1967. Comparative feeding ecology of sea birds of a tropical oceanic island. *Peabody Mus. Nat. Hist.* **24:** 1–131.

BAILEY, A. M. 1956. Birds of Midway and Laysan. *Denver Mus. Nat. Hist. Mus. Pict.* **12:** 1–130.

BAILEY, H. H. 1906. Ornithological notes from western Mexico and the Tres Marias and Isabella Islands. *Auk* **23:** 369–391.

BAILEY, R. 1966. The sea birds of the south-east coast of Arabia. *Ibis* **108:** 224–264.

—— 1968. The pelagic distribution of sea birds in the western Indian Ocean. *Ibis* **110:** 493–519.

—— 1971. Sea bird observations off Somalia. *Ibis* **113:** 29–41.

—— 1972. The effects of seasonal changes on the sea birds of the western Indian Ocean. *J. Mar. Biol. Ass. India* **14:** 628–642.

BAKER, B. H. & MILLER, J. A. 1963. Geology and geochronology of the Seychelles Islands and structure of the floor of the Arabian Sea. *Nature* **199:** 346–348.

BAKER, E. C. S. 1929. *Fauna of British India: Birds,* 2nd ed. London. Vol. 6.

BAKER, R. H. 1947. Observations on the birds of the North Atlantic. *Auk* **64:** 245–259.

—— 1951. The avifauna of Micronesia, its origin, evolution and distribution. *Univ. of Kansas Publ. Mus. Nat. Hist.* **3:** 1–359.

BAKUS, G. T. 1967. Changes in the avifauna of Fanning Island, Central Pacific, between 1924 and 1963. *Condor* **69:** 207–209.

BANCROFT, G. 1927. Notes on the breeding coastal and insular birds of central lower California. *Condor* **29:** 188–195.

BANNERMAN, D. A. 1927. Birds observed on a voyage to Senegal. *Bul. Bt. Orn. Cl.* **47:** 130–133.

—— 1930. *The birds of tropical West Africa.* London.

—— 1968. *Birds of the Atlantic Islands,* vol. 4. *Cape Verde Islands.* London.

BARLEE, J. 1947. *Birds on the Wing.* London.

—— 1956. Flying for business and pleasure. *Shell Aviation News:* 2–9.

BARTHOLOMEW, G. A. 1966. Temperature regulation of the masked booby. *Condor* **68:** 523–535.

BAYNE, C. J., COGAN, B. H., DIAMOND, A. W., FRAZIER, J., GRUBB, P., HUTSON, A., POORE

M. E. D., Stoddart, D. R. & Taylor, J. D. 1970. Geography and ecology of Cosmeledo Atoll. *Atoll Res. Bull.* **136:** 37–56.

Beck, R. W. 1904. Bird life among the Galapagos Islands. *Condor* **6:** 5–11.

—— 1907. Notes from Clipperton and Cocos Islands. *Condor* **9:** 109–110.

Becking, J. H. 1976. Feeding range of Abbott's booby *Sula abbotti* at the coast of Java. *Ibis* **118:** 589–590.

Beer, C. G. 1963. Incubation and nest building behaviour of black-headed gulls. 3. The pre-laying period. *Behav.* **21:** 13–77.

Belcher, C. & Smooker, G. D. 1934. Birds of the colony of Trinidad and Tobago. *Ibis*: 572–595.

Bent, A. C. 1922. Life histories of North American petrels and pelicans and their allies. *Bull. 121 U.S. Nat. Mus.* 343 pp.

Betts, F. N. 1940. The birds of the Seychelles. *Ibis* 489–504.

Bewick, T. 1816. *History of British Birds.* Newcastle.

Bierman, W. H. & Voous, K. H. 1950. Birds observed and collected during the whaling expeditions of the 'Willem Barendsz' in the Antarctic, 1946–1947 and 1947–1948. *Ardea Suppl.* 1–124.

Blackwelder, R. E. 1972. *Guide to the taxonomic literature of vertebrates.* Iowa.

Blake, C. H. 1948. More data on the wing flapping rates of birds. *Condor* **50:** 148–151.

Blanford, W. T. 1898. *The fauna of British India. Birds*, vol. 4. London.

Blyth, R. O. 1930. On the winter distribution of some seabirds. *Brit. Bds.* **23:** 314–317.

Boarman, F. W. 1929. An ornithological trip in the Gulf of Suez and Red Sea. *Ibis*: 639–50.

Booth, E. T. 1887. *Rough notes on the birds observed during twenty-five years shooting and collecting in the British Islands.* London.

Bouet, G. 1955. Oiseaux de l'Afrique tropicale. *Faune Union France* **16:** 1–412.

Bourne, W. R. P. 1957a. The breeding birds of Bermuda. *Ibis* **99:** 94–105.

—— 1957b Review of Sea Report by H.M. Yacht Britannia. Sea Swall, **10:** 14.

—— 1963. A review of oceanic studies of the biology of sea birds. *Proc. 13th Int. Orn. Congr.* Ithaca 1962: 831–854.

—— 1968. The birds of Rodriguez, Indian Ocean. *Ibis* **110:** 338–344.

—— 1971. The birds of the Chagos Group, Indian Ocean. *Atoll Res. Bull.* **149:** 175–207.

—— 1972. Threats to sea birds. *Bull. Int. Counc. Bird Pres.* **11:** 200–218.

—— 1976. On subfossil bones of Abbott's booby *Sula abbotti* from the Mascarene Islands, with a note on the proportions and distribution of the Sulidae. *Ibis* **118:** 119–123.

Bowdish, B. S. 1902. Birds of Porto Rico. *Auk* **19:** 356–366.

Bowman, R. I. & Billeb, S. L. 1965. Blood eating in a Galapagos finch. *Living Bird* **4:** 29–44.

Boyd, J. M. 1961. The gannetry of St. Kilda. *J. Anim. Ecol.* **30:** 117–136.

Brandt, J. H. 1962. Nests and eggs of the birds of the Truk Islands. *Condor* **64:** 416–437.

Brattstrom, B. H. & Howell, T. R. 1956. The birds of the Revilla Gigedo Islands, Mexico. *Condor* **58:** 107–120.

Brisson, M. J. 1760. *Ornithologie ou méthode contenant la division des oiseaux . . .* Imprimeur du Roi, Paris.

Brodkorb, P. 1955. The avifauna of the Bone Valley Formation. *Florida Geological Survey, Report of Investigations* **14:** 1–39.

—— 1963a. Miocene birds from the Hawthorne Formation. *Quart. Florida Academy of Sci.* **26:** 159–167.

—— 1963b. Catalogue of fossil birds, pt. 1. *Bull. Florida State Mus. Biol. Sci.* **7:** 179–293.

Broekhuysen, G. J. & Liversidge, R. 1954. Colour variation in the tail feathers of the South African Gannet (*Morus capensis*). *Ostrich* **25:** 19–22.

——, —— & Rand, R. W. 1961. The South African Gannet *Morus capensis. Ostrich* **32:** 1–19.

—— & Rudebeck, G. 1951. Some notes on the Cape gannet, *Morus capensis. Ostrich* **22:** 132–138.

Brown, R. G. B. 1975. Seabirds of South America and the north west Atlantic. *Proc. 16th Int. Orn. Congr.* Canberra 1974: 716–724.

Brun, E. 1972. Establishment and population increase of the gannet *Sula bassana* in Norway. *Ornis Scand.* **3:** 27–38.

—— 1974. Breeding success of gannets *Sula bassana* at Nordmjele, Andoya, North Norway. *Astarte* **7:** 77–82.

Bryan, E. H. 1942. *American Polynesia and the Hawaiian Chain.* Honolulu.

Bryan, W. A. 1903. A monograph of Marcus Island. *Bernice P. Bishop Mus. Occas. Papers* **2:** 77–139.

Bryant, H. 1861a. Remarks on some of the birds that breed in the Gulf of St. Lawrence. *Zoo.* **19:** 7742–7753.

—— 1861b. *Proc. Brit. Soc. Nat. Hist.* **8:** 65–75.

Brygoo, E. 1955. Observations sur les oiseaux de Tromelin. *Naturaliste Malgache* **7:** 209–214.

Buddle, G. A. 1938. Notes on the birds of Canton Island. *Records Auckland Inst. and Mus.* **2:** 125–132.

—— 1947–50. Contributions to the gannet census. *N.Z. Bird Notes* **2** (4): 69–70; **2** (6): 128–130; **3** (2): 40–42. *Records Auck. Inst. Mus.* **3** (4–5): 195–204; **3** (6): 147–150.

Buller, W. L. 1888. *A History of the Birds of New Zealand.* London.

Cabot, D. In prep. Seabird Populations on the Saltee Islands, Co. Wexford. (Submitted to *Proc. Roy. Irish Acad.*)

Caum, E. L. 1936. Notes on the flora and fauna of Lehua and Kaula Islands. *Bernice P. Bishop Mus. Occas. Papers* **11:** 1–17.

Chance, M. R. A. 1962. An interpretation of some

agonistic postures—the role of 'cut-off' acts and postures. *Symp. Zool. Soc. Lond.* **8:** 71–89.

Chapin, J. P. 1932. The birds of the Belgian Congo, part 1. *Bull. American Mus. Nat. Hist.* **65:** 1–756.

Chapman, F. M. 1900. *Bird Studies with a Camera.* New York.

—— 1908. A contribution to the life histories of the booby *S. leucogaster* and frigate *F. aquila. Tortugas Lab. of Carnegie Inst. of Wash.* **2:** 139–151.

Chasen, F. N. 1933. Notes on the fauna of Christmas Island, Indian Ocean. *Bull. Raffles Mus.* **8:** 51–87.

Cheeseman, T. F. 1888. Notes on the Three Kings Islands. *Trans. N. Z. Inst.* **20:** 141–150.

Clapham, C. S. 1964. The birds of the Dahlac Archipelago *Ibis* **106:** 376–388.

Clapp, R. 1972. The natural history of Gardner Pinnacles, North-western Hawaiian Islands. *Atoll Res. Bull.* **163:** 25 pp.

Clapp, R. B. & Sibley, F. C. 1966. Notes on the birds of Tutuila, American Samoa. *Notornis* **13:** 157–164.

—— & —— 1971a. The vascular flora and terrestrial vertebrates of Vostok Island, South-central Pacific. *Atoll Res. Bull.* **144:** 10 pp.

—— & —— 1971b. Notes on the vascular flora and terrestrial vertebrates of Caroline Atoll, Southern Line Islands. *Atoll Res. Bull.* **145:** 18 pp.

Clarke, W. E. 1902. A month on the Eddystone; a study on bird migration. *Ibis:* 246–269.

Clugston, D. I. 1969. Some observations of seabirds in the Bay of Biscay. *Seabird Bull.* **7:** 32–33.

Coker, R. E. 1919. Habits and economic relations of the guano bird of Peru. *Proc. U. S. Nat. Mus.* **56:** 449–511.

—— 1920. Peru's wealth-producing birds. *National Geogr. Mag.* **37:** 537–566.

Cookson, W. E. 1874. In Hutchinson, 1950.

Cooper, R. P. 1948. Birds of the Capricorns—Great Barrier Reef. *Emu* **48:** 107–126.

Cope, E. D. 1870. Synopsis of the extinct Batrachia, Reptilia and Aves of North America. *Trans. Amer. Phil. Soc. N.S.* **14:** 1–252.

Coppinger, R. W. 1883. *Cruise of the 'Alert'.* London.

Cory, C. B. 1909. The birds of the Leeward Islands, Caribbean Sea. *Field Mus. Nat. Hist. Ornith.* ser. **1:** 193–255.

Coulson, J. C. 1966. The influence of the pair bond and age on the breeding biology of the kittiwake gull *Rissa tridactyla. J. Anim. Ecol.* **35:** 269–279.

—— 1968. Differences in the quality of birds nesting in the centre and at the edges of a colony. *Nature* **217:** 478–479.

—— & White, E. 1959. The effect of age and density of breeding birds on the time of breeding of the kittiwake *Rissa—tridactyla. Ibis* **101:** 496–497.

—— 1961. An analysis of the factors affecting the clutch size of the Kittiwake. *Proc. Zool. Soc. Lond.* **136:** 207–217.

Cowan, P. J. 1972. The contrast and coloration of sea-birds: an experimental approach. *Ibis* **114:** 390–393.

Craik, K. J. W. 1944. White plumage of sea birds. *Nature* (London) **153:** 288.

Cramp, S., Bourne, W. R. P. & Saunders, D. 1974. *The Seabirds of Britain and Ireland.* London.

Crook, J. H. 1965. The adaptive significance of avian social organisations *Symp. Zool. Soc. Lond.* **14:** 181–218.

Cullen, E. 1957. Adaptations in the kittiwake to cliff-nesting. *Ibis* **99:** 275–302.

Cullen, M. S. & Pratt, R. 1976. A census of the gannet nests on Grassholm in 1975. *Brit. Birds* **69:** 88–90.

Curio, E. 1964. Fluchtmängel bei Galapagos—Tölpeln. *J. für Ornithologie* **105:** 334–339.

Daanje, A. 1950. On locomotory movements in birds and the intention movements derived from them. *Behaviour* **111:** 48–98.

Darling, F. F. 1938. *Bird flocks and the breeding cycle.* Cambridge.

Davies, D. H. 1955. The South African pilchard; bird predators, 1953–54. *Rep. S. Afr. Dept. Comm. and Ind.* **18:** 1–32.

—— 1956. The South African pilchard (*Sardinops ocellata*) and maasbanker (*Trachurus trachurus*); bird predators, 1954–55. *Rep. S. Afr. Dept. Comm. and Ind.* **23:** 1–40.

Delano, A. 1817. *A Narrative of Voyages and Travels in Northern and Southern Hemispheres.* Boston.

Dementiev, G. P. & Gladkov, N. A. 1951. *Birds of the Soviet Union.* Moskva (In Russian).

—— &—— 1966. *Birds of the Soviet Union.* Jerusalem.

Diamond, A. J. 1971. The ecology of seabirds breeding at Aldabra Atoll, Indian Ocean. Ph.D. Thesis, Aberdeen.

—— 1973. Notes on the breeding biology and behaviour of the Magnificent Frigatebird. *Condor* **75:** 200–209.

—— 1974. The red-footed booby on Aldabra Atoll, Indian Ocean. *Ardea* **62:** 196–218.

Dill, H. R. 1912. Report on conditions on the Hawaiian bird reservation with a list of the birds found on Laysan. *U.S. Dept. Agr., Biol. Survey Bull.* **42:** 7–24.

Dinsmore, J. J. 1972. Avifauna of Little Tobago Island. *Quart. J. Florida Acad. Sci.* **35:** 55–71.

—— & Ffrench, R. P. 1969. Birds of St. Giles Islands, Tobago. *Wilson Bull.* **81:** 460–463.

Dixon, T. J. 1971. Estimates of the number of gannets breeding on St. Kilda 1969–73. *Seabird Report:* 5–12.

Dobson, R. & Lockley, R. M. 1946. Gannets breeding in the Channel Islands: two new colonies. *Brit. Birds* **39:** 309–312.

Domm, S. B. 1971. The uninhabited cays of the Capricorn Group, Great Barrier Reef, Australia. *Atoll Res. Bull.* **142:** 27 pp.

Dorward, D. F. 1962a. Behaviour of boobies, *Sula* spp. *Ibis* **103b:** 221–234.

—— 1962b. Comparative biology of the white booby and the brown booby, *Sula* spp., at Ascension. *Ibis* **103b:** 174–220.

DOTT, H. E. M. 1967. Number of great skuas and other seabirds of Hermaness, Unst. *Scot. Birds* **4:** 340–350.

EHRHARDT, J. P. 1971. Census of the birds of Clipperton Island, 1968. *Condor* **73:** 476–480.

ELKINGTON, J. S. C. 1930. A bird diary from England to Australia on the S. S. Miamo. *Emu* **30:** 97–101.

ELKINS, N. & WILLIAMS, M. R. 1969. Seabird movements in north-east Scotland 1968 and 1969. *Seabird Report:* 31–39.

EVERMAN, B. W. & RADCLIFFE, L. 1917. The fishes of the west coast of Peru and the Titicaca Basin. *U. S. Nat. Mus. Bull.* **95:** 3–157.

FAIRBRIDGE, R. W. 1966. *The Encyclopedia of Oceanography.* New York.

FALLA, R. A. 1948. Birds of the Solanders. *N. Z. Bird Notes* **3:** 52–55.

FARQUHAR, S. ST. J. 1900. On two nesting places of gannets and terns in the south Indian Ocean. *Ibis* **6:** 63–67.

FIEDLER, R. H., JARVIS, N. D. & LOBELL, M. J. 1943. *La pesca y las industrias pesqueras en el Péru.* Lima.

FISHER, A. K. & WETMORE, A. 1931. Report on birds recorded by the Pinchot expedition of 1929 to the Caribbean and Pacific. *Proc. U.S. Nat. Mus.* **79:** 1–66.

FISHER, H. I. 1951. The avifauna of Niihau Island, Hawaiian Archipelago. *Condor* **53:** 31–42.

—— & BALDWIN, P. H. 1946. War and the birds of Midway Atoll. *Condor* **48:** 3–15.

FISHER, J. 1952. *The Fulmar.* London.

—— & LOCKLEY, R. M. 1954. *Sea-Birds.* London.

—— & VENABLES, L. S. V. 1938. Gannets (*Sula bassana*) on Noss Shetland, with an analysis of the rate of increase of this species. *J. Anim. Ecol.* **7:** 305–313.

—— & VEVERS, H. G. 1943–44. The breeding distribution, history and population of the North Atlantic gannet *Sula bassana*. *J. Anim. Ecol.* **12:** 173–213; **13:** 49–62.

FISHER, W. K. 1903. Birds of Laysan and the Leeward Islands, Hawaiian Group. *Bull. U.S. Fish Commission* **23:** 769–807.

FLEMING, C. A. 1947. Contributions to the gannet census. *N. Z. Bird Notes* **2:** 109–111: 113–114.

—— 1950. Some south Pacific sea-bird logs. *Emu* **49:** 169–188.

—— & WODZICKI, K. A. 1952. A census of the gannet (*Sula serrator*) in New Zealand. *Notornis* **5:** 39–78.

FLEMING, J. 1847. *The Bass Rock: Zoology of the Bass.* Edinburgh.

FORBES, H. O. 1913. The Peruvian guano islands. *Ibis:* 709–712.

—— 1914. The Peruvian guano deposits. *Amer. Fert.* **40:** 44–45.

FORBES-WATSON, A. D. 1969. Notes on birds observed in the Comoros on behalf of the Smithsonian Institution. *Atoll Res. Bull.* **128:** 23 pp.

FORBUSH, E. H. 1929. *Birds of Massachusetts.* Norwood, Massachusetts: 461 pp.

FORDUN, J. DE. 1447. *The Scotichronicon.* Godall's Edition 1759.

FOSBERG, F. R. 1965. Natural bird refuges in the Galapagos. *Elepaio* **25:** 60–67.

FRAPPAS, M. 1820. Rélation d'un voyage fait à Madagascar, à Anjouan et aux Seychelles, pendent les annèes 1818 et 1819. *Ann. Mar. Colon.* **5** (2): 229–273.

FRYER, J. C. F. 1911. The structure and formation of Aldabra and neighbouring islands, with notes on their flora and fauna. *Trans. Linnean Soc.* London—Ser. 2 **14:** 397–442.

GALARZA, N. 1968. Informe sobre estudios ornitologicos realizados en el laboratorio de la Puntilla (Pisco) en Setiembre de 1965/66. *Inf. Esp. Int. Mar., Callao.* IM–**31:** 1–26.

GALLAGHER, M. D. 1960. Bird notes from Christmas Island. *Ibis* **102:** 490–502.

GARCIA, E. F. J. 1971. Seabird activity in the Strait of Gibraltar: A progress report. *Seabird Report:* 30–36.

GASTON, A. J. 1970. Seabird migration off Cape Verde, Senegal, in April 1968. *Seabird Report:* 6–8.

GIBSON, J. A. 1951a. The breeding distribution, population and history of the birds of Ailsa Craig. *Scot. Nat.* **63:** 73–100, 159–177.

—— 1951b. Freak nest material utilised by gannets on Ailsa Craig. *Scot. Nat.* **63:** 193.

—— 1952. The gannets of Holy Island, Arran. *Scot. Nat.* **64:** 178.

GIBSON-HILL, C. A. 1947. Notes on the birds of Christmas Island. *Bull. Raffles Mus.* **18:** 87–165.

—— 1948. Display and posturing in the Cape gannet, *Morus capensis*. *Ibis* **90:** 568–72.

—— 1949. The birds of the Cocos-Keeling Islands (Indian Ocean). *Ibis* **91:** 221–243.

—— 1950a. Notes on the birds of the Cocos-Keeling Islands. *Bull. Raffles Mus.* **22:** 212–270.

—— 1950b. Notes on Abbott's booby. *Bull. Raffles Mus.* **23:** 65–76.

—— 1950c. Notes on sea birds breeding in Malayan waters. *Bull. Raffles Mus.* **23:** 5–64.

—— 1953. Notes on the seabirds of the orders Procellariiformes and Pelecaniformes recorded as strays or visitors to the Ceylon coast. *Spolia Zeylanica* **27:** 83–102.

GIFFORD, E. W. 1913. The birds of the Galapagos Islands, with observations on the birds of Cocos and Clipperton Islands (Columbiformes to Pelecaniformes). *Proc. Calif. Acad. Sci.* Fourth Ser. **2:** 1–132.

GILL, F. B. 1967. Observations on the pelagic distribution of seabirds in the western Indian

Ocean. *Proc. U.S. Natn. Mus.* **123.** No. 3605: 1–33.

——, Jouanin, C. & Storer, R. W. 1970. Notes on the seabirds of Round Island, Mauritius. *Auk* **87:** 514–521.

Glenny, F. H. 1955. Modifications of pattern in the aortic arch system of birds and their phylogenetic significance. *Proc. Nat. Mus.* 104.

Gore, M. E. J. 1968. A check list of the birds of Sabak, Borneo. *Ibis* **110:** 165–196.

Goss, N. S. 1888. New and rare birds found breeding on the San Pedro Martir Isle. *Auk* **5:** 240–244.

Grant, C. H. B. & Mackworth-Praed, C. W. 1933. Description of a new booby. *Bull. Brit. Orn. Club* **53:** 118–119.

Grant, P. R. 1964. The birds of the Tres Marietas Islands, Nayarit, Mexico. *Auk.* **81:** 514–519.

—— & Cowan, I. McT. 1964. A review of the avifauna of the Tres Marias Islands, Nayarit, Mexico. *Condor* **66:** 221–228.

Green, R. H. & Macdonald, D. 1963. The Black Pyramid gannetry. *Emu* **63:** 177–184.

Gray, R. 1859. *The Birds of the West of Scotland including the Outer Hebrides.* Glasgow.

Gross, A. O. 1960. Birds observed at sea during a voyage to and from Africa. *Massachusetts Audubon* **44:** 111–116.

Gudmundsson, F. 1953. Icelandic birds VII. The gannet (*Sula bassana* (L.)). *Nàttùrufraedingurinn* **23:** 170–177.

Gurney, J. H. 1913. *The Gannet, A Bird with a History.* London.

Hadley, C. J. & Parker, S. A. 1965. Field notes on the birds of Santa Cruz Islands, south-west Pacific. *Bull. Br. Orn. Club.* **85:** 154–161.

Haile, N. S. 1964. *Sabak Soc. J.* **11:** 135–137.

Hallinan, T. 1924. Notes on some Panama Canal Zone birds, with special reference to their food. *Auk* **41:** 304–326.

Hanna, G. D. 1926. Expedition to the Revillagigedo Islands, Mexico, in 1925. *Proc. Calif. Acad. Sci.* **15:** 1–113.

Harris, M. P. 1969. Breeding seasons of seabirds in the Galapagos. *J. Zool. Lond.* **159:** 145–165.

—— 1973. The Galapagos avifauna. *Condor* **75:** 265–278.

—— 1974. *Field Guide to the Birds of the Galapagos.* London.

—— 1975. Unusual feeding by blue-footed booby. *Auk* **92:** 601–602.

—— & Hansen, L. 1974. Sea-bird transects between Europe and Rio Plate, South America, in autumn 1973. *Dansk orn. Foren.* **68:** 117–137.

Harrison, C. J. O. 1965. Allopreening as agonistic behaviour. *Behaviour* **24:** 11–209.

—— (in press). The taxonomic status of Milne-Edward's fossil sulids. *Bull. Brit. Orn. Club* **95.**

Hartert, E. 1912–21. *Die Vogel der palaarktischen Fauna*, vol. 2: 833–1764.

Harvey, W. 1651. Exercitationes de Generatione Animalium. Ref. in Gurney 1913, p. 198.

Hellmayr, C. E. & Conover, B. 1948. Catalogue of birds of the Americas. *Field Mus. Nat. Hist. Zoology.* **Vol.** 13.

Henderson, A. C. B. 1974. Seabird movements in Scotland, Autumn 1973. B.Sc. Thesis, Aberdeen.

Hill, M. N. 1963. Ed. *The Sea; Ideas and Observations on Progress in the Study of the Sea.* New York.

Hindwood, K. A., Keith, K. & Serventy, D. L. 1963. Birds of the south-west Coral Sea. *Tech. Pap. Wildl. Serv. Sect. Aust.* **3:** 1–44.

Hirons, M. J., Bellamy, D. J. & Sheppard, C. 1976. Birds on the Chagos Bank. *Nature* **260:** 387.

Hoogstraal, H. 1969. *Ornithodoros* (*Alectorobuis*) *muesebecki*, N. sp., a parasite of the blue-faced booby (*Sula dactylatra melanops*) on Hasikiya Island, Arabian Sea. *Proc. Entomol. Soc. Washington* **71:** 368–374.

Hopkins, J. R. 1969. Seawatching on the coast of Morocco. *Seabird Rep.* 40–42.

Hounsome, M. V. 1967. The Atlantic seawatch 1965. The Gannet. *Seabird Bull.* **4:** 7–20.

Howard, H. 1936. A new fossil bird locality near Playa Del Rey, California, with description of a new species of sulid. *Condor* **38:** 211–214.

—— 1949. New avian records for the Pliocene of California. *Publ. Carnegie Inst. Washington* **584:** 177–199.

—— 1958. Miocene sulids of Southern California. *Contr. Sc.* **25:** 1–16.

Howell, T. R. 1975. Preliminary report to the Cousteau Society on the bird life of Isla Isabela, *Nayarit*, Mexico.

Hutchinson, G. E. 1950. The Biogeochemistry of vertebrate excretion. *Bull. Am. Mus. Nat. Hist.* **96:** 554 pp.

Jardine, W. 1816. *The Naturalist's Library;* IV. *Ornithology. Birds of Great Britain and Ireland.* Edinburgh.

Jarvis, M. J. F. 1970. Interactions between man and the South African gannet *Sula capensis. Ostrich Suppl.* **8:** 497–514.

—— 1971. Ethology and ecology of the South African gannet, *Sula capensis.* Ph.D. Thesis. Cape Town.

—— 1972. The systematic position of the South African gannet. *Ostrich* **43:** 211–216.

—— 1974. The ecological significance of clutch size in the South African gannet (*Sula capensis* Lichtenstein). *J. Anim. Ecol.* **43:** 1–17.

—— & Cram, D. L. 1971. Bird Island, Lamberts Bay, South Africa. An attempt at conservation. *Biol. Conservation* **3:** 269–272.

Jehl, J. J. 1973. Distribution of marine birds in Chilean waters in winter. *Auk* **90:** 114–135.

Jespersen, P. 1929. On the frequency of birds over the high Atlantic Ocean. *Proc. 6th Int. Orn. Congr. Copenhagen* 1926: 163–172.

—— 1932. Observations on oceanic birds of the Pacific. *Vidensk. Medd. frä Foren* **94:** 187–221.

JEWETT, S. G., TAYLOR, W. P., SHAW, W. T. & ALDRICH, J. W. 1953. *Birds of Washington State.* Seattle.

JING-XIAN, L. & ZI-YU, W. 1975. The red-footed booby in the Xisha (Paracel) Islands. *Zoo. Mag. (Dongwuxue Zazhi)* **3:** 40.

JOHNSON, A. W. 1965. *The Birds of Chile and Adjacent Regions of Argentina, Bolivia and Peru.* Buenos Aires.

——, MILLIE, W. R. & MOFFETT, G. 1970. Notes on the birds of Easter Island. *Ibis* **112:** 532–538.

JONES, R. B. 1946. An account of a visit to The Brothers (Jebel Jeir) Islands in the Gulf of Aden. *Ibis* **88:** 228–232.

JORDÁN, R. 1958. Breve nota sobre la ánillación de piqueros. *Bol. Comp. Admin. Guano* **11:** 7–14.

—— 1960. Some results of the banding of guano producing birds in Peru. *The Ring* **23:** 227–230.

—— 1963. Resultados de los censos graficos de aves guaneras efectuado en Noviembre 1960 y enero 1962. *Inst. de Invest. de los Recursos Marinos. Informe* **12:** 1–21.

—— 1964. Las emigraciones y mortandad de aves guaneras en el Otoño e invierno de 1963. *Inst. de Invest. de los Recursos Marinos. Informe* **27:** 1–31.

—— 1967. The predation of guano birds on the Peruvian anchovy. *Calif. Co-operative Fisheries Investig.* **11:** 105–109.

—— & CABRERA, D. 1960. Algunos resultados de las anillaciones de Guanay efectuados durante 1939–41 y 1949–53. Bol. Ciã Admora. *Guano.* **36:** 11–26.

—— & FUENTES, H. 1966. Las poblaciones de aves guaneras y su situación actual. Instituto del Mar de Peru 10: 31 pp.

KAEDING, H. B. 1905. Birds from the west coast of lower California and adjacent islands. *Condor* **7:** 105–111.

KAY, G. T. 1948. The gannet in Shetland in winter. *Brit. Birds* **41:** 268–270.

KENNEDY, J. N. 1917. A little known bird colony in the Gulf of Mexico. *Ibis*: 41–43.

KENNEDY, P. G. 1961. *A List of the Birds of Ireland.* Dublin.

KENYON, K. W. & RICE, D. W. 1958. Birds of Kure Atoll, Hawaii. *Condor* **60:** 188–190.

KEPLER, C. 1969. The breeding biology of the blue-faced booby (*Sula dactylatra personata*) on Green Island, Kure. Publs. *Nuttall Orn. Club* **8:** 97 pp.

KERSLEY, R. 1975. Sea watch movements from Lamba Ness, Unst, 18 to 27 June 1975. *R.A.F. Ornith. Soc.* **10:** In Press.

KING, J. E. & PYLE, R. L. 1957. Observations of seabirds in the tropical Pacific. *Condor* **59:** 27–39.

KING, W. B. 1967. *Seabirds of the tropical Pacific Ocean.* Smithsonian Inst. Washington.

—— 1970. The trade wind zone oceanography pilot study. VII. *U.S. Dept. Int. Sp. Sci. Rep. Fisheries* **586:** 136 pp.

—— 1974. Pelagic studies of seabirds in the central and eastern Pacific Ocean. *Smithsonian Cont. Zool.* **158:** 277 pp.

KIRBY, H. 1925. The birds of Fanning Island, central Pacific Ocean. *Condor* **27:** 185–196.

KURODA, N. 1936. *Birds of the island of Java.* Tokyo.

—— 1960. Analysis of seabird distribution in the north-west Pacific Ocean. *Pac. Sci.* **14:** 55–67.

LACK, D. 1947. *Darwin's Finches.* Cambridge.

—— 1954. *The Natural Regulation of Animal Numbers.* Oxford.

—— 1966. *Population Studies of Birds.* Oxford.

—— 1967. Inter-relationships in breeding adaptations by marine birds. *Proc. Int. Orn. Congr.* **14:** 3–42.

LAMB, C. 1910. A glimpse of bird life on the west coast of Mexico. *Condor* **12:** 74–79.

—— 1927. Notes on some birds of the southern extremity of lower California. *Condor* **29:** 155–157.

LANGHAM, N. P. & WELLS, D. R. 1974. Vertebrates at Pulau Perak in March 1973. In Prep. *Malayan Nature Journal.*

LAVALLE, J. A. 1924. *Estudio de la emegracion y mortalidad de las avas guaneras.* Lima.

LAWRENCE, C. 1972. Some observations of magnificent frigatebirds and red-footed boobies. In MS.

—— 1972. Visual displays of the red-footed booby. In MS.

LAWRY, K. 1926. A seabird's haven. *Emu* **26:** 69–71.

LEACH, W. 1816. Ref. in Gurney 1913.

LEOPOLD, N. F. 1963. Checklist of the birds of Peurto Rico and the Virgin Islands. *Bull. 168 Univ. of Puerto Rico. Agric. Exp. Statn.*

LINDSAY, G. E. 1962. The Belvedere expedition to the Gulf of California. *Trans. San Diego Soc. Nat. Hist.* **13:** 1–44.

LISTER, J. J. 1891. Notes on the birds of the Phoenix Islands (Pacific Ocean). *Zool. Soc. of London Proc.* 1891: 289–300.

LIVERSIDGE, R. 1959. The place of South Africa in the distribution and migration of ocean birds. *Ostrich Supp.* **3:** 47–67.

LLOYD, B. 1926. On the egg-laying of the Grassholm gannets. *Brit. Bds.* **19:** 309–310.

LOCKLEY, R. M. & SALMON, H. M. 1934. The gannet colonies of Iceland. *Brit. Birds* **28:** 183–4.

LOUSTAU-LALANNE, P. 1962. The birds of the Chagos Archipelago, Indian Ocean. *Ibis* **104:** 67–73.

LOWE, P. R. 1909. Notes on some birds collected during a cruise in the Caribbean Sea. *Ibis*: 304–347.

—— 1911. On the birds of the Cayman Islands, West Indies. *Ibis* 137–161.

—— 1911. *A Naturalist on Desert Islands.* London.

MCCASKIE, G. 1970. The occurrences of four species

of Pelecaniformes in the southwestern United States. *Calif. Birds* **1:** 117–142.

MACDONALD, J. D. 1960. Secondary external nares of the gannet. *Proc. Zool. Soc. Lond.* **135:** 357–363.

—— & LAWFORD, P. A. 1954. Sight records of birds in the Pacific: compiled from the bird log kept during the recent cruises of H.M.S. Challenger. *Emu* **54:** 7–28.

McDOWELL, S. 1948. The bony palate of birds. *Auk* **65:** 520–549.

MACGILLIVRAY, W. 1910. Along the Great Barrier Reef. *Emu* **10:** 216–233.

McGREGOR, R. C. 1909. *A manual of Philippine birds.* Manila.

MACINTYRE, D. 1950. The young gannet. *Brit. Birds* **43:** 232.

MACKAY, J. 1723. *A Journey through Scotland.* Ref. in Gurney 1913.

McKEAN, J. L. 1966. Population, status and migration of the gannet *Sula bassana serrator* of Lawrence Rocks, Victoria. *Emu* **65:** 159–163.

—— & HINDWOOD, K. A. 1965. Additional notes on the birds of Lord Howe Island. *Emu* **64:** 79–97.

McNAB, B. K. 1966. An analysis of the body temperature of birds. *Condor* **68:** 47–55.

MADOC, G. C. 1956. The birds observed during two short visits to the Aroa Islands. *Bull. Raffles Mus.* **27:** 150–154.

MAILLIARD, J. 1923. Expedition of the California Academy of Sciences to the Gulf of California in 1921. *Proc. Calif. Acad. Sci.* **12:** 443–456.

MAJOR, J. 1521. *Historia Majoris Brittanniae.* Edinburgh. Ref. in Gurney 1913.

MANIKOWSKI, S. 1971. The influence of meteorological factors on the behaviour of sea birds. *Acta. Zool. Cracov.* **16:** 581–667.

MARCHANT, S. 1958. The birds of the Santa Elena Peninsula, south west Ecuador. *Ibis* **100:** 349–387.

MARKHAM, C. R. 1880. *Peru.* London.

MARTIN, M. 1698. *A late voyage to St. Kilda.* London.

MATHEWS, G. M. & IREDALE, T. 1921. *A Manual of the Birds of Australia.* London.

MATHEWS, G. M. 1913. *Birds of Australia* **2:** 480–503.

MERTON, D. V. 1970. Kermadec Islands Expedition Reports: a general account of birdlife. *Notornis* **17:** 147–199.

MILLER, H. 1847. Geology of the Bass. In *The Bass Rock* by J. M'Crie, Edinburgh.

MILLER, L. 1925. Avian remains from the Miocene of Lompoc, California. *Publ. Carnegie Inst. Washington* **349:** 109–117.

—— 1935. New bird horizons in California. *Publ. Univ. California. Biol. Sci.* **1:** 73–80.

—— & BOWMAN, R. I. 1958. Further bird remains from the San Diego Pliocene. *Contri. Sci.* **20:** 1–15.

MILLIE, W. R. 1963. Brief notes on the birds of San Ambrosio and San Felix, Chile. *Ibis* **105:** 563–566.

MILLIMAN, J. D. 1969. Four south-western Caribbean Atolls: Courtown Cays, Albuquerque Cays, Roncador Bank and Serrana Bank. *Atoll Res. Bull.* **129:** 26 pp.

MILLS, E. L. 1967. Bird records from south-western Ecuador. *Ibis* **109:** 534–538.

MILLS, J. A. 1973. The influence of age and pair-bond on the breeding biology of the red-billed gull *Larus novaehollandiae scopulinus. J. Anim. Ecol.* **42:** 147–162.

MILNE-EDWARDS, A. 1867–71. *Recherches anatomiques et paléontologiques pour servir a l'histoire des oiseaux fossiles de la France.* Paris.

—— 1874. Observations sur les oiseaux fossiles des Faluns de Saucats et la Molasse de Leognan. *Bibl. École Haute Études Sci. Nat.* **11:** 7–12.

—— 1882. Reserches sur la faune des regiones Australes. *Annales des Sciences Naturelles Zoologie* **6:** 36–37.

MILON, PH. 1966. L'Evolution de l'avifaune nidificatrice de la reserve Albert-Chappelier (Les Sept—Iles) de 1950 à 1965. *La Terre et La Vie* 1966: 113–142.

MITCHELL, M. H. 1957. *Observations on birds of south-eastern Brazil.* Univ. Toronto Press.

MOISAN, G. & SCHERRER, B. 1973. Deplacements saisonniers des fous de bassan de L'Ile Bonaventure (Canada). *Terre et Vie* **27:** 414–434.

MOORE, C. C. 1974. Movements of seabirds at Clogher Head, Co. Louth 1971–73. *Seabird Report* **4:** 78–86

MOORE, L. B. & WODZICKI, K. A. 1950. Plant material from gannets' nests. *Notornis* **4** (1): 12–13.

MOREAU, R. E. 1940. Contributions to the ornithology of the east African islands. *Ibis* **4:** 48–91.

—— 1950. The breeding seasons of African birds. *Ibis* **92:** 223–267.

MORGAN, B. & J. 1965. Some notes on birds of the Fiji Islands. *Notornis* **12:** 158–168.

MORRIS, F. O. 1848. *A History of British Birds.* London.

MORRIS, R. O. 1962. Two visits to the Haycocks (Hanish Islands, southern Red Sea). *Sea Swallow* **15:** 57–58.

MORRISON, J. P. E. 1954. Notes on the birds of Raroia. *Atoll Res. Bull.* **33–36:** 19–26.

MORZER-BRUYNS, W. F. J. 1965. Birds seen during west to east trans-Pacific crossing along equatorial counter-current around latitude 7°N, in the autumn of 1960. *Sea Swallow* **17:** 57–66.

MOUNTFORD, M. D. 1972. The significance of clutch-size. 315–323.

MUNRO, G. C. 1944. *Birds of Hawaii.* Honolulu.

MURPHY, G. I. & IKEHARA, I. I. 1955. Summary of sightings of fish schools and bird flocks. *U.S. Fish and Wildl. Serv. Spec. Sci. Rep. Fisheries* **154:** 19 pp.

MURPHY, R. C. 1914. Observations on birds of the south Atlantic. *Auk.* **31:** 439–455.

—— 1923. The oceanography of the Peruvian littoral with reference to the abundance and

distribution of marine life. *Geogr. Rev.* **13:** 64–85.
—— 1925. *Bird Islands of Peru.* New York.
—— 1926. Oceanic and climatic phenomena along the west coast of South America during 1925. *Geogr. Rev.* **16:** 26–54.
—— 1936. *Ocean Birds of South America.* New York.
—— 1967. Distribution of North Atlantic pelagic birds. *Atl. Mar. Environ.*, folio **14.**
——, Bailey, A. M. & Niedrach, R. J. 1954. Canton Island. *Denver Mus. Nat. Hist.*, Mus. Pict. **10.**

Naurois, R. de. 1969. Peuplements et cycles de reproduction des oiseaux de la côte occidentale d'Afrique. *Mém. Mus. Nat. Hist. Nat.* **56:** 312 pp.
Nelson, E. W. 1899. Birds of the Tres Marias Islands. *North American Fauna* **14:** 21–62.
Nelson, J. B. 1964. Factors influencing clutch-size and chick growth in the North Atlantic Gannet *Sula bassana. Ibis* **106:** 63–77.
—— 1965. The behaviour of the gannet. *Brit. Birds* **58:** 233–288; 313–336.
—— 1966a. The behaviour of the young gannet. *Brit. Birds* **59:** 393–419.
—— 1966b. Population dynamics of the gannet (*Sula bassana*) at the Bass Rock, with comparative information from other Sulidae. *J. Anim. Ecol* **35:** 443–470.
—— 1966c. The breeding biology of the gannet *Sula bassana* on the Bass Rock, Scotland. *Ibis* **108:** 584–626.
—— 1967a. Colonial and cliff nesting in the gannet, compared with other Sulidae and the kittiwake. *Ardea* **55:** 60–90.
—— 1967b. Breeding behaviour of the white booby *Sula dactylatra. Ibis* **109:** 194–231.
—— 1968. *Galapagos: Islands of Birds.* London.
—— 1969a. The breeding ecology of the red-footed booby in the Galapagos. *J. Anim. Ecol.* **38:** 181–198.
—— 1969b. The breeding behaviour of the red-footed booby *Sula sula. Ibis* **111:** 357–385.
—— 1970. The relationship between behaviour and ecology in the Sulidae with reference to other seabirds. *Oceanogr. Mar. Biol. Ann. Rev.* **8:** 501–574.
—— 1971. The biology of Abbott's booby *Sula abbotti. Ibis* **113:** 429–467.
—— 1975. Report on the Status and Prospects of Abbott's Booby (*Sula abbotti*) in Relation to Phosphate Mining on the Australian Territory of Christmas Island, August 1974. *Bull. Int. Council Bird Preservation* **12:** 131–140.
—— 1977. Report and recommendations on the status and prospects of Abbott's booby in relation to the British Phosphate Commissioners' mining and conservation policy. Cyclostyled Report.
Nettleship, D. N. 1975. A recent decline of gannets, *Morus bassanus*, on Bonaventure Island, Quebec. *Canadian Field Nat.* **89:** 125–133.
—— 1976. Gannets in North America: present numbers and recent population changes. *Wilson Bull.* **88:** 300–313.
Nichols, R. A. 1943. The breeding birds of St. Thomas and St. John, Virgin Islands. *Mem. Soc. Cubana Hist. Nat.* **17:** 23–37.
Nicoll, M. J. 1904. On a collection of birds made during the cruise of the 'Valhalla' R.Y.S., in the West Indies 1903–1904. *Ibis*: 555–591.
Nielsen, P. 1919. *Dansk, Orn. For. Tidsskr.* **13:** 33–79.
North, A. J. 1912. Nests and eggs of birds found breeding in Australia and Tasmania. *Sydney Austral. Mus.*
North, M. E. W. 1946. Mait Island—a bird-rock in the Gulf of Aden. *Ibis* **88:** 478–501.

Ogilvie-Grant, W. R. 1913. On a small collection of birds from Henderson Island, South Pacific. *Ibis*: 343–350.
Olsen, B. & Permin, M. 1972. The population of gannet *Sula bassana* on Mykinesholmur, 1972., *Dansk Orn. Foren* **68:** 39–42.
Oreel, G. J. & Voous, K. H. 1974. Masked boobies *Sula dactylatra* off the coast of West Africa: a correction. *Ardea* **62:** 130–132.
Owre, O. T. 1962. Nematodes in birds of the order Pelecaniformes. *Auk* **79:** 114.

Pakenham, R. H. W. 1943. Field notes on the birds of Zanzibar and Pemba. *Ibis* **85:** 165–189.
Palmer, R. S. 1962. *Handbook of North American Birds.* New York.
Paris, P. 1921. *Faune de France.* Paris.
Parker, I. S. C. 1970. Some ornithological observations from the western Indian Ocean. *Atoll Res. Bull* **136:** 211–220.
Parkin, D. T., Ewing, A. W. & Ford, H. A. 1970. Group diving in the blue-footed booby *Sula nebouxii. Ibis* **112:** 111–112.
Parrish, B. B. & Saville, A. 1965. The biology of the northeast Atlantic herring populations. *Oceanogr. Mar. Biol. Ann. Rev.* **3:** 323–373.
Parsons, J. J. 1956. San Andres and Providencia, English-speaking islands in the western Caribbean. *Univ. Calif. Publ. in Geogr.* **12:** 84 pp.
Paulik, G. J. 1970. Anchovies, birds and fishermen in the Peru Current. In Murdock, W. W. *Environment, Resources, Pollution and Society*, Stamford.
Peakall, D. B. 1962. Gannet population of Bonaventure Island. *Canadian Field-Naturalist* **76:** 179–180.
Pearce, P. A., Gruchy, I. M. & Keith, J. A. 1973. Toxic chemicals in living things in the Gulf of St. Lawrence. *Proc. Can. Soc. Fish. & Wildl. Biol.* Halifax, Nova Scotia.
Pearson, A. J. 1962. Field notes on the birds of

Ocean Island and Nauru during 1961. *Ibis* **104:** 421–424.

—— 1966. The birds of Christmas Island (Indian Ocean) *Bull. B.O.C.* **86:** 66–71.

PEARSON, D. L. & KNUDSEN, J. W. 1967. Avifaunal records from Eniwetok Atoll, Marshall Islands. *Condor* **69:** 201–203.

PEARSON, T. H. 1968. The feeding biology of seabird species breeding on the Farne Islands, Northumberland. *J. Anim. Ecol.* **37:** 521–552.

PERRINS, C. M. 1970. The timing of birds' breeding seasons. *Ibis* **112:** 242–255.

PERRY, R. 1946. *A Naturalist on Lindisfarne*. London.

—— 1948. *Shetland Sanctuary*. London.

—— 1950. The young gannet. *Brit. Birds* **43:** 343–344.

PETERS, J. L. 1931. *Checklist of Birds of the World*. Vol. 1. Harvard Univ. Press.

PETTITT, R. G. 1969. Seabird movements in northwest Spain. *Seabird Bull.* **7:** 10–31.

PHILLIPS, G. C. 1962. Survival value of the white coloration of gulls and other seabirds. D.Phil. Thesis: Oxford.

PHILLIPS, W. W. A. 1963. The birds of the Maldive Islands, Indian Ocean. *J. Bombay Nat. Hist. Soc.* **60:** 546–584.

POULIN, J. M. 1968a. Croissance du jeune fou de bassan (*Sula bassana*) pendant sa période préenvol. *Naturaliste Can.* **95:** 1131–1143.

—— 1968b. Reproduction du Fou de Bassan (*Sula bassana*) Ile Bonaventure (Quebec) (Perspective ecologique). M. Sc. Thesis. Laval Univ.: 110 pp.

—— & MOISAN, G. 1968. The gannets (*Sula bassana*) of Bonaventure Island, Quebec. Paper presented to 1968 Northeast Fish and Wildlife Conference, Manchester, New Hampshire. 17 pp.

POULSEN, H. 1953. A study of incubation responses and some other behaviour patterns in birds. *Vidensk, Medd. fra Dansk naturh. Foren* **115:** 1–131.

PROBINE, M. C. & WODZICKI, K. A. 1955. A note on the thermal resistance of the feathered layer of gannet skins. *N.Z. J. Sc. and Tech.* **37:** 158–159.

RAIMONDI, A. In Rivero, M. E. 1852. Estudios sobre el Huano. El Interprete del Pueblo. Ref. in Hutchinson 1950.

—— 1856. Memoire sur le huano de îles de Chincha et les oiseaux qui le produisent. *Compt. Rendus Acad. Sci., Paris* **42:** 735–738.

—— 1874. Guano (Nouveaux dépôts). In *Guanos de Tarapaca*. Paris.

—— 1876. *El Peru*. Lima.

RAND, R. W. 1959a. The biology of guano-producing sea-birds—The distribution, abundance and feeding habits of the Cape gannet, *Morus capensis*, off the south-western coast of the Cape Province. *Commerce and Industry Rep.* **39:** 35 pp.

—— 1959b. Conservation of the Cape gannet. *Ostrich Suppl.* **3:** 31–33.

—— 1963a. The biology of guano producing sea birds—composition of colonies on the Cape islands. *S.A. Div. Fish Invest.* **43.**

—— 1963b. The biology of guano producing sea birds—composition of colonies on the southwest African islands. *S.A. Fish Invest.* **46.**

—— 1963c. Seabirds in the southern Indian Ocean. *Ostrich* **34:** 121–128.

REICHENOW, A. 1901 and 1913. *Die Vogel Afrikas:* Vols. 1 and 4. Neudamm.

REINSCH, H. H. 1969. *Der Basstölpel. Die Neue Brehm—Bücherei*: 111 pp.

—— 1971. Die deutsche Dampferfischerei auf Köhler, *Pollachius virens* (L.), 1964–1969 in Nordatlantik. *Sonderdruck aus Bd.* **22:** 184–210.

REITHMULLER, E. 1931. Nesting notes from Willis Island. *Emu* **31:** 142–6.

RICHARDSON, F. & FISHER, H. I. 1950. Birds of Moku Manu and Manana Islands off Oahu, Hawaii. *Auk* **67:** 285–306.

RIDGWAY, R. 1893. Descriptions of some new birds collected on the islands of Aldabra and Assumption, northwest of Madagascar, by Dr. W. L. Abbott. *Proc. U.S. Nat. Mus.* **16:** 597–600.

—— 1895. Birds collected by Doctor W. L. Abbott in the Seychelles, Amirantes, Glorioso, Assumption, Aldabra and adjacent islands, with notes on habits etc. by the collector. *Proc. U.S. Nat. Mus.* **18:** 509–546.

RIDLEY, M. W. & PERCY, R. 1958. The exploitation of sea birds in Seychelles. *Colonial Research Studies* **25** London: 78 pp.

RIPLEY, S. D. 1951. Migrants and introduced species in the Pulau Archipelago. *Condor* **53:** 299–300.

—— & BOND, G. M. 1966. The birds of Socotra and Abd-el-Kuri. *Smithsonian Misc. Coll.* **151:** 1–37.

RIVERO, M. E. de. 1827. Memoria sobre el guano de pájaros del Peru. Ref. in Hutchinson, 1950.

ROBBINS, C. R. 1958. Observations on oceanic birds in the Gulf of Panama. *Condor* **60:** 300–302.

ROBERTS, B. 1934. The gannet colonies of Iceland. *Brit. Bds.* **28:** 100–105.

ROBERTSON, C. J. R. 1969. Community development in the gannet at Cape Kidnappers. Ecological Society Conference.

—— & WILLIAMS, G. R. 1968. A review of gannet research at Cape Kidnappers. Report to Sanctuary Board.

ROBINSON, H. C. 1906. A visit to the Aroa Islands, with a list of the birds found there. *J. Fed. Malay St. Mus.* **2** (1): 8–16.

—— & KLOSS, C. B. 1921. The birds of south-west and Peninsular Siam. *J. Nat. Hist. Soc. Siam.* **5:** 1–87.

ROTHSCHILD, W. 1915. Notes on the genus *Sula*. *Bull. Brit. Orn. Club* **35:** 41–45.

—— & HARTERT, E. 1899. Review of the ornithology of the Galapagos Islands. *Novit. Zool.* **6:** 85–205.

RYTHER, J. H. 1969. Photosynthesis and fish production from the sea. *Science* **166:** 72–80.

SALMON, H. M. & LOCKLEY, R. M. 1933. The Grassholm gannets—a survey and a census. *Brit. Birds* **27:** 142–152.

SALVIN, O. & GODMAN, E. M. 1879–1904. *Biologia Centrali-Americana, Aves.*

SCHAEFFER, M. B. 1970. Men, birds and anchovies in the Peru current-dynamic interactions. *Trans. Amer. Fish Soc.* **99:** 461–467.

SCHREIBER, R. W. & ASHMOLE, N. P. 1970. Sea bird breeding seasons on Christmas Island, Pacific Ocean. *Ibis* **112:** 363–394.

SCHWEIGGER, E. H. 1940. Studies of the Peru coastal current with reference to the extraordinary summer of 1939. *Proc. 6th Pacific Sci. Congr.* **3:** 177–197.

—— 1943. *Pesqueriá y Oceanografía del Péru y Proposciones para su Desarrollo futuro.* Lima.

SCLATER, W. L. 1904. Saldanha Bay and its bird islands. *Ibis* **104:** 79–88.

SERVENTY, D. L. 1952. The bird islands of the Sahul Shelf. *Emu* **52:** 33–59.

——, SERVENTY, V. & WARHAM, J. 1971. *The Handbook of Australian Seabirds.* Sydney.

SERVENTY, V. 1959. Birds of Willis Island. *Emu* **59:** 167–176.

SHARROCK, J. T. R. 1965. The status of immature gannets off Cape Clear Island. *Brit. Birds* **58:** 216–217.

—— 1973. Ed. *Natural History of Cape Clear Island.* Berkhamstead.

SHORTHOUSE, J. F. 1967. Notes on seabirds on Vatu Ira Island, Fiji. *Sea Swallow* **19:** 35.

SHUFELDT, R. W. 1915. Fossil birds in the Marsh Collection of Yale University. *Trans. Connecticut Acad. Arts and Sci.* **19:** 1–110.

SHUNTOV, V. P. 1968. Numerical record of sea birds in the eastern part of the Indian Ocean. *Oceanology* **8:** 494–501.

SIBBALD, R. 1710. *The history of the sheriffdoms of Fife and Kinross.* Edinburgh.

SIBLEY, C. G. & AHLQUIST, J. E. 1972. A comparative study of the egg white proteins of non-passerine birds. *Bull. Peabody Mus. Nat. Hist.* **39:** 276 pp.

SICK, H. 1965. Breeding sites of *Sterna eurygnatha* and other sea birds off the Brazilian coast. *Auk* **82:** 507–508.

SIMMONS, G. F. 1927. Sinbads of science. *Natl. Geogr. Mag.* **52:** 1–75.

SIMMONS, K. E. L. 1967a. The role of food supply in the biology of the brown booby at Ascension Island. M.Sc. Thesis, Bristol.

—— 1967b. Ecological adaptations in the life history of the brown booby at Ascension Island. *The Living Bird* **6:** 187–212.

—— 1970. Ecological determinants of breeding adaptations and social behaviour in two fish-eating birds. In *Social Behaviour in Birds and Mammals.* Ed. Crook, J. H. London.

—— 1972. Some adaptive features of seabird plumage types. *Brit. Birds* **65:** 465–479; 510–521.

SIMPSON, D. M. 1970. Manoek Island. *Sea Swallow* **21:** 40.

—— 1973. Seabird colonies on the rocky islands of Sento Shosho and Sekibo Sho Islet. *Sea Swallow* **22:** 29.

SLADEN, W. J. L. 1953. The Adelic Penguin. *Nature* **171:** 952–955.

SLEZER, J. 1693. *Theatrum Scotiae* Edition 1718. Ref. in Gurney 1913, p. 239.

SLUD, P. 1967. The birds of Cocos Island. *Bull. Am. Mus. Nat. Hist.* **134:** 261–296.

SMITH, R. L. 1968. Upwelling. *Oceanogr. Mar. Biol. Ann. Rev.* **6:** 11–46.

SNODGRASS, R. E. & HELLER, E. 1902. The birds of Clipperton and Cocos Islands. *Proc. Washington Acad. Sci.* **4:** 501–520.

—— 1904. Papers from the Hopkins-Stanford Galapagos expedition, 1898-99. XVI Birds. *Proc. Wash. Acad. Sci.* **5:** 231–372.

SNOW, B. 1960. The breeding biology of the shag *Phalacrocorax aristotelis* on the island of Lundy, Bristol Channel. *Ibis* **102:** 554–575.

—— 1963. Behaviour of the shag. *Brit. Birds* **56:** 77–186.

SORENSEN, J. H. 1964. Birds of the Kermadec Islands. *Notornis* **2:** 69–81.

SPENCER, R. & HUDSON, R. 1975. Report on bird-ringing for 1973. *Bird Study* **22** (Suppl.): 64 pp.

STAGER, K. E. 1957. The avifauna of the Tres Marias Islands, Mexico. *Auk* **74:** 413–432.

—— 1964. The birds of Clipperton Island, eastern Pacific. *Condor* **66:** 357–371.

STARK, D. M. 1967. A visit to Stack Skerry and Sule Skerry. *Scot. Birds* **4:** 548–553.

STAUB, F. 1970. Geography and ecology of Tromelin Island. *Atoll Res. Bull.* **136:** 197–209.

—— 1973. Birds of Rodriguez Island. *Proc. R. Soc. Arts Sci. Maurit.* **4:** 17–59.

—— & GUEHO, J. 1968. The Cargados Carajos Shoals of St. Brandon. *Proc. R. Soc. Arts. Sci. Maurit.* **3:** 7–46.

STEIN, P. 1971. Horuhoru revisited. Longevity of the Australian Gannet. *Notornis* **18:** 310–365.

STODDART, D. R. 1967. The ecology of Aldabra Atoll, Indian Ocean. *Atoll Res. Bull.* **118:** 141 pp.

—— 1970. The ecology of neighbouring islands to Aldabra. *Atoll Res. Bull.* **136:** 1–224.

STONEHOUSE, B. 1962. Ascension Island and the British Ornithologists' Union Centenary Expedition 1957–59. *Ibis* **103b:** 107–123.

STORR, G. M. 1964. Zonation and seasonal occurrences of marine birds in the seas off Fremantle, western Australia. *Emu* **63:** 297–303.

STREETS, T. H. 1877. Some account of the natural history of the Fanning group of islands. *Amer. Nat.* **11:** 65–72.

STRESEMANN, V. & STRESEMANN, E. 1960. Die Hand-schwingenmauser der Tagraubvögel. *J. Orn.* **101:** 373–403.

SVERDRUP, H. V., JOHNSON, M. W. & FLEMING, R. M. 1942. *The Oceans; their Physics, Chemistry and General Biology.* New York.

TAFALL, O. B. F. 1944. La expedición del M. N. 'Gracioso' por aguas del extremo noroeste mexicano. *An. Escuela Nac. Cien. Biol., Mexico* **3:** 331–360.

THAYER, J. E. 1911. A nesting colony of Heermann Gulls and Brewster Boobies. *Condor* **13:** 104–106.

—— & BANGS, O. 1905. The vertebrata of Gorgona Island, Colombia. *Aves. Bull. Mus. Comp. Zool., Harvard Coll.* **46:** 91–98.

THOMPSON, M. C. & HACKMAN, C. D. 1968. Birds of the Tokelau Islands. *Notornis* **15:** 109–117.

THOMSON, A. L. 1939. The migration of the gannet: results of marking in the British Isles. *Brit. Birds* **32:** 282–289.

—— 1964. *A New Dictionary of Birds.* London.

—— 1974. The migration of the gannet: a reassessment of British and Irish ringing data. *Brit. Birds* **67:** 89–103.

TINBERGEN, N. 1952. 'Derived' activities; their causation, biological significance, origin, and emancipation during evolution. *Quart. Rev. Biol.* **27:** 1–32.

TOVAR, H. 1968. Areas de reproduccion y distribuccion de las aves marinas en el litoral peruano. *Bol. Inst. Mar. Callao* **1 (10):** 525–546.

TUCK, G. S. 1966. Operation 'Navado'—first preliminary bird report. *Sea Swallow* **18:** 55–59.

TUGARINOV, A. J. 1947. *Faune de l'U.R.S.S.* Moskva.

TYLER, C. 1969. A study of the eggshells of the Gaviiformes, Procellariformes, Podicipitiformes and Pelecaniformes. *J. Zool. Lond.* **158:** 395–412.

UYS, C. J., DON, P. A., MARSHALL, R. A. S. & WELLS, K. F. 1966. Aspergillosis in Cape gannet, *Morus capensis. Ostrich* **37:** 152–154.

VAN HALEWIJN, R. In Press. Seabirds of the south-eastern Caribbean Sea: distribution, breeding seasons and ecology. *Studies on the Fauna of Curacao and other Caribbean Islands.*

VAN ROSSEM, A. J. 1932. The avifauna of Tiburon Island, Sonora, Mexico. *Trans. San Diego Soc. Nat. Hist.* **7:** 119–150.

VAN TETS, G. F. 1965. A comparative study of some social communication patterns in the Pelecaniformes. *Orn. Monogr.* **2:** 1–88.

—— & P. A. 1967. A report on the resident birds of the territory of Christmas Island. *Emu* **66:** 309–319.

VERHAYEN, R. 1961. A new classification for the non-passerine birds of the world. *Inst. Roy. Sci. Natur. Belgique, Bull.* **37** (27): 36 pp.

VERNER, J. 1961. Nesting activities of the red-footed booby in British Honduras. *Auk* **78:** 573–594.

—— 1965. Flight behaviour of the red-footed booby. *Wilson Bull.* **77:** 229–234.

VESEY-FITZGERALD, D. 1941. Further contributions to the ornithology of the Seychelles. *Ibis* **14:** 518–531.

VEVERS, H. G. & EVANS, F. C. 1938. A census of breeding gannets (*Sula bassana*) on Myggenaes Holm, Faeroes. *J. Anim. Ecol.* **7:** 298–302.

——, —— & ALEXANDER, W. B. 1936–37. A census of gannets on Ailsa Craig. *J. Anim. Ecol.* **5:** 246; **6:** 362.

—— & FISHER, J. 1936. A census of gannets on Ailsa Craig with a new method of estimating breeding cliff populations. *J. Anim. Ecol.* **5:** 246–251.

VOGT, W. 1940a. Islas guaneras. *Bol. Comp. Admin. Guano* **16:** 145–162.

—— 1940b. Conferencias. Una depresión ecológica en la costa peruana. *Bol. Comp. Admin. Guano* **16:** 307–329.

—— 1941. Aves guaneras. *Bol. Comp. Admin. Guano* **17:** 127–168.

—— 1942. Aves guaneras. *Bol. Comp. Admin. Guano* **18:** 3–132.

—— 1946. Report of an airplane inspection trip made over the islands in the Gulf of California and off the Pacific coast of lower California. In *Report on Activities of the Conservation Section, Pan American Union* **4:** 112–119.

—— 1964a. Informe sobre las aves guaneras. *Bol. Corp. Nat. de Fertilizantes* **11 (8):** 9–28.

—— 1964b. Informe sobre las aves guaneras. *Bol. Corp. Nat. de Fertilizantes* **11 (9):** 6–48.

—— 1964c. Informe sobre las aves guaneras. *Bol. Corp. Nat. de Fertilizantes* **11 (10):** 5–40.

VON HEUGLIN, M. T. 1873. *Ornithologie Nordost-Afrika's.* London.

VON HUMBOLDT, A. 1806. Chemische Untersuchung des Guano aus den Inseln der Peruanischen Küste. Klaproth's *Beiträge zur chemischen Kenntis der Mineralkörper.* **4:** 299–313.

VON TSCHUDI, J. J. 1846. *Peru.* St. Gallen.

—— 1852. *Travels in Peru during the years 1838–1842.* New York.

WARHAM, J. 1958. The nesting of the Australian gannet. *Emu* **58:** 339–369.

—— 1961. The birds of Raine Island, Pandora Cay and Murray Island Sandbank, North Queensland. *Emu* **61:** 77–93.

WATERSTON, G. 1968. Black-browed albatross summering on the Bass Rock. *Scot. Birds* **5:** 20–23.

WATSON, G. E., ZUSI, R. L. & STORER, R. E. 1963. *Preliminary Field Guide to the Birds of the Indian Ocean.* Washington.

WELLS, J. G. 1902. Birds of the island of Carriacon. *Auk* **19:** 237–246.

WETMORE, A. 1918. The birds of Desecheo Island, Porto Rica. *Auk.* **35:** 333–340.

—— 1925. Bird life among lava rock and coral sand: The chronicle of a scientific expedition to little known islands of Hawaii. *Natl. Geogr. Mag.* **48:** 77–108.

—— 1926. Observations on fossil birds described from the Miocene of Maryland. *Auk* **43:** 462–468.

—— 1927. The birds of Porto Rico and the Virgin Islands. *Sci. Surv. Porto Rico* **9:** 245–598.

—— 1930. Fossil bird remains from the Temblor Formation near Bakersfield, California. *Proc. Calif. Acad. Sci.* **19:** 85–93.

—— 1938. A miocene booby and other records from the Calvert Formation of Maryland. *Proc. U.S. Nat. Mus.* **85:** 21–25.

—— 1939. Birds from Clipperton Island collected on the Presidential cruise of 1938. *Smithsonian Misc. Coll.* **98:** 6 pp.

—— 1960. A classification for the birds of the world. *Smithsonian Misc. Coll.* 139 (11): 1–37.

—— 1965. The birds of the Republic of Panama. *Smithsonian Misc. Coll.* **150:** 483 pp.

WHITE, S. J. 1971. Selective responsiveness by the gannet (*Sula bassana*) to played-back calls. *Anim. Behav.* **19:** 125–131.

—— & WHITE, R. E. C. 1970. Individual voice production in gannets. *Behaviour* **37:** 40–54.

WHITAKER, J. I. S. 1903. Letter. *Ibis.*

WIENS, H. J. 1962. *Atoll Environment and Ecology.* New Haven.

WILHOFT, D. C. 1961. Birds observed during two crossings of the Pacific Ocean. *Condor* **63:** 257–262.

WILLIAMS, G. R. 1960. The birds of the Pitcairn Islands, central south Pacific Ocean. *Ibis* **102:** 58–70.

WILLIAMSON, W. J. F. 1916. A list of birds not previously recorded from Siam, with notes. *J. Nat. Hist. Soc. Siam.* **2** (1): 59–65.

—— 1918. New or noteworthy bird-records from Siam. *J. Nat. Hist. Soc. Siam.* **3** (1): 15–42.

WILSON, J. E. 1950. Newcastle disease in a gannet. *Brit. Vet. Rec.* **62:** 33–34.

WINTERBOTTOM, J. M. 1969. *Check List of Birds of South Africa.* Cape Town.

WITHERBY, H. F. *et al.* 1940. *The Handbook of British Birds.* London.

WODZICKI, K. A. 1967. The gannets at Cape Kidnappers. *Trans. Roy. Soc. New Zealand* **8:** 149–162.

—— & MCMEEKAN, C. P. 1947. The gannet on Cape Kidnappers. *Trans. Roy. Soc. New Zealand* **76:** 429–452.

—— & MORELAND, J. 1966. A note on the food of New Zealand gannets. *Notornis* **13:** 98–99.

—— & ROBERTSON, F. H. 1953. Notes on the life history and population trends of the gannet (*Sula serrator*) at the Plateau Gannetry Cape Kidnappers. *Emu* **53:** 152–168.

—— & —— 1955. Observations on the diving of the Australasian gannet *S. serrator. Notornis* **6:** 72–76.

—— & STEIN, P. 1958. Migration and dispersal of New Zealand gannets. *Emu* **58:** 289–312.

WOOD-JONES, F. 1909. Fauna of the Cocos-Keeling Atoll. *Proc. Zool. Soc. Lond.* 137–142.

—— 1912. *Coral and Atolls.* London.

WOODWARD, P. W. 1972. The natural history of Kure Atoll, north-western Hawaiian Islands. *Atoll Res. Bull.* **164:** 318 pp.

—— 1975. Red-footed Booby Helper at Great Frigatebird Nests. *Pacific Ocean Biol. Survey Program* **108:** 1–2.

WOOLDRIDGE, D. B. 1974. Observations of seabird movements at Barfleur, Normandy, in the autumn. *Seabird Report* **4:** 87–92.

WORCESTER, D. C. 1911. Hybridism among boobies. *Philippine J. Sc. Sect. D* **6:** 179–182.

WYNNE-EDWARDS, V. C. 1935a. The Newfoundland gannet colony; with recent information on the other North American gannetries. *Ibis* **5:** 584–594.

—— 1935b. On the habits and distribution of birds on the north Atlantic. *Proc. Boston Soc. Nat. Hist.* **40:** 233–346.

—— 1962. *Animal Dispersion in Relation to Social Behaviour.* Edinburgh.

——, LOCKLEY, R. M. & SALMON, H. M. 1936. The distribution and numbers of breeding gannets (*Sula bassana* L.). *Brit. Birds* **9:** 262–276.

WYRKTI, K. 1962. The upwelling in the region between Java and Australia during the south-east monsoon. *Austral. J. Mar. Freshwater Res.* **13:** 217–225.

YOUNG, J. G. 1968. Birds of the Scar Rocks—the Wigtownshire gannetry. *Scot. Birds* **5:** 204–208.

INDEX

'E